Twentieth-Century Literary Criticism

Guide to Gale Literary Criticism Series

When you need to review criticism of literary works, these are the Gale series to use:

If the author's death date is: **You should turn to:**

After Dec. 31, 1959
(or author is still living)

CONTEMPORARY LITERARY CRITICISM

for example: Jorge Luis Borges, Anthony Burgess,
William Faulkner, Mary Gordon,
Ernest Hemingway, Iris Murdoch

1900 through 1959

TWENTIETH-CENTURY LITERARY CRITICISM

for example: Willa Cather, F. Scott Fitzgerald,
Henry James, Mark Twain, Virginia Woolf

1800 through 1899

NINETEENTH-CENTURY LITERATURE CRITICISM

for example: Fedor Dostoevski, George Sand,
Gerard Manley Hopkins, Emily Dickinson

1400 through 1799

LITERATURE CRITICISM FROM 1400 to 1800
(excluding Shakespeare)

for example: Anne Bradstreet, Pierre Corneille,
Daniel Defoe, Alexander Pope,
Jonathan Swift, Phillis Wheatley

SHAKESPEAREAN CRITICISM

Shakespeare's plays and poetry

Gale also publishes related criticism series:

CONTEMPORARY ISSUES CRITICISM

Presents criticism on contemporary authors writing
on current issues. Topics covered include the social
sciences, philosophy, economics, natural science, law,
and related areas.

CHILDREN'S LITERATURE REVIEW

Covers authors of all eras. Presents criticism on
authors and author/illustrators who write for the
preschool to junior-high audience.

Twentieth-Century Literary Criticism

**Excerpts from Criticism of the
Works of Novelists, Poets, Playwrights,
Short Story Writers, and Other Creative Writers
Who Died between 1900 and 1960,
from the First Published Critical Appraisals
to Current Evaluations**

Dennis Poupard
Editor

**Thomas Ligotti
James E. Person, Jr.
Associate Editors**

Gale Research Company
Book Tower
Detroit, Michigan 48226

STAFF

Dennis Poupard, *Editor*

Thomas Ligotti, James E. Person, Jr., *Associate Editors*

Denise B. Grove, Marie Lazzari, *Senior Assistant Editors*

Earlene M. Alber, Sandra Giraud,
Sandra Liddell, Serita Lanette Lockard, *Assistant Editors*

Sharon K. Hall, *Contributing Editor*

Robert J. Elster, Jr., *Production Supervisor*
Lizbeth A. Purdy, *Production Coordinator*
Denise Michlewicz, *Assistant Production Coordinator*
Eric F. Berger, Paula J. DiSante, Maureen Duffy, Amy T. Marcaccio,
Yvonne Huette Robinson, *Editorial Assistants*

Karen Rae Forsyth, *Research Coordinator*
Jeannine Schiffman Davidson, *Assistant Research Coordinator*
Victoria B. Cariappa, Robert J. Hill, Harry N. Kronick, James A. MacEachern,
Linda Mohler, Leslie Kyle Schell, Valerie J. Webster, *Research Assistants*

Linda M. Pugliese, *Manuscript Coordinator*
Donna D. Craft, *Assistant Manuscript Coordinator*
Colleen M. Crane, Maureen A. Puhl, Rosetta Irene Simms Carr, *Manuscript Assistants*

L. Elizabeth Hardin, *Permissions Supervisor*
Filomena Sgambati, *Permissions Coordinator*
Janice M. Mach, *Assistant Permissions Coordinator*
Patricia A. Seefelt, *Assistant Permissions Coordinator, Illustrations*
Susan D. Nobles, *Senior Permissions Assistant*
Margaret A. Chamberlain, Joan B. Weber, *Permissions Assistants*
Sandra C. Davis, Dorothy J. Fowler, Virgie T. Leavens, *Permissions Clerks*
Margaret Mary Missar, Audrey B. Wharton, *Photo Research*

Library of Congress Catalog Card Number 76-46132
ISBN 0-8103-0223-3
ISSN 0276-8178

CONTENTS

PREFACE

It is impossible to overvalue the importance of literature in the intellectual, emotional, and spiritual evolution of humanity. Literature is that which both lifts us out of everyday life and helps us to better understand it. Through the fictive lives of such characters as Anna Karenin, Lambert Strether, or Leopold Bloom, our perceptions of the human condition are enlarged, and we are enriched.

Literary criticism can also give us insight into the human condition, as well as into the specific moral and intellectual atmosphere of an era, for the criteria by which a work of art is judged reflects contemporary philosophical and social attitudes. Literary criticism takes many forms: the traditional essay, the book or play review, even the parodic poem. Criticism can also be of several kinds: normative, descriptive, interpretive, textual, appreciative, generic. Collectively, the range of critical response helps us to understand a work of art, an author, an era.

The Scope of the Book

The usefulness of Gale's *Contemporary Literary Criticism (CLC),* which excerpts criticism on current writing, suggested an equivalent need among literature students and teachers interested in authors of the period 1900 to 1960. The great poets, novelists, short story writers, and playwrights of this period are by far the most popular writers for study in high school and college literature courses. Moreover, since contemporary critics continue to analyze the work of this period—both in its own right and in relation to today's tastes and standards—a vast amount of relevant critical material confronts the student.

Thus, *Twentieth-Century Literary Criticism (TCLC)* presents significant passages from published criticism on authors who died between 1900 and 1960. Because of the difference in time span under consideration *(CLC* considers authors who were still living after 1959), there is no duplication between *CLC* and *TCLC.*

Each volume of *TCLC* is carefully designed to present a list of authors who represent a variety of genres and nationalities. The length of an author's section is intended to be representative of the amount of critical attention he or she has received from critics writing in English, or foreign criticism in translation. Critical articles and books that have not been translated into English are excluded. Every attempt has been made to identify and include excerpts from the seminal essays on each author's work. Additionally, as space permits, especially insightful essays of a more limited scope are included. Thus *TCLC* is designed to serve as an introduction for the student of twentieth-century literature to the authors of that period and to the most significant commentators on these authors.

Each *TCLC* author section represents the scope of critical response to that author's work: some early criticism is presented to indicate initial reactions, later criticism is selected to represent any rise or fall in an author's reputation, and current retrospective analyses provide students with a modern view. Since a *TCLC* author section is intended to be a definitive overview, the editors include between 20 and 30 authors in each 600-page volume (compared with approximately 75 authors in a *CLC* volume of similar size) in order to devote more attention to each author. An author may appear more than once because of the great quantity of critical material available, or because of a resurgence of criticism generated by events such as an author's centennial or anniversary celebration, the republication of an author's works, or publication of a newly translated work or volume of letters.

The Organization of the Book

An author section consists of the following elements: author heading, biographical and critical introduction, principal works, excerpts of criticism (each followed by a citation), and an annotated bibliography of additional reading.

- The *author heading* consists of the author's full name, followed by birth and death dates. The unbracketed portion of the name denotes the form under which the author most commonly wrote. If an author wrote consistently under a pseudonym, the pseudonym will be listed in the author heading and the real name given in parentheses on the first line of the biocritical introduction. Also located at the beginning of the biocritical introduction are any name variations under which an author wrote, including transliterated forms for authors whose languages use nonroman alphabets. Uncertainty as to a birth or death date is indicated by a question mark.

- The *biocritical introduction* contains biographical and other background information about an author that will elucidate his or her creative output. Parenthetical material following several of the biocritical introductions includes references to biographical and critical reference series published by the Gale Research Company. These include *Contemporary Authors, Dictionary of Literary Biography, Something about the Author,* and past volumes of *TCLC.*

- The *list of principal works* is chronological by date of first book publication and identifies genres. In the case of foreign authors where there are both foreign language publications and English translations, the title and date of the first English-language edition are given in brackets. Unless otherwise indicated, dramas are dated by first performance, not first publication.

- *Criticism* is arranged chronologically in each author section to provide a perspective on any changes in critical evaluation over the years. In the text of each author entry, titles by the author are printed in boldface type. This allows the reader to ascertain without difficulty the works discussed. For purposes of easier identification, the critic's name and the publication date of the essay are given at the beginning of each piece of criticism. Unsigned criticism is preceded by the title of the journal in which it appeared. For an anonymous essay later attributed to a critic, the critic's name appears in brackets in the heading and in the citation.

  Important critical essays are prefaced by *explanatory notes* as an additional aid to students using *TCLC*. The explanatory notes will provide several types of useful information, including: the reputation of a critic; the reputation of a work of criticism; the specific type of criticism (biographical, psychoanalytic, structuralist, etc.); a synopsis of the criticism; and the growth of critical controversy or changes in critical trends regarding an author's work. In many cases, these notes will cross-reference the work of critics who agree or disagree with each other.

- A complete *bibliographical citation* designed to facilitate location of the original essay or book by the interested reader accompanies each piece of criticism. An asterisk (*) at the end of a citation indicates the essay is on more than one author.

- The *annotated bibliography* appearing at the end of each author section suggests further reading on the author. In some cases it includes essays for which the editors could not obtain reprint rights. An asterisk (*) at the end of a citation indicates the essay is on more than one author.

Beginning with Volume 12, *TCLC* will include a cumulative index to authors listing all the authors who have appeared in *Contemporary Literary Criticism, Twentieth-Century Literary Criticism,* and *Nineteenth-Century Literature Criticism,* along with cross references to the Gale series *Children's Literature Review, Authors in the News, Contemporary Authors, Dictionary of Literary Biography, Something about the Author,* and *Yesterday's Authors of Books for Children.* Users will welcome this cumulated author index as a useful tool for locating an author within the various series. The index, which lists birth and death dates when available, will be particularly valuable for those authors who are identified with a certain period but whose death date causes them to be placed in another, or for those authors whose careers span two periods. For example, F. Scott Fitzgerald is found in *TCLC,* yet a writer often associated with him, Ernest Hemingway, is found in *CLC.* Each volume of *TCLC* also includes a cumulative nationality index. Author names are arranged alphabetically under their respective nationalities and followed by the volume numbers in which they appear. A cumulative index to critics is another useful feature in *TCLC.* Under each critic's name is listed the authors on whom the critic has written and the volume and page where the criticism may be found.

Acknowledgments

No work of this scope can be accomplished without the cooperation of many people. The editors especially wish to thank the copyright holders of the excerpts included in this volume, the permission managers of many book and magazine publishing companies for assisting us in locating copyright holders, and the staffs of the Detroit Public Library, University of Detroit Library, University of Michigan Library, and Wayne State University Library for making their resources available to us. We are also grateful to Jeri Yaryan for her assistance with copyright research.

Suggestions Are Welcome

Several features have been added to *TCLC* since its original publication in response to various suggestions:

- Since Volume 2—An *Appendix* listing the sources from which material in the volume is reprinted.
- Since Volume 3—An *Annotated Bibliography* for additional reading.
- Since Volume 4—*Portraits* of the authors.
- Since Volume 6—A *Nationality Index* for easy access to authors by nationality.
- Since Volume 9—*Explanatory notes* to excerpted criticism which provide important information regarding critics and their work.
- Since Volume 12—A cumulative *Author Index* listing authors in all Gale literary criticism series and providing cross references to Gale's literary biography series.

If readers wish to suggest authors they would like to have covered in future volumes, or if they have other suggestions, they are cordially invited to write the editor.

AUTHORS TO APPEAR
IN FUTURE VOLUMES

Abercrombie, Lascelles 1881-1938
Adamic, Louis 1898-1951
Ade, George 1866-1944
Agate, James 1877-1947
Agustini, Delmira 1886-1914
Aldanov, Mark 1886-1957
Aldrich, Thomas Bailey 1836-1907
Allen, Hervey 1889-1949
Annensky, Innokenty Fyodorovich
    1856-1909
Archer, William 1856-1924
Arlen, Michael 1895-1956
Austin, Mary 1868-1934
Babits, Mihóly 1888-1941
Bahr, Hermann 1863-1934
Barea, Arturo 1897-1957
Bass, Eduard 1888-1946
Beard, Charles A. 1874-1948
Benét, William Rose 1886-1950
Benjamin, Walter 1892-1940
Benson, E(dward) F(rederic) 1867-1940
Benson, Stella 1892-1933
Berdyaev, Nikolai Aleksandrovich
    1874-1948
Beresford, J(ohn) D(avys) 1873-1947
Bergman, Hjalmar 1883-1931
Bergson, Henri 1859-1941
Bethell, Mary Ursula 1874-1945
Binyon, Laurence 1869-1943
Bishop, John Peale 1892-1944
Blackmore, R(ichard) D(oddridge)
    1825-1900
Blum, Leon 1872-1950
Bodenheim, Maxwell 1892-1954
Bojer, Johan 1872-1959
Bosman, Herman Charles 1905-1951
Bosschere, Jean de 1878-1953
Bottomley, Gordon 1874-1948
Bourne, George 1863-1927
Bourne, Randolph 1886-1918
Broch, Hermann 1886-1951
Byrne, Donn (Brian Oswald Donn-Byre)
    1889-1928
Caine, Hall 1853-1931
Campana, Dina 1885-1932
Cannan, Gilbert 1884-1955
Chand, Prem 1880-1936
Chatterji, Saratchandra 1876-1938
Churchill, Winston 1871-1947
Comstock, Anthony 1844-1915
Corelli, Marie 1855-1924
Corvo, Baron (Frederick William Rolfe)
    1860-1913
Croce, Benedetto 1866-1952
Csáth, Géza 1887-1919
Daumal, René 1908-1944

Davidson, John 1857-1909
Day, Clarence 1874-1935
Delafield, E.M. (Edme Elizabeth Monica
    de la Pasture) 1890-1943
DeMorgan, William 1839-1917
Dent, Lester 1904-1959
DeVoto, Bernard 1897-1955
Döblin, Alfred 1878-1957
Douglas, (George) Norman 1868-1952
Douglas, Lloyd C(assel) 1877-1951
Dovzhenko, Alexander 1894-1956
Drinkwater, John 1882-1937
Dujardin, Edouard 1861-1949
Durkheim, Émile 1858-1917
Duun, Olav 1876-1939
Ellis, Havelock 1859-1939
Erskine, John 1879-1951
Fadeyev, Alexander 1901-1956
Feydeau, Georges 1862-1921
Field, Michael (Katherine Harris Brad-
    ley 1846-1914 and Edith Emma
    Cooper 1862-1913)
Field, Rachel 1894-1924
Flecker, James Elroy 1884-1915
Fletcher, John Gould 1886-1950
Frank, Bruno 1886-1945
Frazer, (Sir) George 1854-1941
Freeman, John 1880-1929
Freud, Sigmund 1853-1939
Fuller, Henry Blake 1857-1929
Futrelle, Jacques 1875-1912
Garneau, Saint-Denys 1912-1943
Gladkov, Fydor Vasilyevich 1883-1958
Glyn, Elinor 1864-1943
Gogarty, Oliver St. John 1878-1957
Golding, Louis 1895-1958
Goldman, Emma 1869-1940
Gosse, Edmund 1849-1928
Gould, Gerald 1885-1936
Gourmont, Remy de 1858-1915
Grahame, Kenneth 1859-1932
Gray, John 1866-1934
Guiraldes, Ricardo 1886-1927
Gumilyov, Nikolay 1886-1921
Gwynne, Stephen Lucius 1864-1950
Hale, Edward Everett 1822-1909
Harper, Frances Ellen Watkins
    1825-1911
Harris, Frank 1856-1931
Hawthorne, Julian 1846-1934
Hernandez, Miguel 1910-1942
Herrick, Robert 1868-1938
Hewlett, Maurice 1861-1923
Heyward, DuBose 1885-1940
Hichens, Robert 1864-1950
Hilton, James 1900-1954

Hodgson, William Hope 1875-1918
Holtby, Winifred 1898-1935
Hope, Anthony 1863-1933
Howe, Julia Ward 1819-1910
Huch, Ricarda 1864-1947
Hudson, Stephen 1868-1944
Hudson, W(illiam) H(enry) 1841-1922
Hulme, Thomas Ernest 1883-1917
Ishikawa Takuboku 1885-1912
Ivanov, Vyacheslav Ivanovich 1866-
    1949
Jacobs, W(illiam) W(ymark) 1863-1943
James, Will 1892-1942
James, William 1842-1910
Jerome, Jerome K(lapka) 1859-1927
Jones, Henry Arthur 1851-1929
Kaye-Smith, Sheila 1887-1956
Khodasevich, Vladislav 1886-1939
King, Grace 1851-1932
Korolenko, Vladimir 1853-1921
Kuzmin, Mikhail Alexseyevich 1875-
    1936
Lampedusa, Giuseppi di 1896-1957
Lang, Andrew 1844-1912
Lawson, Henry 1867-1922
Leverson, Ada 1862-1933
Lewisohn, Ludwig 1883-1955
Liliencron, Detlev von 1844-1909
Lindsay, David 1876-1945
Lindsay, (Nicholas) Vachel 1879-1931
Long, Frank Belknap 1903-1959
Lonsdale, Frederick 1881-1954
Louys, Pierre 1870-1925
Lucas, E(dward) V(errall) 1868-1938
Lugones, Leopoldo 1874-1938
Lynd, Robert 1879-1949
MacArthur, Charles 1895-1956
Manning, Frederic 1887-1935
Maragall, Joan 1860-1911
Marriott, Charles 1869-1957
Martin du Gard, Roger 1881-1958
Masaryk, Tomas 1850-1939
McCoy, Horace 1897-1955
Mencken, H(enry) L(ouis) 1880-1956
Meredith, George 1828-1909
Mirbeau, Octave 1850-1917
Mistral, Frederic 1830-1914
Monro, Harold 1879-1932
Moore, Thomas Sturge 1870-1944
Morgan, Charles 1894-1958
Mori Ogai 1862-1922
Morley, Christopher 1890-1957
Murray, (George) Gilbert 1866-1957
Murry, J. Middleton 1889-1957
Nathan, George Jean 1882-1958
Nelligan, Émile 1879-1941

Authors to Appear in Future Volumes

Nordhoff, Charles 1887-1947
Norris, Frank 1870-1902
Olbracht, Ivan (Kemil Zeman) 1882-1952
Ophuls, Max 1902-1957
Parrington, Vernon L. 1871-1929
Pickthall, Marjorie 1883-1922
Pinero, Arthur Wing 1855-1934
Platonov, Andrey 1899-1951
Pontoppidan, Henrik 1857-1943
Porter, Eleanor H(odgman) 1868-1920
Porter, Gene(va) Stratton 1886-1924
Prevost, Marcel 1862-1941
Quiller-Couch, Arthur 1863-1944
Rappoport, Solomon 1863-1944
Reid, Forrest 1876-1947
Riley, James Whitcomb 1849-1916
Rinehart, Mary Roberts 1876-1958
Roberts, Elizabeth Madox 1886-1941
Rohmer, Sax 1883-1959
Rolland, Romain 1866-1944
Rölvaag, O(le) E(dvart) 1876-1931
Romero, José Rubén 1890-1952

Roussel, Raymond 1877-1933
Ruskin, John 1819-1900
Sabatini, Rafael 1875-1950
Saintsbury, George 1845-1933
Santayana, George 1863-1952
Sardou, Victorien 1831-1908
Seeger, Alan 1888-1916
Service, Robert 1874-1958
Seton, Ernest Thompson 1860-1946
Shestov, Lev 1866-1938
Slater, Francis Carey 1875-1958
Söderberg, Hjalmar 1869-1941
Solovyov, Vladimir 1853-1900
Squire, J(ohn) C(ollings) 1884-1958
Steiner, Rudolph 1861-1925
Stockton, Frank R. 1834-1902
Sudermann, Hermann 1857-1938
Sully-Prudhomme, Rene 1839-1907
Summers, Montague 1880-1948
Tabb, John Bannister 1845-1909
Tey, Josephine (Elizabeth Mackintosh) 1897-1952
Tolstoy, Alexei 1882-1945

Turner, W(alter) J(ames) R(edfern) 1889-1946
Vachell, Horace Annesley 1861-1955
Van Dine, S.S. (William H. Wright) 1888-1939
Van Doren, Carl 1885-1950
Vazov, Ivan 1850-1921
Veblen, Thorstein 1857-1929
Wallace, Edgar 1874-1932
Wallace, Lewis 1827-1905
Walser, Robert 1878-1956
Webb, Mary 1881-1927
Webster, Jean 1876-1916
Welch, Denton 1917-1948
Wells, Carolyn 1869-1942
White, Walter Francis 1893-1955
Wister, Owen 1860-1938
Wren, P(ercival) C(hristopher) 1885-1941
Wylie, Francis Brett 1844-1954
Yonge, Charlotte Mary 1823-1901
Zangwill, Israel 1864-1926
Zoshchenko, Mikhail 1895-1958
Zweig, Stefan 1881-1942

Readers are cordially invited to suggest additional authors to the editors.

E(dmund) C(lerihew) Bentley

1875-1956

(Also wrote under pseudonym of E. Clerihew) English novelist, short story writer, journalist, humorist, autobiographer, and editor.

Bentley is chiefly remembered today as the father of the modern detective novel. Although he was also a successful journalist, and famous in his native England for inventing a form of humorous verse known as the "clerihew," it was as the author of the murder mystery classic *Trent's Last Case* that Bentley achieved international recognition. *Trent's Last Case* was originally devised by Bentley as "not so much a detective story as an exposure of detective stories." Mystery story writers before Bentley had adhered closely to the romantic tradition in detective fiction represented by such writers as Edgar Allan Poe and Arthur Conan Doyle. It was in reaction against this imitative tendency that Bentley wrote *Trent's Last Case*. In *Trent*, Bentley disregarded or ironically reversed many of the conventions commonly associated with the detective genre, such as the infallibility of the detective and the ultimate triumph of reason. However, in doing so, he also introduced an element of wit and realism into mystery fiction that it had previously lacked. Bentley's iconoclastic approach to his subject matter in *Trent's Last Case* paved the way for a new type of mystery novel. As Eric Routley observed, Bentley "stepped in at exactly the moment when the detective story was due either to degenerate into inbred affectation or to establish a true principal of originality."

Bentley was born in Shepherd's Bush, a suburb of London. As a young man he attended St. Paul's School, where he met G. K. Chesterton, who soon became his closest friend. Together they founded an unofficial student magazine that featured poetry in the form of "bad imitations of Swinburne," satire, and nonsense verse. Bentley wrote his first clerihew for this publication. Many years later, this same rhyme, about Sir Humphry Davy, appeared in a slightly amended version in his first book, *Biography for Beginners*, illustrated by Chesterton. Bentley graduated from Merton college at Oxford with a degree in history. Later, he studied law in London and was called to the bar in 1902. He soon abandoned his law career, however, to take a position on the editorial staff of the London *Daily News*. He was a frequent contributor of political articles to such magazines as *The Fortnightly Review*, and his light verse often appeared in the pages of *Punch*. In 1912, Bentley joined the staff of the *Daily Telegraph*, where he remained as foreign affairs editor until his retirement in 1934. During World War II he returned to the *Daily Telegraph* to fill in as chief literary critic. He died in 1956.

Bentley's clerihews, as they appeared in his *Biography for Beginners*, *More Biography*, and *Baseless Biography*, represented a new form of nonsense verse that quickly became popular in England and inspired many imitators. Clerihews, so-called after Bentley's middle name, are formless, four-line verses that often describe a famous person. They are typically absurd or ironic, and, when concerning specific persons, the first line nearly always consists of the subject's name. The principal challenge of the form is thus in the pursuit of suitable rhymes for unrhymable names. Although the word "clerihew"

The Granger Collection, New York

was officially added to the Oxford English Dictionary in Bentley's lifetime, his verses never enjoyed the same popularity in other countries that they did in England. Bentley's humor in his clerihews was necessarily somewhat parochial, and so did not often appeal to non-English readers.

In contrast, *Trent's Last Case* was internationally well-received at the time of its appearance in 1913, and it remains popular today. When *Trent's Last Case* was published Bentley dedicated it to Chesterton, stating that he had written it primarily for his friend's amusement. Chesterton was an avid reader of mystery stories as well as the author of the Father Brown detective stories, and, more importantly, he had urged Bentley in his ambition to write "a new sort of detective story." Although it was not recognized as such by critics, Bentley initially planned *Trent* as a parody of the traditional detective story. In *Trent* Bentley replaced the Sherlockian hero of the popular mysteries with the artist-detective Philip Trent, who, far from being a paragon of order and reserve, facetiously misquotes poetry, falls in love with the prime suspect, and abandons the case. Moreover, Trent's ingenious solution to the crime turns out to be incorrect, and the murderer goes unpunished at the end. In spite of this, the novel was not perceived as a parody, chiefly because Bentley's innovations did more to advance the detective genre than merely to satirize it. Prior to the publication of *Trent*, few artistically successful mystery novels had been written. The manipulation of stock characters and the construction of a clever series of clues were devices more suited to the short story, and, with rare exceptions, writers had difficulty constructing a novel-length tale around them. Bentley was the first mystery writer to conceive of using the psychology of his characters as possible clues to the solution of the crime. He was also the first to utilize a narrative technique that alternated between several different points of view, thus enabling him to play fair with the reader by sharing the detective's thoughts, but not revealing the solution prematurely. These two innovations contributed more to the development of the contemporary detective novel than anything that had appeared since Wilkie Collins's *The Moonstone,* to which *Trent's Last Case* is frequently compared.

Trent's Last Case has been translated into virtually every written language, and critics generally rate it one of the masterpieces of the detective genre. Bentley never duplicated the success of *Trent's Last Case* with any of his other fiction, although his novel *Trent's Own Case,* and the short story collection *Trent Intervenes,* have both been praised by critics for their wit and the polished quality of their prose. Bentley's last book was *Elephant's Work,* a thriller that failed to win critical praise when it appeared. However, in recent years critics have come to regard it as a worthwhile contribution to the genre of suspense fiction.

(See also *Contemporary Authors,* Vol. 108.)

PRINCIPAL WORKS

Biography for Beginners [as E. Clerihew]   (verse)   1905
Trent's Last Case   (novel)   1913
More Biography   (verse)   1929
Trent's Own Case [with H. W. Allen]   (novel)   1936
Trent Intervenes   (short stories)   1938
Baseless Biography   (verse)   1939
Those Days   (autobiography)   1940
Elephant's Work   (novel)   1950
Clerihews Complete   (verse)   1951
The Complete Clerihews of E. Clerihew Bentley   (verse)   1981
The First Clerihews [with Waldo Percy Henry d'Avigdor, Lucien Robert Frederick Oldershaw, Gilbert Keith Chesterton, Edward Chesterton, and Maurice (Grey) Solomon]   (verse)   1983

THE SPECTATOR   (essay date 1913)

Mr. Bentley, whose name is unfamiliar to us in connexion with fiction though there is nothing of the novice in his style of writing, is to be congratulated on a decided success. Indeed, our chief ground of complaint with him is a mere detail of nomenclature. *Trent's Last Case* is such an excellent detective romance that we should like to hear about some of Trent's earlier achievements, and sincerely trust that Mr. Bentley will not adhere to the self-denying ordinance involved in a logical interpretation of the title. For Trent is quite a new personality in the romance of criminology: a man who leads a blameless double life; an attractive humorist with a genius for absurd quotation—"his culture was large and loose, dominated by a love of poetry"; and an unconscious power for getting himself

liked. It is happily said of him that "no one felt on good behaviour with a man who seemed always to be enjoying himself." When we add that his age at the time of the story was only thirty-two, and that it is expressly stated that he had not yet passed the age of laughter and adventure, Mr. Bentley's decision to restrict his further mental activity to art—his second string—or the cultivation of his fireside becomes not only unjust but impracticable.

We have said that there is nothing of the novice in Mr. Bentley's style of writing. He has, however, the engaging optimism of youth which manifests itself in half a dozen different ways. We have been treated of late to several plays and novels, all of them aimed at pillorying the excesses and vulgarities of the modern press. But here we have Mr. Bentley describing the editor of an extremely up-to-date sheet—a man prepared on all occasions to "knock the town endways"—as inspiring the respect of his staff, without a touch of the charlatan, cordial and considerate. If there is one journalistic excrescence which more than any other has stunk in the nostrils of all decent people of late years, it is the amateur "crime investigator"—criminal's ally would be nearer the mark. Yet Mr. Bentley not only assigns this *rôle* to his hero, but shows that it can be played fairly and squarely without "queering the pitch" for Scotland Yard, or disregarding the feelings of relatives of the dead. Some day perhaps Mr. Bentley may give us a satire on the abuse of the opportunities offered to amateur detectives by lavish journalistic enterprise. After all, everything depends on your choice of instruments. Sir James Molloy, the editor of the *Record,* used Trent, not altogether because he was exceptionally clever, but also because he was a sportsman, a gentleman, and a man of independent means.

The case which *ex hypothesi* ended Trent's career as a detective is that of the mysterious and violent death of Sigsbee Manderson, an American millionaire financier. Manderson had inherited wealth, and during his father's lifetime adopted buccaneering methods, generally with success. On his father's death, he "ranged himself," and his millions grew with mechanical regularity. Still this is not to say that he was a popular or genial person. His domestic life was blameless, but he was rather an inhuman though highly efficient machine than a man. He had, it is true, a weakness for being *bien chaussé,* and had begun to dabble in diamonds. Otherwise he had no human redeeming vices, and he was incapable of making a profitable and intelligent use of leisure. A somewhat sinister figure, this American "Colossus," ruthless rather than crooked; of worldwide fame, and yet for all his power unable to inspire affection in a single human soul. . . . He is a well-conceived type of modern millionaire, interesting, formidable, but entirely unattractive. Mr. Bentley has not only drawn him clearly and firmly, but he has shown a thoroughly sound instinct in choosing such a man as the victim. The fact that he inspires no affection or regret or desire to avenge him enables the reader to approach the mystery of his death without any emotional bias in his favour. A really good "mystery" cannot be made out of the murder of a lovable or admirable person. Manderson was neither. He stood for methods which excited hatred amongst millions of working men, and was to this extent always open to assassination. Then he had married a beautiful English wife who was admittedly unhappy. There was presumptive evidence that the murder might have been a *crime passionnel.* One of his secretaries was a handsome young man, who was much in the company of his wife. These are some of the data on which Trent had to exercise his intelligence; but it would discount the joy of perusal to say more than that his task is immensely complicated by his susceptibility to the charms of the widow, and the conflict between his duty to his employer and his chivalrous regard for the widow's feelings. Speaking for ourselves, we find it impossible to develop a lively sympathy for a woman, however attractive, who deliberately married a man such as Manderson out of mere social ambition. But this attitude has not interfered with our enjoyment and admiration of Mr. Bentley's ingenious work. We wonder how many readers will "spot" the sentence, early in the book, in which the identity of the person who fired the fatal shot is first disclosed? (pp. 409-10)

> *A review of ''Trent's Last Case,'' in* The Spectator *(© 1913 by* The Spectator*), Vol. 110, No. 4419, March 8, 1913, pp. 409-10.*

H. DOUGLAS THOMSON (essay date 1931)

[*Thomson's* Masters of Mystery: A Study of the Detective Story, *from which this excerpt is taken, was one of the earliest book-length studies of the mystery story. Thomson's book outlines the history of the genre, and is particularly useful as a guide to English detective story writers.*]

There have been several attempts to civilise the detective story. Realism was the pressing inducement, for the phantasia of the super-sleuth had began to grow stale. The detective story was thus obliged to become domesticated. The introduction of character study was at first not an entirely satisfactory innovation. The *dramatis personae* would behave for the major part of the book rather like W. J. Locke's characters—pleasantly evasive. Then the climax would turn Hyperion to a satyr. In a paragraph the smooth solicitor would be translated to a snarling maniac with an unprepossessing rictus. To this maladjustment, it must be confessed, the detective story is frequently subject. It is the greatest flaw in the theme of ''the most unlikely person.''

Mr. E. C. Bentley, however, in *Trent's Last Case* . . . evaded this bogey of Inconsistency. To do this he had to spirit away his villain by making him the ''murdered'' man, and the posthumous influence of his malignity was just sufficient and no more to take the characters out of themselves. (pp. 147-48)

In some respects the story is unique. The detective Philip Trent—who falls in love with one of the suspects—fails to solve the problem, and the solution is tendered gratis. For this violation of the rules the staggering dénouement is for once ample compensation. It is true that it also causes a second infringement. The ''murder'' turned out to be a less ''sensational,'' but in the circumstances equally exciting, justifiable homicide. In fact, Mr. Bentley turned the tables very neatly. Instead of adhering rigidly to the rules and thus sacrificing his characters, he preferred the human drama and an elastic code. Otherwise the orthodox features are present. For many reasons it is the perfect detective story; and not least for its construction. Indeed, so meticulously is it pieced together, that it fails to discourage the analyst; it even invites the knife. That is at least a defence, however poor, for attempting rather callously to analyse the plot. Suppose we imagine, for the fun of it, the unfolding of the plan.

Could a detective story be worked out . . . from the idea of a man committing suicide, in order to bring to the gallows an innocent man of whom he was blindly jealous? Well, it had been done before. Planting was an old-fashioned dodge. One would have to consider at all events the motive to jealousy. Suppose the villain suspected the dupe of being in love with his wife. On the strength of these suspicions he determines either to commit suicide, or preferably for his own sake to build up a perfect case of circumstantial evidence of robbery, assault, etc., against the innocent party. A straight novel might easily be made out of that triangle. Observe how the entry of the detective complicates matters. Two alternatives at once suggest themselves:—

(1) The detective should arrive at the correct solution of the problem, or,

(2) He should solve the problem as the villain meant it to be solved—by reliance on circumstantial evidence. The second alternative would, however, mean the violation of a perfectly sound canon of detective fiction, the happy ending. Therefore, we must be content with (1).

Now, the circumstantial evidence will be based willy-nilly on an examination of the wife and the innocent ''lover.'' These relations might be described so as to make the reader believe that an illicit love affair was responsible for the ''murder'' of the husband. Or again, it might be hinted that the husband was a brute and beat his wife, and thus the sympathy of modern humanitarianism be enlisted. The latter method would be the more natural one considering the husband's real character. But what was the detective to think?

Then possibly was born Mr. Bentley's great idea—that the detective should fall in love with the wife, that it should be a grand passion. There would be drama in this situation: the detective in love with the wife (or widow), tormenting himself now with the thought that his loved one was guilty of her husband's death, now with the no less agonising suspicion that the dupe had fired the shot from love of her. (One recalls in this context a less dramatic and less artistic situation in *Blackmail*.)

The opening of the story is surprising. As far as the construction goes the first chapter is superfluous. Sigsbee Manderson is dead. Plain, stark fact. No ominous thuds. No shots ringing out in the tenebral stillness. The story might have opened in the offices of the *Record*. Yet, for one reason only it is a brilliant piece of technique. Mr. Bentley, possibly underrating his power of creating the correct atmosphere, evidently determined at the outset to make in an indirect way the most of the dramatic and sensational possibilities.

We are immediately on the tiptoe of suspense. Sigsbee Manderson is dead; the great financier is dead (Sigsbee *is* such a good name for the murdered man. It is also an additional motive to murder.) The world totters at his sudden demise. The ''vortices of finance'' (whatever they are) are in chaos. Thus is the importance of the issues magnified, and one of De Quincey's conditions of a perfect murder ignored. (pp. 149-51)

Now we are in the offices of the *Record*. The press is on the job; the salient facts are coming in. The editor decides to put Trent on the case. It is to be observed that Fleet Street is still regarded as superior in detection to Scotland Yard. This was of course before the latter had seen the commercial prospects in writing ''shop''! Curiously enough Mr. Bentley stoops to the old cliché of making Philip Trent unnecessarily reluctant to ''take up the case.''

The characters have now to be assembled. First comes Mr. Cupples, the genial, who conveniently supplies information about the Manderson ménage. (pp. 151-52)

Trent soon meets Inspector Murch in a spirit of friendly rivalry; and just when we are expecting the death-blow to the old antagonism and a victory for co-operation, the inspector softly and silently fades away. It is now Trent's business to show his mettle. Note-book in hand he creeps from room to room, taking finger-prints and measuring distances in splendid style. As far as the "psychological" aspect of the case goes, Trent starts by suspecting every one. Mrs. Manderson, Marlowe the secretary and intended dupe, Bunner the American, and the butler. As though aware of this, Bunner decides to simplify matters by producing so absurd a theory that he almost cries out to be suspected. All this time Mr. Bentley is working up a strong case against Marlowe and Mrs. Manderson. The first movement closes with the suspects in this order (1) Marlowe; (2) Mrs. Manderson; (3) Bunner.

Mrs. Manderson had yet to make her entrance. The description of Trent's first sight of her is beautifully persuasive. We are immediately sentimental and, like Trent, drawn to her. Then we wonder for a moment if this persuasion was not really meant to consolidate our suspicions. The inquest soon follows, and Mrs. Manderson creates the expected sensation. Trent then ceases to be sentimental and becomes logical. False teeth and a pair of shoes occupy his attention; and we return to the spade work. Trent, despite his logic, is fundamentally an intuitionalist. "Swiftly and *spontaneously* when chance or effort puts one in possession of the key fact in any system of baffling circumstances, one's ideas seem to rush to group themselves anew in relation to that fact, so that they are suddenly rearranged almost before one has consciously grasped the significance of the key fact itself."

The key fact once established, the process of inference proceeds apace. Trent's report is in many ways the most satisfying portion of the book. (Miss Sayers quotes from it at length to illustrate the shifting of the viewpoint from (1) "The Watson viewpoint" to (2) "The detective's" and to (3) "The middle viewpoint.") It is in a way all the more satisfying because, as we find later, the hypothesis was faulty; and it is cleverer in a detective story to appear in these circumstances *plausible to the reader*, than to start from a true hypothesis and delude him by the way. Why this is so, I have never quite been able to understand. The final conclusion, prompted by the circumstantial evidence, is that Marlowe must have been the murderer.

The reader sits back, but finding that there are roughly 150 more pages to the book sits up again, and naturally wonders what the devil has happened. Is Trent wrong after all? Was the deduction of pure reason all at sea? The character of the book now changes. We forget we are reading a detective story. As Trent's love for Mrs. Manderson unfolds, the plot becomes one of character. Yet not for a moment does this development seem out of place. The farrago is exquisitely composed. The third movement ends in the united happiness of the detective and the woman once suspected.

And still suspected, for we suddenly remember that the problem has not been solved. Trent's theory of Marlowe's guilt suffers shipwreck when an intimation of the latter's engagement is brought to Trent's notice; as Marlowe's motive was supposed to be his love for Mrs. Manderson. Trent has now a very good reason for getting to the bottom of the problem. He calls a council of war, and Marlowe is asked to attend. A diabolical suicide is exposed and the fourth wave is spent.

But what we supposed to be the real dénouement was merely a shadow; and Mr. Cupples, dear old Cupples, in the last chapter of all provides the surprise of the book, upsets all calculations and beats every reader on the post. Without this grand finale the story would have had a satisfactory and effective conclusion; but the last chapter raises it to the pinnacle of technique. By this stroke of genius the detective story is emancipated and claims a climax of its very own.

Even from this crude résumé it is not, I hope, impossible to recognise the sterling qualities which won that consensus of approbation. Never have the virtues of the genre been quite so elegantly displayed. The formal problem intertwined with the character problem; the sincerity of the character study; the honeyed morsels of sensationalism; the trail of the red herrings, inside and outside the plot; the naturalness of the "motivation;" the tenseness and also the humour of the situation; and over and above all, that supreme climax. It is rare that a solution hoaxes both the detective and the reader. (pp. 152-55)

H. Douglas Thomson, "The Domestic Detective Story," in his Masters of Mystery: A Study of the Detective Story *(reprinted by permission of William Collins Sons & Co Ltd), Collins, 1931, pp. 144-67.**

CHARLES WILLIAMS (essay date 1936)

[*Williams was a noted English poet and critic, as well as the author of such supernatural thrillers as* War in Heaven *and* All Hallow's Eve.]

[In *Trent's Own Case*] I wonder anxiously if Mr. Trent is becoming a little reckless. He seems to treat words more lightly than he does wines—or at least than Mr. Warner Allen [the coauthor of the book] does wines. I may be fussy. It may be that this is a graver book than the earlier one was. There is no-one quite like our adorable Mr. Cupples. The earlier high sound is, as it were, muted. On the other hand, there is a curious sense of there being 'someone or something behind the arras.' There is an interlude in Dieppe, which has very little to do with necessities of the plot, but enters almost on a town of fantasy: as if between France and England there lay a whole country of the mind, and the roads of Abelard and Racine (and Calvin) ran through the forest of Arden and between the hills of Cumberland, into the distant places of our scepticism and our belief and our poetry. The Hotel of the Little Universe and of the Chimaera . . . I thought Mr. Bentley was going to become all marvellously allegorical and ambiguous, with the Comte d'Astalys, who was descended from the Comte Balthazar the alchemist, by whom the Chimaera was first added to the coat-of arms, and lines of the Odyssey quoted in English and in Provençal. But these things do but tail off into 'private vice and folly,' drugs and madness, and so we come back to England and honest murder.

Yet perhaps Mr. Bentley enjoyed those chapters when he read them over, as I did, . . . as well as all the rest of the book, including the admirably invented episode of the cork of the bottle of Felix Poubelle 1884, and the speech upon corks delivered by Mr. William Clerihew, wine-merchant, of Fountain Court, and the debt we all owe to the Benedictine Dom Perignon, of Hautvillers in Champagne, who rediscovered corks at the end of the seventeenth century ('the century of genius,' as it has—obviously with accuracy—been called). So what with one thing and another, you will see it is altogether a book of high invention and continual savour of good and bad, and wit and poetry, and intricacy and simplicity. (p. 178)

Charles Williams, "Letters to Peter—IV." (reproduced by kind permission of David Higham Associ-

ates), in G. K.'s Weekly, *Vol. XXIII, No. 585, May 28, 1936, pp. 178-79.*

Spectator; *reprinted by permission of* The Spectator*)*, *Vol. 161, No. 5747, August 19, 1938, pp. 312-13.**

NICHOLAS BLAKE [pseudonym of C. DAY LEWIS] (essay date 1936)

[*Nicholas Blake was the pseudonym under which C. Day Lewis, the noted British poet and critic, wrote such popular and highly entertaining detective stories as* The Beast Must Die *and* Malice in Wonderland.]

Mr. Bentley is a remarkable phenomenon. Twenty years ago he wrote *Trent's Last Case,* in which his urbane artistry, perfect timing and tigerish attack established him as the Ranjitsinji of crime fiction. After that one inning he retired, to pop up in *Biography for Beginners* disguised as the most original comic poet of his generation. And now once again Philip Trent is dragged away from his painting to investigate a murder in which two of his friends are involved. His interest in the crime soon ceases to be purely altruistic, for beside the body of the dead philanthropist he finds a razor-blade bearing his own finger-prints! In the dead man's pocket a champagne cork is discovered, with which—and several other vintage points— the learned Mr. Allen deals eruditely. Indeed, the erudition of these collaborators is so wide and effortless that it makes even Mr. Van Dine look like a small-town university professor. *Trent's Own Case* is perhaps not quite so well knit and perfectly rounded as its predecessor. But it has as ingenious a plot, two really wicked characters, the same leisurely Edwardian wit, the same bouquet—dry and ethereal as a very old brandy: you will find yourself sipping slowly at this book, postponing as long as possible the melancholy moment when it shall be finished. But the internal glow will remain; for *Trent's Own Case* is another classic of its *genre.*

Nicholas Blake [*pseudonym of C. Day Lewis*], ''*Trent and Others*,'' *in* The Spectator (© *1936 by* The Spectator; *reprinted by permission of* The Spectator*)*, *Vol. 156, No. 5631, May 29, 1936, p. 992.**

NICHOLAS BLAKE [pseudonym of C. DAY LEWIS] (essay date 1938)

The technique of the detective short-story is a peculiarly difficult one, and only Conan Doyle and Chesterton have consistently mastered it. The main difficulty is to keep the reader guessing, to maintain suspense and create surprise within a severely limited group of characters. Mr. Bentley avoids rather than masters this problem. In his collection of short stories, *Trent Intervenes,* he depends for his effect upon the How, not upon the Who: they are like sums in Arithmetic, whose answer we can guess pretty accurately at the start; the interest lies in the steps towards the foregone conclusion. As we should expect from so distinguished a writer, the plots are neat, economical, and un-fussy. From the literary point of view, they are perhaps a little arid and lacking in colour, but these are to a certain extent the necessary defects of their detective merits. Here we must except the last story, **"The Ordinary Hairpins,"** which describes with great tenderness and delicacy the finding of a famous singer who has disappeared from the world that knew her. Notable also are **"The Genuine Tabard,"** a study in heraldry and deception, and **"The Clever Cockatoo,"** into which Mr. Bentley has infused that atmosphere of creeping uneasiness which made the Father Brown tales so attractive. (p. 312)

Nicholas Blake [*pseudonym of C. Day Lewis*], ''*A Dram of Poison*,'' *in* The Spectator (© *1938 by* The

E. C. BENTLEY (essay date 1940)

[*In the following excerpt from his autobiography,* Those Days, *Bentley explains how he came to write* Trent's Last Case.]

Sometime in the year 1910 it occurred to me that it would be a good idea to write a detective story of a new sort.

The idea of writing any sort of detective story did not occur to so many people in those days as it occurs now. Since the time, during my school days, when Sherlock Holmes burst upon the world there had been a large enough output of detective fiction; but there was in 1910 nothing like the volume of it that is produced to-day, nor did it occupy, I think, any talents of the order of those now engaged in it. (p. 249)

Since the first appearance of Holmes in the *Strand* in 1891 he had been in unchallenged possession of the field: his imitators had stuck faithfully to their model without any approach to its excellence. As a schoolboy, and ever after, I delighted in it as much as anyone; the originality, and the power of good, plain story-telling, were irresistible. If the nature of the detective-story, as of other things, is to be found in its complete development, that was the Holmesian saga. Its very weaknesses were endearing. (pp. 249-50)

Two things about the stories, however, did not move my admiration. One was the exaggerated unreality of the character of Holmes, the educated Victorian who did not know that the earth revolved round the sun, had never heard of Thomas Carlyle, smoked shag, engaged in pistol-practice in the sitting-room, loved music, injected cocaine when things were dull, and so forth. These things were intended to make him more interesting, and no doubt they did so. Victorian fiction abounded in ''rich characters'', and Holmes was the most opulent of all; there was a demand for them. But as life went on, that sort of thing came to jar upon me. It does so still: I do not care about a detective, or any character in fiction, who has been made ostentatiously unlike life, ecentric and ''peculiar'', with the idea of making him interesting. He kills my own interest, usually, as soon as his antics begin. This is a matter of taste, about which not many people, perhaps, feel as I do. (pp. 250-51)

All the same, I did not like those absurdities. And another thing that troubled me was the extreme seriousness of Holmes, and the equal seriousness of his imitators. It is true that they were within the limits of a period when lightness of touch in important persons was not generally tolerated—a period which I most sincerely respect and revere; which it chafes me to see held up to ridicule; but to which I do not and did not belong. Such phases of taste overlap: the one which included me was beginning to like to see great men whole, or as nearly whole as might be. It knew that most men of genius had their lighter moments; that it was, almost, a quality of greatness to have such moments, or more than moments; that even Mr. Gladstone had manifested, at rare intervals, something that could only be described as a sense of humour. So it was that I found the austerity of Holmes and the rest a little wearisome. It should be possible, I thought, to write a detective story in which the detective was recognizable as a human being, and was not quite so much the ''heavy'' sleuth.

Whether it was possible for me was another question. I had never written a novel, or anything narrative beyond the shortest of "sketches" for this periodical or that. I had never wanted to write a novel. But I wanted to write this one now, because I imagined, in my innocence, it would be good fun. In addition to that, as soon as the intention was formed I told myself that it would be a good thing to have another string to one's bow, journalism being what it was. Not that I expected much of a first novel. It must, I suppose, have occurred to me as a remote possibility that the book might be successful, but I certainly had not the smallest confidence in its success—there was no motive of that sort.

So I began to cast about for a plot that had not been used before. (pp. 251-52)

One day I drew up a list of the things absolutely necessary to an up-to-date detective story: a millionaire—murdered, of course; a police detective who fails where the gifted amateur succeeds; an apparently perfect alibi; some fussing about in a motor car or cars, with at least one incident in which the law of the land and the safety of human life were treated as entirely negligible by the quite sympathetic character at the driving-wheel. (p. 253)

Besides these indispensables there had, of course, to be a crew of regulation suspects, to include the victim's widow, his secretary, his wife's maid, his butler, and a person who had quarrelled openly with him.

I decided too, that there had better be a love-interest, because there was supposed to be a demand for this in a full-length novel. I made this decision with reluctance, because to me love-interest in novels of plot was very tiresome. Then it occurred to me that the dragging-in of love-interest by the neck and heels might tend to make the story sprawl; so with an eye to economy of effect I suggested to myself that the love-affair might centre in the suspected widow, and that the amateur detective might be the other party. This wore an air of such supreme absurdity that I thought it would be interesting to see if, by dint of writing, it could be made plausible.

It was not until I had gone a long way with the plot that the most pleasing notion of all came to me: the notion of making the hero's hard-won and obviously correct solution of the mystery turn out to be completely wrong. Why not show up the infallibility of the Holmesian method? The triumphantly incriminated suspect should prove to be innocent after all, and a cleverer fellow than the hero. I was overjoyed at this idea; but I have always had a feeling that if I had mentioned my plan to anyone qualified to give advise on such a matter, he would have been strongly against it. Detective-story fans, he would have said, do not want to be told that the detective hero has made an ass of himself. I thought so myself indeed; and this was another inducement to stick to my own idea, and see if the objections to it could not be, so to speak, written out of existence. In the result, it does not seem to have been generally noticed that *Trent's Last Case* is not so much a detective story as an exposure of detective stories. (pp. 253-54)

> *E. C. Bentley, " 'Trent's Last Case'," in his* Those Days *(by kind permission of Curtis Brown on behalf of the estate of E. C. Bentley), Constable & Co Ltd, 1940, pp. 249-61.*

I. L. BAKER (essay date 1956)

[*Baker's* E. C. Bentley: "Trent's Last Case" *examines the plot, style, and characterization of the classic detective novel. This study is principally composed of chapter-by-chapter plot outlines of Bentley's novel, with annotations explaining literary refer-*ences, place names, allusions to current events of the time, and so on.]

[*Trent's Last Case*] is often estimated to be the one detective story seriously worth considering as literature. We [note] . . . its remarkable plot and climax, its structural compactness and its deft characterisation: but there is more than this, over and above and within all these things, that singles it out among detective fiction, and that is its style, the distinctive manner in which Bentley has chosen to express his thoughts. It is this particularly that has gained the approbation of so many writers, and combines with other merits to produce so agreeable, readable and yet important a book.

It would, of course, be inappropriate to elevate E. C. Bentley into the ranks of the major novelists of his period: *Trent's Last Case* has no pretensions above the light, easily-digested type of fiction to be read solely for pleasure. There is no "social message" here, or subtle interplay of character. Yet, in its characterisation and setting it maintains its reaction to the traditional, the accepted, not only within novel-writing in general, but within the limited field of detective fiction itself. There are no lumps of descriptive detail introducing the characters and the scenes, and clogging the progress of the action. The atmosphere of a person or place is given briefly, in stages, without halting-places in which detail is piled upon detail, hampering the movement of the story, and confusing the impression intended. This was as new in detective fiction as it was in the general history of the novel, at least up to the time of Thomas Hardy (1840-1928). We [note] . . . the neat economical way in which the major characters are introduced, rather as one would see them in real life, making some immediate concentrated impression (Trent bouncing in upon Cupples, Mrs. Manderson on the cliff-verge, Marlowe's tired walk in the grounds of White Gables, etc.) and then slowly unfolding and developing in action. In the same way the setting and background of the story is skilfully suggested, and left to make its own impression: there is no building up of an over-charged atmosphere by vigorous word-painting, and the setting is all the fresher and sharper in consequence. (pp. 24-5)

The absence of "verbal mountains" and digressions, and the avoidance of irrelevant statements (other than deliberate red herrings, of course), which would detract from the general accuracy of the outline of the story, help to make Bentley's style clear. . . .

There are two minor blemishes, however, with regard to clarity and avoidance of ambiguity. In Ch. IV . . . , when Martin is talking to Trent about Manderson's drinking habits, he calls his master "a remarkably abstemious man": and yet he then details "a glass or two of wine at dinner, very rarely a little at luncheon, and from time to time a whisky and soda before going to bed". This hardly qualifies Manderson as abstemious; but this is, of course, a comparative matter. Later, in the same chapter, when he is asked about Manderson's habit of sitting fully exposed to view, Martin says, "But nobody could have seen him who had any business to be there", which is unhappily worded. These are minor blemishes, however. There is, otherwise, nothing in the way of immediate understanding of what you are meant to understand. (p. 26)

From what has already been said it must be clear that Bentley, with his legal training and long years of practising journalism, coupled with deep and wide reading, betrays a sensitivity in his diction, his handling of words: there is often an elegance there which gives pleasure apart from the subject-matter. It is interesting to note, for example, how he handles Trent and Mrs. Manderson. By deciding to introduce a "love" theme at all, Bentley struck out a new freedom for the detective novel: making his detective fall in love with one of his suspects was again the height of unorthodoxy. *Trent's Last Case* is thus the first detective novel in which a real love story is intertwined with the "detective" aspect. All through Bentley indicates and stresses the manliness, the masculinity of Trent, and its counterpart, the gracious femininity of Mrs. Manderson. This is, of course, deliberate exact observation; it is also testimony to a subtlety of word and phrase. Trent is "a long, loosely-built man" who "flings his hat on a chair" and wears "rough tweed clothes" with his hair and short moustache "tolerably tidy"; he pounces on Cupples, seizing his hand in a hard grip; he eats swiftly and abstractedly, strides off, walks rapidly to White Gables, "pokes about" the house assiduously, and even takes his morning bathe terribly seriously: he "dived deep", "swam out to the tossing" sea, swims deliberately across the current, returning "battered and refreshed" to "scale the cliff again". This strain, of a young healthy man living and working to the top of his form physically and mentally, is deliberately maintained throughout the story. Similarly, Mrs. Manderson is depicted as "a very modern figure" of beautiful womanhood. Her whole description (Ch. VII . . .) must be re-read with care, and note taken of the deft incidental touches emphasising her grace and charm. Some examples of this are: "She is full of character; her mind and her tastes are cultivated"; "everybody used to look forward to her coming over in the summer"; "she had at least the resources of an artistic nature"; "her eyes of golden-flecked brown observed him kindly"; re-read her appearance at the coroner's court in Ch. VIII; and the detail of her disposition under other emotional stresses in Ch. X; "in the allurement of evening dress . . . and there was a light of daring in her eyes and cheeks as she greeted him"; "her laugh . . . that sudden rush of cascading notes of mirth"; "she sank on the carpet beside him in a wave of dark brown skirts", and so on.

Such Americanisms as appear are mentioned in sequence in the notes: they are inevitable in the fabric of the story, and are never overdone or "slangy" in the worst sense. Overall there is a humour and urbanity in the writing, a suffused wit, a sort of "bouquet" of charm and ease, particularly in the "preposterous talk" of Trent. . . . (pp. 27-8)

Finally, it is the highest testimony to Bentley's style that, with all its indescribable flavour of ease and naturalness, and without any suspect devices making it falsely lurid, sensational, or over-emotional (common faults of this type of fiction), it is effective. After a series of deliberately false trails, acquitted suspects and positive-seeming "solutions", we still read on, restless, eager, interested and alert, until the last page finally exposes the true culprit. A style less clear or strong would have weakened the interest, and the story, long before its remarkable climax. (pp. 28-9)

> *I. L. Baker, in her* E. C. Bentley: "Trent's Last Case," *James Brodie, Ltd., 1956, 54 p.*

A. E. MURCH (essay date 1958)

[*The following excerpt is taken from Murch's* The Development of the Detective Novel, *which provides especially detailed considerations of such early detective writers as Ann Radcliffe, Bulwer-Lytton, and Charles Brockden Brown.*]

Mr. Bentley, a distinguished journalist, at one time on the staff of the *Daily News* and later with the *Daily Telegraph,* has set down in detail how this remarkable first novel [*Trent's Last Case*] came to be written [see excerpt above]. From boyhood he had delighted in Sherlock Holmes, but came to dislike his eccentricities and his 'extreme seriousness.' He disliked even more the seriousness of Holmes's imitators, and thought it ought to be possible to create a detective who was a human being, 'not quite so much the "heavy" sleuth.' Accordingly, he drew up a list of 'things absolutely necessary to an up-to-date detective story,' added 'a crew of regulation suspects,' and decided to introduce two original features, a love interest and the idea of 'making the hero's hard-won and obviously correct solution of the mystery turn out to be completely wrong.' (p. 203)

Trent's Last Case, unlike most detective fiction of the period, gave an important place to character drawing, the creation of credible portraits of human beings with their changing thoughts and emotions. The detective himself is a cultured man of leisure, a successful painter with an analytical habit of mind, who once solved a murder mystery simply by studying newspaper reports of the case, just as Poe had done in the matter of Mary Rogers. When the great financier, Sigsbee Manderson, is found murdered, Trent is called in, unofficially, to find out what he can of the circumstances.

His deductions are at first based upon his observation of detail—footprints in the garden, clothing and other personal possessions of the dead man and his associates—on 'Serendipity,' in fact, with nothing more scientific than a fingerprint or two. He gains further information from studying the individual characteristics of his suspects, their background, hobbies, casual conversation, even the habitual expression of their features. Intuition, which served Father Brown so well, does nothing to help Trent reach his conclusions. It does, however, restrain him from making those conclusions public. Although his perceptive and logical brain has built up what seems a completely water-tight proof, he feels there is something wrong somewhere, as indeed there is. E. C. Bentley had planned *Trent's Last Case* to be 'not so much a detective story as an exposure of detective stories,' and the same note is struck in the closing lines of the novel itself:—

> The Manderson affair shall be Philip Trent's last case. His high-blown pride at length breaks under him. I could have borne everything, but that last revelation of the impotence of human reason.

But this attempt at 'exposure' did no disservice to detective fiction. What Bentley had, in fact, done was to devise a new method of presenting a detective story. He had broken the convention inherited from Poe, that such a tale must move in ordered sequence like a proposition in Euclid, from 'Given' and 'Required to Prove,' to the logical steps that end with Q.E.D. In *Trent's Last Case* the detective's soundly argued conclusions, which normally form the end of such a story, are given when the tale is little more than half told. What he has proved is true, but not the whole truth. He has discovered facts with great cleverness, but is wrong in the construction he places on those facts. Thereafter, veil after veil is lifted by other hands, still leaving veil after veil behind, until the complete surprise that explains the crux of the mystery is sprung on Trent, and on the reader, in the final pages.

Trent's Last Case, a novel written at a period when the short detective story was still the most popular form of the *genre,* brought to fiction of this kind a more spacious atmosphere, time to consider and reconsider the implications of the evidence, and a new literary excellence. It is that rare thing, a detective story that can be read with pleasure even when the secret is known, for the skill with which the puzzle is devised and concealed, and for qualities that are less frequently found in detective fiction, its sensitive study of character and its delightful prose. (pp. 203-04)

> *A. E. Murch, "The Early Twentieth Century," in her* The Development of the Detective Novel *(© A. E. Murch 1958), Philosophical Library, Inc., 1958 (and reprinted by Greenwood Press, Publishers, 1968), pp. 192-217.**

HOWARD HAYCRAFT   (essay date 1963)

[Haycraft, a perceptive and entertaining critic of mystery fiction, is the author of Murder for Pleasure: The Life and Times of the Detective Story *(see Additional Bibliography), an authoritative study of detective fiction. In a later discussion of Bentley, excerpted below, Haycraft praises him for introducing "easy naturalism and quiet humor" into the detective story.]*

Just 50 years ago—as Europe danced on the brink, unaware that an era was coming to an end—a detective novel was published in London and New York that has been credited with changing the whole course of this popular literary form. The title of this epochal work was **"Trent's Last Case."** . . .

Like many another literary landmark, **"Trent"** was not instantly recognized as such. The critics of the day found the book pleasant and competent enough but failed to sense any special significance; fame was to come gradually. Bentley himself seems to have been well aware of what he was doing, or at least attempting.

From **"Trent's"** inception, he revealed in his warmly human autobiography, **"Those Days"** [see excerpt above], the novel was a conscious reaction against the sterility and artificiality into which much of the detection writing of the day had sunk. (It was not, however, written as the result of a wager with Chesterton—contrary to popular legend—although the author had the encouragement of the creator of Father Brown.) "It does not seem to have been noticed," Bentley wrote, "that **'Trent's Last Case'** is not so much a detective story as an exposure of detective stories. . . .It should be possible, I thought, to write a detective story in which the detective was recognizable as a human being."

It would be over-simplification to suggest that **"Trent"**—reread in 1963—is primarily remarkable for its unremarkableness. Yet the qualities constituting Bentley's chief contributions to the genre are his easy naturalism and quiet humor, which we have long since come to take for granted. Closely related to these is his use of character as a means of detection; often imitated, it has rarely been surpassed. That the detective could be at once both brilliantly right and wrong remains one of the novel's achievements; and the ultimate revelation deservedly stands beside Agatha Christie's "Roger Ackroyd," but without that story's element of trickery. . . .

[A] word of caution as to externals is advisable for the reader meeting **"Trent"** for the first time. Though it need not be read as a period piece, the mores of 1913 were simply not those of 1963, and a little of the difference is bound to show in the minutiae and dialogue, for all of Bentley's advanced ideas and technique. It is a trifle startling, for example, to discover that the motorcar was sufficiently rare in 1913 as to require explanation of the "back-reflector" or rear-vision mirror, which plays a key role in the story. But a little patience with such matters on the reader's part will be repaid by a large dividend of pleasure. (p. 18)

"Trent's Last Case" has survived 50 years, two world wars and a cold war. As long as detective stories are read and enjoyed it is assured of a place on the Select Shelf—beside Poe, "The Moonstone" and Sherlock Holmes. (p. 19)

> *Howard Haycraft, "'Trent's Last Case' Reopened," in* The New York Times Book Review *(copyright © 1963 by the New York Times Company; reprinted by permission), December 15, 1963, pp. 18-19.*

JULIAN SYMONS   (essay date 1972)

[Symons's book Mortal Consequences: A History—From the Detective Story to the Crime Novel *traces the development of the detective story from a specialized puzzle story into the crime novel. In the following excerpt from that work Symons discusses Bentley's strengths and weaknesses as a detective novelist.]*

That the line between the comic and the serious in the detective story is a fine one is shown by [*Trent's Last Case*]. . . .(p. 93)

Writing elsewhere about *Trent's Last Case,* I have said that it is difficult now to understand the high regard in which the book was held, and that "the writing seems stiff and characterless, the movement from one surprise to another, and the final shock of revelation, rather artificial." Perhaps it is a sign of the benevolence of age that this judgment now seems too severe. I think it remains true, though, that the book falls into two parts which are not very well connected. It was dedicated to Chesterton, and Bentley shared at this time Chesterton's radical dislike of the rich, and particularly of rich speculators. The opening treats the death of the millionaire Sigsbee Manderson with an almost savage irony, stressing that "to all mankind save a million or two of half-crazed gamblers, blind to all reality, the death of Manderson meant nothing." His epitaph is provided by the editor of the newspaper, who looks at the large broadsheet announcing "Murder of Sigsbee Manderson" and says: "It makes a good bill."

This ironic note recurs occasionally but is not maintained, and Manderson after being introduced with such a flourish becomes more shadowy as the story proceeds. The major part of the book deals with Trent's investigation and his (as it proves erroneous) discovery of what really happened. Much of this is ingenious, although it depends upon some actions that seem very unlikely, like an innocent man's removal of a denture from the dead Manderson's mouth. Of more importance is the fact that the detection wavers uneasily between a desire to treat the whole thing as a joke and Bentley's impulsion to write seriously about the fact that Trent falls in love with the woman whom he supposes to be involved in the murder. There is a similar uncertainty in the treatment of Trent, who, as Bentley said, "is apt to give way to frivolity and the throwing about of absurd quotations from the poets at almost any moment" and yet, since he is the hero, cannot be regarded as a figure of fun. But perhaps this is still pressing too hard on a book that was acclaimed everywhere as something new in detective stories. The other works in which Trent appears, published more than twenty years later, showed only that Bentley was not able to adapt himself to the further development of the form. (pp. 94-5)

Julian Symons, "The Rise of the Novel," in his Mortal Consequences: A History—From the Detective Story to the Crime Novel *(copyright © 1972 by Julian Symons; reprinted by permission of Harper & Row, Publishers, Inc.; in Canada by Curtis Brown Ltd), Harper & Row, 1972, pp. 91-9.**

ERIK ROUTLEY   (essay date 1972)

[*Routley's* The Puritan Pleasures of the Detective Story, *from which the following excerpt is taken, is primarily concerned with English writers in this genre.*]

It was not surprising that the detective story should for the first generation of its life be confined to the short story form. Detection pure and simple would not stand the strain of a three-volume novel. True, there were the two masterpieces of Wilkie Collins, and there was the unfinished *Edwin Drood*, but these have special qualities. . . . These were real novels of character, and once the detective story had taken off on its new course, following a limited form of plot and leaving character to take care of itself, it was just right for publication in full in literary weeklies. A series of self-contained stories bringing back each time a central character but each making its point quickly and decisively was just what would keep the reading public cliff-hanging. Attempts to draw the detective story out to full length were bound to collapse without the skill of the genuine novelist to sustain them. Doyle managed it only once, in *The Hound of the Baskervilles,* and even that is very brief by the standards of the novel of its day. (p. 119)

The breakthrough that opened the road for the full-length detective novel came from an unexpected quarter, when it occurred to E. C. Bentley, a professional man of letters and a friend of Chesterton, to write a full-length detective story which should at the same time show how it could be done and expose the humbug in the older classics. Here is his own account of it:

> Sometime in the year 1910 it occurred to me that it would be a good idea to write a detective story of a new sort. . . . It was not until I had gone a long way with the plot that the most pleasing notion of all came to me: the notion of making the hero's hard-won and obviously correct solution of the mystery turn out to be completely wrong. Why not show up the fallibility of the Holmesian method? . . . In the result, it does not seem to have been generally noticed that *Trent's Last Case* is not so much a detective story as an exposure of detective stories.

By 1940, when Bentley wrote those words [in his autobiography ***Those Days*** (see excerpt above)], reaction and counter-reaction originated by the Holmes orthodoxy had been too frequent for anybody without a keen historical sense to notice the irony of *Trent*. Readers of that age (or this) would also need to be told how new was the idea of introducing a conventional love-interest into a tale of detection (Holmes's 'most dismal groan' disposed of Mary Morstan as 'love-interest'). But this was, eccentric exceptions apart, the first real detective novel. And what a beauty! Its narrative is conducted in perfect and unaffected English, neither casual nor pompous, as befitted a man whose trade in 1910 was writing. It is sufficient measure of its literary craftsmanship that for the sheer pleasure of reading it you miss the irony of its author's intentions (even the *Last* in the title is an irony). (pp. 119-20)

[The] story marked the coming of age of the detective story; it planted the seeds of humanity, humour and irony which were the qualities it needed to deliver the style from stuffiness. The symptoms of coming of age are all connected with the principle of reacting against one's father while remaining one's father's son. What can be changed, the second generation is prompted to change; what is essential, unless things go badly wrong, he is content to retain. Bentley did a very neat job in reacting without gracelessness. He stepped in at exactly the moment when the detective story was due either to degenerate into inbred affectation or to establish a true principle of originality.

He did not complete the job; that would have been too violent. But he did ask whether the amateur detective must necessarily be a celibate superman, and whether situations must needs be macabre, grotesque and in the ancient sense mysterious. Having said 'No', he set his story in as ordinary a situation, and among as ordinary people, as his imagination could contrive. He made his story as like a novel of 1910 as he could make it.

This, not unnaturally, meant that he wrote, not about fantastic people, but about his own kind of people. In the romantic school of detective writers which he here inaugurated it was the custom for authors to set their scenes in a stratum of society just above that in which they themselves moved, and this is a fashion which Bentley set. (In the Holmes stories there is a certain movement towards high society, which is a product of the romantic element in them against which their immediate successors reacted.) By later twentieth-century standards Bentley's characters are not as ordinary as all that. The assumption that people of this sub-aristocratic, articulate, well-provided kind were the people to whom things worth writing about happened was taken over from the nineteenth-century romantics. But little else was. The detective was so little of a superman that he gets the solution wrong and falls in love with the heroine; and the villain is so far from being a villain that he isn't even punished. (There is another villain who, in the kind of story Bentley was reacting against, would have been the murderer.)

Now this is to question, at an early date, the dogma that detection leads either to legal process or to the death by other means of the culprit. This was a sacred dogma: for the detection reading public was a puritan public and its morality did not wish to be made uncomfortable. In other words, the Bentley reaction against the classical pattern was the opposite of Chesterton's. Chesterton and Bentley between them demonstrate the essential mediocrity of the popular puritan ethic of 1900. Chesterton criticises it by going beyond it to the ethic of the common man, which he equates with that of the Church and claims to be universal where the puritan ethic is sectional and ill-adjusted. Bentley appeals from it not to a more universal ethic but to an individual ethic. The murdered man was a swine—anybody can see that. The murderer (who eluded the detective) was a nice fellow—anybody can see that too. Then judge for yourself, says the author; and in saying that he knocks down one wall of the traditional structure, for the traditional structure is partly supported by the axiom that crime is wrong and punishable. Yes, Holmes did it once or twice (in 'The Blue Carbuncle' and, in a matter of killing, in 'The Abbey Grange'), but Bentley does it for a quite different reason. Father Brown would not lift a finger to deliver a guilty man from punishment—but then he would say that a man was marginally better off if he died penitent than if he lived with the memory of a crime, and that is a different world again. Bentley is a liberal who believes that a man need not die for a justifiable murder, the opinion on the justification being his own and that of like-minded men.

Bentley did write other detective stories. The only other full-length one was written twenty-six years later, in collaboration with H. Warner Allen, and called *Trent's Own Case;* it lacks the distinction of the earlier one and respects more orthodoxies. The corpse here is a highly religious person of repellent habits (named as a Congregationalist and stated to have bequeathed a fortune to the London Missionary Society, a body associated with that denomination until 1966). In the end it turns out not to be murder, so everybody is happy. There are also some short stories, collected under the title *Trent Intervenes,* published in between, which are harmless diversions. The plot of one of them, **'The Clever Cockatoo',** collides head-on with one of Dorothy Sayers's, written about the same time, called 'The Incredible Elopement of Lord Peter Wimsey': this is a strange coincidence which suggests that some real-life episode must have given the idea to both authors, but we do not know what that may have been. (pp. 120-22)

The appearance of Trent, anyhow, generated a fairly strong growth of amateur detective characters, of whom the earliest was probably Philip Macdonald's Anthony Gethryn. The milieu was primarily amiable and conventional. The heroes are not eccentric, they are decently well off, they mix in reasonably civilised society, and they bring to the business of detection no special knowledge, but rather a gentlemanly concern for justice and a readiness to do hard work. It is all very sane and stable, provided that the world of decent men stays put. (p. 123)

> *Erik Routley, "'Coming of Age': E. C. Bentley, Freeman Wills Crofts, John Rhode," in his* The Puritan Pleasures of the Detective Story: A Personal Monograph *(© Erik Routley, 1972; reprinted by permission of The Literary Estate of Erik Routley), Victor Gollancz Ltd, 1972, pp. 119-28.**

JACQUES BARZUN AND WENDELL HERTIG TAYLOR   (essay date 1976)

[*Barzun and Taylor—both respected academic scholars—together produced* A Catalogue of Crime, *the most extensive bibliography of crime fiction ever published. The following is taken from their introduction to an edition of* Trent's Last Case.]

[As] a young man full of modernity [E. C. Bentley] could only laugh at the old mystery story, genteel, melodramatic—and no longer mysterious. The new work [*Trent's Last Case*] came into being without a model and had to wait almost a decade before its lesson was followed, by Agatha Christie.

For Philip Trent, the crime, the detection, and the startling consequences of each are no laughing matter, yet it is the twentieth-century spirit of derision that gives life to his personality and movement to the adventure. As anyone can see, the first chapter about the death of Sigsbee Manderson and the "vortices of finance" is pure parody. Sigsbee, as H. Douglas Thomson has remarked [see excerpt above], is *such* a good name for the financier, besides being an additional motive for murder. Bentley's book is thus the cause of wit in others, because Trent is himself a character out of Stevenson's *New Arabian Nights*, with more than a touch of Oscar Wilde's conversationalists in *Pen, Pencil, and Poison*.

In *Trent's Last Case* the situation, too, is modern. If it were not for three or four instances of deep blushing on the part of beautiful Mabel and something of an awestruck attitude toward the motor car, the story could pass for virtually contemporary with our own unblushing and car-questioning period. The passages in which Trent and Mrs. Manderson account to each other for their earlier actions are done with great skill and great freedom and exhibit a degree of introspection one does not generally associate with the detective genre. Nor are these moments of sustained psychology extraneous to the plot. What makes the work a landmark is precisely the combination of accuracy in reasoning from clues and an emotional predicament arising untheatrically from the very course of the investigation.

Add to this rare mixture the subtle use of the "point of view" in detection, the self-depreciatory manner of the artist-sleuth who uses false poetic tags so apropos, the well-bred tone of the prose, and all that remains to speak of is the ultimate twist by which Mr. Cupples is brought back to our notice in an active role at center stage. Is it a legitimate surprise? That question the reader will not easily settle. As with Mona Lisa's smile, it is hard to come to a conclusion and stick to it. But that in turn only encourages going back to the work again and again. (pp. v-vi)

> *Jacques Barzun and Wendell Hertig Taylor, "Preface" (copyright © 1976 by Jacques Barzun and Wendell H. Taylor; reprinted by permission of Jacques Barzun and Wendell Hertig Taylor), in* Trent's Last Case *by E. C. Bentley, Garland Publishing, Inc., 1976, pp. v-vi.*

BARBARA REYNOLDS   (essay date 1977)

[*Reynold's comparison of Bentley's Trent with Dorothy Sayers's sleuth Lord Peter Wimsey testifies to the influence of the work that has been repeatedly called the first modern detective novel.*]

The recent surge of interest in the life and writings of Dorothy L. Sayers has inspired curiosity as to the origin of her famous detective, Lord Peter Wimsey. . . .

There was one work of exceptional vitality which provided a powerful stimulus for the creation of Lord Peter Wimsey: this was *Trent's Last Case* by E. C. Bentley, first published in 1912. In a conversation which I had with Dorothy Sayers in 1956, I said how much I had enjoyed this book. She said in reply, "I am so glad you admire it. You cannot imagine what a revelation it was when it first came out." I said tentatively that there was something about Trent which made me think of Lord Peter and she replied, "Yes, there is, of course, but with a touch of Bertie Wooster as well."

On a recent visit to Wheaton College, Illinois, I came upon a manuscript draft of a talk by Dorothy Sayers entitled *Trent's Last Case.* Intended for broadcasting, it bears no date or evidence of having been delivered. . . . In this brief talk she confirms the impression which Bentley's book first made on her:

> I suppose everybody has at least heard of *Trent's Last Case.* It holds a very special place in the history of detective fiction. If you were so lucky as to read it today for the first time you would recognize it at once as a tale of unusual brilliance and charm, but you could have no idea how startlingly original it seemed when it first

appeared. It shook the little world of the mystery novel like a revolution, and nothing was ever quite the same again. Every detective writer of today owes something, consciously or unconsciously, to its liberating and inspiring influence.

The obvious differences between Philip Trent and Lord Peter Wimsey have distracted attention from their essential similarities. Lord Peter is the son of a duke; Trent is a painter and a journalist, of independent means but not wealth. They bear no physical resemblance whatever.

Yet on closer observation the two men are found to be so like each other as to seem almost blood relations. Indeed, not only the two detectives but most of the other characters as well could stroll casually in and out of each other's novels and feel at home there. It is true that the gap of twenty years which separates them is widened to a chasm by the First World War, which casts its sombre shadows on Lord Peter, a sufferer from recurrent shell-shock and memories of the trenches. The world of Philip Trent was spared that catastrophe, though the threat was always there in *Trent's Last Case:* "Bellona tossed and murmured as ever, yet still slept her uneasy sleep". Bellona is the goddess of war, whose name Dorothy Sayers was to give to an army officers' club where Philip Trent would not seem out of place as a veteran member.

To judge from a footnote in the Wheaton College manuscript, Dorothy Sayers first read *Trent's Last Case* when she was nineteen years of age. Another eight were to pass before she undertook to write a detective novel herself but she forgot nothing in the interval of "the liberating and inspiring influence" of E. C. Bentley.

Sigsbee Manderson, whose death Philip Trent investigates, is an American financier of worldwide influence, "A gambler of genius," in his early years, he rose, by steady labour in his father's banking business, to a position of power whence he could finance "the large designs of State or private enterprise. Many a time when he took hold . . . he sent ruin upon a multitude of tiny homes." Reuben Levy, the victim in Dorothy Sayers's *Whose Body?*, is also a financier, whose disappearance convulses the Stock Exchange. One of his rivals, Mr. John P. Milligan, an American visited by Lord Peter in Lombard Street, "postponed for a few minutes the elimination from the map of a modest but promising farm". The motive of the crime in both novels is sexual jealousy, nursed as a long-standing grudge which in both cases strains the reader's powers of belief. E. C. Bentley from the outset attributes to Manderson a latent urge towards self-destruction; Dorothy Sayers attributes to Sir Julian Freke an objective, physiological view of morality and in addition finds it necessary to bolster credibility by a footnote in which she quotes from the summing up by Mr. Justice Campbell in the Regina *v* Palmer case of 1856.

Both crimes require for their execution immensely elaborate preparations; investigation in both cases involves details of personal habits as to sleeping and dressing, and deviations from these routines arouse the suspicions of both detectives. In both cases there is one item which defies all explanation: Manderson has gone out of the house fully dressed but without his dental plate, a detail recalled by Sir Julian Freke in his written confession; Levy, as Parker relates, has left his spectacles behind, "without which he can't see a step, as he is extremely short-sighted". The close inspection of Manderson's array of footwear and Trent's connoisseurship of good shoe-leather is par-

alleled in *Whose Body?* by Lord Peter's scrutiny of nine of Levy's hats and, in *The Unpleasantness at the Bellona Club*, his examination of General Fentiman's boots.

The technique of revealing figerprints by means of mercury powder and chalk receives almost identical treatment in *Trent's Last Case* and *Whose Body?* The procedure was still relatively new and a simple demonstration was required. . . .

Coming now to the two main figures, Philip Trent and Lord Peter Wimsey, we observe that both irrupt on to the scene with an exclamation of annoyance. "Hallo, be blowed!" is Trent's first utterance. "Oh, damn!" is Wimsey's. Trent is at once shown to be addicted to quoting poetry or amusingly misquoting it:

> "Where are you?" asks Molloy, on the telephone.
>
> "I am blown along a wandering wind", replied the voice irresolutely, "and hollow, hollow, hollow all delight."

Addicts of Lord Peter can hardly fail to recognize the familiar verbal playfulness. And Trent, like Lord Peter, has a habit of whistling softly under his breath at a crucial moment of perception. (They are both in this respect heirs of Wilkie Collins's Sergeant Cuff.)

A direct portrait of Trent occurs at the beginning of the fourth chapter. Good spirits and a lively, humorous fancy have made him generally popular. In his first case, Trent had succeeded by doing

> very much what Poe had done in the case of the murder of Mary Rogers. With nothing but the newspapers to guide him, he drew attention to the significance of certain apparently negligible facts, and ranged the evidence in such a manner as to throw grave suspicion upon a man who had presented himself as a witness.

Lord Peter resembles him in this: "I love trifling circumstances", he exclaims in *Whose Body?*; "so many men have been hanged by trifling circumstances." And his attention to apparently trifling circumstances enables him likewise to throw suspicion upon a man who had presented himself as a witness.

Among Trent's accomplishments is an ability to speak French fluently and idiomatically, as he does to great effect when he quells the impudent remarks of Célestine, Mrs. Manderson's personal maid. Lord Peter, it will be recalled, converses easily in French in *Whose Body?* with a Russian emigrée in Sir Julian Freke's waiting-room, and his skill in this language is displayed in many of the later novels. The short story "The Entertaining Episode of the Article in Question" even turns on his acute perception of an unexpected use of gender.

Approaching what he believes to be the solution of the Manderson mystery, Trent withdraws his confidence from Mr. Cupples, as Lord Peter temporarily withdraws his from Parker in *Whose Body?* This personal reaction on the part of his detective is ingeniously contrived by E. C. Bentley in order not to reveal the solution too soon; Dorothy Sayers adopts the device for the same reason. Like Lord Peter, too, when he has solved the case (as he believes), Trent is visited with a feeling of self-disgust: "I have done with the Manderson mystery and I wish to God I had never touched it."

Explaining the processes of his mind in his dispatch to Sir James Molloy, Trent stresses the importance of what he calls the "key-fact in any system of baffling circumstances", round which "one's ideas seem to rush to group themselves anew". In the mystery under investigation, the key fact was the possibility that someone had masqueraded as Manderson. . . . Wimsey arrives at the solution of the Levy mystery in an almost identical way. . . .

It was years later that Dorothy Sayers wrote of E. C. Bentley's "liberating and inspiring influence". Liberating from what? From the

> infallible sleuth, with his cut-and-dried clues and cast-iron deductions, [who] plodded mechanically along the trail, always wearisome and always right. . . . The old stock characters were gone, and in their place were real people, Trent the journalist, Marlowe, Bunner, old Mr Cupples and (still more astonishingly) Mrs Manderson, the heroine—all breathing and moving with abounding vitality. . . . There was the amazing, the enthralling novelty. . . . And even the love-story, so often a weak disaster, is, in this masterly book, made moving, credible and integral to the plot.

Thus she recalls the startling originality of the work after which, in the world of the mystery novel, "nothing was ever quite the same again".

Lord Peter's style and method as a detective are strikingly similar to Philip Trent's. It remains to be shown that he resembles him also as a man and a lover. Trent, who has fallen in love with Mrs Manderson, but believes her to be involved in Marlowe's guilt, withdraws from the scene and seeks oblivion as a foreign correspondent: "He saw burnings, lynchings, fusillades, hangings; each day his soul sickened afresh at the imbecilities born of misrule." Lord Peter, sent abroad by the Foreign Office in *Gaudy Night*, confesses to Harriet Vane the sickness of soul he too experiences at all the touch-and-go dangers of international relations. . . .

Trent's passion for Mrs Manderson has come upon him suddenly, not of his seeking. He is taken by surprise by "the insane suddenness of its uprising in full strength and its extravagant hopelessness". Lord Peter, married to Harriet Vane, reflects on the chaos of his personal emotions: "He was filled with a curious misgiving, as though he had meddled in matters too high for him." When the crisis comes, Trent is revealed as no less exuberant and disarming in his wooing than he is in his detection. His declaration of love is eloquent and romantic, but Lord Peter is restricted by his creator to less impassioned appeals until in the last novel, *Busman's Honeymoon*, she unseals "the fountain of delight". Here he is "the lunatic, the lover and the poet", as Harriet calls him, though still with the characteristic touch of self-mockery which he inherits from Trent. . . .

Echoes of *Trent's Last Case* are to be heard in all the Peter Wimsey novels, from the first to the last. They are quite deliberate and unconcealed; it is as though Dorothy Sayers found delight in acknowledging her debt. Anyone who has taken pleasure in E. C. Bentley's book will find that pleasure doubled by the continuing life it enjoys in its successors.

> *Barbara Reynolds, "The Origin of Lord Peter Wimsey" (a revision of a lecture given to the Dorothy L. Sayers Historical and Literary Society in November, 1976), in* The Times Literary Supplement *(© Times Newspapers Ltd. (London) 1977; reproduced from* The Times Literary Supplement *by permission), No. 3919, April 22, 1977, p. 492.*

LEROY PANEK (essay date 1979)

> [*Panek's* Watteau's Shepherd's, *from which the chapter on Bentley has been excerpted, is an examination of the detective story as a literary form as opposed to popular entertainment.*]

Trent's Last Case suited so many readers and writers between the wars because it is a blend of the serious and the comic: Bentley ridicules and appreciates, parodies and imitates. And his principal material is the traditions of the detective story from Poe to Collins to Conan Doyle.

Before coming to *Trent's Last Case,* we need to be aware of what had happened to the detective story when Bentley came upon it. After Conan Doyle's Juggernaut got under way in the 1890's, a number of writers began to create characters and plots exploiting the separate parts of what Eliot calls Holmes' manifold "abilities, accomplishments and peculiarities." The characters of Sexton Blake, Nayland-Smith and others capitalized on the adventure potential in the Holmes stories; Drs. Thorndyke and Craig Kennedy followed up on the scientific potential latent in Holmes; Max Carrados and The Old Man in the Corner developed as eccentric detectives following the pattern set by Conan Doyle. As Raffles might have said, they were *post Holmes ergo propter Holmes*. All of these characters were created in businesslike imitation or serious reaction to the Great Detective in hopes of capturing or sharing some of Conan Doyle's success with the public. Simultaneously, a number of writers, including Mark Twain, realized the unreality, absurdity, and pure comic potential of the "Great Detective." Thus in the early 1900's we get a whole list of comic detectives with names like Herlock Sholmes, Hemlock Shears, Picklock Holes, Shylock Homes, Shamrock Jolnes, Sherlaw Kombs, etc. These detectives appear in stories which were outright comic reductions of Conan Doyle's detective. One only has to look into Mark Twain's "Double-barreled Detective Story" (1902) to get the jist of the full-bodied burlesque of the infallible, unflappable, universally accomplished detective.

What Bentley did when he composed *Trent's Last Case* was to combine both of these reactions to Holmes, the serious and the comic, in a single book which blends parody with imitation and thus satisfies the demands of the intelligent reader who, to relieve his boredom, would like to read detective stories but is put off by their pomposity or embarrassed by their naivete. To this end he shapes the dialogue, the characters, and the plot of *Trent's Last Case.*

In the opening sections of the novel, Bentley presents his detective hero as a man of demonstrated competence but also as a comic character (in the early portions of the novel, in fact, most of the characters and events have a light tone). As the text introduces him to the reader, Philip Trent has all of the qualifications of the renaissance man and, in the context of the detective story, the Great Detective. He became involved in criminology "very much [as] . . . Poe" did by acting as the armchair detective, analyzing newspaper accounts of a crime and finding the solution which the others had missed. As a consequence of this, a newspaper baron made him a special correspondent for crime and he has a remarkable history of success. Not that he does it for the money, mind you, for Trent is a young man of independent means who directs his major energies toward his chosen profession, painting. So far, so good; Trent could have been any of the contemporaries of Sherlock Holmes. Bentley does provide a quick laugh for middle class readers by pointing out that Trent not only paints but also sells his pictures. The real shock, however, comes upon Trent's first entrance. He enters with cap and bells, prattling a language full of burlesque literary allusion and self-conscious parody. Take this example of Trent's speech to Mr. Cupples:

> I should prefer to put it that I have come down in the character of the avenger of blood, to hunt down the guilty, and vindicate the honour of society. That is my line of business. Families waited on at their private residences.

Most of this passage could have come straight out of the thriller with the speaker righteously stating his moral position. The inclusion of the advertisement in the last line, however, overthrows this and gives the reader the signal that the whole passage is facetious.

Trent's persiflage is simply part of his character early in the novel. He is an intelligent young man to whom everything comes easily, who skips through problems and plays at those things at which others must work. This is apparent in his first conversation with his publisher, Sir James Molloy:

> "Trent," said Sir James impressively, "it is important. I want you to do some work for us."
>
> "Some play, you mean."

Precisely the same issue arises when Trent meets the Scotland Yard drudge. . . . His language is simply part of Trent's overall attitude toward himself and toward life.

The whole business of making your hero blithely talk nonsense plays an important part in the detective novel after the First World War, what with Wimsey and Campion as well as the wise-cracking hero of the thriller (especially Simon Templar) and the American hard-boiled story. Part of the impetus of this, of course, comes from writers' attempts to capture current slang in order to build contemporary characters. Then, also, there is the impression of ease and nonchalance when a character under stress can be witty and facetious. Bentley knew this last point because he must have read it in one of friend Chesterton's earliest works, *The Defendant* (1901) in which G.K.C. describes the detective story as a romance and the hero as the "knight errant" who stands

> . . . somewhat fatuously fearless amid the knives and fists of a thieves' kitchen.

Fatuous, but purposely fatuous, is a good way in which to describe Trent early in the novel, and Bentley purposely builds up both his fatuous frivolity and his over-confidence in order to reverse them in the end. One can, in fact, graph the major reversal in the plot by tracking the changes in Trent's speech. The novel closes with his sophisticated poses removed and his nonchalance bridled. At the end he is the Great Detective no more and this is his last case.

Bentley cuts Trent down to human size through two major turns in the plot. The first, and the most famous, shock to Trent's character as the Great Detective comes from the demonstration that his finely wrought analysis of the crime was built on false assumptions and is, therefore, demonstrably wrong. One can hardly go on as the perfect thinking machine after one has produced a faulty product. But before Trent discovers that he is wrong, he falls in love and as a result of the apparent

impossibility of his passion he travels to the continent. In a chapter entitled "Evil Days" Trent suffers from his hopeless love, but he also enters the real world of violence and bloodshed. . . . Playing detective and mouthing witty blather in the idyllic puppet theater makes no sense when compared with man's inhumanity to man. Human misery is something which cannot be punned away or even shut out of the consciousness once it has taken root. The next generation of detective story writers would slowly learn this for themselves, but Bentley knew it in the teens. That is, he knew about the implications of real violence for the detective story. He did not, however, impress this on the form itself, for whatever may happen to Trent's consciousness in the middle of the novel, it does not cloud the end of the story, and the plot remains, in many ways an excellent demonstration of what the Golden Age detective novel should be.

Before *Trent's Last Case* the detective story was written principally as the short story, and this has certain consequences for the writer's purpose. In the detective short story the writer simply does not have the time or space to do more than establish the facts of the problem, render the confusion which it causes in most characters, and expound the solution through the detective hero. In short stories from Poe through Freeman the chief reaction expected in the reader is either confusion or wonder, or both. The novel, on the other hand, provides an opportunity to toy with the reader's reactions. Collins, for instance, sets in motion several lines of false conjecture for the reader to follow (did Rosanna Spearman or Rachael or the Indians steal the Moonstone?) only to undercut them all with the revelations about Franklin Blake's complicity and the guilt of an unsuspected individual. Reversal of expectations lies at the center of *The Moonstone*—and at the heart of *Trent's Last Case* as well. In Bentley's memoir, *Those Days* [see excerpt above] . . . , he writes a rambling and somewhat self-congratulatory chapter on the composition of *Trent's Last Case*. Here he reveals that during the composition of the novel he decided that it would be amusing if Trent's meticulous deductions turned out to be completely wrong. The novel, of course, does exactly this and it reverses our expectations about the detective story in which the hero never fails. On one hand, *Trent's Last Case* defeats readers' expectations about the hero, but on the other hand it confirms them about the detective story through the workings of the plot. The plot confirms our preconceived notion that the detective story will unravel the true facts about the commission of the crime that started the whole business off. Bentley has it both ways.

Trent's Last Case runs on the major reversals in Trent's character, but these are only part of a whole complex of reversals which pervade the plot of the novel. Bentley turns many things upside down during the course of the story and listing all of them would spoil the anticipation; a list of a few of the reversals will show their number and variety:

> 1. In the opening remarks about Sigsbee Manderson, it seems as if he will become a wild speculator on Wall Street and an uncontrolled gambler, but instead he turns into a disciplined financier.
>
> 2. The public believes that Manderson is a stabilizing force in an insecure market, but it is not Manderson but Jeffrey who is holding up the market.
>
> 3. Jeffrey should be safe and successful from his heroic saving of everyone else's bacon, but he fails.

4. Manderson's death should create a crash of epic proportions, but it does not. There is no crash.

5. We expect some moral comment on Manderson's death (*sic transit,* and all that), but Bentley only shows Sir James Molloy gloating over the fact that he can turn it to his own financial advantage. . . .

And there are more reversals than these. Bentley springs surprises at the beginning, middle and end of the novel; it is the principle upon which the book works.

Seeing all of this one can hardly say that Bentley intended to "play fair." Neither this nor about ninety percent of the novels written from 1920 to 1940 intends to take the readers into the writer's confidence and let them solve the crime. If there is anything in the traditional identification of the reader with the hero, then Bentley intends to befuddle, confuse, dupe and surprise. One simply cannot figure out the solution to the crime in *Trent's Last Case* before it is given at the end. Naturally, the whole thing makes some sense after Bentley unwraps the conclusion, but as the narrative unfolds, there are quirks and gaps which make pre-solution based on inductive or deductive logic impossible. For one thing, the story rests on a culprit who does not have a trace of a guilty conscience and who, after the murder, does not think about it at all. . . . Therefore, although Bentley gives us a glimpse into the murderer's consciousness, it does not help us in gaining a solution of the crime—a device which Christie would later make famous in the twenties. Further, Bentley omits a great deal of important material from the first part of the plot and saves it for the summary. A small instance of this comes when Trent fires off a telegram about Marlowe and its contents are withheld. Another, and more important fact that Bentley omits is that Manderson's body has been moved. The moved body is a technique, like disguise, which would be liberally used by writers in the twenties and thirties, and which is ideal for the detective writer's purposes since it means that the murder could have been committed somewhere, anywhere, else, by someone, anyone, other than the chief suspect. It also means that the writer can either mock the use of physical evidence or use the technique of the moved body to shoehorn in even more physical evidence. At any rate, Bentley does not intend to "play fair," he intends to confuse his readers and surprise them with the grand turnabout. The plot, the characters, and much of the effect of *Trent's Last Case* depend on the reversal.

When Bentley began *Trent's Last Case,* the detective story was just that, the detective short story. . . . There had been, however, one well constructed detective novel—Wilkie Collins' *The Moonstone.* When Century accepted Bentley's novel for publication they made him change the hero's name to Trent, and they changed the book's title to *The Woman in Black.* This title is not only more romantic but it may have also been the publisher's play on the title of Collins' first novel, *The Woman in White*—if it was not it should have been, for there is a lot of Collins in *Trent's Last Case.* From one perspective, Bentley's book is simply a remake of *The Moonstone.* Consider the story of *The Moonstone.* The hero, Franklin Blake, who is among other things, a painter, gives up his investigations into the loss of the diamond because of a romantic snub. He lounges about the continent without enthusiasm, returns to England, confronts the woman he loves, and takes up the investigation again. He gathers more facts but cannot solve the theft without the intervention of Ezra Jennings. Now consider the story of

Trent's Last Case. The hero, Trent, who is, among other things, a painter, gives up his investigation into Manderson's death because of his romantic attachment to Mabel Manderson. He travels around the continent, returns to England, confronts the woman he loves, and takes up the investigation again. He gathers more facts (chiefly from Marlowe), but is unable to solve the mystery without the intervention of Mr. Cupples who unravels the whole mystery. Pretty similar. There are some other details too: the Indians in Collins become the hypothetical union thugs lurking about to exact revenge upon Manderson for his shoddy practices in America, and the melancholy Mabel standing on the cliffs reminds one of Rosanna Spearman contemplating the quicksand. From the historical view point, all of this makes sense. Bentley carries the tradition of Collins to a new generation of writers in the twenties and the thirties, and he streamlines the tradition too: he cuts down on the sentiment (which later writers would completely kill off only to rejuvenate), brushes up the character of the hero, and crystallizes the playful manipulation of the reader's expectations.

It is in this last respect, the playful manipulation of the reader's expectations, that Bentley fathers the writers of the Golden Age. Upon opening *Trent's Last Case* one immediately experiences a tone which is aloof, wry, and playful. The opening chapters on Manderson flicker back and forth between objective reportage and gagged satiric laughter, and, although we descend into sentiment in the middle of the novel, the twinkle comes back at the end. Through all of this the book works in the unique roller coaster third person point of view which would become the standard in the twenties, now dipping into characters' minds, now presenting dialogue, now showing facts, now excluding them or covering them up. If one has the patience and knows where to look, *Trent's Last Case* is, indeed, the bible of the detective writer's craft. (pp. 29-37)

LeRoy Panek, "E. C. Bentley," in his Watteau's Shepherds: The Detective Novel in Britain, 1914-1940 *(copyright © 1979 by Bowling Green University Popular Press), Bowling Green University Popular Press, 1979, pp. 29-37.*

GAVIN EWART   (essay date 1981)

[*Ewart is an English writer of satirical and humorous poetry.*]

First written for fun, as a relaxation from school work, Bentley's clerihews were . . . [published] under the pseudonym of E. Clerihew (his mother's maiden name and his own second name). Bentley wrote, in *Those Days,* that they 'had never a popular success': he also wrote: 'I never heard who started the practice of referring to this literary form—if that is the word—as a Clerihew; but it began early, and the name stuck.' Clerihews were written, apparently, by James Elroy Flecker and by Charles Scott-Moncrieff. Like the lost plays of Euripides, these seem to have vanished. (pp. xi-xii)

The clerihew could easily be used for satire, and even satire of great bitterness, but as far as I know it never has been. The element of absurdity was there from the first (Sir Humphry Davy), along with the challenge of names that were hard to rhyme, and it belongs to the clerihew—just as jollity, scurrility and sexiness belong to the classical limerick. It's mainly a question of tone, and the tone of the clerihew is both civilised and dotty.

On page 79 of Frances Stillman's extremely comprehensive and useful transatlantic work of reference, *The Poet's Manual and Rhyming Dictionary* . . . , there is the following definition of the clerihew:

> The clerihew is named in honor of its inventor, Edmund Clerihew Bentley. It is a humorous pseudo-biographical quatrain, rhymed as two couplets, with lines of uneven length more or less in the rhythm of prose. It is short and pithy, and often contains or implies a moral reflection of some kind. The name of the individual who is the subject of the quatrain usually supplies the first line. . . .

This is a sound definition, except that the 'moral reflection' is often entirely absent in Bentley's pieces. Ms. Stillman's own example makes clear another interesting fact about the form. Nobody much except Bentley has ever written really good clerihews. Even W. H. Auden's *Academic Graffiti* are not satisfactory; in fact they are the least effective poems he wrote. . . . [It] is sad stuff for a major poet. A few are up to the highest Bentley standards, but not many. . . . Anachronism is at the heart of a good many of Bentley's, and Auden has this too; Thackeray is rhymed with daiquiri, for example.

Although the word 'clerihew' has passed into the language, it would still be only a fairly literary kind of person who would know what the word meant. Until quite recently, even in the best dictionaries, there was no entry between 'clerify' and 'clerisy'. Definitions of the word 'limerick', on the other hand and naturally enough, have been offered for a long time.

From the very beginning, even in their early days, clerihews were known to the literate; and now, particularly to the editors of anthologies of light verse, the form is a well-known one. In the American William Cole's *The Fireside Book of Humorous Poetry* . . .—to give only one example—there is a section entitled 'The Soul of Wit', described as 'an omnium-gatherum of clerihews, epigrams and other pithy pieces'. One can see at once (as the mammoth is the ancestor of the modern elephant) how Blake's epigram on Sir Joshua Reynolds is the true ancestor of the clerihew:

> When Sir Joshua Reynolds died
> All Nature was degraded;
> The King dropped a tear into the Queen's ear,
> And all his pictures faded.

This has the right element of fantasy, though it is not mild. Blake means what he says—or implies—that Reynolds was a successful fraud. The metre, though, has something in common with that of the limerick. It is still a rhyming epigram and not a clerihew. (pp. xiii-xv)

Clerihews go on being written. . . . In December 1980 the Weekend Competition in the *New Statesman* invited clerihews on existing newspapers and magazines; and in 1981 the *Sunday Times* ran a clerihew competition. Bentley's work is a perpetual challenge. Good clerihews have been written since his day; but the inspired lighthearted silliness and unlikeliness of the originals are not easily come by. (pp. xviii-xix)

Gavin Ewart, "Introduction" (introduction © Gavin Ewart 1981; reprinted by permission of Oxford University Press), in The Complete Clerihews of E. Clerihew Bentley *by E. C. Bentley, Oxford University Press, Oxford, 1981, pp. ix-xix.*

ISRAEL SHENKER   (essay date 1983)

[*Shenker provides a brief comic discussion of the origin of clerihews.*]

The year is 1891, the place is St. Paul's School in London, the daydreamer is Edmund Clerihew Bentley, age sixteen. As he studies Caesar, his eyes glaze. But let him put it in his own words, as he did years later: "By some association of ideas, the process of which I am unable now to recall, there drifted across my mind—like a rosy sunset cloud softening the white majesty of the Himalaya—the valiant figure of Sir Humphrey Davy. The pen was in my hand. Musing, I hardly knew what it was tracing on the page. Then, with a start, I saw that I had written:

> Sir Humphrey Davy
> Detested gravy.
> He lived in the odium
> Of having discovered sodium."

This truant writing, even with Humphry misspelled, was the trace that launched a thousand quips—a new form of poetry to be ennobled in the verse kingdom alongside such peers of the realm as the Spenserian sonnet, the Pindaric ode, and the robust dithyramb. Not suspecting the fame that was to attend his creation, to say nothing of the gnashing of teeth and groans heartfelt that the rhymes would inspire, Bentley noodled on. Innocent of purpose, disdainful of rank, he composed additional tributes. For example:

> Sir Christopher Wren
> Said, "I am going to dine
>   with some men.
> If anybody calls
> Say I am designing St. Paul's."

Fellow-students, including the subsequently illustrious author G. K. Chesterton, look over Bentley's shoulder and wrote their own verses. "Nothing quite so preposterous had occupied our attention before." . . .

When, in 1905, he summoned the old poetic biographies from memory and published a collection entitled **"Biography for Beginners,"** the reticent Bentley truncated the author's name to E. Clerihew. (Clerihew was his mother's maiden name.) He explained:

> I am not without a claim
> To the use of that honourable name,
> Which those who happened to be listening
> Heard bestowed on me at my christening.

He published three more collections, and was confident that they found their way "into the hands of connoisseurs of idiocy everywhere." To wit:

> George the Third
> Ought never to have occurred.
> One can only wonder
> At so grotesque a blunder. . . .

The form may have been outrageous; it was also contagious. British weeklies set their readers to composing what became known as clerihews, and the muse called many to the trial. . . . (p. 148)

In 1971, W. H. Auden filled a volume—"Academic Graffiti"—with his contributions to the genre. . . . There were probably other reasons that Auden never won the Nobel Prize in Literature, since clerihews were eminently respectable, not to say immortal. Chesterton wrote of the "severe and stately form of free verse known as the Clerihew," and the Oxford lords of language included "clerihew" in A Supplement to the Oxford English Dictionary, defining it as "a short comic or nonsensical verse, professedly biographical, of two couplets differing in length.'' In 1981, Oxford University Press published **"The Complete Clerihews of E. Clerihew Bentley,"** describing the poems as ''inconsequential, usually historical, often anachronistic, always biographical . . . benignly satirical and absurdly amusing.'' (p. 151)

> *Israel Shenker, ''Clerihews'' (© 1983 by Israel Shenker), in* The New Yorker, *Vol. LIX, No. 10, April 25, 1983, pp. 148, 151-52.*

ADDITIONAL BIBLIOGRAPHY

Haycraft, Howard. ''England: 1918-1930 (The Golden Age).'' In his *Murder for Pleasure: The Life and Times of the Detective Story*, pp. 112-158. New York: D. Appleton-Century Co., 1941.*

Describes *Trent's Last Case* as the first modern detective story. *Murder for Pleasure* is a classic critical study of the detective story.

Milne, A. A. ''Books and Writers.'' *The Spectator* 184, No. 6366 (30 June 1950): 893.*

Review of Bentley's last novel, *Elephant's Work: An Enigma*.

''A Review of *The Woman in Black*.'' *The Nation* XCVI, No. 2493 (l0 April 1913): 36l.

Praises not only the plot of *The Woman in Black*, but also the felicitous manner in which Bentley used American slang.

Partridge, Ralph. ''The Murder of Nicholas Blake.'' *The New Statesman and Nation* n.s. XI, No. 274 (23 May 1936): 807-08.*

Review of *Trent's Own Case*.

''The Return of Philip Trent.'' *The Times Literary Supplement*, No. 1903 (23 July 1938): 495.

Review of *Trent Intervenes*.

Vicente Blasco Ibáñez

1867-1928

Spanish novelist, short story and novella writer, essayist, and dramatist.

Blasco Ibáñez is the most widely translated and frequently read Spanish novelist after Miguel de Cervantes. He attained his greatest popularity when successful film versions were made of his novels *Sangre y arena (Blood and Sand)* and *Los cuatro jinetes del apocalipsis (The Four Horsemen of the Apocalypse)*. His critical reputation, however, rests upon his earliest novels, which incorporated the literary Naturalism exemplified by Émile Zola into the tradition of the Spanish regional novel.

Blasco Ibáñez was born in the port city of Valencia, which he later vividly recreated in such novels as *Arroz y tartana (The Three Roses)*, *Flor de mayo (The Mayflower)*, *La barraca (The Cabin)*, and *Cañas y barro (Reeds and Mud)*. At sixteen Blasco Ibáñez ran away from home and went to Madrid, where he worked as secretary and as one of the many ghost writers employed by the aging popular novelist Manuel Fernández y González. From Fernández y González, Blasco Ibáñez learned many writing techniques that he retained throughout his career. In particular, he mastered the forceful descriptions of people and places which remain the most widely praised characteristics of his fiction; unfortunately, he also learned the hurried manner of composition that many critics believe is the greatest weakness of his work. Throughout his life Blasco Ibáñez's flamboyant personality competed for public attention with his novels. He was arrested many times, usually for insurrection, sedition, or high treason, and went into voluntary exile several times after clashes with the Spanish political power structure; he fought duels, was elected seven times as the Valencian representative to the *cortes,* the Spanish parliament, and in middle life spent several years in the Argentinean interior attempting to establish a colony. Blasco Ibáñez attained great wealth, largely through the motion picture versions of his novels, and travelled throughout the world. He died and was buried in France, although five years later he was ceremoniously reinterred in his home city of Valencia.

Most critics group Blasco Ibáñez's novels into three periods, though they may differ when naming the specific work which heralds the beginning of each new period. Virtually all agree, however, that Blasco Ibáñez's early regionalistic novels, in which he vividly portrayed the lives of Valencian farmers, fishermen, and peasants, are his finest works. *The Cabin* and *Reeds and Mud* are often considered his best Valencian novels. These portray, with sometimes harsh realism, details of the everyday life of the common Valencian citizen, and led critics to bestow upon Blasco Ibáñez the sobriquet "the Spanish Zola." The novels of Blasco Ibáñez's second period are informed by his increasingly active social and political awareness. *La catedrál (The Shadow of the Cathedral)* and *El intruso (The Intruder)* are considered the best of this period. In these works, Blasco Ibáñez's iconoclastic ideology began to overshadow the elemental characterization and swiftly moving, tragic plots, which were much-praised elements of the earlier regional novels. While many critics disagree about the classification of Blasco Ibáñez's final novels, many concur with Havelock Ellis, who finds in *La maja desnuda (Woman Triumphant)* and sub-

sequent novels a higher level of psychological and analytical development than previously found in the author's fiction. However, critics believe that, following the successful film versions of *Blood and Sand* and *The Four Horsemen of the Apocalypse*, Blasco Ibáñez's fiction became sensationalistic and was in fact aimed at the Hollywood film industry. Several historical novels were written during this final period, including *El papa del mar (The Pope of the Sea)* and *A los pies de Venus (The Borgias; or, At the Feet of Venus);* all are generally dismissed by critics as awkwardly contrived works which attempt to incorporate history into the plots of insipid love stories. Throughout his career Blasco Ibáñez produced several volumes of short stories, including *Cuentos valencianos* and *Luna Benamor*. Critics agree that the best of these stories are those that feature the regionalism of the early novels.

Blasco Ibáñez has been characterized as an author who is more widely known and read outside of his native country than within it. Only his early Valencian novels are highly regarded in Spain. The socially and politically motivated novels of his second literary period, and the psychologically oriented novels of his third literary phase, translated into many European languages almost as soon as they appeared in Spanish, were for the most part regarded by Spanish critics as journalistic fiction intended primarily for exportation to a foreign reading public, and not as serious literary works. It is generally theorized that when Blasco Ibáñez ceased to write about Valencia and sought more cosmopolitan settings for his novels, he lacked interest in the unfamiliar milieu and the result was stock war fiction or romance. However, in his early regional works, Blasco Ibáñez immortalized turn-of-the-century Valencia and its inhabitants. These novels are still considered among the finest local color fiction ever written.

PRINCIPAL WORKS

Arroz y tartana   (novel)   1894
   [*The Three Roses*, 1932]
El juez   (drama)   1894
Flor de mayo   (novel)   1895
   [*The Mayflower*, 1921]
Cuentos valencianos   (short stories)   1896
La barraca   (novel)   1898
   [*The Cabin*, 1917]
Entre naranjos   (novel)   1900
   [*The Torrent*, 1921]
Sónnica la cortesana   (novel)   1901
   [*Sonnica*, 1912]
Cañas y barro   (novel)   1902
   [*Reeds and Mud*, 1928]
La catedrál   (novel)   1903
   [*The Shadow of the Cathedral*, 1909]
El intruso   (novel)   1904
   [*The Intruder*, 1928]
La bodega   (novel)   1905
   [*La bodega (The Fruit of the Vine)*, 1919]
La horda   (novel)   1905
   [*The Mob*, 1927]
La maja desnuda   (novel)   1906
   [*Woman Triumphant*, 1920]
Sangre y arena   (novel)   1908
   [*The Blood of the Arena*, 1911; also published as *Blood and Sand*, 1919]
Luna Benamor   (novella and short stories)   1909
   [*Luna Benamor*, 1919]
Los muertos mandan   (novel)   1909
   [*The Dead Command*, 1919]
Argentina y sus grandezas   (essays)   1910
Los argonautas   (novel)   1914
Los cuatro jinetes del apocalipsis   (novel)   1916
   [*The Four Horsemen of the Apocalypse*, 1918]
Mare nostrum   (novel)   1918
   [*Mare Nostrum*, 1919]
Los enemigos de la mujer   (novel)   1919
   [*The Enemies of Women*, 1920]
El militarismo mejicano   (essays)   1921
La tierra de todos   (novel)   1922
   [*The Temptress*, 1923]
La reina Calafia   (novel)   1923
   [*Queen Calafia*, 1924]
La vuelta al mundo de un novelista. 3 vols.   (travel essays) 1923
   [*A Novelist's Tour of the World*, 1926]
Alfonso XIII desenmascarado   (essay)   1924
   [*Alfonso XIII Unmasked: The Military Terror in Spain*, 1924]
The Old Woman of the Movies, and Other Stories   (short stories)   1925
El papa del mar   (novel)   1925
   [*The Pope of the Sea*, 1927]

A los pies de Venus   (novel)   1926
   [*The Borgias; or, At the Feet of Venus*, 1930]
Novelas de amor y de muerte   (short stories)   1927
En busca del Gran Kan   (novel)   1929
El caballero de la Virgen   (novel)   1929
   [*The Knight of the Virgin*, 1930]
Obras completas. 36 vols.   (novels, short stories, novellas, essays, and drama)   1946

R. H. KENISTON   (essay date 1908)

[*In this early overview Keniston divides Blasco Ibáñez's novels, as do most critics, into three distinct phases: the early regional works, of which* The Cabin *is the best known; the novels which serve primarily as a framework for Blasco Ibáñez's bombastic social protest, including* The Shadow of the Cathedral, The Intruder, *and* La bodega; *and a third period, which Kenniston characterizes as a return to the earlier regional themes, including* The Mob, Woman Triumphant, *and* Blood and Sand. *Most other critics, while concurring with a division of Blasco Ibáñez's career into three periods, do not see in the third phase a return to an earlier style, but a further development of Blasco Ibáñez's skills as a novelist. For a similar discussion of these three phases of Blasco Ibáñez's work, see the essay by Havelock Ellis excerpted below.*]

So much has been written of the awakening of Spain in the last decade, that many persons think of the Spanish nation as already well started on the high-road to religious freedom and prosperity. But as keen an observer as Havelock Ellis finds the typical Spaniard still buried in self-contented indifference, or, at best, but turning in the first restless movement before the dawn. With the exception of Catalonia, whose active, progressive people are abreast of the other nations of Europe in arts, manufactures, and political ideals, the only general evidence of a reaction against the past has thus far been literary—a suggestion of the France of Voltaire, Diderot, and Rousseau in the eighteenth century. . . . With the best writers of the old school cultivating the stage as the medium through which to propagate their theories, there has come into prominence a new group of novelists, less competent as artists, to be sure, but inspired with a more virile craving for progress, a more violent spirit of protest against the torpor of Spain. This intense reaction against the Church, a priest-ridden royalty, and the general somnolence of the people, ignorant and indifferent, is the haunting characteristic of the apostle of this new movement, Vicente Blasco Ibáñez. . . .

The scene of Sr. Ibáñez's early novels is laid in Valencia and the surrounding district. Between 1894 and 1902 he produced six novels and two volumes of short stories, which present a panorama of the life and customs of the region, portrayed with rare insight and intense sympathy. The main theme of all the work of this period is the conflict between the individual and a society deep-rooted in the cruel, selfish prejudices of the past. The best work of this group, **"La Barraca" (The Farmhouse),** is a picture of the life in the *huerta*—the market-garden district outside of Valencia—and the persecution of an honest farmer and his family by his neighbors, who harbor the tradition that the land of which he has become the tenant shall never be cultivated. . . . In marked contrast to these studies of modern perversity stands **"Sónnica la Cortesana,"** a romance of the siege and fall f Saguntum, in which Hannibal appears as one of the characters. From the misery of to-day we are transported into the sumptuous gardens of the Greek courtesan; we live in an exuberant, sensuous atmosphere of youth and beauty; the air is vibrant with a sturdy patriotism.

With his election to the Cortes, Sr. Ibáñez left the novel of manners and in the next three years produced three works—**"La Catedral," "El Intruso,"** and **"La Bodega" (The Saloon)**. . . . [The] plots of the books serve merely as a framework in which to carry his propaganda. Through the long harangues of his anarchistic heroes, Gabriel Luna, Salvatierra, and the doctor, Don Luis, he attacks mercilessly the Church, the Jesuits, and the drunkenness of Spain. Behind these specific objects of his animadversion, lurks the real enemy; it is the people who are to blame; their ignorance and self-seeking are the sources of their subjection and suffering. This, indeed, is the fundamental teaching of all of his novels. (p. 622)

His later works have shown a return to his earlier style. **"La Horda" (The Rabble)** is a picture of the sordid life of the refuse collectors in the suburbs of Madrid, a subject already treated by Pio Baroja in **"La Busca." "La Maja Desnuda"** (from Goya's well known picture), . . . is easily his most artistic production, and fittingly, for it is at once an acute psychological study of the conflict between the artistic temperament and human love and a critique of Spanish art in which Goya's realism is extolled. The last of his novels **"Sangre y Arena" (Blood and Sand)** is a scathing criticism of the bull-fight, "that survivor of the *auto-da-fe*." Despite the vigor of its inspiration, it is distinctly inferior to his previous work.

Blasco Ibáñez is preëminently a preacher of reform. Social justice is his ideal. If we lend him a willing ear, it is in large measure due to his splendid manliness. . . . However little sympathy we may have with his materialism, however Utopian his dreams may be, we cannot but admire and respect him as a man. As an artist he is less deserving of praise. His enthusiastic devotion to Zola and naturalism—a moribund *genre* which has found several tardy adherents in Spain, among them Sra. Bazán and Sr. Valdés—too often leads him into violation of the highest standards of art. He is carried away by his exuberant fancy. But he has an extraordinary insight into life and the human heart; his characters move like men and not like puppets, and his plots, when they are not meant to serve as backgrounds, move with climactic interest. In his style certain characteristics will be obvious even to one who is not a thorough master of the tongue. Leaving aside the question of his Gallicisms and bad grammar, with which he is charged by his Spanish critics, his wonderful force and visualizing power cannot fail to make an impression. His riotous imagery, his lack of grace and elegance, may be in part ascribed to hasty production. (pp. 622-23)

In Spain his popularity and influence have been remarkable. No novelist, except Sr. Galdós, has been so widely criticised or so generally defended. In the rest of Europe he has been rapidly gaining a reading-public since the appearance of **"La Barraca"** in the *Revue de Paris* in 1901, under the title of **"Terres Maudites."** Reviews of his works have appeared in the leading Continental periodicals, and almost all of his novels have been translated into the other languages of Europe, with the single exception of English. The apathy of the English world toward his work may be due to a complacent sense of freedom and prosperity that makes us indifferent to the problems that confront the Continent. To the Spaniard, more than to any other people of Europe, these questions are at present vital. Since Spain is freed from the burden of her colonies, she

may undertake her own upbuilding. It is not easy to foresee the consummation of this process of development and regeneration. At least, in Sr. Ibáñez Spain has a leader whose courage is strong, an apostle whose faith in the future is firm. Whether or not he lives to see the fulfilment of his hopes and ideals, he will have borne no small part in the formation of a new Spain. (p. 623)

> *R. H. Keniston, "An Apostle of New Spain," in* The Nation *(copyright 1908 The Nation magazine, The Nation Associates, Inc.) Vol. LXXXVII, No. 2269, December 24, 1908, pp. 622-23.*

THE NATION   (essay date 1912)

The bull-fight has frequently been described by romanticists in quest of local color, and by humanitarians disgusted with its brutalities; but the picture has always been one-sided and incomplete. It has remained for the Valencian novelist to depict Spain's national spectacle as it actually is, with all its glamour of romance and all its savagery as well. Blasco Ibáñez is, perhaps, the most vigorous present exponent of Zola's moribund naturalistic school. In **"The Blood of the Arena"** (an unhappy rendering of the original title, **"Sangre y Arena"**), he has carefully followed Zola's formula. He has not merely described a few corridas, but has made a minute study of the bull-fight from every conceivable point of view. The rearing of bulls for the arena, the training of matadors, the daily life of the thousand and one hangers-on of the ring, all this and much more claims his attention. He has Zola's skill in describing a crowd, and the French novelist's ability to make literary use of a mass of carefully gathered data. (p. 11)

The book is a terrible arraignment of the national sport, but, unlike the ordinary novel with a purpose, the author's private opinions are not obtruded upon the reader. Facts speak for themselves. It is not until the last sentence of all that Blasco Ibáñez gives the reader a clue to his own attitude; he has advanced in art since writing **"The Cathedral."** By reserving the worst horrors for the last chapter, he clearly intends that the reader shall close the book with a feeling of loathing and disgust; but the author's method is so subtle that, in spite of his well-known advanced views, few foreign reviewers have recognized that the work is an attack upon the bull-fight. (p. 12)

> *A review of, "The Blood of the Arena," in* The Nation *(copyright 1912 The Nation magazine, The Nation Associates, Inc.), Vol. XCIV, No. 2427, January 4, 1912, pp. 11-12.*

HAVELOCK ELLIS   (essay date 1914)

[Ellis was a pioneering sexual psychologist and a respected English man of letters. His most famous work is his seven-volume The Psychology of Sex *(1879-1928), a study which contains frankly stated case histories of sex-related psychological abnormalities and which is greatly responsible for changing British and American attitudes toward the hitherto forbidden subject of sexuality. In addition to his psychological writings, Ellis retained an active interest in literature throughout his life. As a critic, according to Desmond MacCarthy, Ellis looked for the expression of the individuality of the author under discussion. In the excerpt below, Ellis provides a brief biographical sketch of Blasco Ibáñez, as well as a discussion of the novelist's research and writing techniques. Ellis, like R. H. Keniston (see excerpt above), groups Blasco Ibáñez's novels into three phases, but defines the works of the third period as analytic, psychological novels. Ellis notes that Blasco Ibáñez wrote in the tradition of literary Naturalism*

and refers to the sobriquet "the Spanish Zola" which is frequently applied to the Spanish novelist. For other discussions of Blasco Ibáñez's Naturalism see the essays by J. Fitzmaurice Kelly, Katherine Reding, and Sherman H. Eoff excerpted below.]

It is only recently that the novels, even the name, of Blasco Ibáñez became known to English readers. A few years ago the list was long of his translated books in more than half a dozen languages, not one of them in English. Now that *The Cathedral, Sonnica, The Blood of the Arena,* have been published in England and America. . . , it can no longer be said that the best known and the most typically Spanish novelist of to-day is only unknown to English readers.

Even the reader of these translations, however—well as they are executed—may easily receive an inadequate idea of the scope and nature of this novelist's work. An author's latest works, usually the first to be translated, are not always the finest examples of his quality. Moreover, every novelist who is marked by vital exuberance must be considered to some extent in the mass before he can be appreciated. Blasco Ibáñez has published nearly twenty volumes in twenty years, and it is necessary to take a survey of many of these to gain a fair notion of his quality and position. He began as a regional novelist with stories of the tragic and laborious life of the Valencian peasantry among whom he had lived from childhood. *Arroz y Tartana, Entre Naranjos, Cañas y Barro, Flor de Maya, La Barraca* . . . belong to this group. These books are vivid and pungent; they spring naturally out of the writer's experience; they describe persons evidently studied from life and they bring before us in detail a peculiar picture of rural life. They perhaps remain the best books Blasco Ibáñez has written. The vision is narrower than in any of his later books, but its depths and the richness of the sympathy behind it gives them universal interest. One may refer, for instance, to *La Barraca,* published in 1898. This in not only, as it has been called, the finest masterpiece among Spanish regional novels. The struggle of man with the soil, the devotion of the peasant to that soil, the tragic contest between the tenant and the landlord, have never, probably, been so vehemently and poignantly presented in any literature. As a contrast to the monotonous intensity of *La Barraca* may be placed *Cañas y Barro,* published four years later, a picture of life in the malarious rice-fields of the Valencian Lake Albufera, and of the varied types to be found among the workers in this region.

By 1903 Blasco Ibáñez had established his fame as a novelist and at the same time exhausted his personal impressions of Valencia. He now sought to give expression to his spirit of social revolt by studying special aspects of life in Spain generally. We thus have what are termed the "novels of rebellion," including *La Catedral, La Bodega* and *La Horda,* all fighting books, manuals of revolutionary propaganda rather than serene works of art.

La Catedral, in which a struggle between the renovating spirit of modern anarchism and the decaying spirit of conservatism is played out in the cloisters of Toledo Cathedral, is the most translated of all the novelist's books and the first to appear in English, but it is perhaps the least satisfactory. That at all events is its author's opinion; it is too heavy, he confided to a friend, and there is too much doctrine. It is difficult to dispute this verdict. *La Bodega,* a book of similar method, may be regarded as a better example of this group; it presents a vivid picture of the wine industry at Jerez and the invasion into this sphere of the modern labour spirit; the Anarchist Salvoechea is here introduced under a pseudonym as a kind of modern

Christ. In *El Intruso,* which has as its background the iron mines and manufactures of Bilbao, another and more modern phase of Spanish religion is brought forward and the power of the Jesuit set forth. Finally, *La Horda,* the last novel of this group, deals with the parish life of the slums of Madrid.

The later novels of Blasco Ibáñez, beginning with *La Maja Desnuda,* in 1906, are freer and more varied in character; they are more deliberately analytical and psychological than the books of the first period, more artistically impartial than those of the second class. The novelist has become more agile and more self-conscious, to some of us, perhaps, less interesting. In most of these books the author chooses a special panorama and a definite theme which he analyses disinterestedly and indeed often admirably. Thus we have *Sangre y Arena* in which bull-fighting is presented as a problem in the national life of Spain. Again, we have *Los Muertos Mandan* (shortly to be published as *The Tyranny of the Ancestors*), in which, on the background of the lovely Balearic Islands, is presented the great question of tradition, the iron rule of the dead over the living. It is doubtless one of the most vivid and masterly of the novelist's works. Recently Blasco Ibáñez, a great traveller, has been visiting South America and studying the new aspects of life there presented. They form the subject of his most recent books. (pp. 247-51)

Blasco Ibáñez has sometimes been called the Spanish Zola. It is certain that the French novelist has influenced the later development of the Spanish novelist and that in general methods of approaching their art there are points of resemblance between the two writers. Yet the differences are fundamental. Zola was a man of the study who made novel-writing his life-work from the outset; for every book he patiently accumulated immense masses of notes (in which, as he himself admitted, he sometimes lost himself), and in a business-like and methodical manner he wove those notes into books of uniform and often impressive pattern, which becomes the more impressive because it was inspired by a novel doctrine of scientific realism. Nothing of this in the Spanish writer. However revolutionary his social and political outlook may be, he is not revolutionary in methods of art; he has scarcely even mastered the traditional methods; the habits of journalism have taken strong hold of him and his more severe Spanish critics deplore the frequent looseness and inaccuracy of his style. There are passages of splendid lyrical rhapsody, and there are often the marks of a fine and bold artist in the construction of a story or the presentation of a character, but in the accomplished use of the beautiful Castilian tongue Blasco Ibáñez is surpassed by many a young Spanish writer of to-day. Nor has he any of Zola's methodical fervour of laborious documentation. In his early novels he adopted the happy method of drawing on his own vivid early memories of Valencian life and character. More recently his method has been to soak himself, swiftly and completely but for the most part very briefly, in the life he proposes to depict. A week may suffice for this, and the novel itself may be written in a couple of months. Thus for writing *Sangre y Arena* it sufficed him to visit Seville in the company of a famous matador, and the preparation for *Los Muertos Mandan* was a boating expedition round the Balearic coast. . . . Nor are the notes for his books written down; he relies exclusively on his prodigious memory and his intense power of visualizing everything that impresses him. (pp. 254-56)

[His] books are not merely faint reflections of the man who has so carelessly flung them at the world; they are the most interesting documents we can easily find to throw light on the social and industrial questions which are stirring Spain to-day. (pp. 256-57)

> *Havelock Ellis, "Blasco Ibáñez" (originally published in* New Statesman, *Vol. III, No. 60, May 30, 1914), in his* Views and Reviews: A Selection of Uncollected Articles, 1884-1932, first and second series *(reprinted by permission of François Lafitte for the Literary Estate of Havelock Ellis), D. Harmsworth, 1932 (and reprinted by Books for Libraries Press, 1970; distributed by Arno Press, Inc., pp. 247-57).*

THE NEW YORK TIMES BOOK REVIEW (essay date 1918)

[*In the excerpt below, Blasco Ibáñez's novel* The Four Horsemen of the Apocalypse *is praised as "genuine creative literature." The anonymous critic is pleased that "for the first time, a recognized master of fiction, . . . has chosen the war for his theme," and welcomes this first view of the war from a Spanish perspective. For a negative appraisal of this work see the review by Maxwell Anderson excerpted below.*]

Theoretically, taking into account that spirit of aloofness, impartiality, from the heights of which the conscientious novelist is supposed to do his best work, the war story written from the standpoint of neutrality ought to be of high literary value. But—quite naturally—at a time when every man, of whatever nationality, must definitely take sides, one way or another, in the great contest, it is obviously impossible to preserve a neutrality of feeling in a novel having the war for its theme. Nor has there been any conspicuous attempt to surmount this impossibility. . . . But now, for the first time, a recognized master of fiction, who comes of a nation that has so far preserved its neutrality, has chosen the war for his theme, and has given us, in some respects, a novel that, for descriptive interest, knowledge of national character, conflicting national feelings and motives, deserves a place with the foremost of its contemporaries. It goes without saying, however, that this war novel, **"The Four Horsemen of the Apocalypse,"** written by the Spanish novelist, V. Blasco Ibanez, who is generally regarded as second to none among the fiction writers of his country, is very far indeed from being neutral, either in spirit or sentiment. But it does view the war—from the side of the Allies, it is true—through Spanish eyes and with Spanish feeling, and thus occupies a unique place in this kind of fiction.

Those who are familiar with that exquisite bit of fiction by Ibanez, **"The Cabin,"** . . . will look for work very much above the average in **"The Four Horsemen of the Apocalypse,"** and they will not be disappointed in what they find. There is here the same artistic restraint, the same vividness in description, the same naturalness in character drawing that there is in **"The Cabin."** But, while the latter is a perfect specimen of a monochrome study in country life, this takes the world for its canvas and glistens with all the varieties of mood and color that one would expect from the "Four Horsemen"—war, famine, pestilence, and death. . . . [There is] need to emphasize the special niche that [**"The Four Horsemen"**] occupies in the fiction of the war. For Señor Ibanez brings into his story an effective kind of background that, perhaps, only he could have brought—the Argentine hacienda of that humorously drawn, typical Spaniard of the old régime, "Madriaga, the Centaur"—and a series of characters, German, French, Spanish, Russian, for the faithful delineation of which this leading novelist from a neutral nation would seem to be particularly well fitted. The book, in spite of its Spanish viewpoint, is delightfully inter-national in character and interest, at the same time that it is uncompromisingly pro-Ally in sympathy and thoroughly alive to the weaknesses in the German national character. . . . As a work of fiction **"The Four Horsemen"** carries the strongest kind of appeal for those who look for genuine creative literature in a novel. As coming from the pen of one of the foremost writers of Spain, and thus containing, in a sense, an authoritative Spanish view of the war, it has an additional interest just now belonging to few of our recent novels.

> *"Neutral War Fiction," in* The New York Times Book Review *(copyright © 1918 by The New York Times Company; reprinted by permission), September 1, 1918, p. 372.**

ISAAC GOLDBERG (essay date 1918)

[*Goldberg was one of the first English-language critics to write extensively about Latin-American literature, and his* Studies in Spanish-American Literature *(1920) and* Brazilian Literature *(1922) are landmark studies in this field. In the following excerpt, he provides a survey of Blasco Ibáñez's major novels.*]

For a literary career which began only about 1894 and which has included travels and endless translations, not to speak of an ever growing history of the present war, [Blasco-Ibáñez's] labors have been prolific, yet characteristically Spanish in their versatility.

Both the life and the writings of this energetic personality have been devoted to the same high purpose—the abolition of all enemies to progress and freedom. In his attitude toward Church and State, toward the bullfight or the evils of drink, toward the self-blighting ignorance of the very people for whom he has fought, he has been frank and fearless. Naturally such propagandist dynamism shows in his works, which possess the defects of their quality. But they have the virtues too. Blasco Ibáñez is, above all things, a writer of intense, radiant power. He is quick to respond to the picturesque, whether animate in the folk of his beloved Valencia or inanimate in that nature which he has endowed with meaningful life. At his best he triumphs in scenes demanding epic description, until we are overwhelmed with the sense of actuality and feel a strange thrill of actual participation. So absorbed does the writer become in this part of his tale that we are drawn into it with him, and almost unconsciously.

For instance, both *The Four Horsemen of the Apocalypse* and *Sónnica* deal primarily with war, the first with the eventful days of the Marne, the second with the siege of ancient Saguntum by Hannibal; yet in each the author is, so to speak, contemporary with his subject. In each he describes war as the horrible thing it is; not for him the prettified pictures of gold braid and gold medals. At Saguntum you starve with the besieged, you behold them reduced to the verge of cannibalism, you walk with the heroic defenders of the city into the communal funeral pyre rather than surrender to the indomitable Celtiberian. At Saguntum too, in the voluptuous days before the coming of war, you revel in the orgies of Sónnica the courtesan, and it is a tribute not only to the author's powers of reconstructing a past civilization, but also to his virtuosity, that the scenes in Sónnica's abode of pleasure are drawn with an equal measure of realism and actuality. Blasco Ibáñez has a fondness for wealth of detail, but rarely does he overdo it, as in some passages of *Mare Nostrum*. Turn from *Sónnica* to *The Four Horsemen* and you are face to face with contemporary warfare in all its horrors of body and soul. Here, as in the earlier novel of war, the description rises to interpretation. The mud and blood of the trenches becomes almost visible; the characters themselves, rather than acting against a background of war, become merely a detail of the vast mechanism. In this respect the Spaniard stands easily in the forefront of those who have written of the present conflict. He is the Vereschagin of the modern war novel.

Mare Nostrum does for warfare upon the sea what *The Four Horsemen* does for it on land. Its author was from the very first imbued with a strong pro-Ally sentiment. Long a lover of France and republicanism, and long devoted to Zola, from whom he probably drew his descriptive skill, he naturally let this triple love appear in his later works. *Mare Nostrum* is at once an indictment of the German U-boat methods and a trumpet call to Spain. In its interpretative description of the Mediterranean Sea as a background for the action, he has written pages worthy of a Hugo; this part of the novel is epic in its effect.

The weakness of Blasco Ibáñez lies in characterization. This is not so evident in his earlier as it has become in his later novels. Take, for instance, so absorbing a tale as *The Cabin,* which suffers from a rather stiff translation into English but which is none the less superior both to *The Four Horsemen* and to *Mare Nostrum* as a work of art. Although it has been objected that the persons of *The Cabin* are types, yet there is such a throbbing intensity in their presentation that we forget, as we read, to inquire into the matter. Again, take what French and Italian critics look upon as the Spaniard's masterpiece, *Cañas y Barro (Reeds and Mud),* which is as yet unknown in our tongue. This, like the preceding tale, belongs to the regional novel, a genre that has received much attention in Spain, because of the well-defined characteristics of the various parts of the country and the peculiarities of person and place to which they give origin. Here, as in *The Cabin,* it may be objected that the persons are types rather than characters, yet the case for effective characterization is by no means weak. A re-reading of such novels as these makes one ask whether the real field for their author is not in the regional novel rather than in the more profitable, but less artistic, tales of war as exemplified in *The Four Horsemen* and *Mare Nostrum.*

Agreeing at the outset that *The Four Horsemen of the Apocalypse* and its successor were written in a worthy and triumphant cause, let us also agree not to be therefore blind to their artistic defeats. *The Four Horsemen* suffers from two serious drawbacks in this respect. Not only is the characterization weak, but the interest of the novel shifts at a crucial point from one protagonist to another. At first we are led to believe that the tale will concern chiefly Julio Desnoyers and his married sweetheart. Neither of these is distinguished for any depth of mind, yet the war suddenly makes self-sacrificing models of them. Such a transformation may be true; in fact, under the enormous stress of contemporary warfare it must have been so in countless instances. Yet in a novel it is not enough to state the conversion; it should have been prepared, however slightly. Once Julio goes to war the author centers his attention and ours upon Julio's aged father, who having in 1870 run away from military service in France, has returned from South America a wealthy man, only to find himself face to face with another and a greater war. His son's death in a sense redeems his own previous desertion. Throughout, of course, the purpose is plain; take away the marvelous pages of description however, and the story is not only trite but ill managed.

Similar artistic evils beset *Mare Nostrum.* (pp. 415-16)

The later novels reveal another tendency, in which, alas, the Spaniard is not alone. He spins his yarns out to inordinate length. *Mare Nostrum* in particular is filled with a wealth of oceanographical detail, combined with snatches of history, that clearly do not belong in the book, however informative they may be. This is all the more to be deplored on account of the superlative beauty of some of the passages devoted to the Mediterranean. There is no doubt, in one reader's mind at least, that these later tales were written in altogether too great haste. One of the disadvantages of writing war books while the war is in progress is that the possibility of their being rendered anachronistic by the advance of the conflict inspires in the author a greater impatience than usual to get his book out as soon as possible.

Yet for all his faults, Blasco Ibáñez exercises over the reader a fascination that could not be effective but for the presence of high talent. Other novelists are more expert in characterization, yet they attract us far less. Other writers manage a plot with greater consistency, yet we follow them with diminished ardor. There is in all this man does a vehemence that carries us along even over page after page of detail for detail's sake. And although in choice of subject he seems to yield quite readily to the crowd, there is no such concession in the matter of style. He has a habit of extended indirect discourse, for instance, as if to avoid direct quotation. He possesses a love of historical lore and of minutiae in description. He likes to write long chapters, that could easily be split into shorter and more immediately effective ones.

The secret of his power may lie in the projection of his dynamic personality upon all he does. This lover of the glory that was Greece and the glory that is France, this hater of ancient Rome (as displayed in *Sónnica*) and of contemporary Germany, is a good fighter, a passionate lover, a colorful champion, an embodiment of the new Spain, or at least, of one of the phases of the new Spain. And if the reader wishes to know the best that Ibáñez has done in the modern novel, let him turn, after perusing the great descriptive passages of these latest works, to such a tale as *The Cabin* or to *Cañas y Barro.* Here are no pages of padding, no inartistic projecting of purpose through plan, no shifting of interest, no excessive agglomeration of detail, no jerking of manikins. Here is thesis subordinated to—or, better still, fused with—art; here is atmosphere, insight, power, proportion. Here is the real Blasco Ibáñez. (pp. 416-17)

Isaac Goldberg, "Vicente Blasco Ibáñez," in The Dial *(copyright, 1918, by The Dial Publishing Company, Inc.), Vol. LXV, No. 777, November 16, 1918, pp. 415-17.*

M[AXWELL] A[NDERSON]   (essay date 1918)

[*Sharply differing from the acclamatory review in* The New York Times *of* The Four Horsemen of the Apocalypse (*see excerpt above*), *Anderson finds that the theme of global war is too great to be borne by this novel's "slight and anaemic plot." Only the early chapters, set in South America, receive some approval.*]

It is a test of great fiction that it should displace for a time the earth and sky our senses reveal to us and put in their place the moods and ways and seasons of another environment. *The Four Horsemen of the Apocalypse* does this for us briefly in the early South American chapters, but with the transplantation of the Desnoyers family into France the spell is broken, and we know that we have before us—another war book. For the men and women who lived so healthily on their native pampas become, when the German dam breaks over France, mere painted fragments of shingle among the driftwood of a great river. The personalities we had begun to appreciate deteriorate without transition into types upon which Ibáñez may hang typical instances of French heroism and German brutality.

If it is possible to differentiate between literature and journalism, blood-brothers and boon-companions in war and peace, *The Four Horsemen* furnishes a clue to their confused identities. What importance the main portion of the book may have is lent the composition by the magnitude of events treated; the earlier subordinate and obviously unimportant happenings on an obscure ranch in Argentina are flushed with life and firm as material existence because the art of the author was equal to the task of furnishing to this scene the adequate and fitting word. In reporting the war he is a journalist, overwhelmed by his task; in portraying Don Madariaga, despot, philanthropist and centaur of the cattle-plains, he touches the canvas with slow and loving strokes—making out of this minor figure the only developed character in the narrative. In journalism events give weight to words, in literature words rescue events from oblivion. And because this greatest of all wars transcends human imagination it may be that it is and will remain unworkable stuff for artists. Perhaps Ibáñez has done as well as any romancer in our generation may hope to do. (pp. 229-30)

The effective presentation of pageant life, of crowds and communities in flux, is at once the strength of the moving picture—almost its only strength—and the absolute weakness of the novel. In *The Four Horsemen of the Apocalypse* a slight and anaemic plot staggers with the immense luggage of a war that could not long be borne by Atlas himself. In the nature of things it cannot go far. (p. 230)

> M[axwell] A[nderson], *"The War As Excess Baggage,"* in The New Republic *(reprinted by permission of* The New Republic; © *1918 The New Republic, Inc.) Vol. XVII, No. 216, December 21, 1918, pp. 229-30.*

W. D. HOWELLS (essay date 1919)

[*Howells was the chief progenitor of American Realism and the most influential American literary critic during the late nineteenth century. He was the author of nearly three dozen novels, few of which are read today. Despite his eclipse, he stands as one of the major literary figures of the nineteenth century: he successfully weaned American literature away from the sentimental romanticism of its infancy, earning the popular sobriquet "the Dean of American Letters." Through Realism, a theory central to his fiction and criticism, Howells sought to disperse "the conventional acceptations by which men live on easy terms with themselves" that they might "examine the grounds of their social and moral opinions." To accomplish this, according to Howells, the writer must strive to record impressions of everyday life in detail, endowing characters with true-to-life motives and avoiding authorial comment in the narrative.* Criticism and Fiction *(1891), a patchwork of essays from* Harper's Magazine, *is often considered Howells's manifesto of Realism, although, as René Wellek has noted, the book is actually "only a skirmish in a long campaign for his doctrines." In addition to many notable studies of the works of his friends Mark Twain and Henry James, Howells perceptively reviewed three generations of international literature, urging Americans to read Émile Zola, Bernard Shaw, Henrik Ibsen, Emily Dickinson, and other important authors. In his introduction to* The Shadow of the Cathedral, *excerpted below, Howells surveys Blasco Ibáñez' major works and calls this novel "one of the fullest and richest in modern fiction."*]

There are three cathedrals which I think will remain chief of the Spanish cathedrals in the remembrance of the traveller, namely the Cathedral at Burgos, the Cathedral at Toledo, and the Cathedral at Seville; and first of these for reasons hitherto of history and art, and now of fiction, will be the Cathedral at Toledo, which the most commanding talent among the contemporary Spanish novelists has made the protagonist of the romance following. I do not mean that Vincent Blasco Ibáñez is greater than Perez Galdós, or Armando Palacio Valdés or even the Countess Pardo-Bazan; but he belongs to their realistic order of imagination, and he is easily the first of living European novelists outside of Spain, with the advantage of superior youth, freshness of invention and force of characterization. The Russians have ceased to be actively the masters, and there is no Frenchman, Englishman, or Scandinavian who counts with Ibáñez, and of course no Italian, American, and, unspeakably, no German. (p. v)

[Ibáñez writes] fiction of the naturalistic type, and of a Zolaistic coloring which his Spanish critics find rather stronger than I have myself seen it. Every young writer forms himself upon some older writer; nobody begins master; but Ibáñez became master while he was yet no doubt practicing a prentice hand; yet I do not feel very strongly the Zolastic influence in his first novel, *La Barraca,* or *The Cabin,* which paints peasant life in the region of Valencia, studied at first hand and probably from personal knowledge. It is not a very spacious scheme, but in its narrow field it is strictly a *novela de costumbres,* or novel of manners, as we used to call the kind. Ibáñez has in fact never written anything but novels of manners, and *La Barraca* pictures a neighborhood where a stranger takes up a waste tract of land and tries to make a home for himself and family. . . . It is a tragedy such as naturalism alone can stage and give the effect of life. I have read few things so touching as this tale of commonest experience which seems as true to the suffering and defeat of the newcomers, as to the stupid inhumanity of the neighbors who join, under the lead of the evillest among them, in driving the strangers away; in fact I know nothing parallel to it, certainly nothing in English; perhaps *The House with the Green Shutters* breathes as great an anguish.

At just what interval or remove the novel which gave Ibáñez worldwide reputation followed this little tale, I cannot say, and it is not important that I should try to say. But it is worth while to note here that he never flatters the vices or even the virtues of his countrymen; and it is much to their honor that they have accepted him in the love of his art for the sincerity of his dealing with their conditions. In *Sangre y Arena* his affair is with the cherished atrocity which keeps the Spaniards in the era of the gladiator shows of Rome. The hero, as the renowned *torrero* whose career it celebrates, from his first boyish longing to be a bull-fighter, to his death, weakened by years and wounds, in the arena of Madrid, is something absolute in characterization. The whole book in fact is absolute in its fidelity to the general fact it deals with, and the persons of its powerful drama. Each in his or her place is realized with an art which leaves one in no doubt of their lifelikeness, and keeps each as vital as the *torrero* himself. There is little of the humor which relieves the pathos. . . . The *torrero*'s family who have dreaded his boyish ambition with the anxiety of good common people, and his devotedly gentle and beautiful wife,—even his bullying and then truckling brother-in-law who is ashamed of his profession and then proud of him when it has filled Spain with his fame,—are made to live in the spacious scene. But above all in her lust for him and her contempt for him the unique figure of Doña Sol astounds. (pp. vi-vii)

Sangre y Arena is a book of unexampled force and in that sort must be reckoned the greatest novel of the author, who has neglected no phase of his varied scene. The *torrero's* mortal disaster in the arena is no more important than the action behind the scenes where the gored horses have their dangling entrails sewed up by the primitive surgery of the place and are then ridden back into the amphitheatre to suffer a second agony. No color of the dreadful picture is spared; the whole thing passes as in the reader's presence before his sight and his other senses. The book is a masterpiece far in advance of that study of the common life which Ibañez calls *La Horda;* dealing with the horde of common poor and those accidents of beauty and talent as native to them as to the classes called the better. It has the attraction of the author's frank handling, and the power of the Spanish scene in which the action passes; but it could not hold me to the end.

It is only in his latest book that he transcends the Spanish scene and peoples the wider range from South America to Paris, and from Paris to the invaded provinces of France with characters proper to the times and places. *The Four Horsemen of the Apocalypse* has not the rough textures and rank dyes of the wholly Spanish stories, but it is the strongest story of the great war known to me, and its loss in the Parisian figures is made more than good in the novelty and veracity of the Argentinos who supply that element of internationality which the North American novelists of a generation ago employed to give a fresh interest to their work. With the coming of the hero to study art and make love in the conventional Paris, and the repatriation of his father, a cattle millionaire of French birth from the pampas, with his wife and daughters, Ibañez achieves effects beyond the art of Henry James, below whom he nevertheless falls so far in subtlety and beauty. (pp. viii-ix)

I do not know just the order of [*La Catedral*] among the stories of Ibañez, but it has a quality of imagination, of poetic feeling which surpasses the invention of any other that I have read, and makes me think it came before *Sangre y Arena,* and possibly before *La Horda.* I cannot recall any other novel of the author which is quite so psychological as this. It is in fact a sort of biography, a personal study, of the mighty fane at Toledo, as if the edifice were of human quality and could have its life expressed in human terms. There is nothing forced in the poetic conception, or mechanical in the execution. The Cathedral is not only a single life, it is a neighborhood, a city, a world in itself; and its complex character appears in the nature of the different souls which collectively animate it. (p. ix)

[*Le Catedral*] is quite without the love-interest which is the prime attraction of our mostly silly fiction. . . . [And] there is as little dramatic incident as love interest in the book. The extraordinary power of it lies in its fealty to the truth and its insight into human nature. The reader of course perceives that it is intensely anti-ecclesiastical, but he could make no greater mistake than to imagine it in any wise Protestant. . . . [Ibañez is] intensively agnostic. He is the standard bearer of the scientific revolt in the terms of fiction which spares us no hope of relief in the religious notion of human life here or hereafter that the Hebraic or Christian theology has divined.

It is right to say this plainly, but the reader who can suffer it from the author will find his book one of the fullest and richest in modern fiction, worthy to rank with the greatest Russian work and beyond anything yet done in English. It has not the topographical range of Tolstoy's *War and Peace,* or *Resurrection;* but in its climax it is as logically and ruthlessly tragical

as anything that the Spanish spirit has yet imagined. (pp. xii-xiii)

> W. D. Howells, "Introduction" (copyright, 1919, copyright renewed © 1946, by E. P. Dutton & Company; reprinted by permission of the publisher, E. P. Dutton, Inc.), in The Shadow of the Cathedral: A Novel by Vincente Blasco Ibáñez, translated by Mrs. W. A. Gillespie, Dutton, 1919, pp. v-xiv.

UPTON SINCLAIR   (essay date 1919)

[*An American novelist, dramatist, journalist, and essayist, Sinclair was a prolific writer who is most famous for* The Jungle *(1906), a novel which portrays the unjust labor practices, filth, and horrifying conditions of Chicago's meat-processing industry, and which prompted passage of the Pure Food and Drug Act of 1906. A lifelong, outspoken socialist, Sinclair addressed the excesses of capitalist society in most of his works and admired writers, such as Blasco Ibáñez, whose works possessed similar political overtones. In the following excerpt, Sinclair offers praise for Blasco Ibáñez's novels* Blood and Sand, The Shadow of the Cathedral, *and* The Four Horsemen of the Apocalypse. *This and other favorable articles about Blasco Ibáñez and his works by Sinclair (see Additional Bibliography) appeared in* Appeal to Reason, *a Socialist weekly edited by Emanuel Haldeman-Julius.*]

Ten years or so ago I came on a French translation of a Spanish novel called **"The Cathedral."** I had heard of it as a revolutionary book; I thought it was going to be a "muck-raking" of the great ecclesiastical system which for so many centuries has strangled the life of the Spanish people. But I found it a different sort of book than I expected. It is a strange combination of revolutionary protest, with tenderness and love for the old structure and the old system of the past. Can you imagine a social revolutionist who loves a cathedral, who knows every nook and corner of it, and all the queer characters who live within its precincts and draw their sustenance from the church system? Curiously enough, this makes the most effective kind of muck-raking. You realize that the writer actually knows what he is talking about; he disarms all your suspicions, he takes you to live in the cathedral and lets you make up your own mind about it.

I knew that this was a new kind of novel for Spain and a new hope for Spanish life. Quite recently the novel has been translated into English, under the title of **"The Shadow of the Cathedral,"** and half a dozen other books of Blasco Ibanez have also been translated. One of them, **"The Four Horsemen of the Apocalypse,"** telling of the war, has become a "best seller." I have just been reading another, called **"Blood and Sand,"** which is a story of the bull ring and of the bull-fighting sport in Spain. It is just like **"The Cathedral"**; this new and marvelously effective kind of muck-raking. Not once does the author denounce bull fighting, not once does he give you a hint that he is anything but a "fan" for the national sport. He introduces you to a great "torero"; he lets you see how a village boy is drawn in by the excitement, and you see him grow to young manhood and achieve fame and success, you meet his wife and all his relatives and all his friends, including a rich woman of the corrupt aristocracy, and a bandit of the road, and a whole gallery of fascinating people; and then you see him wounded, and broken, and spurned by the crowd, finally killed in a last desperate effort to retrieve his reputation. When you have got through reading that book, you know about the national degradation of Spain, and if you are a Spaniard, you must be ready to join an anti-bull-fighting society!

Upton Sinclair, in a review of "The Cathedral" (re-printed by permission of the Literary Estate of Upton Sinclair), in Appeal to Reason, *No. 1242, September 20, 1919, p. 4.*

J. F[ITZMAURICE-] K[ELLY] (essay date 1919)

[*In this brief overview the critic comments on Blasco Ibáñez's Zolaesque Naturalism and disparages his skill at characterization. For other discussions of Blasco Ibáñez's Naturalism, see the essay by Havelock Ellis excerpted above and the essays by Katherine Reding and Sherman H. Eoff excerpted below.*]

If wide circulation were a decisive proof of merit, there could scarcely be a doubt as to the position of Señor Blasco Ibáñez in contemporary Spanish literature. With the possible exception of Señor Pérez Galdós, who belongs to a previous generation, Señor Blasco Ibáñez is the best-known of Spanish novelists. His originals are read wherever Spanish is spoken, and, where Spanish is not spoken, his works are available in transla-tions. . . .

As Señor Blasco Ibáñez has shown in such early works as **"Arroz y Tartana"** and **"Flor de Mayo,"** he is most familiar with the "orchard of Spain"—with Valencia del Cid and the adjacent district. But he could not be content to move in so narrow a sphere. Even in his first phase there is a trace of the naturalism which Zola brought into fashion, and this charac-teristic has grown more marked with time. Other influences have combined to affect Señor Blasco Ibáñez. Politics have marked out a course for him, and it would be idle to deny that to political causes he owed no small part of the resounding triumph which he won with **"La Catedral,"** and which he repeated with the publication of **"La Horda."** Impressionable in a very high degree, Señor Blasco Ibáñez has naturally not been insensitive to the public events of the last few years. We did not know—we had no reason to suppose—that he had abjured the collectivist views which lay at the root of **"La Catedral"** and the rest. This was no guarantee of his views on matters which touched us more closely. In Spain sympathies are deeply divided, and some leaders of advanced opinions did not hesitate to declare against the Allied Powers. It was, there-fore, a genuine relief to some of us to gather from **"Los cuatro jinetes del Apocalipsis"** and from **"Mare nostrum"** that Señor Blasco Ibáñez was where we should wish him to be—on our side. And that the thesis still retains all its interest for him is evident from the last of his novels.

"Los enemigos de la mujer" is a title which is superficially suggested by the theme of "Love's Labour's Lost." In it we are made acquainted with the story of a fabulously wealthy Prince Lubimoff who, when about thirty-eight, finds his vast fortune imperilled by developments in Russia. Most of the action takes place, not in Navarre, but on the Riviera, and the incidents are very much what we might expect them to be within range of Monte Carlo: intrigues, gambling-scenes, dis-putes as to what "system" (if any) should be followed at the croupier's table, and duels. There are comparatively few at-tempts at character-drawing, and the few that we find are not always successful. . . . On the other hand, the thumbnail sketches of secondary figures like Don Marcos de Toledo and Atilio Castro, are singularly forcible and vivid. . . . We think that persons have less attraction than politics for Señor Blasco Ibá-ñez. It was the German Emperor's fate to be opposed to the novelist in politics, and this brings him within focus. Señor Blasco Ibáñez is perhaps a novelist by accident. He is not so much interested in fictitious personages as in historical char-acters or political propaganda. Having selected the novel as a vehicle for expressing his political opinions, he has by his talent been able to handle the instrument with undeniable skill and ample effect. In his hands romance verges on sociology; greatly as he has succeeded as a novelist, we are by no means certain that he has found his true vocation. This, however, is a matter of speculation; in the domain which he has actually chosen he attains an amount of excellence which justifies his choice. It is commonly alleged that Señor Blasco Ibáñez writes too has-tily. This is true in the case of **"Sónnica la Cortesana."** There are few signs of breathless improvisation in **"Los Enemigos de la Mujer."**

J. F[itzmaurice-] K[elly], "A Recent Spanish Novel," in The Athenaeum, *No. 4676, December 12, 1919, p. 1351.*

T. R. YBARRA (essay date 1920)

[*In a positive review of* Woman Triumphant, *Ybarra finds the novel's style "tense, concentrated, dramatic."*]

["**Woman Triumphant**"] is another of the many novels written by the famous Spanish novelist before the vogue of **"The Four Horsemen of the Apocalypse,"** and now presented, like so many more of his works, in an English translation to satisfy the tremendous demand from the English-speaking world for the books of this remarkable Spaniard, who has been hailed as the writer of the "only great novel of the war." Unlike other writers who, having been swept to fame by one of their works, have suffered cruelly by the resurrection of earlier and inferior works from deserved oblivion, Blasco Ibáñez's fame grows constantly as the works which preceded his war novel appear in translation. There was no question about this writer's position among his own countrymen; now it becomes easier every day for American readers of his books to see how ac-curately Spaniards judged him.

"Woman Triumphant" was, in its original Spanish form, **"La Maja Desnuda,"** deriving its title from that celebrated painting by Goya of a nude woman which hangs close to the main entrance of the Prado Museum in Madrid. It is well worthy of the man who wrote **"Blood and Sand," "The Four Horsemen of the Apocalypse," "The Cabin," "The Dead Command,"** and all those other works which have won enthusiastic approval wherever they have penetrated. **"Woman Triumphant"** has a strange and original theme, tinged with morbidity, driven home with Latin frankness. It is not a pleasant story. There is some-thing repellent in the posthumous love of the artist Renovales for the wife whom he neglected and hated while she was alive, in his obsession by visions of the nude, especially as it is incarnated for him in ultimate perfection by Goya's great pic-ture. His weaknesses, forgivable at first, become ugly blem-ishes that strike the reader as disagreeably as they do his most faithful friend, the eccentric painter Cotoner. . . .

But the novelist's handling of his theme! That is Blasco Ibáñez at his best. The story moves along without flagging; the style is tense, concentrated, dramatic. It seems to throw off as it progresses all non-essentials, all mere decoration and frippery, as a snow plow hurls aside the drifts in its path. There may be contemporary novelists of deeper philosophy, with a keener sense of beauty, finer in moral purpose, more richly dowered with the power to evoke laughter or tears, but Vicente Blasco Ibáñez is the great storyteller of today. In sheer ability to narrate, to make even the minutest analyses of the thought-processes of his characters part of his action, he stands peerless.

"Woman Triumphant" only serves to emphasize those traits which have brought him enthusiastic homage before.

Yet when he decides that the moment has come for descriptive passages, for "fine writing" in the best sense of the word, he does his work with a vigor and splendor of language that once more leave the reader breathless with admiration. And not even in these passages does the onward march flag; the narrative, one feels, has been driven forward with such relentless energy that a reserve momentum has been accumulated, so to speak, more than sufficient to tide the action over such passages, making readers unconscious of any diminution in speed and tensity. The finest descriptive passage in the book is that of the masterpiece seen in dreams by Renovales, the painting which he hopes to paint some day of the divine Greek beauty, Phryne. . . .

In this passage, as elsewhere, the translator has done excellently. But why is the name of the artist's wife always spelled "Josephina"? The Spanish form is Josefina; she should be called either that or plain Josephine. But it is a minor matter. The translation, like the original, is far above the average.

> T. R. Ybarra, in a review of "Woman Triumphant,"
> in The New York Times Book Review (copyright ©
> 1920 by The New York Times Company; reprinted
> by permission), April 18, 1920, p. 198.

LOUISE MAUNSELL FIELD   (essay date 1921)

[*Field provides a review of the novel* The Torrent.]

The political game as it is played in a small town of Valencia and in the Cortes at Madrid forms the background of **"The Torrent,"** a background drawn with a firm, unsparing hand. No boss-ridden American city could show more of corruption, of stupidity and unwillingness to learn than the town of Alcira in Valencia, where "the Brull dynasty had been bossing the district for thirty years with ever-increasing power." The founder of the house, Don Jaime, made money through methods of usury so astute that they won him the liking and respect of the very people he fleeced. His son, Don Ramón, acquired power much as his father had acquired money; Don Rafael, third of the line of Brull, succeeded to a position which had been made for him. He did not himself take any very great interest in "the Party," but his resolute mother, Doña Bernarda, spurred, or rather forced, him on. He was something of a dreamer, very much of a romantic. . . . And he lived the most humdrum of lives under the guidance of the imperious Doña Bernarda—until he met the wonderful, fascinating Leonora, the prima donna who had flamed like a comet across Europe, a great singer, a famous courtesan, one who was, as she herself declared, "the property of everybody—and of nobody." . . . The romance of the ill-assorted pair forms the plot of the book.

There is an abundance of passion in the tale, some wonderful pen pictures of a sweeping, torrential love. But the fact that neither the man nor the woman is in any sense a really big personality—big either for good or evil—rather dwarfs the whole. . . . Both Leonora and Rafael are drawn with skill and vividness; but to a certain extent their limitations impose themselves, unavoidably and, as a matter of course, upon the very interesting book which tells their love story.

It is a story full of intense, splendidly pictured moments. . . .

"The Torrent" is not as long as many of Blasco Ibáñez's novels; it has less of description, less of retrospection, though the gleam of Spain's great past is reflected in many of its pages. The town of Alcira, gossipy, provincial, narrow-minded, steeped in ignorance, with its inhabitants who do not hesitate to tattle and to spy, is presented in sharp contrast to the exquisite beauty of its surroundings, the wondrous "ribera of Valencia," which the Moors, its owners of long ago, called "Paradise." But though the hum of the mean, ignorant little town sounds through these pages, it is important principally as its chatter affects the lives of Rafael and Leonora, who came to feel that they were "two against a multitude," there where "sprightly gossip was the most appreciated of the moral talents." These two, and the passionate love which swept them away like a flood, while it filled them with the very spirit of the springtime and of youth, which once lost, once sacrificed to the claims of ambition and the world, could never be recaptured, are the outstanding figures of Blasco Ibáñez's very interesting novel **"The Torrent."**

> Louise Maunsell Field, in a review of "The Torrent," in The New York Times Book Review (copyright © 1921 by The New York Times Company; reprinted by permission), November 6, 1921, p. 16.

JOHN DOS PASSOS   (essay date 1922)

[*Dos Passos, an American novelist, essayist, poet, and journalist, is best known for his sociopolitical novels of pre-World War II America. His central concerns are social injustice, including the exploitation of the working class, and the injurious emphasis on materialism in American society. The* U.S.A. *trilogy is considered his masterpiece. Strongly political, Dos Passos moved from a left-wing revolutionary philosophy in his youth, to conservatism in middle age. Although the 1950s witnessed a decline in his reputation, in recent years scholars have reaffirmed the artistic merit of his innovative methods and reevaluated his later work. In the following excerpt, Dos Passos provides a negative and somewhat sarcastic evaluation of Blasco Ibáñez's later works, and characterizes the novelist's usually much-praised use of local color as being "a little dragged in at the heels."*]

On the backs of certain of Blasco Ibáñez's novels published by the Casa Prometeo in Valencia is this significant advertisement: *Obras de Vulgarización Popular* ("Works of Popular Vulgarization"). Under it is an astounding list of volumes, all either translated or edited or arranged, if not written from cover to cover, by one tireless pen,—I mean typewriter. Ten volumes of universal history, three volumes of the French Revolution translated from Michelet, a universal geography, a social history, works on science, cookery and house-cleaning, nine volumes of Blasco Ibáñez's own history of the European war, and a translation of the Arabian Nights, a thousand and one of them without an hour missing. "Works of Popular Vulgarization." I admit that in Spanish the word *vulgarización* has not yet sunk to its inevitable meaning, but can it long stand such a strain? Add to that list a round two dozen novels and some books of travel, and who can deny that Blasco Ibáñez is a great universal genius? Read his novels and you will find that he has looked at the stars and knows Lord Kelvin's theory of vortices and the nebular hypothesis and the direction of ocean currents and the qualities of kelp and the direction the codfish go in Iceland waters when the northeast wind blows; that he knows about Gothic architecture and Byzantine painting, the social movement in Jerez and the exports of Patagonia, the wall-paper of Paris apartment houses and the red paste with which countesses polish their fingernails in Monte Carlo.

The very pattern of a modern major-general.

And, like the great universal geniuses of the Renaissance, he has lived as well as thought and written. He is said to have been thirty times in prison, six times deputy; he has been a cowboy in the pampas of Argentina; he has founded a city in Patagonia with a bullring and a bust of Cervantes in the middle of it; he has rounded the Horn on a sailing-ship in a hurricane, and it is whispered that like Victor Hugo he eats lobsters with the shells on. He hobnobs with the universe. (pp. 122-24)

Starting, as Walt Whitman from fish-shaped Paumonauk, from the fierce green fertility of Valencia, city of another great Spanish conqueror, the Cid, he had marched on the world in battle array. The whole history comes out in the series of novels at this moment being translated in such feverish haste for the edification of the American public. The beginnings are stories of the peasants of the fertile plain round about Valencia, of the fishermen and sailors of El Grao, the port, a sturdy violent people living amid a snappy fury of vegetation unexampled in Europe. His method is inspired to a certain extent by Zola, taking from his a little of the newspaper-horror mode of realism, with inevitable murder and sudden death in the last chapters. Yet he expresses that life vividly, although even then more given to grand vague ideas than to a careful scrutiny of men and things. He is at home in the strong communal feeling, in the individual anarchism, in the passionate worship of the water that runs through the fields to give life and of the blades of wheat that give bread and of the wine that gives joy, which is the moral make-up of the Valencian peasant. He is sincerely indignant about the agrarian system, about social inequality, and is full of the revolutionary bravado of his race.

A typical novel of this period is *La Barraca,* a story of a peasant family that takes up land which has lain vacant for years under the curse of the community, since the eviction of the tenants, who had held it for generations, by a landlord who was murdered as a result, on a lonely road by the father of the family he had turned out. The struggle of these peasants against their neighbours is told with a good deal of feeling, and the culmination in a rifle fight in an irrigation ditch is a splendid bit of blood and thunder. There are many descriptions of local customs . . . , a little dragged in by the heels, to be sure, but still worth reading. Yet even in these early novels one feels over and over again the force of that phrase ''popular vulgarization.'' Valencia is being vulgarized for the benefit of the universe. The proletariat is being vulgarized for the benefit of the people who buy novels.

From Valencia raids seem to have been made on other parts of Spain. *Sonnica la Cortesana* gives you antique Saguntum and the usual ''Aves,'' wreaths, flute-players and other claptrap of costume novels. In *La Catedral* you have Toledo, the church, socialism and the modern world in the shadow of Gothic spires. *La Bodega* takes you into the genial air of the wine vaults of Jerez-de-la-Frontera, with smugglers, processions blessing the vineyards and agrarian revolt in the background. Up to now they have been Spanish novels written for Spaniards; it is only with *Sangre y Arena* that the virus of a European reputation shows results.

In *Sangre y Arena,* to be sure, you learn that *toreros* use scent, have a home life, and are seduced by passionate Baudelairian ladies of the smart set who plant white teeth in their brown sinewy arms and teach them to smoke opium cigarettes. You see *toreros* taking the sacraments before going into the ring and you see them tossed by the bull while the crowd, which

a moment before had been crying ''hola'' as if it didn't know that something was going wrong, gets very pale and chilly and begins to think what dreadful things *corridas* are anyway, until the arrival of the next bull makes them forget it. All of which is good fun when not obscured by grand, vague ideas, and incidentally sells like hot cakes. (pp. 125-28)

Next comes the expedition to South America and *The Argonauts* appears. The Atlantic is bridged,—there open up rich veins of picturesqueness and new grand vague ideas, all in full swing when the war breaks out. Blasco Ibáñez meets the challenge nobly, and very soon, with *The Four Horsemen of the Apocalypse,* which captures the Allied world and proves again the *mot* about prophets. So without honor in its own country is the *Four Horsemen* that the English translation rights are sold for a paltry three thousand pesetas. But the great success in England and America soon shows that we can appreciate the acumen of a neutral who came in and rooted for our side; so early in the race too! While the iron is still hot another four hundred pages of well-sugared pro-Ally propaganda appears, *Mare Nostrum,* which mingles Ulysses and scientific information about ocean currents, Amphitrite and submarines, Circe and a vamping Theda Bara who was really a German Spy, in one grand chant of praise before the Mumbo-Jumbo of nationalism.

Los Enemigos de la Mujer, the latest production, abandons Spain entirely and plants itself in the midst of princes and countesses, all elaborately pro-Ally, at Monte Carlo. Forgotten the proletarian tastes of his youth, the local color he loved to lay on so thickly, the Habañera atmosphere; only the grand vague ideas subsist in the cosmopolite, and the fluency, that fatal Latin fluency.

And now the United States, the home of the blonde stenographer and the typewriter and the press agent. What are we to expect from the combination of Blasco Ibáñez and Broadway?

At any rate the movies will profit.

Yet one can't help wishing that Blasco Ibáñez had not learnt the typewriter trick so early. Print so easily spins a web of the commonplace over the fine outlines of life. And Blasco Ibáñez need not have been an inverted Midas. His is a superbly Mediterranean type, with something of Arretino, something of Garibaldi, something of Tartarin of Tarascon. Blustering, sensual, enthusiastic, living at bottom in a real world—which can hardly be said of Anglo-Saxon vulgarizers—even if it is a real world obscured by grand vague ideas, Blasco Ibáñez's mere energy would have produced interesting things if it had not found such easy and immediate vent in the typewriter. Bottle up a man like that for a lifetime without means of expression and he'll produce memoirs equal to Marco Polo and Casanova, but let his energies flow out evenly without resistance through a corps of clicking typewriters and all you have is one more popular novelist.

It is unfortunate too that Blasco Ibáñez and the United States should have discovered each other at this moment. They will do each other no good. We have an abundance both of vague grand ideas and of popular novelists, and we are the favorite breeding place of the inverted Midas. We need writing that shall be acid, with sharp edges on it, yeasty to leaven the lump of glucose that the combination of the ideals of the man in the swivel-chair with decayed puritanism has made of our national consciousness. Of course Blasco Ibáñez in America will only be a seven days' marvel. Nothing is ever more than that. But why need we pretend each time that our seven days' marvels are the great eternal things?

Then, too, if the American public is bound to take up Spain it might as well take up the worth-while things instead of the works of popular vulgarization. They have enough of those in their bookcases as it is. And in Spain there is a novelist like Baroja, essayists like Unamuno and Azorín, poets like Valle Inclán and Antonio Machado, . . . but I suppose they will shine with the reflected glory of the author of the *Four Horsemen of the Apocalypse.* (pp. 128-32)

> *John Dos Passos, "An Inverted Midas," in his Ro-sinante to the Road Again (copyright 1922 by George H. Doran Company; copyright renewed © 1949 by John Dos Passos; reprinted by permission of the Literary Estate of John Dos Passos), Doran, 1922, pp. 120-32.*

R. D. TOWNSEND   (essay date 1923)

Blasco-Ibanez's newly published story [*The Temptress*] is remarkable in its singleness of literary purpose and the precise consistency of its character delineation. Of the woman called the Temptress in the English title of the book, one of the characters who followed her maleficent career said: "She isn't bad, she's merely a woman of impulse whose emotions never had the slightest training, and so she sows evil without knowing always what she is doing, because all her attention has been centered upon herself." This puts the case too leniently: Elena was bad, instinctively as well as by self-indulgence. The devastation she wrought in men's lives, the tearing up morally of one little community, and the temporary destruction of a great reclamation project were cruelly planned point by point to satisfy her craving to watch her victims suffer in their jealousy and passion. Her fall to the lowest degradation was inevitable. The author's realism in portraying evil may not always please, but he certainly cannot be charged in this case with making vice attractive. The South American background of the story is unusual and well brought out. The novel is decidedly one of the author's best books, and from the standpoint of literary execution it is inferior to none of them, not even to his great success, *The Four Horsemen.*

> *R. D. Townsend, in a review of "The Temptress," in The Outlook, August 29, 1923, p. 676.*

KATHERINE REDING [later KATHERINE REDING WHITMORE]   (essay date 1923)

> [*Reding discusses the similarities as well as the differences between the works of Blasco Ibáñez and the French novelist Émile Zola, with whom the Spanish author is often compared. For other discussions of Blasco Ibáñez's Naturalism see the essays by Havelock Ellis and J. Fitzmaurice-Kelly excerpted above and the essay by Sherman H. Eoff excerpted below.*]

No man in the field of contemporary Spanish literature has come before the American public with greater prominence than Vicente Blasco Ibáñez. Our leading magazines have published reviews of his work and in many such articles Blasco Ibáñez has been arbitrarily identified as the "Spanish Zola." This has arisen, no doubt, from a certain frankness in Blasco's manner of giving unpleasant details; but a comparative study of the two reveals fundamental differences in their artistic conceptions as well as in their naturalistic technique.

As disciples of naturalism, Zola and Blasco both devote themselves to portraying society and the controlling forces of the social organism—tradition, prejudice, capitalistic oppression, etc. Thus, we have *La Terre* and *La barraca* presenting a parallel picture of the peasant class. *L'Assommoir* depicts the seething life of the substrata of Paris; *La horda* reveals the condition of the submerged classes of Madrid. *La bodega* also has one point in common with *L'Assommoir,* which is the thesis against alcoholism. In *El Intruso* there is one chapter which contains in a condensed form an account of the miners' life which *Germinal* describes at length. The battle of the Marne in *Los cuatro jinetes del apocalipsis* corresponds in many ways to the battle of Sedan in *La Débâcle.* In the production of both there is a subordination of plot to the description of the milieu. (p. 365)

Blasco's manner of description differs from the French novelist's in that it is more impressionistic. Although he gives details, he does not stop with every person or thing mentioned to tell all of its specific qualities. The introduction of each character is accompanied by a word, a phrase, or a sentence to give an idea of his physical appearance as well as his relation to the action. Often he presents features which are significant because they are indicative of the inner man as well as of his external appearance. It is not that Blasco has not many pages of description—often of extraneous matter, such as the gypsies in *La horda,* whose life and customs have no relation to the story—but he does not dwell with such minuteness upon a single object. This difference is easily explicable by Blasco's method of production. In contrast to Zola's great mass of preliminary notes, Blasco had no record whatever. His keen power of observation was accompanied by a memory which always retained the salient features. But since no memory could hold as many specific details as could a notebook, there is a greater tendency to record the sensation produced, rather than the mere outward aspect of an object. This strengthens, rather than weakens, the power of his description, for the subjective element helps the reader to visualize the scene more completely.

Blasco does not attempt to use the exact language of the people. When the terminology of a certain region is individual, he is naturalistic to the extent of employing these specific terms as far as possible, but the coarse colloquialisms, never.

In addition to the choice of vocabulary, the type of details described marks a striking difference. Many scenes in the Spanish novels are unpleasantly realistic—they make us shudder, but our sense of propriety is not outraged. Nothing, for example, could be more repulsive than the sight of the body of the new-born babe which Tonet had thrown into the lake in *Cañas y barro,* but it is not obscene. It is not that Blasco does not approach the sensual or the erotic. *Entre naranjos* and *Mare nostrum* furnish notable examples of this quality; but his descriptions have the thrill of passion, the carnal pleasure of mutual love. The love element is lacking in Zola, leaving the human being an animal whose instincts are aroused by the presence of an individual of the other sex. Blasco is more voluptuous—Zola more animalistic.

There are features of their description which are alike. One of these is the extensive use of simile and metaphor. Another, the appeal to the senses other than sight. We not only see an object—we feel it, hear it, smell it. Especially is this last sense prominent. Zola accompanies all of his darkest scenes with fitting odors—the dark, dank smell of an old tenement, the asphyxiating odor of decaying flesh in *La Débâcle.* Permeating the atmosphere of *Cañas y barro* is the viscous, fishy smell of the *Albufera* [salt-water lagoon]. (pp. 366-67)

If we compare the manner in which each achieves the "illusion of reality" we see that Zola's method is photographic. . . . In Blasco's production there are admirable descriptions, but a certain looseness in organization diminishes the effect of a vivid representation of life. Sometimes it is propaganda which disturbs the impression, sometimes the presentation is not sufficiently distinct. In the case of Zola, the question is one of accumulative effect; in Blasco, of the intensity of the original impression.

Another phase upon which comparison may be based is the way in which their novels are constructed. Zola is primarily concerned with a social group which, considered as a whole, overshadows the importance of the individual. (pp. 367-68)

Blasco begins with the presentation of three or four characters taken from the center of the action which is to follow. The scene is long enough to give the setting and the nature of the main characters. The events in this chapter are often episodic, having no place in the plot. After this, Blasco reverts, usually one or two generations, and begins the story. He individualizes fewer characters than Zola, so that the social group which constitutes the background, although a definite entity, is incomplete and therefore indistinct. This method has a double effect. It centers more attention upon the leading characters but the setting is more vague. He, too, has the episodic type of plot, but often introduces propaganda to such an extent that he seems to be carried away by the idea and to forget that he is writing a novel instead of a social thesis. There is often a lack of proportion and coördination due, without doubt, to his habit of writing rapidly.

The range of characters which Zola creates is not extended. A monotonous undercurrent of bestiality is ever present, tingeing the better characters with grossness and turning the worst ones into the most consummate of human brutes. They are uniformly simple in psychology, being motivated by a single idea, a single passion, and their aim in life is to satisfy this idea or passion. Since his thesis was physiological, the most common inciting agent is that of the two physical hungers, special emphasis being placed upon sexual desire. Thus, Zola's characters are individuals from whose natures have been taken psychological complexity and spirituality and who, handicapped by unconquerable hereditary weaknesses, struggle in a grim and dreary fight against the blind forces of their environment. There are not great contrasts of strength and weakness, but rather a monotony of little souls and torpid minds.

Blasco Ibáñez excels in the portrayal of virile manhood. It seems, indeed, that by a projection of his own dynamic personality he creates the characters of iron will, his fighters who struggle against great odds. That they must succumb in the end is a reflection of Blasco's own philosophy. Progress is slow and the efforts of one man are unavailing against age-old powers. Therefore the end of life should be action for its own sake and not for the work achieved. In contrast to these are weaklings such as Tonet *(Cañas y barro)*, Juanito *(Arroz y tartana)* and the contrast and interplay of these two types heighten the effect of reality. Although Blasco, too, shows a simplicity in psychological motivation, he does not carry it to the point of making the physiological govern the psychological as Zola tried to do. There is great inequality in Blasco's character portrayal, but the characters of outstanding personality tend to overbalance the effect of the weak and colorless. (pp. 368-69)

The fatalistic element in Blasco is more varying than in Zola and his novels are consistently more hopeful only in his higher conception of human life. When the conquering forces have a recognizable cause, they may be opposed and ultimately overcome. But when they are within the man himself, there is no power which can change them; then is resignation the only open course.

This aspect of morality shows some difference, if not a great one, between Zola and Blasco; but in respect to the common interpretation of morality—grossness—the divergence is marked. Although it was in a spirit of scientific investigation that Zola spread before the reader an array of pornographic details which purported to be entirely true to nature, the dirtiness and obscenity are unfit for artistic purposes. One may accuse Blasco of being plain spoken or indelicate in his novels, but rarely of being gross or vulgar. Certain books contain passages which are, in their sensual suggestiveness, worse, perhaps than Zola's open display of all which society ordinarily reserves for individual privacy, but he does not insist upon tainting every scene with coarseness. His books are rugged and the colors are strong, but indecency does not clog the vivid portrayal of life.

There is no doubt that Zola had a great influence upon Blasco Ibáñez, especially in his earlier works; but, having received suggestions, Blasco did not give them forth in the same form. Rather did he assimilate them, then express them, modified by his own personality, augmented by his individual concepts and experiences, and made thoroughly Spanish. The interpretation of human psychology, the type of characters selected and certain aesthetic touches could belong to no one but Blasco. The relation, therefore, of Blasco Ibáñez to Zola is not that of an imitator, but of one of a common school of literature and only in so far as he portrays sections of Spanish life which correspond to the French scenes presented by Zola, can he justly be called the "Spanish Zola." (pp. 370-71)

> *Katherine Reding [later Katherine Reding Whitmore], "Blasco Ibáñez and Zola," in* Hispania *(© 1923 The American Association of Teachers of Spanish and Portuguese, Inc.), Vol. VI, No. 6, December, 1923, pp. 365-71.**

THE OUTLOOK (essay date 1925)

No one of the fifteen short stories in [*The Old Woman of the Movies, and Other Stories*] fails to attain an obvious effectiveness; Mr. Ibañez is too able and experienced a master of his craft for that. But for the very reason that his best so far transcends the lesser achievements with which he too often contents himself, a critical reader may be moved to impatience. The book contains, for instance, half a dozen war stories, including that which supplies the covering title. Some of them are moving, because the episodes chosen are poignant and the Great War is still near enough to stimulate the reader's responsive imagination. But they are sentimental and theatric rather than in the higher sense tragic; men and women of lesser reputation have achieved finer work in the same field, as, of course, Mr. Ibañez has himself done elsewhere. Nor are most of the other tales of notable quality; but to this there are a few brilliant exceptions. Two especially stand out—**"The Widow's Loan"** and **"The Four Sons of Eve"**—each of which is an almost perfect example of the short story. Both have South American settings, but the latter, perhaps, is the best. In it an old Argentinian laborer relates a whimsical allegory of our first mother and her spoiled favorites, introduces saints, cherubs, archangels, Satan, and the Almighty himself with an amusing naïveté wholly without offense, and reminiscent rather of the colorful and childlike work of primitive religious art or the early mystery plays than of anything more modern.

A review of "The Old Woman of the Movies, and Other Stories," in The Outlook, *August 12, 1925, p. 527.*

LOUIS KRONENBERGER (essay date 1927)

[*Kronenberger comments on the contrast between Blasco-Ibáñez's "great attention to detail" and the careless construction of the novel* The Mob.]

It is not as a novel that **"The Mob"** deserves any great recognition, but rather as a series of portraits and backgrounds. Señor Blasco Ibáñez has to tell of the poor in Madrid, the many kinds of poor who haunt the depths of the city, living lives of squalor, struggling for just the food and lodging which will keep them alive; and with these masses as his background he presents us with a number of vivid and interesting figures who emerge from the rest.

The story of **"The Mob"** is the story of Isidro Maltrata, of a family of beggars and ragpickers and servants, who is early in life more or less adopted by a rich old woman for whom his mother works, educated and petted, only on her sudden death to find himself unprovided for because she leaves no will. He becomes a kind of hack writer, lacking the stamina and perserverance to make good as a reporter or author, who does penny-a-liners, occasional articles, translations. . . .

It is rather his milieu than himself which makes Maltrata interesting. The young rebel and littérateur, arrogant and youthful, who scrapes along from day to day, who takes the young Feliciana as his mistress, though a very lifelike figure, is nothing after all but the young writer the world over. But there is something different, something unique about the Maltrata of the slums of Madrid, coming in contact not with Latin Quarter wastrels of Greenwich Village poseurs or long-haired Bloomsbury poets, but with wretches of the lowest class who in their ignorance and their poverty respect him and regard him as a gentleman; his is not the traditional literary world of young men, but the world of poachers and thieves, of hideous monks in rags, of filthy gypsies and people doomed by their estate never to rise.

And these people appear before us with that peculiar vividness that belongs only to the people of slums. Señor Blasco Ibáñez's publishers compare this book to a Goya painting; and though it never achieves such memorableness, the comparison is good, at least in kind, for here is the material from which Goya draws some of his masterpieces. These pen pictures give us the hopeless filth and waste and unhealthiness which are so strikingly Spanish—the poverty and unenlightenment which often seems as medieval as it is modern. The priest Don Vicente; Maltrata's rag-picking grandmother who hides away the paste stones she imagines are precious jewels; Feliciana's father, going in the dead of night with his ferret and his dogs to kill rabbits and sell them; Maltrata's horrible half-brother; the gypsy colony with their own strange customs—these seem to us to come to us not so much out of a foreign land as out of the past, the dark, evil-smelling past redolent of the crooked streets of Madrid and Paris, the crimes of Villon and his cronies, the villainies of a forgotten underworld. They are vivid, at times almost spectacularly vivid; they are, indeed, portraits rather than people.

Señor Blasco Ibáñez writes in **"The Mob,"** as always, with great attention to detail, careless of the structure of his novel and quite indifferent to the arts of economy and suggestion. He paints a full canvas, satisfying rather than inciting the imagination. His work strikes one, consequently, as it has struck one in earlier novels, as a kind of vigorous and powerful journalism. He always has something to say and he never has any trouble saying it. His novel is a careless composite of scenes and people and places, and he is clever enough to call it **"The Mob"** that it may appear to be the chronicle of all these things. In Isidro Maltrata he has merely supplied us with a protagonist of superior mind who struggles without much success against the fate of the mob to which, by birth, he belongs. That we cannot quite live Maltrata's life with him, which a greater writer would make us do, proves the limitations of Blasco Ibáñez the artist; but the fact that we are always keen observers of Maltrata's struggle proves Blasco Ibáñez to be an expressive and powerful journalist.

Louis Kronenberger, "Ibáñez Explores the Slums of Madrid," in The New York Times Book Review *(copyright © 1927 by The New York Times Company; reprinted by permission), July 24, 1927, p. 13.*

WALTER STARKIE (essay date 1928)

[*Starkie provides a survey of Blasco Ibáñez's major fiction.*]

If we pay too much heed to the later filmed novels of Blasco Ibáñez we shall not understand his mentality. At heart he was always an intense Spaniard, but one from the Mediterranean seaboard, revelling in the gorgeous colours of the Riviera and in the rhetorical profusion in literary style. . . . Nature, by its succession of transverse mountain ranges, has broken the Iberian peninsula into separate sections, and this dislocation has imposed localism and isolation on the inhabitants. It is on account of this localisation that the modern Spanish novel is so interesting to us. We find in it a wealth of local colour that exists rarely in the novels of other more progressive countries, where the tendency has been to evolve a uniform cosmopolitan type of literature. When we read the works of Thomas Hardy we are struck by his deep attachment to the soil of his native Wessex, the soil which he peoples, not only with its modern but also with its ancient inhabitants back to the days of the old kingdom. With this thought in our minds we shall understand the value of the modern novelists of Spain. Ibáñez in his early novels was purely Valencian, and it was only after he left Spain for Europe and the world that he threw off his Spanish personality and became a cosmopolitan writer whose characters may belong to any country or civilisation.

Perhaps the greatest quality of Blasco Ibáñez was his energy. In his life he was the antithesis to the novelist who works away peacefully in some secluded spot. (p. 542)

I should feel inclined to say that rather than a conquistador we should call him a stage conquistador like the braggadocio captain in the ancient *Commedia dell'Arte.* The note of boastfulness runs through all his work, and at times it becomes the veriest gasconading. He always dreamt of splendours heaped upon splendours. . . . All his life Blasco Ibáñez tried to perform impossible feats. He strikes us as one who was always posturing to the world. It was his impulsiveness and his posturing that led him into excesses of vulgarity and bad taste. It was this that led him to publish the infamous libel [*Alfonso XIII desenmascarado (Alfonso XIII. Unmasked)*], in which he attempts to blacken for the world the character of the King of

Spain, who has played so noble a part in creating modern Spain. That pamphlet, though it was translated into English and circulated freely, did more to harm Blasco Ibáñez's reputation than anything he ever wrote, because it showed that he could descend from political argument to the depths of mere personal abuse. In fact all through his life Blasco Ibáñez was not fitted to play the politician. First of all he was a writer possessing a powerful imagination but little reflection. He was a florid orator gifted with facility for pouring out rhetoric, but with little self-criticism. He had none of the subtlety that is needed for the modern politician. There was often a note of generosity in his early political struggles before he became one of the capitalists of literature, but it was vitiated by his lack of restraint. The present writer, in a visit to Unamuno at Salamanca in 1921, asked him what he thought of Ibáñez as an artist. The sage replied that Ibáñez was more an impressionist than an artist. . . . Blasco Ibáñez is read and seen by all the world: his vision of Spain has been multiplied by mass production, and countless people take it as the truth. In this respect he may be considered a creator of the 'stage-Spaniard.' But such a criticism is not altogether just to him. It is true that the man who reads only the novels of Blasco Ibáñez will obtain a limited vision of modern Spain—a vision which does not illuminate the strength and forcefulness of the Spanish people, its infinite variety. Everyone who has read his novels should, then, turn to the works of Pío Baroja, the arch-European, as he calls himself, of the Basque land, to Ramón Pérez de Ayala, the exquisite stylist, or else to Ricardo León, the traditional writer. These writers give us an antidote to the novels of Ibáñez. None of those writers, however, has the literary profusion—we might call it generosity—of Blasco Ibáñez. His works are written by impulse and are the outpouring of his genius. He is like one of those fabulously rich caliphs of the *Arabian Nights* who delight in dazzling their friends by jewel after jewel. His appearance and his speech intensified the impression of generous profusion. (pp. 543-44)

The earliest book is a collection of Valencian stories entitled **Cuentos Valencianos,** which impress us by their realistic touches. They describe scenes and traditions of the province in a terse style that at times recalls Verga's inimitable stories of rustic Sicily. But Blasco Ibáñez does not possess the crisp style of the Sicilian and his powers of suggestion. He is a more florid writer, and he piles on effect after effect. The stories, however, are interesting because they point to the way which the author's genius was to follow. In *Flor de Mayo (Mayflower),* one of the next works to be published, we already see the master hand. The story describes life among the fisher-folk of Valencia, and suggests to our mind Synge's account of the hardy inhabitants of the Arran Isles. But the Mediterranean is a more soft-hearted god than the fierce Atlantic: the fishing-folk of Valencia increase their substance by profitable smuggling expeditions to Algiers, and in this story the hero of the book Pascual nicknamed *El Retor* builds his boat the *Mayflower* on the proceeds of one of such forays. With masterly skill the author sets the scene for his characters, and little by little we penetrate deeper and deeper into the lives of these hardy folk. The most striking description in the book is that given of the terrible storm wherein the ship is doomed and El Retor's son is drowned. No less striking is the scene afterwards when the boy's body is washed up on the rocky coast close to where stand his mother Dolores and the aged grandmother. . . . Such a scene cannot fail to move us by its pathos, though it has not the wonderful simplicity of Synge's *Riders to the Sea,* with its stark tragic setting. . . . Ibáñez does not end his book with the cry of despair: instead he introduces the social thesis. It is not the sea which

is responsible for poor Pascualet's death. 'Over there is the enemy, the true author of the catastrophe': and the sea daughter's great, swollen fist was raised threateningly towards the city as she vomited forth curses: 'Let all those who bargain in the fish market come along. Did they still think fish too dear? At no cheap price is it bought!'

If in *Flor de Mayo* the author described the lives of the humbler folk of the coast, in **Arroz y Tartana** he enters the lives of the bourgeoisie of Valencia. In this book he adopts the system of Zola in *Pot Bouille* and describes with the utmost minuteness of detail the various trades and systems of business. Valencia, even in the Middle Ages, was famous for its 'Calle de Platería,' full of goldsmiths' shops, and its 'Loza Valenciana,' or delf-ware. In spite of the frequent brilliant descriptions, **Arroz y Tartana** is one of the poorest of the regional novels of the author. Far more successful is **La Barraca (The Cabin).** . . . The theme of **La Barraca** is one that reaches the folk of 'La Huerta,' the 'Garden of Spain.' It is a remorseless picture of their relation to the rural problems of Spain. After reading the novel we can understand the pride of race of the Spanish peasant, his superstition and ferocity when roused. With its vivid description of the unpopular landlord, the grumbling peasantry and boycotting, the work reminds us again of many regional novels of Ireland. There is the same pessimism. . . . (pp. 545-47)

The poignant scenes in **La Barraca** make such a strong appeal that we are apt to forget other equally brilliant effects of the novelist's art. Ibáñez writes carelessly as if he had dashed off the proofs to the printer without a correction. . . . Ibáñez is an impulsive writer who writes under the direct inspiration of the visions called up by his fertile imagination. In **Cañas y Barro (Reeds and Mud)** . . . he adopts the same method as in **La Barraca** and sets his story among the humble folk of Valencia, but this time in the district skirting the lake of Albufera, at the little village of Palmar, where the inhabitants gain their livelihood mostly from lake fishing. As in the case of the former novels, the author uses the simplest means to unfold his plot. . . . Ibáñez also tried hard to follow the naturalist doctrine of impersonality in art. But an impersonal art should not smile or weep or show any trace of human sympathy, merely contenting itself with noting down cold objective impressions. As Croce shows, this is an impossibility, and however much writers strive to reconstruct from human documents the psychological processes, sooner or later, if they are artists and not psychoanalysts, they give way to the lyrical side of their personality. Reality is closely studied in **Cañas y Barro:** we see down to the second waistcoat button of those fishermen. With consummate skill the author makes his story spring into being from the Albufera lake just as if he had been a magician capable of calling up visions with his wand. The journey of the little post-boat on the lake full of passengers introduces us to the chief characters of the book. And those characters are no shady beings: they are men of flesh and bone who live a life of their own. . . . No novel in modern literature is so well constructed in its various phases. There is an exact proportion between the different elements. We have as a background the life of the fishing village: then in the foreground stand the protagonists of the drama. Above we have the author's symbolism which explains the moral trend of the work. And this symbolism he suggests through the novel by little touches here and there. When Tonet and Neleta were children they lost themselves one night on the mountain. This casual incident foreshadows their tragic destiny. In the Ibsenian manner Ibáñez often by means of a minor character explains the moral to us. Sangonera, especially, is one of the most striking instances in the book. If we look for Sangonera's ancestors we shall have to go back to early Spanish literature when Celestina the bawd and Lazarillo the Picaresque knave drank and joked their way through their dishevelled lives. (pp. 548-50)

There is no doubt that *Cañas y Barro* is Blasco Ibáñez's masterpiece, even though some critics prefer *La Barraca*. Both books will always be considered as characteristic of Valencia as the plays of the brothers Quintero are of Seville or the novels of Pereda of Santander. The comparison with Pereda is interesting, because as the founder of the realistic school of fiction he has a certain superficial resemblance to our author. He too had the gift of drawing memorable characters. . . . Pereda would not have gone so far in realism as Ibáñez, for he insisted that art should transform reality and make it poetic. He would have objected to the photographic description of unpleasant situations such as we often meet in Ibáñez. Where there is the greatest divergence between the two authors is in the matter of style. The prose of Pereda is majestic, and brings to our minds the saying that Spanish is the language of kings. So broad is the phrase that it seems to be carved in marble, and with such a sense of conciseness that it suggests Tacitus. Blasco Ibáñez has none of that massiveness of style; he always writes in a hurry, without thinking. But sometimes he produces an overwhelming effect on us by the picturesque, untidy, rapid scenes which pass swiftly before our eyes as in a cinema. The scene of the bird-shooting on Albufera lake or else the description of the Festival of the Infant Jesus in the village is unequalled in modern Spanish literature for vigour. At other times he wearies the reader by too long and minute descriptions, and creates so much background that the characters are overwhelmed. It is with regret that we leave this period of Ibáñez's work, for it includes his finest work. The scenes of these early books he never forgot in after-life, and many of the characters are taken from real life. (pp. 551-52)

If the early years of Blasco Ibáñez's life turned his thoughts to his own townsmen and their problems, his arrival in Madrid made him establish closer relations with the outer world. There is thus a vast cleavage between the regional novels and the novels of this second period which we might call novels of the cities of Spain. The early works belong clearly to the school of fiction which sprang up in Spain owing to the influence of Pérez Galdós, the greatest novelist since Cervantes. The novels of the cities, on the other hand, though Spanish in surroundings, are more definitely influenced by French writers such as Zola and the Goncourts. By politics and by temperament Blasco Ibáñez followed in the wake of Zola, and attempted to do for Madrid and Toledo what the Frenchman had done for Paris and Lourdes. The vision of the author widens, and he begins to incorporate social problems, not as passing symbols in his work, but as the central column of the edifice. And this broadening of vision coincides with his definite entry into politics, as if he had then determined to explore the innermost recesses of Spain in order to discover the secrets of tradition and superstition. In successive novels we obtain a vision of a society which had been hidden from our gaze. In *El Intruso (The Intruder)* we descend into the mines near the city of Bilbao and watch the workers living the lives of the mime Nibelung so that capitalists may thrive and wax powerful. Next we pass from Galicia to South Spain, to the city of Jérez, whence the rich wine flows in golden streams to all the world. Then again in *La Horda* the scene changes to the slums of Madrid, where thousands of wretched waifs creep and crawl for a living denied to them by a civilisation of money-grabbers. Not even the

sacred city of Toledo escapes this inexorable investigator, for in *La Catedral* [*The Shadow of the Cathedral*] the author leads us scene by scene into the lives of cardinals, bishops, abbots, curates, even the humblest beggars, who throng round the majestic structure. Such novels lack the wonderful unity of *La Barraca* and *Cañas y Barro*. We no longer feel that the folk are there in the background as an invisible chorus approving and condemning. The author's vision is magnificent in the extent it covers, but it fails to move us because we do not feel the same excitement or passion. He gives the impression of having vacillated between the novel of customs and the novel of social thesis. Like Zola, he wanted to preach a new revolutionary gospel to humanity, and each hero in these novels resembles Pierre Froment in *Paris,* who wants to blow up the church of the Sacred Heart and wipe away the age of superstition. So, too, Luna in *La Catedral* and Salvatierra in *La Bodega* dream of the millennium and theorise in anarchy. They are colourless creatures these characteristic heroes of the modern social novel, and they pass before our eyes like uncertain ghostly phantoms. The desire for antithesis makes the author set as contrast to the theorists other characters who become symbols of brutal reality. They massacre and destroy the illusions of the pale-eyed fanatics and bring down upon them the pall of tragedy. The finest scenes of these books are the descriptions of the life in the various cities. In *La Catedral* . . . the author tries to do for Toledo what Huysmans did for Chartres, and, without rivalling the richness and subtlety of the Belgian, he has succeeded in capturing the atmosphere of the mother-church of Spain. So powerful is his imagination that we become obsessed and even stifled by the huge bulk of the cathedral: it weighs down upon us with all the ponderousness of past tradition as we see it smothered by the swarm of poverty-sticken buildings that cling close to its walls, permitting it to display none of its exterior beauties. Blasco Ibáñez wrote *La Catedral* with the intention of condemning the traditions and superstitions of the past which hang over Toledo. The cathedral to the young revolutionary was a gigantic tumour which 'blistered the Spanish epidermis, like the scars of its ancient infirmities.' He loathes its rich prelates bloated in the dignity and purple, but against his will he becomes little by little fascinated by the place. Gabriel Luna, for all his revolutionary theories, returns for peace to the cathedral: the great silence he found within the immense pile of worked stone caressed him and drew away his thoughts from his own intimate sufferings. The most striking passages in the book are those which describe the life in the 'claverías,' or upper cloister. All along this upper cloister there were doors and windows belonging to the rooms of the college servants which were transmitted from father to son. Ibáñez excels in the description of the queer, grotesque types that pullulate in this upper town. . . . [All] these characters live for us. But not so Gabriel Luna. Whenever Ibáñez thinks of him he pulls out his note-books and we are plunged into digressions on Socialism. (pp. 552-54)

It cannot be said that *La Horda (The Rabble)* is more successful than *La Catedral*. It lacks the beauty of description of the latter, but it is mainly interesting on account of the realistic description of Madrid. Maltrana, like Gabriel Luna, is a delicate lad who has studied deeply but has not been able to make good. There is a hopelessness about all these young people in spite of all their modern thinking. Maltrana falls in love with a girl and goes to live with her, but illness descends upon them: she is taken to the hospital dying, and her body is sent after death to be dissected by students of anatomy. Ibáñez, following his naturalist theories, introduces frequent digressions that weary the reader. In *La Horda* a great part of the book is devoted to a description of the poaching expeditions that are carried out in the royal demesne of 'El Pardo.' These digressions help the author to introduce many vivid secondary characters, but they spoil the construction of the book. The same criticism may be applied to *El Intruso* . . . though it contains many vivid pages describing the life in Bilbao, and the hero, Doctor Aresti, is one of the living characters created by the author. (p. 554)

Many of the novels seem to lack a hero. In *Sangre y Arena,* one of the brilliant works of his middle period, we are much more interested in the crowd of bandits and in the minor members of the bull-ring than in Juan Gallardo or Doña Sol. This novel, which has been dramatised and even filmed, has won immense celebrity for the author because it describes the national spectacle of the Spaniards—bull-fighting. Few writers have ever written more vivacious accounts of the bustling scene, the chattering women, the brilliant colours, the golden sun which beats down on the arena, the brocaded toreadors, the rousing music—all this lives for us through the vivid style of the author. In fact we are really more interested in all the side-shows of the 'corrida' than in the central vision itself. With infinite detail the author analyses the camp-followers, the 'touts' who follow the toreador everywhere as long as he is the public idol. But all this was not the author's purpose in writing the book. Though he gives an account of bull-fighting which finds favour with every 'aficionado' of the art, he sets out with determination to expose all that is tragic in the 'corrida.' (p. 555)

Sangre y Arena is a novel that is definitely Spanish in its scope, and it turned Blasco Ibáñez's attention to other aspects of his country—especially to problems created by race and religion. Spain had in Benito Pérez Galdós a great creator of such a type of novel, and it was not surprising that Ibáñez should try to emulate *Gloria*. In *Gloria* Galdós described the struggle between Christianity and Judaism on a vast canvas that recalls at times Balzac by its intensity. In *Los Muertos Mandan (The Dead Command)* and *Luna Benamor* Ibáñez sets the same problem: in both the hero cannot marry the heroine because she is a Jewess, and nothing is left him to do but renounce the struggle against the forces of tradition. It is interesting to note that the gospel of Ibáñez in 1907 is not more hopeful than that of Galdós in 1877. . . . It is difficult to discover the note of serenity in Blasco Ibáñez, who was not able to abstract himself from the world like Galdós and look down on all the miseries of our condition. Ibáñez never gives us the impression of having lived, like Marcus Aurelius, on a mountain top; he is always struggling in the plain amid the dust and heat, and so he cannot take all humanity in a comprehensive gaze. (p. 557)

At the outset of the war he declared himself on the side of the Allies, and undertook the task of upholding their cause among the neutral nations. Not only did he write flaming articles, but he visited the front on repeated occasions, and as a result produced his most popular work, *Los Cuatro Jinetes del Apocalipsis (The Four Horsemen of the Apocalypse)*. This book had the biggest sale on record, and established Ibáñez as the world's best seller. It is difficult to speak calmly now of a book that described those terrible years of ordeal. As we read its descriptions of scenes of the war period we know how true they were in detail. And yet as a work of literature it is negligible and not worthy to be compared with *Le Feu*, by Barbusse, or *La Débâcle*, by Zola. It is essentially a book written for the American cinema, with its conventional plot and huge scenic apparatus. Countless books appeared during the war describing the contrast between Berlin and Paris and the spy systems of both countries, but Ibáñez paints on a broader canvas than any

of those writers, and by sheer brute force he manages to excite us. The description of the Apocalyptic beast rising from the sea and becoming the terrible symbol of evil for humanity terrifies the crowd like those huge animals that children see in nightmares. There are many cheap and vulgar effects that arrest the attention of the frivolous reader of sensational novels, but there is little to remind us of the former author of *La Barraca* or *Cañas y Barro*. Julio Desnoyers, the young Argentinian, is a sympathetic character, well drawn in contrast to the superficial Margarita, who is only a replica of the familiar Doña Sol. Such a work proved that Ibáñez was definitely moving away from the Spanish novel. In his next work, *Mare Nostrum* . . . , he follows the same course and produces another conventional war novel. . . . *Mare Nostrum,* though it is written around a sensational story, contains beautiful descriptions of the sea which suggest early novels such as *Flor de Mayo*. In fact, so powerful is the author's description of the sea that it becomes the true hero of the book and all the characters become pigmies in stature. As a description of the Mediterranean coast it is most striking, and proves that the author must have visited every creek and bay. . . . After the war in 1919 Ibáñez tried other paths, but always in the world of the cosmopolitan novel, where the characters live amid scenes of gambling and debauchery. In *Los Enemigos de la Mujer (The Enemies of Women)*, where he tells a story of five woman-haters who live at Monte Carlo and who end by renouncing their hate, the stage is set in beautiful surroundings, but there is little to interest the serious reader. It was soon after this that the author undertook his tour round the world in a ship laden with millionaires. He narrated the events of his voyage in a charming three-volume book entitled *La Vuelta al Mundo de un Novelista (A Novelist's Tour Round the World)*. He has not written political or economic studies on the countries he visited, but simply told us what he saw in his own way. . . . In the description of the various countries the author so varies his account by remarks about the history of the several countries that the book is of interest as a guide to his temperament. After his return from that journey he set to work with greater energy than ever on a series of novels which show that he was turning back again towards his native land, this time to study its history of past greatness. In *A los Piés de Venus (At the Feet of Venus)* he tells the story of the Borgias from Spain, showing that Caesar was one of the first men to attempt the task of Italian unity: in *Las Riquezas del Gran Kan (The Riches of the Great Khan)* he devotes his attention to the life of Christopher Columbus, and thus continues his task of writing the history of Spanish America. It is sad to reflect that death has carried him away before he put the finishing touches to that book. We are thus only left with a skeleton of what he would have done for the history of the Spanish world had he been spared. Looking back over his work, we are struck by the vast expanses covered by his imagination. He was a big, untidy genius with no gift of style, but sometimes when his imagination ran riot he would dash off scenes in hot haste that are among the most striking in all the modern literature of Spain. (pp. 557-59)

> *Walter Starkie, "Blasco Ibáñez, 1867-1928," in* The Nineteenth Century and After, *Vol. CIII, No. DCXIV, April, 1928, pp. 542-59.*

J. O. SWAIN   (essay date 1935)

[*Swain opens his essay on the novel* Cañas y barro *by discussing the importance of a fully realised setting in contemporary Spanish fiction. He states that "Vincente Blasco Ibáñez can easily be given first place" among novelists who skillfully employ local color, finding this especially true in the novels with Valencian settings:* Arroz y tartana, The Mayflower, The Cabin, *and* Reeds and Mud. *The rest of Swain's essay recounts his visit to the locale of the novel* Reeds and Mud, *the work he considers Blasco Ibáñez's masterpiece.*]

The student of the modern Spanish novel who visits Spain will find hundreds of interesting places made romantic by some masterpiece of the great output in that literary genre during the past seventy-five years. Fernán Caballero, Alarcón, Valera, Palacio Valdés, Pereda, Pardo Bazán, and Vicente Blasco Ibáñez, all have made famous some village, city, cathedral, river, or province of our always romantic Spain. The more deeply we read into the modern Spanish novel, the more forcibly we are struck by the importance given to local color. The Spanish writer, especially the novelist, apparently cannot or will not separate his work from its background. The background often may even be considered as one of the characters—many times a very important one. For that reason it is seldom possible for one to understand, more than superficially, modern or contemporary Spanish novels without first growing familiar with their settings. . . .

Of the novelists that have made local color do yeoman's duty in their writings, Vicente Blasco Ibáñez can easily be given first place. Especially in his Valencian novels, *Arroz y tartana, Flor de Mayo, La barraca,* and *Cañas y barro*, does the setting play an important rôle. Of these four, the last is the most dependent on its milieu. We may even agree with some critics and say that La Albufera is the only indispensable character in the novel. For we must confess that the author has truly given this lake the dignity of a character. (p. 25)

Of course what Blasco wrote was just a novel. Nevertheless there comes back to me repeatedly the definition of a novel: "A novel is a fictitious story that could have happened." Then I imagine twilight on the lake, Neleta and Tonet alone on Cañamél's boat. Yes, *Cañas y barro* is a story that could have happened. Blasco has created characters in this novel—his strongest woman in Neleta and his masterpiece in the old man, Tío Paloma. But his greatest accomplishment has been to give character and permanency to the Albufera of thirty years ago. The lake may disappear one day entirely, as our materialism, which is present even in Spain, teaches us that there is more money in rice than in eels, but Blasco's Albufera, like Goya's "Majas" or Velazquez' "Don Baltazar," belongs to the ages. He has caught not so much the measurements of the lake, the number of houses on the island, or the number of *arrobas* of eels that may be taken in one night in the famous first-choice place, *la Sequiota,* as he has the spirit of this body of water. He has indeed preserved for the coming generations an idealized conception of a rather commonplace setting. . . . (p. 34)

J. O. Swain "The Albufera Thirty Years After (Memories of 'Cañas y barro')," in Hispania *(© 1935 The American Association of Teachers of Spanish and Portuguese, Inc.), Vol. XVIII, No. 1, February, 1935, pp. 25-34.*

SHERMAN H. EOFF (essay date 1961)

[*Eoff discusses Blasco Ibáñez's "adaptation of French naturalism," which is especially evident in the Valencian novels. For other examinations of Blasco Ibáñez's Naturalism, see the essays by Havelock Ellis, J. Fitzmaurice Kelly, and Katherine Reding excerpted above.*]

The most thorough adaptation of French naturalism in Spain is found in the early, or Valencian, novels of Blasco Ibáñez, whose admiration for Zola was especially strong as he began his novelistic career. Like Pardo Bazán, Blasco Ibáñez was attracted to Zola primarily by the vitality of his art and perhaps to some extent by his sensationalism. In his case, however, it was easier to adopt a naturalistic view of man's place. He was not particularly interested in philosophical ideas, but he was a lover of nature in the raw and personally inclined to co-operate with the spontaneous, natural side of his being. Moreover, he was not restrained by religious convictions from plunging wholeheartedly into the spirit of Zola's exaltation of primal natural forces. As a consequence of this affiliation between intellectual attitude and earthiness of style, he produced a more authentic version of naturalism than Pardo Bazán, at the same time achieving in his novels a stronger artistic consistency than she was able to attain under the handicap of a loyalty divided between art and her philosophical-religious outlook.

The outstanding example of Blasco Ibáñez's naturalism is *Cañas y barro*, of which the author said: "This is my favorite novel . . . it is the one that holds for me the most pleasant memory, the one that I composed with most solidity, the one that seems to me the best rounded" (*redonda*). In this story the novelist grasps the malevolent spirit of primitive nature, holds it at close range, and achieves the sharp singleness of effect that one generally finds in a short story. His procedure is to portray a locale and to impart through his portraiture the suggestion of a sinister transcendent power. The place is the Albufera, a swampy lake region near Valencia, where the inhabitants eke out a wretched existence fishing and cultivating rice. In this setting the people harmonize with their milieu and through it appear to be oppressed by a cruelty that envelops more than their immediate situation. This blending of two levels of reality, the harsh earthiness of immediate surroundings and a fateful overtone of transcendent implications, is maintained throughout the novel. It begins in the initial chapter, where we are introduced first to the filthiness of the mailboat and the brutishness of its occupants, "a nauseating mixture of gelatinous skins, scales of fish that have been raised in the mud, dirty feet, and grimy clothes" . . . ; and then to the awe-inspiring La Dehesa, "the almost virgin forest . . . where fierce bulls pasture and huge reptiles live in the shadows" . . . , habitat of the serpent Sancha who, according to legend, had crushed its one-time friend and companion, a shepherd boy home from the wars.

Within this milieu of coarse physical immediateness veiled with an ominous suggestiveness, Blasco Ibáñez constructs a plot of personal relations, a love story between Tonet, son of the hardworking rice farmer Tío Tòni and grandson of the fisherman Tío "Paloma," and Neleta, his erstwhile childhood companion. The latter has grown up determined to escape from her poverty, and while Tonet was away at war she has married Cañamèl, well-to-do but sickly tavern owner. The author makes a concession to the subject of environmental influence on personality in the second and third chapters, where he gives a retrospective account of Tonet and Neleta's background. This explanatory information, which is dull reading in comparison with the vivid scenes of customs, such as the drawing of lots for favorable fishing positions (chapter 4), is unnecessarily long and may be considered the novel's one technical flaw; for the novel is after all not so much a story of character as it is of situation, in which human beings are pitted against destructive natural forces. Circumstances explain in some degree the spiritless drifting of Tonet and the fierce ambition of Neleta and hence contribute to the plot complication. But they are really secondary to the stronger factors of sex and instinct, which operate at the bidding of an all-powerful Nature that works its will through the medium of local conditions.

In the climactic outcome of the narrative action we are led first to the crisis of the illicit love affair between Tonet and Neleta, which includes the emotional breakdown of the former, the protagonist, and then to the tonal climax bearing on man's haplessness in the clutches of nature. Cañamèl dies, specifying in his will that his widow must not marry or have anything to do with men if she is to keep his property. Neleta therefore refuses to marry Tonet or associate with him openly, and when their child is born she orders her lover to take it to Valencia secretly, hoping thus to evade the spying eyes of Cañamèl's former sister-in-law, who has long suspected her infidelity. Fear and remorse overwhelm Tonet on his way to Valencia, and in desperation he throws the baby in the lake. Some days later during a bird hunt, when his dog discovers the baby's corpse, a viscous, formless mass covered with leeches, he flees from the scene and commits suicide.

In a sense Tonet is a victim of his own weakness, and the gradual intensification of his moral breakdown is a psychological development of considerable interest in itself. But the dominant narrative effect points to the cruelty in the natural world. Neleta is in effect an instrument of nature who crushes individual life just as the serpent Sancha had crushed the shepherd youth. In his last desperate moments Tonet himself compares his lover to the serpent. The love story thus is an occasion for the assertion of a malevolent force in a specific manifestation, and the Albufera is the arena in which the human sacrifice is exacted. In a similarly grim and earthy arena and similarly through the instrumentality of sex, individuality is sacrificed to the monster Nature in Zola's *Germinal*. The tonal theme of human futility, which has been amplified throughout Blasco Ibáñez' story by attention to various examples of wretchedness, notably the vagabond "Sangonera," rises to a climactic height in the final scene, where Tío Tòni buries his son. While his foster daughter, "La Borda," stands by in silent anguish, still concealing her love for Tonet, the father ponders the emptiness of existence and the futility of his struggle with the lake. . . . (pp. 115-18)

Identifying his characters with their immediate surroundings, and these in turn with an enveloping philosophical tone, Blasco Ibáñez achieves a close unity between artistic form and philosophical perspective. . . . [Blasco Ibáñez] assumes a monistic viewpoint and produces strong connecting ties between the human being, his natural habitat, and the intellectual perspective that sees them as one. He therefore succeeds in creating the vivid impression that human ideals can rise only momentarily above the earth, which is their source and their destiny. . . .

Blasco Ibáñez not only creates the vivid portrait of a place in *Cañas y barro,* he combines with it a theme in perfect harmony with the monistic foundations of naturalism. Man is crushed by nature, not in his separateness from it but because he is one with it. On the basis of this oneness the author builds an unusually strong singleness of narrative effect. From an artistic viewpoint, *Cañas y barro* is a gem among modern Spanish novels. (p. 119)

Sherman H. Eoff, "The Deification of Unconscious Process," in his The Modern Spanish Novel: Comparative Essays Examining the Philosophical Impact of Science on Fiction *(reprinted by permission of New York University Press; copyright © 1961 by New York University), New York University Press, 1961, pp. 115-19.*

JOHN DEVLIN   (essay date 1966)

[*Devlin discusses the anticlericalism evident in Blasco Ibáñez's novels. He finds this element most prominent in the novels of social protest:* The Shadow of the Cathedral *and* The Intruder. *Devlin makes comparisons between Blasco Ibáñez and Benito Pérez Galdós (1843-1920), a novelist and major Spanish historian.*]

Anticlericalism in the novels of Blasco Ibáñez is much more intense and vehement than in the work of Pérez Galdós. This intensification is due in part to circumstances of time because the author's creative life spanned the aggravation of the conditions associated with the anticlerical spirit. The intensification is due in part also to the circumstances of the author's life, for, in his youth particularly, he lived close to the pattern of protest and shared in the aspirations of the downtrodden. These aspirations were summed up under the then rather loosely applied and nebulously understood term of "republican." . . . The republican cause became the meaning of his life. He plunged into the labyrinth of socialism, anarchism and syndicalism and became noted for his oratorical abilities in addresses to large groups of workers and peasants. (p. 96)

Critics have tried to divide Blasco Ibáñez' works into various periods. Consequently, there are almost as many divisions as critics. The subtleties of division need not be of concern here beyond the fact that the novels fall into three fairly definite general categories. The "Valencian novels" reveal Blasco Ibáñez, the young enthusiast and sensitive artist. The "Spanish novels" embrace the entire country and probe sociological problems (for example *Sangre y Arena* . . . , which is concerned with bull fighting). The "best sellers" exhibit the author's almost complete sacrifice of art in the interests of popularity. This latter tendency was first strongly manifested in *Los Cuatro Jinetes del Apocalipsis* . . . in which the much travelled novelist and rather self-styled world citizen placed his talents at the service of propaganda. To the first group belong such famous works as [*Arroz y Tartana, Flor de Mayo, Cañas y Barro,* the *Cuentos Valencianos*] . . . , and the masterpiece *La Barraca.* . . . These works are definitely "regional." Their intensity of plot and action and riot of keenly observed local color bring to life the *huerta,* or garden, of Spain, and, in *Flor de Mayo,* the life of the sea-faring folk of the region. In these works anticlericalism is usually incidental and not a main theme.

In *La Barraca* . . . , for example, the author was mainly concerned with his masterfully presented plot and the superb treatment of detail that evokes the plight of the simple people. He stresses their desperate need for education and liberation from prejudices, ignorance and the dead hand of an outmoded social system. The portrayal of "the Water Tribunal" shows the social system at its worst. An anticlerical thread is woven into the pattern of the scene. The Tribunal met to decide water disputes in front of the Cathedral of Valencia. The justice dispensed creaks with the abuses of age and the unrealistic traditionistic policy totally out of harmony with the reality of the peasants' struggle. The Door of the Apostles is described with the author's consummate skill, so frequently demonstrated in his treatment of Spanish monuments. But it seems as if the living judicial figures of the Tribunal merge with the stone apostolic figures in the tympanum. The scene, consequently, suggests the alliance of clerical power with the weight of thoroughgoing traditionalism. If the living set of figures is outmoded, are not the stone representations also? Of what service can religion be in the social struggle of mankind? Blasco Ibáñez does not say this bluntly. But here and elsewhere he leaves his anticlerical symbols ''open'' in such wise that it is very easy to infer from the ''clerical situation'' to religion in general. The tendency to make such an inference is greater because of the vehemence and power of his prose.

Another important instance in *La Barraca* can be found in the death and funeral rites of the little boy, *Pascualet*, nicknamed *Obispillo*. The child's unhappy end had been caused by the equally unhappy confluence of prejudice, filth, and the lack of proper medical and sanitary knowledge. The vigil rites are described with a combination of brutal realism, the power of which is somewhat marred by typically Spanish repetition and over-emphasis. The general impression, however, remains true to the lives of these simple folk. Anguished cries of ''Poor little Pascual! . . . Poor little Bishop!'' are intermingled with the regionalized rites and pious ejaculations. The simple faith of the people emerges vividly amid the macabre ritual. Intermingled in the various episodes is a note subtly suggesting that the comforts of religion—however much they may be believed by simple folk—are empty vain shows.

Another Valencian novel, *Cañas y Barro* . . . , deals with the rice growing people in the swamp and lake district of Albufera. It is a tale of violence, jealousy, and illicit love. Immersed in the vivid projection of his plot and the thoughtfully wrought character studies, the author had little occasion to dwell on anticlericalism. From time to time, however, it does enter—largely through the character Sangonereta, who is a strange combination of drunkard, idealist, and vagrant. It was Sangonereta's habit to sit in the twilight and enjoy the beauty of the lake at sunset, seen through his alcoholic haze. At such times he would meditate upon Christian philosophy. Judging from what we know through other sources of Blasco Ibáñez' attitudes toward religion and clericalism, it is reasonable to assume that he considers the Christian solution to life to be as impractical as Sangonereta himself. In fact, the vagrant seems to personify the author's criticism of the elements of mysticism and impracticality found in certain segments of the Spanish character—qualities which lead people directly into the toils of the rapacious, symbolized by the hydropic inn-keeper, Cañamel. . . . [Passages] in the novel contain acrid criticism of poor taste in liturgical functions, particularly in music. . . . Blasco Ibáñez continually alluded to liturgical bad taste, especially in *La Catedral*. . . . (pp. 96-9)

The author's participation in elected office in the national assembly symbolized an approach to his art on a national rather than a regional basis. This shift of interest, however, brought with it a perceptible decline in artistic achievement. In *La Catedral* the author's descriptive powers are unimpaired. His pictures of the Cathedral of Toledo and his many varied portraits of the people who live within the walls of the community continue to reveal the hand of a master. But in plot and action he slips from his previous heights. In this novel he adopts a technique that he was to follow in many other works. He creates a situation which provides a vehicle for description and conversational debate, the development of which conveys an extrinsic message. The novel form thus becomes a rather obvious instrument of propaganda. As time went on Blasco Ibáñez' plots became more and more threadbare.

In *La Catedral* the situation is the following: Gabriel returns to Toledo to spend his remaining days with his brother, a lay functionary of the Cathedral. Gabriel had been a seminarian who had changed his cassock for the garb of a *carlista* volunteer. Deflected from his vocation he spent some time in Paris where his religious convictions were displaced by revolutionary socialism. Upon his return to Toledo he is tubercular and almost at the point of death due to the many imprisonments and hardships suffered in the revolutionary cause. During his stay at the Cathedral Gabriel holds many conversations in which he alternately develops the tenets of his new creed to the laymen or defends his position against his brother and the other clerical supporters. Thus, he becomes the protagonist of a social theme which the author projects with heavy anticlerical coloring. Here it is difficult if not impossible to separate anticlericalism proper from antireligion. In Blasco Ibáñez' treatment the second seems to follow from the first. The symbolism of the Water Tribunal in *La Barraca* becomes the unambiguous theme of *La Catedral*. The Cathedral and its precincts are a sort of model-to-scale, a *microcosmus,* of Spain. Its beautiful galleries, residences, and porticos are peopled by powerful, predatory prelates and insignificant, quibbling canons. In the immediate shadow of the mouldering but magnificent walls and in the economic orbit of service to the Cathedral live the laymen (both the devout and the external conformists) whose children die of malnutrition and poverty. Gabriel, in his conversations, makes the people aware of their clerical oppression; his is the revolutionary voice amid the pattern of protest. (pp. 99-100)

In his various conversations Gabriel tackles the multiple problems associated with clericalism. By indirection, Spanish fear of the free circulation of ideas—so frequently attended by policies of rigorous censorship—is attacked. . . . Catholic intolerance in history becomes the source of one of Gabriel's meditations. . . . Throughout the work Blasco Ibáñez' historical interpretations leave a pessimistic impression. His view of Spanish history seems as negative as the ideas later developed by Ortega y Gasset.

As the novel progresses these themes, all of which on face value can be classed as anticlerical in the strict interpretation of the word, become charged with a bias that seems to be directed first against Christianity and finally against religion in general. (pp. 101-02)

Like other authors (such as Pérez de Ayala and the writers of the Republican and Civil War Era) Blasco Ibáñez' priests are the antithesis of what would be desireable in servants of a religious cause. His fabulously wealthy, greedy, irascible, and vengeful Cardinal is grievously troubled because the people whisper uncharitable rumors about his ''niece.'' She is his illegitimate daughter whom he dearly loves; rumor slanders her by suggesting that she is his mistress. One usurious priest is a monster of ugliness. . . . The popular indignation against such types is expressed by Tomasa, Gabriel's aunt, who says she believes in the Virgin of the Ciborium and a little bit in God. She disdains clerics more for their pretense of virtue than their defects. (pp. 102-03)

Gabriel's indoctrinating conversations reach their peak and become more like revolutionary sermons in Chapter VII, when he preaches to a motley mixture of lay folk. He claims that the Church is dead and the battle is only with a lifeless form. He maintains that the people cannot understand their lot because they have been fed on rudimentary ideas of the universe propagated by rag-picking Jews. Catholic doctrine taught inside the Cathedral is nothing. So, too, the laws and governing conventions of society. God is humanity and the universe in their constant patterns of change. Man is god. When god was invented the earth had been in existence for a long time. These sentiments succeed in unleashing the revolutionary beast. A group of the Cathedral workers, fired by Gabriel's words, enters to rob the altars of priceless treasures. Gabriel, who is serving as a guard, remonstrates and tries to convince them that their ends cannot be achieved by violence and plunder. He falls mortally wounded at their hands. Thus, Blasco Ibáñez, within the framework of his symbolism, predicted the social disorders and mob violence associated with the pattern of protest in the following decades. It comes as a shock when the author leads Gabriel's life to this lamentable end, because he seems suddenly to disengage himself from the revolutionary in order to stress the inherent social dangers of the people's struggle. He thus fails to identify completely with his protagonist. And he correctly shows that the force of revolution released into the hands of a mob will lead to tragedy.

One of the best descriptive passages in *La Catedral* is the portrayal of the Corpus Christi procession. Gabriel was one of ten bearers of the float on which the huge monstrance rested. He was delighted at this opportunity to see the streets of Toledo and to earn some money; the anomaly of his function caused him an ironic laugh. . . . Blasco Ibáñez' picture vivifies the local color of the ritual amid satirical thrusts at the trappings of Spanish confessional unity. It was a theme which he frequently employed and which drew upon his descriptive skill. There is a similarly interpreted Corpus celebration in *Arroz y Tartana, Flor de Mayo* contains a Good Friday procession which is full of local color and regional prejudices, *Sangre y Arena* contains a Holy Saturday ritual.

El Intruso followed hard upon the heels of *La Catedral* in 1904. Like most of the novels from the author's middle period, it projects a powerful theme of social protest. In this instance poverty and hunger, blighted life and sudden death are portrayed in the mining communities near Bilbao. Amid the cries and imprecations of the poor, the author skillfully weaves a specific and highly controversial motif: the influence of clerics (particularly the Jesuits) in family life—hence the title theme of "the intruder." The central figure of the story is Aresti, a young, highly talented, altruistic doctor who spends his time ministering to the poor. Endowed with an interior calm based upon confidence in the ultimate triumph of "Science and Social Justice" he is able to identify with the aspirations and sufferings of the poor and to stand apart and evaluate with a calculating eye what he conceives to be the causes of a suffering humanity. His disposition is less revolutionary than Gabriel's. His beliefs are basically the same but he realizes that time is not ripe; the masses are stupid and have no real leaders. Hence, he can only bind wounds and believe in the sure advent of a better day when science and social justice will have relegated the saints to the museum.

It would be redundant further to analyze Aresti's beliefs and anticlerical statements because of their underlying similarity with those of Gabriel. The specific theme of "the intruder," however, is most important. . . . (pp. 103-05)

The collaboration between clerical and wealthy elements in the new industrialism is resoundingly condemned. . . . Blasco Ibáñez in *El Intruso* foreshadows the bitterness of the controversy over the Jesuits in the Republic and predicts the violence of the Civil War. *La Catedral* and *El Intruso* are his most powerful anticlerical novels. They also figure among the most violent anticlerical works in the Spanish tradition.

The year following *El Intruso* . . . saw the appearance of two additional powerful novels of protest. They were *La Bodega*

and *La Horda*. The former takes place in Jerez in Andalucía and dwells upon the wine industry and—another side of the picture—drunkenness. Once again the claims of science and social justice are extolled by an idealist. In this instance it is Fernando Salvatierra, an active revolutionary, who raises the standard. The anticlericalism in the novel has the same basic tone. Most frequently it is leveled at the hypocrisy of the greedy and wealthy with whom the clergy frequently make common cause in the novel. . . .

What little action there is in *La Horda* takes place in and around Madrid. The novel presents a motley picture of social outcasts—beggars, poachers on the royal preserves, derelicts, drunken women, prostitutes, etc. These persons wander in and out of the bleak and tragic life of Isidro Maltrana, an impoverished writer and idealist who found his hellenic quest most impractical. There is little anticlericalism in the powerful, dismal pages. Occasionally there is a flash of implication or insinuation when reference is made to the rich. The strongest passage of this sort is found in the final pages. (p. 107)

Blasco Ibáñez devoted the ten years following these novels of social protest to world travels, lectures, and adventurous agricultural experiments in South America. He began to pose as a seer, a sort of prototype of "Papa" Hemingway, whom he strongly resembles. Now his novels opened up to embrace the entire world. The tendency toward propaganda and all-inclusive condemnatory generalizations continued. The year 1916 saw the publication of [*Los cuatro jinetes del apocalipsis*], a work intended largely to stimulate sympathy for the allied cause in World War I.

Blasco Ibáñez' last decades show a steady decline in artistic merit. Many of his late works employ the "conversational frame" of *La Catedral* in ever increasing measure. (pp. 108-09)

In two related novels of the last years the author devoted himself once more to developing an anticlerical theme. By now, however, his anticlericalism has lost any immediate political significance; rather, the novels are simply vehicles for subjective antireligious and pro-Spanish bias. *El Papa del Mar* . . . is built in the "conversational frame" of a sophisticated dalliance on the Riviera. Claudio Borja is in love with a wealthy Argentinian widow, Rosaura. The young gentleman has a Spanish antiquarian's interest in the story of Pedro de Luna, an anti-Pope at the time of the Great Western Schism. In the course of the lovers' travels to Avignon and other historic points of interest, the author sketches, through Claudio, part of the history of de Luna's medieval times. It is the various ecclesiastical recriminations, scandals, and conspiracies, however, which he portrays. A strong predilection for the Spanish claimant to the Papal throne is also evident. . . . The sequel to this novel, *A los Pies de Venus* . . . , continues the history of Claudio's love affair with Rosaura. There enters into the picture Don Baltasar, a *canónigo* who is Claudio's uncle. The priest is a worthy cleric withall, only slightly addicted to over-eating and drinking. Although he looks with the indulgent eye of Latin Catholicism upon Claudio's youthful indiscretions, he wishes to extricate the young man from Rosaura's toils, because the *canónigo* is convinced that Claudio has a mission to perform in life, namely the writing of a history of the Borgia Popes, Claudio's remote ancestors. . . . Into this frame, Blasco Ibáñez weaves the historical pattern of the Borgias and their times. Once again the accent is continually upon scandal, sensation, intrigue, etc. Frequent Renaissance sexual excesses are treated with a lingering emphasis upon detail combined with a puritanical recoil of horror. As in *La Catedral* and *El Papa del Mar* there is a complete void when it comes to understanding of what people of religious sensibilities call the spiritual life. Although accurate in historical detail the author's treatment is tendencious and insensitive to subtlety or variations in shading. . . . [In] Blasco Ibáñez' hands this history becomes a pastiche of excesses and a titillation of pruriency. (pp. 109-10)

It is evident that many of the topics that Pérez Galdós treated in his anticlerical works were reiterated by Blasco Ibáñez. Freedom in educational and intellectual areas is a theme which reappears constantly. The peculiar tendency of the Spanish religious spirit to turn in upon itself and dwell upon past glory, to the neglect of progress and adjustments with the modern spirit, is more vigorously and heavily underlined and anticipates Ortega y Gasset. The republican motif, however, only adumbrated by Pérez Galdós, emerges very strongly in Blasco Ibáñez. Protagonists such as Gabriel in *La Catedral* represent the *potpourri* of various radical philosophies grouped under the vague popular concept of "republican," to which the author himself adhered in his younger days. But Blasco Ibáñez differs even more strikingly from Pérez Galdós on one important point. As a professional champion of liberalism, he would be expected to avoid a doctrinaire viewpoint; yet the tone of his middle and late novels is as doctrinaire as the viewpoints which he condemns. He seems to extend his criticism of clericalism in a way that spreads into a blanket condemnation of religion and the religious spirit. . . . [Many] of Blasco Ibáñez' lesser novels and some of the work of his publishing house must in all fairness be classed as scurrilous. Of course, it is always possible—at times necessary—to ask the question: Where does Blasco Ibáñez end and where do his characters begin? For example, to what extent does the author identify with Gabriel? Is he not merely trying to project an adequate picture of a hardbitten revolutionary type? Doesn't he disassociate himself from Gabriel at the end of *La Catedral* and grimly depict the awful result of revolutionary ideas in the minds of an illiterate mob? The answer is, of course, impossible, if we are looking for exact information, whether dealing with Blasco Ibáñez or Hemingway, or any other author. In this case, however, we must remember that Blasco Ibáñez was primarily a nineteenth century writer and nineteenth century literature is frequently didactic. Blasco Ibáñez was frequently didactic and openly propagandistic. In addition, he had long schooling in revolutionary thought and he was a rebel most of his life. Consequently it would be fair to say that he personally may not have espoused *all* the revolutionary, anticlerical, antireligious ideas that he puts in the mouths of his characters. And it is also fair to say that he probably espoused *most* of them. He remains one of Spain's most powerful, masterful writers. (pp. 112-13)

> *John Devlin, "Anticlericalism in 'Belle Lettres' in Writers for the Most Part Associated with the Pre-Republican Era: Vincente Blasco Ibáñez (1867-1928)," in his* Spanish Anticlericalism: A Study in Modern Alienation *(copyright © 1966 by Las Americas Publishing Company; reprinted by permission of Las Americas Publishing Company, 911 Faile Street, Bronx, NY 10459), Las Americas, 1966, pp. 96-113.*

A. GROVE DAY AND EDGAR C. KNOWLTON, JR.   (essay date 1972)

[This excerpt is taken from a comprehensive survey of Blasco Ibáñez's life and works. The authors provide extensive annotated footnotes regarding details of the novelist's life and critical reputation, extensively translating passages from Spanish-language critical sources.]

Most authors write best about what they know best. This was especially true of Blasco Ibáñez; there is always a close connection between where he is writing and what he is writing about. He began by cultivating his own garden—the beautiful but violent garden of the province of Valencia, with its sun and scenery and its vivid history, for centuries tinged with Arabic culture as well as Christian. The result was a group of six novels and two volumes of short stories which have forever preserved the region as nobody else has done; in fact, one suspects that no other Spanish novelist has presented his homeplace in literature with such completeness. (p. 42) ·

The "Valencian group" is almost always discussed as if the eight books were a planned series comparable to Balzac's *Cómedie Humaine* or Zola's studies of milieu, following the fortunes of a family or "handling" a particular trade or class. Actually, the only thing that these early outpourings of Blasco's genius have in common is that all the settings are in or near the city of Valencia. In style, characterization, theme, and action, they differ greatly from one to another. They all share, however, the author's "descriptionist mania," as one writer termed his frequent rendering of familiar scenes, using the appeals to all the senses which earned him also labels like "colorist," "impressionist," and "landscape painter." (p. 43)

A common quality among the novels and stories is the frequent recourse to violent action that at times verges on melodrama. Underneath the levantine placidity and fatalism lies a smouldering scoria which often erupts when repression becomes unbearable. The only other marked quality found in all these novels except *The Cabin* is the succumbing of a young man to the dominance or mortal power of a woman. This pattern, found also in later novels, is prominent in the very first of Blasco's "serious" novels, [*Arroz y tartana (Rice and a Carriage)*].

This early effort was the only one admittedly written under the influence of Zola. It does have the virtues and defects of the naturalist equation, in which character is the sum of heredity plus environment. The environment of the city of Valencia around 1890 is shown to influence the characters by making misers, spendthrifts, or fools even of those persons who inherited a tough Aragonese temperament.

The title of *Rice and a Carriage* suggests clearly the theme. It is drawn from the quoted first verse of a popular song that might be translated:

> Rice and a carriage,
> Modish all the while—
> And let the ball whirl
> In Valencian style!

This expression ridicules the *petite bourgeoisie* that attempts to dazzle the public by vain show. To ride in a carriage, even though the family must live behind the walls of their home on the cheapest of foods, is the symbol that is supposed to overwhelm the humble classes plodding in the dust. . . . Inevitably, the strain of keeping up with the grandees will lead to sorrow.

The ending is thus predestined, but the story is deftly handled, and the reader soon gets acquainted with the fairly large cast of characters. (pp. 43-4)

Rice and a Carriage is the finest of Blasco's novels from the standpoint of presenting a picture of the milieu he knew best. (p. 46)

This novel lacks the "documentation" of the Zola school; but in its own way it is documented with Blasco's overwhelming recall of his own young manhood. Some scenes, clearly, are digressions, put in for their value as local color. . . . But study shows that quite often the setting of a chapter is more than a bit of scene painting; the background frequently adds irony to the action. (pp. 46-7)

The tone of *Rice and a Carriage* is not completely of the school of Zola. It is a shifting mixture of irony and sentiment. It is fairly objective, even though semiautobiographical. . . .

The main lack in the story is clear motivation. We are told that Uncle Juan is a miser and his sister Manuela is a mad waster, but we are not shown clearly why one is the opposite of the other, and we really never get into their minds. (p. 47)

Heredity and environment still strongly mold the destinies of the characters in *Flor de mayo (The Mayflower)*, but life is tragic rather than mean, and the protagonist emerges as the first of Blasco's stong, simple, honorable, breadwinning heroes. "El Retor" is a classic toiler of the sea, and the Valencian waterfront and the deeps of the Mediterranean on which the fishermen live and die furnish settings that the author knew at first hand. (p. 48)

For suspense and vivid description . . . , Blasco never excelled the final chapter of *The Mayflower*. In the face of a storm which turns out to be the worst tempest in the memory of the oldest seaman of La Cabañal, El Retor madly puts to sea, followed by many other fishing craft. (p. 50)

Characterization is not complex in *The Mayflower,* for these are people with uncomplicated motives. But the story is enriched by sketches of half a dozen minor figures. . . . (pp. 50-1)

The finest aspect of *The Mayflower,* however, as in *Rice and a Carriage,* is the rendering of a milieu—the fishing village and the lives of the Mediterranean seamen. (p. 51)

La barraca (The Cabin), third of Blasco's Valencian novels, became his first universally acclaimed masterwork, to the point that, no matter what he was later to publish, his epithet among lazy critics remained "the illustrious author of *La barraca.*" (p. 52)

The Cabin . . . well deserves all the applause showered upon it. (p. 53)

The frankness and amorality one expects of the Naturalist are frequently found in Blasco's novels, and he probes the "lower depths" without prudishness or avoidance of the dirt, the misery, and the horror. But the theory of Naturalism required its practitioners to hold to a philosophy of pessimistic determinism. Blasco was far from being a pessimist. True, he assumed that in the long run the human race would not triumph. But he was constitutionally an optimist to the end, vigorous in body and enthusiastic in spirit. Nor did he feel that all outcomes were predetermined by a god or the fates. He was a reformer, and anyone that tries to remodel his environment is certainly not a determinist who feels that the human will is helpless to modify a preordained outcome. Most of all, Blasco differs from the simon-pure Naturalist in the choice of characters to enact his theme. The endings of many of his novels show the downfall of the protagonist; but the cause is not usually weakness or lack of free will. Moral flaws are not necessarily hereditary. If the character is broken, the blame rests upon social pressures or circumstance. Sometimes, despite the most tragic pressures,

the character does not break, and a moral triumph is gained. Batiste in *The Cabin* is as strong at the end as at the beginning, and when the pressure becomes unbearable in the narrow-minded village, he survives to go elsewhere, presumably to carry on the fight to live.

If Zola was not Blasco's lifetime master, where can one look for others? Blasco himself gives some cues. He pays tribute, of course, to Miguel Cervantes. . . . (pp. 132-33)

A notable lack . . . in the list of possible influences is the name of any Spanish writer except Cervantes. Blasco's admiration for the author of *Don Quijote* was great, but such a distant influence on style or material would be hard to demonstrate in detail. (p. 134)

Much of Blasco's work is still timely. For example, the motion picture of [*Los cuatro jinetes del Apocalipsis (The Four Horsemen of the Apocalypse)*], filmed in 1921 and dealing with World War I, was remade in 1962 with a setting of World War II, a quarter of a century later, and few changes were needed in the scenario.

Blasco's ideals were high. Far from being a withdrawn Naturalist, objectively reporting on random slices of life, he violently championed many causes that are still alive today. Blasco enlarged his provincial vision until it became a cosmic view. His original mind and gifted imagination were employed in a titanic effort to spread widely his learning, through translating and publishing the works of European thinkers of various countries and philosophies. Like H. G. Wells, the British author whom he resembles in several ways, he embraced the task of becoming a one-man institute of adult education. His sympathy was always with the underdog, but he could portray with compassion the men and women he saw in all strata of society. He was a lover of Mediterranean culture from classical to current epochs, and this background enabled him to expand his scope and become a reliable commentator on Atlantic and American culture as well. His readers around the globe craved such an international view, and he was the most widely translated of all modern Spanish writers. (p. 136)

[He] was a tireless journalist and a magnificent storyteller. From his youth he prolifically poured forth books. His works are the most voluminous in contemporary European literature. Naturally, his product is highly uneven—hence the need for selectivity by the qualified critic. Blasco's fiction covers a boundless range of interests, and his evolution is worthy of scholarly concern. Early stereotyped as a Naturalist of the Zola persuasion, he wrote some of the most impassioned and poignant passages in Spanish fiction. Disdaining "style" as a distraction from the story, Blasco had more than a touch of the poet, and at times his pages are redolent with perfumes and pictorial with images of almost painful beauty. He likewise became one of the masters of Spanish historical fiction, glorifying his country's past. His descriptions of places, impressionistic but precise, have drawn visitors from abroad to view landscapes and edifices he has immortalized (for many people, the province of Valencia will always be Blasco's Valencia). His novels of then contemporary life have become, with the passage of time, valuable sources of social history.

Blasco had a firm theory of the novelist's function, as he explained more than once. He was a craftsman, and his novels often were built on more firm structures than the casual reviewer could perceive. His inborn aesthetic sensibility was sharpened by the need to impress his ideas upon his chosen, broad audience. Working from live models, he created characters who could love and weep and bleed. His ability to depict women is especially notable; they are seldom pretty puppets, and more often vigorous, even masculine, figures dominating their menfolk and impressing their wills on families and even nations. (pp. 136-37)

It is possible that, when success showered on Blasco after the whirlwind sales of the English translation of *The Four Horsemen of the Apocalypse,* his work declined in strength as he led the distracting life of a Riviera celebrity. It would be an error, however, to parrot the usual comment that only the Valencian novels are worthy of serious study. The readers of the world will not soon neglect [*La bodega (The Wine Cellar), La maja desnuda (The Naked Maja), Sangre y arena (Blood and Sand), Los muertos mandan (The Dead Command),* or *Mare Nostrum (Our Sea)*]. The five historical novels of Spanish glorification, to which Blasco devoted the energies of his later years, crowned a career. . . .

Finally, Blasco's themes were often expressed so vigorously that they verged upon propaganda. Yet many of his ideas are still fresh today. Until our generation, or the next one, solves the problems of love, hate, war, race, poverty, art, politics, religion, the dead hand of tradition, colonization, feminism, imperialism, and national loyalties, we should open our minds to the vision of human life found in the fascinating fiction of Vincente Blasco Ibáñez. (p. 137)

> *A. Grove Day and Edgar C. Knowlton, Jr., in their* V. Blasco Ibáñez *(copyright © 1972 by Twayne Publishers; reprinted with the permission of Twayne Publishers, a Division of G. K. Hall & Co., Boston), Twayne, 1972, 167 p.*

JEREMY T. MEDINA   (essay date 1977)

[*Medina analyses and evaluates* Reeds and Mud, *one of Blasco Ibáñez's best known and most critically acclaimed novels. Medina's assessment of the work includes examination of point of view, style, characterization, theme, and structure, as well as the interrelations of these literary elements within the novel.*]

Vicente Blasco Ibáñez's international fame is somewhat unjustified and ill-founded. This situation has arisen because a majority of the public, both in Spain and abroad, have judged him by his later works, ignoring the artistry and power of his Valencian novels. The level of his literary output has varied, to say the least, but in his earlier creations, he left a double legacy which should not be overlooked: a pictorial, concrete realism of strength and beauty and a striking portrayal of human action. These elements are incorporated into novels of sharp contrasts and savage emotions, depicting man's struggle against his instincts and his environment.

This study will attempt to analyze and evaluate what I consider to be Blasco's best work, *Cañas y barro.* . . . Many writers have mentioned particular aspects of this novel, and at least three have made real attempts to scrutinize some of its more prominent features. But there has been no complete analysis of this work in order to clarify systemically its central artistic components and to demonstrate how these aspects function together to produce a harmonious, artistic whole. My assessment of *Cañas y barro* will cover the following categories: (1) point of view and authorial perspective; (2) style, in the sense of language, descriptive techniques, etc.; (3) characterization, (4) theme (ideas); (5) structure; and (6) concluding remarks showing how these aspects relate to one another. (p. 275)

Of the novels written before the Spanish Civil War, this probably represents the most thorough adaptation in Spain of the tenets of French naturalism. The scene is set between 1890 and 1900 in the swamp-lake region of the Albufera near Valencia, an area well known throughout the country for its rice fields and bird game. Blasco's intimate knowledge of the region has been well documented, and the scenes and characters depicted sprang from the author's own acute powers of observation.

The narrative itself is constructed on three levels: (1) the story of three generations (the old fisherman *tío* Paloma, his hard-working son Toni and his rebellious, irresponsible grandson Tonet); (2) the lush, all-pervading atmosphere of the Albufera; and (3) a constant, transcendent feeling of the power of destiny, the irrevocable pressures of an abstract, deterministic force. The plot . . . traces the love affair between Tonet and Neleta from childhood to disaster years later. While the lad is away at war, the latter marries a sickly, but rich tavern owner, Cañamèl, in order to escape her impoverished existence. The subsequent illicit love affair between Tonet and Neleta leads to a series of events in which man is shown to be defenseless against the destructive forces of nature and animal instinct. Tonet suffers an emotional breakdown. Before Cañamèl dies he writes a will stating that Neleta cannot retain their property if she remarries or associates in an intimate way with another man. After Neleta gives birth to Tonet's child, she refuses to see her lover openly and orders him to abandon the child in the city across the lake in order to escape further suspicion of having violated the terms of the will. Instead, fear, remorse and accidents of fate lead Tonet to throw the infant into the lake. When a dog later discovers the baby's corpse, Tonet seeks escape in suicide.

The plot, then, is one of savage actions and strong emotions. Nevertheless, despite the striking and at times shocking turns of events, Blasco himself has restrained from authorial involvement or comment.

Cañas y barro represents one of the first Spanish novels to utilize fully the naturalistic method of authorial *impassibilité.* Our final impression is that of having merely been exposed to a set of circumstances and incidents without being asked to approve or disapprove, without ascertaining completely the author's feelings with regard to his characters or action. The closest Blasco comes to revealing his own emotion occurs during the poignant closing of the novel.

The writer's particular use of perspective is, in fact, one of the most prominent and significant aspects of his realism. At least five techniques are utilized to create a realistic and objective impression. (1) The author's view (and ours) is almost always "within" one character or (as at the beginning) within the people as a whole, and we share completely the knowledge, opinions, ignorance and emotions of that perspective. . . . Dialogue is reported indirectly, through the same technique. And, frequently, there are stylistic changes which accommodate shifts in point of view. . . . (2) Blasco will often place the reader in the position of a newly-arrived, hence ignorant onlooker, revealing what is going on only later in a scene. . . . At times our view of an incident will at first be that of the present moment, but soon jumps to the past for full background detail and explanation, eventually reaching again the original point in time. The episode of the *Fiesta del Niño Jesús* represents the moment where this technique is used most extensively. (3) Blasco frequently utilizes the shifting points of view to reveal more than one outlook concerning the same incident. Thus we witness twice the episode where Neleta opens her window when Tonet whistles from the street below. . . . (4) At times we learn later of things that had happened during a previously described scene, occurrences about which we were originally unaware. We realize after the fact, for example, that Tonet has slipped out during the ''pre-hunting'' party. . . . (5) Finally, Blasco's technique of shifting points of view relates directly to the force of the novel's occasional humor. The juvenile enthusiasm of Don Joaquin during the hunting incident and *Sangonera's* simultaneous ''religious love affair'' with the three *pucheros,* the latter's ''antiwork'' philosophy, Cañamèl's scorn for the doctor's advice against his drinking because ''no podía [Cañamèl] despreciar a los parroquianos,'' [''Cañamèl is not able to turn away customers''] and the priest who watches to see who will spit on his church floor and believes that the question of morals ''residia en el estómago'' [''resides in the stomach''] are the most noticeable elements of humor in the novel. Typically, such scenes offer no subtlety, no refined sense of irony to the reader, but serve primarily (especially in the case of the hunting incident) as comic relief, as a variation in tone from the sense of misery and doom which otherwise pervades most of the novel. Humor provides here a sharp contrast to the action and thus serves to make the plot more forceful and striking. Of particular importance is the fact that the author places the hunting episode between two of the most lugubrious and unpleasant incidents in the novel.

The realism and forceful objectivity that result from these shifting points of view are strengthened by the writer's descriptive techniques. *Cañas y barro,* more than anything else, stands as a series of descriptive passages, revealing the freshness, the spontaneity, the richness, and the sensual power which constitute Blasco's most significant artistic contribution to literature. With only a few exceptions (for example, the description of the tavern . . .), there is no extended, minute *detallismo.* Yet the beauty or destructiveness of nature comes alive before us.

Within these descriptions certain elements stand out. Prominent among these is the graphic appeal to our senses—as, for example, that of smell, more important here than in any novel of Blasco Ibáñez. . . . (pp. 275-77)

Blasco's descriptions are more dynamic than static. Objects ''move'' or ''move themselves'' (reflexive verbs are frequent), rather than being moved by exterior forces. Commentators on his style seem to have overlooked that occasional passages are constructed in chains, with one element building and related to the following, in order to suggest movement. (p. 277)

The reader is frequently struck by the exactness of detail or vivid plasticity of the author's style, of which prominent examples are the description of the progressive increase of the moon's light . . . or the portraits of Cañamèl . . . , Paloma . . . , and Neleta. . . .

Blasco's impressionism is equally visible in *Cañas y barro,* reflecting the painter's eye. . . .

At other moments, Blasco's descriptions are unmistakably naturalistic. The candor and unpleasantness of Zolaesque descriptions are present in such scenes as the depiction of decaying fish. . . . Most famous of all is the scene is which the dog returns with the body of the dead child. . . .

Finally, many of Blasco's descriptions are costumbristic. Indeed, *Cañas y barro,* despite its universal overtones, is one of the most regionalistic creations of modern Spanish literature.

Foremost among such scenes are the opening boat ride, the *sorteo,* the recounting of the legend of the snake Sancha, the *rifla* of the largest eel, the *Fiesta del Niño Jesús,* the *tiradas,* and many minor descriptions of cooking, Sunday processions, tavern games of *truque,* the village archival system, life in nearby Catarroga, vegetation, bird and animal life, etc. In addition the past history of the region is presented and blended into the narrative. It is the deterministic theme, the creation of the man of will (Toni) and the structural relationship between the major costumbristic scenes and the novel as a whole that serve to raise the work above a strictly regionalistic level.

As seen from the previous examples of descriptive techniques, Blasco Ibáñez' style demonstrates a combination of simplicity and rich expressiveness. Some stylistic elements serve in fact to raise the language occasionally to a somewhat poetic level: the frequent use of the imperfect (and conditional) tense to render a feeling of timelessness and pictorial vitality, the use of adjectives in pre-position . . . , and frequent vivid imagery, particularly similes. . . . Not surprisingly, the characters are constantly likened to animals. . . . (p. 278)

Blasco's techniques of characterization rarely allow one to penetrate beneath the superficial level suggested by these animal images. Typically, *Cañas y barro* is a novel of situation, not of character. No figures are presented in depth and none really stands out as a protagonist (a label which might be more accurately applied to the Albufera as a whole). . . . Paloma, Toni and Tonet stand in part as representatives of the past, present and future, respectively. Most personages, with the exception of La Borda, lack any kind of spiritual depth, and all seem to represent dominant passions or vices: laziness (Tonet), drunkenness (*Sangonera*), avarice (Neleta), the will to work and struggle (Toni), and hatred for the changing times (Paloma).

Within the framework of these few dominating traits, the characters are developed in only a very limited fashion.

Tonet is a victim of his own weaknesses: his indifference, his laziness, his hypocrisy, his yearning for adventure, and (by the influence of Neleta) his greed. Caught between the philosophies of his father and grandfather, he is unable to shake off his inertia and irresoluteness and make any decision regarding his life. His suicide, rather than a punishment, should be looked at as a final act of cowardice and self-pity, an escape from facing the future.

Neleta represents feminine avarice, as well as the force and fecundity of nature herself (hence her comparison with the serpent Sancha). Constant references to her eyes suggest her role as a crafty, egotistical cat-figure. She is individualized only by her sexual frustration and an occasional suggestion of real affection for Tonet.

Sangonera is a memorable type, at the same time comic and pathetic, a kind of 19th-century ''hippie.'' His love for nature, his plea that man return to a simple way of life and his refusal to work because labor violates God's commandments suggest that Blasco has put some of Rousseau's perspectives to work in this character's creation. His only concern in life is to have enough to eat and drink, and it is ironic that gluttony is the cause of his death. He, unlike Neleta, dislikes greed and does not eventually oppose nature; in contrast to Tonet he maintains faith in Divine grace. And he alone is happy to the end. In short, he is a modern version of the 17th-century *gracioso,* the comic ''servant'' who nevertheless is able to utter some very wise convictions.

Tío Paloma represents the old way, its customs, its sense of honor, its honesty; as such he is one of the most prominent victims of the novel. His slyness (for example, in avoiding the authorities when he wants to hunt) and his pride (shown by his not wanting anyone to find Tonet's body) are only slight suggestions of individuality.

Toni represents hard work, self-denial, *constancia,* the undying spirit of struggle. He is one of the few characters who demonstrates generosity and love (as evidenced by his final insistence on seeing his son's body). Cañamèl is the greedy, corrupt but deceived "shepherd" of the "fisher-flock." *La Borda* is love and self-sacrifice incarnate, slaving humbly and uncomplainingly for Toni and Tonet. She, only, demonstrates Blasco's occasional capacity for tenderness, as shown in the novel's powerful and touching conclusion. . . . (pp. 278-79)

More important than the attempt to convey a profound level of psychological development is the very fact of the characters' downfall. This in turn brings us to a discussion of theme and, more particularly, to the question of naturalistic intent.

Cañas y barro illustrates the fullness of Blasco's acceptance of the naturalists' deterministic philosophy. Man's struggle against the bestiality of his own instincts and the powerful forces of nature is shown to be a futile one. The death of Paloma's other sons, Cañamèl's sickness (a result of the environment) and Tonet's victimization by Neleta's greed are forceful indications of man's inability to combat these forces. (pp. 279-80)

The use of ironic circumstance appears repeatedly to emphasize the message that man's efforts seem meager indeed compared to the force of an apparently predetermined destiny. Tonet is buried in the land that was to serve as the basis for his and his father's future prosperity; Cañamèl's will thwarts Neleta's greedy ambitions; *Sangonera,* whose only concern in life has been to assure himself enough to eat and drink, is killed by his own gluttony; it is Cañamèl's dog that finds the corpse of the child (which leads to the destruction of the lovers' relationship through the subsequent suicide of Tonet); and, the beauty and impassivity of nature is presented in sharp contrast to the violence and anguish of the suicide scene.

Nevertheless, certain factors would tend to negate the possibility of an *entirely* naturalistic interpretation. The strengths of both Paloma and Toni are exalted. Heredity is not shown to be a significant force, since all three generations differ greatly. Furthermore, despite the causality of the novel's structural components, the plot of *Cañas y barro* lacks the strict logic of Blasco's earlier work, *La barraca.* Tonet's suicide, for example, is not really necessary, since there would be no way to identify the body of the child; sheer coincidence helps to bring about the denouement in that, if the child had not been born *that* night, Tonet would not have seen the hunters around his boat and felt compelled to kill the infant rather than take it to its destination; the suicide, in turn, would not have taken place. The deterministic logic evident in many of the French naturalistic novels is not so predominant here. What we do have is a graphic representation of the hardships of life in the Albufera (lack of nutrition, deaths of the new-born, *paludismo,* etc.), along with a recognition of a certain bestiality native to the human species. (p. 280)

Blasco also seems to express in *Cañas y barro* a condemnation of man's drive to accumulate material goods at the expense of nature and the natural life, a concept which becomes a central theme in some of his later thesis works. As trees fall around the Albufera in order to make way for the tourists or the *bur-*

gueses cazadores, we can detect the author's lament for an age gone by.

The naturalistic elements of the novel's theme mentioned above would seem to relate directly to the work's structure, a pattern which is meant to reflect the inevitability of the *desenlace* [conclusion]. . . . What we actually have, in broadest outline [in *Cañas y barro*], is the pattern followed in many of Blasco's novels: three expository chapters, consisting of one episodic introduction (similar to the *reparto de leche* scene in *La barraca*) together with two sections of retrospective narration. This is followed by the action proper, a causal plot line building directly to a clear climactic point in the penultimate chapter. The main action and subsequent epilogue (*desenlace*) are in turn built upon the movement between three central points in the plot: adultery, infanticide and suicide. The narrative structure may thus be outlined as follows:

   I. *Exposition:*

   A. Chapter 1: episodic introduction (*in medias res*), with a presentation of all major characters and the explanation of the myth of Sancha the snake; the general perspective is that of the people.

   B. Chapters 2 and 3: retrospective narration, progressing from past to present time:

   1. Family background, leading to the revelation of Tonet's laziness; the perspective is generally that of Paloma.

   2. Background, in particular, of the generation of (a) Tonet, (b) *Sangonera* and (c) Neleta. Perspective: generally that of Tonet.

   II. *Rising action:*

   A. Chapter 4: initiation of the "plot" proper: the *sorteo* (leading to Tonet's luck and subsequent relationship with Cañamèl).

   B. Chapter 5: development of the love affair between Tonet and Neleta, leading to adultery (the start of the central complication).

   C. Chapter 6: the *Fiesta del Niño Jesús,* leading to Cañamèl's break with Tonet (due in part to the former's jealousy over the people's praises for Tonet's part in the *Fiesta*).

   D. Chapter 7: development of the relationship between Tonet and *Sangonera,* Neleta's increasing difficulties, Cañamèl's death and will.

   E. Chapter 8: discovery of Neleta's pregnancy; the *tiradas;* the infanticide.

   F. Chapter 9: Don Joaquín and the hunting scene, *Sangonera's* sickness and death, the second hunt and the discovery of the corpse (the climax of the acion).

   III. *Epilogue:*

   A. Chapter 10: Tonet's suicide and burial.

What is remarkable about the novel's structure, however, is its complete unity—a compactness and careful interweaving of interrelated elements which, in view of Blasco's impetuous, tumultuous nature, can only surprise us. The plot is . . . built upon a strict chain of causal links. Thus the child's birth during the time of the *tiradas* leads to the frustration of Tonet's original plans and the subsequent abandonment of the infant in the lake. This in turn causes *Sangonera's* death, since the latter had taken Tonet's place in the hunt and had devoured all of Don Joaquín's food. In order to erase some of the bad memories of *Sangonera* during the first outing, Don Joaquín is taken out a second time, which leads to the discovery of the corpse and the subsequent suicide of Tonet.

Then, too, all three major costumbristic scenes are made integral to the causal plot line. Thus the *sorteo* brings about Tonet's good fortune and leads to the relationship with Cañamèl, which in turn serves to encourage the love affair between the boy and Neleta. Similarly, the *Fiesta* causes Tonet's ejection from the tavern (a contributing factor perhaps to Neleta's subsequent coldness toward him), and the *tiradas* provide the occasion for the climax and dénouement. The psychological and regionalistic elements of the plot are thus carefully blended to function within a single, uninterrupted crescendo (e.g. of pressures in Tonet's life). The chain of events in turn reflects the thematic emphasis upon environmental and deterministic forces.

A series of parallels or corresponding elements serves to lend further unity to the work: the two scenes involving Tonet and Neleta (once as children, symbolically "lost" in the woods, and later in the boat) . . . , and the grotesque parallels between Neleta's pregnant state and *Sangonera's* sickness later.

Certain leitmotifs add to the compact nature of the work's structure. Primary among these are the periodical return to Toni's struggle with the land and the constant presence of the lake itself, the scene of all the novel's major narrative incidents. The repetition of certain images, particularly those relating to man's animalistic nature, serves a similar function.

Finally, Blasco's very skillful use of timing and contrast contributes significantly to the overall effect of the story. The reader notes, for example, how every chapter within the main action ends with a highly dramatic action or revelation, inciting the reader to continue without pause. (pp. 280-82)

Blasco's manipulation of contrasts is equally forceful. Note, for example, the striking difference in tone between the humor of the first hunting scene (where a clear parallel to Don Quijote and Sancho is suggested), and the two deaths which surround it. By the insertion of this moment of comic relief, the reader is lulled into suspecting that the pressures of the environment (or of "destiny") may not win out after all. But he is thrown back into the world of harsh reality with the grotesque description of *Sangonera's* death. On a broader scale, the contrast between the beauty and tranquility of nature and the bestial savagery of man's predicament is present at moments throughout the novel.

We began our analysis by stating that the novel combines three levels of reality: the story of three generations (and in particular of Tonet), the constant presence and influence of the Albufera, and the "transcending," symbolic world of deterministic pressures. Just as these planes of action are brought into artistic harmony, so the major aspects of style, characterization, theme and structure function together to produce a natural and balanced whole. The near flawless causality inherent in the work's structure serves to support the deterministic theme. The stylistic contrasts between impressionistic description and savage action lead the reader to a similar awareness. The constant presence of verbs in the imperfect or conditional tenses enhances our recognition of the intemporality of nature, as well as of man's

inability to mitigate a basically animalistic temperament. The costumbristic descriptions, an important element of Blasco's stylistic approach, serve to clarify the structure of the novel as well as to aid in the delineation of characters.

Above all, the unity of **Cañas y barro** derives from the fact that Blasco wrote with the clear purpose of presenting the people, customs, and *ambiente* of a region without recourse to moralizing. His artistry stems from the rapid, expressive, pictorial and at times poetic presentation of nature, the powerful depiction of the Valencian region and the vigorous portraiture of man's more savage instincts and desires. If Blasco had not strayed from the format and the setting he knew best, he might have attained a more significant place within the history of modern literature. (pp. 282-83)

> Jeremy T. Medina, "The Artistry of Blasco Ibáñez's 'Cañas y barro'," in Hispania (© 1977 The American Association of Teachers of Spanish and Portuguese, Inc.), Vol. 60, No. 2, May, 1977, pp. 275-84.

ADDITIONAL BIBLIOGRAPHY

Bell, Aubrey F. G. "The Realist and Naturalist Schools (Emilia Pardo Bazán, Palacio Valdéz, Alas, Coloma, Picón, Matheu, Blasco Ibáñez, Trigo)." In his *Contemporary Spanish Literature*, pp. 61-102. New York: Alfred A. Knopf, 1925.*
    Places Blasco Ibáñez historically within the tradition of Spanish literature and briefly evaluates his career. In the introduction to this study Bell finds that with "Pérez Galdós and Blasco Ibáñez literature in Spain, literature worthy of the name, became professional for the first time", and finds Blasco Ibáñez's greatest contribution to be his early novels, in which he tempered the French literary tradition of Naturalism with Spanish regionalism.

Boynton, H. W. "A Winter Crop of Novels: *The Pope of the Sea*." *The Outlook* 145, No. 8 (23 February 1927): 248.
    Concisely reviews *The Pope of the Sea*, finding fault with the novel's structure, specifically with the device of imparting history through the extensive monologues of one character.

"Briefer Mention: *The Three Roses*, by Vincent Blasco Ibáñez." *The Commonweal* XVI, No. 26 (26 October 1932): 628.
    Rare negative criticism of Blasco Ibáñez's vivid depiction of the Valencian milieu, finding that the "local color has been employed so thickly that the real city has been lost", that the plot is incidental, characterization poor, and concluding that "the author has contrived a luring volume of tourist's bait but has forgotten he set out to write a novel."

Dendle, Brian J. "Blasco Ibáñez and Coloma's *Pequeñeces*." *Romance Notes* VIII, No. 2 (Spring 1967): 200-03.*
    Contrasts the pro-Catholic attitude of Luis Coloma's defense of Jesuit education with the strong anticlericalism evident in Blasco Ibáñez's novels.

Hind, C. Lewis. "Vincente Blasco Ibáñez." In his *More Authors and I*, pp. 165-69. New York: Dodd, Mead and Co., 1922.
    Takes exception with Blasco Ibáñez's American book publishers who commonly refer to him as "the greatest of living novelists," citing Thomas Hardy, Rudyard Kipling, and Joseph Conrad as greater writers. Hind also praises *The Shadow of the Cathedral* and *The Four Horsemen of the Apocalypse*, but with certain reservations.

King, Georgiana Goddard. "Translating More Ibáñez." *The Bookman*, New York XLIX, No. 3 (May 1919): 345-47.
    Discusses the merits of many different translations of Blasco Ibáñez's principal works.

Livingston, Arthur. "Blasco Ibáñez Leading the Attack on His King." *The New York Times Book Review* (4 January 1925): 5.

> Finds that Blasco Ibáñez's anti-Royalist essays, compiled in *Alfonso XIII Unmasked: The Military Terror in Spain,* provide "certainly one of the most vivid and probably one of the most authentic pictures of political life in Spain."

"Review of *Queen Califa.*" *The Outlook* 138, No. 12 (19 November 1924): 462.

> Finds that the novel *Queen Califa* leads the reader to imagine "that the author had written with an eye on American screen rights"—a common criticism of Blasco Ibáñez's fiction after the successful film versions of *Blood and Sand* and *The Four Horsemen of the Apocalypse.*

Peers, E. Allison. "The Real Blasco Ibáñez." *The Contemporary Review* CXXXIII (May 1928): 599-604.

> Overview of the novelist's career written at his death. Peers, like most critics, finds the early regional novels to be Blasco Ibáñez's "really great works" and dismisses *The Four Horsemen of the Apocalypse* and the later novels as "ephemeral, ostentatious."

"Review of *A Novelist's Tour of the World.*" *The Saturday Review of Literature* III, No. 20 (11 December 1926): 438.

> Cites Blasco Ibáñez's book of travel essays as one of his best works, and finds that it "should rank among the most fascinating travel books of the world."

Sinclair, Upton. "Blasco Ibáñez." *Appeal to Reason,* No. 1263 (14 February 1920): 4.

> Recounts "a couple of afternoons and an evening" spent with the Spanish author. Sinclair characterizes Blasco Ibáñez as "a really great novelist, dealing with modern Spanish life" whose novels each have "a charm and individuality."

Smith, Paul. "Blasco Ibáñez and the Theme of the Jews." *Hispania* 56 (April 1973): 282-94.

> Cites Blasco Ibáñez as the only Spanish author since the sixteenth century to regularly include sympathetic Jewish characters in his fiction. Examining instances of both sympathetically and negatively portrayed Jews in Blasco Ibáñez's fiction, Smith concludes that the author's own attitude toward Jews was ambiguous.

Swain, James O. *Vincente Blasco Ibáñez: General Study, Special Emphasis on Realistic Techniques.* Rev. ed. Knoxville: Graphic Arts, University of Tennessee, 1959, 180 p.

> Slightly revised version of the first doctoral dissertation written on Blasco Ibáñez. In examining Blasco Ibáñez as a literary realist, Swain disagrees with those critics, including Havelock Ellis, Katherine Reding, and Sherman H. Eoff (see excerpts above) who feel the Spanish novelist was greatly influenced by the French Naturalist Émile Zola.

Paul (Charles Joseph) Bourget

1852-1935

(Also wrote under pseudonym of Pierre Pohl) French critic, novelist, short story writer, essayist, dramatist, and poet.

Although often overlooked by critics today, Bourget was at one time praised as "the most original critic since Sainte-Beuve." His *Essais de psychologie contemporaine*—which analyzed the mental and moral characteristics of such writers as Charles Baudelaire, Hippolyte Taine, and Joseph Ernest Renan, all of whom had indelibly influenced Bourget's generation—was a critical watershed, and is considered a prototype for modern psychological criticism. In his revolutionary *Essais*, Bourget attempted to apply the techniques of psychological analysis to literary criticism, interpreting works of literature according to the author's reactions to the moral and philosophical questions of the age. Bourget was also one of the foremost psychological novelists of his time. Armand Singer observes that if "French writers have carried on a seven hundred year love affair with the psychological novel, no one has been more passionately attached to the genre than Paul Bourget."

Bourget was born in Amiens, France. His father was a mathematics professor, and in later years Bourget often attributed his talents to the inheritance of his father's scientific viewpoint and his German mother's poetic sensibilities. As a young man he studied at the Lycée Clermaont-Ferrand and at the Hotel Dieu medical school. He left medical school in 1874, against the wishes of his family, in order to devote his time to writing. At that point his family refused to provide him further financial aid and he was compelled to support himself as a tutor at Lelarges. There he met Ferdinand Brunetière, who, through Bourget's efforts, later became the editor of *La revue des deux mondes* and published some of Bourget's work. Bourget and Brunetière remained lifelong friends. Bourget published his first article, a study of Spinoza, in the journal *La Renaissance* in 1872, under the pen name Pierre Pohl. At this time he aspired to write poetry, and counted as his friends the poets Francois Coppée, Jean Richepin, and Jules Barbey d'Aurevilly. Bourget also frequented Parisian literary circles where he met most of the notable literary figures of the day, including Alexandre Dumas *fils*, Leconte de Lisle, Ivan Turgenev, and Taine, all of whom later became subjects of his criticism. In 1875 Bourget's first book of poems, *La vie inquiète*, was published. This was followed three years later by the verse drama *Edel*. Critical response to the first of these volumes was mildly favorable, but the failure of *Edel* to elicit the enthusiasm of either critics or readers was a bitter disappointment to Bourget. He abandoned the poetic metier but continued to write, working as a drama critic for *Le globe* and *Le parlement*.

In 1881 Bourget's masterpiece, *Essais de psychologie contemporaine*, was published and immediately created a sensation. In composing the *Essais*, Bourget had evolved a style of observing and writing that was based on the newest, most in-depth psychological techniques. He himself called it "a method of psychological analysis applied in turn to talents of writers, problems of general aesthetics, impressions of travel, and varied sensations of nature or art." In the *Essais* and subsequent studies, such as *Études et portraits* and *Pages de critique et doctrine*, Bourget applied this technique to diagnosing the ills

that beset his generation; most particularly he sought "the generating principle" behind the all-pervasive pessimism he observed in the French youth of his day. The success of his new approach encouraged Bourget to apply his analytic technique to other genres. He turned to the novel, believing that it offered the literary equivalent of an examination of conscience. In works such as *André Cornélis*, *Cruelle énigme (A Cruel Enigma)*, and *Mensonges (Lies)*, he attempted to demonstrate how the principles of scientific determinism, as developed by Taine, govern even the most intimate human behavior. In spite of the controversy generated by Bourget's occasionally clinical treatment of sex and erotic psychology in these early novels, and the essential pessimism of the viewpoint they express, these works were extremely popular.

In 1889 Bourget wrote *Le disciple (The Disciple)*. Its publication has been called one of the important events in the intellectual and moral history of France. In *The Disciple* Bourget turned his back on Taine and scientific determinism. Challenging his previous position, Bourget carried determinist ideas to a logical—and some maintain factitious—extreme in order to demonstrate what he termed "the moral bankruptcy of science and materialism." *The Disciple* ignited one of the most memorable debates in French letters, between Anatole France and Ferdinand Brunetière, over the issue of intellectual freedom versus the moral responsibility of authors for the effect of their ideas on readers.

With the publication of *The Disciple*, Bourget ceased to be a detached psychologist examining the inner life of his characters. From that time on he increasingly came to resemble a moralist campaigning for the preservation of a social order. He embraced the political views of the extreme right, advocating a return to monarchy, the reinstatement of the aristocracy, a rigid class structure, and a return to traditional religion; in 1901 he himself was converted to Catholicism. Critical volumes, such as *Nouvelles pages de critique et de doctrine* and *Quelques témoignages* reflect his growing religious and political conservatism. In these works, arguments and observations are often slanted to support his political prejudices, and this proselytizing bent has diminished their interest for today's readers. Bourget's later novels, such as *L'étape*, *L'émigré*, *Un divorce* (*Divorce: A Domestic Tragedy of Modern France*), and *Le démon de midi*, also reflect one or another of his ideological concerns. He had come to believe that it was a novelist's responsibility to instruct his readers. Because of this penchant for didacticism, these later works have dated badly, and, in spite of their clear style, tight plot structure, and the obvious sincerity of their author, are now seldom read. His dramas, such as *La barricade* and *Le tribun*, have suffered the same fate, although they possess many excellent theatrical qualities, including a genuine flair for stage dialogue. His short stories, in which the ideology is a much less intrusive element, have fared better.

Bourget also wrote a number of unconventional and highly popular travel studies. He once explained that he travelled as a psychologist does—immersing himself in the spirit of a country, inventing and interpreting his pleasures as he went along. *Sensations d'Italie* (*Impressions of Italy*) and *Outre-mer* are the best of these volumes. *Impressions of Italy* is notable for its many sensitive observations on Italian art, particularly Renaissance painting. *Outre-mer*, an account of Bourget's travels in the United States, is an enthusiastic survey of American life that was immediately popular. Bourget took note of everything from cowboys to socialites on his American tour, and though he wrote *Outre-mer* at a time when his anti-democratic beliefs were still nascent, he did not fail to provoke controversy. Mark Twain attacked Bourget in *The North American Review* for what Twain perceived as Bourget's presumptuousness in judging American life solely on the basis of experiences gleaned while living among members of the American upper class.

Although critically controversial, Bourget was a great popular success in his lifetime. His works were widely read and discussed. But while many idolized him as a spokesman for the traditional virtues in a difficult and uncertain age, he also had many detractors. His sacrifice of art to ideology in his later career caused many critics to observe that he had outlived his own literary reputation. Today, it is chiefly for his contributions in the field of literary criticism that he is remembered.

(See also *Contemporary Authors*, Vol. 107.)

PRINCIPAL WORKS

La vie inquiète   (poetry)   1875
Edel   (poetry)   1878
Les aveaux   (poetry)   1882
Essais de psychologie contemporaine   (criticism)   1883
L'irréparable   (short stories)   1884

Cruelle énigme   (novel)   1885
   [*A Cruel Enigma*, 1887; also published as *Love's Cruel Enigma*, 1891]
Un crime d'amour   (novel)   1886
   [*A Love Crime*, 1888; also published as *Was It Love?* 1891]
Nouveaux essais de psychologie contemporaine   (criticism) 1886
André Cornélis   (novel)   1887
   [*André Cornelis*, 1887; also published as *The Son*, 1893; and *The Story of André Cornelis*, 1914; and *The Sins of Desire*, 1930]
Mensonges   (novel)   1887
   [*Lies*, 1892; also published as *A Living Lie*, 1896; and *Our Lady of Lies*, 1910]
Le disciple   (novel)   1889
   [*The Disciple*, 1898]
Études et portraits   (essays)   1889
Pastels   (short stories)   1889
   [*Pastels of Men*, 1891; also published as *A Saint, and Others*, 1892]
Les nouveaux pastels   (short stories)   1891
Physiologie de l'amour moderne   (novel)   1891
Sensations d'Italie   (essays)   1891
   [*Impressions of Italy*, 1892; also published as *The Glamor of Italy*, 1923]
Cosmopolis   (novel)   1893
   [*Cosmopolis*, 1893]
Lettre autobiographique   (autobiography)   1894
Outre-mer. 3 vols.   (essays)   1895
   [*Outre-Mer: Impressions of America*, 1895]
Sensations de Nouvelle-France   (essays)   1895
Recommencements   (short stories)   1897
Complications sentimentales   (short stories)   1898
La duchesse bleue   (novel)   1898
   [*The Blue Duchess*, 1902]
Voyageuses   (short stories)   1898
   [*Antigone, and Other Portraits of Women*, 1898]
Drames de famille   (short stories)   1900
   [*Domestic Dramas*, 1900]
Un homme d'affaires   (short stories)   1900
L'étape   (novel)   1901
Monique   (short stories)   1901
   [*Monica, and Other Stories*, 1902]
L'eau profonde   (short stories)   1903
Un divorce   (novel)   1904
   [*Divorce: A Domestic Tragedy of Modern France*, 1904]
Les deux soeurs   (short stories)   1905
L'émigré   (novel)   1907
La barricade   (drama)   1910
Le tribun   (drama)   1911
Pages de critique et de doctrine. 2 vols.   (criticism)   1912
Le démon de midi   (novel)   1914
Le sens de la mort   (novel)   1915
   [*The Night Cometh*, 1916]
Le justicier   (short stories)   1919
Anomalies   (short stories)   1920
Nouvelles pages de critique et de doctrine. 2 vols. (criticism)   1922
Conflits intimes   (short stories)   1925
Le danseur mondain   (novel)   1926
Nos actes nous suivent   (novel)   1927
Quelques témoignages. 2 vols.   (essays)   1928-34
Croire   (unfinished novel)   1935

LAFCADIO HEARN   (essay date 1886)

[Considered one of modern America's leading prose impressionists, Hearn produced a large body of work that is more closely related to nineteenth-century European than American literature. His sketches, short stories, and novellas demonstrate a vision of evil and the supernatural reminiscent of Edgar Allan Poe and Charles Baudelaire. Hearn is also recognized as a perceptive literary critic whose readings and theories reflect his devotion to the beautiful and the bizarre. His lectures on American and European literature, published in such collections as Interpretations of Literature *(1915), are exceptional for their break with the conventions of Victorian criticism, and his essays on Japanese culture long influenced Western perceptions of the Orient. In both his criticism and his fiction Hearn emphasized the emotional effects of art rather than its social and ethical functions. In the following excerpt, Hearn provides an insightful review of* A Love Crime.*]*

Bourget's last masterpiece *Crime d'Amour,* . . . has not, perhaps, surpassed his previous work *Cruelle Enigme,* but has certainly paralleled it. The story is altogether more painfully revolting,—so revolting, in fact, that the reader has almost reached the close before he suspects that the novelist can even attempt to redeem himself by any moral effort above the commonplace. Then, however, comes the surprise,—a surprise unequaled in recent French fiction. The book is absolutely purified by its termination,—one of the most powerfully touching and truthful studies of human nature ever conceived,—a splendid and satisfactory apology for all that preceded it. The story is a sermon,—a magnificent sermon; and one likely to produce infinitely more good than all the pseudo-ethical fiction ever written to fill "a want." It is simply the history of a moral change effected in the person of a corrupt man through the spectacle of a woman's ruin accomplished by himself.

The modern skepticism personified by the chief character of the novel, is essentially pessimistic;—it is less of an anti-religious unbelief than of a hopeless doubting in human nature. When a man begins to doubt the existence of honor, the existence of friendship, the existence of duty, the existence of affection, then the world of course becomes hideous to him. . . . He who trains his mind to perceive the vast evil of human nature must also learn to know the vast goodness in human nature; but after having learned the former in the school of pleasure, he must learn the latter in the school of pain. When Nature maketh the crooked way straight, she is less kindly than the surgeon,—she uses no anaesthetics!

The *blasé* of Bourget's novel receives the lesson through a woman;—but such a lesson may be given in a hundred ways. . . . What a man may not be able to obtain from Reason and what he refuses to receive from theological dogma, may be ultimately forced upon him by the overmastering sentiment of pity,—or what Bourget eloquently calls "that Virtue of Charity, which dispenses with all logical demonstrations and all revelations,—unless it be, indeed, itself the supreme and eternal revelation." The beauty of the French writer's study is not impaired by the fact that it seems to reveal the influence of Russian thought, and that its closing pages recalls Dostoievsky's picture of the unhappy Raskolnikoff, crying out as he kisses the feet of the young outcast: *"It is not before thee that I prostrate myself;—it is to all the suffering of humanity!"* . . . (pp. 153-56)

> *Lafcadio Hearn, "The Religion of Suffering" (originally published in* New Orleans Times-Democrat, *February 21, 1886), in his* Essays in European and Oriental Literature, *edited by Albert Mordell (copy-*

right, 1923, by Dodd, Mead and Company, Inc.), Dodd, Mead, 1923, pp. 153-57.

HAVELOCK ELLIS   (essay date 1889)

[Ellis was a pioneering sexual psychologist and a respected English man of letters. His most famous work is his seven-volume The Psychology of Sex *(1897-1928), a study which contains frankly stated case histories of sex-related psychological abnormalities and which is greatly responsible for changing British and American attitudes toward the hitherto forbidden subject of sexuality. In addition to his psychological writings, Ellis edited the Mermaid Series of sixteenth-eighteenth century English dramatists (1887-89) and retained an active interest in literature throughout his life. As a critic, according to Desmond MacCarthy, Ellis looked for the expression of the individuality of the author under discussion. "The first question he asked himself as a critic," wrote MacCarthy, "was 'What does this writer affirm?' The next, 'How did he come to affirm precisely that?' His statement of a writer's 'message' was always trenchant and clear, his psychological analysis of the man extremely acute, and the estimate of the value of his contribution impartial. What moved him most in literature was the sincere expression of preferences and beliefs, and the energy which springs from sincerity." In the following excerpt, Ellis discusses Bourget's critical masterpiece* Essais de psychologie contemporaine *and explains Bourget's rather specialized use of the terms "decadent" and "dilettante." In discussing Bourget's novels, Ellis praises Bourget, as did Anatole France (see excerpt below) for his skillful treatment of feminine characters.]*

Of the younger generation of French writers Paul Bourget—successively poet, critic, novelist—is the most prominent and perhaps the most interesting. (p. 48)

Bourget first appeared as a poet; he has at intervals published several volumes of poems. In poetry he has been described as *un lakiste Parisien,* an expression which at all events indicates his peculiar complexity; but his poetic work also reveals influences from Baudelaire, from Shelley, from Poe (whose love of mystery appeals strongly to the imagination of modern France), and from less known poets.

These poems, especially, perhaps, the volume called *Aveux,* clearly indicate Bourget's dominant tendency from the first to restless and unceasing self-analysis; they are full of the struggle between life and the ideal, of the immense thirst for life and the irresistible tendency towards the dreams of the ideal, the sense of the sterility of passion and the impotence of life—that pessimism, in short, which was very far from being the exclusive property of young Bourget. "This Satan," he wrote in his first volume, "takes my passions and kills them, and then exposes the mangled limbs of my ideal body—just as a surgeon does with a hospital corpse—and yet, as I see him do it, I feel a strange fascination, rather than anger."

This is youthful, undoubtedly; Bourget's poems are chiefly interesting because they help us to understand the man's personality. As a poet there is a certain ineffectual effort about him; even as a novelist, he fails to leave a feeling of complete satisfaction. It is as a critic—in the volumes of the *Essais de Psychologie Contemporaine*—that Bourget reaches his full development. He has ceased to talk openly of his "membres déchirés" and to lament the sterility of life; his restless and sensitive spirit has at last found adequate occupation in, as he explains it, indicating the examples which "the distinguished writers of to-day offer to the imagination of the young people who seek to know themselves through books.'' So that in his sympathetic and searching examination of these writers, Bourget's Satan is still really analysing, in a more heightened form, the elements of his own nature: this gives a peculiar meaning and personal impress to his work.

In these two volumes, in which there is not a page without some keen critical insight, some fine suggestion for thought, Bourget deals, then, with the psychological physiognomy of certain leading literary figures, chiefly belonging to modern France, and with the psychological atmosphere which has made them possible—Renan, Baudelaire, Taine, Flaubert, Beyle, Tourgueneff, Dumas, Leconte de Lisle, the De Goncourts, Amiel. His aim is thus explained in the Preface: ''The reader will not find in these pages what may properly be termed criticism. Methods of art are only analysed in so far as they are *signs,* the personality of the authors is hardly indicated, there is not, I believe, a single anecdote. I have desired neither to discuss talent nor to paint character. My ambition has been to record some notes capable of serving the historian of the moral life during the second half of the nineteenth century in France.'' . . . The essay on Renan is probably the finest; Renan is peculiarly amenable to Bourget's delicate feminine methods of analysis; the characteristics of Renan's spirit and manner are set down with insurpassable felicity. On the other hand the account of Taine is probably the least satisfactory; Taine's virile (perhaps extravagantly virile) methods, his strong, direct positive grip of things, does not easily lend itself to the sinuous sympathetic methods of Bourget's analysis.

There are at least two points, on which Bourget especially insists, which help to explain his attitude and also much in that contemporary ''moral life'' which he has set himself to analyse. The first of these (introduced in the essay on Baudelaire) is the theory of *decadence.* Bourget uses this word as it is generally used (but, as Gautier pointed out, rather unfortunately) to express the literary methods of a society which has reached its limits of expansion and maturity—''the state of society,'' in his own words, ''which produces too large a number of individuals who are unsuited to the labours of the common life.'' (pp. 48-51)

The second point (discussed in relation to Renan) is indicated by the word *dilettantism.* . . . ''Dilettantism is much less a doctrine,'' Bourget remarks, ''than a disposition of the mind, at once very intelligent and very emotional, which inclines us in turn towards the various forms of life, and leads us to lend ourselves to all these forms without giving ourselves to any. . . .'' These are two of the problems which Bourget develops in these fascinating *Essais,* finding, as he tells us, sometimes an answer of sorrow, sometimes one of faith and hope, most often the former, for his temperament is strongly tinged with pessimism; and for him the two great forces of the modern world, Science and Democracy, have dried up the old sources of the moral life, and furnished none that are fresh.

Bourget's novels are by no means the least interesting part of his work. In novel-writing his style is very simple, very delicate and precise: except for its almost scientific exactness it has nothing of the naturalistic school's burden of elaborate detail. His method, as we should expect, is above all psychological and very sincere. The range of characterisation is not wide; there is usually a man of fairly simple nature, and a background formed of several almost characterless persons. The chief personage is always a woman. In his treatment of these women—Noémie, Claire, Thérèse—lies the strength of Bourget's nov-els. When he turns to them he is at once at home; his own essentially feminine nature enables him to unravel with perfect insight and sympathy the complex and unharmonised natures with which he has endowed them. (pp. 53-6)

One scarcely thinks of calling [*Cruelle Enigme*] a work of art, it is told with such simplicity, such sincerity; the interest, which is always sustained, appears as much that attaching to a psychological ''case'' as to a novel; at every turn we find traces of a singularly fine and delicate observation. Bourget writes with full consciousness that the great novelists of his country—men like Beyle, Balzac, Flaubert—have never hesitated to analyse, keenly and boldly, all the mysteries of passion; he is aware that his own task is a modest one. But how unlike the average English novel! (p. 57)

We are not likely to see in England, at present, any successful union of the French and English novel, because our great English novelists have not touched the facts of life with the same frankness and boldness, and their conception of normal life is unduly restricted. . . . We need, as it has been well said, a synthesis of naturalism and romanticism; we need to reconstitute the complete man, instead of studying him in separate pieces; to put a living soul in the clothed body. It is because they have to some extent done this that the great Russian novelists—Dostoieffsky, Tourgueneff and Tolstoi—are so significant; and Bourget, with his more limited means, seems to be striving towards the same ideal. (pp. 59-60)

> *Havelock Ellis, ''A Note on Paul Bourget'' (originally published in* Pioneer, *October, 1889), in his* Views and Reviews: A Selection of Uncollected Articles, 1884-1932, *first and second series, D. Harmsworth, 1932 (and reprinted by Books for Libraries Press, 1970; distributed by Arno Press, Inc., pp. 48-60).*

ANATOLE FRANCE   (essay date 1889)

[*France is one of the most conspicuous examples of an author who epitomized every facet of literary greatness to his own time but who lost much of his eminence to the shifting values of posterity. He embodied what are traditionally regarded as the intellectual and artistic virtues of French writing: clarity, control, perceptive judgement of worldly matters, and the Enlightenment virtues of tolerance and justice. His novels gained an intensely devoted following for their lucid appreciation of the pleasures and pains of human existence and for the tenderly ironic vantage from which it was viewed. A persistent tone of irony, varying in degrees of subtlety, is often considered the dominant trait of France's writing. In his critical works this device of ironic expression becomes an effective tool of literary analysis. In the following excerpt, France reviews* Mensonges, *praising Bourget for his acute insights into certain aspects of feminine psychology.*]

> Converse not much with the young, nor with strangers.
>
> Flatter not the rich: neither do thou appear willingly before the great. . . .
>
> Be not familiar with any woman; but commend all good women in general to God. . . .
>
> Sometimes it falleth out that a person unknown to us is much esteemed of, from the good report given by others; whose presence notwithstanding is not grateful to the eyes of those who see him.

"The Imitation," Book I., chap. viii.

Having read eagerly to its last page, but not without dejection, M. Bourget's melancholy book [**"Mensonges"**], I immediately glanced at that page in my "Imitation of Jesus Christ" which opens by itself, and I repeated with fervour the verses I have just transcribed. Each of these verses corresponds to a chapter in the new novel. Each of these maxims is a balsam and an electuary for one of the wounds which the able writer has pointed out. (p. 307)

Ah! if M. Paul Bourget's hero, if the young poet, René Vinci, had read over every morning in his little room in the Rue Coëtlogon, the eighth chapter of the "Imitation"; if he had steeped himself in the full meaning of these words: "Do not desire to appear before the great. . . . Be not familiar with any woman"; if he had sought his joy in sadness and his pleasure in renunciation, he would not have tasted the worst of all sorrows, the only sorrow which is truly evil, the sorrow which does not purify, but defiles; and he would not have endeavoured to die the death of the despairing. René Vinci is a poor young man, a poet twenty-five years of age, who successfully produces at the Théâtre-Français a delightful farce, another "Passant." The world of foreigners and Parisians, the drawing-rooms where people talk and play comedies, in a word what is called *the* world, suddenly opened before this young celebrity. He threw himself into it with a childish ardour, and was immediately seduced by what Pascal calls the pomps or gross-nesses of the flesh. The brilliance of these luxurious existences dazzled him. Perhaps he was no great philosopher. I have heard people speaking lightly of him in this respect. They ought rather to have pitied him. Luxury has an irresistible attraction for elegant and delicate natures. . . . René Vinci is . . . [young and candid]. A drop of white-rose perfume is enough to intoxicate him; he loves all the luxury of women. If that is a fault forgive him for it: he is in love and he suffers. Yes, he is in love with a Madame Moraines, of whom M. Bourget has drawn a terribly true portrait. We see her, we feel her, we breathe her, this woman with her delicate features, with her intellectual mouth, with her form at once refined and strong, this woman who conceals the ardent richness of her nature beneath the grace of an apparent fragility. We see her so well that we would almost quarrel over this or that detail with the man who painted her. (pp. 308-09)

When I speak of a portrait, you will of course understand that I mean above all a moral portrait, for the artist is M. Paul Bourget. This portrait is a true one, it is true with that great veracity which at once attests itself. (pp. 309-10)

This book by M. Paul Bourget is a fine and scholarly study. Never before has the author of **"Cruelle Enigme,"** though he has long been a philosopher and a psychologist, shown so great a talent for analysis. Do not forget that there are far more things in **"Mensonges"** than I have indicated. . . . In **"Mensonges"** there is Colette, an actress of the Comédie-Française who inspires a man of letters with a passion "based upon hatred and sensuality." Above all, there are also in this book some observations of a stern reality. Doubtless they are not new, and it is long since they were made for the first time. But does not each generation necessarily do again what those preceding it have done already? What is life except beginning again? Do we not all make, each of us in our own turn, the same saddening discoveries? And have we not a bitter need for a young voice, a new speech, to relate our sorrows and our humiliations? When M. Paul Bourget says: "There are women who have a heavenly fashion of not perceiving the familiarities which we allow our-selves with them," does he not once more unveil an eternal artifice? When he says: "It is a divine pleasure to women to repeat, with certain smiles, truths which those to whom they say them do not believe; they thus give themselves a little of that feeling of danger which deliciously excites their nerves," does he not felicitously renew a precious observation? When he says: "The less women deserve pity the more they love to inspire it," does he not lay bare an important little bit of feminine psychology?

His book, in which we hear the accent of inimitable truth, is despairing from end to end. One tastes in it something more bitter than death. It leaves ashes in one's mouth. That is why I went to the fountain of life. That is why I opened the "Imitation" and read its salutary words. But we do not like to be saved. On the contrary, we are afraid that we are being deprived of the pleasure of ruining ourselves. The best among us are like Rachel, who refused to be comforted. (pp. 312-13)

> *Anatole France, "'Mensonges', by M. Paul Bourget," in his* On Life & Letters, first series, *translated by A. W. Evans (originally published as* La vie littéraire, *Vol. I, Calmann Lévy, 1889), John Lane Company/The Bodley Head Ltd., 1911 (and reprinted by Dodd, Mead and Company, 1924, pp. 307-13).*

ANATOLE FRANCE   (essay date 1891)

[*This essay from France's memoirs presents one half of the famous debate between France and Ferdinand Brunetière (Bourget's friend and editor of* Le Revue des Deux Mondes) *over the question raised by Bourget in* Le disciple: *Should freedom of thought and expression be limited by moral conventions?*]

M. Paul Bourget possesses a quality of mind extremely rare in writers who devote themselves to works of imagination. He has the philosophic mind. He knows how to link ideas together, and keep his thoughts in abstract channels. The quality is noticeable not only in his critical studies, but also in his novels and lyrics. By his method and general bent of mind he belongs to the school of M. Taine, for whom he professes a legitimate admiration, and he is not without intellectual affinity with M. Sully Prudhomme, his senior as a poet.

But he is very far from despising the world of appearances, like the poet of *Bonheur*. On the contrary, he has given proof of curiosity concerning all the forms and changing colours which life assumes in the eyes of the spectator. (p. 53)

M. Adrien Sixte's peaceful existence, described in the first chapter [of *Le disciple*] recalls in more ways than one the life of Spinoza related by Jean Colerus, from whose pages M. Bourget, in days gone by, used to love to quote. . . . (p. 55)

M. Paul Bourget draws us M. Adrien Sixte as a French Spinoza of our own time. . . . (p. 56)

This worthy soul was one of the great thinkers of the century. He demonstrated the doctrine of determinism with a power of logic and wealth of argument unattained even by Taine and Ribot.

M. Bourget gives us a list of the works in which he develops his system. They are: *The Anatomy of the Will, The Theory of the Passions,* and *The Psychology of God.* It must be understood that the last title, in its almost ironic conciseness, means "Studies of the various conditions of the Mind, in which the idea of God has been elaborated."

M. Sixte does not for one moment assume the objective reality of God. The absolute appears to him nonsense, and he does not even admit it to the category of the unknowable. This is one of the characteristics of his philosophy. His strongest claim to be a psychologist "consists in a perfectly new and ingenious explanation of the animal origin of human sensibility." . . . M. Sixte subjects us to Necessity with inexorable severity. He regards free will as a pure illusion. "Every act," he says, "is merely an addition. To say that we are free is to say that the total is greater than the elements added together to make it. This is as absurd in psychology as in arithmetic." (pp. 56-7)

It is impossible for such a philosophy to admit the existence of good and evil, of merit and demerit. . . .

He regards thinking humanity merely as an appropriate subject for psychologic experiment. (p. 58)

To such a degree of inhumanity has a sublime and monstrous zeal for science pushed this simpleminded, disinterested and honest man, this solitary soul who, for the purity of his life, deserves, like Littré, to be called a lay saint.

Unfortunately he has a disciple, young Robert Greslou, who puts the great man's theories into practice. Highly intelligent, highly educated, actuated by a cruel sensuality and an implacable pride, affected by an hereditary neurosis, this latter-day Julien Sorel, a tutor in a noble Auvergne family, coldly and methodically seduces his pupil's sister, the generous and romantic Charlotte de Jussat. . . . (pp. 58-9)

M. Paul Bourget's book presents the problem: are certain philosophical doctrines, such as determinism and scientific fatalism, intrinsically dangerous and baneful? Is the master who denies the existence of good and evil responsible for the misdeeds of his pupil? We cannot deny that this is a weighty question.

Certain philosophies which involve the negation of all morality can enter the order of facts only in the shape of crime. When they are translated into action they come under the jurisdiction of the law.

I, however, persist in believing that thought, in its own proper sphere, has imprescriptible rights, and that any system of philosophy may legitimately be developed.

It is the right, it is even the duty of every scientist who conceives an idea of the universe to express this idea, whatever it may be. Whoever believes that he holds the Truth must express it. The honour of the human intellect is at stake. Alas, our views concerning Nature are fundamentally neither very numerous nor greatly varied; ever since man has been capable of thought he has resolved within the same circle of concepts. Determinism, which frightens us to-day, existed under other names in ancient Greece. There have always been and always will be disputes as to man's moral liberty. The rights of thought are superior to all else. It is man's glory to dare all possible ideas. As regards the conduct of life, that should not be dependent upon the transcendent doctrines of philosophers.

It should be based on the simplest morality. It was not determinism but pride which destroyed Robert Greslou. (pp. 59-60)

In that fine novel *Le disciple,* to which we have already referred, M. Paul Bourget, with an unusual mental agility, raises high moral questions which he does not solve. How should he? Is the conclusion of a poem or a story ever a solution? It is sufficient for his glory, and our benefit, that he has appealed keenly to all reflective minds. M. Paul Bourget has shown us the young pupil of a great philosopher committing an odious crime under the influence of deterministic doctrines; and he has led us to ask ourselves in what degree was the master responsible for his pupil's condition?

M. Adrien Sixte, the master, feels deeply moved. Far from washing his hands of the shame and blood which bespatter even him, he bows his head, humbles himself, and weeps. Even more, he prays. He is not a determinist at heart. What does that mean? It means that the heart is never completely a philosopher, that it is ready promptly to reject the truths to which our minds obstinately adhere. M. Sixte, as a man, was troubled in the flesh. This is all the meaning that I can extract from this part of the story. But is M. Sixte himself to be held responsible for his disciple's crime?

Did he himself commit a crime, in teaching the illusion of free will and the subjective nature of good and evil? M. Bourget has not said so; he could not and ought not to do so. M. Sixte's moral trouble teaches us at least that the understanding alone is not enough to comprehend the universe, and that reason cannot with impunity refuse to acknowledge the arguments of the heart. This idea shines forth like a soft, pure light by which the whole book is illuminated.

M. Brunetière was much struck by the moral character of such an idea, and he has praised M. Paul Bourget in an article whose rigorous argumentation it would be impossible to over-praise, but which, by its doctrine and tendencies, grievously offends against that intellectual liberty and freedom of the mind which one would think M. Brunetière would be one of the first to defend, as he is one of the first to utilize it.

M. Brunetière begins his article by asking whether or not ideas react on morals. It must be granted him that ideas do react on morals, and he takes advantage of this admission to subordinate all philosophic systems to morality. "Morality," he says, "is the judge of metaphysics." Note well, that in thus deciding he does not subject metaphysics, that is, the different theories of ideas, to any particular theory of duty or abstract morality. No, he places thought at the mercy of practical morality, in other words, of the customs of the peoples, their prejudices and habits; in short, to what we call principles. He will appreciate doctrines only so long as they are based on principles. He states this expressly:

"Whenever a doctrine, in the course of its logical consequences, ends by bringing into question the principles on which Society rests, it must be false, and the measure of the error will be seen in the amount of evil which it is capable of inflicting upon Society." A little further on, speaking of the determinists, he says: "Their ideas must be false, since they are dangerous." But it never occurs to him that social principles are even more variable than the ideas of philosophers, and that, far from offering a solid basis to the mind, they crumble as soon as they are touched.

Nor does he reflect whether a doctrine which is to-day disastrous in its first results may not tomorrow be widely beneficial. All the ideas on which Society rests to-day were considered subversive before they became established, and it was in the name of the social interests invoked by M. Brunetière that all maxims of tolerance and humanity were long resisted.

I am no more sure than you yourself of the value of such a system, and like you I see that it is in opposition to the morality of to-day, but who will guarantee me the goodness of this morality? Who will say that this system, unfitted to our present morality, may not some day be in harmony with a higher morality?

Our morality suits us very well; and should do so. Still, it is too humiliating to the human mind to tie it down to customs which never existed yesterday, and will cease to do so to-morrow. Marriage, for example, belongs to the moral order. It is a doubly respectable institution by reason of the interest therein of both Church and State. It should not be deprived of one jot of its power and majesty; but were it the custom in France to-day, as formerly in Malabar, to burn socially important widows on their husband's funeral pyres, assuredly any philosophy which by its logical consequences tended to the abolition of this custom would place a social principle in danger; would it therefore be false and detestable? What philosophy has not been at first condemned when judged by morality? Were not those who believed, at the dawn of Christianity, in a crucified God regarded for that very reason as enemies of the Empire? (pp. 61-4)

To return once more to M. Bourget's interesting novel: do not let us compel good M. Sixte to burn his books because a scoundrel found therein incitements to his natural perversity. Do not let us be in a hurry to condemn this brave man as a corrupter of youth. That, as we know, is a verdict not always confirmed by posterity. Let us refrain from stigmatizing too indignantly the immorality of his doctrines. Nothing seems more immoral than the morality to come. We are not judges of the future. (p. 71)

> Anatole France, "Science and Morals: M. Paul Bourget," in his On Life & Letters, third series, translated by D. B. Stewart (originally published as La vie littéraire, Vol. III, Calmann Levy, 1891), John Lane, 1922, pp. 53-74.

MARK TWAIN (essay date 1895)

[*Twain, considered the father of modern American literature, broke with the genteel traditions of the nineteenth century by endowing his characters and narratives with the natural speech patterns of the common person, and by writing of subjects hitherto considered beneath the consideration of serious art. Twain is often regarded as a humorist and children's writer, though very serious subjects are treated in such perennially popular books as* The Adventures of Huckleberry Finn, The Adventures of Tom Sawyer, *and* A Connecticut Yankee in King Arthur's Court. *Initially a clowning humorist, Twain matured into the role of the seemingly naive Wise Fool whose caustic sense of humor forced his audience to recognize humanity's foolishness and society's myriad injustices. Later, crushed by personal tragedy, economic hardship, and ill health, Twain turned on "the damned human race," portraying it as the totally corrupt plaything of a cruel God. Twain was offended by the impressions of America that Bourget recorded in his* Outre-Mer. *Twain retaliated in this article, in which he attacked Bourget for the superficiality of his observations and the presumptuousness with which he felt they were presented.*]

I take a great interest in M. Bourget's [*Outre-Mer*], for I know by the newspapers that there are several Americans who are expecting to get a whole education out of [it]; several who foresaw, and also foretold, that our long night was over, and a light almost divine about to break upon the land.

> His utterances concerning us are bound to be weighty and well timed.
>
> He gives us an object-lesson which should be thoughtfully and profitably studied.

These well-considered and important verdicts were of a nature to restore public confidence, which had been disquieted by questionings as to whether so young a teacher would be qualified to take so large a class as seventy million, distributed over so extensive a school-house as America, and pull it through without assistance.

I was even disquieted myself, although I am of a cold, calm temperament, and not easily disturbed. I feared for my country. And I was not wholly tranquilized by the verdicts rendered as above. It seemed to me that there was still room for doubt. In fact, in looking the ground over I became more disturbed than I was before. Many worrying questions came up in my mind. Two were prominent. Where had the teacher gotten his equipment? What was his method?

He had gotten his equipment in France.

Then as to his method! I saw by his own intimations that he was an Observer, and had a System—that used by naturalists and other scientists. (p. 166)

The Observer of Peoples has to be a Classifier, a Grouper, a Deducer, a Generalizer, a Psychologizer; and, first and last, a Thinker. He has to be all these, and when he is at home, observing his own folk, he is often able to prove competency. But history has shown that when he is abroad observing unfamiliar peoples the chances are heavily against him. He is then a naturalist observing a bug, with no more than a naturalist's chance of being able to tell the bug anything new about itself, and no more than a naturalist's chance of being able to teach it any new ways which it will prefer to its own.

To return to that first question. M. Bourget, as teacher, would simply be France teaching America. It seemed to me that the outlook was dark—almost Egyptian, in fact. What would the new teacher, representing France, teach us? Railroading? No. France knows nothing valuable about railroading. Steamshipping? No. France has no superiorities over us in that matter. . . . Novel-writing? No. M. Bourget and the others know only one plan, and when that is expurgated there is nothing left of the book.

I wish I could think what he is going to teach us. Can it be Deportment? But he experimented in that at Newport and failed to give satisfaction, except to a few. (p. 167)

If it isn't Deportment, what is left? It was at this point that I seemed to get on the right track at last. M. Bourget would teach us to know ourselves; that was it: he would reveal us to ourselves. That would be an education. He would explain us to ourselves. Then we should understand ourselves; and after that be able to go on more intelligently.

It seemed a doubtful scheme. He could explain *us* to *himself*—that would be easy. That would be the same as the naturalist explaining the bug to himself. But to explain the bug to the bug—that is quite a different matter. The bug may not know himself perfectly, but he knows himself better than the naturalist can know him, at any rate.

A foreigner can photograph the exteriors of a nation, but I think that that is as far as he can get. I think that no foreigner can report its interior—its soul, its life, its speech, its thought. I think that a knowledge of these things is acquirable in only one way—not two or four or six—*absorption;* years and years of unconscious absorption; years and years of intercourse with the life concerned; of living it, indeed; sharing personally in its shames and prides, its joys and griefs, its loves and hates, its prosperities and reverses, its shows and shabbinesses, its deep patriotism, its whirlwinds of political passion, its adoration—of flag, and heroic dead, and the glory of the national name. Observation? Of what real value is it? One learns peoples through the heart, not the eyes or the intellect. (p. 168)

> *The nature of a people* is always of a similar shade in its vices and its virtues, in its frivolities and in its labor. *It is this physiognomy which it is necessary to discover,* and every document is good, from the hall of a casino to the church, from the foibles of a fashionable woman to the suggestions of a revolutionary leader. I am therefore quite sure that this *American soul,* the principal interest and the great object of my voyage, appears behind the records of Newport for those who choose to see it.—*M. Paul Bourget.*

[The italics are mine.] It is a large contract which [M. Bourget] has undertaken. "Records" is a pretty poor word there, but I think the use of it is due to hasty translation. In the original the word is *fastes.* I think M. Bourget meant to suggest that he expected to find the great "American soul" secreted behind the *ostentations* of Newport; and that he was going to get it out and examine it, and generalize it, and psychologize it, and make it reveal to him its hidden vast mystery: "the nature of the people" of the United States of America. We have been accused of being a nation addicted to inventing wild schemes. I trust that we shall be allowed to retire to second place now.

There isn't a single human characteristic that can be safely labeled "American." (pp. 169-70)

Whenever you have found what seems to be an "American" peculiarity, you have only to cross a frontier or two, or go down or up in the social scale, and you perceive that it has disappeared. And you can cross the Atlantic and find it again. There may be a Newport religious drift, or sporting drift, or conversational style or complexion, or cut of face, but there are entire empires in America, north, south, east, and west, where you could not find your duplicates. It is the same with everything else which one might propose to call "American." M. Bourget thinks he has found the American Coquette. If he had really found her he would also have found, I am sure, that she was not new, that she exists in other lands in the same forms, and with the same frivolous heart and the same ways and impulses. I think this because I have seen our coquette; I have seen her in life; better still, I have seen her in our novels, and seen her twin in foreign novels. I wish M. Bourget had seen ours. He thought he saw her. And so he applied his System to her. She was a Species. So he gathered a number of samples of what seemed to be her, and put them under his glass, and divided them into groups which he calls "types," and labeled them in his usual scientific way with "formulas"—brief, sharp descriptive flashes that make a person blink, sometimes, they are so sudden and vivid. As a rule they are pretty far-fetched, but that is not an important matter; they surprise, they compel admiration, and I notice by some of the comments which his efforts have called forth that they deceive the unwary. Here are a few of the coquette variants which he has grouped and labeled:

THE COLLECTOR.
THE EQUILIBREE.
THE PROFESSIONAL BEAUTY.
THE BLUFFER.
THE GIRL-BOY.

If he had stopped with describing these characters we should have been obliged to believe that they exist; that they exist, and that he has seen them and spoken with them. But he did not stop there; he went further and furnished to us light-throwing samples of their behavior, and also light-throwing samples of their speeches. He entered those things in his note-book without suspicion, he takes them out and delivers them to the world with a candor and simplicity which show that he believed them genuine. They throw altogether too much light. They reveal to the native the origin of his find. I suppose he knows how he came to make that novel and captivating discovery, by this time. If he does not, any American can tell him—any American to whom he will show his anecdotes. It was "put up" on him, as we say. It was a jest—to be plain, it was a series of frauds. To my mind it was a poor sort of jest, witless and contemptible. The players of it have their reward, such as it is; they have exhibited the fact that whatever they may be they are not ladies. M. Bourget did not discover a type of coquette; he merely discovered a type of practical joker. One may say *the* type of practical joker, for these people are exactly alike all over the world. Their equipment is always the same: a vulgar mind, a puerile wit, a cruel disposition as a rule, and always the spirit of treachery.

In his Chapter IV. M. Bourget has two or three columns gravely devoted to the collating and examining and psychologizing of these sorry little frauds. One is not moved to laugh. There is nothing funny in the situation; it is only pathetic. The stranger gave those people his confidence, and they dishonorably treated him in return.

But one must be allowed to suspect that M. Bourget was a little to blame himself. Even a practical joker has some little judgment. He has to exercise some degree of sagacity in selecting his prey if he would save himself from getting into trouble. In my time I have seldom seen such daring things marketed at any price as these conscienceless folk have worked off at par on this confiding observer. It compels the conviction that there was something about him that bred in those speculators a quite unusual sense of safety, and encouraged them to strain their powers in his behalf. They seem to have satisfied themselves that all he wanted was "significant" facts, and that he was not accustomed to examine the source whence they proceeded. It is plain that there was a sort of conspiracy against him almost from the start—a conspiracy to freight him up with all the strange extravagances those people's decayed brains could invent.

The lengths to which they went are next to incredible. They told him things which surely would have excited any one else's suspicion, but they did not excite his. Consider this:

> There is not in all the United States an entirely nude statue.

If an angel should come down and say such a thing about heaven, a reasonably cautious observer would take that angel's number and inquire a little further before he added it to his catch. What does the present observer do? Adds it. Adds it at once. Adds it, and labels it with this innocent comment:

> This small fact is strangely significant.

It does seem to me that this kind of observing is defective.

Here is another curiosity which some liberal person made him a present of. I should think it ought to have disturbed the deep slumber of his suspicion a little, but it didn't. It was a note from a fog-horn for strenuousness, it seems to me, but the doomed voyager did not catch it. If he had but caught it, it would have saved him from several disasters:

> If the American knows that you are traveling to take notes, he is interested in it, and at the same time rejoices in it, as in a tribute.

Again, this is defective observation. It is human to like to be praised; one can even notice it in the French. But it is not human to like to be ridiculed, even when it comes in the form of a "tribute." I think a little psychologizing ought to have come in there. Something like this: A dog does not like to be ridiculed, a redskin does not like to be ridiculed, a negro does not like to be ridiculed, a Chinaman does not like to be ridiculed; let us deduce from these significant facts this formula: the American's grade being higher than these, and the chain of argument stretching unbroken all the way up to him, there is room for suspicion that the person who said the American likes to be ridiculed, and regards it as a tribute, is not a capable observer.

I feel persuaded that in the matter of psychologizing, a professional is too apt to yield to the fascinations of the loftier regions of that great art, to the neglect of its lowlier walks. Every now and then, at half-hour intervals, M. Bourget collects a hatful of airy inaccuracies and dissolves them in a panful of assorted abstractions, and runs the charge into a mold and turns you out a compact principle which will explain an American girl, or an American woman, or why new people yearn for old things, or any other impossible riddle which a person wants answered. (pp. 170-73)

When M. Bourget is exploiting [the arts of Generalizations, Psychologizings, and Deductions], it is then that he is peculiarly and particularly himself. His ways are wholly original when he encounters a trait or a custom which is new to him. Another person would merely examine the find, verify it, estimate its value, and let it go; but that is not sufficient for M. Bourget: he always wants to know *why* that thing exists, he wants to know how it came to happen; and he will not let go of it until he has found out. And in every instance he will find that reason where no one but himself would have thought of looking for it. He does not seem to care for a reason that is not picturesquely located; one might almost say picturesquely and impossibly located.

He found out that in America men do not try to hunt down young married women. At once, as usual, he wanted to know *why*. Any one could have told him. He could have divined it by the lights thrown by the novels of the country. But no, he preferred to find out for himself. He has a trustfulness as regards men and facts which is fine and unusual; he is not particular about the source of a fact, he is not particular about the character and standing of the fact itself; but when it comes to pounding out the reason for the existence of the fact, he will trust no one but himself.

In the present instance here was his fact: American young married women are not pursued by the corrupter; and here was the question: What is it that protects her?

It seems quite unlikely that that problem could have offered difficulties to any but a trained philosopher. Nearly any person would have said to M. Bourget: "Oh, that is very simple. It is very seldom in America that a marriage is made on a commercial basis; our marriages, from the beginning, have been made for love; and where love is there is no room for the corrupter."

Now, it is interesting to see the formidable way in which M. Bourget went at that poor, humble little thing. He moved upon it in column—three columns—and with artillery.

"Two reasons of a very different kind explain"—that fact.

And now that I have got so far, I am almost afraid to say what his two reasons are, lest I be charged with inventing them. But I will not retreat now; I will condense them and print them, giving my word that I am honest and not trying to deceive any one.

1. Young married women are protected from the approaches of the seducer in New England and vicinity by the diluted remains of a prudence created by a Puritan law of two hundred years ago, which for a while punished adultery with death.

2. And young married women of the other forty or fifty states are protected by laws which afford extraordinary facilities for divorce.

If I have not lost my mind I have accurately conveyed those two Vesuvian irruptions of philosophy. But the reader can consult Chapter IV. of *Outre-Mer,* and decide for himself. Let us examine this paralyzing Deduction or Explanation by the light of a few sane facts.

1. This universality of "protection" has existed in our country *from the beginning;* before the death-penalty existed in New England, and during all the generations that have dragged by since it was annulled.

2. Extraordinary facilities for divorce are of such recent creation that any middle-aged American can remember a time when such things had not yet been thought of. (pp. 175-76)

As a literary artist, M. Bourget is as fresh and striking as he is as a scientific one. He says, "Above all, I do not believe much in anecdotes." Why? "In history they are all false"—a sufficiently broad statement—"in literature all libelous"—also a sufficiently sweeping statement, coming from a critic who notes that we are a people who are peculiarly extravagant in our language—"and when it is a matter of social life, almost all biased." It seems to amount to stultification, almost. He has built two or three breeds of American coquettes out of anecdotes—mainly "biased" ones, I suppose; and, as they occur "in literature," furnished by his pen, they must be "all libelous." Or did he mean not *in* literature or anecdotes *about* literature or literary people? I am not able to answer that. Perhaps the original would be clearer, but I have only the translation of this instalment by me. I think the remark had an intention; also that this intention was booked for the trip; but that either in the hurry of the remark's departure it got left, or in the confusion of changing cars at the translator's frontier it got side-tracked.

"But on the other hand I believe in statistics; and those on divorces appear to me to be most conclusive." And he sets himself the task of explaining—in a couple of columns—the process by which Easy-Divorce conceived, invented, originated, developed, and perfected an empire-embracing condition of sexual purity in the States. *In forty years.* No, he doesn't state the interval. With all his passion for statistics he forgot to ask how long it took to produce this gigantic miracle.

I have followed his pleasant but devious trail through those columns, but I was not able to get hold of his argument and find out what it was. I was not even able to find out where it left off. It seemed to gradually dissolve and flow off into other matters. I followed it with interest, for I was anxious to learn how easy-divorce eradicated adultery in America, but I was disappointed; I have no idea yet how it did it. I only know it didn't. But that is not valuable; I knew it before. (pp. 177-78)

I wish M. Bourget had read more of our novels before he came. It is the only way to thoroughly understand a people. When I found I was coming to Paris, I read *La Terre*. (p. 179)

> *Mark Twain, "What Paul Bourget Thinks of Us"*
> *(originally published in* The North American Re-
> view, *Vol. CLX, No. 458, January, 1895), in his*
> The Complete Essays of Mark Twain, *edited by*
> *Charles Neider (copyright © 1963 by Charles Nei-*
> *der), Doubleday & Company, Inc., 1963, pp. 166-*
> *79.*

MAX O'RELL [pseudonym of PAUL BLOUET]   (essay date 1895)

[*Max O'Rell took exception to Mark Twain's sarcastic article attacking Bourget's* Outre-Mer *(see excerpt above), and wrote the following article in defense of his countryman.*]

A book, written by a man who has spent six months in a country, on that country and its people, whether by one of the brightest ornaments of modern literature like M. Paul Bourget, or by a professional humorist like Mark Twain, is a joke. M. Paul Bourget has attempted [in *Outre-Mer*] a serious book, a book of opinions, which makes the joke perfectly huge, and Mark Twain does not like it. Now Mark Twain, as a professional humorist, does not appreciate other people's jokes. Professional humorists never do. But I believe that in this case it is M. Paul Bourget who is the humorist and Mark Twain the dull man. (p. 303)

Mark Twain does not like M. Paul Bourget's articles on America. To tell the truth, I do not either. Mark Twain, however, only read the English translation of *Outre-Mer* that appeared in a leading New York paper. The translation is clumsy, and gives no idea of the original. I had this advantage over Mark Twain that I read *Outre-Mer* in French, and I found the sauce almost good enough to make me enjoy the fish. The style of M. Paul Bourget is so beautiful that I can read his books, forgetting the matter for the manner, just as I would listen to Adelina Patti singing scales. (p. 304)

Mark Twain wonders what France could teach America. I may, by and by, enlighten him a little on the subject. "Novel writing?" he exclaims. "No, M. Bourget and *the others* [the italics are mine] know only one plan, and when that is expurgated there is nothing left of the book."

Now, the style of M. Paul Bourget and many other French writers is apparently a closed letter to Mark Twain; but let us leave that alone. Has he read Erckmann Chatrian, Victor Hugo, Lamartine, Edmond About, Cherbuliez, Renan? Has he read Gustave Droz's *Monsieur, Madame et Bébé*, and those books which leave for a long time a perfume about you? Has he read the novels of Alexander Dumas, Eugéne Sue, George Sand, and Balzac? Has he read Victor Hugo's *Les Misérables* and *Notre Dame de Paris*? Has he read or heard the plays of Sandeau, Augier, Dumas, and Sardou, the works of those Titans of modern literature, whose names will be household words all over the world for hundreds of years to come? He has read *La Terre*—this kind-hearted, refined humorist! When Mark Twain visits a garden, does he smell the violets, the roses, the jasmine, or the honeysuckle? No, he goes in the far-away corner where the soil is prepared. Hear what he says: "I wish M. Paul Bourget had read more of our novels before he came.

It is the only way to thoroughly understand a people. When I found I was coming to Paris I read *La Terre*." Fancy my saying: "When I found I was coming to America, I read Mr. W. T. Stead's *If Christ Came to Chicago*." And *La Terre* is a work of fiction; the other is based on facts, and is written by a man who may be called a faddist, but whose sincerity and honesty nobody doubts.

So, Mark Twain read *La Terre*. (pp. 305-06)

If that is all he knows of our modern literature, I may take it that he knows of French life only what was shown him on the Paris boulevards by the guide he had engaged. (p. 309)

M. Paul Bourget's book is pretentious in its aim, and provincial in its execution. In the French original it is like anything M. Paul Bourget writes—a masterpiece of composition and style, and no translation of such a book can do it justice; it is no more translatable into English than the works of Victor Hugo, or than the works of Shakespeare can be into French.

M. Bourget's analysis of character is so subtle that his dissected subject is reduced to threads that often are hardly tangible. On that account the book will pass over the heads of many Americans, and will not be "thoughtfully and profitably studied" by them. It has passed over Mark Twain's head. *Outre-Mer*, however, is the work of a great man of letters, and of a gentleman. If the book will not teach much to the French, or anything to the Americans, it ought to have achieved at least one object—Mark Twain might certainly have derived from its perusal a lesson in politeness and good manners. (pp. 309-10)

> *Max O'Rell [pseudonym of Paul Blouet], "Mark Twain*
> *and Paul Bourget," in* The North American Review,
> *Vol. CLX, No. 460, March, 1895, pp. 302-10.**

HENRY JAMES   (letter date 1898)

[*As a novelist James is valued for psychological acuity and a complex sense of artistic form. Throughout his career, James also wrote literary criticism in which he developed his artistic ideals and applied them to the works of others. Among the numerous conceptualizations he formed to clarify the nature of fiction, he defined the novel as "a direct impression of life." The quality of this impression—the degree of moral and intellectual development—and the author's ability to communicate this impression in an effective and artistic manner were the two principal criteria by which James estimated the worth of a literary work. James admired the self-consciously formalistic approach of contemporary French writers, particularly Gustave Flaubert, an approach which contrasted with the loose, less formulated standards of the English novel. On the other hand, he favored the moral concerns of English writing over the often amoral and cynical vision which characterized much of French literature in the second half of the nineteenth century. His literary aim was to combine the qualities of each country's literature that most appealed to his temperament. After considering various fictional strategies, James arrived at what he thought the most desirable form for the novel to take. Basically objective in presentation—that is, without the intrusion of an authorial voice—the novel should be a well-integrated formal scheme of dialogue, description, and narrative action, all of which should be received from the viewpoint of a single consciousness, or "receptor." In James's novels this receptor is usually a principal character who is more an observer than a participant in the plot. Equal in importance to the artistic plan of a novel is the type of receptor a novelist chooses to use. The type demanded by James's theory is a consciousness that will convey a high moral vision, humanistic worldview, and a generally uplifting sense of life. James's criteria were accepted as standards by a generation of novelists that included Ford Madox*]

Ford, Joseph Conrad, and Virginia Woolf. In the following well-known and frequently quoted letter, James admonished Bourget for what are today recognized as the two major flaws in his fiction: his penchant for authorial intrusions upon the story, and his tendency to dissect rather than create living characters.]

I have received the **Duchesse Bleue,** and also the Land of Cockaigne from Madame Paul, whom I thank very kindly for her inscription. I had just read the Duchess, but haven't yet had leisure to attack the great Matilda. The Duchess inspires me with lively admiration—so close and firm, and with an interest so nourished straight from the core of the subject, have you succeeded in keeping her. I never read you sans voulois me colleter [without wanting to come to terms] with you on what I can't help feeling to be the detrimental parti-pris [prejudice] (unless it be wholly involuntary) of some of your narrative, and other technical, processes. . . . Each of us, from the moment we are worth our salt, writes as he can and only as he can, and his writing at all is conditioned upon the very things that from the standpoint of another method most lend themselves to criticism. And we each know much better than anyone else can what the defect of our inevitable form may appear. So, though it does strike me that your excess of anticipatory analysis undermines too often the reader's curiosity—which is a gross, loose way of expressing one of the things I mean—so, probably, I really understand better than anyone except yourself why, to do the thing at all, you must use your own, and nobody's else, trick of presentation. No two men in the world have the same idea, image and measure of presentation. All the same, I must some day read one of your books with you, so interesting would it be to me—if not to *you!*— to put, from page to page and chapter to chapter, your finger on certain places, showing you just where and why (selon moi!) you are too prophetic, too exposedly constructive, too disposed yourself to swim in the thick reflective element in which you set your figures afloat. All this is a clumsy notation of what I mean, and, on the whole, mal àpropos into the bargain, inasmuch as I find in the Duchess plenty of the art I most like and the realisation of an admirable subject. Beautifully done the whole episode of the actress's intervention in the rue Nouvelle, in which I noted no end of superior touches. I doubt if any of your readers lose less than I do—to the fiftieth part of an intention. All this part of the book seems to me thoroughly handled—except that, I think, I should have given Molan a different behaviour after he gets into the cab with the girl— not have made him act so *immediately* "in character." He takes there no line—I mean no deeper one—which is what I think he would have done. In fact I think I see, myself, positively what he would have done; and in general he is, to my imagination, as you give him, too much in character, too little mysterious. So is Mme. de Bonnivet—so too, even, is the actress. Your love of intellectual daylight, absolutely your pursuit of complexities, is an injury to the patches of ambiguity and the abysses of shadow which really are the clothing—or much of it—of the *effects* that constitute the material of our trade. Basta! [Enough!] (pp. 288-89)

> *Henry James, in his letter to Paul Bourget on August 19, 1898, in his* The Letters of Henry James, Vol. I, *edited by Percy Lubbock (copyright, 1920, by Charles Scribner's Sons; copyright renewed © 1948 by William James and Margaret James Porter; reprinted with permission of Charles Scribner's Sons), Charles Scribner's Sons, 1920, pp. 286-90.*

JULES LEMAÎTRE   (essay date 1905)

[*In this introduction to Bourget's* Cosmopolis, *Lemaître praises Bourget's talent both as a critic and as a novelist.*]

Brunetière says of Bourget that "no one knows more, has read more, read better, or meditated more profoundly upon what he has read, or assimilated it more completely." So much "reading" and so much "meditation," even when accompanied by strong assimilative powers, are not, perhaps, the most desirable and necessary tendencies in a writer of verse or of fiction. To the philosophic critic, however, they must evidently be invaluable: and thus it is that in a certain self-allotted domain of literary appreciation allied to semi-scientific thought, Bourget stands to-day without a rival. His [*Essais de Psychologie Contemporaine, Nouveaux Essais,* and *Etudes et Portraits*] . . . are certainly not the work of a week, but rather the outcome of years of self-culture and of protracted determined endeavor upon the sternest lines. (pp. v-vi)

In fiction, Bourget carries realistic observation beyond the externals (which fixed the attention of Zola and Maupassant) to states of the mind: he unites the method of Stendhal to that of Balzac. He is always interesting and amusing. He takes himself seriously and persists in regarding the art of writing fiction as a science. He has wit, humor, charm, and lightness of touch, and ardently strives after philosophy and intellectuality—qualities that are rarely found in fiction. It may well be said of M. Bourget that he is innocent of the creation of a single stupid character. The men and women we read of in Bourget's novels are so intellectual that their wills never interfere with their hearts. (pp. vi-vii)

Le Disciple and *Cosmopolis* are certainly notable books. The latter marks the cardinal point in Bourget's fiction. Up to that time he had seen environment more than characters; here the dominant interest is psychic, and, from this point on, his characters become more and more like Stendhal's, "different from normal clay." *Cosmopolis* is perfectly charming. Bourget is, indeed, the past-master of "psychological" fiction.

To sum up: Bourget is in the realm of fiction what Frédéric Amiel is in the realm of thinkers and philosophers—a subtle, ingenious, highly gifted student of his time. With a wonderful dexterity of pen, a very acute, almost womanly intuition, and a rare diffusion of grace about all his writings, it is probable that Bourget will remain less known as a critic than as a romancer. Though he neither feels like Loti nor sees like Maupassant—he reflects. (pp. vii-viii)

> *Jules Lemaître, in his preface to* Cosmopolis *by Paul Bourget (copyright 1905 by Robert Arnot; copyright 1923 by Current Literature Publishing Company), Maison Mazarin, 1905 (and reprinted by Current Literature Publishing Company, 1923), pp. v-viii.*

FRANK HARRIS   (essay date 1927)

[*Harris was a highly controversial editor, critic, and biographer who is best known as the author of a maliciously inaccurate biography of Oscar Wilde, a dubious life of Bernard Shaw, and a massive autobiography which portrays Edwardian life primarily as a background for Harris's near-Olympian sexual adventures. A man frequently referred to in colorfully insulting terms by major critics, he was by most accounts a remarkable liar and braggart, traits which deeply color the quality of his works and their critical reception. His greatest accomplishments were achieved as editor of* The Fortnightly Review, Pearson's Magazine, *the* Evening News, *and* The Saturday Review. *As editor of* The Saturday Review *he helped launch the careers of Shaw and H. G. Wells, hiring them as drama critic and literary critic, respectively, during the mid-1890s. Shaw later wrote that Harris "had no quality of editorship except the supreme one of knowing good work from bad, and not being afraid of it." Harris's fame as a critic rests primarily upon his five-volume* Contemporary Portraits *(1915-30), which contain essays marked by the author's characteristically vigorous style and patronizing tone. The following strongly-worded assessment of Bourget's work is one of the most withering offered to date.*]

[Paul Bourget] is not in any sense a great writer; he is not even among the best writers of his generation; he has no distinctive word to men; and yet because he is a Frenchman what he says about letters is always sensible and sometimes exceedingly interesting. Of course, the reason of this is that Bourget is rather an essayist than a creative artist. He patches his stories with scraps of erudition and fringes of conventional frippery. He has been over-educated—educated, that is, beyond his power of assimilation. He smells of the Normal School, and is bookish even in passion. He is therefore at his best in talking of other men's writings, and not when writing himself. (pp. 139-40)

[Bourget's] best book, **"The Night Cometh,"** is much like the others. The characters are all mere types, without individual life, without the whimsies and peculiarities of living people. It is a dead book and a dead book by a Frenchman is more lifeless than any sort of book.

But after all Bourget is a very interesting essayist, and if he had only written about books and works of art instead of trying to create he would have won, I think, a more enduring reputation. (p. 144)

Bourget is not a born story-teller as de Maupassant was, or as Kipling is, but he has learned his craft in a good school, and he is intelligent enough to have turned his reading to fair account. I remember a story called **"La Vie Passe";** it is a little sentimental narrative that lives because it is kindly. It is like a poor, pallid flower on harsh, stony ground. One remarks it because it stands alone and is a little pathetic. It is not worth describing; one just notices it in passing. I turned down pages in the book half a dozen times, and on looking over it I find they are all turned down to mark gross blunders in the story-teller's art. Let me give a couple of examples. Speaking in the first tale of a completely secondary personage, who indeed is dead before the story begins, Bourget says: "His empty chair at table was all that remained of the late Vicenzo Palmi a personage as dead as a Pharaoh"; and then he goes on: "Or as Thouthmasis III., Amenothes II., or King Khouniatonou, son of that Queen Tiyi whose effigy was discovered in 1907 in the Valley of Kings, and is the object of interminable discussions amongst Egyptologists"—an impertinent and deplorable exhibition of untimely erudition. In another story he tells of an automobile accident and a terrible death. He is going to break the news to the woman who loved the dead man, but on his way, all trembling with excitement, he interposes between us and his emotions a page or so of guide-book description of Alpine scenery! The faults are disgraceful—the blunderings of a camp-follower of literature, intolerable to whoever takes his art seriously. (pp. 145-46)

My acquaintance with Bourget was ended by the indiscretion of the lady who had brought us together.

I wrote and told her that Bourget seemed to me second-rate, a sort of small edition of Stendhal without Stendhal's intense interest in life. She wrote this to Bourget and sent me his reply. He wrote: "If Stendhal were alive to-day, he would be one of

my imitators"; "il aurait été un de mes imitateurs." Of course it was only a gesture of wounded vanity, but none the less idiotic. Stendhal's "Le Rouge et le Noir" is one of the half dozen greatest French novels, with a dozen pages in it that no one can afford to ignore, while Bourget has never written a word that will be read twenty years hence. (pp. 148-49)

Frank Harris, "Paul Bourget," *in his* Latest Contemporary Portraits *(copyright, 1927, by Nellie Harris),* The Macaulay Company, 1927, pp. 139-49.

ANDRÉ GIDE (essay date 1930)

[*Many critics regard Gide as among France's most influential thinkers and writers of the twentieth century. In his fiction, as well as his criticism, Gide stressed autobiographical honesty, unity of subject and style, modern experimental techniques, and the author's sincere confrontation of moral issues. The following notes reveal Gide's ambivalent thoughts on his predecessor's career.*]

In *Le Démon de midi*, a remarkable sentence that Bourget puts into the mouth of his Dom Bayle:

All hypocrites began by having the virtues of which they preserve the mark.

(pp. 112-13)

He writes: "They *were* agreed that . . ." I don't remember just where in the first volume. But in the second . . . carried away by his story and paying less attention to himself: "They *had* agreed" which is perhaps wrong, but surely more natural.

His constant references to sacred texts are often hugely comical.

I am full of consideration for this book and deem that the important position occupied by Bourget is in no way usurped. It is even not so pastily written as I thought. There are no deficiencies in the workmanship, or psychological errors; the remarks are always correct and often subtly discerning. But when, leaving *Le Démon de midi* for a moment, I go back to Goethe, I feel at once (and I didn't need this comparison to feel it) how high above the Bourget hillock rise the mountains of real Parnassus. He is not a part of the vast range whose summits, for eternal snow, are always inhumanly bare. Doubtless he congratulates himself on providing up to the very top nothing but arable lands, but I do not think that what is harvested on him long remains very edible. The appetite for his products will pass with his epoch; that utilitarian art is good for but a time and, as soon as it ceases to be useful, arouses no other interest than a historical curiosity. Even the "serious" aspect of his work evokes smiles, and that absence of irony toward himself will soon invite, already invites, the reader's irony. . . . Yes, I believe that Bourget will seem utterly obsolete in twenty years (let us say fifty).

But he makes me realize what a success I could have had with my *Faux-Monnayeurs* if I had been willing to develop my picture somewhat. . . .

I took care to indicate only the significant, the decisive, the indispensable; to avoid everything that was "taken for granted" and where the intelligent reader could fill in for himself (this is what I call the *collaboration of the reader*). Bourget spares us nothing. But the reader is grateful to him for this. (p. 113)

The "verisimilitude" (I believe his word is *vraisemblabilité*) in Bourget is perfect. A disciple of Balzac, he is firmly fixed in reality. He never gets stuck in it as I should surely do if I tried to venture there. (p. 114)

André Gide, in his journal entry of June 23, 1930, in his The Journals of André Gide: 1928-1939, *Vol. III, translated by Justin O'Brien (copyright 1949 by Alfred A. Knopf, Inc.; reprinted by permission of the publisher; originally published in* Journal, 1889-1939, *Editions de la Nouvelle nevue francaise, 1939), Knopf, 1949 (and reprinted by Secker & Warburg, 1949, pp. 112-14).*

WALTER TODD SECOR   (essay date 1948)

[*Secor's survey of Bourget's short stories is taken from one of the few available book-length studies written in English on Bourget's work.*]

The short stories of Paul Bourget are distributed over the length of his literary career. One has only to arrange his works chronologically to realize how well his brief narratives are interspersed between his more brilliant successes in the field of the novel. In his twenty-six volumes of *nouvelles*, he used all varieties of length, ranging from the six pages of *Secum sola*, to the two hundred and ninety-five pages of *Le Luxe des autres*. (p. 50)

In order to explain the impulses which led to this large production of *nouvelles*, it is necessary to take into account the formation of the author's intelligence and character. Bourget's great purpose in writing was to give his "personal impression of life." His temperament, his education, his readings and his environment helped determine the nature of that impression of life. Now, fortunately, with Bourget, one has only to turn to the brief narratives themselves to find one of the sources of this information. By means of the frequent use of the autobiographical method, the author reveals to the reader valuable material. His conception of life and the motives which govern the choice of subject matter are made clearer. A deeper penetration into his inner life is thus brought about by the information he reveals about his ways of thinking and feeling, his tastes, his experiences and his habits. For this reason alone, if for no other, the *nouvelles* are significant. Bourget always used his personal experience by interweaving it with that of the characters of his imagination but this practice is more directly acknowledged in the short stories than in the novels by the use of the first person. Many of the novels are avowedly based on his thoughts but it is in the large group of short stories in which Bourget is the actor-narrator that one discovers information which is necessary for a complete picture of his personality. In most of his first person stories, Bourget indicates by various means whether he himself is the narrator or someone else; consequently, there is rarely any doubt when the first person narrator is Bourget. The things he does in the stories may or may not be true facts. It is what he says about himself as an observer of an action or as a minor character that is important. The *nouvelles*, in addition, offer more of an outlet for his sensibility than do the novels. In the short stories, one comes closer to the feelings of tenderness and sympathy that are behind his observations. (pp. 50-1)

Bourget's earliest *nouvelle* of note, *Céline Lacoste*, appeared on the fifteenth of April, 1874, in the *Revue des Deux Mondes*. It is an illustration of the ideal he presented for fiction in an article published in the same review, called **"Le Roman réaliste et le Roman piétiste."** In this essay, he criticized both the monstrous creations of the realists and the lack of reality found in the opposite extreme, that of the pietists' novels. His ideal for fiction, then given, was a *genre* which would give an exact picture of "the intimate life" and "the exterior world," one which would find beauty in the "study of healthy things and noble sentiments." *Céline Lacoste,* which has as its subtitle, **"Souvenirs de la vie réelle,"** satisfied this program. The *nouvelle* also is illustrative of the author's early taste for psychological analysis of dramas of conscience. . . . Bourget made an about face under the influence of Taine and became briefly an adherent of the principles of Zola. The author of *L'Assommoir* sent Bourget a copy of that novel. To express his thanks, the critic wrote to Zola of his admiration for the work. He also published several articles defending the naturalistic school. A *nouvelle*, *Le Retour,* later called *Jean Maquenem,* published in 1877, is a product of this excursion into naturalism. (pp. 59-60)

In 1880, *Le Parlement* published a *nouvelle,* **Tentation,** which marks a further evolution in the author's ideas, indicating a final break with the naturalistic school. It deals with a young professor's daughter, a product of a completely isolated dream world, who falls in love with a debauched, atheistic writer, who lives near her. . . . The analysis given of her disturbed inner life furnishes evidence that the author is about to leave behind naturalistic tendencies and return to the psychological analyses of *Céline Lacoste.* Bourget soon repudiated his short-lived enthusiasm for naturalism and launched into a literary program in which his originality was to find full expression.

The *Essais de psychologie contemporaine,* published in the *Nouvelle Revue* and then in book form in 1883 definitely established him as a distinguished critic. In his **"Lettre autobiographique,"** he explains how he finally fell upon a field of study which was to be that of his literary career. . . . He conceived the idea that by studying the moral life of the writers who had so influenced the youth of his time, he would discover his entire period with its passions, joys and griefs. His purpose in his two series of essays was to outline the moral portrait of his generation, found in the books by which he had been so deeply influenced.

He had only to transfer his gift for psychological analysis of the very spirit of his time to the narrative field to gain for the *nouvelle* and the *roman,* a new emphasis. . . . (pp. 61-2)

[From] this point on, Bourget, motivated by the desire to "see clearly" into the human soul, adopts as his special province the investigation of the duality of the human being and the controlling forces of his life. . . . In the short story, **Claire,** he calls his work that of the "moral botanist" who conscientiously and scientifically observes cases before coming to any conclusions. . . . It is this insatiable curiosity about the inner life of human beings that made Bourget a forerunner of the literature of psychological analysis in modern times. (pp. 63-4)

With the *Essais* and the early *nouvelles*, Bourget had found a rich vein in which his personal talents could be effectively put to work. He was to go through an evolution which further determines the sources of his short stories. He first turned to the more comprehensive field of the novel. . . . Beginning with *Cruelle Enigme* in 1884, which the public received enthusiastically, *Mensonges, La Physiologie de l'amour moderne* and in 1889, *Le Disciple,* his greatest success and one which stirred up a storm of controversy in the world of letters. *Le Disciple* marks a turning point in the author's evolution, for gradually the moralist had won out over the psychologist. . . . The preface of *Le Disciple,* as is well known, proclaims that it is a writer's duty to point out the cure for the evils of his time. With an almost Jansenistic rigor, Bourget, from this point on, denounces perversities and disorders of human nature and attempts to find the remedy for them. (pp. 78-80)

During this period of his evolution, he had not completely abandoned the *nouvelle* for he published in 1889 a collection of *Pastels,* composed of ten studies of women, written between 1884 and 1888. With a light and delicate touch, the author delves into the intimacy of fragile feminine souls. More than in the novels, the poet in the author finds an avenue of expression in these studies. They are not based completely on life as he observed it but on life as he imagined it to be or as it might have been for the various characters he meets. A poignant emotion of sympathy and understanding for human frailties emanates from the stories. Although the author often deals with the sadness of people who have failed to find any share of happiness in life, the bitter pessimism of some of his novels is not present in the book. The dominant tone is that of charm. The title *Pastels* is aptly chosen for the author could describe in no better way the nuances of colors with which he paints the freshness and grace of feminine beauty. Varied in subject and organization, they demonstrate the critic's successful experimentation in methods of treatment.

They were followed by *Les Nouveaux Pastels* in 1891, a volume which contained ten portraits of men. Just as Bourget, the moralist, began to appear in the novels, the same preoccupation is, for the first time prominent in these short stories. As a scrupulous thinker, he had always been preoccupied with the idea of sin even in his periods of doubt concerning religious matters. The fact that he is thinking more and more seriously that a man can never escape the results of a bad action is shown by the frequency with which he deals with the emotion of remorse in this volume. As a determinist, of course, he would believe that we must reap the consequences of our deeds but he is more and more turning to a religious explanation, revolving around the idea of original sin and the necessity of atonement. God for him is still not the perfect and only remedy for moral sickness although he is gradually approaching that conviction. (pp. 80-1)

Technique of presentation is further developed in *Nouveaux Pastels,* marking a distinct progress over the original *Pastels* of women. The stories are more fully and dramatically organized. The *Pastels* are essentially portraits constructed around some small episode whereas his *Nouveaux Pastels* are exciting narratives, dealing often with violent passions, related with carefully planned steps. . . .

A longer *nouvelle,* **Un Scrupule,** written in 1892, completes the author's period of early development of a technique in the *genre.* (p. 82)

The second main period in the development of Bourget as a *nouvelliste* is one in which he not only perfects his technique, but tries new experiments. The years immediately following his return from America were difficult ones for Bourget. Although he was at the height of his success, he mistrusted himself and his purposes so much that he was not able to produce as much as he would have liked. His analytical mind tended all too naturally to see the dark side of life but at this time particularly he suffered from a constant anxiety and a general lassitude. . . . Although he completed no novels from 1896 to 1900, the four years were very important for the *nouvelle.* (p. 85)

The stories of **Recommencements,** in 1897, demonstrate how well he had perfected his earlier method. Similar to the *Pastels,* they are delicate psychological studies which gain interest and intensity because of the focus on one central character and episode. Their value is increased by the fact that the author broadens his horizon and begins to study numerous and varied milieux, giving the lie to those who say that he understands only aristocratic society. The dedication of **Recommencements** to Charles de Pomairols indicates that the author is recovering from the state of extreme pessimism and is coming closer and closer to a complete acceptance of religious faith. Life's main law is that she is a great ''Re-beginner.'' Although it is heartbreaking to feel that life moves implacably on when loved ones die and that the past slips away from us rapidly, the uninterrupted continuity of life becomes a consoling truth, he believes, when one is able to believe that this patient and invincible labor of the eternal workman must have a meaning.

The second volume, **Voyageuses,** is composed of longer *nouvelles* which permit a more complete analysis of character. They retain, however, the centralized focus upon one revealing moment or episode which is the special characteristic of the *genre.* The stories combine Bourget's special art in depicting delicate personalities of women and his love for foreign lands, which form the background against which each drama takes place. Presented almost in the form of visions, recaptured while perusing his traveling journal, the author has infused them with a poetic charm which is not present in his novels. (pp. 86-7)

Bourget's ideal as expressed to Professor Feuillerat was as follows: ''A long *nouvelle* with compact action but with an extensive perspective and a deeply human meaning.'' This ideal is adequately fulfilled in the third volume of the period, **Complications sentimentales.** There are more important incidents in these stories than in the previous *nouvelles* and the action is more complicated. They would almost be novels but for the dramatic concentration upon a central point. Emile Faguet has stated that the title of the collection of *nouvelles* could be given to all of the works of the author. The writer returns in them to the subject matter of the society novels. . . . The fourth and fifth volumes of this period, **Drames de famille** and **Un Homme d'affaires** are outstanding for they are definite examples of the author's exploration of other fields than that of aristocratic and wealthy society, for the analysis of which he is so well known in his novels. Constructive critics such as Emile Faguet had often suggested that the author apply his excellent faculties of psychological analysis to bourgeois society and the working classes and thus widen the field of his subject-matter. This he now did with marked success for no two volumes draw their subjects from more varied *milieux.* The perfection of the longer *nouvelle* continues in these collections. The form pleased Bourget because it permitted him to give more highly developed psychological studies than in the shorter *nouvelles* without sacrificing the dramatic conciseness of the centralized episode of the *genre.* (pp. 87-8)

In addition, the volumes indicate the author's moral development in this period. The succinct analysis of his own evolution given in the *nouvelle,* **L'Echéance,** written in December, 1898, clarifies his point of view at this time. In the story, Eugène Corbières parents had stolen the money necessary for their son's education. Eugene becomes a successful doctor while the rightful heir of the money is forced, of necessity, into a life of poverty and debauchery. Eugene then discovers the theft of his parents. He feels that he must pay for their crime by a sacrificial life, given without financial remuneration to the service of the poor and sick. . . . Bourget is here on the point of accepting the doctrine of reversibility of merits, one of the principal doctrines of the Catholic church.

At the turn of the century, the critic prefaced the first volumes of his *Oeuvres Complètes* which he took to Plon, with an article in which he insisted that his adherence to the principles of the Catholic church did not represent a conversion but the end of a long progressive development of his thought. He had practiced a methodical doubt in his observation of reality. It was the result of his observations which brought him to the belief that Christianity was the only force that could cure man of his ills. (pp. 88-9)

As a result of this evolution of his thought, the author veered definitely to the social novel and began a whole series of what he named "romans à idées," beginning with *L'Etape* and continuing with such well known works as *Un Divorce, L'Emigré* and *Le Démon de midi.* For the good of humanity, he devotes himself first to the defense of the family, which entails, in his opinion, stable family life, indissoluble marriage and transmission of trade or profession from father to son; second, to the support of a strong religion; and third, to an appeal to tradition, meaning a monarchial or aristocratic state, with a hereditary nobility recruited in all classes and decentralization, which would restore to the provinces their individualized local life.

The third phase of Bourget's creations in the field of the *nouvelle* reflects his attitudes expressed in the novels although not in as strong a fashion as is permitted by the firm argumentation of the latter. Six volumes of *nouvelles* were published in this period before the war. They do not present any new techniques for the author's period of apprenticeship is over but they are significant for the variety of subjects they introduce. *Monique* in 1901 contains several attacks against democracy and the *Droits de l'homme* [*Rights of Man*]. In it, the author presents an idealized portrait of an artisan in furniture, whom he calls a victim of the revolutionary utopia. (p. 92)

By suggesting a return to a monarchical government and tradition, Bourget was bound to meet strong opposition. To the critics of his psychological novel technique were joined those who were in direct opposition to his political and social ideas. He was labeled a reactionary and called a member of the clerical party. Prone to see the dark side of life, he suffered immeasurably from these attacks and became possessed by another gloomy state of pessimism. This unhappy period is mirrored in the *nouvelles* of *L'Eau profonde* in 1902 and the earlier short stories of *Les Deux Soeurs* in 1905. They deal, for the most part, with the evil instincts which conquer the tendencies toward good in life. They are permeated with a melancholy which is constantly depressing. The author succeeds in transferring his poignant suffering over the miscarriage of ideals and ambitions to the reader. (pp. 92-3)

Later volumes of this period, *Les Détours du coeur* and *La Dame qui a perdu son peintre,* give a more favorable impression of humanity, indicating the passing of the dark period for the author. A new source of material is revealed when Bourget uses psychiatry in the analysis and description of passions in *Les Détours du coeur* and *L'Envers du décor.* Bourget, through the influence of Taine, had always studied his characters from a biological point of view, in order to give a total picture of the individual. (p. 93)

Bourget's literary output of novels and short stories was not so great in the period before the war because of his interest in

the theatre and in politics. Most of his work in the latter field found expression through journalistic channels. In 1908, he began a political column in *L'Echo de Paris* called *Le Billet de Junius.* It was in this period that Bourget became intensely interested in writing plays. The experiment was an intriguing one for him because of the evident difficulty of transporting psychological analyses of characters to the stage. In *Un Divorce, La Barricade, Le Tribun* and *L'Emigré,* he gives only an outline study of the characters. Most of his time is given to the opposing arguments of the thesis which each play presents. The moralist is definitely in the foreground in his plays and the psychological interest of his novels and short stories is lacking. His plays were successful, however, mainly because of his instinct for the dramatic situation.

During the first World War, Bourget served his country as best he could through his writing. He published a series of essays called the "Leçons de la Guerre" in *L'Echo de Paris.* The problems that preoccupied him during the war and the postwar period emerge for the greater part, however, in the novels entitled *Le Sens de la mort, Lazarine, Némésis, Laurence Albani, Un Drame dans le monde, La Geôle, Coeur pensif ne sait où il va* and the two volumes of *Nos Actes nous suivent.* A single *nouvelle* of average length, published separately, and two collections, appearing immediately after the war, constitute the fourth division in the history of the author's short story productions. The single *nouvelle*, *Le Testament*, published in a *de luxe* edition in 1919, contains nothing new in subject matter and method of treatment. The stories of *Le Justicier*, however, mark the unfolding of a new moral attitude on the part of the author. Because of the experiences of the war, he becomes less rigorous and severe in his judgment of moral problems. The narratives in this collection are among his best achievements in the *genre.* (pp. 95-6)

The second collection of this period, *Anomalies,* in 1920, again bears the imprint of psychiatry. The scientific element is so conspicuous in these narratives that it injures frequently their artistry. Often they give one the feeling of scientific cases and not the illusion of life which has been the author's aim. . . . In most of his stories, Bourget's abnormal characters do not lose their identity with human beings. One has the feeling, however, that those of *Anomalies* are exceptional people because of the emphasis placed on their mental maladies.

Repetitions of the earlier manner fill the creations of the last period in the history of Bourget's *nouvelles,* covering the last decade of his life, 1925-1935. *Le Danseur mondain, La Rechute* and *Une Laborantine* are the longest of the stories. Other collections, *Conflits intimes, Le Tapin, La Vengeance de la vie, De petits faits vrais, Le Diamant de la reine* and *L'Honneur du nom,* introduce many new environments and subjects, demonstrating the critic's desire to keep abreast of his times. One of the best volumes of his whole career is that of *Conflits intimes* which marks a high point in his contributions to the short story field. (p. 97)

Walter Todd Secor, in his Paul Bourget and the Nouvelle *(copyright 1948 by Walter Todd Secor), King's Crown Press, 1948, 256 p.*

RUDOLPH J. MONDELLI   (essay date 1958)

[*Mondelli examines Bourget's development from a novelist concerned primarily with the intricacies of personal psychology to one whose foremost concern was social problems.*]

At the turn of the twentieth century, Paul Bourget prefaced the first volume of his *Oeuvres complètes* with an article in which he insists that his adherence to the principles of the Catholic Church represents the end of a gradual development in his thinking. He had practiced a methodical doubt in his observation of reality, which brought him to the belief that Christianity was the only force that could cure man of his ills. In a letter to Victor Giraud, dated November 30, 1899, he explains the philosophy underlying his development and his desire that his work be regarded as an "apologétique expérimentale," in essence a method consisting of the complete adherence "au fait," before drawing a conclusion or championing any doctrine. In other words, Bourget maintains that, whatever sociological conclusions he has drawn, they are due entirely to his observations of life, that passion, prejudice, and preconceived notions as to the remedies for society's ills and the source of its vigor and health play no part in his program. (p. 77)

[The works of] Le Play, Balzac and Taine confirmed Bourget's conviction of the role of religion in society. To be a psychologist is not enough for him because once he has discovered the moral laws of life, he feels that they should be interpreted and employed as cures for the troubles of mankind. Bourget's point of view thus becomes social; he is interested in the good he can do for his fellow men. The Catholic Church now is not only his spiritual guide but the buttress of his social opinions.

Bourget likewise became settled in his political doctrine. In 1900 he wrote to Charles Maurras, future author of *L'enquête sur la monarchie* (1900-1909), praising the doctrine of construction and reparation in the treatises of De Bonald, the studies of Balzac, the monographs of Le Play, and Taine's *Origines de la France contemporaine*. De Bonald and Le Play placed their emphasis upon the family as a social cell, for whose moral and material well-being society should strive. Le Play and Taine attempted to uproot what they termed the false dogmas of the French Revolution: systematic liberty, the idea of providential equality, and the right of revolt. Bourget criticized democracy because he felt that it was not in keeping with the laws of science which he had observed: a monarchical form of government seemed best to him.

As a result of the evolution in his thought, Bourget veered to the social novel and began a whole series of what he termed "romans à idées," beginning with *L'étape* and a continuing with *Un divorce* and *L'émigré*. For the good of humanity he devotes himself in these works first to the defense of the family, which entails, in his opinion, stable family life, indissoluble marriage, and the transmission of trade or profession from father to son; second, to the support of a strong religion; and third, to an appeal to tradition, meaning a monarchical or aristocratic state with an hereditary nobility recruited from all classes and with the decentralization which would restore to the provinces their individualized local life.

Bourget considered the main qualities of a good novel to be credibility, "présence," importance of the subject, and "actualité." This last term is of particular importance, because the novelist meant by it the effect of the novel on the reader. He advocated the retention of some of the methods of realism, particularly careful observation and documentation, and considered the crisis as a very important element of the novel, comparing it to the crisis in a disease. Bourget made a distinction between "littérature à idées" and "littérature à thèses." He believed that a novel could suggest or present an hypothesis, but should not presume to demonstrate or prove. He saw that the novelist could not be objective, but claimed that, while

being the editor or organizer of data, he was not to try being a demonstrator. A disciple of Balzac, he was convinced that he wrote "romans à idées." Like Balzac, also, he looked upon his novels, taken all together, as a unified whole, his early novels constituting documentation and statement of the problem, and his later works indicating the causes and underlying laws involved. With this view in mind he believed that he had the right to draw conclusions based on the facts presented in his novels.

The religious and social concepts of Paul Bourget find clear expression in *L'étape*. . . . Speaking of this novel, Ernest Seillière, in *Paul Bourget, psychologue et sociologue,* says: "It seems to me that *L'étape* marks the real turning in Bourget's thought. Here he abandons his almost single concern with emotional mysticism; he now busies himself for a time with social mysticism as the theme of his works of imagination." In *L'étape* Bourget appears an outright Catholic and monarchist: in a word, a traditionalist. Henceforth his creed is that of one religion, Catholicism, and one government, monarchy, without which there can be no stability in this world and no salvation in the next. In this first of his social novels, Bourget tackles the problem which is the base of all his social and religious theories: the conditions of existence of the family. Like De Bonald and Le Play, he is certain that the central unit of society is not the individual but rather the family.

The main thesis of *L'étape* is one of social stability, of the inadvisability of going through different social strata without proper and lengthy transitions. As an author he wished to demonstrate that a sudden change in social status exposes the person who has risen too quickly to difficulties of adaptation, and that a slow progress in social ascent is requisite for the harmonious development of the family. Traditions are necessary for the family as for the individual. Bourget is of the conviction that it is the whole family, instead of the individual, that should progressively rise. In this novel, where Joseph Monneron and his family represent unhealthy social ascent, Victor Ferrand is the *raisonneur*. He is the constant mouthpiece for Bourget. It is he who states that one's life should be the proof of the validity of one's thoughts. Unhappiness results from false ideas just as illness results from bad hygiene. Ferrand states the author's thesis, saying that all the unhappiness of the Monneron family can be ascribed to the fact that it did not develop according to natural laws. It is a victim of the democratic system which substitutes the individual for the family as the unit of society.

The thesis of *L'étape* is, of course, untenable. The social implication which Bourget expounds therein is applied too stringently and rigorously. The book satisfied neither the Catholics, the freethinkers, the royalists, nor the democrats. As in 1889 with *Le disciple,* so too *L'étape* created much controversy. It provoked a lively reaction among the writers, politicians, and clergymen of the period. (pp. 77-9)

Besides this major thesis of social class, there is also in *L'étape* a secondary theme intimately connected with the first. The Monneron children fall into evil and yield to temptation because they have been brought up outside of religion and away from God. Catholicism, for Bourget, is the means of social stability. As a family which has grown contrary to the laws of healthy society, the Monnerons experience the absolute solitude in which members of such a poorly unified group find themselves at hours of crisis. They lack that inner cohesion of traditional households where each generation is but a moment of the same race or an episode in the same history. Julie Monneron faces temptation alone; empty and inefficacious principles, which have replaced sound religious precepts, will not help her. Through Jean Monneron, who is torn between two theories each covering all phases of life, social, political, and religious, Paul Bourget shows the social value of Catholicism. Jean is finally converted after having seen the fruitlessness of his father's teachings and the catastrophes which befall his family. On the other hand he sees the harmony, order, and peace which reign in the Ferrand family; Bourget wishes to illustrate in Monsieur Ferrand that discipline, restraint, and religious faith are necessities.

Bourget's most destructive criticism in *L'étape* is unceasingly directed against the democratic institutions of France. The author firmly believed that the evils of democracy would eventually lead to social and moral bankruptcy. Bourget criticizes democracy, as it was conceived in France, because he feels that it is not in keeping with the laws of science which he has observed. He came to the belief that one of the main laws of science is that of continuity, by which he means an uninterrupted development of all phases of life. For him, continuity is impossible when the people are sovereign, because the power changes with the majority of the electorate. Hence the reaching of democracy in France toward a "universal nivellement" is absurd and unfortunate. Such a leveling is opposed to Nature itself, because "Science demonstrates that the two laws of life from one end of the universe to the other are continuity and selection, a fact to which French democrats reply with the absurd dogma of democracy." Science teaches also that race, which he describes as the energy accumulated by our ancestors, is one of the most powerful factors of human personality. This fact Bourget declares contrary to the formula of the *Droit de l'homme*, which erects man himself as the first element in problems of government. Because of this belief, Bourget maintains that the disorder in public affairs is due in great measure to the parliamentary system and its basis of election. He believes that any state in which the only source of power lies in election by universal suffrage runs a great danger.

In his criticism of the democratic system of general compulsory education Bourget is equally severe. The wholesome family life of France, to be nourished and fortified, must have the support of religion and morality, he says, maintaining that the institution of lay education by democracy has wielded a fatal blow to whatever religious influence the home may have. (pp. 79-80)

[In *Un divorce*], his next novel, Bourget does not cover as much ground as in *L'étape,* which presented an entire *milieu.* *Un divorce* deals with a simple case, limited in its repercussions. By its nature the problem was able to appeal to a wider public. The question of marriage and its possible dissolution touches everyone intimately. The case studied is of such frequent occurrence that the incidents of the plot can be found in the most ordinary life.

Un divorce was published at a time when the question of divorce was the prominent subject of the day. . . . Besides, it was no more than natural that the work should follow *L'étape:* it was Bourget's desire to complete his defense of the family.

In *Un divorce,* Bourget offers an open condemnation of divorce as a social institution. Herein he explains that the Catholic Church must maintain standards for society as a whole which cannot be lowered for a minority. His thesis is that since society is composed of families, as much as these families are worth, so much is society worth. In order that the family develop in normal fashion, it is essential that marriage be not a social link

which can be broken at will but a lasting and permanent institution. History, he says, teaches that all superior civilizations have developed towards monogamy, whereas divorce is successive polygamy. When it exists, certain evil effects inevitably follow: hideous struggles take place between the former husband and wife over a child's sick-bed, a grown son's follies, a daughter's marriage; parents are judged and condemned by their children. Remarriage gives rise to fratricidal hatreds between the children of the first and of the second marriage and to antagonism between children and their step-parents. For Bourget the second marriage of a divorced person is, as the Catholic Church teaches, equivalent to a state of adultery. The Church seems to him the bulwark of family life, its doctrine of indissolubility of the marriage contract one of its surest and most reasonable dogmas.

Bourget attempts to show, in *Un divorce,* that those who live in free union or are remarried following divorce are full of contradiction. They cannot agree with themselves, with their own actions. Albert Darras, one of the protagonists, professes to be guided only by the dictates of his conscience, yet he refuses to give his consent to the marriage of his step-son Lucien to Berthe Planat and denies his wife the right to follow her conscience, when she comes to the realization that she is living separated from God. Lucien desires a marriage in accord with the existing Civil Code, yet he is moved by Berthe, a believer in free union, to agree with her belief. This paradoxical attitude is noted, too, in Gabrielle Darras who, although knowing that she is leading a life contrary to the teachings of religion, considers at various times the idea of finding anew her religious life and of sharing in the sacraments. She would like to be, at the same time, both with and against the Church.

Un divorce, though not as large in scope as *L'étape,* has, however, a force of conviction. Bourget has seen the real motivation of divorce. "For the writer, divorce rests upon just one element: sexual desire, and its satisfaction . . . And like every desire not curbed by a social discipline, it soon becomes noxious . . . In accepting divorce, one is close to accepting free union and even free love," says Paul Mannoni in *Les idées sociales de Paul Bourget.*

Closing the series of novels devoted to the family is *L'émigré.* . . . Although it is inferior to the two preceding works, still it discusses a very important thesis pertaining to the family. Bourget attempts to demonstrate that the French noble families can play an important role in the welfare and civilization of modern France. He presents the character of the Marquis de Claviers-Grandchamp as the mouthpiece for all the ideas which he never ceased to propagate in his articles and addresses. Through the Marquis, he indicates that there can be no growth or strength in a country unless the efforts of generations are added together, unless the living consider themselves a link between their ancestors and their descendants. He underlines three social truths that France should pay heed to: that to endure, families must take root and attach themselves to the soil, keeping the patrimonial domain undivided; that there must be a proper milieu for the maintenance of customs and morals, a milieu which cannot exist without distinct social classes and even the three orders of the Old Regime; that each individual is but the sum of those who have preceded him. All these truths he sees embodied in the noble houses of France. Bourget disapproves of the idleness and inactivity of the nobility. He manifests his regrets that the noblemen refuse to serve modern France, and that France refuses to utilize the services which these men might be able to render. On the contrary, France seeks to persecute, degrade, and ruin them.

L'étape, Un divorce, L'émigré reach the zenith of certitude and are therefore works of contention by means of which the author intends to convince us of three things: that absolute truth is on his side; that justice resides in the institutions which he defends; and that anarchy and ruin belong to the opposite side. Paul Bourget's purpose is not simply to produce works of art, creating characters who appear alive, who feel, who act, and who are his spiritual children who will develop in such a way as to conquer the sympathy of the readers. He is a defender of social and political conservatism, and of the doctrines of the Catholic Church. The characteristic feature of all his social novels is that they treat social problems containing political and religious teachings for the group, as well as moral lessons for the individual. (pp. 81-3)

> *Rudolph J. Mondelli, "The Church, Society, and Paul Bourget," in* Renascence *(© copyright, 1958, Marquette University Press), Vol. X, No. 2, Winter, 1958, pp. 77-83.*

LOUIS AUCHINCLOSS (essay date 1961)

[*An American man of letters, Auchincloss is known primarily as the author of novels of manners, in the tradition of Edith Wharton and C. P. Snow. He is also a respected critic who has written major critical studies of such authors as Henry James, Ellen Glasgow, Henry Adams, and Wharton. Of his own literary scholarship Auchincloss has written: "I find in writing criticism I write more about novelists of the past, and I never write with any other object but to induce my reader to revisit them. This is not to say that I do not read my contemporaries—I do—but I feel less division than many of them do between past and present." Auchincloss disagrees with those critics who praise* The Disciple *and Bourget's later books over his earlier fiction. Auchincloss feels that Bourget was at his best in the early psychological studies of love and jealousy, and that his passion for social reform overwhelmed his literary talent in his later books. See the excerpt above by Rudolph J. Mondelli for an expression of the opposite point of view.*]

James, writing to Charles Eliot Norton in 1892, speaks with great candor of his friend Paul Bourget. "Have you read any of his novels?" he asks. "If you haven't, *don't.*" How this would have pained poor Bourget, who in the dedication of *Cruelle Énigme* had publicly praised the other's *rare et subtil talent!* Yet if we apply James's injunction to Bourget's "serious," as opposed to his "society," novels, it will save us much travail. For, indeed, they express a repellent point of view.

Consider the three most celebrated. *Le Disciple* is the fable of a young man, deeply read in determinist philosophy, who, for reasons somehow attributable to his liberal education, plots the seduction, in cold-blooded steps, of the noble girl who loves him. *Un Divorce* is a warning, equally dire, of the results to be anticipated from the severance of the marriage tie. The heroine's first husband may be a vice-ridden monster, she herself an angel of patience and her second spouse a model of civic virtue—it can make no difference. The outcome is disaster for all. And in *L'Étape* the same stern finger points to the dangers of a too rapid changing of one's class. An atheist professor, born of peasant stock, attempts to raise his children in Paris, away from the soil to which they belong. The result? His son becomes a forger and embezzler, his daughter the victim of a licentious aristocrat. It seems astonishing that such dismal extracts, expressing a social philosophy so appalling, should once have been excitedly discussed in French literary circles, but we tend to forget how much of the royalist "ultra" point of view survived in France sixty years ago. (pp. 127-28)

Bourget was not all his life obsessed with the idea of saving France. In his earlier years he was content to be a novelist and to amuse his reader. The books of this period, *Cruelle Énigme, Un Coeur de Femme, Mensonges* and *Un Crime dōur* were welcomed by a public sated with the dry monotony of a naturalist literature which had concentrated on the physical appearance of things to the exclusion of everything else. Bourget's deft handling of the psychology of love and jealousy came as a needed relief. I know it is the fashion today to downgrade these novels and to laud the graver note which Bourget struck in *Le Disciple.* There seems to be a feeling among certain critics that a writer ought to be given marks if he turns from duchesses to determinism, if, in their condescending term, he "matures." But the only question to me is: does he make determinism more entertaining? I agree with Louis Bertrand that the early period was Bourget's *jardin secret.*

We start in the Paris world of the upper bourgeoisie, but we rise on the social ladder as the novels progress, and from the upper rungs we view palazzos in Rome and villas on the Riviera. *Une Idylle Tragique* takes us to witness a Mediterranean race between three great steam yachts, an American millionaire's, a Russian grand duke's and an English peer's, on the last of which the Prince of Wales himself is a guest. But if the backgrounds are inclined to be lush, the details are still accurate and colorful, the characters vivid, the dialogue crisp and dramatic. The wealth of psychological detail gives to each story a rigorous, ordered framework, sometimes at the expense of reality, but artificial flowers have their claim to beauty. James, who in warning Norton off the novels had to admit their "remarkable qualities," saw the danger of his friend's excess of anticipatory analysis and of his tendency "to swim in the thick reflective element" in which he set his characters afloat. (pp. 129-30)

Adultery is the central theme of this period of Bourget's work. Statesmen, bankers, titled idlers, fashionable artists and their wives are all engaged, in one way or another, knowingly or unknowingly, in playing the dangerous game. To the conscious players it is a completely absorbing occupation which taxes all their ingenuities. For in a Bourget world the astute psychologist has the advantage of being able to predict his victim's reactions and is thus assured of success if he only acts correctly. It is therefore worth his while to spend weeks or even months stalking his quarry. If he is a man, he may pose elaborately as a reformed roué (*Un Coeur de Femme*), calling on his victim throughout a whole season without once declaring himself in order to establish a solid new reputation. If a woman (*Mensonges*) she may go to equal lengths to appear as a loyal, faithful, misunderstood spouse seeking harmless recreation in picture galleries. But when success has been achieved—and it always is—the same procedure is observed by all characters.

Immediately, the man will rent and redecorate an apartment in a district unfrequented by the lady's acquaintance, with a sitting room so that the bed may not be observed, either before or after. When the lovers meet at parties in the great world, they murmur daytime assignations *chez nous.* The lady will dress, on the morning of a rendezvous, in clothes that are easy to remove without the assistance of her maid and proceed to the rented flat in a cab (never, of course, in her carriage). When the rites of love have been celebrated the couple will sip a glass of wine before returning to the more ordinary occupations of their day. In this brief interlude the lady may contemplate her satisfied lover in hazy rapture, if she happens to love him, or with an acid eye if her motive is merely to supplement her husband's inadequate income, or with a troubled conscience if she still has religious scruples. It may occur to her that she takes great risks for fleeting pleasures. It certainly occurs to the reader. For under the good manners of her polished world lurks the constant danger of violence. Sooner or later there will be a confrontation, between husband and lover, or lover and lover, and she will be disgraced, anathematized and spotted with blood. The end of a Bourget novel is like Gerôme's painting, *The Duel after the Ball,* with a dying Pierrot sinking into the arms of his seconds on an early snowy morning while his victorious opponent, also in costume, stalks off to a waiting fiacre. The Bourget heroine is a bewildered, defiant, hunted creature who snatches what pleasure she can in an oriental world of passionate, unreasonable men, knowing that she will one day be indicted and terribly punished for infidelities permissible to their sex but not to hers. What makes one increasingly uncomfortable is one's suspicion and ultimately one's certainty that the author feels her fate to be a just one. It is a point of view that may have received its sublimest expression in Shakespeare, but was not its lowest Jack the Ripper?

James was appalled at the erotic details of these early novels. He would not allow that they were proper subjects for fiction. In a letter to Bourget about **Mensonges** he argues that the essential character of love-making lends itself more to action than to reflection, that the moment a novelist begins to "splash about" in it intellectually, it becomes unhealthy and unpleasant. He accuses Bourget of consecrating to Madame Moraines "and her underclothing" an imagination worthy of a greater cause. And for the sensitive young hero who attempts suicide when he discovers that his mistress, a married woman, is something less than an angel of purity, James has nothing but *"un coup de pied dans le derrière."* That the world is full of such things is all the more reason for the novelist not to flood us with them.

James may have gone a bit far—at least in the eyes of a world of John O'Hara readers—but it was advice from which Bourget could have profited. For somewhere along the line, as happened with Dumas Fils, his denouncing side got out of hand. A modern John the Baptist, he turned his finger of scorn from Salomé to the world that had produced her. Society, in his later novels, has no more traditions and no more roots. A Jew like Hafner can rob his way to fortune and marry his daughter to a Roman prince. An octoroon can be the wife of a famous painter and move in the highest circles. And the morganatic wife of an Austrian archduke can receive her lover in the stateroom of an American yacht. If international society had taken on the worst features of the nations that composed it, the only hope for a Frenchman was to stay in his home, in his class and in his church. For the aging Bourget, the menace of the future must have seemed less Hitler or Stalin than Elsa Maxwell. Small wonder that his last years were depressed and his tales somber. He had allowed the crank to swallow the novelist. (pp. 130-34)

One sees Bourget, with that obsession of French novelists after Balzac to regard their scattered works as a unified *comédie humaine,* grimly considering which aspects of modern degeneration next to treat with his scalpel. The man who in 1885 had written that he and James, in talks about the novel, had finally agreed that all laws pertaining to it boiled down to the need of giving a personal impression of life had long been lost in the reformer and patriot. The older Bourget succeeded only in giving a personal impression of himself.

His nearest return to readable fiction was with **L'Émigré,** in which he drew a vivid and sympathetic portrait of an old mar-

quis, possessed of a great name and chateau, prodigally dispensing his capital to keep up the standards of the *ancien régime* in 1906. The marquis passionately believes in the duty of the aristocracy to close ranks and preserve what is left of the old France for the day when the disillusioned new shall look again to her true leaders. . . . But he also is a generous and trusting friend, a father to his tenants, a princely host, a man of absolute integrity and courage, a comic as well as a tragic character, in short, a magnificent anachronism. We sympathize with him, but never with his creator. It is easier to forgive a Marquis de Claviers-Grandchamp for tracing all the evils of his century to the fall of the Bastille than it is a Paul Bourget. And that is something which a novelist should never forget. Even his own prejudices can be put to work, but they must first be dramatized. (pp. 136-37)

Louis Auchincloss, "James and Bourget: The Artist and the Crank," in his Reflections of a Jacobite *(Copyright 1951, © 1960, 1961 by Louis Auchincloss. Reprinted by permission of Houghton Mifflin Company), Houghton Mifflin, 1961, pp. 127-37.*

ARMAND E. SINGER   (essay date 1976)

[Singer examines Bourget's criticism, poetry, dramas, and travel writings.]

Paul Bourget was indeed polygraphic. Beside his basic career as novelist and short story writer, . . . he enjoyed another as literary critic, and still another as social commentator. While still a young man he was considered a promising poet, and later became a polished composer of journals about his travels to England, Greece, Italy, the Near East, and the United States. A lifelong interest in the stage furnished the excuse for yet another minicareer, this time as dramatist. In each of these fields, with the possible exception of poetry, he was improbably successful.

Among Bourget's earliest literary efforts was poetry, begun in 1872 and published in 1875 with subsequent pieces as **La Vie inquiète.** The earliest section is entitled "Au bord de la mer" . . . , twenty-eight short lyric poems about youth, love, and nature set in Trouville. The form is more or less Parnassian, rather derivative, of uneven value (at their worst, some of the lines are almost doggerel). Two short narrative poems, **"Jeanne de Courtisols,"** and **"George Ancelys"** hint at the kind of plot and milieu he will soon favor in his novels. The later section, "La Vie inquiète," which gives its name to the whole collection, consists of fifty-two more poems (including ten called "Vers le Levant," about a trip to Italy and Greece, that foreshadow his lifelong love of travel). They assume, in turn, the philosophical, esthetic, pragmatic (carpe diem), and mildly erotic outlooks more or less demanded of young poets. . . . It was concerning this first collection that Bourget observed in 1894, "Each poem was sincere and artificial at the same time, each one felt, but not one corresponding to a simple, bare reality." . . . Few writers are so perspicacious about their own literary offspring.

Bourget's second poetic effort was a long verse story called **Edel.** . . . It has a modern Paris setting and his preferred aristocratic characters, the hero a novelist who loves and loses his Danish mistress Edel, takes to debauchery, and ends by telling himself that it was better to have loved and lost his ideal than never to have loved at all, etc. . . . [The] poem was neither a great critical nor a popular triumph.

The third volume of Bourget's verse bears the title **Les Aveux**. . . . The three parts—"Amour," "Dillettantisme," and "Spleen"—continue the bitter despair evinced in **Edel**, particularly "Amour." . . . The verses, like his previous composition, show little if any evidence of the new directions Verlaine, Rimbaud, and Mallarmé had already given French poetry, much less the final hermetic style of the late Mallarmé. These compositions of Bourget's are rational, clear, for the most part quite lacking in unusual metaphors or impressionistic images. They seem autobiographical at first reading, but to me at least have the ring of literary posing. His protestations of debauchery and spleen sound like denatured Baudelaire. (pp. 91-2)

Bourget's poetry was rather better than one might expect from so determinedly Apollonian a character. The Dionysian was hardly his métier.

Said by many to have been a better literary critic than a novelist—on its face a debatable observation—Paul Bourget was at the least distinguished in the field. His encyclopedic interest in divers areas clearly shows here. Rarely is his criticism purely literary, tending almost always to take on religious or social aspects. (p. 93)

[Bourget's **Essais de psychologie contemporaine** consists of] five long studies gathered together from articles appearing 1881-1882 in the **Nouvelle Revue** on the key figures that influenced his generation—Baudelaire, Renan, Flaubert, Taine, and Stendhal. They were followed in 1885 by the **Nouveaux Essais** on Dumas *fils*, Leconte de Lisle, the Goncourts, Turgenev, and Amiel. All ten writers are the subject of what Bourget admits was a "melancholy inquest" into the "profound pessimism" he finds characterizing "these educators of minds and hearts." . . . Bourget's essays, with their use of a newer, more penetrating psychological method, a keener probing into the causes of the malaise that affected the youth of his generation, were the day's sensation. He never quite regained in his later criticism this hold on the minds of the reading public, but he continued to turn out able volumes in the field, ever more socially and religiously slanted, and, unfortunately, more doctrinaire as time went on. The **Études et portraits** appeared in 1889. Volume I of which consists of writers' portraits. . . . The preface noted that the pieces were composed over a fairly long period of time but their real unity lay in "a method of psychological analysis applied in turn to talents of writers, problems of general esthetics, impressions of travel, and varied sensations of nature or art"—in short, the method of the earlier **Essais de psychologie.** Volume III . . . contains socially oriented essays on Balzac, Taine, and Goethe; the second half of the book deals very knowledgeably—his political-social-religious biases kept to a minimum—with ten nineteenth century novelists and poets from Musset and Hugo to Maupassant and Loti.

A more important pair of volumes are the **Pages de critique et le doctrine** . . . and the **Nouvelles pages.** . . . The preface to the **Pages** . . . claims that traditionalism was already present in the thoughts of youth thirty years before, but was suppressed by the scientific preoccupations of writers and critics of the time. By now [Bourget] finds this traditionalism the inevitable conclusion of any student of the literary scene. . . . Such a bias, however accurate, does color Bourget's choice of subject and his judgments, which is not to say that it necessarily ruins his perspective or invalidates his conclusions. He remains as ever penetrating, but he is becoming more predictable. The **Nouvelles pages** of ten years later also begin with a preface, and here Bourget notes that the only unity in his new collection

is the method. Not original with him, he admits, the method is analysis, and its basic tenet is the "search for hypotheses about causes." Given a fact concerning a novel, a philosophical system, the character of a statesman, he will define and situate it, break it down, figure its origins, etc., seek for what Taine called its generative conditions, and finally attach it to the great laws of psychology and society. He claims to have done just that in his **Essais,** his **Études,** and his **Pages de critique,** and again here in these **Nouvelles Pages.** . . . His purpose holds, like Tennyson's Ulysses, though his perspective has gradually changed.

A late collection of literary studies appeared . . . as Volume I of **Quelques témoignages,** in which he includes articles on literary documents (he decries dredging up embarrassing personal documents, scandalous and unverifiable minutiae that prove nothing and cause us to lose sight of the proper use of the great method devised by Sainte-Beuve), on Balzac (a review of a book on his life), Stendhal, Pasteur, Pascal and Renan, Anatole France, and others, ending with some thoughts on Léon Daudet's diatribe *The Stupid Nineteenth Century* (Bourget agrees in principle with Daudet, but pleads notable exceptions). The title of the collection conveys the idea of its contents: testimonies on the occasion of an author's demise, the anniversary of a book about him, or the reprinting of some unusual volume. The selections are not meant to be criticism in the dictionary sense of a decision on the value, qualities, or faults of a work. Not judgments but aids to judgment. . . . Taken as a group, the essays affirm the amazing truth that Bourget remained to the very end a cogent, penetrating literary critic. (pp. 93-6)

In his **Physiologie de l'amour moderne** . . . he introduces a little play in three scenes—he calls it a "petite comédie," or at least, he adds, the scenario of one—quite abruptly and, it seems, merely to illustrate a discussion of jealousy. . . . No masterpiece, the little drama exhibits a good sense of pace, crisp dialogue, and its playable. (p. 96)

La Barricade: Chronique de 1910 [was] first staged January 7, 1910. The subtitle is doubtless a reminiscence of his well-loved Stendhal novel *Le Rouge et le Noir: Chronique de 1830,* both being intended as treatments of a topical theme. Bourget's plot revolves around a workers' strike against a furniture factory owner. (p. 98)

The play was a big success, though it stirred up polemical arguments from a public outraged, either from the left or the right, at Bourget's not taking a firmer stand for or against management or proletariat. The language of the workers sounds reasonably natural, though quite lacking in any of Zola's profanity. The plot, if sensational in spots, is basically credible. Bourget is beginning to write like a professional dramatist. (p. 99)

Bourget followed *La Barricade* with an adaptation of his **"Un Cas de conscience,"** premiering it July 4 of the same year. The new dramatist thus had two plays running simultaneously . . . , the latter done in conjunction with the well-known playwright Serge Basset. Feuillerat and other critics concede that the action is tight, vigorous; the unity of tone is well maintained; there is not a superfluous line. But the plot had been rehandled to its detriment. The wife's character is unnecessarily blackened, and the sick man's evil plan, which gave the original novelette its strength, is not carried out. This concession to the sensitivities of the audience might make good theater, but it weakens the story. . . . The present writer would agree.

Then came *Le Tribun: Chronique de 1911,* first performed March 15, 1911, another story like *La Barricade,* and again, like it, topical. This time it was politics, a subject close to Bourget's heart at the time. Portal, a former philosophy teacher, is now prime minister of France. A socialist, he argues that the social unit is the individual, not the family. During his regime he will loosen the bonds of marriage until it is only a sort of rental contract; suppress parental control in education; remove the power to inherit; combat capitalism. He is, in short, a living casebook of all that Bourget deplores and obviously riding for a fall, though he is completely sincere in his beliefs and a man of good will. (pp. 99-100)

Wearing another of his many hats, Bourget not only travelled extensively, but accounted in writing for most of his major sojourns in foreign lands. . . .

Victor Giraud calls him a great traveller, and with Pierre Loti the most cosmopolitan of French men of letters. Travel books, he continues, look simple, within the reach of all travellers, but really they are most difficult. It is so easy to betray one's mediocrity. Bourget manages to avoid all the pitfalls. He paints himself completely in his accounts; he makes inquests into everything; he seeks out the nature of the English, Italian, or American soul. If he has any limitations, it is in what he seeks, as he admits. He has curiosity, adaptability, and a robust constitution, the three requisites of any traveller. (p. 104)

Beyond the usual reasons most of us have for travelling, beyond even the restlessness that I would claim to see in him, what made of him one of literature's better known vagabonds? Early in his life he wrote of Stendhal that he travelled very personally. Most people travel to get away, he noted, because their habits weary them, they want to put new life into their sensations, leave their sorrows; or they have studied a country in advance and wish to go from the written word to the real fact, test out the book with life, add to their erudition, etc. The first is the way of the idle, the second that of scholars, art critics, and historians. A third way is the psychologist's, and it is rare and difficult. One needs to have both the faculty of inventing one's pleasures and that, even rarer, of interpreting them. One does not read up in advance, but rather throws oneself into the spirit of the new country. This was Stendhal's way. . . . And, I submit, Bourget's own. (p. 105)

Bourget's first pure travel book is Volume II of [*Études et Portraits,* including sections on the Isle of Wight, Ireland and Scotland, the English Lake District, Oxford, "London Sketches," and a final section entitled "Fantaisies"] . . . , consisting of observations on England, France, Italy, Switzerland, and Corfu. In the preface to the original edition he apologizes to the reader for his naïveté, the result of a traveller transported for the first time out of his habitual surroundings. . . . False or genuine, his modesty was unnecessary. He casts an anything but innocent eye on a welter of facets of British institutions and types—country towns and villages, London pubs, theater, clubs, museums, Oxford, English literature. A worthy successor to that perspicacious author of the *Letters on the English,* his eighteenth century compatriot Voltaire. . . . The whole volume remains quite readable to this day, a very nice presage for his more famous descriptions of Italy and the United States to follow in later years.

Sensations d'Italie is the diary of Bourget's honeymoon journey with Minnie David during the winter of 1890-1891, his tribute to the great old Italian painters—Luca Signorelli, Fra Lippo Lippi, Ghirlandaio, Perugino, Pinturicchio—, to the places

associated with the writings of a Byron or a Shelley, and above all to the magic Italian landscapes. It is a beautiful book, a civilized book, delightful in its style and properly appreciative of a country which all his life he loved like a second fatherland. He was seeking "sensations of history, of art, of nature," he says, near the end of the book, which do something good to you and change you. . . . It is a charming book, but it is dead. Literature, painting (rarely architecture), bits of pagan religion and myths, Christianity, especially its artistic manifestations, and nature make for a cultured guide to Italy, but the picture is not balanced. Rarely does he mention a live human being, and never in extension; rarely a child. He never reveals that his wife must have witnessed the things he describes; she never appears at all. There is no noise, no song, no dancing, no crowds, no sweat. He writes "I" a thousand times, never "we"; a honeymoon sans bride. Thus, lived experience is consciously omitted from his account.

How unlike his next travel volume, a little over two years later. *Outre-mer (Across the Sea)* has enjoyed a long and spirited life, actually being still in print in the U.S.A. It chronicles the American way: prostitutes and drunks, the Bowery, plantation life, the public school system and universities (even college cheers), the rich and the poor, big business, a man hunt in the Southern swamps, life on a cattle ranch, the stockyards and slaughterhouses of Chicago, meetings with the great and near great. He visits, among other spots during his eight months overseas, New York, Chicago, Boston, Baltimore, Georgia, and Florida. His eye is sharp, his judgments on the whole sure. He appreciates the hustle and bustle of this new land, so unlike the traditional Europe he knew before. Rarely has France exported so enthusiastic a reporter of life in these United States.

Enroute he detoured to Canada for three weeks, the apparent result of which is a short volume of less than a hundred pages entitled *Sensations de Nouvelle-France,* published in Boston in 1895. It is a curious little book, not at all typically Bourget. The style is not obviously his, the observations are mediocre. Some of the dates are wrong; one town he mentions seemingly does not exist. The Canadian political leader, Honoré Mercier, whom he notes as having died, passed away a year after the period his diary describes. Tentatively I would be inclined to theorize that this little account is hackwork, penned by someone else. In any event, it is an undistinguished record of an uninteresting sojourn in Quebec. (pp. 107-09)

A coda to Bourget's accounts of foreign travel appeared in 1929. . . . The title *Sur la Toscane* suggests another journey to part of his beloved Italy ("gentle and proud Tuscany," he calls it, . . .), in his twilight years. Actually, he seems to have gone no further than southern France in these later years; this is a journey of the mind, and he must make do with images evoked and diminished by "the distance of days." . . . He talks of art, painting, poetry, medieval history. Understandably, there are virtually no descriptions of landscapes. He hopes, in concluding . . . , that these pages of memory are not unworthy of Tuscany, for him "a second and faraway fatherland." (p. 109)

Armand E. Singer, in his Paul Bourget *(copyright ©
1976 by Twayne Publishers, Inc.; reprinted with the
permission of Twayne Publishers, a Division of G. K.
Hall & Co., Boston), Twayne, 1976, 184 p.*

T. H. GOETZ (essay date 1978)

[*Goetz discusses the philosophical question of the moral responsibility of a teacher for the deeds of his pupil that Bourget ad-*

dressed in Le Disciple. *Anatole France (see excerpt above, 1891)
and Ferdinand Brunetière debated this question at length when*
Le Disciple *first appeared.*]

Paul Bourget . . . perhaps more than any other writer or critic
of his time, seemed to be acutely aware of the fact that young
men read and search in literature (understood in the broad sense
of the term) for the answers to the questions which are troubling
them. Between 1883 and 1885, Bourget wrote a series of essays
on such prominent contemporary authors as Baudelaire, Renan,
Flaubert, Stendhal, Taine, Dumas fils, Turgenev, Leconte de
Lisle, Amiel, and the Goncourt brothers. These were collected
and published in two volumes entitled *Essais de psychologie
contemporaine.* Bourget, it should be noted, did not choose
these ten writers with the aim of appreciating the formal literary
values of their works, but to study the impact their works had
had on him and his generation.

This same concern for the basic effect or impact on the reader
of a text is evident in Bourget's novel *Le Disciple*. . . . Bourget's preface to *Le Disciple,* like the speeches of Lysias and
Socrates in Plato's *Phaedrus,* is addressed in a rather abstract
way to an anonymous young man or reader. Moreover, whereas
Plato seeks to illustrate "in the exaltation of the spoken word
over the written, that the quest of truth must be the joint effort
of two minds, the minds of the teacher (or guide) and disciple,
whose love for one another is rooted in their common love of
truth, beauty, and goodness." Bourget, among other things,
sets out to illustrate the particular relationship which exists
between an author and the disciple of his written text. Although
Plato and Bourget may differ on the relative merits of the
spoken word versus the written, central to the thought of both
is the relationship between master (or guide) and disciple, as
well as the moral responsibility of the master in guiding the
disciple in the search for truth.

The question of an author's pedagogical role and the risks of
the reader relationship constitute one of the essential themes
of *Le Disciple.* In a passage describing Sixte's visit to the Palais
de Justice for questioning about the Greslou affair, the magistrate, Monsieur Valette, reveals to Sixte that one of the arguments of the prosecution, brought forward by the old Marquis
de Jussat, was that Robert Greslou had been corrupted by his
reading. . . . Thus, like Socrates, Sixte finds himself accused
of "impiety" and "the corruption of youth." It is difficult to
believe that Bourget did not wish to suggest a parallel between
Sixte and the charges leveled against him and those brought
against Socrates, and at the same time reflect on his own personal identification with the situation in which both Socrates
and Sixte found themselves, for Bourget too had been accused
of the "corruption of youth" by the impact of his cosmopolitan
novels on young minds. . . . By introducing this chain of analogies into his novel, Bourget calls the reader's attention to the
fact that the question of the moral responsibility of the teacher
or writer which is dealt with in his novel is one of the recurrent
problems of moral philosophy.

Even though a reader familiar with Lysias' speech in the *Phaedrus* and Bourget's novel *Le Disciple* might easily come to the
conclusion that Sixte's writings in the novel are comparable to
the function of the Greek rhetorician's speech in Plato's dialogue, it would be wrong to conclude that Bourget agrees with
Plato's view that the written word, like rhetoric, is always
sophistic. On the contrary, Bourget's novel demonstrates that
he has critically rethought Plato's assertion that a writer is an
"imitator, and therefore, like all other imitators . . . thrice
removed from truth." Although his novel is a work of fiction,

Bourget does not view it as a mere imitation or sophistic attempt
at deception, but as an attempt to connect itself with truth, to
make a universal statement about the grave import of the dialectical relationship which exists between an author and his
audience.

In an article entitled "Phenomenology of Reading," Georges
Poulet notes that theories of reading or criticism seem to os-
cillate between two forms of identification and non-identifi-
cation, between "a union without comprehension" and a
"comprehension without union." In the former, he explains,
the reader may identify so completely with what he is reading
that he loses consciousness not only of himself, but also of
that other consciousness which lives within the work. "Its
proximity blinds the reader by blocking his prospect." An
example of the grave disadvantage of extreme proximity in the
act of reading is described by Bourget in his *Lettre autobiographique.* There he notes that his attempts to discover his own
self, as well as to express his own consciousness through the
medium of fiction and poetry, were fragmented into imitations
of all the authors he read. Seeking the cause for his failure to
achieve literary success, he discovered it to be the result of an
"intoxication littéraire" which had the regrettable effect of
preventing him from leading his own life, or expressing his
consciousness in his literary creations. In his autobiographical
poem *Edel* . . . , Bourget is thus discovered in the act of freeing
himself from the tyranny to which his reading and strong assimilation powers had subjected him, when he has the hero of
the poem destroy in a symbolic act the books which had misguided him by failing to help him cut the tie of romantic
idealism. . . . Interestingly, Bourget's description of the young
poet's attack on Balzac for having failed to provide him with
the cutting-edge to shear from his soul the wings of romantic
idealism suggests a parallel to Plato's description of the soul
in the *Phaedrus* in which, as long as the soul's wings remain
undamaged, it travels through the heavens, but falls to earth
if its wings are lost. Literature is a dangerous preparation for
life. Nevertheless, Bourget realized his own case was not unique.
Every bookish adolescent necessarily experiences the disappointment of expectations aroused by his reading. More important, therefore, is the realization that literature plays an
important formative function in the life of the individual and
society.

In *Le Disciple,* Bourget provides an example of a case of literary
intoxication taking place in young Greslou and his friends. . . .
[He examines] the excessive ease with which their young minds
have been penetrated by the sensuous and forbidden thoughts
contained in the great philosopher's book. Like the non-lover
of Lysias' speech in the *Phaedrus,* Sixte (unintentionally, of
course) has succeeded in the seduction of these young minds,
especially Greslou's, by means of verbal persuasion. It is just
this sort of reading which Bourget cautioned against in his
Lettre autobiographique when he stated: "J'ai toujours sontenu
qu'un livre de vérité n'est jamais immoral" ["I have always
maintained that a work of truth is never immoral"] and as
proof of this he noted that no one of his generation was corrupted by such "dangerous volumes" as the verse of Alfred
de Musset, the novels of Balzac and Stendhal, Flaubert, and
the *Fleurs du mal.* The real danger in the act of reading such
works resides, he asserted, in "la précocité de désenchante-
ment" ["too early disenchantment"] and "le déséquilibre in-
térieur" ["interior imbalance"] which they might create in the
imaginations of those who read such works at too early an age
or who lacked the necessary critical consciousness to judge
them properly. This same argument is transposed to the novel

and used by Greslou in his confession to Sixte in which he describes the ordering of some books for the château of the Marquis de Jussat. He intends to use these books to excite the imagination of the young Charlotte de Jussat as part of his plan to seduce her. . . . (pp. 56-9)

In the seventh thesis of his systematic approach to rewriting literary history as an aesthetics of reception and impact, Hans Robert Jauss comes to grips with the fact that the specific social function of literature "can be found only when the function of literature is not understood as one of imitation." True literary history, he concluded, will discover in the course of literary evolution that "truly socially formative function which belongs to literature as it competes with other arts and social forces in the emancipation of man from his natural, religious, and social ties." Bourget was perhaps less concerned with a systematic approach to literary history than Jauss, but his experience of literary intoxication and the "disappointment of expectations" which it occasioned marked a significant moment in his experience of life and left him with the insight that literature is indeed a social force of great significance which can have a profound impact on the natural, religious, and social ties of the reader, especially the young, untrained reader who is not aware that he is the "prey of words," to use a phrase of Poulet. Jauss's assertion of literature's role in the emancipation of the reader from natural, religious, and social ties, however, raises another question. Once his reading has helped man to cut or free himself from these ties, where does this leave him? Bourget actually offers an answer to this question in *Le Disciple,* but at the same time he introduces an important distinction.

As a reader of Lucretius, whom he frequently alluded to in his writings or used as a literary guide, Bourget would have encountered an early example of the social function of literature in Lucretius's use of his scientific poem, *De Rerum Natura,* "to dispel the superstitious fear of the gods and the dreadful fear of death." Using Lucretius as his model, Bourget included in his novel an example of the function of literature as a liberating negation. In *Le Disciple,* for example, it is impossible to miss Greslou's high admiration for Lucretius's brilliant pictorial description in *De Rerum Natura* of religion visualized as a ghoulish head lowering itself upon mortals until defeated by Epicurus, who, having put religion under foot, brings man news that his victory places him on a level with heaven. . . . Bourget also illustrated in his novel how Greslou's reading not only served as the cutting-edge of his ties to religion, but also had the effect of isolating and alienating him from the ties of affection which normally exist between a mother and a son and finally contributed to his breaking the ties of society by causing the death of a young girl who had made the mistake of falling in love with him.

Bourget's understanding of the social impact of literature on a young reader of a certain disposition thus appears to anticipate some of the consequences involved in Jauss's thesis. Since Bourget truly believed that literature was a powerful formative force, he, like Plato, was not blind to the fact that its liberating negation of man's natural, religious, and social ties could pose a threat not only to the individual, but to society and the state as well. On the other hand, and the conclusion of *Le Disciple* supports this assertion, since literature does have a socially formative function, Bourget decided not to exclude it from the state or society because of its possibly dangerous effects (or to advocate book burning as a solution as he had done in his poem *Edel*), but to espouse the Horatian notion of the civilizing effect of literature, and to use his novel as a means to reinforce man's natural, religious, and social ties. (pp. 60-1)

T. H. Goetz, "Paul Bourget's 'Le disciple' and the Text-Reader Relationship," in The French Review *(copyright 1978 by the American Association of Teachers of French), Vol. LII, No. 1, October, 1978, pp. 56-61.*

ADDITIONAL BIBLIOGRAPHY

Drake, William. "Paul Bourget." In his *Contemporary European Writers,* pp. 285-98. New York: John Day Co., 1928.
   A survey of Bourget's career.

France, Anatole. "Paul Bourget: *Un coeur de femme.*" In his *On Life and Letters: Fourth Series,* pp. 21-8. New York: Dodd, Mead and Co., 1924.
   Reviews Bourget's *Un coeur de femme,* offering satiric comments on the novel and on the mentality of the reading public.

Gosse, Edmund. "Some Recent Books of M. Paul Bourget." In his *French Profiles,* pp. 233-58. London: William Heinemann, 1913.
   A critical discussion of several of Bourget's works, including *Outre-mer, L'étape, Complications sentimentales, La duchesse bleue,* and *Voyageuses.*

————. "M. Bourget's Novels." In his *More Books on the Table,* pp. 247-54. New York: Charles Scribner's Sons, 1923.
   Reviews *Ecuyère* and *Un drame dans le monde,* and praises Bourget as the writer most responsible for the decline of Naturalism in France.

Jones, Edward A. "Paul Bourget: Apologist for Traditionalism in France." *South Atlantic Quarterly* XLV, No. 4 (October 1946): 504-10.
   Examines Bourget's works written after *The Disciple,* stressing the author's allegiance to Catholicism, the monarchy, and the family.

Keating, L. Clark. "Mark Twain and Paul Bourget." *The French Review* XXX, No. 5 (April 1957): 342-49.*
   Compares the lives and thoughts of Twain and Bourget.

McFarlane, I. D. "Henry James and Paul Bourget." *The Cambridge Journal* IV, No. 3 (December 1950): 144-61.
   Traces the friendship and mutual opinions of the two writers.

Mondelli, Rudolph J. "Paul Bourget and the Concept of Moral Responsibility." *Canadian Modern Language Review* XVI, No. 4 (Summer 1960): 20-6.
   Revives the Anatole France-Ferdinand Brunetière debate. Mondelli discusses the question of the artist's moral responsibility for the effects of his ideas, a question posed by Bourget in *The Disciple.*

Ross, Flora Emma. "Bourget and Goethe." In her *Goethe in Modern France: With Special Reference to Maurice Barrès, Paul Bourget, and André Gide,* pp. 86-134. Urbana: The University of Illinois, 1937.*
   Examines the influence of Johann Wolfgang von Goethe's thought and work on Bourget.

Singer, Edward A., Jr. "A Disciple of Spinoza." In his *Modern Thinkers and Present Problems: An Approach to Modern Philosophy through Its History,* pp. 65-93. New York: Henry Holt and Co., 1923.
   Discussion of *The Disciple.* Singer notes Bourget's debt to Spinoza for much of the philosophy discussed in the novel.

Stephens, Winifred. "Paul Bourget, 1852." In her *French Novelists of To-Day,* 2d ed., pp. 127-78. London: John Lane, The Bodley Head, 1914.
   Surveys Bourget's work and judges the author to be "a traditionalist, who would efface the work of two revolutions and return to those earlier institutions which hindered rather than encouraged the progress of society and individuals."

Turquet-Milnes, G. "Paul Bourget." In her *Some Modern French Writers: A Study in Bergsonism,* pp. 107-30. New York: Robert McBride & Co., 1921.

> Discussion of the psychological novel. The critic compares Bourget's philosophy to that of Gustave Flaubert, George Eliot, Stendhal, and others who worked in the genre.

Twain, Mark. "A Little Note to M. Paul Bourget." In his *The Complete Essays of Mark Twain,* edited by Charles Neider, pp. 179-89. Garden City, N.Y.: Doubleday & Co., 1963.

> Reprints an article from an 1896 issue of *The North American Review,* written in reply to O'Rell's rebuttal to Twain's earlier essay on *Outre-Mer* [see excerpts above]. Twain mockingly insists that O'Rell's article was dictated by Bourget and that it ignored Twain's points of contention.

Zulli, Floyd, Jr. "T. S. Eliot and Paul Bourget." *Notes and Queries* 13 (November 1966): pp. 415-16.

> Brief speculative article. Zulli points out surprising similarities between Bourget's remarks on Shakespeare's *Hamlet* in his "Reflexions sur le theatre" in *Études et portraits* and Eliot's own essay on *Hamlet.* The critic suggests the possibility of Eliot's indebtedness to Bourget.

Vitaliano Brancati

1907-1954

Italian novelist, dramatist, essayist, short story writer, critic, and journalist.

Brancati's work is predominantly concerned with the effects of Italian fascism. During the first part of his career, he wrote dramas and novels which expressed fervent belief in the doctrines of fascism. In the second phase of his career, Brancati repudiated his former politics and wrote farcical novels and dramas which function both as excellent regional literature and as allegorical critiques of the Fascist party.

Brancati was raised in Catania, Sicily, which served as the setting for most of his later novels. He completed his education in Catania and taught school there for several years before moving to Rome to work as a journalist. While still in his teens, Brancati joined the Fascist party, attracted to the vitality of the movement and sincerely believing that fascism would improve life in Italy. His earliest works—including the dramas *Fedor, Everest,* and *Piave,* and the novel *L'amico del vincitore*—reflect his devotion to the party's tenets. In 1932 Brancati received the Premio Grand Consiglio, a prize awarded annually to the artist who most successfully gave expression to the themes of fascism. By this time, however, Brancati was beginning to question the oppressive nature of the Fascist regime. He was especially influenced by the anti-fascist positions of the philosopher Benedetto Croce and the novelist Antonio Borgese. In 1933 Brancati became a professor at the Rome Normal Institute and published the drama *Don Giovanni involontario.* This was the first of several of his works to be suppressed by government censors for questioning the ethical aims of fascism. By 1935 Brancati had broken completely with the Fascist party and returned to Sicily. The major themes of his works also changed at this time. While political concerns had dominated his early works, social comedy now prevailed. These later works, however, have been interpreted on two levels: on one, they have been read as comedies of manners, lampooning traditional Sicilian mores; on another level, they have been interpreted as subtle denunciations of fascism, with Brancati's attack concealed in symbols and metaphors. Brancati died leaving a final novel, *Paolo il caldo,* uncompleted; many critics believe this would have been his finest work.

Brancati's early works, written while he was an enthusiastic supporter of fascism, have received little critical attention in English. The dramas *Fedor* and *Everest,* and the novel *L'amico del vincitore,* are essentially political allegories which display Brancati's initial devotion to the Fascist party. Robert Dombroski has noted that "Brancati's belief and expression of the myths dear to the regime," "the myths of activity and forceful domination of reality, of manliness and war" were not limited to these allegorical works. The drama *Piave,* for example, is a straightforward piece of propaganda, glorifying the bravery of a group of Italian soldiers, including Mussolini, at the battle of Piave.

Critics are unanimous in finding, with Sergio Pacifici, that the "mature phase of Brancati's literary career . . . coincides with the change of his political posture"; and most also concur with C. Licari Huffman that the novel *Gli anni perduti* "marks the

true turning point in Brancati's artistic, and not merely political, development." The novel opens with the return of a group of young Sicilian men from Rome to their hometown—a recurring theme in the later novels. They become caught up in the scheme of the charismatic Francisco Buscaino to build a sightseeing tower. Progress is slow, many obstacles are encountered, and when the tower is completed thirteen years later an old ordinance is discovered requiring that it be demolished immediately. "That the tower . . . is a symbol of the fascist regime, is clear from a host of allusions to the Duce and to the myths of action, risk, and sacrifice," Dombroski noted. Pacifici has interpreted the tower "as a phallic symbol typical of fascism (which the novelist was repudiating in those years); large and no doubt impressive, it is incapable of performing its most basic function!"

The novel best known to English-language readers is *Il bell'Antonio (Bell'Antonio).* This is the second of three novels set in Sicily and linked by extensive development of the concept of *gallismo*—a term which refers to the Sicilian male's constant preoccupation with and exaggeration of sexual experience. This trait is first treated in *Don Giovanni in Sicilia,* recurs in *Bell'Antonio,* and is further developed in *Paolo il caldo. Don Giovanni in Sicilia* is the story of a typical Sicilian "Don Juan" as interpreted by Brancati: Giovanni's much-vaunted sexual experiences are greatly embellished in his retellings of them to his friends. He marries, believing he has found in his wife the woman who can save him from a life of debauchery that is largely imaginary, only to discover she is as shrewd and scheming as he once was. Antonio, the extraordinarily attractive protagonist of *Bell'Antonio*, maintains a reputation for numerous sexual conquests, despite the fact that he is impotent. Critics generally find that this is Brancati's most pointed satire upon fascism. The elaborate pretenses which Antonio employs to keep his shameful secret are analogous to the lack of real power behind the outwardly vital facade of fascism. Antonio's impotence has been seen as a further development of the symbol of the unusable tower erected in *Gli anni perduti*. In Dombroski's reading "the analogy between political and sexual impotence is structured on the interrelationship between being and appearance: Fascism has no strength save its thunderous proclamations." According to Margherita M. Silvi, in Brancati's final, unfinished novel, *Paolo il caldo*, the theme of *gallismo* is "developed and indeed deepened, achieving a dramatic and moralistic impact" that "gives a measure of Brancati's stature as a mature writer." Other critics have found that in this last work Brancati had evolved a greater artistic depth and command of style.

Despite the fact that Brancati's later works can be read "for the political views they espouse," as Pacifici noted, they are equally rewarding when read "as diverting stories which have the force of broad indictments of antiquated and irrelevant traditions." Readers who lack knowledge of Brancati's political background can take great pleasure in what S. E. Scalia called his "Rabelaisian comicality" and his "broad and abundant" humor.

(See also *Contemporary Authors*, Vol. 109.)

PRINCIPAL WORKS

Fedor [first publication]   (drama)   1928
Everest   (drama)   1930
L'amico del vincitore   (novel)   1932
Piave   (drama)   1932
Don Giovanni in Sicilia   (novel)   1941
Gli anni perduti   (novel)   1941
*Don Giovanni involontario   (drama)   1943
I piaceri   (essays)   1943
Il vecchio con gli stivali   (short stories)   1944
Il fascisti invecciano   (essays)   1946
Raffaele   (drama)   1948
Il bell'Antonio   (novel)   1949
   [*Antonio, the Great Lover*, 1952; also published as
      Bell'Antonio, 1978]
La governante   (drama)   1952
Paolo il caldo   (unfinished novel)   1954

*This work was written in 1933.

S. E. SCALIA   (essay date 1950)

The promise of humor held out by the title of this novel [*Il bell'Antonio*] is amply redeemed as the author of *Don Giovanni in Sicilia* continues with unabated glee and more finished artistry his satire of wenching among the sober playboys of sunny Sicily. The humor is as broad as it is abundant.

Antonio, handsomest of Sicilians, is the picture of virility. This makes it possible for him, with the help of timely lying and pretending, to establish a reputation for sexual prowess that is for years the envy of erotics and the pride of his father, until the annulment of his marriage, unconsummated after three years, turns the envy to hilarious ridicule and the pride to even more hilarious humiliation and resentment.

Over against the farcical figures of Antonio and his father, the author has set the more pretentious ones of Edoardo and Ermenegildo, Antonio's cousin and uncle respectively. They were obviously intended to give metaphysical depth to what might otherwise have seemed sheer lubricity. However, they are as unreal esthetically as they are equivocal conceptually. But no reader disposed to relish Brancati's humor can possibly wish to quarrel with the logic or plausibility of characters that, like the hero himself, are mere pretexts for conversation pieces to carry the author's Rabelaisian comicality. And just as Brancati's characters are mere interlocutors, even so his backdrop is a mere sounding-board. He is a master of racy dialogue.

S. E. Scalia, in a review of "Il bell' Antonio," in Books Abroad *(copyright 1950 by the University of Oklahoma Press), Vol. 24, No. 3, Summer, 1950, p. 296.*

MARGHERITA M. SILVI   (essay date 1956)

The theme of *gallismo,* of the excessive and exclusive interest in women, treated by Brancati in his previous novels, *Don Giovanni in Sicilia* and *Il bell'Antonio,* is [in *Paolo il caldo*] developed and indeed deepened, achieving a dramatic and moralistic impact. Paolo is a Sicilian nobleman whose instinctive sensuality becomes during his youth a conscious search for pleasure as the end purpose of life. As a man in his forties, he sinks into lasciviousness, now developed into a lurid and tenacious vice, exacerbated and augmented by a conflict of conscience. He is a sinner with a Counter Reformation soul, racked by doubts and self revulsion and an authentic yearning for good. A marriage and his activity as a writer seem to change him, but the beast in him soon takes the upper hand and he founders definitely. His character acquires in the long run a symbolic value and his condemnation casts a light of desperate pessimism and sorrow over all of humanity.

This posthumous work—some parts would most certainly have been revised and tightened by the author—gives a measure of Brancati's stature as a mature writer.

Margherita M. Silvi, in her review of "Paolo il caldo," in Books Abroad *(copyright 1956 by the University of Oklahoma Press), Vol. 30, No. 1, Winter, 1956, p. 37.*

LOUIS TENENBAUM   (essay date 1957)

[*Tenenbaum characterizes Brancati as an important representative of Sicilian provincialism in Italian fiction, and examines three of Brancati's novels—*Don Giovanni in Sicilia, Il bell'Antonio, *and* Paolo il caldo*—with reference to their regionalistic, or provincial, point of view. Tenenbaum finds that* Don Giovanni in Sicilia, *in particular, is "perhaps the most dependent on its Sicilian, provincial flavor for artistic realization."*]

Provincialism, which may be equated with regionalism, has been a particularly notable characteristic of Italian prose fiction and is, of course, ultimately related to the facts of Italian geography and history. The most important representative of

Sicilian provincialism in recent Italian fiction is Vitaliano Brancati. . . . The question of the extent to which Brancati was successful in transcending his provincialism in his last, posthumously published novel *Paolo il caldo* . . . has been raised. . . . It must be said, however, that for the most part recent criticisms of Brancati's work undertake to examine it without reference to limitations due to regionalistic or provincial flavor. (p. 233)

A clear and powerful current of sexuality is evident in a greater portion of the Italian prose fiction of the post World War Two period; and, if we think only of Alberto Moravia, it is evident that this current is traceable back quite far into the prewar years. The near ancestor responsible for this orientation in Italian literature is D'Annunzio. In sharp contrast to D'Annunzio's glorification of sexual freedom, Moravia ironically uses sexuality to imprison his characters in a web of intellectual impotence and sterility. Sex is a dispiriting, degrading means by which the Moravian personage tries to assert an intellectual or moral force which he does not possess, while sexuality takes on an unnaturalness and a quality of perversity, offending the taste of many readers by the vulgar framework in which it is presented. Brancati, too, is in reaction to D'Annunzian sexuality; indeed, all the writing of his mature period (from 1935 until his death) is flavored by this retreat from early D'Annunzianism. Brancati chose, however, to satirize erotic excess on its traditional home grounds, the island of Sicily, and as part of a more general comic critique of bourgeois and upper class culture. His approach to sex is conditioned by classical considerations, and his criticism implies a healthy, natural norm which informs his sexual atmosphere. If Moravia's characters are helpless victims of sensuality, *moment* of the Tainian trilogy *race, milieu,* and *moment* is primarily responsible. Brancati, on the other hand, finds that all three factors in Taine's theory are involved in the excessive sexuality of his personages, although of the three he is least concerned with *moment*. Exaggerated eroticism is an inheritance of Sicilian blood and the island's moral tradition; yet it is that environment which somehow prevents the denaturing and vitiation of his fictive world.

In this imaginative re-creation of the erotic atmosphere of Eastern Sicily, and particularly of the bourgeois milieu to which Brancati was born, from the early years of the present century to the 1950's, we are clearly a long way from the Sicilians of Verga's novels or short stories, or Pirandello's *novelle*. His selection of the bourgeoisie and upper classes was significant, for his satire of eroticism does not and cannot deal with elemental, primitive passions. He is engrossed with the manners and morals of the Sicilian classes which are out of the struggle for mere material existence, from the small merchants and professional men through the landowning nobility, choosing to satirize those in whom education and breeding have driven a wedge between sentiments and the senses, those who have uncritically accepted their heritage of erotic preoccupation, or who are unable to resist it effectively. This satire is mildest in *Don Giovanni in Sicilia,* where its principal object, Giovanni Percolla, has the naïveté to fall romantically in love and seek, unsuccessfully it would seem, to dominate his Sicilian indolence and roosterism. In *Il bell'Antonio* the novelist humorously reveals the preoccupation of the Sicilian middle classes with sexual power as a prestige factor. Antonio Magnano's unpremeditated deception of that social grouping and its subsequent discovery of his sexual nonentity are the focal point of its comedy. Characteristically, Brancati centers our attention on Antonio not so much as a romantic impotent, but as a member of a society which laughs at such an unnatural phenomenon. Even those personages who would like to escape from this

aspect of their "Sicilianity," such as Giovanni Percolla after his marriage to Ninetta dei Marconella, and Paolo Castorini who takes up permanent residence in Rome, are not permitted to do so, since the Sicilian reputation for sexual prowess which accompanies them attracts women as bees are drawn to pollen.

For a writer who employs a predominant humor in his literary atmosphere, the danger of lapsing into caricature is ever present. Brancati's fundamental affection for his characters saves him from this pitfall; even at the height of their ridicule, they retain a warmth and glow of humanity. He presents Catanian eroticism, for example, as a kind of adolescence which somehow never turns into maturity. . . . The respective principals of Brancati's three most significant novels, Giovanni Percolla, Antonio Magnano, and Paolo Castorini, are thus portrayed against a fully delineated background, which enables us to appreciate their typicalness and their individualism. We glimpse a Sicily which seems to have been unalterably influenced by the Arab domination of centuries past, when the social separation of the sexes was customary. If for the Arabs such a division was a mark of Woman's inferiority, for Brancati's Catanians it only serves to intensify an exaggerated sexuality which is already a mark of Man's slavery. For with the intensification of his erotic concern, Brancati's Sicilian bachelor type becomes correspondingly more inept and awkward in his sentimental relationships with the fairer sex. . . . Brancati cannot resist a jibe at the Sicilian's sexual renown and thus in *Don Giovanni in Sicilia* we follow our bachelors north to the watering places where their only successes are in situations where they are the hunted and not the hunters, and their Venuses all too often frustratingly on the dilapidated side. At the same time he is mocking the young bloods, Brancati portrays humorously but sympathetically the eternal *disponibilité* of the older generation, which possesses an ineradicable chivalric spirit, often manifested in platonic loyalties of forty years duration to the women of their dreams, or in marriages to prostitutes for whom they were the means of redemption. In the double-pronged irony of *Don Giovanni in Sicilia,* Brancati has (1) his hero fall in love; and (2) succumb to the heroine's determined campaign to "net" him. Much of the humor then hinges on Giovanni's subsequent need to defend his "conquest" from the Sicilian bachelors who were his former associates. A typical Brancati paradox is introduced when, after Giovanni's marriage and transfer to Milan, he finds that it is himself he must defend from the onslaught of mainland women.

The gay, untroubled atmosphere of Giovanni Percolla's story is modified to take on more serious, melancholy qualities in the tragicomic history of Antonio Magnano, hero of *Il bell'Antonio.* The humor is not diminished, but now alternates or is blended with the sadness of his intellectual as well as physical impotence. The fusion is well symbolized in the chapter recounting the visit of the sensual Fascist hierarch to Catania, when the local Party officials welcome him with an orgy at a *bordello.* In the barbed, skilfully placed satire of this chapter Brancati wiped away any taint remaining from his pre-1935 admiration for Mussolini's system. The exaggerated Sicilian emphasis on sex is most unforgettably depicted in the portrait of Antonio's father, Alfio Magnano. . . . (pp. 233-35)

What contributes to the fundamental seriousness of the last novel, *Paolo il caldo,* is the main character's struggle to escape from the erotic web in which he was born. In a sense, Brancati was moving away from his humorous approach to fiction with the composition of this work, in spite of a definite comic flavor still qualifying portions of it. The first and more successful half of the novel describes the decadence of a Sicilian family of the lesser nobility, the Castorinis, through the corruptive effects of sensuality on the intelligence. Sensuality is presented in alternately gay and somber tones, yet ultimately its excessiveness is seen as a vicious defect of the blood, of diabolic inspiration, for it leads to the abortion or destruction of intellectual or spiritual growth. That the situation is universal in its implications is obvious and it is of no essential significance whether the story begins in Sicily or Lombardy. This is not to discount the validity or interest of the presentation of the Castorinis and their relationship to the Sicilian environment. Occasional sympathetic insights into the life of the lower classes reveal previously undisclosed aspects of Brancati's profound humanity, and, incidentally, resemblances to Pirandello and Verga. For example, the contrast of Paolo's egotistic lust with the hopeless, selfless love for him of the family servant Giovanna is narrated by a compassionate observer with a tragic sensibility. This rich vein, however, is not exploited by a Brancati who had no intention of stressing social distinctions as an important element of his pessimistic outlook.

In spite of the direction taken in his last novel, the most distinguishing quality of Brancati's approach to his erotic theme is the comic. Here the efficacy of his Sicilian setting is clearly apparent, for the exaggeration, extravagance, and volubility of Sicilian social behavior and speech lend themselves well to the hyperbolic humor of his fictive world. What more comically vivid and implicit contrast between Sicilian and non-Sicilian woman-chasers than the account of the frustrated Catanian bachelors who find themselves, at one point, in a womanless North Italian mountain resort, and whose voices are clearly heard from the nearby woods one moonlit night threatening to amputate certain useless portions of their anatomy! (***Don Giovanni in Sicilia***). . . . The comedy of middle-aged sensuality threatened by a young, warmer-blooded Don Giovanni is exquisitely rendered in Baron Magri's ever-ready envelope containing the unpaid bills from his current mistress's dressmaker, which he promptly mails to his young, successful rival each time he is forced to bow out (**"I due mondani"**). The humor which permeates Brancati's erotic situations justifies his treatment of the theme; and it is difficult to conceive of this comic treatment against anything but a Sicilian background. Notwithstanding this provincial side of his art, Brancati, by his use of the most important aspect of man's "pursuit of happiness," assures a universal quality to his fiction. His characters, whether they are Sicilian types or individualists, are unfailingly human and representative in their response to erotic stimuli. Moreover, he was careful to clarify character motivations, particularly in his novels, by supplying keen and perceptive insights into sexual psychology. (pp. 235-36)

In contrast to Moravia's sensualists, Brancati impresses us with the ease, inevitability, and naturalness of his presentation of sex. As previously noted, he has the advantage of portraying Sicilians, in a physical setting where sensuality is ever-present, and he has humor to soften the impact of his directness. Two other factors work to Brancati's advantage: his classical reticence to go into details to the embarrassing extent which we regularly find in Moravia, thus giving his erotic descriptions a generality of tone much more acceptable to readers of a certain sensitivity; and the atmosphere of grotesquerie and fantasy which envelops his characters and situations.

Of Brancati's three principal novels with a central erotic theme, ***Don Giovanni in Sicilia*** is perhaps the most dependent on its Sicilian, provincial flavor for artistic realization. The pivotal

importance of Antonio Magnano's impotence in ***Il bell'Antonio*** and Paolo Castorini's contrary defect, *sangue bollente* in ***Paolo il caldo,*** clearly endow these works with a general psychological and moral validity which frees them from a strict dependence on their setting. The increasing seriousness of Brancati's satiric treatment of eroticism in human personality which culminates in the suggestion of diabolic influence in the exaggerated sensuality of his last hero makes one wonder if he would ever have returned to his earlier comic vein. In any case, the deeply rooted moralistic strain in his fiction imbues the erotic themes with an undeniable fundamental seriousness, for, in spite of a somewhat differing literary aesthetic, Brancati resembles Stendhal in his concern and curiosity about an important aspect of the human condition, *la recherche du bonheur*. While his literary gifts are not as extensive as those of a Stendhal, a Proust, a Pirandello, or a Verga, Brancati illuminates the erotic aspects of the human comedy with enlightened irony and compassionate humor. (p. 236)

> *Louis Tenenbaum, "Vitaliano Brancati and Sicilian Eroticism," in* Books Abroad *(copyright 1957 by the University of Oklahoma Press), Vol. 31, No. 3, Summer, 1957, pp. 233-36.*

LOUIS TENENBAUM   (essay date 1964)

[*Tenenbaum summarizes the Italian critical consensus regarding Brancati ten years after his death, and, altering somewhat his earlier critical view of Brancati as a regional writer (see excerpt above), finds that Italian critics have unnecessarily limited their interpretation of Brancati by viewing him strictly as a regional writer.*]

In Italy itself Brancati's reputation ten years after his death, is not yet secure. . . . The consensus of Italian critical opinion on Brancati the literary artist is that he was a writer of undeniable talent, limited to a certain extent by his regional preoccupation, who was cut off in the prime of life when it could reasonably be expected that his inspiration would broaden and renew itself, thus enabling him to achieve a greater measure of excellence.

Brancati's reputation as a novelist and short-story writer during his lifetime could hardly escape being influenced by his role as a polemical and courageous critic of Italian culture of the Fascist and early post-war period. While one can separate these two principal interests and activities of his life, both are characterized by a moral dedication of the highest order. The Catanian writer realized that his essay and journalistic writings took time from "serious" literary effort, but was prepared to pay the price because for him "engagement" was a fundamental tenet of the literary and intellectual creed. He was afraid to gamble on the future, a future which the neglect of the present might render impossible for the artist and the intellectual. There was a special reason for his concern with spiritual and political liberty and with a more rationalistic orientation of Italian culture. Brancati's missionary sense was in compensation for a youthful Fascist enthusiasm which had lasted until he was twenty-eight years old. From 1935 until his death in 1954 his moral life was largely influenced by one consideration: to make up for this early aberration.

Another paradox of Brancati's career is the fact that he has inevitably been classified as a Sicilian writer par excellence, the satirist of a very special Sicilian phenomenon, *gallismo*, when at the same time a closer acquaintance with his work and thought reveals that he is one of the most European of Italian writers. His Europeanism was late-blooming, and came with a kind of desperate intensity after the deep spiritual and moral crisis from which he emerged in 1935, permanently scarred but purged of his enthusiasm for Fascism. The wider intellectual outlook Brancati sought to develop after 1935 was the natural reaction to his awareness of the limitations of his provincialism. . . . Later a number of his detractors failed to appreciate the connection he had established between his personal problem as an artist and the general situation of the arts and the life of the intellect in Fascist and post-Fascist Italy. Consequently they could not understand what lay behind the regular references in his writing, some more, some less direct, to his youthful Fascist errors. Notwithstanding their accusations the Sicilian novelist was not indulging in masochistic breast-beating, but was perfectly sincere in his self-criticism, whose purpose was to provide a salutary lesson to readers of his own and future generations.

As a corollary to his role as a "witness" of the spiritual and moral failings of Italy under Fascism and in the immediate post-war years, Brancati believed passionately in the role of the Italian writer as a goad to and as a voice of the Italian moral conscience. In the disinclination of the Italian people to examine their society critically and honestly he saw his country's most fundamental and serious defect. After 1935 and under the nose of the Fascist censorship he sought courageously to awaken the Italian conscience to the spiritual corruption of the regime and to the intellectual and philosophic dishonesty upon which it was based. His attacks, surprisingly direct at times, were in the form of essays and articles published in newspapers and reviews, in prefaces to books which he edited, and in his own short stories and novels. . . . A reflection of his fundamental optimism (a quality too many of his critics and enemies failed to appreciate or understand) is his . . . continuing even more energetically and courageously in his post-war writing his comic, often satiric portrayal of Italian society and social types. This continuing moral passion produced its fruits in works like *Il vecchio con gli stivali,* a long novella . . . , which in its artistic perfection seems destined to remain as the most sublimely comic commentary on the Fascist experience which will ever be written. It added to Brancati's previous critique of the boredom and stupidities of Italian life under Fascism his biting but affectionate ironies on human behaviour when it fell. His lucid and ironic intelligence continued to probe the weaknesses of Italian society in a mixed comic-serious vein in the novel *Il bell'Antonio,* where he achieved his first successful fusion of the theme of exaggerated Sicilian eroticism with a satirical, sometimes caricatural portrait of Sicilian bourgeois society under Fascism. The six most significant comedies of the Catanian writer's theatre, plays whose themes largely echo those of his novels and short stories, were written in the post-war period. The fact that Brancati found it next to impossible to have them put on an Italian stage is less because of their artistic or theatrical defects than because of a rather widespread reluctance in official and influential circles to permit such a direct mirror to be held up before the face of post-war Italian society. In his last novel, *Paolo il caldo,* which he was completing at the time of his death and was published posthumously, Brancati revealed a changed, more serious approach to character portraiture, although in many respects the work can be considered an updated, post-war-society-centered *Il bell'Antonio.* The novel contains a devastating caricature of artistic and intellectual society in post-war Rome, which perhaps fails as literary art, but which was clearly inspired by the burning moral thirst for sincerity and truth which characterizes Brancati's thought and its literary expression.

Don Giovanni in Sicilia . . . was responsible for Brancati's first large scale success with the Italian reading public and the critics. Its publication established his reputation as an authority on "gallismo" and as a leading comic writer. If "gallismo" can be dismissed as a purely Sicilian social and moral manifestation then the epithet "provincial" used by some of Brancati's critics is justified. However, Italian writers (including Moravia) and film directors in the last twenty years, by the manner in which they have expressed erotic themes, have shown rather persuasively that Brancati was the first to depict, albeit in the somewhat special terms of his native city and island, what they have come to realize is a significant aspect of contemporary Italian manners. Brancati hid the gravity of his charge against Sicilian (and Italian) middle-class society behind the affectionate, baroquely conceived and expressed comicity of his portraits of Giovanni Percolla and his Catanian friends; but the condemnation of the Italians' lack of seriousness and a disciplined moral sense is in the pages of *Don Giovanni in Sicilia* for those who wish to see it. (pp. 4-5)

> *Louis Tenenbaum, "Vitaliano Brancati 1907-1954,"*
> *in* Cesare Barbieri Courier, *Vol. VII, No. 1, Fall, 1964, pp. 3-5.*

ROBERT DOMBROSKI (essay date 1969)

[*Dombroski discusses the protagonists and antagonists of several of Brancati's novels as symbols of political systems. The characters of Giovanni Corda, from* L'amico del vincitore, *and Francesco Buscaine, from* Gli anni perduti, *are interpreted as symbols of the Fascist Party, which Brancati once embraced and later repudiated.*]

After the fall of the regime, [Brancati] published an account of his state of mind during the first decade of fascism. This confession offers us the essential terms of reference to both Brancati's production while an advocate of fascism as well as to the satire and polemics of his mature works. He writes:

> When I was twenty, I was a fascist right down to my hair roots. . . . Perhaps it was on account of my gracility. . . . I admired the more robust and idiotic of my contemporaries and I would have given in trade two thirds of my brain for a well defined bicep. I attributed my frailty to my studies, meditation, and my hatred for that which was practical and useful. I was governed by instinct and intuition. I took up fencing and track, and experienced a feeling of well-being after a workout at the gym—activities unknown to my sedentary and poetical adolescence. . . . I thought fascism to be a religion and fascist Italy, I reputed to be a temple. . . . Fascism was for me a wondrous credo. I experienced the joy of a herded animal; the joy of being in accord with millions of people—to feel what they felt. . . . An optimism of a third order invested me. I felt like the giant of the group even in my solitude. My stupidity played the role of the genius. . . .

And three years later, in his diary:

> I experience deeply in 1927 what it was like for a twenty year old, inclined to meditation, fantasy, and sloth to admire a man of action and violence; to believe that a new delightful morality was about to be born. It tasted like a

glass full of wine. All ideological abortions . . . are as intoxicating as wine because like wine they bring us outside the laws of reality into a sphere which we call the 'new world.' I experienced also the shame which follows upon such drunkenness; the boredom of 1936 and 1937 when it was necessary to look back with shame and write: 'In certain times we should never be twenty'.

When Vitaliano Brancati was twenty, he was writing about Pietro Dellini, the central figure of his first novel: *L'Amico del Vincitore.* This protagonist was apparently conceived as a character-symbol of the old order in crisis, and thus he reflects the state of disillusionment and insecurity, on the author's part, prior to his acceptance of the regime's "new morality." Dellini is a provincial intellectual who has been deceived to believe that his future as a writer and thinker would extract him from the insignificance of the average life. Brancati gradually unfolds his character's awareness of failure, in a process embodying the entire gamut of pseudo-psychological recourses from the initial doubt relating to his identity to the renouncement of traditional ideals; from the failure to feel at ease with new illusions, to a would-be return to the security of youth. Pietro finally abandons himself to a series of "adventures" without any precise scope. He attains firm awareness of his incapacity in the face of "life," and of the uselessness of his existence as well as of the impossibility of any form of regeneration. He meets up with death, of all places, in the snows of the North Pole, in which event, one cannot help notice the banal rhetoric of modern day "contra-passo": Pietro who availed himself too much of reason, freezes to death.

As an effect of the crisis, Pietro gradually gives way to the acceptance of the new hero to whom he is but an insignificant acquaintance. Giovanni Corda, the victor, epitomizes the overturned values: called a fool and dictated to as a youth, he becomes the dictator of Italy. Giovanni is an authentic *figura ducis* and the moral of the story is stated in a typical bombastic and meaningless utterance: ". . . often common minds are very interesting and complex, while geniuses are simple like all powerful machines." So we pass from the awareness of weakness or incapacity to the exaltation of activity. The pensive, melancholy, disillusioned intellectual is replaced by the victor who dominates reality.

Brancati's belief and expression of the myths dear to the regime did not limit itself to this novel, nor were they only shaded by veil of fiction. In 1932, he was awarded the "Premio Grand Consiglio" a prize given to the work which most successfully rendered the themes of the regime in search of intellectual support. The work, in fact, exalts the bravery and patriotism of a handful of Italians (one of which the Duce himself) at the battle of Piave. (pp. 42-4)

The year 1932, the author confesses, also witnessed the beginning of his conversion to anti-fascism. (pp. 44-5)

In [1934], Brancati starts publishing works which begin to reflect his conversion to anti-fascism. The myths exalted in *L'Amico del vincitore* and in the plays *Everest, Fedor* and *Piave,* the myths of activity and forceful domination of reality, of manliness and war . . . are overturned. They are substituted by characters bound up in the problematics of existence whose main refuge from the world is taken mostly in the form of recourse to the passions.

Significant in the author's different outlook is also his return home, from Rome, to Caltanisetta where he wrote in 1933

Singolare avventura di viaggi, a short novel which fell immediate prey to the fascist censorship laws, and thus, within months of publication, was removed from circulation. In the same year, furthermore, the author's play **Don Giovanni involontario** is forced to close after few showings on account of harassing by the "squardristi."

The reasons for the censoring of *Singolare viaggio di avventura* were not directly political for the story makes little or no unfavorable reference to politics. It's publication, on the other hand, was curtailed for "moral" reasons. The work in effect would have had adverse repercussions on the new fascist youth who were being raised according to the ideals of order, patriotism, and "new spiritual mission." Apart from relating the story of two cousins caught up in the delightful frenzy of a carnal relationship, the work attempts to convey willful moral and political indifference. And there is a manifest lack of direction in the protagonist's search for happiness, the result being a return to his awareness that the vitality of life exists precisely in his constant state of anxiety. Life is void of meaning; nothing matters . . . in sum precisely all that which makes the story indeed unique, at least for the year 1934. Brancati recreates therefore a state of crisis in the midst of external order. And in his adversion to the "spirit of the times" he chooses as weapon, the vehicle of return to the uncertainty and exhaustiveness of *fin de siècle* decadentism on the one hand; only, on the other, to temper this "anti-heroic" existence with the irony of one who realizes the futility of every escape.

The **Singolare viaggio** indicates, to be sure, the fundamental direction which the author's narrative is to assume; its terms of reference are clear, even though the language and technique adopted still echos a certain dannunzianesque exaggeration. Reality for the writer becomes commonplace and rationally complex. His future heros will be passive and inactive; their only adventure, that of the dream and sex fantasies. But before arriving at a uniform and artistically successful expression of a world dominated by the spiritually anarchic and indifferent to moral purpose (in contrast to fascist society which solicited for "political order and moral strength,") Brancati writes . . . **Gli anni perduti,** a work in which he prudently endeavours to analogically recapitulate the first ten years of the regime. The novel tells about a group of restless provincial intellectuals unable to decide on any given action. Their world is unimaginative, dominated by boredom and anxiety. . . . (pp. 46-8)

One day into the stillness of the Natàca steps a certain Francesco Buscaino who, viewing the city and its flat dwellings and its people "capable even of yawning on the first night of marriage" decides in a flash that what Natàca needs is a tower from the top of which the inhabitants can "marvel" at the panorama. Buscaino succeeds in gaining the alliance of the city's intellectuals and artists as well as that of the nobility and professions, who all agree on the host of possible benefits which might ensue from a similar project. Consequently, they decide to devote their talent and resources necessary to the tower's construction. As a result, the entire populace works for ten years on the monument only to find out, on the eve of its inauguration, that there exists a law which prohibits the building of towers in Natàca. Boredom again returns to the city, but this time without any compensation whatsoever.

There seems to be little doubt (although many of the work's reviewers wisely overlooked it) that the novel is cleverly written satire of the regime which, symbolized by the tower, is born from the fantasy of a buffoon into a society already sunk into lethargy and depression, thus disposed to innovations of any sort. Buscaino, furthermore, is clearly a Mussolinesque counterpart. When we first meet him, he is already exercising his forceful eloquence. . . . That the tower to be erected is a symbol of the fascist regime, is clear from a host of allusions to the Duce and to the myths of action, risk and sacrifice. . . . Nor is the protagonist's character without the necessary dannunzian mystique. . . . Even the fascist cult for youth is alluded to repeatedly. . . . (pp. 48-50)

Concomitant to his political and literary conversion, in 1937, Brancati makes his definitive change of residence, a decision which should be appreciated in all its honesty. After the fascist victory in Ethiopia, when the regime seemed to have attained a noteworthy solidity and unity,—when even the most politically resistant began to reconsider—Brancati left Rome to return to Sicily and to his old post at the Istituto Magistrale at Catania. There . . . he fmished *Don Giovanni in Sicilia.*

Both the *Singolare viaggio d'avventura* and *Gli anni perduti,* express in direct polemical terms a vision of reality which, in essence, is nothing but a return to the normality of traditional instinctiveness and customs. Artistically, the need reflected is a return to realism. But since the author's sense of reality is ideally at odds with the falseness of official ideals and expression, the narration becomes of necessity political and satirical. Puritan fascism, for example, loudly proclaimed that the life of a good Italian must be serious, austere, and religious; that every action must be subordinated to the creation and maintenance of an ideal praxis. To this, Brancati juxtaposes the theme of *carpe diem* in a world totally preoccupied by sex, both imaginative and real. In his novels, there will be no place for the fascist man of action, nor even for the dannunzianesque super-hero, inexhaustible and bizarre in his sexual prowess. These figures will instead be replaced by anti-heroes like Giovanni Percolla. . . . [In *Don Giovanni in Sicilia*] Brancati celebrates the unique habits and traditional wisdom of a Sicilian middle class whose only ambition in history is to retain its comfortable and peaceful life filled with its major passtime of idle, erotic aspiration and fantasy. But apart from the highly successful comic-satiric motif based upon the gross incongruities between imaginative and real love—which is indeed the work's artistic highpoint—between the lines of *Don Giovanni in Sicilia,* Brancati is giving clever reference to one of his most heartfelt literary themes (one basically also political): the sceptical acceptance of any would-be conversion from tradition. (pp. 50-1)

On the whole, the direct political references in Brancati offer scanty artistic results. This is true especially for works like *Le trombe d'Eustachio* in which the author draws the caricature of a fascist spy with extraordinary sensitive ears and *Raffaele* a play which denounces the standard fascist morality. This is not true, however, of the short story *Il vecchio con gli stivali* in which is revealed the true nature of Brancati's anti-fascism. The story intends to represent the authentic meaning of oppression void of the rhetorical anti-rhetoric of all possible countermyths. The principle character is a meek, colorless, government employee apparently destined to a drab existence. Nonetheless he opposes tenaciously the party's impositions. To keep his job and retain the respect of his family, Aldo Piscitello is forced to become a fascist and to don the emblems of the party: its uniform and boots, the harness which remains indelibly imprinted on the old man's spirit even when its physical presence has disappeared. Thus, in spite of the allied liberation, the old man finishes out his life benumbed and lifeless with no chance for regeneration. Nor can Piscitello justify his innate

anti-fascism by taking recourse to the political animation supplied by an instinctive quest for liberty. (p. 53)

The political motif is explicitly present also in Brancati's penultimate novel, *Il Bell'Antonio.* But here rather than existing side by side [with] the erotic it becomes fused with the latter giving rise to the obvious analogy between sexual and political impotency. Antonio Magnano, a young Sicilian Adonis, has the fame of being an irresistable conqueror of women, whereas in reality he is actually impotent, at least when it's a question of normal marital function (not surrounded by the numerous perils or risks which befall a lover). All goes well until one day he decides to wed. But after three years of marriage, the bond has yet to be consummated. The news of the mishap gradually leaks out and the honor of the whole family is at stake. As a result, Antonio's father, during a bombardment, goes off to vindicate his son's impotency to all ill-famed quarter of the city and there he dies, a prostitute's shoe against his face. Meanwhile Antonio has acquired a sort of affection for his handicap which, in fact, makes him even more charming to the ladies. Then the regime falls and the war ends. The novel ends with Antonio desperately obsessed to at least once "prove himself a man." Applied to the regime, the analogy would go something like this: one who impotent (fascism) but believed to be potent because it enjoys the favours of the various individually potent (those who benefited by it). Thus the link between appearance and reality, and the corollaries of the liability of potency and the impotency of those who oppose the potent and so on.

The *Bell'Antonio* is also the first novel in which the author endeavours to formulate an alternative to the philosophical teaching which conditioned the rise of fascism. And it is Ermenegildo, the old, wise uncle obsessed by an incurable illness, who reflects this attempt. The allusions are to ideal 19th century values. . . . When Brancati speaks of the "past" he is referring to the immediate past, i.e. the 19th century, an epoch of which he mourns the passing, or (more exactly) the disappearance of the simple conditions of life therein. In fact, the Ottocento becomes for him a spiritual and intellectual refuge for one ill at ease with his time and offended by what his epoch caused him to do. (pp. 54-5)

Paradoxically, the conditions surrounding Brancati's initial prefascist involvement: the desertion of the intellectual which resulted from his loss of faith in constitutional government— seem to reappear at the term of the author's cultural experience. When he finished writing *Il Bell'Antonio,* he had already experienced the allied liberation which, also, was characterized by violence and cruelty. . . . The war's aftermath indeed intensified the author's distrust in political systems, and it is without doubt in this sense that *Il Bell'Antonio* should be understood: nothing matters anymore, all historical movements and economic and social systems count but little. The only thing left of which one can be sure is sex. . . . His pessimism with respect to politics is moreover clearly formulated in his diary: "The game of entrusting a civilization to a political formula is capricious, useless, and cruel. . . . A society looks for and finds its necessary remedies in itself . . . never in formulas." His scepticism regarding literary freedom is equally as strong:

> What an unfortunate country! who will be able
> to cure it of its old age, if the physicians are
> either the army or the clergy . . .? In any event,
> be it after the sounding of trumpets or after the
> ringing of bells, if we look toward the door,

invariably we find standing there tyranny either
dressed in black, or in a fez, or in a skull cap.

The negative outlook of this position is clearly revealed in the
author's final novel, *Paolo il Caldo,* the most autobiographic
of his production, unfinished on account of the author's death
in 1954. Paolo too like many of Brancati's past characters is
a hot-blooded Sicilian who ventures out of his native land
toward the more evolved regions of the continent. But where
Giovanni and Antonio, after a short time away from home,
hurry back to maternal consolation, Paolo upon returning home
finds that not even his native city is capable of appeasing his
awareness of having lived a mistaken life. Again the escape
here is too idyllic in nature and it directs itself toward an ideal
of classical values, as in the words Paolo's Roman friend Pin-
suto: "We are classics living clandestinely in an epoch of
decadence. . . ."

In concluding, it can be said that with Brancati we have the
case of a middle class intellectual who, after an initial belief
in the advent of a new activist morality embodied in the fascist
mystique, in turn, rejected the revolutionary mentality of his
youth and fell back on a position politically definable as liberal
conservatism. But rather than being of any one political affiliation, Brancati liked to think himself primarily a moralist. In
fact, in reply to his critics who were accusing him of a certain
political naiveté, the author accepts their opinion stating: "I
know that I judge politics from the point of view of a moralist,
i.e. according to rules which are not its own. It is a mistake
about which I am happy because the rules I apply to politics
are those belonging to an activity which greatly surpasses it."
(pp. 56-7)

*Robert Dombroski, "Brancati and Fascism: A Pro-
file," in* Italian Quarterly, *Vol. 13, No. 49, Summer,
1969, pp. 41-63.*

C[LAIRE] LICARI HUFFMAN   (essay date 1972)

[*Huffman examines some of Brancati's short stories as an introduction to his prose style. She considers the novel* Gli anni perduti
*the turning point in Brancati's career, both artistically and po-
litically, and finds that though* Gli anni perduti *is a political
allegory, it contains valid artistic themes as well, chief among
them being the universal search for happiness. Huffman also
traces the recurring theme of* gallismo—*the Sicilian male's preoccupation with sex—through the novels* Don Giovanni in Sicilia,
Il bell'Antonio, *and* Paolo il caldo.]

Vitaliano Brancati died in 1954, leaving unfinished the novel
Paolo il caldo. In the light of this book the conflicting themes,
the ambiguities of tone, and the formal flaws of his earlier
works are seen as indicative not only of technical uncertainty,
but rather of a complex state of mind which always sought
(and always failed to achieve) an ethical and emotional balance,
a serene even if radical vision of life, which might bring about
a formal composure. *Paolo il caldo* shows the author in his
most extreme moment, having attained such a radical but certainly not serene resolution. For those who had not recognized
the real nature of Brancati's earlier works, *Paolo il caldo* could
only crystallize existing confusions; and indeed there has always been something of a muddle among Brancati's critics,
many of whom have tried neatly to label him as another regionalist or humorist. . . .

[Brancati] is far more than a merely regional writer. (p. 356)

A look at some of Brancati's short stories might well serve as
an introduction to his prose style. In *Il vecchio con gli stivali
e altri racconti,* "Rumori" illustrates the author's predilection
for the fantastic in image and situation, and the beginning of
a gentle satiric vein, which yokes together two sharply conflicting elements, irony and nostalgia. This fascinating brew
remains essentially the same in the later novels; but the proportions change, blend, then separate at every turn.

In the description of the house of the lawyer Giorgio Occhipinti
one notes other tendencies which will also be stylistic con-
stants. The rhythms of the sentences gather up the objects of
environment and then fix them at their most revealing angle,
as well as their most characteristic pose. . . . The novelist
evokes objects and then discriminately "places" them; this is
far from the chronicler's desire simply to catalogue a particular
environment. A detail is not mentioned for its own sake, as a
display of technique: the benign saints who elbow one another
for room, the stuffed shoes, the dangling bulb, all seem to
threaten a metamorphosis into another form of life. These details are important because environment is important: the sounds,
smells and sights of Sicily help form Brancati's style. They
become metaphors of the characters they imprison, indeed they
seem to be alive, and participate in the characters' lives and
in the novel as a whole. If such details become fantastic, so
do the characters, who often become nearly grotesques. But
this is all part of the satire. The method is that of the Dickens
who created Coketown in *Hard Times,* but here without polemic and outrage; both the hero and the environment are sympathetically treated.

Brancati has already given us the metaphors of Giorgio Occhipinti's possible fate in a land of dust and disorder, old forms
and confusion. He has only to describe the metamorphosis of
Giorgio into the "spinzo," the curved figure "possessed" and
invaded by tics and nervous ailments who is fighting an ancient
legal battle based on a petty formality, and who adds his own
noises, the muffled flute-like tones uncontrollably emitted from
his throat, to the "rumori." (pp. 356-58)

Giorgio could well fit in with the gallery of figures Pirandello
created and "allowed to live," like Professor Lamis of "L'Er-
esia Catara" or Judge D'Andrea of "La Patente." These two
are to a degree victims of circumstances beyond their control;
as far as the external world is able to impinge upon them it is
a disruptive force. They are threatened and nearly undone by
incivility and aggressiveness, bureaucracy and superstition. . . . Brancati does not doubt the reality of the physical
world or the threat it poses. The heroes often absorb and reflect
their environment: such is the case of Giorgio, for instance,
who barely escapes this reduction to a totally mimetic function
by the effect of his love for Barbara. The real story lies in the
heroes' escape from or capitulation to the surrounding environment.

In **"Singolare Avventura di Francesco Maria"** . . . D'Annunzio (and concomitantly Fascism) is part of the environment
satirized. Thus the story represents not only stylistic but also
philosophical developments in Brancati's career. Here a young
man caught up in a frenzied world of D'Annunzian fantasies
travels to Catania determined to penetrate to the "marrow" of
life. He meets a girl who shares his energy and spirit and they
exchange some D'Annunzian intuitions. . . . The encounter
dissolves into farce when the girl, like a "petite bourgeoise"
confesses all to her family and a quick marriage is called for.
Neither the girl nor the young man proves to have the necessary
courage to fight a social and moral code so contrasting with

the *élan vital* of the superman. In this sense it is difficult to say which is more heavily satirized, Sicily or D'Annunzio. (pp. 358-59)

It is a well-known fact that Brancati turned his back on both D'Annunzio and Fascism in the thirties. **"Il vecchio con gli stivali"** . . . , more of an anti-fascist political pamphlet than a short story, illustrates Brancati's politically satirical style. But it is *Gli anni perduti* . . . which marks the true turning point in Brancati's artistic, and not merely political, development. Here the themes of southern immobility, with its physical and mental torpor and its decadence, make their appearance. The new themes are not a cover-up, a mere allegory to escape fascist censorship. They are and remain the valid, self-containing themes of the author, and they provide him with the means for expansion to the universal from the particular, while not forcing him to surrender interest in the particular. Thus it is perfectly possible that some of these themes are analogues to political questions. The aggressiveness of the *fascisti* has become sexual pursuit and their corruption has become sensual decadence, but the new themes tend to absorb and transcend political questions. The Sicily of the 1930's and the political conditions of those times are merely reaffirmations of the consistent, unredeemed behaviour of the human animal.

In Brancati this animal happens to be Sicilian, and couldn't be taken for anyone else, because of his customs—the turn that his character takes and the ways he manifests his humanity. But this doesn't mean that we are dealing only with a regionalist writer in the sense of a "costumbrista." Most critics agree that Brancati escaped being a mere chronicler of a limited environment, but they disagree in their analysis of the nature of his expansion. Some have said that Brancati followed the path of Verga; but, although Verga lingered over the Sicilian soil he revealed man atemporally in contention with his Fates. In Brancati Sicily is Sicily, not a spiritual terrain. We must be, and we ultimately are, propelled beyond a restricted zone of experience into an abstract space, but this happens through the catalyst of themes unique to Brancati. It is the theme of "gallismo," a particularly Sicilian phenomenon referring to the bravado and strutting of the Sicilian male, that helps to achieve this universalization for ultimately, in his last, most engaged and pertinent works, Brancati concentrates on the questions that this phenomenon raises: these are the great human questions concerning the nature of honor, love, happiness, fantasy and reality.

In *Gli anni perduti* the theme at hand is Sicilian "pigrizia," the effete restlessness which precludes all action and therefore any possibility of change. This is an ideal topic for satire, which thrives on the unchangeable and unresolvable defects of man. However, Brancati's love for his native soil finds its way into the vivid recreation of Sicily and the all-too-convincing sense of the heat and sultry languor hovering over the darkest and dustiest corner of the most impermeable house serves implicitly to mitigate the faults of his heroes. Perhaps this is what is meant by saying that Brancati is fascinated by the very world which is under his attack. It is this attraction, the ambivalence of spirit, generally considered to be in Brancati's favor, that unfortunately turns on its author and weakens the effectiveness of the satire. Here Brancati is still closest to being a "costumbrista" in this novel about a Sicilian, which might also have been a novel about Man. Its treatment of a failure of character is interlocked with the description of a land and the customs of its people.

The novel opens in Rome with the abrupt decision of Leonardo Barini to return, because he is invaded by a sense of lost happiness, to Sicily. . . . (pp. 360-61)

We see the effect that the return to Sicily has on Leonardo: his latent indolence betrays him to the immobility of the island. The situation is amusing. Little by little our hero simply finds it more difficult to get out of bed. As he settles down under the covers, we search in vain for the brilliant mental peregrinations of Proust's Marcel. Brancati's character is average in intelligence and sensibility, only vaguely unhappy, scarcely able to deal constructively with his difficulties. We remain aloof from him, hardly involved in a problem which could be cured simply by taking vitamins. The author is also at a remove from his character, is so superior in intelligence to him, that he fails to control Barini's thinning out eventually to a type.

Barini's decision makes one think of Vittorini's *Conversazione in Sicilia* . . . and a similar decision; here the hero is haunted by "abstract furies." Yet the movement of this novel gathers ever wider implications as the hero and his pilgrimage acquire symbolic force until everyone, including the reader, participates and is implicated in the last graveyard scene. How different are these "furies" from the "capogiri" of Leonardo, which signal Brancati's main theme explicitly stated and reiterated in *I Piaceri* . . . : the search for happiness, not as a result of an immediate end sought within the framework of the novel, but as an obsessive fantasy, a romantic dream of joy so unalloyed and so uncontested that it resists not only formulation by the heroes but also concretization within artistic form. Short of this euphoric state there is little but vague discontent until those crucial moments when Brancati's heroes, rubbing their eyes and trying to focus on reality, or lying in bed absorbed in themselves and ruminating aimlessly, feel their throats tighten and are invaded by a feeling of exile from a terrestrial paradise. The theme of *Gli anni perduti* more important than all those traceable to the political situations of the time, is that if his characters had thought less about whether they were happy or not, if they had become "engaged," they would have found a measure of contentment. So when the protagonists of the stories glumly contemplate their lot they are severely reprimanded by the others in the story. Through the voice of characters like Lisa Careni in *Gli anni perduti* and Edoardo in *Il bell'Antonio* . . . the author professes that the Leonardos and the Antonios of this world must escape the egotism of their romantic self-absorption. But no alternative to the romantic yearnings of the heroes ever becomes more than a cliché, or is made concrete, allowed cogently to develop within the thematic structure of the novel. As we shall see, the tower, the very symbol of activity and engagement, the answer to Leonardo, is treated farcically. Although this conforms well to the satiric thrust of the novel and its possible political allegory (the tower has been seen as a symbol of the fascist regime), it also sabotages questions raised by the author concerning happiness and personal fulfillment. The unity, the certain direction, the "permission to exist" are all absent; their absence is crystallized by Leonardo's discontent. . . . Enter the "permesso," the main symbol of the novel. Leonardo and his friends, under the leadership of Buscaino (who has come back from his newly found America, and who exhorts his friends to adopt the energy and action he has admired to better Sicily) decide to build a tower to offer a panoramic view of the countryside. But Leonardo's potential source of "interior light" ends farcically as a grandiloquent and futile gesture, grandiloquent because of all the things needed in that country it is *not* a man-made structure to help appreciate a panoramic view, and futile because when it is completed thirteen years later, it is discovered that building laws, long in existence, forbid its use. An absurd and effective twist, but one which ironically weakens the structure of the novel. Construction of the tower, no matter what it may or may not represent, is presented as a strictly Sicilian affair, and the failure to complete it successfully and in a reasonable period of time, the failure to deal with or abolish pointless bureaucratic laws, is the result as much of the ineptitude and nonchalance of the constantly satirized people as it is of outside and inexorable forces.

But where does this leave the hero who has been testing his strength, trying to break out of the neat framework of satire *cum* political fable? Enzo, another character, marks the way. His only possible exit is through madness. This means the character is reduced to a symbol and the solution is a comment on the novel's action. Giovanni, on the other hand, refuses to disappear in the rubble of the demolished tower: he has not been given an expression suitable to his implications, and he remains an infelicitous character within the novel's structure.

Nevertheless, the brilliance of the satire commands attention. Brancati is at his best in describing the bored efforts of Lisa Careni's crowd to amuse themselves. Besides their wealth and because of it, they have one thing in common: superb, precise, complicated watches with which they are all the more able to measure out their boredom. . . . Another object of ridicule—tempered with something of benign amusement—is the matriarchal society of Sicily, represented by Rodolfo's "mammuccia." In this gallery is the rich squire who thinks so much about dying that he has lost his appetite, and Nereggia who is writing a sacred drama on Santa Genoveffa, twenty-one thousand hendecasyllables in length. (pp. 362-64)

Finally there is Leopoldo, who fills his leisure hours observing and studying air bubbles. . . . This is the best of Brancati, his ability to choose images loaded with irony and suggestion. The negative space, the "vuoto" of the air bubble, embodies the theme of the novel, and we note with delight the last devastating ironic turn; the resultant perpetual motion caused by the air movements in the bottle is futilely limited to the space within the bottle, thus paralleling the comings and goings of the Sicilians, perpetual motion leading only to a demolition crew and the remains of a tower. (pp. 364-65)

The characters of *Gli anni perduti* were too lethargic to be threatened by the excesses of sensuality. *Don Giovanni in Sicilia* . . . introduces "gallismo," a theme which will dominate Brancati's later work. *Don Giovanni*, Antonio in the later *Il bell'Antonio* . . . , and Paolo in the final *Paolo il caldo* . . . are all involved in variations of this theme.

Giovanni is an ironic twist of the Don Juan figure. His exploits are imaginary, his conquests non-existent, and as we are told, he has reached the age of forty and never kissed a respectable woman: all this despite, or perhaps because of, his obsession with an idea of love which has dominated even the minutiae of his existence. This *gallismo*, the concept of love as imagined and acted upon by the Southerner, is described by Brancati in *I Piaceri* . . . , where one can find, for example, a detailed description of the art of talking about women. This satiric codification of the southern *ars amandi* provides a humorous commentary on the novels.

Just as the code of love deals with the real and the fantastic aspects of the love experience, so the story is based on the dichotomy between what the hero says, and what really are his exploits, between what he is and what he would be, between what he dreams and what he can cope with; in short between reality and illusions of every sort. When "reality" appears, usually in the form of a woman, Brancati's characters fail miserably to cope with it. To say that they "demeurent tragiquement seuls" ["live tragically alone"] is perhaps to misunderstand the tone of the novel, but it is symptomatic of a problem of interpretation, the question whether and to what extent Giovanni is a victim of society. Certainly this society is judged. The emphasis in fact is so strongly on the caricature of social mores that Giovanni becomes more and more of a puppet as he moves to Milan with his "fair young bride." From this point on the novel degenerates into a somewhat rigid and unimaginative dialectic of north-versus-south.

Giovanni's bride is of course the Donna, the *stilnovesque* lady who has wrought a miracle in him. Brancati doesn't unmask this illusion and it remains unclear whether he is seriously proposing this creature as the object of Giovanni's love or whether he presents her as the ultimate condemnation of "Gallismo," a resulting fantasy life which robs the hero of any link with reality. One hopes that the author will come to terms with questions raised beyond the satire of the novel. In any case, Giovanni returns to Sicily, to the world of dreams and languorous baths after the torture of the cold showers of Milan, unable to cope with his wife or with any world other than Sicily. He now goes to bed and literally pulls the covers over his eyes. A satirical study of mores, or a sympathetic study of one man forced to act within the limits of those mores? One needn't exclude the other. The question whether Giovanni is a victim is not really to the point where land and people are so interlocked that it is difficult to know which more determines the other's nature. Giovanni's immobility is constantly, humourously dwelled on (he says "lina" instead of "luna" for "moon" because he admits the one vowel requires less effort to articulate than the other); and he clearly comes to incarnate the very mores of which he is suffering the consequences. So he is the object of both humor and sympathy. Were he to be wrenched from his environment, dislocated from the structure of the book, he would indeed seem pathetic and lifeless. Like Giorgio Occhipinti he is very much a character created through metaphors.

For Giovanni is saved after all and his return to Sicily is not a return in defeat. Brancati felt strongly that the past, just because it is past, is poetic, more perfect than present time. As Giovanni feels the wool of his old favorite blankets and smells the food cooking in the kitchen, he is to be considered salvaged from a "tragic" end: he is again home, and nothing has changed. This is Brancati at his most nostalgic, attempting to resolve the issues of the novel poetically. Giovanni's situation is resolvable only in this extra-logical tension. He finds peace surrounded and soothed by the very images of his torment. The contradictions remain but the novel has earned its end.

The nature of the novel *Il bell'Antonio* is signaled by the hero's impotence. Rather than provoking an analysis of Antonio's state of mind, it serves as the formal means by which the Sicilian society is unmasked. What Antonio's parents and townsmen feel about him, and how they behave in the light of their discovery, is the major concern of the author. The system of values thus revealed is seen to be an absurd one. It is in the light of the satiric concern that the novel holds together, at least superficially. Within this satiric structure Antonio functions better than Giovanni; but other strains on the structure become apparent.

The world of Antonio and his family—who are freed from financial and other contingencies—is a world obsessed and turned in on itself. In the light of this obsession all things pale. A girl commits suicide for love of Antonio, but this is mentioned only in passing. The greatest crisis for the Puglisi family is that their daughter's marriage is not consummated after three years because of Antonio's "problem." Hence she is, according to them and the Catholic church, living in sin. The whole populace has seemingly little to do but besiege Antonio with letters expressing their condolences, some even offering help, professing "love."

Appearances count more than anything else and beyond this knot of passions and instincts functioning within social conventions a whole field of human experience is negated. We almost never hear a Brancati hero really conversing, really exploring his problems. Words are futile, and imprecations are hurled left and right. . . . All human intercourse seems impossible and gestures seem to confirm this. In a world deprived of rationality the human will has no place. Antonio is basically passive, constantly plunged in sympathy for himself. His actions are negative ones; he pales, he lowers his eyelids, he faints.

Brancati is clearly disgusted by this self-absorption and flabbiness, and he presents the characters of this world through a distorting lens which makes the characters as grotesque as those of Dickens, Thackeray and Dostoevsky at their most telling. (pp. 365-68)

The only truly conscious character, the only voice of reason, is Ermenegildo. He offers an alternative vision, but one which ironically fails to take root in the novel. For Ermenegildo is not certain himself how good and evil are to be distinguished, or whether indeed they can be. This would-be philosopher who presides over and comments on the human comedy at hand is actually nauseated by mankind and by man's condition, two elements which he fails to separate. . . . Ermenegildo's attitudes are echoed and developed in the depressing catalogues of *I Piaceri*. (p. 369)

Turning his back on his philosophy, and also abandoning the sudden idea of a penitent return to the Church, Ermenegildo kills himself. This is the man who has pointed out the need for a rational absolute, who has claimed that only in seeking for it will Antonio find significance. Through his suicide such a point of view fails to become an organic part of the novel, or does so only by negation. Ermenegildo falls prey to an incoherent ideal of pity which confuses man's inherently tragic lot with man's accidental weaknesses. It was with the call for pity, in Brancati's view the only possible common denominator of man's experience, that he summed up man's condition in *I Piaceri*. This stance subverts all others for, unable to leap into faith, Brancati remains mired in pessimism. What man has done, Ermenegildo's essentially a-political comments on the Spanish Civil War make clear, is a sign of man's corruptness and is linked with man's mortality. This "intuition" deals the deathblow to the proposed enlightenment, and is the key to the suicide.

This complex of feelings envelops the whole novel and undermines its promises: it is as if another novel were superimposed upon the satire. But the new vision overwhelms the other ones. Ermenegildo, the enemy of the futility and self-absorption of the world of the flesh, which he condemns as inherently corrupt and irrational, is described in terms of that corruption, is reduced before our eyes to yet another example of the undignified and unredeemable. (p. 370)

Something parallel happens to the political theme of the novel. Edoardo, also disgusted by the world around him in which political meetings take place in brothels and Antonio's choice between fascist or anti-fascist salons depends on the beauty of the women to be found there, decides to participate actively against the fascists. He is sent off to a concentration camp for his views. He cries out that only in a corrupt and flaccid land would impotence have been considered a tragedy, and he too urges Antonio to occupy himself with other concerns. This seems to restore the equilibrium of the novel, to diminish the importance of the self-absorption of the hero, while helping to set up the nice analogy between the aggressiveness of the "mascalzoni" ["rogue"] whose concern is always "farsi onore" ["self honor"] and the political stance of the fascists. Yet Edoardo's actions also negate his point of view. For, shortly after speaking to Antonio, he plunges into a frenzy of eroticism and telephones to apologize, in view of his own weakness and corruptness, for his harshness. (p. 371)

No redemptive emotion, no rationale is placed on a scale against disgust with the non-vital, with disease and the aging process. The intuition of this corruption leads only to suicide or non-action or frustrated eroticism, just as eroticism, blindly obeyed, leads to the intuition of corruptness and subverts the right to judge others. It is with this in mind that we must approach the unfinished *Paolo il caldo*.

At first this novel seems a formal monster. It contains pages of autobiographical rambling, a large extraneous core of satirical analysis of the Roman salon set, and a sometimes humorous recreation of the past in Sicily. Although at the time of Brancati's death the novel still needed to be shaped, it does not lack unity. Certainly its author should not be seen merely as the narrator of "successive incalzanti situazioni"; the events are rather a deliberate, counterpointed progression bearing out an inevitable result. The hero declines, through excessive indulgence of the senses, into uncontrolled debauchery with its concomitant dulling of the mental faculties; and his once similarly inclined family yields to age, sickness, decay and death.

Paolo Castorini, like all his family with the exception of his father, has wallowed in the flesh from his youth, in an extreme, frustrated, uncontrolled eroticism. We see him go from the lusty relationship with a servant girl in Catania to the exasperating need for prostitutes, for any woman of any age. Paolo returns to Sicily from Rome rarely: it is no longer the nostalgic landscape Brancati's heroes used to long for. (pp. 371-72)

Paolo finds himself thoroughly repelled by the sense of corruption in his once loved land and home, and, desiring to renew his life, he marries the daughter of a woman he had once admired and desired. The marriage fails physically and Paolo throws himself with fervor and self-loathing into his old life. At this point the book was cut off by Brancati's death, but he left a note telling the reader that in the last two chapters Paolo, now completely abandoned by his wife and turned in upon himself, declines into near stupidity. Meanwhile we see the family collapse, for the indulgence of the flesh and the inherent corruptness of the flesh are seen as two sides of the same coin: they lead to an identical recognition of absurdity. The only possibility of redemption is for Paolo's father, Michele, but he is "pallido, piccolo, riservato" ["pallid, little, reserved"]. . . . Michele has difficulty in sleeping, in fact all his actions are in contrast to the easy languor of the others. . . . Pale, suffering from low blood pressure, he appears in the dining room to find the rest of the family "red with appetite." . . . Michele represents human reason and is the only bearer of light in the dark land that Sicily has become—the very imagery of the once sun-bathed country has undergone a change. (pp. 373-74)

But Michele, standard-bearer of a possible enlightenment, of constructive humor, of reason, of a new social consciousness, commits suicide, paralleling the fate of Ermenegildo. The author is unable to find a place for him in a world judged to be corrupt. Michele is in fact seen to be not only alienated from his own family but also from the physical world, from himself, by his own nerves and heartbeat which prevent him from participating in life: his ailments, his physical being, prevent the enactment of his rational being.

Brancati clearly wishes to oppose reason to the visceral, but by denying Michele the right to strong nerves, to health, to appetite, he implicitly rejects this real alternative to corruptness. The suicide of Michele and Ermenegildo may be the result of their reason; certainly it is presented as the only reprieve. But according to such a view, reason is the denial of life, not a viable way of dealing with it. Even Camus stopped short of this position: he disclaimed the right to reason to the point of death.

The recurrence of madness and suicide as the way out of the world he created clearly calls for a revaluation of Brancati's "moralism." For most critics have seen him ultimately as a moralist, whether he be a "serious humorist" or a "baroque moralist." Many have spoken of the growing awareness of good and evil, the sense of sin in these last novels, but "moral terror" is perhaps the best definition of Brancati's reaction to his intuition of "the absurd." (pp. 374-75)

[We] have seen how the author always sabotages his would-be vision, how he always adds the last scene, carves the last angle, levels the ideal superstructure the novel has been building towards. In effect, in an implicitly absurd world it is no longer possible to talk of tragedy. Brancati's last novels are existential novels *manqués*. For Brancati explores corruption, decay and nothingness but does not transcend them to the blind and courageous construction of a meaning; he can only suggest such a possibility by negation, outside of the world delimited by his art. Paolo has a sense of terror: he sputters out the "Our Father" on his way to a meeting with a prostitute. Words like "sin," "guilt," "happiness," "reason," and "love" constantly recur. But revulsion at his own flesh never propels Paolo into an enlightened control of himself; and a sense of terror is not a sense of sin, only the intimation of its existence.

Brancati despised the existentialists but remains more pessimistic than they. His attempt to set up a moral system based on reason fails, as this system crumbles away at the slightest probing. Reason, like human love, fails. It cannot survive, for its affirmation of itself is its own negation by suicide, and when it attempts to take a place in the texture of the novel it is hardly viable or attractive in its pale and sickly representation. In the end, the description of *Paolo il caldo* as a "roman noir centré sur l'hérotisme" is appropriate. Out of the rubble of this novel only one glimmer of hope can be gotten, a seeking for light "de profundis." These depths are those of the flesh, the failure of reason, and the drives of the subconscious. They are all in all a view of absurdity, negating salvation. This is not the achievement of a moral vision, merely the positing of its necessity. (pp. 375-76)

C[laire] Licari Huffman, "Vitaliano Brancati: A Reassessment," in Forum Italicum *(copyright © 1972 by* Forum Italicum*), Vol. VI, No. 3, September, 1972, pp. 356-77.*

ROBERT S. DOMBROSKI   (essay date 1979)

[*Bell'Antonio* is] perhaps Vitaliano Brancati's best novel. . . . This English version [translated by Stanley Hochman] captures as well as possible the specific linguistic milieu of the setting and the rather baroque point of view, adopted by the novelist in conveying the Sicilian mentality of his characters. The translation reveals Brancati as a very clever satirist who develops his story along several different levels of meaning, chiefly the political which to be fully appreciated should be viewed against the background of the author's former production, especially *Don Giovanni in Sicilia*.

The blurb on the book's back cover states that *Bell'Antonio* "demonstrates incisively how in a repressive society sexuality is distorted into excess and eventual impotence." Although the observation makes for good packaging in flashing a meaning acceptable to most readers, it is nonetheless misleading, because repressive Fascism in the novel is not so much the cause of the distortion of sexuality as its symptom. Brancati's story aims at representing a real analogy between sexual and political impotence. (p. 462)

Antonio can't quite cut the mustard, a deficiency which in a Sicily totally preoccupied with male sexuality takes on metaphysical significance. Brancati sustains the story's comic tension by overcharging the elements in conflict: Antonio's real impotence and the provincial society's hyperevaluation of potency, the one nourishing and perpetuating the other up to the ludicrous, when Antonio's father in an attempt to vindicate his son's weakness has a heart attack while with a prostitute and dies. Meanwhile, Antonio has learned to live with his handicap which actually makes him all the more attractive to women. The analogy between political and sexual impotence is structured on the interrelationship between being and appearance: Fascism has no strength save its thunderous proclamations. The absence of intellectual qualities in the hero and his total disinterest for everything except his sexuality seem to point to the false virility of Fascism, its fundamental hollowness and capacity for deception. The values Brancati stresses as an alternative to Fascism are the traditional liberal ones which, he has one of his characters state, are at least meant to be substantial.

In sum, however simplistic its politics, *Bell'Antonio* in Hochman's fine translation displays Brancati's fondness for caricature and comic grotesques, a talent which in the history of contemporary Italian narratives is all too often ignored. (pp. 462-63)

Robert S. Dombroski, in his review of "Bell'Antonio," in The Modern Language Journal, *Vol. LXIII, No. 8, December, 1979, pp. 462-63.*

SERGIO PACIFICI   (essay date 1979)

[*Pacifici is the author of several major studies in English of Italian literature, including* A Guide to Contemporary Italian Literature: From Futurism to Neorealism, *and the three-volume* The Modern Italian Novel. *In the excerpt below, he concurs with Claire Huffman (see excerpt above) that* Gli anni perduti *marked a turning point in Brancati's career, and provides an extensive analysis of the novel. Pacifici also discusses the theme of* gallismo *that links* Don Giovanni in Sicilia *and Brancati's last two novels.]*

The mature phase of Brancati's literary career begins in the mid-thirties, and coincides with the change of his political posture. . . . With several books behind him, he set himself to compose *Gli anni perduti* [The wasted years]. . . . [This] novel, by and large, has been unjustly treated by his critics. Claire Huffman, in her sensitive assessment of our author [see excerpt above], calls it "the true turning point in Brancati's artistic, and not merely political, development," a view with which I agree completely. The setting of the novel is the imaginary city of Nataca, a persuasive geographic and social recreation of Catania (spelled backward). The first nine chapters serve to introduce us to a group of young men who have been away to the "mainland," and, having returned home, are so disillusioned by the slow, provincial, unbearably boring life there that they begin making plans to go back North as soon as circumstances will permit. The hero of the story, Leonardo Barini, returns to Sicily because he is nostalgic about his birthplace, but regrets his decision almost as soon as he has carried it out. This is something of a recurrent theme in the work of Brancati, built upon the contrast, and thus contrasting forces, between the North (sophisticated, efficient, open) and the South (repressive, apathetic, closed). Today, such a comparison would be considered justifiably stereotyped. Sicilians can be astute, aggressive, and resourceful; they are also (as depicted by Giovanni Verga and so many of his "followers") hardworking, generous, honest, and very much conscious of their roots. But Brancati's world turns on a different axis, specifically that of the comfortable middle class that spends much of its time fantasizing about afternoon siestas and sex.

In the case of the group of *Gli anni perduti,* an unusual dream is introduced: the building of a tower from which the tourists and the natives will be able to enjoy the magnificent view of the surroundings, a proposal that comes from a certain professor Buscaino, and thus, by virtue of its intellectual sponsor, deemed most worthwhile pursuing. The suggestion is accepted, and some thirteen years later, after overcoming all sorts of difficulties and delays, the project is completed. The end of the story is quite unusual: the tower cannot be opened to the public, and indeed must be demolished, because it violates city ordinances no one bothered to take into account; all that will remain, as a memory of the undertaking, will be a heap of rubble and dust! Ridiculous? Perhaps. But, when seen from a more Olympian perspective, aren't many actions of men absurd and laughable? It may well be that the failure of the project is presented too covertly as one doomed to fail because of the ineptness of its sponsors (all Sicilians), and as such limited in its commentary about human nature in general. However one might choose to see it, it does manage to open the curtain on the motifs that are central in the narrative of Brancati: apathy, indolence, laziness, and a certain sense of futility—conditions presented as being deeply ingrained in the temperament of Sicilians, seldom willing or ready to change their existence.

If the novel is read against the background of Brancati's personal and political evolution, however, the tower can well be seen as a phallic symbol typical of fascism (which the novelist was repudiating in those years); large and no doubt impressive, it is incapable of performing its most basic function! Seen from yet another angle, the long undertaking of building the tower serves as a metaphor of the stuff of which human dreams are made: it is an expression of the understandable human wish to create something that will survive its builders and become a legacy to future generations. An illusion it may well be, but how appropriate that the story should end with the demolition of the tower, and the symbolic consignment of the project to a heap of rubble and dust, an ironic disposal of a dream manufactured by Fascist mentality!

The central "problems" of *Gli anni perduti* reveal the extent of Brancati's debt to the poet Giacomo Leopardi and to the novelist-playwright Luigi Pirandello. Man can escape boredom and forget time by his becoming involved in projects whose difficulties absorb his mind and sap his energy, and thus be spared the metaphysical awareness of the pain of existence. Deep down, man also knows that such compromises are nothing if not illusions, which help us create a special niche in which we may feel relatively safe and protected from the cruelty of human actions. Yet another major theme, sex and eroticism, emerges and blossoms in Brancati's successive novels, constituting a sort of "Trittico Siciliano" ["Sicilian triptych"]: [*Don Giovanni in Sicilia* (**Don Juan in Sicily**); *Il bell'Antonio* (**Antonio the Great Lover**); and *Paolo il caldo* (**Paolo the hot one**)] . . . , left unfinished when Brancati died in 1954, and published a year later, accompanied by a long Preface by Alberto Moravia, Brancati's long-time friend. The theme that links the three novels is *"gallismo."*

Just exactly what is *gallismo?* Taken in its most obvious manifestations, *gallismo,* or "roosterism," is a combination of male exhibitionism and exuberance, conveying the idea of sexual aggressiveness that may be real or imagined. Practiced by men young and mature alike, roosterism is frequently an attitude toward, or even a way of, life, with its rituals and strategies to be employed in amorous adventures, its obsession with women, its constant discussions about past, present, or future sexual exploits—to the point of being turned into a kind of symbol of a way of life. Last, but not least, roosterism accompanies men from their adolescence to old age, becoming a needed crutch for sexual insecurity or a much needed booster for battered or sagging egos, particularly convenient to cover up sexual impotence. Brancati himself, in a survey of the South commissioned by an important newspaper in the immediate post-World War II years, wrote: "[Gallismo] is considered the most noble and heroic act of life. One can be a thief, or flee before the enemy, lie, flatter, bend to tyranny . . . but the act for which one will never be forgiven is that of one's not having sufficiently respected . . . one's own dignity as a rooster."

It would be wrong to think that roosterism is simply an invention of writers or observers of the social scene. On the contrary, it is firmly rooted in the history of Sicily, dating back to the Arab domination and the strict separation of the sexes. . . . If Brancati had limited himself to writing about roosterism, he would have been just another humorous writer. His originality rests not so much on his uncanny ability to depict *gallismo* with a firm hand and a considerable amount of feeling, but on his connecting it, as Claire Huffman observed, with "the questions that this phenomenon raises: . . . the great human questions concerning the nature of honor, love, happiness, fantasy and reality." With *Don Giovanni in Sicilia,* a mordant satire of the social and sexual mores in Sicily, Brancati felicitously blends the erotic motif of his earlier work with that of contemporary politics: roosterism and fascism are now presented as two sides of the same coin.

The hero of the story is Giovanni Percolla who, for the previous ten years, has lived with his three unmarried sisters, Rosa, Barbara, and Lucia. The opening situation reminds us immediately of Aldo Palazzeschi's *Le sorelle Materassi (The Sisters Materassi):* here, too, we have three good, honest spinsters pampering a man who is the substitute figure for the husband they never had. The pleasant, easygoing relationship they have enjoyed for many years is due, to a large extent, to the love and care they have given their brother, ever since the day when, upon the death of their parents, they were recalled home from their grandfather's with whom the three had been living. Giovanni finds himself spending long periods of time in the mainland, ostensibly on business or on vacation, but really trying, together with his best friends Scannapieco and Muscara, to educate himself sexually. Many of the first chapters of the book—the best of the work—depict in gentle, mocking way Giovanni's bashfulness toward women, his excitement at the sight of feminine undergarments, his frequent sessions with his friends talking about sex and women, and last, his adventures with prostitutes. "On the other hand," comments Brancati at one point, "if their experience of pleasure was enormous, that of women was extremely poor. Undressed of the lies, of what they told as having taken place and that had instead been only a wish, or had happened to someone else, their and Don Giovanni's past could be told in ten minutes." (pp. 58-62)

After an extended sojourn in the North, where he has gone for business reasons, Giovanni returns home and one day the inevitable takes place: he falls in love (or so he thinks, at least) with an attractive girl from a fine family. . . . (p. 62)

The depiction of Giovanni's love for Ninetta allows Brancati to touch other aspects of *gallismo*. While Giovanni fantasizes about his falling in love with Ninetta in a romantic way, it is really she who leads him to the altar and, as though this were not enough, stipulates in advance the numerous concessions she will enjoy after the marriage ceremony. (p. 63)

As the novel comes to a close, we find Giovanni back in his sisters' home enjoying the overlong afternoon nap that reminds him of bygone days, while his wife is visiting with her family. The story has come full circle: nothing has really changed, and perhaps it cannot be any other way. Anticlimactic the end surely is: but if Brancati means what he says, then it befits a book that shows that, for all the exposure to a different social milieu, Giovanni remains very much the "Sicilian" he was before his marriage. Since it is impossible to refashion his personality, he concludes that the two will be better off staying with their respective families as long as they remain in Catania!

The simplicity of the novel is somewhat deceptive, for at least two important points are advanced by the book: the first is that it is exceedingly difficult to break certain social and philosophical patterns embedded in the consciousness and life-style of a people since time immemorial. Almost twenty years later, the same point is made with greater intellectual lucidity and ideological depth by yet another Sicilian novelist, Giuseppe Tomasi di Lampedusa, in his masterwork, *The Leopard*. The second point is only obliquely made: the protagonist of the story is presented as an antihero, thus defying the wishes of the Fascist regime, weak, indolent, and apathetic, totally lacking the aggressiveness that was one of the party's chief characteristics. The main character is skillfully used by Brancati to paint an effective canvas of Sicilian manners. The chief element of the author's strategy is what may be called Pirandellian humor, whose objective is not to ridicule or to make us laugh, but to evoke understanding and compassion. The technique is based on the conflict between reality and appearances. Thus, Giovanni, portrayed as "good, serious, cosmopolitan," soon is seen by the reader for what he really is: weak, lazy, devoid of ambitions and ideas, capable only of fantasizing about love affairs that never get off the ground. Comic he may be to a point: for we realize that the culture into which he was

born and educated is largely responsible for molding his character.

Il bell'Antonio (*Antonio the Great Lover* . . .) belongs to Brancati's second, mature period. Written . . . in a climate of hope after the end of World War II and of fascism . . . , *Il bell'Antonio* is the last novel completed by Brancati. The novel takes up, once more, the theme of *gallismo*, fortified by a political motif, this time explicitly presented. The novel is told by a *"cronista,"* or a newspaperman covering city stories, whose professional scruples impel him to be as accurate and objective as possible.

The action is set in 1932, when its hero, Antonio Magnano, is twenty-six. The choice of the time is significant for it coincides with the moment when fascism completed its takeover of power at all levels. Antonio's main asset is his extraordinary physical beauty: ironically enough, it is his handsomeness that proves to be the element that eventually brings out his tragic flaw. . . . As Antonio grows up, his sexual magnetism proves to be irresistible. (pp. 63-5)

[Antonio's] father suggests that he marry Barbara Puglisi, a girl from an affluent local family. Actually, Antonio's father Alfio points out, Barbara "is rich, she loves you, and she is honest." After a suitable period of engagement, the marriage, duly arranged by the respective families, takes place. Three years later, the couple is yet to be blessed by the birth of any offspring, and no one, especially Signor Alfio, is especially happy, let alone proud, of it. But an even more shocking revelation is yet to follow: Barbara's father informs Alfio that his daughter is still a virgin! Since the marriage, in the eyes of the Church, has not been consummated, it must be dissolved. Barbara soon afterwards is wedded to the duke of Bronte, while Antonio, still in love with her, returns to live with his family, and finds in his uncle Ermenegildo an understanding and compassionate consoler. But Signor Alfio finds it difficult to live under the terrible cloud of his son's sexual failure. One evening, in 1943, he ends up in a brothel which is hit during an air raid, and is killed. His death is viewed as a way to erase, however partially, the black mark that Antonio's sexual impotence had made on the family's honor and pride.

The story ends in an anticlimactic if not sordid note: Antonio returns to Catania, expecting to find his home destroyed by the aerial bombardments to which the city has been subjected. Instead, not only does he find his home intact, but in the process of being cleaned up and straightened out by a maidservant, to whom Antonio, in a dream, makes love.

What is the "point" of the novel? The message of *Antonio the Great Lover* is, with some modest changes, the same Brancati makes in his previous work: eroticism considered per se, is clear evidence of the spiritual and emotional emptiness of a human being, a façade shielding a repressive political system. Under such circumstances, proving oneself a man becomes a meaningless exercise in futility. (pp. 65-6)

While it is tempting to read Brancati's novels for the political views they espouse, I prefer to read them as diverting stories which have the force of broad indictments of antiquated and irrelevant traditions of the South that are fundamentally inhuman: the widespread attitude toward sex, the tenacious at times arrogant resolve not to allow any change in the social structure to take place, the unbearable provincialism pervading much of the life and thinking in the *Mezzogiorno*, and, finally, a system of values that puts appearances before truth. My reading of Brancati persuades me that he is more successful when the moral implications are allowed to emerge naturally, not as programmed elements of the plot. My preference goes for a long short story . . . , **"Il vecchio con gli stivali," ["The Old Man with His Boots"]**, considered by many critics to be one of the best pieces by our novelist. The story deals with a modest city employee, a clerk by the name of Aldo Piscitello, who, despite his seniority in the system, has been unable to achieve tenure. When the tale begins, the Fascists have been in power for several years. In their drive to consolidate their hold over the central and municipal bureaucracy, they make membership in the party a condition for employment. Piscitello, warned by the town mayor to enroll, at first balks—for he considers himself a nonpolitical person—but eventually reluctantly accepts the condition imposed by his superiors. . . . The war comes, the Italian and German armies suffer humiliating defeats in Africa, and the American and Allied troops land in Africa and eventually in Sicily. With each day, the horrors of war come closer and closer to Piscitello's town. After a long bout with the plague, he returns home only to find that his job has been taken away from him because of his long and well-known association with the Fascists! The ending of the story is supremely ironic, but not without pathos: the reader, but not the world at large, knows about Piscitello's deep-seated contempt toward fascism and its values, since he has never articulated his opposition to the regime. It is precisely in this stance of non-commitment (or a commitment that remains locked in the mind) that we may well find Brancati's flaw as a novelist. Just like the "old man with his boots," Brancati had neither the passion nor the courage to "see" reality and be resolute enough to take a hand in shaping it. He remained content to trace his own political evolution in his books—from an enthusiastic Fascist in his youth, to a leftist conservative in his mature years. His books reveal him as an acute observer of the social scene of his native island, a writer whose irony and ability to satirize a world he knew intimately commend him to today's reader. What he lacked, as Vanna Gazzola Stacchini pointedly remarks, was the capacity to offer solutions to the problems he posed in his fiction: for this, his own values were ultimately to blame. (pp. 66-8)

Sergio Pacifici, "The 'Southern' Novel," in his The Modern Italian Novel: From Pea to Moravia *(copyright © 1979 by Southern Illinois University Press; reprinted by permission of Southern Illinois University Press), Southern Illinois University Press, 1979, pp. 47-78.**

ADDITIONAL BIBLIOGRAPHY

Knittel, Robert. "The Great Heartbeat." *The New York Times Book Review* (28 September 1952): 4.
    Brief review of *Antonio, the Great Lover* that provides a plot synopsis, and interprets the novel as a satire upon fascism. Knittel concludes that "Mr. Brancati is unquestionably a writer and thinker of eloquence and integrity, whose language has the universality of the true humanist."

Soete, George J. "Political Roosterism." *Library Journal* 103, No. 8 (15 April 1978): 894.
    Favorable review of a new English translation of *Antonio, the Great Lover,* under the title of *Bell'Antonio.* Soete notes that "Brancati brilliantly combines political and sexual themes" and finds that the novel "is a surprisingly accessible, funny book."

H(erbert) G(eorge) de Lisser

1878-1944

Jamaican novelist, journalist, and essayist.

De Lisser is best known for his novel *Jane's Career: A Story of Jamaica*, a work which realistically renders the landscape, language, and customs of early twentieth-century Jamaica and is considered the precursor of modern West Indian literature. The first serious West Indian work of fiction with a black female protagonist, the novel was also innovative for its sympathetic depiction of lower-class rural Jamaican life. With the publication of *Jane's Career*, the literature of Jamaica took on an identity distinct from that of imperial England. For this reason de Lisser is today regarded as a pioneer in the development of Caribbean literature.

De Lisser was born in Falmouth, Jamaica, of Portuguese-Jewish ancestry. Although he had little formal education, by the age of twenty-six he rose to the editorship of the *Jamaican Gleaner*, a position that his father had held before him. During his forty years as editor of the newspaper, de Lisser wrote a regular column expounding liberal political ideas that influenced local as well as international opinion about the island. His interest in politics was also evident in his fiction, which he treated as a hobby rather than a vocation. In his early works, notably *Jane's Career* and *Susan Proudleigh*, de Lisser's identification with the exploited lower classes embodied the tenets of socialism. But fearful of the possible sociopolitical excesses that might accompany Jamaican independence, de Lisser turned from socialism and became increasingly conservative in his political beliefs: he not only propounded a procolonial viewpoint in his works, but his depictions of black characters grew stereotypical, and often savagely contemptuous. De Lisser ended his career writing historical novels that appealed to the tastes of English audiences. He died in 1944.

De Lisser's literary importance rests primarily upon his early novels, particularly *Jane's Career*, a landmark in West Indian literary history. While earlier Caribbean writers mimicked an English style and viewpoint, de Lisser showed an unprecedented awareness of the color divisions, matriarchal family structure, and discontent with rural life that were distinctly Jamaican. An understanding of the lure of the city for rural Jamaicans is contrasted with scorn for the rising mulatto middle class, who are characterized as exploitive, vulgar mimics of white society. Although *Jane's Career* is considered de Lisser's best written and most perceptive work, the conclusion of the novel has been seen by some critics as either careless or inconsistent: when the independent Jane marries a middle-class man and starts a family, it appears that her independence and freedom have been sacrificed for comfort. Her desire to become a mistress with servants of her own is ironic, as she was herself once a servant to an insensitive mistress. Other critics, including John Figueroa, see the ending as realistic; he states, "the novel shows . . . a truly notable achievement on the part of the author in always having Jane, in every situation, so much her own woman."

In *The White Witch of Rosehall*, de Lisser's most popular novel, Jamaica becomes a symbol of primitive life, standing in contrast to the civilized image of England. Corruption, African influences, ancient rituals, and magic slowly impel a staid,

Lee Hunt

civilized Englishman to revert to a long-suppressed, savage state that borders on madness. In this book, the black characters are often portrayed as treacherous or insensitive. Kenneth Ramchand believes that the main interest in the work lies in its exotic sensationalism, with the graphic details of African ritual and voodoo dominating, rather than merging successfully with the story. Ramchand concludes that the novel's exoticism is accompanied by "a revulsion against what is presented as African paganism, and the fictional character's revulsion is shared by the author."

De Lisser's other novels are not well known, but an examination of their plots reveals the author's changing political attitudes: *Susan Proudleigh*, de Lisser's second novel, focuses on the poor in early twentieth-century Jamaica; in *Revenge: A Tale of Old Jamaica*, the black revolutionary Paul Bogle is depicted as a coward while the white governor is characterized as a heroic leader; and in *The Arawak Girl*, de Lisser's last novel, the female protagonist's disdain for Jamaica's Spanish conquerors is presented sympathetically and in contrast to the other Indians in the book, who are viewed with contempt.

De Lisser is today considered a minor author whose contribution to West Indian literature was catalytic. Because his novel *Jane's Career* helped establish a Jamaican literary identity, the study of de Lisser's early work is critical to an understanding of the development of Caribbean literature.

(See also *Contemporary Authors*, Vol. 109.)

PRINCIPAL WORKS

Jane: A Story of Jamaica (novel) 1913; also published as
    Jane's Career: A Story of Jamaica, 1914
Twentieth Century Jamaica (essays) 1913
Susan Proudleigh (novel) 1915
Revenge: A Tale of Old Jamaica (novel) 1919
The White Witch of Rosehall (novel) 1929
Under the Sun: A Jamaican Comedy (novel) 1937
Psyche (novel) 1952
The Arawak Girl (novel) 1958

ESTHER CHAPMAN (essay date 1952)

[*A writer for the* Jamaican Daily Express *and an editor of* The
West Indian Review, *Chapman is an Englishwoman who has lived
in Jamaica. Her own novels, according to Anthony Boxill, "explore in an exotic fashion the problems of colour prejudice and
intellectual sterility in Jamaica." In her review of* Psyche, *Chapman admits that the novel is engaging, but concludes that it is
not as powerful a work as its theme allows.*]

[*Psyche*] was written when its author was suffering from the
illness of which he died. It is readable and the Jamaican background is appealing; but one is conscious of a partial waste of
good material. As I read the book, I all the time had the feeling
that here was a good and powerful theme that should have been
tackled with more strength and vitality. . . .

Psyche is the story of two women in the days of slavery. Psyche
the mother was a slave who was bartered in the market place.
She became the mistress of a white planter, who ultimately
married her. They had a daughter also named Psyche, born
with a light skin. When Charles Huntingdon inherited a title
and went back to England, he (improbably) took the child with
him leaving the mother to invent a story of having been the
nurse of her own child.

The younger Psyche married a French Baron and after the death
of her husband, returned to Jamaica where she gradually became aware of her colour and her parentage.

This romantic theme, set against a background of Jamaica,
England, and France, could have been a rich and variegated
story. If it does not rise fully to the challenge it has itself made,
this is not to say that it fails as a romance. The author has the
courage of the tragedy inherent in the book and in the love
affair in which its younger heroine is involved. The character
of the mother is well realised and even when the story fails to
convince there is still an engaging charm and simplicity about
the outlook of the author.

> *Esther Chapman, in a review of "Psyche," in* The
> West Indian Review, *n.s. Vol. 4, No. 20, September
> 13, 1952, p. 12.*

W. ADOLPHE ROBERTS (essay date 1953)

[*A Jamaican-born novelist and poet, Roberts was the editor of
several American magazines. His most notable works are his non-
fiction studies of the West Indies, which include* Lands of the Inner
Sea *and* Jamaica: The Portrait of an Island.]

Herbert George de Lisser, born in 1878, the most brilliant of
Jamaican journalists and an all-round writer, was nationalistic
as a young man. In his **"Twentieth Century Jamaica"** . . .
he made this assertion: "Politically, the people of Jamaica are
contented enough, but it would be a mistake to imagine that
they are inclined to accept as unchangeable the present system
of Government . . . they are becoming less and less disposed
to be ruled entirely by officials." At other times de Lisser was
intensely conservative. . . .

De Lisser . . . wrote in **"Jane's Career"** and **"Susan Proudleigh"** the first pungent, realistic folk novels in Jamaican literary history, both of them books which will live. His later
costume romances were aimed at the English reading public.

The other British Caribbean territories did not have contemporary writers equal in stature to [Tom] Redcam and de Lisser.
If there were some lesser figures, they did not impinge upon
the consciousness of the region. (p. 16)

> *W. Adolphe Roberts, "The British Possessions," in*
> The West Indian Review, *Vol. 4, n.s. No. 42, April
> 25, 1953, pp. 16-17.**

KENNETH RAMCHAND (essay date 1970)

[*Ramchand examines the evolution of de Lisser's sociopolitical
attitudes and discusses* Jane's Career.]

[H. G. de Lisser's] prose fiction writings examined in order
of publication, reveal changes of attitudes to his raw material
that correspond to a marked extent with his evolution into an
inflexible spokesman for wealth and political conservatism in
his island. Even in an apparently historical novel like *Revenge* . . . for instance, dealing with the Morant Bay uprising
of 1865, de Lisser's attitudes to political and social change in
his own time may be found transferred. His scorn for the rising
browns and light-browns of his own day appears in the presentation of George William Gordon as an unstable mulatto
more intent on making mileage within the existing power structure, than in advancing the revolutionary cause of the Blacks. . . .
If this national hero is a remorseful coward, [another] reverts,
in de Lisser's hands, to savagery: 'Bogle, drunk with blood
and fury, and transformed now out of all semblance to a human
being, had no intention of sparing his enemies.' . . . (pp. vi-
vii)

Revenge was the first of a series of novels dealing systematically with the Jamaican past. Indeed, of the seven novels de
Lisser published after 1918, only *Under the Sun* . . . deals with
the present. The retreat, in his fiction, to what he seems to
have regarded as a safe historical distance was in itself an
expression of de Lisser's alienation from the changing society
around him. If he had no philosophy of history, not even
something as rudimentary as that there are connections between
past and present, it is not surprising, perhaps, that he had no
theory of the historical novel. From his practice, however, a
working formula can be extracted: the historical novel must
contain action, and it must stick to the facts and issues judged
to be significant by historians; the historical novel exists to
personify history, and like a play or concert dresses the agents
in the costumes and customs of the time; to add variety to the
historical matter, the novelist is allowed to introduce a romance
element, like the unrequited love of Paul Bogle's daughter for
the son of a plantation owner. There can be no doubt of the
assiduity with which de Lisser carried out his research, so that
the novels may still be of use in awakening interest in the
history of the periods they deal with. But the romance element

becomes more prominent in successive novels, and the author yields more and more to a temptation to equate action with sensational happenings in an exotic setting. These tendencies come to a climax in *The White Witch of Rosehall* . . . , a story of love, intrigue, of white witchcraft versus black obeah, spell-casting, exorcism, hauntings, floggings, insurrection and strangulation; the characters include a woman who has murdered three husbands, a clergyman addicted to Jamaica rum, several other Europeans made dissolute by the tropics, a black witch doctor and primitive Africans.

De Lisser's anti-nationalistic sentiment, and his reputation as the author of *The White Witch of Rosehall* have worked against the recognition of his first two novels, *Jane's Career* . . . and *Susan Proudleigh* . . . , in both of which the author's attitude to his material is still the attitude of the Fabian socialist he had become for a spell under the influence of Sir Sydney Oliver, governor of Jamaica from 1908 to 1913. *Susan Proudleigh* is the first West Indian novel of emigration; *Jane's Career* is the first in which the central character, the one whose feelings and thoughts are explored in depth, is a Negro.

When it is definitely decided that Jane Burrell is to leave her village and go to Kingston to work in the house of Mrs. Mason, the young girl becomes the envy of her friends. . . . De Lisser's sympathetic awareness of broad changes taking place in the shape of Jamaican society gives resonance to the emotions being expressed in the novel . . . . Villages are being depopulated by emigration to more flourishing parts of the country, or to Panama and Costa Rica, and by the shifting of large numbers of peasants to the attracting urban centre, Kingston. Descriptions of Kingston streets and buildings, and direct references to all these sociological processes occur in *Jane's Career,* but more important than the information itself is the way de Lisser the novelist uses it to give urgency to Jane's quest. . . . Lying behind de Lisser's focus on the particular problems of the young girl, Jane, is his awareness of the emergence of the independent female and the implications of that emergence for the future of West Indian society. Apart from Claude McKay's *Banana Bottom* (1933), Edgar Mittelholzer's *Sylvia* (1953) George Lamming's *Season of Adventure* (1960), the vein opened up by de Lisser remains, curiously unworked in West Indian literature. And, for that matter, the issue still has not been faced by the society as a whole.

Social awareness of another kind lends conviction to Jane's toil in the city. . . . The portrayal of West Indian society as one stratified in accordance with race and colour appears early in West Indian fiction, long before Mittelholzer's *A Morning at the Office* (1950). But two features in de Lisser's representation are worth close attention for the way in which they recur in later West Indian writing.

When Jane runs away from Mrs Mason's house, she shares a room with a virago called Sathyra. In this section of the novel de Lisser filters in description . . . , and through Jane's consciousness, a picture of what it is like to live in a slum yard. . . . In his portrayal of the yard-dwellers, de Lisser constantly reminds us of the rural origins and the dreams of the West Indian urban slum-dweller. (pp. vii-xii)

Mrs Mason's callous treatment of Jane is a particular presentation of the author's intuition that more and more, the exploiter of the West Indian peasant (rural or urban) is the West Indian middle-class or lower middle-class. Mrs Mason's closeness to the people she uses is revealed in the way she can inhabit their point of view in order to predict their behaviour, and in their understanding of her mental process. In a sense, *Jane's Career*

is a diverting essay on the relationship between mistress and maid. But throughout the fun of the haggling over wages, the tactics of dismissal or resignation, the throwing of words, and the outbreaks of quarrels in dialect, de Lisser's satire against Mrs Mason and her class is remorseless. . . . De Lisser's revelation of the gap between the West Indian middle-class and West Indian mass is remarkable because he had arrived at a position whose consequences West Indian writers would only begin to explore and understand almost fifty years after his original probe.

Without de Lisser's social insights, *Jane's Career* would not have been the psychologically convincing novel about growing up that it is. . . . [Jane] is awe-struck in the ostentatiously furnished household of Mrs Mason; and she is confused by the attentions of her employer's itching nephew, Cecil. As we follow Jane's process of coming to terms with her own nature and that of the world around her, *Jane's Career* develops into the first West Indian novel in which the peasant is given full status as a human person capable of spontaneity and a delicacy of response to people and situations, and one involved in a range of thoughts and feelings hitherto denied in literature to the slave or ex-slave.

The theme of growing up, and its connection with the more general issues implicit in the novel are brought into sharp relief in the presentation of Mrs Burrell's visit to her daughter. . . . De Lisser skillfully shows how Mrs Mason insinuates herself into positions that prevent Jane from disclosing her sufferings, and how the rural character defers to the markers of social status displayed in Mrs Mason's house. The author also enters the girl's consciousness to bring out Jane's frustration and anger and jealousy. . . . What the visit crystallizes, however, is the generational gap and the emergence of the independent female. . . . (pp. xiii-xv)

But Jane's dream of freedom turns out to be a dream of comfortable domesticity—a planned family, 'nice' furniture, children washed twice a day, walks with the babies in the afternoon and piano lessons for the young. At the end, she gets married to a respectable young man who takes her to live in a middle-class suburb. The white wedding is to follow. By this time it is clear that the author's irony has turned against Jane. . . . De Lisser's loss of sympathy with his black heroine at this stage can be related to his real-life attitudes. But there is more to be said. The imitative dead-end to which de Lisser ironically drives Jane is the same dead-end now being explored by writers like V. S. Naipaul (*The Mimic Men*, 1967), Garth St Omer (*Shades of Grey*, 1968), and Orlando Patterson (*An Absence of Ruins*, 1966). De Lisser can hardly be blamed for failing to initiate the search for an alternative tradition that is to be found in the differing works of Wilson Harris and L. Edward Brathwaite. But *Jane's Career* already points to cultural dilemmas that make that search more urgent today than ever before in the West Indies. (pp. xv-xvi)

Kenneth Ramchand, "Introduction" (1970), in Jane's Career: A Story of Jamaica *by Herbert G. de Lisser (copyright © 1971 by Rex Collings, Ltd.; reprinted by permission of Africana Publishing Company, a division of Holmes & Meier Publishers, Inc., 1UB Building, 30 Irving Place, New York, NY 10003), Africana, 1971, pp. v-xvi.*

KENNETH RAMCHAND (essay date 1970)

[*Ramchand discusses de Lisser's portrayal of Jamaican racial and cultural differences.*]

As the myth of England as the place of values grew strong, the condition of the West Indies as a spiritual sepulchre became true. H. G. de Lisser's *The White Witch of Rosehall* . . . , set in the Jamaica of 1830's, provides a useful illustration of the contraries. The arrival of a young Englishman Robert Rutherford allows de Lisser to show the difference between the Creole White and the newly-arrived European. Rutherford's liaison with two women (the White Creole, Annie Palmer, and Millie, a coloured girl) and his taking to drink, show the loss of morals in the steamy atmosphere. . . . De Lisser is not a major West Indian artist, but as an illustrator, in the novel form, of the facts and issues in West Indian slave society, he is unequalled. At the end of *The White Witch of Rosehall,* the prolonged contrast between the Creole image of England as home and civilized place, and the picture of Jamaica as the place of corruption, is clinched. (pp. 36-7)

Each of de Lisser's novels is based upon a historical event or set in a specific period: *Jane's Career* . . . deals with Kingston in the early decades of the twentieth century, while his last published, *The Arawak Girl* . . . , is set in the 1490's. Between these two times the other novels are systematically located. A significant pattern may be noticed. In *Jane's Career,* the central character is black, and the scene is contemporary. In *Susan Proudleigh* . . . , set topically in Panama, the central characters are still Negro, but brown-skinned. From this point, however, the novels either draw less and less upon the contemporary scene, or the central characters cease to be Black. This pattern in the *oeuvre* runs parallel with the evolution of the Fabian Socialist sympathizer and critic of colonial rule of 1913 into the arch-reactionary and conservative spokesman of later years: 'From complete self-Government for Jamaica, Good Lord deliver us. Not even Full Representative Government can be considered at a time when, to use a colloquialism, the tail is wagging the dog, and tub-thumping is practically the order of the day.' Not even the Colonial Office would hold this view. . . . (p. 56)

De Lisser's anti-nationalistic position has affected West Indian attitudes to his place in West Indian writing. Most of the novels do not encourage a favourable estimate. But it is necessary to make a claim for *Jane's Career.* It is the first West Indian novel in which the central character is Black; Jane is the first full West Indian fictional heroine; and it is in *Jane's Career* that de Lisser's attitude to his raw material and to his characters comes closest to being like that of later West Indian writers. (p. 57)

West Indian literature would seem to be the only substantial literature in which the dialect-speaking character is the central character. The conventional associations of dialect with comic characters or with characters on the periphery have not been eliminated, but they are disarmed of any stereotyping appearances or effects by occurring among other contextualizations of dialect. (p. 96)

[In] West Indian fiction the two voices [—dialect and standard English—] no longer reflect mutually exclusive social worlds. It increases the delicacy of our reading in fact if we can imagine the narrative sections in a West Indian Standard voice. This kind of delicacy is not always necessary, however, and is hardly called for, in the dialect novels of the White Creole, H. G. de Lisser, where the Negro is still a comic character and not much more, and where the author's attitude of withdrawal is reflected by an exaggerating of the distance between the narrator's language and that of the fictional character. An episode in *Jane's Career* . . . is transitional in West Indian fiction in the way it combines an attitude of social superiority (recurrent in British presentations) with the West Indian's knowledge of the dialect. Jane is about to go to Kingston to pursue a career as a servant girl so she is taken to Daddy Buckram, the village sage. The description of the old man sets the scene in a revealing way:

> Like his audience, the Elder was black; he may have been about sixty years of age, and was intensely self-conscious. His close-cropped hair was turning grey; what chiefly distinguished him from all other men in the village was his glibness of tongue, his shoes, and his collar. . . .

Persuaded into an amused superiority, we witness next the recurrent device of writers handling the dialect-speaking character in a conventional way—a would-be impressive speech by the dialect-speaking character. Authorial markers of dissociation (my italics) are prominent, but de Lisser inscribes his dialect with obvious zest and with a dialect-speaker's understanding of dialect's capacity to absorb miscellaneous material (in this case the Bible):

> 'Jane', he continued *impressively* after a pause, 'Kingston is a very big an' wicked city, an' a young girl like you, who de Lord has blessed wid a good figure an' a face, must be careful not to keep bad company. Satan goeth about like a roaring lion in Kingston seeking who he may devour. He will devour you if you do not take him to the Lord in prayer. . . .

As a speaker of WIS, de Lisser was capable of more varied uses of the dialect than he settled for. But his repeatedly comic purposes merely followed the convention of European writers. In his novels, for all his inwardness with the dialect, the two voices come from two different worlds. (pp. 97-8)

In the novel *Season of Adventure,* [George] Lamming explores the problematic relation to Africa in terms proper to works of fiction. The middle-class West Indian's denial of the masses, and his shame of Africa are seen as obstacles to the fulfilment of the person, and the inauthentic existence of the unfulfilled person is a kind of death. (p. 143)

[It] is possible to locate some major differences in intention and tactics between H. G. de Lisser and Lamming, for in *The White Witch of Rosehall* . . . a main character, Rutherford, witnesses a ceremony. He is accompanied by a friend, Rider. The first thing to notice is that Rutherford is at a distance, not in the crowd. Nevertheless he is given the beginning of an experience:

> A shudder passed through Robert; to his surprise he found that he too was slightly moving his body to the rhythm of the sound. Rider had himself better in hand, but the hypnotic influence of the scene did not leave him entirely unaffected. It had an appeal to the more primitive emotions. It stirred up something in the depths of one's being. He could understand how devotees in pagan lands were moved at times almost to madness by the call and compulsion of their strange and horrible religions. . . .

After the appearance of Kurtz in Conrad's *Heart of Darkness* (1902), episodes dealing with the European character affected by the primitive become a must in the second-rate literature of tropica. Once de Lisser makes the gesture towards this convention, a gap rapidly opens up again between the civilized Englishman and the pagan cultists. Rutherford resumes a function as the enlarging eye upon an exotic rite which it is de Lisser's object to 'write-up'. (pp. 144-45)

The sensational use of an African ceremony in *The White Witch of Rosehall* is accompanied by a revulsion against what is presented as African paganism, and the fictional character's revulsion is shared by the author. (p. 147)

In *The Arawak Girl,* cited less as an easy target than as a convenient illustration, de Lisser portrays the girl Anacanoa both as a fierce nationalist heroine against the Spaniards—persuading us to share her hostile attitudes to 'these brutal palefaced men . . . of another breed altogether'; and as a beautiful and exceptional Indian set apart from a decadent race—so that we approve of her and despise her people in the mass. (p. 166)

> Kenneth Ramchand, in his The West Indian Novel and Its Background (© 1970 by Kenneth Ramchand; by permission of Barnes & Noble Books, a Division of Littlefield, Adams & Co., Inc.), Barnes & Noble, 1970, 295 p.*

MICHAEL G. COOKE (essay date 1973)

[*Cooke provides a balanced critical appraisal of* Jane's Career.]

The re-issue of *Jane's Career,* one of the first volumes in the Colonial Novel Library, doubtless reflects the trend toward fishing in waters outside the literary mainstream. But the novel, implicitly made to respond to a post-dated political adventure, will look outdated, though originally, when published serially in Kingston's *Daily Gleaner,* it embodied an important social adventure, in imaging Jamaica to itself realistically, and evaluatively withal. Thus, if De Lisser fails to jump half a century ahead in terms of political position, he is nonetheless a pioneer in describing the depressed social conditions that cry out for political correction, showing a wide spectrum of people at the mercy of the market, of wilful and unscrupulous employers, and of crippling traditional assumptions. And it is only fair to credit him further with a novelist's, if not a philosopher's perception of the rationalized passivity, the wasteful binges of bad temper, the languor, the narrow-eyed suspicion and selfishness in the Jamaican temperament that break the force of political action.

The trouble is that, for all its local perceptions, *Jane's Career* does not generate a coherent vision. It is a success story, in the mode of the feminine picaresque—Jane, a relatively inhibited and dependent figure, moves or is driven about, though not very widely, in society. But the novel begins by defining success ambiguously, in terms of behavioristic piety ("keeping up" oneself), and again in terms of economic advantage (going to Kingston, wicked but rich). De Lisser does not manage either to fuse or to maintain ironic isolation for his two value systems. He is ironic, to be sure, but with the irony of a patronizing rather than a principled observer, so versed in exposing weakness that he becomes uneasy with real strength. One way or another everybody is scarred with this shallow catholic irony, which is apparently the resort of a mind incapable of handling paradox, and which becomes the veritable source of the character's failure to find a settled good in a paradoxical situation. Jane ends as the equal of her first distasteful mistress in Kingston, but also in vital respects as her reflection. The reward of her singular, Pamela-like devotion to keeping herself up is to be the child-bearing mistress of a man she likes and can in-

fluence, rather than one she dislikes and fears. No matter that he marries her, out of an access of intoxicated nobility; she has effectively resigned herself to having a "friend," the one visible escape from the economic cul-de-sac, and De Lisser ironically makes sure that we do not see the marriage as more than a triumphant event. Character is wantonly sacrificed to scene.

If De Lisser cannot help being co-opted into the interpretive scheme of present-day Jamaica, it seems clear that he had a humble-pretentious eye on another tradition. He is generally content to work in the well-mined vein of Fielding (complete with reflective set-pieces), and Thackeray and Trollope (complete with self-thwarted ironies). Some of his themes recall such predecessors: the city vs. the country, poverty vs. wealth, freedom vs. submission. Some of the formal elevation of the style may go back to them as well, but one feels a personal impulse coming through when De Lisser attributes to barely literate country folk a conversation about "the prevalence of praedial thieves." Oddly enough, he does not show in his characters any sign of this Jamaican love of words in their sumptuousness and musical power.

Jane's Career is subtitled, **"A Story of Jamaica."** One cannot read it without learning something of Jamaica, then and alas! now. The story is told by a man who has paid attention, and who has caught scenes, textures, customs, and a shibboleth or two: this novel, as feminine and mild as it is, remains enough like his notorious *White Witch of Rosehall* to boast recounted earthquakes, superstition, virtual rape, chicanery, criminal charges, quarrels, evictions, strikes, and deaths, just the sort of narrative counters to maintain serial interest and to hold an audience not practised in the reading of fiction. But while De Lisser has been there, one may question whether he has gotten *into* Jamaica. And this goes beyond his failure to combine the features he sees into a mosaic of vision. The real problem is a kind of imaginative prophylaxis, a fruitless muffling of the resonances and relations of what he sees. And he passes this on to his characters. His pride in Jamaica, for example, and his spontaneous fondness for the island break out powerfully in his description of natural scenes. But it is momentary, incidental, and does not get into the stream of narration as a dye, let alone a vital element; and Jane is excluded from even this momentary response, as one who, De Lisser declares, does not notice or care. She is not otherwise that dull; in fact she seems vital, curious, keen, and is powerfully affected by her first sight of Kingston, only to forget it forthwith. One cannot help feeling that she is arbitrarily cut off from a dimension of Jamaican experience, and of her own mind. This is a pity. The contrast of social poverty with natural beauty, even bounty, is part of the story; its near-suppression calls attention away from the story toward the author, and poignantly reveals him as an early case of the disability recently pointed out by George Lamming, a "dread of being identified with the land." (pp. 94-5)

At present, in Jamaica, in the British Caribbean at large, there is a concerted and even artificial effort to become the land's. The writers who two decades ago left home in despair, or desperation, have Antaeus-like returned, or else have proven that they continue to dwell at home in imagination, in a manner untainted with nostalgia. The artificial and the spontaneous run together, in a direction not perfectly foreseen. In this context, De Lisser's hesitancy and inhibitions may well be taken not as personal faults, but as an early thwarted stage of the struggle to belong. This is not to cover up the unfashionable political conservatism which steals into *Jane's Career* in the treatment of the strike, and which asserts itself so strongly in De Lisser's later work. But De Lisser is not so simple, or so homogeneous as a creative writer that he falls into a single place in the history of West Indian literature and consciousness. (p. 95)

De Lisser has his place in the literary scheme. The unsettled definition of that place is partly a factor of the evolution, or under-resolution of the historical matrix. And it is of no use to blame De Lisser for not divining that his story of Jamaica would be attracted into a larger and more positive universe of value and expectation. Credit enough that his story is part of the history of West Indian literature and consciousness. . . . (p. 96)

> *Michael G. Cooke, "West Indian Picaresque," in* Novel: A Forum on Fiction *(copyright © Novel Corp., 1973), Vol. 7, No. 1, Fall, 1973, pp. 93-6.**

ANTHONY BOXILL   (essay date 1979)

[*Boxill provides a short overview and discussion of de Lisser's canon.*]

H. G. de Lisser sums up in his book *Twentieth Century Jamaica* . . . the growing sense of the texture of society as a whole and the sense of the distinctiveness of the Jamaican identity:

> What can be maintained at this point is that the Jamaican of any colour is not precisely like any other man; he is a Jamaican, and has characteristics that are common more or less to all his fellow countrymen. One is not born and brought up in a country for nothing. One does not read the same papers that one's fellows read, hear much the same sort of talk all the year round, come into close contact with all other classes of the people, eat the same food, and enjoy the same recreations, without one's mind becoming assimilated to the minds of one's countrymen.
>
> (p. 37)

In the first chapter of *Twentieth Century Jamaica* he explores the possibilities of Jamaica's future with either England, Canada or the United States. He does not consider independence or nationhood or any form of federation with the other West Indian islands. His preference would be for 'a prosperous Jamaica directly owing allegiance to the mother-country'. (p. 38)

His first two novels are not only the most interesting from a historical perspective: they are his best work. Unfortunately the popularity of *The White Witch of Rosehall* has tended to overshadow them and too many critics have ignored these books. Kenneth Ramchand [see excerpt above], however, has pointed out that '*Susan Proudleigh* is the first West Indian novel of emigration; *Jane's Career* is the first in which the central character, whose feelings and thoughts are explored in depth, is a Negro.' (p. 43)

One wonders what made de Lisser turn from this kind of novel, which pulsated with the life of the folk, to his more shallow middle-class satires and ultimately to historical romance. The answer is probably that as he got older he became more conservative and lost his sympathy for people such as Jane and Susan. Even in *Jane's Career* one gets hints of this impatience in his ridicule of the behaviour of the people at Jane's wedding. *Revenge,* which deals with the Morant Bay rebellion of 1865, lacks the sympathy for the people that Reid demonstrates in *New Day* (1949). And in *The White Witch of Rosehall,* his best-

known work because of its exotic and sensational treatment of the West Indian past, his white man is by far a superior human being to his black man, who is often depicted as treacherous and lacking in sensitivity.

One final point needs to be made about his fiction. All his novels are dominated by resourceful, vital women. Given the importance of women in the West Indian social structure, de Lisser must be credited with doing more than most West Indian writers to explore the effect of this dominant female personality on the West Indian psyche as a whole. (pp. 43-4)

> *Anthony Boxill, "The Beginnings to 1929," in* West Indian Literature, *edited by Bruce King (copyright © 1979 by Bruce King; reprinted by permission of Macmillan, London and Basingstoke), Macmillan, 1979, pp. 30-44.**

MICHAEL GILKES   (essay date 1981)

[*A prolific Guyanese man of letters, Gilkes is the author of three critical studies of West Indian fiction. Below, he examines the questionable triumph of the protagonist in* Jane's Career.]

Jane's Career is essentially about emancipation; and Jane's rise from the poverty and servitude of her role as a domestic can be seen as an emancipation from a form of slavery. Her escape, first from the poverty and restrictions of rural family life and then from a disadvantaged role in society, represents the emancipation of the individual spirit. (p. 23)

De Lisser does not, like most of his contemporaries, romanticize peasant life, nor does he (as Thomas H. MacDermot [under pseud. Tom Redcam] does in *One Brown Girl and—; A Jamaican Story.* Kingston, 1909) sentimentalize his black heroine. Jane is attractive, but she is hardy and realistic. (p. 24)

In Kingston, dazzled by the vigorous life of the city, Jane meets the Mason family, for whom De Lisser reserves an obvious contempt. Mrs. Mason's mulatto pretensions to middle-class respectability are shown to involve little more than a bourgeois clutter of polished furniture and a series of petty squabbles between mistress and servant. The Mason children are uniformly unlovely. De Lisser seems to be criticizing the Masons not because they are householders aspiring, by virtue of their light brown skins, toward the social eminence of the white Creoles like De Lisser himself, but because their role is one of *imperfect,* vulgar mimicry. . . . Cecil, Mrs. Mason's devious nephew, is used by De Lisser to point up Jane's blend of naturalness and sagacity. She keeps his first gift, a three-penny piece, but feels it necessary to give in to his slimy attentions. Jane learns quickly, however, and soon (as Cecil discovers) becomes a wiser, more positive individual. His second gift (a shilling, his acknowledgment of her growing worth) does not interfere with her plan to escape from the household. Jane feels she has earned her shilling: Mrs. Mason's careful counting of the household cutlery reveals that she has stolen nothing.

Her career now reaches its second stage. Her "slavery" has been "abolished" and her roommate, Sathyra, gets her a job on the assembly line of a liquor-bottling factory. She is now a member of an urban group, a labor force with some power. The pay is better, conditions are reasonable, and she has achieved a higher social status. She is now "Miss Burrell" among her fellow-workers, who are also women. De Lisser's descriptions of the humble but enjoyable "bread-kind" and salt-fish meal which Sathyra prepares with Jane's help, their visit to a local dance, the novelty and excitement of Kingston at night, show an observant and sympathetic eye, in spite of his frequently obtrusive, authorial presence. Sathyra's independence of spirit is celebrated without condescension or sentimentality; and when the inevitable quarrel arises and she makes it clear that Jane is unwelcome because she has become a potential rival, Jane, now more experienced in human relationships, takes the initiative. She moves out and "for the first time in her life she was thrown absolutely on her own resources." . . . (pp. 24-5)

The third stage of her emancipation has now been reached. She is free as an individual, has her own room, and is her own mistress. But the corollary of this new freedom is her growing sense of loneliness and isolation. Independence brings its own problems. The new foreman, Mr. Curden, fortyish, married, and respectable, becomes a nuisance, then a threat. Jane finds that to be a single woman, an independent individual in a coercive, patriarchal society, is a complex and worrying situation. She has to use all her experience and wit to keep Mr. Curden at arm's length without endangering her job. It is a measure of De Lisser's fairness and artistic control that he makes Mr. Curden's infatuation with Jane and his growing exasperation with her delaying tactics seem reasonable enough to gain a measure of our sympathy. . . . Vincent Broglie, the brown, marriageable printer's underforeman, has already entered Jane's life, however, so help is at hand. But there is no sudden romantic alliance between Vincent and Jane. He is well off by Jane's standards, not in the least pretentious, and eminently suitable as a husband, but he is more concerned with his role as spokesman for the Printer's Union strikers and with his political future. Jane's attractiveness is noted, but produces no emotional upheaval in his fairly self-regarding life. De Lisser again avoids the trap of romantic cliché by allowing Jane to prick the balloon of Vincent's incipient egotism. She attends the strikers' meeting and observes the proceedings with a practical though not fully comprehending eye. To her the proposed strike seems misdirected. . . . De Lisser . . . [uses] Jane's practical, pragmatic peasant wisdom (". . . You know how Jamaica people stand . . .") to reinforce an authorial disapproval of the half-educated militancy of the strikers; but Jane is drawing upon her own very real experience of the problems of independence. . . . De Lisser seems, at the end of the novel, to have lost sympathy for (or lost interest in) his heroine. The tone has here become somewhat patronizing and one feels that "such a detached attitude at the end does not accord with the involvement in the longer central sections of the novel" [see Ramchand excerpt, above.] But this does not mean that De Lisser's approach has been ironic, or that the last chapter of the book shows merely a failure of sympathy for his black heroine. Rather, it is a failure of imagination, and (under the circumstances) perhaps excusable. De Lisser's knowledge of the rural or proletariat life of Jamaica was, inevitably, limited and circumscribed by his social and political convictions. The fact that he was a white Creole, and therefore identified quite readily with a European world-view, makes his insights into Jane's world the more remarkable. That he could visualize "no higher fortune" for her than a "white wedding" and middle-class respectability is hardly surprising. What *is* clear, and perhaps more to the point, is that Jane, as a married woman and householder, has earned her advance in social status: it is

a genuine emancipation, achieved with dignity and intelligence, and (in contrast to the Mrs. Masons of her world) will help to provide, one feels, the nucleus of an authentic black urban middle class. It is perhaps ironic that De Lisser, resisting the idea of self-government for Jamaica and resenting the rise of the colored bourgeoisie, died in May 1944, only six months before adult suffrage and self-rule were made possible by the granting of a new constitution for Jamaica.

Jane's Career, then, despite De Lisser's last-minute failure—a failure of imaginative vision as much as of sympathy or interest—is an important first novel. It may be seen as analogous to the emancipation of the black West Indian in a white and mulatto-ordered society. Jane's progress from poor peasant to member of an urban work force to middle-class respectability via a white wedding does not necessarily illustrate an amused, authorial irony. In the West Indies, early attempts at cultural indigenization were heavily tainted by an obdurate respect for the values of a white, "pedigree" society. Jane's triumph is a personal and very substantial one in a society still unaware of its true identity and then, as now, reluctant to acknowledge the individual worth and status of its women. *Jane's Career* is the first West Indian novel of substance, the first to have a black central character, the first appearance of a full-fledged fictional heroine.

But Jane's success, her rise from the poverty and restrictions of rural life and urban slum, remains only a private achievement, uncharacteristic of the social class she represents. (pp. 25-8)

> *Michael Gilkes, "Pioneers," in his* The West Indian Novel *(copyright © 1981 by Twayne Publishers; reprinted with the permission of Twayne Publishers, a Division of G. K. Hall & Co., Boston), Twayne, 1981, pp. 23-85.**

ADDITIONAL BIBLIOGRAPHY

Dathorne, O. R. "The Theme of Africa in West Indian Literature." *Phylon* XXVI, No. 3 (Fall 1965): 255-76.*
  General discussion of the subject, mentioning *The White Witch of Rosehall* as a novel that depicts the effects of Haitian voodoo on a white victim.

Drayton, Arthur D. "The European Factor in West Indian Literature." *The Literary Half-Yearly* XI, No. 1 (1970): 71-95.*
  Discusses de Lisser's rejection of the culture of West Indies for that of more "respectable" England.

Figueroa, John J. *"Jane's Career." World Literature Written in English* 12, No. 1 (April 1973): 97-105.
  Discusses the innovative aspects of the novel. *Jane's Career* "is concerned mostly with women, very much with a black maid, and almost entirely with the working classes of Kingston and the peasants of the rural mountains." Figueroa believes that de Lisser's greatest success was in the "mastery of the Jamaican language at many levels" and the consistency of Jane's characterization.

Ramchand, Kenneth. "Decolonisation in West Indian Literature." *Transition* 5, No. iii (May 1965): 48-9.*
  Discussion of the colonial viewpoint in *The White Witch of Rosehall*.

Paul Laurence Dunbar

1872-1906

American poet, short story writer, novelist, librettist, and essayist.

Dunbar is best known for his poetry written in black American dialect. Writing during a period when black Americans were depicted as either weak-minded buffoons or brutal subhumans, Dunbar sought first to win over his audience with the humor of his dialect verse and then to gradually display his abilities as a serious artist in standard English forms. However, his poems and stories written on contemporary themes and in standard English were not popular with white readers, and Dunbar found himself trapped in the undesired role of dialect poet. In recent years there has been a revival of interest in those works of Dunbar that most acutely express his artistic frustration.

The son of former slaves, Dunbar was born in Dayton, Ohio. When Dunbar was twelve years old his father died, and afterward a close bond was formed between mother and son that lasted throughout the poet's life. As a youngster, Dunbar listened to his mother's stories about her life as a slave. Later, as an adult, he incorporated information from these tales into his poetry and short stories. However, because his mother had omitted the more brutal facts of slavery from her stories, Dunbar tended to glorify plantation life, an aspect of his work that has been widely criticized. Dunbar began writing poetry as a child, and teachers recognized and encouraged his talent. As a high school student he continued to write, composing several plays for his drama club. But despite his growing reputation in the then-small town of Dayton, writing jobs were closed to black applicants and he lacked the money to further his education. Although many prospective employers believed he was overqualified for menial jobs, Dunbar eventually found work as an elevator operator. In his spare time he wrote poems and short stories and gave readings that, by popular demand, emphasized his dialect poetry. After one of his readings was enthusiastically received at a meeting of the Western Association of Writers (WAOW), three members visited Dunbar to find out more about the remarkable black youth. Appalled by his predicament, one of the men wrote a press letter about Dunbar and his work that was reprinted in newspapers across the country. Shortly after the article appeared Dunbar was admitted as a WAOW member, and his popularity as a speaker increased. Encouraged, he privately published *Oak and Ivy,* which he sold from his elevator post and after recitals. A Toledo attorney, Charles Thatcher, who was impressed by the book and offered to sponsor Dunbar's college education, was the first of several white benefactors who supported Dunbar throughout his career.

In 1893 Dunbar left Dayton to work with Frederick Douglass in the Haitian Exposition of the Chicago World's Fair. On "Colored Day" he recited original compositions and his audience was the first to give a warm reception to his poetry in standard English. Unfortunately, during the next two years Dunbar suffered career setbacks and his health, poor since childhood, worsened. Unable to support himself and his mother, he considered suicide. However, Thatcher sent Dunbar enough money to sustain him, and later used his influence to help

publish the poetry collection *Majors and Minors.* William Dean Howells, then the most prominent and influential critic in America, praised the dialect poems in this work, noting that Dunbar "reveals in these a finely ironical perception of the negro's limitations, with a tenderness for them which I think so rare as to be almost quite new. . . . It is this humorous quality which Mr. Dunbar has added to our literature, and it will be this which will most distinguish him." While the dialect poems were highly praised, of the standard English poems Howells commented: "Some of these I thought very good, but not distinctly his contribution to the body of American poetry," a verdict that haunted Dunbar throughout his career. Initially overwhelmed by Howells's review and the fame that followed, Dunbar later confessed that he believed Howells had done him more harm than good; the favorable response to the dialect poetry and tentative praise for the standard English poems led Dunbar to believe that if he continued to please audiences and publishers by producing dialect poetry his more serious work would eventually gain acceptance. However, periodicals continually rejected his standard English poetry, requesting dialect pieces instead.

After a trip to England, where he met and collaborated with the black composer Samuel Coleridge Taylor, Dunbar returned to New York and married a poet and school teacher with whom he had corresponded by mail for two years. During this period Dunbar completed his first novel, *The Uncalled,* and collaborated with successful songwriter Will Marion Cook on the musical *Clorindy; or, The Origin of the Cakewalk.* A huge success, the show was the first to feature syncopated music, and the first in which the chorus sang and danced simultaneously. Although Dunbar had agreed to collaborate on future projects with Cook, he was quickly disillusioned with his press reception as "king of the coon shows," and was pressured to quit by his wife and mother, who were insulted by his association with the degrading minstrel tradition. However, he reluctantly fulfilled his obligations, and in the process became acquainted with the artists, actors, singers, and musicians who frequented Harlem's popular theaters. It was during this period that Dunbar gathered material that he later used in short stories and in the novel *The Sport of the Gods.* While in New York Dunbar contracted tuberculosis and began drinking to relieve his physical discomfort. Dunbar's illness worsened in the last years of his life, necessitating intermittent retreats to milder climates. At age thirty-four, separated from his wife and suffering from alcohol abuse and his lingering illness, Dunbar died at his mother's home. He had once described himself as being in the unfortunate position of a "black white man": he wanted acceptance as an artist, not as a representative of his race or a dialect poet, and died believing that his career had been a national joke and a failure.

Dunbar's dialect poetry has long been his most popular work. Dialect was a common literary device in the late nineteenth century, particularly as practiced by Sidney Lanier and Joel Chandler Harris, but Dunbar's work in the genre is considered the most realistic and sensitively handled. Like other dialect writers, Dunbar's dialect work was primarily concerned with humorous situations; however, he portrayed these events with ironic tenderness that conveyed the emotions and thoughts of his uneducated, inarticulate subjects. Even Dunbar's detractors believe that his dialect poetry vividly captures the folklife and beliefs of late nineteenth-century black Americans. However, these critics also note that his dialect poems present a distorted picture of a benevolent plantation past. Dunbar has been accused of subscribing to the "plantation school," a term denoting a turn-of-the-century belief that Southern blacks became homesick and demoralized when they left the safety of the agrarian South for the urban North. While not excusing such beliefs, others have noted that Dunbar was a small town Midwesterner who was not as sophisticated as many of his critics and that he, like so many other Midwestern writers, became disillusioned with city life and was simply expressing his nostalgia for the world he knew as a child. These critics find that his work thus grows out of an emotional longing rather than a reasoned preference for slavery or even a considered view of black Americans.

Although Dunbar's dialect poetry has been his most popular work, it was actually only a small portion of his creative achievement. He wrote many poems in standard English as well as four novels and several volumes of short stories. Dunbar's standard English poems are more concerned with his personal pain and anguish than they are with the created characters of his dialect poetry. These poems consistently examine the nature and possibility of personal freedom in a manner reminiscent of the work of Percy Bysshe Shelley; in fact, Dunbar's standard English poems are often linked to the tradition of Romantic poetry exemplified by Shelley. These technically accomplished lyrics have begun to receive more attention in recent years, even though they have yet to achieve the renown of his dialect verse.

Dunbar's fiction, like his poetry, also reveals his struggle with artistic honesty and commercial success. His early short stories, written for popular magazines, demonstrate his desire to amuse readers and achieve commercial success. In general, these are romantic, sentimental stories of plantation life that stress the folkways of black Americans. These stories convey a sensitive understanding of his characters, but few exhibit any understanding of the problems of contemporary life. Later in his career Dunbar created stories more concerned with racial problems and the inability of white America to perceive black people as human beings. Although some critics believe that Dunbar failed to fully document the harshness of life for black Americans, they note that in these later stories he displayed a powerful naturalistic vision of a people trapped by an unjust social system.

Dunbar's novels also demonstrate an early artistic ambivalence and awakening social conscience. His first three novels featured white characters and are considered poor because Dunbar, unfamiliar with the emotional or intellectual life of his characters, relied on stock figures and situations copied from Victorian novels. Of these works, *The Uncalled* is the most interesting. Considered Dunbar's spiritual autobiography by many critics, the novel examines provincial attitudes toward life and religion in a small Ohio town. His fourth novel, *The Sport of the Gods,* is of interest for being the only novel in which Dunbar depicted a black protagonist. Written two years before Dunbar's death, the novel has generally been interpreted by critics as a celebration of Southern agrarian life and an indictment of the northern migration of black southerners. However, Gregory Candela believes that earlier critics overlooked the irony in the novel, thereby misinterpreting the novelist's intention. Candela contends that Dunbar prepared the reader for a story about dutiful black servants and trusting white employers and then attacked both the hypocrisy of the South and the sinister illusionary glitter of the North.

In general, discussion of Dunbar's work has more often been a reflection of the political and social climate of America than a dispassionate assessment of a literary production. During his lifetime, when most of his readers were white, his humorous dialect poetry was most widely praised. Although well-intentioned, many of these early critics demonstrated patronizing visions of black artists and the lives of black Americans. Similarly, race was constantly a factor—Dunbar was invariably praised as the first great modern Negro poet, while his stature as simply a poet was overlooked. After his death, Dunbar was largely ignored by white critics, but black critics were more inclined to examine Dunbar's total achievement. Benjamin Brawley, for example, noted that many of his standard English poems were unsurpassed by anyone of his era "in the pure flow of the lyrical verse." During the Harlem Renaissance of the 1920s and 1930s black artists rebelled against the minstrel tradition with which Dunbar was associated. For the next three decades Dunbar was most often depicted as a man who had caricatured his race for money and who, with few exceptions, had supported white America's prejudiced view of black people.

It was not until the black literary renaissance of the 1960s that critics began to pay more attention to Dunbar's achievements and, in so doing, resurrected Dunbar as an important voice in American literature. Critics have since made a greater effort to understand Dunbar's compromises rather than simply attack him by using the critical and behavioral standards of a later age. They now find that, as the first black author in America to earn his living by his pen, Dunbar of necessity had to write works that a predominantly white audience would be willing to purchase. Jean Wagner and Peter Revell, in particular, have done much to correct the misunderstandings regarding Dunbar's poetry and have demonstrated the true tragedy of his position—that of a man who hated the only work he could sell, who perceived his own inadequacies, but who could not surmount his feelings of inferiority.

Dunbar's career expresses the dilemma of being black in America, the pain and frustration of living with one race and trying to gain acceptance from another. The ambivalence of his position is expressed throughout his career and is the facet of his work most relevant to contemporary readers. Although his dialect poetry has long been considered his greatest achievement, his later novels and stories, as well as the example of his life, have regained importance in recent years as examples of the compromises exacted from individuals by society.

(See also *TCLC*, Vol. 2 and *Contemporary Authors*, Vol. 104).

PRINCIPAL WORKS

Oak and Ivy (poetry) 1893
Majors and Minors (poetry) 1895
Lyrics of Lowly Life (poetry) 1896
Clorindy; or, The Origin of the Cakewalk (libretto) 1898
Dream Lovers: An Operatic Romance (libretto) 1898
Folks from Dixie (short stories) 1898
The Uncalled (novel) 1898
Lyrics of the Hearthside (poetry) 1899
Poems of Cabin and Field (poetry) 1899
The Love of Landry (novel) 1900
The Strength of Gideon, and Other Stories (short stories) 1900
Candle-Lightin' Time (poetry) 1901
The Fanatics (novel) 1901
In Dahomey: A Negro Musical Comedy [with others] (libretto) 1902
The Sport of the Gods (novel) 1902; also published as *The Jest of Fate*, 1903
In Old Plantation Days (short stories) 1903
Lyrics of Love and Laughter (poetry) 1903
The Heart of Happy Hollow (short stories) 1904
Howdy, Honey, Howdy (poetry) 1905
Lyrics of Sunshine and Shadow (poetry) 1905
The Life and Works of Paul Laurence Dunbar (poetry and short stories) 1907
The Complete Poems of Paul Laurence Dunbar (poetry) 1913
The Best Stories of Paul Laurence Dunbar (short stories) 1938
The Paul Laurence Dunbar Reader (poetry, short stories, essays, journalism, and letters) 1975

W. D. HOWELLS (essay date 1896)

[*Howells was the chief progenitor of American Realism and the most influential American literary critic during the late nineteenth century. He was the author of nearly three dozen novels, few of which are read today. Despite his eclipse, he stands as one of the major literary figures of the nineteenth century: he successfully*

weaned American literature away from the sentimental romanticism of its infancy, earning the popular sobriquet "the Dean of American Letters." Through Realism, a theory central to his fiction and criticism, Howells sought to disperse "the conventional acceptations by which men live on easy terms with themselves" that they might "examine the grounds of their social and moral opinions." To accomplish this, according to Howells, the writer must strive to record impressions of everyday life in detail, endowing characters with true-to-life motives and avoiding authorial comment in the narrative. Criticism and Fiction (1891), a patchwork of essays from Harper's Magazine, is often considered Howells's manifesto of Realism, although, as René Wellek has noted, the book is actually "only a skirmish in a long campaign for his doctrines." In addition to many notable studies of the works of his friends Mark Twain and Henry James, Howells perceptively reviewed three generations of international literature, urging Americans to read Émile Zola, Bernard Shaw, Henrik Ibsen, Emily Dickinson, and other important authors. Dunbar was another writer that Howells introduced to the reading public; his oft-quoted review of Majors and Minors *in Harper's Weekly (see TCLC, Vol. 2) proved to be a major milestone in the poet's career. Howells's introduction to* Lyrics of Lowly Life, *excerpted below, reiterates many of the points made in the earlier review.*]

What struck me in reading Mr. Dunbar's poetry [*Majors and Minors*] was what had already struck his friends in Ohio and Indiana, in Kentucky and Illinois. They had felt, as I felt, that however gifted his race had proven itself in music, in oratory, in several of the other arts, here was the first instance of an American negro who had evinced innate distinction in literature. In my criticism of his book [see *TCLC*, Vol. 2] I had alleged Dumas in France, and I had forgetfully failed to allege the far greater Pushkin in Russia; but these were both mulattoes, who might have been supposed to derive their qualities from white blood vastly more artistic than ours, and who were the creatures of an environment more favorable to their literary development. So far as I could remember, Paul Dunbar was the only man of pure African blood and of American civilization to feel the negro life aesthetically and express it lyrically. It seemed to me that this had come to its most modern consciousness in him, and that his brilliant and unique achievement was to have studied the American negro objectively, and to have represented him as he found him to be, with humor, with sympathy, and yet with what the reader must instinctively feel to be entire truthfulness. I said that a race which had come to this effect in any member of it, had attained civilization in him, and I permitted myself the imaginative prophecy that the hostilities and the prejudices which had so long constrained his race were destined to vanish in the arts; that these were to be the final proof that God had made of one blood all nations of men. I thought his merits positive and not comparative; and I held that if his black poems had been written by a white man, I should not have found them less admirable. I accepted them as an evidence of the essential unity of the human race, which does not think or feel black in one and white in another, but humanly in all.

Yet it appeared to me then, and it appears to me now, that there is a precious difference of temperament between the races which it would be a great pity ever to lose, and that this is best preserved and most charmingly suggested by Mr. Dunbar in those pieces of his where he studies the moods and traits of his race in its own accent of our English. We call such pieces dialect pieces for want of some closer phrase, but they are really not dialect so much as delightful personal attempts and failures for the written and spoken language. In nothing is his essentially refined and delicate art so well shown as in these pieces, which, as I ventured to say, describe the range between appetite and emotion, with certain lifts far beyond and above it, which is the range of the race. He reveals in these a finely ironical perception of the negro's limitations, with a tenderness for them which I think so very rare as to be almost quite new. I should say, perhaps, that it was this humorous quality which Mr. Dunbar had added to our literature, and it would be this which would most distinguish him, now and hereafter. It is something that one feels in nearly all the dialect pieces; and I hope that in the present collection he has kept all of these in his earlier volume, and added others to them. But the contents of this book are wholly of his own choosing, and I do not know how much or little he may have preferred the poems in literary English. Some of these I thought very good, and even more than very good, but not distinctively his contribution to the body of American poetry. What I mean is that several people might have written them; but I do not know any one else at present who could quite have written the dialect pieces. These are divinations and reports of what passes in the hearts and minds of a lowly people whose poetry had hitherto been inarticulately expressed in music, but now finds, for the first time in our tongue, literary interpretation of a very artistic completeness.

I say the event is interesting, but how important it shall be can be determined only by Mr. Dunbar's future performance. I cannot undertake to prophesy concerning this; but if he should do nothing more than he has done, I should feel that he had made the strongest claim for the negro in English literature that the negro has yet made. He has at least produced something that, however we may critically disagree about it, we cannot well refuse to enjoy; in more than one piece he has produced a work of art. (pp. 253-55)

> *W. D. Howells, in an introduction to* Lyrics of Lowly Life *by Paul Laurence Dunbar (copyright, 1895, 1896 by the Century Company; copyright, 1896, by Dodd, Mead and Company), Dodd, Mead 1896 (and reprinted in his* W. D. Howells As Critic, *edited by Edwin H. Cady, Routledge & Kegan Paul, 1973, pp. 252-55).*

POET LORE   (essay date 1897)

[*An anonymous reviewer briefly appraises Dunbar's* Lyrics of Lowly Life.]

[Mr. W. D. Howells] claims to base his admiration of Dunbar upon the absolute value of his work and not upon its comparative value as a negro's [see excerpt above]. But this claim is perhaps somewhat discounted by the fact that he finds his best work to be the negro-dialect poems.

It is not to be denied that these have great charm, combining as they do touches very characteristic of the negro with daintily poetic conceptions. The proverbial laziness of the negro is not in vain when it becomes the inspiration of a little poem like the **'Song of Summer . . .'**. . . . For the other poems, they have a freshness quite befitting a first poet of his race. It is much as if the spirit of the poet looked out upon nature for the first time and saw that it was beautiful, and sang his delight. Often quite perfect in form they have the advantage of not being overloaded, like so much verse we are called upon to read, with ornaments of culture so heavy and costly that the slender thought can but stagger beneath the weight. (pp. 300-01)

> *"'Lowly' Poets," in* Poet Lore *(copyright, 1897, by Poet Lore, Inc.; reprinted by permission of Heldref*

*Publications, a publication of the Helen Dwight Reid Educational Foundation), Vol. IX, No. 2, Spring, 1897, pp. 298-301.**

JOSEPH G. BRYANT   (essay date 1905)

[*Bryant offers high praise for Dunbar's poetic skill, comparing him to the Scottish poet Robert Burns, a master of dialect poetry.*]

[The] sparkling wit, the quaint and delightful humor, the individuality and charm of Dunbar's poetry are not excelled by any lines from the pen of a Negro. No person can read his verse without being forcibly impressed that he is a remarkable man, a genius demanding attention. The New World has not produced a bard like him. Although distinctively American by birth and education, as well as a Negro, yet his prototype is on the other side of the Atlantic. Robert Burns and Dunbar, in many important particulars, are parallel poets. They seem to have been cast in the same mould; with limited educational advantages, both struggled up through poverty, and each wrote largely in the dialect of his clan. He is strong and original, and like Burns, lyrical in inspiration. Probably there never were two men of opposite races, so widely separated by time and distance, and yet so much alike in soul-qualities. With no desire and no doubt unconsciously, he has walked complete in the footprints of the eminent Scottish bard; has the same infirmity, animated by the same hope, and blessed with the same success. (p. 256)

In Dunbar there is no threnody, not even distant clouds arch the sky. Hope and joy are the dominant notes of his song. No poet more effectively warms the cold side of our life and sends sunshine into grief-stricken souls than he. He laughs sorrow away; he takes us into the huts of the lowly and oppressed. There we find, amidst poverty and illiteracy, unfeigned contentment and true happiness; a smile is on every face, and hope displays her brightest gifts. No matter how sorrowful, who can read without considerable emotion **"When de Co'n Pone's Hot," "The Colored Band," "The Visitor," "The Old Front Gate," "De Way Tings Come,"** and **"Philosophy."**

But not all his poetry bubbles with fun, at times he is a serious poet, and appeals strongly to the serious side of life, as does his **"Weltschmertz."** It is full of tender sympathy; it touches chords which vibrate throughout the poles of our nature; he makes us feel that he takes our sorrows and makes them his own, and helps us to bear up when burdened with woe. **"The Fount of Tears," "Life's Tragedy," "The Haunted Oak,"** and the fifth lyric of **"Love and Sorrow"** reveal a high order of poetical genius; he reaches the deepest spiritual recesses of our being. (pp. 256-57)

I prefer **"The Rugged Way"** to Lowell's "After the Burial." **"The Unsung Heroes"** has all the imagination and pathos of Bryant's "Marion's Men;" **"The Black Sampson of Brandywine"** will live as long as his "African Chief." Read Bryant's and Dunbar's **"Lincoln"**—the black poet does not suffer by comparison. I do not in the least wish to convey the impression that Dunbar is a greater poet than Bryant; they move in different parts of the poetical firmament. Each is a master in his respective sphere. As a writer of blank verse Bryant has no equal in America; and as a lyrical poet with a large vein of rich humor Dunbar is without a peer in the Western Continent. (p. 257)

> *Joseph G. Bryant, "Negro Poetry," in* The Colored American Magazine, *Vol. VIII, No. 5, May, 1905, pp. 254-57.**

CHARLES EATON BURCH   (essay date 1921)

[*Burch maintains that Dunbar's poetic forte is humorous dialect poetry, but he also finds a few of Dunbar's poems written in standard English to be worthy of attention.*]

If Paul Laurence Dunbar is to continue to have a place in American literature, it seems to be fairly well agreed that it is to be accorded to him largely because of his poetry written in the Negro dialect. While such a statement is true in the main, it does not define the range of his work. His poetry in literary English has sufficient merit to warrant attention and study; and no survey of his poetry can be considered complete which totally ignores his English verse. . . .

A few admirers of the poet's work have endeavored to establish the fact that his English verse is "pregnant with a depth of thought." To many, however, the application of this view to the greater portion of his poetry is too sweeping. It is only for a very small part of his verse in literary English that such a claim can be made. For Dunbar's lack of broad literary training prevented him from accomplishing any sustained flights in the established media of the language. (p. 469)

"**The Mystery**" and "**The Dirge**" may . . . be included in this small group of selections. . . .

Paul Dunbar was at home in dealing with rollicking humor. His dialect poems show him at his best in this field. However, his English humorous verse is interesting. One might with some justice claim that in dealing with Negro plantation life he was furnished with a wealth of humorous material. But since he had no such help in his English humorous verse, we are forced to conclude that he was of an essentially humorous nature. "**At Cheshire Cheese**" is indicative of what he was capable of doing at times. (p. 470)

Our author was on his own ground when he turned to genuine pathos. His way was not strewn with roses. The few years of domestic happiness were soon overshadowed by the loss of companionship of the one who had exerted a real influence on his life and work. And when we add to this misfortune an enfeebled body it is not difficult to account for a portion of this poetry of pathos. However, there is a danger of overstressing the influence of these circumstances on his poetry. For many poems of this character were written before these forces began to operate in his life. Among the many poems of this character his "**Ships That Pass in the Night**" is perhaps his best effort. It is truly a modest contribution to the world's literature of pathos. (pp. 470-71)

Dunbar had a true appreciation for the beauty of external nature. In our day when the poetry of nature has come into its own and can claim some of the world's greatest poets, there is a tendency to overlook the nature poetry of some of the lesser lights. . . . Dunbar, in his English verse, seldom sounded any new notes; his nature poetry generally follows the paths so well begun in the latter half of the eighteenth century. That he was capable of writing the poetry of the commonplace in nature may be determined from his treatment of Southern plantation life in his dialect poetry. Yet a few nature poems in literary English are worth mentioning. There is a touch of nature in "**The Poet and the Song.**" (p. 471)

"**The Drowsy Day**" is full of suggestions of the gloomy mood of nature. . . .

"**The Sailor's Song**" breathes something of the rugged yet fascinating life of the ocean. . . . (p. 472)

Dunbar was not only the first American Negro to gain a fairly large degree of recognition for his work in creative literature, he was also the first to give a true lyrical expression of the life of the Negro of the plantation. In examining his verse in literary English, one discovers the Dunbar who is proud of the struggles and aspirations of the "New Negro," just as truly as his dialect poetry reveals his sympathy with the lowly life of his people. He never allows any of the larger happenings of his people to pass unnoticed. Often he is found paying a tribute to the departed Negro who has labored in behalf of his people; at times he exults in the victories of the colored soldiers of America, or proudly raises a song in honor of his race. "**The Ode to Ethiopia**" is perhaps better known among the masses of the colored people of America than any other one of his English poems. (pp. 472-73)

Dunbar did not produce any great poems in literary English; however, he did add a few charming poems to the native literature. His was not the role of the great master with the mighty line. But his simple lay is so full of melody, so full of heart, that the lover of literature often leaves the major poet to spend many pleasant moments with him. (p. 473)

Charles Eaton Burch, "Dunbar's Poetry in Literary English," in The Southern Workman, *Vol. L, No. 10, October, 1921, pp. 469-73.*

JAMES WELDON JOHNSON   (essay date 1921)

[*Johnson was a newspaper editor, lawyer, U.S. consul to Nicaragua and Venezuela, and a Broadway songwriter, whose song "Lift Every Voice and Sing" was adopted as the black national anthem. Although he did not make his living as a writer, his literary accomplishments show him to be a novelist, a practitioner of conventional and experimental poetry, a literary and social critic, a historian, and an autobiographer. In addition to "Lift Every Voice and Sing," Johnson is known primarily for the novel* The Autobiography of an Ex-Colored Man (1912), *published anonymously and reissued under his name in 1927. Providing psychological insights into the mind of a black man fleeing from self-understanding, the novel is considered the principal forerunner of the works of the Harlem Renaissance. Concerned in his literary works with the black individual's self-image and role in society, Johnson was labeled an Uncle Tom by later, more militant generations for his conservative approach to social change through education and legislation. Although he did not publish many works, Johnson contributed greatly to the development of a black voice in American literature. In the following excerpt Johnson, a personal friend of Dunbar, highly praises Dunbar's examination of the psychology of black Americans but portrays him as a thwarted genius who desired recognition for his non-dialect writings.*]

Paul Laurence Dunbar stands out as the first poet from the Negro race in the United States to show a combined mastery over poetic material and poetic technique, to reveal innate literary distinction in what he wrote, and to maintain a high level of performance. He was the first to rise to a height from which he could take a perspective view of his own race. He was the first to see objectively its humor, its superstitions, its shortcomings; the first to feel sympathetically its heart-wounds, its yearnings, its aspirations, and to voice them all in a purely literary form.

Dunbar's fame rests chiefly on his poems in Negro dialect. This appraisal of him is, no doubt, fair; for in these dialect poems he not only carried his art to the highest point of perfection, but he made a contribution to American literature unlike what any one else had made, a contribution which, perhaps, no one else could have made. Of course, Negro dialect poetry was written before Dunbar wrote, most of it by white writers; but the fact stands out that Dunbar was the first to use it as a medium for the true interpretation of Negro character and psychology. And, yet, dialect poetry does not constitute the whole or even the bulk of Dunbar's work. In addition to a large number of poems of a very high order done in literary English, he was the author of four novels and several volumes of short stories.

Indeed, Dunbar did not begin his career as a writer of dialect. I may be pardoned for introducing here a bit of reminiscence. My personal friendship with Paul Dunbar began before he had achieved recognition, and continued to be close until his death. When I first met him he had published a thin volume, **"Oak and Ivy,"** which was being sold chiefly through his own efforts. **"Oak and Ivy"** showed no distinctive Negro influence, but rather the influence of James Whitcomb Riley. At this time Paul and I were together every day for several months. He talked to me a great deal about his hopes and ambitions. In these talks he revealed that he had reached a realization of the possibilities of poetry in the dialect, together with a recognition of the fact that it offered the surest way by which he could get a hearing. Often he said to me: "I've got to write dialect poetry; it's the only way I can get them to listen to me." I was with Dunbar at the beginning of what proved to be his last illness. He said to me then: "I have not grown. I am writing the same things I wrote ten years ago, and am writing them no better." His self-accusation was not fully true; he had grown, and he had gained a surer control of his art, but he had not accomplished the greater things of which he was constantly dreaming; the public had held him to the things for which it had accorded him recognition. (pp. xxxiii-xxxiv)

Dunbar was of unmixed Negro blood; so, as the greatest figure in literature which the colored race in the United States has produced, he stands as an example at once refuting and confounding those who wish to believe that whatever extraordinary ability an Aframerican shows is due to an admixture of white blood. . . .

To whom may he be compared, this boy who scribbled his early verses while he ran an elevator, whose youth was a battle against poverty, and who, in spite of almost insurmountable obstacles, rose to success? A comparison between him and Burns is not unfitting. The similarity between many phases of their lives is remarkable, and their works are not incommensurable. Burns took the strong dialect of his people and made it classic; Dunbar took the humble speech of his people and in it wrought music. (p. xxxv)

> *James Weldon Johnson, "Preface" (1921), in The Book of American Negro Poetry, edited by James Weldon Johnson (copyright 1922, 1931 by Harcourt Brace Jovanovich, Inc.; renewed 1950 by Grace Johnson; renewed 1959 by Mrs. Grace Nail Johnson; reprinted by permission of the publisher), Harcourt Brace Jovanovich, 1922, pp. vii-xlviii.**

BENJAMIN BRAWLEY (essay date 1929)

[*Along with Alain Locke and Sterling Brown, Brawley is considered one of the most influential critics of Harlem Renaissance literature. An educator, historian, and clergyman, Brawley is the author of textbooks on freshman English, English literature, and English drama for use at black universities. Most of Brawley's literary contributions are concerned with black writers and artists, and black history. In addition to writing the critical biography*

Paul Laurence Dunbar: Poet of His People, *Brawley is the editor of Dunbar's* Best Stories.]

Incomparably the foremost exponent in verse of the life and character of the Negro people has been Paul Laurence Dunbar. This gifted young poet represented perfectly the lyric and romantic quality of the race, with its moodiness, its abandon, its love of song, and its pathetic irony, and his career has been the inspiration of thousands of the young men and women whose problems he had to face, and whose aspirations he did so much to realize. (p. 64)

"Lyrics of Lowly Life" . . . introduced him to the wide reading public. This book is deservedly the poet's best known. It contained the richest work of his youth and was really never surpassed. (p. 66)

Unless his novels are considered as forming a distinct class, Dunbar's work falls naturally into three divisions: the poems in classic English, those in dialect, and the stories in prose. It was his work in the Negro dialect that was his distinct contribution to American literature. That this was not his desire may be seen from the eight lines entitled, **"The Poet,"** in which he longed for success in the singing of his "deeper notes" and spoke of his dialect as "a jingle in a broken tongue." Any criticism of Dunbar's classic English verse will have to reckon with the following poems: **"Ere Sleep Comes Down to Soothe the Weary Eyes,"** **"The Poet and His Song,"** **"Life,"** **"Promise and Fulfillment,"** **"Ships That Pass in the Night,"** and **"October."** In the pure flow of lyrical verse the poet rarely surpassed his early lines [of **"Ere Sleep Comes Down to Soothe the Weary Eyes"**]. . . . **"The Poet and his Song"** is also distinguished for its simplicity and its lyric quality. . . . (pp. 68-9)

Other pieces, no more distinguished in poetic quality, are of special biographical interest. **"Robert Gould Shaw"** was the expression of pessimism as to the Negro's future in America. **"To Louise"** was addressed to the young daughter of Dr. Tobey, who, on one occasion, when the poet was greatly depressed, in the simple way of a child cheered him by her gift of a rose. **"The Monk's Walk"** reflects the poet's thought of being a preacher. Finally, there is the swan song, **"Compensation."** (p. 71)

The dialect poems suffer by quotation, being artistic primarily as wholes. Of these, by common consent, the masterpiece is **"When Malindy Sings,"** a poem inspired by the singing of the poet's mother. Other pieces in dialect . . . have proved unusually successful, especially as readings. . . . Almost all of these poems represent the true humorist's blending of humor and pathos, and all of them exemplify the delicate and sympathetic irony of which Dunbar was such a master. As representative of the dialect verse at its best, attention might be called to a little poem that was included in the illustrated volume, **"Candle-Lightin' Time,"** but that, strangely enough, was omitted from both of the larger editions of the poems, very probably because the title, **"Lullaby,"** was used more than once by the poet. . . . (pp. 71-2)

The short stories of Dunbar would have been sufficient to make his reputation, even if he had not written his poems. One of the best technically is **"Jimsella,"** from the **"Folks from Dixie"** volume. This story exhibits the pathos of the life of unskilled Negroes in the North, and the leading of a little child. In the sureness with which it moves to its conclusion it is a beautiful work of art. **"A Family Feud"** shows the influence of an old servant in a wealthy Kentucky family. In similar vein is **"Aunt**

Tempe's Triumph.'' "The Walls of Jericho" is an exposure of the methods of a sensational preacher. Generally these stories attempt no keen satire, but only a faithful portrayal of conditions as they are, or, in most cases, as they were in ante-bellum days. Dunbar's novels are generally weaker than his short stories, though "The Sport of the Gods," because of its study of a definite phase of life, rises above the others. Nor are his occasional articles especially strong. He was eminently a lyric poet. By his graceful and beautiful verse it is that he has won a distinct place in the history of American literature.

By his genius Paul Laurence Dunbar attracted the attention of the great, the wise, and the good. His bookcase contained many autograph copies of the works of distinguished contemporaries. The similarity of his position in American literature to that of Burns in English has frequently been pointed out. In our own time he most readily invites comparison with James Whitcomb Riley. The writings of both men are distinguished by infinite tenderness and pathos. But above all worldly fame, above even the expression of a struggling people's heart, was the poet's own striving for the unattainable. There was something heroic about him withal, something that links him with Keats, or, in this latter day, with Rupert Brooke and Alan Seeger. He yearned for love, and the world rushed on; then he smiled at death and was universally loved. (pp. 73-5)

> *Benjamin Brawley, "Paul Laurence Dunbar," in his* The Negro in Literature and Art in the United States, *third edition, Duffield & Company, 1929 (and reprinted by Scholarly Press, Inc., 1972), pp. 64-75.*

VERNON LOGGINS   (essay date 1931)

[*In the following excerpt Loggins surveys Dunbar's career. The critic finds that Dunbar's short stories admirably depict the folkways of black Americans and present the pathos and pain of their position in American society. However, all of Dunbar's novels except* The Sport of the Gods *suffer because they depict white protagonists, and the melodramatic plots cannot make up for Dunbar's poor understanding of the psychology of his characters. Loggins considers Dunbar's poetry his greatest achievement and characterizes the publication of* Lyrics of Lowly Life *as "the greatest single event in the history of black American literature."*]

Dunbar's first collection of short stories, *Folks from Dixie* . . . , contains some of his most characteristic and best work as a writer of fiction. . . . Whatever unity the book as a whole has is told by the title, *Folks from Dixie;* the characters, not all of them colored, are either still in Dixie or once lived there. Two of the stories, "The Ordeal at Mt. Hope," an argument for industrial education, and "At Shaft II," an indirect plea for the Negro to stay out of labor unions, were designed for more than entertainment. The rest are pure tales. "The Colonel's Awakening," the scene of which is laid in Virginia, follows so closely [Thomas Nelson] Page's method of extracting pathos out of the portrayal of the love and devotion of a faithful Negro servant that it might fit well into *In Ole Virginia*. A similar blending of kindliness and romance and sentimentality is in "A Family Feud," a tale of ante-bellum days on two Kentucky plantations. The majority of the stories in the volume, however, show an indebtedness to [Joel Chandler] Harris rather than to Page. Dunbar's knowledge of plantation life in Kentucky probably came from his mother, who passed her childhood and early womanhood as a slave and who was throughout most of Dunbar's life his constant companion. At any rate, he had derived from some source a penetrating understanding of the primitive Negro's superstitions, religious zeal, romance, hu-

mor, and language. . . . And it was his intimate knowledge of the folk ways of Negroes which enabled Dunbar to do some of the strongest work found in his later volumes of short stories, [*The Strength of Gideon, In Old Plantation Days,* and *The Heart of Happy Hollow* . . .].

At the time of its appearance *Folks from Dixie* was by far the most artistic book of fiction which had come from an American Negro. But it was within a year superseded by Mr. Chesnutt's *The Conjure Woman*. Dunbar was certainly more skillful than Mr. Chesnutt as a recorder of dialect, and he perhaps got closer to the real heart of the plantation Negro. However, he created no such character as Uncle Julius, and he never attained Mr. Chesnutt's mastery of treating a folk tale from a subtle and intellectual point of view. Dunbar's stories appealed to the readers of such periodicals as *Lippincott's Magazine,* while Mr. Chesnutt's met the requirements of the more critical *Atlantic Monthly* public.

Among the American writers who have been unable to judge what they could and could not do Dunbar is conspicuous. In 1898, the year of *Folks from Dixie,* he published his first novel, *The Uncalled*. It was to a certain extent autobiographical, an exposition of Dunbar's own ordeal in deciding whether he ought to enter the ministry. Since he was really writing about a personal experience, one cannot help wondering why he did not put himself into the story as a colored man. The action deals with the conflict in the mind of a white youth living in a small Ohio town who feels that he should not become a preacher but who is forced by circumstances into a seminary and then into the pulpit. There is not a single Negro character in the book. As a story about whites written by a Negro it introduces us to the second type of fiction which the Negro of the period attempted. Such a type Dunbar should have painstakingly avoided. All of the bubbling spontaneity which he showed in his tales on blacks is replaced in *The Uncalled* by cheap conventional story-telling, with echoes of Dickens and the popular magazine, and with an English which is often downright faulty. The book came as a great disappointment to Dunbar's admirers. Despite its weakness, it seems to have had some commercial success, and in 1900 Dunbar published a second novel in which all of the characters are whites, *The Love of Landry*. It is a story of Easterners, all treacly sentimentalists, who think that they find the sublime beauty of reality on a Colorado ranch. It was, if that is possible, even a poorer performance than *The Uncalled*. (pp. 314-17)

Dunbar's third novel, *The Fanatics* . . . , is a more successful treatment of white types. While it is a romance of the Civil War, emphasis is not on battle scenes, but on how the struggle affects a small Ohio town which is made up of sympathizers for the South as well as for the North. There is exciting narrative from the beginning. However, interest does not become strong until the "contrabands" come pouring in from across the Ohio River with their queer songs and delightful dialect. Yet entirely too little is made of them. With the exception of a minor character, who provides an interesting climax for the ending of the tale, the Negro appears for no more than atmosphere. (p. 317)

Two of the stories in Paul Laurence Dunbar's *Folks from Dixie,* "The Ordeal at Mt. Hope" and "At Shaft II," have been pointed out as dealing with social problems. They belong to the . . . field in which the Negro novelists and short story writers between 1865 and 1900 ventured, that of fiction offering comment on the social status of the Negro, especially in relation to the white man. It was, as we might expect, the field in which the Negro was most voluminous, and, if not most pleasing, most vigorous. It was also the field in which he was most original.

In his later collections of short stories Dunbar dwelt more and more on racial problems. (p. 320)

Happy Hollow [the fictional setting of the short story collection *The Heart of Happy Hollow*] was not to Dunbar a place for nothing more than sentimental tears and spontaneous laughter. It had its serious side, its sense of wronged justice, its tragedy. In a story of an educated colored youth's ruthless disillusionment, "One Man's Fortune," included in *The Strength of Gideon,* a white lawyer is made to say:

> The sentiment of remorse and the desire for atoning which actuated so many white men to help Negroes right after the war has passed off without being replaced by that sense of plain justice which gives a black man his due, not because of, nor in spite of, but without consideration of his color.

The idea thus expressed was a guiding principle for Dunbar in writing stories on such themes as Negroes exploited by unscrupulous politicians, the economic relations existing between whites and blacks, and the effect of city life on country-bred Negroes. The deep pathos of the truth which it expresses is brought out with force in two stories on lynching, "The Tragedy at Three Corners," in *The Strength of Gideon,* and "The Lynching of Jube Benson," in *The Heart of Happy Hollow.*

But Dunbar's most complete and profound study of the true reality of Happy Hollow came in his fourth and last novel, *The Sport of the Gods.* . . . It is at the same time his most interesting and most imperfect novel. The title hints that Dunbar might have been reading Thomas Hardy, and the story itself more than once shows a naturalistic view of life. (p. 321)

The tragedy is attributed not so much to the wiles of the city as to the ignorant Negro's helplessness when in the clutches of circumstance aggravated by an unfair social system. The novel is structurally about as bad as it could be. A half happy ending is dragged in, and no temptation to submit to melodrama is resisted. Plausibility is in many situations strained to the shattering point. The style is nervous and uneven, typical of that which one might expect from the mind of a man who is suffering from tuberculosis. But there are many patches which are intense, serious, and telling. The description of the first evening which the country Hamiltons spend at a Negro theatre in New York is an effective blending of the Dickensian and the bitter. The horrid tinsel of life as it is portrayed in the Banner Club is saved from the nauseating and repelling only by a grim sort of humor. . . . [An] anonymous critic at the time of Dunbar's death [referred] to *The Sport of the Gods* as a compendium of information for the average American. If it was a revelation to white America, it was a sermon to all America. Dunbar usually lost himself as an artist when he felt strongly the urge to preach, and *The Sport of the Gods* suffers extremely as a specimen of pure fiction. But with the exception of certain perfectly executed short stories, such as "**Jimsella**" in *Folks from Dixie* and "**The Finding of Zach**" in *The Strength of Gideon,* it is of all Dunbar's work in prose the book in which the modern reader would probably find greatest interest.

Dunbar's poetry . . . reveals that there was little bitterness in his nature. Moreover, he was a writer with a broad public to

please. Bold and uncompromising fiction on the Negro problem was not to be expected from him. (pp. 323-24)

The publication in 1896 of Dunbar's *Lyrics of Lowly Life* is the greatest single event in the history of American Negro literature. Dunbar incorporated into the book the best selections from his earlier volumes, *Oak and Ivy* . . . and *Majors and Minors.* . . . Although some of his short stories were thoughtfully conceived and admirably constructed, and although one of his novels, *The Sport of the Gods,* contains such material as should be an inspiration to Negro fiction writers for years to come, his verse is the work which distinguishes him as the universally recognized outstanding literary figure who had by 1900 arisen from the ranks of the American Negro. And *Lyrics of Lowly Life* is in all respects his happiest and most significant volume.

"**Ere Sleep Comes Down to Soothe the Weary Eyes,**" the poem which opens the volume, is a song of the man who sees in the "waking world a world of lies," a theme possibly inspired by Shelley, whom Dunbar counted as his favorite poet. But the book is not a lyrical arraignment of society. . . . One poem after another in the volume proves that Dunbar was a master of spontaneous melody. There is never intricacy of thought nor of imagery, but there is always the song that arouses mood. It was Shelley the melodist and not Shelley the humanitarian whom Dunbar worshipped. And he was natural and sincere enough to distinguish between thoughtful influence and slavish dependence. He came as near to Shelley in "**The Rising of the Storm**" as in any poem he wrote, but . . . he was not submitting to downright imitation. . . . Most of the pieces in *Lyrics of Lowly Life* are in Shelley's English. Many of the subjects—including definitions of life, the mysteries of love and passion, the appeal of nature, and the premonitions of death— are such as one finds often treated in the lyrics of Shelley. If the volume had contained no more, it would have been accounted merely a collection of gentle sentiments sung in pure melody, far superior, to be sure, to anything which any other American Negro poet had done, but not sufficiently strong to be considered a contribution of merit to American literature.

Fortunately, the volume contains a number of selections written in what Howells called the Negro's "own accent of our English." The dialect poems justify the term "lowly life" used in the title. The first which one comes upon is "**Accountability,**" a monologue of an old "darky" who has stolen "one ob mastah's chickens" and who tries to rationalize the morality of the deed. . . . Too infrequently, follow more poems in the language which the Negro's unguided habits fashioned out of English. The soul of the black laborer satisfied with little is expressed with a pure art in "**When de Co'n Pone's Hot.**" . . . "**When Malindy Sings,**" inspired, we are told, by the singing of the poet's mother, is another true expression of Negro character. . . . Equally expressive of the true nature of the lowly Negro are "**Discovered**" and "**A Coquette Conquered,**" humorous love poems; "**The Deserted Plantation,**" a sentimental song of reminiscence, suggestive of the mood of Thomas Nelson Page's "Marse Chan"; "**Signs of the Times,**" a pastoral of autumn; and "**The Party,**" an hilarious descriptive poem.

The dialect poems in *Lyrics of Lowly Life* made the book the artistic, as well as the popular, success which it became. They made the reputation of Dunbar. After all, the teacher who meant most to him was not Shelley, but James Whitcomb Riley. . . . His admiration for Riley led him to include in *Lyrics of Lowly Life* "**After a Visit,**" "**The Spellin' Bee,**" "**A Confidence,**" and a few other pieces written in the dialect of the middle western white farmer. Entertaining, humorous, and highly musical, they might easily be mistaken for Riley's own work. Therefore, there is little excuse for their existence. But in applying Riley's methods to the Negro, Dunbar achieved genuine originality. His strongest predecessors in the writing of Negro dialect verse, Sidney Lanier, Irwin Russell, and Joel Chandler Harris, were detached from their material; Dunbar was a part of his. His realism is better than theirs because it was inspired by sincere feeling and not by the search for novelty; his music appeals to us as more natural because we do not in any way have to associate it with white singers. His Negro dialect verse is today generally accepted as the best which has been written in America. It deserves that consideration, and will probably maintain it. For the picturesque and poetic Negro language which Dunbar knew so well is rapidly passing away; he preserved a record of it at the right time.

A type of pure English verse which Dunbar should have cultivated more intensively is represented in *Lyrics of Lowly Life* by such pieces as **"Frederick Douglass,"** undoubtedly more eloquent than any memorial poem produced by any one of Dunbar's Negro predecessors; **"The Colored Soldiers,"** a stirring tribute to the colored men who fell in the Civil War; and **"Ode to Ethiopia,"** perhaps the most significant of the poems which are not in dialect. . . . The gravest charge which can justly be brought against Dunbar as the author of *Lyrics of Lowly Life* is that he too often forgot the pledge which he made to his race in **"Ode to Ethiopia."** He was endowed by nature "to sing of Ethiopia's glory," but he crowded his first important volume with songs which have little relation to himself and none to his own people. Such songs can be estimated as no more than pretty exercises.

He was twenty-four years old when *Lyrics of Lowly Life* was published, and youthfulness might have been accepted as a reason for the shortcomings of the book. But Dunbar never fulfilled its unusual promise. . . . [Recognition] as a poet prepared the way for the attainment of an ambition which he had long cherished, that for publishing prose fiction. . . . Three volumes of verse followed *Lyrics of Lowly Life*: [*Lyrics of the Hearthside; Lyrics of Love and Laughter;* and *Lyrics of Sunshine and Shadow*]. . . . In spite of the odds which he had to fight against in writing the verse included in these volumes, no one of them falls below the standards which he set for himself in *Lyrics of Lowly Life*. Each, containing pure lyrics, occasional verses on the Negro written in straight English, and dialect poems, is similar in arrangement to the earlier volume. While his prose fiction was being printed in the popular magazines, his verse was appearing usually in such periodicals as the *Century, Harper's,* the *Outlook, Current Literature,* the *Bookman,* and the *Atlantic Monthly.* That he held himself true to the poet within him during the hectic nine years of life which were allotted him after his first great success is a sure mark of Dunbar's genius. If he had in the first place made poets of the soil, such as Burns and Riley, his exclusive masters, and if he had turned his back against popularity, his career would possibly be one of the most singular which American literature has to record.

But it is unfair criticism to expect too much of a Negro poet who lived in the United States in the days when Dunbar lived. The more one considers his work in verse, the more one wonders at his accomplishment. (pp. 344-52)

> Vernon Loggins, ''Fiction and Poetry, 1865-1900,'' *in his* The Negro Author: His Development in America to 1900 (*copyright 1931, 1959; Columbia Uni-*

versity Press; reprinted by permission of the publisher), Columbia University Press, 1931 (*and reprinted by Kennikat Press, 1964*), pp. 305-52.*

STERLING BROWN (essay date 1937)

[*Brown, a noted authority on black literary history, is also a poet, folklorist, and educator. His anthologies and criticism, along with those of his older contemporaries Alain Locke and Benjamin Brawley, are considered among the most important contributions to the understanding of black literature. Brown investigated the folk culture of black people in semirural areas of Virginia, Missouri, and Tennessee, where he taught English courses. As the literary critic for the black periodical* Opportunity *during the Harlem Renaissance, he displayed a deeper understanding of the folk sources of literature than did critics whose lives and works were centered in Harlem and in other northern cities. The poetry in his* Southern Roads *(1932) explores the complex psychology of black people in America as it illustrates the irony of their lives. Noted for his pessimistic realism, Brown is credited with beginning a new era in black poetry by departing from the artificial sentimentality of dialect poetry to discover realistic examples of black life and language. In the excerpt below, Brown contends that Dunbar's fiction failed to confront the reality of slavery and the harshness of Reconstruction life.*]

[Paul Laurence Dunbar's *In Old Plantation Days*] repeats the Thomas Nelson Page formula. Negro house servants comically ape the "quality," or intervene in lovers' quarrels, or in duels between cavaliers. One slave deceives his beloved master into believing that the good times of slavery still prevail. The planters, highbred and chivalrous, and the slaves, childish and devoted, rival each other in affection and sacrifice. These anecdotes of slavery, but a step above minstrel jokes, are all too happy for words, and too happy for truth.

The harshness of Reconstruction and of Dunbar's own time is likewise conventionally neglected in his other volumes of short stories: [*Folks From Dixie, The Strength of Gideon,* and *The Heart of Happy Hollow*]. . . . Freedmen discover that after all their best friends are their kindly ex-masters. In **"Nels Hatton's Revenge,"** an upstanding Negro gives his hard-earned money and best clothes to his destitute master, who had abused him when a slave. The venality of Reconstruction politicians, which certainly existed, is satirized; but the gains of Reconstruction, which certainly exist, are understressed. Probably with due cause, Dunbar feared the rising poor-whites; therefore, like many Negro spokesmen of the period, he idealized the ex-planter class, the "aristocrats," *without* due cause.

Dunbar's fiction veers away from anything more serious than laughter or gentle tears. **"At Shaft 11"** shows the difficulties of Negro strikebreakers; but, afraid of organized labor, Dunbar idealized owners, operators, and staunchly loyal Negro workers who get to be foremen, thus carrying over the plantation tradition formula into the industrial scene. **"The Ordeal at Mt. Hope"** faces the loose-living of a "Happy Hollow," and then is lost in sentimental compromise. Dunbar wrote two stories of lynching, **"The Lynching of Jule Benson"** and the unusually ironic **"The Tragedy at Three Corners."** But Dunbar usually places the hardships of Negro life in the city, as in **"Jimsella,"** with pastoral distrust of the city and faith in rural virtue. Fast livers, quacks, politicians and hypocritical race leaders are occasionally attacked.

The Sport of the Gods . . . , Dunbar's most ambitious novel, is the only one that is chiefly about Negroes. The first of the book is trite, but the latter section, though confused and melodramatic, has a grimness that Dunbar seldom showed. Berry, the innocent victim of a degenerate white man's crime in the South, and his family, the victim of hostile New York, are treated somewhat in the manner of Hardy's tragic laughing-stocks. The book has serious weaknesses, but it gives promise that Dunbar, but for his untimely death, might have become a prose writer of power. Judged by his accomplishment, however, Dunbar in fiction must be considered as one who followed the leader, not as a blazer of new trails. (pp. 77-8)

> Sterling Brown, "Reconstruction: The Not So Glorious South," in his The Negro in American Fiction (copyright, 1937 by The Associates in Negro Folk Education), Associates in Negro Folk Education, 1937 (and reprinted by Kennikat Press, 1968), pp. 64-83.*

STERLING BROWN (essay date 1937)

[*In the following survey of Dunbar's dialect poetry, Brown dismisses Dunbar's vision of the black experience in nineteenth-century America as highly unrealistic.*]

Dunbar was not only the first American Negro to "feel the Negro life aesthetically and express it lyrically," as William Dean Howells wrote [see excerpt above], but also the first American poet to handle Negro folk-life with any degree of fullness. As a portrayal of Negro life, Dunbar's picture has undoubted limitations, but they are by no means so grave as those of [Irwin] Russell and [Thomas Nelson] Page.

Writing in the heyday of the dialect vogue, Dunbar . . . could not completely escape the influences of these two writers, but the shadow of Page, much the lesser poet, fell more darkly upon him. Almost all of Dunbar's poetry about slavery is of the Page school, some of it directly copied. Old slaves grieve over the lost days, insisting upon the kindliness of old master and mistress, and the boundless mutual affection. Treated approvingly, they grieve that the freedmen deserted the plantation, or wish to die so that they can get to heaven to continue serving old master. . . . The master is generally pictured as "smiling on de darkies from de hall," or listening to the corn-song from his veranda with a tear in his eye. In *Parted*, a slave, separated from his beloved, knows that he will come back to her, . . . which seems to be a cruel misreading of history. The very few other poems that admit the distresses of slavery, forget them in memories of cabin dances. **"When Dey Listed Colored Soldiers"** shows Negroes fighting for their own freedom, but love for the gray-clad masters is expressed as well.

These unworthy perpetuations of plantation sentimentalities are fortunately not what Dunbar is known by. He is at his best in his picture of the folk life of his day. He did not know the deep South, but, a willing listener to his mother, an ex-slave, he probably got a good background of folk lore and speech, and he knew small Negro communities of Ohio, Kentucky, Eastern Shore Maryland and the District of Columbia. . . . His fancy is caught by the parties, spelling bees, church services, by nodding and drowsing in front of the hickory fire, by ripened cider ready to be drunk while the back log is slowly burning through. He deals with charming rural love-affairs, from which the bitterness and disillusion of his personal love poetry are noticeably lacking. Farmers brag of an old mare, or welcome the rain so that they can tinker 'round mending harness, or, like Tam O'Shanter, return a bit worse for drink to irate spouses, and lay the blame for the slowness on old Suke, the nag. For these people Dunbar conveys his friendship warmly. Like

Longfellow and Field he does many of his best poems about children (**"Candle-Lighting Time," "Little Brown Baby," "Turning the Children in Bed"**). The slugabed scamp, Lias, is rightly popular with both children and vexed parents.

Though he has written that "it's mighty hard to giggle when dey's nuffin' in de pot," he barely mentions dire poverty. . . . He writes of the countryman's delight in good food, of "wheat bread white ez cotton an' a egg pone jes' like gol' "; of hog jowl, roasted shoat, and all the partitions of the hog; of chickens, turkeys, sweet potato stew, mince pies. One of his poems on possums is a rhymed cooking recipe; one of his less worthy pieces tells of a backwoods suitor winning a wife with a possum. He has a fondness for poetry about hunting and fishing, and the festal seasons of Thanksgiving and Christmas. He is definitely a poet of the happy hearthside and pastoral contentment. Poems that do not show the pleasant life are few. **"Blue"** suggests a vaguely understood melancholy, poems like **"Two Little Boots,"** with the touching quality of Eugene Field's "Little Boy Blue," express the grief of stricken parents, and **"A Christmas Song"** makes use of the folk-saying that a green Christmas means "a hongry churchyard." But explicit revelation of the folk Negro's hardships is absent.

Dunbar's best qualities are clear. Such early poems as **"Accountability"** and **"An Antebellum Sermon"** show flashes of the unforced gay humor that was to be with him even to the last. With a few well-turned folk phrases he calls up a scene as in **"Song of Summer."** . . . Except when unexplainably urged to write Irish dialect or imitate Riley's "Orphant Annie," or to cross misspelling with moralizing as in **"Keep A Pluggin' Away,"** his grasp upon folk-speech is generally sure. His rhythms almost never stumble and are frequently catchy: at times as in **"Itching Heels"** he gets the syncopation of a folk dance. Most of all he took up the Negro peasant as a clown, and made him a likeable person.

Unlike Irwin Russell, whose views of Negro life and character are those of an outsider on a different plane, Dunbar, writing more from within, humanizes his characters and gets more of their true life. There is still, however, a great deal omitted. His picture is undoubtedly idealized. Believing with the romanticists that "God made the country and man made the town," . . . he left out many of the more unpleasant aspects of life. His backsliders are guilty only of such "sins" as dancing after joining church, or of comic fisticuffs. More serious is his omission of the hardships that the Negro folk met with as much in Dunbar's day as in ours. Reasons for such omission may have been Dunbar's own kindheartedness and forgivingness, or his lack of deep acquaintance with the South. Or it may have been the influence of his literary school, his audience and his publishers, or of the professional conciliators who in that day guided racial expression. Be the reason what it may, one of these or all, the fact of omission remains. Dunbar concentrated upon a pastoral picture. No picture of Negro life that is only pastoral can be fully true. (pp. 32-6)

> Sterling Brown, "Dunbar and Traditional Dialect," in his Negro Poetry and Drama (copyright 1937 by The Associates in Negro Folk Education), Associates in Negro Folk Education, 1937 (and reprinted in his Negro Poetry and Drama and The Negro in American Fiction, Atheneum, 1972, pp. 32-44).

VICTOR LAWSON (essay date 1941)

[*Lawson examines Dunbar's short stories and novels, concluding "Dunbar's prose adds up to four volumes of weak short stories,*]

*usually in the plantation tradition, and four novels, none of which
is good enough to be called 'second-rate'."*]

To understand the picture of life among Negroes given by
Dunbar's short stories, we have but to see how he—softened . . . whatever may have been evil; enlarged the scale of
life, increased proportionately the colors, showed gentlemen
perfected in courtly grace, gay girls in loveliness, and slaves
in immeasurable devotion. And, we might add, life of Negroes
in the North was maladjusted, full of longing for the old South,
with no greater woes than those that might be encompassed by
a brief range of genteel laughter and tears. (p. 82)

The most clearly and truly plantation tradition characters in
Dunbar's short stories were, white: the genial, kindly overlord,
the dashing belles and duelling cavaliers, and the unkind, un-
gentlemanly, and at least in the spirit of the thing un-southern
overseers; and colored: mammy, *the proprietary;* and slave,
the contented. There were characterizations in other trends
among the whites: a scheming master educating a slave for his
own gain and fuming when the slave makes his escape, or a
doty septuagenarian or bereft belle stranded by a receding tidal
wave of war—but the latter two are of the tradition, and the
former is an exceptional character who seldom appears. Characterizations other than those named among Negroes, however,
were more than exceptions. Affectionate wives and husbands,
brothers loyal to each other, self-respecting church workers
appeared so frequently in Dunbar's stories of plantation life as
to constitute a strain of mild common man, sentimental, "genteel," but sympathetic portraiture running through the special
pleading for the South. Unfortunately the sympathetic portraiture often ceases to be *that* and becomes truckling burlesque. The ministers, as much in Parker, spiritual middle-man
of the Mordaunt plantation who appears in several stories of
Old Plantation Days, as in those who appear in but one story,
are quaint, funny people to a great extent rather than powerful
uneducated men, purveyors of saving or betraying opiates
(evaluated in relation to times and needs) that more thoughtful
and frank commentators have made them.

The Negro characters *off* the plantation were human enough in
their genteel way, their humanity being betrayed by the great
loyalty to the South which militated against their own interest.
(pp. 87-8)

Dunbar's short stories deal with Negroes on plantations, and
in keeping with the plantation tradition his Negroes were proprietary, bossy and well-loved mammies, loyal slaves, comical
or at least strangely unhampered banjo twaddlers and preachers.
A few instances of well-placed loyalty or affection and a general tendency to make Negroes human, if piquant in fiction,
shows a drawing away from some elements of the plantation
tradition. It is noteworthy that the brute Negro, a favorite with
some southern propagandists, was absent from Dunbar's short
stories, but it is unfortunate that other elements in his work
make this absence one to be commented upon.

The proprietary mammy "bossing the whole household
round . . ." comfortably established with special privileges,
belongs to the plantation tradition, and with it, to Dunbar.
(p. 97)

The familial pride of the proprietary mammy continued with
freedom. Even when Mima was forced to sell "the old place"
to a northerner, Mammy Peggy forced her to conceal her poverty and distress from the stranger. Only when Northcope revealed himself as Mima's brother's friend was the Mammy's
pride appeased.

Such was the proprietary mammy. The master owned the plantation, but the slave nearly owned the master. Here was the
blown up aura of plantation kindliness. . . .

Akin to the proprietary mammy was the contented slave. . . .
He was so proud he didn't want to be free. Most loyal to his
master of all the slaves in Dunbar's stories is Gideon, the hero
of the title story in *The Strength of Gideon.* He was the perfect
example of that loyalty which militated against the slaves'
better interests, referred to in *The Fanatics.* (p. 100)

"Nelse Hatton's Vengeance" turns out to be the vendetta of
those who will inherit the earth. Hatton certainly must have
had cheek, for, when pressed, he turned the other. In this story
of an ex-slave's meeting with his former master, many years
after the Civil War, and his kindnesses to the former master
after a moment of passionately angry remembrances, Dunbar
fails fully to develop either by direct analysis or ample suggestion the dramatic possibilities—the servant's and master's
recognitions, the master's possible fear, the servant's probable
anger, the inner debates of the former slave—and hence fails
to write the gripping story some one might do; not necessarily
a melodramatic one, but perhaps one simply pathetic. . . .
(p. 104)

Most unpardonable is Dunbar's burlesquing of the ministry,
which group often expressed in sheer poetry the faith that made
the black man whole in a world he could call only in small
part his own. Brother Parker, the Negro minister of the Mordaunt plantation, who filled a role of ignoble lackey similar to
that of rural clergymen in eighteenth century England, was the
butt of several of Dunbar's joke-book stories. Off to tend the
sick, Brother Parker falls in a puddle and ruins his trousers.
He borrows a pair at the home of a sick woman, continues to
church, delivers his sermon, and is embarrassed when a pair
of cards falls from his pocket. The owner of the pants appears
in time to clear Parker of the sin implied by the cards. (pp.
104-05)

Other stories, **"The Trial Sermons on Bull-Skin"** and **"Mt.
Pisgah's Christmas Possum,"** are sad attempts at humour treating with buffoonery the groups which gave the world very
great music, perhaps greater than that of any other religious
group but the Catholics. When the religious thinker, Dunbar
of *The Uncalled* and **"Weltschmerz,"** conceived of the "Psalmist and his brethren sitting at a 'possum feast with the con-
gregation of a rival church looking enviously on" he was sac-
rilegious; he made a mockery of a faith of which he could see
the beauty very clearly.

Following into the rialto of the half-world such writers as Poe
and Twain, Dunbar did several stories on diddling. His accounts of investment companies in which one man was the
company suggest the character of business as it is among Negroes, though Dunbar is Amos 'n' Andy rather than middle-
class crisis in his tendencies. There are amusing stories of
conjuring and courtship, in which the Negroes' "credulity"
and "mawkishness" are paraded, but in which understanding
is lacking on the part of the author. Such stories are **"Dandy
Jim's Conjur Scare," "The Conjuring Contest,"** and **"The
Deliberation of Mr. Dunkin."** Dunbar's humour in these stories is on the side of minstrel joking. Dunbar's works "created
a vogue" as one writer says. But there was waiting for them
an audience which wished to welcome a quaint and curious
black man whom it would not have to call "mister." To this
audience Dunbar was a friend.

Dunbar wrote a few stories which broke with the plantation
tradition and pseudo-gentility. Sometimes in stories truly of

the tradition he introduced the unusual (that is, the generally true). Sometimes he made complete departures from mythic apology in writing of the South. Sometimes he wrote of the North without regret for the melon-patch or ire at the sinful city. In **"The Memory of Martha"** the human affection of Uncle Ben for his wife transforms the first impression one has when he reads that Ben was an excellent banjoist. . . . Uncle Ben stops playing when his wife dies. He takes up his banjo once more, several years later, to please his master and guests. Ending with the hymn "Hark! From the Tomb," which he played when Martha died, he himself dies. The brother-love of Jim and Joe, shown by Jim's stealing of food to feed his brother, who fled rather than be *given* (traditionally, he is not sold) to Mr. Groby (who is not quite a gentleman) and Jim's return from hiding to save Joe from a beating, command respect. **"The Wisdom of Silence,"** a very traditional story in which the master proves the freed Negro's best friend, saving him from loan sharks, admits the picture of a prosperous, talkative Negro being burned out by envious whites. Marred by "gentility" but untouched by plantation tradition is **"Viney's Free Papers,"** which tells of Ben's struggles to buy freedom for himself and his wife. Viney, the first to become free, plans to go North leaving her husband a slave, but is gripped by a gratuitous last minute repentance which rings with a hollow sound. (pp. 107-09)

Dunbar depicted the colored college graduate, the politician, the sincere and sometimes thoughtful preacher in a few stories. He showed the sparsity of positions for educated Negroes. At least once, in **"A Council of State"** as well as in a few lines of **"The Fanatics"** he touched the taboo subject of color discrimination within the Negro group. He showed by what indirect routes and spurious appeals the Negro vote was corralled. Stories such as these had factual accuracy.

The favorite stories of Dunbar, telling of happy days, hot-blooded duels, warm romance, regret in the North for happiness in the South, despite the occasional exceptional stories . . . , placed his work in the plantation tradition. Lacking in bare actualness, the stories also were not even clever. The stock Negro characters probably existed in kind, if not degree, but they were not the only, or the main, or the most profound characters to be found in Negro life. (pp. 115-16)

Dunbar's novels, like the short stories, were fourth-rate. They do not contain the distorted picture of Negro life which makes possible protracted, if unfavorable, criticism. But the ideas around which the stories center, partially conventional, reflect the author's ability to think independently and coherently. Literary history in a restricted sense would be interested more in the novels for completeness than for merit, but a biographer would have to consider a real religious and philosophic basis of tolerance, disconcertingly but patently distinct from Dunbar's Pollyanna optimism, revealed in the novels. The ideas expressed may not have been Dunbar's. He must have been able to grasp them, however. (p. 124)

The story [**The Uncalled**] might have been set in another town, or among Negroes rather than whites, without great change. Out of the character of strict Methodist orthodoxy, however, arises the psychological conflict which could have taken place in another town, or with Negro Methodists, but which could not have taken place without the straightjacket which Methodist orthodoxy appears as in the story.

The main characters, united in family and outward love, but bitterly opposed in outlook on life, are clearly drawn, Miss

Prime's narrowness being *her's,* and not palpably that of an author who could conceive character only narrowly. Freddie Brent's rebellion, sublimated into the protest of a religious radical, results in revelation of shifting character, expressed in prose that is, in a few paragraphs, quite excellent. (p. 125)

The Uncalled is amateurish and trite in some places. The characterization of Freddie as a child is episodic, and the episodes are overworked. Freddie's arrival on a river bank to rescue his minister's daughter twenty yards ahead of everyone else is no mean feat. The coincidence by which Freddie meets his long absent, drunken, and reformed father is a possible improbability.

Yet these early incidents prepare the way for better-written climaxes. . . . *The Uncalled* is weakly told in many parts. Yet a few passages . . . reveal Dunbar as one not incapable of excellent prose or intense, independent thoughts. In essence, it is the romantic tale of Nature *versus* Art.

The Love of Landry is trivial. Unlike **The Uncalled,** it is not redeemed at all by powerful passages towards the end, or anywhere else. Dunbar wrote the book for his own amusement, using a Colorado setting which he knew, to some extent, from a visit. (pp. 126-27)

As in **The Uncalled,** the lines giving thoughts expressed by a leading character come closest to able writing.

The Fanatics tells a story of strained ties and family loyalty tested and re-examined under pressure of the State to side with it against all public enemies. . . . [The] "message" of the novel becomes: "The ideals of brotherhood and love are more to be followed than demands of the State." The shattering of these ideals is a greater catastrophe than defeat, and the approbation of the ideals among the enemy is greater than victory. This is the theme of *Antigone,* and while **The Fanatics** is not even a middling-good novel, Dunbar's development of the theme, presupposing a previous self-clarification, adds another hint of independent reflection already glimpsed in a few poems, and from time to time in the prose. (pp. 127-28)

The Sport of the Gods, in which Dunbar wrote of Negroes as main characters but broke with the "plantation tradition," is naturalistic. Dunbar need not have had any more definite idea of social protest than Hardy in this story of a world in which all must end ill. Nevertheless the story debunks southern "gentility." But the mishaps of Berry Hamilton's family, however Hardyan, are too close to the evils which cropped up in Dunbar's short stories of the romantic sinful town to prove he had gotten free of the old pattern entirely. (p. 130)

The novel, however much of the romantic sinful town it retained, however much it may have been a mere exercise in naturalism, gave a warranted rebuff to "that strange, ridiculous something we misname Southern honour, that honour which strains at a gnat and swallows a camel . . ."

Dunbar's prose adds up to four volumes of weak short stories, usually in the "plantation tradition," and four novels, none of which is good enough to be called "second-rate." Three of the novels are about white characters mainly. While it may be argued it was better to write about whites than to malign Negro character as in most of the short stories, that three out of twelve or more books is a small number for a Negro on whites, that the people of **The Uncalled** could have been made Negro by adding a word here and there, since their significant characteristic was Methodism of which Negroes could have partaken—yet Dunbar was not the great spokesman of the aspirations of Negroes he has often been called, and in spite of the apology for his defection contained in *The Fanatics* the novels are unfortunately in the direction of his shallow optimism with regard to race relations, and his repudiation of a praiseworthy canon of realists of his time: write the truth. (pp. 131-32)

> *Victor Lawson, in his* Dunbar Critically Examined *(originally a thesis presented at Howard University in 1941; copyright, 1941 by the Associated Publishers, Inc.), Associated Publishers, 1941, 151 p.*

J. SAUNDERS REDDING (essay date 1949)

[*Redding is a distinguished critic, historian, novelist, and autobiographer. His first book,* To Make a Poet Black *(1939), is a scholarly appraisal of black poetry that includes a historical survey as well as biographical information about individual poets. As one of the first anthologies of its type to be authored by a black critic, this book is considered a landmark in criticism of black writers. Redding's fiction and histories can be both educational and disturbing.* They Came in Chains: American from Africa *(1950) traces the history of black people in America without the over-emotionalism evident in other such histories by black scholars. Written in a fluid style, it has been called a creative story as opposed to a dry catalogue of historical facts. As the editor of anthologies and histories that include* Cavalcade: Negro American Writing from 1760 to the Present *(1971), Redding has made innovative contributions regarded by some as essential to a total picture of American literature. In the following excerpt, he discusses Dunbar as a writer who pandered to white racists' conceptions of black Americans.*]

There is this about literature by American Negroes—it has uncommon resilience. Three times within this century it has been done nearly to death: once by indifference, once by opposition, and once by the unbounded enthusiasm of its well-meaning friends. (p. 137)

[Indifference] had threatened even before the turn of the century. Dunbar felt it, and the purest stream of his lyricism was made bitter and all but choked by it. Yearning for the recognition of his talent as it expressed itself in the pure English medium, he had to content himself with a kindly, but condescending praise of his dialect pieces. Time and again he voiced the sense of frustration brought on by the neglect of what he undoubtedly considered his best work. Writing dialect, he told James Weldon Johnson, was "the only way he could get them to listen to him." His literary friend and sponsor, William D. Howells, at that time probably the most influential critic in America, passing over Dunbar's verse in pure English with only a glance, urged him to write "of his own race in its own accents of our English" [see *TCLC*, Vol. 2]. (pp. 137-38)

Enough has been said about the false concepts, the stereotypes which were effective—and to some extent are still effective—in white America's thinking about the Negro for the point not to be labored here. History first, and then years of insidious labor to perpetuate what history had wrought, created these stereotypes. According to them, the Negro was a buffoon, a harmless child of nature, a dangerous despoiler (the concepts were contradictory), an irresponsible beast of devilish cunning—soulless, ambitionless and depraved. The Negro, in short, was a higher species of some creature that was not quite man. (p. 138)

There can be no question as to the power of the traditional concepts. The Negro writer reacted to them in one of two ways. Either he bowed down to them, writing such stories as would do them no violence; or he went to the opposite extreme and

wrote for the purpose of invalidating, or at least denying, the tradition. Dunbar did the former. Excepting only a few, his short stories depict Negro characters as whimsical, simple, folksy, not-too-bright souls, all of whose social problems are little ones, and all of whose emotional cares can be solved by the intellectual or spiritual equivalent of a stick of red peppermint candy. It is of course significant that three of his four novels are not about Negroes at all; and the irony of depicting himself as a white youth in his spiritual autobiography, *The Uncalled,* needs no comment. (p. 139)

> *J. Saunders Redding, "American Negro Literature," in* The American Scholar *(copyright © 1949, copyright renewed © 1976, by the United Chapters of Phi Beta Kappa; by permission of the publishers, the United Chapters of Phi Beta Kappa), Vol. 18, No. 2, Spring, 1949, pp. 137-48.**

EUGENE ARDEN (essay date 1959)

[*Arden discusses* The Sport of the Gods *as a forerunner of the novels of the Harlem Renaissance.*]

The Harlem novel has . . . come of age. The setting now lends itself to good and bad fiction, to delicate psychological exploration or to social propaganda, and addresses itself both to special readership and to the general public.

I propose to look back, however, and describe something of the beginning of Harlem fiction, and to remind the reader of a nearly-forgotten but nearly-great novel which was the forerunner of the whole school. The novel I speak of is Paul Laurence Dunbar's *The Sport of the Gods* . . . , the first novel to treat Negro life in New York seriously and at length.

A naturalistic novel, *The Sport of the Gods* embodies something of the "plantation-school concept," which implies that the Negro becomes homesick and demoralized in the urban North. The inexperienced youths in this novel, Joe and Kitty Hamilton, migrate from the South to a treacherous New York environment which deterministically produces their degeneration and disaster. . . . (p. 25)

The attitude of the Hamiltons toward New York and their experiences in the city follow a familiar pattern, reminiscent of all "evil city" folklore. In *The Sport of the Gods,* New York at first represents a promised land of freedom, where the protagonists expect to shed their troubles and start a fresh happy life. . . . But fate in this naturalistic novel is inexorable, and the forces of the city, so alluring and yet so disastrous to the inexperienced, quickly demoralize Joe and then his sister Kitty. A visit to the Banner Club—"a social cesspool"—starts Joe's decline, and a place in the chorus starts Kitty on a life which includes "experiences" obviously leading to no good end for her.

At the time Dunbar wrote this novel, there was not yet a Harlem as we know it today. Just after the turn of the century, most of New York's Negroes lived in cramped quarters near the Pennsylvania Railroad Station (the region to which the Hamilton family went on arrival), or else wedged in amongst the Irish on San Juan Hill. Another colony existed on West 53rd Street, but the Negroes there were mainly stage folk, musicians, and journalists—and even there the over-crowding was notorious. (p. 26)

In fiction, Carl Van Vechten was the first to capitalize successfully on the new, swarming Harlem [of the 1920s], though he and his imitators were really following the lead of Dunbar in treating the comparatively unworked scenes of Harlem low-life. Indeed, Van Vechten expressed the indebtedness of his *Nigger Heaven* (1926) to Dunbar's *The Sport of the Gods* by writing that Dunbar

> described the plight of a young outsider who comes to the larger New York Negro world to make his fortune, but who falls a victim to the sordid snares of that world, a theme I elaborated in 1926 to fit a newer and much more intricate social system.

That ''intricate social system,'' however, gets lost in the sensationalism of *Nigger Heaven,* which paints Harlem with too obvious a gusto. (p. 27)

Perhaps the most important thing to say about the Harlem novel is the most obvious: a new character in American fiction was created. Just as the plantation Negro was typical of Nineteenth Century fiction, so in our own day the prototype was the Negro in an urban, industrial environment. There he was confronted with new pressures evolving from a new *mise en scène* and a set of social imperatives different from those which had once dominated his tradition. (p. 31)

> Eugene Arden, ''The Early Harlem Novel,'' in PHY-LON: The Atlanta University Review of Race and Culture, *Vol. 20 (copyright, 1959, by Atlanta University; reprinted by permission of* PHYLON*),* Vol. XX, No. 1, First Quarter *(March, 1959), pp. 25-31.*

JEAN WAGNER   (essay date 1963)

[*A French author and critic, Wagner has written on the works of black and Southern writers of the United States, with a particular interest in the fiction of Flannery O'Connor. A student of American slang and dialects, Wagner is the author of the doctoral dissertation* Black Poets of the United States *(1963). Translated into English in 1973, this book is regarded as one of the most authoritative and innovative tools available for the study of black American poets and poetry. In the following excerpt from that work, Wagner studies Dunbar's poetry and discusses his attitudes and vision as revealed in his poems, providing explanations for many common misunderstandings regarding Dunbar and his work.*]

Paul Laurence Dunbar is probably the black poet it is most difficult to evaluate fairly, and one has a strange but inevitable feeling of embarrassment in turning to him. Even after the lapse of half a century, his contradictions and his complexity have yet to lose their disconcerting quality.

''Ambiguous'' is the word that spontaneously occurs to anyone who sets out to characterize him, and the adjective does sum up the man and his work. Ambiguous, to begin with, is his popularity with whites and blacks alike; ambiguous, too, is this southern-style poetry written by a black man from the North a quarter-century after Emancipation; ambiguous, finally, is the destiny which decreed that he should pass into posterity, in spite of all, as a poet of his people.

But to be born black, and a poet, in the United States in 1872— was that not ambiguous at the outset? (p. 73)

Dunbar runs the gamut of . . . backward-looking optimism, from mere praise of the good old days to the actual hymning of the Old South. . . . [It] is important that we know to what degree it may be inferred that Dunbar had adopted a certain philosophy of history—important since he is in fact no neutral or foreign observer who takes a stand before certain historical

facts in which he had no direct involvement. To the contrary, Dunbar is the son of former slaves who had felt slavery's yoke; yet he is willing to use the same colors as did his former masters to depict conditions in the Old South.

Following in the footsteps of Stephen Foster and Thomas Nelson Page, Dunbar does indeed offer us, for the most part, pleasing views of the old plantation. The masters are kind, the slaves are happy and filled with devotion, and as they give expression to their reciprocally tender feelings, they both feel how the tears spring to their eyes.

''A Corn Song'' is the very embodiment of such traditional stereotypes. The master is sitting on the big white veranda, which is bathed in the warm light of the setting sun; in the distance one can hear the song of the slaves as they return from the corn fields, physically weary but light of heart and holding their heads high. The inevitable tear falls in the final stanza. . . . (pp. 80-1)

Dunbar has a special liking for happy domestic scenes in which, after a day of strenuous labor, the slave who has no quarrel with his lot idealizes men and their srroundings. Thus the couple in **''Chrismus Is A-Comin''** bend adoringly over their child and find him more handsome than any of the master's children. . . . (p. 82)

To do Dunbar justice, however, it must be noted that on occasion he does offer us brief glimpses of the miseries of slavery which the plantation literature had totally ignored. But they are only glimpses, and their effect is rapidly eliminated by the resurgence of optimism.

Typical in this respect is **''Parted,''** the lament of a slave who has been separated from his beloved because his master has just sold him and a boat is taking him deeper into the South. To appreciate Dunbar's handling of this theme, one must bear in mind the terror that the threat of being ''sold down the river'' aroused in a slave, for this was the direst punishment that could be inflicted on the insubordinate. But the slave of **''Parted''** goes off almost light-hearted, confident that God, who can read lovers' hearts, will one day bring them together again. . . . (pp. 82-3)

To see things in this way is, as Sterling Brown discerningly remarked in his consideration of this poem, ''a cruel misreading of history'' [see excerpt above].

Less grave is the separation suffered by Samuel in **''When Sam'l Sings.''** His wife works on a plantation twenty miles away, and he returns gay as a lark every time he has been able to visit her. (p. 83)

But to the poet's credit is a certain integrity in his presentation of the subject. This sets him off markedly from the plantation school and is something that, to the best of our knowledge, has not hitherto been stressed. For, in the first two stanzas of [**''The Old Cabin''**], Dunbar actually indicates in the clearest possible way just what the function of memory is: spontaneously suppressing the evil recollections, while hastening to dredge to the surface only the happiest images. In this way he appears to be saying, as though to defend himself in advance, that *he* cannot be accused of having kept silent about the horrors of slavery; that, on the contrary, his poems are extraordinarily faithful renderings of the psychology of the former slave, who has a natural tendency to forgive and forget. Nor does it seem to us that there is any bad faith in Dunbar's implicit defense. Yet it cannot be denied—and here, in spite of everything, the poet may deserve reproof—that the reader takes away with him a much stronger impression of the agreeable recollections, since the others occupy no more than one of the six stanzas in the poem. (p. 85)

As for **"Speakin' o' Christmas,"** a poem more in the manner of Riley than of Page, it looks back longingly on the old-time Christmas for the reasons that always lend glamour to times past, while **"Long Ago,"** more or less in the same vein, has a certain relationship with the spirit of "Auld Lang Syne."

On the basis of this, it might seem that Dunbar had simply borrowed from the literature of his own day, especially from Riley, the general notion that the good old days were preferable to the present. He perhaps fused this nostalgia with an idealized picture of the plantation borrowed from the Page school, which also expressed much the same nostalgia, though for reasons of its own. In addition, . . . Dunbar tended to tone down the more outrageous features of the plantation school's portrait, particularly by inserting brief evocations of slavery's abominations.

Unfortunately, there are other poems whose topic is not the antebellum plantation but the post-Emancipation one. Here Dunbar, in a way that is astonishing for a man of his race, espouses the southern ideology as we have seen it expressed in *Befo' de War* by Page and Gordon.

The most equivocal poem in this group is undoubtedly **"When Dey 'Listed Colored Soldiers."** The blue uniform of the North and the grey uniform of the South are juxtaposed, without its being entirely clear that the poet's sympathies are not extended to both. The happenings evoked by the young Negro woman in the poem occurred during the Civil War, after the Emancipation Proclamation, on a plantation situated in territory already occupied by the northern armies. She recalls the grief she felt at the imminent separation when 'Lias, her beloved, came to tell her that he was leaving to fight on the northern side. At first she would have wished to stop him, but how could she not approve his decision to earn his newly granted liberty on the battlefield? And she felt proud of him, standing so strong and so handsome in his splendid blue uniform with its shiny buttons!

Her two masters, father and son, had already left for war, wearing grey uniforms, of course; seeing her mistresses cry at the news of their death, she had cried also. Then she was told that her 'Lias, too, had fallen somewhere in the South.

One cannot fail to see that Dunbar has chosen a highly delicate topic, since he lets his young freed girl shed the selfsame tears for her masters and her 'Lias, whose status in life and whose loyalties were in conflict, without making any mention of the personal affection she might have felt for any of them. Here Dunbar is dancing on a tightrope, and he sheds a revealing light on the art of compromise he had to practice to avoid angering either of his two publics, the black or the white. The reader can but lament his embarrassment. (pp. 85-6)

The scene evoked by **"Chrismus on the Plantation"** is a dreary Christmas Eve. On that day the old master, impoverished by the war, calls together the freedmen he has been paying since the Emancipation and informs them that he is ruined. He is forced to sell the plantation, and it breaks his heart that he must dismiss them. The former slaves shed tears, and in the master's eye too a tear glistens.

At this moment Ben steps forward to speak in the name of them all. Does their master, he asks, think they have no gratitude? Now that he is poor, are they going to forget all his past kindness? If that is the effect liberty has, well, let Mr.

Lincoln take back "his" liberty! Come what may, they will never abandon their master, and even if he cannot pay them, the strength of their arms will still be able to obtain from the old plantation everything they need to support everyone. . . . (p. 88)

This apologia for the plantation . . . verges on a neighboring theme which may also serve to throw some light upon it. We refer to a certain longing for the South that finds expression even in Dunbar's earliest poems. The two themes cannot always be readily distinguished and are sometimes presented together, as we have seen with the longing for the plantation and longing for the days gone by. Nevertheless, they are markedly different in character. In the case of the plantation, the basis is the comparison drawn between past and present, while longing for the South springs from the opposition, sometimes only implicit but always undeniable, of North and South and extends beyond that to contrast urban and rural existence. This last aspect . . . allows the theme to emerge from the purely ideological character it had, when connected with the plantation, and to acquire a certain documentary value concerning the psychology of the freedman who heads for the North.

This is the very context of **"Goin' Back,"** which takes the form of a monologue in which a freedman, who has gone to live in a northern town after the Emancipation, explains how his homesickness, after thirty years' absence, is now taking him back to his native Kentucky. (pp. 88-9)

This longing for the South seems to have had a more down-to-earth validity in some other poems, where it occurs together with the expression of hostility for the city. The objection might be raised that this feeling, far from being a mark of realism, is on the contrary pulled right out of the romantics' stock in trade. Yet this is not entirely the case, for the loathing of the city felt by the mass of those freedmen who had settled in the North, like the hero of **"Goin' Back,"** must be interpreted in the first place as the expression of their disillusionment in contact with city life, and as a symptom of their difficulty in adapting to urban conditions. As a corollary, their longing for the South indicates no desire for romantic escapism or for a return to nature; it is simply a commonsense reaction in favor of a livelihood less painfully gained and better remunerated.

In Dunbar's own case, his dislike of the city is also, assuredly, the reaction of the tuberculosis victim against the city's noise and pollution. . . . [It] may be added that this anti-city bias borrows its forms of expression from the romantics. (pp. 90-1)

One may legitimately wonder how much Dunbar's idealization of antebellum society corresponded to his personal convictions. In other words, had Dunbar himself come to accept in some respects the Southerners' theories? Or was he merely bowing to the taste of the day and utilizing these views with an eye toward achieving speedy popularity?

The first thing to bear in mind is that Dunbar, who was born seven years after the Civil War had ended, had no extensive, direct knowledge of the South. (p. 92)

Whether he had them from his mother or from the old men in Howard Town, the pictures of the Old South that Dunbar had garnered were in either case already partially winnowed, perhaps deliberately, perhaps through the normal functioning of the memory mechanism. Thus, in contrast, the biased exaggerations of the plantation school may have appeared less shocking to him than they do to the twentieth-century reader.

Yet it cannot be denied that Dunbar might well have eliminated the ambiguity in which he was content to leave the real feelings of the freedmen, for the tenderness they expressed for the South of another era was that of an old man for the familiar scenes of childhood, or of a country-dweller transformed into townsman for his bygone rural life—and not in the least a longing for the state of slavery.

Allowance must also be made for the sense of inferiority and the self-contempt that prolonged oppression inevitably imposes on the oppressed class. As a consequence, this class espouses in some measure the mythical portrait of itself drawn by the oppressors. (p. 93)

This phenomenon was assuredly at play in the case of Dunbar and his informants, so he cannot be blamed entirely for presenting his fellows in an unfavorable light. He simply presented them, quite often, as they really were. (p. 94)

Dunbar did not set out to challenge his era; to a very considerable extent he headed in the same direction. And the current was running in favor of accommodation and useful compromises, not toward futile outbursts of nationalism and rebellion.

Thus the plantation tradition in Dunbar's work must be looked on as essentially "the mark of oppression." This theme of maladjustment is, in the last analysis, the price he paid for his fame.

It may seem paradoxical, at first glance, to speak of race consciousness in connection with a poet who . . . so closely espoused the attitudes of white people toward his own race. His attempts to make his avowed feelings match the norms of the plantation tradition and of the minstrels would indeed be the negation of all race consciousness, had not the poet sensed with poignant sharpness the ambiguities and the total disarray of the situation in which he found himself. (pp. 94-5)

The strength of the emotional factors that tie Dunbar to the South and to everything it represents; the necessity of writing for a twofold public with differing requirements; the uncertainties of an era when the Negro's political and social status was rapidly evolving and, sometimes, beating a retreat—all these things made it highly distressing, if not entirely impossible, for the poet to make such a choice. Through all the hesitations, ambiguities, and differences that mark his evaluation of both past and present, what chiefly becomes apparent is the consuming urge to equality and integration in the mainstream of American national history.

By taking over and adopting a considerable portion of the plantation tradition, Dunbar was already manifesting a certain attitude toward the problem of the past. But fundamentally he realized that this was a way of deceiving himself, and no more than an escape from the distressing features of the present. So this past seemed to him, at one time and another, to be a devil's gift that followed him like a specter and which not even the passage of time could exorcise. . . . (pp. 95-6)

[We] know that his view of the present grew gloomier in his last years, as shown by a number of poems in the 1903 collection. In those difficult times he turned beyond the grave to invoke Frederick Douglass, whom he looked on as the great leader of the race, and to ask him for help. . . . (p. 97)

These poems, so modest in presentation, are important in our eyes for the changed perspective they reveal in Dunbar and for the kind of awakening of a more precise historical sense that can be divined. Here the happy days are no longer placed in a past bathed in glory and borrowed from others, but in a future which the black race can attain solely through its own efforts.

Dunbar's eyes, in spite of this, remain fixed on the past, and he sets out to people it with heroes of his race, whether real or legendary. Nevertheless, his way of choosing them is a proclamation of loyalty to America rather than to his race, and their example serves as a plea to the nation that the black be recognized as a full-fledged American. (p. 98)

"The Colored Soldiers," while it sings of "those noble sons of Ham . . . the gallant colored soldiers / Who fought for Uncle Sam," is unusual in addressing white America directly. The poet begins by reminding whites that, at the outset of the war, the services of blacks had been contemptuously refused. Then he mentions several battles in which black troops took part, and sketches a savage portrait of the combatants. . . . The final two stanzas broach the question of equality of the races. . . . But here too he persists in his timidity, expressing no open indignation at injustice and limiting himself to dropping hints.

He is more successful in the sonnet addressed to Robert Gould Shaw, the only son of a rich and famous New England family, who agreed to head the 54th Massachusetts Regiment, made up entirely of blacks. He and they were slaughtered while attacking Fort Wagner, near Charleston, on July 18, 1863. In this sonnet, Dunbar was able to disguise his emotion and restrain his bitterness and disillusionment, until in the last three words of the last line he gives them free rein. Why, he asks in a long apostrophe of the young hero, had he left family and studies to confront death [in vain?] (p. 99)

What authentic heroes of the race can then be found in Dunbar's work? Alexander Crummell, the black missionary to Africans and builder of churches? Frederick Douglass and Booker T. Washington, between whose achievements Dunbar scarcely seems to distinguish? This is truly a sparsely populated gallery of heroes, and one which does not go back very far in the history of the race since, actually, it coincides with the independence of the United States. Nor is there a genuine rebel among them, though Dunbar had sung the praises of men who refuse to compromise with injustice and stand alone as they brave the elements. . . . (p. 100)

But these exalted hopes come from a man easily swayed by conflicting impulses; they are a counterweight to his sense of inferiority and his frustrations. Dunbar's real heroes are those modest and conformist individuals who know and remain in the place to which the decisions of the majority entitle them. . . . Between the intransigence of a Frederick Douglass and the modesty of a Booker T. Washington, he inclines toward the latter. . . . (pp. 100-01)

These aspects of Dunbar's personality . . . explain why he wrote so few poems protesting the injustice and violence that were victimizing his fellows. The poet was not unaware of the state of affairs, and had even suffered personally during a race riot in New York in July, 1900. But if we overlook the kind of implicit protest to be found in the . . . poems that recall the deeds of Negro soldiers, there are only a few poems of outright protest.

The most lyrical of these is assuredly the poem inspired by the action of a young Negro woman, Mary Britton, a teacher in Lexington, Kentucky, who rose up in the state assembly and delivered a passionate speech against a bill providing for segregation in public transport. The rhetorical force of the first two stanzas echoes in some measure the indignation expressed by Milton in his sonnet on the slaughtered Piedmontese. . . . Yet here too the protest remains indirect, for it is addressed to God and not to men, while the tone is that of prayer rather than denunciation. (pp. 101-02)

There can be no doubt that financial considerations affected [Dunbar's] attitude. But the pressure of public opinion cannot be held altogether responsible for the poet's failure to resolve the conflict of loyalties that was tearing him apart.

In connection with this psychological entanglement, the outstanding work is certainly **"To the South: On Its New Slavery."** The title leads one to expect a protest directed against this new form of slavery, made up of disfranchisement, peonage, and the lynchings that became steadily more frequent as the South shook off its defeat. But a reading of the poem utterly disposes of such expectations. The first stanza, with its grammatical inadequacies, plunges us at once into total confusion. Besides, the tone does not suggest protest but is, rather, that of a son speaking affectionately to his mother. The irresistible conclusion is that in his heart the poet had established a hidden equivalence between his mother in the flesh and this southern earth, uniting the two in the same excessive and almost unnatural love.

Any thought of reproach is soon abandoned, and the "new slavery" of the title yields to a mere "weakness" in the body of the poem, with praise for the Old South far outweighing the blame. So we slip back imperceptibly into the plantation tradition. The two stanzas that contrast the happiness of the slave in the past and the despair of the freedman in the present treat the latter, and not the slave, as a pathetic prisoner. . . . What is retained from the poem is the immense outpouring of tender feeling at the end, and the fictitious conflict between the poet and the South is thereby reduced to a harmless lovers' quarrel. . . . (pp. 103-04)

Nothing could more accurately depict the ambivalent nature and the real limits of Dunbar's racial consciousness.

While ill at ease in its relationship with the major themes of race, Dunbar's personality was especially suited to harmonize with the more modest themes of the life of the people. The *New York Times* called him "a true singer of the people—white or black." This explains not only his precocious affinity with such poets as Riley, but also his more compromising kinship with the southern poets and the wordsmiths of the minstrel songs who had set out, earlier than Dunbar, to portray the Negro in their own fashion. (pp. 104-05)

If these relationships were to be overlooked, one would risk losing at the same time all that lies behind the specific worth and delightfulness of Dunbar's popular poetry. The reader will not be able to re-create for himself the rhythmic and dramatic integrity of these poems unless he uses his voice and his imagination to reawaken the underlying sound and rhythm and even the actual setting, which Dunbar never failed to provide in his recitals. Never far removed from song, stage show, and popular entertainment, these works are designed not for reading but for live performance. (p. 113)

We have yet to speak of what is, it must be confessed, the most engaging aspect of Dunbar's poetic work—that in which, as a genuine lyric poet, he gives vent to the cry of pain torn from him by the tragic destiny of his brief existence. For over his entire life there hovers the dramatic feeling of a double falling short and a double failure: one his work, the other his love. . . . (p. 118)

Black critics have been unanimous in wishing to present Dunbar as a writer who was victimized by the prejudices, and even by the indifference, of his public. . . . Striving first of all for popularity, he had risked playing the buffoon before his public, hoping that, once the audience had been won over, he could turn about and gain a hearing for the more serious things he believed he must say to them. Not until too late did he realize that he had entered into a pact with the devil—for the public, once they had come to know him as a buffoon, would refuse to see him as anything else.

This is one facet of Dunbar's tragic situation which it would be futile to deny, and which has inspired several of his most moving poems. **"Sympathy"** is the heartfelt cry of a poet who finds himself imprisoned amid traditions and prejudices he feels powerless to destroy. . . . (p. 119)

But the tragedy of Dunbar cannot be restricted to the dimensions of what was imposed upon him from outside, and it is going too far to accuse his readers of systematically underestimating his poems in standard English and of accepting only his works in dialect. Most of his poems in English share several basic defects with many other works of the same period, not the least of which are banality and a lack of sincerity. Dunbar was not blind to them. Indeed, it is at those moments, when he perceives his own inadequacies and measures the distance separating his goals and his abilities, that his situation appears to him in its true light and lets him glimpse his tragedy as one of failure. He had taken Shelley as his model, but his lyric flights had neither the momentum nor the ardor of Shelley's. . . .

This conviction of failure was not due entirely, perhaps, to the faltering powers of his lyricism; it may have originated in equal measure in his awareness that he had not been the poet his race deserved, and had not truly sung its virtues. (p. 120)

Dunbar's pessimism, though it may have been deepened by public indifference to certain portions of his work, is essentially the manifestation of his feeling of inferiority. In any event, it precedes the publication of his first volume, where a number of poems give it expression.

"A Career" may be said to prefigure the failure that Dunbar would later view as his. This poem, with its two unequal parts, contrasts the poet's aspirations and the reception given by the world. . . . (p. 121)

Even in the last of his poems, written at a time when he had achieved a degree of resignation, the same pessimistic outlook persists. Thus his pessimism is an absolutely central attitude; it is not always very convincingly patched over by the facade of beautiful, exhibitionistic optimism which he and his ethnic brothers prefer to present to the world. (p. 122)

Jean Wagner, "Paul Laurence Dunbar," in his Black Poets of the United States: From Paul Laurence Dunbar to Langston Hughes, *translated by Kenneth Douglas (translation copyright 1973 by The Board of Trustees of the University of Illinois; reprinted by permission of the author; originally published as* Les poètes nègres des Etats-Unis, *Librairie Istra, Paris, 1963),* University of Illinois Press, 1973, pp. 73-125.

ROBERT BONE   (essay date 1965)

[*Bone, critic and educator, is the author of the informative critical histories* The Negro Novel in America *(1958) and* Down Home:

A History of Short Fiction from Its Beginnings to the End of the Harlem Renaissance *(1975). A student of Afro-American, English, and American literature, with a special interest in Shakespeare, Bone has said of himself: "A white man and critic of black literature, I try to demonstrate by the quality of my work that scholarship is not the same thing as identity." In the excerpt below, Bone examines Dunbar's novels and defends him from charges of being a literary Uncle Tom.*]

While most of the early [Negro] novelists were concerned in one way or another with racial protest, Paul Laurence Dunbar went his own way, seeking to amuse rather than arouse his white audience. Viewing Dunbar's literary career as a whole, it is impossible to avoid the conclusion that his chief aim was to achieve popular success by imitating the plantation tradition. Most of his poems and short stories, as well as one of his novels, fall safely within the broad tradition established by Thomas Nelson Page. Whenever Dunbar had something to say which transcended the boundaries of the plantation tradition, he resorted to the subterfuge of employing white characters, rather than attempting a serious literary portrait of the Negro. The net effect of his work, therefore, was simply to postpone the main problem confronting the Negro novelist. (pp. 38-9)

Dunbar's first and most successful novel, *The Uncalled* . . . , is widely regarded as his spiritual autobiography. It is the story of a young white man who rebels against his Puritan heritage, and against his guardian's grim determination to make him a minister. (p. 39)

Perhaps by virtue of its autobiographical content, *The Uncalled* ranks a notch above most of the early novels. It is relatively free of melodrama, and not without some attempt at characterization. Conflict and resolution take place on a psychological plane, rather than at the elementary level of plot. The principal setting of the novel is the small Ohio town of "Dexter," before the advent of industrialism. Dunbar's realistic description of these transplanted Yankees, with their narrow religion, their small-town gossip, and their frontier humor, adds a local-color dimension to the book. In short, the characters, setting, and theme of *The Uncalled* are well within range of Dunbar's provincial consciousness.

Most of this writer's important themes are foreshadowed in his first novel. The conflict between the Natural (Freddie) and the Artificial (Hester) is basic to Dunbar's agrarian values, in which nature plays a vital part. In Freddie's experiences in Cincinnati there is a hint of the provincial distrust of the "wicked city." A sense of fate, of forces beyond human control, pervades the novel. . . . [The] note of fatalistic surrender, which appears frequently in Dunbar's novels, may be traceable to his illness, and perhaps it accounts for his supine response to Negro life in America.

The Love of Landry . . . is by far the worst of Dunbar's novels. It hinges on the romantic separation of two lovers by a class barrier, resulting from the fact—so unpalatable to Victorian sensibilities—that the hero works with his hands. . . . Insofar as the novel can be said to have a theme, it opposes the freedom of the Western plains to the stuffiness of the Eastern seaboard. . . . Landry's romantic retreat from civilization to his ranch in Colorado has its parallel in Dunbar's spiritual retreat from the conditions of modern life to the old plantation.

Dunbar's third novel, *The Fanatics* . . . , is a well-disguised attempt at racial protest, so carefully veiled that only the subtlest of readers will grasp the point. The novel has an historical setting in an Ohio town during the Civil War. (pp. 40-1)

The Fanatics is ostensibly an attack upon sectional chauvinism, as well as an abstract plea for toleration of differences and recognition of individual worth. The closing paragraph of the novel reveals the brand of fanaticism that Dunbar actually has in mind. A minor character, Nigger Ed, comes home in glory from the wars: "And so they gave him a place for life and everything he wanted, and from being despised he was much petted and spoiled, for they were all fanatics." North and south, Dunbar is saying, may have reconciled their differences, but both sections are united and fanatical in their determination to keep the Negro in his place.

This oblique protest is self-defeating, however, because the medium is corrupted in advance. Pandering to the prejudices of his white audience in order to gain a hearing, Dunbar resorts to caricature in his treatment of minor Negro characters. In order to flatter Southern pride, he singles out Bradford Waters' "New England fanaticism" for special condemnation. In contrast, his old-fashioned Southerner, Stephen Van Doren, is presented sympathetically: "'Come boys,' he said, addressing the negroes, and they grinned broadly and hopefully at the familiar conduct and manner of address of the South which they knew and loved". . . . Such a passage is its own best commentary. Far from altering the attitudes of prejudiced whites, Dunbar merely reinforces them.

The Sport of the Gods . . . is the only Dunbar novel whose main characters are colored. Like several of Dunbar's short stories, the novel reiterates the plantation-school thesis that the rural Negro becomes demoralized in the urban North. The first five chapters develop, not altogether credibly, the trial and imprisonment of Berry Hamilton, a loyal servant who is falsely accused of theft. The remainder of the novel traces the effects of this disgrace on the Hamilton family. Forced by the hostility of a small Southern community to migrate to New York City, the family soon disintegrates in that sinful metropolis. By the time Berry is released, he finds his son in jail, his daughter (worse than dead) on the stage, and his wife married to another man.

Dunbar's ulterior motives are revealed in a long didactic passage, which begins by warning of "the pernicious influence of the city on the untrained Negro." To be sure, Dunbar concedes, "The South has its faults—no one condones them," but in spite of the most flagrant injustice (like Berry's), it is preferable to the sidewalks of New York: "Good agriculture is better than bad art . . . brown-jeaned simplicity is infinitely better than broad-clothed degradation . . . better and nobler for them to sing to God across the Southern fields than to dance for rowdies in the Northern halls." Thus at the height of the post-Reconstruction repression, with the Great Migration already under way, Dunbar was urging Negroes to remain in the South, where they could provide a disciplined labor force for the new plantation economy. His only fear was that the stream of young Negro life would continue to flow Northward, a sacrifice to "false ideals and unreal ambitions."

Before dismissing Dunbar as an Uncle Tom, it is well to recall that he was the first Negro author in America who tried seriously to earn a living from his writings. Dependent for his income on the vagaries of the market, he was not overly disposed to challenge the prejudices of his white audience. On a deeper level, his midwestern agrarian values coincided at many points with the anti-industrial bias of the plantation tradition. His horizon was the village. A provincial and a romantic, he was a stranger to the pressing problems of the rising Negro middle class. Escape from industrial civilization is the dominant motif in his writings. Through his dialect verse and his plantation tales, even more than his novels, he sought refuge in the Golden Legend of the South. Nevertheless, despite his narrow social horizons, Dunbar produced one novel, *The Uncalled,* which is superior to the political tracts of his more sophisticated Negro contemporaries. (pp. 41-3)

> Robert Bone, "Novels of the Talented Tenth: Paul Laurence Dunbar," in his The Negro in America (© 1965 by Yale University Press, Inc.), revised edition, Yale University Press, 1965, pp. 38-43.

KENNY J. WILLIAMS   (essay date 1970)

[*In a study of Dunbar's novels and short stories, Williams divides Dunbar's fiction into three types: the romantic tradition, the plantation tradition, and the naturalistic tradition, and assesses the strengths and weaknesses of each.*]

For a well-known poet Dunbar produced an unusually large body of fiction, and it can be divided primarily into two types. There are those stories in which he appeared to concern himself mainly with white characters and their world, stories which do not deal with specific aspects of Negro life. In some of these stories the characters could have been anybody and the situations frequently applicable to white and black alike. Those who look at this fiction and deplore the lack of Negro characters are inadvertently supporting the thesis that the Negro artist must and should produce either works which are within the mold of social protest or which are circumscribed not only by the time and place but also by the race of the author. Dunbar was not, in this fiction, intent upon renouncing his race neither was he attempting to ignore those problems which he saw daily but rather he was operating within the framework of his own belief that the literary artist who happens to be a Negro is not bound by the limitations of purely racial subjects. (pp. 156-57)

As a first novel, [*The Uncalled*] suffers from the usual self-consciousness which one tends to ascribe to such works. In many ways it appears to be autobiographical in the sense that the protagonist, Frederick Brent, is faced with the problem of whether or not to enter the ministry, a question which Dunbar also faced. The novel is set in Dexter, a small town in Ohio, and the central action surrounds Frederick's need to find himself. In spite of his own wishes he does attend a seminary and become a minister, but eventually he rejects the life of hypocrisy for a more meaningful life. The purpose of *The Uncalled,* if this popular slick magazine story can be said to have a purpose, is the revelation of the pettiness and deceitfulness which exist in a small town. The central theme focuses upon Frederick's growing awareness of himself and of the world around him. (p. 157)

The Love of Landry appeared in 1900. The characters are white easterners who go West. The attitude of some white Americans is briefly introduced with no attempt on the part of the novelist to either deny or support the portrayal presented. While on the westbound train Mildred Osborne, the protagonist, comments rather sadly upon the life of a porter, and her father scoffs at her for being sympathetic. . . . (p. 158)

The major action is set in Colorado, and once the characters, especially Mildred Osborne, get there, they begin to lose the superficialities which had bound them to the East and to civilization. They become "real" people once again as they become aware of the beauty of nature, a beauty which eluded

them in the East. The story is not at all spectacular. Dunbar uses an old ruse for having his characters "find" themselves, but in terms of the back-to-nature tradition which he uses in the novel, it is as successful as any of this type. Most certainly, the novel demonstrates all of the weaknesses of the romantic novel at the turn of the century.

His third novel, *The Fanatics* . . . , does touch more upon racial questions, but once again primarily from a "white" point of view. The novel deals with the conflict between two families in a small town in Ohio. Bradford Waters and his family are Union sympathizers, and Stephen Van Doren and his family support the Confederacy. The conflict between these two families is symbolic of the general conflict in the border town which is almost evenly divided between northern and southern supporters. (pp. 158-59)

As a story dealing with the effects of the Civil War upon a community, the novel demonstrates once again that Dunbar understood the psychology of the small town and that he understood the self-righteous northerner even better. (p. 159)

As is typical of the romantic and sentimental novel, the characters of Dunbar's novel are overdrawn. The Negroes who stream into the town as refugees from the war are used primarily in the local color tradition; only Nigger Ed, the town crier who goes to war, emerges as a warmly human character. Dunbar, the author, remains detached from all of his characters as he views the fanatics on both sides; yet he demonstrates quite clearly the hypocrisy of the North as well as the paradoxical position in which most Negroes are forced in northern communities. And he concludes that the North is really no different in attitudes from the South. (p. 160)

The second type of fiction which Dunbar wrote was in the plantation tradition after the manner and formula of Joel Chandler Harris, Thomas Nelson Page, Irwin Russell, and George Washington Cable. In four collections of short stories, [*Folks From Dixie, The Strength of Gideon and Other Stories, In Old Plantation Days,* and *The Heart of Happy Hollow*], . . . Dunbar presents a sentimental picture of the Old South. His portrait of ante-bellum days is similar to those which followed the conventional local color methods. This tradition presented imagined characters in typical situations when the South was thought of as being divided into two classes: the slaves and the masters. Seldom are the unpleasant aspects of life displayed. Of all of the men who dealt successfully with this world of masters and slaves, Dunbar was the only non-southerner in the group. As the observant outsider, Dunbar never permitted his characters to become clowns merely for the sake of humor. Even though he really did not know the characters about whom he wrote, from his mother's stories he was able to present them sympathetically and gently; his plantations stories (as much of his dialect poetry) show more obviously the influence of James Whitcomb Riley than they do of the plantation school of southern writers. When Dunbar wrote of the days following the Civil War when Negroes were migrating in large numbers to northern cities, he was insistent upon the contrast between the more pleasing side of life in the South with the harshness of life in northern cities. This was partially due to Dunbar's own belief in an agrarian way of life as opposed to that in an industrial community.

His first collection of short stories, *Folks From Dixie,* is most apparently influenced by the then-popular plantation tradition. Many of the stories are set in Kentucky where his mother had been enslaved. While the stories are typical of their genre,

Dunbar demonstrates a far more sensitive understanding of his characters than Russell, Page, Cable, or Harris ever did. Thus while most of the twelve stories of the collection are traditional in the sense that they portray—in a large measure—the happy and contented relationship between master and slave, the differences (both social and intellectual) between house and field slaves, the narratives are presented with far greater knowledge of some of the basic problems which existed before and after the Civil War. Dunbar, who did not have first-hand knowledge of either slavery or those days following in the South, was content to employ the usual stereotypes: the young master or the considerate master who sold his slaves only in a financial crisis, the beautiful mistress who spent much time in the slaves' quarters taking care of the ill and educating the young, the poor white overseer who was hated by master and slave alike, the house slaves—especially the "Mammy" and the butler—who controlled everybody and everything in the "Big House," and the general aura of gentility which pervaded the idea of southern life and manners.

Although his stories in this collection included in varying degrees all of these stereotypes, he did analyze such themes as the effects of religion and church life in such stories as **"Anner Lizer's Stumblin' Block,"** **"The Ordeal at Mt. Hope"** which was also a strong plea for industrial education. . . . He further explored the exploitation of Negroes by Negroes in such stories as **"Aunt Mandy's Investment,"** and in **"Jimsella"** he presented the problem of life in the North, a problem which he was to treat at greater length in *The Sport of the Gods*. Just as **"The Ordeal at Mt. Hope"** is a form of social protest so also is **"At Shaft 11"** where Dunbar pleads with Negroes to stay out of labor unions. The success of these stories, once one passes the superficialities of the local color tradition, is in Dunbar's ability to distinguish the true meaning of the actions of his characters from those actions which are assumed for the sake of expediency. No white writer of the plantation tradition was ever able to do this.

The Strength of Gideon and Other Stories consists of twenty stories. . . . A number of the narratives of this collection deal with the inability of Negroes to adjust to northern urban environments and with the role of Negroes in politics during the days of Reconstruction. **"An Old Time Christmas,"** **"The Trustfulness of Polly,"** **"The Finding of Zach,"** **"The Faith Cure Man,"** **"Silas Jackson,"** **"The Finish of Patsy Barnes,"** and **"One Man's Fortune"** portray the disillusionment with life in the North. **"One Man's Fortune"** is especially interesting today for it deals with a young man who had listened to all of the injunctions to "get an education" only to discover that education has little or no value for him. He becomes aware that society still looks at him as a Negro rather than as a man. Dunbar makes it clear that the initial efforts toward aiding the freedman after the Civil War was soon replaced by a general spirit of indifference. Political aspirations are treated realistically in **"Mr. Cornelius Johnson, Office Seeker,"** **"A Mess of Pottage,"** and **"A Council of State."** In **"The Ingrate"** Dunbar sympathetically presents the story of a slave who has escaped to Canada but who later returns to the United States in order to join the Union Army and to help others gain their freedom. The story, which is probably patterned after the life of his father, is significantly one of his strongest attacks on the institution of slavery.

With *In Old Plantation Days* Dunbar returns to the basic type of *Folks From Dixie*. While in his second collection of short stories Dunbar introduced far more realistic portrayals of char-

acter and situations as well as more stories of social protest, his third volume re-echoes the traditionalism of the first. Stuart Mordaunt's plantation is the background for most of the stories which adhere to the conventional concept of good masters, happy and contented slaves, and cruel overseers. A very few of the stories, most notably **"A Judgment of Paris,"** **"Silent Samuel,"** and **"The Way of a Woman,"** deal with those days of adjustment in northern cities after the Civil War.

Dunbar concerned himself more with racial problems in *The Heart of Happy Hollow* than he had done in his earlier collections. . . . It is ironic that Dunbar should have called his village "Happy Hollow" because if one can say true happiness existed here, it was of the most hollow variety. People groped for a method which would alleviate, no matter how briefly, the problems of their lives in an environment which was essentially hostile. For this reason the small things of life took on added significance as the characters were bound together in their search for anything which would help them. The people of Happy Hollow were a serious lot, laughter was seldom, tears came often as they were often forced to mask their true feelings in order to survive. They were exploited by the unscrupulous and ignored by the supposedly sympathetic. With no one to whom they might turn, they lived—or rather, they existed—from day to day. The pathos of the collection is perhaps best exemplified by **"The Lynching of Jube Benson."** Dunbar firmly believed, as he demonstrated in so many of his stories, that the role of the writer was to tell a good story; consequently, he did not view fiction as primarily a social instrument. Yet, in spite of the functional restrictions which he placed upon his own work and upon himself, probably nowhere in American literature has the protest against lynching been more plaintively revealed. The anger and rancor occasioned by the action is submerged in the author's own sense of disbelief which is passed on to the reader who shares in the shock of the action. (pp. 160-65)

Whatever the shortcomings of this story may be, no man committed to the plantation tradition could have told it.

Dunbar's last novel [*The Sport of the Gods*] is neither a "white" novel nor is it truly in the plantation tradition. . . . While the situations described are not always believable, it is the most naturalistic of all of Dunbar's fiction. The Berry Hamilton family is forced by circumstances to move away from home because Berry has been accused of stealing money from his employer's brother and for which he is sentenced to ten years in prison. Before his trial, which is a farce, he is rejected not only by Maurice Oakley, his employer who knows that he has always been a good and honest worker, but also by the Negro community which fears reprisals if anyone should show mercy or sympathy for the Hamiltons. Dunbar does not find white rejection unusual, but he attacks those Negroes who are afraid to support Hamilton or to acknowledge his integrity. (p. 172)

Thus victimized by both Negro and white society, Hamilton goes to prison, and his wife and two children escape to New York City in a search for anonymity. In the city they are caught in a web of conditions over which they have no control, and the closely-knit family is doomed to defeat. Pathetically each character tries to hold the ideals which he had maintained in his southern home, but the urban environment is too much and takes its toll as these unsuspecting people go down one by one. (p. 173)

Throughout the novel Dunbar makes it quite clear that the "cheerful" journey to the devil is not really the doing of the characters themselves but rather is a result of the hypocrisy and deceitfulness of a society which can imprison a man because he is black thus forcing the man's family to face a world for which the members of the family are not prepared. Underlying the action of *The Sport of the Gods* is a powerful message to white and black America. (p. 174)

[With Dunbar, for] the first time an American Negro writer gained widespread acceptance with the reading public. He wrote at a time when the romantic tradition was still currently in vogue and when realism and naturalism were just beginning to make an impact. Romantic though much of his work is, there is in his fiction a growing awareness not only of the social problems of America but most specifically of the problems created by an urban society. The city as an evil force reached its culmination in *The Sport of the Gods,* but throughout his writing career he attempted to deal with the influence of the city upon men. By veiling his views of life and masking his ideas of society frequently behind raceless or white characters, he was able to produce in rapid succession four novels which enjoyed a measure of success. With great understanding Dunbar, in his short stories, became the interpreter of various facets of Negro life in America. Committed to the popular in fiction, he took the well-liked plantation tradition which was not original with him and made it peculiarly his own. While one may smile or even laugh at some of the antics of his slave characters, one can never forget that beneath the humor there is the unspoken assertion: I, too, am a man. (pp. 174-75)

> *Kenny J. Williams, "The Masking of the Poet," in her* They Also Spoke: An Essay on Negro Literature in America, 1787-1930 *(coyright © 1970 by Kenny J. Williams; reprinted by permission of the author), Townsend Press, 1970, pp. 153-215.*

ADDISON GAYLE, JR. (essay date 1971)

[*In the following excerpt from his biography of Dunbar,* Oak and Ivy, *Gayle examines Dunbar's lifelong concern with the possibility of attaining personal freedom and the resulting pessimism the poet felt when he was unable to direct his literary career or create the works of art he dreamed of. For Gayle, Dunbar's failure represents a personal and literary tragedy.*]

In 1888, while [Dunbar] was still a student, the Dayton *Herald* published his poem, *Our Martyred Soldiers,* which was followed five days later by another of his poems, *On the River.* Neither of the poems was written in dialect. They were both written in standard English, as was the case with most of his early poetry. His first real attempts at creation were written in the English spoken by his mother, father, neighbors, and classmates. (p. 22)

As with most juvenilia, the early poems [in *Oak and Ivy*] foreshadowed the themes and conflicts of his later works. In such poems as *October,* the poet sang to nature with the passion and enthusiasm that would increase as he grew older. (pp. 28-9)

Here, too, could be found the first tribute to race. Dunbar's first call to his people to "strive ever onward" was given in *Ode to Ethiopia.* Other poems hinted at what was to become the major conflict of his life. This can best be seen in *A Career.* This poem is more than juvenilia; in a sense it is almost a prophecy—the young poet seemed able to see beyond the present and capable of knowing and analyzing the future. . . .

Despite the importance of *A Career* to Dunbar's development as a poet, few of his biographers have realized its full implication. Had they done so, they might have noted that Dunbar's most serious poems in *Oak and Ivy* were written in standard English and that the poet himself was less than pleased with the success of his dialect pieces. (p. 29)

Humorous and dialect poetry paid. It was what the editors wanted. One had confided to him at the Chicago World's Fair, "I'll take anything you write in dialect." And so he wrote dialect. More and more. Much of his new work was in the dialect vein. This decision was not made solely in the interest of making a quick profit. Most of his biographers have attributed to him a sophistication that he did not possess. He was, in reality, a small-town Midwesterner in thought and outlook. This accounts in part for his animosity towards the big city. He was incapable of divining the sinister forces at work in the society; and he believed that once he had established himself as a poet through the medium of dialect, his white audience would accept whatever he offered in a poetical vein. (pp. 37-8)

[*Majors and Minors*] was an improvement over *Oak and Ivy.* There were one hundred and forty-eight pages in *Majors and Minors*—more than twice the number in *Oak and Ivy.* . . . Of these seventy-four poems only eleven had previously appeared in *Oak and Ivy.* Once again, the poems in standard English dominated the book. Of the seventy-four, only twenty-six were in dialect, and these were placed in a special section entitled "Humour and Dialect." The title *Majors and Minors,* like the title *Oak and Ivy,* was meant to be a guideline for his readers.

Perhaps they would see, as he did, that the term majors, meant to designate the selections he considered serious works of art, reported, however subtly, the truth that burned with such volcanic fury within his breast. Perhaps they would feel something of the agony of spirit and mind suffered by those who were forced, as in the poem *We Wear the Mask,* to ". . . smile, [while] O Great Christ, our cries / to thee from tortured Souls arise." Perhaps they could understand his veiled plea for sympathy in the *Poet and His Song.* . . . Were there not readers whose souls were in tune with his? Could they mistake the despondent tones of *Ere Sleep Comes Down to Soothe the Weary Eyes* as an elegy for physical instead of creative death—that death of artistic sensibility, more meaningful to the poet than physical death. . . . (pp. 42-3)

But the world did not understand. It turned its attention to the minors—the humorous and dialect pieces—and, because of them, made the poet famous. *The Party, A Banjo Song, When De Co'n Pone's Hot,* and *The Deserted Plantation,* among others, became the overnight favorites of his readers. These poems received the heartiest applause during readings, while those "of deeper note" were accorded only polite, condescending recognition. Whatever his personal pain, whatever his private conflict, they were unimportant as long as he produced lines such as those from *A Banjo Song,* which spoke not of pain or conflict, but of contentment and joy. . . . (p. 43)

However, [*Lyrics of Lowly Life*] was important in a much more meaningful way: it brought him national fame and a national audience.

That a great deal of this acclaim was due to William Dean Howells is a point beyond dispute. . . . In terms of form, the book was a mixture of poems in standard English and dialect. The difference between this arrangement and that of the previous books—and it was probably due to the ingenuity of the editors—was that the dialect pieces were not separated into special sections. (p. 71)

The book [*Lyrics of Lowly Life*] opens with a poem in standard English, *Ere Sleep Comes Down to Soothe the Weary Eyes,* and closes with the dialect poem from which Howells had quoted at length, *The Party.* Perhaps the most important poem in the volume is *Unexpressed.* It had previously appeared in *Majors and Minors* and received little notice by the critics. Yet, it is fundamental to an analysis of the crisis that Dunbar was undergoing. (p. 80)

In the summer of 1898, *Clorindy,* the musical which [Dunbar] had worked on with Will and John Cook, opened at the Casino Roof Garden in New York. Dunbar and his wife were present on opening night. . . . As Dunbar listened to the lyrics that he had helped to write, he felt a sense of embarrassment. The musical was in the worst of the minstrel tradition. Not only were black people laughing at themselves, they were also performing on stage, offering themselves as objects for the laughs of others. The tunes for which he had written the lyrics were not much more offensive than some of his dialect poems—although, in these he had avoided making his people into buffoons. Still there was a great deal of difference between writing a poem and reciting it, and watching the same poem acted out on a stage. The all-black cast, including the great Afro-American star Ernest Hogan, was very talented and performed well. However, the musical was not a serious work. The titles of the songs illustrate this fact: **"The Hottest Coon in Dixie," "Love in a Cottage Is Best," "Who Dat Say Chicken in a Crowd."** In addition, among his contributions was **"A Negro Love Song,"** which he had written in a humorous vein. Listening to it now, in this setting, it sounded not humorous, but ridiculous. *Clorindy* caused Dunbar to doubt the claim to fame which others made for him. In his own eyes he had not achieved success and never would. (pp. 87-8)

Dunbar desired freedom from restrictions above all else; as did his fictional counterpart, Freddie Brent [in *The Uncalled*]. Both were restricted by tradition, and neither thought he could win his fight against "blind fate." By the end of *The Uncalled,* however, Freddie would win his fight, and Dunbar, through identification with his character would win a victory also. As Saunders Redding has noted, Dunbar not only wrote about white characters, he became the white characters about whom he wrote. Paul Laurence Dunbar is Freddie Brent and Freddie Brent is Paul Laurence Dunbar. Freddie is trapped in the town of Dexter; he is forced to obey the dictates of Hester Prime; he attempts to live down his past. At the time *The Uncalled* was written Dunbar was forced to be the kind of poet he did not want to be; he was forced to obey the dictates of his critics; he, too, was attempting to live down his past. (pp. 97-8)

The Uncalled fails as a novel because the events are unrealistic; for example, Freddie's accidental encounter with his father at the temperance meeting. In addition, the language is artificial and the characters are romanticized. However, these are the reasons for the failure of Dunbar's fiction in general. The collections of short stories, *The Strength of Gideon, Folks from Dixie,* and *In Old Plantation Days* all fail for the same reasons: none is true to life, the situations in each are implausible, the language is artificial, and the characters are way outside the range of possibility.

Folks from Dixie consisted of twelve short stories, and with the exception of **"At Shaft 11,"** each deals with an aspect of the plantation tradition. **"At Shaft 11,"** which tells of a labor strike in a coal-mining town, and **"Jimsella,"** the story of a young married couple, who after leaving the South encounter great difficulty in the North, are the only two stories in the volume that contain elements of reality. (p. 99)

Lyrics of the Hearthside, dedicated to Alice, was released in February of 1899. . . . [Dialect] poems and those in standard English were separated from each other as they had been in the earlier books, *Oak and Ivy,* and *Majors and Minors.* The desperate struggle he waged with his own spirit—against a world he dared to fight openly—is here revealed more clearly than in the previous volumes. Here, in lines that tell of love, joy, melancholia, struggle, and death, is the stuff of his life, his inner-self, the material of his poetic essence. Of all these themes, he began to write most frequently of death. This was not a new theme for him. He had written of death, of the end of life, in *Oak and Ivy, Majors and Minors* and *Lyrics of Lowly Life.* However, for the most part, these poems had merely been speculations about death—youthful investigations of a world that attracts because it is unknown.

Now, his statements on death took on a maturity of form. He wrote of it with a passion and an understanding peculiar for a young man of twenty-seven. Death was still unknowable. Yet he looked upon it now as not being very far away, a mystery soon to be a mystery no more, the unknowable destined eventually to make itself known. Even in the love poems there is this longing for escape, for release from the earthly pain that only death can bring. No volume of his works is more despondent than *Lyrics of the Hearthside;* no lines appear in any of his other writings so filled with resignation and despair. (p. 110)

Lyrics of the Hearthside is the "fruitage" of the years spent wrestling with his conscience after Howells' review, of his experiences in England, and of the uncertainty concerning his marriage. At that time he had needed a love such as that called for in *Love's Apotheosis,* and there is little doubt that Alice fulfilled that need.

This belief that love might act as a barrier between him and the world is found in other poems in this volume. At times he seems to conceive of love as being more than emotion, more even than a bond between two human beings. With the world closing in on him, out of despair, he makes love an instrument—sometimes even a weapon—to be used in combating his many enemies. It is this sense of love as weapon that one finds in the poem, *Love's Phases.* . . . (pp. 111-12)

However, the poems that stand out in the first part of the book are those in which the poet looks at death through older eyes. The most beautiful, and perhaps the saddest of all his poems, is *When All Is Done.* It is also the most personal. Here, more than anywhere else, the poet poured pain, anguish, despair, and heartbreak into one loud, long wail for the release which only death could bring. . . . (p. 113)

Beside such poems as these, those in dialect are mere ornament. Yet here, in this book, are included some of Dunbar's most popular dialect poetry: *Little Brown Baby, Angelina, Whistling Sam, At Candle-Lightin' Time, Temptation,* and *How Lucy Backslid.* However, not even the dialect poetry was free of the theme of death. . . . (p. 114)

[He] worked diligently on the novel, *The Love of Landry.* The editor had asked for "a light novel," and this book filled the bill. It was a love story and took place in Colorado. (p. 120)

Once again, despite . . . a slight plot, Dunbar manages to impose his personal experiences on the novel. Each of the major characters represents some aspect of Dunbar's experiences: Arthur Heathclift, the English suitor for the hand of the heroine, a man who "smells of civilization," is a character modeled after Englishmen whom the poet had met during his stay in England. Heathclift is, to be sure, a poor stereotype of an Englishman, yet he represents Dunbar's idea of a civilized man. John Osborne is the kind, considerate father. He reminds one of the equally kind and considerate Doctor Tobey. Dunbar cherished Tobey's friendship as small boys cherish their relationship with their fathers. There is Aunt Annesley who attempts to interfere in the romance between Landry and Mildred, just as Alice's parents had attempted to interfere in their romance. Mildred, the heroine, suffers from tuberculosis. Like Dunbar, she is forced to come to Colorado to regain her health. Landry Thaler whose name, Landry, reminds one of land, is a man of the earth. Once a part of the frustration and chaos of the city, he has forsaken urban America and come back to nature. With such characters—each symbolizing different aspects of his character—Dunbar wrote a novel in which he, once again, deals with the theme of personal freedom.

Like the characters in his first novel, *The Uncalled,* the characters in his second novel are also white. However, where Freddie Brent, the hero of *The Uncalled,* sought freedom from the iron grip of Hester Prime, Mildred and Landry, heroine and hero of *The Love of Landry,* seek freedom from the civilized world. The novel depicts a conflict between the civilized world and the world of nature: "Nothing," the author states in the novel, "is quite so conceited as what we call civilization. And what does it mean after all except to lie gracefully, to cheat legally and to live as far away from God and nature as the world limit will allow." (pp. 120-21)

The peace that [Dunbar] sought in life, the freedom, came only when he created out of a sense of reality as he knew it, when he created in his white characters images of himself. *The Love of Landry* is a poor novel. But as the account of a poetic spirit seeking escape, seeking release from the bars and cages of life, of a dying soul attempting to lessen the impact of pain upon the still living, it is a remarkable accomplishment.

The Strength of Gideon and Other Stories, with few exceptions, is not remarkable, although this second book of short stories is an improvement over the first. The improvement is due to the fact that Dunbar went beyond the plantation tradition and dealt with aspects of his own personal problems, and one story, **"One Man's Fortune"** is as close to an autobiography in the short story genre as Dunbar ever came.

There is no hint of a shift, however, in the opening story of the book. **"The Strength of Gideon,"** the title story, tells of the loyalty of the slave Gideon to his master during slavery and to his master's family after the abolition of slavery. (p. 125)

"One Man's Fortune" is [a] story based upon material of which the author had firsthand knowledge. The story deals with aspects of his own life and focuses on the disappointments of a young black man. Although the young man is educated, he still finds that the doors of opportunity are closed to him. (p. 128)

Not only is **"One Man's Fortune"** autobiographical, it also evidences the distance Dunbar had traveled since the optimistic days of *Oak and Ivy.* Like Halliday, he had believed that race was an artificial barrier. He had believed that men could rise above the limitations imposed because of race. Like Booker T. Washington, he had believed that one need only build a better mousetrap than his neighbor, and irrespective of color, the world would beat a path to his door. Yet, because of his skin, severe limitations had been placed upon him. He had been forced into special areas of the literary world just as his people had been forced into special jobs, special neighborhoods, and special associations. (p. 130)

The disappointments, the bitterness, the hostility—all were to be found in *The Strength of Gideon and Other Stories* neatly tucked between the narratives of the plantation tradition. (p. 131)

The Fanatics was published in 1901, and the reception it received was disappointing. He had spent countless painful and sleepless nights laboring over the plot of the story. He had crossed out phrases, torn up whole pages, and rewritten entire sections. He wanted the novel to stand as a monument to his contribution to literature. He had chosen his theme well. The sectional strife of the Civil War—when a nation was internally torn, when the conflict of loyalties between North and South were often reflected in private households, affecting the relationships between son and father, brother and brother—was not far from the memory of the reading public of 1901. (p. 137)

As he had done before in *The Uncalled* and in *The Love of Landry,* he sought to work out his personal problem through the medium of fiction. The theme, peculiar to his other novels, runs through this one also: the constant demand for freedom, the assertion that man must be released from all restrictions. (p. 138)

The Fanatics is a bad novel; it is far worse than *The Love of Landry.* The reason is that Dunbar was attempting to reconcile too many disparate elements. He wanted to reconcile North and South, Waters and Van Doren, Robert and Mary. In addition, he wanted to reconcile Nigger Ed with the town and, through Ed, the black men who sought refuge in the town. The result is that the attempt at reconciliation fails. For all of Dunbar's attempts to portray Nigger Ed as a changed character, he remains a buffoon at the end of the novel. More important, however, there is no reconciliation between the escaped slaves and the town. They are the most alienated group in *The Fanatics.* Unwanted by the North, mistreated by the South, they are men without a country. Whatever union may eventually come about as the result of peace between the two warring factions of the nation, there will be no union with the new freedom except on the terms that prevailed during slavery. (pp. 140-41)

[Dunbar] was forced to conclude that the world belonged not to the Nigger Eds or the escaped slaves, but instead to the Van Dorens and the Waterses. The blacks had places in it, but these places were selected and defined by others. The nation that had made Nigger Ed a buffoon was unlikely to raise him to the status of human being. The nation that had fooled itself into believing it had fought a war to free the slaves, was not likely to extend its generosity further.

The Fanatics was one of Dunbar's most fervent pleas in prose for compassion and understanding. It was his most eloquent appeal for peace. As a failure, therefore, the novel ranks among his most pessimistic. In failing to reconcile the conflicting forces in the novel, he failed also to reconcile those within himself. (p. 141)

In 1902 he published what was to be his last novel. *The Sport of the Gods* is a product of the years of illness. (p. 150)

The Sport of the Gods marked a new turn for Dunbar in many ways. For the first time he dealt with blacks as major figures in a novel; he made the environment which produced crime and degeneracy the novel's chief villain. In no other novel does the city come under as fierce an attack from Dunbar's pen. The city is portrayed as the center of evil, vice, sin, and corruption. Into this hellhole falls the family of Berry Hamilton, a victim of the southern plantation system, whose daughter and son are ruined by this hostile environment. (p. 151)

The emphasis upon the city as a place of corruption is not new to Dunbar's fiction. In the short stories, **"The Truthfulness of Polly"** and **"Jimsella,"** he had already dealt with the evil influences of the city on his characters. Part of this animosity toward the city stemmed from his romance with nature, from a belief that the country life was far superior to that of the city. What is important in this book is that the emphasis on destiny is more pronounced here than in his other books; it is as though the poet had irrevocably resigned himself to "cruel fate." (pp. 152-53)

Within Dunbar, however, there remained elements of both the realist and the dreamer. The realist in him cried out in bitterness—in despair—as evidenced in . . . [his] poem to Frederick Douglass. . . . The dreamer cried out in hopeful if not optimistic tones: "Heart of the Southland, heed me pleading now," he began the poem, *To the South,* which he subtitled **"On Its New Slavery."** The poem is a plea. The poet enumerates the long list of deeds warranting better treatment for black men and women. . . . After . . . words of despair concerning lost love, he goes on to scale the heights of sentimentality. In lines that Du Bois would certainly have called whining and loathesome, Dunbar calls the South's attention to the former loyal servant in stanzas that rank among the most disgusting in black poetry. . . . (pp. 158-59)

The contradictions between these two poems are magnified in the volume *Lyrics of Love and Laughter*. . . . In it are included the poems of the years of depression and tension, of the sojourn in Colorado, of the search for health, of the breakup of his marriage. For the first time in a book of poetry, his dialect poems are almost as numerous as those in pure English. Unlike the poems in *Lyrics of the Hearthside,* they are intermingled. One finds, therefore, such poems as *The Poet,* Dunbar's most important statement on dialect poetry and the one that evidences his opposition to the writing of it, sandwiched in between two poems written in dialect, *In the Morning* and *Li'l' Gal*. The bitterness and despondency illustrated in *Douglass,* by the lament that the hero is no longer present to lead the race, is obscured by the tribute to Booker T. Washington. . . . The most striking contradiction of all is that between *To the South* and *The Haunted Oak*. *The Haunted Oak* paints a portrait of the South which no words can erase.

Despite serious shortcomings in selection, there were poems in *Lyrics of Love and Laughter* that rank among those in previous volumes. One of the most important is *Life's Tragedy*. Here the poet weaves the twin tragedies of his life into a poetical pattern. Since the age of six when he first began to put words on paper in stanzaic form, his dream had been that of every poet: to sing the perfect song, to write a poem so complete in meter, rhythm, and message that it would stand forever as a well-wrought work of art. (pp. 159-61)

Life's Tragedy laments his inability to attain these goals. Yet, he is despondent not because they were unattained, but because he had come so close to attaining them. . . .

Lyrics of Love and Laughter was not his last book. An illustrated volume of poems, *Howdy, Honey, Howdy,* and *Lyrics of Sunshine and Shadow* followed. However, neither measured up to its predecessors. . . . (p. 161)

> *Addison Gayle, Jr., in his* Oak and Ivy: A Biography of Paul Laurence Dunbar *(copyright © 1971 by Addison Gayle, Jr.; reprinted by permission of Doubleday & Company, Inc.), Doubleday, 1971, 175 p.*

NIKKI GIOVANNI (essay date 1972)

[*Giovanni is a contemporary black American poet and writer of children's books widely known for her dramatic oral presentations of her work. Although her early poetry was noted for its militant appeals for social change, in recent years she has been more concerned with the struggles of individuals for survival, reflecting her belief that the black community is made up of diverse individuals with individual needs rather than a collective body with common concerns. Because of this belief and her admiration for Ayn Rand's concepts of rational self-interest and extreme individualism, Giovanni stood apart from the mainstream of black literature in the 1970s. In the following excerpt, Giovanni stresses Dunbar's achievements as an individual poet and criticizes those who would regard him as a representative of his race.*]

Paul Laurence Dunbar is a natural resource of our people. He, like all our old prophets and preachers, has been preserved by our little people. Those who could command words and images, those whose pens thundered across the pages, those whose voices boomed from lecterns, those who set policy for our great publications then, as now, were quite silent. Not ever quite knowing what to do about one of America's most famous poets, when they spoke his name it was generally to condemn his dialect poetry—as if black people aren't supposed to laugh, or more as if Dunbar's poems were not the best examples of our plantation speech. One gets recitation after explanation of Dunbar's poetry, his love of his "white poems," his hatred of his need to please the white critics, but something rings quite hollow to me. I refuse to believe Paul Dunbar was ashamed of **"Little Brown Baby, come sit on my knee."** The poem has brought too much happiness to me. I categorically reject a standard that says **"A Negro Love Song"** should not make me feel warm inside. If Dunbar is only a poet with a gift in jingle tongue then there is no need for a critique. He is clearly much more. (pp. 243-44)

Dunbar preserved a part of our history. And accurately. It would be as foolish to say all blacks struggled against slavery as it would be to say all acquiesced to it. The truth lies somewhere in the blending. Perhaps Dunbar's greatest triumph is that he has survived all those who would use his gift for their own dead-end purposes.

Every artist, should he create long enough, will come full cycle again and again. The artist is a political animal as well as a sensitive being. Like any person the artist is a contradiction. Dunbar will speak of the good ole days, then say **"We Wear the Mask."** The message is clear and available to us if we invest in Dunbar the integrity we hope others will give us.

It seems somehow strange to me that critics are so colorless—despite claims to deeper insights should they share an ethnic or religious background with the subject. . . . [In] Dunbar's case, he was black enough for the white but not white enough for the blacks. (pp. 244-45)

Dunbar . . . is peerless. There is no poet, black or nonblack, who measures his achievement. Even today. He wanted to be a writer and he wrote. He survived, not always well, by his pen. He probably did not want to be hassled by his peers, who through Dunbar's efforts were enjoying greater attention. He probably was plagued by as many doubts as any other person. Yet he dared to persist in hope. (p. 245)

Nikki Giovanni, *"Afterword"* (reprinted by permission of the author; originally a lecture delivered at the University of California, Irvine, in 1972), in A Singer in the Dawn: Reinterpretations of Paul Laurence Dunbar, *edited by Jay Martin, Dodd, Mead & Company, 1975, pp. 243-46.*

PETER REVELL   (essay date 1979)

[*In the conclusion to his critical biography of Dunbar, excerpted below, Revell examines misconceptions and historical fallacies regarding Dunbar and his work, demonstrating that he should be considered as a man attempting to confront the unique problems of his time, and not judged by the standards for art and behavior of a later age.*]

If we examine Dunbar's work as a whole we cannot help being forcibly impressed by the contrast in attitudes between one part and another. No black American writer more clearly exhibits the basic dilemma of all black Amerian writers until the last two decades of the nation's history—that of living with and for a particular section of the populace with a unique origin and experience, while writing for as large a part of the national audience as would be likely to accept the writer's work. Other American writers have written intimately and devotedly of the experience and beliefs of particular ethnic groups within the American nation—one might instance Willa Cather's Bohemian farmers or, in recent years, Isaac Bashevis Singer's east European Jews—but their experience is invariably, with minor variations of detail, a part of an American pattern of experience, one usually of voluntary migration followed by struggle, hope, and the final realization of a new perspective in their lives which is the measure of their Americanness.

The peculiar institution of slavery sets the experience of the black community apart from this basic American pattern. The involuntary migration of its origin, the involuntary racial mixing that followed this, the struggle to achieve freedom in a land dedicated to freedom, and the more bitter and prolonged struggle to make a true reality of that freedom once it had been given are elements of a different pattern, one that is wont to make the basic American pattern seem like a form of duplicity. The black experience bred the virtues of survival, and survival itself often required a kind of duplicity, which might equally take the form of a false conciliation to white demands upon the race while working to subvert them, or an overt concession to such demands or expectations in the hope of surviving to a better day. (pp. 162-63)

Reflecting the immense range of attitudes among black leaders is the wide variety of style, approach, and treatment of subject to be found in Dunbar's work. Commentators on it can never hope to agree, because there are so many Dunbars and he can be revered or abused, according to which aspect of his work is felt to be predominant and the expression of his real beliefs. But the only real certainty is the ambiguity and ambivalence of his work. "My position is most unfortunate," he once remarked, "I am a black white man." As a black man living in a white world, a black writer working for a predominantly white audience, ambiguity and ambivalence were a necessary condition of life and work. It suggests a certain unhistorical

shortsightedness on the part of many critics who are irritated by these qualities and demand consistency as though they had a right to expect it. Dunbar wrote as he was, and he was, to an important degree, like any Afro-American of his time, what the white establishment allowed him to be.

Among the many possible images of Dunbar, two came to predominate during his own lifetime and for a decade or so after his death. These are both partial and distorted images, and the expectations they gave rise to have contributed to the critical confusion about Dunbar. The first is that of Dunbar as "the Poet Laureate of the Negro race." We can discern the beginnings of this image in Howells' praise of the poet in that most influential review of *Majors and Minors* [see *TCLC*, Vol. 2], the review that first brought Dunbar as a literary phenomenon to national attention. Howells' began the unfortunate critical habit of comparing Dunbar's dialect poems with those of Burns. (pp. 163-64)

Not only did [Howells'] words draw undue attention to the Negro dialect poems, which Dunbar had considered humorous and "minor" and relegated to the back of the volume, but they stamped the serious Dunbar of the poems in literary English (which included in this volume **"We Wear the Mask,"** the **"Ode to Ethiopia,"** and **"The Colored Soldiers"**) as "least himself," as not writing from the point of view of his own race. We may contrast with Howells' words some words of Dunbar in a letter to H. A. Tobey written in 1895. He wanted, he said, "to be able to interpret my own people through song and story; and to prove to the many that after all we are more human than African." Howells attempts to categorize Dunbar as the Robert Burns of his race by stating that in the dialect poems he writes of the fundamental truths of black human nature which Howells considers to be, except in rare instances, within the limited range "between appetite and emotion." The end result of this intended praise is doubly damning, for not only is Dunbar credited with being a spokesman for his race, a larger claim than he himself would make, but he is held to speak authentically only in the dialect verse—in much of which . . . the stereotypes of character and situation imposed by minstrelsy and the plantation tradition provide the vehicle for what is said. (pp. 164-65)

The second false, or at least partial, image of Dunbar that prevailed in his lifetime was one that he helped to create and worked hard to maintain, though it was much against the grain of his talent. This was the image of Dunbar as the interpreter of the Southern "darky," the author of tales in the plantation tradition or of stories depicting the buffoonery or peculiarities of darky types in the postbellum South, as an extension of the plantation tradition. . . . Dunbar was virtually forced into story-writing in the mold of Thomas Nelson Page in order to achieve publication in the large-circulation magazines. The result was to provide a kind of endorsement from the black race for the version of Southern black experience offered in Page's stories. Page had frequently constructed his stories so that the narrative, and the account of the social structure implied by it, was spoken in the words of a slave or former slave. Dunbar, as a black writer working in the style of Page, might be thought to be an independent black witness to the truth of Page's version. Editors and reviewers of white newspapers and periodicals were not slow to seize upon this advantage, and to acclaim the authenticity of what were very often stereotypes of character and thought that had been long before established by white writers. Over the years of Dunbar's writing career, the *New York Times* followed this line fairly consistently in its reviews, invariably anonymous, of his work. (pp. 166-67)

These . . . reviews in a most influential newspaper indicate clearly enough the kind of problem Dunbar faced in gaining acceptance for his work from white editors and readers. The comments are . . . valid in respect of a considerable proportion of Dunbar's work, though they ignore much else that is probably a better indication of Dunbar's real aims in writing of his race. (p. 168)

Dunbar certainly wanted commercial success and worked hard for it. After returning from his visit to England he found himself in demand as a writer of "impressions" for the magazines. He wrote to a friend that he was "only sorry that I am not in a position to resist the demands made upon me. . . . When one is just over the first flush of youthful enthusiasm and beyond the first glow of youthful dreaming, how sordid and cynical and commercial we grow." Dunbar was prepared to concede much for this success, but did so in full awareness of what he was conceding, and never ceased to agonize over the misuse of his talent that he felt was forced upon him by publishers and readers. Some of the most interesting products of Dunbar's last years may be seen as attempts to break free of these frustrations. The naturalism of *The Sport of the Gods* and the attempt at an ironic comedy of upper-class white life in some of the Ohio pastorals (long before Booth Tarkington worked this field) are indications that Dunbar wanted and tried to extend his range and break free of the old forms. In 1898 he wrote of wanting to "go to work in real earnest on my novel which will deal with the educated class of my own people," but this work, unfortunately, was never written, or at least no trace of it has survived. Its theme may simply have been beyond Dunbar's powers. Still, he did attempt, in a variety of ways in poems and stories, to present an account of the life of America's black citizens which would benefit them both directly, by inculcating pride in their race and its history and heritage, and indirectly, by emphasizing the common humanity of black life, the humor, courage, resource, and resilience that the difficult circumstances of the black citizen's life constantly brought out.

Dunbar in general preferred this image-building, yea-saying approach to the question of working for the benefit of his race. When he essays protest, as he does with conspicuous success in a number of stories and poems, it is usually by the oblique method of irony—and he can be at times bitterly ironic. Overt protest he confined to his occasional contributions to newspapers, the most powerful example being his letter on race riots and lynchings printed in the *Chicago Daily Tribune* for July 10, 1903. There can be no suggestion that Dunbar avoided overt protest because of what this might cost him in commercial appeal. His newspaper contributions were widely reprinted, in the fashion of the day, by other newspapers, particularly in the northern states where most of his readership lay. It seems probable that Dunbar did not write poems or stories of overt protest for two reasons. First, and most obviously, he would have found great difficulty in getting them printed. Like Sutton E. Griggs, he might have had them printed at his own expense, but this would have required another career from which to make a living, and would also have drastically limited the audience for his work. A second reason, less obvious and less certain, is that Dunbar may have felt that overt protest distorted the whole structure of a work of art, making it a vehicle for propaganda in which the effective purveying of the message is the predominant purpose. But Dunbar was willing to accept other forms of distortion, as his stories in the plantation tradition well testify.

The real man beneath the ambiguities and inconsistencies of Dunbar's work has always been visible to a discerning few— in his own time, for example, to James Weldon Johnson and in our time to Gwendolyn Brooks. Yet it is perhaps surprising to find Richard Wright, the embodiment of the spirit of overt protest in the 1930s and 1940s, writing with insight and understanding of the "fatal conflict" in Dunbar. . . . (pp. 171-72)

That Dunbar "turned his eye from the horror of lynching and race riots [as Wright stated] is to be doubted. He went to a good deal of trouble, and risked the goodwill of an influential editor, to have his poem on lynching, **"The Haunted Oak,"** printed in the *Century*. . . .

[The] work of any black writer flourishing decades ago inevitably acquires through the years a function as sociological documentation, by which the writer is judged to stand or fall according to his ability to fulfill certain requirements invented long after the time in which he wrote. Though this is conspicuously true of Dunbar's work, the attempt must be made to judge it by impartial standards. . . .

Dunbar was not at any time a great innovator. Negro dialect poetry had existed long before his time, not only in the work of Gordon and Page, or of Irwin Russell, but in black writers like Daniel Webster Davis and James Edwin Campbell. In her work on minor black poets of the nineteenth century, Joan R. Sherman has recorded that "during the century between Phillis Wheatley and Paul Laurence Dunbar, over 130 black men and women published some ninety volumes and pamphlets of poetry plus hundreds of poems in black periodicals." (p. 173)

Yet Dunbar's work was so manifestly better, so much wider in range than that of any of his predecessors, that he totally supplants them. . . . In technical ability, the expertise necessary to handle intricate forms with accomplishment, Dunbar stands high among nineteenth-century American poets without regard to race. Some of his poetry in literary English, and in particular some of the sonnets and odes, though not works of genius, can be placed without hesitation in the first rank of work by American poets, again without regard to race, in the second half of the nineteenth century. At his best he is a better poet, a more serious writer, than writers of the second rank such as Bayard Taylor, Charles W. Stoddard, or Thomas Bailey Aldrich. His work in dialect frequently remains fresh and vigorous, not as a realistic representation of black life in its time, but as a lively recreation—much as the stories of Chesnutt's *The Conjure Woman* recreate the black folklore of their time in a form readily acceptable to white readers. The authenticity of the emotion and the charm of the language redeem the spuriousness of much of the material. What finally counts is the vitality of the individual poem, and there are enough of these—poems like **"When Malindy Sings," "Li'l' Gal,"** and **"A Negro Love Song"** which are sure to survive.

Many critics since the 1940s and particularly within the past ten years have found new meaning in Dunbar's work by recognizing his limitations honestly and at the same time taking into account the constricting social and psychological influences of his time. Admitting these limitations, they find enough evidence of realism and protest in his work to show a writer working against formidable odds to present some measure of the truth without "losing his voice" as Chesnutt did, without sacrificing his popularity, and without becoming merely a writer of protest. (pp. 173-74)

Peter Revell, in his Paul Laurence Dunbar *(copyright © 1979 by Twayne Publishers; reprinted with the permission of Twayne Publishers, a Division of G. K. Hall & Co., Boston), Twayne, 1979, 197 p.*

EMEKA OKEKE-EZIGBO (essay date 1981)

[*Okeke-Ezigbo discusses Dunbar's conception of dialect poetry, his perception of self that made the role of dialect poet hateful to him, and compares his dialect poetry to the innovative work of Robert Burns and James Whitcomb Riley.*]

Although perceptive scholars such as Professor Darwin Turner have labored to annul the myths impeding the proper evaluation of Paul Laurence Dunbar's poetry [see *TCLC*, Vol. 2], some of the old myths have not only persisted, but new ones have unfortunately developed, as critics—some with obviously good intentions—endeavor to reassess the much misunderstood poet. This essay is an effort to come to terms with some of these myths by examining Dunbar's poetic practice and growth and placing Dunbar in a clearer perspective vis-a-vis James Whitcomb Riley, Robert Burns, James Russell Lowell, and Geoffrey Chaucer. If, however, Dunbar happens not to fare too well in the comparisons, it is not just because he was a black writer who had to contend with the peculiar, harsh racism of America; but, more importantly, because "Dunbar considered himself superior to the uneducated slaves and freedmen." Invariably, Dunbar's condescending attitude toward the black folks conditioned his stance on "Negro dialect." This aspect of the poet's psychology, often overlooked by critics, will be underscored here, because it is central to his literary predicament. (p. 481)

It was as an elevator boy that Dunbar privately published his maiden collection, *Oak and Ivy.* . . . His next collection, *Majors and Minors,* fell into the hands of William Dean Howells, who reviewed it in the *Harper's Weekly* of June 27, 1896 [see *TCLC,* Vol. 2]. Howells' enthusiastic review catapulted Dunbar to immediate national fame. . . . When we note that from 1800-1885 not one magazine reviewed an Afro-American's poetry, Dunbar's breakthrough becomes more significant.

Dunbar's use of Riley as the master model for dialect verse virtually determined the scope and technique of Dunbar's dialect poetry. For one thing, Dunbar probably inherited his dislike of Whitman from Riley, who, hating "free verse with uncompromising ardor," declared that Whitman's poetry "has positively refused, and still refuses, my applause." Riley cherished poetry of *heart* appeal, and discredited Whitman for being "more of a poet at soul than at heart." Incidentally, Riley's appeal to the heart tended to be rather "lighthearted"; in consequence, Dunbar, through his mentor, inclined more toward hearty jingles than toward the *soul-forceful* verse ("skillful phrases"), which a freer poetic form could have engendered. Dunbar thus unwittingly limited himself to "poetry of the heart"—a circumscription that will revolt him later, but for which he is largely culpable since it is a direct result of his offhand rejection of "skillful phrases." (pp. 482-83)

Furthermore, Dunbar apparently learned from Riley, or shared with him, the tendency to hanker after public approval. . . . The danger in writing with "one eye and ear on the audience" [as Riley suggested] is that the writer, like a catchpenny salesman, supplies the audience with whatever it demands—including stereotypes of the Negro.

Moreover, Dunbar apparently learned from his "mentor" to regard dialect writing as an engagement that demanded serious technical care. Riley's conviction seems to be that the writers who stick to traditional poetic diction are those whose elitist aloofness has rendered them unfit to record the living speech of the common man. (pp. 483-84)

Riley's emphasis on meticulous representation of the dialect demands that the poet who aspires to write perfect dialect must first embark on a vigilant field trip, understandably on foot and by ear, and acquaint himself or herself thoroughly with the way of life and speech traits of the common people. Dunbar, accordingly, saw the need to learn more about the blacks whose speech he intended to represent in dialect poetry. . . . (p. 484)

Dunbar, therefore, was "vigilant" and eclectic in his search for cultural material for poetry. When "one evening in Washington" Dunbar "heard from an old Negro the story of a nephew in Alabama who had been falsely accused of a grave crime," the poet exclaimed, "That is too good a story to be forgotten." A nondialect poem, **"The Haunted Oak,"** was written on the subject.

Dunbar's childhood acquaintance with Afro-American lore parallels Robert Burns' childhood intimacy with Scottish lore and songs. Burns learned from his Mother's Maid. . . . In a similar vein, Dunbar learned Afro-American lore from his mother. . . . (p. 485)

From his mother and also from his diligent observation, Dunbar acquired a substantial intimacy with black people that gave him an artistic surefooting on materials relating to Afro-American culture. The poet's closeness to his cultural material lends a certain bountiful naturalness and spontaneity to his writing, so much so that although a critic was moved to remark that Chesnutt's "Uncle Julius' dialect is labored" and that "it is easy to see that Mr. Chestnutt had not had a lifelong familiarity with the speech of the Southern Negro," the same critic was impressed enough to proclaim that Dunbar's "Negro dialect verse is today generally accepted as the best which has been written in America" [see excerpt above by Vernon Loggins]. (p. 486)

That Dunbar was "early drawn to Shelley, Keats, Tennyson . . . and gave most of his poetic career to writing their kind of poetry," does not obviate the fact that "Negro dialect" was his more immediate and natural medium. Burns, too, was early drawn to Pope, Thomson, Gray, and Milton; but just as Burns, who was half foreign to the English tongue, was least effective when he followed the genteel tradition of eighteenth-century English poetry, so was Dunbar, also a half foreigner to the English language, least effective when he essayed the language of Keats and Shelley. (pp. 491-92)

Although American racism is peculiarly cruel and enervating, Burns' dialect was as much subject to demeaning social pressures as Dunbar's. The significant difference between Burns and Dunbar is not that "Burns' dialect was standard, a native tongue," as Redding argues [see *TCLC,* Vol. 2]. Rather, it is that Burns was *proud* of his dialect whereas Dunbar was *ashamed* of his, because he felt superior to the uneducated Slaves and freedmen who spoke the "Negro dialect." A comparison of their book titles will immediately reveal the difference in cultural attitude between the two poets. Dunbar's first book is titled *Oak and Ivy* (The Strong and the Weak), while Burns' is *Poems Chiefly in the Scottish Dialect.* To say, as Redding does, that Burns' dialect was "standard" and "understood by all the Scots," is to lose sight of the division between the Gaelic and the non-Gaelic elements in Scottish civilization, as well as the fact that the Lowland Scots and the Highland Scots did not understand each other. Redding's disclosure that if

Dunbar had "imitated the speech of the North Georgia Negro and uttered it among the Geechees of South Georgia or the Gullahs of South Carolina, he would not have been understood," is scarcely startling. The mutations of dialects and the fact that these splintered dialects seem to be mutually unintelligible to speakers from the same ethnic group was not peculiar to Dunbar's Afro-American. A similar "fate" befell the Scots. As David Daiches notes from his somewhat patrician perspective, "The Scots language gradually ceased to be a language and became a series of dialects; for when there is no literary standard of purity a language will always so disintegrate."

In the light of this, Dunbar could have played the role of a remedying agent by utilizing the advantage of his immense popularity to instill a literary standard for "Negro dialect." Had Dunbar undertaken such a pioneering task, he could have more closely resembled Chaucer rather than Burns. (pp. 492-93)

Although Dunbar's was the age of "Jim Crow" and "the Klan," the same period witnessed a literary movement in America whose major impulse—not its adjunct follies—was favorable to the development of a genuine Afro-American vernacular literature. The patriotism which guided Chaucer also guided Burns; no doubt, Dunbar could have gained inspiration from both poets. For hardly any great writer has things laid out in perfect order for him. Burns, for instance, had to contend with the literati of Edinburgh, who advised him to give up writing in Scots and model himself on Shenstone or Homer. Burns resisted the pressure and stuck to Scots. (pp. 494-95)

Dunbar was off to a good start in the business of fashioning a distinctive Afro-American literary dialect. Not only was he cognizant of the different features of the various dialects, but he also was perceptive enough to "differentiate dialect as a philological branch from Negro minstrelsy." He had the advantage of knowing the black people well: "I believe I know my own people thoroughly. I know them in all classes, the high and the low." Far from being "scant," Dunbar's knowledge of "Negro dialect" was profound enough to encourage him to declare "modestly": "I simply came to the conclusion that I could write it ("Negro dialect") as well, if not better, than anybody else I know of, and that by doing so I should gain a hearing, and now they don't want me to write anything else but dialect." Sterling Brown agrees, after all, that Dunbar's "grasp upon folk speech is generally secure" [see excerpt above].

Why, then, did Dunbar have a limited success as an Afro-American poet? It would seem that this was because he belittled the folk speech upon which he had a sure grasp, in pursuit of the rather pretentious and certainly elusive "standard English." In effect, therefore, Dunbar's final lament is the soul-wrenching agony of the writer who has basically pursued a mirage rather than genuine artistic growth, the misguided self-reproach of the Ephraimite for his futile effort to pronounce "shibboleth." . . . (pp. 495-96)

> *Emeka Okeke-Ezigbo, "Paul Laurence Dunbar: Straightening the Record," in* CLA Journal *(copyright, 1981 by The College Language Association; used by permission of The College Language Association), Vol. XXIV, No. 4, June, 1981, pp. 481-96.*

HOUSTON A. BAKER, JR.   (essay date 1981)

[*A poet and educator, Baker has contributed critical interpretations of black literature to anthologies and periodicals, including*

Phylon, Black World, and The Virginia Quarterly Review. *In addition, he is the editor of critical volumes on African, Caribbean, and black American literature. In the excerpt below, he examines Dunbar's most significant novel,* The Sport of the Gods.]

Mythic and literary acts of language are not intended or designed for communicative ends. That is, rather than informational or communicative utterances that assure a harmonious normalcy in human cultures, they are radically contigent language events whose various readings or performances occasion inversive symbolic modes of cognition and other non-quotidian human responses. Considered in these terms, *The Sport of the Gods* must be taken as a phenomenon different in kind from the communicative, historical document. The novel's conditions of existence are found not in the determinate circumstances of an historical moment, but in what Jonathan Culler calls "the institution of literature." What is implied by Culler's phrase, however, is not the familiar disjunction between "literature" and "life." For an "institution" is, finally, a conventional or systematic behavioral pattern that is valued by a human community. To distinguish literature as an institution is to focus on the systematic linguistic behavior conventionally entailed among human beings by a particular kind of discourse. The justification for concentrating on language lies in the fact that the medium for literary works of art is language and in the fact that the linguistic behaviors associated with literary discourse are, in my view, different from those surrounding the speech of everyday contexts. (p. 130)

The title of Dunbar's work finds its reference not in the historically documented betrayals and confusions of American Reconstruction, but in the domain of literature. The blinded and deceived Gloucester remarks in *King Lear,* "As flies to wanton boys are we to the Gods; / They kill us for their sport." The origin and nature of the world, this utterance implies, are functions of capricious supernaturals. The mythic universe of discourse is thus invoked as an explanation of man's failings: Man is nothing special; he is a toy in the ludic world of the gods. (p. 131)

That Gloucester, whose incredible folly is matched only by that of his aged counterpart Lear, is the character who summons "the sport of the Gods" as an explanation reinforces a reader's decision to concentrate on human agents and actions in understanding Shakespeare's drama. Similarly, having followed the controlling voice of the narrator from the first to the concluding line of *The Sport of the Gods,* a reader knows there is little need to summmon incomprehensible supernatural powers to explain the human affairs represented in the novel. For the characters of Dunbar's work are, finally, the victims of their own, individual modes of processing reality. Their failings are the paradoxical results of their peculiarly human ability (and inclination) to form theories of knowledge. The narrator's recourse to what seems a mythic dimension (an invincible "Will"), therefore, like Gloucester's evocation of the Gods in *Lear,* not only stands in ironic contrast to the novel's representations of a mundane reality, but also suggests an authorial awareness on Dunbar's part that is crucial to a full understanding of his narrative. (p. 132)

It is tempting . . . to label Dunbar's narrative a minor romance of the South, to salvage what one can of historical import and move on. I have already suggested, though, that such an approach forecloses the possibility of an adequate account of the novel as a literary work of art. The act of theft, which is central to the story, for example, cannot be comprehended in its textual implications unless one apprehends the narrative's implied view of human understanding. *The Sport of the Gods* is essentially a discourse, I think, on the fallibility of human habits of thought. Maurice Oakley offers a case in point.

Considering himself a shrewd businessman beyond the reach of sentimentality, Oakley takes what he considers an analytical position on his servant's alleged theft. He says: "I shall not condemn any one until I have proof positive of his guilt or such clear circumstantial evidence that my reason is satisfied." . . . Only the flimsiest "circumstantial evidence"—the fact that Hamilton has more than the amount of the reported theft in a savings account and the fact that he has access to the half-brother's bedroom—is available. Yet, it is sufficient to satisfy the master of his servant's guilt. Indeed, Oakley's vaunted empiricism and proclaimed analytical bent are no more than linguistic masks. They are verbal shows that conceal a sentimental and prejudiced ("No servant is beyond suspicion," he says) . . . fantast. Having received Franks' confession letter from Paris later in the text, he sits and weaves elaborate fantasies of his brother's abilities. . . . When such sentimental musings are shattered by the actual contents of the letter, Oakley has no way of processing reality. His mental operations are at an end. Bereft of his governing fancy, he goes mad, weeping "like a child whose last toy has been broken." . . . (pp. 132-33)

The black servant who suffers the consequences of Oakley's weak intellect is a man falsely accused. The text, however, does not grant him the status of a noble victim where human understanding is concerned. Instead, the narrative implies that Berry Hamilton has been as driven by a misleading abstract idealism as his master has been controlled by a groundless fantasy. Berry has conducted his life in accordance with an ideal of frugal, convivial Christian respectability that he takes as the moving force of the white world occupied by his employer. He feels that by conducting his life in harmony with this ideal, he will transcend the limits that mark the black life of his own community. He has set his goals and established his "fictional finalisms," however, without considering the nearly mindless state of Maurice Oakley and his class. For in the servant's world view, the white world of the masters represents "quality." "It's de p'opah thing," he says, "fu' a man what waits on quality to have quality mannahs an' to wair quality clothes." . . . The paradoxical results of the servant's idealism achieve apt representation when he is sentenced to ten years of hard prison labor as a function of his life of industrious thrift. The bank account signaling adherence to his ideal is the evidence that condemns him in the eyes of the world.

The very existence of the "theft" that disrupts the Oakley estate is, thus, contingent upon a fragile psychological economy. A prejudicial fantasy and an infirm idealism offer its conditions of possibility. And Oakley's mode of processing experience is so prevalent among his fellow white townspeople and so forceful as a mode of explanation that no one is able to see that the servant is not "really" a thief. The town concurs that Hamilton could not have accumulated thirteen hundred dollars by honest means. . . . (pp. 133-34)

The black townspeople respond in the manner of their white overlords. There is an immediate audit of the books Berry has kept as treasurer of his lodge, the Tribe of Benjamin. And the black A.M.E. church promptly expels him from membership. Finally, the servant's response to events surrounding him is not unlike Oakley's response to his brother's letter. "The shock," we are told by the narrator, "had been too sudden for him,

and it was as if his reason had been for the time unseated." . . . (p. 134)

In the fictional world that *The Sport of the Gods* establishes with the representation of a theft, men and women are undone by their limited and limiting modes of perception. They are incapable of seeing any object, person, or event steadily and whole because their cognitive strategies always mandate a partial view. At its most absurd level of representation this human inadequacy is captured by the denizens of the Continental Hotel. Horace Talbot, Beachfield Davis, and Colonel Saunders gather at the "Continental" (a devastatingly ironic label of sophistication in view of their discourse) to drink and to discuss the topics of their own and of southern days past. The adequacy of their means of apprehending the world reveals itself in their reflections on black Americans. Talbot advances what he calls his "theory" with the claim that blacks are irrepressible children who are unprepared for a "higher civilization." They have been mistakenly liberated from their bondage, says Talbot, by well-intentioned northerners. "Why gentlemen," he intones, "I forsee the day when these people themselves shall come to us Southerners of their own accord and ask to be reenslaved until such time as they shall be fit for freedom." . . . Beachfield Davis, by contrast, suggests that blacks suffer a condition of "total depravity." His evidence for the claim is the fact that one of his servants once used Davis' finely bred hound dog for possum hunting. Finally, Colonel Saunders' epistemological mettle is revealed when he retracts even his speculative remark that Berry Hamilton may be innocent. The three characters who occupy the Continental stand as parodic representations of "choice spirits of the old régime." . . . They are men who take pride in a manner of ordering experience that blinds them to their own patent absurdity. Even Oakley, who is one of their number, refers to them as "a lot of muddle-pated fools." . . . (p. 135)

The black counterparts of such unknowing whites are found in New York's Banner Club, a northern parallel to the Continental Hotel. Pretense, self-deception, masking, and indolence are the norm at the Banner Club. It is here that Berry's son Joe meets Hattie Sterling (who is anything but "sterling"). The chorus girl's fast-disappearing physical beauty is sufficiently masked to attract the young man's idolatry. . . . Joe has been primed for this ecstatic response to a cosmetic beauty by his experiences among the "quality" young whites of the South. . . . Like his father, Joe is undone, in part, by his adoption of what he feels is a suitable white standard of conduct. When he finally realizes how his naive enthusiasm and sense of triumph in gaining Hattie's attention have played him false, he becomes what the text describes as a "Frankenstein." Manipulated and shaped by misleading ideals, the young Hamilton is driven to murder. . . . When the boy's mode of understanding the world is destroyed, he is left a prey to madness.

Kitty and Fannie Hamilton fare little better than Joe in their choice of constructs for ordering experience. The girl's reaction to her first view of the New York stage is described as one of enchantment. . . . Her mode of understanding life is fixed in this narrative moment. Her vision and sympathies hardly extend beyond her own theatrical world when the novel draws toward its climax with Joe's act of murder.

The unfortunate ends to which the characters come in *The Sport of the Gods* are the logical results of their misguided modes of understanding the world. The narrator of the novel, however, does not situate this human failing in a single geographical setting, nor does he suggest that it is solely the function of an unalterable and determinate set of historical events. Men and women in the city are as prone to misapprehensions of experience as are those in the country. The events of an implied historical progression (the "old days") may have left a legacy of inexact ideas and fragile ideals, but all of human life is not helplessly shackled by these false constructs. There is release from erroneous habits of thought in a domain that transcends the ordinary course of affairs. This redeeming area of human action is signed by the first line of the novel, which introduces the implicit subject of the narrative. From the outset, we are thus alerted that the text which follows is a "fiction" whose implied goal is to avoid the "monotony" of a traditional pattern of narration. This oft-repeated narrative pattern has been called the "Plantation Tradition."

By inference, I suggest that the narrative strategy of *The Sport of the Gods* moves from its announced subject of "fiction" to an implicit *reductio ad absurdum* of the Plantation Tradition. The desire of Oakley and his confreres to see their mode of life raised to acclaim by an idealizing art conditions the pallid and deceptive romanticism of the southern artist. This reciprocal relationship is ultimately responsible for the true theft of the novel. Berry Hamilton's liberty and rightful earnings are the genuine items of theft. Their appropriation by southern justice is a function of the distorting modes of perception that both condition and gain support from the fictions of the Plantation Tradition.

The "surplus value" accumulated by the servant is seen by the South as a theft. Basing its conviction of the servant's guilt on the prevailing stereotypes of an idealizing fiction, the town is incapable of perceiving the genuine theft. Oakley offers a parodic illustration of this conditioned myopia. . . . The implication . . . is that the black American who honestly assumes values lying beyond a subsistence level of existence—that lie beyond the status prescribed for blacks as happy servitors—is "unthinkable." The art in which Oakley and his class place their entire faith supports such staunch ignorance. In a sense that constitutes a striking indictment of the southern businessman and his art, the black servant is the hapless victim of a fiction. (pp. 135-37)

As integral to the narrative strategy of *The Sport of the Gods* as the work's representation of the implications of a Plantation Tradition is the novel's implicit critique of black American popular art in the North. On the day the Hamiltons arrive in New York, their landlady suggests an evening out to them. "Why, yes," says one of the occupants of the rooming house, "what's the matter with tomorrer night? There's a good coon show in town. . . . [The] narrator of *The Sport of the Gods* characterizes them as theatricals combining "tawdry music and inane words." . . . Their audiences are described as "swaggering, sporty young negroes" . . . who move about the theatre as though they were the "owners" of the shows. Later in the text, Kitty is represented as dropping "the simple old songs she knew to practise the detestable coon ditties which the stage demanded." . . . The coon show, finally, comes to stand in the narrative as the emblematic and ordering mode of perception for northern blacks.

At their first show, the Hamilton family capitulates to the vision of life that the coon show represents. Kitty gives way to the enchantment noted earlier. Her brother Joe is not only impressed by the pomp and swagger of the black audience, but also by the appearance of the women of the chorus. . . . Mrs. Hamilton at first has reservations, but these give way before the vigor of the performance. . . . All of northern black life,

The Sport of the Gods implies, is a stage—the province of a gaudy coon show. And the lives guided by this "tawdry" means of processing experiences stand in contrast to those that are governed by what the text refers to as the "old teachings and old customs" . . . of black southern life. The irony of this contrast, however, is that the "customs" and "teaching" associated with singing to God "across the Southern fields" have provided no security for the lives of the Hamiltons, nor have they in any sense enabled them to withstand the allure of a northern coon show. Even more ironic, of course, is the fact that the coon-show representations that win them over are not radically different from the representations of the Plantation Tradition. The opening scene of the show they attend is one of jovial, energetic black picnickers on holiday, singing their contentment to the world. The turn-of-the-century black theatrical, then, is hardly an art—a means of understanding life— that can redeem the theft perpetrated by plantation fiction. What is needed for this task, *The Sport of the Gods* makes clear, is a new "idea," a new theory that will produce a dramatically different reading of life. Skaggs, the yellow journalist of the novel, is the character who arrives at such an idea. . . . His "idea" is that he can uncover the genuine theft and set matters right in print. It is this construct that he slowly nurtures. . . . What Skaggs' theory amounts to is a speculative ordering of unaccustomed propositions, and the editor calls it "a rattle-brained, harum-scarum thing." . . . Yet the editor is alert to the universe of discourse that the reporter is invoking, for he adds, "Yes, it [the theory] looks plausible, but so does all fiction." . . . Earlier, the narrator has commmented that Skaggs is one with a penchant for the "bizarre." . . . He is also described as a person whose "saving quality . . . was that he calmly believed his own lies while he was telling them, so no one was hurt, for the deceiver was as much a victim as the deceived." . . . The reporter, in fact, begins his relationship with Joe by telling the boy an elaborate lie about his white boyhood on a southern plantation. By the end of *The Sport of the Gods,* however, he has ferreted out the crime perpetrated by the Plantation Tradition and its artist. Skaggs' narrative progress, therefore, involves the introduction of a new and revealing perspective into the universe of fictive discourse. I think he both represents (as a "monumental liar") and inhabits (given the text's strategies on the subject of "fiction") this universe of discourse in the world of *The Sport of the Gods*. (pp. 138-40)

The "Will" referred to in the narrative's final tableau, . . . is, in my view, the force that generates a new mode of fictive discourse. The author of *The Sport of the Gods,* however, seems patently aware that the text's representation of the redemptive potential of fiction is, in itself, but one proposition in a fiction. His narrator self-consciously announces "fiction" as a subject of the narrative in the opening line of the novel. What I am suggesting is that Dunbar knew there was no such thing in the world of actual human events as a "limitless" freedom—mythic or otherwise. He knew that his own novel would not have the kind of immediate effect on the context in which it emerged as Skaggs' story has on the novel's fictive world of southern governors and northern readers. The black author realized, in short, that actual fictions operate within the "institution of literature" and are, like myths, marked by certain constraints. . . . *The Sport of the Gods,* viewed in terms of his observation, is Dunbar's symbolic "acting out," as it were, of the effects on American life and letters of a supreme, revelatory fiction that will enable human beings to see life steadily and whole, that will enable them to break free from both their "artistic" and "ordinary" modes of structuring experience.

The novel, thus, explores the proposition that a literary tradition governed by plantation and coon-show images of Afro-Americans can be altered through an ironic, symbolic, fictive manipulation of these images and of the tradition in which they have played a formative part. (pp. 141-42)

> *Houston A. Baker, Jr., "The 'Limitless' Freedom of Myth: Paul Laurence Dunbar's 'The Sport of the Gods' and the Criticism of Afro-American Literature" (© 1981 by the University of New Mexico Press; reprinted by permission of the author; a revision of a lecture entitled "'The Sport of the Gods' As a Literary Work of Art" originally delivered at Morgan State University in 1978), in* The American Self: Myth, Ideology, and Popular Culture, *edited by Sam B. Girgus, University of New Mexico Press, 1981, pp. 124-43.*

ADDITIONAL BIBLIOGRAPHY

Allen, Walker. "Paul Laurence Dunbar, A Study in Genius." *The Psychoanalytic Review* XXV, No. 1 (January 1938): 53-82.

Interprets Dunbar's genius as "some frustrated craving or attempted solution of some insurmountable problem." Allen views Dunbar as a complex personality burdened by an "intense devotion" to his mother, emotional immaturity, and sexual, racial, and physical inferiorities, among other neuroses typical of creative genius.

Brawley, Benjamin. *Paul Laurence Dunbar: Poet of His People.* 1936. Reprint. Port Washington, N.Y.: Kennikat Press, 1967, 159 p.

Critical biography based on the poet's letters, and personal interviews with his mother, former wife, friends, and acquaintances.

Brown, Sterling A. "The Literary Scene: Biography." *Opportunity* XV, No. 7 (July 1937): 216-17.

Reviews Benjamin Brawley's *Paul Laurence Dunbar: Poet of His People.* Brown states: "The biography before us . . . is uncomfortably close to Horatio Alger. . . ." Brown feels that Brawley provides little evidence to support the critical generalizations and "debatable dogma" he presents.

Candela, Gregory L. "We Wear the Mask: Irony in Dunbar's *The Sport of the Gods.*" *American Literature* XLVIII, No. 1 (March 1976): 60-72.

Unique interpretation of Dunbar's novel. Candela feels that the "good satire" in the novel is more relevant than the "bad melodrama" dwelt on by many critics of Dunbar's *The Sport of the Gods.* He believes that Dunbar, rather than being on the "outside of black authors' march toward literary criticism," should more justly be considered "in the vanguard as a novelist able to mix the seemingly inflexible elements of melodrama with the consciousness of an ironic mask that the black people in America know so well."

Cunningham, Virginia. *Paul Laurence Dunbar and His Song.* New York: Dodd, Mead & Co., 1947, 283 p.

Considered one of the most authoritative biographies. The book, which contains dialogue attributed to letters, scrap books, and personal reminiscences, traces the poet's life, presenting a picture of a dutiful son, loyal friend, and brilliant writer. Racial problems and controversies are given only passing mention.

DuBois, W. E. Burghardt. "Negro Art and Literature." In his *The Gift of Black Folk: The Negro in the Making of America,* pp. 287-319. Boston: The Stratford Co., Publishers, 1924.*

Brief history of black American writers. DuBois calls Dunbar "the undoubted laureate of the race," who became a national figure by raising dialect from the "minstrel stage to literature."

Hughes, Langston. "The Negro Artist and the Racial Mountain." *The Nation* CXXII, No. 3181 (23 June 1926): 692-94.*

Examines racial influences upon black writers. Hughes mentions Dunbar as an early artist who was viewed as a "freak" despite the "quaint charm and humor" of his dialect verse.

Johnson, James Weldon. In his *Along This Way: The Autobiography of James Weldon Johnson.* New York: Viking Press, 1933, 418 p.*

Personal reminiscences. A personal friend and admirer, Johnson recalls Dunbar's refined manners, commanding voice, and the seriousness with which he approached his craft. Johnson also recalls the poet's biting sarcasm, childlish lack of discipline, and his regrets about the small amount of work he completed.

Martin, Jay, ed. *A Singer in the Dawn: Reinterpretations of Paul Laurence Dunbar.* New York: Dodd, Mead & Co., 1975, 255 p.

Lectures and memorial poems presented at the Centenary Conference on Paul Laurence Dunbar at the University of California, Irvine, in 1972. Contributors include Arna Bontemps, Addison Gayle, Jr., Nikki Giovanni, Saunders Redding, and Darwin T. Turner, among others.

Wiggins, Lida Keck. "The Life of Paul Laurence Dunbar." In *The Life and Works of Paul Laurence Dunbar,* by Paul Laurence Dunbar, pp. 25-136. Naperville, Ill.: J. L. Nichols & Co., 1907.

Biography and collected works. The first complete biography of Dunbar is colored by the admiration of Wiggins, a Dunbar family friend. W. D. Howells's famous introduction of Dunbar's *Lyrics of Lowly Life* is reprinted, and the poems and short stories are illustrated with photographs.

Wright, John Livingston. "Three Negro Poets." *The Colored American Magazine* (April 1901): 404-13.*

Brief biography that praises the successes of Dunbar, Daniel Webster Davis, and James D. Corrothers for depicting black characters in ways different from the derogatory portrayals by white predecessors.

Hanns Heinz Ewers

1871-1943

German novelist, short story writer, scriptwriter, dramatist, poet, essayist, and critic.

Ewers was the author of several novels and short stories that are considered among the classics of twentieth-century Gothic and occult fiction. *Der Zauberlehrling (The Sorcerer's Apprentice)*, *Alraune*, and the anthology piece "Die Spinne" ("The Spider") have particularly earned the esteem of specialists in Gothic literature for their grotesque imagination and for their depictions of the darkest aspects of human nature. The principal theme articulated throughout Ewers's major works is that humanity's most vital impulses are also its most barbaric, and that these impulses are nurtured solely by the exercise of cruelty. Characters are most intensely alive in Ewers's fiction when engaged in some destructive and brutal endeavor.

Ewers was born in Düsseldorf, Germany. His father was a painter and his mother a translator. His literary career began with the publication of *Ein Fabelbuch*, a collection of rhymed satires written in collaboration with Theodor Etzel. The work was well received and the ensuing publicity led to Ewers's association with a literary vaudeville theater. In 1901, Ewers founded his own vaudeville theater and traveled throughout Germany, Hungary, Austria, and Switzerland. When the troupe was disbanded, due to expenses and to its provocation of censors, Ewers continued his travels. He lived in India for a time, and the outbreak of World War I found him in the United States, where he was interned during the war. Ewers's novels, particularly the trilogy comprised of *The Sorcerer's Apprentice*, *Vampir (Vampire)*, and *Alraune*, had gained him considerable public notoriety as well as respect among critics. In the early 1930s, the underlying philosophy in these works—that a primitive will directs human affairs—had an immediate appeal for the Nazis, conforming with the *Blut und Boden* ("blood and soil") conception of the Third Reich. The Nazis' regard for Ewers was reciprocal, and he stated that he found in the party the "strongest expression of the Powers of Darkness." Ewers went on to write a nationalistic novel, *Reiter in deutscher Nacht (Rider of the Night)* and a fictionalized biography of the Nazi martyr Horst Wessel. Later, however, Ewers's emphasis on the vicious and perverted expression of human drives, a purportedly "Jewish" theme, caused his works to be placed on the Nazis' "List of Harmful and Undesirable Authors." Aside from these facts, information on Ewers's life is scant or obscure.

In his highly laudatory monograph on Edgar Allan Poe, Ewers assumed that Poe's works were inspired by alcohol and defended the use of "poisons" in the creation of art. "Must not the mind be 'poisoned' in order to produce works of art?" he wrote. "Such intoxication is no delight, it is an unbearable torture; consciously desired only by him on whose brow the living mark of art is branded." Like his American counterpart, the German author also subjected himself to the "intoxications" of an art of horror. His earliest works in this vein were the short stories found in such collections as *Die Besessenen* and *Das Grauen*. As in most of his other Gothic writings, Ewers constructed many of these stories around perverse and bestial incidents. In "Die Mamaloi" ("Mamaloi"), for ex-

ample, a German businessman living in Haiti willingly becomes involved in the ritual slaughter and sexual practices of a local voodoo cult. Other stories, such as "Die Tomatensauce" ("Tomato Sauce"), also develop the theme that the line dividing primitive and so-called civilized societies is a very thin or nonexistent one. In "Die Hinrichtung des Damiens" ("The Execution of Damiens") appears another theme common to Ewers's fiction: the hidden layer of sadism lying beneath a veneer of romantic love. The narrator's awakening comes when he discovers that the British noblewoman with whom he was in love is attentive only to a slim book that describes in gruesome detail the tortures undergone by the would-be assassin of King Louis XV. Ewers's most famous treatment of the theme of sadism occurs in the short story "The Spider." The main character's masochistic subservience to a mysterious woman and his eventual suicide under her direction has been condemned by some critics as puerile demonism while others have praised it as a tour de force of psychological horror. Concerns similar to those in Ewers's short stories are developed at length in his novels, especially his trilogy.

Gabriel Ronay has stated that "Ewers went well beyond Poe . . . in his conscious exploitations of the cruelty and blood-madness that had swept across Europe." Possibly the most symbolic and artistically successful evidence for this statement is the first work of his trilogy, *The Sorcerer's Apprentice*. The protagonist, Frank Braun, is an erudite adventurer proud of his ability to incite others to mystical frenzies in which he, a jaded and cynical man, is incapable of losing himself. Braun's sojourn in an isolated Italian village illustrates Ewers's philosophical tenets, in particular the close relationship between religious ritual and humanity's hunger for butchery. Through mass scourgings and both voluntary and involuntary crucifixions, the villagers of Val di Scodra discover what Frank Braun considers the essence of mystical experience: reversion to a divine condition prior to and below human consciousness, a metamorphosis "down to God." While Braun has set these events in motion, through psychological manipulation and hypnosis, he is repelled at their outcome and remains the sole exemplar of human morality. In *Alraune*, Frank Braun again acts as the parent of a sequence of bizarre catastrophes. On this occasion he arranges for the creation of the title character, Alraune, who is the supernatural offspring of a newly executed murderer and a prostitute. Alraune is a human incarnation of the mandrake plant, which according to legend is grown from the seed of a hanged man and nurtured by the earth. Her subsequent career of sadism and tragedy is Ewers's most extended statement on the destructive power of erotic forces. Don Ryan, an early critic, noted that in *Alraune* Ewers "intended his heroine to stand as a protagonist of the female principle in nature; that power omnipotent, unreasoning, demanding everything and destroying all." The final work of the trilogy is *Vampire*. The depiction of a German citizen who is—unconsciously—a vampire was viewed by critics in the 1930s as indicative of that country's mentality at the time, one that was seeking justification in myth and legend for a worldwide blood rite. In his essay on Ewers, Ronay explains the symbolic values that the vampire had taken on in German fiction: "Those returning from the grave were not frightening figures of horror, but superhuman *Übermenschen* heralding the destruction of the decadent old world and the creation of a New Order based on blood."

Although Ewers wrote widely outside the Gothic genre, it is his work in this form which has secured his reputation. Believing, as did Poe, that art and imagination, even of the most macabre bent, were the only sources of beauty, Ewers wrote: "Reality is ugly—and to the ugly is denied all right of existence. Dreams are beautiful, and are true because they are beautiful, and therefore I believe in dreams as the only reality."

(See also *Contemporary Authors*, Vol. 109.)

PRINCIPAL WORKS

Ein Fabelbuch [with Theodor Etzel]   (satire)   1901
Edgar Allan Poe   (essay)   1905
  [*Edgar Allan Poe*, 1917]
Die Besessenen   (short stories)   1908
Das Grauen   (short stories)   1908
  [*Blood* (partial translation), 1930]
Der Zauberlehrling   (novel)   1909
  [*The Sorcerer's Apprentice*, 1927]
Alraune   (novel)   1911
  [*Alraune*, 1929]
Vampir   (novel)   1921
  [*Vampire*, 1934; also published as *Vampire's Prey*, 1935]
Nachtmahr   (short stories)   1922
Reiter in deutscher Nacht   (novel)   1932
  [*Rider of the Night*, 1932]

"The Execution of Damiens"   (short story)   1962;
  published in *Selections from the Pan Book of Horror, No. 3*
"The Spider"   (short story)   1979; published in *Wolf's Complete Book of Terror*

ADÈLE LEWISOHN   (essay date 1916)

[*Lewisohn was the translator of Ewers's monograph* Edgar Allan Poe; *the following excerpt is taken from the introduction to that work.*]

One of the reasons for Hanns Heinz Ewers' influence upon German verse and prose is his wonderful sense of the value of words, of their colors and sounds, which he shares with the masters of all times. His instinct leads him toward the strange, the unexpected. The actions in his books take place in the human soul—that land of dreams which unites our soul to the world-soul.

The conception of the **"Alraune"** or **"Mandragora,"** his most famous book, antedates Pythagoras. It is a fable of the plant that shrieks when plucked. Ewers combines this story with the science of our times and creates a tale of a strange passion, with no intent to intoxicate but rather to explain. This book has affected not only the literature of Germany, but the literature of France. . . . (p. v)

I cannot quote from any of his poems for they are as yet untranslated. In the series called **"The Soul of Flowers,"** in a manner so simple as to be almost ingenuous, he has declared in exquisite language that if the rose is the flower of love in all the universe it is because this thought caused it to become what it is.

His **"Sorcerer's Apprentice, or, the Devil Hunters"** is a powerful performance. A community of peasants in an Italian mountain village repeat among themselves the whole of the passion of Christ until the final crucifixion. A simple peasant girl is hypnotized into believing herself a savior and taking the sins of the world upon her shoulders. Of this work we can truly say that nothing that is human is alien to it. (p. vi)

[Ewers'] conclusion is that the occult is so deeply rooted in our spiritual natures that the mind is our actual body, and the imagination our real mind—that as a phenomenon of nature there exists nothing more holy or more spiritual than the carnal.

At a time when Poe was comparatively little understood Ewers was his most sympathetic German interpreter. He is able to mirror the soul of Poe because they are intellectual kinsmen. Both are at home in "the misty mid-region of Weir," both dwell "out of Space, out of Time." Both have explored the realm of Horror. In fact, Ewers has gone beyond Poe because to him was revealed the mystery of sex; to Poe sex always was a sealed book. However, his attitude toward Poe, as shown in [**"Edgar Allan Poe"**] is almost that of a worshiper. (p. vii)

> *Adèle Lewisohn, "Introduction" (1916), in* Edgar Allan Poe *by Hanns Heinz Ewers, translated by Adèle Lewisohn (translation copyright, 1916, by B. W. Huebsch), Huebsch, 1917, pp. v-vii.*

THE NATION (essay date 1917)

The translator [of *Edgar Allan Poe,* Adèle Lewisohn, (see excerpt above)] tells us that Ewers "has gone beyond Poe because to him was revealed the mystery of sex." But slightingly as Mr. Ewers thinks of America, we have not had to wait for him to open that mystery. And in this maudlin little rhapsody he is not dealing with sex at all. He is only celebrating the effect of poisons and intoxicants upon the human brain. He is only pointing out the elements of the artistic consciousness. He is only giving us another fragrant whiff of German *Kultur.* "The time will come," he prophesies, "when the highroads of our sober art, only scantily lighted by the melancholy lamps of alcohol, will be riduculed. A time for those to whom intoxication and art are inseparable ideas, who as a matter of fact will only recognize the distinction in the art brought forth by intoxication." Till that blessed time comes, it will be difficult for any one to appreciate the *Einfluss* of Mr. Ewers, unless he is himself, as Cicero says, *bene potus.*

> *A review of "Edgar Allan Poe," in* The Nation *(copyright 1917 The Nation magazine, The Nation Associates, Inc.), Vol. CIV, No. 2701, April 5, 1917, p. 410.*

HENRY B. FULLER (essay date 1917)

[In *Edgar Allan Poe*] Herr Ewers sends forth his work from the Alhambra. On his opening page the fountains babble and the nightingales sing from out the laurels. On his last page the nightingales are still warbling; and through the intervening spaces the author himself sings—and sings rather "wildly well"—a somewhat more than "mortal melody." It is impassioned; it is unboundedly generous. It is elegiac too.

For Poe—such is his plaint—never knew the Alhambra. This privilege was allowed Washington Irving, "that model of English conventionality," who was able to dream at will under the magic spell of the Alhambra moonshine. What might not Poe have done in the same environment? And what *did* he do— what did he *have* to do—in bleak and empty America? He drank. The Dionysiac state which might have been reached so happily under one set of conditions had to be reached most unhappily and disastrously under another. Only thus could the poet, as he was situated, "create new *art values.*"

What is the artist? The artist, says Herr Ewers, is the first explorer. The eternal land of our longing lies dreamily before us in grey misty clouds. There is no beauty, as Poe himself says, quoting Lord Bacon, without some strangeness; or, as glossed by Arthur Symons, some unexpectedness, some novelty. The artist is the man whose tormenting desires are so great that he "must emerge from the realm *which we know.*" He enters first; then come the hordes of investigators and surveyors—the "land registrars and rent collectors," as our author disdainfully calls them. And what gives entrance? The so-called poisons, narcotics, are as potent as other means to lead us beyond the threshold of the unconscious. If one succeeds in getting a foothold in this other world, and has the native capacity for profiting by a state of ecstasy, he creates a new work of art, and is, in the noblest sense, an artist. And such, believes Herr Ewers, was Poe *in excelsis.*

Yet no intoxicant in the world, he goes on to say, can develop in a man qualities which he does not possess. Thus "the Griswolds and the Ingrams could take any amount of wine, could smoke any amount of opium, could eat any amount of hashish; nevertheless they would be unable to create works of art."

One wonders just where our author, in his fiery zeal, would place certain other of Poe's American critics of the New England tradition, or near it; the eminent essayist who called him the "jingle man"; the eminent novelist who spoke of his "very valueless verses." But Herr Ewers ranges himself promptly with the European commentators: with Arthur Symons, who calls Poe a genius among various American talents—one who, because he was "fantastically inhuman, a conscious artist doing strange things with strange materials," has failed to make many realize how fine, how rare was the beauty which—an anticipator of Verlaine and of Mallarmé—he brought into the world. . . . (pp. 433-34)

We do not exactly warm to Herr Ewers when he declares himself happy in being a German, because "Germany's great men were permitted to be immoral—that is, not quite as moral as the good middle class and the priests"; or when he adds that the German knows that Goethe "was not so very moral," yet "does not take that fact too much to heart." Nor do we quite rise to our author when he announces that "later investigation" has rehabilitated Byron, so that he can now be accepted as "moral" and therefore be read by the hypocritical English. Nor do we relish his prophecy that Oscar Wilde will presently be put through the same process. Nor do we quite apprehend how Poe's one personal failing, or weakness, should cause him to be dragged so summarily into Herr Ewers's improvised court of "morality." Poe assuredly was, as our author himself is made to declare, "a gentleman from top to toe," albeit a peculiarly unfortunate one; and we are not at all certain that this new friend of his—whom, the more we linger on him, the less, on general grounds, we like—has made the misfortune of our poet and gentleman appreciably less. (p. 434)

> *Henry B. Fuller, "An Idol of the Parnassians," in* The Dial *(copyright, 1917, by The Dial Publishing Company, Inc.), Vol. LXII, No. 742, May 17, 1917, pp. 433-34.*

DON RYAN (essay date 1929)

How far can the mind of the bizarre artist go toward the creation of tangible evil?

Pretty far, if we recall the long list of these flowers of evil, ranging from the reasoned atrocities of the Marquis de Sade down through Poe and Baudelaire to Huysmanns. And it is in this category that the work of Hanns Heinz Ewers falls, both by virtue of his quest for sin and his quest for beauty.

Given a groundwork of religious faith, the desire to revolt and the spark of creative genius, and the result is often a work of appalling beauty. Much of the fiction that Ewers has written bears this impress. "Alraune," his latest book to reach us in an English translation, is regarded by most critics as the best work of this perverted genius. Personally the writer gives preference to "The Sorcerer's Apprentice," but only because of the more detailed and sustained horror of the latter work.

And it is not meant in any wise to discourage the prospective reader of "Alraune." This flagrant tale contains enough of horror to make it an ideal Christmas gift for some aged and wealthy relative by whose sudden demise we might worthily profit.

"Alraune" is the child of a perverse thought—a challenge to the Almighty. Her mortal conception was engineered by snatching the procreative power of a murderer at the moment he is guillotined and transferring it to the body of a shameless woman of the streets. Over the child of this fell union hangs the influence of the mythical mandrake—the gallows flower of medieval legend—the root of which, formed like a man, brings riches to its owner just as surely as the early death which it makes inevitable.

The tale records the fate of Alraune's six lovers, including the perverted old scientist who carried out the experiment that made her; the narrow escape of the man whose idea it was to bring her into the world; likewise what happened to her feminine admirers, for Alraune's diabolical attraction existed for both sexes.

The orgies of the last chapters are enough to bar the volume from censor-ruled communities were it not for Ewers's delicate restraint.

This book, in fact, is not for the public whose morals the censors are trying to protect. It is for the minority of readers who delight to follow the same formula in reading that Ewers and his school pursue in writing, namely the quest of beauty—in evil, in decay, in death. If you are of the reading elect you will revel in the grandeur of Ewers's gloomy Schwarzwald. For "**Alraune**" is a book to be read more for style than content—although there is a lingering suspicion in the mind of the writer that the author intended his heroine to stand as protagonist of the female principle in nature; that power omnipotent, unreasoning, demanding everything and destroying all.

> *Don Ryan, "Hanns Ewers Creates a Subtle Flower of Evil," in* New York Evening Post, *(reprinted by permission of the* New York Post; © *1929 New York Post Corporation), November 23, 1929, p. 14 M.*

THOMAS TERWILLIGER (essay date 1929)

[*Alraune*] is rooted deep in medieval love of the grotesque. We are asked to follow pagan superstition into modern science and to watch the forces of evil, blown like pollen on hot winds from the southern deserts, unite poisonously with reason and with biological fact. Yet in this union Ewers insists by his very form upon the supernatural, which finds its shape in folklore and grotesque fairy tale. Three times he embodies in his story an intermezzo which rings like poetry or music, and each of these short passages surpasses the tale itself in its intensity of expressed desire and in its sense of fatality.

Here Ewers comments upon his own work, and repeats like the theme of a song the story of the birth of Evil in the deserts, whence it is blown north to inflame mankind. His key is fancy and brooding nightmare; against this science can make slight headway. Reality lies in the dream, the allegory of incarnate evil born of thought; and we believe the physical fact less than the mental fever of its birth. The plot, by its repeated coincidences, bears weight only in so far as we are intentionally credulous, while the desires that move the plot tower more impressively because they are described with the validity of art.

So, too, the stewing, fuming evil which nurtured the Idea in Frank Braun and the Act in his uncle is painted with really masterly colors; this first picture cannot be forgotten, though it should be partly forgotten for the sake of the whole. No other part of Alraune's history seems so hideous or so poisonous as her origin, before she was even compounded. Nothing that she does seems to rise to the intense horror of the first union, so that she appears almost human after all and we can almost explain her scientifically by heredity and environment—

both dark enough—as a girl who was not given the opportunity of an equal test. Her story sounds a little too much like any depressing psychological novel, and so she loses her original fairy power. Possibly her author knew this; at least his intermezzo and finale show an increasingly violent struggle to convey a picture of lust and nightmare. The result is not a great novel; but it is a weird tale, parts of which have been told with poetic beauty.

> *Thomas Terwilliger, "Root of Evil," in* New York Herald Tribune Books *(© I.H.T. Corporation; reprinted by permission), December 15, 1929, p. 2.*

PAUL ALLEN (essay date 1934)

Blood seeps through [the pages of "**Vampire**"]; long before the protagonist stares horror stricken at his mutilated mistress we have come to know the feel, the smell, and almost the taste, of the blood this vampire has lived on. And we are as terrified as Frank Braun for, unlike "Dracula" and "The Werewolf of Paris," this horror is to be known in our own time, our own city, among the people we know. . . .

But it is not this conception of a vampire that gives the book its power. That has been done before and again in thrillers. It is when we face the maggot in Frank Braun's brain that we feel the impetus of the book. It is the fear of the unknown that carries the horror. For when the author weaves in and out of this tale the old myths of the blood-goddess we have the desperate feeling that he has touched powers of malignant evil that are still about us. The myth is an expression of an ancient and terrible reality; perhaps a truth about human nature from which reason turns aside.

It is this revulsion of the reason rather than any revulsion of the emotions that makes the book hold us with such compulsion. It is that which makes us grateful that the book is dull in spots, and sometimes even ridiculous, for then we have surcease. For the author may hold us for page after page of lore from "The Golden Bough" and we believe; but nothing will convince us that high life in New York City is as he paints it, except in a servant girl's dream. And when he writes of the great mission of the Jews and their power, one can but agree and wonder that he is not bitter about the return the Fatherland has made to them. But when he persists in thinking the English were stupid and the Americans essentially selfish children in 1916, we feel that time and tide should have changed all that. It is when he reverts to that power he used so successfully in "**The Sorcerer's Apprentice**" that he is the magician again, able to terrify us in spite of ourselves with the realization that forces of evil beyond our control can clutch at us and destroy us. Read other horror books about vampires for the thrill, but with this one be prepared for a psychological experience.

> *Paul Allen, in his review of "Vampire," in* New York Herald Tribune Books *(© I.H.T. Corporation; reprinted by permission), September 30, 1934, p. 22.*

THE NEW YORK TIMES BOOK REVIEW (essay date 1934)

Vampire fiction has usually been invested with an esoteric, medieval atmosphere—to invoke shudders—which in Herr Ewer's novel ["**Vampire**"] is advantageously missing. Absence of the familiar attributes, however, is filled with a good deal of the usual hocus-pocus anent cabalism, sorcery, precious stones, devil worship, astrology, mythology, soothsaying and the like which does not seem to fit harmoniously into the generally modern design of the story. The ancient, legendary subject is here treated from a fresh angle—that of an involuntary, unconscious sufferer from the terrifying malady—which, it is needless to say, does not completely lift the tale out of incredibility or lend it perceptible semblance of the possible. . . .

The author strives his utmost to clarify and impart the sense of terror that obsesses his chief character, but fails, if valiantly, to do so. Frank never more approximates actuality than do the childish bogies which relentlessly torment him. Perhaps the story's failure may be laid to the fact that vampires have always belonged to supernatural literature and that it is impossible successfully to bring them into the alien fold of the realistic novel. A necessarily unfavorable opinion of the book in no degree alters our admiration of Ewers's past novels, our particularly high regard for **"The Sorcerer's Apprentice"** and the more recent **"Rider of the Night."**

> *"The Vampire Theme,"* in The New York Times Book Review (© 1934 by The New York Times Company; reprinted by permission), November 4, 1934, p. 24.

JERRE MANGIONE (essay date 1934)

Ewers finished [**"Vampire"**] several years before anyone took the Nazis seriously—before he even guessed that one day he would be among the few German writers of any consequence who could be nice to Hitler. Yet if **"Vampire"** had been written under the Führer's leadership it could hardly have been more in tune with the theme songs of the Nazis; its pages fairly drip with the mysticism, nationalism and symbolism dear to their hearts. Ewers did have the poor taste to make his heroine half-Jewish, but partly redeemed himself: such of her as wasn't Jewish was very pure, and Aryan. At any rate, his novel, **"Vampire,"** will be found much to the taste of those who thrill to such writers as Poe and Huysmans (I am thinking particularly of "Là-Bas"). Ewers has the same macabre passion for the sinister, the same neurotic obsession for details designed to hit the senses or turn the stomach. In between horrors, he likes to turn philosopher and mystic. He solemnly lets you know, with flourishes savoring of "East Lynn," that German patriotism is a first cousin of Divinity or, better still, that the World War came about because "humanity had become stricken with a wild fever and had to drink blood to make themselves well and young again." In the face of such sweeping explanations, his plot seems rather anemic. Frank Braun, under the influence of his half-Jewish mistress Lotte, becomes an important German agent in this country during the War. He is instrumental in persuading Pancho Villa to attack the American border, but his greatest handicap in life is a feeling of emptiness. This comes over him at regular intervals. Only Lotte understands that it is nothing more than a craving for human blood. And only she, of all the women he knows, is willing to feed him the necessary "red milk." Braun, poor innocent, does not realize he is a vampire until the end of the story. (pp. 82-3)

> *Jerre Mangione, in his review of "Vampire," in The New Republic (© 1934 The New Republic, Inc.), Vol. LXXXI, No. 1043, November 28, 1934, pp. 82-3.*

WOLFGANG KAYSER (essay date 1957)

[*Kayser's 1957 study* The Grotesque in Art and Literature *was the earliest attempt to compose a critical history of the grotesque as a distinct category of aesthetics. Kayser traces the evolution of the term "grotesque" from its first application to an ornamental style in Roman architecture through its various manifestations in the works of nineteenth and twentieth-century authors and artists, among them Edgar Allan Poe, Franz Kafka, and the Surrealist painters. Kayser defines the grotesque as "the estranged world." By choosing the modifier "estranged" Kayser intends to distinguish a merely non-naturalistic world, as in the traditional fairy tale, from one in which once familiar objects, characters, situations are altered in some demonic and uncanny way. While Kayser manages a precise description of the nature and function of the grotesque in art and literature, he concludes that its sources and ultimate meaning are unknown. The grotesque, he concludes, "is primarily the expression of our failure to orient ourselves in the physical universe," and the motive behind the artistic creation of the grotesque is the "attempt to invoke and subdue the demonic aspects of the world."*]

H. H. Ewers's works by no means lack the pathos of a metaphysics which seeks to generalize the individual, sensational event. Man is a "blind creature" surrounded by a "night of terror"; life (in a fictitious conversation with Oscar Wilde) is the "dream of an absurd being." (p. 142)

[In Ewers's work] one is struck by its limitation of scope, since Ewers is preoccupied with perverting the commonly accepted notions about man's love life. The narrator's attention is constantly drawn toward sexual perversion. Ewers tries to reinforce and substantiate such practices by referring to corresponding biological phenomena. Repeatedly, he tells his readers how the female spider entangles her male partner and sucks his blood in the act of copulation. (He also reports the case of a snake who started to devour her partner during that act.) The novella *Die Spinne (The Spider)* from the volume *Die Besessenen* [*The Possessed*] develops this motif into a story mysteriously located between the human and animal world.

The story begins with the words: "When the medical student Richard Bracquemont decided to move into room seven of the little Hotel Stevens, Rue Alfred Stevens 6, three persons had hanged themselves on the crossbars in that very room on three successive Fridays." These suicides are all the more mysterious since every speculation about the underlying motives has proved vain. The student wants to solve the puzzle. The rest of the story is told through the entries in his diary. Increasingly, he falls under the spell of a woman who lives on the other side of the narrow lane. She is described as possessing both human and animal characteristics. When in the act of spinning, her fingers (she wears long black gloves) rapidly intertwine, the observer is reminded of the motion of insect legs, especially since she wears a tight-fitting black dress with violet dots. In the material she is weaving one discerns "strange patterns" of "fabulous creatures and grotesqueries." Subsequently when the student presents the story of the spider as a personal experience, the reader begins to foresee the outcome but is entranced by the account of the gradual paralyzation of the hero's will. The diary ends at the point at which the student rises in order to hang himself. The narrator later informs us that a black spider with strange violet dots, which had crawled out of the mouths of his predecessors, was sticking squashed to his lips. We are also told that the apartment across the street had not been inhabited for several months prior to this event.

The grotesque elements in this story lack significance insofar as they subserve the sensational effect. But there is no trace of metaphysics or biology. Nothing is hidden behind the event; the logic of its construction is easily apprehended. The criterion of re-readability, recommended in English literary criticism, proves useful with regard to the stories of Ewers . . . ; they do not bear a second reading, and their grotesqueness is hollow. Ewers, however, is familiar with the grotesque and constantly employs it. In his novel **Der Zauberlehrling** [**The Sorcerer's Apprentice**], a whole mountain village is drawn into the "witches' sabbath and dance of all delusions." (Ewers is always preoccupied with erotic perversion.) But the grotesque never comes into its own, for—as our analysis has shown—a third element is needed in addition to the enticements offered by crime and love: the observation of a soul in the process of being estranged from itself and thus ineluctably bound for destruction. (pp. 142-43)

> *Wolfgang Kayser, "The Grotesque in the Twentieth Century," in his* The Grotesque in Art and Literature, *translated by Ulrich Weisstein (translation copyright © 1963 by Indiana University Press; originally published as* Das Groteske, seine Gestaltung in Malerei und Dichtung, *Gerhard Stalling Verlag, 1957), Indiana University Press, 1963, pp. 130-78.**

THE TIMES LITERARY SUPPLEMENT   (essay date 1965)

[The stories of **Die Spinne**] shocked and excited Germans before the First World War, when Hanns Heinz Ewers constituted himself the herald of a fantastic, Satanist movement in literature that looked back to Poe, Villiers de l'Isle Adam, Huysmans and—ultimately—the Divine Marquis. The protagonists of Ewers's stories were much given to expounding their philosophy and experience of life in passages such as this:

> I know the Venus which turns into Eros, which dons furs and wields the scourge. I know Venus as a Sphinx bloodthirstily driving its talons into the tender flesh of infants. I know the Venus that wallows voluptuously among mouldering carcasses, and that which, at a Black Mass, splatters the priest's revolting sacrifice over the virgin's white body . . . I know, what few know, the strange attractions of Sodom . . . I know the most perverted (or should I say: the purest?) Venus of all, that which marries men to flowers!

Time has not improved these stories; their heavy philosophizing, the journalistic reportage style which suddenly lands us in passages of nauseatingly sentimental fine writing, the dashes of pornography and commercialized algolagnia, the general nastiness of it all lead one to wonder why Ewers could not have been left to moulder in well-deserved oblivion.

It is not, perhaps, irrelevant to recall that when Hitler came to power in 1933, Ewers—despite his professed championship, in earlier years, of Heine and other Jewish writers—showed himself ready and eager to serve him with his pen. The Nazis themselves, in fact, regarded their champion with suspicion— they thought his work an insult to German motherhood, mixed up, somehow, with Expressionism and other degenerate movements of that sort; but we may well feel, with the wisdom of hindsight, that the atavism, cruelty and pseudo-philosophy of these unpolitical, consciously "fantastic" tales helped to prepare the spiritual climate of the Third Reich.

> *"Pumped Up Sewage," in* The Times Literary Supplement *(© Times Newspapers Ltd. (London) 1965; reproduced from* The Times Literary Supplement *by permission), No. 3295, April 29, 1965, p. 333.*

GABRIEL RONAY   (essay date 1972)

> [*Ronay relates the mythology of vampires, as popularized by Bram Stoker's novel* Dracula, *to the war-minded nationalism of Germany, viewing Ewers's fiction as an expression of this mixture of politics and mysticism.*]

The Transylvanian vampire and the myth of the un-dead returning from the grave to feast on human blood had fallen on fertile soil in Wilhelmin Germany. The eighteenth century ghost stories and tales of the macabre, which still had a vast following, were reinforced by *Dracula* and, in accordance with the laws of cross-fertilisation, produced a horror fiction with a difference. The vampire's predeliction for the blood of young females was greatly emphasised, lending the German stories a heavy sexual undertone. And the widespread preoccupation with Nordic myths and Teutonic blood rites, introduced into the vampire stories by the German practitioners of horror, gave the horror fiction an unexpected political significance.

The new generation of mystic nationalists, who found an elective affinity with Edgar Allan Poe's notably reactionary philosophy, welcomed Stoker's vampire as the consummate expression of the power of blood. To them, the drinking of human blood was not merely a rediscovery of the magic of forgotten Nordic rites, but also the realisation of the mystical Life Force. Those returning from the grave were not frightening figures of horror, but superhuman *Übermenschen* heralding the destruction of the decadent old world and the creation of a New Order based on blood. The convergence of horror fiction and political literature in Germany lent the Dracula myth new dimensions.

The writings of Hans-Heinz Ewers reflect most clearly the close link between the blood-fixated mysticism of the literary precursors of National Socialism and the vampire Dracula conjured up by Bram Stoker. His life—from 1871 to 1943—spanned the high tide of German nationalism. His horror trilogy, completed around the First World War, [**The Sorcerer's Apprentice, The Vampire,** and **Alraune**], contained all the dark, shapeless Nordic mysticism and exultation of Teutonic blood rites that were to become so dear to the ideologists of the Nazi order. It also incorporated elements of barbarous cruelty—conspicuously missing from Stoker's horror fiction—which bear the hallmark of the historical Dracula. There is no incontrovertible proof that Ewers was acquainted with the Rennaissance German news-letters describing Vlad Dracula's horrible deeds but, during his researches into the ethnic origins of Rumanians and what he saw as the corruption of the once dominant Latin and Finno-Ugrian races, he could not have missed the Impaler.

On the eve of the First World War, Ewers became the most devoted and sympathetic interpreter of Poe's genius, but his eulogy of the American master of horrors was mixed with overtones of strident German nationalism. In the first English language publication of his essay on Poe he was, aptly enough, described as eminently suited to mirror the soul of Poe because they are intellectual kinsmen. Both are at home in the "misty mid-region of Weir", both dwell "out of Space, out of Time". Both have explored the realm of Horror. In fact, Ewers has gone beyond Poe because to him was revealed the mystery of sex' [see Adèle Lewisohn's essay excerpted above]. Blood-crazed sex would, however, have been a more correct definition.

Indeed, Ewers went well beyond Poe—well beyond Stoker, too—in his conscious exploitation of the cruelty and blood-madness that had swept across Europe. The mystic aura and

Teutonic fanaticism of his heroes spoke of the Valhalla, that special, reassuring corner of everlasting Germanic glory, and his horror tales provided defeated post-world war I Germany with the perfect escapism capable of thrilling and diverting the disillusioned masses.

At the same time, like all other patriots, Ewers was dreaming of a new, Siegfried-like, Teutonic hero capable of reanimating a drained Germany and restoring her lost glory and national honour. Stoker's un-dead Dracula, sustained by the magic power of human blood, inspired Ewers in the creation of his vampire hero. The choice of the vampire Dracula as the model for his un-dead German hero was in part due to the Transylvanian's claim to be the representative of 'a conquering race' and Stoker's reference to Dracula's blood link with Attila the Hun. 'Here in the whirlpool of European races', says Stoker through his un-dead Dracula, 'the Ugric tribes . . . found the Huns, whose warlike fury swept the earth like a living flame, till the dying peoples held that in their veins ran the blood of those old witches who, expelled from Scythia, had mated with the devils in the desert. Fools, fools! What devil or what witch was ever so great as Attila, whose blood is in these veins?'

The un-dead vampire with Hun blood in his veins, and endowed with all the Teutonic trappings of Wagnerian imagery, was, however, not conceived in a dream. It was born in the nightmare of defeated Germany. It haunted and thrilled Germany, and Ewers's two vampire books were vastly successful, as was *Nosferatu,* a straight film version of the un-dead Transylvanian vampire.

In *The Vampire* and *Vampire's Prey,* Ewers also explored the netherworld of man's killer instincts. In his scheme of things, man's blood-fixation, like his yearning for supernatural powers, was all part of his heritage. The mystical potential of man's mind, when fully realised, could become the physical extension of his senses, transcending the limitations of the mortal body. In a strange and suggestive way his horror fiction contained the promise of an alternative existence.

This mystical approach to the nature of man's bloodthirstiness could also accommodate the newly emergent racialist theories of German nationalists. Ewers made the carrier of vampirism, 'this ancient affliction of mankind', a wandering Jewess, and extended the nightmare existence of bloodsuckers to become synonymous with life in decadent Europe. The German reincarnation of the Transylvanian vampire became the infected Everyman of the twentieth century, carrying blood-madness in his veins.

"The blood madness, it must have started somewhere, although we do not know where, but it is contagious and infects all the people who came into contact with it", Frank Braun, Ewers's un-dead Everyman in *The Vampire* tells Lotte Levi, the Jewish girl who has initiated him into blood-sucking. "They all want blood, blood, blood. Just as you did."

> She smiled a wan smile. "I know, my beloved. But do you think the millions of soldiers in Europe know more? They are unaware of their wild madness, of their thirst for blood—just as you were."

> "But they don't want to drink blood, Lotte," he countered.

> "Are you so sure of that? Are you sure they don't? That none of them wanted to, not even wanted without realising it?"

> "I, too, dreamed of blood—of rivers of blood in which to drown our enemies! And that I grew above it I owe to you! The storm seized all the leaves and tossed them about near the ground, but it carried me high up into the clouds and beyond—up to the stars. Ask a hundred, a thousand, a million people, but not one of them will be able to tell you how it happened. They don't know because they were merely swept along by the storm. They saw red, all of them, as I did and you did. The time is red—red with blood, and in you it simply revealed itself more strongly, more divinely, if you like. Humanity had become stricken with a wild fever and had to drink blood to make themselves well and young again."

The mixture in the writings of Ewers of sacreligious lust, excessive cruelty and the exultation of pre-Christian Germanic forms of worship greatly attracted the ideologists of the National Socialist party who were in search of a new religion. The attraction was mutual. The creator of the Vampire Everyman, too, appears to have delighted in the ancient magic of the Nazi symbol, the party's blood rites and worship of cruel Teutonic traditions.

Although the spiritual kinship between the Nazi belief in revival through bloodshed and Ewers's purification through the sacrifice of innocents is obvious, it must be said [in all fairness] that these themes were present in Ewers's writings long before the advent of Nazism in Germany. His belief in wild cruelty as a necessary means of bringing men of lower civilisations nearer to their god, expressed in 1911, sprang from the same mystic sense of nationalist superiority that nearly thirty years later justified the establishment of Nazi torture chambers and gas ovens. In *The Sorcerer's Apprentice,* written in the peace of Wilhelmin Germany, he also anticipated the Nazi holocaust:

> This rage of bloodthirsty madness, this sight of bloody, tormented sacrifices, this intoxication of strong wine, this fevered dancing and this restless, deafening music—by all such possible means men drew and flung themselves into the depths, down to the last abysses, down to the original consciousness of the world, to the *blind will* that was its innermost being.

In *The Sorcerer's Apprentice* Ewers describes with great psychological realism the blood-crazed Devil Hunters of a small Italian mountain village out to exorcise the evil in their midst. The parallel with the exorcism of 'political evil' in the Germany of the 1930s by the blood-crazed stormtroopers of Hitler is just as evident as the close affinity between the hypnotic power Hitler came to hold over the German masses and the prophet's ability to stir up the Italian village and give it hope of purification through the sacrifice of an innocent maid. The girl, hypnotised into believing that she is a saint, eventually takes upon herself the sins of the world and is crucified.

While presaging the spirit of the Nazi New Order, the story also contains all the ingredients that assured through the centuries the survival of the Dracula myth. The possessed villagers in the book do not drink ordinary wine: their prophet's prayerful hands actually transform their drink into the Saviour's blood. Their frenzied fanaticism, the tortures in the hope of salvation, and the ritual sacrifice of innocents differ from the deeds of Vlad Dracula or Ivan the Terrible only in their politico-religious scope. The meaning attached to the blood rituals, together with the sadistic flagellations and the orgiastic communions, forms, however, an integral part of the new twentieth century Teutonic religion. The hysterical passage on the frenzied mass flagellation and religious copulation of the Devil Hunters could have been taken, twenty or so years later, for a factual description of one of the storm trooper initiation rites. . . . (pp. 156-61)

Ewers could no more lay the spirit he conjured up in 1911 than the sorcerer's apprentice of the fable could his. It led the creator of Germany's vampire saviour to Hitler's movement. The road to the Brown House was a straight one for Ewers, without moral impediments or ethical misgivings. Adolf Hitler's personal friendship helped Ewers in bridging the gap between horror fiction and Nazi political literature.

In 1932 he undertook to write the story of Horst Wessel, the SA leader killed in a street battle with the communists. Hitler saw the book as a committed piece of writing, capable of edifying Germany's National Socialist youth. Ewers justified, both to himself and his great literary following, the writing of a Nazi propaganda book with one sentence: 'Horst Wessel had to die so that Germany could live.'

In an epilogue to *Horst Wessel*, dated September 15, 1932, he wrote: 'It is my pleasurable duty to thank all those who have helped me in the writing of this book. First and foremost I'd like to thank the Fuehrer of the German freedom movement—Adolf Hitler; for it was he who suggested a year ago in the Brown House that I should depict "the battle for the streets", to write a chapter of German history.'

After the consolidation of Nazi power, Hitler fell out with Ewers: he was put on the blacklist of forbidden authors, and his books were swept out of public libraries. The German visionary of horror became an embarrassment to the Nazis. Even Ewers was out of space and out of time in the apocalyptic reality of the Third Reich. Both the myth and its creator had outlived their usefulness, for Hitler was about to unleash another cycle of 'blood madness' which was to last for a thousand years. In the six years it lasted more blood was spilled than the master who had conjured up the German vampire monster could have dreamed of in all his nightmares. (pp. 162-63)

> *Gabriel Ronay, "Germany: Vampire Horror Fiction, Blood and the Nazi Myths," in his* The Dracula Myth *(copyright © 1972 by Gabriel Ronay; reprinted by permission of the author), W. H. Allen, 1972 (and reprinted as his* The Truth about Dracula, *Stein and Day, 1972), pp. 156-63.**

JACK SULLIVAN (essay date 1981)

Solidly in the German Gothic tradition of Hoffman, Tieck, and Meinhold, Ewers surpasses them in sustained terror. To the romantic supernaturalism of his predecessors, he added a strain of dark psychology from Poe and Freud and a languid decadence from Huysmans and Baudelaire. The desolating power of his work, however, is distinctly his own. . . . The most original Ewers novel is *Vampire*, which tells of the unconscious vampiric blood-lust of Frank Braun, a charismatic German patriot living in New York during World War I. Of Ewers's short horror stories, the most famous is **"The Spider,"** a splendid tale that presents a distillation of Ewers's style and major themes in a narrative of spellbinding intensity. Ewers was fond of femme fatale creations, and in **"The Spider"** he gives us one of the most nightmarish and original evil females in literature, a spidery woman with quivering nostrils and dark eyes full of light, who appears in black gloves and a black dress with purple dots before she lures men to a grisly death. In one scene, the doomed hero watches in appalled fascination as a female spider in his room attracts, flirts with, and finally devours a male spider, prefiguring what is to happen to him. Ewers's characteristic mingling of ecstasy and revulsion in a single death wish is evident throughout. (p. 243)

> *Jack Sullivan, "Psychological, Antiquarian, and Cosmic Horror: 1872-1919," in* Horror Literature: A Core Collection and Reference Guide, *edited by Marshall B. Tymn (reprinted with permission of the R. R. Bowker Company; copyright © 1981 by Xerox Corporation), Bowker, 1981, pp. 221-75.**

ADDITIONAL BIBLIOGRAPHY

Eisner, Lotte H. "The Spell of Light: The Influence of Max Reinhart." In her *The Haunted Screen: Expressionism in the German Cinema and the Influence of Max Reinhart*, pp. 39-74. Berkeley and Los Angeles: University of California Press, 1973.*

    Analysis of the film *The Student of Prague*, for which Ewers wrote the script. Eisner calls Ewers's script "a much more restrained piece of work than his novel *Alraune*."

Lovecraft, Howard Phillips. "The Aftermath of Gothic Fiction." In his *Supernatural Horror in Literature*, pp. 45-51. New York: Dover, 1973.*

    Classifies Ewers as a writer "who brings to bear on his dark conceptions an effective knowledge of modern psychology," and states that the novels *The Sorcerer's Apprentice* and *Alraune*, along with the short story "The Spider," "contain distinctive elements which raise them to a classic level."

Wolf, Leonard. "Dracula's Grandchildren." In his *A Dream of Dracula: In Search of the Living Dead*, pp. 225-38. New York: Popular Library, 1977.*

    Descriptive summary of *Vampire*, concluding with the comment that "Ewers's 1921 novel, crammed as it is with astrology, extensive sexual decadence and a 'redeeming' blood vision of German-Jewish destiny is particularly unnerving to read."

André (Paul Guillaume) Gide

1869-1951

French novelist, novella writer, dramatist, diarist, critic, autobiographer, essayist, and poet.

Although credited with introducing modern experimental techniques to the French novel, Gide is more highly esteemed for the autobiographical honesty of his work, which depicts the moral development of a modern intellectual. His work is recognized for its diversity in both form and content, yet critics have also noted that his characters are consistently manifestations of his own moral and philosophical conflicts. For this reason, Gide's commentators often attach as much importance to biographical detail as they do to artistic method.

Gide was born in Paris in 1869. His father, a professor of Roman law at the University of Paris, died when Gide was only eleven years old. Consequently, Gide was raised by his domineering and highly protective mother, a strict Calvinist whose family background was Norman and Catholic. In later years Gide often attributed his divided nature to this mixed southern Huguenot and Norman Catholic heredity. Gide attended the École Alsacienne and the Lycée Henri IV in Paris, but frequently required private tutoring at home because of his delicate health. As a young man, Gide traveled to the Middle East in an attempt to break away from the stifling Calvinist atmosphere of his home. There, the exotic locale and surroundings inspired him to pursue previously denied sensual pleasures; in Algiers, Gide discovered and celebrated his bisexual inclinations for the first time. However, his early religious training continued to haunt him, and he became obsessed with resolving the struggle between the puritan and the libertine in his nature. After his return to France, Gide married his cousin Madeleine, with whom he had been in love since he was thirteen years old. Their attachment was deep and unremitting, and Gide described it as "the devotion of my whole life," but the marriage was traumatic for them both. Although Gide expressed an overwhelming spiritual need to share his life with his cousin, and she provided him with a source of stability, her strict Christian values often conflicted with his unconventional lifestyle. Many of his mature works were inspired by the difficulties that he experienced in this relationship. *La porte étroite (Strait is the Gate)* and *L'immoraliste (The Immoralist)*, in particular, portray characters who are carried to destructive extremes of behavior by forces within their natures similar to those that Gide saw in himself and in Madeleine. All of Gide's works are in some way reflections of his emotional struggles, and critics agree that one source of Gide's genius lay in his ability to translate the contradictions and complexities of his nature into art. Two works which effectively delineate the conflict in Gide's personality are *Les cahiers d'André Walter (The Notebooks of André Walter)*, a poetic treatment of the theme of spiritual love, and *Les nourritures terrestres (The Fruits of the Earth)*, a lyrical paean to sensuality.

Another important factor in Gide's development as a writer was his concern with social issues. Although Gide was wealthy and occasionally exhibited a conservatism consistent with his privileged position in society, his social conscience was awakened early by his travels to Chad and the Congo in the 1890s.

What he saw there of the natives under Dutch and Belgian rule prompted him to write a controversial attack on the practice of colonialism. In the 1920s he was again embroiled in controversy when *Corydon*, his notorious defense of homosexuality, appeared. Gide turned to communism in the 1930s as did many other intellectuals who saw it as an acceptable compromise to the conflict between the rights of the individual and the need for more equitable social and economic opportunities. However, Gide found a visit to the Soviet Union in 1936 disillusioning. Upon his return he published his negative impressions of the Communist experiment in his *Retour de l'U.R.S.S. (Return from the U.S.S.R.)*, and was bitterly criticized by many of his former associates for his "betrayal." During World War II, when Gide was in his seventies, he once again took a social stand when he left occupied France rather than succumb to pressure from the collaborationist Vichy regime to lend his support to the Nazi cause. Gide died in 1951.

Throughout his literary career Gide adapted his style to suit his subject matter, resulting in an unusually wide variety of works. Such early efforts as *The Notebooks of André Walter* and *The Fruits of the Earth* are rich in metaphor and lyric beauty, as befits works concerned with an impressionable young man's first encounters with life. The poetic prose contained in these books clearly reveal the influence upon Gide of Stéphane Mallarmé and the Symbolists. Gide abandoned Symbolism, however, in favor of a simpler, more classical style when he began experimenting with themes and forms drawn from the Bible and Greek mythology. Gide also discovered the works of Johann Wolfgang von Goethe, and was influenced by the German writer's classicism. All of these factors played an important part in the development of Gide's mature style. For example, he made use of ancient myth in such works as *Philoctète, Le Prométhée mal enchaîné (Prometheus Misbound)*, and *Thésée (Theseus)*, his celebrated study of the problems of the mature artist; while his drama *Saül* and *Numquid et tu . . . ?*, a series of meditations on the New Testament, are both based on biblical materials. Critics have also noted logical and formal similarities between Gide's *récits*, or psychological narratives, such as *Strait is the Gate* and *La symphonie pastorale (The Pastoral Symphony)*, and biblical parables. Some believe that his farcical *soties*, such as *Paludes (Marshlands)* and *Les Caves du Vatican (Lafcadio's Adventures)*, are derived from the same source.

Gide's most ambitious and stylistically elaborate achievement was the novel *Les faux monnayeurs (The Counterfeiters)*, a work that owes a great deal to Gide's reading of Fedor Dostoevski. *The Counterfeiters* is an experimental novel, the form of which is derived from patterns in music. In it, Gide attempted to reproduce the unstructured chaos of everyday life through the use of meaningless episodes, conversations that are left unfinished, and Dostoevskian interruptions of action at moments of great intensity. Linear chronology is abandoned as several unrelated stories occur simultaneously. The novel's theme, as Justin O'Brien has noted, is entirely Dostoevskian: the demoniacal role of the intelligence and the power of convention to counterfeit life. Although Gide's innovations in *The Counterfeiters* were important to the development of the French novel, he did not continue to pursue that experimental vein. Later works, such as *Oedipe (Oedipus)* and *Theseus*, are written in a severely classical style with none of the inventive audacity of Gide's earlier works.

One of Gide's primary artistic and philosophical concerns was authenticity. He discussed his life in a way that has been called self-consciously candid and exhibitionistic by some critics, while others see religious overtones in the "unremitting search for self-correction and self-purification." Alfred Kazin, in discussing the psychology of Gide's highly confessional works, observed that "he would like to be both free and good, and failing both, had compromised by being honest." The much-discussed Gidean notions of "sincerity"—which Germaine Brée has summarized as signifying the "struggle of human beings with truths compulsively followed"—and *"disponibilité,"* which Gide interpreted as, "following one's inclinations, so long as they lead upward," were products of this lifelong passion for self-awareness. However, Gide's critics are quick to point out that although he used forms conducive to autobiographical honesty, such as first person novels, journals, and personal essays, Gide did not reveal himself completely in his works. There are significant omissions in the *Journals*, and the characters in his fiction, although they are based in part on himself, often distort the image of the artist even as they disclose it. This occurs because Gide's method in his fiction was to create a character abstracted from a single aspect of his personality. Thus the nature of his characters often varied widely from work to work. Moreover, Gide was constantly reexamining his assumptions, so it is not uncommon for successive novels to portray contradictory beliefs and situations. Still, Gide's shifting concerns did not reflect indecisiveness, as early critics

charged. Rather, they were the external evidence of his continual dialogue with himself.

Although he was well-known and respected among his fellow writers, Gide was unrecognized by the general public until the 1920s, when his involvement as founder and editor of the prestigious *La nouvelle revue française* led to his discovery by a postwar generation of youth who rejected social conventions and embraced both his restless search for spiritual values and his belief that life should be lived to its emotional and intellectual fullest. His influence on the generation of Albert Camus and Jean Genet was enormous, and, though he rejected existentialism, he was unarguably one of its forerunners. The importance of his examination of private morality and its effect on society was recognized in 1947 when, after a lifetime of neglect due largely to his public confession of homosexuality, he was awarded the Nobel Prize for literature.

Critics today are divided in their assessment of Gide's novels. While some see them as dated and of only minor interest for contemporary readers, others, such as Henri Peyre, maintain that the perfection of Gide's style and the sincerity with which he set out to expose social, religious, artistic, and sexual hypocrisy guarantee the novels a permanent place in twentieth-century literature. There is far more consensus among critics about the value of Gide's voluminous *Journals*. Despite the charges of narcissism that are often raised in discussions of the *Journals*, most critics agree with Philip Toynbee that Gide's "greatest talent was for portraying himself against the carefully delineated background of his time," and that the *Journals* today retain "all the interest for us which can be earned by a patient sincerity, an eager curiosity, and a brilliant pen."

(See also *TCLC*, Vol. 5 and *Contemporary Authors*, Vol. 104.)

PRINCIPAL WORKS

Les cahiers d'André Walter (novel) 1891
   [*The Notebooks of André Walter*, 1968]
Les poèsies d'André Walter (prose poems) 1892
Le traité du Narcisse (essay) 1892
Le voyage d'Urien (novella) 1892
   [*Urien's Voyage*, 1964]
Paludes (novella) 1895
   [*Marshlands* published in *Marshlands and Prometheus Misbound*, 1953]
Les nourritures terrestres (prose poems) 1897
   [*The Fruits of the Earth*, 1949]
Philoctète (drama) 1899
Le Prométhée mal enchaîné (novella) 1899
   [*Prometheus Illbound*, 1919; also published as *Prometheus Misbound* in *Marshlands and Prometheus Misbound*, 1953]
Le Roi Candaule (drama) 1901
L'immoraliste (novel) 1902
   [*The Immoralist*, 1930]
Prétextes (essays) 1903
   [*Pretexts*, 1959]
Saül (drama) 1903
La porte étroite (novel) 1909
   [*Strait is the Gate*, 1924]
Isabelle (novella) 1911
   [*Isabelle* published in *Two Symphonies*, 1931]
Les caves du Vatican (novel) 1914
   [*The Vatican Swindle*, 1925; also published as *Lafcadio's Adventures*, 1928]

La symphonie pastorale (novella) 1919
  [*The Pastoral Symphony* published in *Two Symphonies*,
  1931]
Dostoïevsky (criticism) 1923
  [*Dostoevsky*, 1925]
Corydon (dialogues) 1924
  [*Corydon*, 1950]
Les faux monnayeurs (novel) 1925
  [*The Counterfeiters*, 1927; also published as *The Coiners*,
  1927]
Si le grain ne meurt (autobiography) 1925
  [*If It Die*, 1950]
Numquid et tu . . . ? (meditations) 1926
Voyage au Congo (travel essays) 1927
  [*Travels in the Congo*, 1930]
L'école des femmes (novella) 1929
  [*The School for Wives*, 1929]
Oedipe (drama) 1931
  [*Oedipus* published in *Two Legends: Oedipus and
  Theseus*, 1950]
Retour de l'U.R.S.S. (travel essays) 1936
  [*Return from the U.S.S.R.*, 1937; also published as *Back
  from the U.S.S.R.*, 1937]
Journal, 1889-1939 (journal) 1939
Journal, 1939-1942 (journal) 1946
Thésée (novella) 1946
  [*Theseus*, 1948]
The Journals of André Gide, 1889-1949. 4 vols. (journals)
  1947-51
Journal, 1942-1949 (journal) 1950
Et nunc manet in te, suivi de journal intime (journal)
  1951
  [*Madeleine*, 1952]
Le journal des faux monnayeurs (journal) 1951
  [*Logbook of the Coiners*, 1952]
My Theatre (dramas and essays) 1951
Ainsi soit-il; ou, Les jeux sont fait (memoir) 1952
  [*So Be It; or, The Chips Are Down*, 1959]
The Return of the Prodigal (essays and dramas) 1953

REMY DE GOURMONT (essay date 1896-98)

[*Gourmont was a prominent man of letters in late nineteenth and
early twentieth-century French literature. One of the founders of
Le Mercure de France, which for a time served as a forum for
the Symbolist writers of the period, Gourmont was a prolific
novelist, short story writer, dramatist, and poet. His creative
works, however, were never as highly regarded or influential as
his literary criticism. These works, particularly* Les livre des
masques (The Book of Masks), *are important for Gourmont's
sensitive examinations of the Symbolists and for his adherence to
a critical style that made him a significant influence on modern
English and American poetry and led T. S. Eliot to call him "the
perfect critic." As critic Glen B. Burne explains: "Symbolism
meant for [Gourmont] the absolute freedom of the artist to follow
and express the impulses of his individual sensibility." Gourmont's criticism also follows this criterion of subjectivity, reflecting a sensibility that combined a keen artistic intuition with a
background of scientific learning. Both were employed throughout
the body of his literary and philosophical writings. His most
esteemed intellectual achievement was in articulating the concept
of the "dissociation of sensibility," a method of thought whereby
familiar ideas—such as the idea of liberty or justice—could be*
abstracted from their conventional meanings and associations,
chiefly in order to separate sentiment from truth. This type of
intellectual discipline, along with a mystical temperament which
he shared with the Symbolists of his generation, make clear Richard Aldington's description of Gourmont as "a mixture of a Romantic artist—poet and novelist—and an eighteenth-century phil-
osophe." In the excerpt below, Gourmont discusses Gide's
"originality of soul," and observes that the promise shown by
Gide in his first work, Les cahiers d'André Walter, had been
fulfilled in Paludes.]

In 1891 I wrote as follows apropos of the **Cahiers d'André
Walter,** an anonymous work: "The diary is a form of good
literature and perhaps the best for some extremely subjective
minds. De Maupassant would make nothing of it. For him the
world is like the cover of a billiard table; he notes the meetings
of the balls and stops when the balls stop, for if there is no
further material movement to be perceived, there is nothing
more to be said. The subjective soul feeds on itself through
the reserve of its stored sensations; and, by an occult chemistry,
by unconscious combinations whose numbers approach infinity, those sensations, often of a faraway past time, become
changed and are multiplied in ideas. Then are narrated, not
anecdotes, but the very anecdotes of oneself, the only kind that
can often be retold, if one has the talent and gift to vary their
appearances. In this way has the author of these copy books
worked and thus will he work again. His is a romantic and
philosophic mind, of the lineage of Goethe. One of these years,
when he will have recognized the helplessness of thought against
the onward course of things, its social uselessness, the scorn
it inspires in that mass of corpuscles named society, indignation
will seize him, and since action, though illusive, is forever
closed to him, he will wake armed with irony. This oddly
enough, is a writer's finishing touch; it is the co-efficient of
his soul's worth. The theory of the novel, stated in a note of
page 120 is of more than mediocre interest; we must hope that
the author upon occasion will recollect it. As for the present
book, it is ingenuous and delicate, the revealer of a fine intelligence. It seems the condensation of a whole youth of study,
dreams and sentiment, of a tortuous, timorous youth. This
reflection . . . rather well sums up André Walter's state of
mind: 'O, the emotion when one is quite near to happiness,
when one has but to touch it,—and passes on.' "

There is a certain pleasure in not having been deceived in one's
first judgment of the first book of an unknown person. Now
that André Gide has, after several intelligent works, become
one of the most luminous of the Church's Levites, with the
flames of intelligence and grace quite visible around his brow
and in his eyes, the time nears when bold discoverers will
discuss his genius, and, since he fares forth and advances,
sound the trumpets of the advancing column. He deserves the
glory, if anyone merits it (glory is always unjust) since to the
originality of talent the master of minds willed that in this
singular being should be joined an originality of soul. It is a
gift rare enough to justify speaking of it.

A writer's talent is often nothing but the terrible faculty of
retelling, in phrases that seem beautiful, the eternal clamors
of mediocre humanity. Even gigantic geniuses, like Victor
Hugo or Adam de Saint-Victor were destined to utter an admirable music whose grandeur consists in concealing the immense emptiness of the deserts: their soul is like the formless
docile soul of deserts and crowds; they love, think, and desire
the loves, thoughts, desires of all men and of all beasts; poets,
they magnificently declaim what is not worth the trouble of
being thought.

The human species, doubtless, in its entire aspect of a hive or colony, is only superior to the bison species or the kingfisher, because we are a part of it; here and there man is a sorry automaton; but his superiority lies in his ability to attain consciousness; a small number reach this stage. To acquire the full consciousness of self is to know oneself so different from others that one no longer feels allied with men except by purely animal contacts: nevertheless, among souls of this degree, there is an ideal fraternity based on differences,—while social fraternity is based on resemblances.

The full consciousness of self can be called originality of soul,— and all this is said only to point out the group of rare beings to which André Gide belongs.

The misfortune of these beings, when they wish to express themselves, is that they do it with such odd gestures that men fear to approach them; their life of social contacts must often revolve in the brief circle of ideal fraternities; or, when the mob consents to admit such souls, it is as curiosities or museum objects. Their glory is, finally, to be loved from afar and almost understood, as parchments are seen and read above sealed glass cases.

But all this is related in *Paludes,* a story, as is known, ''of animals living in dusky caverns, and which lose their sight through never being used''; it is also, with a more intimate charm than in the *Voyage d' Urien,* the ingenuous story of a very complicated, very intellectual and very original soul. (pp. 175-79)

> Remy de Gourmont, ''Gide,'' in his The Book of Masks, *translated by Jack Lewis (originally published as* Le livre des masques, *1896-98), J. W. Luce and Company, 1921 (and reprinted by Books for Libraries Press, 1967; distributed by Arno Press, Inc.), pp. 175-79.*

HERMANN HESSE   (essay date 1933)

[*Recipient of the Nobel Prize in literature for 1946, Hesse is considered one of the most important German novelists of the twentieth century. Lyrical in style, his novels are concerned with a search on the part of their protagonists for self-knowledge and for insight into the relationship between physical and spiritual realms. Critics often look upon Hesse's works as falling into the tradition of German Romanticism, from the early bildungsroman* Peter Camenzind *to the introspective* Steppenwolf *to the mystical* Das Glasperlenspiel (Magister Ludi), *his last major work. Magister Ludi is generally held to epitomize Hesse's achievement, delineating a complex vision which intermingles art and religion to convey a sense of harmony unifying the diverse elements of existence. This work, along with such earlier novels as* Siddhartha, *established Hesse's reputation as an author who to many readers and critics approximates the role of a modern sage. In the excerpt below, Hesse provides a brief review of Gide's dialogue, Corydon.*]

The four dialogues [in ''**Corydon**''], beginning with a natural history of love and ending with a kind of metaphysic of love, contain Gide's confession to pederasty and at the same time constitute the most significant contribution to this theme made in our time. They not only vindicate pederasty by freeing it from the character of perversion or crime; they divest the whole theme of that false solemnity and moralism into which it was forced by the middle class and the law. Over and above all this, they become a theory of love in general.

> *Hermann Hesse, ''André Gide: 'Corydon' '' (1933; originally published as ''André Gide,'' in his* Schrif-

ten zur Literatur, Suhrkamp Verlag, 1970), *in his* My Belief: Essays on Life and Art, *edited by Theodore Ziolkowski, translated by Denver Lindley with Ralph Manheim (reprinted by permission of Farrar, Straus and Giroux, Inc.; translation copyright © 1974 by Farrar, Straus and Giroux, Inc.), Farrar, Straus and Giroux, 1974, p. 336.*

RÉGIS MICHAUD   (essay date 1934)

[*In this survey of Gide's work through 1932, Michaud discusses Gide's role as a moralist and as a thinker. Citing Gide's motto of ''no limits, no definitions,'' Michaud argues that Gide's iconoclasm and anarchy, together with his sincerity, helped bring the nineteenth-century tradition to a close.*]

From his *Cahiers d'André Walter* (1891), to his drama *Oedipe* (1932) André Gide's literary career has run uninterrupted for forty years. (p. 79)

The *Cahiers d'André Walter,* written at twenty, showed him tortured by contradictions in feeling and thought, between platonic love and the erotic impulse, between mysticism and the critical sense. He called the Bible, Spinoza, poetry and music to his rescue, and he heroically strove to find a new and personal means of expression. The success of the book did not come up to his expectations, but it brought him into touch with the late Parnassians and the Symbolists, with Herédia and Mallarmé. It marked the beginning of what may be called his Symbolist period, the period of his lyrical treatises from *Le Traité du Narcisse* to *Les Nourritures terrestres.* Gide had found all the fascination of the visible world and was already bent on brooding much over himself. Like Narcissus he went to look at himself in the water of the springs, but the water flowed, and how could he grasp and hold the flowing phantoms? And which is true, the water or the images in the water?

Gide was already passionately searching for reality through appearances, and reflection was as dear to him as dreams. He was a poet with a conscience, intent on finding some faith beyond images and words—some faith beyond his books. How pallid, dull and prosaic life was, Gide told half sarcastically, half tragically in *Paludes,* a smart handbook of disillusion. There Tityre did not find any better solace than to fish for worms in the mud while wishing to leave everybody and everything behind. There, as in his other treatises, Gide longed for something new, something unforeseen and gratuitous. To start on a journey somewhere and to stop nowhere! Urien, in *Le Voyage d'Urien,* went on an imaginary journey and reached the polar sea only to wish that he had never been there. The plight of this world was ennui and the only duty was evasion. Anything was better than to live in the dark caves and become blind because of not knowing how to open one's eyes. He had found one of his leit-motifs.

Gide himself, however, did not sail for the Arctic, but in 1893 through southern Italy he left for Algeria, where he spent two years, and we owe to this journey *Les Nourritures terrestres.* This book is Gide's song of songs, a symphony in two movements, an allegro at the beginning and an andante at the end. This hymn to the joy of life ends as a dirge on the vanity of all things. To escape from his scruples he had then come to a capital decision. He would surrender to instinctive life without any reserve and disregard all he had been told to obey. He bathed in cold springs, courted shepherds, loafed in the oases, sang the roundelay of desires, the lure of the desert, and listened to the cynical teachings of Ménalque. He tried, as he declared, to gain his freedom of mind through a thorough exhaustion of all his senses. To cleanse body and soul and be born anew, to find eternity in the bliss of every second, this was the first part of the symphony. Then, alas! came the funeral march and the passionate pilgrim returned empty-handed. Desire was all, provided that it was never fulfilled; traveling was fine if only one stopped nowhere. No thirst could be quenched, no beauty could be grasped, and Gide advised his disciple Nathanael to throw away his song of songs when he had read it. There was nothing to seize and nothing to love; at least one could remain free and ready to start again. Who knows but that wisdom meant giving away all things and above all the desire of possession? Who knows but that self-renunciation was the sum of all wisdom?

Gide dramatized his North African experience in his novel *L'Immoraliste* . . . , the meaning of which is clearly indicated by the title. In this book he went searching more and more for what he called "the complete possibilities of man," and, as he declared, for the full disposal and employment of oneself through the painstaking exercise of his mind. Could one be daring enough to "turn the page," renounce morals, and be born anew? A man was the only law unto himself. Let him stretch to the utmost all his energies, good and bad, to reach happiness. Culture has killed life; let us revive it through instinct. The story took us to Normandy and to Algeria. Michel, the hero, was married without love to Marceline, and Marceline was an obstacle in his path. Michel was a scholar, but life had become dearer to him than books, and all the dearer as he was threatened with consumption. He would leave all behind, shed the "old man" and exert himself beyond good and evil. Michel answered the call of the wild and lost his moral sense systematically. Health came back to him in the oases, where he consorted with young Arabs. At the advice of his tempter, Ménalque, he shed all his prejudices and his education.

We then see him practising his new ethics on his Normandy estate, where he went so far as to play the poacher at his own expense. He had discovered the dark side of life and went back to Africa to perfect his experience. What would become of poor and devoted Marceline in the company of such a superman? The question was hardly worth debating at this stage, and he let Marceline die in order to better find himself and be happy. But happiness did not come, and at the end of the book Michel had lost all his enthusiasm. Lonely and empty-handed he sent an S.O.S. to his friends in Paris to help him start on a new journey—to what destination we are not told. Would he start again for the sake of starting, as Gide recommended in his treatise on the prodigal son (*Le Retour de l'Enfant prodigue*), or would he learn at last the lesson of self-sacrifice and renunciation as taught in *Philoctète* and *Le Roi Candaule*? Gide never converted his characters; he left them to their fate and wrote new books.

The leit-motif of renunciation versus self-love was the theme of *La Porte étroite,* where once more Gide staged the conflict of instincts and Christian morals. The story reads as a plea for spiritual versus natural love, for sanctity against passion, until we come to the end of the book to learn from Alissa's journals that pride had been her real motive in refusing Jérôme. She really loved him and would have been his had he been daring enough. Both were victims of their scruples. Their story was the tragedy of timidity and pride parading under the disguise of mysticism and platonic love, the tragedy of hypocrisy. Thus the book shows us Gide already in possession of most of his major themes and already very deft in handling his double-edged tactics. His casuistry could already be summed up in a

doctrine of salvation through surrendering to one's instincts. The only true morals taught the integral fulfilment of instinctive desires and the necessity of exploring the worst in man unhampered. No limits nor tabus must be set to personal experience, and only when all his possibilities have been tried can man be put on his road to God.

That Gide insisted on preaching his new morals under the disguise of the gospels shows well what grasp his Puritan education had on him. Even at the time of his most romantic escapades he never parted with his Bible. Long before he wrote his comment on the gospels in *Numquid et tu* and his book on Dostoievsky he had found in the Scriptures a text on which he became very fond of commenting. "He who will save his soul shall lose it" was already quoted in *La Porte étroite* as the A B C of Christianity as interpreted by Gide, and it came back in all his books. In Gide's interpretation it teaches the renunciation not of evil but of good, and especially the doing away with self-respect. It holds sin to be a safer way to perfection than so-called virtue, for virtue is always pride. Sin teaches humility, which is the only approach to God. Let us try our worst instincts, were it only to know that they exist; let us revel in all that is dark and sinister in us, so that at the end of our distress we can find true good and clamor for it. Of all sins hypocrisy is the greatest and all the thoughts in us must be confessed. Let us not shun temptation but rather court it.

Temptation, sin, renunciation, confession, humility—Gide's vocabulary, if not his thoughts, is so far orthodox; and so is the homage he pays to the devil. Evil is no empty word for him; as for Dostoievsky, whom he so much admires, evil is a synonym for the evil one, Satan, in whose existence he confessedly believes and whom he restores to his rights in his last books.

Gide knows well that his moral program runs counter to accepted standards, and this explains the stand he has taken in his later books. *Les Caves du Vatican, Les Faux-Monnayeurs,* are a denunciation of hypocrisy and deceit in a light or a tragic mood. Public morals are a system of tabus meant to forbid man an access to his dark side, a system of conventions intended to hide and disguise man in his own eyes. It puts a premium on duplicity and makes people live a double life as cheaters and counterfeiters. Society has been prospering on the interdiction of what is most personal and original in the individual man or woman. It has made a law of conformity and encouraged every individual to force upon others a false and ready-made portrait of himself. Most personalities are not natural but manufactured, and, as Gide would have us believe, "we live counterfeited." Nobody dares to be himself and there is no prospect of change and progress in what we are. In a world where everybody cheats, an honest man can only be a mountebank. So let us not be duped.

Against social hypocrisy Gide staged his doctrine of "actes gratuits"—of gratuitous and free actions—and he intrusted the defense of his doctrine to one of his most puzzling characters, young and unconventional Lafcadio. Gratuitous actions are the keystone of his ethics and the consistent conclusion of his plea for individual freedom. They set aside causation and motives in conduct and proclaim the right of every man to invent *ex tempore* his actions. They are, to his mind, an efficient weapon to break the moral and social structure and evade what is called responsibility. When he saves a girl from fire or throws an old man out of a train Lafcadio can neither be rewarded nor punished, since he acted without intention. There can be a legal sanction to his acts, according as they are beneficial or harmful to society, but he cannot be judged, since there is nothing to judge. Did not the gospels say, "Judge not, that ye be not judged"? (See his *Souvenirs de la cour d'Assises,* some personal recollections of the criminal courts.) Any act to be pure must be personal, entire and immediate. Forethought and pre-vision forestall innocence. Pride begins when a man reflects too long before he acts and asks himself questions about what he must or can do. Such action is a sin and a challenge to God. If you cannot act, be content with thinking, and maybe somebody will come to translate your thought into a deed, a poor imitation of what could have been an original masterpiece. Act first and think afterward, as does Lafcadio. Your action then cannot be labeled or pigeonholed, and it does not bind you to any laws and standards. Spontaneity is better than ethics. Gide himself, however, qualified his own theory and felt the flaws in his system when he had Lafcadio contradicted by an opponent and left in a quandary in respect to his own acts at the end of the book.

Les Caves du Vatican was called a "sotie" or light farce by the author. Irony ran on a high key from the beginning to the end of the book. Fantastic as it seemed, Gide had not invented the great Vatican swindle, but had found it in the newspapers. Thenceforth he fondly collected the casual news in the papers— what the French call *faits divers*—especially criminal cases, as a key to the study of human behavior undisguised. He did it especially to write *Les Faux-Monnayeurs,* the central and final episodes of which were found in the newspaper columns. In that book, according to his own confession, he tried to "demonetize beautiful feelings" and dramatize the way social and moral constraints check and stifle our best possibilities. It is a tragedy of appearances, of what is and of what seems to be. So far Gide had not dared to call his stories novels, but *récits.* Now at fifty-five he went systematically into fiction writing, and composed what may be considered the great book of the post-war period, pouring into it, as he said, all he knew of life. The title, as translated into English, tells the true meaning of the book. It takes us among counterfeiters, young and old, in a literal and figurative sense. It is a searching investigation of duplicity, a game where cards have been falsified and where every player cheats himself and others. Some do it unwittingly, others deliberately. It is the book of Gide's sympathies and antipathies, a mirror of his life and of that of his times. He took a cruel revenge on his Puritan boyhood, his parents and educators, and made an excruciating study of delinquent youth. What a Mephistophelian epic, what an assault on conformity, what a lie given to the traditionalists, and what a dissection of the human heart!

Gide's most original trick in the book was to give it to us to read just as it was being thought out and written by the author himself, who was present in the story. Reality, Gide told us, interested him only so far as it was turned into a work of art, and so it was, under our very eyes. Edouard's journal in the book (supplemented by *Le Journal des Faux-Monnayeurs*) was a treatise on the art of fiction written by a novelist eager to conciliate the French tradition and modern and foreign models. Concerning psychology we were told that there were new depths to explore of which French novelists had not been aware, and Edouard's views in this respect were endorsed by a professional psychoanalyst in the novel. Concerning art Edouard took the stand against realism and claimed that fiction must put side by side art and reality. His first duty was to be methodically concrete, but particulars had no value to him unless they were made universal. This was the classical method, than which none was ever more perfect.

This example illustrates very well Gide's favorite method and that inner necessity which forced him always to mix thought with art and fill with comments the margins of his books, an original but not, perhaps, an ideal process. Notes and comments cannot well make up for that perfect fusion of art and life which has been achieved by the great classicists.

Taken all together *The Counterfeiters* is Gide's great work, a sinister and cynical book for those readers who fear to enter the inferno of life, but nevertheless containing some gleams of hope. The devil roams at large in its pages, but there are some guardian angels, and young Bernard, the hero, is not altogether unsympathetic. Gide took up counterfeiting again in his novelettes, *Isabelle, La Symphonie pastorale, L'École des Femmes,* and *Robert.* There, once more, men and women played at blind man's buff and cheated each other more or less knowingly. The blind maid in the Symphony was a transparent symbol of the moral blindness of the minister, her guardian. The *School for Wives* and *Robert* drew two contradictory portraits of a man who forged his identity to the woman he loved.

The critical and personal character of Gide's works must not be overemphasized to the detriment of his positive and more general teachings. We may well conclude from his own confessions in and outside his books that his stories are, to a large extent, his own story and an *apologia pro vita sua,* a record of his evasions. As elusive a personality as his could not be held in a book, but it was there just the same, and critics traced his leit-motifs back to the idiosyncrasies and anomalies which he confessed so candidly in his autobiography. They hinted that perhaps he was a hypocrite himself and used sophistry to hide his abnormalities behind the gospels. Evasion, instability, gratuitous actions and the gospel of sincerity at any cost were the consequence of his personal obsessions and were desperate efforts to cover his morbid propensities.

Yet the value of Gide's books cannot be made to depend only upon his confessions. In the form of exhortations and maxims they are a pathetic plea in favor of a new life. They recommend a free exploration of human resources beyond tabus and barriers. Away with hypocrisy, let us shun happiness and foreclose all our mortgages; let man arise, confess his sins, gird his loins and start on a new journey. Let him live a dangerous life, court risks and adventures and find new gods. Invention is better than imitation and heresy than conformity. Nothing is simple in life; let us like and cultivate our complexities. Who knows but that the impulses we call abnormal, strange and morbid can put us on the way to new discoveries and creations?

"I say that man was made to grow, not to stop," quotes Gide from Browning. Man has not said his last word, and his soul can still expand. Let an author write not to please but to stir and disturb. Let him push his fellow men toward new destinies through the forbidden lands of life.

These formal books, treatises, dramas, farces and novels represent only one phase of Gide's literary activities. They show the point where his secret thoughts came to the surface, but they were fed by many rivulets under ground. He has turned into art only a part of his thoughts. There is a large collection of diaries, letters, notes and essays which must be read to know him fully. Art to him comes only second to thought, and while most writers have put themselves wholly in their books, Gide has kept the best of himself for his marginalia. His influence spread largely through these side issues. It grew slowly at first and unofficially, but little by little he emerged as an intellectual leader. . . . His real triumph came after the war at the age of fifty, and he presided over the brilliant 1920-1930 decade. Then his early books were reprinted and his position could no longer be challenged. He could go undisguised in public and preach or shock as he liked. He did so by publishing his autobiography, *Si le Grain ne meurt,* and *Corydon,* in which he put into practise his doctrine that all thoughts must be confessed.

The young insurgents flocked around his banners and proclaimed him their master. It seemed that he had been twenty-five years in advance of the new generation and that he had drawn its portrait before it was born. Here were the new revoltees with their restlessness, their anarchy and their critical awareness. *The Counterfeiters* was a true epic of the new times. Gide at fifty was still young for liberty, and he hailed the new revolutions, stretched his hand to Dada and renounced all the past. His hour had come, altho he knew many contradictions and fell a prey to bitter attacks (at the hands of MM. Henri Massis and Henri Béraud especially). He was not yet at the end of his journey. He had shown the way toward new standards, toward sincerity, integrity, the joys of life and of self-sacrifice. Midway between Nietzsche and Dostoievsky he had announced the advent of a new man. "Sprung out of the unknown," exclaimed Oedipus, "no more past, no more models. Nothing to lean on. All to be created, fatherland, ancestors to be invented and discovered. Nobody to imitate but myself." Oedipus had slain the Sphinx; there were no more sphinxes; the solution of our problems was within ourselves.

Gide so far had paraded as a rugged individualist. His journey to the Congo in 1925 made a Socialist of him after seeing civilization at work. A man could not be happy alone, and everybody must have his fair share of worldly goods and "nourritures terrestres." He came back from Africa with two books purposely written in a prosaic and matter-of-fact way. He had found men among the savages and savages among the civilized white men. . . . Men were the same everywhere and there was no exoticism in Gide's eyes. Pierre Loti's nostalgia was not his; he spent most of his time investigating the conditions in that part of France's colonial empire, and his reports were none too pleasant. (pp. 80-93)

As a writer Gide has acted as a disintegrating force in French literature. His literary evolution has followed closely his moral evolution. He renounced one by one all literary adornments to reach a sort of asceticism. He left behind all artistic writing as it was practised in his early days. He flirted with Parnasse and with Symbolism and soon renounced them. Herédia and Mallarmé could not be his masters, and as he advanced in life he gave up more and more imagism and lyricism to adhere to the naked truth and the naked style. To music, which was so dear to him, he preferred design. To his mind classicism alone made an art of necessity. Classicism acted, in regard to romanticism, as an instrument of control and sublimation. Romanticism gave the emotions and that inner ardor without which there can be no art, but classicism provided the discipline and the rules. (pp. 93-4)

In regard to his contemporaries none contributed more than he to bringing to a close the nineteenth century tradition and to alienating the new generation from the literary leaders in the first two decades of the new century. This he did through his searching criticism of some of the leaders of the pre-war period, ruining, for instance, Paul Bourget's traditionalism through his attack on family standards, challenging Barrès's position in regard to the "uprooted," dismissing Anatole France as a writer without a conscience and Romain Rolland as a sentimentalist. Call no man your master, but if you need models, follow the

example of such men as Stendhal, Baudelaire, Rimbaud, Dostoievsky or Whitman. Writing must put us on our road to life and to freedom, and it must renew itself as everything else. The World War spared nothing; it destroyed cathedrals and factories and upset standards; why should words and the art of writing be spared? How despair of the future when such artists as Proust and Valéry were alive? No limits, no definitions—this, in the last analysis, is Gide's motto. Let it also be a warning to his readers and critics. (pp. 94-5)

> *Régis Michaud, "The Leadership of André Gide,"*
> *in his* Modern Thought and Literature in France, *Funk*
> *& Wagnalls, 1934, pp. 72-95.*

ELIZABETH M. RODRIGUE   (essay date 1937)

[*Rodrigue examines the classical aspects of Gide's writings, in particular his ability to "create wide implications with a paradoxical economy of means."*]

André Gide has often expressed his opinions on the subject of classicism. According to him, there is, latent in every mind, a struggle between classicism and romanticism. A work of art shows the triumph of form, pure and restrained, over the romantic elements constituting the subject matter. Gide writes that 17th century French art "was entirely one of restraint", whereas contemporary literature, under the pretense of rendering human feelings effectively, emphasizes the unusual instead of stressing harmony and order. He believes that the French genius expressed itself best in classical art, and that, in contemporary literature, he André Gide, represents classical tradition, at its best.

Classicism, in 17th century France, could well be defined, according to Henri Peyre, as a "refined stylization of life", characterized by a conscious search for clarity, intellectual as well as technical.

This definition appears almost identical with that given by André Gide. With his own conception of classicism as a starting point, it seems interesting to raise the following questions: Considering his most representative works, do we find that André Gide only expresses the individual Ego? Or, on the contrary, has he proved that one may find universal truth by studying one's mind, thereby drawing universal implications?

André Gide finds a perfect definition of the work of art in the following lines of Baudelaire:

> Là tout n'est qu'ordre et beauté,
> Luxe, calme et volupté.

> [There all is order and beauty,
> Luxury, calm, and voluptuousness.]

These lines, he maintains, provide sufficient material for a treatise on Aesthetics. The artist is but an arbitrator, a witness. His subject matter must be a particular topic, treated with enough power so that it may imply a general idea. The reader, the critic, will supply the actual generalizing, provided there be a possibility of it.

The essential quality of restraint is emphasized by Gide in several of his writings. To him, Reason is the most important literary guide, for a "work of art is a work of reason", and "whatever is not useful is harmful." (pp. 95-6)

Gide was influenced by Symbolism in his early works, in *Les Nourritures Terrestres* especially. According to Ramon Fernandez, "Gide wrote in the symbolist manner as one would practice scales . . . then was formed his unbending poetic conscience, and then he conceived of his task as an artist. He also became fully aware of the trends of his imagination and of his literary gifts, that he was to develop, thereafter, in complete independence.

Les Nourritures Terrestres "may be defined as a study of universal desire fulfilled—and this fulfillment is nothing less than the world in general." This accounts for the impressionistic method followed by the author. Under a lyrical appearance, the book is a classification of human sensations, comparable to the minute observations of naturalists or psychologists. The main character, or rather, Gide himself, in expressing his sensations, follows a subtle technique of sentence construction, which would be a fascinating study, were it approached from a musical point of view.

The lyrical tendencies that André Gide developed during the symbolist period of his career, were to find a more complete expression in *L'Immoraliste*. A definite organization may be found in this book, but a lyrical melody pervades it entirely. Gide here expresses the experiences of a convalescent, Michel, whose volition attains not only to health but—more important—to full awareness of health, and, thus, to happiness. The climax of this upward surge is an ecstatic physical harmony. When once this height of joy is reached, however, a lack of balance—a discordant note—slowly invades Michel's personality. His selfish thirst for joy gradually disintegrates his once-attained harmony. (p. 97)

In *L'Immoraliste,* Gide links a subject matter of dramatic intensity: the human search for happiness and its tragic consequences, with a restrained, skillful and melodious form.

His next book, *La Porte Etroite,* is a complete contrast to *L'Immoraliste* in subject matter. André Gide now portrays the search for spiritual and religious harmony, here desired as intensely as physical harmony was, in *L'Immoraliste.* Alissa, the heroine, creates a tragedy of universal implications, by sacrificing her human love to her religious aspirations. One may compare *La Porte Etroite* to *La Princesse de Clèves* for its purity of passion, its restraint in style, and its grave and beautiful tone.

In the diary, where Alissa notes her struggles toward the attainment of religious serenity, Gide has reached the purest form of his genius, and, according to him, the most satisfying medium of expression.

After *L'Immoraliste* and *La Porte Etroite,* André Gide synchronizes the two opposed ideals of aesthetic harmony and religious serenity in *La Symphonie Pastorale,* the three forming a psychological trilogy. The entire book is written in the form of a diary, and Gide achieves an amazing feat of psychological skill by making an objective use of the pronoun "I". (p. 98)

The brevity and the concentration of the narrative seem rather disturbing to the reader; the progress of the action is almost excessively compact; but, following his technique, Gide expresses only what is essential, and, through successive readings, one penetrates into a wealth of implications, revealing a masterful skill. . . .

The last three books of Gide form a second trilogy. In *L'Ecole des Femmes,* Geneviève publishes her mother's diary; her father answers in *Robert;* in the third book, Geneviève, the heroine, relates a few episodes of her adolescence and of her family life, inter-mingled with personal reflexions, answering Gide's own thesis on the emancipation of women.

A few pages give us as much information about the life of this family as would an intimate acquaintance with them. (p. 99)

This is indeed true classicism, according to Gide's own definition. With a paradoxical economy of means, one could not create wider implications.

André Gide finds the narrative to be his most satisfactory form of expression, but he has also experimented with the novel. To him, this genre is essentially a conflict between artistic reality and worldly facts; it cannot be constructed after a definite plan but must "progress at random"; the facts themselves dictate to the writer; and the latter must remain "objective and impartial".

One finds in *Les Faux-Monnayeurs* a great number of characters, intermingled actions, spontaneous dialogues, well-balanced scenes, melodious descriptions, clever sketches. It is the novel of adolescent beings, and that of a novel in the making, the latter being treated as a scientific experiment. The author, with the curiosity of a biologist, watches the characters offered him by life itself; they sometimes deceive him by unexpected or even valueless reactions.

Les Faux-Monnayeurs may be considered as an attempt to synthesize the various literary ambitions of the author into critical experiment. It precedes *L'Ecole des Femmes* by three years, and *Geneviève* by ten, which tends to show that Gide returned to the short narrative after having completed an experimental study of the novel.

As shown in his most recent narratives, he has perfected a new mastery, a serene and chiseled style, and an infallible feeling in selecting forceful traits with unerring precision.

A judgment of André Gide's works considered as an entity is not possible. However, up to the present time, his writings show a great diversity, ranging from impressionistic treatises to the novel and to stylized narratives. He observes the technical and psychological laws of traditional classicism, necessary to a harmonious order, and, with such traditional restraint, he probes contemporary problems of universal significance, in which he constantly strives for the attainment of absolute technical mastery. (pp. 99-100)

> *Elizabeth M. Rodrigue, "Andre Gide, Exponent of Classical Tradition in Modern French Fiction (originally a paper read at the Modern Language Association, Chicago, on December 29, 1937), in* The French Review *(copyright 1938 by the American Association of Teachers of French), Vol. XII, No. 2, December, 1938, pp. 95-100.*

CARLOS LYNES, JR. (essay date 1941)

[*Lynes discusses Gide's highly original experiments with novelistic form in* Les faux monnayeurs. *Although he praises Gide for his inventiveness, Lynes finds fault with the novel for its lack of continuity on a chapter to chapter basis. Although Gide did this deliberately out of his "unwillingness to compromise the spontaneity of his future responses by his present choice," Lynes believes it was an error in judgement on Gide's part because, in so doing, he lost his grip on the reader's imagination.*]

Few writers of any age have been more consciously and acutely aware of the problem of form in the novel and few have provided us with more complete records of their wrestling with the difficulties of transforming the reality of experience into the autonomous reality of fiction than has the author of *Les Faux-Monnayeurs.* If Gide has failed in this work to achieve a real masterpiece of the novel, he has nevertheless given us an extraordinarily interesting and enlightening book—a critical novel or a critique of the novel which, together with the *Journal des Faux-Monnayeurs* in which the author notes the problems, the doubts, and the tentative solutions which he formulated during the period of gestation of his fiction, deserves our closest scrutiny.

It is possible now, a generation after the appearance of *Les Faux-Monnayeurs*, to consider the novel itself and Gide's theory with detachment, an attitude which most critics—French as well as foreign—have been loath to accord a work that seemed to outrage moral and critical conventions alike. Because of the moral implications of all his writings, Gide has been the constant prey of the moralistic critics, and . . . it was only in 1938 that Jean Hytier produced his brilliant analysis of Gide's art by heeding the author's own advice: "Le point de vue esthétique est le seul où il faille se placer pour parler de mon oeuvre sainement" ["The aesthetic viewpoint is the only one necessary in order to speak of my wholesome works."].

It is this point of view that must be adopted, of course, if we wish to learn anything from Gide about the problem of form in the novel. One fact only must be noted about Gide the man, which is that his whole life has been an effort to realize and to harmonize all the rich and conflicting possibilities which he felt within himself—to reconcile these possibilities not by suppressing some of them in accordance with a convention imposed from without or an ideal set up from within but by including them all in a synthesis, a "perilous balance," which would be authentic and sincere, vital and mobile, the perfect realization of a man within the limits set by his own physical and spiritual nature. To what extent Gide the man has approached this goal need not concern us directly here, though human limitations being what they are and Gide's problem being more difficult than most because of the anomaly which he has revealed to us so frankly in *Si le grain ne meurt* . . . it seems obvious that achievement of this goal in his life could be but partial. In fact Gide soon understood that complete realization was no doubt impossible in life, but he believed that it could be attained, virtually at least, in the work of art.

This conception of the work of ar as the reconciling of opposites and the resolving of discords in a form that recognizes and respects the variety and complexity of experience was not new, of course, but it was something which too many writers and literary schools had in practice forgotten. Gide was unable even to approach this goal at first, all the more so because he began his literary activity under the aegis of symbolism—not what Mr. Edmund Wilson has called the "conversational-ironic" type of symbolism represented by Laforgue and Corbière but rather the "serious-esthetic" kind of symbolism turned inward represented by Verlaine. This turning inward gave Gide one kind of reality—a kind which the naturalists had too long neglected—but it was only one element in the complexity of experience.

Aside from their intrinsic esthetic value, Gide's writings during the long interval between his youthful symbolistic writings (which began to appear in 1891) and *Les Faux-Monnayeurs* (1926) reveal the author's groping toward the kind of artistic synthesis which he early recognized as his goal. Before attempting such a synthesis in a comprehensive literary form, Gide preferred to prepare himself by treating the elements separately, first in the little compositions that he calls "traités" and later in the short fictions that he designates as "récits" or "soties" rather than as novels. Or doubtless it was not really

a matter of preference but simply the fact that until late middle age he hesitated even to attempt the difficult problem of harmonizing in a single work themes as varied as the ones stated separately in *L'Immoraliste, La Porte étroite, Isabelle,* and *Les Caves du Vatican.* When he published *Isabelle* . . . he planned a preface to explain that this book, as well as *L'Immoraliste* and *La Porte étroite,* is termed a "récit" because it does not correspond to his conception of the novel. Similarly, in the dedication of *Les Caves du Vatican* he asserts that he does not wish people to take his fictions as novels and then accuse him of violating the rules of the genre. . . . He feels that his short fictions, which he insists are "ironical" or "critical," represent conflicting tendencies or possibilities of his own nature—tendencies coexisting and held in check in Gide the man but here isolated as a pathologist might isolate bacilli for study and placed under a light so clear and direct that each element stands out in sharp relief. The criticism and irony are only implicit in the individual fictions, partly because Gide understands that the work of art itself is the only proper solution to the "problems" that it raises, but above all because the real criticism of *L'Immoraliste* lies in *La Porte étroite* just as the criticism of *La Porte étroite* is found in *L'Immoraliste.* Gide understands, moreover, the close relationship among these works as well as his own inability, at the time of their composition, to harmonize their diverse themes in the complex unity of a real novel. (pp. 175-78)

Realization of such a synthesis, granted that the artist's experience is sufficiently rich and his attitude sufficiently comprehensive and profound, is essentially a problem of form, since form—in all the arts—is what has been called "the artistically expressive organization . . . of the medium in which it has its being." (p. 178)

All this implies no shallow "art for art's sake" doctrine or exclusively formalist esthetic, however, nor any belief in a priori patterns of composition, especially in the novel, which has always enjoyed more freedom than any other literary type. Gide would certainly subscribe to Percy Lubbock's assertion that "The best form is that which makes the most of its subject—there is no other definition of the meaning of form in fiction." Yet in France during the late nineteenth and early twentieth centuries there had developed a type of "well-made" novel which, fortified by the academic prejudice that the French alone know how to "compose" and that such formal "composition" is essential to literature, tended to crystallize in a strict conventional mold into which the individual novelist was expected to stuff whatever material came to hand instead of actively shaping his experience into the unique form required by the subject. Against this kind of unintelligent, inartistic doctrine Gide rebels—Gide the master of style and composition himself and the exponent of the vital kind of "classicism" which he defines as the integration of the totality of the moral, intellectual, and emotional preoccupations of one's age in a synthesis allowing all the elements to assume their proper reciprocal relationships. . . . He is unwilling to accept any such ready-made frame for his own composition because he understands that the true novelist is a poet or "maker" whose task and privilege it is to shape his material into the specific form which *is* the novel just as surely as the form *is* the statue. (pp. 178-79)

Les Faux-Monnayeurs is all the more interesting for the study of Gide's esthetic of the novel because it is, in a much truer sense than any of Zola's fiction, an "experimental" novel—a work in which the real subject is largely the novelist's effort to transform the reality of experience into the ideal reality of the work of art. . . . Though published separately, the novel itself and the *Journal des Faux-Monnayeurs* were so closely linked in the author's consciousness that he thought more than once of pouring the *Journal* into his imaginative creation and attempting to fuse the two in a still more complex synthesis. Yet the novel was already sufficiently complex, for by a curious "doubling" of his subject (a type of composition already used, though less elaborately, in several earlier writings) Gide places within *Les Faux-Monnayeurs* a novelist who is writing a novel with the same title as Gide's and who, in turn, plans to place a novelist in *his* story.

This doubling of the subject is one of the elements in the solution which Gide gives to the problem of the point of view in his fiction. As Henry James and Percy Lubbock have shown us, the "post of observation," or the point of view from which the story is presented, largely determines the form which a novel assumes. Gide recognizes this fact in several passages of the *Journal des Faux-Monnayeurs* and he has his novelist Édouard, too, note its importance in his effort to narrate little Georges Molinier's abortive theft of a book from one of the stalls along the Seine. (pp. 179-80)

Gide's specific solution to the problem of the point of view depends ultimately, perhaps, upon what Professor Rogers would have called his "basic organization," that is, upon the general pattern which he gives to life and experience. More immediately, however, it depends upon the subject of the particular novel as he envisages it, with appropriate modifications as the work develops. The two extremes in the method of presenting the subject matter of a novel are direct narration—a sort of "pictorial summary," as Percy Lubbock phrases it—from the point of view of the author, and the type of rigorously dramatic presentation that gives not an account or a report of what has happened but a direct sight of the matter itself while it is passing. Modern fiction generally lies between these extremes, where there is room for the greatest variety and freedom, the only requirement for the novelist being that the presentation he adopts should be the one which makes the most of the subject.

For the subjects of works like *L'Immoraliste, La Porte étroite,* and *La Symphonie pastorale,* Gide found the first-person narrative by a character in the story admirably suited, but when he wishes to harmonize a number of varied and conflicting themes within the structure of a single complex novel the problem of the point of view again presents itself. At first he considers having Lafcadio, the hero of *Les Caves du Vatican,* serve as narrator for *Les Faux-Monnayeurs,* but he soon doubts that everything can be presented from the highly individual point of view of this youth. Then he thinks of using Lafcadio's diary for certain chapters, Édouard's *Journal* for others, and perhaps the files of a lawyer for still other chapters. Finally he decides that he cannot entirely avoid the use of impersonal narration, since his novel is to consist of so many strands of action, but he modifies and supplements this traditional method so abundantly that his novel acquires a highly original structure with a texture of unusual richness. Because he knows himself to be much better at making others speak than in speaking directly himself, he presents much of the story by means of dramatic dialogues and even allows the characters to take over the narration of events which he prefers not to tell in impersonal narrative or in dramatic scenes. Moreover, the same happenings are sometimes presented from different angles by different characters and Gide welcomes the slight distortion which re-

sults because it calls for the active collaboration of the reader to correct the image. Sometimes letters assist in telling the story and here again Gide is glad to relinquish direct narration from the author's point of view for what he considers a more objective method.

An especially large part of the story is presented indirectly by means of the *Journal* of Édouard. Gide's use of the *Journal* for this purpose has been criticized by Jean Hytier, who points out that it introduces a confusion in the structure of the novel without any important compensation. Édouard's "reality" is the story told by Gide and what one expects to find in his *Journal* is, on the one hand, reflections on the problems encountered in writing his novel which by contrast with the "real" events of Gide's story would show how the reality furnished by experience is transformed by the artist into something which is his own unique creation. But Gide disappoints us in this expectation, under the pretext that Édouard is an "amateur," a "raté" who will never be able to write his novel at all because he lacks the faculty of being able to give himself up wholeheartedly to reality outside himself. As a result, Édouard's *Journal* is used partly as a means for Gide to consider the esthetic of the novel without having to commit himself fully on any point and partly as a medium for the indirect presentation of incidents in Gide's own story from a rather detached point of view similar to but not identical with the author's point of view.

But even this diversity in the method and point of view finally seems insufficient to Gide. After re-reading *Tom Jones* he decides that, in spite of Flaubert's example and the advice of Martin du Gard, he will intervene directly in his novel to comment on the characters and action. This he does in numerous instances, notably in the final chapter of Part Two, which is entirely given over to the author's review of his characters. Gide handles this method rather more subtly and critically than did the eighteenth- and nineteenth-century novelists who had used a similar technique, and it becomes a factor in the deliberate rejection of "realism" that he wishes his novel to be. To make this break with realism even sharper, he tries to introduce epic elements in *Les Faux-Monnayeurs* and, though most of these attempts, especially with respect to the fantastic or the marvelous, fall rather flat, he occasionally strikes a minor epic note in such a passage . . . where he intervenes with poetic omniscience to survey the story from on high. . . . (pp. 180-82)

Of fundamental importance to his conception of form in the novel is Gide's rejection of any a priori plan, any set mold into which the material has to be stuffed according to fixed patterns or rules. (p. 182)

This rejection of the traditional framework and the conventional "plot" does not mean, of course, that the novel for Gide is to be a formless, undisciplined growth, but only that "form" and "content" are to be wrought into a unique organic whole outside of which neither element has any relevant meaning. Composition is of first importance in a book, Gide believes, but he adds that the best procedure is to "laisser l'oeuvre se composer et s'ordonner elle-même, et surtout ne pas la *forcer*" ["allow the work to compose and order itself, and above all not to *force* it"]. . . . He recognizes that because of the variety and complexity of the themes which he seeks to harmonize in *Les Faux-Monnayeurs* it is necessary in some way to "établir une relation contue entre les éléments épars" ["establish a cohesive relation between the separate parts"]. To do this he wishes, in Édouard's words, to make of his novel something like Bach's *Art of Fugue*. . . . (p. 183)

In this attempt, I think, he is not completely successful. As Gide himself recognizes, there are two centers to *Les Faux-Monnayeurs*—the objective story and Édouard's effort to convert this "reality" into a novel. Moreover, since we are given no glimpse of Édouard's accomplishment (except in his tentative narration of Georges Molinier's attempt to steal the book), the two centers never really coincide. And the relationship among the different strands of the narrative is tenuous and sometimes arbitrary, so that one cannot help believing that Gide—who is admirably gifted for the "récit"—lacks the specific ability required to integrate these separate themes in a contrapuntal texture from which they could not easily be detached. Gide himself was acutely aware of these difficulties and in the early stages of the composition of his novel he revealed his misgivings about the new task before him. . . . He was in any case unwilling to adopt the facile, ready-made solution that a conventional "plot" would have provided. Nor could he bring himself now to break his conception up and treat the various stories in separate "récits" (though he admits that without the influence of Martin du Gard he might have had recourse to this). We may be grateful that Gide did stick to his determination to make his novel a complex synthesis of his experience, for even if *Les Faux-Monnayeurs* is not the great masterpiece of the novel that we might wish, it is still the most complete expression of a great artist.

The question of the "roman pur" ["pure novel"] which comes up in *Les Faux-Monnayeurs* and in the *Journal des Faux-Monnayeurs* need not detain us long, for like the debate over "la poésie pure" ["pure poetry"] which has caused so much French critical ink to be expended, it leads only to a sterile impasse if it is pushed very far.. . . If Gide chooses to eliminate from his own fictions everything except the inner life of his characters there is no reason why he should not attempt to do so, but neither is there any reason why his taste in this matter should be set up as a general rule for the novel. Gide seems to realize this, for after discussing the problem of the "roman pur" in the *Journal des Faux-Monnayeurs* he decides to place these ideas in Édouard's *Journal* because in this way he can avoid committing himself definitely on all the points raised, however judicious some of them may seem to him at the moment.

The final point that I wish to discuss is the reason for the disconcerting, even slightly irritating, impression made upon the reader of novels by the form of *Les Faux-Monnayeurs*. The characters in the book are admirably introduced and awakened to a life of their own and the individual chapters of the story have a vitality which reveals Gide's exceptional narrative and dramatic gifts. Yet from chapter to chapter, and accordingly in the work as a whole, there is a sense of discontinuity, of failure on the author's part to "follow through" once he sets his characters on their feet and his themes in motion. The effect on the reader is a vague dissatisfaction that prevents the novel from firing his imagination and possessing him utterly in the way that the greatest masterpieces of fiction tend to do. This effect is not due to carelessness or ineptitude in Gide but rather to a deliberate principle of his esthetic of the novel. Gide was certainly not taking the easy or the popular way, for the rule that he set himself in *Les Faux-Monnayeurs*—"ne jamais profiter de l'élan acquis" ["never to profit from acquired momentum"]—made it almost as difficult for him to launch each chapter as it was to get the book itself under way.

This peculiar method of composition, which tends to take away the reader's spontaneous pleasure in the narrative in proportion as it is applied more rigorously, undoubtedly corresponds to a basic element in Gide's attitude toward life—to his desire to be always sincere, "authentique," "disponible," and not to commit himself by his present choice in such a way that the spontaneity of his future actions may be in any way impaired. The fullest expression of this attitude occurs in the early *Nourritures terrestres* . . . , but to a marked degree the tendency has remained characteristic of Gide the artist and the man throughout the years. (pp. 183-85)

The result of this attitude and of this method of composition is that though Gide suggests infinitely rich possibilities in the characters and action of *Les Faux-Monnayeurs*, he does not go very far in developing them. Here too one must recognize something intentional. . . . (p. 186)

[In] the specific case of *Les Faux-Monnayeurs*, I think, Gide's application of his theory, sincere as it is, gives the impression of a somewhat too conscious technique, almost a tour de force, and the pleasure which the reader derives from collaborating with the novelist to follow through his leads verges on the pleasure that is derived from sheer mental gymnastics. . . . It is possible that Gide is too much of an artist to take his place among the greatest novelists, though I do not wish by this remark to suggest that artistry and craftsmanship are less desirable in the novel than in other literary types. But as Gide himself realized, even though he has expressed confidence that his novel will eventually win praise for the very things which critics still question, the type of composition that he adopted in *Les Faux-Monnayeurs* was a risk. . . . It was, in fact, a sort of wager, and unfortunately Gide did not emerge so clearly the winner that his work may be termed an unqualified success as the great novel, the rich synthesis of the author's experience in the complex unity of a solid masterpiece, which he strove so hard to achieve.

In view of this incomplete success, we may ask in conclusion, what is the lesson to be learned from Gide—from his theory and his practice—with respect to the problem of form in the novel? On the one hand, it seems to me, Gide has proved that for any novelist who is a sincere and serious artist the old, conventional, stereotyped "form" which the Paul Bourgets and the Henry Bordeaux' accepted without question is gone forever. The novelist may not care to discard "plot" or he may develop his fiction in such a way that this element loses its traditional identity; the important thing is that the novelist, no less than the poet, is an imaginative artist whose task and privilege it is to create for each subject a form that will fuse so inseparably with the matter that a work of art in all its specific objectivity comes into being. This valuable lesson, which each new generation of writers and critics needs to have brought before it in concrete examples, was especially appropriate for the generations that have looked to Gide as a courageous master.

But on the other hand, Gide's attempt to achieve a great novel in *Les Faux-Monnayeurs* shows clearly that it is not enough for the novelist to be an intelligent, skillful, sensitive artist and to reject the old forms for a new design showing rare inventiveness and superb craftsmanship. What is necessary is something at the same time simpler and much more difficult, for the novelist's success depends upon his making the reader accept his creation as living and true—not, of course, true only in the narrow realistic sense, but true in that the artist so captures our imagination that we cease to regard mere reason as the sole criterion of truth and attend to his creation with all our faculties at once. In *Les Faux-Monnayeurs*, Gide fails to an appreciable degree in this essential matter, it seems to me, and this in spite of his admirable effort to synthesize his experience in the complex structure of a single work and in spite of the exceptional artistic and intellectual gifts which he brings to the task. This failure, moreover, strikes me as a failure to achieve a perfect solution to the problem of form, since it comes largely from the author's conscious artistic procedure of refusing to "follow through" either his characters or his story. This refusal, I have noted, is a manifestation of one of the basic traits of Gide's make-up—his unwillingness to compromise the spontaneity of his future responses by his present choice. In a novelist, no less than in a man of action, such a trait is a handicap if it becomes dominant, and the result in this instance is that while *Les Faux-Monnayeurs* is the work most fully representative of its author and one of the most interesting pieces of fiction in an age that has produced the writings of Thomas Mann, Marcel Proust, and James Joyce, it fails to sustain that mysterious quality of life which would place it among the real masterpieces of the novel. (pp. 186-88)

> *Carlos Lynes, Jr., "André Gide and the Problem of Form in the Novel" (copyright, 1941, by Carlos Lynes, Jr.), in* The Southern Review, *Vol. VII, No. 1, Summer, 1941 (and reprinted in* Forms of Modern Fiction: Essays Collected in Honor of Joseph Warren Beach, *edited by William Van O'Connor, Indiana University Press, 1959, pp. 175-88).*

E. M. FORSTER (essay date 1943)

[*Forster was a prominent English novelist, critic, and essayist, whose works reflect his liberal humanism. His most celebrated novel,* A Passage to India, *is a complex examination of personal relationships amid the conflicts of the modern world. Although some of Forster's critical essays are considered naive in their literary assessments, his discussion of fictional techniques in his* Aspects of the Novel *is regarded as a minor classic in literary criticism. In the excerpt below, Forster argues that Gide's thought belongs to the humanist tradition because he possesses the four characteristics of a humanist: "curiosity, a free mind, belief in good taste, and belief in the human race."*]

Gide is an old man now. He has written a number of novels including *The Immoralist*, his most disquieting work, *The Caves of the Vatican*, expressing his pagan side, and *The Narrow Gate*, which expresses his Protestant pietistic side. He has also written criticisms and plays, and a fascinating and frank autobiography of his early life, he has kept journals, been active at conferences, helped to run the chief French literary magazine. And now he is an old man. And when his country collapsed three years ago he might naturally have done what some French writers actually did—that is to say, collaborated with Hitler or at all events with Vichy. He refused. Retiring to unoccupied France, he continued to express truths which he alone, owing to his prestige, was able to get into print. Instead of playing for safety, he used his high position to uphold still higher the torch of freedom. Then Hitler advanced again and occupied the south. Gide got away to Tunis, and when the Allied Armies captured it this spring they found him there. He has honoured us as well as his own country by his conduct, and he has advanced the republic of letters.

Yet I do not want to present Gide as a hero. He would not wish it and he isn't the type. He is not a hero. He is a humanist.

The humanist has four leading characteristics—curiosity, a free mind, belief in good taste, and belief in the human race—and all four are present in Gide. His curiosity—he is always enquiring, he's interested in society and its breakup, in his own character and other people's, in virtues and in vices too: in forgery as much as in the ecstasies of the saints: in self-denial and in self-indulgence. And secondly, he has a free mind. He is indifferent to authority, and he is willing to pay the penalty for independence. For example, he once went to the Congo, and he was so disgusted by economic imperialism and its exploitation of the African Negro, that he became a communist, at some personal inconvenience. Later on he went to Russia, and what he saw of communism there compelled him at even greater inconvenience to renounce it. I'm not saying either of these decisions is correct. I only want to point out that here's a man with a free mind, indifferent to authority, indifferent sometimes to logic, indifferent to everything except what he believes to be true. He has remained an individualist in an age which imposes discipline. His third characteristic is that he believes in good taste. Gide is a literary man, not a scientist, not a prophet, and his judgments tend to be esthetic. He's subtle and elusive—sometimes annoyingly so—he sets great store by charm, he's more interested in harmony than in doctrine.

Fourth, he believes in humanity. He is not cynical about the human race. And consequently—for it is a consequence—he has no class prejudice and no colour prejudice. I remember so well the last time I met him: it was in an international congress of writers at Paris in the 'thirties, and he had to make a speech. A tall, willowy figure, he undulated on the platform above the vast audience, rather full of airs and graces and inclined to watch his own effects. Then he forgot himself and remembered the human race and made a magnificent oration. His thesis was that the individual will never develop his individuality until he forms part of a world society. As his thought soared, his style became fluid, and sentimentality passed into affection. He denied that humanity would cease to be interesting if it ceased to be miserable, and imagined a social state where happiness will be accessible to all, and where men, because they are happy, will be great. At that time the menace of Fascism was already darkening our doorways, and it seemed to us, as we listened to Gide, that here was a light which the darkness could not put out. It is not easy, in a few words, to give a picture of a very complicated individual; let me anyhow make it clear that he reacts to the European tragedy as a humanist, that the four characteristics of humanism are curiosity, a free mind, belief in good taste, and belief in the human race, and that he has been prepared to suffer for his beliefs: they have not been just for the study and the cloister; and consequently men honour him. (pp. 228-30)

> *E. M. Forster, "Gide and George" (1943), in his* Two Cheers for Democracy *(copyright 1951 by E. M. Forster; renewed 1979 by Donald Parry; reprinted by permission of Harcourt Brace Jovanovich, Inc.; in Canada by Edward Arnold Ltd.), Harcourt Brace Jovanovich, 1951, pp. 228-31.**

JEAN COLLIGNON (essay date 1951)

[*Collignon discusses the meaning and importance of sincerity in Gide's life and work.*]

No pastime is more appealing to unemployed critics than collecting instances of contradictions in André Gide's words. This is a game where one scores at every other page; and a safe one, at that, for the opponent not only puts up no fight whatsoever, but also invites continuous attack; to such a shocking extent that the critic begins to suspect that he has been charging against windmills. Gide composedly and repeatedly emphasizes the two sides of an endless dialogue. Whoever is naive enough to confess surprise will be confronted with the disarming answer: Such contradictory statements express successive and equally sincere thoughts.

Now the epithet ''sincere'' is puzzling for anyone interested in Gide; and therefore of paramount importance. For, without sincerity, the successive and contradictory statements would testify only to some deceitful intention in the author. Of course, one can always, like Massis, tax Gide with hypocrisy, infer that he must be either a mountebank or a preacher in immorality; whereupon, nothing remains but to dismiss him without further ado, except to warn gullible readers against the evil influence of his talent. Unfortunately, there are those who, convinced they will like him in spite—not to say because—of his weaknesses, would nevertheless have a much better conscience, if assured that Gide *can* actually be trusted. So far, they have assumed that he could. What would happen to their faith, should his sincerity be exploded? The question constitutes the cornerstone of Gide's validity, primarily as a thinker, but, to a certain extent, as an artist. Unless a positive answer is given, what a futile attempt, indeed, to ask why Gide could ever write such diptychs as *l'Immoraliste* and *la Porte étroite, les Caves du Vatican* and *Numquid et Tu, Retour de l'URSS* and *Retouches à mon Retour de l'URSS?* Any discussion of their origin, composition and significance must appear fruitless, if the honest reader is not shown, beforehand, that each of the widely different messages represents the expression of equally authentic opinions of Gide's.

Once aware of the vital importance of the question, one cannot help feeling bewildered by its magnitude and difficulty. To be fair, an answer should be complete, that is, an investigation of the whole of Gide's word is required. And concurrently, a day-by-day account of Gide's spiritual biography should be available, as a screen on which to project each work to test its sincerity. Such an attempt being impossible here, we must be satisfied with a few indications.

Naturally enough, one is tempted to turn to Gide himself, expecting that a man so permanently interested in his mind and art might provide some first hand information. But over-conscientious readers are bound to be shocked when coming across passages—in his diary and elsewhere—where Gide either confesses that, on the whole, he is not immoderately concerned with total sincerity or frankly admits that he is full of hypocrisy. At which point, the two possible answers would be: a) Gide is only trying to scandalize his readers and force them to lay down the book, not to think, but to be disgusted, thus showing that he pooh-poohs the readers' opinions, or b) Gide is actually honest when confessing his dishonesty, in which case it seems rather paradoxical that he should be sincere only when asserting he is not sincere; in all likelihood, he ought to be sincere on other points as well.

But now, we are confronted with other statements to the effect that Gide is anxious to write exactly and exclusively what he thinks or feels. Thus another door bangs right in our face. Gide will offer no information. There is no objective reason to believe or disbelieve his statements about his sincerity or hypocrisy. But if we like him, we are tempted to believe he is sincere, especially when he gives us the lie; and vice-versa.

Such is the seemingly unescapable conclusion of any limited attempts to discuss Gide's sincerity: an interrogation mark, or just an impression; and to remain content with the hope that, some day, a long-lived and indefatigable scholar will present us with the spiritual biography already mentioned. But on second thought, we see that an attempt of this kind is bound to fail. A day-by-day account of Gide's thoughts would at the same time be too much and too little. For we are not exceedingly anxious to become acquainted with the detail of his thoughts, when, on February 29 of a certain leap-year of the early twenties, he enters in his diary that he caught a cold riding *La Flèche d'Or* between Nice and Paris; but we are emphatically interested in knowing accurately and completely what feelings, images, memories, ideas etc . . . were revolving in his mind when he wrote a sentence like this: ''The number of things that are better left unsaid increases for me every day.'' As far as we can judge, no critic will succeed in providing the adequate material. Unfortunately (or fortunately) the question of Gide's sincerity is beyond the scholar's reach. Gide himself does not know. If he is at all interested, he will have—willy-nilly—to ask the Lord.

Nevertheless, on a strictly private level, we realize that we will not be satisfied without an answer. And if we are fond of Gide and try to analyze our impressions when reading his work, we discover that we believe him to be sincere, even though, in a number of cases, he may be suspected of some hypocrisy. All we can try is what most critics indulge in, without admitting it, namely to rationalize our impressions. And there is no small comfort in noticing a striking similarity between our uncertainty and Gide's baffling statements on the question. There must lie the only available basis for a personal evaluation of Gide's sincerity.

The origin of the uncertainty could very well be explained by the lack of a proper definition for ''sincerity''. Here again, Gide fails to help. As if better to confuse the issue, he declares at one point that he does not know what it means. This is no false modesty or some clever way to dodge the difficulty. But rather an admission that, although realizing the full content of the concept ''sincerity'', he becomes more and more aware that it is impossible to understand how one *can be* sincere. Especially in the case of a writer in whom two aspects of sincerity have to be considered: internal and external, honesty with oneself and honesty with the reader.

Obviously enough, we cannot deal with the question of internal sincerity alone, since what we might know of it originates in what Gide himself tells us, which inevitably involves external sincerity. And yet, all the time, he seems to try to overcome the obstacle and present us with some material on which to test his internal sincerity. Any book of his stands, as it were, like a screen between the reader and the idea of himself that Gide wants to give. For instance, telling the story of Jérome and Alissa under the accomplished form of the *récit* involves various operations: 1) considering a number of possible episodes, analyses etc . . . ; 2) selecting the best among them; 3) considering a number of possible artistic means to translate the selected episodes, etc. . . . into words; 4) selecting the proper means of expression. Thus the book, when eventually published, represents *one* selection among many possible books. Now we know how Gide has always hesitated before any kind of choice, or rather before the eliminations that any choice implies. Quite naturally therefore, in the case of Alissa, he has tried to present a fuller, more complete, more direct account of her feelings in the ''Journal d'Alissa''. This closing chapter of *la Porte étroite,* for which Gide confesses some partiality, is an attempt to tell us, at one point, what the whole book might have been, had not the author chosen, with the self-imposed discipline of the *récit,* a method of transcription less direct, that is, less completely sincere.

We might make the same remarks concerning the Minister's diary in *la Symphonie Pastorale,* Edouard's diary in *les Faux-Monnayeurs,* and finally concerning *le Journal de Faux-Monnayeurs.* Eventually, we might consider the whole of Gide's works as books that would tend to assume the form of diaries, but that assume it only on specific occasions, and as examples, because aesthetic considerations—as important in the eyes of Gide as the desire to be sincere—compelled him to adopt more accomplished forms such as the novel, the dialogue, the drama etc. . . . Any sympathetic reader will be impressed by Gide's earnestness in such efforts. But on closer investigation, even the diaries read like pathetic, rather than convincing, attempts to reach an elusive sincerity. Although theoretically less adulterated by aesthetic preoccupations, the mere act of writing them means selecting and eliminating, just as in *la Symphonie, la Porte étroite* or *les Faux-Monnayeurs.* Granted that they can be more sincere than the books themselves, they suffer none the less from the inevitable inaccuracy linked with the process of translating man's thoughts into words. Gide himself has been aware of that fallacy and has refrained from making a more extensive use of the diary form in his books.

Whatever the case may be, even if we admit—in the face of multiple evidence—that a diary constitutes a direct, complete and honest transcription of Gide's thoughts, we are now confronted with a new difficulty. For, at the start, Gide knows, not himself, but only *an idea* of himself. As a sincere man, he tries to make this idea of himself coincide as closely as possible with his own authentic self. Now, in tracing his efforts, we may notice two different methods. At times, sincerity with himself is achieved, or at least attempted, through relaxation, almost complete abandon to both impulse and instinct. As if the only way to take a glimpse at his real nature was to remove all obstacles between it and his perception of it, mainly moral obstacles (scruples, remorse etc. . . . .) and simply to yield to the mood of the instant. Such an attitude characterizes *les Nourritures Terrestres, l'Immoraliste, les Caves du Vatican, les Nouvelles Nourritures,* and numerous parts of the *Journal.* And there is no doubt that it represents a considerable part of Gide's writing. Here again the question of ascertaining to what extent the real Gide is represented in such books remains beyond our reach. But on one point at least we may have our doubts: How can we assert that, within Gide's personality, the level of impulses and moods is the deeper, the more permanent one, rather than the more superficial and fragile? For, in releasing instincts and impulses, perhaps he only opens the door to what, in him, is modeled by education, habits and circumstances. Perhaps he unduly throws light, not on his innermost self, but on that part of himself which he shares with other men living under similar conditions. Sincerity through relaxation may be the least revealing form of sincerity.

Gide is well aware of the danger. Besides, his aesthetic principles are so adverse to facility, he is such an emphatic exponent of the classical striving towards perfection, and he has tried so constantly to fashion his life into his most accomplished work of art, that we can hardly imagine him as content to focus his attention on the incidental and peripheral aspects of his personality. That such curiosities excite him, we cannot doubt: as such, in the first place; and secondly because to omit or even

to overlook them would be sheer dishonesty. But he must be interested in another way of coming into contact with his authentic self. Perhaps those supposedly superficial and less personal elements do constitute, on the contrary, Gide's truer self, the one which lies deep under the crust of habits and prejudices. Since we know that he has suffered under the weight of what Pascal called "second nature," we can look at *les Nourritures* and similar books as recording, not relaxation, but an effort to remove the superficial layer and uncover the true, unspoiled self. In fact, *les Nourritures* show the same marks of effort as a supposedly much tenser book like *la Porte étroite.* Yet the former is an attempt to lessen tension, the latter an attempt to increase tension. Sincerity in the former is not a lower variety of sincerity in the latter. They only differ in that, at first sight, the kind of sincerity we come across in *les Nourritures* seems—erroneously and on account of its specific object—easier to reach and less fruitful. Gide however referred to both categories when he said that sincerity appeals to him only when it is "difficilement consentie," that is, granted only after a struggle.

But precisely because "difficilement consentie," sincerity is again endangered. An idea or feeling, discovered at great cost, then examined at some length, assumes undue importance, becomes magnified, that is adulterated. The longer we focus our attention on it, the sooner we realize that it may not be entirely authentic, but partly a product of our imagination. Trying to make sure that we are sincere prevents us from being sincere. Thus does the famous image of Gide always writing in front of a mirror assume its full significance. In order to know himself, Narcissus is obliged to look at his reflection in the water; who can warrant that he will not fall in love with himself, cease to know himself and stop being sincere? Writing in front of a mirror is a self-destroying, though indispensable, method.

Gide knew this long ago; and did not have to wait for Claudel's haughty and hasty condemnation in a recent interview. But, at a time when Claudel could still believe in Gide's sincerity because he showed some inclination towards Catholicism, Gide himself had pointed out, in a much deeper way, the ultimate failure of sincerity: in our mind, what is imaginary cannot be distinguished from what is real: "Psychological analysis lost all interest for me from the moment that I became aware that men feel what they imagine they feel. From that to thinking that they imagine they feel what they feel was a very short step . . ." The idea was so pregnant that Gide dared not (or did not care to) carry it to its conclusion. Because it affirms nothing less than the impossibility of knowing whether what we now think is genuine or spurious.

At this juncture, a logical mind would comment: Why then indulge in so many psychological analyses? Why not give up entirely? We can, to a certain extent, imagine a tentative answer: Gide admits that he is never sure about what he thinks, or, more accurately, he never knows whether what he thinks represents his own self, temporarily or permanently, partly or entirely. Any psychological analysis should bear the label: "Not guaranteed"; and absolutely, is of little value. But, relatively, it is priceless, as an effort. Because, when all is said about the shortcomings of sincerity, it remains that, for Gide, the problem is not to decide whether his own deep permanent self is better embodied in Jérome or Alissa, or Prometheus, or Lafcadio, or the Prodigal Child, or Edouard. The capital thing is that, in all cases, they are all trying to be themselves, and that he, Gide, is trying to be himself in the process. What part of

Gide's personality does the ideal of relaxation or the ideal of tension appeal to? That is an idle question. What does matter is that, out of sheer, unrewarding sincerity, with either ideal prevailing at the time, Gide is striving to find one aspect of himself. A fervent and hopeless craving for sincerity: such is his own eagle. But the chances of Gide ever killing the bird and eating it are rather negligible. Because if sincerity was to be rewarded by some unquestionable results, the whole edifice of Gide's works might very well be seriously endangered. Sincerity must be at the same time indispensable and unattainable. And if we like men, not for what they are, but for what devours them, we will experience an exquisitely Gidian delight at seeing the Master in such a predicament. (pp. 44-50)

Jean Collignon, "Gide's Sincerity," in Yale French Studies, Special Issue: Andre Gide *(copyright © Yale French Studies 1951), No. 7, 1951, pp. 44-50.*

IRVIN STOCK   (essay date 1951)

[*Stock is an American critic, dramatist, and short story writer. In the following excerpt, he discusses the meanings of the two central symbols—the devil and counterfeit money—in Gide's novel* Les faux monnayeurs.]

If **Les Faux Monnayeurs** is a confusing novel, the reason is that it contains more of life than any other ever written. This is not to say more of life's *experiences,* but rather more of those formulae, ideas, "truths" by which the human mind defines experience and prescribes for it. The realm of ideas is the realm of Gide's art. A cliché of criticism has it that a concern with ideas must result in some violence to life's rich complexity. From such a danger Gide has been saved, however, by the peculiarly Protestant sincerity with which he has always examined a self too wide and too much in motion for any formula that stood still. To this has been due a mistrust of formulae equal to his interest in them. The tension between these two movements of his mind, in fact, may be regarded as itself the formula for his entire career and many of his works may be regarded as attempts to discredit some cherished principle, cherished, that is, by himself.

In **Les Faux Monnayeurs** this tension receives for the first time its total expression. Unlike the works which preceded it (and in this respect, perhaps, his "first novel"), it examines not a single formula and the situation in which its rising and falling truth may be tested, but a life-like multiplicity of both. Moreover, following out to its extremity his own logic, he has provided the novel with a second level, a level below that on which the narrative we watch—the parade of its "truths"—takes place. On this level, that of Edouard's composition of his own *Faux Monnayeurs,* we are shown the formula-making process itself. It is the function of the second level to cast doubt upon the first. **Les Faux Monnayeurs** tries to answer then, by thus facing it head on, the ultimate question of Gide's intellectual life: in a world which the human mind can only grasp after subduing it to formulae, but in which both observer and observed are so complex and changing that none can do their relationships justice, what is the formula in which men *can* come to rest? We may well watch with suspense the result of such an experiment since the problem is not only Gide's, but that of the modern mind in general, of which his own, divided and self-rejecting, is an adequate symbol.

The subject of **Les Faux Monnayeurs,** as Edouard defines it, is precisely this "rivalry between the real world and the rep-

resentation we make of it to ourselves. The manner in which the world of appearance imposes itself on us and the manner in which we try to impose on the outside world our own interpretation, this is the drama of our lives." In other words, the novel's subject is no other than Gide's own struggle to write it, which is to say, his own effort to understand his life truly, to find a unified structure of ideas which will permit him to transpose it without loss of value into coinage of the mind. How is this to be done? Gide begins by denying himself the single insight—or homogeneous cluster of insights—which, conscious or unconscious, forms the core of all other novels and by which its material is organized in advance. To keep his novel true to its subject, he leaves it *open,* as in fact the mind which would preserve its relevance and justness must remain in life. "It is essentially out of the question for a book of this kind to have a plan," Edouard observes. "Everything would be falsified if anything were decided beforehand. I wait for reality to dictate to me." If the book's confusing variety sometimes suggests that it is in his narrative that Gide has left himself thus free, this is not, however, on the whole, the sense actually intended. Too many of the story patterns come out "right". The freedom Gide has chiefly made use of is the freedom to *change his mind,* to permit every new development to suggest some new measure by which people and events, true and false, good and evil, healthy and moribund are to be understood. This is what accounts for the novel's terrible difficulty. There is no one whose point of view it is always safe for the reader to trust—even Edouard is finally discredited—and no principle emerging as the moral of any particular episode and seized by the panting reader as a possible theme, which it will be safe to apply to all others. We do in fact come at last to one which seems durable. But this is so only because it is itself an open door to all others, and far from solving the endless problem, offers rather a touchstone by which to measure a given solution's varying adequacy.

I have said that the picture of Edouard's struggle must cast a doubt on the result of Gide's. This is not the only reason for doubt. Since the clash between reality and our formulae must necessarily be endless, how could Gide's attempt to write a book which will justly formulate his material ever come to an end? Edouard's does not. At the close of Gide's novel, Edouard's is still unfinished. In the **Journal des Faux Monnayeurs** Gide suggests it will never be finished because Edouard is incapable of a "veritable devotion" to anything. "He pursues himself incessantly and through everything." But what is Gide's own peculiar distinction if not this incessant pursuit of himself, which is only a search for his true reactions to what is being observed? The other name for this pursuit is integrity. It is Edouard's extravagant integrity that will keep him forever at work. To stop seeking further at any moment of apparent understanding would mean a closing of his book to life, where the search is necessarily continuous, which would, precisely, invalidate it as an embodiment of his theme. Gide, then, has put a limit to his own integrity in stooping to finish the book we have. It is a betrayal by which all its truth stands forever compromised. But if he has cheated us, as all novelists must, he has done what none has ever done before. He has helped us to find him out.

The narrative of the book, then, is the realm of its (intentional) confusion, as Edouard's attempt to formulate it in a coherent novel is the source of its unity. But even for the confusion, or rather for the processes which engender it, Gide has found formulae to help us grasp them, and his chief symbols for these are the counterfeit and the devil. Without understanding the full, the developing import of each it is impossible to understand the book.

The counterfeit gold coin begins, of course, by symbolizing the false, the inauthentic individual: a major preoccupation of Gide's career. "I should like," says Bernard, "all my life long at the very smallest shock to ring true. Nearly all the people I have known ring false." In the light of this, characters like Pastor Vedel, professionally virtuous, or the literary parasite de Passavant are immediately understandable as examples of the counterfeit. Nor do we see only "evil" pretending to be "good," but also the reverse, as when Armand, basically in love with virtue, apes out of despair, a nastiness he loathes. And between these poles will be found many other degrees and variations of the process.

But the circle of suspicion widens. Even thoughts and feelings we entertain in all *sincerity* may be counterfeit, taken for granted once and for all because we believe, says the villainous cynic, Strouvilhou, "everything we see in print." In literature, he tells us—and surely by extension in all the media from which we learn what to feel and think, as we learn the only language we know—"feelings may be as arbitrary as the conventions which the author believes to be the foundation of his art." They may "ring as false as counters, but they pass current . . . A man who should offer the public real coins would seem to be defrauding us . . . If I edit a review," he continues, "it will be in order to prick bladders—in order to demonitize fine feelings, and those promissory notes which go by the name of words." Though Strouvilhou is a monster, we may not shrink from the truth of what he says.

We come next to a complication more audacious still: the symbol ceases to be pejorative. Bernard has told us of his indignation at hearing a tourist boast of robbing the customs. "'The State is nothing but a convention,' he said too. What a fine convention it would be that rested on the bona fides of every individual!" Though even the conventions upon which society rests are not so much true as believed to be true, like the counterfeit coin not yet found out, we are not therefore justified in denying them full value. Their value is the value they elicit from us, which we unite to grant them. It is by such counterfeits that we organize the multiple possibilities of human nature in a desired direction. Objectifying thus the best in ourselves, we are sustained at the ennobling level by what we have created.

With the road thus opened, there is no place to stop. For Edouard, "ideas of exchange, of depreciation, of inflation gradually invaded his book." Whatever his mind rests on begins to appear to him, good or bad, as a kind of currency with questionable backing. Remember indeed how he defined the very subject of his book. What emerges at last is the suggestion that *all* the ideas and images by which we represent reality, and by which we must perforce live, are a species of counterfeit, waiting like Bernard's gilt-covered coin of glass to be seen through and discarded. The real culprit is the human brain which cannot with the best will in the world truly represent reality. When, in the light of this, we turn back to Bernard's description of the false coin, every modest phrase swells with meaning. "Just hear how true it rings . . . I was taken in by it this morning, just as the grocer who passed it on to me was taken in himself, he told me. It hasn't quite the same weight, I think, but it has the brightness and sound of a real piece; it is coated with gold, so that all the same it is worth more than two sons; but it is made of glass. It'll wear transparent. No, don't rub it . . . One can almost see through it as it is." For coin read the ideas, indeed the axioms, of any epoch or any individual, which, until time has rubbed their value away, ring wonderfully true, and are passed, innocently or not, from grocer to customer to whom you will, and on through a whole society. If we had not arrived at the point from another quarter, we would see from this that the chief counterfeit with which Gide presents us is the novel itself, as he is the chief of its counterfeiters. The novel pretends, as fiction must, to represent reality, a pretension to which it is itself designed to give the lie. And the failure of Edouard is due simply to his unattainable desire to make of his own a coin of solid gold.

Gide, however, is no mere skeptic. Though he shirks none of the difficult obstacles, he insists always on moving beyond despair. There is a chink in the darkness of Bernard's description. The coin "is coated with gold, so that all the same it is worth more than two sous." There *is* a way of being true that our counterfeits possess, even if that truth, with rubbing, must prove impermanent. The formula for it will be the same as that by which we outwit the devil, and we will come to it in its place.

"I should want one (character), the devil," Gide wrote in the *Journal des Faux Monnayeurs,* "who would circulate incognito throughout the book." This character is indeed the most important of all. If we examine a few of his appearances, we will find that he gives himself away.

It is the devil who leads Vincent to gamble with the money intended for Laura, and then helps him to invent an ethic to "legitimize" his behavior. For Vincent "continues to be a moral being, and the devil will only get the better of him by furnishing him with reasons for self-approval." Edouard, in confiding little Boris to old Azais as for an interesting experiment, has allowed curiously flimsy reasons to conceal dangers he should have foreseen. His sophisms "must be promptings of the devil, for if they came from anyone else he would not listen to them . . . There often lies hidden behind the good motive a devil who is clever enough to find his profit in the very thing one thought one was wresting from him." And, "Have you noticed," asks the wretched La Perouse, "that in this world God always keeps silent? Or at least, at least . . . however carefully we listen, it's only the devil we can succeed in hearing." Finally, in a fragment of dialogue in the *Journal des Faux Monnayeurs,* we learn that though one can only regard the devil as a childish substitute for the rational solution of certain psychological problems, "the devil himself would not speak otherwise; he is delighted; he knows that he hides nowhere as well as behind these rational explanations." And his first words are bound to be: "Why do you fear me? You know I don't exist."

The devil thus delineated is the *self.* He is the voracious, sly inextinguishable self, whose sole motive in every situation is the free gratification of appetites, but who must adopt, to overcome a variety of fears and scruples, an appropriate variety of disguises. This metaphor is complemented by an earlier one of Gide's. I do not love man, he said, but only that which devours him. What devours the self is a love of and aspiration toward something other, by which the self is used up, and which subordinates the gang of its clamorous short-sighted appetites. For the self's immediate gratification the latter would destroy each other, destroy their own power of enjoyment, destroy the man. We need not be told, after the labors of depth psychology, how wonderful is this devil's cleverness. There is no principle, however self-denying, that he cannot find a way either to outwit or to turn to his own advantage. Indeed, the freezing suggestion of La Perouse is that every audible voice is his, that we are incapable of hearing—in a self-less motive—the voice of God. Why does the devil delight to be regarded as a fiction? Because those who leave him out of their calculations, leave out, that is, the immeasurable subtlety of their selfishness, will perforce accept those reasons which the devil provides to ''legitimize'' their behavior. On this account scientific explanations are of course best of all. Screened by such authority from the gullible conscience, the liberated appetites may proceed to gorge themselves in perfect peace. As the case of Edouard showed us, however, reasons need not be iron-clad if they come to grant us our desire.

In the novel we are presented with four kinds of relationship to the devil—two based on denial of him and two on his recognition. The virtuous and the simple are his victims through denial. The first (Vedel and Azais) because they are convinced that, though he exists for some, he has no place in behavior like theirs, covered by all the rules of virtue. They yield to him with all the gusto of self-righteousness, having equated their desires with the will of God. The simple, on the other hand, like Douviers, whose ''goodness'' is so sincere and modest Edouard feels cheap to treat it with irony, yield not out of pride in their virtue, but because they lack the imagination to suspect their own good motives, to fear another, a darker side to every act and profession.

The second pair begins with the Passavants and the Lady Griffiths, who may well be considered to grant the devil's existence since they deny rather the possibility of any other master. These are less his victims than his infatuated votaries, votaries, that is, of their own untrammeled appetites. They demonstrate, moreover, how dangerous are those appetites, in the merely liberated self, leading to the absolute inferno of ennui and ultimately to the destruction of the individual. Finally, there are the wise, to whom Edouard, like most of us, can belong only intermittently. . . . The wise are those who acknowledge the existence of the devil as adversary. Granting his existence, they are in possession of a clue with which to penetrate an infinity of disguises, a clue which prevents the natural carelessness of equating him with one or two of his forms. Too often we lull ourselves by such questions into believing that these forms are all we have to fear, whereas to know the devil who is their protean essence is to beware of him everywhere, in every form, and even the least likely. We are put on guard against *all* our reasons, that is, against ourselves.

In the *Journal des Faux Monnayeurs* Gide writes: ''The renunciation of virtue through abdication of pride.'' The wisely virtuous man must give up the pride of confidence in his virtue. Suspicious of himself, he is at least free at every moment to modify his behavior when, in spite of the handsomest justifications, he finds himself doing evil. Skeptical of reasons, he learns to judge by results. He is forearmed against the danger that his most disinterested profession may only mask the selfish motive, the devil, which renders it other and less than it appears, which renders it *counterfeit*. It is thus the two metaphors come together in organic—not arbitrary—unity. The devil is the glass beneath our gold.

One thing remains to be said. We have seen that, though the devil is evil, it is positively wisdom and health to get to know him. Moreover, the speaker in Gide's dialogue expresses approval of Goethe's insight that the profoundest genius must be partly demonic, and in his *Dostoevsky* Gide himself coins the maxim: ''The Fiend is party to every work of art.'' This is no contradiction. Electricity too is a murderer unless recognized

and controlled. Is not the artist preeminent among those who see through the counterfeits of word and deed to the hidden self who is their true author? And what gives him the clue to this *other* side, if not an intimate acquaintance with the devil in himself. It is precisely the artist's knowledge of the horrors that lie potential within his own breast that provides his art with its third dimension.

At the moment when Bernard, wholly self-liberated, must decide in which direction to proceed, an angel comes to hint that the devil's is not the only path before him. The principle which accomplished his liberation, that the self has a higher authority than whatever would prevent it from knowing or being itself, has begun to grow equivocal in its implications. Freedom alone provides no measure for the value of his acts nor any guide for his aspirations. For reasons which will grow clear, the angel cannot bring such a measure or such a guide, but what he does is more important: he awakens a desire for them.

Look again at the story of the angel. You will see that from the moment when he appears with a foot so light it might walk on water—*like the foot of Jesus*—his every act and effect involves sympathy for others. By the same token, it is when Bernard is seized by a contrary feeling, contempt, that the angel temporarily disappears. The angel is that in us—or elsewhere—which opposes the devil-self and would make of it a sacrifice to God. Jesus provides the form of this angel for many, and a chief sign of his influence, as in the novel, is love, generosity, the substitution of another's self on the altar where one had worshipped one's own. Actually, however, the form of every man's angel is unique, adapted as it must be to the unique self it will oppose; this is the reason Bernard cannot see the other angels wandering in the church. In their night long wrestling, neither conquers. Not Bernard, because, as this chapter's significant first sentence tells us, he is one ''for whom there is no greater joy than to rejoice another being,'' that is, because his selfishness can never wholly conquer his generosity. And not the angel either, because selfishness is after all inextinguishable. Yet the *conscious* struggle accomplishes the highest object one may hope for from it: it brings Bernard to maturity, which means to an awareness of the issues and conditions of life, in short, to a knowledge of good and evil. His struggle is that of every young man evolving, after the self-absorption of childhood and against his own ''interests,'' a conception of virtue, and a goal more worthy of his gifts than personal aggrandizement.

But the angel's gift of maturity is not an answer; it is a question. The next day, seeking a definite rule for his life, Bernard goes to Edouard for advice. The ensuing dialogue contains the ripest Gidian wisdom. The novelist has nothing definite to offer. All he can say, when pushed at last to rock bottom, is this: ''It is a good thing to follow one's own inclination, provided it leads uphill.'' Indefinite—but the little sentence is far less modest than it looks. For even an angel who brings us the knowledge of good and evil cannot be expected to define a goal whose pursuit will guarantee our virtue. Of what value is a single fixed goal for men who are various and in constant motion? My goal will not be yours, and the goal which led me upward today will tomorrow hold me back. Dynamic to match the dynamism of life, Edouard's formula is, in fact, the only one which can keep us moving forever in the general direction of a God necessarily and properly impossible to pin down. Both its elements are essential, the first, that the self—yes, the devil-self—be frankly consulted, and the second, that the result lead uphill. Whenever the two are at war the devil wins an advantage. For just as the heedless gratification of the self means the devil's triumph, so does the most virtuous program which involves its falsification or denial, since the self will only explode at last into rebellion against all virtue. (The fate of Armand brought up by the blameless Vedels.) Every right act, in short, must be a collaboration between the devil and the angel.

This concluding formula has implications as wide as the skepticism which preceded it. Though every image of reality is counterfeit, we need not despair, there remains a basis for choice among them. That basis is the self's needs, honestly acknowledged. Not absolute truth, but relevance to man's changing needs determines the value of his mind's coinage, as it is the growing irrelevance of that coinage, through changes in men and their situations, which rubs away the layer of gold, and enables us to see through it like glass. The bringer of a new truth is simply the man who has become aware of needs which the old was not designed to satisfy. His will not be more permanent (insofar as it pretends to be it is a counterfeit like all the rest) but only more suitable. It is proper, then, that each age and each man, in some degree, make counterfeits of their own for the solution of their own felt problems, provided only that they are restrained from capitulation to unbridled appetite by endless care that the solutions lead always uphill. When will the often wearisome necessity for such care, for continuous fresh examination and evaluation, come to an end? When can we find rest in currency of pure gold? Never. For then change should have ceased, which is to say, we should be dead.

But *this* truth at least, the formula Gide does arrive at, this is gold, is it not? Alas, no. It is only the ultimate truth of the novel's first level, that of its material, of Gide's life. But the book's subject was precisely the impossibility of representing life truly. The only answer it gives us then is this: examine this final coin for yourself. Has the gold rubbed off it yet? Not yet? Then you don't know yet that it is false. Apply to it, as you must to every principle, the test itself advises. And when it ceases to conform to your personal needs—or to lead you upward—throw it away.

That formula (the conclusion of its first level) and this willingness to grant that it too is provisional (the conclusion of its second) is the moral of Gide's great novel, and the final equilibrium of the conflict in his thought with which our examination began. But as Gide's problem is the portion of free minds everywhere in our tormented self-conscious epoch, so its solution too extends in relevance beyond the book. It is such a moral, if any, that can be for all of us at once the safeguard of our freedom and the guarantee of its health and fruitfulness. (pp. 72-80)

> *Irvin Stock, "A View of 'Les Faux Monnayeurs',"* in Yale French Studies, Special Issue: Andre Gide *(copyright © Yale French Studies 1951), No. 7, 1951, pp. 72-80.*

JUSTIN O'BRIEN (essay date 1951)

[*O'Brien is an American critic who has written extensively on modern French literature and has translated important works by André Gide, Albert Camus, and Paul Valéry. In the excerpt below on Gide's fictional technique, O'Brien traces the origin of many of the plot and narrative techniques that Gide used in* Les faux monnayeurs *and earlier works.*]

Just what does Gide mean by a *récit*? The word signifies merely a narration and is by no means so exact a designation as *conte* or *nouvelle*. It is vague and not very committal. All his tales have certain elements in common: (1) concentration of action, (2) limitation to two, three, or four characters with almost no incidental figures, (3) a personal form of narration by one of the interested parties, and (4) a directness and simplicity of style. In other words, the tale as Gide conceives it is a narrative of crisis, an active type of fiction, close in form to the famous seventeenth-century novel *La Princesse de Clèves* or even to the French classical tragedy of Racine. It is highly dramatic because of the concentration of action and because of the narration by one of the actors. It is noteworthy that *L'Immoraliste (The Immoralist)* is told entirely by the chief protagonist to a group of friends who may be able to help him. On the very first page he says: "I am going to tell you my life simply, without modesty and without pride, more simply than if I were talking to myself." *La Porte étroite (Strait Is the Gate)* is again a direct narrative made by the principal actor Jérôme, who begins: "Some people might have made a book out of it; but the story I am going to tell is one which it took all my strength to live and over which I spent all my virtue. So I shall set down my recollections quite simply. . . ." But at one point in Jérôme's account he is obliged to describe the most intimate emotions of his beloved, which he could not possibly have known. Hence Gide has him discover her journal after her death and that journal is incorporated verbatim into the novel. *La Symphonie pastorale (The Pastoral Symphony)* is entirely in the form of a journal kept by the principal male character, the Pastor himself. On the very first page the Pastor notes: "I will take advantage of the leisure this enforced confinement affords me to think over the past and to set down how I came to take charge of Gertrude." The use of direct narration and especially of the diary form has obvious advantages and disadvantages. Its appearance in so many of André Gide's works—even in [*Les Faux-Monnayeurs (The Counterfeiters)*] he will have a novelist character commenting on events in his own diary— suggests that the journal is Gide's form *par excellence* and that his imaginative works might almost be considered to be extracted from his own *Journals*. It would be more just to say that the habit of spiritual self-scrutiny contracted during his pious childhood and reinforced by the fairly regular keeping of his own diary has caused him to make his characters indulge in the same practice.

Thus Gide repeatedly risked the dangers of narration in the first person singular. By the time *The Immoralist* appeared Oscar Wilde had already warned Gide never again to use the pronoun "I," but Gide was to flaunt that advice so consistently that in 1921 Marcel Proust had to repeat it to him. It would be hard to imagine, indeed, what his work would be like were it less personal—and one might even say less confessional. Autobiographical elements in *The Immoralist* are so numerous that the author has suffered ever since from the identification of his hero with himself. . . . Yes, Michel was torn from the very heart of his author but this does not mean that Michel is Gide. In one of the most significant letters written by that great letter-writer, whose entire correspondence will doubtless not become known for many years yet, he stated his theory of the creation of a character. It so happens that he related that theory to this particular novel, stating: "That a germ of Michel exists in me goes without saying. . . . How many germs or buds we bear in us which will never flower save in our books! They are 'dormant eyes' as the botanists call them. But if one intentionally suppresses all of them *except one* how it grows! How it enlarges, immediately monopolizing all the sap! My recipe for creating a hero is quite simple; take one of these buds and put it in a pot all alone, and one soon has a wonderful individual. Advice; choose preferably (if it is true that one *can* choose) the bud that bothers you the most. In this way you get rid of it at the same time. This is probably what Aristotle called katharsis.'' Others have expressed the same theory, even going so far as to see works of imagination as safety valves preventing the writer from indulging in the excesses which symbolize his characters. Bergson, for instance, remarked that ''Shakespeare was not Macbeth nor Hamlet nor Othello but he would have been those various characters if circumstances and the consent of his will had brought to a state of eruption what was but an inner urge.''

Gide's theory of katharsis holds of course not only for Michel but also for his other characters. In general, each of the short tales presents a single protagonist who represents the monstrous flowering of one of the buds in the author. Has not Gide said of himself: ''I am a creature of dialogue; everything in me is at war and in contradiction''? In *Strait Is the Gate* a very different bud is produced: the heroine Alissa, who is so close in many ways to Mme André Gide that we tend to forget she is a projection of the author. Alissa is the excessively pious young person afraid of life whom Gide might have been had he never transcended his adolescence. . . . By a series of subtle touches, Gide unfolds the obsessive character of Alissa and reveals her motivation. At one point she asks her diary: ''Was that sacrifice really consumed in my heart? I am, as it were, humiliated to feel that God no longer exacts it. Can it be that I was not equal to it?'' From such a doubt it is but a step to the decision to make the sacrifice anyway, simply to prove that she is capable of it. Commenting on his novel years later, Gide noted that whenever she thought of Jérôme, there welled up in Alissa a sort of unconscious and irresistible burst of heroism. And he adds: ''Absolutely useless heroism.''

In *The Pastoral Symphony*, still a third bud reaches fruition. Here it is the Pastor with his lamentably good intentions, his sanctimonious hiding behind the Scriptures, and his blind self-deception who reflects a facet of his creator. (pp. 92-5)

[It] was easy for André Gide to put himself in the position of the hero of his *Pastoral Symphony*. Around this figure he constructed a parable of blindness in which the spiritual blindness is so much more dangerous than the physical blindness. Subtly and yet emphatically by repetition Gide established a parallel between Gertrude's actual blindness, her state of innocence, and the Gospels on the one hand, and on the other, lucidity, the state of sin, and the Epistles of St. Paul.

It is important to note a variation of the diary form in *The Pastoral Symphony*. Obviously the Pastor would not and *could* not have recounted the whole story after the final tragedy. Or if he had, he would inevitably have transferred to its beginning the state of mind with which he witnessed its end. Hence Gide makes him begin to keep his notebook in the middle of Gertrude's evolution, recording at the start events that began two and a half years before. On 10 February he makes his first entry and on 30 May, his last. Meanwhile, on 8 May events catch up with his diary, and from that point on the Pastor is recording the *present* as it unfolds. This skillful technique gives to the tale an extraordinary mounting intensity that could have been achieved in no other way. (p. 95)

Judging his work from the inside, Gide is pleased to emphasize the differences between his *Faux-Monnayeurs* and all the rest of his fiction. In an ironic and unused preface for that novel he declared that he had not classified his earlier works as novels for fear they might be accused of lacking some of the essentials

of the *genre,* such as confusion, for instance. In the novel itself he makes his novelist Edouard reflect that his earlier tales resemble those basins in French parks, precise in contour, but in which the captive water is lifeless. ''Now,'' he says, ''I want to let it flow according to the slope, at one moment rapid and at another slow, in meanders that I refuse to foresee.''

Between *The Pastoral Symphony* and *The Counterfeiters*, Gide gave a series of lectures on Dostoevsky in 1921 and 1922. Rereading the great Russian, he noted certain similarities between Dostoevsky and himself; he found the same type of irresolute, half-formed, contradictory characters to which he has always been drawn himself; he recognized his own familiar themes: the relation of the individual with himself or with God, the demoniacal role of the intelligence, the challenge to conventional ethics and psychology, the value of an audacious deed, the opposition of thought and action and of carnal and emotional love, the influence of convention in counterfeiting us. He became aware that Dostoevsky, too, invariably expresses ideas in relation to individuals, depicts the particular to achieve the general, intentionally interrupts action at its most intense, and creates a painting with a specific source of light rather than a lifeless panorama.

But the break at this point in his career is less abrupt than he implies. In actual fact *The Counterfeiters* covers less ground both spatially and temporally than most of the tales. *The Immoralist* includes scenes in Paris, North Africa, Italy, and Normandy; *Strait Is the Gate* is laid in Rouen, Fongueusemare, Paris, Havre, and Aigues-Vives (near Nîmes); only *The Pastoral Symphony* with its limitation to La Brévine and nearby Neuchâtel rivals the economy of *The Counterfeiters*, which takes us out of Paris only for a brief stay at Saas-Fée in Switzerland. It is equally surprising to note, in view of the novel's complexity, that the action of *The Counterfeiters* is concentrated within a few months, whereas *The Immoralist* records three years, *Strait Is the Gate,* twenty years, and *The Pastoral Symphony,* two years and nine months of life. Furthermore, for all their precise contours, not one of the tales is as balanced in composition as *The Counterfeiters* with its eighteen chapters and 220 pages of the first part exactly paralleling the eighteen chapters and 225 pages of the third part.

The complexity and ''confusion'' of the novel must be attributable, then, to the number of characters or rather to the number of plots, since the twenty-eight characters are necessitated by the multiple plots. Now, André Gide has noted most loyally in his *Journals* for 1928 that his friend Roger Martin du Gard gave him ''the advice to gather together the various plots of *Les Faux-Monnayeurs,* which, had it not been for him, would have formed so many separate 'tales.' '' . . . Just now—after noting in passing that even more than the example of Dostoevsky was required to renew Gide's fictional technique—it is more important to emphasize the persistence, nevertheless, of certain elements within that technique.

From June 1919 to June 1925—that is, during the actual writing of *The Counterfeiters*—Gide kept a separate notebook in which to record ''inch by inch,'' as he said in English, the progress of his novel. That fascinating and invaluable [*Le Journal des Faux-Monnayeurs (Journal of ''The Counterfeiters'')*], which has never been a part of Gide's monumental *Journals,* was first published in French the same year as the novel. . . . In it the author presents the problems encountered in composition, his hesitations and false starts, and the solutions he has found to his difficulties. The novelty of his approach throughout and his little youthful thrill of triumph at each new problem overcome prevent the reader from noticing how many of the apparent technical innovations had already found their place in the earlier tales. For instance, the first entry in *The Journal of "The Counterfeiters"* reads: "For two days I have been wondering whether or not to have my novel related by Lafcadio. Thus it would be a narrative of gradually revealed events in which he would act as an observer, an idler, a perverter." Is this not again the first-person narration of the tales? To be sure, a month later Gide abandoned this plan after writing some pages of Lafcadio's journals; yet in doing so he added: "But I should like to have successive interpreters: for example, Lafcadio's notes would occupy the first book; the second book might consist of Edouard's notebook; the third of an attorney's files, etc." Surely this is the same technique as in *La Porte étroite* where, at a certain point, Jérôme's account is broken to admit the diary of the dead Alissa.

In fact, it was not until much later that it occurred to Gide—possibly as a result of rereading *Tom Jones*—to resort to impersonal narration with frequent interventions of the author. As late as May 1924 he noted: "The poor novelist constructs his characters; he controls them and makes them speak. The true novelist listens to them and watches them function; he eavesdrops on them even before he knows them. It is only according to what he hears them say that he begins to understand *who* they are." . . . "I should like events never to be related directly by the author, but instead exposed (and several times from different vantages) by those actors who will be influenced by those events. In their account of the action I should like the events to appear slightly warped; the reader will take a sort of interest from the mere fact of having to *reconstruct*. The story requires his collaboration in order to take shape properly." But this is already true of the tales. That there are two points of view in *Strait Is the Gate*—thanks to Jérôme's account and Alissa's diary—is obvious. In *The Immoralist,* although there is but one narrator (Michel) who is trying to report himself objectively, he is nevertheless judged by his wife, Marceline, and by his friend, Ménalque, not to mention the Arab youth Moktir; and Michel strives to record those judgments—with the inevitable result that the reader has to re-establish the truth. Likewise in *The Pastoral Symphony* where the lamentable Pastor is judged by his wife, his son, and the blind girl he loves.

After *The Counterfeiters,* when Gide writes *L'Ecole des femmes (The School for Wives)* and its two sequels, *Robert* and *Geneviève,* he somewhat mechanically presents three views of the same family conflict, one to a volume, much as he had toyed with doing in *The Counterfeiters.*

Perhaps the most generally acknowledged originality of *The Counterfeiters* is that of a novel within the novel. As the author noted in *The Journal of "The Counterfeiters"*: "Properly speaking, the book has no single center for my various efforts to converge upon; those efforts center about two *foci,* as in an ellipse. On one side, the event, the fact, the external *datum;* on the other side, the very effort of the novelist to make a book out of it all. The latter is the main subject," he continued, "the new focus that throws the plot off center and leads it toward the imaginative. In short, I see this notebook in which I am writing the very history of the novel, poured into the book in its entirety and forming its principal interest—for the greater irritation of the reader." With Edouard's journal this is precisely what Gide has done. It was a brilliant idea to set Edouard the novelist at the center of the novel, both an observer and an actor in the events, engaged in grappling with the problems posed by the translation into art of those events. Yet this was far from a new idea with Gide. His very first work, published in 1891, shows a young romantic hero writing the novel we are reading. And in his *Journals* for 1893, Gide has noted: "I wanted to suggest, in the *Tentative amoureuse,* the influence of the book upon the one who is writing it, and during that very writing. . . . Our acts exercise a retroaction upon us. . . . In a work of art I rather like to find transposed on the scale of the charcters, the very subject of that work. Nothing throws a clearer light upon it or more surely establishes the proportions of the whole. (pp. 96-100)

In *The Counterfeiters* this apparent narcissism reaches its height when Gide puts a novelist resembling himself at the center of the novel, engaged in writing a novel to be entitled *The Counterfeiters* and recording and commenting the action in his diary as it unfolds. Such a device offers the incalculable advantage of narration by indirection, for "a character may well describe himself wonderfully while describing someone else or speaking of someone else—according to the rule that each of us really understands in others only those feelings he is capable of producing himself"—as *Journal of "The Counterfeiters"* points out. Thus it is that the progress of Michel in *The Immoralist,* or of the Pastor in *The Pastoral Symphony,* becomes apparent to us through his wife's attitude toward him *as reported by him himself.* . . . Hence, Gide is stating a principle that has always been his when he says in *Journal of "The Counterfeiters"*: "It is appropriate, in opposition to the manner of Meredith or James, to let the reader get the advantage over me—to go about it in such a way as to allow him to think he is more intelligent, more moral, more perspicacious than the author, and that he is discovering many things in the characters, and many truths in the course of the narrative, in spite of the author and, so to speak, behind the author's back."

Many of us have long admired the ending of *The Counterfeiters* with Edouard's suspensive remark: "I am very curious to know Caloub." And indeed, in his workbook the author notes: "This novel will end sharply, not through exhaustion of the subject, which must give the impression of inexhaustibility, but on the contrary through its expansion and by a sort of blurring of its outline. It must not be neatly rounded off, but rather disperse, disintegrate. . . ." This too is less new than Gide would have us think. Do not the earlier novels likewise blur off, leaving the reader to reflect at length on the situation and emotions of the chief protagonist? Particularly in *The Immoralist* and in *Strait Is the Gate,* when the end is reached, the reader feels better informed—thanks to the technique of indirection—than does the bewildered narrator. Consistently André Gide has allowed the reader the illusion of getting the advantage over him.

It is by no means necessary, or even advisable, to attempt to diminish *The Counterfeiters* in order to build up the earlier tales. That there is a difference is only too apparent. The example of Dostoevsky and the capital advice of Roger Martin du Gard suffice to explain Gide's new orientation in the years 1919 to 1925. But three points must not be forgotten: (1) that as early as 1908 Gide had already sketched a portrait of *Dostoyevsky According to His Correspondence,* (2) that between 1909 and 1914 in the newly formed group of the *Nouvelle Revue Française* the conversation and writings of intimate friends as Jacques Rivière, Roger Martin du Gard, Jean Schlumberger, and Albert Thibaudet had centered about the aesthetics of the novel, and finally (3) that in 1914—directly between *Strait Is the Gate* and *Isabelle* on the one hand and *The Pastoral Sym-*

phony on the other—Gide had brought out *Les Caves du Vatican* (badly titled in one English language edition as *Lafcadio's Adventures*). That thrilling novel—for it is a novel despite the author's timid and misleading classification of it as a *sotie*—has more in common with *The Counterfeiters* than with the tales that precede and follow it. Comprising almost the same multiplicity of plots and contrapuntal composition as the later novel, it is narrated in the third person by a very conscious writer who even indulges in Fieldingesque or Sterne-like apostrophes and asides to disclaim omniscience and responsibility; and it unfolds swiftly with all the complexity and compulsion of a novel of adventure. Furthermore, it comprises a microcosmic novel within the novel, which Julius is writing almost at the dictation of Lafcadio. Clearly it is a tryout of the techniques to be used ten years later in *The Counterfeiters*. Nothing is more natural than that Gide should have begun *The Counterfeiters*, in his first draft, with the journal of Lafcadio, the charming and elusive hero of the earlier novel. His later rejection of Lafcadio reflects his characteristic desire not to take conscious advantage of momentum acquired in an earlier work.

Yet, as we have seen, it was impossible not to benefit from unconscious momentum in the form of the fictional techniques patiently elaborated over the preceding twenty-five years. Some readers will always prefer the concentrated, gemlike tales of Gide's early maturity, whereas others will choose the exasperatingly living, Dostoevskian qualities of *The Counterfeiters*. But, whatever their differences, the men and women who have the good fortune to read those works a century from now will doubtless not hesitate for a moment to recognize the same hand in all of them. (pp. 100-02)

> *Justin O'Brien, "Gide's Fictional Technique," in* Yale French Studies, *Special Issue: Andre Gide (copyright © Yale French Studies 1951; reprinted by permission of* Yale French Studies*), No. 7, 1951 (and reprinted in his* The French Literary Horizon, *Rutgers University Press, 1967, pp. 91-102).*

HERMANN HESSE   (essay date 1951)

[*Hesse discusses the ideological concerns of Gide's work.*]

Gide was an author who approached his problems, so similar to mine, in so completely different a fashion, and his noble independence, stubbornness, and constantly renewed self-control of the unwearying truth-seeker continued to please me and in a strange way seem related to me. Principally Gide's development took the course of release from the pious world of faith and religious attitudes; it was the way of one overgifted and much too strictly and morally raised, who can no longer bear the narrowness and knows that the world is waiting for him, but nevertheless is not minded to sacrifice the sensibility of conscience won through that upbringing. Of course, his struggle for freedom is not simply in the intellectual sphere; it has to do with the senses as well, which demand their rights, and from the revolt of the senses against control and tutelage there emerges and grows clear the character of *enfant terrible*, of joy in exposing and stripping bare, in trapping the pious in their piously labeled lusts and depravities—in short, that element of malice and aggressive love of revenge which without doubt is a part of Gide's character and constitutes for many of his readers his most fascinating and seductive aspect. But important though this motive was in André Gide's life, however much he may have been tempted and seduced into unmasking the righteous and baffling the philistines, there was in this noble

spirit something greater, impelling him toward fruition and maturity, than the ability and enjoyment of startling and shocking his readers. He was on the dangerous path of every genius who, after breaking out of a for him unbearable tradition and morality, finds himself dreadfully alone and leaderless in the face of the world and searches on a higher level for a substitute for the lost security, seeks for models or norms that can correct and heal the far too exposed condition of the unfettered individual. So we see him all his life interested in the natural sciences and studying them, and we see him exploring the world of cultures, languages, and literature with a diligence and tenacity that evokes our astonishment and admiration. What he has won in this laborious, lifelong, chivalrous battle is a new kind of freedom, a freedom from dogma and partisanship, but in constant subjection to the service of truth, in constant striving for knowledge. In this he is a true brother to the great Montaigne and to that poet who wrote *Candide*. It has always been difficult to serve the truth as an individual without the protection of a system of faith, of a church, of a community. In serious and exemplary fashion André Gide has pursued this difficult course. (pp. 335-36)

> *Hermann Hesse, "André Gide" (1951; originally published as "André Gide," in his* Schriften zur Literatur, *Suhrkamp Verlag, 1970), in his* My Belief: Essays on Life and Art, *edited by Theodore Ziolkowski, translated by Denver Lindley with Ralph Manheim (reprinted by permission of Farrar, Straus and Giroux, Inc.; translation copyright © 1974 by Farrar, Straus and Giroux, Inc.), Farrar, Straus and Giroux, 1974, pp. 334-36.*

HAROLD MARCH   (essay date 1952)

[*March's reading of Gide's well-known récit,* La porte étroite, *is considered representative, and most critics agree with his assessment of the novel's meanings. However, Loring D. Knecht's essay excerpted below provides an interesting alternative to the standard reading.*]

[It] was chiefly the remembered Madeleine of his childhood that Gide put into the portrait of Alissa [in *La Porte étroite*] and in so doing he drew to such an extent on his recollections that in none of his works of fiction is there a closer parallel with persons and events of his own life. Jérôme, the male protagonist, is Gide, or rather occupies the position of Gide; Alissa, Jérôme's cousin, two years his senior, has the role of [Gide's wife] Madeleine; Gide's sister-in-law Jeanne Rondeaux takes the name of his mother Juliette; Valentine is not represented and the boys Edouard and Georges unite to become Robert in the novel. Jérôme's father, like Gide's, has died, and . . . Fongueusemare, the scene of much of the action, is Cuverville undisguised. The crucial incident of Gide's returning to the rue Lecat and discovering the family drama that was causing Madeleine such suffering is reproduced in the novel with scarcely a change, and takes place as in real life at Le Havre; and Jérôme's love for Alissa, clarified like that of his creator by this event, has the same character of religious adoration and protective tenderness unmixed with physical desire.

Yet despite these striking parallels (and more could be mentioned) Gide felt able to say many years later: "If in *L'Immoraliste* I still put large segments of myself, I have since then absented myself from my tales"; and he went on to cite *La Porte étroite* as an example. The apparent paradox can be justified by the fact that in this book, as had not been the case in the earlier ones, the central theme of sacrifice is not his own problem, and the interest centers not upon Jérôme-Gide but upon Alissa-Madeleine. Moreover Alissa, although obviously inspired by Madeleine, cannot be identified with her. As in *L'Immoraliste* Gide isolated and studied a potentiality of his own nature, so in *La Porte étroite* he took Madeleine's tendency to self-sacrifice, suggested its implications, and pushed it to an extreme not reached by the original. (pp. 150-51)

The immediate way to take [the] story [of *La Porte étroite*] is to see in it nothing but the description of a pathological case. Alissa has a masochistic craving for suffering, but this is not all: both she and Jérôme are natural solitaries, at their exalted best when separated and writing letters to each other, but constrained and uneasy when proximity summons them to translate their flights of imagination into the realities of personal relations. Alissa does not really love Jérôme, nor anyone else; all she loves are her own emotions, which she is trying to intensify by discipline and selection.

This interpretation is to some extent justified not only by the book itself but by the author's statement of his intentions. Gide meant to paint the portrait of a woman's soul, "of a Protestant soul in which is enacted the essential drama of Protestantism." This drama, impossible in authoritarian Catholicism, lies, as Gide explained to Claudel, in the fact that Protestantism "starts the soul on unforeseen ways which can lead to what I have shown. Or else to free-thinking. It is a school of heroism, of which I think my book brings out the error rather well; it lies precisely in a sort of higher infatuation. . . . But it can also be accompanied by true nobility."

This last sentence reveals the difference between the purely pathological interpretation and Gide's intention. In his view Alissa was mistaken but hers was a noble error; he wanted to show not so much the aberrations of an individual as the dangers inherent in Protestantism. Alissa was the victim of her religious education, and as such she had to enlist the sympathy, not the contempt, of the reader. "I was afraid," Gide continued in his explanations to Claudel, ". . . that detached from all exterior motivation this drama might appear paradoxical, monstrous, inhuman; hence the invention of the double plot, the fear of buying her happiness at another's expense—hence particularly the 'sin' of the mother, causing a vague need of expiation." And in a letter to another correspondent he called the book "a critique of Protestantism or of Christian abnegation, and critique does not mean satire—I use the word in the Kantian sense."

The book contains, in addition to its "double plot," an implicit dual judgment on its theme. We find, if we accept the author's evaluation, that Alissa's ideas contain something which cannot be immediately condemned and dismissed. They seem less like unadulterated errors than distorted truths; Gide is able to create this impression because he shares some of her beliefs and can present them with a persuasive sincerity. When Jérôme says for himself, "I sought of the future not so much happiness as the infinite effort to attain it," we are not particularly surprised at meeting one of Gide's basic attitudes because Jérôme to a certain extent represents him in the book; but Alissa too says much the same thing when she confides to her journal, "I wonder now whether it is indeed happiness that I want or a moving toward happiness." Gide's own also are her words, "We are not born for happiness," and her appropriation of the quotations, "God having reserved us for something better" and "All that is not God is incapable of fulfilling my expectation."

Another theme close to Gide's heart suggests itself and whether or not the reader accepts it he cannot help being seriously impressed by the question it raises. Is the quasi-religious character of youthful love merely a disguise for sex? When Jérôme and Alissa listen with exaltation to the solemn words about the strait gate are they only poeticizing a physical urge to reproduction? Or, without denying the little disputed observation that sex and religion are related, can one invert the relationship and say, not that the religious element in love is sex deflected, but that romantic love furnishes a temporary and illusory stopping place for the religious urge to enlarge the self, merge it with something beyond?

Claudel's answer to these questions is the one Gide wanted: "The gross literature of the past century is misleading on the subject of the deeper emotions. No, sexual satisfaction does not satisfy the passion of love, it shrinks it, it is sometimes the caricature of it, usually a deformation and always a transformation. The impulse to 'refusal' is deeply rooted in the heart of a woman. . . . There is no richer or more complex dramatic subject, nor one more pathetic for the masculine soul; hence the interest for us of all the books where we watch the struggle of passion against duty. . . . The power of your book lies in the fact that there is no external duty, but only an inner voice."

Gide does not condemn Alissa's initial aspiration and he does not intend us to do so. On the other hand he does not condone the extremes to which her basically sound impulse led her, and in this unfavorable judgment lies his criticism of Protestantism. At the outset we have a basic character in which lives the broadly human urge to expansion beyond the limits of the self, and we have an environment which gives to the point of aspiration the name "God" and surrounds it with precepts of self-mortification. It is this environment which bends the young twig so that, instead of growing straight and true as nature intended, it ends in deformity.

Here is the charming early Alissa, waiting in the garden for Jérôme:

> She was by the wall at the end of the orchard, picking the first chrysanthemums which mingled their perfume with that of the dead leaves of the beech grove. The air was saturated with autumn, the sun barely warmed the trellises, but the sky had an oriental purity. Her face was framed, almost hidden, in a large Zealand headdress which Abel had brought back from a journey and which she had put on at once. She did not immediately turn at my approach, but a faint start which she could not repress told me that she recognized my step; and already I was bracing myself, encouraging myself against her reproaches and the severity of the look she would give me. But as I drew close and as, timidly, I was already checking my pace, she, without at first turning her face toward me but keeping it down like a stubborn child, stretched out to me, almost behind her, a hand that was filled with flowers, and seemed to invite me to come. And as I, making a game of it, stopped at this gesture, she turned at last, took a few steps toward me, and raised her face, and I saw that it was full of laughter.

And here is the later Alissa in the same garden:

> She was extraordinarily changed; her thinness and her pallor wrung my heart. Leaning heavily

on my arm she pressed against me as if she were afraid, or cold. She was still in full mourning and probably the black lace which she had put over her head and which framed her face accentuated her pallor. She was smiling, but seemed to be about to faint.

There is no obstacle between them except her idea that God has reserved them for something better. She gives back to Jérôme her most prized possession, a small cross of amethysts that he gave her, and she tells him to marry someone else and give it later to his daughter. At this Jérôme breaks out, "Alissa! Whom could I marry? You know that I can love only you," and he seizes her in his arms and kisses her. For a moment she seems to yield; then her eyes close, and she says in a gentle voice, "Have pity on us, my friend. Do not spoil our love."

The contrast is sufficiently striking to suggest a doubt. Could the lovely natural girl of the beginning really have turned into the fanatical recluse of the end? Do the delicate music of Gide's style and the poetry of tender reminiscence which saturate the early part of the book lull us into accepting unnoticed a basic disharmony? Perhaps the sentimental interest of the story contributes to the same end: a deathless but unfulfilled love is always appealing, and in *La Porte étroite* there are two of them, Alissa's and Juliette's, both for Jérôme—though why that slack and moody young man should inspire such devotion is a little hard to understand.

Yet if we look more closely we become convinced that the total picture of Alissa is consistent. The potentiality of the fanatic is within the charming girl just as the skeleton and skull underlie her young flesh; her end can be foreseen from her early reaction to the sermon on the strait gate, and the progressive revelation of her motivation is both subtle and convincing.

But this is not to say, necessarily, that the ideas of the book carry conviction. Its charm lies in the early part, where Gide is recalling the scenes and even the events of his own youth, his own emotions and aspirations, above all his love for Madeleine. Here he is on sure ground. But also he is dealing with accessories; the real nub of the book, its theoretical justification, is in the later part, where tender memories are of no use to him. Madeleine was unshakable in faith and moral principles, but, as Gide later remarked, "her kindness tempered all this, and what I say about it would surprise those who have known only the gentle radiation of her grace. I have met fierce puritans: she in no way resembled them." Her self-abnegation was natural, not puritanical; what was negative and privative in it came from her character rather than from her religion. Her clinging to the home ground, her distress at travel, her emotional vulnerability, her instinct of retreat: these were temperamental weaknesses, not religious aberrations. In giving Alissa Madeleine's self-abnegation Gide cut it off from its original source, and to explain it anew he had to strike out for himself.

The resulting (but largely implicit) arraignment of puritanism is in its general terms an old story now; we have become satiated with such attacks. It is still interesting, however, in what it reveals of Gide's own problems, for it hinges on the question of sacrifice, and its relation to self-loss. Sacrifice undertaken from the motive of self-esteem, or as a move in the acquirement of merit, is poisoned at its source; it is only valid when it can scarcely be called sacrifice at all, when it arises spontaneously from the realization that there is no sep-

arate good, that the individual's happiness is, and can be no other than, the good of others. (pp. 156-62)

The theoretical kernel of the book is in the journal and letters of Alissa, of which Gide wrote to a friend in 1909, "I am *very pleased* with the journal of Alissa and with nearly all her letters"; this satisfactory result was obtained, he later claimed, by subordinating himself to the demands of the character he had created. . . . (p. 162)

The account of Alissa's solitary search for God by prayer and meditation was objective in the sense that it did not correspond to a present preoccupation of the author; as he recorded while writing it, "It is an anachronism in the midst of all that we think, feel, and want today. No matter; I have to write it."

But Gide was no stranger to an effort like Alissa's; it was just such a quest that he had described in *Les Cahiers d'André Walter,* and the aspirations of his youthful hero ended, like those of Alissa, in doubt. There are of course great differences between the two books. *La Porte étroite* is immeasurably superior to Gide's first book in literary art, as is only to be expected. Moreover Alissa is morally superior to André Walter, and beyond the reach of his primitive temptations.

And yet there is a basic similarity between the two books. What André Walter wanted was a state of continuous religious exaltation, of which he had had foreshadowings but to which he thought his impurity was a bar. He therefore wanted in addition divine intervention in his temptations, and when it was not forthcoming he concluded that religious aspiration was illusory. Shorter-lived and more victorious is Alissa's struggle against sensuality; but self-love, which is its essence, is with her to the end, and happiness is for her, as for André Walter, the final objective.

For that matter it would be hard to prove that happiness in one form or another is not what everyone basically desires. But happiness may be repressive or expansive, separative or unitive. To seek for a happiness definable in terms of pleasurable emotions is quite a different matter from the mystic's longing for self-loss and union with the Absolute because it is a demand of his deepest nature without whose satisfaction he can find no resting place. When Alissa writes " 'All that is not God is incapable of fulfilling my expectation.' O too human joy which my imprudent heart desired. . . . Was it to wring this cry from me, Lord, that you have reduced me to despair?"—she is far beyond the elementary petitions of André Walter.

And yet her appropriation of the mystical cry of Pascal is belied by the whole course of her conduct and preoccupations. Never does she forget herself, the state of her own soul, and she moves into a steadily shrinking area of sympathies and interests. The true mystic may be and often is physically isolated, and he always believes that the Kingdom of Heaven is within him; but a progressive spiritual isolation can result only in the defeat of his quest.

It is surely gratuitous to reproach Gide, as some have done, for having failed to give us a picture of true mysticism in this book, since his obvious intention is to depict false mysticism. The question of whether there is a true mysticism is simply not raised, and the existence of false varieties is not in dispute. Similarly unraised is the problem of the transcendent existence of God. Alissa dies in doubt, with perhaps a slight balance in favor of disbelief, but the author does not personally commit himself on his own beliefs. He has created a powerful atmosphere, he has made a credible character, and he has suggested certain problems, without answering them. Beyond that, in this book, he has not chosen to go. (pp. 163-65)

Harold March, in his Gide and "The Hound of Heaven" *(copyright 1952 University of Pennsylvania Press), University of Pennsylvania Press, 1952, 421 p.*

ENID STARKIE (essay date 1953)

[*Starkie was an English literary critic and the author of numerous studies of nineteenth and twentieth-century French writers. Her works include* Baudelaire, Arthur Rimbaud, André Gide, From Gautier to Eliot, *and a two-volume study of Gustave Flaubert. In this excerpt from her critical study* André Gide, *Starkie discusses Gide's complex psychological makeup and his role as a moralist who "had aspirations towards spirituality, asceticism and puritanism; but also leanings towards sensuality, self-indulgence and sin."*]

In spite of its many contradictions there is one striking characteristic which runs through Gide's work in all its many phases, a deep embedded shining seam; his quality as a moralist, passionately interested in the problem of sin, what it is and where it hides itself, especially in the apparently virtuous and complacent. He describes himself as watching people coming out of Church on a Sunday, and he says that their thoughts are freshly washed and ironed by the sermon they have just heard and put away tidily in their minds, as in a cupboard. 'I would like to rummage in the bottom-drawer', he declares, 'I've got the key'. This bottom-drawer is the hidden part of man's nature. As a young man, when he looked at civilisation, he was appalled by the pressure of outworn codes on the individual personality—the Church, society, political theories—, and he considered that, in his attempt to conform, the individual was obliged to develop an outward personality, a counterfeit personality. Discovery of our unacted desires, emancipation from the counterfeit personaiity, Gide thought, would bring freedom and fulfilment to the individual. It is the inner personality, beneath the counterfeit one, which he always tried to reach; that inner reality where good and evil overlap as in a marriage of Heaven and Hell. In reaching that inner personality he stirs up its troubled depths, drags up from the thick overlaying mud the hidden motives. This is for him the really fertile soil, the one which, in a state of nature, is overrun by exuberant vegetation and which must be cleared before it can be cultivated. He considered that those who had first studied man's nature did so only where it was most easily accessible and that only very gradually did psychologists come to realise all the hidden possibilities in man. All the troubled, tortured and distressed beings are those who interest Gide because he believes that more can be expected from them, when the subterranean forces have been liberated and subdued, than from the complacent. So he studies cases of disconcerting behaviour, cases of apparent wrong-doing; he observes all the idiosyncracies, the nervous tics, as signs which reveal the hidden obsessions; he studies all these unconscious gestures just as a detective might look for fingerprints, or analyse grains of dust or tufts of hair. Most of the characters in Gide's writings have some maladjustment, or psychological flaw, which drives them to their doom, and often to the destruction of others as well. (p. 9)

Gide was a man who found his own harmony and movement in a duality of polarisation. He needed this perpetual motion to obtain power for creation, just as some writers need to sin to gain the dynamic force of remorse. He had aspirations towards spirituality, asceticism and puritanism; but also leanings towards sensuality, self-indulgence and sin. It was not the contrast and clash between *Spleen* and *Idéal,* which we find in Baudelaire, man's longing for purity and beauty in conflict with his inevitable proclivity towards sin and vice. That was not Gide's problem; his was one of equilibrium and balance. It was necessary for him to find that one point between both poles where he could freely balance, like a see-saw, from one to the other, backwards and forwards, with equal attraction to each, refusing the necessity for blame or remorse when he came down on the side of what is called vice. Yet, at the same time, he desperately needed sanction and approval, and to feel always that he was right. When composing **Corydon** he was not content with merely gaining freedom and immunity for his own instincts, he needed as well the sanction and support of science and history. In the same way, when he had finally accepted atheism, he claimed confirmation for his lack of faith in the Bible itself. This curious twist of his nature was the cause of the accusation of intellectual dishonesty which has so often, unjustly, been made against him. But it came rather from the deep uncertainty in him which no amount of success, no amount of experience, could cure. He needed intellectual sanction to feel that he was right, and to be right was what he wanted more than anything else. But he would not compromise in order to achieve it, and this led him into the contradictory state of desire for martyrdom, which is, in fact, an inverted way of being right. Unable to believe in himself without assurance, he was forced into that vacillation and twisting which are the most characteristic aspect of the Gidian personality. (pp. 56-7)

Although Gide was particularly interested in his own problem as an individual, he was passionately interested as well in the larger problem of individualism in the world today. This brought him many of his readers in all parts of the world, those who seek a remedy to our present discontents. The problem of our time, as Gide sees it—the real crisis of our age—is how to reconcile the inalienable right of the individual to self-development, and the urgent necessity for the diminution of the misery of the masses. In these days of collectivity and mass-thinking, when security from the womb to the tomb is the goal, there is the danger that the individual may be strangled in the ever-increasing coils of bureaucratic red tape. For Gide there was no contradiction between belief in the individual and belief in the community—he had hoped to find the reconciliation in Communism—but he would not sacrifice the sanctity of each individual human soul, since he believed that only by being truly himself could man be of service or value to others. He had a horror of the slow ruminating of the herd, pedigree or otherwise, chewing over the same cud of ideas. He preferred to wander and be lost rather than follow the well mapped-out paths. He had the pride of the one lost sheep, safe in the knowledge that the Eternal Shepherd will scour the hillsides to look for him, and that there will be more rejoicing in Heaven at his being brought safely back to the fold, than for the ninety-nine which never strayed.

In his sixty years as a writer there had been a constant evolution in Gide's style of the same order as the transformation which occurred in his thought. At first he was a poet, preoccupied with himself, using language to express personal lyric feelings—there are some who regret the disappearance of this personal artist—and eventually he became a moralist with a style of pure and sober classicism. In his early writings he adopted the musical manner of the Symbolists and favoured 'la chanson grise', which gave full freedom to his imagination. By the end of the First World War, however, he had banished all extraneous ornamentation from his style. One need only compare *La Symphonie Pastorale* with the early works to realise the difference. The complete simplicity of the language now matches the dazzling whiteness of the snow. Later his language became still more stripped and bare as he perfected the art of Racine, of expressing most by saying least, a strict form containing and restraining deep emotion.

Although all through his life Gide went out with eager anticipation towards the future, he remained, after he reached maturity, classical and universal in the truest meaning of the expression, and became a repository of the past, to protect it against destruction. European civilization for him, in spite of Christianity, grew from Graeco-Roman roots; and, although he was interested in foreign literatures, reading and absorbing much from such writers as Dostoevsky, Shakespeare, Blake and Nietzsche, he nevertheless felt deep down that it was in French classical culture that it had reached its most perfect flowering.

After an examination of sixty years and eighty odd volumes of Gide's writings the impression remains that he is a moralist, psychologist and stylist rather than a pure novelist or dramatist. Each of his novels is an attitude which he adopts for the sake of argument, of speculation—he tells us so himself—and that makes him less of a novelist than a moralist; less of a novelist than an investigator. He does not concern himself with creating complex characters giving the illusion of life; he is less interested in *men* than in *man,* in the classical sense. 'Man is more interesting than men', he says, 'it is he whom God has made in his own image'. He is less anxious to make an amalgam of contradictions than to isolate some special characteristic. He is a chemist who isolates certain substances to obtain their purest essence. Each of his works is a chemical experiment in purifying some particular quality or vice which he pursues to its logical conclusion.

La Porte Étroite is probably Gide's most perfect and moving book, but his *Journal* is perhaps his most characteristic and original. It is a work unique in French literature—indeed in any literature; a treasure-house of discussion on every artistic and intellectual movement, on every moral problem, of more than sixty years. As a whole it may lack form and unity—indeed how could it be otherwise, with its million words dealing with so many topics and phases of life; but individual passages are amongst his finest writing. He has written few pages of greater beauty, simplicity and poignancy, than his description of the death of the writer Charles-Louis Philippe, and his funeral amongst the simple peasants who were his family. (pp. 57-9)

The tangled skein that is Gide will one day have to be unravelled. There is in everyone, however many the contradictions, one main thread which runs through everything, outlining the individual pattern and making it clear. In Gide it will be found to be a spiritual thread. All through his life, in spite of lapses—even in these lapses—it has been spiritual values that he has always sought, albeit sometimes in the byways. Proust had called his own work, the work of his life-time, *A la Recherche du Temps Perdu;* Gide might have called his *A la Recherche d'une Âme*. 'All our thoughts which have not God for object', he said, 'are of the realm of death'.

Gide's ultimate fate will be to be considered as a moralist in the great French seventeenth-century tradition—the tradition of La Rochefoucauld and Pascal—whose integrity and nobility of thought, whose purity and harmony of style, give him an immortal place amongst the great masters of French literature. (p. 60)

Enid Starkie, in her André Gide *(reprinted by permission of the Literary Estate of André Gide), Bowes & Bowes, 1953, 63 p.*

ALFRED KAZIN (essay date 1955)

[*A highly respected American literary critic, Kazin is best known for his essay collections* The Inmost Leaf *(1955) and* Contemporaries *(1962), and particularly for* On Native Grounds *(1942), a study of American prose writing since the era of William Dean Howells. Having studied the works of "the critics who were the best writers—from Sainte-Beuve and Matthew Arnold to Edmund Wilson and Van Wyck Brooks" as an aid to his own critical understanding, Kazin has found that "criticism focussed many— if by no means all—of my own urges as a writer: to show literature as a deed in human history, and to find in each writer the uniqueness of the gift, of the essential vision, through which I hoped to penetrate into the mystery and sacredness of the individual soul." In the excerpt below Kazin argues that Gide's* Journal, *because it is the record of an "unremitting search for self-correction and self-purification, by a succession of small efforts" is essentially a religious work that arose as a product of Gide's "Protestant prudence and French introspective rationalism."*]

Gide is now seventy-eight, and he has been keeping a journal since he was eighteen or nineteen. He began it as a literary exercise and once wrote that he kept on with it to give himself practice "in writing quickly." He has always tested his life and ideas on it, and he has probably never written a sentence in it without shaping it for publication. Like all writers' journals, it has been a "savings bank," in Emerson's phrase, for future work. Such books are dictated as much by prudence as by self-fascination, and it is hard to say of many passages in this one whether Gide was lamenting his life or rehearsing a passage for some unwritten book, since for a writer so consumed by literature there is a constant injunction not to lose a shred of experience. Even in his moments of severest agony, Gide has never forgotten to write well; when a careless passage is forced out of him, he usually instructs himself to repair it. There is probably a good deal of his real life that he has sacrificed for the point and leanness of that amazing style that has been the admiration of even his enemies and his recompense for a certain thinness of imagination. Yet I am sure that Gide has given himself to his journal more freely than to any other book, or idea, or passion. Begun as an exercise, kept up in illness, in travel, in flight from work and as a constant stimulus to work, with many a grumble against its tyranny over him, it has become not only his best book but the symbolic center of his life—its armory, its apology, its supreme justification. If he has surprised himself by living so long, surely one reason has been his unwillingness to finish it.

Journal keepers are a strange breed, and with all their faults are less given to complacency than most people. There have been many writers greater than Gide who kept inferior journals, and many who were incapable of the journal's traditional complaints of failure. It is absurd to imagine Balzac writing a journal (what for?) as it is to imagine Amiel writing anything else. . . . Perhaps, to carry on a journal in our time, a writer must have a certain vital anxiety about himself and a realization that his personality is his chief literary resource. The great journal keepers have been extreme Protestants, brought up to account for every minute of their time to a watchful God—our early literature is crammed with them—and Frenchmen, in whom the introspective rationalism of their literary tradition has encouraged the keeping of *cahiers*. Gide is both Protestant and Frenchman, and more, a human being who from early childhood realized that he was "different" and that he could find freedom and consolation only in that dialogue with oneself of which every sincere journal consists.

The continual interplay of these elements makes Gide's *Journals* unique. He is a writer whose real gift has always been for the modeling and modulation of his personal experience rather than for any central originality as a thinker or artist, and in these notes all his ability for moral speculation and the abrupt *pensée* is turned on himself, his work, his friends, the cockpits of literary Paris, and his longing for God. One never knows from passage to passage where the burden of his concern will fall next—whether it will be on himself as a "sinner" who needs to flout the outward law but is afraid that pleasure unhinges him for work, or on his superlative keenness for spotting weakness or falseness in his own writing and that of everyone else, a gift that is sometimes indistinguishable from his desire to write a masterpiece that will redeem him from the gnawing sense of his personal unworthiness. He is either noting scraps for future work, or reproaching himself for wasting time, or getting back at critics, or mourning over his sins, or encouraging himself to sin (those Greeks!), or trying unanticipated flights of thought to get the most out of himself, or finishing salon conversations in which someone else, it is clear, got the upper hand. The book is his confessor, with his ever-present Bible his only spiritual tool, for while he venerates Jesus, he is unable to believe in any church, Catholicism being "inadmissible" and his ancestral Protestantism "intolerable." It is also a register of all his reading (he is as careful to make a notch for each new book read as was Justice Holmes or John Quincy Adams), of his progress at the piano (he cannot play if anyone is listening), and of letters to unfriendly critics that he will never mail. The journal is even a character in his life and work. We find him addressing it as his taskmaster, his conscience, the shadow of that outer world he hopes to escape when he enters the journal's happy chaos. When he is idle elsewhere, he can be busy here; when he is writing, or even unexpectedly happy, he complains that he notes in this book merely his bad days—will history misjudge him? But only the journal is adequately flexible and easy to contain all his contradictions; only its privacy will force him to the bottom of his own mind. A good deal like Eliot's Prufrock, he is constantly asking himself "Do I dare?," and, having dared, he attacks his failings with Puritan indignation. He is an unresting student—even after he had reached seventy, he was still memorizing long lists of German words, and he later incurred the wrath of the party-line patriots, who already disliked his views on Russia, when he revealed that he had been studying his beloved Goethe during the Occupation of France—but even here he sadly comments on his inability to rely sufficiently on himself; all those books he must finish are only a way of getting him "ready" for his work. His greatest wish has always been to let himself go, to confess the heresies of his mind and his sexual cravings to the limit. But two injunctions stand on opposite sides of him—the command of Jesus that a man must "lose his life" in order to save it, and the ethic of supreme liberation he worships in the Greeks, in Blake, Keats, Goethe, and Nietzsche. It is interesting to note that his passion for Socrates was not shared by Blake and Nietzsche—*he* needs them all. He would like to "renounce" his life, and, in a famous passage written in 1916, during his religious crisis, notes his wistful belief that "it is in perfect abnegation that individualism triumphs . . . self-renunciation is the summit of self-assertion." Yet, like another La Rochefoucauld, he notes

with his little smile that "vice" is "more imperious than any duty." Actually, he has never expected liberation but has characteristically sought the literary text for liberation. If he had achieved the Greek ideal, he would never have defined so correctly, and with typical French *justice*, the limits within which man actually lives. He would like to be both free and good, and, failing both, has compromised by being honest. He is not noble and does not pretend to be. There is many a feline thrust at Francis Jammes (too cloying), at his friend Paul Valéry (makes too many demands on his intelligence, is almost inhuman), at Paul Claudel (too self-righteous, like so many Catholics he knows). And there is a particularly cold portrait of Marcel Proust, whose boldness about his own homosexuality shocked Gide; we are not surprised, in a later passage, to find him peevishly criticizing Proust's syntax. Yet, with all this, he never allows us to forget that, despite everything he feels lacking in his own life and talent, he is a European and that his great tradition has been to translate every experience into an idea.

What is it that drives a man to keep a journal so long? Each writer starts with his own need, but surely the reasons are always the same—the struggle against death and for time, the need to use one's life to the uttermost. Recording one's days somehow saves them from extinction, and if one is a writer, there is always the hope that they will be reused in the tasks that lie ahead. There is nothing so moving in all Gide's works as this struggle with himself to maintain the victory over life. "I cling desperately to this notebook," he writes in one passage. "It is a part of my patience; it helps keep me from going under." In another: "It is time to learn once more to prefer the events that choose men to those I should have chosen myself." The journal is thus an accounting of necessity and a training in necessity. He notes that Briand's secretary, whom he dislikes, is the perfect type of climber: "He succeeds by means of patience, of minute economy, of hygiene." Add "moral" before "hygiene," and this "minute economy" becomes the very pattern of Gide's own journal. Even as he is repeating to himself Jesus's command to "lose" one's life, he is saving his in little ways, improving it, sharpening his mind on the classics, and constantly turning the whetstone of his style. It is this unremitting search for self-correction and self-purification, by a succession of small efforts, that reveals the essentially religious source of the journal. To this must be added the candor of a man who knows that he will always stand outside conventional society; and this would give a special pathos to his book if he were not always able to use up the dead matter of his days in other work. Work fills every gap, and if he cannot work, he must tirelessly analyze why. It is not until one has lived through so many days of Gide's life that one realizes how much modern man has replaced faith in another world with work in this one. Gide is never so Protestant as when he is counting up in every minute of his time, and never so modern as in his belief that work will fill the spiritual vacuum. But if the ideal success has escaped him, there is always his journal. And so, consuming his life, he still has it. (pp. 149-54)

Alfred Kazin, "The Journal Keeper," in his The Inmost Leaf: A Selection of Essays *(copyright 1948; renewed 1976 by Alfred Kazin; reprinted by permission of Harcourt Brace Jovanovich, Inc.), Harcourt Brace Jovanovich, 1955, pp. 149-54.*

GERMAINE BRÉE (essay date 1963)

[*Brée is a French-born American critic and translator. Her critical works are devoted to modern French literature and include*

Marcel Proust and Deliverance from Time, Gide, *and* The French Novel from Gide to Camus. *Concerning her work as a critic, Brée has written: "I do not consider myself a writer and should probably be classed among the 'academic' critics . . . I have no particular critical method and am, in fact, an eclectic. Each writer seems himself to suggest to me the method of approach I should use as I attempt to elucidate the kind of book he has written. . . . I attempt, with a good deal of difficulty, to communicate what seems to me essential about each, rather than to prove, attack or praise." In the following excerpt from her critical study of Gide, Brée discusses Gide's constant efforts to perfect the form and language of his art. She also defines what she believes to be his principal theme, that is, "the struggle of human beings with truths compulsively followed."*]

"My ideas do not naturally follow each other logically," Gide wrote in 1900. "They come all together or not at all." Gide is no logician; nothing is less systematic than his thinking.

> Take things for what they are.
> Play with the cards one holds.
> Insist upon being as one is.

> This does not keep one from struggling against the lies, falsifications, etc., that men have imposed on a natural state of things, against which it is useless to revolt. There is the inevitable and the modifiable. Acceptance of the modifiable is in no wise included in *amor fati*.

> This does not keep one, either, from demanding of oneself the best, after one has recognized it as such. For one does not make oneself any truer to oneself by giving precedence to the less good.

These few lines offer the sum total of Gide's wisdom. It had already been at work underneath the maze of confused speculation, personal anxiety and inhibitions of the early *Journals*. It took Gide many years to free his thought from the purely disquisitional and present it directly without excuse or justification. His convictions, slowly come by, do not obtrude upon the reader, persuasive rather by their singularly unpretentious air. Gide's Theseus found that the greatest danger he encountered was not the Minotaur, but the labyrinth. Gide steadily fought against the lure of all labyrinthian speculation.

When stated as above, Gide's thought may seem limited and rather sibylline. To what "things" is he alluding? What does he mean by the "cards" we hold? What is the "natural state of things"? What Gide really requires of us of course is that we reformulate all the great questions, a healthy state of mind all too rare at the turn of the century. But how and on what grounds? Gide's pragmatic ethic is founded on two basic precepts: we must refuse to compromise our "becoming" either by failing to see beyond the present moment or by yielding to the attractions of the many-faceted mental lie. One can be grateful to Gide for stubbornly warning against all forms of doctrinaire contagion and for pointing out the dangers we run when we fail to think and decide for ourselves. There is a commitment to noncommitment in Gide that is a welcome contrast to the noisy and questionable commitments of partisan thought. Yet this would not be a sufficient reason to take his works seriously. Gide's wisdom proposes a dynamic form of individual opportunism kept within bounds by a sense of human dignity: one should follow one's inclination, but, he insisted, upward. His innate optimism led him to trust that each human being would sift out for himself what was best, given the circumstances. His art of living is addressed to individuals and

brings a warning rather than direction to an age whose vital preoccupations and deepseated anxieties concern collectivities rather than individuals.

But Gide attracts because behind the precepts one always finds the man. His ethic was formulated by him, for himself, and he worked at perfecting it to the very end—a fine example of intellectual vigor and moral dignity. (pp. 1-3)

Gide's personal ease and fine sense of balance, quite rare in the often crass brutality of our own time, may temporarily, perhaps, hide the firmness and integrity of his critical approach and its value as example and discipline. In the long run it will emerge as the very foundation of his reputation. From *Fruits of the Earth* to *New Fruits of the Earth,* Gide eliminated all direct messages from his work. His extraordinary ability as author was to probe and reveal indirectly the devious ways of human consciousness in relation to everyday existence. And in this chosen realm Gide concentrated upon a topic of no small consequence: the struggle of human beings with truths compulsively followed.

True, Gide's excursions into the labyrinths of the subconscious are limited when compared to the audacities of the surrealists who came after him or the revelations of psychoanalysis. But he did not write merely to liberate himself or to express his new insights. Gide is first and foremost a disciplined artist whose distinguishing mark is the control he achieved of form and language. He was gifted to an extreme degree with the ability to develop complex and very finely structured narrative patterns. Whether "récit," "sotie" or novel, all his work reflects the same artistic conscience and ability. In this respect Gide has influenced the course of the French novel more than Proust. Seeking to expose certain forms of self-deception, Gide posed the deeper-lying question of the limits of the mind at grips with the actual experience of life. Yet as an artist he was committed to mold experience into form. This struggle of Gide's with himself as an artist gives his works their particular dynamism and humor. Each mold is set aside in turn as the artist watches, with elation, life spilling out of the form he had tried to impose upon it while he as an artist inevitably seeks another mold. Gide's ideas are always ideas of form, aesthetic in nature and not political or ethical. To keep form and content in strict equilibrium is an artistic discipline which Gide untiringly imposed upon himself. Hence the fundamentally restrained, or classical, understatement and objectivity of each work.

At one stage in his life Gide felt with some violence that several centuries of civilization had set up between himself and the world of reality a screen of beliefs and rules that was fast proving dangerously inadequate. This was the true scandal to which the discovery of the world of homosexuality had awakened him. His first step was to dare to appraise and liberate his desires; his first advice to others was of the same order. But this brought him face to face with moral chaos. From this perplexity arose the supple Gidian game of thought and experience by means of which Gide fashioned himself and his work in terms of the reality he grasped. He felt that the culture of which he was an inheritor need not be bankrupt, if only it was willing to come to terms with the modern world. A cautious heir of that culture, Gide was not a revolutionary. His was a warning voice, intent on revitalizing gestures and formulae so that they might become acts and living expressions of belief.

"I believe that what most pushed me to write was a pressing need for sympathy." This attempt to establish contact with the reader is perhaps the weakest part of Gide's work. It explains the more superficial, artificial mannerisms in which he indulges. But it was also one of the sources of his creativity. In a sense Gide uses a "proposition" as a starting point for his work, such an intellectual proposition as might come up in casual conversation. Gradually he shapes a concrete fictional situation which has this proposition as its momentum and orientation. The story establishes the relation between reality and the character's conceptions of reality, and then reveals the dangers lurking behind the proposition, however plausible it might seem. This is Gide's way of conversing, through art rather than abstract debate.

A book or a fictional situation for a book begins for Gide where there is a break in the "balance . . . between the real world and the mind's creation." In the course of his stories, the original proposition—"the mind's creation," in other words— is little by little limited, qualified, reduced and finally demolished, as all of the mind's creations in a Gidian world must necessarily be. This seems to have imposed upon Gide's novels the "strangulation" which he sometimes deplored.

Gide's work was bound to change in the process of creation, tracing as it did the modifications of an idea in contact with life. The change of direction always takes place at the very center of a Gidian work, as the story reaches its peak. The general movement of each story thus seems to have depended not on a decision arbitrarily made but on Gide's inner sensitivity. There Gide's evolution was unusual. Because he knew how prone he was to letting himself be carried away by emotions, he reacted by imposing a strict self-discipline on his writing. Temperamentally inclined toward torment, resolutely he pursued the happiness which comes from equilibrium, a Goethean happiness, the kind of happiness his *Theseus* achieves. Emotion and discipline were combined in Gide's search for the new forms of expression he developed with a "sort of musical logic" that in the case of *The Counterfeiters* he compared to a fugue. The conflicts between intelligence and sensibility, characteristic of many French post-symbolists, became, for Gide, powerful incentives to create subtly balanced, carefully modulated works. The "adversary," whether Claudel, for example, or simply the "other" within himself, played a really essential part in the genesis of the best of his works, more as instigator than as foe. Since Gide's ideas came all at once, sometimes giving him the impression that his entire life-work was alive in him and had been from his youth on, the impetus needed to start work on any one idea had to come from outside. The Mephistophelean outer suggestion is then taken in hand, and Gide sets up the mechanics by which it can go into action and through which its weaknesses are uncovered. Where Michel and Alissa sink into tragedy, Gide, like his Theseus, moves on. Gide's elusive humor, a rarity in our emphatic age, makes it clear that art, after all, simply plays with the substance of life; it "proposes" whereas life "disposes."

Gide is one of the rare French writers since Rabelais for whom humor is one of the mainsprings of creativity. On the whole, critics seem singularly blind to the peculiar modalities of Gidian wit and the unique corrective they bring to his more easily recognized and less original use of irony. The mechanism of the sotie, with its ludicrous characters and burlesque debates, travesties we quickly recognize, is the most patent form of Gide's humor. But a gentle amusement underlies the tragic ironies of the récits and suffuses the atmosphere in which the counterfeiters in the novel go about their dastardly work. Humor rescues Gide's work from pathos and moralizing, giving it its particular air of lightness and fantasy.

"But a special joy," said Gide, "comes from the discord between the real and the imaginary." Gide's humor is a form of that special joy. He could not take tragically as does a Sartre the discrepancy between his Zeus and Prometheus—Zeus representing the natural order. Prometheus man's consciousness— prone though he is to take Prometheus's side. Zeus' tranquil disregard of Prometheus's grandiose schemes and consequently the ludicrous scaling down to size he inflicts on the best of these, seemed to Gide both moving and grotesque. The double perspective that this sense of discord introduces determines the subtle play of light and shadow in every Gidian work. To attack Gide on the ground that he evades all issues is absurd. Writing, for Gide, was not a form of demonstration. A book embodied the play of idea and sensibility peculiar to Gide in contact with certain facets of his own experience. Situations and themes are used over and over again, but serve only as might the seven notes of the scale. Each work echoes the others, refers to them, yet they never interpenetrate; each is closed to the others and in itself complete—"full as an egg," as the baffled protagonist of *Marshlands* had dreamed. Many readers think they have drained the liqueur from a Gidian work when actually they have scarcely sipped. Gide requires the reader to penetrate the meaning of his works. He does not explain them.

There is nothing superficial about Gide's thought, but its real expression lay in the creation of literary forms, almost as difficult to explain verbally as are musical forms or abstract paintings. Gide was right to claim that his works could be sanely evaluated only from the point of view of art, "a point of view never taken by the critic, or almost never. Besides it is the only point of view that excludes no other." The end of his remark suggests that Gide did not propose to divorce aesthetic value from all others. So far as his work was concerned, he knew that its significance would appear only through an understanding of the forms he had fashioned.

Language, for Gide, was strictly subordinated to the intent at work in the form. Word by word, sentence by sentence, it had to reveal a dynamic structure. Gide, a natural virtuoso with language, did not reach perfection by an easy path. In *André Walter* he had wallowed in an apparently spontaneous patchwork of borrowed rhythms and imagery, to say nothing of imitative rhetoric. But under the aegis of Mallarmé he soon learned to lay aside oratory and hackneyed metaphor in favor of more subtly suggestive rhythms and a new complex imagery. (pp. 3-8)

Not until Gide succeeded in separating his heroes from himself was he able to fashion his style, his language, in relation to the musical logic of each individual work. *Strait Is the Gate* is a fine example of Gide's control of language, with its two carefully differentiated registers for Jerome and Alissa. After *Strait Is the Gate* Gide was in search of an unobtrusive variety of tone, a carefully controlled spontaneity approximating the modes of spoken language without adopting its loose syntax and vagaries. Narrative gave way to dialogue in an attempt to create an entirely self-sustained four-dimensional world which the reader might approach from every side. The autonomy sought by Gide required an increasingly demanding control if the work was to convey what he wanted to say. He used all the resources of a language he had thoroughly mastered to shape a new, subtle and personal register. But in a sense his very subtlety in the use of a term, the slight twist he gave by an imperceptible change in the place of an adverb, and the tight control he kept over each word give his work its rather mannered, dated clothing. Gide's works are like the man. They are newer, more powerful, more imaginative than is at first apparent under their rather fastidious garb.

Gide's works are so deeply rooted in a fast-disappearing culture that a whole re-education may be necessary before they again find a large reading public. Like Vergil's works, so dear to Gide, his own may find a place only on the library shelves of a few subtly sensitive individuals. Gide's freedom from grim disillusion or revolt, his humor and optimistic enjoyment of life seem more compatible with less harassed times than our own. To relate and reveal is a modest ambition, less dramatic than to denounce or explicate. The discovery of the ''other'' in us is now a worn-out theme; the fight against the closed world of deterministic materialism, though still with us, has long since gone beyond the simple forms it assumed at the turn of the century. The grain of folly Gide instilled in his characters, which carried them to the extremes he himself carefully avoided, seems very mild today. Yet in its solitary independence, the work of André Gide remains unshaken. In its entirety it is one of the outstanding literary achievements of our time. (pp. 8-9)

> *Germaine Brée, in her* Gide *(copyright © 1963 by Rutgers, The State University; reprinted by permission of Rutgers University Press; originally published in a different form as* André Gide: L'insaisissable protée, étude critique de l'oeuvre d'André Gide, *Belles-Lettres, 1953), Rutgers University Press, 1963, 302 p.*

ROBERT F. O'REILLY (essay date 1965)

[*O'Reilly argues that Gide's* Paludes *was a turning point in his career because it was the first work in which he did not wholly identify himself with the narrator. Instead, the narrator of the tale is a semiconscious, somewhat unreliable witness to the events he describes, and the reader must weigh his statements carefully to detect Gide's implicit image. Gide employed this device frequently in his later fiction.*]

Paludes . . . stands out as both an emotional and an artistic pivot for [Gide]. A close re-examination of *Paludes* is valuable for several reasons. *Paludes* represents a clearly defined point of departure from Gide's earlier works, presents significant developments in Gide's narrative techniques, and prepares the inseparable relationship between theme and structure which characterizes Gide's later works.

A satire of Gide's early works, *Paludes* represents an emotional change in the young artist. Supercharged with symbols, *Paludes* is a satire of the earlier symbolic works and in particular of the *Traité du Narcisse*. The *Traité* describes the artist's quest to disengage from the symbolic nature of phenomena a representation of truth and to pursue the Platonic world of pure beauty and crystalline perfection by means of the work of art. Overrun by twisting vines and spongy moss from stagnant ponds, *Paludes* satirizes the emotional landscapes of the *Voyage d'Urien*. The *Cahiers d'André Walter* are similar in many respects to the story of *Paludes*. However, the tone of *Paludes* is one of controlled irony whereas irony is lacking in the *Cahiers*. This use of irony or the lack of its use indicates particularly in Gide's work the perspective from which the author views the events and characters which make up the work. The introspective André Walter obsessed by the pursuit of an ideal and the representation of this ideal in his symbolic novel *Allain* is akin to the hero of *Paludes*. Both are motivated by a need to compensate for certain shortcomings in their respective personalities, and both are possessed by an idea which distorts

their lives and escapes self-examination. The function of the projected novel *Allain* is to testify to the emotional struggle experienced by the young Walter, not in a traditional nineteenth century novel form but in a symbolic novel, angel versus beast, the soul versus the flesh, thereby giving to the novel the two dimensional effect of both a specific and a general significance. In much the same fashion the narrator of *Paludes,* who, like André Walter, is also writing a novel, attempts to extract from his own personal life the story motivating his novel and to generalize in a symbolic way the meaning behind it, so as to preserve its validity for all men and to ensure its permanence as a work of art. . . . However, the principal female character in *Paludes,* Angèle, does not differ substantially from Gide's earlier female characters. In fact, she presents distinct analogies with the earlier heroines. Poorly defined and enigmatic, this character appears to have no other function in the work than that of an emotional springboard for the hero. Like many of Gide's heroines Angèle represents an intellectualized notion of womanhood. She is the symbol of a particular emotional gap in the narrator's life. It isn't until *La Porte étroite* that the Gidean heroine is treated on a par with Gide's heroes. Alissa is the first Gidean female character to emerge from multiple points of view and to be presented ironically and critically.

In tone and form *Paludes* is the creation of an author who views his work from a critical perspective. The voyage to North Africa provided the emotional distance and freedom necessary for an objective appraisal of an earlier phase of Gide's life, which is represented by the confining, stifling, social and literary atmosphere in *Paludes*. . . . Gide's ability to examine objectively and critically certain phases of his past life demonstrates a dual function of *Paludes*. It is above all a self-contained artistic whole for the reader and a necessary aesthetic and emotional step forward for the author of the *Nourritures terrestres* and the later works. This principle of the retroactive and self-contained work of art, which finds its first important expression in *Paludes,* becomes an important aesthetic quality of the whole body of Gidean literature following *Paludes*.

In brief, *Paludes* is the story of an unnamed hero who keeps a diary. In turn, he is writing a novel entitled *Paludes,* whose hero Tityre also keeps a diary. The work involves three authors, Gide, the hero of *Paludes,* and Tityre, all similar yet separate and distinct from one another.

Paludes was a significant advance in Gide's search for an adequate art form. Gide presents his nameless character from several points of view. The journal and notes kept by the hero of *Paludes,* the ''Journal of Tityre,'' the characters of Hubert, Angèle, and Richard, and the social and literary atmosphere of Angèle's salon bring the character of the narrator into sharp focus. It is through the journal and notes kept by the first person narrator that the reader grasps these various points of view which act as mirrors reflecting a character in several dimensions. Gide has introduced into this work a semiconscious narrator who tells his story in the first person but without full knowledge of the ramifications of his narration. Gide as the real author of *Paludes* and the reader view the main character from a certain perspective which is denied the first person narrator. It is through this device of withholding certain knowledge from the first person narrator that a situation of dramatic irony is established. This use of dramatic irony produces a work which is self-critical, self-correcting, and self-contained. . . . Irony in *Paludes* creates a fluctuation of emotions moving from the ridiculously comic to the pathetically serious. This constantly shifting perspective, this alternation of aesthetic distance, indicates a real author who is both sympathetic with and critical of his main character. Moreover, these devices indicate an author who is trying to convey to his readers the proper perspective from which he wishes the work to be read.

Immersed in the monotony of a humdrum existence, the narrator is shown contributing to the very ineffectualness which he is trying to combat. The extent to which the narrator is trapped by routine is comically and unconsciously reflected in his journal. Hemmed in by a continuous parade of repetitions in his daily life, the hero's journal is a sort of atonal record. It reports the narrator's existence in a monotonous and concise style and indicates the hero's rigid posture through the use of recurring expressions and repetitive vocabulary. Submerged by notes, agendas, programs, literary and social obligations, the hero moves in a closed circle which confines his existence. In fact, the work follows a circular pattern from beginning to end, which culminates in the circular imagery at Angèle's *soirée*. The narrator's notes at the end of the work coincide almost exactly with the beginning of the *sotie* completing the vicious circle of events which circumscribes the narrator's life. . . . A comparison of the opening lines of *Paludes* . . . with the closing lines of the *sotie* illustrates in brief major themes of the work. The monotony and the circular pattern of the narrator's life is captured through the use of similar vocabulary and dialogue in almost identical passages. The narrator's rather placid existence is contrasted with the physically active lives of his friends, and further, the narrator's pathological concern for his health is revealed through the gesture of closing windows to prevent a cold draft. . . . The circular imagery of the work occurs most noticeably during Angèle's literary *soirée*. The literary gathering pivots around the narrator and the question "*Paludes? Paludes?*—qu'est-ce que c'est?" Angèle moves in circles among her guests, a small ventilator revolves noisily in the background, and even the narrator's arguments are circular. (pp. 236-40)

The narrator's life is cluttered by a number of small details which stultify his desire to break away and to become a man of action. Drinking tea instead of milk for breakfast, rising at eight instead of six o'clock, preparing an agenda of the day's activities and then disregarding it are ways in which the hero tries to vary his existence. These small and petty events take on the dimension of action for the narrator, and are only possible for the hero because they lack real importance.

The narrator's desire to become a man of action and to emulate his friend Hubert in this respect is reflected in the triangular relationship of Hubert, Angèle, and the narrator. Hubert is portrayed as a character of great strength and endurance and as a man with wide and varied interests. In this sense Hubert's life is contrasted with the narrator's rather narrow and timid existence. Aware of this contrast and afraid of its influence on Angèle, the narrator demonstrates a distinct jealousy towards this possible rival for Angèle's affections. This contrast between the two characters is brought out in two narratives, "La Chasse à la panthère" and "La Chasse au canard." Hubert's narration is simple, straightforward, and concise, revealing the strong silent man of action engaged in a dangerous hunting expedition. Hubert's story is purposely toned down, demonstrating in a simple manner a large scale adventure. Afraid of the effect of Hubert's story on Angèle and not wanting to be outdone by his rival, the narrator relates in an overblown style a hunting experience of his own. It is comic because of the obvious desire to thrill his companion by inventing a novelistic situation. The duck hunt is juxtaposed to Hubert's story, thus

displaying the contrasting personalities of the two men. The hero's method of narration is complex, embellished with highly descriptive language, sadly inappropriate for a duck hunt, and bogged down by incidental details. The indiscriminate nocturnal setting for the hunt is an obvious invention which gives the narrator an opportunity to set the desired tone and to demonstrate his descriptive prowess. Told in a grandiose style, the duck hunt reveals the narrator's propensity for exaggeration, his concern for details and incidentals, and his preference for activities much less vigorous than hunting, as shown in his fear of firearms and in his distaste for a smoky hut. These contrasting narratives re-emphasize in a rather burlesque and comic fashion certain fears and character traits which contribute to the hero's basic ineffectualness.

Satire and irony in *Paludes* take their points of departure in the "Journal of Tityre." It is around this sketchy narrative which forms the focal point of *Paludes* that the story gravitates, and it is from this enigmatic core that the events of the story radiate towards a circular limit imposed by the hero and in turn reflect back upon him. While writing about Tityre the narrator lacks the objectivity, the spatial, temporal, and emotional distance necessary for his work to be critical and not merely autobiographical. The problem which the narrator encounters is aesthetic as well as emotional. The story of Tityre is conceived of as a complex symbol of the entire society surrounding the narrator. Tityre's story is similar to the narrator's and yet separate, typical of Richard's type of existence, in contrast to Hubert's, and representative of the social and intellectual atmosphere of Angèle's salon. (pp. 240-41)

The hero faces a problem in writing this symbolic novel. He conceives of the work of art as an ideal totality. . . . This desire of the hero to conceive and seize the work of art as pure and perfect form exists only in the hero's imagination but never materializes in the constantly evolving story of Tityre. The dilemma and frustration of the hero is that of the artist who is unable to see the totality of the work of art because he is actively living the experiences which he wishes to fictionalize and to objectify.

The narrator of *Paludes* sets out to present a contemptible example of man's resignation and stagnation in the face of social and moral convention. Surrounded by swamps and stagnant ponds, Tityre is at first content with his "tour entourée de marais." Tityre's contentment with his life depends on not choosing to search outside the oppressive and stifling environment around him, and it is for this reason that the narrator wishes to disengage himself from his fictional creation, to separate himself from all men similar to Tityre, and to examine critically this particular type of existence. It appears, therefore, that the work of art as conceived by the narrator is a type of indirect action which should act retroactively on the narrator and the reader to produce a positive effect from a negative cause, and that it is, as well, a prelude to a more direct form of involvement on the personal and social levels. (pp. 241-42)

In the effort to make Tityre repugnant to readers, the narrator attempts to show him as a victim of and as resigned to moral and social pressures which influence his life. Tityre is forbidden to hunt ducks by the Church under penalty of sin and is warned by his doctors for reasons of health not to eat the ducks living in the swamp as they are carriers of a certain swamp fever. In lieu of his ducks Tityre is advised to eat worms. Symbolically, Tityre's acceptance of worms manifests his resignation to moral and social stagnation. . . . The fever of which the doctors speak exerts an influence on the symbolic story of Tityre and is a satiric comment on the narrator's personal life. For Tityre this fever would be a liberation from convention, but would also be the beginning of the mental and physical anguish of the misfit who is not content with his stagnation yet forced to live with it. For the narrator of *Paludes* the fever is implicitly autobiographical and represents his own mental anguish and his genuine concern for physical suffering which is manifested as one of the obstacles on the path to an active life. The act of both opening and closing windows, the former a grandiose symbolic gesture of liberation, the latter a fear of a cold draft and a concern for physical well-being, constitutes a similar physical fear for the narrator and a further obstacle to possible liberation. This obstacle which creates a type of impotence for the narrator in his own life is transferred to the fictional character Tityre.

The story of Tityre undergoes a slow and subtle transformation. Originally conceived as a critical study of a particular type of existence, Tityre finds a genuine satisfaction in the life that he leads. He finds consolation in being able to integrate his own morose personality with the lugubrious landscapes which surround him. Tityre's story becomes more complex as his sadness is revealed along with his sterility. But even then Tityre remains content because he feels a sympathetic bond of friendship between himself and the surrounding environment. (pp. 242-43)

Tityre in this respect differs from and is more successful than his author. He makes the choice of harmoniously integrating his sadness with the landscapes. Tityre does not try to change his sadness, accepts his impotence, and searches for a sympathetic *âme-soeur* which he finds in the surrounding swamps and bogs. It is significant that the story of Richard immediately precedes the beginning of this change in Tityre. Richard's contentment with his mediocrity and his love for his wife Ursule and his children are symbolized in Tityre's integration with the natural elements and announces in another respect the quest of the narrator in search of a similar emotional relationship. . . . The narrator is even more solitary than his fictional creation at this point. He has no sympathetic marshes but indicates his desire to pursue this *âme-soeur* in the character of Angèle by convincing her of his loneliness and finally by engaging her in his suffering. Perhaps as an echo of the relationship between André Walter and Emmanuel, the hero of *Paludes* wants to create from the character of Angèle a sympathetic mirror reflecting his own sadness. As the breach between the hero and his fictional creation Tityre becomes more apparent and as chances for escape through the work of art are reduced, the narrator's efforts to convert Angèle are more pronounced. The hero's attempt to find consolation and compensation in Angèle are revealed particularly through Richard's story, through the hero's jealousy of Hubert and psychologically through a dream in which the hero pursues the elusive figure of Angèle. Several times Angèle comes close to tears, but it is only in the final pages of the work that the author achieves his goal by making Angèle cry and thereby establishing a sort of mutual understanding through sadness. (pp. 243-44)

Tityre in fact raises a critical eye and chastizes the narrator for meddling in his happiness, thus raising the question of the validity of the work of art as a critical probe into the workings of the individual psychology. . . .

A further stage in Tityre's journal shows the character still trapped in a circular type of existence from which he is unable to escape because of his own ineffectualness. However, the landscapes described by Tityre have assumed poetic proportions seemingly indicating an analogous progression in Tityre's happiness and contentment. (p. 244)

The narrator's desire to hide these pages of Tityre's journal from Angèle because of Tityre's apparent happiness is further proof of the narrator's own loneliness and his need for a companion in his sadness. . . . Even though Tityre's apparent happiness is not the narrator's personal happiness, it is the result of the narrator's creation and his personal desires. In this sense the narrator appears to be searching for an escape in his fictional world as the character of Tityre takes on an autonomous dimension. Tityre is a composite of the narrator's life and at the same time separate from it.

In the final phase of Tityre's development he is portrayed as a prophet and as a doctor with the power to instruct men and to cure them of their illnesses. His adventure is similar to that of his author in that his words have no impact on his listeners. In order to demonstrate the curative powers of his wonder drug, Tityre takes on the sickness of his fellow men but with the understanding that he can cure himself. Again the desires of the narrator are manifested in the successful integration of his fictional hero into a community of men. Tityre is no longer a misfit but a part of a society of men from which he may distance himself at his will.

The aesthetic problem for the narrator of *Paludes* is both serious and comic. His enigmatic novel lacks interest and significance for his friends and is constantly misinterpreted. The story of Tityre even escapes the narrator. Originally conceived as a critical work, Tityre becomes a model of life reduced to its primordial elements. The novel aspires towards a pure form, detaches itself from its author and reduces his role to that of mere spectator. The harmonious relationship which Tityre finds in his simple world between external phenomena and subjective emotion, instead of becoming an aesthetic escape for the narrator, becomes a critical and ironic comment on the disproportionate existence which results from the narrator's fanatic obsession with his stagnant and monotonous life.

The direction which the story of Tityre takes reveals the important Gidean theme of contingency. It raises the questions of the degree to which the individual is dependent on others for existence and the extent to which the individual is dependent on himself for the course and quality of his life. Implicit in Tityre's story is the idea that the individual has a choice in deciding the direction of his existence. From the narrator's own fictional creation, the meaning is clear—choice is an ever present commodity which may be exercised even under the most oppressive and stifling conditions. Since the narrator continues to endure the society in which he lives, he does it by choice, indicating that his suffering is also of his own choosing. The degree to which the narrator is responsible for his own suffering and the degree to which society is responsible are questions which Gide leaves open for the reader.

The world of *Paludes* is as static as the stagnant ponds which surround Tityre. Although temporal and spatial relationships are suspended and rigorously controlled by the day to day agenda of the first person narrator, the evolving story of Tityre represents a flux, the faint glimmer of a variation in the hero's life. But this flux occurs only in the realm of fiction and is not transposed into the narrator's life. The story of Tityre is critical insofar as the narrator ignores the possibility of choosing to integrate the worlds of fiction and of reality. Gide's own point of view resounds through the story of Tityre. And in such later works as *Les Caves du Vatican* and *Les Faux-monnayeurs* the problem of flux is more explicitly posed in terms of constantly shifting temporal and spatial relationships. After *Paludes* the problem of choice remains constant for all Gide's heroes. Without exception the Gidean hero is faced with a relative universe in which myriad permutations and combinations require characters who can adapt. The structure of Gide's fictional worlds is composed of a constant flux of events. This apparently loose structure, the constant shifting of events, is critical of the rigidity of the Gidean hero. Irony in Gide's works emerges from the interaction of a particular type of structure, an apparently arbitrary arrangement of events, and the characters portrayed, rigid automatons unable or unwilling to adapt to a relative world. The relative universe surrounding Gide's characters demands a provisory code of existence, a denial of absolutes and the acceptance of shades of interpretation.

In *Paludes* it is apparent that Gide was already developing and perfecting many of the technical narrative devices which were to characterize such later works as *Le Prométhée mal enchaîné*, *L'Immoraliste*, *La Porte étroite*, *Les Caves du Vatican* and *Les Faux-monnayeurs*. The relationship between Gide and the fictional hero of *Paludes* is a prelude to the later works. The hero of *Paludes* is an autonomous character keeping a diary which corresponds in certain respects to Gide's own life but who is different and detached from Gide's personal life. Similarly the Gidean hero of the *récits* is to some extent attached autobiographically to the real author, Gide, but evolves in a certain direction conforming to his own designs and seemingly without the author's intervention. Needless to say, the hero of *Paludes* is not Gide in that he is a fixed fictional creation directly controlled by the explicit dramatic irony of Gide. The constant shift in perspective through the various narrative devices of *Paludes* reveals the real author's point of view which is clearly critical.

The use of burlesque satire mixed with pathos is a device which Gide repeats in the later *soties*. In general the *soties* conform to a pattern in which the interest of the work depends to a large extent upon the drama of exterior events and situations rather than on the interior drama of character analysis as is the case in the Gidean *récits*. The characters of the *soties* are shaped by external factors explicitly burlesque and comic, revealing implicitly the personal drama of the characters. It is the double irony of *Paludes* that the main character is also the narrator who, while describing through his own journal the burlesque and comic situations of his existence, is unknowingly self-critical.

Also important, however, is Gide's use of the semiconscious narrator. The semiconscious narrator in Gide's work defines a hero who tells his own story and in so doing gives enough information for the story to become self-critical and self-contained, indicating the possibilities the hero has for understanding or alleviating his problems. The real author, Gide, remains objective and establishes distance from these first person heroes by refusing to judge them socially or morally, and he is only critical insofar as he establishes a tone of dramatic irony or as he reveals to the reader certain possibilities or choices that the hero might have followed. Gide's first person narrators face the problem, therefore, of adding up the events of their lives in order to explain the particular quality or course of their existence. The hero of *Paludes*, like Michel, Alissa, and Jerôme, lacks this capacity for synthesis, which could give his life new directions and new dimensions. It remains for the reader to be aware of and to synthesize the objective and subjective forces acting on Gide's characters.

The Gidean work of art is elusive and resists simple definition. As Gide indicated in the preface to *Paludes,* a book is a collaboration between the author and the psychology of the individual reader. The unfinished aspect of each Gidean work, the unanswered questions, is a tantalizing invitation to return again to Gide with renewed vigor and interest. (pp. 245-47)

Robert F. O'Reilly, "The Emergence of Gide's Art Form in 'Paludes'," in Symposium (copyright © 1965 by Syracuse University Press; reprinted by permission of Heldref Publications, a publication of the Helen Dwight Reid Educational Foundation), Vol. XIX, No. 3, Fall, 1965, pp. 236-48.

ANDRÉ MAUROIS   (essay date 1965)

[*Maurois was a French man of letters whose versatility is reflected in the broad scope of his work. However, it was as a biographer that he made his most significant contribution to literature. Following the tradition of Lytton Strachey's "new" biography, Maurois believed that a biography should adhere to historical facts regardless of possibly tarnishing the images or legends of biographical subjects. Furthermore, he felt that biography should delve into the psychological aspects of personality to reveal its multiplicity, its contradictions, and its inner struggles, and that a biographical work should be an interpretive expression of the biographer. Most of Maurois's works have been translated into English and many of his biographies were widely read in America, including* Ariel: The Life of Shelley *(1923) and* Proust: A Biography *(1949). In the following excerpt from his memoir of Gide, Maurois discusses the moral doctrine of* Les Nourritures Terrestres.]

Like *Thus Spake Zarathustra*, **Les Nourritures Terrestres** is a gospel in the root sense of the word—glad tidings. Tidings about the meaning of life addressed to a dearly loved disciple whom Gide calls Nathanaël. The book is composed of Bible verses, hymns, *récits*, songs, rounds, held together on the one hand by the presence of Nathanaël and on the other by the doctrine Gide *seems* to be teaching him. I say *seems* because we shall shortly see that Gide would accept neither the idea of teaching nor that of doctrine.

Besides Nathanaël and the author, there is a third character in **Les Nourritures,** one who reappears in *L'Immoraliste* and who is in Gide's life what Merck was in Goethe's or Mephistopheles in Faust's. This character, whom Gide calls Ménalque, has sometimes been identified with Oscar Wilde, but Gide told me it wasn't Wilde at all. Ménalque is, indeed, no one unless perhaps one aspect of Gide himself, one of the interlocutors in the dialogue of Gide with Gide that comprises his spiritual life.

The core of the book was a *récit* by Ménalque, one not far different from a *récit* Gide might have given after his African rebirth. . . . (pp. 83-4)

This *récit* contains the essence of the "tidings" of **Les Nourritures.** First a negative doctrine: flee families, rules, stability. Gide himself suffered so much from "snug homes" that he harped on its dangers all his life.

Then a positive doctrine: one must seek adventure, excess, fervor; one should loathe the lukewarm, security, all tempered feelings. "Not affection, Nathanaël: love . . ." Meaning not a shallow feeling based on nothing perhaps but tastes in common, but a feeling into which one throws oneself wholly and forgets oneself. Love is dangerous, but that is yet another reason for loving, even if it means risking one's happiness, *especially* if it means losing one's happiness. For happiness makes man less. "Descend to the bottom of the pit if you want to see the stars." Gide insists on this idea that there is no salvation in contented satisfaction with oneself, an idea he shares with both a number of great Christians and with Blake: "Unhappiness exalts, happiness slackens." Gide ends a letter to an *amie* with this curious formula: "Adieu, dear friend, may God ration your happiness!"

It would be a mistake to view the doctrine of *Les Nourritures Terrestres* as the product of a sensualist's egoism. On the contrary, it is a doctrine in which the Self (which is essentially continuity, memory of and submission to the past) fades out and disappears in order that the individual may lose himself, dissolve himself into each perfect moment. The Gide of *Les Nourritures Terrestres* does not renounce the search for the God André Walter was seeking [in *Les Cahiers d'André Walter*], but he seeks him *everywhere,* even in Hell: "May my book teach you to take more interest in yourself than in it, and more in everything else than in yourself!"

There are many objections that might be made to this doctrine. First one might object that this immoralist is at bottom a moralist—that he does teach even though he denies it, that he preaches even though he hates preachers, that he is puritanical in his anti-puritanism, and finally, that the refusal to participate in human society ("snug homes . . . Families, I hate you!") is actually another form of confinement—to the outside.

Gide is too intelligent not to have anticipated this kind of objection. He raises it himself in *Les Faux-Monnayeurs.* In describing Vincent's development, he writes: "For he's a moral creature . . . and the Devil will get the best of him only by providing him with reasons for self-approval. Theory of the totality of the moment, of gratuitous joy . . . On the basis of which the devil wins the day." A subtle analysis of his own case: the beast has found a new way of playing the angel who plays the beast. If the Immoralist weren't a moral being, he would have no need to revolt.

One might further object that this is the doctrine of a convalescent, not a healthy man. . . . But again Gide has taken care to raise this point himself in the very intriguing preface he later added to the book, and to point out further that at the time when he, the artist, wrote *Les Nourritures Terrestres,* he had already, as a man, rejected its message, for he had just got married and, for a time at least, settled down. Moreover, he followed *Les Nourritures* with *Saul,* a play which can only be interpreted as a condemnation of seekers after the moment and sensation. Thus, Gide's wavering course between the angelic pole and the diabolic pole is not at all broken by *Les Nourritures Terrestres.*

How should it be when at the end of the book the master himself advises his disciple to leave him. . . . (pp. 85-6)

But why doesn't Gide require of himself the same rejection he so strongly urges on his disciple? And if he has a horror of any and all doctrine, why isn't he horrified by his own? *He is much too much Gide to be Gidean.* He always protested against people's habit of reducing him to a rulebook when he had attempted, contrarily, to create a rulebook for escape. This is Gide's supreme and perilous leap, the leap that makes him impossible to pin down. What others might find to condemn in him, this Proteus condemns in himself.

This brings up an extremely interesting question. Why is this subtle, Protean doctrine which constantly denies itself, why

after thirty years is this powerful and dangerous book, still such a source of joy and enthusiasm to so many young men and women? Read Jacques Rivière's letters to Alain-Fournier; read in Martin du Gard's *La Belle Saison* the account of the hero's discovery of *Les Nourritures Terrestres;* listen, finally, to some of the young people about you. Many of them intensely admire this book—with an admiration quite beyond the literary. Here is why.

With the discovery of the harshness of life, the magical and sheltered days of childhood are followed, with nearly every adolescent, by a period of rebellion. This is the first adolescent "stage." The second stage is the discovery—*despite* disillusionments and difficulties—of the beauty of life. This discovery ordinarily occurs between eighteen and twenty. It produces most of our young lyric poets.

The special thing about Gide's character, its originality and its force, is that, having been retarded in natural development by reason of the constraints of his upbringing, he went through this second stage when his mind was already relatively mature, the result being that this *retardation enabled him to express the discoveries common to all young people in more perfect form.* In other words, young people are beholden to a retarded and unregenerate adolescent for having so well expressed what they feel. Thus, the necessity, the universality, and the likelihood of endurance of a book like *Les Nourritures Terrestres.* A disciple (as in Wilde's fine story) is someone who seeks himself in the eyes of the master. The young look for and find themselves in Gide.

Readers will find this same lesson in immoralism in *Le Prométhée Mal Enchaîné.* . . . Gide calls this book a *sotie,* a Middle Ages term used to denote an allegorical satire in dialogue form. Prometheus *thinks* he is chained to the peaks of the Caucasus (just as Gide once was by so many shackles, barriers, battlements, and other scruples). Then he discovers that all that's needed is to *want* to be free, and he goes off with his eagle to Paris where in the hall of the New Moons he gives a lecture explaining that each of us is devoured by his eagle—vice or virtue, duty or passion. One must feed this eagle on love. "Gentlemen, one must love his eagle, love him so he'll become beautiful." The writer's eagle is his work, and he should sacrifice himself to it. (pp. 87-9)

André Maurois, "André Gide," translated by Carl Morse (originally published under a different title in De Gide à Sartre, *Perrin, 1965), in* From Proust to Camus: Profiles of Modern French Writers *by André Maurois, translated by Carl Morse and Renaud Bruce (copyright © 1966 by André Maurois; reprinted by permission of the author and the author's agents, Scott Meredith Literary Agency, Inc., 845 Third Avenue, New York, NY 10022), Doubleday & Company, 1966 (and reprinted by Weidenfeld and Nicolson, 1967), pp. 71-95.*

LORING D. KNECHT (essay date 1967)

[*Knecht offers an alternative to the standard reading (see Harold March's essay above) of Gide's* La porte etroite. *Knecht argues that the récit may be read in such a manner that the blame for the tragedy falls on Jérôme and not on Alissa as most critics maintain. Knecht makes this point by enumerating the many flaws in Jérôme's character, and by proving that Jérôme is not, in all cases, a wholly reliable narrator.*]

It is all too tempting on first acquaintance with Gide's *La Porte étroite* to see in it only the pathetically tragic tale of a young girl who believed too wholeheartedly that "virtue is its own reward." Not too surprising, for this seems to be the reaction Gide intended to elicit. He protested against the view of some critics that he had "evolved" to a more sympathetic moral and religious attitude since 1902 and the publication of *L'Immoraliste*. He insisted repeatedly that he sought rather to make the work a criticism of a certain furiously deplorable protestantism, a puritanism that curiously evokes Jansenism, a misplaced sense of heroism which he characterizes as a sort of "cornélianisme gratuit." This last must certainly apply to Alissa rather than to Jérôme. . . .

Yet, it does appear strange that, although most have seemed keenly aware of the "elusive Proteus" that is Gide, few if any have been finely enough attuned to the subtly elusive ambiguity of this particular *récit*. Alissa has been reduced to too much of a "deliberate simplification," a girl who destroys the possibility of realizing her normal potential as a woman by a precocious and rather unnatural renunciation of earthly happiness in favor of a heavenly ideal. A drama of mistaken virtue, giving the Gide of *L'Immoraliste* the chance to balance the earthy excesses revealed in that work with a work criticizing the excesses of ascetic, unearthly puritanism. (p. 640)

This *récit* would then be the simply and artlessly told account of the distillation of a religious essence which, burning too brightly, devours its own flame with ever-increasing intensity as Alissa withdraws bafflingly and by almost imperceptible degrees, but in "a single direction" from the real world of Jérôme, the man she loves. The final irony: without her love, Jérôme, she can not finally find peace in her saintly sacrifice (for she had thought to remove herself as a barrier between Jérôme and God) and dies alone, bereft of even the God she had adored. A classical debate between love and duty, duty to her religion, to her God, one might suppose. No. As is the case with the Princess of Clèves in Madame de La Fayette's seventeenth-century novel, the real motivation lies elsewhere than in an apparent sense of duty.

If we are to assess the true center of gravity of *La Porte étroite*, its true density, we must be fully alert to the startling contrast presented in the very beginning of the novel between the character of Jérôme and that of Alissa. We must be conscious of the harmonics of every word as we hear now the informed hints of the Narrator (an older Jérôme recounting the story ten years after the death of Alissa), now the reactions and uncomprehending reflections of the younger Jérôme quoted directly from the midst of the action. The earliest portraits of Jérôme and Alissa are crucial in this respect. Here Gide has given us the point of departure with disarming frankness and honesty. There is a most charming air of freshness and naturalness in our first impression of Alissa as furnished by the Narrator. . . . (pp. 640-41)

And what of our introduction to Jérôme? His first real portrait is preceded by the significant incident between Jérôme and Alissa's mother, the Creole Lucile Bucolin. This passionate, this gay and loose woman inspires a physical terror of women in the young Jérôme (about fourteen or fifteen years old) when she lasciviously caresses him one hot summer day. . . . Jérôme has been soiled by premature physical contact with Woman in the person of his wayward Aunt Lucile. This harm, its effect on Jérôme, will be important in determining the future course of his relationship with his cousin Alissa. (p. 641)

Much has been made of the religious symbolism in this novel that is overtly suggested by the quoted Bible verses. For example, Jérôme's seeing the door to Alissa's room as the *narrow gate*, a kind of *press* through which he must pass with effort. However, when the true role of Jérôme has been penetrated more deeply, the possibility of a Freudian symbolism becomes even more likely than that of a purely Christian symbolism. For Jérôme, the possibility of a movement toward sexual fulfillment seems indeed painful, an almost impossible goal demanding great effort. That he specifically connects the symbol with the door to Alissa's bedroom could well be significant.

The importance of these symbols in giving a "timeless dimension" to the novel has been pointed out. . . . It now seems possible to see in them an aid to uncovering a more specific truth. The symbol of the garden reappears constantly. So charming, warm, and inviting in the early descriptions, the garden (as Miss Brée suggests) seems definitely hostile to Jérôme when he returns there for his final meeting with Alissa. The dog barks at him. There is a new gate and a new gardener. The garden is still Alissa's, but it is as though Jérôme no longer has a right to be there. But it is not so much that the two lovers can not move beyond the garden's confines (as Miss Brée also suggests); it is rather that, because Jérôme has failed to cultivate the garden, it no longer responds to him. He has left it fallow, so he is finally shut out, finally shut out of the place where he had been so welcome, of the life that had tendered toward him its every passion.

If *La Porte étroite* does not have universal appeal, it may well be in part because it has little movement. It is static . . . , but precisely because it had to be, because the character that Jérôme had to be stifled all normal movement. This substantive reality is admirably reflected in the tempo that Gide has given to the work. All progression is either illusory or artificial. We remain at the static point of Jérôme's arrested development. It is not the "restraint and purity of line" that Gide has given to the work that has eliminated "spontaneity and richness" in the characters as has been suggested. . . . It is the inescapable fact that Jérôme could not be what he was not that banishes spontaneity, not only from the action, but from the style—but only from the style of the parts having to do with Jérôme himself. Spontaneity has not been banished from the letters of Alissa and from her diary in spite of all Jérôme's influence to the contrary. Tragically, there was, however, a forced suppression of her spontaneity in her face to face relationships with her cousin. Perhaps the reason that Gide did not like the parts he wrote for Jérôme . . . is that he somehow felt his own suppressed guilt too clearly reflected in him. If the style of all parts of the *récit* that proceed from Jérôme is dull, it represents a dull, obtuse side of himself which he detested and which he could only bring himself to recognize fully and overtly forty-three years later in *Et nunc manet in te*. His fundamental, almost unconscious honesty, not to mention his artistic integrity, somehow forced him to project a truer light on a story that had been a more simply conceived criticism of a certain mystical tendency. This dual and contradictory inspiration of *La Porte étroite* is reflected not only in the tortuous meanderings of its story line, but also, and just as basically, in the fundamental differences in tone, rhythm, and tempo between the two stylistic registers, that of Jérôme and that of Alissa.

The key to the understanding of the direction of the novel (which is neither single nor simple) lies in the rejection of the "tragedy of renunciation" interpretation in favor of that of resignation born of loss of hope. Need we point out that *renunciation* and *resignation* are not the same?

La Porte étroite must be seen to be a confession almost as much as *Si le grain ne meurt* or *Et nunc manet in te*—a confession whose most important element is expressed through the character of Jérôme rather than in the more obvious mystical tendency which Alissa may give the appearance of incarnating. To confess more openly than he did would have been detrimental to the plot line, for the impression of Jérôme's blindness had of necessity to be maintained. Just as in *L'Immoraliste*, the Narrator's main problem is reflected in his "inconscience" ["lack of awareness"] and "aveuglement" ["blindness"]. Rather than balancing each other's excesses, *La Porte étroite* and *L'Immoraliste* are in reality two manifestations of the same problem.

Jérôme kills Alissa just as surely as Michel kills Marceline in *L'Immoraliste*. (p. 648)

> *Loring D. Knecht, "A New Reading of Gide's 'La Porte Étroite'," in PMLA, 82 (copyright © 1967 by the Modern Language Association of America; reprinted by permission of the Modern Language Association of America), Vol. LXXXII, No. 7, December, 1967, pp. 640-48.*

H. J. NERSOYAN (essay date 1969)

[*Nersoyan discusses Gide's "passionate atheism," contending that it was characterized by his intense concern with the answers to three questions: "Why is there anything?" "What is sacred?" and "Why should I love my neighbor?" Nersoyan concludes that Gide was not really an atheist, but a mystic because of his convictions that humanity was not alone in the universe, and that the center of history is outside of history.*]

Gide, who combined French and German characteristics, was attracted by the God-man relationship theme in Russian novels, and versed in what Charles de Gaulle would refer to as Anglo-Saxon literature, *lived* the utter defeat of God and his victory. To say that he was an atheist or a humanist at any period of his life is not only an injustice (for he did not want to be pigeonholed above all) but also nearsightedness. He simply mirrored the theological revolution taking place around him, and his use of several names in reference to the "more hidden" or "secret" reality—such as "virtue," "Future," and, most significantly, "Em."—reflects the confusion that is bound to reign wherever and whenever ideas are being remodeled and reshuffled to be rearranged in a way as to express new tastes and moods.

From the perspective of religious sensitivity Gide was probably the greatest creative writer of his generation, at least in his own country. He was drawn to religionless Christianity under the more delicate phrase, "unity of spirits without arbitrary unification." (pp. 3-4)

Gide used every means at his disposal—from insult to sarcasm to persuasion—to do away with Protestant puritanical and Catholic dogmatic rigidity. The Church's exclusive claim to given-once-and-for-all truths and her alliance with the secular powers were his constant targets. Both puritanism and dogmatism kept the individual in a straitjacket and hampered free development. This was a travesty of Christ's teaching, and bred hypocrisy and falsehood. But unlike so many others Gide did not, in the process of his denunciation of the churches' manipulation of men, introduce a basically non-Christian view of man. Man was not to him merely a material organism put together to function according to certain physical laws.

Gide recognizes that man is an isolated being, aware of his isolation, and unable, left to himself, to overcome this predicament. He can be saved or know himself, that is, recognize his own position in a spiritual community, after a struggle, one may even say after a process of self-emptying or *kenosis*. This process of reconciliation is through the artist who has himself a privileged position vis-à-vis "the ideal world." Reason does not reconcile a man to the foundation of his being because any reality beheld by reason is an *object*. Reason disjoins us from that with which it puts us into contact. Reconciliation is not through belief either, if *belief* means assent to the proposition that someone up or out there made me, watches over me, requires obedience to propositions he vouchsafes to men of his choice, and controls my destiny. When a god is defined in this way (or, to say the same thing in different words, when a god is set up over the whole world, in heaven) he becomes an answerer of metaphysical questions who allows no dissent, and a legislator. He robs individual man of his freedom, a development which means, in less image-ridden language, that men would rather escape their freedom than assume the responsibility of its exercise.

Gide took upon himself the task of telling men not to be afraid of their freedom, to be themselves, a precept which was always accompanied by the warning that the end of individualism is not an assemblage of disparate individuals. Rather, there is a plateau of fellowship where all individuals will stand in communion, equal to each other, but that fellowship is to be attained only through the realization of one's own potentialities. Self-realization is a means to an end, and the method to be used toward self-realization is receptivity, openness to the reality that both continues and envelops one. The method is to make of oneself, to use St. Paul's phrase, an earthen vessel. Gide was ostensibly opposed to Paul and there is no reference in his writings to the fourth chapter of the Apostle's second letter to the Corinthians. But he must have surely read it more than once, and must have liked *earthen*, not only because of its association with the earth, but also because *earthen* must have agreed with his ideal of renunciation. The word *ideal* is used here advisedly. Gide was born to wealth and is not known for his generosity. But the ideal of renunciation remained with him. It echoes Marx's warning against things whose private accumulation makes a thing out of the owner himself.

Gide may appear to advocate limitless receptivity and the other side of the coin, namely uninhibited self-expression. *Any* experience is welcome if you happen to be there to experience it. Do anything you feel like doing. Such suggestions are less startling and appear less callow when placed within the whole context of Gide's opus. They are, on the one hand, the exaggerated statements of his principles of receptivity and sincerity; on the other hand they may be meant to drive home the Dostoevskian conjecture that when God is dead everything is possible—or permissible. Yet Gide, though he remained the champion of zestful living, advocated neither anarchy nor irresponsible self-abandonment to sensuality.

A Gidian opinion that could be used against this last observation is the separation of love and sexual desire. Gide maintained that they do not involve each other. This is the curious consequence of a belief that he ostensibly rejects repeatedly: the separation of soul and body. He was brought up to believe that a good Christian must chastise the body in favor of the soul. His manner of opposing the theory that the body is evil was precisely to advocate the desire-love dichotomy in the sense that they both must and can be accepted, even when they happen not to be directed to the same object. Gide's point, in effect, is this: do not deny yourself a physical satisfaction if the only obstacle in your mind thereto is someone's commandment against it. Such a commandment may not be valid because the body must be welcomed and pleasure is not bad.

Gide frequently invites his listeners to give in to temptation. Close scrutiny of his text reveals that this is not an invitation to lasciviousness. After allowance is made for the show of daring that a champion of dissent must make, the reader realizes that Gide himself gives in to temptations involving pleasure in pursuit of a sort of unblocking of the self by way of entering into fuller communion with the surrounding reality. Here again morality to Gide turns out to be a means to a religious end. If we compare the end pursued to health, his position may be illustrated as follows: if a drug will make you healthy, do not refuse to take it just because it happens to be sweet. A health-giving drug *need* not be bitter. Painful repression and chastisement of the body do not guarantee spiritual freedom, or salvation.

Gide's general criteria for the goodness of an act are drawn with sufficient clarity, though they get less attention: an act in order to be good must be based on a principle that does not involve a denial of nature; it must contribute to the esthetic improvement of the world, and it must be useful to society, "society" including of course the doer of the act. These criteria do not add up to hedonism, let alone sensualism. Authenticity and constant determination to surpass oneself are dominant keynotes in a dynamic morality based on these principles. The advice that keeps surfacing is, "detect in yourself such traits as will make you surpass in excellence the generality of men, and do not shrink from the privations and effort required to develop them." It may be argued that the majority of men do not have such seeds of greatness in them, and many of those who do, do not have the leisure to pursue their preferences. The Gidian morality is for an élite. And it is largely for those who have their lives ahead of them. Its danger is that its emphasis on individual preferences may be adopted by men who are not already sensitivized by moral training or education or art, that is, by those who act impulsively as detached individuals and not as responsible members of society.

A circumstance Gide did not consider with enough care is that commands such as "do not destroy," "do not steal," "do not lie," "do not snoop," are not so much prohibitions, ways of leveling down individuality, as attempts at developing in the individual a sense of social responsibility. They are attempts at instilling respect for human life and for the rights of others. While it is obvious that there is no salvation or advance without the insubmissive, it is equally obvious that without the submissive—that is, without those who keep the law—there would be no society to save, no society worth carrying to a higher degree of perfection. And even this manner of viewing the scene is wrong. There are not some men who are submissive and others who are not; rather, all men are insubmissive in some respects and submissive in others. Submission and insubmissiveness are dialectically balanced at every level of their occurrence.

But it is somewhat futile to insist on these and other possible shortcomings in Gide's ethics. He did not have a detailed blueprint for the ideal society. He sought first the kingdom of God and had the carefree assurance that the rest would be given. Moreover, it is a mistake to think of him as a teacher. Gide is not a teacher. Gide is rather an example, or rather a case. The question is: "How did *he* live? He knew his vocation,

sought constantly to perfect his craft, questioned agonizingly the moral implications of his "inclination," and followed it only after he had honestly satisfied himself that it was according to the inevitable order of things, according—in another *façon de parler* ["manner of speaking"]—to a superior Will. He *accepted* what had to be. And even within its limits sought to improve the world. Moreover, indulgence in this inclination had salubrious effects on him, or so he thought, and did not damage anyone else.

Gide found the solution to his predicament as "this" man at the projected juncture of the vertical and horizontal dimensions of life. He foresaw a state of affairs where the vertical *Why* would no longer be a question different in nature from the horizontal *How,* a sort of paradise where the Dionysian and Apollonian, or such perennial kin-yet-opposites as love and justice, would no longer be in conflict. He overcame in joy his own inner conflicts. In joy too he overcame the tedium of life. He overcame that tedium in transtemporal joy and in the good *use* of time, which is work. . . . It is almost with fanaticism, but not always with ease or a sense of justification, that he appears to have insisted on being the man he thought he was destined to be, or to have done the work he knew he was destined to do. And the fervor which informs his writings, along with the example of his life, led many a beholder into paths which seem startling, but only at first sight.

Had Gide written in the forgotten language of Christianity, few people would have listened to him, and he would have been even less instrumental as he in fact was in leading many to the Christian faith. As he used symbolisms of his own without departing from the view that the center of history is outside history, Gide may be said to have strengthened Tertullian's famous claim that the soul is Christian by nature! He remained a Christian in yet another sense. Christianity is revolutionary not only because, as Gide said, it places the Kingdom of Heaven within man, but also because of a theme that permeates the Gospels: the last shall be first, and the first last. Thus Christianity is revolutionary not for any one of its teachings, but because it is the storehouse of a power of constant change. It seeks the demolition of *any* established order, regardless of its name and claims—including the Church—as soon as it becomes a den of thieves, that is, a locus and a vocabulary where one hides oneself not only from others, but also from oneself while pursuing selfish ends. Gide did not see this point about the revolutionary aspect of Christianity quite so clearly, but it was built into his mind, and it may account for his lasting appeal to youth. Nor is the Christian revolution an immature, headlong rush, heedless of damage and blood, toward some utopia. It contains within itself its own principle of criticism, inasmuch as its source is love.

Gide's use of secular terms to put forth an essentially religious attitude is, looking at it from the other side, the crystallization of religious—he would surely authorize us to say Christian—feeling on symbols that are not publicly acknowledged to stand for the sacred. This raises some problems. Does the substitution of secular for forgotten religious symbols mean that man's awareness of God's presence is inescapable, and that when one set of symbols become inoperative another set will necessarily replace them? Or does the rejection or replacement of the conventionally sacred symbols usher in the age of total secularity?

In Gide's case, the former of these alternatives appears to be true. The reality which he felt he must manifest without deflecting it in himself, which he nevertheless longed "to touch," is not limited to man, and Gide is not a humanist—or if the claim must be made that he is, then the already unmanageably large meaning of humanism must be extended further still. To Unamuno's question, Is man alone in the universe? Gide's unmistakable answer is No. He was a contemplative with a clear sense of ontological contingency. Reality to him was sacred, or had a sacred dimension, as we can gauge from the holiness that Em. (whom Gide loved) acquired in his mind in the course of his life. He hoped for an eschatological consummation without *relying* on a supernatural intervention which would set things right. He realized, in other words, that if there are no logical grounds to declare the world meaningful, there are no logical grounds to declare it absurd either. He opted for meaningfulness with what can only be described as an act of faith.

Gide was of course no theologian. The systematic investigation of the concept of God and of the nature of belief was not his responsibility. It is the critic's job to show how the experience of the creative writer blossoms forth—or does it die out?—in the theories of the systematic thinker. Gide's symbols were private or personal, and this guaranteed in a way his own and everyone else's religious freedom. This is in line with the view that authenticity consists in living out one's freedom, revealing oneself to oneself, in the process, as rooted in the larger reality. The fulcrum of human fellowship must not be external, Gide constantly insisted, because then it turns into an idol, which, itself being a mortal thing, is no bulwark against the fear of death. Nor should men belong to circles where loyalty is restricted to entities less than the universal.

There are two Gidian attitudes which in the minds of the unwary pass for atheism: anti-idolatry and mysticism. Anti-idolatry which may well subsume nearly everything said so far was the stated mission of his life. This is an indication of his ineradicable Protestantism. The Protestant principle, Tillich has written, is to protest against any absolute claim made for a relative reality. The God of Christendom, as a relative reality, was to Gide just another idol. He could not through this old idol overcome his alienation.

Gide's mysticism is manifest in *Les Nourritures Terrestres (The Fruits of the Earth)*. This book seems to be a radical departure from his first published work, *Les Cahiers d'André Walter (The Notebooks of André Walter)*, but the difference is largely one of literary maturity and language. In the new world of symbols adopted for *Les Nourritures Terrestres* Gide states the same fundamental concern and the same sort of answer to that concern: he wonders whether he is nothing but a "gathering together of sensations," and the answer is: "my life is always THAT, plus myself." The reader must reflect that "THAT" is potentially dissolvable in reality without a residue; but then there is "myself." Later in life, the hope of a "prodigious" relationship with the reality wherein he would both keep and not keep his selfhood was entertained by Gide under the category of love. The opposite of love—disruption—he saw as the work of the Devil.

To Gide, the isolated individual, no permanently held conviction brought solace. He overcame that isolation, a symptom of his solitariness, only in occasional heightened experiences. In these experiences he transcended time and space. As he remembered subsequently, at such moments his dichotomies, his sense of isolation were conquered. They remained the yearned for, focal points of his existence. This is the mystical way, a conclusion which is reinforced by his declaration made as late as 1942 that "solitude is bearable only with God." In this way

the very difficulty connected with being, and yet not being, conscious of oneself in the Whole, vanishes.

The meaning of the word *theism* is undergoing radical changes at the hands of contemporary theologians. We must likewise modify our understanding of *atheism*. An atheist can no longer be described as a man who refuses to believe in the existence of a disembodied Spirit beyond the firmament. A cool atheist is someone who considers the following questions trivial: Why is there anything? What is the sacred? Also, perhaps, Why should I love my neighbor? These questions are trivial to the cool atheist in the sense that they are not genuine questions. They seem to promise to take the questioner beyond (or below or above) himself to the source of his being, but this promise is illusory. Actually, the cool atheist says, there is no source to be taken to and no point in asking these questions at all.

These questions were constantly present in Gide's mind, and he sought the answers by way of satisfying deeply existential needs. The charge of atheism leveled against him is therefore inaccurate, even if understandable. Atheism—in the old sense—and mysticism have often been not-so-strange bedfellows. (pp. 4-11)

H. J. Nersoyan, in his André Gide: The Theism of an Atheist *(copyright © 1969 by Syracuse University Press, Syracuse, New York), Syracuse University Press, 1969, 210 p.*

G. W. IRELAND   (essay date 1970)

[*Ireland considers* Les caves du Vatican *a turning point in Gide's career because Gide made his first in-depth exploration of the concept of gratuitousness in this work. Ireland also notes that* Les caves du Vatican *marked the first appearance of an idea of central importance in all of Gide's later writings: the quest for certainty. See the excerpt above by Regis Michaud for additional discussion of Gide's themes.*]

L'Immoraliste and *La Porte étroite* prolong, in Gide's works, a tradition whose previous high-points had been *Les Cahiers d'André Walter*, *Le Voyage d'Urien*, *Les Nourritures terrestres*, and the plays of the nineties. The atmosphere in which these works breathe is rarefied. They are exquisitely written in a style which, whether elaborate or chastened, is manifestly self-conscious, deliberate, carefully wrought. They execute arabesques; they trace profiles; they are, to use Gide's own expression, 'dessiné'. Side by side with the works in this tradition, however, and indeed within these works themselves, there are signs of artistic ambitions of a very different order.

From the very beginning of his career Gide was acutely conscious of the temptation which a certain 'rhétorique' represented for him. In the opening pages of his first book he denounces this temptation in terms which leave no doubt as to the strength of his feelings on the subject. . . . Heartfelt though this declaration of principle appears to be, however, it is scarcely carried into practice in *Les Cahiers d'André Walter* itself; but from *Les Poésies d'André Walter* onwards we see Gide reaching at intervals for a form of artistic expression—less contrived and more spontaneous than the plaintive cadences of the *Cahiers*—closer in its form as in its substance to the exciting chaos of life itself. Even in such beautifully wrought works as *Le Traité du Narcisse* or *La Tentative amoureuse*—and still more in *Le Voyage d'Urien*—this tendency asserts itself if only in the form of a subversive influence. The colloquialisms of the *Poésies*, the author's 'asides' to the reader in *La Tentative amoureuse*, his apostrophizing of 'Madame', much of the humour in *Le Voyage d'Urien*—these are so many gestures, among others, aimed at liberating author and reader alike from a universe of discourse which is patently felt at times to be oppressively closed.

By the time *Isabelle* was completed, Gide's impatience with the rarefied nature of so much of his writing had been growing for a considerable time. From the very beginning . . . there had been gestures of revolt. . . . [The] writing of *La Porte étroite* served only to exacerbate Gide's irritation. *La Porte étroite*, he assures a correspondent, 'm'exaspère deux pages sur trois'. (pp. 249-50)

Isabelle, as we have seen, was in part an attempt to break out from the enclosed moral universe of the works which had preceded it. In part, too, it was an attempt to achieve a certain novelty of manner. In both respects, however, *Isabelle* had proved an unsatisfactory compromise. This was particularly true of its style; and Gide duly records in his *Journal* his dissatisfaction with his achievements in this direction. (p. 250)

Despite its early origins . . . *Les Caves du Vatican* was clearly intended, in Gide's mind, to make a break with what had gone before and to mark a new departure in his work. Its novelty was to be threefold.

In the first place, it was to follow and improve upon the example set by *Isabelle* in moving away from a purely subjective investigation of the author's own moral situation. *Isabelle* had, to be sure, accomplished something in this direction by taking as its starting-point a *fait-divers* in which the author was not personally concerned. But the incident in question was still, in a sense, too close to the author's own experience to mark a decisive break. (pp. 251-52)

The starting-point of *Les Caves du Vatican* was to be a *fait-divers* of a different kind—a random incident culled from the public domain, with which the author had no connection of any kind. Towards the end of 1893 a curious rumour began to circulate in Europe, which eventually found its way into a number of French newspapers. The story was nothing if not sensational. It alleged nothing less than that the Pope, Leo XIII, had been kidnapped by a group of high Church dignitaries, acting in concert with the Freemasons, and that he was being held prisoner in the Vatican dungeons. A pamphlet purporting to give details of the affair was published in Saint-Malo, and this document found its way into Gide's hands. Whether or not the rumour had deliberately been launched with that end in view, it furnished the opportunity for a large-scale confidence trick by means of which large numbers of faithful Catholics were persuaded to subscribe funds for a Crusade which was to restore to liberty the unfortunate Vicar of Christ—which funds, it goes without saying, were diverted to more secular ends.

Gide was intrigued by the story and gathered what information he could relating to the affair. . . . Here indeed lay ready to hand the basis for a lively farce—a theme as far removed as possible, or so it seemed, from the kind of subject on which Gide was then engaged and with which he was already growing impatient.

Gide's comments on the style of *La Porte étroite*, for example, or *Isabelle* make abundantly clear in what way the style of *Les Caves du Vatican* was to mark a new departure in his writing. The style of *Les Caves du Vatican* was to forsake the delicate half-tones, the cunningly modulated rhythms, the carefully defined nuances which characterized these works. It was to be

more spontaneous, brisker, less contrived—closer to life. . . . What Gide clearly has in mind is something very much more than a technical adjustment in his art. He is not proposing to substitute one form of artifice for another; but to dispense with artifice altogether, in an attempt to draw closer to the animating power with which life spontaneously manifests itself. This does not mean that he must write badly. It is enough that he should not sacrifice spontaneity to any conscious effort to write well. He may even write with a certain elegance, but that elegance will be like that of Lafcadio: 'parfaitement naturelle, comme une seconde sincérité'. (pp. 252-53)

Gide's labours met with a considerable amount of success. The story of the Pope's captivity and of the confidence trick to which it gave rise is very skilfully made to provide the framework for what is, at one level, a tolerably lively farce. If the comic characters in the book are not especially memorable they are at least bravely attempted; and if some of the humour is at the rather schoolboyish level of fleas, bed-bugs, and comical-sounding proper names, there is also, here and there, a certain amount of genuinely refreshing verbal fun.

Even if none of these effects is in fact very spontaneous, there is no denying that in the book as a whole Gide did succeed in giving to his prose a more impersonal colouring and a brisker gait than it had had hitherto and that, to that extent, *Les Caves du Vatican* does bring something new to the Gide canon. The desire for spontaneity of manner—even if frustrated—is, moreover, inseparable in Gide from a quest for spontaneity of a far more fundamental kind; and although this quest itself was by no means new to Gide's work, the comprehensiveness and the concreteness with which it was now to be pursued was to be the third important element of novelty in *Les Caves du Vatican*.

This theme . . . has a long history in Gide's work, and from the beginning the notion of spontaneous action is associated with a corresponding stylistic freedom. When Adam, in *Le Traité du Narcisse*, provides the earliest example in Gide's work of such an action, by breaking a branch from the tree Ygdrasil, the abruptness of his subversive gesture is matched by the spontaneous disorder of the words in which he voices his protest. . . . Central though Adam's action may be, however, the reader's attention is soon drawn away from it, in *Le Traité du Narcisse,* by other considerations. Indeed it appears just possible that Gide himself may not at the time have grasped its implications fully. The problem of uninhibited action, at all events, remained close to the surface of his preoccupations during the years that followed. In *Les Nourritures terrestres* it appears as the desire to act 'sans *juger* si l'action est bonne ou mauvaise' ['without *judging* if the action is good or evil'] In the context of *Les Nourritures terrestres* this desire is presented primarily as the manifestation of a lyrical impulse which it is not the business of the book to examine; but even in the form in which it is there expressed, Gide's attitude to actions unmotivated by antecedent or prospective moral judgements is substantially different from that which had determined Adam's gesture in *Le Traité du Narcisse*. Indeed it represents the opposing tendency in a system of polarity which persists throughout Gide's work.

For a number of Gide's protagonists unmotivated action is ultimately a means of acquiring a moral status. Their desire is not merely to act but to provoke by acting consequences for which they are not only willing but eager to accept responsibility. This is true in varying degrees both of Adam and Saül, to take only these examples; and Gertrude, in *La Symphonie pastorale,* is obliged, like Adam, to put behind her a form of

Paradise in order to recognize and face a moral dilemma on the only terms on which her actions can achieve moral significance. (pp. 254-55)

If Adam's action corresponds very closely to the form of existential choice by which, for Sartre, the individual asserts and defines his freedom—guaranteeing the authenticity of his act by recognizing the true nature of that freedom—Gide's protest in *Paludes* is directed against the very notions of freedom and authenticity that such a conception implies. His hero's ambition, indeed, is to free himself from the conditions which impose on the agent an existential choice of this kind. Such a choice, for example, takes into account the fact that our freedom to act is circumscribed by our own mortality. Characteristically, Gide's protagonist shrinks from the necessity of admitting such a limitation. . . . (pp. 256-57)

What one might call the Sartrian quality of the writing [in *Paludes*] should not mislead the reader. True, it makes it clearer than ever that Gide and Sartre are covering the same ground; but they are moving in opposite directions—Sartre towards the identification of the agent with his act, Gide towards the separation of the one from the other, Sartre towards the grounding of the personality in total commitment, Gide towards the dissolution of the personality in total freedom. (p. 257)

It is the tragedy of Michel [in *L'Immoraliste*] and of Alissa [in *La Porte étroite*] that they are imprisoned within a project to which an initial act of choice commits them once and for all. Each has—to use the vocabulary of *Paludes*—to 'entretenir' an action once committed; and this necessity is sufficient in itself to make that action 'insincère'. In each case the personality of the agent is surrendered to the act: the act devours the agent. . . .

The waiter, in *Le Prométhée mal enchaîné*, looks to the 'acte libre' or—to use his alternative expression . . .—the 'Acte autochtone', to defend the integrity of the personality against this form of exhaustion.

If he fails to make out his case, if he fails, above all, to provide a convincing illustration of the point he is striving to make, he does reveal, and perhaps communicate, to the reader the fascination which the very idea of 'l'acte gratuit' held for his creator. This was clearly not an issue on which Gide could easily admit failure; and in *Les Caves du Vatican* he returns to the attack. (p. 260)

Gide seeks, in *Les Caves du Vatican*, to illustrate his argument by means of an example. To this end he will act as the novelist in the book proposes to do. When the suggestion is made to the character in question that it is not difficult to provide motives for an imaginary crime, the novelist replies that he does not *want* to find motives for the crime. . . . He has only to create a protagonist whose actions will neither be determined nor deterred by family ties, educational conditioning, professional responsibilities or career ambitions, social pressures or established moral codes. And so Lafcadio is born.

Like Voltaire's Eldorado, which owes most of its well-being to its total isolation, Lafcadio owes most of his advantages to the exceptional character of his situation. As a bastard he is freed from family ties by having, in practice, no family. Born of a French diplomat and a Rumanian courtesan and brought up in a number of different countries by a series of 'uncles', he is exempt from any feeling of patriotism. Nor, of course, is he the product of any consistent educational system. His natural elegance and superior attainments make him a misfit

in the lower classes of society, while the circumstances of his birth and the modesty of his condition exclude him from the higher. He has no profession and therefore no professional responsibilities or ambitions; but a timely legacy relieves him of the necessity of earning a living. He has no religion and no conventional moral code. In particular, the nature of his sexuality is carefully shown to be ambivalent.

Travelling, more or less at random, between Rome and Brindisi, Lafcadio finds himself sharing a carriage with an inoffensive middle-aged man whose perfect anonymity is unrelieved by any distinguishing characteristic and between whom and himself there exists, so far as either of them knows, no connection of any kind.

At once bored and intrigued by his companion, Lafcadio allows his imagination to wander. 'Le tapir' is experiencing some difficulty in putting on his collar, and Lafcadio toys for a moment with the idea of coming to his assistance. Then, with the same apparent casualness, he allows himself to indulge a fancy of a very different kind. How easy it would be, he tells himself, to murder his fellow traveller by pushing him out of the carriage-door! He could, of course—or so he tells himself—have no motive for doing so; but it is precisely in this apparent lack of motive that the interest of the proposition lies. His first thought is that such an unmotivated crime would be a considerable embarrassment to the police; but this consideration is too secondary to detain him for long. It is not even the act as such that interests Lafcadio. It is about himself that he is curious. . . . Even the idea of putting the matter to the test by means of an unmotivated murder had occurred to him before. On that occasion he had obligingly carried the haversack of the old lady whom he had contemplated strangling, just as on this occasion he had been about to assist his victim to fasten his collar-stud. In each case, it is suggested, either outcome might equally have been possible. A supposition of this kind, however, requires to be tested. It is all very well, Lafcadio tells himself, to try to imagine what would have happened if he had actually begun to tighten his grip on the old woman's throat; for imagination, by its very nature, *predicts*, and, in practice, it is always the unpredictable that occurs. Since, moreover, it is the unpredictable alone that offers any real interest, it is necessary to do more than imagine: it is necessary to act. . . . [In] order that the unpredictable may be reaped the unpredictable must be sown. And so Lafcadio, after a last appeal to chance (if he can count slowly to twelve without seeing a light in the countryside he will abandon his project), pushes his companion out of the train.

As an example of gratuitous action this murder is so decidedly unimpressive that it scarcely seems necessary to insist at length on the inadequacy of its claims in this respect. It might appear, moreover, that Lafcadio's character and situation are so obviously conceivable only on paper that the psychological interest of any action he may perform must be very slight.

The book, however, does not stand or fall by Gide's success or failure in his attempt to define and illustrate the 'act gratuit'. *Les Caves du Vatican*, indeed, marks a decisive development in Gide's art, the implications of which were to be more far-reaching than he himself perhaps realized and which certainly went beyond what he had consciously hoped to achieve at the outset. (pp. 262-64)

The text of the book . . . betrays signs of uncertainty of purpose and direction on the part of its author. Gide's intense preoccupation at the time of writing *Les Caves du Vatican*, with what one might call the classical novel tradition results, for example, in the presence in the book of an element of parody so pervasive as to be distracting. [W. Wolfgang] Holdheim, subdividing the traditional novel into characteristic types, shows that *Les Caves du Vatican* contains clearly discernible elements of the family novel, the realistic 'society' novel, the edifying novel, the *Künstlerroman,* the picaresque novel, the detective story, the romance of chivalry, and the straightforward love story. It is possible to find in the book echoes of Cervantes, Fielding, Defoe, Lesage, Dostoievsky. . . The list is endless. Professor O'Brien has even elaborated an ingenious parallel to support his claim that the book, as a whole, is a direct parody of Wagner's *Parsifal!* However we may assess the merits of the various claims that have been made in this connection, and however much—or little—importance we may attach to any one of them, we can scarcely fail to appreciate the difficulty involved in fusing so many and such various promptings into a unified creative purpose, let alone into a coherent artistic design. . . . [In] *Les Caves du Vatican,* Gide was acutely conscious of the difficulties which confronted him. . . . [He] confesses to having found himself confronted, in the course of writing the book, with problems which he had not foreseen and to which he cannot be sure that he has invariably been able to provide a wholly satisfactory solution.

The most conspicuous, perhaps, of these problems concerns the *status* of the characters in the book. Gide's original intention, he tells us, had been to make them merely stock types, lay figures, ciphers in an allegorical satire to which the personality of the individual as such was largely irrelevant. In the course of writing the book, however, he found his characters acquiring, spontaneously, as it were, a real life of their own, which made them less than perfectly tractable to the author's designs. (pp. 266-67)

The reader may well feel that this tendency is not, in practice, carried very far—that Gide's characters, in the main, retain quite firmly their status as *fantoches.* . . . In whatever strength these elements of realism—of 'sang réel' ['real blood']—are felt to be present in the book, the mere fact of their presence in a work which is committed in principle to fantasy is sufficient to create problems of registration which are not always easy to resolve. One of the devices to which Gide has recourse, in grappling with these problems, is formally to separate his characters from their creator in such a way as to permit what is virtually a dialogue between them and him. He addresses them directly, but at a distance, creating a perspective in which his remarks, while formally recognizing his characters' autonomy, at the same time comment ironically on their pretensions. . . . (pp. 267-68)

Alternatively, the author affects, as it were, to turn his back on his characters in order to dialogue directly with the reader. . . . (p. 268)

The effect of such devices is similarly ambiguous. They do appear to make the characters independent of their author (or him of them); but they suggest that the author meets the reader on a plane of reality to which his characters have no access.

There are swift transpositions in the style itself from, for example, a key of overt mockery (in the presentation of Carola Venitequa, for example, or Amédée Fleurissoire) to a key of simple dignity (in the case of the same characters) or even of covert passion (as in the declarations of 'Defouqueblize').

Fascinating as these devices are, however, and resourceful as Gide proves himself to be, it is perhaps doubtful whether the problems created by the co-existence in the book of registers so distinct can be adequately solved by purely formal means. Hytier, for example, sees in Gide's failure to reconcile them satisfactorily in the case of Lafcadio the central weakness of the book. (pp. 268-69)

But the book's weakness is also its strength. The existence of the double register (or of the plurality of registers) which made the writing of it so arduous and which makes the reading of it so bewildering is the result neither of chance nor of caprice. The book, as it stands, is the outcome of Gide's unwillingness—even more than of his inability—to commit himself to any one point of view or to confine himself to any one plane of perception. The effect of ambivalence—more exactly, of polyvalence—which is obtained by the complexity of the registration in Gide's writing is not an effect of vagueness. It is an extension of significance amounting to something in the nature of an emancipation. By creating between the author and his creations, between his creations and each other, and even between his creations and their actions the type of ironical distance to which we have referred, Gide is able to escape from the form of lyrical commitment which, as in his earlier works, could only, in the last resort, lead back to its point of origin in himself. *L'Immoraliste* and *La Porte étroite,* for example, could claim a form of objectivity only by offering a synthesis of commitments already reconciled in their author. Now Gide can dispense with both the reference of each commitment to himself and the arresting effect of the return to himself in a pre-ordained synthesis. He is free, indeed, to look afresh at the whole question of commitment, and it is perhaps in the discovery of this freedom that the significance of *Les Caves du Vatican* is above all to be sought. From the very beginning, it is to this conclusion that the book leads.

For, if the starting-point of the book is a *fait-divers,* this *fait-divers* is transformed, in the book itself, into a *fable*—a fable which is clearly announced in its title. Germaine Brée's account of this fable is a little summary; but it is richly suggestive. To her, certainly, belongs the merit of pointing out (for the first time?) that the book is, after all, about the Papacy! The significance of this observation would no doubt have been lost on fewer readers if Gide had been allowed by Claudel to print the epigraph that he had hoped to borrow from him: 'Mais de quel Roi parlez-vous et de quel Pape?' ['But to what King did you speak, and to what pope?'].

The argument of Gide's fable is disarmingly simple. A Pope on earth should, by definition, be a repository of infallible truth, divinely guaranteed. But, of course, the authenticity of the Pope would, in its turn, require to be guaranteed: one could have confidence in the infallibility of the Pope's pronouncements only if one could be infallibly certain that one was dealing with the one infallible Pope. This would require, of course, a generalized infallibility on this point which, even historically, has not always been given and which, at any rate, the kind of rumour on which Gide's fable is based would be sufficient to call in question. But a Papacy which is open to question is not a Papacy at all. In simple terms, therefore, the end of our quest for certainty is not certainty but the wisdom accruing from our experience of the quest. Our experience of belief itself does not differ radically in kind from any other form of experience.

Nothing could be more Gidean than this conclusion. For what at first appears to be only a defeat—and what is in fact a defeat—may equally be regarded as a victory. The realization that certainty must elude our grasp is only bitter to the extent that we require certainty. Certainty, on the other hand, has a distinctly negative aspect. It puts—or it would put—an end to our seeking. Is it not, perhaps, better to travel hopefully than to arrive? For if nothing is certain, all things are possible. The world of certainty is a closed world: the world of possibility is open, endless . . . and inviting.

It is this underlying invitation, conveyed to a whole generation of readers in terms of an association of the idea of sincerity with the notions of iconoclasm and anarchy, which made the book so influential in the post-war world of the twenties, in much the same way as the conjugation of similar notions in Sartre's *Nausée*, say, or Camus's *Étranger*—both, of course, lineal descendants of *Les Caves du Vatican*—fired the imagination of another post-war generation. (pp. 269-71)

> *G. W. Ireland, in his* André Gide: A Study of His Creative Writings *(© Oxford University Press, 1970; reprinted by permission of Oxford University Press), Oxford at the Clarendon Press, 1970, 443 p.*

STEVEN S. CURRY   (essay date 1982)

[*In the following excerpt Curry discusses the nature of time and personal identity in Gide's early works, and the manner in which these themes evolved in his later works.*]

In his first signed work, *The Treatise of Narcissus*, Gide describes the River of Time into which Narcissus gazes as a "fatal and illusory river where the years pass and flow away." Narcissus, fixed in the present moment on the bank of the river, sees his reflection on the surface of the river as it flows from the future into the past. The figure of Narcissus poised over his image becomes emblematic of a human dilemma which occupies much of Gide's attention in his later works; this is the dilemma of identity fostered by the schizophrenic character of time: I see myself *in* time while not in time myself, but I feel myself *of* time I cannot see. "For Narcissus," Marshall Lindsay suggests in a recent article, "it is time that retains him captive in the present and in the world of appearances, and in the River of Time he discovers not truth but his own image." Lindsay continues, "it is fairly evident in *les Cahiers d'André Walter* and *le Traité du Narcisse* that at the beginning of his career, Gide regarded time as an obstacle, even as an adversary." If this is so, then time is an obstacle Gide was unwilling to meet head-on, an adversary he was unwilling, or perhaps unable, to confront. For neither Narcissus nor André Walter enters time; Narcissus, to borrow an expression from Professor Lindsay, "Contemplates the River of Time without getting wet," and André Walter attempts to transcend time in a Platonic ecstasy—both seek to glorify the moment outside of time; Narcissus, in a sense, is a historian, while André Walter is a mystic seeking the eternal.

In the early works, the Gidean hero strives to avoid, indeed to escape, the flow of time, which he sees as an illusion. Yet, he experiences it as something which stands between his worldly self and his ideal self; it is an abyss, somehow to be bridged. However, in the later works—for which *Theseus* is the paradigm, though somewhat after the fact—the Gidean hero learns that his identity lies in the reconciliation of these two "selves," and that his reconciliation can only be achieved by filling the abyss; that is to say, by fully immersing himself in time and living to its accompaniment. The consequences of this act are, to say the least, startling, for a twofold transformation occurs. Not only does the hero realize his identity, but the character of time changes as well. Ironically, perhaps, this double trans-

formation is prefigured in *The Treatise of Narcissus* itself—whether or not Gide was aware of the prefiguration when he wrote the work is a moot question. The key, first of all to the problem of identity, is evident in the original legend of Narcissus. Narcissus *is* Narcissus not because he ponders his own reflection, but because he attempts to possess it; he becomes Narcissus only by annihilating Narcissus. If it is indeed into the River of Time, as Gide would have it, that Narcissus plunges himself into, it is not the same river which consumes him.

Gide describes the river as "fatal and illusory." Because Narcissus stands outside of the river, its time is not lived-time, not human time as it is experienced, but rather it is history, objectified and mechanical, fatal and illusory. The River of Time is fatal in two ways: first, it is fatal *to* Narcissus, because he dies in it and, second, it is fatal *for* him, because—since death is inevitable—he fulfills his destiny. More significantly, though, the River of Time is illusory in two ways as well: first, because its illusion is itself an illusion; that is, the image of himself which at first appears to be merely an illusory image is, in the final embrace, the gateway to Narcissus' essential "reality"; second—and here a paradox, which only begins to unveil itself in *Theseus,* enters—as long as Narcissus is external to the river, it flows from the future (its source) into the past; but the instant he enters the river, its temporal flow reverses: the source becomes the past, and the current runs toward the future. Time ceases to be history or observed time—mechanical, systematic, and causal—and becomes lived-time, the time of human experience. Without exploring further here the ramifications of this transformation, it is sufficient to say that duration, not history, ultimately becomes the object of Gide's consideration.

Prefigured, then, in the story of Narcissus is the transformation which appears in Gide's works from *The Notebooks of André Walter* (ca. 1890) to *Theseus* (1946). The transformation may be summarized this way: where Narcissus seizes the ideal only to encounter the reality, Theseus encounters the reality only to seize the ideal. In essence, Gide lays the foundation for this transformation in the works from *The Immoralist* (1902) to *Lafcadio's Adventures* (1914) and, at the same time, provides a record of the evolution of the problem of time and identity from the last century halfway into this one.

Time in the nineteenth century, [Georges] Poulet writes [in his *Studies in Human Time*], was conceived as an "immense causal chain"; and, "a world of causes and effects becomes an illusory world, a world that vanishes like the mist in shreds of duration, some of which, the more hallucinatory, last a little longer than others." The crisis of identity provoked by such a world view is not difficult to understand; in a world where one feels his origins, hence his meaning, receding as quickly into the oblivion of the past as time itself, a morality of the instant would seem to be the only viable source of significant experience. As Lindsay suggests, "it is only within the individual moment, separated from the rest of time, that man is in total possession of his life, that he is in direct contact with the world, and that he can attain God." Such is the morality of André Walter and of the speaker in *The Fruits of the Earth*; such is the morality of illusion.

Lindsay concludes his discussion of "Time in Gide's Early Fiction" with the following: "the importance of the experience described in *The Fruits of the Earth* is that it brought Gide into contact with the moment, and made him undertake to embrace it"—not unlike, one is compelled to interject here, Narcissus—"the moment, in turn, freed [Gide] from the symbolic timelessness of his early works, permitting him later to exploit temporality in a manner far more subtle and varied.'' Also, one might add, it permitted him to enter the twentieth century.

The twentieth century brought with it a different theory of time, which required a different morality. With Bergson's declaration to the effect that ''duration is the only reality,'' experienced-time is accorded the rank of an existential imperative—time cannot be avoided, it cannot be imagined or rationalized; it can only be lived, for the experience of time takes time. As it concerns individual identity and morality, however, the ''new'' time is still a breeding ground for illusions: since duration is a perpetual becoming, it requires choice and responsibility in the free act of the creation of the self. Poulet recommends this aspect of Bergson's philosophy as his greatest contribution to the thought of this century:

> [Existence] is a free adaptation of past resources to present life, in view of the future. . . . there is no longer any opposition between moment and duration; no longer any trace of deterministic fatalism; but in place of the hiatus between the actual feeling of existence and the profundity of existence, there is the possibility of a mutual communication, of a relationship between the moment and time. . . . duration is something other than history or a system of laws . . . it is a free creation.

This ''freedom'' to create being is one of the dominant concerns of Gide in the *récits* which follow *The Fruits of the Earth.*

The opposition between moment and duration, or moment and history, which characterizes the early works is replaced, in the middle and late works, by a duration which exists as a fleeting shadow between the past and the future—perhaps this shadow is in some ways analogous to the recurring image of the desert, where ''Between desire and ennui our disquiet balances'': the ennui of the past and the desire for the future. Being, as a self, is achieved when one captures, defines, and then releases the shadow to reach for the next, and so on. Being is becoming; the shadow is becoming (or the failure to become). The unrealized self lies within the shadow which falls between the motion and the act, between the idea and the reality. The despair created by the freedom implied in the shadow, as well as the uncertainty evoked by its obscurity, paralyzes many of Gide's characters and destroys others. In the conclusion of *The Immoralist,* Michel sounds the note of despair which will reverberate through Gide's works until *Theseus* appears in 1946: ''. . . give me some reason to live. I myself no longer know where to look. I may have liberated myself, but what does it matter? This useless freedom tortures me.'' The movement in Gide's writings, from *The Immoralist* through the *récits* and *romans* to *Lafcadio's Adventures,* is a movement toward understanding the shadow—first by peering into it, finally by plunging into its shining obscurity.

Gide's works, on this level, are an exploration of time and identity. In the end, the task of his principal characters—like the task of narration itself—is to define the shadow as the scene of this becoming, without spatializing time. For the shadow is the time and the place where, in Narcissus' act of an instant, the river of history and the river of duration meet, defining the essential moment of self-knowledge; identity is created in the meeting of the past and future, in the instant the self annihilates itself. (pp. 233-36)

Steven S. Curry, "Into the Shadow of Hesitation: Time and Identity in Gide's Middle Fiction," in

Twentieth Century Literature (copyright 1982, Hofstra University Press), Vol. 28, No. 3, Fall, 1982, pp. 233-51.

ADDITIONAL BIBLIOGRAPHY

Ames, Van Meter. *André Gide.* Norfolk, Conn.: New Directions Books, 1947, 302 p.
> Literary biography with particular emphasis on the predominant ideological and moral influences that affected Gide's work.

Camus, Albert. ''Encounters with André Gide.'' In his *Lyrical and Critical Essays,* edited by Philip Thody, translated by Ellen Conroy Kennedy, pp. 248-53. New York: Alfred A. Knopf, 1969.
> Personal reminiscences. Camus praises Gide for his humanism.

DuGard, Roger Martin. *Notes on André Gide.* London: Andre Deutsch, 1953, 107 p.
> A remembrance of Gide by his close personal friend, the Nobel Prize-winning novelist Roger Martin DuGard.

Ellmann, Richard. ''Corydon and Menalque.'' In his *Golden Codgers: Biographical Speculations,* pp. 81-100. New York: Oxford University Press, 1973.
> Speculative biographical essay. Ellmann attempts to reconstruct Gide's relationship with Oscar Wilde.

Falk, Eugene H. *Types of Thematic Structure: The Nature and Function of Motifs in Gide, Camus, and Sartre.* Chicago: University of Chicago Press, 1967.*
> Study of the interrelationship of theme and structure in the works of Gide, Albert Camus, and Jean-Paul Sartre.

Holdheim, William D. ''The Dual Structure of the *Prométhée mal enchaine.*'' *Modern Language Notes* LXXIV, No. 8 (Dec. 1959): 714-20.
> An analysis of the peculiar structure of Gide's *Prométhée.* Holdheim believes that the structure of the *Prométhée* holds the key to the work's meaning.

Knight, Everett W. ''Gide.'' In his *Literature Considered as Philosophy: The French Example,* pp. 91-127. London: Routledge and Kegan Paul, 1957.*
> Examines the manner in which Gide's thought anticipated the development of existentialism.

Laidlaw, G. Norman. *Elysian Encounter: Diderot and Gide.* Syracuse: Syracuse University Press, 1963, 251 p.*
> Comparative study.

Lottman, Herbert R. ''André Gide's Return: A Case of Left Bank Politics.'' *Encounter* LVIII, No. 1 (Jan. 1982): 18-27.
> Account of Gide's travels in the Soviet Union. Lottmann describes the reaction of the left-wing intellectuals in France to Gide's publication of his unfavorable impressions of Communism.

Mann, Klaus. *André Gide and the Crisis of Modern Thought.* New York: Creative Age Press, 1943, 331 p.
> Biographical and analytical study written by Gide's close personal friend, Klaus Mann.

McLaren, James. *The Theatre of André Gide: Evolution of a Moral Philosopher.* New York: Octagon Books, 1971, 117 p.
> Examination of the psychological significance of the biblical and mythological figures in Gide's works.

O'Brien, Justin. *Portrait of André Gide: A Critical Biography.* New York: Alfred A. Knopf, 1953, 390 p.
> Biographical and critical study by one of the principal translators of Gide's works.

O'Neill, Kevin. *André Gide and the Roman d'Aventure: The History of a Literary Idea in France.* Sydney, Australia: Sydney University Press, 1969, 76 p.

Traces the crucial role that Gide played in the development of the theory of the ''roman d'aventure'' in France. The focus of the study is Gide's *Les caves du Vatican*.

Painter, George D. *André Gide: A Critical and Biographical Study*. London: Arthur Barker, 1951, 192 p.
    Examines the relationship between Gide's life and work, and the relationship of his works to one another.

Rossi, Vinio. *André Gide: The Evolution of an Aesthetic*. New Brunswick, N.J.: Rutgers University Press, 1967, 198 p.
    Study of technique in Gide's fiction. Rossi theorizes that the two most important influences on the development of Gide's aesthetic were the classical myth and the biblical parable.

Stoltzfus, Ben. *Gide and Hemingway: Rebels against God*. Port Washington, N.Y.: National University Publications, 1978, 97 p.*
    Comparative study. Stoltzfus maintains that ''the invisible thread connecting Gide and Hemingway is their need to assert a purely human stamp against the forces of an implacable destiny,'' that is, their humanism.

Weinberg, Kurt. *On Gide's ''Prométhée'': Private Myth and Public Mystification*. Princeton: Princeton University Press, 1972, 145 p.
    Interpretation of Gide's *Prométhée* based on ''hermeneutical principles derived from Gide's idiosyncracies; his changing attitudes which leave intact the dichotomy of his Arcadian libertinage and his obsessive Calvinism'' within the context of his total work.

(Marguerite) Radclyffe Hall

1886-1943

English novelist, poet, short story writer, and essayist.

Hall is best remembered for her portrayal of female homosexuality in the novel *The Well of Loneliness*. While her early poetry and novels had met with some success, *The Well of Loneliness* and the sensationalized obscenity trial surrounding it received worldwide attention. Many contemporary critics still neglect Hall's other works, dwelling instead upon the autobiographical and propagandistic elements of this novel. However, the honesty and compassion so often noted by critics in *The Well of Loneliness* are also primary characteristics of Hall's total body of work.

Born in Hampshire, England, Hall was raised by a capricious mother and a temperamental Italian stepfather. By turns, she was ignored or subjected to emotional and physical abuse by her parents. Hall looked to her maternal grandmother for affection and developed a strong interest in animals, nature, music, and the arts. Later, as an adult, she became an excellent horsewoman and raised show dogs. A natural pianist, Hall's talent was nurtured by her stepfather, a music instructor, but she had neither the discipline nor the desire to become a professional musician. At about age seventeen, Hall inherited a great deal of money from the father she had seen only twice, and with whom she shared a remarkable similarity of interests. New financial independence enabled her to purchase a house for herself and her grandmother, and to travel throughout Europe, where she discovered a sympathetic lesbian community. Though educated in Germany and at Kings College in London, Hall had little interest in a career until her grandmother encouraged her to publish some of the poems she had written as lyrics to accompany her piano compositions. The privately published collection of love poems *'Twixt Earth and Stars* was followed by four other collections. Ladye Mabel Batten, who became Hall's artistic advisor and lover, introduced her to London's preeminent literary circles to help advance her poetic career. Batten also encouraged Hall to write fiction as her poetry grew increasingly autobiographical and erotically explicit. In 1924 she published two novels: *The Forge*, a slight but successful work, and the more serious *The Unlit Lamp*, which guardedly addresses lesbianism and incest. After the death of Batten, Hall, who had converted to Catholicism during their relationship, asked the church for permission to engage in psychic research. As a member of the Council of the Society for Psychical Research she tried to contact Batten, whose death she felt she had hastened by flaunting her infatuation with Batten's young cousin Una Troubridge. These aspects of Hall's life—lesbianism and a devout belief in Catholicism and psychic phenomena—influenced her later writing. Troubridge, the wife of an English naval officer, devoted her life to making influential literary connections for Hall and providing pleasant surroundings to further the career of the woman she believed was a genius.

In 1926 Hall won the respect of critics and other writers with *Adam's Breed*, an autobiographical novel about a lonely man's struggle for material success and for acceptance by others. With Troubridge's approval, Hall began writing *The Well of Loneliness*, a product of her desire to argue for public under-

standing of homosexual behaviour. However, upon publication the novel was tried for obscenity and banned in England. Among the members of the literary community who supported Hall during the trial were Leonard and Virginia Woolf, Bernard Shaw, H. G. Wells, Aldous Huxley, and Hugh Walpole. Others refused to admit their support for fear of ruining their reputations by association with a controversial subject. Hall continued to write and travel, spending time in Italy, France, and the English countryside. For years she catered to the invalid Troubridge, but Hall's own frail constitution succumbed to serious illnesses in the last years of her life, resulting in repeated surgery. In 1943 she died of cancer and was buried in a plot provided for herself, Batten, and Troubridge, all of whom she felt certain would be reunited after death.

The Well of Loneliness, which many critics view as Hall's autobiographical attempt to justify her life, is an impassioned portrait of a homosexual woman. Although *The Unlit Lamp*, written two years earlier, addresses lesbianism in a cautious way that went almost unnoticed at the time of its publication, *The Well of Loneliness* depicts the love affair of an older woman and young girl with frankness and honesty. Although the book contains virtually no erotic content and adheres to the precepts of the Victorian romantic novel despite attempts at realism, some critics viewed it as enticing propaganda, as well as an artistic failure. Rebecca West, for example believed that

"Radclyffe Hall's aim . . . was not to find the inner truth about the lives of Stephen and Mary; it was to excite the reader to certain friendly emotions." And Leonard Woolf observed that despite Hall's obvious sympathy with and understanding of the characters, which he saw as well-individualized, she had created "creatures of intellect, and for the reader [they] have no emotional content." Woolf did, however, feel that "as a study of a psychology which is neither as uncommon nor as abnormal as many people imagine, the book is extremely interesting." In the mode of the Victorian romance, the protagonist's family lineage is impressive, as are the personal qualities of the main characters. The protagonist Stephen gives up her lover to a male friend and rival, sacrificing her own happiness in Christlike martyrdom. This sacrifice is interpreted by Jane Rule as Hall's complete acceptance of the "negative teaching of her class and time" that women are inferior, and men's rights to power are preordained. Throughout the novel, Rule observes, women are weak in character or power, while men are strong, powerful, and insightful, an atmosphere established by the juxtaposition of the reactions of Stephen's parents to the child at the beginning of the novel. Although considered an artistic failure by many critics, *The Well of Loneliness* is widely acknowledged as a liberating influence on social attitudes towards both homosexuality and the subject matter acceptable to the serious artist.

The Unlit Lamp and *Adam's Breed* also depict individuals fighting against society's strict demands for conformity. In *The Unlit Lamp*, a woman's desire to be free to express her intellectual gifts is thwarted by a guilt-sustained devotion to an invalid mother, who wins a struggle with the girl's tutor for her undivided attention and care. *Adam's Breed* depicts a man's struggle for success and love, with his gradual disillusionment prompting a mystical search for life's meaning. The religious and mystical implications in *The Well of Loneliness* and *Adam's Breed* become the central focus in *The Master of the House*, which describes the life of a modern carpenter's son who accepts literally the teachings of Christ and who leads a life that parallels Christ's, ending in death by crucifixion. While most critics agree that Hall handles the subject well, Lovat Dickson has noted that "modernizing Christ's life diminishes the glory and brightness of the myth."

Hall's poetry is not as widely read as her fiction. Critics find that her early love poetry, collected in *'Twixt Earth and Stars*, exhibits the falsely poetic language of a novice. Hall's technical skills increased in subsequent collections, and so did the autobiographical content which, by the time of the third collection *Poems of the Past and Present*, included allusions to friends and love affairs. *Songs of Three Counties* celebrates unspoiled nature and is heavily influenced by Hall's concern with her newly-found religion. Many of her poems are distinguished by a musical quality that frequently resulted in their use as lyrics by notable composers.

Hall is generally viewed as a minor author with deep feelings of compassion and a desire to work out her personal problems through literature. Criticized by some for using protagonists to fulfill her own fantasies, Hall nonetheless illustrated through her characters the inner conflict of people who do not fit into acceptable social roles. *The Well of Loneliness*, Margaret Lawrence has observed, "doomed [Hall] to be remembered in her own time only as a student of sexual inversion." However, Clifford Allen has stated that while "it is doubtful whether posterity will place her in the first rank . . . her true position is that of an honest writer, and not a purveyor of dirty books."

PRINCIPAL WORKS

'Twixt Earth and Stars   (poetry)   1906
A Sheaf of Verses   (poetry)   1908
Poems of the Past and Present   (poetry)   1910
Songs of Three Counties, and Other Poems   (poetry)   1913
The Forgotten Island   (poetry)   1915
The Forge   (novel)   1924
The Unlit Lamp   (novel)   1924
A Saturday Life   (novel)   1925
Adam's Breed   (novel)   1926
The Well of Loneliness   (novel)   1928
The Master of the House   (novel)   1932
Miss Ogilvy Finds Herself   (short stories)   1934
The Sixth Beatitude   (novel)   1936

THE NEW YORK TIMES BOOK REVIEW   (essay date 1926)

With **"Adam's Breed"** the headwaiter comes, if not into his literary own, at least somewhat into prominence. Miss Hall tells here the life story, literally from birth to death, of Gian-Luca, by blood, Italian; by birth, English; by profession, a waiter. (p. 9)

"Adam's Breed" is a very unusual story, exhibiting a definite talent, but compounded, too, of weakness, of artistic mismanagement, of sentimentality. Success is mixed with failure; for every virtue there is a defect, for every well-done page a poor one. The first part of the book moves along with a great deal of interest, with the ability to create character and give piquancy to a career neglected in literature. Somehow, though the reverse might superficially seem to be true, the perfect waiter, the automaton at the Doric, is much more real than the struggle with a newly awakened soul. For the last part of the book degenerates into high-falutin' sentimentalism. There is no beauty, no reality about Gian-Luca's struggle: it seems predetermined and does not ring true. Miss Hall's talents do not run to psychology; she is much better off creating people in outward terms. That is why her groups, such as the people of the Italian quarter with their superficial relations and typical emotions, have a naturalness approaching truth where her individuals fail to be specific. And her book is by far too long, too loose in form, too lacking in emphasis. The overwhelming influence of Gian-Luca's grandmother on his life, for instance, is not clearly expressed. Miss Hall has aimed at too much. One's reach should exceed one's grasp, perhaps; but had Miss Hall written the life of a head waiter, and implied his inner feelings rather than sought to express them with so much detail, she would have written something far more original and piquant than a biography which comes a trifle closer to failure than to success. (pp. 9, 17)

> *"Life of a Head-Waiter," in* The New York Times Book Review *(copyright © 1926 by The New York Times Company; reprinted by permission), May 23, 1926, pp. 9, 17.*

HAVELOCK ELLIS   (essay date 1928)

[*Ellis was a pioneering sexual psychologist and a respected English man of letters. His most famous work is his seven-volume* The Psychology of Sex *(1897-1928), a study which contains frankly stated case histories of sex-related psychological abnormalities and which is greatly responsible for changing British and American attitudes toward the hitherto forbidden subject of sexuality. In addition to his psychological writings, Ellis maintained an active interest in literature throughout his life. As a critic, according to Desmond MacCarthy, Ellis looked for the expression of the individuality of the author under discussion. "The first question he asked himself as a critic," wrote MacCarthy, "was 'What does this writer affirm?' The next, 'How did he come to affirm precisely that?' His statement of a writer's 'message' was always trenchant and clear, his psychological analysis of the man extremely acute, and the estimate of the value of his contribution impartial. What moved him most in literature was the sincere expression of preferences and beliefs, and the energy which springs from sincerity." In the following short preface to* The Well of Loneliness, *Ellis highly praises Hall and her controversial novel.*]

I have read *The Well of Loneliness* with great interest because—apart from its fine qualities as a novel by a writer of accomplished art—it possesses a notable psychological and sociological significance. So far as I know, it is the first English novel which presents, in a completely faithful and uncompromising form, one particular aspect of sexual life as it exists among us to-day. The relation of certain people—who while different from their fellow human beings, are sometimes of the highest character and the finest aptitudes—to the often hostile society in which they move, presents difficult and still unsolved problems. The poignant situations which thus arise are here set forth so vividly, and yet with such complete absence of offence, that we must place Radclyffe Hall's book on a high level of distinction.

> *Havelock Ellis, "Commentary" (copyright 1928 by Radclyffe Hall; copyright renewed © 1956 by the Literary Estate of Radclyffe Hall; reprinted by permission of François Lafitte for the Literary Estate of Havelock Ellis), in* The Well of Loneliness *by Radclyffe Hall, Covici, Friede, 1928.*

LEONARD WOOLF (essay date 1928)

[*Woolf is best known as one of the leaders of the "Bloomsbury Group" of artists and thinkers, and as the husband of novelist Virginia Woolf, with whom he founded the famous Hogarth Press. The Bloomsbury Group, which was named after the section of London where the members lived and met, also included Clive and Vanessa Bell, John Maynard Keynes, Lytton Strachey, Virginia Woolf, Desmond MacCarthy, and several others. The group's weekly meetings were occasions for lively discussions of philosophy, literature, art, economics, politics, and life in general. Although the group observed no formal manifesto, Woolf and the others generally held to the tenets of philosopher G. E. Moore's* Principia Ethica, *the essence of which is, in Moore's words, that "one's prime objects in life were love, the creation and enjoyment of aesthetic experience, and the pursuit of knowledge." Deeply interested in promoting the growth of experimental, modern literature, the Woolfs founded the Hogarth Press in 1917 "as a hobby," and through the years their efforts enabled the works of many new, nontraditional writers, such as T. S. Eliot and Robert Graves, to appear in print for the first time. A Fabian socialist during the World War I era, Woolf became a regular contributor to the socialist* New Statesman *and later served as literary editor of* The Nation and The Athenaeum, *in which much of his literary criticism is found. Throughout most of his life, Woolf also contributed essays on economics and politics to Britain's leading journals and acted as an advisor to the Labour Party. During the decency trial of* The Well of Loneliness, *the Woolfs offered to provide Hall's bail, not understanding that the book, not the author, was on trial. In the excerpt below, Woolf examines the novel as a work of art and as a discussion of the subject of female homosexuality. He concludes that* The Well of Loneliness *fails*

as a work of art because it lacks the emotional realism appropriate to the subject.]

"The Well of Loneliness," by Radclyffe Hall . . . , is a novel which will certainly cause a good deal of discussion. . . . Her present book invites consideration from two points of view: as a work of art and because of its subject. I will deal first with its subject. . . . The sexual life of Miss Hall's heroine is that which has been ascribed, traditionally and probably without foundation, to the greatest of the world's poetesses. The daughter of Sir Philip Gordon, of ancient family and the owner of Morton Hall, she is born a Sapphic or Lesbian, a woman who falls in love with and is physically attracted, not by men, but by women. The cause of this perversion of the normal sexual feelings is represented in this book to be pre-natal. Sir Philip and his wife, Anna, were passionately desirous of a son and heir; they convinced themselves before the child's birth that it was going to be a boy. Stephen, the daughter, has the body of a woman, but the mind and instinct of a man. . . .

As a study of a psychology which is neither as uncommon nor as abnormal as many people imagine, the book is extremely interesting. It is written with understanding and frankness, with sympathy and feeling. The chief of those "unsolved problems," to which Mr. Havelock Ellis [see excerpt above] refers, is, of course, caused by the instinctive and barbarous attitude of society, and particularly British society, towards the abnormal. The county families feel instinctively that there is something not quite right about Sir Philip's daughter—and "something not quite right" means in plain English something morally wrong. When Stephen's relations with Angela Crossby, the wife of the Birmingham hardware manufacturer, are disclosed, Stephen's mother turns from her with horror and loathing. She is a moral pariah, and the scandal has to be hushed up, just as if she cheated at cards or forged a cheque. This moral attitude of the world and the reaction from it upon the mind of Stephen are well described in the book. Another problem, internal to the psychology of the invert (as Miss Hall rather strangely calls her heroine), is touched upon in the book, but is not dealt with so firmly or clearly. The reader is left in some doubt whether, in Miss Hall's view, the tragedy of Stephen's life is or is not partly due to a certain barrenness and sterility in her relationships, whether, in fact, her heroine is not condemned by fate—in other words by herself—as well as by society to drink of the well of loneliness.

Miss Hall's subject will be considered "unpleasant" by many people; as treated by her, it is far less unpleasant than many of the subjects of popular novels. But I must leave the subject for the novel. Miss Hall has written her book as a novel, and she is obviously a serious novelist who asks to be judged by high standards. According to those standards, the book is a failure, and why it fails is an interesting question. Up to a point it has great merits. Miss Hall is one of a large number of women writers who obviously have very considerable gifts for novel writing. She can construct a plot, tell a story, think of characters and make them sufficiently distinct and interesting, describe scenes vividly, set people talking. She has a much quicker, subtler, and, I think, more sincere, feeling for the psychology of her characters than have most male novelists of her calibre. And yet the book fails completely as a work of art. There are many reasons for this, but one of the chief reasons is that Miss Hall loses the whole in its parts, and is so intent on the stars that she forgets the heavens. Her book is formless and therefore chaotic. Its shape should have been given to it by the psychology of Stephen and by her tragic relation to society—that is clearly Miss Hall's intention. But the leaven of this central idea does not remain a creative principle for long in Miss Hall's mind or in the novel. The first 150 pages are good, for there the yeast is still working; but after the death of Sir Philip the novel becomes a catalogue, almost a ragbag. Incident is added to incident, and character to character, and one sees the relevance which Miss Hall intended each to have to the theme of the book. But their relevance is intellectual, not emotional, and therefore not artistic. They remain discrete patches which never join to form a pattern. Instead of the book gathering way as it goes, it loses it, and Miss Hall labours heavily in that terrible trough which is the middle of every long book. It is emotionally that the book loses way, and a sign of this is Miss Hall's use of language. At the beginning the language is alive; the style is not brilliant or beautiful, but it is quick and vivid, particularly in the descriptions of hunting. But as the book goes on, life and emotion die out of the language, and Miss Hall drops into journalese or the tell-tale novelist's clichés, when she wants to heighten the emotion. "They sat down close together. They were weary unto death. . . ." "Came a queer, halting voice. . . ." ". . . fared forth in the motor to visit divers villages. . . ." These are small points, but they show unmistakably a failure of the emotional impetus. It is the same emotional failure which is noticeable in Miss Hall's characters. Her characters are interesting, carefully constructed, and individualized. And yet disconcertingly they hardly seem to be persons. They appear to be the creations of the intellect, and for the reader they have no emotional content. The consequence is that one does not feel the emotions appropriate to their tragedy or comedy.

Leonard Woolf, in a review of "The Well of Loneliness," in The Nation and The Athenaeum, *Vol. XLIII, No. 18, August 4, 1928, p. 593.*

DESMOND MacCARTHY   (essay date 1928)

[*MacCarthy was one of the foremost English literary and drama critics of the twentieth century. He served for many years on the staff of the* New Statesman *and edited* Life and Letters. *Among his many essay collections* The Court Theatre 1904-1907: A Commentary and a Criticism (1907), *which is a detailed account of a season when the Court Theatre was dominated by Harley Granville-Barker and Bernard Shaw, is especially valued. According to his critics, MacCarthy brought to his work a wide range of reading, serious and sensitive judgement, an interest in the works of new writers, and high critical standards. In the following excerpt, MacCarthy attacks the suppression of* The Well of Loneliness.]

Miss Rhoda Broughton, at the end of her life, used to say amusingly, 'When I began to write I was a Zola, now I am a Charlotte Yonge'. There was not, of course, an improper word in her novels, but the heroines were described as feeling passionately when in love, and even as falling in love with a man before he was in love with them. There are many people still alive who remember in their youth the works of Charlotte Brontë being withheld on that account. It seems startling at first sight, but those who locked up copies of *Jane Eyre* were prompted by the same feelings as those who now have just banned *The Well of Loneliness.* They wished that *Jane Eyre* should not be read because it made people, especially young people, aware that women existed whose experience of love is passionate. They did not wish knowledge of facts to spread for fear that readers should recognize the emotions described. They knew these facts themselves, but they conceived it was bad for the community that they should be more generally

known. In the case of *The Well of Loneliness* the passion described is abnormal; it is the story of a woman who falls in love with another woman. That there is a very small percentage of human beings of both sexes whose love-life is centred on members of their own sex is a fact about human nature which is well known; why should it not be generally known? What harm can a book do which deals with the unfortunate complications which result from such aberrations? Here and there it might suddenly reveal a reader to herself. It might again suddenly explain to a reader of another kind the behaviour of some one else towards her. Why should this be bad for them? Is there not, on the contrary, a possibility that such a book may be of service, helping them to recognize traits in themselves and in others, and so know more surely where they are? Again, if it is true that these abnormal tendencies are mixed, as in the case of normal instincts in normal people, with emotions which the abnormal person recognizes as the noblest he, or she, is capable of feeling, ought not their fellow human beings to know this? If people are treated as inhuman monsters, they become monsters; and what is more serious, those who mistakenly think themselves abnormal (in youth this mistake is easy) conceive themselves as only fitted to associate with those who really are. The fear that if such novels are not at once suppressed the book-market will be flooded with them, is empty. A curiosity sale is soon over. . . . History shows that only those communities have flourished in which men were allowed to pool their experience and comment freely on life, and that the suppression of freedom is a graver risk to civilization than the circulation of any particular book to morality. (pp. 340-41)

Desmond MacCarthy, "Literary Taboos" (reprinted by permission of the Literary Estate of Desmond McCarthy), in Life and Letters, *London, Vol. 1, No. 5, October, 1928, pp. 329-41.**

ROBERT MORSS LOVETT   (essay date 1929)

[*Lovett, American scholar and educator, edited* The Dial *and was associate editor of* The New Republic. *In the excerpt below, he calls* The Well of Loneliness "*a beautifully written piece of propaganda for the right of a woman to love one of her own sex [and] for social tolerance.*"]

Miss Hall introduces to serious consideration new ramifications of the sexual motive which open the way to new varieties of fiction. In the place of the organic absolutes, male and female, she recognizes the principle of relativity. An individual may be male in respect to this person and female to that, a fact which complicated enormously the problem of selection. In place of the triangle of man, woman, and intruder, she suggests a polygon of innumerable facets, a condition as appalling to the reader of fiction as the introduction of non-Euclidean geometry into his comfortable tridimensional world. If the human race showed only six well-defined sexes, like the strawberry, the complications would outrun the tether of the ordinary novelist, and demand an epic poet like Erasmus Darwin, to write something on the scale of his "Loves of the Plants." But the possibilities of transmutation in the field of sexual relativity far outrun this feeble effort of the imagination to deal with them.

Miss Hall resembles in seriousness the nineteenth century novelists whom she transcends. Her novel of last year, **"The Well of Loneliness,"** was a beautifully written piece of propaganda for the right of a woman to love one of her own sex, for social tolerance of the sexual invert, as earnest it would seem as the pleas of Charles Kingsley for the working-class, and far more beautifully written than "Alton Locke," **"The Unlit Lamp"** is an earlier work and treats of the same theme more guardedly. In the latter the conflict of the heroine is circumscribed; she is the victim not of society, but of her family. The book might be read as a rather powerful rendering of a motive which was becoming prominent in fiction at the close of the last century, that of the conflict of generations, of which Turgeniev gave the classic example in "Fathers and Sons." But in the case of Jean Ogden as in that of Mary Olivier and of the hero in "Sons and Lovers," there is a definite sexual element in the struggle. Jean is male toward her friend Elizabeth and toward her mother; both are in love with her, and mother, with the support of traditional loyalties and social inhibitions, wins. It is a real tragedy in that Jean, the victim of this abominable incest, is a real person and a beautiful one, but there is nothing of true reality and beauty in her yielding to the convention of maternal affection and the authority of the dead hand. This shifting of values, literary and vital, shows how far we have moved from the nineteenth century and its ideal of renunciation. The book should be issued in a special edition for Mother's Day, to be sent by young Euphues as a "cooling card for all fond mothers"—instead of trying to say it to them with flowers, or teaching them to reach for a sweet instead of a fag. (pp. 132-33)

> Robert Morss Lovett, "Incestuous Mothers," in The New Republic (© 1929 The New Republic, Inc.), Vol. LX, No. 772, September 18, 1929, pp. 132-33.

REBECCA WEST (essay date 1931)

[*West is considered one of the foremost English novelists and critics to write during the twentieth century. Born Cecily Isabel Fairfield, she began her career as an actress—taking the name Rebecca West from the emancipated heroine of Henrik Ibsen's drama* Rosmersholm—*and as a book reviewer for* The Freewoman. *Her early criticism was noted for its militantly feminist stance and its reflection of West's Fabian socialist concerns. Her first novel,* The Return of the Soldier *(1918), evidences a concern that entered into much of her later work: the psychology of the individual. West's greatest works include* The Meaning of Treason *(1947), which analyzes the motives of Britain's wartime traitors—notably, William Joyce ("Lord Haw-Haw")—and* Black Lamb and Grey Falcon *(1942), a record of the author's 1937 journey through Yugoslavia. West's literary criticism is noted for its wit, aversion to cant, and perceptiveness. In the excerpt below, West, a personal acquaintance and admirer of Hall, contends that while the literary community respected and supported the author, they found it difficult to defend* The Well of Loneliness, *which West believes was written specifically to garner sympathy for the protagonists and people like them.*]

Everybody who knows Miss Radclyffe Hall wants to stand by her. But they are finding it far from easy to stand by **The Well of Loneliness,** for the simple reason that it is, in a way which is particularly inconvenient in the present circumstances, not a very good book. The first part is factually interesting; the second part is far below the standard the author has set for herself in her other books. A novel which ends a chapter with the sentence "And that night they were not divided" cannot redeem itself by having "they" mean not what it usually does. Now, no one believes that a book ought to be suppressed because it is badly written; but it unfortunately happens that the qualities which make this book a poor one are precisely these that have been used dialectically in tussles with the censorship over other books.

When a book of great literary merit is denounced the first line of defence always is to point out that that kind of book, which conscientiously analyzes a human experience and gives its findings honestly, cannot do those who read it any harm, since it adds to the knowledge of reality by which man lives. It has always been emphasized that far more harmful are books written sentimentally, that is to say written by persons who do not pass their subject matter through their imaginations and report on the results, but who describe their subject matter without investigation in terms they think likely to cause certain emotions in their readers. It is to that last category that *The Well of Loneliness* unhappily belongs. Miss Radclyffe Hall's aim in writing was not to find out the inner truth of the lives of Stephen and Mary; it was to excite in the readers certain friendly emotions toward the lives of Stephen and Mary. The book constantly gives us a sense of fictitious values, of "Cry, damn you, cry," hokum. Hence considerable dismay is being felt by those who are compelled by their belief in a free press to wrestle with the authorities over the suppression of this book, but who realize perfectly well that this is the kind of book they have denounced again and again in the course of other tussles with the censorship. (pp. 7-9)

As a fiction reviewer of long experience I know that the life of *The Well of Loneliness* would not have extended beyond four months. By that time it would have vanished completely from the shelves of the Times Book Club and the hearts of the people. Nor, during that time, could it conceivably have done what the narrowest mind could have considered much harm. It would have been read chiefly by wondering adults, most of them above the age when conversion is likely. Its effect on the young might have been bad, for a priggish adolescent might have had its first emotional stirrings clarified and sanctified and therefore fixed by those pages. But such children are unlikely to come into possession of a high-priced novel which their parents would be reluctant to give them; and the sophisticated adolescent who has a way of coming into possession of everything it wants would hardly enjoy anything so like the earnest novels Miss Elizabeth Robins wrote in the 'nineties. I would be willing to bet my entire life ration of caviare and Berncastler that had *The Well of Loneliness* not been suppressed it would have made but little dint on the Day of Judgment.

Now the case is altered. *Time and Tide,* a weekly journal largely written and read by women, published an irritated letter from "A Modern Mother" who tells that she had read **The Well of Loneliness** when it first came out and decided that she preferred her fifteen-year-old daughter not to read a recommendation of homosexuality, and that she had been able to see that the book came into the house and went out of it without her daughter knowing. Since then, however, the book has been censored. In consequence, the newspapers have every day over a long period of time shown placards and published articles which have thrust on every child who can read full knowledge of the existence of female homosexuality, and a newspaper costs a penny, whereas the book cost fifteen shillings. This is a very serious charge against the authorities: particularly when one considers the tendency of wholesome youth to side with the rebel. The imprisonment of Oscar Wilde was the best propaganda that was ever put in for male homosexuality, and now that the government has supplied female homosexuality with a handsome, noble, and intrepid martyr the word Lesbian will in no time suggest to the young girl something other than the friend of Catullus who had bad luck with a sparrow. (pp. 10-11)

Rebecca West, "Concerning the Censorship" (originally published in a slightly different form as "A
London Commentary," in The Bookman, New York,
Vol. LXVIII, No. 5, January, 1929), in her Ending
in Earnest: A Literary Log (reprinted by permission
of A D Peters & Co Ltd), Doubleday, Doran & Company, Inc., 1931, pp. 6-12.

L.A.G. STRONG   (essay date 1932)

[*The novelist Strong offers a generally negative review of* The
Master of the House.]

Miss Radclyffe Hall's new novel raises a difficulty. Her story
of the reluctant carpenter-saint of Saint-Loup-sur-mer bears an
external resemblance to the story of our Lord, of whom Christophe, as set forth on pages 135-138, evidently feels himself
to be a reincarnation. I am not clear to what extent Miss Radclyffe Hall encourages his idea, but the episode of the stigmata,
the emphasis upon carpentering, upon the divine power which
makes him refuse the advances of Aeliana, and his ultimate
(literal) crucifixion on active service in Palestine, show that at
any rate the parallel has been in her mind. It is hard to see
what is gained by it. *The Master of the House* is a solid, full
story about a little Provençal seaport which was transformed
by a Paris furniture dealer into a fashionable resort, and then
emptied by the War. Bound up with its fortunes are the life
histories of the cousins Jan and Christophe, the carpenter Jousé,
and the drunken cobbler Eusèbe. The War part is maybe less
convincing, but the story stands very well on its own legs:
whereas, by adding this weight of symbolism to it, Miss Radclyffe Hall makes it totter dangerously, and keys the reader's
attention to an inconveniently high pitch. Like all her work,
The Master of the House shows a high seriousness of purpose,
but the aforementioned high pitch makes more obvious her
occasional characteristic lapses into sentimentality, and the
death of the dog furnishes an unfortunate parallel to the death
of the racehorse in an earlier work.

L.A.G. Strong, in a review of "The Master of the
House," in The Spectator (© 1932 by The Spectator;
reprinted by permission of The Spectator), Vol. 148,
No. 5410, March 5, 1932, p. 342.

H. E. BATES   (essay date 1934)

[*Bates was one of the masters of the twentieth-century English
short story and the author of* The Modern Short Story *(1941), an
excellent introduction to the form. Bates was also a respected
novelist and contributor of book reviews to the* Morning Post *and*
The Spectator. *In the excerpt below, he finds little to praise among
the short stories in* Miss Ogilvy Finds Herself.]

Miss Radclyffe Hall's short stories [in *Miss Ogilvy Finds Herself*] are . . . disappointing. She possesses considerable talent
and much courage, but she would seem to be essentially a
novelist, ill at ease with a shorter and more exacting form.

The stories seem to sprawl loosely over the pages and her style
is in places singularly careless and drab. Of the five stories
Fraülein Schwartz seems to me the most successful. "Fraülein
Schwartz was little and round and fifty, with neat greying hair
and a very high bosom," and had lived for some years in
Raymond's Private Hotel in Pimlico. She is a patriotic, sentimental creature who, though loved by everyone, devotes all
her own love to a starving kitten. The story is a study in
loneliness; but it also criticizes society, and there is something

extremely ironical about the fact that the Fraülein, surrounded
by so-called friends, should find solace in the kitten she picks
up on the doorstep.

H. E. Bates, in a review of "Miss Ogilvy Finds
Herself," in The Spectator (© 1934 by The Spectator;
reprinted by permission of The Spectator), No. 5516,
March 16, 1934, p. 426.

PETER QUENNELL   (essay date 1934)

[*In the excerpt below, Quennell concludes that* Miss Ogilvy Finds
Herself *provides strong evidence that Hall cannot be considered
a purveyor of indecent literature.*]

Miss Ogilvy Finds Herself has a special interest. Every newspaper moralist who joined in the ridiculous hue and cry after
The Well of Loneliness should be obliged to digest the whole
of Miss Radclyffe Hall's new production, and thereupon do
public penance with a copy of the volume and a printed re-
cantation securely padlocked around his neck. A sentimental
novelist who, in perfect good faith, once stumbled on an important but excessively controversial theme, Miss Radclyffe
Hall has now justified her artistic integrity by publishing a tale,
among four companions, which, far from deserving to be likened to a phial of—was it arsenic, spirits of salt or fabulous
cantharides?—can only be compared to a very mild and entirely
harmless sleeping-draught. The story ["**Miss Ogilvy Finds Herself**"] is wonderfully and touchingly foolish. (p. 414)

Peter Quennell, in a review of "Miss Ogilvy Finds
Herself," in The New Statesman & Nation (© 1934
The Statesman & Nation Publishing Co. Ltd.), n.s.
Vol. VII, No. 160, March 17, 1934, pp. 414, 416.

THE TIMES LITERARY SUPPLEMENT   (essay date 1936)

[*An anonymous reviewer for* The Times Literary Supplement *offers a balanced assessment of* The Sixth Beatitude.]

Miss Radclyffe Hall's new novel [*The Sixth Beatitude*] is, in
effect, a lively and unsentimental account of life in a row of
insanitary old cottages belonging to the town of Rother on
Romney Marsh. The title of the novel is an implication that
chastity of body and purity of heart are not synonymous, for
Hannah Bullen, the heroine of the story, is the unmarried mother
of two children by different fathers, and in the course of the
story is driven by the urge of life to consort habitually with an
earthy but virile gardener and once, during a hopping holiday,
with a consumptive young piano-tuner, less credible than the
gardener, who expires after the experience. Hannah Bullen,
daily servant when she can get a job and the mainstay of her
whole wilful and grubby family, is certainly an admirable creature as portrayed by her creator, a faithful daughter, a loving
mother, a capacious worker and an honest character with a
touch of unexpressed poetry in her feeling for the Marsh. Miss
Hall, whose inspiration seems to flag a little towards the end,
brings Hannah's life to a tragic close, but her death while
rescuing another woman's children from a fire adds nothing to
her stature. She is the author's idea of *un coeur simple*, whose
rugged language did not belie her fundamental goodness. However, it is perhaps less Hannah herself than her surroundings
and belongings which arrest the reader's attention. The uncompromising picture of the Bullen family—Granny in her
second childhood, Mother with her gin-drinking and indigestion, Father with his ulcered leg, brother Alf on the dole,
brother Tom bettering himself by marriage, Doris and Ernie

the children, with their internal quarrels and family loyalty, the squalor of their cottage and their disgust at the prospect of leaving it for a council house, their lurid expressions and their exchanges with their neighbours—would have profoundly distressed Mr. Bowdler; but is, if not Shakespearian, a very creditable study in a regionalism which, apparently to the author's regret, is doomed to fade before the sanitary inspector and the surveyor.

Miss Hall certainly conveys, without any special pleading or attitudinizing, the native richness of speech and character that can exist in a row of old hovels in an old town, the warmth that somehow makes the dirt, cold and bickering bearable, and the loyal affection that can bind even two verminous old men to one another. But possibly the light in which she presents them, if bright, is a little too dry. The everlasting beauty of Romney Marsh, tradition and the urge of the blood are none of them enough to make the Bullens or Croft's Lane admirable, so that one's enjoyment of them is made slightly uncomfortable by reflections from which the author resolutely abstains.

> *"A Heroine in a Hovel," in* The Times Literary Supplement *(© Times Newspapers Ltd. (London) 1936; reproduced from* The Times Literary Supplement *by permission), No. 1785, April 18, 1936, p. 333.*

GWEN LEYS   (essay date 1936)

[*In a review of* The Sixth Beatitude, *Leys mentions several of the commonly expressed criticisms of Hall's books.*]

Untutored, amoral, and burdened with more than her share of the world's tribulations, Hannah Bullen takes her uncharted way through the pages of [**"The Sixth Beatitude"**] toward that vision of God which, according to the sixth beatitude, rewards the pure in heart. Hannah is thirty when we meet her, a strong, steadfast woman whose strength gives her a sort of dignity, "the dignity of toil." She lives in Croft's Lane, a tumbledown alum alley of a small, south-of-England seacoast town, where she labors patiently on behalf of her oddly assorted family, descended from gypsies and laborers. . . .

Miss Hall has made her sympathetic and credible, but unfortunately, like many good souls, Hannah inclines to be dull. That **"The Sixth Beatitude"** is an entertaining novel is no thanks to its central character. It is the other people in the Lane—dirty, sly, old Granny, the vindictive Mrs. Roach, Jumping-Jimmie, Watercrease-Bill, Father, who needed new teeth, and the rest—who give this story its bite, its fight and its character.

Mrs. Hall is relentlessly determined to be grim. She rattles very loudly the skeletons which wait, ready to leap out, in the closets of the poor.

> *Gwen Leys, in a review of "The Sixth Beatitude," in* New York Herald Tribune Books *(© I.H.T. Corporation; reprinted by permission), April 26, 1936, p. 10.*

MARGARET LAWRENCE   (essay date 1936)

[*In the following examination of* The Well of Loneliness *and* The Master of the House, *Lawrence praises Hall for her role as a priestess of culture—one who pleads the cause of one segment of society to another, more powerful segment.*]

[Though] the artiste may contain the mystic, and though the mystic may be essentially an artiste, there is a motif of reconciliation in the written work of a mystic, and an altered motif of interpretation in the writing of the artiste. The mystic is focused upon life for its meaning. The artiste is focused upon life for its simple being. They may meet and blend in individual cases. It is this possibility of meeting and blending which is baffling to any set division. Yet the separated qualities which do meet and blend can be resolved to their origins in the cause of any tentative catalogue of type. In enclosing a group of the great women writers under the listing of priestesses I have listened for a conciliatory undersound. In all cases they are gently calling the attention of their readers to something they wish to be understood. They are both healing and teaching. In the other writers this sound is so submerged as not to be audible. The difference is almost negligible, yet distinct enough to make it a difference. (p. 318)

Radclyffe Hall is an example of the inability of the public, even of the reading public, to hold more than one idea about one writer. She published *The Well of Loneliness,* and it doomed her to be remembered in her own time only as a student of sexual inversion. All the beauty and power of her prose was, in general, lost in the popular reaction of horror to her theme. The book was banned by opinion terrified by a frank study of abnormality. It refused to consider the book as a valuable document set down in parable form. It does not happen to be a valuable document when considered psychiatrically. It opens with a curious psychiatric error. The writer submits an artistic theory concerning the peculiarity of her heroine. She assumes that a girl child could be born out of the normal sexual plan because of the prenatal influence of her parent's desire for a boy. If this were so, nearly every girl would be born out of the normal sexual plan. . . . For some reason Radclyffe Hall avoided the traumatic shock findings of the psychiatric investigators in relation to the sexual invert, or if she did not avoid it in thought, she could see no way apparently of dramatically presenting shock in the course of her story. The heroine grows up longing to have been a boy, and when she comes to sexual maturity she discovers in herself the normal male's attraction to the female. The tragedy goes on from there.

But she did manage to get over one documentary contribution— that the whole problem of Lesbianism needs to be considered coolly and justly in relation to the present doings of women in the world. (pp. 323-24)

Apart altogether from its psychiatric implications, *The Well of Loneliness* produces an artistic impression which is somewhat similar to the artistic impression of the Greek tragedies. The Greeks accepted inversion in all its variations as being of excellent dramatic substance. The Greeks were able to separate their intellectual curiosity from their instinctive regard for the preservation of the normal, which fact alone makes them stand out in history a superior people. Radclyffe Hall set herself the mission of portraying to the normal the sufferings of the invert in society. She pleads for pity and for understanding. She says that mankind, having only just begun to find the laws relating to sex, may in a relatively short time discover that there are biological accidents producing inversion. Her heroine she presents as a victim for our sympathy. The pity note in the book is pity that goes out to all creatures who are not able, through her theory of biological accident, or through the psychiatric theory of trauma, to partake of normal experience.

There is pity also for the race which, through its terror of the abnormal, punishes the victims, and may thereby lose valuable services in fields that are other than racial. She believes that these people, because of their peculiarity, have something else to do for the race than to continue it. She stresses their acutely sensitized nerves—the nerves that always go with beings of high capacity. She dwells upon the invert's susceptibility to sound. Radclyffe Hall herself writes with mystical sensitivity to tone. Her phrasing shows it. Her words are put down in relation to their sounds set against other sounds. She produces by this means a disturbing emotional effect.

The importance of her fictional comment upon the situation of the invert lies in this—that inasmuch as inversion, by reason of its distortion of nerves, can at least be tentatively held to be a nervous disorder, the invert should not be treated as a pariah, but rather as a person who through no fault of his or her own is suffering from nervous excitement coming from the kinetic response of the whole human fabric to change. It can be drawn from her story that only the highly sensitized members of society take shock acutely enough to be disorganized away from the normal, and that in the long run it is only the highly sensitized members of society who are in the spiritual sense valuable. The race goes on. The normal people see to that. But art and religion and thought and science have always been maintained in the race by the variously abnormal, and meanwhile they suffer tortures through being unable to adjust themselves to normality.

The priestess tone in Radclyffe Hall developed through the tone of the invert. She comments in her story upon the attraction of the invert to religion, and that very comment in itself suggests a world of inquiry concerning the old historic orders of the priestesses and concerning the priestess temperament itself. It may be that the attraction of any young girl to any order of the priesthood, implied or actual, presupposes inversion certainly to the extent of a marked shrinking from normal experience. Radclyffe Hall fulfilled the essentials of her priesthood when she wrote *The Well of Loneliness.* She showed the invert striving to find reconciliation to her fate. She pleaded with the world for understanding and patience and sympathy concerning its inverts. And having fulfilled that mission she has moved deeper into her destiny.

Her latest book, *The Master of the House,* portrays a man so enamored with the Christ that he himself partakes of the earthly experience of the Christ even to the extent of suffering upon a cross during the war. It is a study which goes into the phenomena of the stigmata and the indrawing of the personality regardless of time or place within the very details of the lives of the saints. It is a purely mystical presentation of the idea that what we love, we are. The hero, loving the Christ, becomes step by step a Christ. This is the intangible law behind the symbol of the sacrament.

The Master of the House, like *The Well of Loneliness,* deals with inversion. While the heroine in the one book lives the life of a man within the body of a woman, the man in the other book lives the life of a Christ within the body of a mortal. Neither of them has any concern with normal experience. They should be kept together and read together. They are part of the same mysterious saga. Some process was started which had to be fulfilled in crucifixion. Radclyffe Hall in her studies has come to the edge of something that is not as yet comprehended. She puts her observations into parables because parables suggest rather than proclaim. These things happen, she believes. A woman gets tangled biologically with the being of a man, and maybe also spiritually. She loves women instead of men. A man gets attached spiritually to the being of a Master, and

maybe also biologically. He loves mankind instead of an individual. The woman begins to look like a man. She wears the clothes of a man. She acts like a man. The man begins to look like the Master. He wears in his flesh the marks of the Master's suffering. He takes it upon himself to live in his mortal flesh the life of the Master. Both of them are under some impulse neither they nor anyone else can understand. Yet both are sane; and both in their way are great. The woman was great artistically; the man was great in spirit.

The work of Radclyffe Hall, including these two books and two others which also touch upon the spiritual mystery, *Saturday's Child* and *Adam's Breed,* is serious, profound and beautiful work, in no way doctrinaire, yet thoroughly indoctrinated. Her emotion is still yet deep. She is like a quiet pool of great depth. She is ageless. It is work that might have come out of Greece. It is work that might have come from India. It seems to have nothing to do with the modern Western world and the flair of that world for the nonchalant, the bizarre and the funny. It has nothing to do with Victorian sentiment. It has nothing to do with Elizabethan delight in living; neither has it anything to do with eighteenth-century sophistication; nor yet anything to do with the romance that belongs to all centuries. She is preoccupied with the mysteries, as the priestesses were, and she pities the human race as it passes them by for things that can be added up and multiplied and subtracted and divided. (pp. 327-30)

Margaret Lawrence, ''Priestesses,'' in her The School of Femininity: A Book for and about Women As They Are Interpreted through Feminine Writers of Yesterday and Today, *Frederick A. Stokes Company, 1936 (and reprinted by Kennikat Press, 1966), pp. 311-38.**

CLIFFORD ALLEN   (essay date 1950)

[Allen discusses Hall as a writer of autobiographical works of fiction and offers a fervent defense of The Well of Loneliness.*]*

Radclyffe Hall as a novelist is interesting because it would seem that most of her work is an exploitation of her personal problems rather than the technically superior use of objective factors. Her novels are either autobiographical, as for example *The Well of Loneliness,* or wish-fulfilling. The main characters are taken from her own fantasies and only the minor, less important ones, are drawn from observation of other people.

This woman, for she was a woman in spite of her masculine name, was born in Bournemouth and published five volumes of verse in the years between 1905 and 1915. Then in 1924 she produced her first novel. This was *The Unlit Lamp* and although well reviewed caused little stir at the time. It is the story of a young girl who was born into the narrow, genteel world which Radclyffe Hall must have known so well in Bournemouth: the world of retired civil servants, superannuated army officers, middle-class ladies with a small private income, and so on. The description of the girl in the book might have been drawn from her own mirror, it is so like as to be almost photographic. (p. 185)

It is not difficult to realize that Joan is emotionally abnormal and that she will never settle down happily. The characteristic which one sees in all of Radclyffe Hall's novels, this emotional abnormality which makes the chief characters thresh themselves into misery, is bred from the fact that there is always parental incompatibility. Colonel Ogden, Joan's father, is a stern tyrant and her mother is a timid, fearful woman who cannot stand up to him. This old martinet dies and Joan is left with the responsibility of the weak-willed mother. Although she wishes to escape into a wider world and study medicine she is frustrated by her emotional conflicts—she is tied hopelessly to her mother and Elizabeth, the woman who has been her tutor. (p. 186)

Adam's Breed is the story of a young boy who is illegitimate. His mother, the daughter of English Italians who own a provision shop in Soho, dies when the child is born. He is brought up by the grandparents but his grandmother, Teresa, is hard and unloving towards him because he has caused the death of her beloved daughter. This arouses emotional conflict in his mind and he feels lonely and inferior. He learns that he is illegitimate but never knows who is his father. . . . He dies of neglect and perhaps significantly his body is placed in a stable until burial.

Finally Radclyffe Hall was exposed to the glare of a cruel publicity by her novel, *The Well of Loneliness*. This was subjected to scurrilous attacks from one of those journalists who gain personal notoriety by perpetually discovering something foul to rake up. (pp. 186-87)

It is well now to re-examine this book and see how horrifying it really is after the lapse of twenty years. Firstly, it is apparent that the book is autobiographical. The main character, Stephen, is a girl whose parents wished intensely for a boy and so was given this inappropriate name (perhaps like the author). From the beginning she showed masculine characteristics and it is apparent from the story that the author has made her mold herself upon, or introject, her father. She grows up homosexual as a result and no doubt the process of her development has been drawn a great deal from the author's own experience. This sexual abnormality inevitably leads to trouble. Stephen rejects marriage and so is forced to face the struggle of life as best she can. She serves during the First World War and then manages to form a satisfactory emotional relationship with a younger woman. Finally she relinquishes this girl so that she can marry the man she herself might have wed.

Now, one might ask, how far could such a work ever have been considered obscene? The trouble is, of course, that the word "obscene" is not properly defined in law. Like "infamous conduct in professional respect," "conduct unbecoming to an officer and a gentleman" and similar phrases it really means whatever authority wishes it to mean. (p. 187)

If a book presents abnormality in such a way as to entice the innocent into trying some practice likely to harm them, then that is obscene; if not, if it presents only the truth then it is not obscene to normal minds. If we use this criterion, which is the only sensible one, with regard to a book like Radclyffe Hall's *The Well of Loneliness,* how far is it obscene? Does it describe homosexual practices so that young, pure, innocent girls are likely to feel a longing to try them? It does nothing of the sort. On the contrary it shows the unhappiness, the misery, the long drawn-out search of an abnormal woman to find a modicum of joy. Like all Radclyffe Hall's books it is basically honest. She may have had faults in style, she undoubtedly fell occasionally from the novelist's detachment and indulged in sentimentality with regard to her characters, but on no occasion did she indulge in dishonesty, never did she describe things falsely or cast a gloss over what was real. She never pretended that homosexuality led to other than unhappiness. It was her very honesty which led to her book's being banned.

It is well worth rereading this author's books if only to study her complex psychology. . . . It is mainly owing to Radclyffe Hall's stand that public opinion has accepted a widening of the novelist's range and a less hypocritical attitude has been taken regarding things which everybody knows exist. It is doubtful whether posterity will place her in the first rank but now that she is dead it is easier to put her in true perspective. Her true position is that of an honest writer and not as a purveyor of dirty books. (p. 188)

> *Clifford Allen, "The Personality of Radclyffe Hall" (originally published in* International Journal of Sexology, *Vol. IV, 1950), in* Homosexuality and Creative Genius, *edited by Hendrik M. Ruitenbeek (© copyright 1965 by Astor-Honor, Inc.; reprinted by permission of ASTOR-HONOR, INC., New York, NY 10017), Astor-Honor, 1967, pp. 183-88.*

V. S. PRITCHETT (essay date 1961)

[*Pritchett is highly esteemed for his work as a novelist, short story writer, and critic. He is considered one of the modern masters of the short story, and his work is a subtle blend of realistic detail and psychological revelation. Pritchett is also considered one of the world's most respected and well-read literary critics. He writes in the conversational tone of the familiar essay, a method by which he approaches literature from the viewpoint of a lettered but not overly scholarly reader. A twentieth-century successor to such early nineteenth-century essayist-critics as William Hazlitt and Charles Lamb, Pritchett employs much the same critical method: his own experience, judgement, and sense of literary art, as opposed to a codified critical doctrine derived from a school of psychological or philosophical speculation. His criticism is often described as fair, reliable, and insightful. In the following essay, Pritchett finds Hall to be of more value as a liberator of thought than as an artist.*]

Allowing for its crudities, the sexual revolution has been one of the few blessings in the life of this century. In its beginnings it was loudly Puritan, most drastic when it was most religious, and all the more religious for having got sex out of the meddling hands of the clergy.

The ferocity and absurdity have gone; the residual gain from the sexual revolution has been the extension of human sensibility and understanding. If *The Well* seems now painfully lofty in its archaic style—the constant use of the word 'betoken' tells us all—and unbearably solemn in an enthusiastically *déclassé* way and not even 'modern' in a generation that made an unlucky fetish of 'modernity', it did awaken the sympathetic reader to the emotional perplexities of the invert's life. Society dresses up its sexual morality in clichés. At least Miss Hall cut some of that creeper away. In doing so she occasionally cut more than was good for her case:

> All things they would be the one to the other,
> should they stand in that limitless relationship:
> father, mother, friend and lover, all things—
> the amazing completeness of it; and Mary, the
> child, the friend, the beloved.

The invert is emotionally ambitious. The writer has just complained of the selfishness, arrogance and possessiveness of men in the heterosexual relationship! It looks as though Genet is right: the cult of sex isolated from the rest of life becomes the cult of dominance and power: one is the crushed, the other the crusher. Miss Hall was honest enough to end her book on the note of defeat and the cry for help and pity, but her sense of the Cause and Crusade made her fatally humourless as a novelist. (p. 925)

V. S. Pritchett, "Lesbos Unbound," in New Statesman *(© 1961 The Statesman & Nation Publishing Co. Ltd.), Vol. LXII, No. 1605, December 15, 1961, pp. 925-26.**

MARGHANITA LASKI   (essay date 1968)

[In the excerpt below, Laski, an English critic, novelist, and biographer, calls The Well of Loneliness *"a nauseating novel," adding that "the book reeks with self-pity, and the style has the worse faults of its period."]*

In 1928, after James Douglas's broadside in the *Sunday Express* where he declared he would sooner give a healthy boy or girl a phial of prussic acid than *The Well of Loneliness,* the book was prosecuted under the Obscene Publications Act. Under the law as it then stood, the magistrate was justified in refusing to hear any of the defence witnesses. The book was ordered to be destroyed, and, on Appeal, the verdict was upheld. The following year, a case against the book was brought in New York, but there the charge was quashed.

Since that time the book has, of course, like other 'banned' books, been easily available to anyone who badly wanted it, but except as 'The classic novel of lesbian love', which is how Corgi describes its paperback edition, few people could have done so. It is a nauseating novel. Una Troubridge, Radclyffe Hall's most permanent lover, has explained that 'John', as she was called, decided to write the book 'on behalf of a misunderstood and misjudged minority', a motive for novel-writing that has seldom proved valuably fructifying. In fact, as a plea for sympathy, the book is less effective than Graham Greene's throwaway vignette of the lesbian journalist in *Stamboul Train.* What *The Well of Loneliness* turned out to be was a kind of lesbian's *Sheik.* . . .

The book reeks with self-pity, and the style has the worst faults of its period: for instance, the climactic sentence of a book which, like *Fanny Hill* (but alas, like it in no other way) never uses a dirty word: 'Stephen bent down and kissed Mary's hands very humbly, for now she could find no words any more . . . and that night they were not divided.' Nothing but dangerously undiscriminating compassion or prurience could justify the republication of this bad, embarrassing novel. (p. 322)

Marghanita Laski, "Ghetto Press," in New Statesman *(© 1968 The Statesman & Nation Publishing Co. Ltd.), Vol. 76, No. 1957, September 13, 1968, pp. 321-22.**

JANE RULE   (essay date 1975)

[Rule, American novelist, critic, and civil libertarian, calls Hall a courageous woman. In the excerpt below, taken from her Lesbian Images, *Rule finds the importance of* The Well of Loneliness *in the revelation of "the honest misconceptions about women's nature and experience." Nonetheless, Rule concludes that Hall's novel, often referred to as the "lesbian bible," is "really no better for women than the* Bible *she would not reject."]*

The Well of Loneliness by Radclyffe Hall, published in 1928, remains *the* lesbian novel, a title familiar to most readers of fiction, either a bible or a horror story for any lesbian who reads at all. There have been other books published since, better written, more accurate according to recent moral and psycho-

logical speculation, but none of them has seriously challenged the position of *The Well of Loneliness*. Often a book finds momentary identity only by negative comparison with that "noble, tragic tract about the love that cannot speak its name." Along with the teachings of the church and the moral translations of those teachings by psychologists, *The Well of Loneliness* has influenced millions of readers in their attitudes toward lesbians.

Radclyffe Hall's intention was to write a sympathetic and accurate book about inversion. She was already a novelist and poet of some reputation, and, if she had neither the craft nor the power of insight of her contemporary D. H. Lawrence, she shared his zeal for educating the public. . . . *The Well of Loneliness* was . . . not only a novel intended to give insight into the experience of inverts but also to justify Radclyffe Hall's own life. She must have been the more pressed to defend the innocence of her nature because she was a Catholic, apparently thoughtfully and deeply committed to most of the doctrines of the Church. . . . There is no final evidence for how she reconciled her sexual life with her faith. There is only the testimony of those closest to her that she had resolved the conflict for herself. (pp. 50-1)

Though Stephen Gordon, the main character in *The Well of Loneliness,* shares few of Radclyffe Hall's own experiences, she is Radclyffe Hall's idealized mirror. Both recognized from childhood their essential difference from other females. Both had early emotional ties with female servants. Both were fine horsewomen and successful writers. Neither had any erotic interest in men. Both affected the same masculine style and manners. But Radclyffe Hall gave Stephen basic securities she herself lacked, a father who loved and understood her, a childhood on a fine estate, good health, and a sound education. Stephen was also very tall, a mark of masculine power and beauty Radclyffe Hall probably envied, though it is said of her that she always gave the impression of being a good deal taller than she was. Of all the good fortunes they did not share, Stephen's opportunity to serve England in the war was in Radclyffe Hall's eyes the greatest because she was a patriot and did not indulge in the political sophistication and skepticism of other more intelligent and subtle minds of her generation. Yet the one great blessing of Radclyffe Hall's own life, the faithful love of both Mabel Batten and Una Troubridge, she did not allow Stephen, who is required to give up the woman she loves to a man who can provide the protection and social acceptance Stephen can never offer. Stephen's final selfless gesture is undoubtedly calculated to strengthen reader sympathy, to allay moral doubts, and to deepen the tragedy of inversion. But for Radclyffe Hall herself, neither God nor man could interfere with her sexual life. She was not of a temperament for such a sacrifice.

A canny propagandist in plotting an unhappy ending, Radclyffe Hall also worked hard to provide a background of psychological information, intended to deepen understanding and acceptance for her main character. The books of both Karl Heinrich Ulrichs and Krafft-Ebing are in Mr. Gordon's library, and it is from them that he learns to understand and help his only and beloved child. Ulrichs not only argues that inversion is congenital and natural, but also that legal and social recognition should be given such sexual love, permission to marry granted to people of the same sex. Krafft-Ebing, taking issue with Ulrichs, grants that some inversion is congenital but insists that the cause is pathological rather than physiological, traceable in every case to inherited degeneracy. . . . It is clear that, though Radclyffe

Hall took a great deal of information from Krafft-Ebing, she is on Ulrichs' side of the argument.

Stephen must be established as a congenital invert to escape Krafft-Ebing's moral condemnation. There is no sign of insanity in Stephen's family history. The only causes of inversion are obviously physiological. Stephen is broad-shouldered, slim-hipped, unusually tall, with a striking resemblance to her father. That she is not unique is carefully underlined in the physical descriptions of a group of inverts she meets in Paris. "One had to look twice to discern that her ankles were too strong and too heavy for those of a female." Or "one might have said a quite womanly woman, unless the trained ear had been rendered suspicious by her voice . . . a boy's voice on the verge of breaking." Not trusting the reader to take this evidence alone, Radclyffe Hall makes general assertions about inverts, calling them "those who, through no fault of their own, have been set apart from the day of their birth." Or she lets Stephen's tutor, a repressed invert herself, say to Stephen, "You're neither unnatural, nor abominable, nor mad; you're as much a part of what people call nature as anyone else; only you're unexplained as yet—you've not got your niche in creation." Stephen is described as "like some primitive thing conceived in a turbulent age of transition." Stephen's father wanted a son, then christened his female child Stephen, but these facts are offered not so much as suggestive of conditioning as some deep insight of his own into the real nature of his child.

Society's attitude toward the invert is presented by Stephen's mother, who is from the first offended and repelled by a child she does not understand. She objects to her husband's desire to raise Stephen as if she were a boy, but he, in what is presented as his real wisdom, overrules her. Stephen is allowed to ride horseback astride. She is encouraged in masculine virtues. Her father says, "And now I'm going to treat you like a boy, and a boy must always be brave. I'm not going to pretend as though you were a coward." Later, when he feels her education is being neglected, he says, "You're brave and strong-limbed, but I want you to be wise." In giving Stephen so unusually supportive a father, Radclyffe Hall is insisting that the accepted invert grows into a fine, moral person who can survive even the rejection of a mother. After her father's death, her mother discovers Stephen in an affair with a married woman in the neighborhood. "And this thing that you are is a sin against nature." How accurately Radclyffe Hall anticipated the attitude of many of the critics when the book appeared, who would have liked to drive her into silence as Stephen is forced to leave her home, which has meant so much to her, able to take only her loyal and understanding tutor with her.

The husband of the woman Stephen so unwisely loved is given speeches like, "How's your freak getting on? . . . Good Lord, it's enough to make any man see red; that sort of thing wants putting down at birth, I'd like to institute state lethal chambers." But his viciousness is seen as part of his general incapacity as a man.

Men, in *The Well of Loneliness*, are capable of the highest courage and insight. Stephen's father is "all kindness, all strength, all understanding." Martin, the young man who befriends Stephen and then unfortunately falls in love with her, has "a man's life, good with the goodness of danger, a primitive, strong, imperative thing." In him Stephen feels she has found a brother. "He spoke simply, as one man will speak to another, very simply, not trying to create an impression." And Stephen has "longed for the companionship of men, for their friendship, their good will, their understanding." When Stephen rejects Martin, she unwittingly rejects the tentative acceptance of the community which has developed during the period of their friendship. "He it was who had raised her status among them—he, the stranger, not even connected with their country. . . . Suddenly Stephen longed intensely to be welcomed and she wished in her heart that she could have married Martin." Years later, when he appears again in Stephen's life and falls in love with Mary, the young woman Stephen herself loves and lives with, Stephen recognizes his superior power, as a man, to protect Mary. "I cannot protect you, Mary, the world has deprived me of my right to protect; I am utterly helpless, I can only love you." Her father has taught her all the male virtues, "courage and truth and honor," and she rejects their vices, "Men—they were selfish, arrogant, possessive," perhaps as much because she has no social right to them as because she finds them morally repugnant. Without those vices, she has no choice but to become a martyr to her love.

Though Stephen cannot claim social equality with men, in some ways she sees herself as superior to them, not only in rejecting their vices but in having the curious virtues of ambivalent sex. "She seemed to combine the strength of a man with the gentler and more subtle strength of a woman." "Those whom nature has sacrificed to her own ends—her mysterious ends which sometimes lie hidden—are sometimes endowed with a vast will to loving, with an endless capacity for suffering also." "But the intuition of those who stand midway between the two sexes is so ruthless, so poignant, so accurate, so deadly as to be in the nature of an added scourge." Echoing Krafft-Ebing, Radclyffe Hall claims also for the congenital invert remarkable intelligence, great passion, and intense religious feeling. Stephen was born on Christmas Eve. Radclyffe Hall followed *The Well of Loneliness* with a novel about a contemporary Christ with whom she felt it easy to identify after her own social crucifixion. During the writing of it, stigmata appeared on the palms of her own hands.

Neither she nor Stephen ever identifies with other women. Stephen's first love, Collins, the second maid, is a stupid, dishonest creature whom the child, Stephen, can forgive anything "since despising, she could still love her." "I'd like to be hurt for you, Collins, the way that Jesus was for sinners." Stephen's mother is loved by her father because she is restful, beautiful, passive. Stephen's own effort to make a relationship with her mother is protective and courtly. Stephen's tutor is made a sad example of. "She was what came from higher education—a lonely, unfulfilled middle-aged spinster." When Stephen first falls seriously in love with a married woman, Angela is described as "idle, discontented, and bored and certainly not overburdened with virtue." She "listened, assuming an interest she was very far from feeling." Mary, the lover for whom Stephen sacrifices her own happiness, "because she was perfect woman, would rest without thought, without exultation, without question, finding no need to question since for her there was now only one thing—Stephen." "Mary, all woman, was less a match for life than if she had been as was Stephen." Devoted to Stephen, subservient, with all wifely virtues, she cannot stand the social isolation of her life with Stephen, would have grown bitter at the judgments Stephen has the strength to rise above, for she has no work of her own as Stephen does, no identity of her own. She is simply a woman.

Occasionally Stephen does crave to be normal. "While despising these girls, she yet longed to be like them," but these are only moments of despair when she feels rejected in the company of men who have a preference for "killing ivy." Much more often, she longs to be a man, to take her natural and superior place among those of the sex she admires. Radclyffe Hall even asserts that Stephen "found her manhood," though always she knows that, trapped in a female body, she is a freak, and in the final contest between Stephen and Martin, even the dog can tell that Martin is the true man. Stephen has nothing left now but her work. "She must show that being the thing that she was, she could climb to success over all opposition," but she will go on being plagued by the doubt, "I shall never be a great writer because of my maimed and insufferable body." (pp. 54-9)

On the sexual market, it is still better to be narrower-shouldered, broader-hipped, and shorter than Stephen, but those "defects" would not convince anyone that a woman is a born invert. And though intelligent women are still a threat to some men, no one would see in intelligence a signal for diagnosing inversion. As for the freedom of behavior Stephen craved, there isn't a woman today who doesn't prefer trousers and pockets for many activities, and only the Queen of England still occasionally appears in public riding sidesaddle. If few women have desired a masculine name in private, a great many have used male pseudonyms in order to win honor for their work in public. (p. 59)

Obviously Radclyffe Hall so accepted that very teaching of her class and time she could not imagine a woman who wanted the privilege and power of men unless she was a freak.

Though *The Well of Loneliness* was viciously attacked for its sympathetic idealizing of the invert, giving it greater importance at the time than it deserved, its survival as the single authoritative novel on lesbian love depends on its misconceptions. It supports the view that men are naturally superior, that, given a choice, any woman would prefer a real man unless she herself is a congenital freak. Though inept and feminine men are criticized, though some are seen to abuse the power they have, their right to that power is never questioned. Stephen does not defy the social structure she was born into. Male domination is intolerable to her only when she can't assert it for herself. Women are inferior. Loving relationships must be between superior and inferior persons. Stephen's sexual rejection of Martin, though it is offered as conclusive proof of her irreversible inversion, is basically a rejection of being the inferior partner in a relationship. Her reaction is one of "repulsion—terror and repulsion . . . a look of outrage." In her relationship with Mary, Stephen is "all things to Mary; father, mother, friend and lover, all things, and Mary is all things to her—the child, the friend, the beloved, all things." The repetition of "all things" is not persuasive enough to cover the inequality of the categories. When Stephen decides not to fight for Mary, she gives her to Martin much as one would give any other thing one owns. And though her altruism is sometimes associated with her female gender, it is more often likened to the virtues of Christ. It is courageous or foolhardy for a woman to behave like a man, but, since she accepts herself as a freak, since in fiction if not in life she is made to give up the ultimate prize, she is no political threat to anyone. The natural order of things is reasserted, and she is left on the outside, calling to God and to society for recognition. (p. 60)

Radclyffe Hall was a courageous woman, and *The Well of Loneliness* is an important book because it does so carefully reveal the honest misconceptions about women's nature and experience which have limited and crippled so many people.

Radclyffe Hall did think of herself as a freak, but emotionally and intellectually she was far more a "womanly woman" than many of her literary contemporaries. She worshiped the very institutions which oppressed her, the Church and the patriarchy, which have taught women there are only two choices, inferiority or perversion. Inside that framework, she made and tried to redefine the only proud choice she had. The "bible" she offered is really no better for women than the Bible she would not reject. (p. 61)

> *Jane Rule, "Radclyffe Hall," in her* Lesbian Images *(copyright © 1975 by Jane Rule; reprinted by permission of Doubleday & Company, Inc.), Doubleday, 1975, pp. 50-61.*

LOVAT DICKSON   (essay date 1975)

[Dickson, an English biographer and autobiographer, makes extensive use of letters, written to and by Hall, as well as personal reminiscences of friends and acquaintances, in her biographical and critical work Radclyffe Hall at the Well of Loneliness: A Sapphic Chronicle, *from which the following excerpt is taken.]*

[Homosexuality] has now become an open subject freely discussed, and is no longer something to snigger over, or condemn as criminal. For that enlightened attitude, books among other causes have to be thanked. It was Radclyffe Hall's urgent desire to have the subject dragged into the open light of day that made her write *The Well of Loneliness*. It isn't a great literary work, but it is a book of importance in the history of the unending struggle with censorship. It was the stone that loosened the avalanche. (p. 21)

The Well of Loneliness does not set out to glorify the joys of deviant sex, and legitimacy wins out all along the line. In the end, Stephen sacrifices her Mary to Martin, and Stephen Gordon is left alone, crying out to God 'Give us also the right to our existence'.

The answer was then an outraged 'No' from authority. Nearly fifty years after the trial which condemned *The Well of Loneliness*, we would seem to have reached the goal at which she aimed. But Radclyffe Hall asked for sympathy and understanding, not for indifference, which is all we have brought ourselves so far to offer. (p. 23)

The frustrated emotions stirring within [Radclyffe Hall] drove her to fierce exercise and to poetry, which was meant no more at first than to provide the words for songs she wanted to compose at the piano. By 1907 she had enough of these poems collected to make a small volume ['*Twixt Earth and Stars*]. (p. 36)

The poems in this first volume are not remarkable for the originality of their subjects or the depth of their thought, but they do have a musical quality which attracted the song-writers of the time, ever on the look-out for lyrics to satisfy the incessant demand for songs for the piano. No less than twenty-one of the poems in this little volume were set to music before the end of the year by Mr Hubert Bath, Mr Cuthbert Wynne and Mr Easthope Martin, all well-known composers of accompaniments for songs. . . . (pp. 36-7)

What gives this little collection a touch of its own is the sequence which closes it called '**A Sea Cycle**'. These sixteen poems describe the beginning and end of a love-affair on a sea voyage. The poetry romps. The language is rhetorical, Swinburnian in emphasis and ardour, but curiously false to our ears. That is not the way contemporary lovers talk. . . .

We can hardly bear it. And yet, reading these sixteen poems at a gulp, one has the impression that the emotions described in this fantastic language were actually felt and that the parting was pain. If not a poet there is someone here who feels deeply, memorializing a rapture that has fled. (p. 37)

A Sheaf Of Verses . . . shows a considerable advance in technique over the first book, and is more interesting to anyone who knows about the author for its now often quite explicit description of lesbian love. The conventions had not changed so much as the author had done. Ladye [Mabel Batten] had drawn her out, pulled her from behind the poetic diction which had covered her shyness and uncertainty in the first book. There are still dewdrops and rosebuds; breezes are still tender. But now for the first time Sapphic love is celebrated . . . and for the first time, with increasing confidence and power, the passion of those first years of their association is struck for all to hear. . . . (pp. 40-1)

A still further collection, *Poems of The Past and Present,* was ready in 1910, and this time it was issued by a publishing firm . . . at their own risk. Here the assurance has grown marked, the variety of the metre is exhilarating, the images no longer conventional and stiff. The love poems are even more explicit, in some cases openly revealing to their friends who knew where they had been, for they were travelling much at this period. A pleasing note of detached irony gives both a lightness and a new depth to the verse. (p. 41)

The nispero tree, with its fruit gleaming gold from afar but bitter to the taste, is taken as a symbol of lesbian love. The wounded cries of the lovers at the barrenness which is the inevitable end of their passion is echoed again and again. . . .

Three years were to pass before in 1913 she had yet another collection ready for publication. *Songs of Three Counties* was the title she chose for the book. . . . She was by now becoming something of a figure, for her songs were being taken up by well-known concert singers in France and Germany as well as England, and were being reprinted profitably as sheet-music. . . . And now Robert Coningsby Clarke, Coleridge Taylor and Liza Lehmann set these poems to music.

The new volume was more deliberately rustic in note, and suggests the influence of A. E. Housman's *A Shropshire Lad.* This is perhaps because it commences with a series called **'Rustic Country'**, and ends with one of her most accomplished lyrics, **'The Blind Ploughman'.** (p. 42)

A religious note has entered her poetry. Ladye had been born a Catholic, and John [Radclyffe Hall's nickname] had recently been received into the Catholic Church, and much of the verse in this volume reflects not only the lover of earth but the lover of a God newly found. (p. 43)

From Swinburne's influence through Housman's; to that of Bridges' perhaps, with her next book, *The Forgotten Island:* this seems to be the chart of her course. No, not Bridges, except for the classical allusions, but the author of the *Indian Love Lyrics* which were the rage of 1913, and which, put to music, throbbed forth from the open windows of English homes all through that summer before the outbreak of war. *The Forgotten Island* was to have appeared in the autumn of 1914, but delayed by the war, it did not come out until 1915. From this point on she was to turn to prose, encouraged to do so by Ladye who perhaps was sensitive to the autobiographical element which could not be kept out of so individual a poet's celebrations of love.

John had already turned her hand to short stories. . . . (pp. 43-4)

The Unlit Lamp [is] the story of Joan Ogden—and of the struggle between her mother and her woman tutor, Elizabeth Rodney, for her body and her mind. (p. 109)

It is by the standards of the time a good first novel, conveying with noticeable skill for a beginner subtleties in human relationships that could only have been observed by someone of acute sympathies. For what we see here is an early demonstration of an attitude on the author's part towards sexual relationships between women. *The Unlit Lamp* is in fact an experimental run of the theme of *The Well of Loneliness.* . . .

It had taken two years to write *The Unlit Lamp,* and another two to find a publisher for it. It took only five months to write *The Forge,* and it was accepted by the first publisher who saw it. *The Unlit Lamp* had reflected the author's deepest interest. *The Forge* is a quite skilfully-presented social comedy, pointing a moral. It only *pretends* to be serious. (p. 110)

[At a dinner-party one evening, John told May Sinclair and Rebecca West] of an obsequious waiter she had seen that day at a restaurant, busy at his task of keeping the customers at his group of tables satisfied. She said 'I would like to write a novel about the life of a waiter who becomes so sick of food that he allows himself nearly to die of starvation'. . . . The novel which, when she started it, she had meant to call *Food,* [became] the story of a simple man in search of God: it was called *Adam's Breed.* (p. 114)

Adam's Breed belongs unmistakably to the period in which it was written. One could hardly conceive a book with this theme becoming today the instantaneous success that it was on publication. (p. 115)

Radclyffe Hall did genuinely believe that she was now in a position to help her fellow-sufferers by presenting their plight sympathetically in a novel. But she was wrong in thinking that only an invert could write truthfully about the suffering of inverts. It was to be the attempt to treat the abnormal as normal that was so to shock authority when the book was published. Far from helping her fellow-sufferers, her action was temporarily to stiffen opposition and close the ranks against the oppressed minority whom it had been her aim to help. (pp. 125-26)

It is only in these present times that it has become the habit to boast of obscure beginnings and early hardships. Fifty years ago when the author of *The Well of Loneliness* set out to tell her own story, the Victorian romantic idea still dominated the novel, and it was no more than natural for the novelist to claim for the Gordons of Bramley greater prominence than had ever been known by the Radclyffe-Halls, who had descended by way of clergymen, private tutors and doctors. . . .

The background to *The Well of Loneliness* at least is authentic. Sir Philip Gordon's large estate, not very far from Upton-on-Severn, is in the district where Radclyffe Hall had her hunting box. This was the country over which she had hunted, and about which she had written with such feeling in *Songs of Three Counties.* She knew it as well as if she had been born there, and as love of the land was to play a large part in the story, the childhood chapters are important in bringing us to a sympathetic understanding of Stephen Gordon's warped nature and her strange upbringing. (p. 128)

When Stephen has her first childhood 'pashes', they are directed towards women. She falls in love, not with one of the grooms but one of the housemaids, Collins. The silly girl responds instinctively, kisses her, and is unconsciously attracted to the child. Stephen becomes passionately attached to Collins, but one day, glimpsing her in the arms of one of the footmen, a blind rage seizes her, and she throws a broken flowerpot and cuts the man's face open; then runs sobbing to her father bewildered and frightened. These and other incidents are taken straight from the young life of Marguerite Radclyffe Hall. . . .

John had always been a compulsive novel reader, and it was natural for her to invent the sort of background common to so many of the late Victorian and Edwardian novels she had read as a child and a young woman. Her own absent father whom she did not meet until she was fifteen, and saw again only on his deathbed, whose wealth provided everything by which she and the Visettis lived, was invested with the pitying, understanding love, not to mention the title, which were Sir Philip Gordon's; and her mother, there before her eyes every day, a bad-tempered, unsympathetic, spoilt and silly woman . . . living with the equally silly Alberto Visetti, was elevated to the position of wife to Sir Philip and hard, unsympathetic mother to Stephen Gordon. (p. 129)

In 1914 the war comes. Stephen joins the Breakspear Unit—a Unit of Englishwomen attached to the French Army Ambulance Corps, and here she meets Mary Hamilton. When armistice comes she returns to the house in Paris, taking Mary Hamilton with her. For some weeks Stephen makes no physical advances to Mary. A sense of honour stops her, even though the girl makes no secret of her desire for it; and the strain on both of them is intense. Although the language in which this protracted restraint is presented is novelettish, the sense of strain is vividly conveyed, and the reader sees some of the handicaps of perversion. (p. 132)

But *The Well of Loneliness* is not just a cry of pain from the deprived abnormal, asking only to be understood; it tells the truth of what abnormal love is like, the dry aftertaste of passionate love when it cannot create, when it is sterile. (p. 133)

The ignominious rejection of her book by authority seemed to [Radclyffe Hall] proof that compassion had gone out of the world. She began to think of a character in a setting such as this who might possess that ancient virtue, and whose life and death might reawaken the world to what it had lost. (pp. 187-88)

[In *The Master of the House* the] very name of the family, the Bénédits, suggests the close analogy she wanted to draw with the Holy Family. Christophe is to be the boy who grows up into the modern suffering figure. His father is the carpenter Jousé, his mother Marie, his young friend and cousin Jan, who is to be the modern John the Baptist. Her story as she designed it was to begin in Provence and end in Palestine during the First World War when Christophe and Jan, taking part in the campaign to liberate the Holy Land from the Turks, are sent out on night patrol, and Christophe meets his end, retreading Christ's way to Calvary.

There is nothing intrinsically wrong imaginatively, and nothing scientifically unacceptable, in assuming that a simple peasant's son in Provence might be on a plane in time with a spirit who had lived terrestrially two thousand years earlier in a similar family and in similar circumstances. We now accept that time is relative, and although our views on what happens when the body and the soul part company at death differ widely, at least

the Christian view is that the soul lives on. . . . That sense of the continuity of the soul would justify the conception of a powerful psyche continuing to vibrate, and someone now living might be tuned in on those vibrations. He who had been the carpenter's son in Nazareth two thousand years before might strike responsive chords in the carpenter's son in Provence. On that assumption the story of *The Master of the House* is based.

The trouble with such a theme is literary acceptance, not intellectual approval of a possible scientific phenomenon. Modernizing Christ's life diminishes the glory and the brightness that myth has attached to it. (pp. 188-89)

Radclyffe Hall catches the simplicity and innocence of her Christophe, but these are the marks of any lonely child's life. There is an attempt to lighten the solemnity with 'the introduction of a mischievous younger brother to Christophe, and a drunken old fisherman, and a designing widow looking for a husband, all of whom play important parts in the plot. But their presence and their actions do not make up for the excessive weight that must be given to Christophe's holiness if the link with another carpenter's Son is to be made credible, and if the end of the story, repeating the pattern of Christ's sacrifice, is to be accepted as showing what compassion can do to help in a world dedicated to self-destruction. (p. 190)

One sees, looking at it from this distance, that the book in fact fails through over-earnestness, a mood antipathic to the time in the early thirties when it was published. (p. 194)

> *Lovat Dickson, in his* Radclyffe Hall at the Well of
> Loneliness: A Sapphic Chronicle *(© Lovat Dickson
> 1975; reprinted with permission of Lovat Dickson),
> Charles Scribner's Sons, 1975, 236 p.*

A.O.J. COCKSHUT   (essay date 1977)

[*Cockshut, an English critic and literary essayist, calls* The Well of Loneliness *a landmark novel in which the lesbian world is viewed from within. Cockshut argues that while the decency trial generated by the novel may be viewed in terms of the changeability of social mores, there are more important implications when that trial is viewed as a restatement of the period delusion that "everyone could be good without really trying, and everything inevitably improved all the time."*]

With *The Well of Loneliness* . . . , we enter for the first time a world directly corresponding to that created by the male homosexual writers . . . , the lesbian world seen from within. It is not surprising that the book has something of the air of a propaganda piece. Radclyffe Hall had already published several books, in which no direct lesbian hint had been given. (p. 204)

The plot is well-drawn to give the main lines of the problem. We have the incurably masculine heroine, Stephen; the old woman, acting as nurse, who has a chaste devotion to her, and sad memories of her youth and the world's condemnation; the beloved, who is married and not really lesbian in temperament, but in search of glamour and excitement; and finally there is the young girl of unformed and indeterminate sexual temperament, attracted by the masculine style of heroine, now in uniform and doing war-work. In the background there is a mother who fiercely rejects her, and a father who tenderly fears that his wish for a son has been ironically answered, since he guesses his daughter's nature and probable destiny.

The first love, the married Angela, soon takes fright and retreats to her husband, blaming all her own vagaries on Stephen. (pp. 204-05)

Here the married Angela is treated as a coward, a slave of convention, a rejector of life and freedom for returning to her husband.

Yet it is doubtful whether, after all, that is quite what the book as a whole is saying. The masculine idea of the lesbian prison is not exclusive to the male writers; it is found in a different form here. In fact, there are two lesbian prisons in Radclyffe Hall's world; there is the prison of the tortured lesbian's own heart and the prison of the world's misunderstanding and contempt. The book's ambiguity, its failure, despite all its rhetoric and emotion, to make a clear impression on us, is due to a failure to be sure where one prison ends and the other begins. At times the author writes as if the lesbian problem was created entirely by an uncomprehending world. The condition and the life to which it leads are natural, if only people could see and admit this. But at other times, the condition appears as a curse that cannot be understood. There is a religious current in the book (Catholic in its tendency) and here too we meet the same ambiguity. Can the condition be somehow reconciled with God's laws, so that lesbians can live innocently before God? Or is some great renunciation more painful and more complete than any achieved by heterosexuals, positively demanded of them?

All these painful ambiguities are seen in the second lesbian encounter. Stephen is now thirty-two, and has still not experienced lesbian passion in full physical form. Mary, her girlish young friend, is willing to give herself completely. . . .

> Stephen bent down and kissed Mary's hands very humbly, for now she could find no words any more . . . and that night they were not divided.

The last four words are perhaps the most significant and the most enigmatic in the whole book. The phrasing is biblical, and there is a reminiscence of David's lament over Saul and Jonathan. It is perhaps unlikely that Radclyffe Hall (in no way a subtle artist), considered deeply the precise nature of the allusion made. A passage which refers to death, and to dying together as a kind of fulfilment, is transposed into a sexual union. Was there a deliberate or an unconscious reference to the powerful old pun, which treats sexual union as the 'little death'? Or is the connection merely accidental? Since the biblical passage alluded to is a lament over the dead, does the use of it here carry menace of death, or of separation and disaster which will be the death of love? It is hard, perhaps impossible to say. But one thing is clear. The biblical phrase spreads a veil of traditional dignity; it saves the necessity either for a detailed physical description or for an embarrassing vulgar euphemism. The act which was immoral according to traditional moral principles, and obscene, unnatural and disgusting in the eyes of the workaday world, has been endowed with another traditional sanctity. It is a sanctity of literary style as well as of religion.

The opening words of the next chapter tell us that to both the act seemed 'natural' and 'fine'. But again, this reads more as defiant assertion under the influence of the senses than as something which can really be believed and lived out by the protagonists. And if the protagonists have doubts, inevitably author and reader will have stronger ones.

The book ends with a renunciation. The man who loves and wishes to marry Mary comes to Stephen and confesses that she has defeated him. Mary is hers, and he will go away. Stephen then invents a lying tale of her own infidelity in order to force Mary to leave her, and go off with the man for ever, which she does. What does this mean? Does it mean that Stephen at last, fortified by prayer, perceives the sinfulness of the life they are leading, and renounces it, and thus leads Mary to renounce it too? Or does it mean that she senses that Mary is not strong enough to go on for ever outfacing public opinion? Or that she realizes that Mary is really heterosexual in temperament? Or is it rather an act asserting a strong moral claim? Is the author showing a woman of unalterably lesbian temperament making the greatest sacrifice of all; and proving thus that lesbians also are capable of the highest moral attainments which the world reveres, and of which only a few, of whatever sex or temperament, are ever capable?

Again it is hard to say, but the last alternative seems nearest the mark. If we select it, we read the ending as a brave statement that no inborn abnormality can take away from a human being the possibility of moral greatness. Its importance as a statement, almost a manifesto, possesses moral importance far in excess of its rather dubious literary merits. Radclyffe Hall, in her own overlush and perhaps embarrassing way, is reasserting an ancient doctrine that the respectable English world had forgotten, denied or despised. It is the doctrine stated in the words of her contemporary Von Hügel thus:

> It is simply of faith that every human being is provided by God with graces sufficient for salvation.

From this point of view the storm of protest and controversy that the book raised has a line of symbolic value. The England of 1928 believed, on the whole, in the words of T. S. Eliot . . . 'that if one was thrifty, enterprising, intelligent and prudent in not violating social conventions, one ought to have a happy and successful life'. This belief is, of course, a manifest delusion, and it is a delusion which people will fight with all their strength to retain. Seen in this light, the controversy over *The Well of Loneliness* has an interest much wider and more lasting than at first sight appears. If it is seen as a mere argument over 'decency', it is quickly dated. Standards of decency are always changing, and cannot be convincingly linked with any fundamental moral principle. If it is seen as an episode in the decline of the facile humanistic optimism of a nation favoured by sea power, coal, iron and empire to believe that everyone could be good without really trying, and everything inevitably improved all the time, it has much more than a period interest. (pp. 205-08)

A.O.J. Cockshut, "The Lesbian Theme," in his Man and Woman: A Study of Love and the Novel 1740-1940 *(copyright © 1977 by A.O.J. Cockshut; reprinted by permission of Oxford University Press, Inc.; in Canada by William Collins Sons & Co., Ltd.), Collins, 1977 (and reprinted by Oxford University Press, New York, 1978), pp. 186-208.**

STEPHEN BROOK (essay date 1981)

[*Brook favorably discusses* The Unlit Lamp.]

Radclyffe Hall is best known for *The Well of Loneliness,* a Lesbian novel banned for obscenity in 1928. Unlike Joyce and Lawrence, her reputation gained no lustre from the prosecution and she remains a dim figure, excluded from literary recognition. That this obscurity is undeserved is established by this re-issue of her first novel, **The Unlit Lamp**. . . . It concerns the struggle for Joan Ogden, born into a shabby, genteel army family, waged by her mother and her governess, later friend, Elizabeth Rodney.

Elizabeth is a bluestocking, austere but devoted to her gifted pupil. Mrs Ogden, on the other hand, is weak and self-pitying, and uses her vulnerability to manipulate her daughter. Joan and Elizabeth make repeated plans to leave the dreary seaside town where they live and set up house together in London to pursue a medical career. Each time the plans are thwarted, either by financial difficulties or by Mrs Ogden's psychological warfare. The mother is no ogre, which is why the portrait is so brilliant. Her manipulations are only half conscious: 'Her mother's very devotion was a weapon turned ruthlessly against her daughter, capable of robbing her of all peace of mind.' . . .

Bitter writing, but complex too; for the achievement of **The Unlit Lamp** is that no one is let off lightly. (p. 21)

Perhaps the vision is too desolate, but there's no denying the passion of the writing, and the subtlety of feeling. It is not just sexual convention that defeats Joan and long-suffering Elizabeth, but small-town snobbery, misplaced loyalty, and financial hardship. **The Well of Loneliness** may be polemic, but the less sensational **The Unlit Lamp** is a powerful and detailed portrayal not just of Lesbian love, but of how the emotional needs of three flawed women are finally irreconcilable. (pp. 21-2)

Stephen Brook, "Three Women," in The Spectator *(© 1981 by* The Spectator; *reprinted by permission of* The Spectator*), Vol. 246, No. 7961, February 7, 1981, pp. 21-3.**

ADDITIONAL BIBLIOGRAPHY

Brittain, Vera. *Radclyffe Hall: A Case of Obscenity?* New York: A. S. Barnes and Co., 1969, 185 p.

> Recounts the obscenity trial of *The Well of Loneliness*. Of Hall's controversial book Brittain writes: "I am still impressed by its passionate honesty and the author's courage in presenting her case to a hostile and intolerant public. I still feel that she had a real appreciation of beauty, shown especially in her vivid small vignettes of country scenes and that her quality of compassion was quite exceptional."

Troubridge, Lady Una (Vincenzo). *The Life of Radclyffe Hall.* New York: Arno Press, 1975, 189 p.

> Personal reminiscences. Hall's constant companion for nearly thirty years, Troubridge provides biographical details with affectionately biased criticism.

Marie (Adelaide) Belloc Lowndes

1868-1947

(Also wrote under pseudonym of Philip Curtin) English novelist, autobiographer, short story writer, dramatist, and biographer.

Lowndes is best known for her crime and suspense novels, and she was one of the earliest authors to weave the facts of actual murder cases into her plots, most notably in *The Lodger*, which was based on the Jack the Ripper murders.

Lowndes was the oldest daughter of a French father and an English mother. As a child, she had little formal education; however, since her family lived alternately in England and France, she was bilingual, and acquired at an early age an appreciation for French as well as English and American literature. As an adult, Lowndes worked as a journalist and magazine writer, again dividing her time between France and England, though she considered herself to be French and lived in France during most of her early career. Lowndes was in her late thirties when she wrote her first novel, and she subsequently published a work of fiction or drama every year for the rest of her life. Among her later works are four volumes of autobiography—*"I, Too, Have Lived in Arcadia": A Record of Love and of Childhood*, *Where Love and Friendship Dwelt*, *The Merry Wives of Westminster*, and *A Passing World*. Her autobiographical works reveal, as Lowndes herself wrote in her *Diaries and Letters*, that she "knew *all* the writers" as well as many important politicians and socialites of her era. These volumes provide a revealing glimpse of the early twentieth-century European literary and social scene. Lowndes also wrote an insightful biography of her younger brother, the English author Hilaire Belloc.

Lowndes's earliest novels and short stories were primarily character studies, described by a critic for *The Bookman* as "careful and minute studies of people and situations, characterized by a Continental boldness of theme." After the critical and popular success of her first suspense novel, *When No Man Pursueth*, Lowndes wrote mainly novels and stories of crime and suspense. Her chief interest always lay in examining the motives behind the crimes she portrayed in her fiction. She wrote: "What has always seemed to me to be of paramount interest in either a true or an invented story of murder is contained not in the word 'Who?' but in the word 'Why?'" While the most common method of engaging reader interest in crime and suspense fiction was to keep the identity of the malefactor a secret, Lowndes frequently reversed this device in her fiction. She revealed the identity of the criminal at the outset of the story and sustained a high level of suspense by depicting day-to-day relations between people—one of whom is suspected by one or more of the others of having committed a crime. L. P. Hartley found that this method was used to best advantage in the novels *The Chink in the Armour* and *The Lodger*. In *The Lodger*, Lowndes's best-known work, the Buntings rent a suite of rooms to a seemingly perfect tenant—a quiet, retiring man whose only recreation is an occasional outing of several hours' duration. During the period he occupies their rooms, a series of horrible murders takes place, and Mrs. Bunting—as well as the reader—begins to suspect that the lodger may be the killer. Although perhaps more

familiar today through its dramatic version or its two screen adaptations, *The Lodger* remains a classic suspense novel and its author an interesting figure in the history of the literature of crime.

(See also *Contemporary Authors*, Vol. 107.)

PRINCIPAL WORKS

The Philosophy of the Marquise (novel) 1899
Barbara Rebell (novel) 1905
Studies in Wives (short stories) 1909
When No Man Pursueth (novel) 1910
Jane Oglander (novel) 1911
The Chink in the Armour (novel) 1912; also published as
    The House of Peril, 1935
The End of Her Honeymoon (novel) 1913
The Lodger (novel) 1913
Studies in Love and Terror (short stories) 1913
Good Old Anna (novel) 1916
Why They Married (short stories) 1923
What Really Happened (novel) 1926
The Story of Ivy (novel) 1927
Who Rides on a Tiger (novel) 1935
Lizzie Borden: A Study in Conjecture (novel) 1939

THE SPECTATOR (essay date 1899)

Comedy and satire are effectively blended in the entertaining series of dialogues to which Mrs. Belloc-Lowndes has given the title of *The Philosophy of the Marquise*. Three ladies, one French and two English, who have been schoolmates in their girlhood at Boulogne, renew their friendship as middle-aged widows with married or marriageable children. The scene is laid first in the town house of Mrs. Furleigh, the wealthiest and most worldly of the three, and then in the country house of one of her married daughters, a smart, slangy, and uncompromisingly "up-to-date" young lady. Mrs. Butler-Green, Mrs. Furleigh's impecunious sister, a pensioner on the bounty of her bachelor brother, with her three daughters, and a mixed assortment of semi-detached couples and detrimental bachelors, are included in the house-party, in which the Marquise de Rabutin—the French widow—shines conspicuous by her tact, her grace, and her *bonhomie,* amid the jostling crowd of selfish pleasure-seekers. The society to which we are introduced is the reverse of edifying, but Mrs. Belloc-Lowndes, while resolutely effacing her own personality, contrives that her characters shall reveal themselves in their true, and for the most part contemptible, colours with remarkable skill. The little book, in short, has frankness, audacity, and even wit. . . . The scenes at the Bishop's luncheon-party and in the newspaper office are admirable pieces of what we believe is called "high-class descriptive reporting."

> *A review of "The Philosophy of the Marquise," in* The Spectator *(© 1899 by* The Spectator*), Vol. 82, No. 3700, May 27, 1899, p. 758.*

THE SPECTATOR (essay date 1910)

It is to be hoped that although Mrs. Belloc Lowndes gives her new novel [*When No Man Pursueth*] the sub-title **"An Everyday Story,"** the incidents therein related do not often happen in English country life. Her book is concerned with a group of people living in Surrey in a set of houses built on peculiar lines by one owner. These houses are all small, all picturesque, and all connected with each other by telephone. But "Sunniland," as the settlement is called, is not a village, for it possesses no shops, no public-house, and no police. Into this community come three strangers, who give themselves out to be husband, wife, and sister-in-law, and before he has made much progress with the story the reader will share the suspicions of George Glyn, the young doctor, that the *soi-disant* brother and sister are slowly poisoning the wife. The interest of the plot lies in the struggle which goes on in the young doctor's mind as to what he is to do. He is leaving the village for his honeymoon, and his *locum tenens* by no means agrees with him in his diagnosis of the case. The picture of George Glyn, and his hesitations and perplexities, is well done, and the reader will feel some relief when, at the end, the problem

is taken out of his hands and the villains of the piece are discovered in their full iniquity. . . . The book is well written, and the minor characters clearly drawn. The interview between Glyn and the fashionable London doctor, and the latter's change of front when he discovers that the *locum tenens* concerned is his own son, are cleverly managed.

> *A review of "When No Man Pursueth," in* The Spectator *(© 1910 by* The Spectator*), Vol. 104, No. 4262, March 5, 1910, p. 387.*

H. L. MENCKEN (essay date 1910)

[*From the era of World War I until the early years of the Great Depression, Mencken was one of the most influential figures in American letters. His strongly individualistic, irreverent outlook on life and his vigorous, invective-charged writing style helped establish the iconoclastic spirit of the Jazz Age and significantly shaped the direction of American literature. In the excerpt below, Mencken offers a brief, favorable review of* Studies in Wives.]

In most of [the stories in **"Studies in Wives"**] the note is tragic, and in a few it is positively horrible; but in all of them one observes the sure hand of a practised and accomplished fictioneer. The best of the stories is **"According to Meredith,"** an account of a trial marriage's unexpected termination. Mrs. Lowndes has a sort of grim, ironic humor; she knows how to give her characters reality; she is well worth reading.

> *H. L. Mencken, in a review of "Studies in Wives" (copyright, 1910, by John Adams Thayer Corporation; used by permission of the Enoch Pratt Free Library of Baltimore in accordance with the terms of the will of H. L. Mencken), in* The Smart Set *(copyright, 1910, by John Adams Thayer Corporation), Vol. XXXI, No. 3, July, 1910, p. 158.*

MARGARET SHERWOOD (essay date 1911)

Jane Oglander, unlike the tales that waver in the telling, is an instance of a direct, centred plot, which, in both the major and the minor strands, clings to the same theme. The heroine, a woman of fine inner charm, is betrothed to General Lingard, whom she deeply loves; he falls victim to a foolish, beautiful woman of the vampire type, Athena Maule, whose disillusioned husband, cynic and philanthropist, administers to her an overdose of chloral to save the situation. Athena has ruined other men, and the story of one of them, Bayworth Kaye, a young soldier, runs side by side with the main plot. The book is not extraordinary, but it has interesting character-contrasts: the silent, loyal Jane; the foolish, selfish Athena; and Mrs. Kaye, whose dry and wordless affection for her son makes one of the most appealing phases of the book. The plot is as daring as it is logical, a rather startling instance of consistency in character, and of character manifest in action that seems plausible, for the outcome is artistically, if not ethically, justified. (p. 565)

> *Margaret Sherwood, "The Makers of Plots" (copyright © 1911 by Margaret Sherwood; reprinted with permission of The Atlantic Monthly Company, Boston, Mass.), in* The Atlantic Monthly, *Vol. 108, No. 4, October, 1911, pp. 557-68.**

THE BOOKMAN, NEW YORK (essay date 1912)

[Mrs. Belloc Lowndes's] first venture in fiction, *The Philosophy of the Marquise,* was a novel in dialogue form . . . , which found scant favour with the critics. . . . *The Heart of Penelope,* which followed in 1904, revealed its author as a writer of serious intent and unsuspected strength; and *Barbara Rebell,* published a year later, caused a leading English review, previously hostile to her, to declare enthusiastically, "there is more breadth and largeness about Mrs. Belloc-Lowndes than any other woman novelist we can call to mind."

For several years longer, in volumes like [*The Pulse of Life, The Uttermost Farthing,* and *Studies in Wives*] . . . , Mrs. Belloc-Lowndes continued to cultivate the same vein of fiction, careful and minute studies of people and situations, characterised by a Continental boldness of theme,—as for instance, *The Heart of Penelope,* in which the central idea is whether a mother has the right to commit murder, in order to save her daughter from dishonour. These volumes brought her a steadily increasing *succès d'estime,* but not a wide public. Suddenly, in 1910, she abandoned her previous field in favour of the novel of crime and mystery, and achieved a surprising success with *When No Man Pursueth,* in which, in a charming and sunny setting of Surrey landscape, two villains, a frank, genial male villain, and a pale, gentle, and truly womanly villain, conspire slowly to poison their respective wife and sister. It is interesting to note that this formula, a man and woman, apparently quite inoffensive, but really partners in crime, in a setting apparently redolent with the joy of living, also serves as the substructure of Mrs. Belloc-Lowndes's new volume [*The Chink in the Armour*]. . . . (pp. 351-52)

> *A review of "The Chink in the Armour," in* The Bookman, *New York (copyright, 1912, by Dodd, Mead and Company, Inc.), Vol. XXXV, No. 4, June, 1912, pp. 350-53.*

FREDERIC TABER COOPER   (essay date 1912)

[*An American educator, biographer, and editor, Cooper served for many years as literary critic at* The Bookman, *a popular early twentieth-century literary magazine. In his review of* The Chink in the Armour, *excerpted below, Cooper notes the "care and minuteness" with which Lowndes portrays even minor characters. While many critics have praised Lowndes's characterizations, Cooper finds that painstakingly depicted minor characters detract from the presentation of central figures in Lowndes's fiction.*]

The Chink in the Armour, by Mrs. Belloc-Lowndes, is another of those stories of mystery and crime to which she so unexpectedly turned her considerable literary talent a couple of years ago. The setting of the story is a miniature Monte Carlo, which we are asked to accept as existing in close proximity to Paris. The central event is the disappearance of a young Polish lady, a confirmed gambler, who on the eve of her mysterious vanishing is known to have won enviable sums at baccarat. And the story is seen chiefly through the eyes of a young Englishwoman, who has come to this gambling resort out of friendship for Anna Wolsky, whose disappearance keenly distresses her, and the mystery of which she solves, almost at the cost of her own life. The trouble with the book is chiefly the fault of too great transparency. It would take a rather dull-witted person not to see through the transparent friendliness of the mysterious cosmopolitan couple, the Wachners, to whom we are introduced early in the story. . . . Mrs. Belloc-Lowndes has a theory, and a rather unfortunate one, that all the characters in a story, regardless of their relative importance, should be drawn with equal care and minuteness. She has a curious and illogical idea that this method represents our experiences in real life, failing to realise that the people we meet are never seen with

uniform clearness, but always in a steadily diminishing perspective, until the least important of them melt away into the indistinguishable ranks of the unknown crowd. It is interesting to glance over the various reviews of Mrs. Belloc-Lowndes's several volumes. Over and over again, one finds the same criticism advanced by reviewers of all sorts and conditions, namely, that her central characters do not stand out as they should,—and here and there a critic more perspicuous than the rest suggests that it is because she has obscured her canvas by devoting a disproportionate space to the personages of secondary importance. All this is pathetically true; and her besetting sin is again in evidence in the present volume. Her portrait painting is always admirable; but she will never produce a novel of the first magnitude until she learns to practise a more rigid scheme of proportion. (p. 414)

> *Frederic Taber Cooper, "Mankind in the Mass and Some Recent Novels," in* The Bookman, *New York (copyright, 1912, by Dodd, Mead and Company, Inc.), Vol. XXXV, No. 4, June, 1912, pp. 409-15.*

THE NEW YORK TIMES   (essay date 1913)

There is a certain cool quality to these stories ["**Studies in Love and in Terror**"] by Mrs. Belloc Lowndes which well suits their title of "**Studies.**" Not once does the author herself become excited, even though several of her plots are more than a little melodramatic, and her calmness proves contagious. In each of the five tales which compose this volume there are moments when the reader's pulse ought to quicken—the heroine's midnight walk bearing her gruesome burden on "**St. Catherine's Eve,**" the departure of the boats from the wrecked channel steamer, the tragic payment of "**The Price of Admiralty,**" to mention only a few but never once does it lose its regular beat on account of anything printed upon these pages. And yet, the stories are not uninteresting.

It is curious, this complete absence of dramatic value where dramatic value has apparently been so sedulously labored for. The stage-setting is in general well chosen, the actors carefully and appropriately costumed; they make the proper gestures and do their hard-working best to achieve climaxes, but somehow the whole thing fails, in theatrical parlance, "to get across."

> *"Love and Terror," in* The New York Times *(copyright © 1913 by The New York Times Company; reprinted by permission), August 17, 1913, p. 438.*

THE NEW YORK TIMES BOOK REVIEW   (essay date 1914)

In her last novel, "**The End of Her Honeymoon,**" Mrs. Belloc-Lowndes kept her readers in a pleasant state of mystification until the final chapter. In "**The Lodger,**" there is a reversal of this method. Before the story is half told the clue to its mystery is purposely disclosed, and the interest of the reader is thereafter intensified by the accumulating horrors, which he is himself led to add to the strange situation first suggested to his mind. And then there is the tantalizing feeling that this very obvious clue, furnished by the author, may be nothing more than a clever "blind," the key to a solution that is quite unrelated to the particular fact or series of facts intended to be solved. All this, of course, testifies to the skill of Mrs. Belloc-Lowndes as a writer of mystery stories. In this department of fiction, indeed, she can be depended upon to produce work of a very excellent quality—work that has just that touch of reality, that feeling of "atmosphere" that gives to a novel of this character genuine and permanent value.

"The Lodger" is rich in just this kind of excellence. The setting for the story is admirably simple. A retired serving man and his wife have invested their savings in a small house in an unpretentious London neighborhood. For their income they are dependent on such lodgers as can be induced to rent the four rooms that are set apart for the purpose. . . . And then there happens in, just in the very nick of time, an eccentric sort of gentleman, who is abundantly supplied with money and for whom the rooms offered by the Buntings have a peculiar attraction.

Mr. Sleuth is the singular name of this eagerly welcomed person. He rents all four rooms of the Buntings at a rate fixed by themselves and turns out to be an acquisition that would arouse the envy of the most prosperous of boarding-house keepers. This Mr. Sleuth is apparently confined to two occupations, an occasional experiment in chemistry or a daily study of two books, the Bible and Cruden's "Concordance." For the rest his manner of life is quite like that of a retired gentleman of moderate means and simple tastes, and he fits in admirably with the Bunting menage. . . . And then something happens, something with which the Buntings have no apparent connection, but which absorbs their attention and excites their horror, as it does that of all their neighbors.

The series of singular crimes giving rise to this popular excitement will be recognized at once by the reader as those which stirred London some years ago, which baffled the police of that period, and which have never been satisfactorily, or, rather, definitely solved to this day. . . . In the hands of so skillful a writer of stories as Mrs. Belloc-Lowndes, the theme furnished by these famous crimes from London's underworld becomes an unforgettable contribution to the type of fiction that owns Poe for its supreme master. Her book is a splendid bit of work in the art that creates mystery in literature.

> *"Mrs. Belloc-Lowndes's Story of Famous Crime,"* in The New York Times Book Review *(copyright ©
> 1914 by The New York Times Company; reprinted
> by permission), February 22, 1914, p. 82.*

FREDERIC TABER COOPER   (essay date 1914)

The Lodger, by Mrs. Belloc-Lowndes, is easily the best of the various mystery stories that this writer has produced. The real merit of it lies in the quietness with which it opens, without a hint of anything gruesome or uncanny; and then little by little we begin to connect certain events and places and to realise the utter grimness of a situation innocently brought about by a respectable middle-aged woman renting a room to a strange lodger. He seemed to have come to her like a special dispensation of Providence. That very evening she and her husband, who had once been respectable family servants but were now too old to go back to their former work, had been reckoning up just how many shillings stood between them and abject poverty; and then the husband, yielding to that illogical desire which often comes when funds are low, to redeem his self-respect by some reckless expenditure, actually steps out of the house and pays a penny, one of their few, precious pennies, for an evening paper. You see, just at this time all London was excited by a series of atrocious and inexplicable murders. . . . Now if he had not gone out for that paper, he would not have left the light turned high in the front hall and the Lodger would have passed the house without seeing the sign

announcing furnished rooms. . . . So, happy in the possession of a month's rent in advance, the landlady descended to the dining-room to interrupt her husband in his perusal of the latest details of a fresh murder in Whitechapel. Well, there is the situation; and the fine art by which, without unnecessary haste, without a word too much or too little, you are led to form a mental connection between the grim headlines of the newspaper and the identity of the Lodger upstairs entitles Mrs. Belloc-Lowndes to cordial recognition as an adept in this type of fiction. It satisfies the reader's desire to be kept in a state of sustained suspense; and, what is much rarer, it satisfies him equally when the final disclosures have all been made. The only weak point in the whole volume is the somewhat melodramatic and unlikely coincidence of having all the parties concerned meet by chance in the Chamber of Horrors at Madame Tussaud's Wax Works. (pp. 209-10)

> *Frederic Taber Cooper, "The Art of Looking On and
> Some Recent Novels,"* in The Bookman, New York
> *(copyright, 1914, by Dodd, Mead and Company,
> Inc.), Vol. XXXIX, No. 2, April, 1914, pp. 207-10.**

H. W. BOYNTON   (essay date 1916)

The *Good Old Anna* of Mrs. Belloc Lowndes shows the war coming to another quiet nook of England, the cathedral town of Witanbury. But here we have to deal with a special war-problem. . . . *Good Old Anna* is a spy story, its implication being that every German in England, naturalised or unnaturalised, is likely to be in some way connected with the spy-system. Mrs. Otway is the widow of a canon, who lives pleasantly at Witanbury with her one daughter and a German servant of many years' standing. When war comes, Mrs. Otway is advised by friends to get rid of Anna. But the lady thinks this is preposterous, cannot imagine doing without Anna, or Anna's wishing to do without her. . . . [Anna's] sympathies are with the Fatherland; and with every day bringing news which affects them differently, her relation to the Otways becomes inevitably awkward. Still, it is unconsciously that she becomes, in effect, a spy and a conspirator. . . . The results are serious for England and, incidentally, involve the supposed death of her young mistress's betrothed. All this gives leeway for Mrs. Belloc Lowndes's sort of thing—an odd blend of sensational incident and the ladylike manner. Poor Old Anna is brought to book in the end and, despairing of making out a case, hangs herself in her cell, while young romance effects its kiss-curtain hard by. (pp. 259-60)

> *H. W. Boynton, in a review of "Good Old Anna"
> (reprinted by permission of the Literary Estate of
> H. W. Boynton), in The Bookman, New York, Vol.
> XLIV, No. 3, November, 1916, pp. 259-60.*

L. P. HARTLEY   (essay date 1926)

> [*Hartley was an English novelist, short story writer, and critic
> who contributed criticism to* The Spectator, The Observer, *and*
> The Saturday Review, *among other publications. In the excerpt
> below, he favorably reviews* What Really Happened.]

There are two kinds of murder story: one which obtains its effect by concealing to the last the identity of the murderer; the other which makes it plain from the start who is the murderer and who his intended victim. The second kind works up to the crime, relying for its thrill on pure narrative, while the first puts the crime at the beginning, and, for the most part, works backwards. Mrs. Lowndes is perhaps the best exponent we have of the delayed murder: **'The Lodger'** and **'The Chink in the Armour'** bear comparison with 'Uncle Silas,' the most noteworthy example of this genre.

In **'What Really Happened,'** Mrs. Lowndes has departed from her usual method. She gives us first of all the trial and the judge's summing up. Then, going backwards, she traces the history of the murdered man, his wife and his housekeeper, and shows how the judge was very naturally mistaken in his imputation of guilt; and lastly she returns to the trial and the jury's verdict. To some this will be the least satisfactory section; it lacks the finality that we are accustomed to associate with stories of this kind. But it is in tune with the rest of the book, which, in spite of its superficially sensational character, is a sincere (and successful) attempt to portray the mental processes which find an outlet in murder. We may criticize the motive as being insufficient, but we cannot say that it is uninteresting or impossible or unconnected with life. Mrs. Lowndes has been at great pains to make her setting convincing, and the crime is subdued to the characters, who pull their own weight and appeal to us by what they are as well as by what they have become involved in. Mrs. Lowndes has a wide knowledge of the world; she keeps her eye fixed on the object and never assumes that because a murder has been committed, the ordinary small events of life are going to cease. And in scores of instances where an inferior writer would have been content to fall back on the broad effects of sensation—in the scene, for example, of Mrs. Raydon's arrest—she goes behind stock emotions and patiently disentangles real ones. **'What Really Happened'** is not one of her greatest thrillers, but it is a very readable, entertaining, solid and well-devised novel.

> *L. P. Hartley, in a review of "What Really Happened" (reprinted by permission of Curtis Brown, Ltd.; copyright © 1926 by L. P. Hartley), in* The Saturday Review, *London, Vol. 142, No. 3690, July 17, 1926, p. 74.*

EDWIN MUIR   (essay date 1927)

[*Muir was a distinguished Scottish novelist, poet, critic, and translator. In his critical writings, Muir was more concerned with the general philosophical issues raised by works of art—such as the nature of time or society—than with the particulars of the work itself, such as style or characterization. In the following excerpt, Muir finds "an undeniable rough force of characterization" to be the only positive element of* The Story of Ivy.]

"The Story of Ivy," like most of Mrs. Belloc Lowndes's stories, is powerfully told. Her style has no grace, her view of life is uninteresting and illiberal, but she has an undeniable rough force of characterization, and set beside the figures in the other novels in this list, Ivy is vividly and hatefully alive, a vulgar, grasping, pathetic little adventuress. The strange thing about the book is that having so much truth, it should have no significance. After reading about Ivy, after seeing how true she is, we do not want to hear anything more of her again. The reason for this is that Mrs. Lowndes shows no proportion, no profound sense of an order of significance in human experience, the presence of which is more essential in a work of art even than truth to life.

> *Edwin Muir, in a review of "The Story of Ivy," in* The Nation and The Athenaeum, *Vol. XLII, No. 10, December 10, 1927, p. 404.*

WILL CUPPY   (essay date 1935)

Straight on the recommended list goes this high-pressure romance [**"Who Rides on a Tiger"**] about a young girl's mistake, a villain's passion, the Duchess of St. Erth's ball, antimony in the corpse, a strong man's love, the secret cavity in a jewel case and who did in poor rich Mrs. Castledyne at Lady Jane Blunt's party at Jerricks. . . .

Personally, though there are crowds of young folks, we concentrated on the older characters, including the aged and spiteful Dowager Duchess of St. Erth, Lady Jane and old Lord Alfred Lelant, who dwells at Jerricks in what we took to be some sort of domestic relationship to Lady Jane. We kept hoping he was at least Lady Jane's cousin or something, but Mrs. Belloc Lowndes finally comes out and explains him this way: "Of late years he had spent a good deal of his life at Jerrick's, being cosseted by his early love, for he had always been delicate, in the comfortable way that an elderly couple who are not married are now allowed by British public opinion to dwell together in platonic amity." We are no prude, but we wonder whither British public opinion is drifting—and what's more, we doubt it. One may add that **"Who Rides on a Tiger"** is Mrs. Belloc Lowndes's best story in years—maybe her best since her thrice celebrated **"The Lodger."** It's a heady mixture of love, gooseflesh and the upper classes in just the right proportion.

> *Will Cuppy, in a review of "Who Rides on a Tiger," in* New York Herald Tribune Books *(© I.H.T. Corporation; reprinted by permission), April 21, 1935, p. 10.*

MAY LAMBERTON BECKER   (essay date 1939)

In her most important novel since **"The Lodger,"** Mrs. Belloc Lowndes has at last provided the Borden Case [in **"Lizzie Borden: A Study in Conjecture"**] with one feature it has hitherto lacked for the purpose of fiction—a reasonable, even a convincing motive. She gives it one that makes the whole thing fall into line.

It is indeed the persistence of the human mind in refusing to be satisfied, when the incredible has happened, until some believable reason has been found for it, that has kept young and on the boil as old a case as this, a crime in which this matter of motive has long been the only mystery. For the solution of the mystery, the author seeks in the hidden life of the Sphinx of Fall River—the woman whose plump and placid photographs, whose thirty pretty frocks, whose trip to Europe, are matters of record along with matters more grim. If this woman ever did have a love affair, any one who has followed the case as carefully as students of Bordeniana always do follow it will be forced to grant that this is precisely the kind she would have had, and probably the only kind she could have had. . . .

The hero of this love affair, and all those concerned in its maintenance, are inventions of the author, such as quasi-biographical fiction seems increasingly to encourage. They are supplied, one gathers from the preface, because they have to be there if the crime is to make sense. "Necessity is the mother of invention. I present a group of characters, trusting that my readers will agree that this invention is surely the legitimate child of what I hope some will feel to be an absolute necessity." All the rest of the novel—which closes before the trail begins—keeps to the facts, and the whole thing keeps to the spirit of time and place. Speaking as one whose grandfather subscribed to his home town paper, "The Fall River News," all through the *cause célébre*, I can testify that it has caught not only the look of the place but the feel of it. People in this novel do not "talk New England dialect," but neither did well-to-do citizens of Fall River in 1892. Life was calm and quiet on Second Street at the outset of the '90s, like the opening chapters of this story, like still water with torpedoes in it.

"The nineteenth century left us two great unsolved murder mysteries," says the author, "one centering in a man, the other in a woman. Around these two, controversy has raged for a lifetime, and still goes on. Books yet are written, discussion may at any moment break out, on the Mystery of Edwin Drood and the Mystery of Lizzie Borden. Though one of these is a character in fiction and the other a character in real life, the mystery in each case will be penetrated, if at all, by the same method. It will be solved by surmise, by conjecture based on the evidence." In any event, this "study in conjecture" has put Lizzie Borden into fiction to stay.

> *May Lamberton Becker, in a review of "Lizzie Borden: A Study in Conjecture," in* New York Herald Tribune Books *(© I.H.T. Corporation), April 23, 1939, p. 8.*

CLIFTON FADIMAN   (essay date 1942)

[*Fadiman became one of the most prominent American literary critics during the 1930s with his often caustic and insightful book reviews for the* Nation *and the* New Yorker *magazines. He also managed to reach a sizable audience through his work as a radio talk-show host from 1938 to 1948. In the excerpt below, Fadiman finds Lowndes's first volume of autobiography to be a "charming idyll."*]

Mrs. Belloc Lowndes, the sister of Hilaire Belloc and author of **"The Lodger,"** has, in her honorable old age, written a quiet book of memoirs called **"'I, Too, Have Lived in Arcadia.'"** They deal with a French-English childhood as it was lived around 1870, and that, my dears, was a long, long time ago. One can only say that Mrs. Belloc Lowndes' book, despite its plethora of family history, has a Victorian grace, a sweet decorum, that may appeal even to some of the brash youngsters of our own un-Arcadian day.

The best chapters deal with the War of 1870 (the Germans were just the same then, as the correspondence in this book shrewdly demonstrates) and with the tender romance of Bessie Parkes, great-granddaughter of the scientist Joseph Priestley, and Louis Belloc. The doctors denied the invalid Louis the possibility of paternity, but within a brief time the Anglo-French union of the two lovers produced Hilaire and the little Marie, who writes this book. It all makes a charming idyll, reminiscent in flavor of "The Barretts of Wimpole Street." (pp. 49, 51)

> *Clifton Fadiman, "Josephus, Columbus, and Others" (copyright © 1942, 1969 by Clifton Fadiman; reprinted by permission of Lescher & Lescher, Ltd.), in* The New Yorker, *Vol. XVIII, No. 2, February 28, 1942, pp. 49, 51.**

RAYMOND MORTIMER   (essay date 1943)

Mrs. Belloc Lowndes raised a touching and impressive monument of domestic piety in her book *I, too, Have Lived in Arcadia.* In a second volume [*Where Love and Friendship Dwelt*] she now continues the story. Again we are enveloped in the

hothouse climate of French family life: we admire the refinement and sensibility, we wonder at almost monstrous flowers of self-sacrifice, we catch even an occasional glimpse of the resentments inevitable in so cabined an environment. Some sagacious Frenchmen consider that the strength of the family spirit, in France as in China, has not been an unmixed blessing to the nation. But Mrs. Lowndes is visited by no such uncomfortable thoughts, doubtless because her own family was exemplary no less in public service than in domestic manners. Her English mother and her French grandmother had great nobility of character, and it is striking to find relations with a daughter-in-law sustained with so complete a reciprocity. That this new book contains no further extracts from their correspondence must excite disappointment. Students of the period will find in it, despite an occasional inaccuracy, a picture of absorbing interest. . . .

[To] anyone interested in the past the most delightful chapters of Mrs. Lowndes's book may well be those devoted not to the famous but to her French relations and their friends. For these conjure a whole vanished world of the *haute bourgeoisie*—men and women in many ways conventional to the point of narrowness but conspicuous for their dignity, their courtesy and their sense of honour, a society respectful of tradition, contemptuous of ostentation, compact of integrity, and resolute in fulfilling duties. This is a world little known to the English, because the great French novelists have almost all preferred to treat the more picturesque lives of a vestigial aristocracy, a rapacious *demi-monde* or a martyred proletariat. But it was from this world that sprang almost all the men of genius to whom the Third Republic owes its imperishable fame.

> *Raymond Mortimer, "Very Heaven," in* The New Statesman & Nation *(© 1943 The Statesman & Nation Publishing Co. Ltd.), Vol. XXVI, No. 657, September 25, 1943, p. 206.*

GORDON HAIGHT   (letter date 1943)

[*Considered one of the world's leading authorities on the life and works of George Eliot, Haight became acquainted with Lowndes during World War II through an exchange of letters. A friendship was formed, although Haight and Lowndes actually met but once. In the following excerpt, Haight expresses admiration for* Where Love and Friendship Dwelt. *The appreciative review to which he refers, from the* New York Herald Tribune Weekly Book Review, *is by May Lamberton Becker, who wrote, in part: "With the appearance of the second volume of Marie Belloc Lowndes' chronicle of friendship and of love, it is clear that one of the great memoirs of our time is in process of publication."*]

Dodd Mead sent me *Where Love and Friendship Dwelt* the first day it was published, and I read it with the most intense interest. It is completely absorbing to me, crammed with most fresh and intimate observations of literary people and of life itself. I am happy to see that the reviewers recognize its importance too; I enclose the article from the *New York Herald-Tribune*, which even if the publishers have sent you a copy of it, you will be glad to have.

The chapters I found most exciting were those on Verlaine and de Goncourt, and Zola, which are exceedingly vivid and give me the feeling of being present, that is the test of real writing. But the more domestic parts of the book are of deep interest to me too. What you have to say of the French institution of *l'ami de la maison* was very curious to me, for I think its like is seldom seen in America and perhaps even in England. Mlle de Montgolfier, I suppose, is a sort of representative of it in the Belloc family.

Gordon Haight, in a letter to Marie Belloc Lowndes on October 3, 1943, in Diaries and Letters of Marie Belloc Lowndes: 1911-1947, *edited by Susan Lowndes (© Susan Lowndes Marquis 1971; reprinted by permission of the author and Chatto & Windus), Chatto & Windus, 1971, p. 247.*

THE NEW YORKER   (essay date 1956)

[*The Young Hilaire Belloc,* a] reminiscence of Belloc's youth, young manhood, and early middle age was written by his sister, who died in 1947, and put into final shape by her daughter. Although Belloc is the focal personality, the book is an affectionate memoir of the whole astonishing family—the French father; the English mother, who was a writer and a friend of Robert Browning and George Eliot; and all the French, English, and French-English relatives—and serves as a graceful bridge between two centuries (or three, for one of the intimates of the household had lived through the French Revolution) and between two cultures. It takes Belloc from his precocious childhood through his youthful, happy, and tragically destined marriage and well into his career in politics and letters. An admirable piece of portraiture.

A review of "The Young Hilaire Belloc," in The New Yorker (© 1956 by The New Yorker Magazine, Inc.), Vol. XXXII, No. 3, March 10, 1956, p. 142.*

ERNEST HEMINGWAY   (essay date 1964)

[*Hemingway was one of the most influential and well-known American novelists of the twentieth century. Critics generally regard his distinctive writing style—terse, lucid, and unornamented—as his greatest contribution to literature. Hemingway's style grew out of his early newspaper writing and was further developed under the influence of Gertrude Stein, Sherwood Anderson, and Ezra Pound. With F. Scott Fitzgerald, E. E. Cummings, and John Dos Passos, Hemingway was part of a group of disillusioned American writers who lived in Paris during the 1920s and were collectively known as the "lost generation." Hemingway is best known for such novels as* The Sun Also Rises, A Farewell to Arms, *and* The Old Man and the Sea. *In the following excerpt from* A Moveable Feast, *his memoir of life in Paris, Hemingway recounts a conversation with Stein on literature. Georges Simenon, mentioned by the critic, is one of the world's most prolific writers of detective fiction.*]

[Miss Stein said] "If you don't want to read what is bad, and want to read something that will hold your interest and is marvelous in its own way, you should read Marie Belloc Lowndes."

I had never heard of her, and Miss Stein loaned me *The Lodger,* that marvelous story of Jack the Ripper and another book about murder at a place outside Paris that could only be Enghien les Bains. They were both splendid after-work books, the people credible and the action and the terror never false. They were perfect for reading after you had worked and I read all the Mrs. Belloc Lowndes that there was. But there was only so much and none as good as the first two and I never found anything as good for that empty time of day or night until the first fine Simenon books came out. (p. 27)

Ernest Hemingway, "Une Génération Perdue," in his A Moveable Feast (copyright © 1964 Ernest Hemingway Ltd.; reprinted with permission of Charles Scribner's Sons), Charles Scribner's Sons, 1964, pp. 23-32.*

THE TIMES LITERARY SUPPLEMENT   (essay date 1971)

Mrs Belloc Lowndes was one of that monstrous regiment of writing women who flourished in Edwardian England and gave to that period something of its unique literary quality. Most of them are forgotten now. . . . Yet at their best they produced competent, readable fiction for a large, and largely female, public. They were, one gathers, an altogether professional lot, who worked hard at their trade, dined together in an amiable literary society, and had no illusions about immortality. Of their huge number of novels, only one survives: *The Lodger* remains as a minor classic of suspense, the single monument to all that labour.

The story of that society has already been told by Mrs Belloc Lowndes in her excellent memoirs, *The Merry Wives of Westminster* and *A Passing World.* She was in many ways the ideal memoirist of that world; she was well-connected and knew everybody, she was tirelessly social (she seems to have dined out nearly as often as Henry James did, often at the same table), and she was a shrewd observer. She was reticent about herself and discreet about her friends, but within these limitations of good breeding she was a wise and worldly historian of her times.

Compared with the memoirs, the *Diaries and Letters* makes a minor volume, but it is nevertheless of continuous interest. It records the small change of literary life, the kind of gossip and anecdote that might have been heard in the society Mrs Belloc Lowndes frequented. Reading it, one can see why she was so sought after as a dinner guest, for the book is like conversation, and it would be excellent company over the clear soup. Sometimes it turns on serious and public affairs: it gives a valuable tea-table view of the First World War, the rumours, the anxieties, the indiscretions of politicians in society; it provides a close-up of the abdication crisis that is full of interest; it is excellent on the 1945 election. Other entries are trivial but amusing: Sir Edmund Gosse rebuking a girl who had called him *Mr Gosse*, Margot Asquith snubbing a house full of guests, and a story of Lady Tredegar, who had, says Mrs Belloc Lowndes, "the unusual gift, perhaps the mania, for making chaffinches' nests".

A book like this is the raw material of careful literary history. Here the reputations have not been sorted out; Alice Duer Miller stands with Virginia Woolf; Charles Morgan and Yeats-Brown and Bennett and L. P. Hartley are all present as acquaintances, people one meets on a weekend. Not that there are no sharp literary judgments, for example of *Brideshead Revisited*—"I thought the Catholics in the book quite unrealistic, like cats with 2 heads"—but they are the judgments of the moment. Reading them, one recovers the time, the literary life being lived.

Like most good gossips, Mrs Belloc Lowndes assumes that her audience knows a good deal of the background; hence much is assumed, or omitted for reasons of discretion. The reader who is not well-informed on English politics and society may find some entries baffling and teasing, and yearn to know the whole story (for example, when Mrs Belloc Lowndes remarks, apropos of an engagement, "I think Magdalens often make excellent wives").

The editor, who seems to have inherited her mother's discretion, is of little help in such matters; she has worked hard at identifying persons named, in a *Who's Who* sort of way, but she has provided almost no additional information. But in spite of such editorial limitations, the book is a delight, and one is glad to have further insight into the mind of this remarkable woman, who at the end of a long, hard-working life could begin a letter . . . : "I can't tell you how odd everything is." Fortunately, she *could* tell us, and her report of the oddness of life is worth having.

"View from the Tea-Table," in The Times Literary Supplement *(© Times Newspapers Ltd. (London) 1971; reproduced from* The Times Literary Supplement *by permission), No. 3629, September 17, 1971, p. 1108.*

ADDITIONAL BIBLIOGRAPHY

D[ixon], D[orothy]. "Marie Adelaide (Belloc) Lowndes." In *Catholic Authors: Contemporary Biographical Sketches, 1930-1947,* edited by Matthew Hoehn, pp. 439-40. Newark: St. Mary's Abbey, 1947.
   Brief biographical and critical sketch, listing some of Lowndes's best known works.

"Mrs. Lowndes, 79, Novelist, is Dead." *The New York Times* (15 November 1947): 17.
   Obituary, giving a brief outline of Lowndes's life and noting some of her most famous novels.

John McCrae

1872-1918

Canadian poet.

McCrae is best remembered for his poem "In Flanders Fields." Published and widely circulated during World War I, the poem elicited from Allied soldiers and civilians an emotional response unparalleled by any other twentieth-century war poem. While many war poems were written by more celebrated poets, critics believe that this poem most successfully captured the sentiments of an emotionally charged historical period.

McCrae was born in Guelph, Ontario, into a middle-class family of Scottish descent. His youthful interests—literature, painting, ships, and nature—continued to hold his attention in adulthood. Talented in many fields, McCrae chose to study medicine at the University of Toronto. After graduation he practiced pathology at Montreal General Hospital and McGill University, where many of his poems appeared in the McGill *University Magazine.* Throughout his medical career, McCrae sought the company of writers and artists, and kept abreast of trends in contemporary literature, becoming an active member of Montreal's prestigious Pen and Pencil Club. McCrae's diverse and active life was interrupted twice by war: he served as a medical officer in both the Boer War and World War I. During World War I, he anonymously submitted "In Flanders Fields" to *Punch.* The poem opens in a Flemish cemetery, grown over with poppies and watched over by soaring larks. The Allied war-dead then speak, recalling their short lives and the similarity of their hopes and actions to those of all people. The poem concludes as the dead call upon the living to continue the struggle against the enemy, and to thus insure that their own young lives will not have been lost in vain. Overwhelming, unprecedented reader response to the poem led to its use as an inducement for new recruits, and many papers carried sympathetic poems written in answer to the patriotic plea of the dead in the original. McCrae continued to serve in the field, and later, at a general hospital. Two years after the publication of "In Flanders Fields," he died of pneumonia and massive cerebral infection while serving at a general hospital in France.

Blending three of McCrae's favorite themes—religion, patriotism, and untimely death—"In Flanders Fields" also demonstrates his mastery of the rondeau, "a form upon which he had worked for years and made his own," according to Andrew Macphail. McCrae had employed both the themes and style of "In Flanders Fields" in earlier poems, but none received such popularity. The structural rigidity and auditory demands of the rondeau are not discernible in "In Flanders Fields," and Macphail believed that "no other medium could have so conveyed" McCrae's idea. Harriet Monroe disagreed, however, finding the fifteen-line rondeau too slight for the subject, preferring instead the technique of "The Anxious Dead," in which McCrae employed quatrains to treat a similar subject from the point of view of a living soldier. "The Night Cometh," another rondeau, is often compared to "In Flanders Fields." Aside from structural affinity, they have in common haunting voices from the grave, peaceful beginnings that build to dramatic appeals by the dead, and, finally, a return to silence and peace.

The timeliness of "In Flanders Fields" was the primary reason for its popularity: it was published when the morale of Allied forces, faced with almost certain defeat, was at its lowest. However, perhaps the emotional impact of "In Flanders Fields" owes more to McCrae's use of identifiable symbols: the poppy—a blood-red symbol of sleep and death; the white crosses, which suggest numerous allusions to the crucifixion of Christ, including the willing sacrifice of promising young lives, and resurrection; and the torch, a light-giving, purifying symbol passed from a fallen fighter to another who will continue the sanctified crusade. It is generally agreed, as Andrew Macphail has noted, that "In Flanders Fields" gave "expression to a mood which at the time was universal, and will remain a permanent record when the mood is passed." H. E. Harmon has observed that "nothing in all literature ever did so much to fire the western world to the cause of liberty."

(See also *Contemporary Authors,* Vol. 109.)

PRINCIPAL WORKS

In Flanders Fields, and Other Poems   (poetry)   1919

H[ARRIET] M[ONROE] (essay date 1919)

[*As the founder and editor of* Poetry, *Monroe was a key figure in the American ''poetry renaissance'' which took place in the early twentieth century.* Poetry *was the first periodical devoted primarily to the works of new poets and to poetry criticism, and from 1912 until her death Monroe maintained an editorial policy of printing ''the best English verse which is being written today, regardless of where, by whom, or under what theory of art it is written.''*]

[Now] and then some poem lifts the emotion of the moment into song, thus winning a chance of survival after the moment has passed. John McCrae achieves this in the much-quoted *In Flanders Fields*—achieves it by sheer simplicity and concentration in the expression of a moving and tragic appeal. Another poem on the same motive—a living soldier's address to *The Anxious Dead*—is perhaps still finer, and its quatrains fit the subject better than the too slight rondeau form of the first. (p. 221)

McCrae, who was about forty years old and a Lieutenant Colonel in the Canadian medical service when he died of pneumonia in France, will be remembered for these two poems, and possibly also the sonnet on death, *Mine Host.* (p. 222)

> H[arriet] M[onroe], ''Other Poets of the War,'' in Poetry (© 1919 by The Modern Poetry Association; reprinted by permission of the Editor of Poetry), Vol. XIV, No. 4, July, 1919, pp. 220-25.*

H. E. HARMON (essay date 1920)

[*Harmon, finding little merit in McCrae's early poems, attributes the ''fervor,'' ''force,'' and ''appeal'' of* ''In Flanders Fields'' *to ''a soul stirred to its very depths.'' For contrasting opinions regarding McCrae's early poetry and the influence of inspiration in his work, see the excerpts below by Lewis Wharton and A. H. Brodie.*]

[Dr. John McCrae] witnessed the steady, onward march of the enemy, the almost hopeless heroism of his comrades to stay the German pressure; he saw the warm earth hide its shame in the scarlet glory of the poppy; and out of this harrowing experience this great poem [*In Flanders Fields*] was born. It is the outgrowth of personal observation, of intense feeling, and hence its every line rings true to the subject matter, because it came from a soul stirred to its very depths.

Dr. McCrae had served for a while in the Boer war and afterwards had written some verse, but nothing to indicate that he could ever be the author of *In Flanders Fields.* (p. 10)

And yet in the slender volume, which has now been published and which shows the bulk of his poetic contribution to the world's literature, but one poem will live and that will live with the best.

In Flanders Fields was first published in London *Punch*, December 8, 1915, and bore no signature. Evidently the author did not realize the literary value of his work, but it was not long in finding its way to the great throbbing world without, all afire with feeling for what was going on in northern France. It was the most widely copied poem of the war. It was read from thousands of platforms in England and France to stir the fire of enthusiasm for recruits. And when America was finally drawn into the great struggle, it became national in its appeal for help, and thousands went to the front to hold high the torch thrown back by dying heroes. Perhaps nothing in all literature ever did so much to fire the soul of the western world to the cause of liberty. Its every line was a bugle note and men went forward filled with a new enthusiasm for the cause which America had espoused.

Few indeed may seem the burning lines of such a poem, yet thousands were stirred by its fervor, by its force, its appeal—and it sent all the power of a new, strong nation against a common enemy, and made the armistice of last November a possibility. (p. 12)

> H. E. Harmon, ''Two Famous Poems of the World War,'' in South Atlantic Quarterly (*reprinted by permission of the Publisher; copyright © 1920 by Duke University Press, Durham, North Carolina*), Vol. 19, No. 1, January, 1920, pp. 9-17.*

J. D. LOGAN AND DONALD G. FRENCH (essay date 1924)

[The] Canadian poetry inspired by the world war cannot be depreciated as 'twinkling trivialities' either in substance or in form. All the best of it is good poetry—originally conceived, winningly suffused with beauty of sentiment, rich in noble ideas and spiritual imagery, engaging in verbal music, and technically well-wrought. If the formal finish of Canadian Poetry of the world war is not always quite the equal of the British and American poetry similarly occasioned, still the altogether most famous and most popular poem of the war and most likely to perdure in the popular memory, is neither the sonnet of the English soldier-poet, Rupert Brooke, *The Soldier,* nor the poem of the American soldier-poet, Alan Seeger, *I Have a Rendezvous with Death,* but the lyric of the Canadian soldier-poet, John McCrae, *In Flanders Fields.* Further, special circumstances, special sentiments, and special color and form went to making the poem by McCrae the supreme lyric of the world war, and the popularity of *In Flanders Fields* affected the appreciation of other Canadian poetry of the late war to such a degree as to cause the popular imagination, as well as the critical sense of the cultured, to estimate all other Canadian poetry of the world war as so far below McCrae's exquisite lyric as to be second-rate in substance and form. This is not so. Save that they do not embody a special form and are not as musically insinuating as McCrae's, the best of other Canadian poems of the world war are as nobly conceived, as spiritually subduing or exalting, and as technically finished as *In Flanders Fields.* (p. 345)

> J. D. Logan and Donald G. French, ''The War Poetry of Canada,'' in their Highways of Canadian Literature: A Synoptic Introduction to the Literary History of Canada (English) from 1760 to 1924 (*copyright, Canada, 1924 by McClelland and Stewart, Limited, Toronto; used by permission of The Canadian Publishers, McClelland and Stewart Limited, Toronto*), McClelland and Stewart, 1924, pp. 339-53.*

LEWIS WHARTON (essay date 1926)

[*Wharton disagrees with H. E. Harmon's assertion that* ''In Flanders Fields'' *was an accident of inspiration (see excerpt above). Wharton states that ''such a perfect thing could never have been built by an unpractised hand,'' and cites* ''The Night Cometh'' *and* ''Passing of Père Pierre'' *as earlier examples of McCrae's poetic skill.*]

To most people (I would almost add ''unfortunately'') [John McCrae's] name is associated with one poem only—his world-famed and immortal *In Flanders Fields.* This, however, is most unfair. It is true that the success of that exquisite appeal, expressing as it did in ideal form the most engrossing thought of the moment, was immediate and overwhelming. But two other things are equally true. In the first place, such a perfect thing could never have been built by an unpractised hand. Secondly, it is the aim of the writer of these few lines to establish that John McCrae wrote at least one other poem every whit as beautiful and inspiring.

In order to show that the magnificent workmanship of *In Flanders Fields* was not entirely the accident of a fortunate inspiration, let us notice the construction of his *The Night Cometh,* published in 1913. . . .

Compare [it] with *In Flanders Fields* and it will be seen that the form is identical. Of that poem much has been written. Here we will only pause to note the peaceful opening, the haunting voice from many graves, the sudden appeal and the final return to the sleep-bearing poppy. . . . (p. 237)

Let us now turn to another poem [*Passing of Père Pierre*], written more than ten years before. . . .

Comment on these beautiful lines seems something perilously like sacrilege, but it is difficult not to ask whether thought could be better expressed or imagery be more appropriate. It is difficult to imagine that the golden pages of literature can contain anything more affecting. We have to watch the "incense-mist" and the light that blindly groped its way: we see so clearly the saintly man whose path had been what men call "lonely," and yet not really so because God had been with him and had been his guide.

It has been said, almost in a tone of self-reproach, that there is a certain sameness in the poems of John McCrae and it is indeed true that almost all of them deal with the subjects of death, sorrow, and weariness. In his writings, to quote his own words, we ever hear "the half-hush'd sobbings of the hearts that weep."

Surely, however, this is not at all strange in the case of a doctor who happened to be a poet, or, perhaps we should say, of a poet who happened to be a doctor? He was a busy man who had not time to write much. He only did so when his thoughts would not be denied. He never thought it necessary, like the professional or incorrigible poet, to scan the tree-tops or horizon frantically for poem-subjects. He always found them ready to his hand and, in this connection, it is noticeable how often he refers to the manner in which death so often snatches the laborer from his unfinished toil. . . .

No sketch dealing with the life and work of John McCrae would be complete without mentioning his love of children and it is very fitting that the physician, so beloved of the young, should have written of the raising of the dead child by the prophet Elijah. (p. 238)

In taking leave of this poet, large of stature and still more large at heart, we may mention what was, apparently his favorite quotation: "What I spent, I had; what I saved, I lost; what I gave, I have." (p. 239)

> Lewis Wharton, "Who's Who in Canadian Literature: John McCrae," in The Canadian Bookman, Vol. VIII, No. 8, August, 1926, pp. 237-40.

LIONEL STEVENSON   (essay date 1926)

[*A respected Canadian literary critic, Stevenson was also the author of five biographies, each highly acclaimed for the author's scholarship, wit, and clarity. In the excerpt below, Stevenson discusses McCrae's poetry and praises his accomplishment.*]

"In Flanders Fields", or a sonnet like [Archibald] Lampman's "There is a beauty at the goal of life" derives neither advantage nor disadvantage from its formal strictness when compared with the simplest metres of [Bliss] Carman or Duncan Campbell Scott.

That which endowed John McCrae with such potency was primarily of course . . . the intensity of emotion, the clarity of vision, in which true poetry is brought forth. It is to the secondary quality of the poem that we must confine our attention, the quality which makes it so difficult for us to realise the strictness of the form. And this quality is supreme simplicity. Every word is brief and entirely familiar; not a phrase is distorted or far-fetched; with utmost directness, with rigorous economy, the poet conveys his thought and emotion in the words that seem inevitable; their pellucid clarity opposes no barrier to our communion with the mind of the poet.

This is the very crux of the situation. Most of our writers are hampered by their riches: their vocabulary is too extensive. It is not expression which they should cultivate, but repression. **"In Flanders Fields"** and its equally brief sequel are the fruit of twenty years' apprenticeship. Throughout that period the pages of the best Canadian journals were open to John McCrae, yet his whole production scarcely fills a slim volume. Contrast that with the bibliographies of our other writers—writers of fiction particularly, but of verse also to a large extent. The inference need not be elaborated. (pp. 66-7)

> *Lionel Stevenson, "The Fatal Gift," in his* Appraisals of Canadian Literature *(copyright, Canada, 1926 by The Macmillan Company of Canada Limited; reprinted by permission of the Literary Estate of Lionel Stevenson), Macmillan, 1926, pp. 63-71.**

V. B. RHODENIZER   (essay date 1930)

[*A Canadian literary critic and book reviewer, Rhodenizer wrote the biocritical* A Handbook of Canadian Literature *from which the following excerpt is taken.*]

From [McCrae's] university days to the end, his one poetic theme was death, the tragic inevitability of which was deeply impressed on his sympathetic and refined nature by his experiences as a physician and by his historical and actual knowledge of war. He felt especially the tragedy in the death of those who die in the midst of a life work which they are pursuing with joyful zest. Some of his best poems make the dead anxious that the living shall continue the uncompleted task. McCrae was a very conscientious craftsman, and the relatively few poems that constitute his single posthumously published volume have a finish that ranks them high as specimens of Canadian poetic art. (p. 236)

> *V. B. Rhodenizer, "Canadian Poets since Service," in his* A Handbook of Canadian Literature *(copyright 1930 by Graphic Publishers Limited), Graphic, 1930, pp. 232-42.**

A. H. BRODIE   (essay date 1972)

[*Brodie views "In Flanders Fields" as a natural progression in McCrae's poetic expression and defines three periods in McCrae's artistic development.*]

Whilst the work of McCrae's earlier years, say before 1900, though reflective, maintains a more or less personal note and occasionally, such as in *The Hope of My Heart,* degenerates into the merely sentimental, the poems written after that time introduce a distinctively morbid note which expresses itself in symbolisms of death and subsequent union with God. At the same time McCrae combined his morbidity with verses containing patriotic sentiments which, in their lack of depth, strike the modern reader as absurd and affected. It is as if only the experience of a renewed emotional upheaval such as the Great War could bring McCrae's poetic powers to the point of producing *In Flanders Fields.*

On the face of it, McCrae's early years had been normal for a young man of a comfortably off but not overly rich family. He had been born in 1872 in Guelph, had gone to the University of Toronto in 1888, had spent a brief but apparently unfortunate year as resident master at the Ontario Agricultural College, had returned to Toronto and graduated from there in biology in 1894, in medicine in 1898, and took up appointments at McGill University and Montreal General Hospital in 1900. It was during these years that such of his work that can claim to be of interest was produced. The first of the available pieces . . . , *Unnamed Poem,* is a puzzling little thing about "two tiny wee maidens" launching "A little toy ship from the shore". Needless to say, the sea claims its victims, boat and maidens. Whatever symbolism the poem may contain in the form of golden sunsets, darkening night and "little graves by the shore" is lost on the uninitiated reader.

The earliest of McCrae's poems printed in the Macphail collection are the already mentioned *Hope of My Heart, A Song of Comfort* and *The Shadow of the Cross,* all three quite obviously the outcome of some deep emotional experience suffered by the youth of 22. *The Hope of My Heart* commemorates the death and burial of a girl child. . . . The occasion seems trivial now, the similes and sentiments employed commonplace, but the motto *Delicta juventutis et ignorantius eius, quaesumus ne memineris, Domine* lends poignancy to the second stanza. . . . (pp. 13-14)

On examination, the other poems of the same year bear out the impression of an emotional experience. *A Song of Comfort* moves from personal appeal to reflection. Its subject symbolises the mutability of human existence whereby the winds of summer, autumn and winter comfort some unnamed dead whose only season had been spring. There is a transference of thought here whereby human life is equated with the four seasons (a commonplace image) of which the object has only experienced the best. There is little doubt that McCrae's own experience created a feeling of guilt which caused him to find therapeutic relief in poetic form. This guilt complex, evident throughout the work of his pre-1900 period, is accentuated by a piety which remained with him throughout his life. (p. 14)

Hence it is perhaps little surprising that his verses are permeated by what might with some justification be called "mystical experiences." The third poem of the year 1894, *The Shadow of the Cross,* merges the personalised aspect of love, with which McCrae had been battling before, into the wider symbolism of Caritas, the true love that passes all understanding. In spite of any fusion of Love and Caritas he might achieve periodically however, the introspective brooding on past events to which McCrae was prone poetically is repeatedly in evidence. *Unsolved* and *Penance* return again to the problem of lost human companionship! . . . Significantly, the only way McCrae seems to be able to come to terms with such problems is through

death, yet, as shown in *Penance,* never death without guilt. . . . Whenever he refers to experiences that might have effected a fundamental change of life it is in the spirit of nostalgic longing of one who regrets the might-have-been, but was not strong—or courageous?—enough to conquer. Such poem is *Then and Now,* perhaps the only piece that approaches what might be termed "love poetry" and certainly the only one that closes on a note of self-conciliation. At no time does McCrae appear able to detach himself from that morbid brooding introspection, that pre-occupation with death, which was in evidence already in the *Unnamed Poem.* By 1897 technique and imagery had advanced far enough to leave the infantilism of the earlier piece behind, but one wonders whether the sentimentalism of *Slumber Songs* is really an improvement. . . . (pp. 14-15)

Parallel to this impersonalising of past emotion runs the broader development indicated already in *The Shadow of the Cross.* Thus the remaining pieces of that period in McCrae's life are more or less contemplative and achieve in their ending that near mystic fusion indicated before. As a genre they surpass in no way the sentiment or imagery common to so much of Victorian religious verse. Like all compositions of that nature each piece is the outcome of a particular mediation on the relationship between God and man. In McCrae's case we have evidence of such meditative periods before composition, though slender, in the reminiscences of some of his friends. . . . (pp. 15-16)

Likewise it is said that McCrae owed the inspiration to *In Flanders Fields* to the death of his friend and the contemplation of the poppies blooming amongst graves of the fallen. No doubt that this was indeed the case. The critic however is interested in more than the momentary causes of his subject's inspiration. As McCrae, as all his poems show, appeared to be infatuated with the image of death, so *In Flanders Fields* will be found not to be just the result of a temporary situation but a logical link in a poetic chain.

Of the contemplative poems of the years 1895 to 1898 *Anarchy* alone appears worthy of particular note. In contrast to the others, which are conciliatory in their conclusions in that a final equation of Death and Peace is achieved, *Anarchy* presents as near an apocalyptic version of crime and punishment as McCrae was capable of. . . . It is difficult to fathom what may have lain behind this particular piece. According to the date it belongs to McCrae's Toronto period, but one doubts whether the Toronto of seventy years ago could justify an apocalyptic vision. It is a sign that McCrae's imagination appears to have been capable of response to colourful stimulation which makes the poetic manifestations of his second period more plausible. But between the two lay his experience as a serving officer in Africa. (p. 16)

We can date the beginning of the new direction in McCrae's poetry as early as 1898 with the appearance of *The Song of the Derelict,* not a difficult poem to understand, but an unusual piece to fit into the McCrae pattern. Not unlike many of Sir Henry Newbolt's seapieces of the same period, it is the monologue of one of the by-gone fighting ships now derelict, recalling the glory of old and the rollicking "swing of the sea". A splendid piece for the compilers of school-boy anthologies! The last stanza contains that curious reference to Death bringing peace to the troubled after toil, which another poem of the same year, *The Harvest of the Sea,* had treated, a little paradoxically perhaps, but in a somewhat more adult fashion. Both are in many respects re-statements of a mood that had already been set up in pieces like *In Due Season* and *Mine Host:* Death as the final liberator from toil.

There is no apparent reason for McCrae's melancholia. According to testimony, he was a convivial well-liked man, a good mixer. . . . It looks then as if his verses express a side of his character that presumably surfaced only when alone during the meditative processes preceding poetic composition. This hypothesis would offer one explanation for the gap in publication lasting ca. four years, during which he saw service in South Africa, followed by a period of social life in Montreal. . . . But with resumed publication the new direction of his thought becomes evident. One wonders a little how much of this new patriotic note that creeps in may have been due to his fortuitous meeting with the then High Priest of the Empire. On February 25th 1900, McCrae wrote from Capetown:

> We met the High Priest of it all, and I had a
> five minutes' chat with him—Kipling I mean.
> He visited the camp. He looks like his pictures,
> and is very affable.

Pieces like *Isandlwana* and especially *The Captain,* or even his last poem *The Anxious Dead,* do not fit wholly into the contemplative melancholic pattern of his "surrounding" poetry of which *Upon Watts' Picture, "Sic Transit"* is a suitable illustration. It is fundamentally a poem of resignation in which the poet renounces participation in life. . . . Without actually seeing the picture in question one cannot judge how much of the general *Weltschmerz* of the poem is due to the pictorial inspiration, there is however no doubt that Watts' representation must have struck a chord that responded in suitable manner. In the pieces of the post-1900 period the intense personal involvement of previous poems subsides. A wider view has now become possible, in which the fragrance of death as universal panacea lingers on in almost every verse. *The Dying of Pére Pierre, The Pilgrims, The Warrior, The Oldest Drama* all attempt to distance the problem of Death and Conciliation from the personal level into the realm of general application. McCrae becomes a preacher, an Ecclesiastes whose message is the vanity of human endeavour, the inevitability of struggle and the final dissolution and peace in death. At times his expression is deeply pessimistic as in *The Night Cometh*. . . . At other times his verses express what is for him a decided note of optimism. . . . One cannot, in justice, maintain that his phraseology is fresh, his imagery untarnished, his thought profound in the majority of his poems. However there is no discernible reason at all why McCrae should have cultivated morbidity. . . . Only after McCrae's first experience in France does Macphail record the change in temperament which had been foreshadowed in his poetry. . . . In 1915 *Punch* published *In Flanders Fields.* Tempers are still apt to run high in any discussion of the piece, which is technically competent and emotionally attractive to those to whom the war of 1914-1 is still a reality. It appeals to a sentiment which is patriotic and picturesque; it contains sufficient religious undertones to elevate it into the realm of faith rather than reason. As part of McCrae's work it fits into the pattern of his development. Stanza one contains the mood, the scene setting, utilising the by then accepted symbol of the Flanders poppy, supported by the cross, the images of death and resurrection set against the continuity of nature overlaid by the destructive forces of man. Stanza two, in its direct appeal, plays on the most fundamental emotion, the identification with the subject, containing at the same time McCrae's favourite themes—death and the vanity of human endeavour. Stanza three then transfers the appeal to the patriotic

level, the continuity of the struggle against the "foe", who by fortuitous arrangement remains unnamed, thereby allowing the reader scope for his own interpretation. The closing lines shift to a direct appeal, not only in the *sensus literalis* of the war in question but also in the *sensus moralis* which the wider application of the word "faith" implies. Again, the skilful use of the word "sleep" with its double meaning, coupled with the re-iteration of the opening image of the Flanders poppy, endows the whole with that semblance of universality to which the poem owes its continued use fifty years later. (pp. 17-19)

> *A. H. Brodie, "John McCrae—A Centenary Reassessment," in* The Humanities Association Bulletin, *Vol. XXIII, No. 1, Winter, 1972, pp. 12-22.*

PAUL FUSSELL (essay date 1975)

[*In the following excerpt from his award-winning study* The Great War and Modern Memory, *Fussell finds "In Flanders Fields" to be badly flawed because the peaceful opening section jars with what the critic deems a warmongering conclusion.*]

The most popular poem of the war was John McCrae's **"In Flanders Fields,"** which appeared anonymously in *Punch* on December 6, 1915. Its poppies are one reason the British Legion chose that symbol of forgetfulness-remembrance, and indeed it could be said that the rigorously regular meter with which the poem introduces the poppies makes them seem already fabricated of wire and paper. It is an interesting poem because it manages to accumulate the maximum number of well-known motifs and images, which it gathers under the aegis of a mellow, if automatic, pastoralism. In its first nine lines it provides such familiar triggers of emotion as these: the red flowers of pastoral elegy; the "crosses" suggestive of calvaries and thus of sacrifice; the sky, especially noticeable from the confines of a trench; the larks bravely singing in apparent critique of man's folly; the binary opposition between the song of the larks and the noise of the guns; the special awareness of dawn and sunset at morning and evening stand-to's; the conception of soldiers as lovers; and the focus on the ironic antithesis between beds and the graves where "now we lie." Not least interesting is the poem's appropriation of the voice-from-the-grave device from such poems of Hardy's as "Channel Firing" and "Ah, Are You Digging on My Grave?" and its transformation of that device from a mechanism of irony to one of sentiment.

> In Flanders fields the poppies blow
> Between the crosses, row on row,
>   That mark our place; and in the sky
>   The larks, still bravely singing, fly
> Scarce heard amid the guns below.
>
> We are the Dead. Short days ago
> We lived, felt dawn, saw sunset glow,
>   Loved and were loved, and now we lie
>   In Flanders fields.

So far, so pretty good. But things fall apart two-thirds of the way through as the vulgarities of "Stand Up! Stand Up and Play the Game!" begin to make inroads into the pastoral, and we suddenly have a recruiting-poster rhetoric apparently applicable to any war:

> Take up our quarrel with the foe:
> To you from failing hands we throw
>   The torch; be yours to hold it high.

(The reader who has responded to the poppies and crosses and larks and stand-to's, knowing that they point toward some trench referents, will wonder what that "torch" is supposed to correspond to in trench life. It suggests only Emma Lazarus.)

> If ye break faith with us who die
> We shall not sleep, though poppies grow
> In Flanders fields.

We finally see—and with a shock—what the last six lines really are: they are a propaganda argument—words like *vicious* and *stupid* would not seem to go too far—against a negotiated peace; and it could be said that for the purpose, the rhetoric of Sir Henry Newbolt or Horatio Bottomley or the Little Mother is, alas, the appropriate one. But it is grievously out of contact with the symbolism of the first part, which the final image of poppies as sleep-inducers fatally recalls. (pp. 248-50)

> *Paul Fussell, "Arcadian Recourses," in his* The Great War and Modern Memory *(copyright © 1975 by Oxford University Press, Inc.; reprinted by permission of Oxford University Press, Inc.), Oxford University Press, New York, 1975, pp. 231-69.**

ADDITIONAL BIBLIOGRAPHY

Brown, E. K. "The Development of Poetry in Canada." In his *On Canadian Poetry*, 2d. ed., pp. 28-87. Toronto: Ryerson Press, 1944.*
    Mentions "In Flanders Fields" as "the one masterpiece" written by Canada's war poets. Brown praises McCrae's poem as one in which "careful art, studied moderation in tone, and intense as well as perfectly representative emotion are fused to produce a moment's perfection."

Cook, Howard Willard. "John McCrae." In his *Our Poets of Today*, pp. 88-90. New York: Moffat, Yard & Co., 1918.
    A short, biocritical sketch of McCrae's life and work.

Macphail, Andrew. "John McCrae: An Essay in Character." In *In Flanders Field, and Other Poems*, by John McCrae, pp. 47-141. New York: G. P. Putnam's Sons, 1919.
    Biographical and critical essay.

Pierce, Lorne, "Biographical Sketch." *The Canadian Bookman* VIII, No. 8 (August 1926): 239-40.
    A short, appreciative biographical sketch. A bibliography of McCrae's publications is also included.

——. "English Canadian Poets: The Post-War Period." In his *An Outline of Canadian Literature: French and English*, pp. 88-112. Montreal: Louis Carrier & Co, 1928.*
    A biocritical sketch which finds "In Flanders Fields" to be "one of the three or four poems born of the war which will never die."

Harriet Monroe

1860-1936

American editor, poet, essayist, critic, autobiographer, biographer, journalist, and dramatist.

As the founder and editor of *Poetry*, Monroe was a key figure of the American "poetry renaissance" that took place in the early twentieth century. *Poetry* was the first periodical devoted primarily to this genre. From 1912 until her death, Monroe provided in *Poetry* a much needed forum for poets, whose work was often ignored or used only as page filler by other magazine editors. During Monroe's editorship, the poetry of T. S. Eliot, D. H. Lawrence, Carl Sandburg, and William Butler Yeats, among many others, appeared in the United States for the first time in the pages of *Poetry*.

Monroe was the second of four children born to an ambitious Chicago lawyer and his retiring wife. She left high school at sixteen due to severe illness; upon her recovery, she completed her education at a Georgetown, D.C., convent school. After graduating, Monroe returned to Chicago, where she worked as a journalist and, briefly, as a teacher. Monroe published some poetry in Chicago and New York periodicals, and in 1888 was commissioned to write a dedicatory ode for a new auditorium in Chicago. Two years later—shortly before the publication of her first volume of poetry, *Valeria, and Other Poems*—she was commissioned to write an ode commemorating the four-hundredth anniversary of Columbus's landing in America, to be read chorally at Chicago's Columbian Exposition in 1892. *Valeria* received little critical attention, but the "Columbian Ode" attracted much notice, particularly when Monroe sued the New York *World* for publishing the text of the poem without permission. Monroe was awarded five thousand dollars in damages in a landmark decision that helped to establish the rights of authors to control their own works. Monroe continued to work as a free-lance journalist, contributing theater and art criticism to publications in Chicago and New York. She published a biography of her brother-in-law, John Wellborn Root, a noted Chicago architect, and a volume of verse dramas, *The Passing Show*, which were never produced. She also travelled extensively, visiting Europe several times and exploring the American West. It was shortly after a European vacation in 1911, during which she had first read the poetry of Ezra Pound, that Monroe conceived the idea of a poetry magazine.

In preparation for the first issue of *Poetry*, published in 1912, Monroe spent months reading the works of many contemporary poets writing in English. She also singlehandedly obtained pledges of financial support from over one hundred prominent Chicago business-people. Over fifty American and British poets received her "poet's circular," explaining her proposed editorial project, requesting submissions, and stressing in particular three points. First, contributors would be free of the restrictions of the popular periodicals that assumed their readers were uninterested in poetry and therefore included verse only occasionally. Second, Monroe would impose no limitations of length, style, or character—good poetry of any sort would be considered for publication. Last, all contributors

would be paid. One immediate response came from Ezra Pound, who, situated in London, was in contact with many poets living in Europe. He enthusiastically became *Poetry*'s first foreign correspondent. While he and Monroe never met, they worked closely through the medium of hundreds of letters over the three years of Pound's official association with the magazine. Pound submitted to Monroe his own works, as well as poems by Lawrence, Eliot, Yeats, John Gould Fletcher, Rabindranath Tagore, and H. D. Critical controversy still exists regarding Pound's contribution to *Poetry*. D. D. Paige, editor of a volume of Pound's letters, grudgingly grants Monroe credit for being the first in America to publish Pound, Eliot, H. D., Robert Frost, and others; however, he also suggests that "Pound had to overcome in her an inertia of ignorance" and further, that "Pound had to overcome as well her narrow conception of poetry." In a study of "little magazines" contemporaneous with *Poetry*, Reed Whittemore accords Monroe little more than the status of fund-raiser for a magazine that was vivified by Pound's association. More recently, however, Monroe's biographer, Daniel J. Cahill, finds that "there is no doubt that Harriet Monroe was the one person responsible for adroitly maneuvering her magazine into a position of influence and greatness." Other critics, too, have pointed out that editorial discretion always lay with Monroe, and that she by no means always needed Pound's opinionated editorial advice. Ellen Williams cites the "absurdity" of the critical contention that

"*Poetry* was vital only so far as it expressed the choices of Ezra Pound. . . . The editorial choices which created *Poetry*'s brilliant record were Harriet Monroe's."

The two outstanding characteristics of Monroe's editorship most often cited are her catholicity and her partisanship toward American writers. Her eclecticism—the "open door" format she instituted at *Poetry*—was the keynote of her somewhat amorphous editorial policy and has been seen by many critics as the saving grace of the magazine. The second issue of *Poetry* contained the editorial "The Open Door," in which Monroe briefly stated her intention "to keep free of entangling alliances with any single class or school" of poetry. She promised to print "the best English verse which is being written today, regardless of where, by whom, or under what theory of art it is written." Monroe always strove to maintain *Poetry* as a reflection of the current literary scene, and not as a means of shaping it. Some critics, including Donald Davidson, have maintained that Monroe's eclecticism was due to a lack of real critical judgment on her part. However, the demise of countless "little magazines" devoted to single poetic movements, and the continued existence of *Poetry* as a periodical with a reputation for artistic excellence, would seem to have vindicated Monroe's decision. That Monroe tended to favor and to promote American poets—Midwestern poets, in particular—has been noted by Pound, Conrad Aiken, Leonard Brown, and many other critics. This tendency sometimes led Monroe to give prominent place and unjustified praise to essentially minor poets. However, Monroe was as often correct in her support of American artists; an impressive discovery which earned the poet, Monroe, and "the futile little periodical" *Poetry* a scathingly harsh review in *The Dial*, was the *Chicago Poems* of Carl Sandburg.

"It is the fashion now to jeer at such phrases as 'poetry renaissance'," Malcolm Cowley wrote at Monroe's death, "but there really was something of the sort in 1912, and Harriet Monroe and *Poetry* had a great deal to do with it." As a poet, albeit a little-known one, Monroe saw that early twentieth-century poetry was receiving little of the popular encouragement accorded the other fine arts. She set out to champion the "Cinderella of the arts," supplying a forum that showcased the art of poetry and for the first time provided poets with remuneration comparable to that garnered by other artists. Perhaps of equal importance, by producing a publication devoted to poetry, Monroe helped to create a discerning audience for that neglected literary form, fulfilling Walt Whitman's dictum that "to have great poets there must be great audiences too," a phrase which appeared on every issue of *Poetry* that Monroe edited. A fellow editor and contributor to *Poetry*, Eunice Tietjins, has called Monroe a "matrix," saying that she "gathered up and bound into herself all the threads that went to make up the great Middle Western revival of poetry."

(See also *Contemporary Authors*, Vol. 109.)

PRINCIPAL WORKS

"With a Copy of Shelley"   (poetry)   1889; published in
    journal *The Century*
Valeria, and Other Poems   (poetry)   1891; also published
    as *Valeria, and Other Poems* [revised and enlarged
    edition], 1892
"The Columbian Ode"   (poetry)   1893

John Wellborn Root: A Study of His Life and Work
    (biography)   1896
You and I   (poetry)   1914
*The New Poetry: An Anthology of Twentieth-Century Verse
    in English* [editor; with Alice Corbin Henderson]
    (poetry and criticism)   1917; also published as *The
    New Poetry: An Anthology of Twentieth-Century Verse
    in English* [revised and enlarged edition], 1923, 1932
The Difference, and Other Poems   (poetry)   1924
Poets and Their Art   (essays)   1926; also published as
    Poets and Their Art [revised and enlarged edition],
    1932
A Book of Poems for Every Mood [editor; with Morton
    Dauwen Zabel]   (poetry)   1933
Chosen Poems   (poetry)   1935
A Poet's Life: Seventy Years in a Changing World
    (autobiography)   1938

WILLIAM MORTON PAYNE   (essay date 1892)

[*The longtime literary editor for several Chicago publications, Payne reviewed books for twenty-three years at* The Dial, *one of America's most influential journals of literature and opinion in the early twentieth century. In the excerpt below, he examines Monroe's* Valeria, and Other Poems.]

The English drama in heroic verse has had a curious history. . . . Emerging in our own century from its long entombment, it has once more given us, from "The Cenci" of Shelley to the historical dramas of Lord Tennyson and Mr. Swinburne, a series of the noblest poems in our literature, but with the striking difference that their appeal is made solely to the reader, not to the spectator. . . . This shifting of ground is, on the whole, fortunate, for it insures the perpetuation of a great poetical form, whatever may be the fate of the stage, and it gives us from time to time examples of careful workmanship in dramatic verse that would find no *raison d'être* under a system that necessarily linked all work dramatic in form with the stage. Miss Harriet Monroe's "**Valeria**" is an example of such workmanship. It is a tragedy in five acts, the scene being a small Italian state of the fourteenth century. It deals with love and hatred, with intrigue and attempted revolution, and offers, in the character of Valeria, a triumph of subtle delineation. The subordinate characters are fairly well defined, although the men are sometimes a little womanish. In construction it is skilful,—although we are not quite sure of the propriety of doing away with the Prince by means of a poison so slow that, administered in the third act, it does not complete its work until the close of the fifth. On the other hand, we are quite sure of the admirable effectiveness of the close of this same third act, considered by itself, as well as of many touches here and there. . . . The verse of the play is, in the main, excellent, and shows careful study of the best models. There are lines that we regret to come upon. . . . But the verse is generally fluent and harmonious. . . . The interspersed lyrics are less successful than the blank verse of the play. "**Valeria**" is accompanied by a number of miscellaneous poems of varying excellence. One of the best is the sonnet "**With a Copy of Shelley.**" The Chicago Auditorium cantata is better than such perfunctory things are apt to be, and, considering the prosaic nature of the subject, something of an achievement. There is much of the influence of Shelley, and a little of the influence of Rossetti, in these miscellaneous pieces. The volume, as a whole, is distinctly creditable to the author, and is one of the very few books produced in the West that fairly belong to literature. (pp. 358-59)

> *William Morton Payne, in a review of "Valeria, and Other Poems," in* The Dial *(copyright, 1892, by The Dial Publishing Company, Inc.), Vol. XII, No. 142, February, 1892, pp. 358-59.*

WILLIAM MORTON PAYNE   (essay date 1892)

[*Monroe's "The Columbian Ode" was included in a revised edition of* Valeria, and Other Poems *in 1892. A year later, it was itself published between hard covers. In the excerpt below, Payne examines the work.*]

Miss Monroe, it will be remembered, was selected by the Committee on Ceremonies of the World's Columbian Exposition to write the dedicatory poem for the exercises to be held in the Exposition buildings on the four hundredth anniversary of the discovery of America. Upon the occasion of those exercises, last October, portions of the poem were read to the vast audience assembled, and other portions, set to music by Mr. George W. Chadwick, were sung, with orchestral accompaniment, by a chorus of five thousand voices. Under the circumstances, it was, of course, impossible to make any estimate of the literary value of the poem, and its publication in the present volume first gives us an opportunity to pronounce upon its merits. The fact that Miss Monroe's poetical work, at the time when she was honored with the invitation of the Exposition authorities, had received circulation only among a limited number of her friends, naturally caused the public to feel misgivings as to the wisdom of the selection, and to ask why some poet of national reputation, such as Mr. Whittier or Mr. Stedman, had not been chosen to do so important a work. But the poem, as now published, justifies both itself and those by whom it was commissioned; it is a dignified and noble production, equal to the occasion, and probably equal to anything that could have been obtained had the authorities looked for their poet beyond the horizon of Chicago. This fact, which is not surprising to the few who have known for some time the quality of Miss Monroe's work, must be both a surprise and a satisfaction to the wider public. If the great exhibition, on its artistic side, shall offer nothing less creditable than this ode, it will deserve the warmest congratulations that its friends know how to frame.

The structure of the poem has evidently been the object of much care, and it is a little curious that the one marked fault of the work should be a defect in its architectonics, a neglect of the careful perspective that has been elsewhere faithfully observed. The poem begins with an invocation to Columbia describing the procession of nations come to do her homage. Then comes a song of the unknown world and the quest of the Genoese, and a further personification of Columbia as the ideal of the new civilization. . . . The subduing of the New World is the subject of the next division of the ode, and tributes follow to the two great figures of American history—Washington and Lincoln. Finally, we have the prophetic section of the work. . . . The lyrical movement of the poem reaches its climax in the closing chorus, with its simple and stately rhythm. . . . (pp. 346-47)

> *William Morton Payne, in a review of "Valeria and Other Poems," in* The Dial *(copyright, 1892, by The*

Dial Publishing Company, Inc.), Vol. XIII, No. 155, December 1, 1892, pp. 346-48.

WALLACE RICE   (essay date 1913)

[*In a general attack on modern poetry—especially the work of Ezra Pound—Rice scolds* Poetry's *editors for publishing "poor prose" under the guise of "good poetry."*]

Though no one can quarrel with literature in its highest form, nor with any periodical devoted to such a cause, one must regret that "Poetry" is being turned into a thing for laughter. No one need offer any particular criticism of the earlier work of Mr. Ezra Pound; it is as he prefers it. But with the practical identification of "Poetry" and Mr. Pound one may pick a very pretty quarrel, since it involves not only a lowering of standards, but a defense of the thesis, unusual in "A Magazine of Verse," that poor prose must be good poetry. (p. 370)

The attitude of "Poetry" toward poetry is that of Mrs. Mary Baker G. Eddy toward Medical Science. Yet, if poetry have no technic and, left formless thereby, is at one with illiterary prose, why devote a magazine to it? Every newspaper, programme, advertisement contains similar English—and English quite without false pretence. . . .

The editors of the usual magazines have their own standards, and many of the singers of the day know their best work to be at variance with these standards. It was hoped that "Poetry" would search out these poets and such poems, many of them of much significance and beauty.

So far there has been little done in these directions. The quest has seemingly been for the bizarre, for the astonishing, for the novelty for novelty's sake, even for the shocking. The paper of the magazine has been poor, the type that of the newspapers, the cover and form inadequate to the dignity of the cause, the proofreading heedless. The editor too seldom allows a number to go out without containing her own verses, though these show a steady retrogression from a once high standard. Her own sense of self-criticism in abeyance, Mr. Pound was bound to occur. (p. 371)

> *Wallace Rice, "Mr. Ezra Pound and 'Poetry'," in* The Dial *(copyright, 1913, by The Dial Publishing Company, Inc.), Vol. LIV, No. 645, May 1, 1913, pp. 370-71.*

E[DGAR] L[EE] M[ASTERS]   (essay date 1915)

[*Masters was one of the first major twentieth-century American authors to use the theories of modern psychology to examine human thought and motivation. A prolific writer, he is best known for the monumental poetic cycle* Spoon River Anthology, *a collection of free-verse epitaphs of the men and women buried in a small-town churchyard. In its sardonic attack on provincial dullness and spiritual sterility,* Spoon River Anthology *strongly influenced the literature of the 1920s. Monroe quickly recognized the worth of Masters's work and became a key figure in the critical defense against attacks on the poet's free-verse style and his Naturalistic vision. In the excerpt below, Masters—himself a frequent contributor of reviews and verse to* Poetry—*offers a generally favorable appraisal of Monroe's* You and I.]

Miss Monroe, both as editor and as creator, has done so much for the art of poetry, in the several capacities of encouraging beginners and by way of setting a high example in poetical production, that any volume of hers commands attention. *You and I* may continue something of her manner of style as it was shown in the *Columbian Ode;* but it also expresses her sympathy with the feeling of to-day. *The Hotel,* the initial poem in the book, makes one wish that she had given us more free verse. Her catholic attitude toward the revolutionists in verse, the Imagists and Futurists, is not a matter of liberal taste alone; it is a matter of genius for mingling perception and philosophy with a musical skill all her own. We wonder, with this poem before us, why she has clung so largely to the choral and symphonic effects of her earlier work. It is not a question of her failure to make good use of these forms. But we incline to the belief that in the free measures, and as to certain phases of modern life, her vision would find closer expression, for which opinion *The Hotel* is ample proof. On the other hand, some of Miss Monroe's lyrics of the swifter and intenser sort justify her large adherence to rhyme and the classical methods *Nancy Hanks* and *The Childless Woman* are among these successes. The music of the latter with its antistrophic movement and impression of double rhyme is unusual indeed. . . . (pp. 188-89)

There is subtlety and a lyric quality in *The Wonder of It* not to be passed over. These things we say with the conviction that the author's artistry, if not the realization of her conceptions, shows at its best in her odes rather than in her lyrics. She seems to require dithyrambic lines and a soft diffusion of color for the complete out-pouring of her gifts. But we predict that her growing realism and the gradual emancipation of her art, here evident, from classical expletives and exclamation, will drive her closer to the living flesh of future subjects, rhyme or no rhyme. Rhyme must give way more and more where it results in spiking a subject about with javelins that do not pierce the heart of the theme.

Anyone who has practiced the art of poetry and mastered its literature measurably as well as Miss Monroe has can well understand the irresistible temptation to treat subjects of modern life with something of the majestic form by which the ode is distinguished. (pp. 189-90)

Miss Monroe's poems such as *Night in State Street, The Ocean Liner, Our Canal,* have varied music and loftiness of conception; but they do not seem to measure up to her sense of realism. . . . [It] seems to us that simple quatrains or free verse would have given us more perfectly what was so clearly before her eyes. (pp. 190-91)

There are pictures and music in abundance throughout the book, and a wide variety of subjects treated; there are fugues and simple melodies, and sonnets of power. The double sonnet *Pain* is unforgettable, both for feeling and sound. (p. 191)

> *E[dgar] L[ee] M[asters], in a review of "You and I," in* Poetry *(© 1915 by the Modern Poetry Association; reprinted by permission of the Editor of* Poetry*), Vol. V, No. 4, January, 1915, pp. 188-91.*

CARL SANDBURG (letter date 1915)

[*Sandburg was one of the central figures in the "Chicago Renaissance," an early twentieth-century flowering of the arts, which vanquished the myth that the American East was the only center of legitimate creativity and established the Midwest as the home of major writers, sculptors, and painters, as well as an important source of artistic subject matter. A lifelong believer in the worth of the common, unsung individual, Sandburg expressed his populist beliefs in poetry and songs, and in his Pulitzer Prize-winning biography of Abraham Lincoln. A frequent contributor to* Poetry,]

he was impressed by Monroe's essay "The Fight for the Crowd," *which describes* "the difficulty of finding and winning over a public for art, for ideas, while the great headlong tolerant American crowd huddles like sheep in the droves of commercial exploiters."]

My Dear Harriet Monroe:

After that editorial of yours on **"The Fight for the Crowd,"** I must leave the Miss off in addressing you—for the same reasons that I don't like to call Tagore a Mister. This editorial I rewrote into a free verse form, parts of it, and sent on to Bill Reedy of the *Mirror.* It was you at your stormiest and is an authentic page of your autobiography.

> *Carl Sandburg, in a letter to Harriet Monroe on March 20, 1915, in his* The Letters of Carl Sandburg, *edited by Herbert Mitgang (letters copyright © 1968 by Lilian Steichen Sandburg, Trustee; reprinted by permission of Harcourt Brace Jovanovich, Inc.), Harcourt Brace Jovanovich, 1968, p. 102.*

CONRAD AIKEN (essay date 1917)

[*An American man of letters known primarily as a poet, Aiken was deeply influenced by the psychological and literary theories of Sigmund Freud, Havelock Ellis, Edgar Allan Poe, and Henri Bergson, among others, and is considered a master of literary stream of consciousness. In reviews noted for their perceptiveness and barbed wit, Aiken exercised his theory that* "criticism is really a branch of psychology." *His critical position, according to Rufus A. Blanshard,* "insists that the traditional notions of 'beauty' stand corrected by what we now know about the psychology of creation and consumption. Since a work of art is rooted in the personality, conscious and unconscious, of its creator, criticism should deal as much with those roots as with the finished flower." *In the following review of* The New Poetry, *Aiken scathingly attacks Monroe for her ignorance of modern poetry and for the favoritism she displayed toward American poets.*]

While in some respects **"The New Poetry"** is the best American anthology in many years—if not the best to date—in other respects it is very disappointing. There are two types of anthology: the comprehensive, which aims to embrace all that is typical of the period chosen or all that is important in it; and the highly selective, which (guided of course by a fallible personal taste) aims at a small representation of the best. Miss Monroe's anthology is of the first class rather than of the second, which, in the present reviewer's opinion, is a mistake at the outset; and a second mistake lies in the fact that while apparently comprehensive it is very imperfectly so. It is fairly comprehensive as regards American poets, but makes lamentable omissions as regards the English. Not only are such poets as Masefield, Brooke, Gibson, Hodgson, Flint, Lawrence; de la Mare, and Bottomley very scantily and often poorly represented by comparison with our native poets; but, what is worse, the work of Lascelles Abercrombie (considered by both Brooks and Gibson the most significant poet in England today), of James Elroy Flecker, and of William H. Davies, is omitted entirely. . . .

In short, the faults which have for four years been conspicuous in Miss Monroe's magazine of verse are again conspicuous here. The policy of "Poetry" has been unfortunately provincial in tone; toward all that she has felt no sympathy with Miss Monroe has manifested too frequently a cocksure intolerance. In one of the first issues of "Poetry" (1912) an article appeared which maintained that at the moment no poetry worthy of serious consideration was being written in England. If one remembers that at this time Masefield's "Dauber" had just appeared in "The English Review" (following his other two narratives), that the first volume of "Georgian Poetry" was being arranged, and that, in general, Masefield, Brooke, Gibson, Abercrombie, de la Mare, and Davies were doing their best work, one at once perceives in Miss Monroe the kind of limitation against which one must be on guard. These English poets were easily ignored—they were far away, they had no hearing in America. At the same time our very numerous American poets, particularly those of the Middle West, and those who manifested that moderate degree of radicalism of which the essentially conventional Miss Monroe was capable, were coming in for garlands—the bad and the good alike. Throughout, the editors of "Poetry" have displayed an amazing lack of discrimination—both as regards aesthetics and ideas. So extraordinarily have they mixed bad with good, mediocre with brilliant, that, in the last analysis, they have stood, in any appreciable degree, for little or nothing.

These remarks are almost equally applicable to the anthology which Miss Monroe has now compiled. **"The New Poetry"** is, to begin with, astonishingly copious. Barring the signal omissions mentioned above, it offers a taste of almost everything. It is only when one turns to this or that individual poet that one discovers how shabbily many of them are represented—even, too, Miss Monroe's own favorites. How is one to explain the fact that none of Vachel Lindsay's moon poems is included, while that ephemeral jingle, "General William Booth," leads his group? Amy Lowell, too, though amply, is poorly represented. (p. 389)

And so it is throughout. . . . It seems almost as if Miss Monroe had a peculiar instinct for choosing a poet's second-best.

What is the secret of this? Is it merely bad taste? Partly, of course, if not largely; but there is also, further, the fact that Miss Monroe has tried desperately to live up to her title (in so far as it represents an idea) and at the same time to those canons of poetry which are more enduring. Miss Monroe does not realize of course how much of a traditionalist she is ethically and emotionally; in at least a part of the aesthetic field, she is really a traditionalist, and in consequence as much of the "old" as of the "new" is here represented, and, on the whole, with the same strange unevenness of taste. The result, as all these remarks have been implying, is a performance singularly confusing and inconsistent, singularly lacking in tone or character. It is neither old nor new, good nor bad, selective nor comprehensive. It devotes twenty pages to Pound (who leads in point of space) and none to Abercrombie; sixteen to Lindsay and Masters; five to Masefield; six to Gibson; while such poets as Fletcher, Robinson, and Frost trail far behind Miss Lowell in space allotted—far behind the editress herself. Are these ratings to be taken literally? Is the amount of space granted a poet totally unconnected with his relative importance? And why, if this anthology is intended to disclose only the "new" in poetry (in Miss Monroe's sense) does it contain the distinctly traditional work of Josephine Preston Peabody, the punctilious lyrics of John Hall Wheelock, Joyce Kilmer, Louis Untermeyer, and many less well-known but almost equally adroit makers of verses pleasantly conventional? Why have the more acid and powerful of the Spoon River daguerreotypes been omitted—along with the more magical? The only answer is that Miss Monroe, if she is really a radical at all, is chiefly so as regards form; as regards the material of poetry (and to any genuine well-wisher of poetry this is the important thing), she suffers from many of the curious inhibitions, for the most part

moral, which played havoc with the Victorians. The truth must not be told when it is disagreeable or subversive. One's outlook on life must accord with the proprieties. Above all, one should be a somewhat sentimental idealist—anthropocentric, deist, panpsychist, or what not, but never, by any chance, a detached or fearless observer. Frost cannot give us his "Home Burial" here, nor Masters his "Arabel," or "In the Cage," nor Brooke his "Libido." Realism is pardonable in Miss Monroe's eyes only if it is decorative.

In short, Miss Monroe, like many another anthologist, has willed the good and achieved the evil. An anthology of the new poetry which shall be equally fair to English and American poets, to realists and romanticists, is much to be desired. But a tangle of personal predilections, biases, editorial necessities, dimly seen ideals, and half-resisted nepotisms and the reverse, has proved too much for the editor. And the result is a disappointing half-success—a provoking half-failure. (pp. 389-90)

> *Conrad Aiken, "The Monroe Doctrine in Poetry," in* The Dial *(copyright, 1917, by The Dial Publishing Company, Inc.), Vol. LXII, No. 741, May 3, 1917, pp. 389-90.*

WILLIAM LYON PHELPS   (essay date 1918)

[*Phelps spent over forty years as a lecturer at Yale. His early study* The Beginnings of the English Romantic Movement *(1893) is still considered an important work and his* Essays on Russian Novelists *(1911) was one of the first influential studies in English of the Russian realists. From 1922 until his death in 1943 he wrote a regular column for* Scribner's Magazine *and a nationally syndicated newspaper column. During this period, his criticism became less scholarly and more journalistic, and is notable for its generally enthusiastic tone. In the following excerpt, Phelps notes Monroe's greater skill as an editor than as a poet.*]

Harriet Monroe's chief services to the art of poetry are seen not so much in her creative work as in her founding and editing of the magazine called *Poetry*. . . . In addition to this monthly stimulation—which has proved of distinct value both in awakening general interest and in giving new poets an opportunity to be heard, Miss Monroe, with the assistance of Alice Corbin Henderson, published in 1917 an anthology of the new varieties of verse. Certain poets are somewhat arbitrarily excluded, although their names are mentioned in the Preface; the title of the book is **The New Poetry**; the authors are fairly represented, and with some sins of commission the selections from each are made with critical judgment. Every student of contemporary verse should own a copy of this work.

In 1914 Miss Monroe produced a volume of her original poems, called **You and I**. There are over two hundred pages, and those who look in them for something strange and startling will be disappointed. Knowing the author's sympathy with radicalism in art, and with all modern extremists, the form of these verses is surprisingly conservative. To be sure, the first one, **The Hotel**, is in a kind of polyphonic prose, but it is not at all a fair sample of the contents. Now whether the reading of many manuscripts has dulled Miss Monroe's creative power or not, who can say? The fact is that most of these poems are in no way remarkable either for feeling or expression, and many of them fail to rise above the level of the commonplace. There is happily no straining for effect; but unhappily in most instances there is no effect. (pp. 283-84)

William Lyon Phelps, "Sara Teasdale, Alan Seeger, and Others" (originally published in a different form as "The Advance of English Poetry in the Twentieth Century," in The Bookman, *New York, Vol. XLVII, No. 4, June, 1918), in his* The Advance of English Poetry in the Twentieth Century *(reprinted by permission of Dodd, Mead & Company, Inc.; copyright, 1917, 1918 by Dodd, Mead and Company, Inc.), Dodd, Mead, 1918, pp. 277-311.**

DONALD DAVIDSON (essay date 1926)

[*Davidson, with John Crowe Ransom, Allen Tate, and Robert Penn Warren, was a member of the Fugitive Group of Southern poets from 1915-28. The stated aim of the Fugitives was to create a literature utilizing the best qualities of modern and traditional art. After 1928, the four major Fugitives joined with eight other writers, including Stark Young and John Gould Fletcher, to form the Agrarians, a group dedicated to the preservation of the Southern way of life and traditional Southern values. The Agrarians were concerned with social and political issues as well as literature; in particular, they attacked Northern industrialism as they sought to preserve the Southern farming economy. Ransom, Tate, and Warren eventually left Agrarianism behind and went on to become prominent founders of New Criticism. Davidson, however, was fiercely partisan to the Agrarian cause and continued to promote the values of the Agrarians throughout his career. Davidson firmly believed that the antebellum South was the best of all possible worlds: for that reason his poetry and critical writings have been alternately characterized as anachronistic, as a voice from the past unwilling to submit to the anonymity of modern life, or as the conscience of a lost civilization. In the excerpt below, Davidson provides an essentially negative assessment of the magazine* Poetry *in his review of Monroe's* Poets and Their Art. *Davidson believed that Monroe lacked any definitive critical principles, and that this absence of critical judgement led her to champion with equal enthusiasm poets of unequal talent and importance.*]

"To have great poets there must be great audiences too," is the quotation from Whitman carried as a motto on Harriet Monroe's *Poetry: A Magazine of Verse.* . . . In Miss Monroe's behalf it must be said that she has worked to create this "great audience" and has accomplished more, possibly, in this direction than any other of the propagandists for poetry, with the possible exception of Mr. Louis Untermeyer. She has done American poetry a good service because she had the foresight to establish her magazine at exactly the time when it was needed, and the courage to publish writers who needed an introduction to the public. She has argued for poetry, lectured for it, and tried to stimulate respect for it. She has also written some poetry, a goodly selection from which you will find included in her anthology, *The New Poetry* just as you will find a goodly selection from Mr. Untermeyer's poetry included in his anthology, *Modern American Poetry.* Oh, well, fair enough! We can forgive anthologists for including themselves if they will only include enough other people. And here I do not have to discuss Miss Monroe as a poet.

It is her recently published book, ***Poets and Their Art,*** that stands for the most important part of Miss Monroe's career—that is to say, her function as editor of the first magazine in the United States to be devoted entirely to poetry and discussion of poetry. This book, consisting of essays taken in large part from *Poetry's* editorial pages, is not only, as she suggests, a record of *Poetry's* adventures, of great names published and good causes sponsored. It is a very illuminating picture of Miss Monroe. She reveals herself in all her vices and virtues even

more clearly than she reveals the poets she discusses. (pp. 121-22)

I heartily recommend Miss Monroe's book to all who have only a mild interest, or no interest at all, in poetry: it will start them thinking: it will tease them onward. . . . Miss Monroe's book is a measure of the propagandizing service which she has done for the finest of the fine arts.

That service, however, lies pretty largely in the past. It is a book of memories, a backward glance to the stirring days of 1912 and thereabouts, when Harriet Monroe was energetically introducing us to newcomers who have since become leaders. Harriet Monroe is still apparently living in that past, and her magazine is running by sheer momentum only. One finds news, gossip, reviews in *Poetry* these days, but very few good poems. Miss Monroe is not now "discovering" Lindsays, Sandburgs, and Masterses of a new day. Her magazine is diluted with fripperies, minor wails, schoolgirlish platitudes. It is decaying.

Another disappointing fact is that Miss Monroe, in spite of honesty, diligence, and independence of mind, is not really a critic. Other than her vague but determined defense of free verse, her somewhat opportunist championing of poetry as a factor in the national life, what claims can she make to the title of critic? It will be impossible to discover in her book any body of principles such as we might have expected her to be maturing in her fourteen years' experience as editor and student of poetry. Compare her book, for instance, with critical volumes like T. S. Eliot's *The Sacred Wood* or even Conrad Aiken's *Skepticisms,* which is mainly a book of reviews. These volumes have a solidity and purpose which Miss Monroe's does not possess.

Delightful as these essays often are, they rarely get down to bedrock. They play earnestly over the surface of poetry. They introduce us with a pleasant feminine urbanity to a series of notables, breathing recollections, recording tilts and encounters, volleying opinions and dogmatic preferences which have little systematic dogma to uphold them. They represent crusades rather than analyses. They show a fondness for neatly turned phrases which have more of the flavor of the tea-table than of the critic's study. I note, in the essay on Robinson, references to the "meaty richness" of Robinson's produce, "the exquisitely tender and beautiful 'Mr. Flood's Party'" (Miss Monroe likes the word "exquisite"). . . . Frost's "The Hill Wife" has an "exquisitely delicate pathos." Millay's lyrics are "ineffably lovely." And so on! Furthermore, the volume is notable for its exclusions as well as its inclusions. Miss Monroe has space for the fifth-rate Marjorie Allen Seiffert and a pack of minor feminine singers, but nothing at all to say for Conrad Aiken, E. E. Cummings, John Crowe Ransom, Louis Untermeyer, John G. Neihardt, Robinson Jeffers, and William Ellery Leonard. Elinor Wylie gets only a narrow corner in Miss Monroe's gallery of women poets, and T. S. Eliot . . . , is strangely yoked in discussion with Lew Sarett, who has written some charming but mild lyrics about the Indians. In short, Miss Monroe has fought for poetry nobly but blindly. She has wanted to be a general, but her strategical capacities are thin. She claims to be the friend of poetry and of poets, but has little of real importance to say to them. She is an enterprising editor who by courage and a happy combination of circumstances was able to launch a much-needed and, in the beginning, a notable magazine; but time has shown in her and in her followers of the Chicago group grave weaknesses which deny her claims to leadership in the field of poetry.

Without meaning to imply disparagement, I wish to record my belief that Miss Monroe has essentially the club-woman mind. This is, up to a certain limit, a very fine thing. . . . It signifies an earnest public spiritedness, an active and real interest in art, intellectual curiosity, zeal for "the good life." But in its dealings with literature, especially when it sits in judgment and proposes to make itself into a critical force the limits of its seriousness are evident. (pp. 122-24)

Miss Monroe's book is, like a clubwoman's diary, too much a record of sensation. It might be entitled *Poets Whom I Have Met*, for it is the zest of her editorial adventures that seems to underlie her reactions and estimates. And I am not without some suspicion that, if American poetry for the moment shows an inclination to languish, and if the great poetic revival in which Miss Monroe participated seems to falter when it should be at its climax, Miss Monroe and those who have followed similar methods are partly to blame. They have made much of false issues, and now are without issues. They have been concerned with sensations rather than ideas, and are now jaded prophets, without a cause. They have arrogated to themselves power and dictatorial robes, and now, bereft of authority, have only the illusion of past triumphs to clothe their nakedness. I would not take away from Miss Monroe one iota of the credit that is due her as a leader, but it is time to recognize that leadership has passed or ought to pass into other hands. Her magazine should either be revitalized or it should be discontinued. (p. 125)

> *Donald Davidson, "Critics and Commentators: Harriet Monroe" (originally published in* The Tennessean, *August 1, 1926), in his '*The Spyglass': Views and Reviews, 1924-1930, *edited by John Tyree Fain (copyright © 1963 by John Tyree Fain), Vanderbilt University Press, 1963, pp. 121-25.*

EZRA POUND   (essay date 1930)

[*Pound is regarded, with T. S. Eliot, as one of the greatest innovators and influences in twentieth-century Anglo-American poetry. He was instrumental in editorially and financially aiding Eliot, Wyndham Lewis, James Joyce, and William Carlos Williams, among other poets. His own* Cantos *are among the most ambitious poetic cycles of the century, and his series of satirical poems* Hugh Selwyn Mauberley *is ranked with Eliot's* The Waste Land *as a significant attack upon the decadence of modern culture. An American, Pound considered the United States to be itself a cultural wasteland, and he spent most of his life in Europe. He was* Poetry's *European editor for several years, a period during which he introduced Monroe to the works of several new, major poets and urged their publication in the magazine. The two editors quarreled frequently, as Pound considered Monroe to be too conservative and provincial of taste, while Monroe believed that Pound promoted Imagist poets to the near-exclusion of all others. In the excerpt below, Pound expresses his opinion of Monroe and of* Poetry, *and seems to verify Ellen Williams's sardonic appraisal of his aggrandized self-image in regard to the magazine: "He, Ezra Pound, originated everything in the files worth printing, while Harriet Monroe was a good-hearted donkey who provided the means for printing his movement, but also presented annoying obstacles to its effective promotion."*]

The active phase of the small magazine in America begins with the founding of Miss Monroe's magazine, *Poetry*, in Chicago in 1911. (p. 689)

Miss Monroe and her backers recognized that verse, to be of any intellectual value, could not be selected merely on the basis of its immediate earning capacity. This idea was not new, but it was not at that moment functioning vigorously in other editorial offices.

I don't know of any other constructive idea that is directly traceable to the Chicago office. (p. 691)

Miss Monroe never pretended to adopt either a contemporary, European, or international criterion. Certain principles that Europe had accepted for eighty years have never penetrated her sanctum. It is possible that recognition of these ideas would have prematurely extinguished her magazine. On the other hand, she may never have grasped these ideas. She has repeatedly protected her readers; i.e., she has assumed that the intelligence of her readers is so far below that of the authors whom she has printed that the readers are at certain points not permitted to read and to judge for themselves what the writers believe.

We Europeans consider this an insult to the reader; and "we" (the author . . .), as an American, consider it a pessimistic lack of confidence in our compatriots.

Miss Monroe has occasionally mutilated a work by excisions and has occasionally failed to see the unity of a longer work and given it in fragments.

Nevertheless, she has done valuable service by reason of the purity of her intentions. She meant to provide a place where unknown poets could be printed; she has done so. Where new ideas and forms could be tried, she has done so. She has provided a meal ticket when the meal ticket was badly needed.

She has printed on her own motion Mr. Lindsay's "General Booth Enters Heaven."

She has printed, after six months argument with me, Mr. Frost.

She printed (after Marion Reedy had with great difficulty persuaded him to write *Spoon River*) some poems by E. L. Masters.

She printed, after six months argument with me, Mr. T. S. Eliot's *Prufrock*.

She printed me a year or so after Mr. Mencken had done so.

She printed without protest the early work of "H. D." and of Aldington; work by Yeats, F. M. Hueffer (Ford).

She also mutilated my "Homage to Sextus Propertius" at a time when I had to take what I could get, and long after I had ceased to regard *Poetry* or its opinion as having any weight or bearing or as being the possible implement or organ for expressing any definite thought. (pp. 691-92)

> *Ezra Pound, "Small Magazines," in* The English Journal *(copyright © 1930 by the National Council of Teachers of English), Vol. XIX, No. 9, November, 1930, pp. 689-704.**

LEONARD BROWN   (essay date 1933)

[*In this examination of the second revised edition of* The New Poetry: An Anthology of Twentieth-Century Verse in English, *Brown discusses the philosophical conventions of poetic movements from Romanticism through Imagism.*]

By issuing a revised edition of this anthology of contemporary poetry, Miss Monroe has performed an important labor of our time. Other collections may show fewer poets more fully, or persistently maintain a higher level of verse; and a few, by a policy of rigid exclusion and the exercise of a correct judicious taste, may stand as permanent monuments to the finest poetic talent of the last thirty years. But only this book gives us the illusion of living again in the midst of that fever of verse which was so characteristic of the first quarter of our century, of witnessing, so far as it is now possible to witness, the poets of the last two generations at work. In this respect Miss Monroe is superior to Mr. Untermeyer as an editor.

The New Poetry is hardly criticism, as would be a more rigidly exclusive volume (and indeed such notes as Miss Monroe includes, both from her own essays and from essays by others who have been associated with her in editing *Poetry*, are largely acclamatory rather than critical); but Miss Monroe's anthology is certainly an incitement of criticism. For it makes clear that the possibility of re-examining the poetic output of the last thirty years, with the critical intention of revealing the poetry as it has come to stand, should be entertained. Accordingly the question is whether contemporary poetry is an extension of an older convention, or, on the other hand, a new movement within a great tradition. (p. 43)

Although Miss Monroe neglects, in her notes, to point out adequately the differences between our contemporary romanticists and Mr. Eliot's generation, and fails, critically, by indiscriminately acclaiming as ''new'' such contemporary poetry as abjures nineteenth-century ''poetic'' diction, she more than rewards us by representing all contemporary poets justly. Given the poetry, we may criticize it for ourselves. (pp. 62-3)

> Leonard Brown, "Our Contemporary Poetry," in The Sewanee Review (reprinted by permission of the editor; published 1933 by The University of the South), Vol. XLI, No. 1, Winter, 1933, pp. 43-63.*

EZRA POUND   (essay date 1936)

[This brief essay, and the one by Wallace Stevens which follows, appeared in a special issue of Poetry devoted to the memory of Harriet Monroe [see Additional Bibliography]. In comparison to his earlier opinions (see excerpt above, 1930), in the following elegiac essay Pound offers a more considerate view of Monroe.]

The death of Harriet Monroe will be felt as a personal loss by everyone who has ever contributed to her magazine. No one in our time or in any time has ever served the cause of an art with greater devotion, patience, and unflagging kindness. The greater and more frequent one's differences of view about that art, the greater opportunity one had for weighing these qualities in her. (p. 137)

Measuring by space and time, the elasticity of her perceptions and the freshness of her interest were those of a great editor, and as no one more acrimoniously differed with her in point of view than I did, so, I think, no one is better able to testify to her unfailing sincerity, to the unfailing purity of her intentions.

We will not see another such patience, another such kindliness in her place. Even in matters of detail, considering the contingencies, I have never contended that she was specifically wrong for a given time, and in the possibilities of the situation. In the give and take of untrammeled correspondence the total comprehension of this, between her and myself, must be considered, and no fragment of that correspondence can be properly judged save in relation to the totality, from 1910 or whenever it was to the present.

The new generation of the 1930's can not measure, offhand, the local situation of 1910. An exclusive editorial policy would not have done the work of an inclusive policy (however much the inclusiveness may have rankled one and all factions).

It is to Miss Monroe's credit that *Poetry* never degenerated into a factional organ. Her achievement was to set up a trade journal in the best sense of the word. You might say it preceded the guild sense—if you even now see any signs of that component of civilization emerging in the American disorder.

During the twenty-four years of her editorship perhaps three periodicals made a brilliant record, perhaps five periodicals, but they were all under the sod in the autumn of 1936, and no other publication has existed in America where any writer of poetry could more honorably place his writings. This was true in 1911. It is true as I write this. (pp. 137-38)

> Ezra Pound, "Vale," in Poetry, Special Issue: Harriet Monroe (© 1936 by The Modern Poetry Association), Vol. XLIX, No. 3, December, 1936, pp. 137-38.

WALLACE STEVENS   (essay date 1936)

[A major American poet, Stevens blended an elegant, sometimes shocking style with the thematic concerns of a philosopher. Influenced by the French Imagists and Symbolists, his poetry is noted for its recondite vocabulary, original metaphors, lavish imagery, and spirit of agnostic searching. Stevens was one of Monroe's discoveries; virtually unknown, he submitted a group of poems titled ''Phases'' to Poetry's War Poem Contest in November 1914, at which time Monroe published them. She later wrote: ''I was alone in the office when this group arrived almost too late for the War Number. I remember my eager reassembling of the page proofs to make room for two pages—all I could squeeze in—by this master of strange and beautiful rhythms.'' Below, Stevens applauds his former editor for bringing the same consideration to her work that she exhibited toward others in her private life.]

Her job brought Miss Monroe into contact with the most ferocious egoists. I mean poets in general. You could see her shrewd understanding adapt itself to her visitors. When they had left her office she remained just as amiable. (p. 154)

No one could have been more agreeable, yet she had not a trace of the busy welcomer. She wanted more time so that she might know you better. She would go along to lunch and then invite you to her house for dinner. She did the most she could for you and gave you the best she had. To cite not too exalted an instance, I remember that on one occasion she produced after dinner as a liqueur a small bottle of whiskey which she said was something like ninety years old, almost colonial, as if stored up for that particular winter's night. . . .

All this reflected itself in *Poetry*, which might so easily have become something less than it was: something less in the sense of being the organ of a group or mode, or of having a rigid any-other standard. It was notably a magazine of many people; it was the widest possible. She made it so. (p. 155)

> Wallace Stevens, in a memorial essay to Harriet Monroe, in Poetry, Special Issue: Harriet Monroe (© 1936 by The Modern Poetry Association), Vol. XLIX, No. 3, December, 1936, pp. 154-55.

MARY M. COLUM (essay date 1938)

[Colum, who contributed criticism regularly to such publications as The New Republic *and* The Saturday Review, *was called "the best woman critic in America" by William Rose Benét in 1933. Others, however, have noted that Colum sometimes allowed personal prejudice to color her critical judgement. In her autobiography,* Life and the Dream, *Colum displays great personal animosity and bitterness toward Monroe (see additional bibliography). In the excerpt below, she provides an extremely negative assessment of Monroe's contribution to literature, claiming that Monroe's devotion to literature was due to her unmarried, childless state.]*

After the summing up, the late Harriet Monroe's autobiography—*A Poet's Life*—is dull and tedious. It reads like the account of the life of a very serious, though not very inspired, schoolmarm, without much poetry in her soul in spite of her official connection with that art. But Miss Monroe was a good editor and had the pioneer characteristics of resourcefulness, ambition, self-sacrifice, and courage. She had, in addition, an intuition almost like that of a businessman's for a good investment. . . .

The first intuition that brought her real returns urged her to present herself at the office of the organizers of the Chicago fair of 1892 and propose to write an ode of dedication to the fair. She got the commission, wrote the poem, and demanded $1,000 but she encountered great opposition to having the ode read. However, her determination was greater than that of the members of the committee, some of whom appear to have had a sense of poetry. Before she was through with them, all her demands were accepted. . . . In addition to the $1,000, she got $5,000 more—damages from a New York paper for printing the work without permission. In short, she got $6,000 for a poem that at best was but a literate, dull affair.

Twenty years later, in her fifties, she accomplished another piece of salesmanship that was even more remarkable. She persuaded a number of Chicago businessmen to endow a magazine for poetry, with her as editor. Ezra Pound, who had great passion for poetry and little personal ambition, offered himself as European editor without pay. Through him she got the work of some of the finest European poets, practically all the best-known ones. Through herself and her colleagues she got the work of all that group of poets who burst on America in the second decade of this century—Robinson, Masters, Frost, Millay, Sandburg. She thus gave an organ to some of the finest poets of the day.

She came to know a great deal about poetry because she had a love of it and an open mind. Her life covered the span of the most interesting part of Chicago's development, and her autobiography could have been very interesting if she had had any power of gauging the value of her materials. She devotes pages and pages to the doings of uninteresting relatives, spends other pages pointlessly hitting at people who did not share her own estimate of her work. A little self-knowledge of the kind that Somerset Maugham has, a little sense of humor, would have lightened this chronicle.

Miss Monroe's very lack of humor sometimes produces Rabelaisian effects, as when she solemnly records the compliment paid to her father by the madam of a house of prostitution, whose lawyer he was.

Another attorney called during a visit of this client to Mr. Monroe and, apparently knowing the lady, inquired jocosely, "Do you throw in the privileges of the house?"

The lady replied: "Mr. Monroe is a gentleman; and when I want that kind of lawyer I will go to you."

One can see that the material here for a diverting narrative is considerable, if the author had used it instead of filling her book with so much literary data. Poetry somehow emerges from these pages as a branch of ponderous and artificial *Kultur* rather than the rhythmical expression of ardent life.

> *Mary M. Colum, "The Stuffy Side of Experience," in* Forum and Century *(copyright, 1938, Events Publishing Company, Inc.; reprinted by permission of Current History, Inc.), Vol. XCIX, No. 5, May, 1938, p. 280.*

HORACE GREGORY AND MARYA ZATURENSKA (essay date 1946)

[Gregory and Zaturenska are both noted American poets. They were married in 1925 and have coauthored several works, including the important study American Poetry 1900-1940, *from which the excerpt below, praising Monroe's contribution to America's early twentieth-century "poetry renaissance," is taken.]*

To a marked degree, Harriet Monroe's little magazine, *Poetry* . . . , was actually the "poetic renaissance." The circular announcing its arrival created an air of excitement among readers of poetry that compared favorably with the publicity that attended William Butler Yeats's announcement of an "Irish Renaissance" in the 1890's. To the poets, Harriet Monroe wrote:

> *First,* a chance to be heard in their own place, without the limitations imposed by the popular magazine. . . . *Second* . . . All kinds of verse will be considered—narrative, dramatic, lyric—quality alone being the test of acceptance. . . . *Third,* besides the prize or prizes above mentioned, we shall pay contributors.

Here was an offer not to be resisted, and the flame ignited by Harriet Monroe spread to other periodicals, and fanned by quickening winds of sporadic enthusiasm, it ran into far and sometimes contrary directions. (pp. 141-42)

But of all the ventures occasioned by the so-called "poetic renaissance," *Poetry* commanded a central position within them, devoting special issues of the magazine to divergent and contrasting groups of poets, and for three-quarters of an active and controversial decade, the influence of Harriet Monroe's championship of poetry "as the highest, most complete human expression of truth and beauty" was felt and echoed in editorial offices throughout the country. (p. 142)

Harriet Monroe had few pretensions as a critic, and throughout her life she held an attitude of sharp distrust toward painters who talked too much about their art and poets who had too many theories concerning poetry. . . . Harriet Monroe had put her trust in the resources of her own imagination and intuition, and since she also possessed the gift of common sense—that rarest of all human senses—she made few mistakes in feeling or in judgment. It was in this spirit that she became a brilliant editor, willing always to accept verse that contained the "individual, unstereotyped rhythm, the surprises, and the irregularities, found in all great art because they are inherent in human feeling."

To Harriet Monroe there was no lack of consistency in publishing the work of poets whose taste and intentions seemed at a far distance from her own; she had had the courage to publish the poetry of many writers long before it had become fashionable to do so, and with this knowledge and assurance, she continued to edit *Poetry* up to the date of her death in 1936. Meanwhile the early impulses and enthusiasms that had attended the founding of her magazine had begun to change their temper soon after the close of the First World War. It would not be too far-fetched to say that the "poetic renaissance" came to a final conclusion with the publication of T. S. Eliot's poem, "The Waste Land," in the November, 1922, issue of *The Dial*. From that moment onward, Harriet Monroe's position seemed to represent all the fervor, the warmth, the native quickness, and innocence that defined the hopeful attitude of Middle Western America before the war, and readers of "The Waste Land" became aware of something from another world than that of the "new" poetry of which Miss Monroe was so ardent a champion. The unrest and the spiritual malady that had become prevalent in the large cities of Europe and of the United States seemed to speak out in voices so disturbing that it was no longer possible to ignore them, and another day beyond the period of the "poetic renaissance" had well begun. (pp. 146-47)

It is only by an extremely selective reading of her *Chosen Poems* . . . that one may discern the intelligence, the dignity, the grace which combined to make her personality a memorable one; again one sees her as if in glimpses behind the screen of her active life. . . . (p. 148)

> *Horace Gregory and Marya Zaturenska, "Harriet Monroe and the 'Poetic Renaissance'," in their* A History of American Poetry, 1900-1940 *(copyright, 1942, 1944, 1946, by Harcourt Brace Jovanovich, Inc.; copyright renewed © 1974 by Horace Gregory and Marya Zaturenska; reprinted by permission of the Estate of Horace Gregory and Marya Zaturenska), Harcourt Brace Jovanovich, 1946, pp. 141-49.*

MORTON DAUWEN ZABEL   (essay date 1960)

[*Zabel is a poet, critic, and prominent scholar. He became acquainted with Harriet Monroe in 1926 when he began contributing to her magazine,* Poetry, *and in 1928 Monroe asked Zabel to become her associate editor. Zabel assumed editorship of* Poetry *for a year after Monroe's death in 1936, and continued to make frequent contributions thereafter. Later in his career, Zabel was influential in increasing the study of North American literature in South America. During the mid-1940s he held the only official professorship on North American literature in Latin America. He spent two-and-a-half years lecturing throughout Latin America, and wrote two widely used American literary histories in Portuguese and Spanish.*]

Though few lives in the past hundred years have been allowed to remain untouched by "history in the making", there are always some in which the shape of a century seems to have been a matter of conscious instinct from the outset, impelling them to the risks that defy the safety of convention and to the courage or curiosity that makes it possible to add something of value to the given resources of experience. The greatest lives in any century show that instinct, but so do some of the others. Harriet Monroe's life arrived at a distinct and substantial achievement of its own, a positive contribution to the finer prosperity of its era. (p. 242)

During the last two years of her life she devoted most of her spare time to the writing of her autobiography. She wrote the last chapters she completed on the ship that took her to South

America, and she left it unfinished when she died. The manuscript was typed and assembled by Miss Udell; it fell to my lot to write its concluding chapters; it was published as *A Poet's Life* in 1938. For twenty-two years I had not opened its pages. Now that I do so I find what any reader is likely to discover in them: not one of the great autobiographies of our time but a deeply sincere and moving chronicle that revives the voice and presence of "H. M." as she lived: the spirit of expectancy and generous humanity that impelled her from her girlhood, the trials of doubt and discouragement she survived, the honesty of her feeling and impulses no matter what their results in disappointment or satisfaction, the undiscouraged resolution that carried her through five decades of struggle to the moment when, past the age of fifty, she conceived the great project of her life, launched her magazine, and played a major part in bringing a new age of poetry to birth.

The event and the year with which her name will always be associated was her founding of *Poetry* in October 1912. (p. 243)

Today, almost half a century later, it is doubtless easier for students or historians of that now-distant period, using the convenient hindsight of five decades, to add up her errors, doubts, misapplied confidences, and mistaken enthusiasms than to count her triumphs. But this is only to say that her present judges live long after an accomplished fact while she lived inside it, squarely in the middle of a venture long before its success was assured. It was she who took the risks; put herself in the middle of a merciless limelight and the pitched conflict of a new age of poetic innovation; had to read and judge manuscripts that had not yet been subjected to the exhaustive analysis and evaluation of a new age of criticism; exposed herself to thankless recrimination as well as to exhilarating discoveries for which no publicity had prepared her; had to exercise the vigorous eclecticism of choice which is always more difficult to maintain than a privileged selectivity; and saw to it that her magazine survived and paid its bills while most of its more reckless or defiant contemporaries indulged themselves in the pleasures of unpaid accounts, recurrent bankruptcy, and aesthetic martyrdom. She made her mistakes and adhered to her personal loyalties, but of what modern editor or magazine, even those that have boasted severer principles than hers, can this not be said? She was always willing to take the risks of her generosity, even when she knew these led her into errors from which a stricter distaste or selfishness might have saved her. She gave her journal one of the most difficult things a magazine can achieve for itself—a personal character, an intimate editorial personality and quality. As is usual with generous natures, she was most impugned, lampooned, or vilified by those for whom she had done most. She made no habit of nursing resentments or grievances, rejecting arguments, or avoiding conflicts with her associates. She was past the age for these practices when she became an editor. Her sense of humanity and justice had been toughened by bitter experience; and the best lesson her co-workers took from her was the example of her balanced judgment and her unresentful openness to suggestion.

"Her job brought Miss Monroe into contact with the most ferocious egoists", Wallace Stevens said in 1936: "I mean poets in general" [see excerpt above]. She thus laid herself open to becoming not only the publisher but the scapegoat of the many talents who appealed to her editorial hospitality. Though it was one of the most impressive aspects of her intelligence that she, who was born and conditioned to so different an age of poetry, could have re-created herself and become one of the most enthusiastic sponsors of a new era in the art, she was wise enough to know that enmity is a fate that no editor can hope to escape. Ten years ago when a collection, highly manipulated, strategically edited, and tactfully selected, of Pound's letters was published, Miss Monroe, who had been the first American magazine editor to recognize his talent and his gift for discovering or instigating new forces in the arts, was made to figure as one of the scapegoats in his career. Some careers seem to need more scapegoats than others, but this was not the role in which Pound himself cast her when, in one of the noblest moments of his life, he wrote his tribute to her in 1936 [see excerpt above]. . . . If she had her doubts about ''Prufrock'' when Pound first sent it to her in 1915, she had earned her right to her doubts as well as her enthusiasms; and if some of the finest manuscripts she published in those years came from Pound, many others came from now-distinguished poets for whom he had no use or sympathy whatever and whom she had to recognize and discover for herself. Our present wisdom after the fact is our easy privilege. Hers before the fact of within the fact was another matter altogether and a far more difficult one, but it was her skill in sustaining it that gave her her own kind of sanity and balance, and that brought her to her success.

But most of what has been said thus far has concerned Harriet Monroe's public life, her editorial function, and to anyone who came to know her closely this is only a part of her story.

The most arresting feature of any achievement is how much it costs in self-judgment and self-limitation; how much secret hope or ambition has to be sacrificed to it; how strictly it is held in reserve by the individual destiny; and how the one guarantee of its arrival is that the striver refuse to submit to the finality of any reversal that denies the force that impels him. Harriet Monroe knew a long ordeal of this kind in her life, and it was only made acute by the zest she brought to her experiences, the deceptive forms of success she had gained or been deluded by, the years of deferred hope she weathered, and the tenacity these bred in her nerves and intelligence. This is the personal drama she conveys in her autobiography. She also conveys it in her verse which, if it failed in the greatness she so resolutely strove for, still reveals a spirit that had its own peculiar honesty and probity. It was these that brought her idealism intact through fifty years of American experience during which so many careers and characters were aborted by crasser standards of success or willing forms of disgust and discouragement. They gave her memories the charm of an enthusiasm that quickened the lives of her friends and listeners to the day she died. Her practical hard-headedness never deprived her of her contact with an older and more innocent American idealism which had a great deal to do with the shaping of her personal career and with the energy she brought to the founding of *Poetry*. These matters were once more familiar in these pages than they may be today. (pp. 247-49)

Morton Dauwen Zabel, ''H. M.: In Memory, 1860-1936'' (1960), in Poetry *(© 1961 by The Modern Poetry Association; reprinted by permission of the Editor of* Poetry*), Vol. XCVII, No. 4, January, 1961, pp. 241-54.*

ELLEN WILLIAMS   (essay date 1971)

[*Williams blasts the ''absurdity'' of the tradition that Monroe was a timid and inept editor whose magazine only attained vitality through the contributions of foreign correspondent Ezra Pound. This tradition was established by Pound himself, who assumed*

the editorial ''we'' in his first letter to Monroe (see Additional Bibliography). Subsequent critics, such as D. D. Paige, editor of a volume of Pound's letters, Reed Whittemore (see Additional Bibliography), and Noel Stock, Pound's biographer (see Additional Bibliography), have all presented a picture of Pound struggling to overcome Monroe's intellectual limitations when convincing her to print such poets as T. S. Eliot and W. B. Yeats. Ignoring Monroe's stated purpose in creating Poetry—*to provide a forum for such poets, who could not gain hearings elsewhere—these critics have portrayed Monroe as little more than an able fund-raiser for a publication which was great only insofar as Pound was associated with it.*]

When the origins of twentieth century poetry emerged from the eclipse which obscures the not-quite-recent past, the reputation of the editor who had been the chief promoter of the *new movement* suffered a peculiar reversal. Harriet Monroe figures in many accounts as the editor who almost refused to print *The Love Song of J. Alfred Prufrock,* yielding reluctantly, after six months of bullying persuasion from Ezra Pound, to give T. S. Eliot his first publication outside college magazines. *Poetry* magazine . . . had undeniably a brilliant record. Not only had it been the first paper to promote Ezra Pound and his school of Imagistes—comprising in 1912 such poets as Hilda Doolittle and Richard Aldington, and briefly including John Gould Fletcher—but it had given first magazine publication or first American publication to a number of other significant poets: William Carlos Williams, Marianne Moore, and Carl Sandburg, as well as Eliot. . . . *Poetry* gave Robert Frost his first new American publication after his English success of 1913. . . . *Poetry's* publication of [the] transitional Yeats material is particularly interesting because it links the change in the Irish poet to the vigorous development of American poetry.

The most immediately sensational of the new American writers, Edgar Lee Masters, was also associated with *Poetry* at the beginning of his celebrity. Although his *Spoon River Anthology* was published [elsewhere] . . . , *Poetry* was quick to recognize its merits and to promote it, and became Masters' defender against conservative protest about his free verse manner and his realistic material. (pp. 77-8)

[A] labor of historical re-creation is necessary for appreciation of Harriet Monroe's strength as an editor. No reader today can be expected to count it remarkable that she consented to publish T. S. Eliot's great poem, or recognized a peculiar beauty and rhythmic originality in Wallace Stevens' small early poems. She saw in Ezra Pound a powerful poet and an immensely stimulating literary intelligence, and promoted him both as a poet and as a critic: her perception now seems elementary. At the most, one could say that Miss Monroe was right in a high percentage of her enthusiasms.

But after that the retrospective judgment of her would grow more and more negative. After all, she was displeased by the conclusion of *Prufrock,* and apparently wanted to suggest alterations to Eliot, a move vetoed by Pound. If her recognition encouraged Stevens at the beginning of his career, it hardly helped that career when she printed *Sunday Morning* in a fragmented version in 1915, omitting three of the eight stanzas apparently because she did not see the poem as a whole, but as eight separate poems on a common theme. If her appreciations were catholic and her tolerance of irascible poetic genius inexhaustible, so that she was over a long period before 1920, a sounding board and a publication outlet for William Carlos Williams, Stevens, Pound, Masters, and others, one finally must come down to the fact that her own particular prize *discovery* among the new American poets was Vachel Lindsay.

Indeed, the observer who expects precision in editorial matters might describe Harriet Monroe's entire career as the prolonged experience of failure. It began in the failure of her own poetic work. At the age of fifty-one, in 1911, she was led by the accumulated frustrations of a lifetime of half-success in her own art to conceive of *Poetry* as an outlet for the most neglected of the arts. . . . She did not create *Poetry* to be the triumphant vehicle of a *new movement*, of a *Poetry Renaissance*, which it quickly became. *Poetry* began as the vehicle of embattled idealism, developed out of Miss Monroe's refusal to accept the logic of her own literary career, and the universal judgment that American poetry was too thin and too derivative to merit serious attention.

If Miss Monroe had an editorial platform in the magazine— the cast of her mind, neither sharply critical nor analytical, weighed against any very explicit program—it was expressed in the motto from Whitman which she posted on it: *To have great poets there must be great audiences, too.* She hoped that her magazine might go beyond the encouragement of the artist by modest recognition and frugal payment, that it might reach out to the great shapeless mass of the American people, creating a reciprocal relation between the artist and his public from which not only great art but a great civilization might grow. Her most ambitious goal for the art she nurtured was the reformation and the redemption of American society at large. This goal was purely an ideal—her circulation never exceeded 2,000 readers altogether in the early years—but it was so outrageously in conflict with Ezra Pound's poetic ideals that his service as foreign correspondent was punctuated by explosive quarrels. Pound was the more easily upset, because his own temperament seems antipathetic to the very idea of rhetoric, to any suggestion of an audience and its expectations. . . . Since the *new movement* terminated in a poetry which is notoriously inaccessible to the man in the street, Harriet Monroe's aspirations for her audience seem ironically absurd today. (pp. 78-9)

The pathetic failure of Miss Monroe's hopes for the poet in American society has fed the tradition that *Poetry* was vital only so far as it expressed the choices of Ezra Pound, operating in London as foreign correspondent during the years 1912-1919. This rather widespread tradition, which skips over the fact that Pound curtailed his contribution to the magazine after mid-1914, pictures Harriet Monroe as an obstacle to the promotion of the new movement, an editor requiring constant bullying, prodding, lecturing from Pound. . . .

The absurdity of this tradition is plain when one considers that Miss Monroe was under no obligation to accept counsel from Ezra Pound or from anyone else. The magazine and its capital support, contributed by individual guarantors whom she had found in Chicago, were entirely under her management. If she had been in the least degree hostile to the new movement, she would very early have broken the connection with Ezra Pound. His irascible outbursts gave her plenty of occasion. The editorial choices which created *Poetry's* brilliant record were Harriet Monroe's, although Pound scarcely saw it in that light. . . .

Harriet Monroe brought to the new movement an inexhaustible and disinterested zeal. She was sensitive on an intuitive level: she had a very high batting average as an acceptor of significant poets, whatever hesitations may be charged against her, and whatever the excesses of her political idealism. If she was doubtful about the early Eliot, she did print *Prufrock* at a time when other editors had rejected it as *queer to the point of*

madness, and she was much more responsive to the early Stevens than Pound. (p. 80)

Editorial control of a magazine of verse, at that particular moment in history, was an unparalleled opportunity, one to stimulate any amount of daydreaming and retrospective second guessing, and Harriet Monroe was sufficient to it. The new movement needed the galvanic stimulation, the sense of revolution, which Ezra Pound knew how to communicate. It needed the critical discriminations which Eliot and others began to suggest in 1917. But it also needed the perceptive, disinterested, zealous service which Harriet Monroe was able to render. While she managed to sustain a balance at the center, in the period before literary politics thickened, poetic careers grew diverse, and *Poetry* became the prisoner of its own past successes, her magazine was the focus of a veritable renaissance— a renewal of the poetic art in America which seems more astonishing every year. In that renewal Harriet Monroe was instrumental, and she should be remembered in the glow of the romance which it held for her. (p. 82)

Ellen Williams, "Harriet Monroe" (copyright 1971 by Ellen Williams), in The Antigonish Review, *Vol. II, No. II, Summer, 1971, pp. 77-82.*

DANIEL J. CAHILL   (essay date 1973)

[*Cahill's* Harriet Monroe *is a valuable study of her life and career. In the following excerpt he surveys both her poetry and her editorial work.*]

Harriet Monroe was, first, a poet and, second, an editor of uncommon sensibility. She would like, we feel sure, to be remembered for her achievements in that order. History has, however, honored her more dynamic and tangible role of editor. As the founder of *Poetry,* she infused a new vitality into the American poet; she encouraged a new seriousness and a new confidence in the art. Most significantly, she gave the poet a voice, a place from which he could speak with dignity. For Miss Monroe, poetry was not a "cloistered virtue" to be kept pure from the ravisher of time and men. If poetry was ever to achieve a new vitality, believed Miss Monroe, it had to distill that energy from contention and truggle; it had to be a statement of man's responses to human experience. Throughout the decades of her editorship, she fostered this new adventure in poetic statement; therefore, her place as a shaping force in the making of modern poetry is secure. (p. 130)

Miss Monroe's success as an editor has been ascribed to a number of personal and ideological attitudes. There is no doubt that the continued success of *Poetry* derived much from the firmness and stability of its editor, but such characteristics only account for the superficial motives. Her deepest source of insight was her own poetic sensitivity. From her youthful days, she cared for poetry—for its special magic in words and for its unique satisfactions of mind. To be an active poet was the deepest and most abiding commitment of Miss Monroe's life. Because she was a poet first, she was a sensitive critic of poetry.

As a poet, there is a marked development in her work—a movement from the derivative to a mature and characteristic voice. The early poetry and her foray into poetic drama are less distinguished because they represent a young poet's search for her proper medium. The interesting quality of these poems and plays is the note of experimentation, a willingness to launch out in untried directions. This is especially true of her efforts in drama. The plays are inevitably bounded by the limitations of the American theater in the 1890's; but, within that frame-work, Miss Monroe tried to insert some realism of subject matter, to make the plays deal with the real problems of men and women and not some artificially conceived remote and romantic characters. Her efforts are minor when pitted against those of Ibsen and Shaw; but she was, nevertheless, aware of the rising tide of Realism in drama. Her plays were written in a highly transitional moment in American drama, which only reluctantly shed the trappings of a heroic "poetic drama" for the later Realism of the twentieth century. If Miss Monroe's plays are not fully achieved works, it is because they are a part of national drama in a state of change—written too early for their Realistic content and too late for the waning vogue of high "poetic" drama.

A similar judgment may be conferred upon her early poetry. Too many of the poems are caught up in the tangle of the "romantic diction" of the "genteel" tradition. After the success of her **"Columbian Ode,"** . . . Miss Monroe struck a more contemporary tone in her work—both in diction and in subject matter. Most of the poetry reprinted in this study was composed after the founding of *Poetry;* it reflects her work after she had been freed of satisfying the demands of commercial publishers. The diction is no longer false, and the themes are no longer tailored to any noble preconception of what poetry should be and do.

Almost all of Miss Monroe's poetry is occasional, prompted by some public or private event. The individual lyrics are marked by a fine perception and technical sophistication; the more descriptive poems—especially those of individual cities—are evocative of the unique historical spirit of place. In judging the quality of her poems, we must recognize that, if her range is personal and limited, the works still have the solidarity and excellence of a good minor poet. She was consistently innovative in her poetic technique, and she sought constantly to make a meaningful statement of life. She had little tolerance for intellectual indirection or for a negative view of life. As a poet, she consciously sought new avenues of expression, and she encouraged the same adventurous spirit in other young poets. Her poetry is a minor contribution to the revolutionary spirit of twentieth-century literature. As for *Poetry*, it, to cite Vernon Watkins, "was the first mouthpiece of poems which have turned the course of our literature!" (pp. 130-32)

> *Daniel J. Cahill, in his* Harriet Monroe *(copyright ©1973 by Twayne Publishers; reprinted with the permission of Twayne Publishers, a Division of G. K. Hall & Co., Boston), Twayne, 1973, 148 p.*

ABBY ARTHUR JOHNSON   (essay date 1975)

[*Johnson decries the "sexist allusions" that have "obscured Monroe's contributions" as a poet and as an editor. She cites in particular Noel Stock (see Additional Bibliography), and Mary M. Colum (see excerpt above and Additional Bibliography), as critics whose sexist interpretations of Monroe's life and works have led them to critically misrepresent her.*]

As Monroe conducted her work, her feminism began to surface explicitly in her editorials and in some of her editorial policies. She saw herself not as an aging "spinster" but as a woman capable of helping the poet who did not fit society's mold. Often that poet was a woman. . . .

The autobiography reveals that Monroe considered traditional feminine roles extremely limiting. She said her grandmother "had that uncomfortable possession, a mind" and conse-

quently hated "housework" and lacked "everything she must have secretly longed for." She understood that the marriage of her own father and mother suffered because each grew up in a conventional way, he well-educated, she barely literate. (p. 34)

From adolescence, Monroe desired a life style which would encourage the fullest intellectual and artistic development: "I cannot remember the time," she wrote, "when to die without leaving some memorable record did not seem to me a calamity too terrible to be borne. . . . As she matured, she became more realistic about her literary ambitions. She maintained her dedication to art but also pursued some "ordinary human happiness." At times she even spoke wistfully of the marriage that never occurred and the child that was never conceived. She was not a simple woman.

In her *Poetry* editorials, she furthered her criticism of conventional female posturing. She occasionally directed her attack to the "club-mentality" she saw everywhere: "it was the same familiar crowd of women . . . somewhat too well dressed and well fed for a tempered human weapon in this democratic age; the same rather wistful crowd of housed and guarded souls, holding resolutely to the material goods they felt sure of, and casting about doubtfully and frugally for half-suspected spiritual joys."

Such women did little to encourage creativity in themselves and in their associates. As they failed, society failed. Such a conclusion led Monroe to a sweeping indictment of a culture which inhibits the natural and artistic development of one half of its members: . . . "clothes are the only form of artistic self-expression of which nine-tenths of our young girls are keenly aware. . . . Joy in clothes is better than no creative joys at all, but why shouldn't these girls have been led to sing, dance, rhyme, carve, make toys or furniture, textures or garments, or even delicious dishes—to create something of their own?"

Monroe's comments rankled many. In 1920, a writer for the Philadelphia *Record* accused her of chauvinism: "The vigorous male note [is] now seldom heard in the land," he declared, "and almost never at all in the pages of *Poetry: A Magazine of Verse,* the most pretentious publication in the country devoted solely to that important branch of letters. *Poetry* is edited by a woman . . . and most of its contributors are feminine. . . ."

To respond, Monroe surveyed the numbers of *Poetry* issued between April, 1919, and March, 1920. She published her findings in the *Record,* as well as in her own journal: "Before indulging in self-reproach, I was led to look up the facts. I find that during the past year . . . *Poetry* has printed verse from 105 contributors, of whom 64 were men and 41 were women. Counting the pages of these twelve numbers, I am astonished to discover that of 373 devoted to verse, 247 were filled by men and 126 by women, the proportion being almost exactly two to one." She concluded: "the facts compel me to accuse myself of injustice toward my own sex."

In the years following, she tried to right the balance by encouraging women poets whenever legitimately possible. She expressed great pleasure, for example, when women finally captured significant literary prizes. (pp. 35-6)

With a series of essays, she discussed the work of Amy Lowell, Sara Teasdale, Majorie Seiffert, H. D. and Edna Millay, those women helping her disprove Byron's line: "Man's love is of life a thing apart,/'Tis women's whole existence." She praised

Edna Millay for "Thursday," "The Penitent," "The Not Impossible Him" and "The Betrothal," poems cleverly upsetting "the carefully built walls of convention which men have set up around their Ideal Woman, even while they fought, bled and died for all the Helens and Cleopatras they happened to encounter!" She heard Millay articulating the frustrations of countless housewives. . . . (p. 36)

She devoted the September, 1926, issue to a "Women's Number" and featured work by Marion Strobel, Beatrice Ravenel, Sara Bard Field, Charlotte Arthur and Margery Swett Mansfield, among others. Some of the contributions were distinctly feminist and thereby avoided by most contemporary journals. With "Captive," for example, Marion Strobel could never have gained a hearing in, say, the *Atlantic Monthly*. . . . (p. 37)

[Monroe] knew that a periodical dedicated to feminist verse could never survive the 1920's. Moreover, she never planned such a journal, desiring instead to print the best new poets, male and female. She explained that "no deprecatory significance is intended" by the September *Poetry;* "we are thinking of issuing a *Men's Number* to enforce whatever contrasts of mood and method may be found to exist between the two great fundamental human groups." Monroe never developed the "Men's Number" and never edited another "Women's Number." She continued to highlight feminist verse, but she maintained discreet intervals between these publications.

On the twenty-second anniversary of *Poetry,* two years before her own death, Monroe recalled her heroines, women who "stand out in my memory with peculiar distinctness." She mentioned Edna Millay, Sara Teasdale, and her associate editors, Alice Corbin Henderson, Helen Hoyt, Eunice Tiejens, Marion Strobel and Jessica North. These women instructed her in the richness of the feminine past: "to know well such women . . . has been so rich an experience of feminine character that all women of history and myth and fiction become more luminously alive." (pp. 38-9)

When Monroe began to talk of retirement, in the early 1930's, Pound complimented her after his own fashion. He expressed his surprise, to begin with: "I forget how old you think you are, but you are good for another ten or fifteen years anyhow." He would discuss retirement, though, since she was in that mood. First and foremost, he believed *Poetry* a valuable journal, one that should survive Monroe's departure. . . . (p. 42)

Poetry survived by encouraging new and frequently unpopular verse. Among the numerous editors of literary periodicals, Harriet Monroe was one of the few to make a substantial contribution to the shape of 20th Century poetry. (p. 43)

> *Abby Arthur Johnson, "A Free Foot in the Wilderness: Harriet Monroe and 'Poetry', 1912 to 1936," in* Illinois Quarterly *(copyright, Illinois State University, 1975), Vol. 37, No. 4, Summer, 1975, pp. 28-43.*

ADDITIONAL BIBLIOGRAPHY

Aldington, Richard. "War Poems and Others." *The Egoist* I, No. 23 (15 December 1914): 458-59.*
  A mixed review of *You and I.* A member of Pound's Imagist coterie, Aldington concludes his assessment with the statement: "I am frankly out of sympathy with a good deal of the volume—

but that is my misfortune. But the book contains many spirited efforts."

Bond, Judith. "Dear Miss Monroe." *Manuscripts* XIII, No. 2 (Spring 1961): 34-44
  Presents examples of letters Monroe received from many renowned people in all areas of the arts. Bond provides historical background and anecdotes about each letter and its writer. Letters from Frank Lloyd Wright, Edna Millay, Ezra Pound, and T. S. Eliot, among others, are quoted.

Colum, Mary. "Chicago, 1915" and "Literary Critic." In her *Life and the Dream,* pp. 220-31, 367-77. Garden City, N.Y.: Doubleday & Co., 1947.*
  Intersperses acknowledgment of Monroe's achievement in founding and editing *Poetry* with extraordinarily insulting personal remarks about Monroe herself. Colum makes the insupportable claim that Monroe was jealous of her (Colum's) "critical reputation" and accuses Monroe of spreading lies about the Colum family.

Gerber, Philip. "Dear Harriet . . . Dear Amy." *Journal of Modern Literature* 5, No. 2 (April 1976): 233-42.*
  Account of the long professional relationship between the poet Amy Lowell and editor Monroe. Gerber quotes from several of the hundreds of letters that the two women exchanged. What emerges is the portrayal of an antagonistic relationship in which the only common ground was their "mutual interest in promoting the New Poetry."

Gregory, Horace. "The 'Unheard of Adventure': Harriet Monroe and *Poetry.*" *The American Scholar* 6, No. 2 (Spring 1937): 195-200.
  Elegaic tribute to Monroe. Gregory provides a brief overview of Monroe's editorial policies, noting especially her eclecticism in accepting widely varied types of poetry for the magazine *Poetry.*

———. "Brookline and the World." In his *Amy Lowell: Portrait of the Poet in her Time,* pp. 1-92. New York: Thomas Nelson & Sons, 1959.*
  Discusses the "poetic renaissance" in England and the United States in the five years preceding 1912 and the first publication of *Poetry,* and examines Monroe's contributions to this renaissance.

Kramer, Dale. "Harriet Monroe: *Poetry's* Muse." In his *Chicago Renaissance: The Literary Life in the Midwest, 1900-1930,* pp. 200-15. New York: Appleton-Century, 1966.
  Favorable biocritical study of Monroe's life and career, focusing upon her determination to found a journal devoted to poetry.

Lowe, Robert Liddell. "Edwin Arlington Robinson to Harriet Monroe: Some Unpublished Letters." *Modern Philology* LX, No. 1 (August 1962): 31-41.*
  Prints excerpts from letters exchanged between Robinson and Monroe. Robinson was a recipient of the "poet's circular" sent by Monroe to American and British poets in an attempt to interest them in her proposed periodical.

Pound, Ezra. *Letters, 1907-1941.* Edited by D. D. Paige. New York: Harcourt, Brace, 1950, 358 p.*
  Contains a response, dated 18 August 1912, to Monroe's "poet's circular." Pound reacts enthusiastically to Monroe's projected poetry magazine. By the close of his letter, Pound is addressing Monroe in the editorial "we" and making policy suggestions.

Stock, Noel. *The Life of Ezra Pound.* New York: Pantheon Books, 1970, 472 p.
  Contains scattered references to Monroe. Stock propagates the view, held also by Reed Whittemore (see Additional Bibliography) and others that Pound was the vital force responsible for the success of *Poetry.* This claim is refuted by Ellen Williams (see excerpt above).

Whittemore, Reed. *Little Magazines.* Minneapolis: University of Minnesota Press, 1963, 47 p. *
  An account of the history of the magazine *Poetry,* ascribing primary editorial significance to Ezra Pound and portraying Monroe's importance merely as a fund-raiser for the publication. Whittemore

severely criticizes *Poetry's* policies ''for evading responsibilities'' because the magazine was apolitical.

Williams, Ellen. *Harriet Monroe and the Poetry Renaissance: The First Ten Years of 'Poetry.'* Urbana: The University of Illinois Press, 1977, 312 p.

   Examination of Monroe's efforts to found the first journal devoted solely to poetry in the United States that includes a brief biography of Monroe. Williams examines closely the personal relationships between Monroe and such contributors as Ezra Pound, Vachel Lindsay, Amy Lowell, and many others, through the many extant letters still on file in *Poetry's* offices.

Zabel, Morton Dauwen, editor. *Poetry* LXIX, No. 3 (December 1936).
   Special issue dedicated to Monroe. The magazine contains reminiscences by Helen Hoyt, Marion Strobel, Marianne Moore, Malcolm Cowley, and Morton Dauwen Zabel, as well as encomiastic poems by Edgar Lee Masters and John Gould Fletcher.

Robert (Edler von) Musil

1880-1942

Austrian novelist, novella writer, dramatist, essayist, and poet.

Although Musil is little known outside of literary and academic circles, he is considered by many critics to be among the greatest novelists in modern literature, primarily because of his voluminous novel *Der Mann ohne Eigenschaften (The Man without Qualities)*. This work occupied him for twenty years but was never completed. The novel's protagonist, Ulrich, the "man without qualities," has been interpreted as a paradigm of the modern individual and the novel's setting—decadent pre-World War I Austria, with the Austro-Hungarian empire on the brink of collapse—has been seen as symbolic of the whole of twentieth-century existence.

Musil was born in Klagenfurt, Austria, to an aloof, intellectual father and an emotionally unstable mother. While his father devoted himself to a successful career as a professor of engineering, Musil's mother maintained a forty-year liaison with a teacher who lived with the family. Critic Frederick G. Peters wrote that this strange domestic triangle "had a profoundly adverse effect upon [Musil's] psychological development." Musil was a troubled and withdrawn child who had to be taken out of the third grade for half a year to recover from a nervous breakdown. His father enrolled him in a military academy when he was twelve, and two years later sent him to the senior military academy at Mährisch-Weisskirchen, which Rainer Maria Rilke had attended a few years earlier. Both writers later recounted that they suffered greatly from the rigorous regime of the school and from harrassment by older students. Rilke claimed that he always meant to write about his ordeal at the school, but was never able to carry out his intention. Musil, however, used his experiences there as the basis for his first novel, *Die Verwirrungen des Zöglings Törless (Young Törless)*. At seventeen, he decided to forgo the military career mapped out for him by his father and began to study engineering, in which he took his degree. Musil later entered the University of Berlin to study philosophy, psychology, and mathematics, and in 1908 submitted his dissertation on the epistemology of the physicist and philosopher Ernst Mach. In 1911 Musil married, and in the same year published his second book, *Vereinigungen (Unions)*, containing the novellas *Die Vollendung der Leibe (The Perfecting of a Love)* and *Die Versuchung der stillen Veronika (The Temptation of Quiet Veronica)*. His father obtained for him a post as librarian at the Technical University of Vienna, which he occupied for two years before moving back to Berlin to become an editor of the periodical *Die neue Rundschau*. During World War I Musil served as an officer, and after the war held various semimilitary positions with the Austrian Foreign Ministry and the War Office. In 1922 he lost his job due to governmental cutbacks, and afterward lived as a freelance writer, often in extremely impoverished circumstances. Financial pressure, coupled with the tremendous intellectual and emotional stress of composing the massive novel *The Man without Qualities*, led to another nervous breakdown in 1929. Patrons in Berlin and Vienna provided some financial support, and Musil tried repeatedly, but without success, to find a sponsor to aid in his emigration to the United States. In 1938, just before the Nazi invasion of

Vienna, Musil and his Jewish wife fled to Switzerland. He died there four years later, embittered by continued poverty and lack of public recognition, his vast final work unfinished.

Musil's first novel, *Young Törless*, examines the crises in the life of a schoolboy. Musil critic and biographer Burton Pike has summarized the novel as "an examination of the psychology of an adolescent and, perhaps even more, an examination of the psychology of an adolescent representing a general type of human psychology at a particular stage of development." In *Young Törless* Musil defines an adolescent as someone who has not yet constructed the fiction of character, and Törless has been seen as a precursor of Ulrich, the man without qualities. Törless is described early in the novel as having no character (or personality or ego, depending upon the translator) of any kind. His part in the sadistic treatment of the hapless, "soft" Basini is often viewed as a preparatory stage to Törless's development and to his achievement of greater self-knowledge. Because Musil appears to sanction his protagonist's cruelty toward a weaker classmate, the novel has been interpreted in terms of Nietzsche's philosophy of a superior individual who is above conventional morality. Critics also find Freudian themes in *Young Törless;* in fact, Harry Goldgar has said that it may be "the earliest novel of any sort in any language to show specific Freudian influence." However, other critics, notably Frederick G. Peters and Yvonne

Isitt, dispute this claim. Peters cites evidence from Musil's diaries and journals that Musil possessed only a minimal grasp of Freudian thought, and that he rejected much of what he did understand. Isitt states that pertinent Freudian works were not even published at the time of the novel's composition.

Musil produced two volumes of novellas, *Unions* and *Drei Frauen (Three Women)*. In the two novellas which appear in *Unions, The Perfecting of a Love* and *The Temptation of Quiet Veronica*, Musil presented his central characters by describing their successive mental impressions of various situations. Musil's style in writing these two novellas has been likened to impressionism in painting. The closest stylistic literary comparison is to the stream of consciousness technique as employed by James Joyce and Gertrude Stein. In an attempt to render the feelings of his female characters to his readers, Musil used what has been described as a "stream of emotions" and intended the reader of these novellas to respond to them emotionally, rather than intellectually. Musil told his stories through images and metaphors, omitting the usual fictional elements of plot, physical description, and conventional narrative. Both novellas focus upon the attempts of a central female character to reconcile the varying demands of physical and spiritual love. Claudine, in *The Perfecting of a Love*, reaffirms the bonds of her marriage through a meaningless sexual encounter with an animal-like stranger. Veronica, in the second novella, denies her own sexuality and seeks a purely spiritual union. At one point she believes she has attained this; upon discovering she was mistaken, some critics believe she becomes insane, though Musil's surrealistic narration makes any definitive statement regarding *The Temptation of Quiet Veronica* difficult.

The novellas in Musil's second collection—*Grigia, Tonka,* and *Die Portugiesin (The Lady from Portugal)*—have male protagonists, with the eponymous characters, all women, serving as antagonists. The respective protagonists—an engineer, a scientist, and a soldier—each become involved with an enigmatic woman in a relationship which ultimately demands that the man seek a reconciliation between the rational and the nonrational aspects of life. Only the soldier, through his marriage to the Portuguese lady, achieves a synthesis between the two. The protagonist of *Grigia* cannot strike a balance between the empiricism of his profession and the "andere Zustand"—the mystical state of "other reality"—of the valley where he has gone to work, which is embodied in his peasant mistress. *Grigia* concludes with his death. The protagonist of *Tonka* is a scientist who does not attempt a reconciliation between the rational and nonrational, but chooses scientific reason over mystical faith in his lover, and the result is her death. The three male-female relationships explored in the novellas in *Three Women* are often critically interpreted as the antecedents to the union between Ulrich and his sister Agathe in *The Man without Qualities*, a relationship whose success or failure cannot be conclusively judged because of the work's unfinished state.

Musil also wrote a drama, *Die Schwärmer*, and a farce, *Vinzenz und die Freundin bedeutender Männer*. While *Vinzenz* figures less prominently among Musil's works, *Die Schwärmer* shares a central concern with *The Man without Qualities*: the dilemma of modern humanity faced with the realization that reason and science are insufficient to sustain human relationships. The protagonist of *Die Schwärmer*, Thomas, is another prototype of the man without qualities. In the drama he is referred to as the man of possibilities: lacking all characteristics, he potentially possesses them all. Thomas is, like many of Musil's male characters, a coolly rational man who is set in opposition

to a man of personal warmth, Anselm, but one who is a fraud and a failure in both business and society. Anselm is, in turn, an early type of the character of Arnheim, the antagonist and foil to Ulrich in *The Man without Qualities*.

The Man without Qualities appeared in three volumes over a thirteen-year period, and as it is thought that Musil began the novel in 1922, he devoted about two decades to this unfinished work. As early as 1931 the initial volume of *The Man without Qualities* was described in *The Times Literary Supplement* as the "first part . . . of a monumental work." At the novel's center is the collapse of the Austro-Hungarian empire and its significance as the end of an epoch. However, other elements have been pointed out which are equally important to the structure of the novel. The first of these is the central character, Ulrich, the man without *Eigenschaften*—a difficult term for translators, who have settled upon "qualities"; however, in the same context the word has been alternately translated as "characteristics," "attributes," "properties," and "capacities." Ulrich's age, his background in philosophy, the sciences, and his military experience are all Musil's own, making the novel autobiographical to some extent. Ulrich, the man of multiple possibilities, has decided to spend a year keeping himself apart while speculating upon which possibility to pursue. His dilemma is seen as representative of the existing social conditions in pre-World War I Europe. Musil depicts a panorama of Austrian, and by extension, European, society in decline. At the same time he shows his quintessential modern European struggling to reconcile the rational with the nonrational aspects of life through his relationship with his sister Agathe. Another important feature of the novel is the presence of the psychotic murderer Moosbrugger, whose upcoming trial is a common topic of conversation. Wilhelm Braun wrote that Moosbrugger is "representative of the mood and the scope of the work" and that he is symbolic of the disintegration of the European people prior to World War I. There is no way of knowing what form the novel would ultimately have taken if Musil could have brought *The Man without Qualities* to a conclusion. In the third volume of the novel, Musil has Ulrich approach a union between "Moglichkeitssinn" and "Wirklichkeitssinn" ("possibility" and "reality") in his physical and spiritual union with his sister Agathe.

As Musil's works become better known through increased critical attention, they are met with an enthusiastic response from critics and readers who find in Musil an author with an idiosyncratic approach to fiction, yet one who addressed his works to basic human problems: whether the morality of a past epoch can be applied to a new age; how the individual is to find an ideal balance between the many alternatives presented by life; and how the modern individual is to deal with the potentially limitless possibilities now available. Denis de Rougemont summarized current opinion when he wrote that Musil's work "will continue to rise on the horizon of European literature."

(See also *Contemporary Authors*, Vol. 109.)

PRINCIPAL WORKS

Die Verwirrungen des Zöglings Törless (novel) 1906
   [*Young Törless*, 1955]
*Vereinigungen (novellas) 1911
   [*Unions* published in *Tonka, and Other Stories*, 1965]
Die Schwärmer [first publication] (drama) 1921
"Isis und Osiris" (poetry) 1923; published in journal *Die neue Rundschau*

Vinzenz und die Freundin bedeutender Männer [first
      publication] (drama) 1923
Drei Frauen (novellas) 1924
   [*Three Women* published in *Tonka, and Other Stories*,
      1965]
Der Mann ohne Eigenschaften. 3 vols.   (unfinished novel)
      1930-43
   [*The Man without Qualities.* 3 vols., 1953-60]
Nachlass zu Lebzeiten (essays) 1936
Gesammelte Werke in Einzelausgaben. 3 vols.   (novels,
      novellas, essays, journals, dramas, and letters) 1952-
      57
Tonka, and Other Stories (novellas) 1965; also published
      as *Five Women,* 1966

*This work includes the novellas *Die Vollendung der Leibe* and *Die
Versuchung der stillen Veronika.*

**This work includes the novellas *Grigia, Die Portugiesin,* and *Tonka.*

THE TIMES LITERARY SUPPLEMENT   (essay date 1931)

[*This is one of the earliest English-language reviews of* The Man
without Qualities, *written more than twenty years before the first
translation from the German appeared.*]

[Robert Musil] attracted some attention by his stories before
the War. . . . But widely noticed he cannot be said to have
become until the appearance of this first part, over a thousand
pages, of a monumental work [*Der Mann ohne Eigenschaften*]
which, apparently, is to sum up Austrian society before the
catastrophe of Sarajevo. English readers have already had from
Germany a somewhat similarly planned large-scale novel—an
indictment of society—in Lion Feuchtwanger's "Success," but
Musil's work, in spite of its constant irony, has more political
impartiality than that prolonged polemic against Bavarian conditions; his characterization, also, is finer, his analysis more
subtle. Types of Austro-Hungarian aristocracy and bureaucracy
live here, side by side with a type of German intellectual for
whom it is not difficult to recognize the model, with an intense
individuality. When completed this should be the prose-epic
of the Hapsburg Monarchy hastening to its decay.

The "man without qualities" around whom the action of this
very long story turns is one Ulrich—his surname is not given.
He is not so colourless a personality as might be thought from
his creator's description. Ulrich, briefly, is a physically and
mentally normal young man who has shed all prejudices, has
reached a degree of detachment from the commonplace actuality of life which those who wish to praise him will call
idealism, those who wish to abuse him will dismiss as cynicism
or unpractical fantasy. He possesses, in spite of his title, the
"Möglichkeitssinn," the sense of the possibilities of life; other
men possess a "Wirklichkeitssinn," a mere sense of the concrete realities of the moment. For example, confronted with a
criminal, he will be incapable of taking the harsh view of the
realist; still less will he play the sentimentalist. For him the
crime will be regarded as the visible sign of a defect in the
social organism, open to correction. For him life is not "given,"
it is not just *there*; it is a process of becoming, as is his own
personality. . . .

[There is] a promise to the reader that in the second volume
he will develop a more positive interpretation of his view of

life. So far, both in his own person and in his attitude to the
people with whom he has come into contact, he has provided
a brilliant sceptical commentary on and a destructive critical
analysis of the philosophy and the mental and social and political prejudices which brought Europe to disaster.

> *"An Austrian Novel,"* in The Times Literary Sup-
> plement (© *Times Newspapers Ltd. (London) 1931;
> reproduced from* The Times Literary Supplement *by
> permission), No. 1555, November 19, 1931, p. 914.*

THE TIMES LITERARY SUPPLEMENT   (essay date 1949)

[*This lengthy review is credited by many critics with providing
the primary impetus toward a critical examination of Musil in
England and America. For a negative opinion of this review, see
Anthony West's essay excerpted below.*]

Robert Musil, the most important novelist writing in German
in this half-century, is one of the least known writers of the
age. Only two modern novelists compare with him in range
and intelligence—Proust and Joyce; and the indirect light they
cast on him also illuminates "the cultural situation." The popularity that Proust has attained suggests that modern Europe
finds it easier to acknowledge the greatness that is sick. Joyce,
whose private language made his later work even less accessible than was the autobiographical subjectivity of Proust, is
also the object of a cult; and this although both men reckoned
with the world's indifference. Musil must have reckoned with
it too, but for different reasons; his writing is not exclusive
and not bitter. Above all it is not sick. That his chief work,
Der Mann ohne Eigenschaften, with its inimitable ring of authority, its strength and lucidity remains out of print, except
for a privately published posthumous third volume, is a disgrace to German publishing. . . .

In spite of the general disadvantage of comparing unique works—
and comparison with Joyce did, understandably, exasperate
Musil himself—the practice can be useful. For thus to compare
two contraries is to disengage pecularities and common qualities that place the writer not merely at the head of his contemporaries but, as Hazlitt said of Wordsworth, "in a totally
distinct class of excellence." Work like Joyce's and Musil's
is on a borderline; comprehension and comprehensiveness have
been strained to the limits of what can be said. Both the book
that ends "A way a lone a last a loved a long the" and the
book that begins "There was an atmospheric depression over
the Atlantic. . ." are gigantic fragments corresponding to an
element in the nature of their time. . . .

The richness and largeness common to the work of both writers,
the architectural control of design, the preoccupation with history as it exists in the eternal present—all this, analysed further,
reveals the differences between them. Joyce, a philosophic
artist, in his over-lifesize day and night packed history into a
nutshell: a gigantic nut, too hard for most teeth to crack. The
huge day is one in which it is easy to get lost, as in a world.
How big is a day in reality? And what sort of day is it that
contains all history, including the present day? Musil, a philosopher turned artist, did not use mythological means; he
treated reality not as something to pack back into the Yggd-
rasilian pod, but like those Japanese paper pellets which when
laid on water slowly unfold in delicate and astonishing patterns.
Musil's method is an unfolding, with a transparent depth as of
still water under the floating pictures. A witness to the decline
and fall of an ancient empire, he records not only historical
events and social habits but illumines layer after layer of the

causes underlying them. Here time is not twenty-four hours but one year; the scene not a decaying outpost of another civilization but the imperial heart of Europe; the hero not the "enemy" always on the fringe, but the elect man born at the centre of things and shedding his "properties." Musil, expert in two kinds of abstraction both inadequate as art itself is, turns imperfection to imaginative account; in his third quality, that of the artist, he makes a world of irony and tragedy. It is a whole world in terms of a single year, and it poses the menacing questions: How long is one day of such a year? How long is that which seems to be only a year? The achievements of Joyce and of Musil—so closely related and yet so different—are like two hemispheres trying to join, but unable to do so. They do not combine to form the whole unity, a comprehensible world. But the defeat to which such books witness is only partial. In so far as it is the reader's defeat, and not the writer's, it is the defeat inherent in life. (p. 689)

[Musil's] writing has a wit, restraint and understatement that recall passages of Butler rather than of *The Egoist,* to which this book has been compared. For Meredith's style is diamond, Musil's plate glass; it is for looking through. But ***Der Mann ohne Eigenschaften*** is both an extraordinarily amusing and an extraordinarily difficult book. Its sheer length demands unusual powers of intellectual endurance from the reader if he is to enter into the experience, which is as large and dazzling as life. For it was not written for the reader any more than it was written against him; it was simply written in disregard of the average. Hence in its very likeness to life it is so steep that the reader who goes up the rock face needs, in every sense, a good head. That it is both edifying and entertaining is incidental. Musil sought to get right to the bottom—or, rather, to the top—of life. As in life itself, the work's difficulty and danger is intrinsic; like everyday life, acceptance makes it finally endurable; its weight is, after all, in proportion to its bulk, it is intense and manifold, informative and reflective, refreshing in its exactitude, reconciling in its long-sighted humour.

These are high claims, but not too high. The book's length is not only horizontal, in pages; it is also vertical, each page being capable of such extension and elaboration that the implicit number of the whole rises into infinity. (pp. 689-90)

[Musil's] gift for defining and calculating, the highly evolved mind's capacity to reduce everything to essentials and relate everything to principles, applies not only to the material but to the texture of the book. There is no artificial restriction, apparently no "construction"; there are no distinct threads of plot and sub-plot, any more that there are in life. Everything is alive; therefore everything is, as if in spite of itself, a living symbol of life itself. The result is a work of art, a world created by an artist; and it is a real world because it is limited by its own nature, by time and the fact that it is seen from one point, grouped round one man. . . .

Just as the hero who has shed his qualities and become a man without properties is a man potentially with all properties, so, logically enough, the book contains all actions and no action—the cancelling out of action in its own futility. . . .

Two main themes run side by side, an abyss between them: the *Parallelaktion,* the activities of the campaign committee organizing the Emperor's seventieth jubilee (to be held in 1918, concurrently with Wilhelm II's thirtieth), and the case of the sexual maniac Moosbrugger, on trial for murder. The *Parallelaktion* embodies the real action, or rather, inaction—a campaign that never gets started, symptomatic of that Austria where the feeling always was "es muss etwas geschehen" ("something must be done") and where what happened was usually only what could not be helped, in other words "es ist passiert" ("it just happened"). The counterbalance to all this latent eventfulness is personified by Ulrich, who becomes the committee's honorary secretary. He is a passive philosopher of a style that can only be the product of a centuries-old culture, and perhaps only in its last hours: himself a finishing touch to a way of life that has a doubting smile for everything, knowing that life itself is something that always slips beyond the scope of human planning and "ist passiert."

Figures from many sections of society are involved in the jubilee campaign, which sets out to show the world that there are not only brand-new, spit-and-polish empires, but venerable ones that can look on their cracks as on honourable scars. For one endless, breathless, feckless year the campaign, a gigantic symbol of human foolishness, an enterprise like a dinosaur, becoming more and more desperately idealistic, ambles on towards 1914 and Sarajevo. The inevitability of its failure is apparent in every feature of those who, having created it, are unable to live up to their own idea, now prismatically split into innumerable ideas.

The story that is not told might be compared to a dry, invisible river that is yet intensely perceptible as a current of will. . . .

Sombre and terrible in the background is Moosbrugger, whose trial is a national sensation, taking on a symbolic quality as compulsively as things in reality do: the shadow-side, the lurking terror that night must fall. The paradox behind Moosbrugger is that he is the first movingly human figure to rise beside the hero: his is the child's soul innocently taking on itself the maniac's act of blood. Moosbrugger often feels the world grow "too tight" for him; if he is not to stifle, he must destroy, and instinctively he identifies pain with woman. At other times he identifies himself with the essence of being; then he dances the planetary dance of life's eternal motion. But although he is a bogy, a threat to the existence of society, he is not repulsive. It is strange how touching this grisly figure is, how at the very end, after incarceration and escape from an asylum and in the midst of a drunken, brawling life, he seems to be a large, sad animal, always behind bars and made vicious by the presence of the bars. He is the "I" against "Them," the others who for all their sharp and subtle differentiation make up a collective total. A society of Moosbruggers is unthinkable; and the essence of the case against him is, of course, that he forces society to see the Moosbrugger in itself. To escape this awareness they all take refuge in law, crown, country, "the spirit of the age" and the *Parallelaktion,* their own version of the rhythm of life. . . .

But the two figures in the foreground do not occupy all the space. In the third volume the reader feels the closeness of the impending war, the menace of it in everything, though particularly in the unrelieved erotic tension between brother and sister. In the last chapter, which Musil was writing on the day of his death, Ulrich and Agathe lounge in deck-chairs on the lawn of the high-walled garden all day, moving round with the sun, in utter solitude, like mysterious substances in the alchemist's retort from which the miracle is hoped for. . . .

Although the surface is satire on a society in decay, and under that one system of knowledge after another, one manner of life after another, is dissected and discarded, many readers will also apprehend an esoteric pattern lying deeper still. Paradoxically, negatively, the book is an *Entwicklungsroman,* an adventure of quest and initiation, operated by stripping off skin after skin of illusion. But like every great work of art it is more than its creator consciously intended. In one of the last dialogues the banker Fischel utters deceptively simple words which in their context cause a tremor of shock: "Money has a mind of its own." So have books. It is fascinating to see the novel's shape looming out, making its own way ahead, independent, alive and growing. Yet Musil worked not like a mystic, but like an abnormally well-equipped anthropologist, with a mind as accurate as a spirit-level. It is the mind of the Man of No Properties, from whom the lines of light radiate to the other figures, showing by contrast how inessential properties and dignities of every kind are. When it becomes possible to stand back from the book and see it as a whole characters and events suddenly turn out to be elements in a new myth, built upon a very ancient order. . . .

A friend of Musil's said of *Der Mann ohne Eigenschaften:* "All formal truth has its complement on the mythological side, but myth cannot be manufactured; it is something one recognizes later." If this great work can be regarded as something like a miracle play in whch the mystery is indicated by the very lack of anything mysterious, the explanation lies in Musil's own words: "This book has one passion that is nowadays somewhat out of place in the realm of *belles lettres;* the passion for rightness, precision." (p. 690)

"Empire in Time and Space," in The Times Literary Supplement *(© Times Newspapers Ltd. (London) 1949; reproduced from* The Times Literary Supplement *by permission), No. 2491, October 28, 1949, pp. 689-90.*

EITHNE WILKINS AND ERNST KAISER (essay date 1952)

[Musil's primary English-language translators, Wilkins and Kaiser, provide a critical overview of Musil's life and works. They find that in some way every aspect of Musil's biography and literary output lead up to the massive and incomplete novel The Man without Qualities.*]*

[In 1906] Musil's first book, the novel *Die Verwirrungen des Zöglings Törless,* appeared, bringing him some degree of recognition, even of international notice. This helped to make him decide that he would decline all of several opportunities to make a career as an academic philosopher (there was an opening for him at Munich University as well as at Berlin) and would live as an independent writer.

In *Törless* there is doubtless a good deal of his experiences at the military academy at Weisskirchen. No one can tell to what extent the influence of that environment in his schooldays was decisive in making him, not a professional philosopher or psychologist any more than an army officer or an engineer, but an artist. We do not know to what extent the weird and terrifying experiences of the boy Törless correspond to those of the boy Robert. When Musil was asked whether the book was a portrait of that period of his life, he is said to have answered, laughing, that what he had written down was nothing compared to the reality. Yet although neither *Törless*—a seemingly heartless and yet passionate book that is an extraordinary study of torture and misery, a microcosmic prefiguration of the Nazi world—nor the much later and utterly different *Mann ohne Eigenschaften* is intended as autobiography in the strict sense, Törless, the schoolboy, and Ulrich, the Man Without Qualities, must both be regarded as aspects of Musil himself. We can

draw conclusions as to Musil's own boyhood and development from the fact that no adult Törless ever came into existence: he would have been a monster. . . . So we need to superimpose on the image of Törless that of the boy that Ulrich remembers having been, if we are to get a picture of the writer in his early life, and see the origins of the psychological constitution that was the driving-force of that great engine of a mind. The ruthlessness, the sceptical curiosity, and the romanticism of Törless, and the intellectual integrity, even severity, of Ulrich who, among other things, 'should have become a pilgrim', are obviously part of the one pattern. Both characters are austere and yet sensual; in both the personal aloofness is counterbalanced by irony and searing humour, as well as by a capacity to come to terms with violence; and both, however much they may seem to refrain from action of any kind, are actually on a quest—a quest for truth, for the first-hand thing, the immediate and ultimate experience. But the important difference is that in Ulrich's remembrance of his schooldays the sordid aspect is shed. Retrospectively that boyhood underwent a change: it was purified of its anguish and guilt, portrayed in a reconciled mood by the writer of the later and greater book.

It would be a mistake, however, to believe that because the element of ruthlessness in Musil's character did not develop in the way foreshadowed in *Törless* it was therefore no longer there. It was always there, but it became constructive. There was an, as it were, ruthless impulse to go on from soldier to technician, mathematician, philosopher, in order to arrive finally at art, so turning it all to creative account. This impulse became organised into a single purpose. It became an uncompromising determination to say what he had to say, no matter where it would get him, and no matter what the obstacles were in his way. There is ruthlessness, although not only that, in these words from one of his note-books: "I state my case, even though I know it is only part of the truth, and I would state it just the same if I knew it was false, because certain errors are stations on the road to truth. I am doing all that is possible on a definite job in hand."

Just as all his studies were necessary to give him the equipment for his unique literary undertaking—the intellectual apparatus of a technician, scientist and philosopher, all of which the Man Without Qualities is also—so too, inevitably, his earlier writing, however significant in itself, was even more significantly the clearing of the way for *Der Mann ohne Eigenschaften.* It was a number of experiments with material that was to take final shape in his main work.

In 1911 a small volume containing two exquisitely written stories, *Vereinigungen,* was published. It is interesting to see how in the first story, *Vollendung der Liebe,* a pattern that is recurrent in Musil's work—the tensions between intellect and feeling, and above all erotic feeling, which sometimes becomes suffocatingly intense—is treated entirely in terms of sex: the intellectual man, representing the mind itself, who is later almost always to be the protagonist, here recedes into the background immediately, leaving the scene to the woman, and it is she who goes through the whole experience, the critical ordeal, triumph over which is necessary to make their relationship complete. Apart from *Törless,* however, the work that shows the shaping of the *Mann ohne Eigenschaften* most clearly is *Die Schwärmer,* a play that was published in 1921. Musil himself often declared that these two works were 'the direct way' to the *Mann ohne Eigenschaften.* (pp. x-xii)

[Musil's] smaller writings, which have a fascination all their own, are incidentally valuable for revealing something one might not single out from the immense wealth of *Der Mann ohne Eigenschaften*: Musil's pin-point observation of natural detail and the way he uses it—the seated, lolling cows in the field, gazing towards the dawn, working their jaws as though in prayer; the stream, where it runs over a stone, looking like an ornamental silver comb; the little cat dying of mange and the sense of helpless guilt it arouses—to illuminate the relations of things, as though with a light at once from without and from within. . . .

Der Mann ohne Eigenschaften, which occupied Musil all the rest of his life, was begun early in the 'twenties, and the first volume was published in 1930. The work remained unfinished. Even so, it is one of the longest novels in literature. (p. xiv)

Musil, whose favourite reading among the novelists was Dostoievsky, Tolstoy, and Balzac, in his writing kept to tradition. He was not an innovator. That was not his function in literature. Perfunctory references to his work in surveys of modern German literature as, for instance, part of the 'aftermath of Expressionism' are misleading and nonsensical. He was the writer above all others who summed up and finished off the classical novel of tradition. *Der Mann ohne Eigenschaften* is indeed magnificently classical in its inclusiveness, its unhurried sweep—as though some vast bird, slowly wheeling at a great height, were taking its bird's-eye view of the revolving world. Not only does it comprehend infinitely many aspects of life, all bristling and rippling with ideas and glittering with wit, but it gives the reader the feeling that he is moving steadily through years, even decades, of experience. Yet the whole book's action takes place within the framework of less than one year. (On the face of it, this may seem a counterpart to Mr. Bloom's one day, as to the one night of H. C. Earwicker, and in the wider literary-historical sense it is; this remains true in spite of the fact that the comparison annoyed Musil, who did not care for Joyce's work.) The book was to end with the outbreak of the first world war; but it lingers on the brink in a way that is evidently due to something inherent in the situation and even stronger than the artistic plan. The story of the preparations for a nation-wide festival to celebrate the Austrian Emperor's jubilee and permeate the world with the spirit of 'our grand old Austrian culture' (which many of the characters would certainly, if they had known our current expression, have called 'the Austrian way of life') could not go on, of course, after the outbreak of the war that was to end the Austrian Empire. Yet even this end is never reached. It is as though it could not come about. (pp. xiv-xv)

Musil, in spite of looking back on it all afterwards and seeing it fall into shape all the more clearly for the clarity of his scientific mind, could never, in the chronology of what he was writing, and however much everything he wrote was always *to* the point, actually reach the point of fatality. Here, it must be, lies the inner reason why the book remained unfinished. It may even be that this unfinishedness is its real form. . . . The blood and destruction of the years 1914-1918 were the manifestation, Musil recognised, of something that could not be fully said in terms only of blood and destruction. The war was in the last resort an anti-climax. And Musil was not a moralist. Showing the origins of the untold catastrophe says more, on the highest level of expression, about the evils and stupidities of the world than could be done by developing them in their historical chronology; and in that sense this novel is also, as has been said more than once, a contribution to the *Geistesgeschichte* (history of ideas) of our era. That is not to say that the blood-curdling and hair-raising aspect is left out:

it is there, of course, as much in the petrol fumes and asphalt of a spring day in town as in the peculiarly horrible murder of the prostitute by the journeyman carpenter Moosbrugger. But what Musil was concerned with was a far larger problem than merely that of depicting the new dark age, which he had known and symbolically expressed long ago in *Törless.*

It would be useless to attempt a synopsis of *Der Mann ohne Eigenschaften,* not only because of its length and complexity, but also because the real action lies not on the surface, in what the characters do (though that is often dramatic enough), but within, in their states of mind, the fluctuations of their emotions, their theories, and the counterpoint between the thoughts and behaviour of them all, in themselves and in relation to each other, especially to the Man Without Qualities himself, who is the nucleus, and in relation to the demands of the indefinable pattern of this world we live in. There are two main themes bound up with each other. The first is the imposing Campaign, 'Collateral' because it is in competition with a similar campaign in Germany—that new-fangled empire snobbishly, jealously, and nervously disliked. It involves the most diverse people. . . . Almost all of them are in frantic and vain search for a guiding idea, for some formulation of their vague yet fervent conviction that the Good, the True, and the Beautiful must be realisable upon earth. Ulrich, the man who has given up his 'qualities' as an ascetic might give up the world, and who against his intentions drifts into becoming honorary secretary to the Campaign, is the one serious character among them. He is the only one who recognises that no such ideal can be realised, and against the background of his irony it becomes apparent that the Campaign is a farce, a caricature quest for the Grail.

The second theme is the *cause célèbre* of Moosbrugger, the sexual maniac and murderer, whose fate—hanging or confinement in an asylum—is in the balance. The problem is that of the individual's responsibility before the law. What we are confronted with is the Good, the True, and the Beautiful in reverse. Only if those categories could be established could Moosbrugger's fate be settled in terms of true justice. The lack of the great idea, of any idea at all, not only indicates all the evil, the false, and the hideous, on a scale that dwarfs Moosbrugger, the monster; it not only reveals that there are no standards by which his crime can be measured; it also reveals that there are no measurements for crime on any scale, and hence it implies that the *débâcle* is inevitable. So the Moosbrugger case drags on without getting anywhere, precisely like the Collateral Campaign, of which it is, indeed, the sombre reflection. (pp. xvi-xviii)

A third, subsidiary theme, linking up with both these, is that of Walter and Clarisse, Ulrich's friends since his extreme youth, whose tragedy is that Walter is the intellectual and artistic Jack-of-all-trades and not the genius that Clarisse insists he ought to be. She is a harsh, inspired little creature ('like the month of March', Ulrich says) with a streak of madness. Her growing frustration brings about a growing preoccupation with Moosbrugger, into whom she projects partly Ulrich—whom she suspects of being the man all of one piece that Walter is not—and partly herself, her vision taking on the dream-like outlines of the hero-genius, of all that she yearns for but hates when it is presented to her in Walter's impassioned play of Wagner. And this oneness is in fact what Ulrich also yearns for but, floating in his 'interim scepticism', does not care to do anything about. It is the reason why he also is deeply bound up with Moosbrugger, that embodiment of all sinister qualitites, who is complementary to the utterly sane Man Without Qualities. (p. xviii)

Just as this book ends without an end, at Musil's death, so too it has no plot that is important merely as a plot. . . . We can get a glimpse of the writer's development and of his work in progress, and so of the story of the story, not only in the evolution of the boy Törless into Ulrich, but in particular from the plays, the characters of which irresistibly transform themselves into those of *The Man Without Qualities,* growing in both size and significance with the enlarging of the scope. A glance back over this development is extraordinarily illuminating, for what it shows is a steady re-shuffling and re-grouping of characters and their functions—as though according to some pre-established plan that the writer was compelled to follow—towards the achievement of the final constellation. What we then see is not the story of the Collateral Campaign or that of the murder case, both of which are told in detail, but that elusive thing, the story of Ulrich himself—the story that is 'not told'.

In *Die Schwärmer* the hero is the man of intellect, the professor who loses his wife to the good-for-nothing charmer, Anselm, and seems to gain his wife's sister as a partner for a possible new life, surmounting that betrayal and going on to something beyond the terms in which the betrayal could be committed. In the farce *Vinzenz* the hero is the man of intellect and the good-for-nothing charmer fused into one, the combination producing the 'brilliant failure' who finally parts from Alpha, the *Freundin bedeutender Männer,* with the sardonically picaresque resolve to 'take service with a society lady or a financier'. In the novel this combination of intellect and feeling is carried a long stride further. Ulrich is the man above intellect. He refuses to go on, from being a 'promising young man', to become a professor; he refuses to take sides or commit himself or indeed 'be' anything but a dilettante in feeling, quite unattached and independent. His neutrality is stressed by the fact that his surname is never mentioned. He does not earn a living. He is not married. The conflict between him and his main antagonist, Arnheim, the Prussian high-financier . . . is therefore not motivated by jealousy or ambition; it is a matter of pure antagonism between two temperaments, two conceptions of the world, two styles of living. Arnheim's offer may be read as a higher mockery built on the mockery of *Vinzenz's* conclusion, with the difference that what in *Vinzenz* was an ironically coloured wish-dream born of despair now becomes reality; but Ulrich, who stands out much bigger against a much more gravely threatened world, is, because of all he is and is not, constitutionally unable to accept what was never offered to his more light-hearted and also more desperate forerunner. Similarly, what is the final chord of the farce becomes, in the novel, an incident of less importance. To Ulrich, whose sole occupation lies in reducing everything to its essentials, the megalopolitan Arnheim's unspeakable wealth, culture, and reputation as a thinker are all the more preposterous because so much 'idealism' is involved in them. Arnheim in contrast sincerely believes that one owes it to the world to get on in the world. This is the secret of his success. It is this, too, that helps to make him so solemnly fascinating to the high-minded Diotima.

There is a curious parallelism in the male and female characters of the plays. Just as the hero and his antagonist of the *Schwärmer* fuse into one in *Vinzenz,* so the two women of the drama merge into the one woman Alpha. It is equally significant that the new combination of mind and feeling, Vinzenz, is confronted

with no single antagonist, but with a whole assembly of types: The Man of Learning, The Politician, The Musician, The Reformer, and so on. So too at the end of the farce there is no Omega to Alpha. In the novel there is therefore necessarily a new beginning, and it is made with a whole series of women: Leona, the Junoesque night-club artiste who sings risqué songs 'with a housewifely air', Bonadea, the maternal nymphomaniac, Diotima, as chaste and beautiful as she is eager to be intellectual, and Clarisse, the dementedly unmaternal, the vicarious artist. With all of them, it is as though Musil were experimenting in order to work up towards the final achievement, Agathe, which means 'The Good'. This is not the place to go into the significance of names *(nomina sunt numina),* but it is interesting to notice that two of these women are called by nicknames that are classical allusions, instead of by their real names, and also to see the parallelism between, on the one hand, Maria and Regine, one the professor's wife, the other his wife's sister—who, it is clear as the curtain falls, will either commit suicide or become his mistress—and, on the other, Agathe, Ulrich's sister, who, when the novel breaks off, seems to have become his lover. The mystical implications of 'Maria Regina' and Agathe, the ultimate heroine, the perfected female principle, need not be stressed. That the brother-sister relationship was fascinating to Musil is known; yet to take this development as either a piece of sensationalism or the result of a morbid compulsion would certainly be wrong. On the ritual incestuous love between brother and sister, with all its sacramental implications, a great deal has been written by those far better qualified to discuss it than the present writers, and there is no need to say more about it here. But there is no getting over the fact that from this point of view the splitting up of the female characters for the sake of achieving a higher unity precisely in the sister takes on a startlingly symbolic aspect, and that by following his feelings the Man Without Qualities steps out of life's ordinary conditions into a realm accessible only to divine heroes and kings.

Of the antagonist in the drama only straw-men, types or qualities, remain in the farce. And now these condense into two new characters, forming, together with the Man Without Qualities, a new pattern. Ulrich has absorbed the intellectual-erotic conflict into his own being, but to compensate for this he has his Moosbrugger like a shadow stalking after him. His one antagonist is Arnheim, the bachelor millionaire, who has his own little shadow in his Negro servant-boy, Soliman, whom—at least according to Soliman's own boastful, hate-ridden fantasies—he has robbed of his liberty. Arnheim is the big man, the public figure, all-powerful, universally admired. Ulrich is nothing of all that; his existence is essentially private. At the same time, he is the only one who sees through Arnheim. And as Ulrich admits the importance to himself of Moosbrugger, it seems as if this must be applied by analogy to Arnheim's case, only that Arnheim cannot admit his bondage to Soliman. For although Ulrich and Arnheim cannot come together, in a peculiar way they do correspond to each other. Walter, the other antagonist, is all the more hostile to Ulrich since he knows of Clarisse's feelings and is jealous, even frightened, of what may happen. (pp. xix-xxii)

It is only after seeing something of the pattern throughout Musil's writing that one can approach the question as to what he was really getting at—not his conscious intellectual intentions alone, but his attitude as a whole, all he was in his life and work 'making for and *meaning*'. Nobody seems to know to what extent he was conscious of this pattern, which—apart from the preoccupation it indicates—takes on an increasingly mythological aspect, a pattern of submerged values that barely creates a ripple on the surface realism. The problem is difficult, because Musil was, after all, a realistic writer. And this brings us to the question of the reality he was ultimately dealing with. (p. xxiii)

[Because Musil] was, consciously, above all a realistic writer, it is safest to say only that he was reluctant to enter into controversy about such things. For however he strove to overcome the limitation of the human mind by artistic means, he had to face and admit them intellectually. He himself personified the eternal antagonism between the scientist and the artist, the one holding fast to facts, guarding the frontiers of the mind, the other charged with the mission of overstepping those frontiers, of breaking out of the confinement of matter and mind by the force of his vision and so enlarging the world of experience. Musil may have been a resolute positivist for the sake of intellectual truth, but that does not mean that he enjoyed the self-imposed restrictions. In the very last years of his life, in exile and solitude, he was, as he himself wrote, under the pressure of the outer crisis going through a crisis within, and he was making notes for what he called a 'layman's theology'.

This is not necessarily to suggest that he was trying to put a name to something that he always regarded warily. (pp. xxiv-xxv)

If one looks back, in *Der Mann ohne Eigenschaften,* to the first volume from the last it seems superfluous any longer to raise the question whether Ulrich—whose way of thinking was 'not so much godless as God-free'—became a 'daylight mystic' against Musil's will, so detaching himself from his creator. Does not all the evidence force us to assume that his experience is also Musil's? And that brings us right back to the question whether Törless's experiences at school were Musil's own. Remembering the answer Musil gave to that question, we almost expect the answer here too to be: What is written down is nothing compared to the reality.

To whatever extent Ulrich is Musil's mouthpiece, he is certainly his eyepiece. And Musil was so many-sided that his view of the world should perhaps be described not as a bird's but as a fly's-eye view. It is into some vastly magnified, many-faceted fly's eye, with countless images mirrored in it, that the reader finds himself gazing.

Among Musil's pet philosophical notions was that of the fly-paper: man is irresistibly attracted by the sweet smell of life, as the fly is by that of the fly-paper, and each is doomed, with every movement of attempted escape, to sink a little deeper, so perishing in the sweet stickiness. With this allegory in mind one may wonder whether he felt himself indeed to be the superfly with the gigantic facet-eye. Yet to take the fable of the fly-paper as the core of his ideas would be as wrong as to take the farce of the Collateral Campaign, or even the tragedy of Moosbrugger, for the central idea of *The Man Without Qualities,* as it would be equally wrong to take the book as a whole for the teachings of a modern mystic. Musil is no more a mystic merely because he knows and says a great deal about mysticism than he is a philosopher who merely uses the form of the novel for the propagation of his ideas; moreover he is extremely entertaining on a high comic level, as neither a teacher of esoteric wisdom nor a professional philosopher commonly is. But neither is he a satirist or a humorist only. All these qualities combine in him, each transparently illumined by the others, each making the others a little sharper and more real. The sum of all the components making up this highly unusual man re-

mains less than the whole, the *Gestalt,* which is reflected in this highly unusual book. (pp. xxv-xxvi)

Eithne Wilkins and Ernst Kaiser, ''Foreword'' (1952), in The Man without Qualities, Vol. I *by Robert Musil, translated by Eithne Wilkins and Ernst Kaiser (reprinted by permission of Coward, McCann & Geoghegan, Inc.; in Canada by Martin Secker & Warburg Limited; translation copyright © 1953 by Eithne Wilkins and Ernst Kaiser), Coward-McCann, Inc., 1953, Secker & Warburg, 1953, pp. ix-xxxv.*

HUGH W. PUCKETT   (essay date 1952)

[*Puckett discusses some of the major characters, events, and themes of* The Man without Qualities.]

To give any succinct conception of what **Der Mann ohne Eigenschaften** is like is a difficult task. The thread of narrative is all but invisible. There is an agglutination of events none of which may be called major; they are hung on a skeletal idea of a most ironic sort and are held together by the sheer force of the author's personality. . . .

Musil's book amounts to his version of an intellectual history of Austrian society in the year 1913. This is then before the great cataclysm, which is not anticipated by these people. (p. 412)

In its subordinate material **Der Mann ohne Eigenschaften** contains plots enough for many novels. The story of Walter, the somehow impeded musical genius, would stock a *Künstlerroman.* He conforms to convention sufficiently to hold an office job, but after hours he paints ineffectively, and he welters in music, playing Wagner endlessly and never getting to organize his own musical ideas. His frustration is the greater since he is confronted continually with the chilly logic of his boyhood friend, Ulrich, and is needled by his irresponsible wife, Clarisse. The latter is herself a fit theme for a piece of psychological fiction so favored in our time, as is also Gerda Fischel, pathetic product of a mixed marriage, confused and unhappy victim of the turbulent intellectual currents of the age. Furthest out on the psychopathic fringe is the murderer, Moosbrugger. If Musil's book does not turn into another *Der Fall Maurizius* it is not because he is not aware of legal injustice but because ''man's inhumanity to man'' is for him just one more of the absurdities in our society.

Of course, the heart of this novel is Musil himself depicted in the character of Ulrich. The fiction that he has no qualities is quickly dispelled by the author, although the really characteristic qualities remain somewhat imponderable and intangible. (p. 414)

External appearance, of which Musil shows himself constantly and intensively aware, is naturally not the real factor in Ulrich's character. . . .

Soul is a word that Musil shies away from; he thinks it is used for something that escapes our conception. . . .

This somewhat cavalier treatment of the soul stands in great contrast to what Ulrich thinks of *Geist.* This quality, which distinguishes man from the lower orders and is his one chance of progress, interests Musil beyond all else. It is the stuff of which he has built all his works but its application here where he is giving an intensified glimpse into the intellectual history of his time has special significance. (p. 415)

For this ever searching man *Geist* is the divining rod and the measuring stick of experience. In the constant fluidity that is the kaleidoscope of life it has learned through the centuries that vices may become virtues and virtues may become vices, and if in a lifetime we cannot make an honest man out of a criminal it is just because we are awkward at it. Good and bad . . . are not things one can isolate and nail fast forever. . . .

It is evident that Ulrich may be a man without characteristics but not without character. His presence is felt in every group he enters. And yet he is never a leader. . . . Ulrich is sure to make a disconcerting remark in any discussion—not just some chance monkey wrench hurled into the machinery to attract attention, not some witty mot uttered for its own sake, but a question or comment which makes the others pause and sort out their thoughts. No one is quite at ease with him and since he is sui generis he has no intimates, but also no enemies since he stands in no one's way. His character has the quality of that *Geist* that he emulates: it views the scene from an eminent coign of vantage and quietly pervades it all.

Der Mann ohne Eigenschaften is one more document in the battle against collectivisim. Ulrich notes with some chagrin the passing of individuality. . . . Of old, men were swept away like the grass of the field by act of God, by pestilence, fire, or sword, not all mankind but groups, and there was still always room for individual action. Some odd persons even today give life a personal touch without bothering about the significance of it. . . . But these people are out of step and appear absurd to those who live by regular and universal standards. (pp. 416-17)

I am not sure that Musil had such faith in his ideas that he thought he could affect conversions to them. Argued in a vacuum they are convincing enough; in fact, he reasons practically everything out of existence on which our society is based. It is obvious that this does not make him happy. Like Archimedes he knows that to move the world one must have a place outside it to stand, and his mother wit tells him that that is no proper place for a member of the human race. He freely calls the Austria he lives in a fool's paradise, *Kakanien, pays de cocaigne,* but he portrays it not so much with satire as with irony; that is, far from being outside the sphere he is showing, he feels that his fate is wrapped up in the common fate. For all his strictures he treats his characters with kindly indulgence. They may be stupid but he loves them. So it comes about that his superiority engenders no arrogance, only some sadness. (p. 417)

Whatever Ulrich may say about the soul he has some sort of faith to which he, non-conformist and individualist though he be, can subscribe. . . . In the midst of many distractions Ulrich surrounds himself with the writings of all the mystics and peruses them in search of the good way of life. So did Musil himself, who in his later years was preparing a lay theology.

The tolerance Musil shows in spiritual things is markedly absent where matters having to do with his profession are concerned. Straight indeed is the way and very selective the gate to his poetic heaven, and few be they that enter in. His judgments are rendered sparingly and when given, tend to be sweeping rather than meticulous. In some of his essays, e.g. *Eine Kulturfrage (Nachlaß bei Lebzeiten. . .),* he makes sport of the popularity of the word *Dichter* [''poet''], generally coupled with superlatives; the genus is rare and who can say with assurance that he has seen one? (pp. 417-18)

For [Musil] Rilke is the poet of the perfect poem, in which statement ''perfect'' is not a superlative but refers to the com-

plete integration of image, matter, and form. Such striking words might be just fulsome praise in another writer, but in Musil they come from deep conviction. Indeed, of all possible influences on him, that of Rilke may be the most certain; not only in his view of life but even in style. No other writer's work teems with such an array of poignant figures of comparison as that of Musil and one tastes here time and again the flavor of Rilke imagery.

Musil is himself not a writer about whom storms of opinion rage. One can scarcely find a piece of adverse criticism of him, but on the other hand there is very little written about him at all. . . . But one thing is significant: those who like Musil put him at the top. (pp. 418-19)

Hugh W. Puckett, "Robert Musil," in Monatshefte *(copyright © 1952 by The Board of Regents of the University of Wisconsin System), Vol. XLIV, No. 8, December, 1952, pp. 409-19.*

ANTHONY WEST   (essay date 1953)

[*West is the author of several novels—some of them fictionally detailing his own life as the son of illustrious parents, Rebecca West and H. G. Wells—that are concerned with the moral, social, psychological, and political disruptions of the twentieth century. As a critic he has written a study of D. H. Lawrence in addition to his many reviews published in various magazines. In his attack on the laudatory review of* The Man without Qualities *that appeared in a 1949* Times Literary Supplement *(see excerpt above), West accuses Musil of imitating Anatole France and concludes that Musil "was not much of a writer."*]

The resurrection of the Austrian writer Robert Musil's long and unfinished novel, **"The Man Without Qualities,"** . . . a decade after its author's death is one of those mysterious literary events for which logic provides no explanation. The book was fading gently into an obscurity even greater than the one it had enjoyed during its author's lifetime when, four years ago, a Judgment Day trumpet was blown on the front page of the Literary Supplement of the London *Times* [see excerpt above]. The notes of the horn rang out loud and clear, and all the more startlingly because they were sounded by a normally sober publication. Musil, the critical essay declared, was (it was then 1949) the most important novelist in Germany in the past half century; only Joyce and Proust compared with him in range and intelligence, but while Joyce was obscure and Proust was sick, Musil was neither; his writing had an inimitable ring of authority, it had strength, it had lucidity; and it was a disgrace to the German publishing business that he was out of print. (p. 69)

[The] novel itself is a staggering surprise. There is not the slightest reason for comparing it to the work of either Joyce or Proust. It belongs, in fact, to an earlier literary epoch, and it is the work of an imitator and not an innovator. **"The Man Without Qualities"** is modelled, not far short of plagiarism, on a group of Anatole France's novels, of which ''The Wicker-Work Woman'' and ''The Amethyst Ring'' are perhaps best known. They describe the adventures of a M. Bergeret on the fringes of the Dreyfus case and of the secular political maneuvers of the various candidates seeking appointment to the vacant bishopric of Tourcoing. Herr Ulrich, Musil's man without qualities—intelligent, cultivated, and sensitive, an ironic and detached spectator of his own small successes and disappointments, and a thoroughly ineffectual and yet extremely shrewd critic of other people's follies and illusions—is a replica of M. Bergeret in everything but nationality. Ulrich's attempts

to win clemency for a maniac sex murderer called Moosbrugger, who has been condemned to death even though he is
insane, at once parallel Bergeret's Dreyfusard activities and
duplicate an episode in which Bergeret makes some unconventional observations on the penal code after a sex crime has
been committed next door to the bookshop he frequents. There
is a much stronger resemblance between the proceedings of
the committee organizing the Emperor Franz Josef's Seventieth
Jubilee in Musil's novel and those of the candidates intriguing
for the see of Tourcoing. These resemblances, however strong,
might seem merely coincidental if it were not that Musil has
taken over both the deceptively inconsequential anecdotal and
episodic narrative technique France perfected in the Bergeret
books and the method of oblique social criticism they so successfully employ. France's delicate comedy of manners is really
a tragedy "about" the weaknesses of the Third Republic, and
Musil's novel is "about" the intellectual and moral paralysis
of the Hapsburg regime in Austria. The story that does not get
told is the story of the failure of the Hapsburg regime to adapt
to the modern world in any way, the failure that made Austria
the point of weakness in Europe and led to the collapse of the
nineteenth-century house of cards.

It was bold of Musil to attempt to tell such a large story, but
in literature mere good intentions are worth nothing. The fact
is that Musil was not much of a writer. The non-functioning
simile, in which things that have no similarities are compared,
is a sure sign of bad writing, and Musil goes as far with it as
it is possible to go: "Walter's tenderness collapsed like a souf-
flé taken out of the oven too soon;" "The piano behind his
back lay open like a bed that had been rumpled by a sleeper;"
"His emotion splashed on to the keys like big drops of rain."
Musil claimed that his work was not popular because he was
ruthless in his pursuit of precision, so the comparison of the
hardness and the immutable internal order of the piano with a
rumpled bed shows a real blindness. It is the clue to the major
defect in his writing. Musil was not an observer or an analyst
like France, much less like Joyce or Proust. He dealt in his
own intellectual concepts and was persuaded that when he
wrote about them, he was describing life. As the biographical
introduction shows, he had enough intellectual arrogance to be
well satisfied with the arid and undistinguished product of this
approach. His arrogance enabled him to botch even the almost
foolproof technique he borrowed from France; he continually
elbows his characters off the page, and nearly every chapter
of his novel reveals a diagonal drift away from fiction into
philosophic essay writing. . . . (pp. 69-70)

This may look a great deal better in German than it does in
English, in which it looks neither like part of a novel nor like
sense. Even allowing for the translators, who are capable of
devising "seated, lolling cows in the field, gazing towards the
dawn," it must be said that the great Musil revival will not
do, that there is no spark of vitality in his work to keep it from
its well-earned obscurity. (pp. 70, 72)

> *Anthony West, "Out of Nowhere," in* The New Yorker
> *(© 1953 by The New Yorker Magazine, Inc.), Vol.*
> *XXIX, No. 23, July 25, 1953, pp. 69-70, 72.**

HANS MEYERHOFF   (essay date 1954)

> [*Meyerhoff discusses the affinities he finds in Musil's works—*
> *though he deems them slight—with Marcel Proust's depiction of*
> *a decaying social order in* Remembrance of Things Past. *Joseph*
> *Strelka (see Additional Bibliography) also discusses Musil's use*
> *of the theme of social decay.*]

[Comparing] Musil with Proust and Joyce, or calling him, as
an American reviewer did, "a sort of day-light Kafka," is
critical nonsense. . . . If we are looking for critical comparisons, Musil, I think, had certain affinities with Henry James
and with Gide: with James, in his style and composition, the
social setting, and perhaps outlook on life; with both James
and Gide, in his intense intellectualism.

As a matter of fact, Musil's most significant contribution, his
achievement as well as his failure as a writer, lies in the ingenious treatment of the theme of the intellectual in the modern
world. And it is this aspect of his work which I wish to discuss
primarily.

To satisfy the conditions of a halfway accurate report, however,
I must at least mention two other topics which are usually
singled out by critics as providing the thematic structure of
The Man Without Qualities: the portrait of a society in decay
and, running counterpoint to this social theme, the portrait of
a psychotic sex murderer, called Moosbrugger. The former is
largely responsible for the comparison with Proust. Musil depicts the decline of the Austrian Empire during the last year
before the outbreak of World War I. The picture reveals a
keen, critical intellect at work and is drawn along amusing,
satirical lines. But it is not comparable to Proust's work—
either in the vast scale on which the latter reconstructed the
Swann and Guermantes ways of life, or in Proust's quest for
time lost and the "eternal essences" through which it might
be recovered, or, most importantly, in the abundance of memorable, unforgettable characters and situations created by Proust.
Nobody will go away from Musil's book remembering the
"feel" of the world he describes—in fact, there are no sights,
smells, or any other qualities of direct sensory experience in
it at all—nor the "feel" of the characters as in Proust. In Musil
it is not what the characters are like which is memorable as in
Proust, but rather what they say or think. (pp. 99-100)

The Man Without Qualities . . . is Musil's designation of the
hero, only known by his first name Ulrich. Ulrich is the prototype of the intellectual bringing to bear the full powers of
his (or Musil's) critical intelligence upon an analysis of himself
and the actions, motives and ideas of the people around him.
This function of *The Man Without Qualities* has earned the
work . . . critical clichés; for example, that it is a "psychological novel" or, in Mr. Geismar's words, a "distinguished
novel of ideas," again inviting comparisons with Proust and
Joyce. I have never understood what the term "psychological
novel" means, or for that matter, the term "social novel."
What novel is *not* a psychological and social document? Anyway, as far as Joyce is concerned, the comparison is . . . quite
superficial. Musil did not invent, as Joyce did, a new literary
technique to exhibit unconscious psychological motivation, nor
did he embark upon the ambitious project of Joyce's later works
to achieve an aesthetic fusion of complex psychological, social,
historical and mythological elements. The translators [Wilkins
and Kaiser] call attention to the fact that the action in *The Man
Without Qualities* is compressed within the time-span of one
year analogous to Joyce's use of one day or one night [see
excerpt above]. They might have added that, like Joyce, Musil
began his career as an artist by writing a portrait of himself as
a young man based upon his recollections of the years spent
in the barracks of a military academy, not so different from
Joyce's experiences in the Jesuit College of Belvedere House.
But these are trivial points. Musil did not care for Joyce's
work; and this attitude makes sense. His own work was altogether different from Joyce's, a much more self-conscious,

reflective, intellectual analysis of psychological processes and ideas than a concrete, dynamic presentation of them in the lives and actions of people.

The result, of course, may be called a "novel of ideas"; but it is worth noting that even the ideas Musil deals with, or the way he deals with them, further restrict the significant scope of the work. *The Man Without Qualities* is primarily a work about an intellectual, addressed to intellectuals. This explains why its appeal and contribution is definitely limited—unlike, say, *The Magic Mountain,* also a novel of ideas, but of a much wider scope—while its reputation is extremely high among those who can identify with it because they feel it was written especially for them. (pp. 101-02)

Hans Meyerhoff, "The Writer As Intellectual," in Partisan Review *(copyright © 1954 by Partisan Review, Inc.), Vol. XXI, No. 1, January, 1954, pp. 98-108.*

ALAN PRYCE-JONES (essay date 1955)

[*In his preface to the translation of* Young Törless *by Eithne Wilkins and Ernst Kaiser, Pryce-Jones discusses the themes of Musil's first novel and contrasts its depiction of a German school with school-life in England.*]

[*Young Törless*] was first published in Germany in 1906, under the title *Die Verwirrungen des Zöglings Törless.* "*Verwirrungen*" mean "perplexities"; and since the scene is set in a military school—the very one, we may suppose, that was attended both by Musil himself and by Rilke—the scope of the novel is at once made clear. We are in for a bout of adolescent *angst,* none the less painful for being set in a framework of dead Imperial glory.

And in fact *Young Törless* is a most alarming book. For it is very much more than it at first appears—a pungent and corrosive school story. Musil has managed, with the sure touch of genius, to construct a parable on the subject of power, and above all on the misuse of power. And since he himself approaches this subject in a spirit of liberal humanism he has much to say that is particularly apposite to the events of our own times: in effect he is writing a miniature history of those bodeful currents of thought and action which have twice plunged Central Europe into a disastrous war since his novel was published. (p. v)

[An] English reader is likely to be held up by certain divergences between the accepted norms of school life in England and in Germany. Looking warily into the opening pages, he will find that the Central European schoolboy has a disconcerting gift for introspection. The purely physical aspect of school life is missing: we have no idea what the school looks like, for instance, and no idea of the relationship between boys and masters. Where an English school would have been conjured up in full array—set in its elms, as alert as a Stilton cheese, and reeking of Jeyes Fluid and cabbage—the German school has not so much as a name. It simply acts as a funnel down which is poured a selection of personalities: or perhaps the metaphor should be that it is a puppet stage upon which are enacted the larger passions of the outside world of full-sized people.

Everyone is articulate; everyone knows his part. In place of the brisk interests of an English schoolboy, of the games and the open smut, we are given mysterious hints of a very different world. The gossip is ontological, the recreations are consis-

tently dejected. Walking by dirty cottages with their swords clattering on the cobbles, the boys at Törless's school escape from a claustral world only into the smoky darkness of a dubious tavern, compared to which the *gemeines Beisl* of *Der Rosenkavalier* is as grand as the Ritz. Otherwise they are the slaves of a military ritual inside the school, and much of their free time is spent in a secret attic—the kind of hide-out which appeals to a Germanic love of the mysterious, and a torture-chamber as well, into which much of the action of *Young Törless* is confined.

There are two main themes in the book: one, a painful process of self-discovery, and the other a brutal narration of bullying. It must not be thought, however, that Musil uses either of these themes complacently. He is not a writer like Mr. Aldous Huxley, out to shock us for our own good; nor is he prone to linger a moment longer than necessary over the tribulations of adolescence. On the contrary, what strikes powerfully home is his rare detachment. This gives his short book an unexpected force. It is alarming, yes; and alarming with all the economy of a thunder-clap. Musil himself is totally aloof from the action of his personages. The noise of the thunder rumbles briefly and terribly, the whole book is heavy with a sense of threat; but there is never a moment when the threat becomes explicit.

This makes the closing scene all the more effective. After the bullying, the discovery, the sacking, Törless himself is taken away from the school by his parents. At the moment of leaving his perspective is restored:

> He had the memory of a tremendous storm that had raged within him, but all he could muster by way of explanation for it now was entirely inadequate. . . . And the thing that had been there even before passion seized him, the thing that had only been overgrown by that passion—the real thing, the problem itself—was still firmly lodged in him. . . . All this, and the rest besides, he saw remarkably clear and pure—and small. It was as one sees things in the morning, when the first pure rays of sunlight have dried the sweat of terror, when table and cupboard, enemy and fate, all shrink again, once more assuming their natural dimensions.

The book is written in just that sweat of terror, and the dimensions of its incidents are swollen to unbearable size. Accustomed as we are to the comparatively civilised atmosphere of our own public schools—to the rabbit-keeping and the potter's kiln, the Gothic cool of the chapel and the stout ring of studded boots on linoleum, the coloured waistcoats and the strawberry-messes for tea, the alcaics ground out by the fireside and the evening passages full of the smell of burning toast—accustomed to this, we shall find Törless's school absurdly barbaric. And we must remember, too, that it was a very consequential school—a kind of Eton, or perhaps from its military connection a Wellington, perched away on the Polish frontier of the Austro-Hungarian Empire.

But where a lesser writer than Musil might have limited his theme to a horrified depiction of this barbarity, the poetic gift which emerges in his fables, and above all in *Der Mann Ohne Eigenschaften (The Man without Qualities),* lifts the narrative of *Young Törless* above it theme. This book becomes the story of all young, trapped creatures, and Törless the prototype of bewildered adolescence. We forget that we have gone back fifty years, and moved from England to Bohemia. The novel is a good one, and that is enough. (pp. vi-viii)

Alan Pryce-Jones, in his preface to Young Törless
*by Robert Musil, translated by Eithne Wilkins and
Ernst Kaiser (copyright © 1955 by Pantheon Books,
Inc.; reprinted by permission of the publisher; in
Canada by Alan Pryce-Jones), Pantheon Books, 1955
(and reprinted by Noonday Press, 1958), pp. v-viii.*

WILHELM BRAUN (essay date 1960)

[*One of Musil's most prominent critics, Braun discusses the psychology of Moosbrugger and the function of this character in the overall thematic structure of* The Man without Qualities.]

Even though Robert Musil's novel *Der Mann ohne Eigenschaften* has been frequently commented upon during the last few years, many difficulties that bar the understanding of the work remain. . . . Some critics such as [Herman] Pongs, [Günter] Bloecker, and K. A. Horst have favored the hero of the novel, the man without qualities, above all other characters; they have examined Ulrich and the various concepts that he stands for. . . . It is with this problem in mind that we undertake a study of Moosbrugger. For he, perhaps more than any other character, excluding the hero, is representative of the mood and scope of the work. In Moosbrugger's fate the whole disintegration of European man is mirrored. Moosbrugger is the lonely man par excellence, the man without parents, without home, without tradition, without faith, the "unbehauste Mensch" of our time. He is also insane, the murderer of a prostitute, a schizophrenic, and a split personality. His trial becomes symbolic for the inability of an antiquated European system of morality to judge his actions. In this context, Moosbrugger's particular problem, his quest for justice, becomes that of his whole generation. Musil has gone to great lengths to account for Moosbrugger's state of mind, and it is here that we can observe both the causes for his breakdown and also the germs for a possible synthesis. Thus Moosbrugger's problem moves on many levels at once. It is at the same time social, moral, psychological, and philosophical, for it is both Moosbrugger's and our world that is held up to judgment.

In an almost morbid manner Musil intensifies the dichotomy between Moosbrugger's appearance and his crime. In so doing he has again given expression to a fundamental problem of our time. For Christian Moosbrugger, whose name perfectly evokes an Alpine "mossy brook" atmosphere, full of peace and contentment, is really a horrible murderer. To stress the dichotomy mentioned above, Musil has lent him a face "blessed by God with all the signs of goodness." Moosbrugger radiates a feeling of righteousness that even hardened reporters find difficult to connect with his crime. In a dry, matter-of-fact tone Musil introduces the courtroom protocol that relates the devastation that Moosbrugger has wrought upon another human being, and in this manner Musil stresses the problem of a split personality which Moosbrugger embodies.

The simplest explanation is, of course, that Moosbrugger is mad. But since he is lucid at other times, particularly during his trials, he presents a special problem to the psychiatrists, who have "declared him normal quite as often as they had declared him not responsible for his actions." . . . Musil here pokes fun at the medical profession in the service of justice, unable to make up its mind whether the prisoner is sane or not. No doubt Moosbrugger is a deeply disturbed human being. By tracing the cause and the course of his predicament it might be possible to account more fully for his disease.

Musil provides us with many data about Moosbrugger's past to explain his plight. Moosbrugger grew up a poverty-stricken wretch; he was so poor that he never spoke to a girl. All he could do was look at them even later, when he was an apprentice and during his wanderings as a journeyman. In time this privation colors Moosbrugger's mind. His desires become unnatural, full of frustration, pain, and despair. Moosbrugger's relations with women have moreover been embittered as a result of a traumatic experience he suffered when he was sixteen years old. He was then an apprentice living with his master, and other apprentices induced him to approach his master's wife in an unseemly fashion. . . . From being hostile to women he moves to being hostile to the law and its institutions. His life becomes a "battle for his rights" . . . , a battle to assert himself.

Moosbrugger is thus basically antisocial. He never comes to terms with this world, and the world and the community are best exemplified by women. From his perspective Moosbrugger sees women only in the form of "processions" . . . , as religious groups. He never experiences them as individuals. The socio-religious characteristics that Moosbrugger applies to his chance meetings are significant, for in this manner he identifies women with the two forces that he hates. Women are his enemies. "The giggling women-folk were in a conspiracy against him; they all had their fancy-boys, and a steady man's straightforward way of talking was something they despised, if they did not take it for a downright insult." . . . Moosbrugger abhors women not only because he is sexually repressed, not only because of his traumatic experiences, but as representatives of mankind as he encounters it and suffers from it. "Women are women and men. Because men chase after them". . . , Moosbrugger remarks at one point, and thus characterizes the universality of the feminine symbol. In his mind women stand for society and for mankind; his enmity is pinpointed at them. He seems, then, at least formally justified when he claims that he had never committed murder for the pleasure of it, "because he had always been inspired with feelings of disgust for all these females." . . . So deep is this ingrained aversion of Moosbrugger that Musil compares it to the basic animal urge to kill, like that of a cat "sitting in front of a cage in which a fat, fair-feathered canary is hopping up and down, or striking a mouse, letting it go, and striking it again, just for the sake of seeing it run away once more." . . . Moosebrugger's hatred for mankind is a deeply instinctive reaction, on a level close to that of an animal and not subject to any rational explanation and guidance. (pp. 214-16)

It is with this background in mind that we must consider Moosbrugger's ugly deed. And Moosbrugger must be given due credit for making an almost superhuman attempt to escape from committing murder. "He took long strides, and she ran along beside him. He stopped, and there she stood like a shadow. He was drawing her along after him, that was it. Then he made one more attempt to scare her off: he turned round and spat into her face, twice. But it did not help; nothing could affront her." . . . Moosbrugger cannot escape her, for she represents his suppressed sexual desires, a part of himself, that will sooner or later take revenge on him.

In a larger context, the prostitute, a woman, becomes representative of the mankind that Moosbrugger hates. For he becomes certain "that some fancy-man of the girl's must be somewhere about—for else how would she have had the courage to follow him in spite of his annoyance?" . . . And for mankind Moosbrugger has only one answer. He pulls out his knife "for surely he was being got at, perhaps they were again about to attack him." . . . Even though Moosbrugger makes a second, pitiful attempt to escape violence, it is just as futile as the previous one. He cannot get rid of her. . . . Musil clearly outlines the connection in Moosbrugger's mind between his repressed sexual urges, his phobia of women and of society. The prostitute, from whom he cannot escape, is part of himself, his second, sexual and social self. (pp. 217-18)

Musil shows that Moosbrugger's murder of the prostitute is really a symbolic suicide. For, as we have pointed out, Moosbrugger identifies the prostitute not only with his suppressed sexual feelings, but also with society, and thus with his social self. She is part of himself. . . . By killing the prostitute, Moosbrugger exterminates a part of himself; his deed is thus both murder and suicide.

In addition to this detailed analysis of Moosbrugger's crime, Musil devotes a great deal of space to show what goes on in Moosbrugger's mind during and after the trial. And it is from these descriptions that we derive more insight into Moosbrugger's mental state. Moosbrugger is only at times insane. "An irresistible urge from time to time cruelly turned his personality inside-out." . . . Thus Moosbrugger experiences alternate sane and insane periods. The real trouble lies in the fact that Moosbrugger values his disease more than his healthy periods. "Although obviously it was his diseased nature that was the cause of his behaviour and set him apart from other human beings, to him it felt like a stronger and higher awareness of his own personality. His whole life was a struggle—laughable and horridly clumsy—to extort acknowledgment of this." . . . By giving precise evidence of what ails Moosbrugger, Musil attempts to describe the symptoms of his troubles and it is by means of this analysis that Musil integrates Moosbrugger within the intellectual framework of the novel. (pp. 218-19)

[A] significant aspect of Moosbrugger's imbalance, which occurs even in his saner periods, is his attitude towards metaphors. For an example of that kind of thinking Musil lets Moosbrugger choose the word "Eichenkatzl," the Austrian dialect term for the High German "Eichhörnchen." The literal translation of *Eichörnchen* is "oakpussy," of *Eichkatzl*, "oaktree cat." For Moosbrugger however, these two words are examples of a number of concepts used interchangeably for one another. "If an oakpussy is not a cat and not a fox and not puss, the hare that the fox eats, one doesn't need to be so particular about the whole thing; somehow or other it's patched together out of all of it and goes scampering over the trees." . . . Thus Moosbrugger lacks somehow a logical, unequivocal sense which would permit him to distinguish precisely between objects. It has been his experience, as he puts it, "that one could not pick any one thing out all by itself, because each one hangs together with the next one." . . . (p. 220)

It seems then that Musil wants to show that Moosbrugger thinks in a manner more related to the metaphor, for it is precisely in the metaphor that the sliding of borders, the mixing of concepts occurs. (p. 221)

A corollary to this examination of Moosbrugger's mode of thinking can be found in his reaction to other people. When Moosbrugger was in good mood he would look into the face of a man and there would see his own face "as it would gaze back at him from among the minnows and bright pebbles in a shallow stream." . . . Thus when in a happy frame of mind, Moosbrugger overidentifies himself with the world, and again in a manner that lacks clear limits and definite outlines. His

perceptions have the uncertainty and haze of a reflection in water. On the other hand when Moosbrugger is unhappy, all he has to do is to look briefly into the face of a man and he realizes "that it was the same man with whom he had always got mixed up in a row, everywhere, no matter how much the other one pretended to be a different person each time." . . . One can say that Moosbrugger's kind of thinking colors his social relationships. It shows the very same extremes in overidentification and oversimplification.

For Musil, Moosbrugger's predicament is representative of a general attitude in man. Our whole relationship with other people depends upon our emotions and is subject to the same mechanisms of identification with those we love, and a kind of oversimplification for those we seem to hate. "All of us quarrel with the same man almost every time. If one were to investigate who the people are with whom we get so senselessly entangled, it would surely turn out to be the man with the hook to which we are the eye." . . . When we hate, our emotions of hatred somehow seem to bring this oversimplification about. And when we love, Musil claims that recognition does not matter at all. "How many people look into the same loved face day in day out, but when they shut their eyes could not say what it looks like." . . . In this case the emotion seems to be overwhelming, and therefore recognition not necessary. And starting with these observations, Musil goes on to stress the importance of emotions in our life. "To what changes things are unceasingly exposed, according to habit, mood, and point of view! How often joy burns out, and what is left is an indestructible core of sadness! How often a man calmly bangs away at another whom he could just as well leave in peace! Life forms a surface that pretends it has to be the way it is, but under its skin things are thrusting and jostling." . . . From his analysis of Moosbrugger's modes of thought, Musil draws this important conclusion regarding the influence of our emotions upon our actions.

At this point it might be useful how Musil's description of Moosbrugger's modes of thinking and feeling compare with those of some of the other characters in the novel. Our attention is immediately drawn to Ulrich, the hero, who in chapter 116 makes some very significant pronouncements regarding his own emotional development. (pp. 221-22)

As far as human history goes back Ulrich perceives two fundamental human attitudes, which he does not call power and love, but unequivocality and metaphor. Unequivocality "is the law of waking thought and action, which prevails equally in a compelling conclusion in logic and in the mind of a blackmailer driving his victims along before him, step by step." . . . It is the basis of the rational, legal, scientific type of thinking that has made man of the twentieth century the kind of being he is. Musil insists that it stems "from the exigency of life, which would lead to doom if conditions could not be shaped unequivocally." . . . Metaphor on the other hand "is a combining of concepts such as take place in a dream; it is the sliding logic of the soul and what corresponds to it is the kinship of things that exists in the twilit imaginings of art and religion." . . . And Ulrich extends this attitude to all relations of man to himself and to nature which are not yet purely objective—they can only be understood by means of a metaphor.

Ulrich's development had thus stressed the emotional mode of "power" or "unequivocality" and had suppressed that of "love" or the "metaphor." With this we may now compare the character of Moosbrugger. For in his case, too, an imbalance of an extreme kind, has taken place. Moosbrugger's dark, inhuman, criminal periods are times when his unequivocal attitudes have gained complete hold over him, when he oversimplifies his hatred for the one single person, when he is unable to perceive metaphors in their true meaning. On the other hand, his normal state is characterized by an overdose of metaphorical thinking which equally unbalances him. It is the imbalance of these two modes of feeling and thinking which are the cause of his mental breakdown, and his split personality. (p. 223)

[If] we consider the chapter ''Moosbrugger Dances'' and relate it to the history of its protagonist and to the novel as a whole, it may be possible to recognize its special significance. In Moosbrugger, Musil has gone to extremes to demonstrate the split between unequivocal and metaphorical thinking. Moosbrugger's mental disease can be explained in this manner. But Musil goes on to show that even Moosbrugger is capable of experiencing something akin to ''der andere Zustand''—albeit under conditions similar to hallucination, a mystical unity with the world, and thus Musil points towards the universality of mystical experiences. It is Moosbrugger's special misfortune that ''he had never managed to find the point, midway between his two states, where he might perhaps have been able to stay.'' . . . Once again in this tragic character Musil attempts to stress the necessity of reestablishing a union of the two faculties of the mind, of unequivocality and the metaphor. (p. 225)

By anchoring Moosbrugger securely to the intellectual structure of his novel, Musil has intensfied the organization of his work in a manner quite unique in the history of modern German letters. (p. 230)

> *Wilhelm Braun, ''Moosbrugger Dances,'' in* The Germanic Review *(reprinted by permission of Joseph P. Bauke), Vol. XXXV, No. 3, October, 1960, pp. 214-30.*

BURTON PIKE (essay date 1961)

[*In his* Robert Musil, *Pike opens with a chapter, excerpted below, which summarizes the characteristics common to Musil's major works. Chapters devoted to each of the major works follow, including one on the drama* The Visionaries, *which Pike claims is a significant work.*]

As a whole, Musil's fiction might best be characterized as *Ideendichtung,* a poesy of ideas. (I am using ''poesy'' here as the closest equivalent in English to *Dichtung.*) . . . What and how [his characters] *think* and *feel* is always at the center of Musil's novels, stories, and plays; with few exceptions, deeds in his works are so laden with psychological introspection that they lose the name of action.

The primary orientation of *Ideendichtung* is, I would say, toward the general idea underlying an individual problem or attitude. While this orientation is challenging and fruitful in the hands of a writer as talented as Musil, it tends to produce at times, even in his writings, a preoccupation with theory at the expense of the work. (p. 17)

Musil's emphasis on presenting his characters by showing the succession of their mental impressions has naturally led his readers to conclude that the core of his work is psychological. This Musil emphatically, if not too effectively, denies. (p. 18)

[The] essential subject matter of Musil's fiction is not the psychological, sociological, or political themes, however important they may at first seem, but the process of an individual searching for an ideal balance between himself and the world,

or more specifically between his inner and outer selves. None of Musil's major characters ever find this balance. . . . None of Musil's protagonists succeeds in establishing real contact between his inner and the outer world, each of which exists for itself. In Musil's works the realm of inner existence is the higher reality; like the school in *Törless,* the external world usually remains sketchily peripheral, the source of sensory impressions and social action for the characters. But it is on the inner workings of the sensory mechanisms and the reactions produced by them in the form of feelings and ideas that Musil's powerful microscope is focused. In *The Man without Qualities* a further dimension is added: inner existence is looked at not impressionistically, as in *Unions,* but from a generally detached, clinical viewpoint. (pp. 18-19)

Whatever may happen to them in later years, when the works in which they figure end, Musil's major characters are almost pitifully bewildered by their failure to reconcile their inner and outer lives. Life has defeated them. . . . (p. 19)

The dichotomy between the inner and the outer life is reflected in the areas of life on which Musil chose to concentrate in his fiction. . . . Both social and erotic experience are primary means of individual expression, and a person's identity is largely determined by his position in regard to his inner existence (of which the erotic is the most personal area) and to his outer, social life. This dichotomy between the inner and the outer life is sharpest in *The Man without Qualities,* but it is basic to the characters in all Musil's works. Whether this split is as well defined in life as Musil maintains is a moot point, but in his writing it does serve a valuable mechanical function: it focuses his ideas and orders the encyclopedic mass of material which, in *The Man without Qualities,* is almost overwhelming.

In view of Musil's whole abstract orientation toward fiction it is natural that external action in his works is minimized. Action is minimized in his shorter works, and sometimes replaced entirely, by an impressionistic depiction of successive mental states. In the fiction written between his two novels Musil's usual technique is to proceed by a subtle association of feelings in the mind of a character on a semi-conscious plane. This unorthodox but effective procedure, in which the reader often finds himself baffled rationally but responding emotionally, reaches its most extreme point in Musil's writings in **''The Temptation of the Silent Veronika.''** Thereafter, and especially in *The Man without Qualities,* Musil gives only the results of these associative processes of feeling in his characters. The sea of inner life is seen from a somewhat greater distance in the later novel; clarity and rationality predominate in this work, and ''essayism'' displaces impressionism. (pp. 20-1)

On the one hand, then, Musil's psychological orientation was obviously toward the theoretical rather than the concrete, toward the typical and general rather than the particular and individual. On the other hand his works show an intense preoccupation with the fates of individual people. What is at stake in the cosmic game is not a general principle, but Törless' life, Thomas' life and Ulrich's life. Much of the intensity of this preoccupation seems due to autobiographical forces . . . ; but whatever its source, this conflict in Musil's works between the general and the individual is a central paradox. The tension which springs from this paradox gives Musil's writing heartbeat and pulse.

But the heart itself lies deeper than the paradox. I think it is to be found in a kind of fear underlying the articulation and articulateness of the work, a Pascalian sense of the dread silence above and beneath the chatter of mankind. In a way the most interesting phenomenon in all Musil's works is not what is said, but what is not said or only half articulated. . . . (p. 22)

The orientation of Musil's fiction toward feelings and ideas suggests some of the problems raised by this approach to literature. The most basic of these problems deserves special emphasis. The reader of any of Musil's works will at once be struck by its impersonality; this is true even of his diaries. But this impersonality is a surface quality; underlying it is a strong passion, and the tension which these two forces create is evident both in Musil and in his work. (p. 23)

Musil himself stated the paradox of his approach to literature succinctly (it is implicit in almost everything he wrote) in his definition of literature as "a boldly, logically combined life. A production or deductive analysis of possibilities, etc. It is a fervor that consumes the flesh down to the bone for an intellectually emotional goal." An *intellectually* emotional goal—there is in Musil a consistent refusal to recognize emotion as a valid quality in itself, an insistence on the superiority of the intellect. But Musil's passionate concern for his Törless, his Thomas, his Ulrich, and ultimately himself undercuts the too often and too strongly stated attitude of detachment toward his material. . . . Precisely this polarity makes Musil's fiction come alive. The extreme tension between the personal and the impersonal seizes the reader's imagination. It arises perhaps from the fact that Musil lived in his writing. His personal life stands very much in the background; he did not pour his energy into brilliant letters or diaries, or extensive social intercourse. He held himself largely aloof from the bright world of Vienna, and after the early twenties withdrew almost entirely into *The Man without Qualities*. More, I think, than is the case with any other modern European writer, the expression of Musil the man is to be found in his work.

The conflict between the individual and the world is emphasized in Musil's writings in a very curious way. Except for the first story of *Unions* ["The Completion of Love"], the titles of all his works involve personal characteristics. In addition, the titles of his two novels focus on individuals: *The Confusions of Young Törless* and *The Man without Qualities* are thus consistent in this respect with "**The Temptation of the Silent Veronika,**" *The Visionaries, Vinzenz and the Girl Friend of Important Men,* and *Three Women* ("**Grigia,**" "**The Portuguese Lady,**" "**Tonka**"). (pp. 24-5)

One is not surprised to find that a skeptical moralist in whose work ideas play such a central role should have a strong utopian orientation. This is centered in the mystic vision of a millennium in *The Man without Qualities* and is likewise implied, on a somewhat less exalted level, in the endings of *Törless* and "**Tonka.**" Utopia was for Musil a dynamic rather than an absolute ideal, a direction rather than a goal. (p. 26)

But Musil's conception of utopia is nowhere very clear. He seemed to think in utopian terms as a compensation for the frustration and irrationality shown by mankind in its daily rounds. . . . The utopian direction of Musil's thought is closely connected with his concept of *werden,* of "becoming"; I shall return to this point shortly.

Against the background of these general characteristics of Musil's fiction some of the general qualities of his characters can be placed. The most salient of these qualities is the paradoxical nature of the characters: they are alive but pale, weak but impressive. While reading about them one has no very clear impression of what they are like; after closing the book one

finds it hard to forget them. . . . As fictional characters, then, these people lack vividness and focus, although at the same time one cannot deny that there is even in Musil's minor figures an opaquenss, an ambiguity such as one is conscious of in living people, which gives them an unexpected and attractive depth. (pp. 27-8)

Musil's characters also share a common basic problem, which may be stated as follows. Life has meaning only insofar as the individual finds for himself a place in relation to the society in which he lives. Before he can do this, however, he must find himself, and Musil focuses his attention on this latter process. The slice of time he deals with in all his works is a period of mental uncertainties and unsettling confrontations for his characters; habitual patterns of thought and action are dislocated and new ones must be thought out. The individual, in other words, has first of all a commitment toward himself; as soon as this is realized he can go on to become effective in the world. (Musil's basic criticism of the character of Arnheim in *The Man without Qualities* might be that he has become effective in the world without fulfilling this commitment.) Musil ends his works at this point. Törless, the "he" of "**Tonka,**" Thomas, indeed all of his protagonists except Veronika and Ulrich—*The Man without Qualities* is unfinished—face by implication a more comprehensive and subtly better life at the end of their respective stories than they did at the beginning. (p. 28)

Underlying this approach to fiction is the assumption that one cannot *be* something, but must *become* something. The verb *werden,* to become, is the hidden spring in Musil's works. It is not precisely the traditional concept of *werden,* a rather hazy tenet of faith in the dynamic process on the part of the early German Romantics; in Musil it is closely related to the term "possibility," as well as to a conception of utopia and the search for a new morality. Becoming implies change; possibilities can only be appreciated by a person who is aware of change; they can only be realized by a person who is capable of change. There is in each of Musil's works but one character who knows this, a doubter, a seeker, a "dreamer" in the sense in which Thomas uses the term in *The Visionaries.*

One can only become something in reference to a fixed standard; social values, for instance, must remain constant in order for an individual to change in reference to them. In his earlier writings Musil operated on this basic assumption. The school in *Törless,* the school and the official hierarchy in "**The Completion of Love,**" even the feudal framework in "**The Portuguese Lady**" are expressions of this fixed order of the world. Indeed it is with this fixed pattern that the emotional fermentation of Musil's characters conflicts: they feel that they do not belong in it. But in *The Man without Qualities* Musil seems to have shifted his ground. Only after the First World War did he begin to work on this novel in earnest, and he was busy with it through a disastrous inflation and a second cataclysmic upheaval of traditional European values beginning with the rise of Hitler and culminating in the Second World War. In other words Musil fastened in his great novel upon a fixed social order *after its fall.* The result is a complete transformation into irony of the elaborate social structure of the Austro-Hungarian Empire which is the novel's framework—and also of Ulrich's search for his identity within this framework. (pp. 29-30)

One effect of this in *The Man without Qualities,* as opposed to the effect of the stable frames of social reference in Musil's earlier works, is to give even greater weight to the theme of the individual, specifically to Ulrich's doubts about himself and his relation to the world. In an established order of things possibilities are irrelevant, and important, one might say, only to the rare individual who feels psychologically left out of this order. But in a disintegrating order possibilities become frighteningly real. Instead of automatically progressing from one well-marked station in life to another, the individual suddenly finds that he has to choose among many possibilities. The external falls away, the internal emerges with all its existential problems. In Musil's large second novel, it should be added, this is seen as a human problem and not a class question. . . . (pp. 30-1)

Another prominent characteristic of Musil's personages is what might be termed a "common isolation." They react not to other people but to their own thought processes, and consequently are always either estranging or bewildering others. . . .

This common isolation of Musil's personages is brought home by their sensory contact with the world, which leads not to physical action but to mental reaction, not to communication with others but to communication with self. In conversation they talk at rather than to each other. And, especially in *The Man without Qualities,* there is often a disconcerting lack of connection between a dialogue and an accompanying action which mirrors the lack of connection between mind and body, individual and environment.

The characters in Musil's works, consciously aware of the world through their sense perception of it, are by the same token made aware of their isolation from others. (p. 31)

One might say that the basic *donnée* of Musil's characters is a sense of exclusion in an increasingly complicated and basically indifferent world. The infinite space that terrifies Musil by its silence is the vacuum between a person and his neighbor in a social context which makes the individual seem increasingly irrelevant. (p. 32)

What seems to have interested Musil most in the problem of character was to establish some new method by which the individual could establish contact with himself and with other individuals. Basically he was seeking a new language to express in art the inner life of the emotions. Here he comes closest to an American writer who also began with psychology and was trying to do the same thing: Gertrude Stein. The most frequent process Musil uses in his fiction is not an association of words or ideas (the direction of Joyce) but, as has been indicated, an association of feelings (the direction of Stein). (pp. 32-3)

After the dust has settled around *The Man without Qualities,* Musil's only serious play, *The Visionaries,* may one day be considered his finest work. It contains in distilled form, and with the greater strength of a distillation, most of the important elements of the later novel as well as many of its subordinate concerns. It is true that *The Visionaries* lacks the broad perspectives of *The Man without Qualities.* Unlike the novel the play does not present a society on the brink of dissolution; but it might be argued that Musil's talent was better suited to the smaller scope of this drama which presents a household on the brink of dissolution. Both works have as their central concern Musil's statement of the dilemma of the modern man of intellect, the man who has tamed nature through reason's child, science, only to realize that when it comes to human relationships reason and science are not enough. Furthermore, although the setting and dialogue of *The Visionaries* are nonrealistic, the play's characters are more convincing, even on reading, than are those in any other of Musil's works. Partly as a result of

this, Musil here comes closer than he does anywhere else to directly involving the reader in his cogent but peculiar statement of the emptiness of modern life. (p. 71)

[*The Visionaries*] is a serious sophisticated play with a comic element; Musil labeled it simply *Schauspiel* ("play"). It would appear at first glance to belong in the company of Molière's *The Misanthrope* and Hofmannsthal's *The Difficult One (Der Schwierige),* but it differs from such works in at least two fundamental respects: it is concerned with thought rather than social convention (although bourgeois social attitudes are satirized in the character of Josef), and hence cannot be described as a "comedy of manners," and the play's unsettling actions and implications have the effect of removing it completely from the domain of comedy.

The relationships in Musil's play serve only to delineate the psychological and metaphysical postures of the individual characters; the dialogue is rather on the level of thought process than of social relations, somewhat in the manner of T. S. Eliot's *The Cocktail Party.* The people in *The Visionaries* hardly engage in conversation in the usual sense, but speak their own attitudes. Consequently the dialogue is atomistic as well as partially abstract, and this reinforces the isolation of the individual figures in a context of minimal physical action. *The Visionaries* displays what might be called a Racinian existentialism in the intensely painful isolation of its protagonists, whose frequent and hard collisions with each other produce—or reveal—only frustration. Relief of sorts in this savage mental struggle is provided by the stock-comic "virtuous" character of Regine's companion Fräulein Mertens . . . , and by the seriocomic detective Stader, to whom are given some of the basic philosophical statements of the play. (pp. 72-3)

The body of the action of the play involves attempts by the other figures to explain the character of Anselm. The total effect of these expressions is prismatic; the others see Anselm from their own individual perspectives and in their own individual terms. This again reinforces the strong feeling of personal isolation which runs through the play. (p. 91)

Anselm, present or absent, dominates the entire play. Hurtling into the established order of the two households (Josef's and Thomas') of his childhood friends, he has upset the mental checks and balances that had allowed Josef and Regine, and Thomas and Maria, to live with each other in a *modus vivendi.* The implication of this upset is that a *modus vivendi* is not good enough, however much pain may be caused by its dislocation. Anselm's function, unpleasant though both it and he himself may be, is yet felt by the other characters to be necessary as a kind of psychological cathartic. And in facing up to themselves more clearly, they accept Anselm, ultimately, on his own terms.

The presentation of Stader as a comic figure is masterful. The basis of this presentation is irony; Stader takes himself seriously while the audience is allowed to feel superior to his unconsciously clownlike pretensions to "scientific" stature. The proprietor of the detective bureau of Newton, Galileo, and Stader might best be described as seriocomic in relation to the other figures. His position in the economy of the play is basically a serious one; a detective orders and interprets people's external actions, and is hence a behaviorist par excellence. His vocation, that of a kind of lay scientist, depends exclusively on a rationalistic approach to human action. Like Josef, Stader is out of place in Thomas' household. He too tries to apply to the actions of the principals standards which here have no relevance, or rather which do have relevance but not in his terms. (pp. 93-4)

The question arises as to the ultimate pessimism of Musil's view of life as here presented, for the "creative condition," whatever that may be, seems a small dike to erect against the raging sea of dissolving values and relationships in *The Visionaries*. In an ultimate sense one might say that the play is deeply pessimistic; but "pessimistic" and "optimistic" are judgments based essentially on an evaluation of action and character in moral terms. If "good" succumbs to "evil" in a work one might justly speak of pessimism. But as this discussion of *The Visionaries* has brought out, the only such value judgments in the play are delivered by a minor character, Josef, and are satirized in him. Anselm and Maria are not doing a "bad" thing in coming together, but only facing the truth about themselves. In losing their illusions, however, the major figures do not change or develop, but come to realize what they are; and as has been indicated what happens to them is the almost mechanical consequence of what they are. Thomas is excluded in this process as surely and as indifferently as a chemical precipitate in a test tube. It is his awareness of this fact (and who should be better aware of it than a scientist?) that best explains his bitterness.

This is indeed Darwin's struggle of life observed in the social and erotic spheres, and sophisticated and cosmopolitan ones at that; a struggle in which conventional standards of morality are seen as simple-minded. The tragedy of the play, a kind of tragedy of despair, is that Thomas is left alone. Being the kind of person he is, he has to end alone. But in this terrifying Pascalian loneliness is the feeling that it is at least an honest loneliness. Regine too, in announcing her decision to return to Josef, says that she has come to appreciate the meaning of sacrifice. (pp. 94-5)

Burton Pike, in his Robert Musil: An Introduction to His Work *(© 1961 by Cornell University; used by permission of the publisher, Cornell University Press), Cornell University Press, 1961, 214 p.*

YVONNE ISITT (essay date 1964)

[*In this survey of Musil's works, Isitt provides her own translations for the various quotes from the novellas and novels. Isitt negates the claim made by Harry Goldgar (see Additional Bibliography) that* Young Törless *was influenced by Sigmund Freud's writings; she indicates that Freud was unpublished at the time.*]

There was an imminent duality about Robert Musil. It ranged about his career as a spirit of indecision, filtered through his mind as an agonisingly keen awareness of the irony of human existence, and revealed itself in his work as a constant ambivalence. It was distilled finally into the positive thought of a "morality of possibilities", the product of Ulrich, the man without developed "qualities" only because his vast potential was coupled with a fundamental and prohibitive integrity. His was a make-up, shared by Musil himself, which dictated that any quality propagated independently and for its own sake, detached itself at once from an ultimate cause, became a cause in itself, and was at once useless. "Ich bin auf das Äusserste vielseitig ungebildet" ["I am downright uneducated all round"] was how Musil once described himself. Ulrich might have said the same thing. Their common creed forbade them to become talented, for consciously to develop a talent involved the decision to act, which in turn involved the deception of a shift of emphasis from all things generally, to one thing particularly.

The only honest way to live was in unceasing recognition of an infinity of possibility, void of a finite scale of judgment, refusing to admit right and wrong as absolutes.

Many critics have called Musil most things, but few, until comparatively recently, a good author. His concern for the abysmal dichotomy of his own and all life, and his constant endeavour to force this recognition into a pattern by which he, and man, could live, hoodwinked numbers of them. They called him psychologist, pervert, "educational Philistine". (p. 238)

[Musil] sought tirelessly to forge a link between the two realities of the human mind, which, as he experienced it, was divided against itself; the reality of the understanding, and a strange, "other" reality of the senses. That is why he has so often been called a psychologist, because he was concerned with the vaguries of thought and feeling, locked apart without mutual means of communication. His own thought on the subject often descended like a depth-charge into the realm of human experience, but wrangling with the problems of motivation and behaviour at this level was a task which admitted only sparse results. One day, for example, Musil sat down to begin writing something under contract, which he anticipated would take him some six weeks, but which he finished only after two years of what he described as "verzweifelte Arbeit" ["despairing work"]. The result was the two Novellen published as *Vereinigungen*. . . . With his mind focused simultaneously on the twin poles of a dual reality, his literature could do little else but attempt to establish a bond between them.

Törless enters the battle as Musil's first and youngest hero (*Die Verwirrungen des Zöglings Törless* . . .). Like Ulrich, he reflects many of Musil's own traits, but at a much earlier age. For Törless is at school. He arrives there as a boy, and at first experiences a huge emptiness inside him which he can analyse as loneliness. He writes home with fervour, stretching out to a childhood which has suddenly forsaken him. . . . Törless is standing at the point where two worlds meet, the world of the child and the world of the adult. And this is where Musil's ambivalence begins. Törless reflects the crushing irony of a young mind which finds suddenly it can no longer live by sensing, but which has not yet grasped that it must understand. He is unconsciously beginning to intercept the images which invade his mind with a growing critical capacity. If Freud had already published at this time, Musil would have had a store of relevant vocabulary on which to draw (although it is far more likely that he would have elected to fight his own battle!), for in Freudian terms Törless was leaving the world of conceptual reality, and entering that of perceptual reality. But Freud was not to publish for several more years, and the ironic experience of Törless is depicted in searching terms with a poignancy that a static vocabulary could never have achieved. Although the style of *Törless* has been claimed as the first example of Expressionism in German literature, and the apparent theme, homosexuality in a military academy, would seem to be pretty revolutionary, the ironic experience of the boy, which is revealed at a much deeper level, harks back as far as the Romantics. (pp. 239-40)

[Musil] shared the "double-vision" which resulted from the awareness of a deep dichotomy. It is the prevailing attitude to life presented by Austrian literature; the interplay of the magical and the real world in the *Zauberstück*, the interaction of magic and morality in the *Geisterstück*, the combination of spontaneity and rehearsed composition, of farce and pathos, so typical of Nestroy and Raimund, the incongruity of man as Franz Grillparzer sees him, guiltless in his original estate, but degraded and dislocated by the world at large, and, from one of Musil's contemporaries, the complete dissociation of Hofmannsthal's Maria / Mariquita. Because he was primarily an analyst, Musil transposed this inconclusive state of mind, which most Austrians had chosen to present within the momentarily total, but thereafter irretrievable, world of a drama, into the medium of the novel, where it could be scrutinised and examined. This is true even of his two dramas, for they take no advantage of the fully-emancipated, horizontal representation of life which the stage can command, but remain rather within safer, novellistic bounds, where the characters can retreat at will into the vertical world of their own subjectivity. Thus the need for action is superfluous, since progress through the plot is made possible only by the clash and reaction of inner events which subordinate outward circumstance to themselves. In *Die Schwärmer* . . . the characters are ranged in two parallel lines, so to speak, which represent duelling attitudes to life. (p. 242)

A first hint of the moveable moral scale of right and wrong, which is to be the guiding light of Ulrich's ethical philosophy, appears in this play as the characters seek to integrate themselves. But it has not yet been objectivised by Ulrich, and appears here still in its subjective form as a moral code graded by emotional intensity. An emotion so intense that it no longer answers to the circumstance which gave rise to it, but becomes autonomous, is the only force Musil is able to designate at this stage of his development, to attempt to form an honest and uncultivated link between the divided spheres of his experience of reality. In moods of intense anger or fear, the distinctions of personality are fused together in subjection to one overall cause, and only the emotion engendered continues to exist as a united, autonomous force. The distinctions of body and soul disappear for Thomas in his paroxysm of fury and disgust at the attraction he sees between Maria and Anselm, and which he expresses through a series of powerful, biological images. . . .

An expression of tremendous sensuous potency is released through a flood of lyrical language—a poetic device which in itself indicates the fusion of physical and emotional aspects into the one intensity of the situation. The same fusion is evident in Anselm's "suicide", which is faked with the involvement of such emotional expenditure that it is indistinguishable from a real one. The incident gives Thomas his first impression of a scale of judgment extending in both directions into an infinity which by definition can know no absolutes. He is beginning to understand what it means to live with such intensity; later he may even understand Regine's cryptic pronouncement that all such people, she calls them "dreamers" (Träumer, the word has an unusual significance for Musil) share in a certain condition of creation and carry "den feurigen Tropfen" ["the fiery drop"] of creation in some degree within them. (p. 243)

Vinzenz (*"Vinzenz und die Freundin bedeutender Männer"* . . .) is a grotesque extension of Thomas. Thomas only senses the unity which intense emotion can provide, Vinzenz has converted the feeling into an intimate and useful part of his knowledge. This is betrayed by the farcical scepticism with which his view of life is coloured, and which allows him to distort the infinite moral code which Thomas senses, into the sheer expediency of living a lie. Inspired perhaps by Anselm's "suicide", he advises Bärli, who intends to shoot Alpha and then himself, to use blank shots, for this will enable him to experience the murder and suicide he plans, without the inconvenience of police enquiries and hearses which would nat-

urally ensue for others if the act were really to be committed! The suggestion is ludicrous because the play is a farce and because the author has not yet reached the stage where he feels that his infinite moral code can sincerely be implemented within society. This is to be Ulrich's task. Vinzenz' interests do not yet lie with mankind, but very much with himself, and he adopts the code of living a lie because it is useful to him personally. The device he uses for coercing reality into his own framework of expediency is language. He describes himself, when Bärli questions him about his profession, as "ein Wortemacher"—a maker of words. For Vinzenz, words have the power to seal over the crevices and divergencies which normally appear between experiences to rend them apart and to cause disunity in life. (p. 244)

Vinzenz, like *Die Schwärmer* is an intellectual extract. In these two dramas, the attempt to unify opposing realities, to destroy ambivalence of experience, is made through the philosophy of the characters concerned, and indicates Musil's gradually increasing objectivity in his approach to the problem which in *Törless* had gripped his understanding in a vice, making him as much a victim of the deadly irony as Törless himself, and as ardent a seeker of its resolution. There was no objective distance between the author and the character he created, and the situation therefore suffered the further irony of the blind leading the blind. But as Musil develops as a writer, not just as a thinker, so the objective distance grows as he employs his literary craftsmanship to pummel a shape into the philosophies which in *Törless* had seemed so annihilating. In his first novel, language had been used simultaneously with thought, both being parallel expressions of the same ideas. Language described thought, and when thought ran out or hit against a brick wall; so did words, and were supplemented by the series of dots and dashes which probably earned *Törless* the Expressionist label it did not really deserve. By the time Musil published *Vereinigungen* . . . , the role of language had become integral to the total expression of the work. It was no longer a simultaneous reflection of the ideas and actions it set out to express, but rather a natural extension of them. It too, has become autonomous; an entity able to conceive and propagate ideas in its own right, but which draws its strength initially from the ideas of fusion and communication with which Musil is concerned. The result is a dramatic adhesion of form and content. From the point of view of taxing his abilities as a writer, this method of trying to assemble a total and integrated reality was probably the most difficult Musil ever undertook.

He was concerned in these two Novellen, with horizontalising the vertical reality of subjectivity, through language. He made concrete those abstract experiences of Törless which he had previously only been able to circumscribe, or else forced to interrupt with dots and dashes when they defied analysis, by forcing them into the limits of flexible verbal and compound nouns. He caught and held a series of motions or reflections or experiences in the tangible form of a single word, and yet allowed that word to contain the pent-up potential of the whole series. . . . In their desire to live a unified existence the characters seem unwittingly to have exchanged their human properties for others from a more natural world, where they mingle together with greater ease and freedom. This desire for freedom of self-integration, the desire to attain a perfect state of balance, is something of which Claudine, heroine of *Die Vollendung der Liebe,* is acutely aware. Like Törless, she too unexpectedly senses the freedom and agility which the ironic circumstance could provide for her. She is given to looking back into the past, but on one particular occasion as the separate worlds of her past and present experience join, she notices something new and enormously free about their meeting. . . . "Gleichgewicht", a state of perfect integration and balance, is the operative word not only for what Claudine senses, but for what all Musil's major characters hope to attain. It is the central concept which backs the whole of his literature. But his characters are not seeking a merely satisfied matrimony of body and soul, where neither is assaulted unduly by the other, but a state so deep, so central, so immovable, that it can only be the very fulcrum of their existence. Had Musil been well acquainted with depth psychology he might possibly have called it the "deep centre". But Musil stood at the beginning of this new system of designation, as a member of the *avant-garde,* although he is likely to have found the beginnings of such thought in the writings of Ernst Mach, about whom he had written his doctoral dissertation. He could only circumscribe in his way, that same devastating, ironic awareness of all things which he shared with Schlegel, Novalis, Solger, Kierkegaard, Nietzsche, Thomas Mann—to name only the most important. Each had his methods of circumspection, and Musil had his. In *Vereinigungen* and *Drei Frauen* he was perhaps more direct and more concentrated than any of them, for the density of these works is truly amazing. In his attempt to unite the ambivalent realities in *Vereinigungen,* he creates a complex world in which physical things take on abstract properties, and abstract things take on physical properties. But such an intermingling of the spheres is often too grotesquely frightening to be the longed-for harmonious synthesis. . . . The reader feels himself being drawn into depths where inanimate objects become anthropomorphised, into a realm which appears to be a subtle integration of the physical and the abstract, and yet which proves itself a constantly vulnerable victim to the "unending, plenitudinous chaos" of Freidrich Schlegel's irony. It is an extreme world in which the characters play no active part and are forced to submit themselves to the complex functionings about them. . . . Although the mental and physical aspects of this world are so freely interchanged, there is no real indication of that "Gleichgewicht" which is for ever being sought. For the deeply emotional world Musil creates here is a perversion, in which circumstances have taken charge of character; a destructive, misshapen setting in which man cannot possibly continue to exist. Ulrich, in *Der Mann ohne Eigenschaften* is to attempt to temper this destructiveness through a morality forged of man's own reckoning, which sets up man's will-power as his ruling force. Musil has not yet achieved the degree of objectivity necessary for such an approach. His characters still find themselves overpowered by the frenzy of an ill-synthesised existence from which they are unable to break free. They become conscious at these moments of a bewildering rhythm of movement which dominates the outside world and alienates them from all human responsibility. (pp. 246-49)

In a sense Musil uses these two Novellen as ground to bed out Ulrich's scheme of an infinite morality. In them we are first introduced to the subjunctive world of possibility; a way of comprehending made functional only by the comparitive forms "wie wenn" ["like"] and "als ob" ["as if"]. . . . The characters live, comprehend and experience comparatively. Sometimes they themselves become meaningful only through the medium of a comparison. . . . (p. 251)

In *Drei Frauen* . . . this literary device is contracted from a comparison to a symbol, as Musil's increasing objectivity draws the conditions of synthesis more tightly together. These symbols are so tight, that they do not merely represent, but replace. Grigia's cow is a reincarnation of herself, in "*Tonka*" the

horse "gehört dazu", it belongs integrally to the young man's evocation of Tonka, and in *Die Portugiesin* the sick, mangy kitten is the counterpart of all three characters. (pp. 251-52)

Neither the juxtaposition of symbol and reality however, nor the tight construction of these three tales, can approach the final resolution. They represent the most paradoxical of all Musil's writing, for the characters actually reside within that impenetrable region between mythology (in the very broadest sense of the word as a mysterious, inviolable unity) and logic; the women darkly representative of the one, and the men answerable only to the other. Each tale depends for its very existence on a primeval indecision, on a fundamental incapacity to find an explanation. Did Grigia escape from the cave, and was Homo left to die there? Was it even a real cave in which they found themselves, or is the whole situation a symbol? What or who was the little cat; could it really have been God as the Portugiesin suggests? Was Tonka guilty or innocent? Each question, the very axis of each tale, remains essentially unanswerable. The stories are not only a reflection, but a faithful representation of Musil's ambivalent attitude, although the close texture of the work, and the intricate manoeuvres, indicate that he has intervened with a greater objectivity than ever before. The characters are therefore less terrorised by the insoluble situations; Herr von Ketten even heralds something of Ulrich's willpower as he finally overcomes his illness and his suspicion. The dreadful immediacy of *Törless* has disappeared, as has the wandering formlessness of *Vereinigungen.* The three heroes are no nearer to explaining the ironic duality of their lives, but the intensity of their experience has decreased. Homo is left to die alone, but not in agony. Herr von Ketten is allowed to live on with his beautiful wife in their castle where "no noise penetrated beyond the walls". The nameless hero of *Tonka* looks back on the whole unexplained episode and realises the benefits with which the "tiny, warm shadow" of that past experience has endowed him.

Musil's experience of irony as expressed in all these works has been in some degree akin to the Romantic conception of it. This is not true of *Der Mann ohne Eigenschaften,* although the basic dichotomy still remains to be resolved, because between *Törless* and *Der Mann ohne Eigenschaften* Musil's field of vision had widened proportionately as the objective distance between him and his major characters increased. As he became less painfully involved with each of them personally, so a natural shift of emphasis ensued from the individual to society. The hero of *Der Mann ohne Eigenschaften* is a man whose concern for himself only stems from his far greater concern for society. The code he seeks for his own life shall be a pattern for others, and his search for it causes him to forego his own character in order that he might potentially incorporate all characters. . . . (pp. 252-53)

Over the years, the development of Musil's writing reflects that same development of a purposive dealing with the ironic paradox of life which is evident in the span of ironic writers between Friedrich Schlegel and Thomas Mann. It ranges from a totally paralysed and incapacitated acceptance of the ambivalence of the human condition, to the broad ethical vision, forged of an unqualified acceptance of moral responsibility, which we find in *Der Mann ohne Eigenschaften.* The plans for the novel were begun before the publication of *Törless,* and yet Musil died leaving it unfinished. He had entrusted his entire life to this monumental and precarious attempt to lay the ghost of polarity and dissociation, by taming his awareness of irony until it could be welded in as an integral part of an ethical, human pattern. It is doubtful whether he would have been able to do this without the courageous attempts of Solger and Kierkegaard to fight back the destructive fire of irony to a distance at which it could be contemplated and analysed. It is practically certain he could not have done it without the Nietzschean Übermensch having demonstrated the possibility of human supremacy over the ironic circumstance. But Ulrich is not in the clouds of Zarathustra's mountain, exhorting the people, he is down with them in the failing days of the Austro-Hungarian empire, living their daily life and thrusting an ethical purpose into it in an attempt to save it. He is not the all-capable Übermensch, but the all-possible human. (pp. 253-54)

Musil was a mathematician, but his talent was constantly disjointed by a deeply mystic yearning. The explanation of God lay somewhere between the two. The developing schools of psychological thought in Vienna around the turn of the century, suckled by Sigmund Freud, Arthur Schnitzler, Franz Wedekind, and encouraged indirectly by the supposedly "absolute" philosophy of Ludwig Wittgenstein, attracted his interest, but they never persuaded him to accept them as a fundamental means of analysing the human psyche. Austrian, Expressionist, mathematician, psychologist, mystic; Musil was all of these and none of them. He lived in an eruptive era which suffered two world wars with all their inclusive chaos and fanaticisms. Musil steered a course through it, navigated entirely by his own conscience, which was indeed, the harshest judge of all that he undertook. Its iron rigours scrutinised his every thought and action, so that he could accept nothing unreservedly but was forced always to weigh up the merits of the opposing argument. It forbade him to join the ranks of any particular literary movement or political party, although he was never out of touch with current developments in these fields. A communal doctrine of which he could accept only a part could never become the mainstay of his life. Ultimately, the high integrity of his own conscience was the only code to which he could conform, and this owed obeisance to nothing which invaded it from without. It was a strong creed but a lonely one, which would not allow Musil to bow to the phases of popular taste. His work does not present the waxing and waning reflection of the so-called spirit of the age, but a constant drive forwards; he refused to ride the waves of circumstance, but tried to course his way through them. The only way he could be of use to others was by being intensely loyal to himself, and it was this mode of living and thinking which fashioned the extreme and brave individuality which was his, and around which increasing numbers of admirers have assembled. The inner dual which forms its well-worn cornerstone causes his writing to exercise a dichotomous fascination over its readers. On the one hand we can only stand in deep awe of his unerringly courageous attempts to pour his experience into a unifying mould of synthesis, whilst at the same time we feel ourselves dragged down into the vortex created by the insolubility of his cause. He fought his battle anonymously, but Musil's bravery has posthumously gained him a name which represents an unusual sanity and positive line of attack within modern German literature. (pp. 260-61)

> *Yvonne Isitt, "Robert Musil," in* German Men of Letters: Twelve Literary Essays, Volume III, *edited by Alex Natan (© 1964 Oswald Wolff Publishers) Limited), Wolff, 1964, pp. 237-66.*

V. S. PRITCHETT   (essay date 1964)

[*Pritchett is highly esteemed for his work as a novelist, short story writer, and critic. He is considered one of the modern masters of the short story whose work is a subtle blend of realistic detail and psychological revelation. Pritchett is also considered one of the world's most respected and well-read literary critics. He writes in the conversational tone of the familiar essay, a method by which he approaches literature from the viewpoint of a lettered but not overly scholarly reader. A twentieth-century successor to such early nineteenth century essayist-critics as William Hazlitt and Charles Lamb, Pritchett employs much the same critical method: his own experience, judgement, and sense of literary art, as opposed to a codified critical doctrine derived from a school of psychological or philosophical speculation. His criticism is often described as fair, reliable, and insightful. In an examination of* The Man without Qualities, *Pritchett compares the character of Musil's protagonist Ulrich with that of Italo Svevo's Zeno from the novel* Confessions of Zeno. *The characters of Ulrich and the novel's antagonist Arnheim are also contrasted. Pritchett compares the lucidity of Musil's style favorably with that of Anatole France and Marcel Proust, although in a later essay (see Additional Bibliography) he disavows the possibility of Proustian influence on Musil.*]

[*The Man Without Qualities*] is a wonderful and prolonged firework display, a well-peopled comedy of ideas, on the one hand; on the other, an infiltration into the base areas of what we call "the contemporary predicament." There is the pleasure of a cleverness which is not stupid about life: "Even mistrust of oneself and one's destiny here assumed the character of profound self-certainty," Musil wrote—not altogether ironically—of the Austrian character and these words suggest the conflict which keeps the book going at its cracking speed. Of course, Musil's kind of egoism had a long run in the first twenty years of the century and he has been—the translators tell us—written off by the standard German literary histories. Musil's tongue does indeed run away with him, but it is stupid to denigrate him. Proust and Joyce, with whom he has been exaggeratedly compared, approached the self by way of the aesthetic imagination; Musil reconstructs egos intellectually. What ideas do our sensations suggest? What processes are we involved in? If Musil has come to us regrettably late, if he sticks for his subject matter to the old pre-1914 Vienna and has some of that period flavor, he is not stranded there. The revival of Henry James has taught us that writers who live passively within history may be more deeply aware of what is really going on than those who turn up in every spot where the news is breaking.

The nearest parallel to Musil is not Proust but Italo Svevo in *The Confessions of Zeno*. Musil is very much an intellectual of that strain. The two writers represent opposite sides of the same Viennese school. They are restless, headlong psychologists and skeptical talkers, to some extent café writers. Like Zeno, the Ulrich of *The Man Without Qualities* is a gifted and self-consuming man. He burns up his experience. But whereas Zeno is a hypochondriac, a man of endless self-doubt, the clown of the imagination and the heart, whose great comic effect is obtained by the pursuit of folly with passionate seriousness, Ulrich is a healthy, athletic, extraverted and worldly character whose inquiring brain captivates and disturbs men of action. He is a mind before he is a sensibility. He has only to appear for others to behave absurdly; his irony muddles them; his perception alarms. Musil's achievement is to make this formidable character tolerable and engaging. (pp. 446-47)

Musil has been compared with Proust—though, if the translation is to be relied upon, he does not write as well—yet, where Proust seeks to crystallize a past, Musil is always pushing through that strange undergrowth to find out, if possible, where he is, where life is tending, and what is the explanation.

His book is a crab-wise search for a future, for what has not yet been given the sleeping draught. (p. 448)

Consciousness was Musil's real subject, not the "stream" but the architecture, the process of building, stylizing and demolishing that goes on in the mind. (p. 450)

[Musil is] subtle, light, liquid, serious. He is, no doubt, a bit over-fond of himself, perhaps a bit too tolerant to the "I" who is never brought up against anything stronger than itself; a bit too much on the spot, especially in the love affairs. What the novel does show is that the habit of intellectual analysis is not stultifying to drama, movement or invention, but enhances them. . . . Some critics have discerned what they believe to be a mythological foundation to this novel, in the manner of *Ulysses;* the density, suggestiveness and range could support the view. For it is cunningly engineered.

The second volume of **The Man Without Qualities** sustains the impression of a major writer of comedy in the Viennese manner, and of an original imagination.

A French friend of Musil's, M. Bernard Guillemin, has been good enough to add something to the comments I made on the mysterious English title of this novel. What Musil meant by "a man without Qualities" (*Mann ohne Eigenschaften*), he says, was "a man completely disengaged and uncommitted or of a man in quest of nonaccidental attributes and responsibilities self-chosen—the German counterpart of Gide's "*homme disponible*" though there is nothing of Gide in Musil's work. In the later volumes, it is said to have worried Musil himself, that a character as disengaged as Ulrich is, will eventually become isolated and bypassed by life. The sense of adventure which exhilarates the early volumes becomes paralyzed in the later ones, where the intellectually liberated man is not able to take the next step into "right action." It is significant that Musil's novel was never finished. He had spun a brilliant web of perceptions round himself and was imprisoned by them. (pp. 451-52)

The most irrelevant criticism made of him by some Germans and Austrians is that his kind of café sensibility is out of date. It may certainly be familiar in Schnitzler and Svevo, but Musil's whole scheme prophetically describes the bureaucratic condition of our world, and what can only be called the awful, deadly serious and self-deceptive love affair of one committee for another. And he detects the violence underneath it all. In only one sense is he out of date: he can conceive of a future; of civilized consciousness flowing on and not turning back, sick and doomed, upon itself. (p. 457)

> *V. S. Pritchett, "An Austrian: A Viennese," in his* The Living Novel & Later Appreciations *(copyright ©1964, 1975 by V. S. Pritchett; reprinted by permission of Literistic, Ltd.), revised edition, Random House, 1964, pp. 445-57.*

HERBERT W. REICHERT   (essay date 1966)

[*Reichert examines the influence of the writings of the German philosopher Friedrich Nietzsche on* The Man without Qualities.]

Any attempt to determine Nietzschean influence in **Der Mann ohne Eigenschaften** should begin with a consideration of the central character, Ulrich, since the huge though fragmentary novel is ultimately concerned with his search for a purpose in life. (p. 12)

Ulrich's indecision and confusion ultimately lead him to set aside one year in which to determine whether life can be meaningful. In the course of this experiment, which is the actual concern of the novel, he investigates several widely divergent, utopian possibilities.

The first of these utopias is correlated with an attitude of dionysiac abandon. Although important to Achilles and Anders, as the hero was variously called in early versions of the novel, the dionysiac solution to life's problems appeals to Ulrich only on rare occasions and he usually considers it a dangerous seduction leading to insanity.

He gives more serious consideration to the second possibility, termed the "Utopie des Essayismus," which is a rational attempt based on Nietzschean relativism to straddle and bracket ever more closely the unattainable truth. However, when no positive results seem forthcoming, Ulrich turns again to irrationalism and together with his twin sister Agathe, seeks to attain a mystical serenity in the "Utopie des andern Lebens," based on an attempt to blend platonic and erotic love. During the course of his involvement with this obviously antisocial utopia, treated in the novel in a section entitled "Die Verbrecher," and rooted in Nietzschean immoralism, Ulrich becomes disillusioned with subjective ethics and terms them a passing fad. According to later fragments, the paradisiacal existence *à deux* turns out unsatisfactorily, and a third utopia is envisioned termed the "induktive Gesinnung," which once again is socially directed and takes into account the daily problems of existence and the need for getting along with one's fellow men. Nevertheless, even in this final utopia, certain basic Nietzschean elements are in evidence, such as the dual morality which distinguishes between the masses and the inspired few.

Whereas none of these utopias directly reflect Nietzsche's Weltanschauung, all are presented in a Nietzschean framework. (pp. 12-13)

To begin with Ulrich then, he has been endowed with many traits of the Nietzschean superman. . . . Ulrich possesses the Nietzschean characteristics of masculinity and aggressiveness, disdain for pity, egotistical self-esteem, respect only for equals and not for traditions; that he is endowed with a nihilistic propensity, a distrust of the good and an attraction to the forbidden, a dislike for social duties and a will to create his own duties; that he is imbued with arrogance, ruthlessness, indifference, and a strong sense of mission. Ulrich's two prototypes in early versions of the novel mentioned above, Achilles and Anders, consider themselves to be a kind of "little Napoleon," who under other circumstances might have become a Mongolian general. . . . Despite their cynicism, however, all three protagonists are filled with an intense desire to improve mankind. Thus, one early fragment significantly bore the title, *Der Erlöser,* and while still a young man Ulrich had viewed the world as a great laboratory. . . . (pp. 13-14)

As the title of the novel suggests, Ulrich is a complete relativist who distrusts all such concepts as *Geist, Seele* and *Leben,* analyzing them endlessly without ever reaching satisfactory conclusions. (p. 14)

Such relativism is closely related to nihilism, and so it is not surpising to find that Ulrich holds the world to be devoid of goal or meaning. . . . Ulrich is of the opinion that mankind is in a transitional state that may endure till the last days of our planet. . . .

Ulrich's nihilism encompasses an awareness of Nietzsche's concept of the eternal recurrence. At the death of his father, which occurs significantly between two utopian adventures, Ulrich is plunged into a darkly pessimistic mood. Looking at his dead father's face, he senses the possibility that everything is only an eternal repetition and circular movement of the mind. . . . (p. 15)

The tragic realization of life's futility imbues Ulrich and his predecessors with a deep sense of isolation. Monsieur le vivisecteur, the first prototype, feels that he is frozen deep under polar ice . . . , a close parallel to Nietzsche's icy high noon of revelation or the icy wastes referred to in his poem "Vereinsamt." Ulrich is more communicative than the others, but he is still a lone wolf, unmarried and unemployed, who contemplates life with passive irony.

Paradoxically enough, but like his forerunners and like Nietzsche, Ulrich remains deeply concerned with the need for a complete revaluation of moral values. He rejects conventional morality. . . . Just as Zarathustra detests the notion of the smugly virtuous "letzte Mensch" who steers a careful middle course to avoid exertion, Ulrich disdains the modern tendency to regard strong feeling as a psychopathic. . . . (pp. 16-17)

True morality must take into account the flux of reality, the "Beweglichkeit der Tatsachen." . . . It has to recognize that reason cannot probe the depths of "das wahre Leben." According to Ulrich, morality lies not in conduct according to rules but in carrying out one's acts "mit ganzer Seele." (p. 17)

To emphasize the invalidity of conventional mores, Ulrich frequently discusses murder, which in bourgeois eyes is conceived as the extreme crime. For him the fifth commandment . . . is not to be taken as an inviolable law. . . . Not only are there valid exceptions to this law but in less clearly defined cases the reactions of the average newspaper reader are often in part sympathetic. . . . The act itself is not what matters, since a murder may be either a crime or a heroic deed. . . . The decisive factor is whether one acted from inner necessity or not, since a truly moral person could never let himself be guided by an external law. . . .

Imbued with this attitude, Ulrich is able to contemplate murdering his arch-opponent, the pseudo-idealist Arnheim. (p. 180

The morality of murder is embodied most clearly in the case of the sex-murderer Moosbrugger, which constitutes an earlier and more significant motif than the much discussed Collateral Campaign; the latter was, by the author's own admission, only a development of the Moosbrugger motif permitting the introduction of additonal characters. . . .

When the strong, benign-looking carpenter Moosbrugger committed murder, he acted in harmony with his innermost need. An abnormal upbringing had made him extremely shy in the presence of women and this shyness later developed into an insane fear, inducing him to react in a frenzied and sadistic manner when approached by a prostitute. He came to believe that he was being persecuted by female spirits and ultimately sought refuge in insanity. The law court, with its psychiatric staff, sentences Moosbrugger to death for slaying a prostitute, but Ulrich is convinced that "immoralists" such as Luther and Meister Eckhart would have judged the case in a more profound manner and set the carpenter free. . . . (p. 19)

Moosbrugger has both a passive and an active function in the novel. He not only serves to point up criticism of existing society and mores, but on the symbolical plane he also offers a solution to man's dilemma. Indeed, grotesque as it may seem, he represents the first irrational utopia Ulrich considers, a release from the stultifying bonds of reason and moral responsibility into frenzied dionysiac abandon, so well described by Nietzsche in *Die Geburt der Tragödie*. Clarisse and, to a lesser extent, Ulrich and Bonadea, see in Moosbrugger an answer to the problem of decadent civilization.

Clarisse links Moosbrugger with the ecstatic mood of dionysiac music which Musil, like Nietzsche, distrusted for its enervating effect on the will to live. Clarisse, it will be remembered, is a vigorous young pianist who thrills unduly to rapturous music and whose greatest wish is to continue to play endlessly. . . . When Ulrich gives her a set of Nietzsche's works, she becomes a confirmed if superficial Nietzschean, advocating will and genius. . . . Now, more than ever, she exults in frenzied dreams of perfection, so that her husband fears for her sanity and hates Ulrich for encouraging her to yield to this heady seduction. . . . (pp. 19-20)

Another important character related to Moosbrugger is the nymphomaniac Bonadea, who personifies the sexual element in the dionysiac mood. She wants Ulrich to help free Moosbrugger, i.e., to identify himself with the latter, as she would like Ulrich to assume the murderer's innocence and sense of irresponsibility. . . . Like Moosbrugger, Bonadea violates conventional morality without remorse and from a consuming desire. She seeks to convert Ulrich to her own sensuality and wants him to follow his instincts. . . .

The Moosbrugger motif, perhaps all-important in the earliest versions of the novel, recedes into the background of the later versions when confronted with the more serene utopia embodied in Ulrich's sister, Agathe. . . . (p. 22)

Ulrich's charming sister also possesses the "eine Tugend" praised by Zarathustra, that complete harmony between act and intent which Musil termed "ein ganz Begreifen." Like Moosbrugger, she embodies an ideal of the irrational and the instinctive, and has a fair share of Bonadea's earthy sensuality, being only more passive and serene. She has had an unhappy second marriage and shares Ulrich's nihilistic views and his desire to escape the misery of daily existence. . . . The two spend countless hours discussing questions of morality, during which time Agathe comes to accept Ulrich's relativistic *Lebensmoral*, largely because it articulates what she already believes.

Without a twinge of conscience, Agathe commits what normally would be considered a serious crime; she forges her father's last will and testament. She does so to prevent her husband from sharing in her inheritance and possibly interfering with her present way of life. From her point of view her act is entirely justified, but the theorist Ulrich is horrified, chiding her that even Nietzsche had adjured his "freie Geister" to adhere to certain outer laws so that they might maintain their inner freedom. . . . (p. 23)

Nietzsche's ideas are apparently rejected . . . but even here Nietzschean nihilism and immoralism remain the central theme. Agathe embodies these concepts just as all the other characters mentioned, excluding at times the vacillating Ulrich.

Concerning Musil's rejection of certain aspects of Nietzsche and Nietzscheanism, it would appear that the mystical Austrian wanted to dissociate his interest in Nietzsche completely from the customary will to power interpretation of the latter. To this end he introduced into the story the Nietzschean writer Meingast, presumably a caricature of Ludwig Klages, who comes down from "Zarathustras Bergen" to spend several weeks with Walter and Clarisse. In his advocacy of an irrational hierarchy based solely on power, Meingast is presented as a pompous, superficial and lascivious person. . . . (pp. 24-5)

An even more comprehensive rejection of Nietzsche seems implicit in the disillusionment experienced by Ulrich and Clarisse in the insane asylum, where the orgiastic exhibitionism of the insane brutally ridicules the romantic idea of dionysiac ecstasy. One inmate is actually an ironic portrayal of the insane Nietzsche. He is described as a man in his late fifties, obviously from the upper class, with bushy hair and a spiritualized face. His sickness is depressive *dementia paralytica;* the psychiatrist Siegmund whispers to Clarisse, "Ein alter Syphilitiker.". . . (p. 25)

To judge from the novel as published by the author, it would appear that Musil had gone the way of many other writers of his generation, such as Thomas Mann, Hermann Hesse, Stefan George and Georg Kaiser, who were at first captivated by the possibilities inherent in the new immoralism but who gradually became suspicious of an anarchistic morality. If one also takes the early fragments into consideration, the hero may be seen to have evolved from a Cesare Borgia type of ruthless superman to a mystical immoralist who ultimately rejects Nietzscheanism as a passing fad.

The published portion and early fragments comprise, however, only a part of Musil's work on the novel; there are also the later fragments on which he continued to work until his death in 1942. One cannot disregard these fragments on the ground that they were not final copy or that they were not published by the author himself, since Musil had wanted to publish more of the novel and was thwarted by lack of funds, the Nazi ban on his writings, and the difficulties of emigré existence.

In these later fragments there are indications that Musil contemplated having his hero explore the possibilities of a third utopia. (pp. 25-6)

According to one late fragment, the utopia of the inductive attitude was to make a clear distinction between the morality for the many and the morality for the few. . . . The distinctly Nietzschean flavor of such a dual morality is further enhanced by the fact that the elite few were to utilize Ulrich's *Geniemoral.* . . . Even the morality for the many has Nietzschean overtones. . . .

The morality for the many is discussed in such Nietzschean terms as *Dekadenz, Ressentiment, Macht,* and *das Böse* . . . . Nietzsche is himself frequently referred to. . . . (p. 26)

There is little doubt that the novel expresses Musil's own basic viewpoints. This is apparent both in the autobiographical nature of the hero and in the fact that the novel, including early versions and late fragments, was a life's work covering the period 1898 to 1942. It appears equally evident that Nietzsche, and not similarly oriented thinkers in whom Musil was simultaneously absorbed, was the principal inspiration for the ideas discussed above. (p. 27)

> *Herbert W. Reichert, "Nietzschean Influence in Musil's: 'Der Mann ohne Eigenschaften'," in* The German Quarterly *(copyright © 1966 by the American Association of Teachers of German), Vol. XXXIX, No. 1, January, 1966, pp. 12-28.*

LEON L. TITCHE, JR.   (essay date 1966)

[*Titche discusses the theme of hermaphroditism and the mythological framework of Musil's one published poem. The Isis and Osiris myth is also discussed by Lisa Appignanesi (see excerpt below), as representative of "the integration of the self."*]

The subject of hermaphroditism may not as yet be firmly entrenched as a motivating theme in scholarly research, but it does have an advantage in promoting lively commentary. (p. 165)

Robert Musil's poem "Isis und Osiris" displays the hermaphroditic theme within a solid mythological framework. This theme was a source of fascination and deep involvement for Musil and is prominent throughout his diaries and prose works, the most important of which is, of course, *Der Mann ohne Eigenschaften.* What in "Isis und Osiris" is the union of two persons into one being becomes in *Mann ohne Eigenschaften* the frustrated striving by Agathe and Ulrich for this attainment: the physical and spiritual union of brother and sister into one being. The beautiful chapter in *Der Mann ohne Eigenschaften,* "Die Reise ins Paradies," where Ulrich and Agathe experience a mystical consummation of their love, may be regarded as one end-product of the Isis-Osiris poem. The other is the character of Clarisse, proclaiming herself to be *"der grosse Hermaphrodit."* In her character and in the ideas which she espouses can be found vestigial concepts of medieval theology, especially the view then subscribed to by some thinkers who conceived of God as an androgynous entity. This poem therefore serves as a basis for Musil's later works. . . . (pp. 165-66)

The poem "Isis und Osiris" consists of five stanzas, each elucidating the Isis-Osiris myth and employing the three themes which exist in the cult-worship of Osiris: his death, dismemberment, and resurrection. However, this mythological outline is but a conscious frame for that which lies within it—the true image of the poem, an additional interpretation sketched by Musil, that of the *unio mystica,* the androgynous state which Carl Jung cites as "a symbol of the *unity* of the personality." This theme is immediately evident as one begins to analyze the poem.

The opening stanza depicts Osiris in death surrounded by *"des Sonnenrades Nabe,"* an image which brings to mind the symbol of the *Uroboros* or of the *rota* which the alchemist has ascribed to Mercury perceived by Jung as "the hermaphrodite . . . who divides into two in the classic dualism of brother-sister . . ." It is at this point, the very beginning of the poem, where the basis is established for the eventual unification of Isis and Osiris their assimilation into one being, the perfect circle, the self-devouring serpent.

In the second stanza, Isis removes her brother's genitals, eats them, and in exchange gives him her heart. This is the dismemberment phase in the myth. This does not follow the traditional belief that Osiris was hewn into fourteen pieces which were then scattered, all being recovered by Isis except for the genitals, which were eaten by fish. Departure from this indicates Musil's inclination toward the emphasis of the androgynous goal. This symbolic communion possibly has a religious reference. If one strips away the liturgical aspects and the doctrines of transubstantiation and consubstantiation from the rites of Christian Communion, there remains only the blood and the body, two separate components united in the symbol of one action relating to one person. The ritual contained in Mithraism, where actual blood and flesh were consumed, is, at least from the evolutionary standpoint, somewhat closer to the Isis-Osiris myth than to Christianity. This sacrifice to a god-head, who in Mithraism and in early Christian teachings was considered to be androgynous, certainly forms some basis for this poem.

The resurrection of Osiris occurs in the third and fourth stanzas, and with this attainment of a mystical apotheosis the fusion into the hermaphroditic state is also achieved. The storm that now begins arises from the union of the brother and sister into the androgynous state. It is as though two unstable elements have violently fused into one stable compound. . . . (pp. 166-67)

The synthesis has taken place. The perfect state of the hermaphrodite is complete. This higher realm not only indicates the perfection of self, but also a more refined and stable order for those who fall under the rule of the hermaphrodite. As separate beings in the first stanza, Isis and Osiris dominate a sterile wasteland and an effete civilization. This atmosphere is depicted by the desert with its red wind and the shores devoid of ships. Yet, as the androgynous union is complete, the forest looms to announce this union; the once arid land has now become fertile. (p. 167)

[The] mythical Osiris who marries his sister Isis has been resurrected in the poem as man-woman. The male attitude is stressed more than the female—it is the *conscious* attitude, the overt depiction of the male, whereas the female counterpart lies deeper. As Jung points out, ''The primordial image of the hermaphrodite should reappear in modern psychology in the guise of the male-female antithesis, in other words, as *male* consciousness and personified *female* unconscious.'' This is very typical of Musil. His male characters, while being consciously masculine in action, at the same time possess remarkable female insight; they are capable of extreme sensitivity, and many times bear traits bordering on the effeminate. (p. 168)

The last line of the poem completes the circle and restates the harmonious junction of the hermaphrodite. The *anima* is the dominant feature. Thus the hermaphrodite now relates to the female unconscious, and calling the hermaphrodite ''Isis'' implies this epicene union of brother and sister and not the goddess as a separate female entity. . . . [The] assimilation of Isis and Osiris into one being, into the perfect circle, marks the mastery of Musil's creation. (pp. 168-69)

Leon L. Titche, Jr., '' 'Isis und Osiris': An Interpretation of Robert Musil's Poem'' (originally a paper presented at the University of Kentucky Foreign Language Conference in 1966), in Kentucky Foreign Language Quarterly *(© University of Kentucky), Vol. XIII, No. III, Summer, 1966, pp. 165-69.*

FRANK KERMODE (essay date 1966)

[*Kermode is an English critic whose career combines modern critical methods with expert traditional scholarship, particularly in his work on Shakespeare. In his critical discussions of modern literature, Kermode has embraced many of the conceptions of structuralism and phenomenology. Kermode characterizes all human knowledge as poetic, or fictive: constructed by humans and affected by the perceptual and emotional limitations of human consciousness. Because perceptions of life and the world change, so does human knowledge and the meaning attached to things and events. Thus, there is no single fixed reality over time. Similarly, for Kermode, a work of art has no single fixed meaning, but a multiplicity of possible interpretations. In fact, the best of modern writing is constructed so that it invites a variety of interpretations,* all of which depend upon the sensibility of the reader. Kermode believes his critical writings exist to stimulate thought, to offer possible interpretations, but not to fix a single meaning to a work of art. True or ''classic'' literature, to Kermode, is thus a constantly reinterpreted living text, ''complex and indeterminate enough to allow us our necessary pluralities.'' In the following excerpt Kermode discusses Musil's novellas in* Five Women.]

The Man Without Qualities is unlike the other great novels of its period in about everything except its stature. Ironical, deeply serious, acute and extravagant, extremely personal and yet nowhere—on the surface at any rate—obscure, it is a work of fantastic intelligence, of pervasive eroticism, of completely original mysticism. It cannot be described in a paragraph, but it is an experience which no one who cares for modern literature should be without. He may be exasperated but he must see that this book, unfinished, extravagant, tiresome as it is, is the real thing. And the earlier stories will help him to do so.

Three Women (''Grigia,'' ''The Lady from Portugal,'' ''Tonka'') was published in the middle of a great literary period and stands comparison with its contemporaries. *Unions,* thirteen years earlier, has rather more the character of the *fin de siècle* (as indeed may be said of *Death in Venice*), but Musil valued it highly, perhaps because it contains, in a different blend and without irony, the same constituents—a nervous obliquity, a mystique of the erotic, a deep interest in the borders of the human mind, those uneasy frontiers with the human body and with inhuman reality—that go to the making of ***The Man Without Qualities***.

Musil's is notoriously a world in political collapse, the end of a great empire; but more central to his poetic writing (at times he makes one think of a prose Rilke) is the sense of a world in metaphysical collapse, a universe of hideously heaped contingency, in which there are nonetheless transcendent human powers. These he represents always by the same complex and various image of eroticism, which reaches its fullest expression in the big novel. ***The Man Without Qualities*** has among its themes nymphomania, incest and sex murder, not at all for their prurient interest but as indices of the reaches of consciousness. Moosbrugger, the murderer, thinks, when he is not killing, that he is by his personal effort holding together the world; the story of the love between Ulrich, the book's hero, and his sister was, according to Musil, to take us to the ''farthest limits of the possible and unnatural, even of the repulsive''; and yet if one theme can be called central in ***The Man Without Qualities*** it is this one, and nobody could think Musil anything but overwhelmingly serious in his treatment of it. Erotic ecstasy is beyond good and evil ''all moral propositions refer to a sort of dream condition that's long ago taken wing'') and exemplifies the power of our consciousness to cross the borderline formerly protected by what are now the obsolete fortresses of traditional ethics and metaphysics.

Throughout his career Musil explored this borderline. He kept a notebook on medieval mysticism and labeled it ''Borderline Experiences.'' It interested him that the mystic, speaking of his incommunicable experience of God, will usually do so by analogies with erotic pleasure. Ulrich, a considerable authority on love-making, decides that the transformation of a sane man into a frothing lunatic by the pleasures of the bed is only ''a special case of something far more general''—namely, our ability to undergo a quasi-erotic metamorphosis of consciousness which gives us what is in effect a second state of consciousness interpolated into the ordinary one. Like E. M. Forster, whose greatest novel, *A Passage to India*, came out in the same year as ***Three Women,*** Musil believed that the heightening of consciousness which makes possible the order and the perceptions of good fiction has something in common with erotic feeling; and meaningless contingency is the enemy of novels as well as love. For Musil the two metamorphoses of consciousness—art and love—ran together, and the sheer polymorphousness of the erotic was the subject as well as the analogue of his fiction.

To some extent this was already the case in *Young Törless,* and it is altogether so in the stories [in *Five Women*]. All have erotic themes, and most are concerned with female eroticism and with love as a means to some kind of knowledge. Here, as in the later novel, love is extremely various and free of the considerations of parochial ethics. In "**Quiet Veronica**" it is bestial, in "**The Perfecting of a Love**" it is profligate. "**Grigia**" and "**Tonka**" are variants of the medieval *pastourelle*—the seduction, in "**Grigia**," of a peasant girl by a man of higher social class, and in "**Tonka**" of a shopgirl by a student; but in either case the sexual situation is a figure for what is beyond sex. To study the behavior of people in love is, for Musil, to study the human situation at its quick. Even when there is only delighted animality, or when, as in "**Tonka**," there is an avowed absence of love and of intellectual communion, in a milieu of poverty and disease, sex remains the central ground for Musil's study of the potentialities of human consciousness.

The earliest of these stories is "**The Temptation of Quiet Veronica**," which appeared in an earlier and very different version as "**The Enchanted House**" in 1908. One's first thought is to relate this story, in its later form, to the literature of the Decadence; but its opaque surface, and the erotic feeling which occasionally pierces it, reflect Musil's preoccupation with the penetrating of reality by consciousness under the stimulus of sex. In short, it is not a failed attempt at the literature of neurasthenia, but a perhaps overworked statement of what we have seen to be Musil's principal theme. What we remember is not the pathology but Veronica's sense of her own body as she undresses, and Johannes, on the point of suicide, sensing himself as somehow rooted in the randomness of life. "**The Perfecting of a Love**" has a stronger and more visible story, and again there is a touch of romantic agonizing—"voluptuous enervated horror . . . nameless sin." But there is also much to distinguish it from run-of-the-mill decadence: the sharp picture of the amber twist issuing from a teapot on the first page; the detached view of Claudine dressing ("all her movements took on something of oafishly sensual affectation"); the sexuality of the stranger, which causes "a scarcely perceptible displacement of the surrounding world." Finally sex, represented as a defense against the "horribly gaping contingency of all one does," achieves a low and commonplace realization in the hotel cut off by snow; and from a body disagreeably swelling with lust emerges an image of love and union. "**The Perfecting of a Love**" cost Musil more nervous effort than any other work, and it is curiously central to his achievement. It is entirely lacking in the worldly irony and the "essayism" with which, in the great novel, he tried to relate its themes to the whole surface of modern life; but it is for all that a work which, in its uncommunicative, oblique fashion, expresses an understanding of human capacity, an intelligent and modern creativeness, comparable with those displayed in the contemporary writings of Lawrence and Thomas Mann.

By the time *Three Women* was published, thirteen years later, Musil had given up this somewhat hermetic manner, though he had not, as yet, developed the ironical discursiveness of *The Man Without Qualities.* Standing between his early and late manners, this book nevertheless has the same preoccupation with the erotic metamorphosis of consciousness and might also have been called *Unions.* The difference from the earlier work could be expressed as a new willingness to find a place in his stories for straight narrative (the "low, atavistic" element in fiction which Forster comically deplored and which troubles most experimental novelists). Not that this simpler form of satisfaction has the effect of making the stories simple, considered as a whole. They are still parables, and still, in the manner of parables, refuse to submit themselves to any single interpretation. In "**Grigia**," Homo is distinguished from the peasant community by his association with urban technology as well as urban civility; there is a futile rape of the land as well as easy seduction of women. Homo rediscovers the pleasant animality of sex, and with it a love for his absent wife and perhaps even for death. The climax of the tale has an insoluble ambiguity; but it is worth noting that ambiguity is a property not only of the narrative but also of the texture of the book. There are many passages of strange resonant poetry, for instance the description of behavior of hay when used as a lovebed. "**Grigia**" has the obliquity of high intelligence and idiosyncratic creativity. So too has "**The Lady from Portugal**," though its parable announces itself more clearly because its elements—love and union, spirituality and sickness—are placed at a great historical distance. And if "**Tonka**" is the best of all the stories, it is so not in virtue of its more down-to-earth theme, but because one senses in it a stricter relation between the narrative and the texture.

The story of "**Tonka**" seems almost commonplace beside the others, but that is only because of its superficial resemblance to the stories of Zola or the De Goncourts or George Moore. It treats of the quasi-mystical aspects of sex in the least promising of relationships. The liaison is of apparently low power; there is nothing involved that can be called love, indeed there is hardly any discernible communication between the pair. On the other hand there is a curious lack of amorous or spiritual self-aggrandizement, there is goodness and nature. Above all there is guilt, but even guilt somehow escapes the conventional categories and remains as it were unattached to real personalities. When Shakespeare's Cressida was unfaithful, Troilus could not believe his senses: "This is and is not Cressida." In the same situation Tonka steadfastly *is* Tonka, the "nobly natural" shopgirl who has nevertheless quite certainly been unfaithful. These ambiguities reflect the ambiguities of human reality; Musil once wrote that he saw no reason in the world why something cannot be simultaneously true and false, and the way to express this unphilosophical view of the world is by making fictions. As Tonka's lover notices when he debates with himself the question of marrying or leaving her, the world is as a man makes it with his fictions; abolish them and it falls apart into a disgusting jumble.

All these stories have obvious autobiographical elements, roots in Musil's personal life; but much more important is their truth to his extraordinarily intelligent and creative mind. They are elaborate attempts to use fiction for its true purposes, the discovery and registration of the human world. As with all works of genius, they suggest a map of reality with an orientation at first strange and unfamiliar. And though it is true that the experience of *The Man Without Qualities* is one involving a more permanent change of consciousness in the reader, these works also require his serious attention. (pp. 8-13)

Frank Kermode, "Preface" (copyright © 1966 by Dell Publishing Co., Inc.; used by permission of Delacorte Press/Seymour Lawrence), in Five Women *by Robert Musil, translated by Eithne Wilkins and Ernst Kaiser, Delacorte Press, 1966, pp. 7-13.*

WALTER H. SOKEL (essay date 1967)

[*Sokel compares and contrasts works by Heinrich Kleist, Søren Kierkegaard, and Robert Musil dealing with modern man's attitude toward faith.*]

Kleist's "The Marquise of O." (1806/1807), Kierkegaard's *Fear and Trembling* (1843) and Musil's **"Tonka"** (1904-1924)—reflect a significant development in modern man's attitude toward faith. All three works deal with situations in which faith contradicting human reason and experience is the problem. In all three the suspension of common sense in favor of an irrational and absurd trust is the challenge that constitutes the point of departure. Yet the terms in which the problem is posed in each work and the solution given (or withheld) delineates a shift which makes comparison a means for gauging a profound and symptomatic change in the spiritual history of Western man.

Two of these works are narratives and one is an essayistic discourse. At first sight, doubts may arise as to the legitimacy of comparing works so dissimilar in genre. However, a closer look at our three authors will go far to dispel these doubts. If we imagine a line separating the writer of narrative fiction from the philosophic essayist, we can say that Musil inhabits the immediate border area on the one side of the line, Kierkegaard that on the other. . . . Kleist and Musil turned to imaginative literature because philosophic discourse proved inadequate for the spiritual and moral problems they wished to express. Despair in the possibility of discovering truth by intellectual means preceded the birth of the writer in Kleist, while for Musil narrative fiction was a means of exploring questions posed by morality, psychology, epistemology, and religion. At times he regretted his defection to literature and saw his great novel, **The Man without Qualities,** as a cowardly substitution for the directness of philosophical treatise or essay.

> Wouldn't it have to be said that I simply lacked the courage to present my philosophical preoccupations as systematic reasoning. . . .

This is not denying the fact that Kleist and Musil were artists first of all, and indeed artists of the highest rank; yet it should be apparent that such authors have a place in the history of thought as well as in the history of *belles lettres*, and can be compared to essayistic thinkers like Kierkegaard.

Nevertheless, for the purposes of this comparision, there is, naturally, a closer affinity between Kleist and Musil than there is between either and Kierkegaard. Apart from the common genre of the *Novelle* or tale, there is a striking likeness of theme between "The Marquise of O." and **"Tonka."** Both narratives deal with the (at least initially) unexplained pregnancy of an unmarried young woman who claims not to have had sexual intercourse at the time she conceived. Thus both tales raise, or seem to raise, a fundamental question. Should one give credence to the laws of nature or to the word of a human being? We cannot, it seems, believe both. If we choose to trust reason and experience, we must forego faith in the innocence and honesty of mankind represented in these two highly trustworthy women characters. On the other hand, if we put our trust in them, we are forced to a *sacrificium intellectus* and must cease to believe in the explicability and rationality of phenomena.

This is the fearful dilemma in which Kleist and Musil place the characters, and with them, the reader, of their stories.

This dilemma symbolizes the conflict between religion and the scepticism inherent in modern rational thought. Both stories touch upon the fundamental tenet of Christianity—belief in the miraculous conception of Christ. Faith in it is one of the elements that illustrates the discrepancy between Christianity and common sense. In these two stories trust in a woman's word constitutes a parallel to that faith in the word on which Christianity is based. The emerging consciousness of a contradiction between this faith in the word and the knowledge of the world as derived from science ushered in the crisis of religion which has characterized the last three centuries, and to which both Kleist's and Musil's tales seem to allude.

Yet the two stories, initially so alike, exhibit a very profound difference. In Kleist's work, nature vindicates faith; the seemingly miraculous receives a natural explanation. In Musil's tale, written almost exactly one century later, the mystery remains unexplained. The gap between faith and rationality is never bridged. (pp. 505-07)

In Musil's story, the protagonist has an affair with a girl named Tonka. She, too, becomes mysteriously pregnant. At the time of conception, her lover had been away, and he cannot possibly be the father of her child. Yet Tonka vows that she has been completely faithful to him. He loves her and knows that she is not the type of girl likely to lie and deceive. However, he cannot make himself believe her, since such a belief would be absurd. At best, he can act as if he believed her, while in fact he does not. His problem is aggravated by the illness Tonka contracted. It could have entered her bloodstream only from the father of the child, either directly or through the embryo. The doctors, however, have been unable to detect a trace of this sickness in him. The disease seems to make her unfaithfulness a certainty. The only alternative would be parthenogenesis—a mystical conception. Tonka dies of her illness before the child is born. No explanation of the puzzling plot appears.

The outcome of the plots—re-establishment of harmony and certainty in Kleist, persistence of perplexity in Musil—is not the only significant difference between "The Marquise of O." and **"Tonka."** The whole nature of the problems and the terms in which they are posed are radically distinct in the two works. Crucial in this is the difference in narrative perspective. "The Marquise of O." shows essential stretches of the narrative from the point of view of the heroine. . . . Consequently, the problem of the story differs essentially from that of **"Tonka."** (pp. 507-08)

Kleist's Marquise of O. presents the problem of faith and the absurd this side of Kierkegaard; Musil's **"Tonka"** carries it beyond. Significant is the shift in perspective. In Kleist's story the problem is viewed from inside, from the inner experience of the heroine. Only if we share her perspective can we comprehend her unshakable certainty. Since she is sure of her memory, she *knows* that her belief in her innocence must be right. The question is simply this: has she knowingly committed the act that brought about her pregnancy? And the answer can be a definite "no." For her past actions are known to her and, therefore, to the reader, who views the problem from her perspective. Tonka's lover, on the other hand, is in the position of the Marquise's parents or Mary's contemporaries. He can never have the Marquise's certainty, since it is not his memory of his own actions but the authenticity of another's claim he must accept. For him the possibility of deception always exists. His faith must be a venture; it involves the risk of being duped. Only because of this risk can it properly be called faith as distinct from knowledge. As absolute commitment to his mistress, his faith would be "die Vollendung der Liebe" (to quote the title of another of Musil's works)—the perfection or completion of love. At the same time, it would entail the *sacrificium intellectus* and the threat of making a miserable fool of him. This establishes its close parallel to Kierkegaard's interpretation of Christian faith as paradox and suspension of the universal. In contrast to Kierkegaard's Abraham and Mary, Musil's protagonist is not prepared to make the sacrifice of the universal, here embodied in *common* sense, which is the result of universal human experience. As a lover, he yearns for the ability to believe; as a modern man, an engineer and scientist, he cannot allow himself to satisfy his yearning. The division between emotional need and mental scepticism cannot be overcome. Musil's tale presents itself as a parable of modern man's relationship to faith.

If Tonka's claim is true, she resembles Mary—the mother of God. If we pursue this parallel, we find that this time Christ is not born. Tonka does not live to give birth to her child. The "miracle" is literally still-born; indeed, it kills itself. For assuming the conception is a miracle, so is the disease which kills her and the unborn child. In Musil's parable, there are two sides to the miraculous, and they cancel each other. The result of the miracle of burgeoning life is disease and death. (pp. 510-11)

> Walter H. Sokel, "Kleist's 'Marquise of O.', Kierkegaard's Abraham, and Musil's 'Tonka': Three Stages of the Absurd As the Touchstone of Faith," in Wisconsin Studies in Contemporary Literature (© 1967, Wisconsin Studies in Contemporary Literature), Vol. VIII, No. 4, Fall, 1967, pp. 505-16.*

JUAN GARCÍA PONCE   (essay date 1968)

[*García Ponce provides an extensive comparison of the principal works of James Joyce and Robert Musil.*]

One way to evaluate Joyce and Musil, is to compare their chance similarities and innate differences. Viewed in the perspective of time, the careers of Musil and Joyce parallel and diverge at several points, thus creating a suggestive set of contrasting patterns containing some of the finest moments of modern literature. Both represent the culmination point of two cultures and both belong to nations somewhat marginal within their own cultures. Though writing in English, Joyce thinks of himself always as an Irish writer, and Musil, writing in German views himself as an Austrian writer. The national traits so clearly delineated in their works to a degree stand between them and their mother tongue. Also, both belong to Catholic countries that exist within a Protestant tradition. Moreover, each in a totally different way turns against his original faith. But even though Joyce finally comes to reject his maternal religion (maternal in the national as well as in the familial sense) in the name of art, his original faith remains as a vital cultural antecedent throughout his work. By contrast Musil, starting from a strictly positivistic education, adheres finally to the German idealistic tradition, though in a contradictory and personal manner. This strained relation with their cultural world creates a peculiar tension in their works. For Joyce, preoccupation with Catholicism will forever be a motive for rebellion and a source of personal reassurance. For Musil,

enticing idealism canopies reality, opposing or characterizing it. Thus the Luciferian "I will not serve" of Stephen Dedalus is a guideline that leads Joyce to the cyclical conception of time and history in *Finnegans Wake;* Musil asks himself at the end of *A Man without Qualities:* "What remains in the end? Does there exist a sphere of the ideal and another of the real? Directive images and the like? What an unsatisfactory answer! Isn't there a better one?" (p. 75)

Quite apart from the different explications applicable to their works, undoubtedly this Catholic-Protestant difference appears in Musil and in Joyce as a kind of inherent substratum. Joyce is clear. Even when traveling in landscapes of night and dreams, when descending into the dark depths to grasp the ultimate organic form of language, Joyce evidences the type of Catholic and scholastic clearness of which Santayana speaks. Musil is obscure. Even when he dazzles us with the shadowless brilliance of his logical discourse in the attempt to illuminate the subterranean world and its hidden roots, Musil . . . remains metaphysically immersed in darkness. His symbols, in this sense, are contradictory even though unintentionally so. Joyce proceeds from the rational to the irrational, always sees the general in the particular, which makes of him a humanist in spite of himself, so to speak. His world has the fluidity of water, the heavy gravity of the earth and is feminine when the mother image dominates. Musil always looks for the particular in the general. Proceeding from irrational intuition he tries desperately to attain a higher reason. His world, governed by the spirit in freedom, is winged, expands in its aerial flight, appears to be eminently masculine, and is a closed world in contrast to Joyce's open world.

These basic differences, easily discernible in the early writings of both authors, shed considerable light on their mature works. Today Joyce is known as the author of *Ulysses* and *Finnegans Wake* and Musil of *The Man without Qualities.* Their other books achieve definition and true meaning through these great works by dint of the new values and perspectives they acquire in retrospect as precursors. Musil and Joyce both seem intent on channeling their creativity into massive and global works which contain their complete thought. Their achievement is similar to that of another great contemporary novelist: Marcel Proust. In this their trajectory differs from that of other equally great artists. To do justice to Joyce, Proust or Musil we need only to refer to them as the authors of *Ulysses, In Remembrance of Things Past,* and *The Man without Qualities.* But to do justice to the works of Lawrence, Conrad or Faulkner, one has to mention several titles. And the same can be said of those works of Joyce and Musil written prior to their definitive works. Viewed in relation to the latter, the former assume the suggestive characteristics of preludes which anticipate the theme and hint at what is to come. (p. 76)

The works of Musil, before they expressed the real Musil— that is before Musil became the writer he would become—like the early works of Joyce, reveal a number of similarities, elements in common and significant differences. . . . (p. 77)

Both Joyce and Musil cultivated the short story, drama, essay and short novel, with more or less obvious autobiographical intent, before doing *Ulysses* and *The Man without Qualities.* . . . Musil's first work was a disturbing and peculiar novel, *Young Törless.* Although in a different context, this book has its counterpart in Joyce's *A Portrait of the Aritst as a Young Man.* Likewise, *Exiles,* Joyce's only dramatic work, has affinities with the two dramatic works of Musil, *Visionaries* and *Vinzenz and the Girl Friend of Important Men,* not only on account of their *genre* and style but also because of their profound meaning and thematic development. Finally Joyce's short stories, *Dubliners,* equate with those of Musil's **Unions** and **Three Women.** The essays written by both during the period preceding the creation of their great novels likewise reveal their basic concerns, those of Musil's more than Joyce's, and their indirect way of coping with them. (p. 78)

Musil, in his stories, probes increasingly into experience by focussing entirely on the inner motivation, thus bypassing external reality completely to keep it from obtruding on the descriptive exteriorization of the inner self which, in his judgment, alone truly defines the relationship between the individual and reality. Furthermore, whereas in Joyce action in each successive work implies an increasing adaptation of language to verbal representation of subjective action, in Musil it consists in the desire to establish a gap between the function of language and its object, the result being a diaphanous reflexive clarity, in which subjective processes are expressed through the juxtaposition of daring images and metaphors and a tightened sharpening of the conceptual aspect of the narrative development. So, from the beginning, their works point the direction their creators will take and indicate the nature of what it is that they seek. Subsequently, in their works for the theater, both will elect a strictly realistic and traditional form, somewhat reminiscent of Ibsen and Strindberg. The revolutionary character of their intent will find focus in the nature of their themes struggling for expression in a refractory style. In this sense, the dramatic works of both appear especially suggestive and disturbing in that, on account of this conflict between form and content, the traditional theater reaches a supreme degree of tension. The closed structure of these works clashes with the kind of conflict that the style strives to express. But the implication and basic meaning of these conflicts, which already foreshadow those in the later great books of these two artists, are best observed if studied comparatively in their development through the early works, the latter being already outstanding because of the high level of their artistic merit. (p. 79)

As we have suggested, **Young Törless** is partially a developmental novel with a structure similar to that of *A Portrait of the Artist as a Young Man,* but in a different sense. In this respect, the work falls within an essentially German narrative tradition extending from *Wilhelm Meister* to *The Magic Mountain* and more recently to *Joseph and his Brothers.* In this type of fiction we follow the various stages of development a young man goes thorugh in his life to attain the understanding he processes from the sum total of his experiences. But in **Young Törless** this symbolical journey, usually always a repetition and illustration of that of Odysseus and which normally covers several years, takes place in a few months and never gets anywhere in particular. From the beginning pages of the novel, the style anticipates the tense tautness of the action, in which everything is reduced to essentials. The dry direct language moves forward jerkily in brief and concise paragraphs. In immediate contrast stands the open and evocative style of *A Portrait* by Joyce, moving along in vast rhythmic waves. Joyce moves slowly, stopping to enjoy the sense and color of words and seeking his characters through them; Musil plunges us forthright into a cutting, acerbating reality in which description is reduced to a minimum. The action in **Young Törless** does not proceed marginally, intent on registering the echoes and atmosphere of a city for the purpose of showing how it shapes the characters; rather it is confined to a small town almost lost on the Austro-Russian border; moreover we see very little of the town itself. The writer limits himself to depicting the tan-

gential relations of the poor peasants with the privileged students of the military academy to which the town owes its social importance. After a stirring and significant scene between a prostitute and two of the chief protagonists of the novel, the story ends inside the academy which, the author admits is no other than the one which he, and a few years previously, Rainer Maria Rilke, had attended. Thus, the knowledge of this emphasizes conclusively the close relationship between the student Törless, protagonist of the novel, and its creator; however, in spite of this circumstance, we do not find in the work any portrait of the artist as an adolescent. In contrast to Joyce, Musil does not find the answer in art as a vocation. In the final analysis the meaning of Törless' experience will be something different. Before the student gets involved in the episodes that constitute the novel's nucleus, Musil says of Törless that "at that time it seems that he had no character at all," and that when impelled by a vague instinct to write imitating authors he had read, the effort had no effect on him because in his state of mind "his spirit lived only in action, so to speak." This characteristic is the one that interests the novelist above all else. However, when Törless has been through the terrible things that change him to a degree, experience matters only for itself. In **Young Törless** what interests us is the nature of the experience, whereas in *A Portrait of the Artist as a Young Man* obviously what matters is the personal decision the protagonist reaches, the novel being the story of a vocation which, when decided upon, provides a solution.

These dissimilarities within a similar frame of reference tell us a great deal about the later development of Musil and Joyce. The ending of *A Portrait* is clear. . . . The ending of **Young Törless** is ambiguous. . . . (pp. 80-1)

In a certain sense, it is valid to assume that from Törless, changed by time and new experiences, with more maturity and a deeper and therefore more disquieting philosophy, will emerge Ulrich, the protagonist of **The Man without Qualities.** Parenthetically, it is not without significance that in the first novel we only know the hero's family name and in the second only his given name. Musil will subsequently explore, in a search characterized by even greater intensity, the problems left unsolved in his first novel. (p. 81)

> *Juan García Ponce, "Musil and Joyce," translated by Boyd Carter and Eileen Carter (translation copyright, 1968, The University of Tulsa; originally published in an expanded form as "Musil & Joyce," in Revista de Bellas Artes, No. 13, January-February, 1967), in James Joyce Quarterly, Vol. 5, No. 2, Winter, 1968, pp. 75-85.***

HENRY HATFIELD (essay date 1969)

[Hatfield views the brutal and aberrant experiences of the protagonist of Young Törless *as ultimately positive in their effect on his emotional and psychological growth. For an interpretation of this work that discusses the destructive aspects of Törless's experiences, see the excerpt below by Jeffrey Meyers.]*

To encounter Robert Musil among the Central European writers of the earlier twentieth century is a refreshing surprise: none of the clichés applies to him. He is not romantic, not sentimental; he does not make a cult of youth, music, the soul, or nature. No "mere rationalist," he was keenly aware of the depths of the unconscious; this very awareness made him all the more convinced of the value and necessity of logic and clarity. One might call him the anti-Hermann Hesse: (p. 35)

To be sure, Musil was no isolated phenomenon. Although Vienna was a center of neoromanticism in literature, music, and painting around the turn of the century, there were countervailing tendencies: the names of Freud, Schnitzler, Mach, and Wittgenstein spring to mind. Musil was trained as an engineer and a mathematician and wrote a dissertation on Mach. Precision and detachment characterize all his work. Yet he was well aware that only one hemisphere of life had proved accessible to scientific methods. He was obsessed by the hope, Utopian as he called it, of achieving a combination and interpenetration of rational and nonrational elements—not a "synthesis" in the bombastic Hegelian sense. A "secretariat of precision and soul" was one of his formulas for this quest. In other words, the "night side" of life, the irrational elements, the emotions and intuitions, are not to be underrated—Musil was as convinced of their importance as were Rilke and Hofmannsthal—but to be explored, accurately and coolly. Sober observation, not "dialectics," and mathematics, not *Geistesgeschichte,* are needed. Of the twentieth-century German writers known to me, Musil is the closest to Freud in lucidity of thought and intellectual courage.

Of course this great combination is the major theme of Musil's enormous but never finished *The Man without Qualities*. . . . It also figures importantly in his other novel, *Young Törless*. . . . Since the latter book, somewhat overshadowed by its giant successor, is fascinating both in itself and as a pioneering work of fiction, it is worth discussing in its own right. *Törless* is amazingly ahead of its time in its subtlety of psychological analysis, its freedom from both sentimentality and sensationalism, and its frank treatment of sexual matters, including in this case homosexuality and sadism. Although less brilliant than *The Man without Qualities,* it is formally far more successful: in Musil's magnum opus the essayistic sections tend to overwhelm the book as well as the reader.

Young Törless is essentially the analysis of a critical period in the life of an adolescent. Törless, sixteen years old, is a student at an aristocratic military academy, located in the eastern flatlands of the Austro-Hungarian Empire, not far from the Russian border. His experiences are extremely unpleasant, in fact potentially ruinous, but he survives: he is a brilliant, sensitive but not a weak youth. (Presumably there is some autobiographical substructure.) *Törless* has something in common with the traditional *Bildungsroman,* but its protagonist, basically a realist, is no Wilhelm Meister or Parzival. Similarly, while the theme of *Törless* links it to the "school novel" of the period, which depicted the sufferings inflicted on defenseless boys by unfeeling schoolmasters, its tone is radically different. Musil has not written an emotional protest against the educational establishment, as Hesse did in *Unterm Rad (The Prodigy)* and Emil Strauss in *Freund Hein,* nor a satire like Heinrich Mann's *Professor Unrat (Small Town Tyrant)*. Musil's aim was rather to describe, *sine ira et studio,* the ordeal of Törless. Clearly, the narrator's sympathies are with his hero, but he does not load the dice. The threat to Törless does not come from the school as such, but partly from contemporary society as reflected in his companions, still more from forces within himself. He is changed; to some extent he "grows up"; but this is an educational novel with a difference. Possibly the protagonist's name is symbolic: he becomes less of a fool, is partially rid of folly—*der Torheit los*. Perhaps the closest analogy—though not a very close one—is Joyce's *Portrait of the Artist as a Young Man.*

There are two levels of action: the external, dealing with Törless' psychological "confusions," and the internal, concerned

with his intellectual adventures. Actually the two planes merge into one. Whenever Törless is really stirred, whether by an attractive body or such an enigmatic concept as the square root of minus one, he feels a thrill which Musil clearly links to sexual excitement. To Törless a challenging mathematical concept is as stirring as an erotic adventure. Not more so: he is not unduly bookish and regards his teachers (who are his social and intellectual inferiors) with a mixture of contempt, pity, and curiosity.

On the literal level, the action centers on Törless' relations with three of his schoolmates: Beineberg, Reiting, and Basini. The first two, larger and somewhat older than the protagonist, attract him partly because of their bad reputations: he is bored and has yet to develop any real independence of character. . . . Basini, a miserable youth, is completely in the power of Reiting and Beineberg, who have found out about a theft he committed and blackmail him ruthlessly. He is their slave, the object of their sadistic and homosexual aggressions. Reluctantly fascinated, Törless observes their "experiments" and for a while takes some part in them.

Musil's characterization contrasts the two bullies very strikingly. Beineberg is a pretentious pseudo intellectual, sincere but hopelessly unbalanced, in a sense even stupid. Unfortunately, this type occurred all too often in what one might call the Wagner-through-Hitler period of German culture, as the criticisms raised by Heinrich and Thomas Mann, Karl Kraus, Broch, and Musil himself attest. Musil preserved several further examples in *The Man without Qualities,* "like flies in amber." (pp. 35-8)

Reiting, for his part, is devoted to power for its own sake: he is a completely unscrupulous "operator," whose greatest pleasure lies in intrigue. When the mood takes him, he stirs up trouble quite gratuitously. As clever (in his way) as he is cruel, he deduces Basini's theft from circumstantial evidence and browbeats him into confession. . . . The unpleasant pair is especially dangerous to Törless, in that each possesses, in a distorted form, characteristics of the protagonist: Beineberg has Törless' intellectual speculations, Reiting his ambition.

If Beineberg with his "philosophizing" seems to anticipate figures like Alfred Rosenberg and Hitler himself, Reiting suggests the opportunistic, activistic type of Nazi—men like Goering or Ernst Röhm. (Probably the latter sort is a bit less despicable.) Basini completes the vicious circle: the predestined victim, soft, masochistic, weak rather than evil. Although Musil himself wrote that *Törless* foreshadowed National Socialism, I do not believe that he specifically foresaw, in the first years of the twentieth century, the rise of German Fascism. Rather, he was aware, as few if any others were at the time, that there were forces in contemporary Austria which pointed toward sadistic tyranny. The secret room where Beineberg's and Reiting's activities are focused is located "like a forgotten relic of the Middle Ages, away from the warm, clear life of the classrooms.". . . In its theatening archaism it suggest the unconscious mind but has political overtones as well. . . . Even when the whole disgrace has come to light, the students unite to put all the blame on Basini, who is expelled. As Robert Minder remarks, this final turn of the screw anticipates the attitude of many Nazis in 1945: the guilty testify to each other's innocence.

In this sense, many details in *Törless* do indeed have a prophetic ring today. (pp. 38-40)

Törless is narrated almost entirely in the third person. Although we often perceive the cadets and their doings through the eyes of the hero, a highly intelligent adolescent, the narrator sometimes steps away from the story, as it were, to comment on it. At one point we are told of a development which took place years after Törless' "confusions" were things of the past: "Later, after Törless had surmounted (*überwunden*) the events of his youth, he became a young man of very subtle and sensitive intellect.". . . (p. 40)

Törless survives his sordid entanglements relatively unscathed and is in fact strengthened by his brush with evil. When Törless, years later, tells a friend about his "confusions," he admits that the episode was degrading but does not feel ashamed. Instead, he values it for having preserved him from the illusion of an "all too secure and tranquil healthiness" . . . , from naïve smugness. Musil does not draw any specific moral conclusions; he seems to treat Törless' experiences as one might regard an unpleasant but not too serious illness. One is reminded of Menninger's remark that a patient who has emerged from a mental illness is stronger than he was before its onset. Although *Törless* is in a sense a *Bildungsroman*, its cool tone and relatively neutral point of view set it off from most educational novels. (p. 41)

Törless' final self-assertion is that of a young man who has emerged, not gloriously but decisively, from his first ordeal. There are hints that he may become a writer, a mathematician, perhaps a philosopher, but he is seen primarily as a gifted young man, not as "the artist." Doubtless there will be other confusions, but one senses that these will be more worthy of him. He has put the Beinebergs and Basinis behind him. By accepting and articulating his conviction that reality is Janus-faced, he has conquered his fear of it. (p. 48)

> *Henry Hatfield, "An Unsentimental Education: Robert Musil's 'Young Törless,'" in his* Crisis and Continuity in Modern German Fiction: Ten Essays *(copyright © 1969 by Cornell University; used by permission of the publisher, Cornell University Press), Cornell University Press, 1969, pp. 35-48.*

LISA APPIGNANESI (essay date 1973)

[*Appignanesi examines Musil's "pronounced effort to include the feminine in the decidedly male world of theory and intellect" of which he wrote. She finds that a study of Musil's major works reveals his in-depth investigation of feminine attributes, "an attempt to reveal the core and the components of that which is essentially feminine."*]

In Robert Musil's highly intellectual and masculine universe it is almost surprising to find such a large number of female characters of central importance. . . . It would seem that in such a hard-minded world, woman, with what has become known as her social frivolity and intellectual vagueness, would be out of place and the effort made to understand her would be minimal. Yet, it is clearly the case that Musil, in *The Man Without Qualities* through his major hero, Ulrich, does make a pronounced effort to include the feminine in the decidedly male world of theory and intellect. In fact, one might say that the impingement of the feminine into Ulrich's or Musil's lucid world of scientific strictness and exactitudes could be charted from the very opening of *The Man Without Qualities* when the first woman, Leona, enters this encyclopedic universe. (p. 82)

It is in her opaqueness that Leona's femininity lies and as Ulrich moves up the hierarchy of women in this book, this opaqueness increases: all the women he comes into contact with become more and more difficult to apprehend.

From Bonadea's mixture of morality and nymphomania, he moves to the bewildering idealism of Diotima, the incipient madness of Clarisse and finally to the ordinariness yet complete extraordinariness of his sister Agathe, whom Ulrich feels he must fathom if he is to understand himself. Hence, just by glancing at territory yet to be explored, it becomes evident that Musil's emphasis on the feminine arises from an attempt to comprehend even those spheres which cannot be grasped intellectually and form a wish, perhaps, somehow to harness the energies found in these realms in order to find a total solution for the human condition. Musil, in his scientific exactitude and his completeness must explore those areas which are paradoxically closed to scientific investigation. He must demystify the 'other'; and this otherness for the moment can, without further explication, be called 'femininity'.

Yet, for all his lucidity and hard-mindedness, there is something in Musil which inclines him precisely toward this sphere of the 'feminine', because Musil is essentially the philosopher of possibility or of manifold potentiality, of that which cannot as yet be logically defined. When Ulrich embraces the concept of 'Essayism' as that most beneficial for understanding the world and himself, he is, in a masculine context, selecting the approach of most integrity for trying to capture the multitudinous possibilites reality offers to the mind. Essayism for Ulrich is that form of exploration which sees everything from many points of view without ever comprehending it fully 'for a thing wholly comprehended instantly loses its bulk and melts down into a concept'. Essayists are the masters of the floating life within and their domain lies between religion and knowledge, between example and doctrine, between *amor intellectualis* and poetry.

This inclination toward Essayism can be taken as Musil's own from the many indications to this effect in his notebooks, and what it reveals is precisely a thinker who would like to see the ultimate union of 'precision and soul' or rather 'exactitude and spirit', what many of Musil's critics call *Ratio und Mystik*. Ulrich's definition of Essayism permits not only that kind of exactitude which insists on a thing being seen from all sides and in all of its relationships, but also on the potentiality involved in the unfixed world of spirit and poetry. The first half of this union is definitely the male's for Ulrich is the man of precision *par excellence*, the man of empirical reality continually tempted by possibility. It is necessary to remember, however, that even though Musil depicts Ulrich in the first pages of *The Man Without Qualities* as a man of possibilities and attributes to him a conscious Utopianism and a total lack of the sense of reality, the author's irony is directed at his hero. Musil himself points out the inconsistencies of his hero's viewpoint, for Ulrich can theorize about possibility but cannot necessarily live by it. He is firmly grounded in an intellectual reality and only tempted by *Möglichkeiten* (possibilities). This is the situation of the arch male in the Musilian universe.

The second half of the conjunction between precision and soul lies in the region of the feminine, as is made clear by Ulrich's attempted union with the most important female in the books hierarchy, Agathe. Well-versed in depth psychology, Musil was fully aware of the masculine and feminine components that go to make up the total being. . . . What becomes evident . . . and provides a working formula, is that in the relativistic and highly realistic world of Musil's works, if the masculine represents that reality which is continually tempted by possibility, the feminine is then that possibility which must always be tested by reality.

Musil's desire for completeness—for a synthesis between the dialectical opposites of mysticism and reason—is evident in his choice of the myth of Isis and Osiris as a symbolic substructure for his central work and as the subject of his only poem. This myth represents the integration of the self, for Isis and Osiris, female and male, are tied together in all possible ways through their incestuous relationship. Brother and sister, husband and wife, and finally mother and son, they provide the fullest mythical marriage of opposites. What is important . . . is the totality of the Isis figure who reveals the feminine in a good many of her possible manifestations and who takes the male into herself first as wife, and then more explicitly as mother, thereby attaining the peak of feminine selfhood. In his encyclopedic scope, Musil systematically investigates the various manifestations of the Isis figure and their significance.

If in the mythical substructure of Musil's work there is a union attained between male and female as such and between their respective elements within the human entity. . . , this union is never fully resistant to the daylight world of dry wit and irony where Musil would like to place it. Musil's daylight and masculine world has an intellectual anguish at its very foundation which ultimately will not allow it to accept fully any total solution, any completeness. The exact pursuit of various points of view, which is basic to Ulrich's Essayism, can never totally relinquish its aversion to forming anything which is a concept and hence complete. Nor can it ever fully give in to the feminine 'spirit' qualities, to unlimited and nameless possibilities not controllable by intellect alone—except under the light of the moon, the night-time world of dream. (pp. 82-5)

[For] Musil the essential feat of fiction [is] the possibility of integration offered by and through fiction's flexibility. In fiction the *unio mystico* can take place: that synthesis of masculine and feminine, of intellect and soul can exist. But if fiction is to encompass the entire sphere of 'real' relations to self and society, then this synthesis can only be momentary. It cannot have duration as a total solution.

For Musil the self—like any other object in the orbit of the sensible world—exists as an object, something seen from the outside looking in. Thus the inner world and the outer cannot fully unite. Much as Musil seems to desire this solution or synthesis, he cannot—perhaps because of his intellectual integrity and strictness—allow Ulrich to live it, except in certain isolated moments of mystical ecstasy. Ulrich, the male dominated by intelligence, must remain that form of reality which is eternally tempted by possibility but can never arrive at a fixed solution of any problem.

Ulrich's inability to arrive at any absolute is paralleled by the book itself, *The Man Without Qualities,* which similarly can find no real 'end' since the dialectical oppositions which it initiates between being and possibility, male and female, reason and mysticism, are not capable of synthesis in the kind of world Musil insists on describing as totally relativistic. (pp. 85-6)

> Lisa Appignanesi, ''Robert Musil: Femininity and Completeness,'' in her Femininity & the Creative Imagination: A Study of Henry James, Robert Musil & Marcel Proust (© 1973 Lisa Appignanesi; reprinted by permission of the author), Vision Press, 1973, pp. 81-156.

C. E. WILLIAMS   (essay date 1974)

[*In his chapter on Musil included in his study* The Broken Eagle: The Politics of Austrian Literature from Empire to Anschluss,

Williams examines Musil's political essays and relates them to his novel The Man without Qualities.]

The editorial of the *Soldatenzeitung* for 15 April 1917 bore the title **'Vermächtnis'** (Testament). This was to be the last number of a periodical which had circulated for over a year among the Austrian troops on the Italian Front, and the editor took the opportunity to sum up his past policy and to underline the tasks facing the nation. . . .

The writer of this leading article was Robert Musil. (p. 148)

The *Soldatenzeitung* was not the only platform from which Musil expressed his opinions on the issues of the day. As a detached but perceptive observer, he contributed essays to various journals on the state of politics under the Empire, on the implications of the War, on the meaning of peace and the challenge of the postwar world. I believe that these essays are directly related to Musil's culminating literary achievement, his monumental novel, *Der Mann ohne Eigenschaften.* The War plainly reinforced many of those insights into the state of European culture which were eventually woven into the warp of his novel.

Like the majority of his contemporaries, Musil experienced an intense elation at the outbreak of the War. Like many others, he accepted the propaganda argument that Germany had been deliberately encircled and threatened with political extinction. He saw the War in terms of an act of self-defence on the part of the Central Powers. Where Musil differs from Hofmannsthal, Bahr, Schnitzler or Zweig, is in the value he attached to this initial experience of patriotic feeling. The corruption, incompetence and cowardice which appeared to him to have subsequently dominated public life failed to influence Musil's assessment of that original mood. On the contrary, the unique experience of the first few days was heightened in retrospect by a knowledge of what followed. Musil's reaction was intensified by a sense of dissatisfaction with his work and career, which in 1914 appeared to him to be in danger of stagnation. (p. 149)

By about 1917 . . . he saw the War as an explosive liberation from a stagnant culture. This idea was developed in the essays **'Die Nation als Ideal und Wirklichkeit'** . . . and **'Das hilflose Europa oder Reise vom Hundertsten ins Tausendste'**. . . . Musil observed in the reactions of his contemporaries to the pressures of war, whether on the battlefield or in civilian life, a wide range of human behaviour which pointed to the flexibility and fluidity of the human personality. The banal assertion that a man could be a hero one day and a coward the next, was for Musil of far-reaching consequence. It confirmed that individual behaviour was determined not by an immutable ethical code possessed of an absolute validity, but by psychic idiosyncracies and environmental pressures. Musil postulated the need for a revaluation of the traditional Judaeo-Christian morality. . . . (Musil's contemporary, the novelist Hermann Broch, saw in the War the final proof of the 'decline of values', of the fragmented nature of the modern world with its ruthless single-minded devotion to totally discrete, self-contained areas of activity.) Musil's imaginative probing of the 'dark gods' in his novel *Die Verwirrungen des jungen Törless* . . . clearly anticipated this theme. The young cadet's *nostalgie de la boue* shown by his relationship with the prostitute Bozena, and his escape from the oppressive, constricting values of bourgeois society into her arms; his vision of the proximity of the world of reason, morality, progress and success—and the underground world of perversion, debauch, blood and filth; his awareness of the effortless transition from the one to the other; the whole contrast between the amoral depravity of the adolescents and the unsuspecting respectability of the adults—all this foreshadows the 'liberation' of July and August 1914. However, the insight is not fully rationalised until after the War. Musil thus proceeds from the analysis of the individual psyche to the critique of culture.

An heir to Nietzsche's criticism of contemporary values, Musil tried to show that the War was the concluding stage of a prolonged cultural decline, caused by the inability of the civilisation of the nineteenth and early twentieth centuries to keep pace with its own evolving knowledge of the natural world. Scientific advance and a scientific way of thinking had undermined the traditional ground of our being. Yet out of lethargy, or fear, we had not accepted the consequences of this development. In religion, morality, jurisprudence, psychology, politics and even in science, we clung to outmoded conceptions of the world and of human nature. We deliberately closed our eyes to the fact that our actual conduct bore little relation to our cherished values, that our habitual ways of thinking about the world bore little relation to our scientific progress. From this discrepancy between our capacity for knowledge, or the true conditions of our existence—and our reluctance to meet the cultural challenge they posed, sprang the malaise which characterised European life before 1914. Systematically our lines of thought had been invalidated: first rationalism, then idealism, then positivism; yet we persisted in outworn traditions. Consequently, beneath the surface appearance of order and progress lay confusion, doubt and insecurity. The revolt against intellectualism was a symptom of the malady. But Musil defended the intellect on the ground that it destroyed only that which was already rotten at the core, and that far from being corrosively analytic, it offered the hope of ultimate synthesis.

The cultural scene up to 1914, then, was marked by a fatal hollowness, and a loss of direction and purpose, which contemporary politics mirrored in its confusion and cynicism. From this point of view, the War seemed to represent an escape from a peace that had become intolerable. Musil wrote of a 'flight from peace' and of a 'revolution of the soul'. He noted that 'in 1914 people were literally bored to death' and again, 'the age simply perforated like an ulcer'. Despite the strong echo of Ernst Jünger's peacetime frustrations, Musil did not share Jünger's militarism. He did not believe that war of itself furnished any kind of solution. Musil was closer to the position of Karl Kraus, who maintained that in the War European culture, far from being renewed, had escaped the executioner by committing suicide. (pp. 150-52)

In an essay entitled **'Politik in Österreich'**, written in 1913, Musil had highlighted the peculiar unreality of Austrian politics before the War. . . . Musil also claimed that the Empire lacked any idealistic inspiration. Six years later, in 1919, he added that because of the uncertainty attending the decadal renewal of the Compromise with Hungary, Austria's economic and technological progress had been seriously impeded. . . . Musil felt that politics had become a convenient outlet of confusion and frustration, a means of evading the real dilemma of the age, which was moral and philosophical, not political. The passion which politics aroused was a mere camouflage for a lack of personal involvement and true concern. Politics had become a game, a method of whiling away the time, pending more important developments. Musil denied that the ideology of supranationalism formed an ethical or cultural ideal: he saw

it for what it was, a political response to the challenge of emergent nationalism.

This semi-official doctrine, particularly as we have seen it adopted by such apologists as Hofmannsthal or Joseph Roth, claimed that Austrian culture was a unique synthesis of German, Magyar, Slav and Latin cultures within the framework of the Habsburg Empire. To Musil, on the other hand, in 1919 no less than in 1913, the Empire revealed only the co-existence of diverse cultures, not a cultural symbiosis. In an area too long befogged by idealisation and nostalgia, Musil brought his lucid and sceptical gaze to bear. . . . (pp. 152-54)

A lack of purpose and direction, a paradoxical lack of true involvement, confusion and insecurity—these are the features of Musil's description of the Habsburg Monarchy in its closing years. Alienation, paradox, self-delusion, the hollowness of accepted values and ways of thought—such are the features of Musil's critique of European culture as a whole. In the initial flood of elation in 1914 Musil believed that a new, more authentic mode of life had emerged from the ruins of prewar culture. At the end of the War he again experienced an intense joy of expectation, a fervid faith in a new world. (p. 162)

Der Mann ohne Eigenschaften did not progress as far as August 1914, as was originally planned. Thus the novel does not evoke the elation and communal unity which moved Musil so intensely in the first days of the War. One wonders, however, if this experience does not impinge indirectly upon the portrayal of the mystical union enjoyed by Ulrich and Agathe. I do not wish to suggest that this mystical relationship is a direct transposition of Musil's political experience. Moreover, the personal relationship between the hero and his sister is explored more deeply, more exhaustively and above all more creatively than the political emotion. Again, the novel invokes religious and philosophical overtones in a manner barely implied by the description of national unity. Yet the nature of the two experiences is undoubtedly analogous: the escape from individuation; the intensification of one's awareness of self and the merging of the self with a greater whole; the overcoming of separation in space and succession in time; and the consummation of an emotion which the concept 'love' can only approximate. The path which Ulrich and Agathe will tread is described as one 'which in some ways was related to the world of those possessed by God . . .'. . . . For all its immanence, the quality of the experience is seen to be religious, it is 'mysticism in broad daylight'. Similarly, Musil called the wartime patriotic feeling a 'religious' or 'mystic' experience. There is a common denominator: the private and the national experience share a detachment from everyday life, the receding of ordinary cares and concerns, and a sense of well-being arising from disinterestedness.

The quasi-mystical mood of August 1914 was shortlived. It was followed by disenchantment—though for Musil its validity was never questioned as a consequence of what followed. Now the course which Ulrich's relationship with his sister was to take cannot be ascertained with certainty because the novel remained unfinished and we lack a definitive text. . . . Perpetual mystical communion (Ulrich at one point conjures up the image of a 'permanent vacation' from everyday reality) would be inconsistent with the theory of essayism, of the partial solution. . . . And Musil's notes suggest a progression from the 'utopia' of the quasi-mystical union to a utopia 'of the inductive way of thought', that is, to the abjuring of social withdrawal.

The mystical experiment is sometimes presented as Ulrich's escape from the intolerable isolation and detachment imposed upon him by his critical insight into conventional values, and by his *Möglichkeitssinn*. His faith in the eventual triumph of the mathematical mind proves cold comfort amid the miasma of modern culture. (pp. 182-84)

The largely non-literary analysis to which I have subjected *Der Mann ohne Eigenschaften* does not, I believe, violate its aesthetic integrity. . . . Musil explained, where Kafka or Trakl articulated their private nightmares—and because this attempted explanation is fundamental to the novel, the critic is justified in examining the author's treatment of the historical background, and in discussing the validity of some of his arguments in non-aesthetic terms. Musil's endeavour to 'explain' leads him on occasion into a 'prosy' seriousness, and—in the later sections of the novel—to a concern which ultimately vitiates the total achievement. There, in the dialogues between Ulrich and Agathe, the novelist abandons the traditional interests of narrative fiction and concentrates upon the process of thinking, the activity of consciousness. In doing so, he tries to discover common ground between literature and psychology: but the attempt—or the very endeavour—meets with only limited success. As Heine remarked of Jean Paul, it is more a question of cerebration than of ideas. The real achievement of the novel lies in the earlier chapters, in the comedy of manners, in the critique of European culture, in the evocation of the aura of Kakanien. (pp. 185-86)

> C. E. Williams, "Robert Musil: Vanity Fair," in his *The Broken Eagle: The Politics of Austrian Literature from Empire to Anschluss* (copyright © 1974 C. E. Williams; by permission of Barnes & Noble Books, a Division of Littlefield, Adams & Co., Inc.), Barnes & Noble, 1974, pp. 148-86.

JEFFREY MEYERS (essay date 1977)

[*In contrast to Henry Hatfield (see excerpt above), Meyers views the experience of the protagonist in* Young Törless *more as a destructive and alienating ordeal than as a constructive episode in his psychological development.*]

Young Törless. . . , by Mann's contemporary Robert Musil, is an interesting contrast to *Death in Venice* and provides a useful transition to [Marcel Proust's] *Cities of the Plain* and [T. E. Lawrence's] *Seven Pillars of Wisdom*. Wilde, Gide and Mann are all concerned with the aesthetic and idealistic aspects of homosexuality, though they frequently express them through their moral complements: decadence and guilt. But in Musil, who is more realistic in his description of inversion than practising homosexuals, there is no platonic transfiguration of the theme, no exotic culture, no ambiguity, no apologetics, no sympathy. His book is spare, harsh, brutal, arid and thoroughly negative. (p. 53)

Musil uses the sado-masochistic aspect of inversion, which fills the moral vacuum at a boys' school, to emphasize the cruelty of power. Though icily objective, *Young Törless* prepares us for the painful and perceptive self-scrutiny of Proust and T. E. Lawrence.

In *Young Törless* Musil portrays the inner life of a sensitive adolescent at a crucial moment of his psychological development and describes his brutalizing experience with homosexuality. Musil imposes severe limitation on his extremely abstract and cerebral book, and achieves concentration, intensity and power at the expense of character and plot, the traditional

concerns of the novel. For there is virtually no description of the physical setting or the life of the school, the parents and teachers are left deliberately vague, the whore is a cliché, and even the boys have an unusual taste for theoretical mathematics, philosophical speculation and metaphorical language. (pp. 53-4)

The essence of the novel, Törless' relationship with the unfortunate Basini, who is caught stealing and subjected to torture by Törless' companions, Reiting and Beineberg (whose big ears stick out like his sword), is closely related to all the major themes: political, maternal, military, religious and sexual. Both Božena and Basini, who represent the Slavic and Italian minorities who are dominated by the Austrians, are contrasted to the Germanic ethos of Törless and his friends, and compared to each other. (p. 55)

Like the army, the cloistered atmosphere of the school provides no acceptable outlet for the boy's sexual desires—'seething, passionate, naked and loaded with destruction'—and they are inevitably forced into whoring and homosexuality. Basini, who is both weak and effeminate, with 'a chaste, slender willingness, like that of a young girl', is the perfect sexual victim. His weakness stimulates the sadistic impulses that spring from repressed sexuality and from the military ethos of brutality and power. Basini, who provides the same fascination as a naked woman, becomes the personification of the flagellants and martyrs when he is tortured and bloody. His 'sacrifice' is supposed to have a 'purifying effect', but his religious passion aggravates the torturers' sexual guilt at the same time that it stimulates their sexual excitement.

The fact that Basini is guilty of a crime allows Reiting and Beineberg to justify his humiliation on moral grounds and to punish him for their own sexual offences; and his interrogation soon leads to torture and to homosexuality. The boys' hatred is unleashed on the degraded yet pliant Basini, a 'rotten swine' who has forfeited his right to exist, in a secret, concealed room behind a locked door that is approached by a narrow tunnel and smells of unopened trunks—an obvious symbol for the unconscious.

At first Törless is merely an observer who is perplexed and uncomfortable about his passive relation to the suffering Basini and puzzled by the 'queer fascination' that the boy holds for him. This fascination is clarified when Törless realizes that, like Reiting and Beineberg, he is sexually aroused by Basini's suffering. Törless makes an unsuccessful attempt to discover an answer to his perplexities through the study of mathematics and philosophy, and an unrewarding discussion with his teacher. But the real illumination comes when Basini confesses his homosexual relations with Reiting and Beineberg, and seeks the friendship of Törless, mainly for protection and partly because he desperately needs the love of a kindred spirit. . . . Musil is unusually frank about homosexuality, which is manifested in sadism and symbolizes perverted power.

Törless has cultivated an ability to 'see things in two different ways' and is 'torn between two worlds': the everyday world of respectable citizens (like his parents) and the other world of darkness, mystery and blood (his school). He is both revolted and fascinated by 'the various little vices that boys went in for', yet oscillates between agony and rapture, shame and desire, lucidity and illusion. (pp. 55-6)

When Törless learns that he is being used by Basini as a means of escape from his tormentors, his feelings turn to straightforward repugnance. . . . The conclusion of this disturbing novel is negative and rather cynical. Basini, unable to endure further torture, gives himself up, is condemned by the school and expelled. Törless, morally and aesthetically disgusted by the treatment of Basini, runs away, is brought back and tries to explain his feelings to the teachers. Musil attempts to describe all the experience of the novel in terms of Törless' feelings, but his 'new and aimless craving' and 'flood of dark stirrings' are never defined. The hopelessly baffled teachers, who re-affirm the banality of evil by passively accepting it, suggest that Törless leave the school to be educated privately. He re-turns home radically changed and alienated from his mother, but we never learn precisely how his experience has affected his character and his life. Reiting, Beineberg and the evil sym-bolized by the homosexual rites in the secret attic remain un-touched and entrenched. Though it is tempting to read retro-spective meaning into the novel, after the horrors of German militarism in the two world wars, the homosexual theme of **Young Törless** is not strong enough to bear the allegorical im-plications which, unlike those of Musil's major work, **The Man Without Qualities,** are sounded but not developed. (p. 57)

> *Jeffrey Meyers, ''Mann and Musil: 'Death in Venice' (1912) and 'Young Törless' (1906),'' in his* Homo-sexuality and Literature 1890-1930 (© *Jeffrey Mey-ers 1977), The Athlone Press, 1977, pp. 42-57.**

DAVID S. LUFT (essay date 1980)

[*In his* Robert Musil and the Crisis of European Culture, *Luft places Musil in precise relation to his historical and cultural milieu. The excerpt below provides a discussion of what Luft considers Musil's most creative literary period, the years 1918 through 1933.*]

[Musil's] maturity as a creative writer between 1918 and 1933 was important primarily for the process of conceiving and writ-ing **The Man without Qualities,** but this novel is only the most conspicuous product of his most creative period. Moreover, Musil's significance lies not only in his individual works, but also in the understanding which informs them: he emphasized ''the utopian assumptions'' of his work, that the ''individual works are always occasional!'' Just as strongly as Musil re-sisted systematic philosophy and reductionist psychology, he argued *for* a theoretical literature. (p. 158)

Musil's characteristic predicament as a writer was to find him-self in a middle zone between the ''so-called intellectual'' and the ''so-called man of feeling.'' Resisting the drives for unified formulas and positions of rest, Musil offered a more flexible model of the mutuality of thinking and feeling. (p. 159)

In his plays—**Die Schwärmer** . . . and **Vinzenz** . . .—and in his theater criticism, Musil explored the mystery of individu-ality in relation to the fixed roles of bourgeois culture. In the novellas and stories of the mid-1920s, particularly in **Drei Frauen** . . . , he overcame the problems of **Vereinigungen** and found his way to the purity of the symbolic story. In the pro-cess, Musil formulated his mature aesthetics and his phenom-enological reduction of the romantic tradition in terms of ''the other condition'' (*der andere Zustand*). He also gave new clar-ity to his understanding of the novel's function of mediation between the ideological art of his dramas and the formalism of the novellas. The war had provided the framework for his conceptions for a novel and after 1918 his sketches evolved with steady intensity, until by 1924 he was ready to write. Since Musil devoted the remainder of the decade to **The Man**

without Qualities, the range of his creativity is most apparent in the early 1920s.

The extraordinarily productive years between 1918 and 1924, which firmly established Musil's stature and reputation as a *Dichter,* represent a crucial period of maturation. As he emp-tied himself into his art, Musil seems almost to have died inwardly—working through the feelings of doubt and despair which had inhibited his writing before the war. This struggle to become humanly mature culminated in 1924 with the deaths of his parents, the loss of economic security in the inflation, and the task of writing his novel. (pp. 159-60)

The goal of Musil's art was the ethical person, the motivated human being who creates meanings out of himself. In writing **Die Schwärmer** Musil developed a model of this type which he considered schematically valid for all his work. The creative person is characterized by his intense awareness of isolation and of the mystery of individuality. Musil described this person as ''undefined, beyond truth and right, and metaphysically restless''; he is experienced by others as ''asocial,'' as an ''unfeeling dreamer'' who is ''exclusive, passive in relation to what exists as well as the improvements, contemptuous of reality, and opposed to both ideals and illusions.'' This type of the other person was the guiding paradigm for the protag-onists of Musil's plays—Thomas and Vinzenz—and the point of departure for the sequence of heroes for his novel—Achilles, Anders, and Ulrich. While the outlines of the type remain throughout the 1920s, there is a clear evolution from the se-riousness of Thomas and the rebelliousness of Achilles to the ironic hero who emerges in Vinzenz and Ulrich. Musil defined this creative type in opposition to the normal or uncreative person, who was ''defined, true, righteous, sympathetic, so-cial, metaphysically secure, inclusive, active, real, and com-mitted to Sunday-ideals, illusions, realities.'' The enemy of the creative person was all the authorized conditions of the soul which had become rigidified in the conventions of bour-geois culture under the guidance of the mandarinate and the norms of bourgeois morality. (pp. 160-61)

Musil's vision of the poet and the realities of bourgeois culture in the 1920s intersected in his relationship to the theater, both as a dramatist and as a critic of the Vienna stage. Whatever the occasional achievements of specific poets, directors, or actors, Musil concluded that the theater had become the most rigidified of bourgeois cultural institutions, victimized both by the routine of cultural convention and by the demands of the marketplace. Film had access to undreamed-of-technical free-dom and the chance to create a new audience; the novel was relatively formless and less dominated by the problems of sell-ing tickets; theater seemed to have the worst of both worlds. . . .

Musil disliked any art which depended on standard metaphors, images, and emotional scenarios, instead of building life fur-ther. He saw the theater of his day as an arena of manipulation which worked for effects and drew on the emotional habituation of the audience rather than the creative power of the poet. . . . Musil believed that the poet's task was to see new things, to notice the way human beings actually experience their lives. . . . (p. 169)

Musil believed that the problems of the theater were sympto-matic of the crisis of bourgeois culture as a whole—a crisis of the values and institutions of the eighteenth century. . . . In the eighteenth century the theater had been part of a vital social experience, helping to focus the transforming cultural energies of the ideology of *Bildung*. But *Bildung* had ''lost its social nimbus,'' not simply because of the emancipation of the working class, but because of the spiritual ossification of the educated classes and their mandarin elite. This situation of cultural decline in the midst of social heterogeneity gave the theater its quality of sheer spectacle. Musil believed that in an age without valid rules for the feelings or authentic bases for action, people were all too likely to seek release in the spectacle of great gestures. His preference for inaction over pseudo-action, for authentic feelings over manufactured ones, made him seem like an unfeeling man of reason and a bad dramatist. He wanted to lead his culture back to the preconditions of drama, but he wondered how to ''lead a people whose ideal is the strong man without many words, the reserve lieutenant''; this heroic type of the leader was hailed by critics ''in whom the spirit now clamors like the noise in class when the teacher unexpectedly has to go out.'' Given the disintegration of the motivating power of culture, the poet was left to create a drama which reflected the new spiritual situation. . . . (p. 170)

This vision informed Musil's attempt in *Die Schwärmer (The Visionaries)* to turn modern theater away from tragic drama to investigate the bases of motivation. As the major connecting link between his early and late art, *Die Schwärmer* expressed Musil's conviction that ''life ought to be motivated in the extreme, and thus also the drama.'' In dramatizing the tension between the creative person and the inauthenticity of normal reality, Musil focused primarily on the basic form and value in bourgeois culture—marriage—and secondarily on the other main form of the encapsulation of the ethical-aesthetic self—the profession. The plot involves nothing more than an exchange of lovers, but the real substance is the explication of the creative person and the problems of leading a motivated life. The figures gather at the home of Thomas and Maria to discover the truth about the adventures of Anselm and Regine. As in **''Das verzauberte Haus''** and again in *Vinzenz* and *The Man without Qualities,* the house is the central spiritual symbol. Here it stands for the world of the creative person, for the will to be different, for the antagonism toward the normal, uncreative person and the world of ordinary reality. (pp. 170-71)

[Musil's] brief involvement with the theater as a critic and playwright was enough to remind him that in his generation the main vehicle of the spirit was not the theater but the novel. The novel left more freedom for the spirit, both formally and substantively. The preoccupation of theater with heroic action and feeling left too little room for the truths of impersonality which were made more apparent by the structure of modern life, however much sentimental theater liked to evade them. . . . (p. 177)

Musil found his greatest artistic fulfillment in the forms of the novella and the novel, but his experience with theater marked the initial phase in his development of the ironic voice and the satirical emplotment. He discovered that the old tragedies were dying out, and with *Vinzenz* he began to move away from anger and pathos. . . . Musil had begun to find his way to the satiric magic and ironic objectivity that made it possible for him to write a great social novel; he had also found his way to the absolute beginning of his own personal life, to the novella, and to the crystallization of his aesthetic vision. (pp. 177-78)

The Man without Qualities explores what Musil took to be the typical ideological difficulties of his generation. The explicit setting is Vienna 1913, and Musil's brilliant portrayal of Austrian elites suggests that his central theme is ''the cultural and moral decline of the ruling classes before the First World War.'' For Musil, however, the old Austria was simply ''an especially clear case of the modern world,'' a model for the larger theme of the transition from traditional-bourgeois society to modern, pluralistic, mass culture. Moreover, he was concerned not so much with politics as with the spiritually typical, not so much with the decline of Austria as with the birth of a spirituality commensurate with modern science. Kakania is a paradigm of European culture in Musil's generation, and the implied setting for this adventure of the mind is the flow of European culture in the first third of the twentieth century. Musil explores the manifold relations within this culture between knowledge and love, male and female, evil and good, power and intimacy, intellect and feeling. The mode of portrayal is impersonal, objective, ironic—allowing the contradictions to speak for themselves and showing the interdependence of the characters within the structure of a culture in crisis. The assumption of Musil's portrayal is that only by driving the dissolution of dead ideology to its limit, to the pure whiteness of leveled-out, devalued reality, can the constructive possibilities of a new culture be liberated.

Ulrich, the man without qualities, lives in the historical reality of pre-war Austria but he is also the extreme case of modern consciousness, intensely aware of the fluidity of the world and of his own identity. His disinterested objectivity makes him an ideal ironic hero, free to bring his scientific audacity to bear on the forms of culture. His inability to take his own qualities personally allows his intellect to play with his feelings and to suspend the conventions of social reality. At the same time, Ulrich functions as a ''kind of statistical midpoint'' for a huge cast of characters who display the nuances of ideological variation and analogy. (pp. 214-15)

This novel, however, is not a systematic presentation of a complete model of the world. Its meaning lies not in a final yield of truth or narrative resolution, but in the transforming process of reading itself. This exegesis of the text of a failed culture eschews firm order, and its open ideology offers at most a way of proceeding under particular historical circumstances. Musil does illuminate patterns and relations within the flow of culture, but to see this novel as a fixed totality—whether as a story or philosophy—would make it simply another abstract version of the stabilized hopelessness that it seeks to overcome. Musil offers a complex texture of analogies, shattered moments, and reawakened meanings, always fluidly moving the process forward. His essayistic mode seeks to stay in touch with both intellect and feeling, while giving partial solutions to lived experience. *The Man without Qualities* captures the spiritual predicament of a generation, but it gives its meanings with a richness and indirection which underscore the incommensurability of *Dichtung* and criticism. (pp. 216-17)

David S. Luft, in his Robert Musil and the Crisis of European Culture: 1880-1942 *(copyright © 1980 by The Regents of the University of California; reprinted by permission of the University of California Press), University of California Press, 1980, 323 p.*

ADDITIONAL BIBLIOGRAPHY

Bedwell, Carol B. ''Musil's 'Grigia': An Analysis of Cultural Dissolution.'' *Seminar* 3, No. 2 (Fall 1967): 117-26.
    Innovative interpretation of Musil's novella Grigia ''as an analysis of the factors leading to cultural dissolution.'' Bedwell discusses the psychological interpretations of the novella provided by Burton Pike, Ernst Kaiser, and Eithne Wilkins (see excerpts above), and

by Lida Kirchberger (see Additional Bibliography below), but finds a more profitable analysis of the story from the point of view of sociology rather than psychology.

Boa, Elizabeth J. "Austrian Ironies in Musil's *Drei Frauen*." *Modern Language Review* 63 (1968): 119-31.
Interpretation of the three novellas in *Three Women* as a "radical critique of the most Austrian of preoccupations": the search beyond appearances "to an absolute value which will guarantee the reality of experience." Boa disagrees with Lida Kirchberger's Freudian interpretation of *Three Women* (see Additional Bibliography below).

Braun, W. "Musil's 'Erdensekretariat der Genauigkeit und Seele': A Clue to the Philosophy of the Hero of *Der Mann ohne Eigenschaften*." *Monatshefte* XLVI, No. 6 (November 1954): 305-16.
Analysis of the philosophy of Ulrich, the protagonist of *The Man without Qualitites*, as "an alternative to grappling with the whole novel." Braun finds Ulrich to be a scientific personality who thinks inductively on every subject. Quoted material from the novel which is central to Braun's discussion is not translated into English in this essay.

Braun, W. "The Temptation of Ulrich: The Problem of True and False Unity in Musil's *Der Mann ohne Eigenschaften*." *German Quarterly* XXIX, No. 1 (January 1956): 29-37.
Finds the main theme of the first volume of *The Man without Qualities* to be Ulrich's rejection of the false unity offered by Arnheim, the novel's antagonist.

Cohn, Dorrit. "Psyche and Space in Musil's 'Die Vollendung der Liebe'." *The Germanic Review* XLIX, No. 2 (March 1974): 154-68.
Stresses the novella's focus on the heroine's consciousness. This review is somewhat inaccessable to English-language readers because quotes central to the discussion are given in German.

Goldgar, Harry. "The Square Root of Minus One: Freud and Robert Musil's *Törless*." *Comparative Literature* XVII, No. 2 (Spring 1965): 117-32.
Attributes to *Young Törless* the likely distinction of being "the earliest novel of any sort in any language to show specific Freudian influence." Quotes from the novel are not translated in this essay. Frederick G. Peters (see Additional Bibliography below) concludes that "Goldgar's analysis of *Young Törless* from the perspective of Musil's knowledge of Freud's work is unconvincing."

Heald, David. "'All the World's a Stage'—A Central Motif in Musil's *Mann ohne Eigenschaften*." *German Life and Letters* n.s. 27, No. 1 (October 1973): 51-9.
Discussion of the sense of self-conscious awareness displayed by Ulrich and other characters from Musil's novel *The Man without Qualities*.

Holmes, F. A. "Some Comic Elements in Musil's *Der Mann ohne Eigenschaften*." *German Life and Letters* n.s. 18, No. 1 (October 1964): 25-9.
Brief discussion of some comic elements in *The Man without Qualities*, which several critics, such as V. S. Pritchett, have mentioned. All of the examples which Holmes quotes are given in the original German with no English translation provided.

Johnstone, Walter E. "The Shepherdess in the City." *Comparative Literature* 26, No. 2 (Spring 1974): 124-41.*
Comparative analysis of the characters of Lena, from William Faulkner's *Light in August*, and Tonka, from Musil's novella *Tonka*.

Kirchberger, Lida. "Musil's Trilogy: An Approach to *Drei Frauen*." *Monatshefte* LV, No. 4 (April-May 1963): 167-82.
Freudian interpretation of the three novellas contained in *Three Women: Tonka, Grigia* and *The Portugese Lady*. This essay is referred to by Carol B. Bedwell (see Additional Bibliography above) and by Elizabeth J. Boa (see Additional Bibliography above), who dismisses it as an "arbitrary interpretation" of "Freud's interpretation of the casket motif in *The Merchant of Venice*."

Kirchberger compares these three novellas by Musil to Flaubert's *Trois Contes*.

Mayer, Hans. "Robert Musil: A Remembrance of Things Past." In his *Steppenwolf and Everyman*, translated by Jack D. Zipes, pp. 14-34. New York: Thomas Y. Crowell Co., 1971.
Reminiscence of Musil that includes some critical discussion of *The Man without Qualities*.

Paulson, Ronald M. "A Re-examination and Re-interpretation of Some of the Symbols in Robert Musil's *Die Portugiesin*." *Modern Austrian Literature* 13, No. 2 (1980): 111-21.
Warns against a religious interpretation of Musil's novella *The Portuguese Lady* despite the "prominence of religious symbolism" in the work.

Peters, Frederick G. *Robert Musil, Master of the Hovering Life: A Study of the Major Fiction*. New York: Columbia University Press, 1978, 286 p.
Lengthy study of Musil's major fictional works.

Pritchett, V. S. "Books in General." *The New Statesman and Nation* XLVII, No. 1204 (3 April 1954): 442-3.
Review of the second English-translated volume of *The Man without Qualities*. Pritchett echoes his earlier comparison of the character of Ulrich with that of Italo Svevo's Zeno (see excerpt above), notes the comic elements of the novel, and disavows the possibility of Marcel Proust or André Gide being an influence upon Musil.

Rose, Marilyn Gaddis. "Musil's Use of Simile in *Törless*." *Studies in Short Fiction* VIII, No. 2 (Spring 1971): 295-300.
Examines Musil's use of simile in his first novel to relate the protagonist's feelings to a larger social context.

Rougemont, Denis de. "New Metamorphoses of Tristan." In his *Love Declared: Essays on the Myths of Love*, translated by Richard Howard, pp. 39-76. New York: Pantheon Books, 1963.*
Comparison of the theme of passion in three modern novels: Vladimir Nabokov's *Lolita*, Boris Pasternak's *Doctor Zhivago*, and Musil's *The Man without Qualities*.

Sjögren, Christine Oertel. "An Inquiry into the Psychological Condition of the Narrator in Musil's *Tonka*." *Monatshefte* LXIV, No. 2 (1972): 153-61.
Approaches an analysis of *Tonka* with the assumption that the unnamed narrator suffers from a psychological aberration, making an objective interpretation of the novella impossible.

Strelka, Joseph. "The Afterglow of Imperial Austria: Robert Musil." *Germanic Review* LIV, No. 2 (Spring 1979): 49-53.
Places Musil within his historical context, at the close of the Austrian Hapsburg monarchy. Strelka discusses Musil's two novels, *Young Törless* and *The Man without Qualities*.

Titche, Leon J., Jr. "The Concept of the Hermaphrodite: Agathe and Ulrich in Musil's *Der Mann ohne Eigenschaften*." *German Life and Letters* n.s. 23, No. 1 (October 1969): 160-68.
Interprets Musil's novel *The Man without Qualities* from the basis of the hermaphroditic myth presented through the relationship of Ulrich and Agathe. Titche finds insight into Musil's use of this theme in the poem *Isis und Osiris* (see excerpt above).

Von Nardroff, Ellen. "Robert Musil's Concept of the Poet and Writer." *Modern Austrian Literature* 4, No. 1 (Spring 1971): 23-30.
Examination of the role and nature of the poet as interpreted from Musil's essays, articles, diaries, and notes. The critic finds that Musil believed "the poet should be a model of personal as well as intellectual responsibility"; and finds also that Musil's two best-known protagonists, Törless and Ulrich, though not poets, "illustrate nevertheless Musil's concept of what the ideal poet should be."

White, John J. "Mathematical Imagery in Musil's *Young Törless* and Zamyatin's *We*." *Comparative Literature* XVIII, No. 1 (Winter 1966): 71-8.*
Examines the use of the Kantian concept of mathematical infinity as an image in the two novels mentioned.

Frederick (William Serafino Austin Lewis Mary) Rolfe

1860-1913

(Also wrote under pseudonyms Baron Corvo, Frederick Baron Corvo, and Fr. Rolfe, among others) English novelist, short story writer, poet, historian, and essayist.

Rolfe was a novelist whose works more than usually reflect elements of his bizarre life and eccentric personality, and they are most often appreciated for their integration of autobiographical fact and highly imaginative fantasy. The novels *Hadrian the Seventh, The Desire and Pursuit of the Whole*, and *Nicholas Crabbe* have been called the confessional apologias of a paranoid personality. In these and other works, Rolfe displayed a gift for depicting inflated conceptions of himself as well as for heaping eloquent abuse on those whom he judged enemies. This libelous quality, along with obviously homosexual overtones, caused publishers to reject many of his works, and several remained unpublished until after his death. An additional obstacle to acceptance of Rolfe's works was the extraordinary and elaborate prose style in which he wrote them. Invective, odd bits of knowledge, vivid descriptions, and unusual spelling and punctuation are the stylistic trademarks of "Baron Corvo."

Born in London, Rolfe was the oldest of a piano manufacturer's six children. Drawn to the Church at an early age by a religious faith that approached fanaticism, the zealous youth tattooed a cross on his chest when he was fourteen years old. Although he was raised in a dissenting Protestant household, Rolfe converted to Catholicism when he was twenty-six because he believed that he could best serve Christ as a priest. However, complaints from fellow students about his debts and unconventionality led to Rolfe's dismissal from the Scots College in Rome, where he had been accepted as a probationary candidate for the priesthood. Rolfe's rejection is seen by many critics as the turning point in his life, evinced throughout his works by his relentlessly bitter treatment of clerics and by the fictional vindication of himself in the novel *Hadrian the Seventh*. After his dismissal, Rolfe pledged a twenty-year oath of celibacy to prove himself worthy of his chosen vocation.

Except for brief periods at Oxford, Oscott, and Scots College, Rolfe's formal education ended at age fifteen: he subsequently worked as a boys' school instructor, private tutor, photographer, furniture designer, gondolier, and painter. Although he had earlier written some poetry, Rolfe did not begin pursuing a literary career until the early 1890s, when he produced the short stories that appeared in the *Yellow Book*. At that time the *Yellow Book* was still enjoying notoriety as a publication devoted to Decadent art and literature, and Rolfe's contributions to the magazine, later collected as *Stories Toto Told Me*, brought him a modest amount of attention. However, he never earned the financial rewards or critical notice he thought he deserved, and was often plagued by financial difficulties, depending on friends and acquaintances for subsistence. While his charm endeared him to influential families and collaborators, he demanded unquestioning financial and emotional support from all; anything less was interpreted by Rolfe as betrayal, warranting reprisals in the form of public and private attacks. Rolfe's biographers often comment on his self-destructive urge to turn benefactors into enemies. During

a life of continuous personal difficulties, Rolfe found an emotional haven in the city of Venice, where he could live among remnants of the Renaissance world he admired. He preferred to suffer poverty in Venice rather than return to England, and this city plays an important part in his later works. During much of this period Rolfe was unable to publish his works or receive money from former friends. He died destitute, bitterly blaming his "enemies" to the end for his demise. Letters, manuscripts, and photographs discovered after his death support the assessments of Rolfe as a man who was both pious and demonic. Revealing his activities as a pederast and panderer, these disclosures color the criticism of his works.

Rolfe's first important book, *In His Own Image,* incorporated the stories collected in *Stories Toto Told Me* with several more featuring the same central character, Toto. Based on Christian and pagan legends, these stories are told from the point of view of a naive Italian youth, said to be an idealized composite based upon boys Rolfe met in Rome. In these early stories Rolfe's stylistic and thematic penchants are already in evidence: verbosity and word coinage, harshly critical evaluation of the Catholic Church, idealization of youthful beauty, and mythical fantasy distinguish the collection. Initial interest in the stories arose from a controversy over their purported irreverence. While many critics believed the stories were intentionally critical of ritual and superstition in the Roman Catholic Church, others felt they showed an understanding of the unique Italian approach to Catholicism.

While almost all of Rolfe's fiction contains autobiographical elements, the novels *Hadrian the Seventh, Nicholas Crabbe,* and *The Desire and Pursuit of the Whole* directly parallel the author's life. George Arthur Rose, the protagonist of *Hadrian,* and Nicholas Crabbe, protagonist of the other two novels, share with Rolfe his physical appearance, his sense of superiority, and his vengefulness. Written in elaborate, often affected language, these novels exhibit Rolfe's love of archaic diction and spelling and frequent use of Greek and Latin phrases, stylistic traits that some critics find distracting. The novels mix fantasy with details from the author's life. *Hadrian,* considered Rolfe's masterpiece, has been called by Shane Leslie "the oddest and perhaps vividest Apologia or Autobiography of present times." Commonly viewed by critics as a wish-fulfillment dream, this novel follows the fictional career of George Arthur Rose, who is elevated from failed seminarian to the papacy, and reflects Rolfe's twenty-year period of suffering after his rejection from the priesthood. In an uncommon interpretation, G. P. Jones minimizes the importance of the wish-fulfillment aspect of the novel to examine its dream and waking imagery, which he believes are used to create a self-conscious and highly complex work of art, rather than a self-indulgent exercise in egotism. *Nicholas Crabbe,* also based on Rolfe's life, is intended as a sympathetic portrait of a friendless, misunderstood man. The name "Crabbe" emphasizes the central, repetitive symbol of the story: the protagonist's defensive gestures toward those who approach him, his reckless refusal to loosen his grasp on an offender, and the hard shell that protects the vulnerable inner man. In *The Desire and Pursuit,* Crabbe finds love and happiness with the androgynous, servile orphan Zildo-Zilda. A.J.A. Symons calls the love affair "charming" and believes the imaginative aspects of the story to be those of a "romantic dream-tale." But W. H. Auden finds it a "terrifying," abnormal daydream interwoven with nightmare. Along with Cecil Woolf, Auden believes that Rolfe's honesty unintentionally makes Crabbe an unsympathetic character who imagines "all of his complaints against his victimizers." While these two novels inspire the same kind of critical controversy as Rolfe's other works, most critics also agree that they contain one of his greatest achievements as a literary artist: his fresh and vivid rendering of Venice.

In addition to these highly autobiographical novels, Rolfe also wrote fictionalized history. Although these historical novels are stylistically similar to the autobiographical works, some critics feel they are superior, owing to a higher degree of detachment. As in most of Rolfe's works, style dominates, while characterization is one-dimensional, except for the one character who represents Rolfe himself. *Hubert's Arthur, Don Renato,* and *Don Tarquinio* are typical: the central character, a youth of about fifteen, is flawless in every aspect; an older admirer, usually the narrator, is presented with contradictions and eccentricities that make him more "real" than the absolute good or evil personalities the protagonist meets during his perilous quest for glory. An exception, *Chronicles of the House of Borgia,* is a history which presents an admiring portrait of the Borgias, placing the blame for their infamous reputation on malignant enemies.

After Rolfe's death, interest in his life and work was almost nonexistent until the appearance in 1934 of A.J.A. Symons's "experimental" biography, *The Quest for Corvo.* The manuscripts, letters, and personal information uncovered by Sy-

mons showed Rolfe to be a religious, passionate man of extremes. When he had money, he spent it freely; when he was without it, he lived in squalor. Although he never lost his desire to become a priest, he freely indulged his erotic inclinations during his years in Venice. Graham Greene saw the dichotomy in what he termed a "sincere, if sinister, devotion to the Church," and felt that Rolfe's physical appearance, violent passions, and ingratitudes "have about them the air of demonic possession. . . . But the devil too is spiritual, and when Rolfe wrote of the spirit . . . he wrote like an angel." While Rolfe's works appeal to a limited readership of highly specialized taste, his volatile personality and its expression in his writing provide one of the most engrossing character portraits in modern literature.

(See also *Contemporary Authors,* Vol. 107.)

PRINCIPAL WORKS

Tarcissus: The Boy Martyr of Rome in the Diocletian Persecution (poetry) 1880
Stories Toto Told Me [as Frederick Baron Corvo] (short stories) 1898
Chronicles of the House of Borgia [as Frederick Baron Corvo] (history) 1901; also published as *A History of the Borgias,* 1931
In His Own Image [as Frederick Baron Corvo] (short stories) 1901
Hadrian the Seventh [as Frederick Baron Corvo] (novel) 1904
Don Tarquinio: A Kataleptic Phantasmatic Romance [as Fr. Rolfe] (novel) 1905
The Weird of the Wanderer [with Charles Pirie-Gordon] (novel) 1912
*The Desire and Pursuit of the Whole: A Romance of Modern Venice (novel) 1934
**Hubert's Arthur [with Charles Pirie-Gordon] (novel) 1935
The Cardinal Prefect of Propaganda, and Other Stories (short stories) 1957
***Nicholas Crabbe; or, The One and the Many [as Fr. Rolfe] (novel) 1958
Letters to C.H.C. Pirie-Gordon (letters) 1959
Letters to Leonard Moore (letters) 1960
Letters of Baron Corvo to Kenneth Grahame (letters) 1962
Letters to R. M. Dawkins (letters) 1962
****Don Renato (novel) 1963
Without Prejudice: One Hundred Letters from Frederick Rolfe, Baron Corvo, to John Lane (letters) 1963
The Venice Letters (letters) 1966
The Armed Hand, and Other Stories (short stories, sketches, essays, and criticism) 1974

*This work was written in 1909.

**This work was written in 1908.

***This work was written in 1904.

****This work was written in 1908.

THE BOOKMAN, London   (essay date 1901)

[*In His Own Image*] is a book made only for devout and intimate lovers of Italy. To all others it must seem a farrago of impossible inventions. To the real Northerner it must also sound blasphemous. It is not blasphemous; the writer is a religious man, after the good fashion of the South, where angels and saints, and even the Higher Powers, are of such unquestioned reality that to speak of them familiarly is the only natural thing to do. On the other count, we admit the tales, or rather their setting, to be full of exaggeration. The magnificent Frederico and his boys are not human at all. He is a god, and they are beautiful fauns and wood and water spirits, the embodiments of grace, the reminders of Nature before the Fall. Their life seems a long idyll. As a painter near Rome, with a band of boyish attendants, you can hardly realise him. And Toto—and the whole book is Toto—is no mortal lad. He is Apollo. He is Genius given shape. Not even in the most favoured land of all the earth at this hour can you quite soberly believe in Toto. But it is an exaggeration of a reality. The grace, the charm, the wonderful power of speech, of flashing images in a word—powers almost entirely absent from present-day literature in Italy—are still the possession of her uncultured people. How Toto has been preserved from the cynicism of the day—for he makes fun of the good Sampietro as a son of the Church may, if only he be devout enough at heart—is not explained. Perhaps because he is a poet, one of those great ones, who think that poetry is for every-day living, and not to shut up inside little printed books. But there he is, a fascinating, impossible, fantastic, and most amusing person, with the manners of a great lord, the wisdom of Pan, and the sensitiveness of a delicate woman—the flower of an old civilisation that long ruled the world by its genius. As for his stories of *frati* and saints, and people wise and foolish, they are delicious. This unconventional, attentive, and vivacious reporter has done them justice, and made alive to us, while we are under his spell, some part of the very soul of Italy. (pp. 93-4)

> *A review of "In His Own Image," in* The Bookman, *London, Vol. XX, No. 117, June, 1901, pp. 93-4.*

THE TIMES LITERARY SUPPLEMENT   (essay date 1904)

[*Hadrian the Seventh: A Romance*] is a strange, and in some ways a striking, book—fantastic, and in that sense only a romance; for there is no concession to love in the story of George Arthur Rose, an Englishman, who, by a curious set of circumstances, is elected Pope, and after a short reign full of surprises for the world, is shot by an assassin. The writer declares himself in a note "to be an obedient son of the Holy Catholic Apostolic Roman See"; but he would seem to hold revolutionary views as to the Papal system—its wealth, its temporalities, its isolation, and its methods. It is the work rather of an incisive, keenly observant pamphleteer than of a novelist, save for the fertile and minute realism of its style.

> *A review of "Hadrian the Seventh: A Romance," in* The Times Literary Supplement (© Times Newspapers Ltd. (London) 1904), No. 132, July 22, 1904, p. 231.

SHANE LESLIE   (essay date 1925)

[*An article by Leslie in the* London Mercury *sparked new interest in Rolfe and his works. The excerpt below is taken from Leslie's introduction to Rolfe's* In His Own Image, *later retitled* A History of the Borgias, *and analyzes the writer's style and themes. De-*

scribing Hadrian the Seventh *as Rolfe's masterpiece, Leslie calls that novel "the oddest and perhaps vividest Apologia or Autobiography of present times."*]

As a writer Rolfe first swam into notoriety by the stories, which originally appeared in the famous *Yellow Book*. These were reprinted in book form as Number Six in the Bodley Booklets; and by James Douglas were described as "the most amazing, fantastical, whimsical, bizarre, erratic, and hare-brained of books." To these six Rolfe added twenty-six similar tales, and let them be published under the title of **"In His Own Image."** . . . (p. xiii)

The stories in **"In His Own Image"** were variously received. To the oldfashioned orthodox they appeared pungently irreverent, but certain converts to Catholicism distributed them under the title of "the fifth Gospel" as the complete reaction from British Pharisaism and Hypocrisy. . . . The *Twentieth Century Review* saw "a beautiful fancy that seduces one into thinking it quite the most delightful thing, which, of course, it isn't, but is very nearly, really." Catholic readers were publicly outraged or delighted surreptitiously. The *Tablet* thought him "unfortunately very amusing." *Church Bells* hoped that "the author's object may be to throw some light upon the superstitious doctrines of modern Rome!"

These tales are unique, and though very uneven, they are very original. They represent a natural comminglement of the Pagan and the Christian tradition in the form of modern Italian folklore expressed through the medium of a rather fantastic youth. But at times it is difficult to say whether it is Toto or Corvo who is speaking. The naïveté is always Toto's, but the subtlety is sometimes Rolfe's.

"The Epick of San Georgio" is a Christianisation of the legend of Perseus. Others are based on such incidents as the rebuff given by an English duchess to King Bomba (**"About the Holy Duchess and the Wicked King"**), or the blessing by Pius IX of an Anglican Bishop (**"About Papa Feretti and the Blest Heresiarch"**). Others are popular fantasies making furious fun of the Capucins and Jesuits. Most of them are rollicking but exquisite pictures of "the gods" or saints and their emotions in Paradise. . . . The style is only blurred in places by Rolfe's incurable love for fancy coinages and his individualistic spelling. A sentence like "His lampromeirakiodia obeyed each rythmic call" only leaves the reader with an irritated impulse towards the Greek Lexicon. (pp. xiii-xv)

On a point of mediaeval spelling or of wilful indentation he would challenge a legion of printers' devils. Artifex rather than artist, he was not a Lord of Language, but a would-be tyrant of words, and words seemed to turn and tyrannise over him. His classical verbalisms amused scholars, but none dared to ask what he meant by "tygendis" or "technikrym." Ouche, birth-flare, lickerishly, liripipe, flyfot, noluntary, solert or talpine, are good English, though rare. But tolutiloquent, contortuplication, fumificables (for tobacco), zaimph, aseity, purrothrixine, banaysically, remain to trouble commentators. The only meaning attachable to "rose-alexanrolith" might occur to a Chinese mind as a portmanteau-word for the London pavements on Alexandra Day. He was very fond of the word *precipitevolissimevolmente*, which would have made his literary epitaph. (pp. xv-xvi)

In preserving the correctness of Greek spelling Rolfe outdid the Historian Grote.

This artificial facility found vent in his renderings of the Rubaiyat. "Saprous bones," "somatick atoms" and "aimaterose heart'' seem legitimate classicisms; but ''methystine lake'' requires some explanation as a term for drunkenness. Rolfe brought out the humour and sarcasm which Fitzgerald missed as well as all the coloured epithets such as ''tulip-tinctured, xanthine, rubine'' necessary to illuminate what he called ''diaphotick verse.'' Rolfe provided an interesting if roundabout way of reaching both the poesy and philosophy of Umar, but as in the case of Fitzgerald the reader unread in Persian can only guess which poet he is reading. (p. xvi)

It remains difficult to place Rolfe in literature. He possessed a morbid sense of the picturesque and garish which totally and drug-like undermined his historical sense. When he wrote *A History of the Borgias* he could rejoice in such sentences as the following rocket of racy realism: ''So the Senior Branch in the line of the direct descendants of the murdered Duke of Gandia, bastard of the Lord Alexander P. P. VI, withered in sumptuous obscurity!'' Savonarola, whom he hated as a Puritan and a Salvationist, he summed up as a ''director turned dictator,'' the subtlety of which epigram he urged in hectic and violent correspondence. (pp. xvii-xviii)

A History of the Borgias is a vivid attempt to rehabilitate Pope Alexander the Sixth from the secular infamy which ''unproved suspicion, kopriematous imagination and ordurous journalists'' had combined to heap upon his tiara. (p. xviii)

The book is not sustained, and it is difficult to read continuously, for it is a collection of striking monographs loosely fastened together on such subjects as the Ceremonial of Papal Conclaves, Calumny as a fine art, the theory of Cardinal-Nephews or Nepotism, Art under the Borgias, the Science of Poisoning or Venom, Cardinalitial Privileges, the full meaning of Excommunication. . . .

Sometimes he shows the touch of Tacitus, which is the same in a modern or classical historian, whether it is a statement of mockery or of truth, or of both. Caesar Borgia, we learn, ''hanged all those who betrayed to him, loving the treachery, hating the traitors.'' Lucretia Borgia ''had observed that the lack of money is the root of all evil, and at that root she struck!'' . . .

Sometimes he uses the antithesis of epigram. Of the Borgian and Victorian centuries: ''Now we pretend to be immaculate, then they bragged of being vile.'' In the history of poisons: ''The Dark Ages were the ages of Simples. The Age of the Renaissance was the age of Compounds.'' (p. xix)

It is Rolfe's obsession and research for weird detail rather than his character-drawing that makes *A History of the Borgias* interesting. Whence did he ferret out his list of practical jokes permissible on ladies in the Borgian era? Could he have invented the recipe for getting rid of unwelcome guests of strewing harp-strings cut small on hot meat so as to writhe like worms?

Hadrian VII with the possible exception of the Book on the Borgias is Rolfe's masterpiece, with all its uneven mixture of news-cuttings, canon law, ecclesiastical scenes, archaic diction and Rolvian propaganda. It might be summed up as ''If I were Pope,'' to take a place beside Richard le Gallienne's ''If I were God.'' There can be little doubt that Rolfe is describing some of his life, and all his likes and dislikes. The sense of a foiled vocation to the priesthood always lay at the back of his own defeated life. His hero is himself, George Arthur Rose, who broods for years over his rejection from Maryvale (Oscott) and St. Andrew's College (Scots College, Rome), wondering ''why,

O God, have you made me strange, uncommon, such a mystery to my fellow creatures?'' (pp. xx-xxi)

Hadrian VII saves the necessity of writing Rolfe's life. He was undoubtedly his self-confessor with ''reddish-brown hair turning to grey'' and ''tattooed on the breast with a cross,'' who wore his grandfather's silver spectacles to write ''his wonderful fifteenth-century script.'' . . . He believed all the while that the ''salient trait of his character, the desire not to be ungracious, the readiness to be unselfish and self-sacrificing, had done him incalculable injury.'' *Hadrian VII* is the oddest and perhaps vividest Apologia or Autobiography of present times. (pp. xxi-xxii)

> *Shane Leslie, in an introduction to* In His Own Image *by Frederick Baron Corvo, Alfred A. Knopf, Inc., 1925 (and reprinted in* A History of the Borgias *by Frederick Baron Corvo, Carlton House, 19??, pp. v-xxiii).*

JOSEPH WOOD KRUTCH (essay date 1925)

[*Krutch is widely regarded as one of America's most respected literary and drama critics. A conservative and idealistic thinker, he was a consistent proponent of human dignity and the preeminence of literary art. His literary criticism is characterized by such concerns: in* The Modern Temper *(1929) he argues that because scientific thought has denied human worth, tragedy had become obsolete, and in* The Measure of Man *(1954) he attacked modern culture for depriving humanity of the sense of individual responsibility necessary for making important decisions in an increasingly complex age. In the excerpt below, Krutch attributes to Rolfe the outward affectations of the eccentric intellectual, with none of the talent or literary genius of those he emulated.*]

The least interesting thing generally about the minor writers of the Eighteen Nineties is their works. They wrote like men of small though occasionally respectable talents, but they acted like transcendent geniuses, for they adopted all the eccentricities which the possession of genius can excuse, claimed all the privileges of the superman, and shrank to moderate size only when they seated themselves at their desks to write. . . .

''Baron Corvo,'' more original than any of his works, was no exception to the rule. He was born Frederick Rolfe, and he began his career as a school teacher; but he quickly degenerated into an eccentric sponge who lived sometimes by his wits but usually upon the means of others, and who reviled his benefactors in the sacred name of Art for not giving him more and for not putting up more gladly with his insolent pretensions. . . . [His] desire to be an artist was greater than his capacity to become one. . . . Though he contributed to the *Yellow Book* and doubtless thought himself on that account certainly immortal, his contemporaries neglected him, and both Holbrook Jackson's ''The Eighteen Nineties'' and Osbert Burdett's ''The Beardsley Period'' also know him not. (p. 694)

In addition to the present volume [**''In His Own Image''**], which consists of a number of mildly entertaining anecdotes and legends dealing with priests, monks, and saints in the traditionally familiar manner of the Italians, ''Baron Corvo's'' principal works are a satiric novel called **''Hadrian the Seventh''** and **''The Chronicle of the Borgias''**—for Corvo, being true to type, had to profess the usual admiration for the arch-villains of the Renaissance. He had, it seems, some classical learning, which he used chiefly for the formation of the outlandishly Greek and, sometimes, merely fantastic words which strew his writings, and he was capable of an occasional ingenious phrase like that in which he says that Caesar Borgia "hanged all those who betrayed him, loving the treachery, hating the traitors"; but the general effect produced by both his matter and his manner is usually extremely mild. **"In His Own Image"** is intended to be highly original, fantastic, and daring; actually it is rather conventional, slightly tame, and completely innocuous. (pp. 694-95)

Corvo copied the affectations of his age and followed its intellectual fashions, but there seems to be no evidence that he even intuitively understood their direction or their meaning. If Wilde was a forerunner he, it would appear, was scarcely more than a characteristic by-product. In another age he could not have existed, and in his own he was hardly noticed. (p. 695)

> *Joseph Wood Krutch, "A Dim Diabolist," in* The Nation *(copyright 1925 The Nation magazine, The Nation Associates, Inc.), Vol. CXX, No. 3128, June 17, 1925, pp. 694-95.*

D. H. LAWRENCE   (essay date 1925)

[*Lawrence, regarded as one of the twentieth century's most important novelists, produced the first modern psychological novels. A proponent of freedom of expression, especially sexual expression, Lawrence's novels often treat the conflict between human sexuality and what he considered dehumanizing modern industrial society. In the excerpt below, taken from his* Selected Literary Criticism, *Lawrence calls the protagonist of Rolfe's novel* Hadrian the Seventh *a farcical character because his insight does not keep him from acting in helpless, sometimes ridiculous ways. However, Lawrence does not feel that this "destroys" the novel, which he calls "too extraordinary and daring ever to be forgotten."*]

In *Hadrian the Seventh,* Frederick Baron Corvo falls in, head over heels, in deadly earnest. A man must keep his earnestness nimble, to escape ridicule. The so-called Baron Corvo by no means escapes. He reaches heights, or depths, of sublime ridiculousness.

It doesn't kill the book, however. Neither ridicule nor dead earnest kills it. It is extraordinarily alive, even though it has been buried for twenty years. Up it rises to confront us. And, great test, it does not "date" as do Huysmans's books, or Wilde's or the rest of them. Only a first-rate book escapes its date. (p. 149)

Hadrian the Seventh is, as far as his connexion with the Church was concerned, largely an autobiography of Frederick Rolfe. It is the story of a young English convert, George Arthur Rose (Rose for Rolfe), who has had bitter experience with the priests and clergy, and years of frustration and disappointment, till he arrives at about the age of forty, a highly-bred, highly-sensitive, super-aesthetic man, ascetic out of aestheticism, athletic the same, religious the same. He is to himself beautiful, with a slim, clean-muscled grace, much given to cold baths, white-faced with a healthy pallor, and pure, that is sexually chaste, because of his almost morbid repugnance for women. (p. 150)

The first part of the book, describing the lonely man in a London lodging, alone save for his little cat, whose feline qualities of aloofness and self-sufficiency he so much admires, fixes the tone at once. And in the whole of literature I know nothing that resembles those amazing chapters, when the bishop and the archbishop come to him, and when he is ordained and makes his confession. Then the description of the election of the new pope, the cardinals shut up in the Vatican, the failure of the Way of Scrutiny and the Way of Access, the fantastic

choice, by the Way of Compromise, of George Arthur Rose, is too extraordinary and daring ever to be forgotten.

From being a rejected aspirant to the priesthood, George Arthur Rose, the man in the London lodgings, finds himself suddenly not only consecrated, but elected head of all the Catholic Church. He becomes Pope Hadrian the Seventh. (p. 151)

And what's the good of being Pope, if you've nothing but protest and aesthetics up your sleeve? Just like the reformers who are excellent, while fighting authority. But once authority disappears, they fall into nothingness. So with Hadrian the Seventh. As Pope, he is a fraud. His critical insight makes him a politician of the League of Nations sort, on a vast and curious scale. His medievalism makes him a truly comical royalist. But as a *man,* a real power in the world, he does not exist.

Hadrian unwinding the antimacassar is a sentimental farce. Hadrian persecuted to the point of suicide by a blowsy lodging-house keeper is a bathetic farce. Hadrian and the Socialist "with gorgonzola teeth" is puerile beyond words. It is all amazing, that a man with so much insight and fineness, on the one hand, should be so helpless and just purely ridiculous, when it comes to actualities.

He simply has no conception of what it is to be a natural or honestly animal man, with the repose and the power that goes with the honest animal in man. (p. 152)

He is assassinated in the streets of Rome by a Socialist, and dies supported by three Majesties, sublimely absurd. And there is nothing to it. Hadrian has stripped himself and everything else till nothing is left but absurd conceit, expiring in the arms of the Majesties.

Lord! be to me a Saviour, not a judge! is Hadrian's prayer: when he is not affectedly praying in Greek. But why should such a white streak of blamelessness as Hadrian need saving so badly? Saved from what? If he has done his best, why mind being judged—at least by Jesus, who in this sense is any man's peer?

The brave man asks for justice: the rabble cries for favours! says some old writer. Why does Hadrian, in spite of all his protest, go in with the rabble?

It is a problem. The book remains a clear and definite book of our epoch, not to be swept aside. If it is the book of a demon, as the contemporaries said, it is the book of a man-demon, not of a mere *poseur.* And if some of it is caviare, at least it came out of the belly of a live fish. (p. 153)

> *D. H. Lawrence, in a review of "Hadrian the Seventh" (originally published in* The Adelphi, *Vol. III, No. 7, December, 1925), in his* Selected Literary Criticism, *edited by Anthony Beal, William Heinemann Ltd, 1955, pp. 149-53.*

W. H. AUDEN   (essay date 1934)

[*Auden has been called the most influential modern poet since T. S. Eliot. Politically a leftist, Auden was in the forefront of a new generation of British poets, and wrote satirical poems of social protest strongly influenced by Marxism, but later rejected Marxism as an impediment to individual freedom. Throughout his career he continued to reject the precepts of the bourgeois class into which he was born. While Auden's early works reflect his belief in the necessity for poetic impersonality, later works address the isolation of the individual, the inevitable loss of love, and the*

modern individual's search for salvation. In his foreword to Rolfe's
The Desire and Pursuit of the Whole, *from which the following
excerpt is taken, Auden considers Nicholas Crabbe a self-portrait
of Rolfe that unintentionally depicts him as a paranoid homosexual
with wholly imaginary enemies. Calling the novel a mixture of
nightmare and daydream, Auden observes that the author's love
of Venice saves the story from being totally oppressive.*]

A gift for literary expression can embarrass its owner for it is
always revealing his nature to others without his consent or
even his knowledge. Banalities and platitudes are effective
masks which can be worn by any face and it is impossible to
guess the character of the wearer through them; but a genuine
style, however 'artificial' or 'impersonal', however intended
to conceal, is the creation of the unique face behind it and its
'unlikeness' to the latter is never arbitrary. *The Desire and
Pursuit of the Whole* is as striking a proof of this as I know.
In writing it, Rolfe certainly expected that his readers would
see life as Crabbe sees it, that they would take his side, agree
that he was the innocent genius victim of a gang of malicious
boobies, 'bullocks stamping on the fallen', and share his indignation. Thanks to Rolfe's remarkable talent, however, the
reader has the very different and, for him, much more interesting experience of knowing that he is looking at the world
through the eyes of a homosexual paranoid: indeed, so brilliantly does the author draw his own portrait that one is more
likely to be unjust to him and dismiss all his grievances as
imaginary which, in one instance at least, the behaviour of
Bonsen (Benson), was not the case. (p. v)

The Desire and Pursuit of The Whole interweaves a nightmare
and a day-dream. The figures in the nightmare really existed
in Venice or England but appear distorted into sinister shapes
by Crabbe's rage and suspicion: Zildo never was on land or
sea but is as accurate, as 'realistic' a revelation as one could
find anywhere of what, in all its enormity, every human ego
secretly demands of life. One of the triumphs of the book, one
which Rolfe certainly did not consciously intend, is that, though
Zildo and the 'enemies' never meet, the relation between the
two worlds is made so clear: a person who surrenders himself
so completely to such a day-dream without acknowledging its
absurdity is bound to make his daily life in the world a nightmare.

I cannot agree with Mr. Symons [see excerpt above] that the
Zildo story is 'exquisite' and 'romantic'; to me it is quite
terrifying. Crabbe begins by telling us, blandly, that for a long
time he could not make up his mind whether his Other Half
was a person or a position, a statement which is surely as brutal
as anything in Rochefoucauld. Granted that Half-Two is a
person, what properties must it possess? Well, physically, of
course, It must be a seventeen-year-old boy because that is
Crabbe's physical type; but a boy, unfortunately, is not capable
of an absolute and life-long devotion to a middle-aged man
with no money, a boy will grow up and become hirsute and
coarse-featured and, furthermore, neither Church nor State will
permit you to marry one; consequently, Zildo, the boy, is
declared Zilda, the girl, by fiat: It throws snowballs overarm
but knows when to stop because Half-One is getting bored. It
must be a poor orphan because it must owe its life, livelihood
and education to Half-One; but, since It must be worthy of
such a union, It must be descended from a Doge. Lastly, It
must be, like the Miltonic Eve, a servant but by choice not
fate, finding in the service of Its master Its 'perfect freedom'.

The characteristics of this day-dream which are abnormal and
peculiar to Crabbe should not conceal its generic likeness to

the reader's; on the contrary, they should help to prevent the
latter from thinking of his own as 'romantic'.

A paranoid goes through life with the assumption: 'I am so
extraordinary a person that others are bound to treat me as a
unique end, never as a means'. Accordingly, when others treat
him as a means or are just indifferent, he cannot believe this
and has to interpret their conduct as malignant; they are treating
him as an end, but in a negative way; they are trying to destroy
him. (pp. v-vi)

Rolfe-Crabbe had every right to be proud of his verbal claws.
Like most suspicious people, he had a sharp eye; more than
most he knew how to describe what he saw. For instance, the
'blubber-lipped Professor of Greek with a voice like a strangled
Punch' happens to be a friend of mine and I can vouch for the
remarkable accuracy, within its unkind limits, of the description. A large vocabulary is essential to the invective style, and
Rolfe by study and constant practice became one of the great
masters of vituperation; when he uses a rare word or a neol-
ogism such as 'banausic' or 'bestemmiating' it is never out of
place, and he is equally at home in ornate abuse. (pp. vii-viii)

[In] real life it is said that the recipients trembled when they
saw an envelope or 'a severe postcard' addressed in Rolfe's
handwriting.

If there were nothing in *The Desire and Pursuit of The Whole*
but Rolfe's nightmare and his daydream, it might be too depressing to read except as a clinical study; luckily there is a
third story behind both which is a real love story, the story of
Rolfe's love for Venice. Just when we are beginning to think
that we cannot take any more clapper-clawing and megalomania, Crabbe suddenly notices where he is and becomes quiet,
self-forgetful, truthful and happy. (p. viii)

Rolfe arrived in Venice in the summer of 1908. . . .

Whatever else about him was distorted or sham, his passion
for the city was genuine. . . . Venice was for him The Great
Good Place, a city built by strong and passionate men in the
image of their mother, the perfect embodiment of everything
he most craved and admired, beauty, tradition, grace and ease.

As we read the extraordinary and magnificent twenty-fifth and
twenty-sixth chapters of this book, in which Crabbe, friendless,
homeless, penniless, delirious for lack of food, wanders day
and night through the streets, we cease to laugh at or pity him
and begin to admire. Faced with the choice of going home or
dying in the place that he loves, he will choose to die, and
behind all his suffering there is a note of exaltation. Like his
author, Crabbe is more than a little crazy, more than a bit of
a scoundrel, and a most dreadful nuisance, but he is neither a
wet-leg nor ignoble. (p. ix)

W. H. Auden, in a foreword to The Desire and Pursuit
of the Whole: A Romance of Modern Venice *by
Frederick Rolfe (Baron Corvo), Cassell and Company, Limited, 1934 (and reprinted by Cassell and
Company, Limited, 1953), pp. v-ix.*

A.J.A. SYMONS (essay date 1934)

[*Symons, an English biographer and bibliophile, is best known
for his experimental biography* The Quest for Corvo [*see Additional Bibliography*], *which traces the life and career of Frederick
Rolfe. The book, based on years of painstaking research, is considered a brilliant modern biography and essential to students of
Rolfe. In his introduction to Rolfe's* The Desire and Pursuit of the
Whole, *from which the following excerpt is taken, Symons calls*

the novel "an admirable and astonishing book, a characteristic product of its author's genius, full of his unflagging zest for life and phrases, with hundreds of memorable and beautiful passages and sentences."]

The Desire and Pursuit was written with extreme care. There are in existence four manuscripts, each showing variations of text, each rejoicing in the elaborate caligraphy that was Fr. Rolfe's pride and hobby. Rolfe is, of course, identifiable with his own hero Nicholas Crabbe, and the method of the book is to submit Crabbe to the adventures and misfortunes of his creator (to the point of including actual and paraphrased correspondence) while superimposing these extracts from reality upon a charming imaginary love-affair with a hero-heroine of anomalous sex. Such a method, though it shows the completeness of Rolfe's self-dramatization, could hardly be expected to produce a perfect work of art; and it has not. **The Desire and Pursuit** is an incongruous compound of an exquisite, romantic dream-tale with undramatic and sordid details from Rolfe's life. And it is these actual details from life that seem improbable and out of place in the book. Rolfe's artistry conveys conviction when he narrates the adventures of Crabbe in his boat during the earthquake, and the discovery of Zildo, which are pure inventions; but the letters exchanged between the youthful Lieutenant of the Order of Sanctissima Sophia and the angry Nicholas, which are true, seem flimsy and exaggerated travesties. Nevertheless, when all that can be urged against **The Desire and Pursuit** has been weighed, it remains an admirable and astonishing book, a characteristic product of its author's genius, full of his unflagging zest for life and phrases, with hundreds of memorable and beautiful passages and sentences—as in the sage remark that 'Only beggars can be choosers,' or the Rochefoucauld-like severity of 'his closest friend or enemy—they are much the same in the long run,' or such descriptions as 'the rain streamed down in frigid lances.' There are not many writers who can say better things. Those who think otherwise are advised to try.

And Rolfe's punctuation is beautiful throughout. It was characteristic that he should take pains with his commas and semi-colons, as he did with the shape of his letters when he wrote. In many ways, indeed, the essential Rolfe reveals himself. . . . (pp. xiv-xv)

The Desire and Pursuit of the Whole, like all Rolfe's books, was written by a man who was nearly starving. That in itself is not a recommendation; starving men may write good books or bad ones. But at least there is likely to be fire and feeling in what they write, and this book is no exception. It shows the intense passion of Rolfe's defeated but indomitable soul, his zest for life, his love of words and learning, his paranoia, and the twists and crannies of his strange mind, with the reflected exactness of a spiritual mirror. (pp. xv-xvi)

> *A.J.A. Symons, in an introduction to* The Desire and Pursuit of the Whole: A Romance of Modern Venice *by Frederick Rolfe (Baron Corvo), Cassell and Company, Limited, 1934 (and reprinted by Cassell and Company, Limited, 1953), pp. xi-xvi.*

GRAHAM GREENE (essay date 1934-35)

[*An English novelist, short story writer, and essayist, Greene is one of the most widely read and highly respected living writers. A convert to Roman Catholicism, he writes novels that examine the relationship between God and humanity in a world dominated by evil. While his Catholic world view allows for the possibility of miracles and God's redemption, Greene's works reflect his*

religion in a non-dogmatic way, using Catholicism as a system of organization and dramatization, a set of symbols rather than literal truths. Deeply psychological, his works depict an anti-hero's struggle against evil in the search for salvation. In his The Lost Childhood and Other Essays, *from which the following excerpt is taken, Greene finds Rolfe's* Hadrian the Seventh *to be evidence of the author's "sincere, if sinister, devotion" to the Catholic church, and says that Rolfe has about him "the air of demonic possession."*]

[If] ever there was a case of demoniac possession it was Rolfe's: the hopeless piety, the screams of malevolence, the sense of despair which to a man of his faith was the sin against the Holy Ghost. 'All men are too vile for words to tell.'

The greatest saints have been men with more than a normal capacity for evil, and the most vicious men have sometimes narrowly evaded sanctity. Frederick Rolfe in his novel **Hadrian the Seventh** expressed a sincere, if sinister, devotion to the Church that had very wisely rejected him; all the good of which he was capable went into that book, as all the evil went into the strange series of letters . . . written at the end of his life, when he was starving in Venice, to a rich acquaintance. (p. 173)

These were the astonishing bounds of Corvo: the starving pander on the Lido and the man of whom Mr. Vincent O'Sullivan wrote to his biographer: 'He was born for the Church: that was his main interest.' Between these bounds, between the Paradise and the Inferno, lay the weary purgatorial years. . . . (p. 174)

· · · · ·

It is the measure of the man's vividness that his life always seems to move on a religious plane: his violent hatreds, his extreme ingratitude, even his appearance as he described it himself, 'offensive, disdainful, slightly sardonic, utterly unapproachable', have about them the air of demoniac possession. **The Desire and Pursuit of the Whole,** the long autobiographical novel of the last dreadful years in Venice, . . . has the quality of a mediaeval mystery play, but with this difference, that the play is written from the devil's side. The many excellent men and women who did their best, sometimes an unimaginative best, to help Rolfe, here caper like demons beside the long Venetian water-fronts: the Rev. Bobugo Bonsen (known on the angels' side, as Monsignor Benson), Harry Peary-Buthlaw, Professor Macpawkins, Lady Pash. It is instructive and entertaining to see the great and the good for once from the devil's point of view.

And the devil has been fair. . . . The facts (the correspondence with Bonsen and Peary-Buthlaw, for example) appear to be quite truthfully stated; it is Rolfe's interpretation which is odd. Offer the starving man a dinner or the homeless man a bed and instantaneously the good deed is unrecognizably distorted. The strangest motives begin obscurely to be discerned. Is it that one is seeing good from the devil's side: 'The lovely, clever, good, ugly, silly wicked faces of this world, all anxious, all selfish, all mean, all unsatisfied and unsatisfying': or is it possibly only a horribly deep insight into human nature? (pp. 176-77)

One says that he writes from the devil's side, because his shrill rage has the same lack of dignity as Marlowe's cracker-throwing demons, because he had no humility ('he came as one to whom Mystery has a meaning and a method, as one of the intimate, and fortunate, as one who belonged, as a son of the Father'), and because, of course, he had a Monsignor among his enemies. But the devil, too, is spiritual, and when Rolfe wrote of the spirit (without the silly rage against his enemies or the sillier decorated style in which he tried to make the best of a world he had not been allowed to renounce) he wrote like an angel; our appreciation is hardly concerned in the question whether or not it was a fallen angel. . . . (p. 177)

· · · · ·

Hubert's Arthur . . . is a laborious experiment in imaginary history. The assumption is that Arthur was not murdered by King John but escaped and, after recovering a treasure left him by Richard Lion-Heart, won the crown of Jerusalem and finally, with the help of Hubert de Burgh, the chronicler of his deeds, gained the throne of England. Originally Rolfe collaborated with Mr. Pirie-Gordon, but after the inevitable quarrel he rewrote the story during the last months of his life. The style, we are told, 'was meant to be an enriched variant upon that of the *Itinerarium Regis Ricardi* and of William of Tyre, with an admixture of Maurice Hewlett.' Hewlett, alas, in this appallingly long and elaborate fantasy is too much in evidence, and perhaps only a knowledge of the circumstances in which it was written, to be gained from Mr. Symons's biography [see Additional Bibliography], gives it interest.

For if Rolfe is to be believed (a very big assumption) he brought this book to its leisurely decorative close at the very time when he claimed to be starving in his gondola on the Venetian lagoons. (p. 179)

That to me is the real dramatic interest of *Hubert's Arthur.*

For on the whole it is a dull book of small literary merit, though it will be of interest to those already interested in the man, who can catch the moments when he drops the Hewlett mask and reveals more indirectly than in *The Desire and Pursuit of the Whole* his painfully divided personality. Reading his description of St. Hugh, 'the sweet and inerrable canorous voice of the dead', one has to believe in the genuineness of his nostalgia—for the Catholic Church, for innocence. But at the same time one cannot fail to notice the homosexual and the sadistic element in the lushness and tenderness of his epithets.

When he writes in the person of Hubert de Burgh: 'They would not let me have my will (which was for the life of a quiet clergyman). . . . So once every day since that time, I have cursed those monks out of a full heart,' one pities the spoiled priest; when he describes Arthur,

> the proud gait of the stainless pure secure in himself, wholly perfect in himself, severe with himself as with all, strong in disgust of ill, utterly careless save to keep high, clean, cold, armed, intact, apart, glistening with candid candour both of heart and of aspect, like a flower, like a maid, like a star,

one recognizes the potential sanctity of the man, just as one recognizes the really devilish mind which gives the formula for a throat-cutting with the same relish as in his book on the Borgias he had translated a recipe for cooking a goose alive. (pp. 180-81)

> *Graham Greene, "Frederick Rolfe" (originally published as "Edwardian Inferno," "From the Devil's Side" and "A Spoiled Priest," in* The Spectator, *Nos. 5512, 5554 and 5606, February 16 and December 7, 1934, and December 6, 1935), in his* Collected Essays *(copyright 1951 © 1966, 1968, 1969 by Graham Greene; reprinted by permission of Laurence Pollinger Ltd. for Graham Greene),* The Viking Press, *1969, pp. 172-81.*

MARVIN MUDRICK (essay date 1954)

[*Mudrick, literary biographer and essayist, contends that Rolfe's* Desire and Pursuit of the Whole *is a bad, affected, adolescent novel and an unintentional burlesque of the theme of virtue versus wickedness found in the traditional English novel.*]

Contemporary best-sellers and would-be-best-sellers . . . are at the end of one major tradition of the English novel. It might be called the bourgeois-humane tradition: it accepts the bourgeois (including the Marxist) assumptions about human nature; and what it above all requires, and tries to confirm, in the reader is an active sympathy toward the author's favorite characters. It started with Fielding and achieved its apotheosis of deserved popularity with Dickens; its first axiom is that events and characters are fixed, in unchallengeable commonsense terms, as decisively good or evil; and its suspense resolves itself, through a series of illustrative rather than developing episodes, into the question: Will virtue (*i.e.,* the "sympathetic" characters) triumph? (p. 626)

The Desire and Pursuit of the Whole is, like most bad novels, in the same tradition; but it is so stubbornly, and so unintentionally, a burlesque of Plot Number One of the tradition—virtuous hero versus wicked, or at least indifferent, world—as to explode into the wildest comedy, incidentally illuminating similar but solemnly accepted burlesques. The boy-girl slave-heroine is Italian; and the author, anticipating by a generation (the book was written about 1909) another cropped-headed boy-girl, thoughtfully translates her into pidgin-Hemingway: "'Sior, he is a brave, and very beneficent; and, as for me, I am appassionated for pictures'"; and into this kind of dialogue, interchangeable with any Hemingway "love" scene:

"It was yours."
"Then you are me, and I am you."
"Sissior. My beloved is mine and I am his."
"When did you know that?"
"Sior, when but as soon as I knew that you had seen me."

It is tempting to let quotes do the job unaided: except for those who share Mr. Auden's prefatory compassion [see excerpt above], the novel is unfailingly uproarious. The hero describes the heroine unclothed, "the form of a noble boy, in all but sex": "Where should he find a simile for the generous spread of her candour and softness and firmness and long strong vigorous pallor, for her naïve freshness and innocent unusedness, for her unstained stainableness?" On the hero as a buried horse: ". . . he was . . . saddled with an unploughed field of female, seventeen years old, shaped like a boy and having a boy's abilities." On his virtues: "His was the knightly soul; and his deeds were the deeds of a champion fighting the battles of others, neglecting his own" (the hero's time, by the way, is taken up almost exclusively with his ferocious orations, by mail and in person, against anyone somehow getting in his way or keeping his books unpublished). . . . Corvo's style is not only startling for its expanses of pure adolescent fantasy-language but animated by new past tenses—"swang," "slank," "ununderstand"—and such interesting words as "operose," "diorthotic," "fastidy," "suspicacious," "amoenely." Now and then he sounds enough like S. J. Perelman to convince us, nearly, that he's kidding: "Crabbe hardened in his cane arm-chair, afflicted by verification of his instinct. There came a mouth-taste of sour milk mixed with very bad egg and rancid oil in a rusty old meat-tin; and a warm ache gasped inside of him. It was, of course, indigestion, caused by angry contempt temporarily paralyzing intestinal muscular action—peristalsis, in short. He commanded boiling water, and moodily sipped the potion.''

Corvo was no doubt paranoid . . . ; but the image of him that persists (he and Crabbe are identical, and the book is autobiography spattered with Nietzschean and erotic daydreams), behind all his airs, sponging, edginess, his spitting tantrums and arcane gibberish, is after all only the image of the wistful arty homosexual, who doesn't ask for much: just the grateful acknowledgment of his superiority. It would be impolite, however, to ask the publisher what sort of reader (apart from the unexpected sort who takes it as burlesque) he expects this reprint to gratify. (pp. 629-30)

> *Marvin Mudrick, ''Rugby, Fastidy and a Live Tradition,'' in* The Hudson Review *(copyright © 1953, copyright renewed © 1981, by The Hudson Review, Inc.; reprinted by permission), Vol. VI, No. 4, Winter, 1954, pp. 626-33.*

CHRISTOPHER SYKES   (essay date 1968)

[*In his preface to Rolfe's* Stories Toto Told Me, *from which the following is excerpted, Sykes, an English fiction writer and essayist, examines Rolfe's style and finds this collection to be the product of the only happy period in the author's life.*]

All Corvo's fictional writing has a stronger element of autobiography than is the usual case. It is never very difficult to relate his inventions to known experiences, or to the wild hopes which sustained him, and the daydreams which consoled him. The stories [in *Stories Toto Told Me*] . . . seem incontrovertibly to reflect one of the few happy and (so far as anyone knows) guiltless periods of his life, that which he spent after leaving the Scots College, when he lived in the Sforza-Cesarini household. . . . There is a sweetness and absence of bitterness, a gaiety too, about these stories, which is not typical of Corvo, and even when, usually through Toto, he girds at the clergy, especially at the Jesuits, he attacks with so much more of farce than of his accustomed, venomous rancour, that good feeling persists. The whole thing is fun. Only in one story does one hear, amid so much reflection of happiness, an echo of the misery from which Corvo's tormented and probably not quite sane temperament made complete escape impossible at any time. The passage occurs in the opening paragraphs of . . . **''About Some Friends''**. (p. 14)

Corvo is very difficult to ''place'' in our letters. That he was published in *The Yellow Book* suggests quite rightly that he belonged to the self-consciously ''decadent'' school of our late nineteenth-century literature of fantasy. The Toto stories clearly owe something to Oscar Wilde's lovely *Happy Prince* stories, but one should not pursue the relationship further, and to see in him a literary disciple of Wilde is clearly wrong. He was a word-coiner to an extreme extent which can at times remind one of the absurd Richard Le Gallienne and other *Yellow Book* luminaries, especially the brilliant young Max Beerbohm; but again the resemblance should not lead one on to see more in it than that. In his *Yellow Book* days Max could with a grave face use such a word as ''pop-limbo'' as if it were normal currency, and he was capable of describing how Edward VII, as Prince of Wales, would ''watch at Newmarket, the scud-a-run of homuncules over the vert on horses. . . .'' But there was always a fund of common sense in Max, such as was remarkably absent in Corvo. No reader doubts that ''pop-limbo'' in the context means ''nonsense'', or that the second quotation above refers to the Prince watching jockeys competing in a horse-race. But when Corvo in all seriousness uses such terms as ''tolutiloquent'', ''contortuplication'', ''fumificables'', ''zaïmph'', ''aseity'', ''purrothrixine'', or ''banaysically'', the minority of his readers who remain feeling quite at home with all this erudition grows minute to invisibility. He and Max and Wilde had something in common, but it was very little. As in life, he belonged nowhere. He cannot be described in terms of a group, or even in terms of his own period, except in one respect where Corvo can be said to have been symptomatic of his day. That is in regard to his ardent if erratically followed religion, and it finds expression in these stories. (pp. 15-16)

Some Catholics were understandably shocked at these stories which threw such an absurd light on Roman Catholic belief, and some Protestants rejoiced at an exposure of the folly and superstition of Rome. But, so far as one can judge, such was not the majority reaction. Catholics were much more apt to delight in this picture of a simple, illiterate, beautiful Italian boy, with his indestructible faith and piety all expressed in the saintly fantasies and legends of the Roman peasantry. They smiled at the ignorant extravagances, but hardly in disapproval, and if there was evident exaggeration and caricature in Corvo's record of Toto (we shall never know who was his model), they felt that they were those of a friend and fellow-worshipper. If there was superstition revealed in the stories, with their amazing confusions of Catholic tradition and pagan myth, and with their fanciful retelling of the creation and fall of man according to the Book of Genesis, this was not likely to distress most of his Catholic readers, the majority of whom were enthusiastic converts. Nor were the typical Catholics who lived during that amazing revival of the old faith in England likely to find their Englishry affronted by Toto. They were the reverse of nationalistic, inclining to be not only *plus papale que le pape* [holier than the pope], but more Italian than the Italians. Revelations of superstition were not likely to shock people whose practice was dominated by devotionalism, and who never heard superstition denounced from the pulpit. What they were likely to find in the Toto stories was delightful evidence of the cosy spiritual atmosphere surrounding the lives of humble people who lived at the centre of the Faith. Corvo reflected a prevalent Catholic mood. One should perhaps think of the stories as being greatly extended and greatly sophisticated versions, contrived by a writer who had something of real genius in him, of those tales which are the subject of demure merriment among pious people, and have for long been commonplace in clergy houses and behind convent walls. If the merriment is demure this does not mean that it excludes wit, humour and penetration. Corvo's singular talent shows how much of all three can be contained within what might be thought (especially in our foul-mouthed yet conventional age) to be a fatal limitation.

The stories, as a reader must notice, are uneven in quality. The form is a precarious one and depends for success, far more than most fiction, on a precise estimate of hit or miss, and without any comfortable half-way house between. (pp. 17-18)

[The] variety within the small compass of the Toto stories (though it is true that they deal with eternity) is one of the most surprising and interesting things about them. Consider only the charm of slightness in . . . **''About the Original Fritter of Sangiuseppe''**, the almost Hieronymous Bosch quality of . . . **''About Beata Beatrice and the Mamma of Sampietro''**, the fierce power in . . . **''Why the Rose is Red''**, and the poetic splendour of . . . the extraordinary Christianized version of the tale of Eros and Psyche which Corvo gave under the title **''About Divinamore and the Maiden Anima''**. (p. 19)

Christopher Sykes, ''Preface'' (1968; © in the Preface, Christopher Sykes, 1969; reprinted by permission of A D Peters & Co Ltd), in Stories Toto Told Me by Frederick Baron Corvo, William Collins Sons & Co. Ltd., 1969 (and reprinted by St. Martin's Press, 1971), pp. 9-22.

SERGIO PEROSA (essay date 1971)

[*Perosa is an Italian literary critic, translator, and editor. In the excerpt below, he minimizes the critical emphasis on Rolfe's autobiographical wish-fulfillment, and, surveying his novels, reconsiders the relationship of the man to the characters and the artist to his creation. For a similar reevaluation of the wish-fulfillment interpretation of Rolfe's fiction see G. P. Jones's essay excerpted below.*]

Now that [Frederick Rolfe's] works are available, one has to reconsider the relation between the man and the writer, his biography and his fiction, his fiction and his times. Rolfe is often very much present in his fiction, writing about his story of deprivations and humiliations, yearnings and retaliations. But it is exactly here that one has to distinguish what refers to the man from what refers to the writer, what is mere expression of personal obsessions from what acquires specific artistic and historical significance through literary transposition.

Two facts must be kept in mind. If Rolfe's autobiographical fiction is often a direct expression of the defenseless and alienated self, it shows on the other hand revealing links and coincidences with the historical experience of the Decadent Movement. Secondly, the main characteristics of his historical, or pseudo-historical fiction, can often be related to the ideals and the forms of Decadent literature and reveal striking experimental aspects which foreshadow some important trends of twentieth century fiction.

Rolfe himself, in his prologue to *Nicholas Crabbe,* tells us that his fictionalized history falls into four divisions: The period of his previous incarnations (*The Weird of the Wanderer*); the period when he was driven out into the wilderness (*Hadrian the Seventh*); the period when the vernacular multitude came about him (like bees) and were rapacious (*Nicholas Crabbe*); the period when Love brought him wings wherewith to flee away and be at rest (*The Desire and Pursuit of the Whole*). In these four novels the autobiographical transposition throws light both on the man and on the writer, and in at least two cases achieves artistic fulfilment exactly on the ground of a close relationship between art and life.

The Weird of the Wanderer is, in fact, an idle and patched-up work, ''being the papyrus records of some incidents in one of the previous lives of Mr. Nicholas Crabbe.'' At first King Balthazar in Thebes and in Egypt under the Roman rule (with a timepiece and a revolver to subdue his enemies), then Odysseys on his quest for the Treasure of Hades, then again King of Moxoene, while waiting to become what he always is—Nicholas Crabbe the Impossible—this stale and insufferable character is endowed with only a few traits of Rolfe's personal obsessions: the wish for a magical initiation as a substitute for priesthood, the sense of superiority and the drive for self-assertion. But the book moves along mechanically from papyrus to papyrus with a display of fake-erudition and no real hold on the reader. One is reminded of a second-rate *Connecticut Yankee in King Arthur's Court,* with none of the humour of the original, burdened with cheap spiritualism and pseudoliterary elegance.

This book was an escape into elaborate formalism. Rolfe's true escape lies in the creation of a personal myth of retaliation and self-assertion in the unencumbered realm of imagination. The outcast of society, the failed priest imagines and projects himself as Pope, Pontifex Maximus and ruler of the world, in *Hadrian the Seventh*—impossible and improbable realization of a day-dream. From the abyss of utter destitution, from the hatred and rancour of the outcast driven out into the wilderness, emerges the figure of a pope with artistic and autocratic leanings, whose task is not to regenerate the world and the souls of men, but to impose an absolute order on all nations before paying the price of martyrdom for it.

Thanks to a series of extraordinary circumstances, the hero of the book (George Arthur Rose), suffering under the burden of Rolfe's own humiliations and deprivations, finds himself called to the Holy See. As his acceptance is motivated by a paranoic desire for self-assertion, so the activity of the new, improbable Pope Hadrian VII is motivated by a kind of political-aesthetic drive to establish an autocratic order on the world. The fascination of this book lies in the mingling of private malice and imaginative grandeur, of personal revenge verging on the absurd and the majestical dimension of a day-dream which acquires, as it were, evidence and substance of reality, thanks to the imaginative power which sustains it. It is obvious that the story must end in a melodramatic way, and in fact the ending is the weakest part of the book; and this is exactly because the renewed interference of autobiographical elements breaks the autonomy of the day-dream which only the iron law of the absurd can keep together. Hadrian VII is an original and unparalleled character only in his complete adherence to myth. His greatness—and credibility—lies in the imaginative projection of the day-dream, in the solemn celebration of the outcast who, by sheer force of will, asserts himself as the chosen one.

Obviously, the Chosen One is fleeing away from the world even as the world rejects him in real life. *Nicholas Crabbe* is the chronicle of the terrible life of deprivation led by Rolfe in London, and must be read as the reality of nightmare against the escape into wish-fulfilment. Almost directly autobiographical, it is a painful record of struggles and humiliations in his daily encounters with ''the vernacular multitude about him'', and it depicts the parable of the One who, in his opposition to the rapacious Many, finds himself in the end ''all alone with The Alone'' (*The One and The Many* is the subtitle of the book). Through a series of invectives, squabbles and explosions of impotent rage, Nicholas Crabbe's total withdrawal from the world is here enacted, and the slightly sinister ceremony of his surrender is staged. We are told that ''Crabbe grimly drew in his eyes and folded his claws and retired into his cave''; in fact, the crab with which Rolfe identifies himself, both on the semantic and on the symbolic level, is soft inside; and even ''his carapax seemed to soften''. It thus becomes a suitable figure of his retreat into the cave of the self, which is the real theme of the novel.

Again driven out into the wilderness of isolation, Nicholas Crabbe courts humiliation and defeat. It is only in *The Desire and Pursuit of the Whole* that Nicholas Crabbe *redivivus* can assert himself and triumph over humiliation and defeat or, indeed, thanks to humiliation and defeat. In this beautiful ''Romance of Modern Venice'' the motif of redeeming and liberating Love blossoms on the ashes of squalor. The One and The Alone seeks here the platonic completion in The Whole, finds or finally recognizes the other half with which to reunite, and celebrates the ritual of reconciliation and regeneration.

He discovers the natural habitat of the Venetian lagoon and the labyrinthine city into which to retreat, according to the inborn habit of the crab. He wages always and forever his private war with real or hypothetical enemies, gradually shuts himself away from human society, descends into the private world of the boat where he lives and which becomes at once house and womb, cradle and tomb of the broken flesh, floating on the waters beyond life and time. But for the first time the spirit resists the triumphs in the city of death which is also a city of rebirth—he goes through the pang of conscience to discover a truer self, experiences sea-quake, storm and rain, struggles in the mud, but finds in the city of waters the stimulus to regeneration, the possibility of overcoming dejection and isolation.

This is made possible because of the literal and symbolic encounter with Zilda-Zildo, the androgynous girl dressed in male attire, who, saved from sea-quake and earthquake, becomes Crabbe's faithful servant and companion, looks after him and his boat, and interposes between him and the difficulties of the world. In Zilda-Zildo—an extraordinary fictional creation—Rolfe-Crabbe finds his specular image and his completion, physical salvation and the riches of love. Above all, he achieves a contact and a reconciliation with reality, the measure of self-discovery (not self-assertion) that is needed so that from the abyss of destitution and deprivation the encounter with The Other and the completion in The Whole may be possible.

In the city of mists, on the rain-drenched *fondamenta,* under the precarious shelter of bridges, in the livid lagoon or in the flowery paths of the graveyard-island, the earthly fears of Rolfe-Crabbe are consumed because of the redeeming devotion of the androgynous girl. The softening of the crab, which still reaches out uselessly with his claws, verges sometimes on sentimentality. But what matters here, again, is the imaginative projection of a private myth, the intense realization of the most poetic day-dream in the midst of the daily nightmare. Wish-fulfilment celebrates its poetic triumph, tenderness is achieved, the escape from the world and from time is poetically and symbolically attained in a novel which is still saturated with the paranoic rage of the eternal outcast.

In a private and personal way, these novels represent the consummation of the historical experience of the Decadent Movement. In that "Edwardian hell" (according to Graham Greene's definition) in which Rolfe struggled for life, his cultural awareness clearly reveals a Decadent matrix. Rolfe had, in fact, begun his literary career within the Decadent movement, contributing his **"Stories Toto Told Me"** to the *Yellow Book* in 1895-6 (twenty-six more tales were added in 1900 to make up the volume *In His Own Image*). These short stories were told by a young boy, Toto, in a sunny southern Italy that had all the traits of Arcadia, the land of happy seclusion, and dealt with surrealistic episodes, hagiographic adventures, and popular fantasies, in a setting which is somewhere between heaven and earth.

Rolfe's idea was to retell the stories of Catholic saints in the manner of Greek mythology and to confer human character and motivations to their heavenly activities. In so doing, he was often on the verge of irreverence, but he succeeded in giving a tone of homely fairy-tale to these stories of adolescent saints who play and cavort in flowery paradises, come down to earth alone or in groups to play tricks on mortals, and are good-humouredly checked by the Heavenly Father. The rural and Arcadian atmosphere of the autobiographical frame made acceptable such a meeting between heaven and earth. Irony

and humour were sustained by the colloquial language and the primitive sensitivity of Toto, exploiting the grotesque and the picturesque, relying on mock-simplicity and contrived naturalness.

The work is in line with typical aspects of the Decadent Movement: the affectation of mock-simplicity, the cultivated recourse to primitivism, the worldly taste for fairy-tales, the insistence on exotic or surrealistic effects, and on a kind of hedonistic and aesthetic Christianity with pagan undertones. Here the coincidence with Decadentism is immediate. In the autobiographical novels, it is basicly a matter of adhering to the more flamboyant aspects of the historical experience: the raw exoticism and the mannered classicism of *The Weird of the Wanderer;* the fascination exerted by ecclesiastical pomp in *Hadrian VII,* with its colorful conclaves, solemn processionals, and the mixture of aesthetic and ascetic traits in the protagonist; the painful retreat from the world and the assertion of the One against the Many in *Nicholas Crabbe,* as in *The Desire and Pursuit of the Whole,* which moreover revived that ideal setting of the Decadent adventure—Venice—and, not least, the figure of the androgynous adolescent, which had haunted the Decadent imagination from Pater to Wilde.

A further link with Decadentism lies in the adoption of fluid and "open" narrative forms, of artificial structures and frames, in the use of a precious, elaborate, overly refined kind of language. Structural and linguistic artifice is a distinctive trait in Rolfe's autobiographical fiction. It becomes a supporting element and sometimes a central concern in his pseudo-historical narratives, which are indeed qualified by its presence both in a Decadent, and in a purely experimental way. In all these works, moreover, we are clearly confronted by colorful and impressionistic renderings, and these aspects must be further explored in order to grasp the real significance of Rolfe's fiction. (pp. 112-16)

As far as the method of composition was concerned, impressionism led to a juxtaposition and montage of impressions—so many tesserae of a mosaic; while colouring style, it also fragmented structure. . . . (p. 116)

The theory of art as articraft and artifice—long before Viktor Sklovskij and the Russian Formalists—had been expressed by Oscar Wilde in *The Decay of Lying* (1889), with its celebrated display of paradoxical aphorisms to the effect that life and nature imitate art (the "supreme reality", as we read in *De Profundis*) while life is a "mere mode of fiction". Similar ideas of pure formalism and artificial decoration are also to be found in Max Beerbohm's *A Defence of Cosmetics* (1894) and *The Happy Hypocrite* (1897). All this obviously expressed an opposition to contemporary realistic trends. There is no doubt that Rolfe—who in a letter of 1908 wrote that he detested realism, because artists must create ideal models—shared, however unconsciously, these views, finding in Pater, moreover, a theoretical and practical advocacy of ornate style, that latinate prose that Pater extolled as the appropriate style of the period.

The peak of Rolfe's artificiality, in this sense, is to be found in his pseudo-historical narratives, which also present revealing coincidences with two other aspects of Decadent literature: a peculiar interest in particular periods of the past, rediscovered and re-experienced in contemporary terms, and an avowed preference for *romantic* modes of expressing them. If Ruskin, the Pre-Raphaelites and William Morris rediscovered the Middle Ages, the Decadents took to Byzantium and a late Latin culture on the verge of Christianity, to a Renaissance glowing with lights and shadows which marked the revival of the artistic and the pagan sensibility, the rediscovery of classical man, the fulness of the life-drive. In both cases, it was a question of ages of transition and conflicts, in which contemporary concerns seemed to be reflected. (pp. 116-17)

In *Nicholas Crabbe* Rolfe had written of "his singular and proper handicraft, which actually was rather solid and very brilliant and picturesque historical fiction based on unusually extensive researches in historical fact." More of an artifex than an artist, of a manipulator than a creator (as he was himself to recognize in a letter), a mystifier by nature as well as by cultural choice, Rolfe began writing about history on commission. His *Chronicles of the House of Borgia* . . . aim at dismantling the negative interpretations of the Borgias and at restoring the main figures to their proper dignity and stature. The care with which he pursues his aim can only attenuate the historical truth; what matters, however, is Rolfe's way of confronting the Renaissance (the same Renaissance, in spite of his attacks, as that of Burckhardt and J. A. Symonds) in such a way as to give a colorful picture of it and to celebrate the vitality and the self-assertion of the new man who rediscovers the energy and the zest for life of pagan classicism. (p. 118)

The Renaissance hero is celebrated in his vitalism and in his "corruption" as master of his own destiny, free and pleasure-seeking, artistic and pagan, capable of restoring the Church itself to its authority and splendor. Authority and splendor, of course, in the world; and here we go back to Rolfe's (and the Decadents') obsession with ecclesiastical pomp and aesthetic Christianity.

But, as the central image of the fire indicates, the picture is achieved through the juxtaposition and the montage of numberless picturesque touches, colorful and impressionistic details, violent or idyllic moments, careful renderings of people and places. The canvas—or tapestry—is, as it were, broken and fragmented into a sequence of impressionistic episodes, sketches and ecstatic moments; it reveals the elaborate and chiselled formal texture, the precious stylistic embroidery, of a purely artificial creation. Going back to the Renaissance was for Rolfe a way of counteracting the present. The contemporary relevance lies, in fact, in the taste for manipulation and mystification, for the elaborate texture and a sort of fake linguistic mimesis.

These elements become preponderant in the two pseudo-historical romances that followed, and in fact grew out of, the *Chronicles of the House of Borgia*. In *Don Tarquinio* and in *Don Renato* one is confronted by a complete impressionistic fragmentation and re-construction of the historical material, thanks to the "latitude" and freedom allowed by the romance. The absolute artificiality of structure and language makes them not only representative of the period, but also typical of twentieth century experimental fiction.

Originally, *Don Tarquinio* was to have been a short tale "embodying every act of a man of fashion of the [Borgia] era during a certain four-and twenty consecutive hours. It was to be written brilliantly, giving the life and the atmosphere of the time so that any modern (reading it) could live it for himself." It grew, however, into a full-length work to which the most artificial of forms is given by means of the interplay of three technical devices. The first lies in the fact that Rolfe pretends to be merely translating a manuscript written in 1523-27 by Don Tarquinio Drakontoletes Poplicola of Santacroce, which tells

of his extraordinary adventures one day in 1495 that led to the lifting of the Great Ban on his Family. Secondly, as the original is supposedly written in a sort of Italian jargon of the times, the "translation" reflects its composite nature and its syntactical and idiomatic oddities, adopting in brief a sort of English macaronics. The third element of artificiality is given by the impressionistic form of the romance.

As the subtitle specifies, *Don Tarquinio* is "a Kataleptic phantasmatic Romance". The reference is to Zeno, the stoic philosopher, and to the principle that "the truth is that which every man may acquire from the apprehensive nature of perfectly cultivated senses: or, as Zeno the Stoic saith, the test of truth is the Kataleptic Phantasm. For this cause"—Don Tarquinio-Rolfe goes on to say—"I will write history from the evidence of my proper senses alone, and not from the idle reports of ungoverned and ungovernable tongues." At the end we are told again that he has not been "concealing anything which his own senses perceived; and he saith, that this is the manner in which history ought to be written." This is nothing else than a perfect definition, from the inside, of the impressionistic romance; truth and history can only be recreated through the direct impressions of perfectly cultivated senses, and in a personal way. In the same way, and in the same years, we might remember, F. M. Ford proclaimed that he would rely on impressions, not on facts. In Jamesian terms, Rolfe's romance, for the fun of it, has cut the cable that ties the balloon of experience to earth.

Truth and verisimilitude, in other words, are pursued and achieved within the framework and in terms of Decadent artificiality. Rolfe's coloristic and imaginative power pervades a romance which is constituted of a sequence of brief episodes, descriptive moments, idyllic scenes, picturesque details and decorative touches. Young Don Tarquinio in exile moves young Cardinal Deacon Ippolito d'Este to pity and becomes his follower; excursions on river boats alternate with football games, swimming contests in the Tiber with boxing matches, refined conversations with exquisite meals. . . . Paragons of the new man who cultivates spiritual beauty together with physical fitness, Don Tarquinio and Don Ippolito move lightly among the pleasures of the country and the bustle of papal Rome. Fresh loves blossom; against the background of majestic palaces and sumptuous dinners, readings from the classics and delicate bathings, among swarms of pages and *famigli*, we catch glimpses of Lucrezia Borgia and Pope Alexander VI; we hear of the Emperor's raids. (pp. 118-20)

The image, and the active life of the Renaissance such as the Decadent soul envisages, half in admiration and half in dismay, is made to unfold before our eyes as in a living panorama.

"Live your life as if it were a work of art", someone says in the book, in keeping with so many similar statements of the *fin de siècle*. Life is an image, or a function, of artistic perfection, and the thin story is only a pretext for the display of significant moments and admirable incidents, for the description of manners, for the picture of characters caught in the poses or the frantic activities of triumphant humanism. The wish-fulfilment of historical imagination predominates over any other interest, and this time, too, language achieves the condition of a realized wish-fulfilment in a purely artificial triumph of manipulation. One is reminded of what F. M. Ford was doing in the *Fifth Queen Trilogy*. There is the projection of the present into the past, in keeping with the "romantic classicism" of the times, but it is the achievement of Rolfe's impressionistic romance that makes of this literary "fake" a representative example of Decadent literature and linguistic experimentation.

Things are further complicated in **Don Renato**. Here too we have the convention of the historical "source" (Dom Gheraldo's Diurnal or diarium for the years 1528-30 and Don Renato's Letter to his father, A.D. 1545), and a direct reference to a contemporary fact: Rolfe's discovery, in 1890, of Dom Gheraldo's bones in a trap in Palazzo Santacroce in Rome. Here too Rolfe pretends that he is translating the source into English macaronics; that is, a purely artificial language, for which we need a glossary at the end of the book. Here too, the narrative mode is that of the impressionistic romance which aims at giving us "an ideal content" (according to the subtitle).

But there is something more, which makes of **Don Renato** the most artificial of Rolfe's narratives. In 1902 he had written in a letter that his romance was an attempt at writing historical fiction in a new way. In the first of the introductory epistles which open the book, "Of the Efficient Cause", while examining some previous examples of historical fiction—from Walter Scott to Charles Reade, from Mark Twain to Sienkiewicz—Rolfe emphasizes the need for a linguistic form that would strike the reader for its novelty and strangeness and give the impression of verisimilitude. Thackeray's *Henry Esmond,* in his opinion, failed because its language was "dyspathetic to the form", whereas "historick romance must be true, apparently if not actually, accidentally if not essentially, implicitly if not explicitly." The Form of it must be appropriate to the Matter, language to subject-matter; it must mimic, that is, the linguistic texture of the hypothetical source.

Truth and verisimilitude, again, lie in linguistic and structural artifice. Hence, the form of the personal journal or, indeed, Diurnal, being the most direct and immediate way for collecting impressions, whose montage can give us the perception and *feeling* of the story, and the creation of an artificial language which is supposed to make the story sound true, while in fact it is contrived, made-up, invented at each step. These two aspects are further stressed by the fact that Dom Gheraldo himself is obsessed with problems of style, and prone to linguistic experimentation. (pp. 120-21)

What matters is the painstaking registration of events and moments, details and impressions which form an image of Renaissance life in an aristocratic household and in the streets, bustling with people and activities, unruly youths and authoritative men, soldiers and priests.

If the story of Don Renato and Marcia (who have escaped death) continues, and if an epilogue is provided by the discovery, centuries after, of the bones of Dom Gheraldo, his Diurnal is literarily and structurally at the centre of the book, the interest of which lies in the creation of an impressionistic pseudo-historical romance and in the linguistic experiment that it makes possible.

This experiment is twofold, as has been hinted. As Rolfe explains, the hypothetical, holograph source is written in a mixture of Latin and Renaissance Italian (of which four examples are given, that is, invented by Rolfe). . . . While keeping (i.e. inventing) the parts in pure Latin, Rolfe "translates" the Italian macaronics into English macaronics, using English terminations for Latin words and reproducing the "archaic" spellings and idioms, the syntactical idiosyncrasies of the "original".

But all this, of course, is in fact purely literary pretense and linguistic invention on the part of Rolfe—a completely artificial

construction, all the more so if one keeps in mind the greater difference existing between English and Latin than between Italian and English. But here lies the strength and the fascination of his linguistic "fake"; hence the tension of total, self-sufficient invention that sustains the book and that places it among the forerunners of more radical twentieth century attempts at purely linguistic creation (from Joyce to the most recent writers of the neo-avant-garde in Europe, with the obvious distinctions to be made in terms of artistic achievement, as in the case of Joyce). It is not the mere use of archaic language, common enough with the Decadent writers, that may interest us at this point, but the attempt at creating a complete, self-sufficient, artificial and autonomous linguistic universe.

If we consider, moreover, that Dom Gheraldo, within the terms of the already described linguistic framework, is given in his journal to a display of stylistic versatility—writing in Seneca's tragic style or in Juvenal's low style, in Virgil's epic and Ausonius Magnus' descriptive style, in Catullus' idyllic or in Cicero's oratorial style—we may say that Dom Gheraldo (and Rolfe behind his shoulders) sees every episode in strictly and purely linguistic terms, reduces any given fact to the question of its verbal rendering. His—and Rolfe's—obsession is primarily a linguistic obsession, and the book itself may be seen as an attempt at creating a fictional reality out of the mere linguistic substance, or surface.

One says 'surface' because the experiment is carried out half jokingly and half in earnest. Rolfe himself speaks of comic affectation. It is, after all, the connection with Decadentism that motivates such a display of superficial brilliancy. But the Decadent interest in the Renaissance goes beyond itself, generates a linguistic obsession which is typical of later experimentalism. There is something more than the mere *pastiche,* as noted; there is the effort of breaking all barriers and creating a self-sustaining, autonomous linguistic universe. This perhaps is Rolfe's final escape from the actual world. It is in this light that one can read and interpret Rolfe's pseudo-historical fiction as anticipating, in its own peculiar way, our contemporary concerns in the novel.

There are other examples of Rolfe's interest in pseudo-historical fiction. . . . With Harry Pirie-Gordon he wrote a long pseudo-historical romance, **Hubert's Arthur,** according to the new principle, set forth in **The Desire and Pursuit of the Whole,** of writing history as it should have been, and might as well have been, but was not. Assuming that Arthur, Duke of Armorica, heir to the throne of England, historically murdered in the Tower of London in 1203, had *not* been murdered but had escaped instead, with the help of Hubert de Burgh, Rolfe leads us into a new venture in the realm of imagined, and indeed invented, history. Not only imaginatively recreated according to the romantic principle, history is *corrected* and modified. The balloon of historical, and fictional, experience has been set loose in the most drastic way, and the freedom and "latitude" of romance is here, again, verging on the absurd.

The book is, however, as heavy and as idle as **The Weird of the Wanderer;** if it represents the most radical example of mystification and manipulation on the part of Rolfe, it remains on the level of pure play, with none of the structural and linguistic achievements of the previous works. While stressing Rolfe's fidelity to a fictional method, it adds nothing to his artistic or historical significance. It is in such works as **Don Tarquinio** and **Don Renato** that we can better appreciate, nowadays, his originality and his modernity. There the Decadent matrix nourishes what will become twentieth century experimental forms;

there the outcast and the fallen angel of autobiographical fiction achieves measure and reconciliation in a purely artificial, autonomous world of fictional pretense. Rolfe's true liberation was in the realm of imaginative abstraction vitalized and held together by a linguistic tension. (pp. 121-23)

Sergio Perosa, "The Fiction of Frederick Rolfe 'Baron Corvo'," in MOSAIC: A Journal for the Comparative Study of Literature and Ideas (copyright © 1971 by the University of Manitoba; acknowledgment of previous publication is herewith made), Vol. IV, No. 3 (Spring, 1971), pp. 111-23.

CHARLES WRIGHT (poem date 1971)

[Wright is an award-winning American poet. The following poem, entitled "Homage to Baron Corvo," is based on Rolfe's years in Venice.]

Of all the poses, of all the roles,
This is the one I keep: you pass
On the canal, your pope's robes
Aflame in a secret light, the four
Oars of your gòndola white
As moth wings in the broken dark,
The quail-eyed fisher boys
Sliding the craft life a coffin out to sea;
The air grows hard; the boat's wake
Settles behind you like a wasted breath.

*   *   *

(For months, Corvo, you floated through my sleep
As I tried to track you down:
That winter you lived in a doorway;
The days and night on these back canals
You spent in a musty blanket.
Your boat both bed and refuge—
And writing always
The book, the indescribable letters . . .
Was it the vengeance only
That kept you alive, the ripe corkscrew
Twisted and deep in the bottle's throat?

One afternoon—in the late spring—I went
To San Michele, to see
The sealed drawer that holds your name,
To take you flowers, as one
Is moved to do for the dead, and found
Not even a vase to put them in.
Leaving, I spread them on the lagoon,
Ungraftable shoots of blood. There is, you said,
A collusion of things in this world. . . .)

*   *   *

And so you escape. What books there are,
Old hustler, will never exhume you,
Nor places you stayed.
Hadrian, Nicholas Crabbe, you hide
Where the dust hides now,
Your con with its last trick turned,
Stone nightmare come round again—

Fadeout: your boat, Baron, edges
Toward the horizon, a sky where toads,
Their eyes new fire,
Alone at the landings blink and blink.

(p. 14)

Charles Wright, "Homage to Baron Corvo" (originally published in The Southern Review n.s., Vol. VII, No. 3, July, 1971), in his Hard Freight (copyright © 1973 by Charles Wright; reprinted by permission of Wesleyan University Press), Wesleyan University Press, 1973, p. 14.

JOHN TYTELL (essay date 1972)

[A Belgian literary critic, poet, and essayist, Tytell interprets Rolfe's novels as a struggle in the transition from a nineteenth to a twentieth-century sensibility. Rather than ascribing to him the doctrine of art for art's sake, Tytell views Rolfe as a rejected artist whose art can only be nurtured by isolation.]

The facts of Rolfe's fascinating life . . . serve to separate him from the aesthetic, "decadent," *Yellow Book* tradition of the eighteen-nineties, even though he received his first important publication there. Rolfe's fiction is not concerned with "art" as a subject, or even with the art of living; his life seems to have been too much of a struggle and his primary interest was often in obtaining its necessities. He can be better related to the tradition of the *poète maudit* (although some might substitute the term *poète manqué*), the rejected artist cast aside and ignored by the mainstream. And Rolfe seems to belong to a particular branch of this tradition, a branch perhaps best illustrated by the early careers of such writers as De Quincey, Francis Thompson and the young George Orwell (in the "Down and Out" phase), the kind of writer who, nurtured by isolation, seeks rejection for the sake of his art. (p. 70)

In an age of realistic novels, Rolfe chose to write romances. His novels may be divided into two categories, those of "historical" and of "modern" romance. The historical romances consist of *Hubert's Arthur,* about a thirteenth-century war for succession to an English throne, and two novels, *Don Tarquino* and *Don Renato,* which deal with the lives of noblemen in sixteenth-century Italy. The modern romances are *Hadrian the Seventh,* and two novels which deal with a persona, a writer who represents Rolfe. *Nicholas Crabbe* presents the early career of this writer (whose name is identical with the title), and *The Desire and Pursuit of the Whole* continues his career in Venice. The experiences connecting these novels are profoundly autobiographical. In this sense, Rolfe anticipates the major motivation for the novel in our time. His use of his own life and personality can reveal much about the misuse of the autobiographical impulse in modern fiction. (p. 72)

Each of Rolfe's novels is dominated by one central figure, primarily a projection of the author, whom we may term the "Corvo Hero." In the historical romances, Rolfe's hero has the psychological purpose of achieving denied recognition. The historical heroes, Tarquino and Arthur, conquer directly through the manly characteristics of physical prowess and courage. The hero of the modern romances, Nicholas Crabbe, is faced with the same non-recognition, but with a significant difference. Arthur can regain his kingdom by defeating his enemies on the field of combat; Crabbe is constantly frustrated by forces with which he cannot cope, and his strategy becomes the passive course of persistence in writing. Crabbe, at the end of *The Desire and Pursuit of the Whole,* does receive the recognition that Rolfe never actually achieved. What is important, how-ever, is that the medieval fantasy becomes the counterpart of Crabbe's distinct societal antipathy. Rolfe, judging from his letters, was an impetuously active man. His action led to no advance of his interests. The result, for Rolfe, was the retreat to a medieval fantasy.

There is no psychological portrait of the heroes in the historical romances, only an externalized view of their predicaments and the manner of their triumphs. In the modern romances, how-ever, there exist a number of significant details. In *Nicholas Crabbe,* the hero has "a horror of those next to him" . . . and is possessed by an "unreasoning instinct, against anything like near relations with his fellow creatures." . . . Hadrian ex-presses a similar attitude: "His feeling for his fellow creatures was repugnance pure and simple," . . . and he writes of a "complete psychical detachment from other men," . . . after a series of personal setbacks which leave him "denuded of the power of loving anybody." (pp. 77-8)

These characteristics should not suggest that Rolfe created an early version of the alienated hero (as Joyce did with Gabriel Conroy and Dedalus); Crabbe is a better example of what might be called the lesser case of the "harassed hero," comparable to figures like Jake in Iris Murdoch's *Under the Net.* The theory that Rolfe's heroes function in his novels to compensate for the paranoia in the creator is easily documented. In each of the novels, the hero is beset by enemies, and battles against unconquerable odds. . . . (p. 78)

In the historical romances, the hero triumphs; at the end of *Nicholas Crabbe,* the hero is left in abject desolation; in *Hadrian the Seventh,* he has exerted power and is assassinated (fulfilling the fantasy implications of Rolfe's early boy-martyr poem); and at the end of *Desire and Pursuit of the Whole,* after the most prolonged difficulties, the hero publishes his books. Dur-ing the process, the Corvo Hero develops a protective shell, a device which reappears in the novels as an identification with the characteristics of the crab. The letters testify fully:

> My own characteristics are those of the crab. Inability to feel except when I'm changing my shell; inoffensiveness till I'm attacked: and then, the most violently amazing ability of nipping and pinching other people's rawest and most secret sores and Tenacity, the faculty for hold-ing on even at the expense of my claws.

The imagery of the modern romances is marked by a series of comparisons to the lives and habits of crustaceans, and this is most evident in *Nicholas Crabbe.* . . . And the situation of the crab in its natural surroundings is analogous to Rolfe's anti-social attitudes, as expressed in his fiction. The central irony of *Hadrian the Seventh* (though, perhaps, quite unintentional) is that a man who cannot feel at all for his fellow human-beings, a man who expresses the greatest disdain and contempt for them, is asked to act as their spiritual father, the guiding link from God to man. Hadrian, as George Arthur Rose, aris-tocratically exclaims that he finds most people "repulsive," because of ugliness in either person, manner, or mind. (pp. 78-80)

Rolfe's point of view can be narrowed to the objection to what he would call "modernism." In a Prefatory Note to *Hubert's Arthur* he admits that "it is our most singular anxiety to avoid incurring any taint (however faint) of Modernism." Most of what Rolfe calls modernism is associated with the development of democracy, the merger of the individual with the group, the

rise of the lower classes, and the general change in manners and mores. . . .

In *Nicholas Crabbe,* Crabbe attacks "modern mealimouthness notions" . . . and the "fear of individual singularity." (p. 80)

Nicholas Crabbe, who is writing a book called "Towards Ar-istocracy," is, like Carlyle, always conscious of the threats of democracy. Rolfe's attitude is most fully expressed in *Hadrian the Seventh.* On its first page, he quotes d'Annunzio's "Old legitimate monarchies are everywhere declining, and Demos stands ready to swallow them down its miry throat." . . . Demos, for Hadrian and for Crabbe, is represented by the newspapers. Rolfe, in *Nicholas Crabbe,* writes that most of the papers "chattered and shrieked and squeaked platitudes and shibboleths and stereotyped plates," . . . and throughout *Had-rian the Seventh* the newspapers publicize the counterattack to Hadrian's policies.

As Pope, Hadrian is especially active against socialism, which Rolfe seemed to fear as the successor in evil to democracy. In *Hadrian the Seventh,* a novel which Rolfe claimed was "de-liberately written for the many," Rolfe attempted to satirize English socialism through his description of the witless Jere-miah Sant (which seems to stand for cant), and the Socialist members of the "Liblab Fellowship." The members are a bit too simple-minded to be credible, and they are routed by Had-rian: their attempt to discredit and defame him is foiled. Rolfe's position is clear when he retires the female pawn of the bribing Sant, Mrs. Crowe, to "Baboon Street."

Hadrian the Seventh is the only novel of Rolfe's to demonstrate any social awareness, and this awareness is reactionary. Writ-ing about ten years before the First World War, Rolfe begins his novel with a series of news clippings (actually anticipating by some time a technique for which the American writer John Dos Passos became famous), articles which picture the unrest of the era and almost predict the outcome. Later in the novel, Hadrian offers an analysis of European power blocks and sug-gests a cockeyed scheme for redistribution of world power. Rolfe understands the German need for "lebensraum" as no other Englishman (and certainly no Frenchman) ever has. The novel is openly pro-German and Kaiser William bursts into the context of the novel with an impassioned speech against so-cialism.

In the historical romances, Rolfe's social position is implicit as he praises the virtues of an aristocratic world. In the modern romances, this order has been replaced. . . . In all of Rolfe, there is little sign of the social deprivation that Wells describes, or the spiritual deprivation that Lawrence was later to describe. (pp. 81-2)

[There] are certain patterns in the historical novels which bal-ance the whole picture of Rolfe's fiction, which reflect deeper aspects of his personality and vision.

The heroes in *Don Tarquino,* in *Don Renato* and in *Hubert's Arthur* are all exactly the same age, fifteen years old. (Zilda, the girl who plays boy in *Desire and Pursuit of the Whole* is sixteen, and Kemp in *Nicholas Crabbe* is over twenty; however, they only accompany the heroes of their respective novels.) Each of the historical heroes is equipped with a kind of su-perhuman strength and endurance which enables him to regain a stolen birthright; Rolfe clearly stresses the youth, the vigor and the ability to act of the hero.

In each novel, before gaining victory, the hero is in some way defiled or tortured, reminding us of Swinburne's love of flagellation, of primitive initiation rites, and the horrors of Gothic fiction. Don Tarquino is exposed before the papal court after the ordeal of an exhausting ride on horse-back. Arthur undergoes a crucifixion attempt until saved at the last minute, but not until Rolfe has included some quite gory details. Scenes of slaughter and torture and physical prowess are most evident in **Don Renato:** one scene, describing the driving of a sword into the eye of a captured infidel, is particularly graphic, . . . and in another scene Rolfe elaborately presents the details of a murder and the execution of the murderer by strangulation. . . . The historical romances are replete with a violence that is sublimated as mere suffering in the modern romances. The connection between the historical and the modern romances is explained by Rolfe's fantasy of personal assertion: the aggression evident in the historical romances offers a release for Rolfe's imagination which he could not realize as Crabbe.

There is much evidence, also, to indicate that Rolfe wrote all his novels as one book, one personal myth expressing his own quest for recognition. There are a number of links between all of the novels which serve to connect them more fully. **Hubert's Arthur,** for example, is a mnauscript which has been found among the literary remains of one Nicholas Crabbe, a "well-known but grossly misunderstood and over-rated writer . . .". . . . And it is in **Hadrian the Seventh** that an apparently inconsequential relationship between a snake and a goose—a formula which is translated as a key password in **Hubert's Arthur**—is fully explained. . . . These inter-references infiltrate the pages of all of Rolfe's novels, forming a kind of interior *roman a clef*. In **Nicholas Crabbe,** references are found to several of the characters in **Don Tarquino,** and the term "Katapleptic Phantasm," the subtitle of **Don Tarquino,** is defined. In **Don Renato,** the death of Tarquino is described, as well as the explanation of why Crabbe prefers Thackeray's *Henry Esmond* to *Vanity Fair*—because it was nearly an historical romance. The note itself is significant, since it shows Rolfe bridging the time-gap between the historical and modern romances.

In a number of such particulars the novels refract upon one another but, ultimately, they all reflect their creator. Early in **Nicholas Crabbe** Rolfe writes that Crabbe knew George Arthur Rose, who becomes Hadrian. . . . Whether he wrote of thirteenth-century England, of sixteenth-century Italy, or the England and Italy of his own day, Rolfe wrote a similar story. Rarely has a writer plunged his own paranoid vision of harassment and failure so totally into his work.

This intense illusionism, however, is not without its cost for Corvo's craft. Rolfe, enduring his pain with classical stoicism, risks sentimentality because of the unrelenting quality of his self-exposure. The writer, as T. S. Eliot proposed in "Tradition and the Individual Talent," must continually surrender himself "as he is at the moment to something which is more valuable. The progress of an artist is a continual self-sacrifice, a continual extinction of his personaltiy." The pity for which Rolfe pleads in each of his novels is a barrier to the kind of detachment Eliot proposes, the sophisticated artistic mask which our age has demanded of its writers. Of course, many of the most successful of modern writers have used their lives as subjects for fiction. The great task with the autobiographical element is to render it convincing as fiction: Lawrence, Joyce, and Hemingway find different ways to dramatize their life experiences, while a writer like Thomas Wolfe often falters in the same attempt. The difference between a writer brazenly re-

lieving his pain, therapeutically confessing his life while unable to transcend and transform it into something even more meaningful, more universal and less particular, has been clearly demonstrated to us in the comparison of *Stephen Hero* and Joyce's revision in *Portrait of an Artist*.

The nature of Rolfe's involvement with his subject is indicated by the tortured, spastic, uncontrollably eccentric style, the attempts to leap beyond the boundaries of expression because words themselves could not be sufficient for what he felt. And did the style out of order warp the ability to see, or were both style and vision the results of common pressures forcing the writer away from more direct expressions of his condition and toward wish-fulfillment and fantasy? Rolfe's fiction is the mirror of an assailed, perverted, lost soul who desperately attempts to project his torment as art. His insistent, vociferous vision is almost too explosive for development, too fiery for the dramatic dynamics of the novel. As a novelist, therefore, Rolfe is handicapped by the limitations of personality; as Corvo, his Byronic ardor presents numerous elements of fascination. (pp. 82-5)

> *John Tytell, "Frederick Rolfe and His Age: A Study in Literary Eccentricity," in* Studies in the Twentieth Century *(copyright 1972 by Stephen H. Goode), No. 10, Fall, 1972, pp. 69-89.*

G. P. JONES   (essay date 1974)

[*Jones, in an opinion diverging from the main body of criticism on Rolfe, finds the qualities of daydream and wish-fulfillment in Rolfe's novel* Hadrian the Seventh *to be underrated in their complexity, which he characterizes as "more deliberate and functional than has generally been appreciated." For a similar re-evaluation of the wish-fulfillment reading of Rolfe's fiction see Sergio Perosa's essay excerpted above.*]

It has often been said—usually in passing and with barely disguised contempt—that Frederick Rolfe's semi-autobiographical and speculative novel, **Hadrian the Seventh,** is a daydream or a wish-fulfilment fantasy, as if there were something ultimately discreditable about the fact. Even fervent admirers of the novel have on occasion felt compelled to modify their enthusiasm when faced with the charge. . . . [While] **Hadrian the Seventh** undoubtedly exhibits the unrealistic and dreamlike qualities associated with such terms as "day-dream" or "wish-fulfilment fantasy," those qualities are considerably more complex in meaning and their presence in the novel is more deliberate and functional than has generally been appreciated.

We may distinguish between three modes of dreamlike experience incorporated in the novel. The first and most obvious of these is what we may call the personal dream. The authorial *persona*, the despised and neglected George Arthur Rose, is metamorphosed by a series of near-miraculous coincidences and extraordinary circumstances into the magnificent Pope Hadrian VII. Rolfe is thereby enabled through his protagonist to establish and sustain a forum for vicarious rehabilitation and self-vindication. The second species of dreamlike experience is what may conveniently be called the public dream, which springs out of and complements the personal dream. It consists of Rolfe's providing through his revolutionary pontiff a formula for the spiritual and political regeneration of the Roman Catholic Church, a regeneration which in turn allows the Vatican to act as the initiator and co-ordinator of the author's grandiose utopian solution to the political problems of the contemporary world that have been examined in the course of the novel. The public dream is no less important than the personal dream, but it has been accorded far less critical attention than the latter, basically because Rolfe's commentators have usually been more interested in his emotions than in his ideas. The third and least obtrusive type of dreamlike experience embodied in the novel is what may be termed the artistic dream, the provision within the boundaries of the novel of a vantage point from which the whole structure is seen to be illusory and which thereby serves to cast a quality of ironic reservation over the whole work, modifying the sensationalism and speculativeness of the two substantive dream elements, the personal and the public dream.

The crudest of the dreams, the one that has been universally recognised though not always with approval, is the Walter Mittyish dream of personal aggrandisement. By creating a protagonist who resembles himself in appearance, speech, habits, sensibility, personal history and general circumstances, Rolfe vicariously samples the fruits of respect and recognition and savours the fictional exercise of the unique and awesome power of the papacy. The basic improbability of the personal dream is patent. The alienated author-hero of the work is rescued from the oblivion of his lonely garret by two prominent members of the Roman Catholic hierarchy in England, full reparation is made to him for his past sufferings at the hands of lay and clerical Roman Catholics, he is restored to the bosom of the Church, and his priestly vocation is recognised at last. And all this is merely the prelude to the elevation of George Arthur Rose, alias Frederick William Rolfe, to the Chair of Peter. In personal terms, here is the author's hyperbolical expression of what he conceives to be his potential, for if George Arthur Rose is the reflection of Rolfe's disappointing past and present, Hadrian is the projection of his untried capacity, of the future achievements that will wipe out the failures of the past. The election of Rose to the position of supreme authority within the Church is Rolfe's extravagant metaphor for the recompense merited by his past misfortunes (especially the failure of Church authorities to ratify his sense of vocation). The papal accomplishments of Hadrian are Rolfe's metaphor for what he might do in actuality if he were offered the opportunity of exercising his talents on a less elevated level of endeavour (as a simple priest, for example). Both metaphors function as the paranoiac's boastful assertion of his capabilities and his tacit appeal for help and understanding.

Fairly obviously, the personal dream is a compensatory one. Rolfe makes amends to himself for past and present disregard by placing his surrogate in a fictional position where respectful attention is granted him without its being demanded and where success is self-evident. And at the end of the novel even larger claims are made as the fictional Pope becomes a fictional martyr to the cause of international peace and co-operation. While he is at the peak of his success and courted in person by the monarchs of the world, Hadrian is assassinated by the fanatical arch-socialist, Jerry Sant. The episode not only constitutes an ambitious method of authorial ego-inflation and a dramatic means of imaginatively compensating for the aimlessness and obscurity of his private life, it virtually amounts to self-canonisation. (pp. 109-11)

The personal dream does not, however, consist solely of self-glorification, nor is it merely Rolfe's elaborate method of thumbing his nose at those who have not recognised his potential in lower walks of life. The novel is certainly compensatory and self-vindicatory, but it is also confessional. As well as using the work to proclaim what he might do if he were given the chance, Rolfe uses it as a means of explaining himself

and his dubious past, though the explanations are characteristically delivered *de haut en bas* ["from on high"]. Through his protagonist, he obsessively rehearses his past trials and tribulations and attempts to provide justification for his sometimes questionable conduct, justification that is made less humiliating by virtue of the fact that the authorial *persona* is in a position where he could, if he so desired, simply refuse to offer explanations.

The confessional dimension of the personal dream is most clearly seen in the latter part of Chapter 22 of *Hadrian*. Symbolically removing the papal ring, the author-hero steps outside his papal role in order to reveal and justify himself to the assembled curial cardinals in response to the libels published against him by a segment of the English press, journalistic attacks which correspond very closely to those directed against the author himself (under his pseudonym of Baron Crovo) in 1898 by the Aberdeen *Daily Free Press*. Like Rolfe's, Rose's name is blackened by malicious publications concerning his "Pseudonym: begging letters: debts: luxurious living: idleness: false pretences as to means and position." Unlike Rolfe, however, Rose-Hadrian has a forum and an audience for detailed refutation of the libels, not to mention a position in the world that inspires confidence in his veracity.

Though the episode is daring and powerful, it is less than totally persuasive, for it frequently becomes a little too evident that the author's self-respect has caused him to place the actions and motives of his surrogate in an unrealistically favourable light, while placing those of his detractors in the worst possible light. Here and elsewhere, Rolfe's confessionalism is a trifle specious. While his painstaking analyses of his actions, motives and emotions often bristle with intimacy and with convincing particularity of circumstance, the totality of their candour remains in doubt, the confessional process being more reminiscent of the manufacturing of plausible excuses than of the revelation of unvarnished truth. The shortcoming is characteristic of Rolfe whenever he writes about himself, and the type of special pleading that is sporadically observable in *Hadrian* is much more prevalent in his two other semi-autobiographical novels, *Nicholas Crabbe* and *The Desire and Pursuit of the Whole*. Whether calculated or not, this disingenuousness can become annoying. It is less prominent and less annoying in *Hadrian* than in the two other novels because alternative thematic focuses are provided in *Hadrian* (as they are not in *Nicholas Crabbe* and *The Desire and Pursuit of the Whole*), the compulsive energy generated by the purely personal issues being tempered and directed into more productive channels by the exigencies of the ecclesiastical and political themes, by the discipline imposed by the public dream.

The public dream is far more extensive in scope than the personal dream, but it is executed along similar lines. Like the personal dream, its starting point is literalistic, a simulation of contemporary international reality. Like the personal dream, it moves rapidly from the real world into an imaginary world, a world in which ideals may be realised and in which final solutions may be achieved, a world in which the Church can be reformed overnight and in which international tensions can be dissipated at a stroke. The exposition of ecclesiastical and political reality is admittedly sensational and the conclusions derived from it are admittedly speculative. What has not been generally appreciated, however, is that the political analysis provided by Rolfe as the foundation for his speculative flights and hortative reforms is deeply rooted in contemporary actuality, as it must be if the novel is to be anything more than a frothy entertainment, if it is to have any purchase on the real world and its problems. The real world is premised and described at the outset, and it is the shortcomings of the real world that are exposed, analysed, derided, sermonised over and finally resolved by Rolfe's semi-serious blueprint for the future roles and relations of Church and State.

The public dimension of the novel commences with Rolfe's semi-documentary commentary on the anarchical political forces and the socialist theories that he sees as threatening international peace and social stability. He provides a compelling if biased sample of the state of international affairs by presenting a selection of newspaper articles through which his protagonist is browsing. . . . Under the repressive czarist regime of turn-of-the-century Russia, riot and insurrection were endemic; and although the political symptoms on which Rolfe bases his fictional extrapolations did not at that time lead to the outright revolution that he foresees and dramatises, he anticipates the Russian revolution by some dozen years. (pp. 111-13)

While we are being persuaded by Rolfe's alarmist and reactionary interpretation of conditions in Russia (and, by extension, in the world at large) to accept the necessity of a radical solution to the situation described, we are presented with a parallel symbol of disorder in ecclesiastical terms. The Church is leaderless after the death of the Pope, and the College of Cardinals, split by factional dissension, is unable to decide on a successor. At first sight the two situations may appear to have little in common, but they are in fact simply two facets of the single problem of maintaining a firm hierarchy of authority in modern society. The key to the solution of both the ecclesiastical and political manifestations of the problem is the new factor introduced into the equation, Rolfe's outrageously unorthodox and fundamentalist Pope, whose aim is first to cleanse the Augean stables of the Church and then to use the Church as a lever to move the world. . . .

Various far-sighted institutional reforms are effected by Hadrian as Rolfe's symbols of the responsibilities of the Church in the modern world, the two major symbols being Hadrian's renunciation of the Vatican's claim to sovereignty over the old Papal States and his renunciation of institutional wealth by dispersal of the Vatican treasures. Both are imaginative measures calculated to underline the institutional hypocrisy, the distorted scale of values, and the conflict of interest between matters spiritual and matters temporal that prevented the Church in the late nineteenth century from fulfilling what Rolfe saw as its rightful role as moral guardian and spiritual mentor of the temporal world. By casting off these temporal millstones, Rolfe's fictional papacy terminates its competition with the secular powers and is thereby enabled to exercise to the full its tutorial functions in the international arena. (p. 113)

Observing the degeneracy into which the Church has allowed itself to sink by perpetuating the mistakes of the past, and observing that the impasse that has developed between Church and State is largely the result of the Vatican's political intransigence and spiritual arrogance, Rolfe proposes revolutionary reforms that will regenerate the Church, restore its self-respect, and re-establish its moral authority in the eyes of the world. (p. 114)

The other major ecclesiastical innovation introduced by Hadrian is the renunciation of institutional wealth and the auctioning of the Church's treasures, with the proceeds being devoted to financing public works and charitable foundations for the benefit of the Italian people. As an application of the spirit of Christian charity, as an imitation of apostolic poverty, and as a means of countering rampant materialism in the Church, the concept of renouncing institutional wealth and applying it to philanthropic purposes has impeccable credentials, even if it is wildly improbable as a practical measure. The massive wealth of the Church has always been a prime target of its opponents, and from within the Church Rolfe concedes that its opponents are right, that institutional wealth is irreconcilable with the values professed by the Church. Hadrian's dispersal of the Church's possessions is a modern driving of the money-lenders from the temple, an aggressive reassertion of basic principles and priorities. It is the dream of the Christian ideal by means of which the institutional actuality is criticised and deplored.

In spite of the practical improbability of the measure, its presentation is cunningly and plausibly handled, in such a way as to make it appear entirely feasible and indeed rational. Throughout the novel, it is part of Rolfe's effect to blend the mundane and the extravagant, to present revolutionary proposals in an elaborately casual manner. In this case, the plan arises plausibly enough out of the well-established ascetic nature of the protagonist; and in its implementation great care is taken by the author to reduce the scheme to the dimensions of a mundane problem of logistics by painstaking enumeration of the ways and means of disposing of such huge quantities of bullion. The treasures of the Vatican are to be divided into three categories, "the historic, the artistic, and the merely valuable," and the differing requirements of prospective purchasers are to be considered. . . . Nor are the technical and ecclesiastical problems of such a sale ignored: they are anticipated and settled in Hadrian's dialogue with the cardinals. . . . Without such details the suggestion of dispersing the Vatican treasures would indeed appear thoroughly unrealistic and impracticable; with them it becomes a distinct possibility.

The major flaw in the fictional presentation of the innovation is not any implausibility or improbability relative to the scheme itself but the fact that insufficient reasoned opposition to Hadrian's reforms and their premises is provided within the novel. There is opposition aplenty, but it is not reasoned opposition. Consequently there can be no rational dialogue between contrary opinions, no qualifications of Hadrian's projects. Ecclesiastical conservatism, as embodied particularly in the form of the fictional Secretary of State, Cardinal Ragna, is allowed no attractive counterarguments; and though conservatism is frequently as unthinking and automatic as the responses of Cardinal Ragna, not all of it is. By allowing the opposition no valid arguments, Rolfe discredits opinions contrary to his own too glibly, and the endorsement of his own ideas that is thereby achieved is forensically suspect in that alternative opinions have not been considered, displayed, and either accommodated or refuted. Like the fictional cardinals, the reader is presented with a series of *faits accomplis:* Rolfe writes as Hadrian rules— by *fiat*. (pp. 115-16)

Rolfe's opinions in the complementary sphere of secular politics are almost entirely instinctive, emotional and irrational. In contrast to his ecclesiastical progressivism, in the political realm Rolfe is a thoroughgoing reactionary, embodying all the characteristic middle-class fears of egalitarianism and "mobocracy" that flourished in England at the time. That the papacy has traditionally been philototalitarian in its political sympathies lends colour to the fictional Pope's reactionism, but it does not make it any more intellectually reputable.

To adherents of socialism touched on in the novel, Rolfe consistently attributes the crassest and most venal of motivation, as is especially evident in his portrayal of the British socialist, Jerry Sant, and in the fictional Kaiser's denunciation of German socialists. By dramatising the results of the imagined overthrow of legitimate authority in Russia and France, and by providing the reader with a totally biased examination of socialist aims in England and Germany, Rolfe would have it accepted unquestioningly that anarchy, rapine and slaughter are the inevitable results of the extension of the democratic principle. Throughout the novel, the claims of democracy are equated with the demands of the most extremist brand of Jacobinism, to such an extent that the author's reactionism is frequently reminiscent of a Tudor sermon against the sinfulness of rebellion. In one of his several Epistles, for example, Hadrian inveighs against resistance to established authority with: "A rebel was worse than the worst prince, and rebellion was worse than the worst government of the worst prince that hitherto had been." Such neo-feudalistic utterances as this are indicative of the nostalgic political oversimplification that Rolfe indulges in throughout the novel. He reduces consideration of the delicate nexus of social organisation, duties and privileges to the level of blatant sloganising in support of the autocratic principle. Similarly, socialist ideals concerning the international brotherhood of man are peremptorily dismissed by Hadrian's insistence on individual and national uniqueness, by his assertion of the benevolence and necessity of the competitive mechanisms of nationalism, and by his fostering of the recognition in the international sphere of hieratical principles of privilege and precedence. These factors shape Rolfe's Draconian solution to what he perceives as the international crisis: the division of the world into five competitive spheres of influence to be paternalistically governed by the "aristocratic" powers (England, America, Japan, Germany and Italy)—"the only nations, in which the 'facultas regendi' survived in undiminished energy."

The notion is not quite as startling as it must have seemed to contemporary readers of *Hadrian.* However much the specifics of the solution may be a reflection of the author's wishful political thinking, the general outlines do correspond fairly closely to the accelerating modern tendency for nations to coalesce into power blocs, with smaller nations becoming *de facto* protectorates of their more powerful allies. It is, indeed, a recurrent paradox of Rolfe's political theorising that while his ideological premises are generally naive and simplistic, his analysis of contemporary political phenomena and his anticipation of the consequences of current political trends are usually remarkably accurate, as is witnessed not only by the general shape of his drastic solution to the international challenge of socialism, but also by the accuracy of his predictions about the outcome of political unrest in czarist Russia, about the impending dissolution of the Austro-Hungarian Empire, and about the expansionist impulse of Imperial Germany. His speculations in these and other areas were verified by historical fact, albeit not until after his death in 1913. (pp. 116-17)

The third mode of dreamlike experience incorporated in *Hadrian,* that has been referred to earlier as the artistic dream, is the most subtle and perhaps the most important in terms of the total aesthetic effect of the work. (p. 117)

Throughout the work the reader periodically encounters passages which covertly refer him not to the autonomous fictional world of the novel, nor to the real world outside it, but to the private world of the novelist in the act of composing—not in the self-conscious act of recording as a narrative figure (a device resorted to fairly frequently in Rolfe's other novels),

but in the act of creating, of giving independent existence to his visions. The process is analogous to the not uncommon experience of a sleeper's being aware that he is dreaming in the middle of a dream; and the implications of the analogy are far from inconsiderable.

In the opening section of the novel, the predominantly literalistic "Prooimion," the reflections of the protagonist on the unnamed book he has been reading and the resolutions that arise therefrom refer directly to Rolfe's own situation and to the composition of *Hadrian* itself. George Arthur Rose reflects that the unnamed book's commercial success demonstrates that there must be a large market for "books about the Good." Therefore, he continues, "Why not do one of that sort instead of casting folk-lore and history before publishers who turn and rend you? The pity is that the Good should be so dreadfully dowdy."

Rolfe is here discussing the inspiration for *Hadrian* within the boundaries of the work itself. The "folk-lore and history" cast before ungrateful publishers correspond respectively to Rolfe's *In His Own Image,* published by John Lane in 1901, and *Chronicles of the House of Borgia,* published by Grant Richards in the same year. The book that the author resolves through his protagonist to write is *Hadrian the Seventh,* with its primary themes of the Good in political life (Aristos) and in private life (human and divine love), the Good being made somewhat less "dowdy" than usual by the exotic papal setting. In isolation this allusion to the genesis of *Hadrian* may appear cryptic and inconsequential; but when taken in conjunction with the novel's repeated allusions to dreaming, it assumes a certain importance.

The first part of the Prooimion, in which George Arthur Rose is alone save for his cat, closes with the words "he fell asleep." A typographical indication of hiatus follows, and is followed in turn by the abrupt arrival at Rose's lodgings of two prelates, Cardinal Courtleigh and Bishop Talacryn, with their dramatic offer to the spoiled priest of holy orders and of financial compensation for past injustices. This episode is the first step in the revelation of the chain of events leading to Rose's elevation to the papal throne. That everything that occurs after the protagonist's falling asleep and the indication of hiatus is to be understood as taking place in a dream is too crude a statement to characterise the delicate ambivalence of the connection between the first and second parts of the Prooimion. Nevertheless, the analogy between dreaming and the exercise of the creative faculty should be borne in mind, particularly in view of Hadrian's admonition to one of his companions to "read books, (write them too perhaps,) and dream dreams, (and certainly write those)." The injunction subtly refers the reader to the author himself in his creative dreaming and composing, thus adding a further dimension to the novel while casting over it a cloak of ironic reservation that qualifies its hyperbole. (pp. 118-19)

Similar hints of ironic detachment are scattered through the novel. After Rose has been accepted into the priesthood and monetary restitution has been made to him on behalf of the Church by Cardinal Courtleigh, his first act, writing a quixotic cheque to the prelate for donation to a charity of his choice, is provocatively described as "the act of a man awakening from a vivid dream and automatically doing what he had resolved, before falling asleep, to do. In effect, it was by way of being a pinch of a kind to himself." On one level the metaphor in an appropriate expression of the character's bewilderment and an impudent warranty of the authenticity of the fictional experience; but on another level it is quite the reverse, an expression of the writer-dreamer translating his dreams from the private terms of the imagination to the public terms of fiction and quietly mocking himself and sharing the joke with the reader as he does so. (p. 119)

The dream-vision metaphor is built up by slow accretion of suggestion rather than by explicit statement. The cumulative effect is to render it incontestable that Rolfe is deliberately creating an ironic analogy between the activities of author and protagonist on different planes.

Toward the end of the novel, as Rolfe prepares the ground for Hadrian's death, but also as the author-dreamer prepares to emerge from the creative trance, he reverts to the dream metaphor, or at least to a phenomenon closely related to it. Hadrian's period of psychic disturbance is described in terms reminiscent of, though not directly compared with, the vague inconsequence and otherness of dreaming experience. The effect of his mental state is to give him the impression that he is not quite in step with reality, that he is living in a world that is not quite synonymous with the material world. . . . The disconnectedness experienced by the protagonist is a metaphorical equivalent for the disorientation experienced by the author at the point of equilibrium between the dreaming world of imagination and the waking world of reality, as he prepares to dissolve the one and return to the other.

Significantly, Rolfe goes on specifically to link the effects of this hallucinatory state with the protagonist's writing and drowsing over his work. . . . (pp. 120-21)

[The] dream-vision device, with its culminating return to unchanged actuality, challenges the reader to consider whether the fictional theorems ought to exist outside the author's dream. Here, says the author, is the ecclesiastical and political ideal; but shouldn't it have an actual as well as fictional existence?

If this is day-dreaming, it is day-dreaming of a far higher and more purposive order than has generally been realised. The naive, compensatory order of day-dreaming doubtless enters into the case, as we have seen, but the compensatory functions of the personal dream are firmly controlled by its equally important confessional function, by the thematic demands of the ecclesiastical and political material (the public dream), and, most particularly, by the tacit reservations generated by the ironic dream-vision metaphor (the artistic dream). To dismiss the work as merely a day-dream is to ignore much of its thematic substance and to disregard the subtle controlling mechanism which the author develops in order to preserve a measure of detachment from his speculations. To dismiss the work as merely a day-dream is as myopically peremptory a judgement as to dismiss such notable examples of the dream-vision mode of expression as *The Divine Comedy* or *The Book of the Duchess* or *The Taming of the Shrew* on the same ground. Of course the elevated comparisons are ludicrously disproportionate with respect to assessment of a novel written by Frederick Rolfe, but the substance of the analogy holds nonetheless, and it should perhaps persuade us to consider whether there may not be rather more technical sophistication, more artistic responsibility, and more self-deprecating wit in *Hadrian the Seventh* than have hitherto been admitted by admirers and detractors alike. (p. 122)

> G. P. Jones, "Frederick Rolfe's Papal Dream," in MOSAIC: A Journal for the Comparative Study of Literature and Ideas (*copyright © 1974 by the University of Manitoba; acknowledgment of previous*

publication is herewith made), Vol. VII, No. 2 (Winter, 1974), pp. 109-22.

KENNETH CHURCHILL   (essay date 1980)

[*In an essay in his* Italy and English Literature 1764-1930, *from which the following excerpt is taken, Churchill sees Rolfe's interest in Venice and its artistic traditions as a desire to escape what he felt was a drab, unexciting present, and calls Rolfe's The Desire and Pursuit of the Whole "the most harrowing, and most powerfully creative, of all pictures of Venice."*]

Corvo's first Italian works were the idyllic Toto stories, which began to appear in *The Yellow Book* in 1895 and were collected as *Stories Toto Told Me* . . . and *In His Own Image*. . . . These offered a delightful new version of Italian life. Most of the characters are religious, either priests or saints in heaven, and Toto tells of their amusing little quarrels: the rivalry of the Jesuits (who always come off worse) with the other Orders, and the squabbles of the saints, which are frequently settled by the intervention of a benign, paternal figure of God. The stories are narrated in a naïf, childish manner, with abundant monosyllables, and the English occasionally retains an attractive Italian turn of phrase to give a pleasant impression of spontaneous translation. . . . The effect is altogether charming, recalling somewhat the primitive representation of religious legend in the early Italian painters, and giving a very different, and more sympathetic, view of Italian attitudes to religion than had usually been the case before. (pp. 171-72)

In the next stage of his Italian work, more colourful and less serene than the Toto period, Corvo entered Symonds' own province, the Renaissance. (p. 172)

His first Renaissance writing was the incomplete *Chronicles of The House of Borgia* . . . , abandoned and disowned by Corvo after disagreements with his publisher. Its best chapter, on *The Legend of The Borgia Venom*, displays not only an intimate knowledge of the period, but an immense fascination with the intricacies of the Renaissance search for a super-poison: the constant implication is that an age which could devote so much effort and ingenuity to such immoral and exhilarating activity offered a scope to the individual talent which made it a far more worthwhile time in which to live than later centuries had become. This feeling led to Corvo's two major attempts at recreating the atmosphere of so eminently attractive a period, in *Don Renato. An Ideal Content*, written about 1902 though not published until 1963, and *Don Tarquinio. A Kataleptic, Phantasmatic Romance*. . . . Though it had remained unpublished, and Corvo was apparently unaware of it, these books are effectively sophisticated developments of Swinburne's *Tebaldeo Tebaldei*. Like that work, their major literary debt seems to be to Browning: they are extended dramatic monologues in prose. They are supposedly translations, into a deliciously rich English style, of two sixteenth century macaronic manuscripts. . . . Corvo's constant emphasis in manufacturing these documents is on the beauty of the age—in its art, its literary style, the beauty of its women and young men, and of their clothes, and the fascination of its science, its occult arts, and of the intricacies of its religious ritual and Machiavellian statecraft. It is, of course, a violent age, but the element of danger, in the luscious day-dream that these two works constitute, only adds to its excitement: and at the very worst it is only a small price to pay for the freedom and exhilaration of living in an age where individual excellence was the supreme virtue, allowed to shine untarnished by the corrosive mediocrity which seemed to Corvo responsible for the drabness of his own day. (pp. 172-73)

Corvo went to Venice in 1908, and apparently in the following year wrote most of *The Desire and Pursuit of The Whole. A Romance of Modern Venice*. . . . The atmosphere of Venice is totally integrated into the texture of the novel. The city is the perfect setting for Crabbe's sufferings. Others might provide the contrast between the superficial glamour of cosmopolitan society and the squalor to which Crabbe retreats to hide his anguish and his hunger, but no other city offers also the potent image of his pulling away in his little boat to suffer his lonely days and nights amid the desolation of the most deserted parts of the lagoon. No image of the artist starving in his garret is as moving as that of Crabbe drifting on the lagoon, refusing to accept defeat; it is the profoundest cri de coeur of neglected genius and the most harrowing, and most powerfully creative, of all pictures of Venice. (p. 174)

> Kenneth Churchill, "Italy and the English Novel, 1870-1917," in his Italy and English Literature: 1764-1930 (© Kenneth Churchill 1980; reprinted by permission of Macmillan, London and Basingstoke), Macmillan, 1980, pp. 162-81.*

ADDITIONAL BIBLIOGRAPHY

Benkovitz, Miriam F. *Frederick Rolfe: Baron Corvo*. New York: Putnam's Sons, 1977, 332 p.

Biography. Benkovitz states: "No attempt is made here to examine [Rolfe's] literary origins or to place him among his contemporaries." Rolfe's letters, fiction, and essays are used to study the man. In addition to new material, Benkovitz also uses information from earlier Rolfe biographies by A.J.A. Symons and Donald Weeks (see Additional Bibliography below).

Glucker, John. "Metrical Patterns in Rolfe." *Antigonish Review* 1, No. 1 (Spring 1970): 46-51.

Examines the "strange, poetic style in the last few lines of each chapter" in Rolfe's *The Desire and Pursuit of the Whole*. Glucker believes this illustrates "Rolfe's real acquaintance with the classical languages, their literature, and the more technical sides of these literatures."

Jones, G. P. "Frederick Rolfe's Historical Gallimaufry." *Papers on Language and Literature* 14, No. 1 (Winter 1978): 95-108.

Discussion of Rolfe's historical romances. Jones contends that these works are neglected because, in them, "Rolfe goes out of his way to cultivate unorthodox spellings, obsolete words or forms, and archaic meaning," which are a barrier to the "uninitiated" Rolfe reader. However, Jones says of the historical romances: "Notwithstanding . . . unevenness of execution, it is still rather odd that so little attention has been paid to so substantial a body of material. . . . [It] was his historical writing that he regarded as a vocation."

Rank, Hugh. "The Reforms of *Hadrian the Seventh*." *Renaissance* XXI, No. 1 (Autumn 1978): 10-16, 40.

Discussion of novel *Hadrian the Seventh*. While Rank views the work as "a literary curiosity which has a continuing fascination because of its extended self-portrait of a paranoid personality," he believes that "Hadrian's papacy offers valuable insights into some of the transitional developments of the reform movements."

Symons, A.J.A. *The Quest for Corvo*. Rev. ed. East Lansing: Michigan State University Press, 1955, 314 p.

First full-length biography of Rolfe. The 1934 edition of this work sparked new interest in Rolfe and his works. Symons chronicles his own painstaking, obsessive search for facts among myth and legend, and his discovery of unpublished works and letters. Symons was subsequently responsible for the publication of Rolfe's *The Desire and Pursuit of the Whole, Hubert's Arthur*, and *The Songs of Meleager*. Long considered the definitive biography of Rolfe, *The Quest for Corvo* is still regarded as an invaluable resource by other critics.

Weeks, Donald. *Corvo: Saint or Madman?* New York: McGraw-Hill Book Co., 1971, 449 p.

Biographical analysis. Weeks, a collector of Rolfe's works, attempts "to see the man beyond his manuscript and printed pages." To this end, Weeks traveled to London and Venice, visiting Rolfe's former schools, homes, and acquaintances.

Woolf, Cecil. In his introduction to *The Armed Hands, and Other Stories*, by Fr. Rolfe Baron Corvo, pp. 8-12. London: Cecil & Amelia Woolf, 1974.

"[A] selection from Rolfe's uncollected stories, sketches, essays, book reviews and miscellaneous writings. . . ." Woolf sees the short stories as a mixture of truth, fantasy, and pure biography. He further examines possible reasons behind Rolfe's projection of himself into his works.

———. In his introduction to *The Venice Letters*, by Fr. Rolfe Baron Corvo, edited by Cecil Woolf, pp. 7-13. London: Cecil & Amelia Woolf, 1974.

Reprint of Rolfe's notorious letters. Woolf minimizes Rolfe's homosexual obsession for boys, a feature many critics find most fascinating about these letters written by Rolfe to Masson Fox. Instead, Woolf sees in the letters "that like most people of all sorts of sexual concerns, Rolfe wanted a body, without personal commitment, and yet also a person, a human being. . . . It is this concern for involvement that adds depth to the *Venice Letters*."

ISAAC ROSENBERG (letter date 1917)

[*In another letter to Marsh, Rosenberg discusses one of his most famous poems, "Daughters of War."*]

I think with you that poetry should be definite thought and clear expression, however subtle; I don't think there should be any vagueness at all; but a sense of something hidden and felt to be there; Now when my things fail to be clear I am sure it is because of the luckless choice of a word or the failure to introduce a word that would flash my idea plain, as it is to my own mind. I believe my Amazon poem ['**Daughters of War**'] to be my best poem. If there is any difficulty it must be in words here and there[,] the changing or elimination of which may make the poem clear. It has taken me about a year to write; for I have changed and rechanged it and thought hard over that poem and striven to get that sense of inexorableness the human (or inhuman) side of this war has. It even penetrates behind human life for the 'Amazon' who speaks in the second part of the poem is imagined to be without her lover yet, while all her sisters have theirs, the released spirits of the slain earth men; her lover yet remains to be released.

> *Isaac Rosenberg, in a letter to Edward Marsh on July 30, 1917, in his* The Collected Works of Isaac Rosenberg: Poetry, Prose, Letters, Paintings and Drawings, *edited by Ian Parsons (© The Literary Executors of Mrs. A. Wynick, 1937 and 1979; reprinted by permission of the author's Literary Estate and Chatto & Windus), Chatto and Windus, 1979, p. 260.*

F. L. LUCAS (essay date 1926)

[*Lucas was an English man of letters who is best known as the editor of John Webster's works and as a literary critic. He was also the longtime poetry critic of the* New Statesman. *Lucas wrote extensively on classical Greek literature, and his poetic ideal stressed, according to John Sparrow, "the proper appreciation of the relation between form and matter, feeling and its artistic expression, which inspired alike the poetry and the criticism of the Greeks." Noted for what another critic termed the "eighteenth-century" qualities of "bluff common sense and man-of-the-world manners" in his criticism, Lucas was antagonistic to modernist trends in poetry and criticism, a position which frequently placed him at odds with his scholarly adversary and fellow Cambridge don, F. R. Leavis. In the excerpt below, Lucas reviews Rosenberg's* Poems, *a collection edited by the poets Laurence Binyon and Gordon Bottomley.*]

If devotion sufficed, [Isaac Rosenberg] would have done great things; but the reader [of his poems] encouraged in his expectations by Mr. Laurence Binyon's introductory memoir, and by a certain quality in Rosenberg's own quoted letters, may find with disappointment in the poems themselves not much fulfilment and only a fading promise. For the earlier pieces are certainly more attractive than the later. It is true that they are full of echoes of other styles. . . . But Echo is a deceiving nymph, and 'there is imitation in the planting of cabbages,' and he was young. It would be absurd to damn such writing as 'unoriginal'; what matters is that it is charming; less remarkable things have grown and are growing to a reputable age in anthologies.

But the poems of Rosenberg's war period show a change for the worse. As he grows and comes more under contemporary influence, as he struggles harder and harder to realise his own passionate ambition and the generous hope of those who had backed him, yet feels himself crushed and numbed by army

life and the miseries of the front, his ear and his vision seem to grow blunter, his voice shriller and harsher and more strained in its effort to surmount the clangour of his day—until it snaps into sudden silence. (pp. 205-06)

The change was, no doubt, partly due to the vampire-sucking of the war, the failing vitality felt in his later letters—'all through this winter I have felt most crotchety,' 'my memory, always weak, has become worse,' 'all I do is without energy and interest.' But there were other causes, in himself, in his time. Mr. Binyon's account of his painting, as now confounding its skill in the covetousness of tangled symbolism, now sacrificing its own qualities in vain efforts after a more modern realism, applies exactly to his later verse. '**The Louse-Hunt**' is tiresome and '**The Dying Soldier**' ballad-doggerel. . . .

'**Moses**' and '**The Unicorn**,' on the other hand, are fantastic without beauty, wild without strength, obscure without depth. . . . (p. 207)

Rosenberg's idea of poetry as 'an interesting complexity of thought,' while it serves to describe some kinds of it, is a perilous guide for practice. To emulate Donne, or Fulke Greville even, by setting out to be complex is not much better than hoping to become a Beethoven by eschewing barbers. 'Poets,' said Nietzsche—in this, as in other ways, often a poet himself—'make their water muddy, that it may seem deep'; if so, the less poets they. Unfortunately Rosenberg, to take his own favourite image of the star in the puddle, became too lost in troubling the puddle, became less complex than perplexed, less subtle than incoherent. From his letters one catches the ring of the Hebrew passion of the young Disraeli shouting in the teeth of the derisive Commons: 'Ay, and though I sit down now, the time will come when you *will* hear me'; but in reading his last verse one thinks rather of the impatient despair of the painter in the story flinging his sponge at the refractory canvas. That experiment may have succeeded once—not more.

Rosenberg's work will hardly win long remembrance, but that need not mean it was wasted. How many of the legion of our modern poets are fools enough to hope to score a century for their memories? Rosenberg was at least poet enough to write to please himself, for the sake of self-utterance, without looking to poetry for her loaves and fishes. . . . Under the hedgerow last year's thrush lies mute forgotten dust; but who asks if his singing was in vain? (pp. 207-09)

> *F. L. Lucas, "Isaac Rosenberg," in* New Statesman (© *1922 The Statesman Publishing Co. Ltd.), Vol. XIX, No. 491, September 9, 1922 (and reprinted in an enlarged form in his* Authors Living & Dead, *Macmillan, 1926, pp. 205-09).*

D. W. HARDING (essay date 1935)

[*Harding collaborated with Gordon Bottomley in preparing the 1937 edition of Rosenberg's* Collected Works. *It was largely through Harding's efforts that Rosenberg's works once again became available to the public; when Harding took up Rosenberg's cause in 1934, the 1922 edition of* Poems *had been out of print for years. The article from which this excerpt was taken originally appeared in* Scrutiny, *a magazine for which Harding was, at that time, an assistant editor. Harding is generally acknowledged to be Rosenberg's most perceptive critic.*]

What most distinguishes Isaac Rosenberg from other English poets who wrote of the 1914-1918 war is the intense significance he saw in the kind of living effort that the war called out, and the way in which his technique enabled him to present both this and the suffering and the waste as inseparable aspects of life in war. Further, there is in his work, without the least touch of coldness, nevertheless a certain impersonality: he tried to feel in the war a significance for life as such, rather than seeing only its convulsion of the human life he knew.

Occasionally, it is as well to say at once, he seems to simplify his experience too much, letting the suffering be swallowed up, though at his best he knows it never can be, in glory; this happens in **'The Dead Heroes'**, and to some extent in **'Soldier'** and **'Marching'**. By themselves these poems might have implied a lack of sensitiveness; actually they were in him only one side of an effort after a more complete sensitivity. He could at least as easily have written only of loss and suffering. . . . (p. 91)

The significance which the war held for Rosenberg might have been anticipated from his dissatisfaction with the pre-war social order (especially acute, it seems, in South Africa where he was living when the war came). The poem he wrote on first hearing of the war makes evident at once his deep division of feeling. . . . (pp. 91-2)

His dissatisfaction with pre-war life had already shown itself in his work, notably in the revolt against God which appears in several passages, God being taken as someone responsible for the condition of the world and its established order. . . . (p. 92)

In **'Moses'**, . . . he was engrossed with the theme of revolt against a corrupting routine; he presents Moses at the moment of breaking free from the comfort of the usual and politic by killing the overseer. Rosenberg never fully defined his attitude to violence as distinct from strength, though there is a hint in his letters that **'The Unicorn'** might have approached this question. In **'Moses'** he accepts violence because it seems a necessary aspect of any effort to bring back the power and vigour of purpose which he felt the lack of in civilized life. . . . (pp. 92-3)

It was because of this attitude to the pre-war world that Rosenberg, hating the war, was yet unable to set against it the possibilities of ordinary civilian life, and regret them in the way, for instance, that Wilfred Owen could regret them in 'Strange Meeting'. When Rosenberg wanted to refer to an achieved culture—rather than merely human possibilities—against which to measure the work of war he had to go back to remote and idealized Jewish history, producing **'The Burning of the Temple'** and **'The Destruction of Jerusalem by the Babylonian Hordes'**. More usually he opposed both to the war and to the triviality of contemporary civilization only a belief in the possibilities of life and a hope derived from its more primitive aspects. . . . The root is the most important of the symbols which recur throughout his work, and birth, creation, and growth are his common themes.

These and related themes were to have been worked out in the unfinished play, **'The Unicorn'**. But there they would have been influenced vitally by the war, and Rosenberg's account in letters of what he intends the play to be helps to reveal the significance of the war to him. The existing fragments point to his plan having changed more than once, but the letters show something of what he aimed at. The play was to have included a kind of Sabine rape by a decaying race who had no women and yearned for continuity. . . . At the same time he wanted the play 'to symbolize the war and all the devastating forces let loose by an ambitious and unscrupulous will' (which might have been essentially the will of Moses seen in a slightly dif-

ferent light). Moreover, 'Saul and Lilith are ordinary folk into whose ordinary lives the Unicorn bursts. It is to be a play of terror—terror of hidden things and the fear of the supernatural.' It would, in fact, have been closely related to **'Daughters of War'**. . . . (pp. 93-4)

The complexity of feeling . . . which would probably have been still more evident in **'The Unicorn'**, is typical of the best of Rosenberg's war poetry. His finest passages are not concerned exclusively either with the strength called out by war or with the suffering: they spring more directly from the events and express a stage of consciousness appearing before either simple attitude has become differentiated. They express, that is, what it is tempting to call, inaccurately, a 'blending' of the two attitudes. It can be seen in [the poem **"Dead Man's Dump"**.] . . . It is noteworthy here that Rosenberg is able and content to present contrasted aspects of the one happening without having to resort to the bitterness or irony which are the easier attitudes to such a contrast. One sign and expression of his peculiar greatness consists in his being able, in spite of his sensitiveness, to do without irony. The last two lines of the . . . [fifth verse] come from a keyed-up responsiveness to the vividness of violent death in war, but the passage possesses nothing of nationalist-militarist rapture; it is 'the half used life' that passes. . . . (pp. 94-5)

Rosenberg seems to have been specially impressed by the destruction of men at the moment of a simplified greatness which they could never have reached before, their destruction by the very forces that had made human strength and endurance more vividly impressive than ever. This conception of the war he tried to express through the fiction of some intention being fulfilled in the destruction. . . . From this it was a short inevitable step to the suggestion of some vague immortality for these lives. . . . (p. 95)

'Daughters of War' develops the same group of ideas. 'Earth' gives place to the more active symbol of the Blakesque Amazonian spirits who take as lovers those who have been released from Earth. . . . The Daughters, their voices (as Rosenberg says in a letter) 'spiritual and voluptuous at the same time', are a symbolic expression of what he felt ought to be a possible plane of living. They are an embodiment of the God-ancestralled essences, but he feels now that they can be reached only through the sacrifice of men's defective humanity, that they bring about 'the severance of all human relationship and the fading away of human love'. This was an idea that he had been feeling towards in **'Girl to Soldier on Leave'**. It is only for warriors that the Daughters wait, for the simplification of living effort which Rosenberg saw in the war impressed him as a first step—a step back—towards the primitive sources of life, 'the root side of the tree of life'. Death in itself was not his concern, but only death at the moment when life was simplified and intensified; this he felt had a significance which he represents by immortality. For him it was no more than the immortality of the possibilities of life.

This immortality and the value he glimpses in the living effort of war in no way mitigate his suffering at the human pain and waste. The value of what was destroyed seemed to him to have been brought into sight only by the destruction, and he had to respond to both facts without allowing either to neutralize the other. It is this which is most impressive in Rosenberg—the complexity of experience which he was strong enough to permit himself and which his technique was fine enough to reveal. Naturally there were some aspects of the war which he was not able to compass in his response: maiming and lingering death he never treats of—he thinks only in terms of death which comes quickly enough to be regarded as a single living experience. Nevertheless the complexity he did achieve constituted a large part of his importance as a poet.

To say that Rosenberg tried to understand all that the war stood for means probably that he tried to expose the whole of himself to it. In one letter he describes as an intention what he obviously achieved: 'I will not leave a corner of my consciousness covered up, but saturate myself with the strange and extraordinary new conditions of this life. . . .' This willingness—and ability—to let himself be new-born into the new situation, not subduing his experience to his established personality, is a large part, if not the whole secret of the robustness which characterizes his best work. ('Robustness' is, as the fragment on Emerson indicates, his own word for something he felt to be an essential of great poetry.) It was due largely, no doubt, to his lack of conviction of the adequacy of civilian standards. In **'Troopship'** and **'Louse Hunting'** there is no civilian resentment at the conditions he writes of. Here as in all the war poems his suffering and discomfort are unusually *direct;* there is no secondary distress arising from the sense that these things *ought not* to be. He was given up to realizing fully what *was.* He has expressed his attitude in **'The Unicorn'**. . . . (p. 97)

It was Rosenberg's exposure of his whole personality that gave his work its quality of impersonality. Even when he imagines his brother's death he brings it into a poem which is equally concerned with the general destruction and the circumstances of life in war, and which ends with a generalization of his personal suffering. . . .

The same quality is present, most finely, in **'Break of day in the trenches'**. . . . There is [in this poem] a cool distribution of attention over the rat, the poppy and the men which gives them all their due, is considerate of all their values, and conveys in their precise definition something of the impersonal immensity of a war. For Rosenberg the war was not an incident of his life, to be seen from without, but, instead, one kind of life, as unquestionable as any life.

Without attempting a systematic survey of Rosenberg's use of language, it is perhaps useful to discuss briefly one feature of his writing which must seem important even in a first approach to his work, partly because it contributes largely to his obscurity. It is that in much of his most interesting work he was only in a very special sense 'selecting words to express ideas'.

Usually when we speak of finding words to express a thought we seem to mean that we have the thought rather close to formulation and use it to measure the adequacy of any possible phrasing that occurs to us, treating words as servants of the idea. 'Clothing a thought in language', whatever it means psychologically, seems a fair metaphorical description of much speaking and writing. Of Rosenberg's work it would be misleading. He—like many poets in some degree, one supposes—brought language to bear on the incipient thought at an earlier stage of its development. Instead of the emerging idea being racked slightly so as to fit a more familiar approximation of itself, and words found for *that,* Rosenberg let it manipulate words almost from the beginning, often without insisting on the controls of logic and intelligibility. An example of what happened occurs in a prose fragment on Emerson and a parallel phrase in a letter. In these he tries two ways of describing some quality that he feels in Emerson: at one time he calls it 'light dancing in light', at another, trying to be more explicit and limit further the possible meanings of the phrase, he writes

'a beaminess, impalpable and elusive only in a circle.' The elements of this idea are apparently 'lightness' and 'elusiveness' and also 'endlessness, continuity within itself' of some kind, and these elements he feels also to be inseparable and necessary to each other.

He would of course have worked further on this before considering it finished. Much of the labour he gave to writing—and he is known to have worked extremely hard—was devoted, as his letters show, to making these complex ideas intelligible without sacrificing their complexity. . . . It is the creation of ideas which he takes to be his task as a poet; speaking of the cause of the faults in his poems he insists . . . that it is not 'blindness or carelessness; it is the brain succumbing to the herculean attempt to enrich the world of ideas'. And he is reported to have worked constantly towards concentrating more and more *sense* into his poetry, disturbed at the thought of thinness or emptiness. But how remote this was from implying any respect for mere intellectual exercising in verse is evident not only from his poetry but also from his own description of what he aimed at: poetry 'where an interesting complexity of thought is kept in tone and right value to the dominating idea so that it is understandable and still ungraspable'. . . . (pp. 98-100)

It remains 'ungraspable'—incapable of formulation in slightly different terms—because Rosenberg allowed his words to emerge from the pressure of a very wide context of feeling and only a very general direction of thought. The result is that he seems to leave every idea partly embedded in the undifferentiated mass of related ideas from which it has emerged. One way in which this effect came about was his rapid skimming from one metaphor to another, each of which contributes something of its implications—one can't be sure how much—before the next appears. . . . The compression which Rosenberg's use of language gave him is therefore totally unlike the compression of acute conversation—such for example as some of Siegfried Sassoon's verse offers—in which a highly differentiated idea is presented through the most effective *illustration* that can be found. Rosenberg rarely or never illustrated his ideas by writing; he reached them through writing.

With this as his attitude to language it is not surprising that he should have had the habit of reworking phrases and images again and again, developing out of them meanings which were not 'the' meaning he had originally wanted to 'express' with them. Emerging, as they seem to have done, from a wide context of feeling, his more interesting images carried with them a richer or subtler meaning than Rosenberg could feel he had exhausted in one poem, and he would therefore use them again in another. This happened with 'Heights of night ringing with unseen larks', a phrase that first reports an actual incident during the war, and is then used by the Nubian in **'The Unicorn'** to contrast the mystery-exploiting femininity of his own girls with the vividness of Lilith. . . . It is this reworking of images—developing first one set of possibilities and then another—which gives one the impression of Rosenberg's having as it were modelled in language.

The idea of a sack for the soul is similarly reworked and developed. It occurs twice in **'Moses'**: first simply, 'we give you . . . skin sacks for souls', as a contemptuous description of the Hebrew slaves; then the soul sack becomes the body and the habits of ordinary life to be thrown off in Moses' spiritual development. . . . And finally the emptiness and collapsedness of the sack allows it to be used of the bodies of the dead flung on the earth. . . . (pp. 100-02)

'God-ancestralled essences' in turn reappear in **'The Unicorn'**. . . .

All this may only amount to saying that when Rosenberg got a good phrase he tried to make the most of it, though it equally suggests what an interesting process making the most of a phrase may be. Naturally, too, it need not be supposed that Rosenberg was unique or even—among poets—very unusual in treating language in this way. What is unusual, however, is his willingness to publish several uses of the same phrase or image (and there are many more instances than I have quoted), so that what may be a fairly common process is, in Rosenberg's work, available for examination. Moreover, although the process may be familiar in the writing of poetry, it is by no means usual in ordinary language, and there can be no doubt that it has special significance as a means of exploring and ordering the affective sources from which we draw our more manageable mental life. (p. 103)

> *D. W. Harding, "Aspects of the Poetry of Isaac Rosenberg," in* Scrutiny *(reprinted by permission of Cambridge University Press), Vol. III, No. 4, March, 1935 (and reprinted in his* Experience into Words: Essays on Poetry, *Chatto & Windus, 1963, pp. 91-103).*

SIEGFRIED SASSOON   (essay date 1937)

[*Sassoon was himself an important war poet, and the verses he wrote expressing the horror of war strongly influenced the poetry of Wilfred Owen. In his foreword to Rosenberg's collected works, Sassoon describes Rosenberg's poetry as both "scriptural and sculptural," and praises his rough-hewn, forceful imagery.*]

It has been considered appropriate that I should say something about the poems of Isaac Rosenberg. I can only hope that what I say, inadequate though it may be, will help to gain for him the full recognition of his genius which has hitherto been delayed. In reading and re-reading these poems [in *The Collected Works of Isaac Rosenberg*] I have been strongly impressed by their depth and integrity. I have found a sensitive and vigorous mind energetically interested in experimenting with language, and I have recognised in Rosenberg a fruitful fusion between English and Hebrew culture. Behind all his poetry there is a racial quality—biblical and prophetic. Scriptural and sculptural are the epithets I would apply to him. His experiments were a strenuous effort for impassioned expression; his imagination had a sinewy and muscular aliveness; often he saw things in terms of sculpture, but he did not carve or chisel; he *modelled* words with fierce energy and aspiration, finding ecstasy in form, dreaming in grandeurs of superb light and deep shadow; his poetic visions are mostly in sombre colours and looming sculptural masses, molten and amply wrought. Watching him working with words, I find him a poet of movement; words which express movement are often used by him and are essential to his natural utterance.

Rosenberg was not consciously a 'war poet'. But the war destroyed him, and his few but impressive **'Trench Poems'** are a central point in this book. They have the controlled directness of a man finding his true voice and achieving mastery of his material; words and images obey him, instead of leading him into over-elaboration. They are all of them fine poems, but **'Break of Day in the Trenches'** has for me a poignant and nostalgic quality which eliminates critical analysis. Sensuous frontline existence is there, hateful and repellent, unforgettable and inescapable. And beyond this poem I see the poems he might have written after the war, and the life he might have lived when life began again beyond and behind those trenches which were the limbo of all sane humanity and world-improving imagination. For the spirit of poetry looks beyond life's trenchlines. And Isaac Rosenberg was naturally empowered with something of the divine spirit which touches our human clay to sublimity of expression.

> *Siegfried Sassoon, "Foreword" (foreword © The Executors of Siegfried Sassoon, 1937; reprinted by permission of the Literary Estate of Siegfried Sassoon), in* The Collected Works of Isaac Rosenberg: Poetry, Prose, Letters and Some Drawings *by Isaac Rosenberg, edited by Gordon Bottomley & Denys Harding, Chatto and Windus, 1937 (and reprinted as* The Collected Works of Isaac Rosenberg: Poetry, Prose, Letters, Paintings and Drawings, *edited by Ian Parsons, Chatto and Windus, 1979, p. ix).*

F. R. LEAVIS   (essay date 1937)

[*Leavis is an influential contemporary English critic. His critical methodology combines close textual criticism with predominantly moral, or social-moral, principles of evaluation. Leavis views the writer as that social individual who represents the "most conscious point of the race" in his or her lifetime. More importantly, the writer is one who can effectively communicate this consciousness. Contrary to what these statements may suggest, Leavis is not specifically interested in the individual writer per se, but more concerned with the usefulness of his or her art in the scheme of civilization. The writer's role in this vision is to promote what Leavis calls "sincerity"—or, the realization of the individual's proper place in the human world. Literature which accomplishes this he calls "mature," and the writer's judgement within such a work he calls a "mature" moral judgement. From the foregoing comments it should be clear that Leavis is a critic concerned with the moral aspects of art, but a number of his contemporaries, most notably René Wellek, have questioned the existence of a moral system beneath such terms as "maturity" and "sincerity." Leavis's refusal to theorize or develop a systematic philosophy has alienated many critics and scholars from his work. Both Leavis and Irving Howe (see excerpt below) point to similarities between the works of Rosenberg and D. H. Lawrence. Leavis explains this in terms of the two writers's "radical and religious interest in life," while Howe believes that each writer experienced an apocalyptic sense of "living at a moment of historical disintegration."*]

My criticism against [*The Collected Works of Isaac Rosenberg*] is that it doesn't contain as introduction the essay that one of its editors, D. W. Harding, contributed to *Scrutiny* for March, 1935 [see excerpt above]. Such an introduction would very much have improved Rosenberg's chances of obtaining, at last, the recognition due to him, and is the more to be desired in that the volume, being exhaustive, includes a bulk of work that isn't in itself strikingly significant. Not that it's a question of vindicating a slender talent; 'genius' is the word for Rosenberg, who has all the robustness of genius. But the history of his reputation brings home to one that it is easy to be too optimistic about the chances original genius may expect of getting recognized.

To begin with he had a measure of luck. Circumstanced as he was, how easily he might have escaped all notice, and, dying an insignificant Jewish private with a few pieces of illegible scrawl in his tunic pocket, have disappeared for good (he was killed in 1918), a total loss to English poetry. But he had gained the attention of several representative figures in Georgian letters; patrons who, though the spirit of Rosenberg's work was hardly congenial to what they themselves stood for, kept in benevolent touch with him. And in 1922 the small selection of his verse made by Gordon Bottomley (it was introduced by Laurence Binyon) came out. It is disquieting now to think that that volume did not establish Rosenberg's reputation; did not, although the book was reviewed and Rosenberg became an anthology poet—one of the five hundred, and further distinguished as 'one of the war-poets.' The history is the more significant in that Mr. T. S. Eliot (it was the occasion of my noting Rosenberg's name as one to remember) mentioned him in a Poetry Bookshop Chapbook [see additional bibliography] as a poet who would have received notice if criticism had been performing its function.

But it is one thing to feel that here is something strange, original and interesting, and another to recognize its nature and significance. I recall the conviction that Mr. Eliot expressed years later regarding Marianne Moore: 'that Miss Moore's poems form part of the small body of durable poetry written in our time; of that small body of writings among what passes for poetry, in which an original sensibility and alert intelligence and deep feeling have been engaged in maintaining the life of the English language.' I think that something of that kind might have been said, and with far more appropriateness, of Isaac Rosenberg. But, though I knew Gordon Bottomley's selection and was 'interested' in Rosenberg, I cannot pretend that it had ever occurred to me to say anything like it. And I confess this with the less confusion since even Mr. Eliot, who stopped to call attention to Rosenberg, appears to have left him with the passing mention. (pp. 229-30)

[Perhaps] it is still worth while to insist on Rosenberg's astonishing force of originality. It was a force that, after the past decade's changes in poetic fashions, it is not immediately easy to appreciate. . . . His early work shows the influence of Rossetti, Swinburne, Francis Thompson, and other poets of the nineteenth century. As for contemporary influences, since he was born in 1890 it will be realized that his debt here, in respect of emancipation and stimulus, cannot have amounted to much. . . . Yet when, in 1916, Rosenberg writes . . .

> Simple *poetry*,—that is where an interesting complexity of thought is kept in tone and right value to the dominating idea so that it is understandable and still ungraspable,

he is describing the spirit of his efforts in poetic technique over the past several years.

He could not, of course, have arrived at this notion of poetry, and at the astonishing technical skill that has been so little appreciated, had he been mainly preoccupied with earning fame as a poet. There are those sentences quoted by Mr. Harding from a letter of 1916 . . . :

> I will not leave a corner of my consciousness covered up but saturate myself with the strange and extraordinary new conditions of this life, and it will all refine itself into poetry later on.

This is the voice of the young man who already before the war was expressing in poetry, not a revolutionary's or social reformer's, but a radical dissatisfaction with civilized life. His interest in life, in fact, is radical and religious in the same sense as D. H. Lawrence's. It has to be added that we must credit him, on the evidence of his best work, with an extraordinarily mature kind of detachment such as is not characteristic of Lawrence—to say this first gives the right force to the ob-

servation that of the two Rosenberg was much more an artist. (pp. 230-31)

It is fortunate that we have [Rosenberg's] letters. Without them, impressive as the poetry is, we could not have realized the extraordinary heroism lying behind it. Not that there is anything obviously or consciously 'heroic' in them. They are matter-of-fact, unexcited and businesslike. . . . The quiet detachment of [the letters] is one aspect of the intensity, the intense disinterestedness, of genius. The spelling and punctuation (rightly preserved by the editors wherever they had the original text) only serve to make the genius more apparent.

It is still, perhaps, not superfluous to insist that the 'imperfections' and obscurities of Rosenberg's poetry are not, as some even of his friendly correspondents (one reads between the lines) seem to have thought, of the same order as his faults of grammar, punctuation and spelling, or in any way analogous to them. If he was, like Blake, 'uneducated,' he was also like Blake in ways in which Blake had the advantage over most educated people; and he appears to have worked more persistently at his problems of poetic technique than Blake did. (pp. 232-33)

The 'form,' it should be plain beyond all question, is achieved, and the world of ideas enriched, at any rate in **Break of Day in the Trenches, Returning We Hear the Larks, In War, Dead Man's Dump** and **Daughters of War,** which are great poetry. In **Moses, The Amulet** and **The Unicorn** he was extending his technical experimenting in the creation of myth. To dismiss these draft-fragments, as reviewers have done, with the comment that Rosenberg hadn't got very far in the mastery of dramatic form is not intelligent. They show a richly promising ability to develop into more inclusive organizations the achievements of his verbal technique as exhibited in his best poems. . . .

[The total effect of **The Collected Works of Isaac Rosenberg**] should be, not only the recognized enrichment of the English language by a dozen pages of great poetry, but also the enrichment of tradition by a new legend. And Rosenberg belongs, not with Chatterton, but rather with Keats and Hopkins.

In short, a debt of gratitude is owing for the prolonged, tedious and devoted labours that went to the editing of this volume, the classical status of which, as a rare document of invincible human strength, courage and fineness, should not have to wait long for general recognition. (p. 234)

> *F. R. Leavis, "The Recognition of Isaac Rosenberg," in* Scrutiny, *Vol. VI, No. 2, September, 1937, pp. 229-34.*

DAVID DAICHES   (essay date 1950)

[Daiches, an English scholar and critic, has written extensively on modern English literature and is a widely recognized authority on Scottish literature. In the excerpt below, he compares Rosenberg to Dylan Thomas for his "fiercely colorful imagery," and for the similar manner in which the two poets make use of their national and religious backgrounds.]

[Rosenberg's] early poems have a rich, almost lush, vocabulary and a startling sensuous violence: his problem was to learn to control his images and subtilize his rhythms without losing his characteristic strength and liveliness. It is interesting to trace the development of this control, to note the gradual shedding of images suggesting the overgrown romanticism of a poet like Beddoes in favor of a more astringent verse. Yet he never seems to have come under the influence of Hulme or Pound or the other preachers of a spare, sinewy verse who were active in London just before and at the beginning of the First World War. He was not moving towards anything reminiscent of "Prufrock" or even the controlled ironies of Wilfred Owen's war poetry. He had begun as a painter . . . and this perhaps accounts for his fiercely colorful imagery, so different from the pallid precision of the Imagists. If he had lived he would not have become just another poet in the Eliot group, but would have developed into a poet much more like some members of the Apocalypse group who emerged in England immediately before the Second World War. One can almost see in him something of Dylan Thomas.

The parallel with Thomas (inaccurate, of course, as all such parallels are bound to be) can be drawn not only on the basis of the violence and richness in the verse of both poets, but also with respect to their use of national and religious background. Thomas uses Welsh folklore and Christian symbols together and distills a strange magic by peppering both with Freud and surrounding the whole with a profound personal emotion. Rosenberg did something similar with his Jewish background. He drew on this background readily; he is in fact one of the few English Jewish poets whose poetry quite unmistakably owes much of its quality to Biblical and other Hebrew sources; but he uses this material in an original, mythopeic manner, casting his own ironies and modernities around it until it develops an atmosphere quite different from anything to be found in Hebrew literature. His verse-play **Moses,** Biblical in theme yet so un-Biblical in mood and imagery, effectively illustrates this point: a more obvious example is his poem **"God,"** with its deliberately shocking point of view. . . . Rosenberg carried his strong, sensuous imagery into his war poetry, to produce a few fully realized poems (such as the well-known **"Break of Day in the Trenches"**) which project the individual experience with a combination of violence and precision. His rhythms are subtler now, his imagery less congested, an almost conversational idiom has come to temper the poetic surge. . . . The grotesque violence of **"Louse Hunting"** well illustrates the combination of movement with pictorial quality that is to be found in his war poems. . . . (pp. 91-2)

Yet he had not abandoned, even when at the front, the rich romanticism of his earlier work. At the time of his death he was working on **"The Unicorn,"** a verse play which he described as "a kind of 'Rape of the Sabine Women' idea." . . . This is Rosenberg's "Waste Land," but so different from Eliot's! What we possess of it are only drafts and fragments, including a lament at the prospect of extinction which sounds the "Waste Land" note quite explicitly, and in a wholly original manner, and the first tentative revision of a preliminary draft. (p. 92)

Had Rosenberg lived to develop further along the lines on which he had already moved, he might have changed the course of modern English poetry, producing side by side with the poetry of Eliot and his school a richer and more monumental kind of verse, opposing a new romantic poetry to the new metaphysical brand. (p. 93)

> *David Daiches, "Isaac Rosenberg: Poet," in* Com- *mentary (reprinted by permission; all rights re- served), Vol. 10, No. 1, July, 1950, pp. 91-3.*

FRIEDA CLARK HYMAN   (essay date 1960)

[*Hyman focuses her discussion of Rosenberg's work on his role as a Jewish poet.*]

With [Isaac Rosenberg's] own language we ask, who was he, this 'half used life,' from whom 'the swift iron burning bee drained the wild honey' of his youth? On the basis of what he left us we know he was a genuine poet; according to some, a genius. Siegfried Sassoon saw him as ". . . a fruitful fusion between English and Hebrew culture." There is no doubt he grew up in both civilizations naturally, organically. The man who could write **Daughters of War,** as pagan as Wagner's Ride of the Valkyries, could also wonder at the paradox of anti-Semitism in eight quiet lines he called **The Jew.**

Rosenberg was like a 'tree of life', an image he used in **Daughters of War.** Like the tree, he absorbed all ingredients of sun, air, soil, and alchemized their chemistry into his art. That he was aware of this transmutation, is no secret. . . . [In] a letter to a Miss Seaton . . . we are permitted an insight into the power and passion this man offered his Muse;

> I am determined that this war, with all its pow- ers for devastation, shall not master my poet- ing; I will not leave a corner of my conscious- ness covered up, but saturate myself with the strange and extraordinary conditions of this life, and it will all refine itself into poetry later on.

This single-mindedness was characteristic of the whole of his brief life. Were he not so stubborn, he might have submitted to the tyrannies of poverty and illness. He was one of eight children born into an impoverished home. His familial rela-tionships were warm to be sure, but they could not generate the pounds and shillings his needs demanded. Life, he admit-ted, in his poem **Aspiration** . . . was: "a rose within the mirrors with the fragrance of it hid." He was helped in some measure. But it was mainly his will and drive that broke the mirror, and felt "The scented warm lit petals of the rose."

The seizing upon life, bending, shaping it to man's needs and goals, despite every obstacle, is a central theme for Rosenberg. He is to state and restate it in more virile and defiant language. It is not fortuitous that he chose Moses of his play **Moses** as an exemplar of the prime shaper of destiny. For Moses was a Messiah, his Messiah. He delivered his people from slavery, and whipped them into that nation whose influence on Western civilization can be matched only by Greece. (pp. 141-42)

But [Rosenberg's] . . . **Moses,** is not the Moses of the Bible. To Trevellyan he wrote: "Moses symbolises the fierce desire for virility, and original action in contrast to slavery of the most abject kind."

Certainly Moses was revolted by slavery. But Rosenberg's **Moses** is fashioned with more English clay than Hebraic. He is virile, to be sure, but he lacks the moral force of the Biblical man. (p. 142)

Moses, this Moses, therefore, ". . . will ride the dizzy beast of the world", his road, his way. The Biblical Moses would ride it God's way. Indeed, because God commands him, (Ex-odus IV, 16) this Moses goes first to the elders to seek their cooperation. At the crossing of the Sea of Reeds, according to the Midrash, Nachshon, elder of the tribe of Judah, plunges first into the terrifying waters. But unto Rosenberg's Moses, youth, not age, responds. . . . An old Hebrew, on the other hand detests him, seeing him only a roué, who, by fornicating with Koelue, has unleashed upon them her father Abi-naoah. . . . The baby, as pure and innocent at birth as it can ever hope to be, is replaced by the monstrous Taskmaster. And what irony in the name. Abinoah: Father of Rest.

Yet the old Hebrew can hear the voice of Moses as Messiah. And here Rosenberg's intuition is right on two counts. First, because aural keenness is the earmark of Israel. In Deut. IV, 15, Israel is reminded it ''. . . saw no manner of form on the day that the Lord spoke. . . .'' It only heard. Secondly, it is difficult for age to respond to the glory of man's potential. It's blindness, or bitterness, stems from its own impatience. Age has so little time.

In *Soldiers Twentieth Century,* and *Girl to Soldier on Leave,* two of his **"Trench Poems"**, the group which comprises the best of his work, this theme of Moses is restated. In the former, Rosenberg reveals to the soldier what power he possesses, and how it should transform him. . . . In the latter, the soldier, the Titan . . . has stripped himself of all ties as Moses did of Koelue, of Pharahô, even of humanity. Indeed, the girl releases him, understanding he has ''looked through death at'' her eyes. He has ''tempted a grave too much.''

The problem of the war for Rosenberg, however, had to be seen in a different frame, a mythic frame, if he was to deal with it adequately. He does exactly this, in *Daughters of War,* the poem he considered his best. Nevertheless, this theme of the superman and his special destiny, is woven into its stanzas, as we shall see. It took him about a year to write. He strove: ''. . . to get that sense of inexorableness the human or (unhuman) side of this war has. It even penetrates behind human life, for the ''Amazon'' who speaks in the second part of the poem is imagined to be without her lover while all her sisters have theirs.

It does truly penetrate behind human life, going back ''by the root side of the tree of life''. The situation Rosenberg creates echoes the apocalyptic tone of war. The Amazons he visualizes, are women who will have only the best, the hero. (pp. 143-44)

The soldiers who come to them are ''clean of the dust of old days'' in this underground world. They forget their past within the embrace of the powerful Archangels. The end, as Rosenberg wrote, ''. . . is an attempt to imagine the severance of all human relationship and the fading away of human love.'' Heroes alone achieve such dimensions. Heroes like his new 'Titan' his 'splendid rebel,' may achieve such a reward. No trace here of the Hebrew ideal: the moral giant, who must love man in order to love God. Rather, if we listen carefully, we may hear the same challenge Moses flung as he sundered himself from Koelue. . . . (p. 144)

In *The Unicorn,* his last play, his hero is Tel, an almost supernatural creature, except for the ''warm human-like grasp of his hand''. Actually, he is a prince of a decaying race, who with his men, snatch the women of a neighboring country. Significantly, the woman Tel seizes, is named Lilith, the name of a female demon. (Indeed, in *The Amulet,* a play which experimented with the plot of *The Unicorn,* Lilith says: ''Sorceress they name me.'') Again as in *Daughters of War,* it is as though mighty men must mate with special women.

The Unicorn throbs with the pulse of the unknown. Nevertheless Rosenberg demands man live fully . . . while at the end of the play Tel cries: ''Small dazzling face I shut you in my soul''. Despite the Hebraic names of *The Unicorn;* Enoch, Saul, Lilith (taken from the Babylonian) its theme contradicts the Hebraic code. Not that the Jew, like Tel, has not considered the mysteries of man; nor stressed continuity. But the weapon Tel and his men employ to assure continuity is force; force and the terror it inspires.

Why did the theme of *The Unicorn* intrigue Rosenberg? It was never truly finished; and the sections and fragments that exist belong to several different conceptions of the play. Was it because the war marked mankind as a decaying species? (pp. 144-45)

It is not difficult to sense the horror of the trenches. It is inevitable the poet should seek an answer to this madness. If so, would this kind of 'Rape of the Sabine Women' stay the process of dissolution. Of course, without woman, there is no hope; no birth, no rebirth. . . . (p. 145)

But the reproductive power is not insurance against obliteration. Certainly we of the nuclear age have recognized this. The pollution of the ocean, the great reservoir of food, is an uncomfortable possibility. The shadow of complete extermination hangs over us like a Damoclean sword. Not that we should be amazed. The earth cannot contain so much innocent blood and remain quiescent. The debt must yet be paid.

The Unicorn is weird, terrifying, and as indefinable as its title. It has no Jewish roots. Nevertheless, Rosenberg was still searching his past for his future work. We know he intended to write a play about Judah Maccabee. To Bottomley he wrote in 1917; ''Judas as a character is more magnanimous than Moses''.

One thinks immediately of Moses praying for Israel, spurning a nation from his own seed (Exodus XXXII, 10-13); or of his answer to Joshua concerning Eldad and Medad: ''. . . art thou jealous for my sake; would that all the Lord's people were prophets, that the Lord would put His spirit upon them'' (Num. XI, 29); or of his prayer for Miriam who had libelled him: ''Heal her now O God, I beseech Thee''. (Num. XII, 13); and the conclusion of the poet is to say the least debatable. But what is a fact, is that Judah Maccabee the ideal of the knight errant for all Europe. . . . The knight errant is gallant, brave, and supposed to be of pure heart. Certainly the Arthurian knights were committed to justice. But their weapon was the sword; their deeds against tyranny always physically heroic.

It cannot be denied the Jew knows man must be redeemed from physical as well as spiritual despotism. The Exodus, his great historical beacon, reminds him of this constantly. . . . It is overemphasis that diminishes its Hebraic quality. It is Exodus without Sinai. If it were not so, if indeed physical deprivation could destroy where would Israel be today?

We shall never know how Rosenberg would have developed his Maccabeean hero. However we do know, despite the tempestuous character of *Daughters of War,* and *The Unicorn,* that he was revolted by brutality, and like most of his contemporaries, disenchanted with the war he fought.

In a *Worm Fed on the Heart of Corinth,* he says plainly, ''the incestuous worm'', the canker of corruption, shall rape England as surely as it did Helen of Troy, or the great cities of history. Never could he have written the [opening] lines of Rupert Brooke's . . . *Soldier.* . . . (pp. 145-46)

Rather he is aware of the crossroads of the whole world where in his *Dead Man's Dump,* ''friend and foeman'' are stretched out forever. It is because one of these dead cries: ''. . . as the tide of the world . . .'' breaks over his sight, that all the dead become one. This is the cosmic view of all visionaries, whether poet, scientist, or prophet. . . .

The tone of *Dead Man's Dump* is more remarkable, if we recall Wilfred Owen's description of the dead, as "... the most execrable sights on earth." For Rosenberg the dead are:

> . . . sunk too deep
> For human tenderness . . .
> Joined to the great sunk silences.

A more explicit example of the poet's vision is in *Break of Day in the Trenches*. "Droll rat", he says,

> . . . they would shoot you if they knew
> Your cosmopolitan sympathies. . . .

We are reminded instantly of Wilfred Owen's *Strange Encounter,* which brings the fashioned enemies, these "strange friends face to face". But Rosenberg's art is of a subtler kind. It is the rat who joins them; the rat is the arbiter of society. Irony is here, as it is not in *Dead Man's Dump.* But it is not bitterness.

He is surprisingly free from rancor. We must agree with Harding [see excerpt above] that "detachment" is Rosenberg's unique quality. Certainly we should expect resentment in the **"Trench Poems"**: *The Immortals* and *Louse Hunting.* The debasing and demonic features of trench life, its swarms of lice, would goad a simpler soul to malevolent language. But Rosenberg sees this, not only with a flash of humor, especially in *The Immortals,* but with wry mockery! The "supreme littleness" of the louse, is, after all, triumphant over "supreme flesh".

Yet *In War* another **"Trench Poem",** when he imagines the death of his brother, he does give way to despair. This emotion is created out of its own antithetical ingredients. The whole poem from its dull, numbed beginnings, to the vexing duty of digging a grave in the "sun's heat", builds with architectural soundness into a solid organic structure. War is brought home to the reader with feral force. . . . (p. 146)

The most telling of all his **"Trench Poems"** for me, is *Returning, We Hear the Larks.* I agree with Beth Zion Lask, that this one poem would have insured Rosenberg's fame. (pp. 146-47)

[It] opens with a knell-like quality. Sombre . . . sinister . . . the adjectives of life amid death. Man has his life, but as though it were lent to him, and the debtor waits impatiently. The mood continues into the next stanza. The poison-blasted track evokes much of his life, that was, or might have been poisoned: the humiliations of charity; the limitations of disease; the obsessive sense of frustration of a seed-packed flower in a windless land. The last line of this stanza, "on a little safe sleep", pulls us down to a kind of peace. We are almost relieved.

It is exactly at this moment he experiences what can only be called an epiphany in the Joycean meaning. This revelation cannot be captured by words. That is why we have, what borders on the inarticulate: "joy—joy—strange joy". But the poet's power asserts itself in the very next line. "Lo!" the vision is caught, suspended in time and space. "heights of night": space is limitless. Where does it begin; where can it end? "Ringing", he cries; and we hear a symphony of bells, of vibrant spires ascending. . . And then, of course, the birds, the unseen larks. The word "unseen", intensifies the mystical nature of birds. It is not only that they can sing, can soar, but they can do this behind the cloak of darkness, behind screens we cannot penetrate, but can only imagine.

His next line, "Music showering on our upturned list'ning faces", reminds us instantly of Whitman, who, we know Ro-

senberg had read. But Whitman in his "Down from the shower'd halo", draws everything about him; receives all of life as rain. Rosenberg captures this one moment. It is pure for that moment. It is the whole meaning of man's destiny for him. What it is we may try to understand. But we know it is what makes man, man, and life endurable.

Immediately reality invades. The transcendent instant is gone. "Death could drop from the dark", he says, and surely the trench with its fire, filth, lice, indecencies, are the appurtenances of death. Yet song dropped; and because of the presence of death, that song, potentially so true and beautiful, becomes: a blind man's dreams on sand where the tides rush in; or that image so meaningful to Rosenberg, a girl's streaming hair, lovely, but mysterious and dangerous.

Something of this theme is put neatly by Mallarmé in a letter to Henry Cazalis, (1865): "As far as I am concerned, the only thing a self-respecting man can do is to keep looking up at the sky as he dies of hunger". Rosenberg may or may not have known Mallarmé; but he surely knew his own history: knew the unabating persecution, the "Death" that "could drop from the dark".

I could be accused of pushing too far, to say this poem is also the story of Israel. But we have Rosenberg's own words as witnesses. In his essay, **"Romance at the Baillie Galleries"**, he discusses the work of two Jewish artists: "Yet though these causes (which made the Jew a race, and unmade him a nation) have deprived us of any exclusive atmosphere such as our literature possesses, they have given that which nothing else could have given. The travail and sorrow of centuries have given life a more poignant and intense interpretation, while the strength of the desire of ages has fashioned an ideal which colours all our expressions of existence."

He was, as we know today, wrong about the causes which unmade the Jew a nation. But he was right about the "ideal". The "poison-blasted track" was the path history provided for Israel. Indeed, according to all the logic and laws of history, Israel should have disappeared into the dust as surely as Moab, Edom, Babylon, and Assyria. But for the Jew death and song dropped together. (pp. 147-48)

The "unseen larks" renewed flesh and spirit over and over again. True, with their notes the dull beat of doom could drum, the iron-soled boots could march. But the song, the song of joy, was the more powerful. In it the Jew heard the future, the Messianic age. Which, indeed, is the song of Israel, and the secret of her survival.

This poem, is in some degree, a crystallization of his *Night and Day.* . . . [Rosenberg's] language in *Night* is lush compared to the stricter syllables of *Returning We Hear the Larks;* the thought more diffused. But the prophetic awareness of evil is present, as is man's weakness, and his despair.

In *Day* he wonders where the birds have flown. And like the prophets who swim in his blood, he sets out to find them. First in the city, among men, then, as the prophets did, away from man, to listen to the lessons of his own heart. In the fastness of nature, he learns of hope, of love, of beauty. (pp. 148-49)

The vision the larks brought to a more mature mind, is seen in these earlier poems. Though heartsick and worn in the trenches, struggling always to understand the paradox of man and God,

Rosenberg was never quite either of "The ardent gaze of God" or of the knowledge that:

> For him whose eyes do look for Him
> He leans out through the seraphim
> And His own bosom draws him to.

It is well to remember this when we come upon the terrible accusation Rosenberg made against God in the poem *God*. It has been explained as a sociological one. But no matter how explained, "Ah, this miasma of a rotting God" is a frightful blasphemy. That it is born out of agony for man, does not mitigate it. That it is the voice outside of society, lashing society's values, does not attenuate its fury. . . .

Let us trace [Rosenberg's] relationship to God through his poetry, and see to what conclusions they lead.

In *Night and Day* . . . Rosenberg acknowledges that bond between God and man, not only that expressed by Judah the Pious, but by all Hebraic tongues, from Abraham on. In *On Receiving News of the War* . . . God is impotent and bereft before man's deeds. . . . (p. 149)

In *God Made Blind* . . . God is defeated by love. But this love is "the poured rays of God Eternity". Indeed the only hoist that can raise man up to God's level is love. In *The One Lost* . . . , man is capable of hiding from God on Judgment Day, if he mingles with love's dust. Both these poems are, however, defiant; preparing us for his following phase.

The next year (1916) he rages. In *God* he is bitter, rebellious, scornful, scurrilous. In the "Trench Poems", (1916-1918), he is no longer judgmatic; he is wiser with a bittersweet wisdom. In *In War* he cries for his dead brother: "God! God! it could not be." In *Dead Man's Dump* man is God-ancestralled. Always in hope, in anger, in blasphemy, in knowledge, God exists. In this, Rosenberg is all Jew.

But the most cogent clues the poet gives us, are in his two plays, *Moses* and *The Unicorn*. . . . [The] poet who cries to God out of his despair, who sees man as God-ancestralled, gives us the unequivocal clue [in *The Unicorn*]. It is the throat, the tongue, the voice which blasphemes; never the spirit. His own testimony must satisfy or dissatisfy us, according to our predilections.

What is incontestable, is that the poet returned to his ancient roots whenever he evoked the ideal state. . . . In his "Trench Poems", the three strongest of his Hebraic poems appear: *The Burning of the Temple; The Destruction of Jerusalem by the Babylonian Hordes;* and *Through These Pale Cold Days*. (pp. 149-50)

Rosenberg was only one of a group of poets, who hating the war, did their best work during and despite its inhuman conditions. Nor is this surprising. War strips man of all but the barest physical needs, as well as of illusion. It purges, and the true metal emerges. But for the others, the war could be seen against brighter years, for Rosenberg, war was not a different life. It was but another aspect of life, to be lived fully. The contrasts were not as sharply drawn in his mind. Not only his own life gave him no bright canvass, but the history of his people added its shadows. Only his internal world was unlimited. The war, though it impinged on his external life, (his letters hint at many punishments brought on by the absentmindedness engendered by thought) could no more affect that quiddity of being, than had poverty and illness. Like all winged minds, Jewish or not, he could soar there, and did.

It is tempting to compare Rosenberg to Tchernichowsky: both sought meaning in all histories; both believed in man, in his power and spirit; both turned back to the ancient age of Jewish glory. Nevertheless, Rosenberg's dismay at anti-Semitism found release, not in anything resembling a *Baruch of Mayence*, but in eight syllogistic lines he entitled *The Jew*. . . . It may be that had he lived to see the Nazi horror, he would have found more tempestuous words. Or would he have directed them against God alone?

We shall never know. Man, especially the artist, is many-faceted. What he created once is no guarantor of his future creations. All one may say is, he was a great poet. If T. S. Eliot decries the indifference to Rosenberg by the world, as the evidence of the bad state of contemporary criticism, we must, nevertheless, be grateful with Leavis [see excerpt above], that his poetry survived at all.

Earth, to use the imagery of *Dead Man's Dump*, took him, in the strength of his "strength suspended—stopped and held." But he has shaken more than "grass," and we who read his poems, still feel his "half-used life pass" by. (pp. 150-51)

> *Frieda Clark Hyman, "The Worlds of Isaac Rosenberg," in* Judaism *(copyright © 1960 by the American Jewish Congress), Vol. 9, No. 2, Spring, 1960, pp. 141-51.*

JOSEPH COHEN   (essay date 1960)

> [*Cohen, who later wrote* Journey to the Trenches: The Life of Isaac Rosenberg *(see Additional Bibliography), in this excerpt takes issue with critics for their neglect of Rosenberg. He also disagrees with most critics in their assessment of Rosenberg's work, stating that Rosenberg was neither a Georgian, as Horace Gregory maintains (see Additional Bibliography), nor a "consciously Jewish" poet, as F. R. Leavis describes him (see excerpt above), but a romantic who evolved in his later work into a classicist.*]

Beginning with T. S. Eliot in 1920 [see additional bibliography], critics have called attention to Rosenberg and emphasized the significance of his poetry without telling us precisely why we should read it and bless his memory.

The explanation for Rosenberg's neglect is as obvious as that neglect is churlish. Practically every critic who has examined his poetry has assumed that because he died young, leaving only a small quantity of mature verse, most of it on war, that there was no unified development in his poetic thought. They credit him with some achievement but claim that his performance was uneven and static, its limits carefully marked. Within those limits Rosenberg has been classified as an "isolationist" poet, a Georgian poet, a war poet, a "consciously" Jewish poet, an "unconsciously" Jewish poet, and a romantic poet. Readers have had no consistent series of signposts to guide them, and those that have been put up all point in different directions.

Several critics have refused even to erect signposts, maintaining that Rosenberg is unclassifiable, but those who have erected the single ones have seemed dissatisfied with their directions and have hinted that there may be other yet unelucidated routes to the understanding of Rosenberg's work.

Before seeking another route, let us see which of the previously erected signposts misinform us. To begin with, Rosenberg was neither more nor less an "isolationist" poet than any other poet who has ever written a line of genuine verse. At the same time, he was not a coterie poet either. To call him a Georgian is simply to recognize that he reached his maturity in the second decade of the twentieth century. To those Georgians who knew him, he was little more than a literary freak. And as for his being a war poet, he made it clear before his death that he did not think of himself as a soldier with a poetic mission, as did both Rupert Brooke and Wilfred Owen.

Certainly Rosenberg was a Jewish poet in that he made both a "conscious" and an "unconscious" use of his religious heritage in his writing. However, he never "aspired to become a representative poet of his own nation" as Laurence Binyon maintained in his well-intentioned but superficial Introduction to Rosenberg's *Poems* published in 1922. On the contrary, there is reason to believe that Rosenberg rejected Judaism's fundamental tenet, the belief in a patriarchal deity, in favor of a pre-Hebraic matriarchal mythology. In any case, he was not orthodox and he could not have been a Jewish poet in any traditionally acceptable theological frame of reference.

We are left with one signpost, romanticism, and the hint of another one, still undisclosed. It takes only the merest glance at the poems to see that romanticism is not only a direction for the reader but is indeed Rosenberg's high road to poetry. But he had a low road too, and it is down that road that the unmarked signpost points. That one should be marked *classicism*. For it was Rosenberg's fate always to be attracted by ambivalent concepts, and any understanding of his work must be based largely on the knowledge that in the last four years of his life when he wrote the poems on which his reputation rests he was unable to choose decisively between romanticism and classicism. Much of the time he used both simultaneously.

The strong romanticism in Rosenberg's poetry developed through his love for the Romantic poets whom he imitated, particularly Shelley, Keats, Tennyson and Browning; his upbringing in an atmosphere where hope eternal fired the imagination of the East European Jews who had settled in Whitechapel; and his rebelling against the socially and religiously restricted ghetto which encompassed him. His classicism, on the other hand, came about through his constant struggle to impose order on his writing; his Hebraic fatalism that manifested itself in a pessimism that grew out of his seeing constantly his hopes thwarted by a cosmic machinery from which he could not escape; his attraction historically to his classical Jewish background, obtained from a study of the Bible; and his response to the impact of the war which made him see clearly the value of contemplating the finite world and using its materials in the conceptualization of poetic images.

Both romanticism and classicism held Rosenberg with such force that he was never able to ignore one or the other. The bulk of his poetry is romantic, but the poems composed after 1915 are essentially though not wholly classical. Since his ambivalent progress coincided with T. E. Hulme's concern with the same subjects, and since there is the possibility that Hulme's ideas were known to Rosenberg, it may prove worthwhile to examine his poetry against the background of Hulme's "Romanticism and Classicism." However, I do not wish to suggest . . . either that Hulme's bias against romanticism is justified—clearly he misjudged its role in the twentieth century—or that his classical principles are to be regarded as the norm for classicism. His definitions of classicism simply have a peculiarly direct relevancy to Rosenberg's later development, just as his observations on romanticism relate cogently to Rosenberg's earlier development.

Hulme began his now famous essay (written in 1913 but not published until after his death) with a consideration of the late eighteenth century atmosphere that nurtured romanticism. Out of it came the "religious enthusiasm" that he called "the root of all romanticism," as well as the idea that human progress would be assured once society brought about the destruction of "oppressive order" which interfered with man's drawing upon his "infinite reservoir of possibilities." Though Hulme had the French Revolution in mind, this same religio-political milieu existed in the Whitechapel of Rosenberg's youth, filled as it was with immigrant Russian Jews who had escaped the Czar's "oppressive order" and who now looked optimistically to a bright future for their children where ambition and vision and industry would spell individual success. This attitude, deeply ingrained in Rosenberg's thought when he was a youth, contributed to his seeing the world largely in romantic terms.

Unlike those who planted the seeds of this romanticism within him, Rosenberg did not, however, think of "oppressive order" simply in terms of fierce Russian Cossacks and horses in the synagogue; he saw it symbolized also in the Old Testament figure of God. This stirred his rebellious nature, which had been molded early by constant privation and frustration. It was to be expected that he would rebel, but his rebellion becomes significant when we observe that the method he employed (as we shall see . . . in considering his poem **"God Made Blind"**), was precisely the method Hulme described as natural for the romantic. Hulme wrote that the romantic will not believe in God, so he begins "to believe that man is a god." This led Hulme to define romanticism as "spilt religion." Since much of Rosenberg's rebellious poetry is poor in quality, Hulme's definition is remarkably appropriate.

"Spilt religion" finds its source in the romantic's view of man as an infinite being, and Hulme wryly observed that the romantic was always talking about the infinite. In his pre-war poetry and prose, Rosenberg talked of little else. Moreover, Hulme argued that the romantic recognizes always a "bitter contrast" between man's estimate of his capabilities and his actual attainments, which results in gloom. Rosenberg's early poetry is filled specifically with this kind of gloom. Hulme argued further that the "whole of the romantic attitude seems to crystallise in verse around metaphors of flight." These metaphors tumble over one another in Rosenberg's verses.

At one time in his youth, Rosenberg's world picture was apparently enveloped in romantic terms. He once composed an informal essay on the symbolism of a door knocker, which begins: "This is essentially an age of romance. We no longer dream but we live the dream. Romance is no more a dim world outside the ordinary world, whose inhabitants are only poets and lovers, but [it is a world] wide, tangible, and universal." At the same time, Rosenberg's theme in a number of poems was the neo-Platonic quest for "the glory of the heavens celestially in glimpses seen." . . . This theme, which Rosenberg took from Shelley and Keats, fitted in well with his view of man as an infinite being seeking celestial perfection. As Hulme observed, the infinite being achieves this perfection by becoming god himself. Rosenberg's **"God Made Blind"** illustrates fully his use of this concept. . . . (pp. 129-34)

This idea was sufficiently important to Rosenberg in 1914 that he used it as the basis for the arrangement of **"Youth,"** a pamphlet of poems published privately in 1915. The idea was outlined in a brief introduction, and **"God Made Blind"** appeared in the section where the transformation takes place.

The concluding poem in **"Youth"** Rosenberg called **"Expression."** It represents the fullest flowering of his romanticism. In a sense it is a manifesto stating vigorously the poet's faith in an imagination freed from "oppressive order." . . . (p. 134)

For all its unrestrained enthusiasm, **"Expression"** is actually Rosenberg's farewell to romanticism as the dominating force in his poetry. He would continue to hold in contempt "oppressive order" in its theological context and, indeed, seek a mythological substitute for it, but by late 1915 he was beginning to differentiate successfully between an all inclusive "oppressive order" and a more limited one which combined unity, simplicity, and clarity in matters of style and expression. He began to see clearly the values in the ancient classical restraints. He was not ready to "leave [a] place" for them, but he did refer to them as a "superb and grave / Magnificent throng." It was not long afterward that Rosenberg crossed over, hesitantly, to his low road of classicism. (p. 135)

"Daughters of War" is a good example of Rosenberg's working on two different principles. His material is primarily classical, but his treatment is both classical and romantic. The soldiers who become the Amazons' lovers are first described in a classical context: they were before their deaths "fixed and limited" . . . but once dead, their spirits romantically transcend the finite to become enamoured of the Amazons. . . . Subsequent lines revert to the classical and meet Hulme's requirements for classical verse in that they are "all dry and hard," and they have "an actually realised visual object." . . . Rosenberg moves back to the dry hardness and to the finite through employing classical fatalism to convey to the reader "that sense of inexorableness the human (or unhuman) side of [the] war has." . . . (pp. 136-37)

"Daughters of War" is one of twenty so-called "trench poems" which, with the privately published play **Moses** and the draft of another short play, **"The Unicorn,"** comprise the bulk of Rosenberg's mature poetry. With the exception of parts of **Moses,** these works are more classical than romantic. Rosenberg no longer reaches totally out of himself, inflating the microcosmic to macrocosmic proportions, seeking through rebellion to escape his destiny. In the trenches he was learning resignation. (p. 137)

The war forced on him an orderliness and a continuity his life had lacked. His earlier romantic flights of the imagination gave way to the somber consideration of the finite, his trench poems offering testimony to the changes. There was no sense of rebellion left in him. Unlike the trench poems of Sassoon where rebellious thrusts abound, or the trench poems of Owen where rebellion takes the form of repeated insistence upon the useless sacrifice of human life, Rosenberg's trench poems are simply acknowledgments of man's particularly unfortunate situation on the Western Front. Though Rosenberg never acquiesces, he does not make his verse a poetry of personal appeal. He is classically composed, resolute, disinterested, one of the impersonal many who suffer. There are numerous examples: In **"Marching"** the "iron cloud" rains "immortal darkness" on *all* "strong eyes"; . . . in **"The Troop Ship,"** Rosenberg sees himself merely as one of the "Grotesque and queerly huddled / Contortionists" seeking sleep . . . ; in **"Louse Hunting,"** he is one of the "Nudes—stark and glistening, / Yelling in lurid glee"; . . . and in **"Break of Day in the Trenches,"** he points to the individuality of the "queer, sardonic rat" in order to emphasize by contrast how man has lost his own identity in combat, returning again to his figure in **"Marching"** of the vision of death reflected in the eyes of all the soldiers. . . . Taken together, these poems aptly and precisely illustrate

Hulme's arguments that in classical verse "man is always man, and never a god," and that "man is an extraordinarily fixed and limited animal whose nature is absolutely constant."

Hulme had emphasized, moreover, that the classical poet "remembers always that [man] is mixed up with the earth." Throughout the trench poems Rosenberg consistently binds his soldiers to the earth but never in the way that Wordsworth would have argued that the common man ought to be close to the soil. **"From France"** describes the "heaped stones . . . with grass between and dead folks under"; . . . **"Break of Day in the Trenches"** speaks of the "haughty athletes . . . Sprawled in the bowels of the earth"; . . . **"In War"** is concerned with grave-digging. . . . (pp. 138-39)

Through impersonality, passivity, and the acceptance of man's finiteness, Rosenberg's poetry became a predominantly classical memorial to the war-dead rather than a romantic protest. Man's fundamental dignity and his quiet courage in the face of destruction are simply recorded in the carefully limited images of war Rosenberg presents. This approach, incidentally, was the one taken by the World War II poets. Though they were nurtured on Owen, it was Rosenberg's classical pessimism that they imitated.

This same classical pessimism is found in verses which deal with subjects other than the Western Front. In the months before his death Rosenberg returned occasionally to biblical themes. These poems are marked by their detachment and restraint, and one entitled **"The Destruction of Jerusalem by the Babylonian Hordes"** illustrates how accomplished Rosenberg was becoming in manipulating classical materials in a thoroughly classical framework. . . . (p. 139)

Accompanying this return to ancient Hebrew materials are numerous allusions from Greek and Roman literature. Where the pre-war poems never went to Greece or Rome for subject-matter, the trench poems allude to Mars, Helen, Paris, the Amazons, Circe, Zeus, and Prometheus. Furthermore, **"The Unicorn,"** Rosenberg's unfinished drama, has for its theme, as he described it, "a kind of 'Rape of the Sabine Woman' idea." . . . (p. 140)

The purpose of **"The Unicorn,"** as Rosenberg wrote to Winifred Seaton, was "to symbolize the war and all the devastating forces let loose by an ambitious and unscrupulous will." . . . (pp. 140-41)

An examination of the draft of **"The Unicorn"** suggests that, some romantic elements in it notwithstanding, it is Rosenberg's strongest bid for unity along classical lines. Using a Roman myth he superimposes on it Hebraic and Egyptian elements. His chief protagonist, Saul, is Hebrew, his antagonist, Tel, Nubian. His theological system is a combination of Hebraic and Greek fatalism; Saul seeks his security in the conventional Old Testament God, while Tel symbolizes but does not understand the compulsive, irrational force of fate in action. . . . Just before seizing Lilith, Tel comes to understand that he can avoid his fate through procreation with a human female. Addressing Lilith as he sweeps her up, he tells her that the storm has passed into his veins, and that a "Crude vast terrible hunger overpowers" him, motivating his action.

Saul accuses God for the catastrophe of Lilith's rape and abduction and his own imminent death, but nowhere in the play does Rosenberg permit him to contest God's will. Rather he bows to that will, going to his destruction without any reason to believe in infinite purpose, love, or salvation, for he sees clearly that the energy of the universe is invested and regenerated in the forces of terror and violence.

In amalgamating these primarily classical materials, in depicting for us a fixed, limited, and finite Saul, in remaining faithful to the limits he has set for himself, in producing images of terror that lead Saul to self destruction rather than to rebellion or self-pity, in giving us powerfully created, actually realized visual objects, in following the classical unities of time and space, Rosenberg gives us his most convincing demonstration of the classical approach to the composition of poetry.

Deploring Rosenberg's death in combat, we may observe that it was particularly unfortunate that he was cut off in the midst of putting **"The Unicorn"** into final shape. What he would have done with the approach it emphasizes had he lived, however, remains one of those uselessly intriguing imponderables that forever surround the poet who dies young and suddenly. But what he did produce along classical lines is sufficient, I believe, for us to resolve the problem of his classification as a poet. By birth and by faith he was a Jew, by chronological and historical reckoning he was a Georgian and a soldier who wrote verse; but most of all, he was a poor romantic whom circumstance was transforming into a remarkably good classically inclined poet at the same that it was speeding him to his death. (pp. 141-42)

> Joseph Cohen, "Isaac Rosenberg: From Romantic to Classic," in TSE: Tulane Studies in English (copyright © 1960 by Tulane University), Vol. X, 1960, pp. 129-42.

DENNIS SILK (essay date 1965)

[*Silk discusses Rosenberg's preoccupation in the later poetry with the themes of power and energy. Silk states that Rosenberg depicted misused energy leading either to chaos or to destruction, with new life as the end result. In the* Trench Poems *Rosenberg related this idea of energy unleashed to both the war itself and to the feminine principle in nature.*]

In the dramatic fragment which gives its title to [Rosenberg's pamphlet **"Moses"**], the extraordinary movement of the verse is based on two opposing principles. In some passages, Rosenberg's verse acquires a stone or monumental quality, though softened by his subtle rhythm. This sense of the ponderable quality of things, of their weight, their resistance, their cutting power, is among contemporary poets to be found only in Robinson Jeffers, but in Jeffers it is too often combined with an obsessive interest in unconscious matter, or matter repudiating consciousness of any kind, any commerce with thought, any volition. With Rosenberg things are moving always to some end; there is a sense of energy, propulsion, destination. The opposing rhythmical principle is one of sharp and emphatic movement. Moses' first soliloquy contains the following verbs: *torn, broken, prick, crack, boil, grip, break, drive, catch.* Rosenberg's prescription for a drawing characterizes this rhythm. "You look at a drawing. Can I read it? Is it clear, concise, definite? It cannot be too harsh for me. The line must cut into my consciousness, the waves of life must be disturbed, sharp and unhesitating. It is nature's consent, her agreement that what we take from her we keep."

The theme of **"Moses"** is the proper use of the will and imagination, when expressed in action. The fusion of these is Power, Power to break through and down, to create a new life, to destroy the old. Moses had been trapped by an imitation marvel, the pleasures of sensuality. Now he has grown beyond it;

he wants instead "the huge kiss of power." His genius will utilize the trapped energies of the Israelite bondmen, "the mauled, sweaty horde" (surely there is a reference here to contemporary Anglo-Jewry, lost either in commercial brutality or pointless over-sensitivity). Rosenberg's Moses is a very free variation on the theme of the hero of *Exodus*—he is sick of priests, of forms, of the miasma of a dying god, yet the Biblical Moses is a great inventor and codifier of priestly forms. He is superb, with nothing of the Biblical Moses' meekness. His power will substitute a new consciousness for the old inertia, but what this consciousness will contemplate is not defined. Only the magnificence of the expectation is there.

Moses speaks a new fierce language. The occasional residual archaicism, oddly embedded there, suggests a pre-Raphaelite caught between swing-doors by a Vorticist, and horribly pummelled. The syntax has been clarified by its relation to the central concept of Power. Rosenberg's earlier obscurity had been caused largely by the fact that more than most poets, even in a period riddled by doctrines of the image as the basic poetic unit, he thought in terms of the image. This cast of thought must have been encouraged by his working habits as a painter. Laurence Binyon describes an early canvas which "was saturated with symbolism and required a good deal of explanation. . . . [Though] the whole work had grown impossibly complex with its convolutions of symbolic meaning." Now overmuch imagery, unless held down by a governing impulse, leads to a slush of sensation for its own sake, and to a bombardment of the governing impulse by the accidents of life. This is what occurs in a number of Rosenberg's earlier poems, particularly in the middle period. The governing impulse behind **"Moses"** is Rosenberg's grasp, at a level beyond the rational or the emotional, of the nature of Power. This governing impulse gave him control of his images, and taught him how to use the normally short-winded Imagist method for longer works. What Rosenberg did is in direct contrast to what happens in Ezra Pound's "Cantos," with their deification of the image at the expense of the intellect, and their consequent passivity in the face of experience.

Rosenberg is nowhere more Jewish, or rather Hebraic, than in the active and dynamic quality of his thinking. In fact, his essentially Hebraic mind is expressed more in how he thought, and the expression it took, than in what he thought. Thorlief Boman, in his comparison of Greek and Hebrew thinking, has several remarks very pertinent to Rosenberg, who habitually, because of his Jewish endowment, sought out possibilities in English that exist more fully in Hebrew. Boman writes: "If Israelite thinking is to be characterized, it is obvious first to call it dynamic, vigorous, passionate, and sometimes explosive in kind: correspondingly, Greek thinking is static, peaceful, moderate and harmonious in kind." Again: "In any case, Hebrew, a language exceptionally unusual in our experience and to our manner of thinking, betrays in many respects the idiosyncrasy of the Israelite psyche. The verbs, especially, whose basic meaning always expresses a movement or an activity, reveal the dynamic activity of the Hebrews' thinking." (pp. 462-64)

Rosenberg took pleasure in almost any display of energy, in a wild louse-hunt behind the lines in France, in marching soldiers, in a man straining to lift a cart-wheel deep in mud. Misuse of it might unleash chaos, as in his poem on the destruction of the Lusitania, or it might breed the horrors of trench-warfare. The risk seemed to him worthwhile, when balanced against the chances of new life (although there is in him a poet's hatred of chaos). He constantly protests against the miseries of army life, and maintains that misery drove him to enlist, but he seems at least half-consciously to have chosen military life in order to follow the unleashed energies to their source. (p. 464)

This preoccupation with Power explains why, together with the more immediate poems of trench life, he could write **"Moses,"** **"Daughters Of War,"** and the **"Unicorn"** fragments. None of them seems so immediately relevant to the conditions of life in France as the poems of Owen and Sassoon, or some of his own Trench poems. Yet they are engaged, at the deepest level, with war and the energies generating it.

In **"Moses,"** the man who is the vehicle of Power has to go beyond what Blake calls the "shadowy female." A year later, Rosenberg, with an intensified knowledge of what appears to be a visionary experience never once directly alluded to outside his poetry, thought differently. In his greatest poem, **"Dead Man's Dump,"** and in **"The Daughters Of War,"** his own favorite poem, the energies generating chaos or a new life are traced to their source in a supernatural female will. This will, heroic and demanding, spiritual and voluptuous, destroys to quicken.

In **"Dead Man's Dump,"** a wire-laying party passes with its limber over the bodies of the dead in battle. A grimly physical description alternates with a religious invocation of the supernatural female will. (pp. 464-65)

The casual reader who has not penetrated to the unity underlying Rosenberg's last work may interpret the [beginning] stanza as a conventional apostrophization of Mother Earth. This interpretation becomes difficult with the more explicit stanza commencing "Maniac Earth!" which for some reason was excluded from the 1922 Binyon edition but silently inserted in the 1937 Bottomley and Harding edition. [In a footnote, Silk explains that "**Dead Man's Dump**' is generally printed in anthologies without this crucial stanza."] When **"Dead Man's Dump"** is related, as it must be, to the wild **"Daughters of War,"** such an interpretation isn't possible.

This poem is the other side of the legend in *Genesis* of the Sons of God who saw the daughters of men that they were fair. A race of supernatural Amazons need for their fulfillment "the sons of valour," "the earth men" who will be joined to them by death. War then is the instrument for this fusion of mortal and immortal. The Amazons compete with the mortal lovers of these men. (pp. 465-66)

One can work out the approximate date for this poem from Rosenberg's letters to Edward Marsh; he was working on **"Dead Man's Dump"** and **"Daughters of War"** at roughly the same time. In **"Dead Man's Dump"** the dark and negative aspect of the Amazonian will is emphasized. The title itself is savage and derisive, the dead are emptied out, diminished, whether they go back into, or sexually enter, the earth, or lie abandoned on its surface. In **"Daughters Of War"** there is more of creative terror, the sense of a difficult enlargement of men's faculties. Earth, in **"Dead Man's Dump,"** waits morosely for her prisoners: the Amazons wait "in sleepless passion for the sons of valour." Two worlds that need one another, must meet.

Rosenberg writes about **"Daughters Of War"** in a letter to Edward Marsh: "The end is an attempt to imagine the severance of all human relationship, and the fading away of human life." Such a severance of all human relationship occurs at the end of **"Dead Man's Dump,"** with its great and terrible de-scription of the man who dies at the moment the wiring party reaches him.

It occurs in **"Girl to Soldier on Leave."** Here the girl addresses her lover, who is a kind of Titan enlarged by his sufferings and released from servitude to an ignoble civilization. The girl is losing in her competition with death, and behind death stand the Amazons. She figures in **"Daughters Of War,"** she is one of the mortal women who lose their earth-men to this fierce supernatural will. Her Titan lover will soon be dead, when the last gyve of heroic life is loosened, and he is fetched home by his Amazonian lover.

Rosenberg's final conception of this female supernatural will follows a series of poems written over a number of years, in which, on the whole, he is kinder to Christ than to Jehovah, but kind finally only to the Daughters of War. Rosenberg's first thought, in thinking of God, usually equated with Jehovah, is how to trick Him. In **"Spiritual Isolation,"** God flees from him as from a leper. In **"Invisible Ancient Enemy of Mine,"** Rosenberg would even amass all of the world's pain, thus cheating God by leaving none for life. In **"God Made Blind"** we cheat God by keeping Him ignorant of our amorous joy. Then, when our joy has become too evident to conceal, we can cheat Him with it, for what can God do when we have grown to be a part of love, which is itself God? (Here Rosenberg charmingly contradicts himself, for in the earlier part of the poem God is jealous of our love, but to trick Him at the end He has to be made into an embodiment of it.) In **"The One Lost,"** a lover mingles his dust with that of the beloved, so that Jehovah at Judgment Day can't find it. In the only considerable poem of the series, the very beautiful **"God,"** He is just a cowardly bully Whom one must hit back at. . . . Finally, in **"Moses,"** the miasma of a dying god is to be removed, to make way for a new consciousness. The pain inflicted by God is the work of a spiteful bully: inflicted by a Goddess, it becomes necessary suffering.

Just as an earlier series of poems about God culminates in the explosion of **"Moses,"** in the same way a series of earlier poems preceding and leading directly to **"Dead Man's Dump"** and **"Daughters Of War"** are tentative attempts to cope with the visionary experience of the two later poems.

This experience had best be related to what is known of Rosenberg's life, or can be deduced from his poetry. In Maurice de Sausmarez' note on Rosenberg's drawings and paintings, he refers to his "frailty and sensitiveness at this time [*circa* 1911] . . . the taunting he suffered at the hands of a colleague Guevara until Kramer, who had been learning to box, entered the lists as his champion." De Sausmarez recalls how "his literary ambitions, his continual anxiety about making a living and his natural seriousness set him always somewhat apart." This reinforces the impression made by the poems of a lonely person leading a hard ascetic life. It is difficult to believe that Rosenberg's early love-poems, with their impossibly idealized conception of a woman's nature, were written for a real person. A later cluster of poems, which includes **"A Warm Thought Flickers,"** **"First Fruit,"** **"I have lived in the underworld too long,"** and **"Auguries,"** suggests a relationship entered into, potentially liberating, and turned away from. I believe that Rosenberg's straitened conditions, his ambiguous status, his natural taciturnity, made it difficult for him fully to reveal himself to a woman. The pressure built up by his love-longing probably precipitated the visionary experience at the back of **"Auguries,"** **"The Female God,"** **"The Poet (III),"** **"At Night,"** **"In a concentrated thought a sudden noise startles,"** and possibly several other poems difficult to pin down because of obscurities of syntax. They lead to the last poems and dramatic fragments, in which the earlier intuitive knowledge is confirmed by later battle experience.

In "At Night," supernatural horsemen, amorous, violent and secretive, sexually assault a sleeper's world. (This poem has obvious connections both with "Daughters Of War" and the "Unicorn" fragments.) In the fragment "In a concentrated thought," the sky itself vibrates with sensuality, "Helpless, obscene and cruel." In "The Poet," at a moment of silence, the street dies to "an essence, a love spirit." In "The Female God," there is an appalled submission to the erotic supernatural will underlying the other poems.

The dividing line between visionary experience of this sort and sexual repression is difficult to draw. It is easy to dismiss as a dishonest deferment of pleasure, or as overreaching symbolism. For me, finally, Rosenberg's experience and his attempt to shape it go beyond personal unhappiness or poetic symbolism.

Rosenberg uncovers in these poems the workings of a supernatural Amazonian will, in need of, and actively seeking out, human lovers transfigured by death in war. In the last year of his life, this will, as represented in his late dramatic fragments, becomes more humanized and in part transformed, so that it is difficult to distinguish in his conception between the superhuman intervening in human life, and human necessity raised to a superhuman pitch.

Between 1917 and his death he wrote three related fragments, "The Amulet," and "The Unicorn" (in two separate versions). They are baffling in their incompleteness, often contradictory, but contain, among a good deal he would certainly have revised, some of his best work. A systematic account of these fragments is impossible, but certain ideas do emerge which are obviously related to the Amazonian cluster, and develop or depart from it. All of them have a vaguely Hebraic or Semitic background, with characters given Hebrew names or roots—Lilith, Saul, Tel, Enoch, Dora—all of them are studies in barrenness.

In "The Amulet," the protagonists are Lilith and a giant Nubian, who goes back ultimately, maybe, to the naked African in "Moses." They are ambiguous figures. Lilith is at once Eve's predecessor, Lilith Queen of Devils reviled by men, and a desperate wife deprived of her husband Saul's love. I don't believe this ambiguity was intended by Rosenberg. Rather, he attempted to humanize the Amazonian figure of the earlier poems, but with only partial success. The characterization of the Nubian, to whom Lilith bares her heart, is equally ambiguous. He is a kind of miracle-worker, possessing Golden Age wisdom, the gift of happiness, spices to make the brain run wild, bewitching conversation, and a jade amulet to restore lost love. Rosenberg's directions run: "He is an immense man with squat, mule-skinned features, his jet-black curled beard, crisp hair, glistening nude limbs, appear to her like some heathen idol of ancient stories." Yet Lilith wonders whether he is "Law's spirit wandering to us / Through nature's anarchy." Perhaps, even, he had met Moses. And the Nubian is sexually unawoken. Aroused in a shattering way by Lilith, apparently for the first time his glacial coldness is troubled. The lawmaker and the coldness are incompatible with the earlier miracle-worker, with his spices, his amulet to restore lost love, his glistening nudeness. I suggest that Rosenberg was wavering between his conception of Moses as a man going beyond sex-

uality, and his older knowledge, now intensified by battle, of the Daughters of War. The Nubian's soliloquy at the end, when he discovers his passion for Lilith, suggests in its rushing but jagged rhythm a soliloquy of Moses. But Moses turned beyond love, while the Nubian is reaching out for it. A strange reversal.

In the first of the two "Unicorn" fragments, Saul and Lilith appear again, but in a new setting. Saul has been describing to a bookseller his encounter with a unicorn. . . . Whereupon the unicorn rushes by, again terrifying him. It is, at one level of interpretation, the symbol of Saul's barren love for Lilith, of the unused and dammed-up love he had never, because of his taciturn cold ways, sufficiently revealed. . . . At another level it carries out Rosenberg's intention, as defined in a letter to Edward Marsh: "Saul and Lilith are ordinary folk into whose ordinary lives the Unicorn bursts. It is to be a play of terror, terror of hidden things and the fear of the supernatural." The unicorn gone, Saul hurries home to Lilith, afraid he may die before revealing his love. The first "Unicorn" fragment ends at this point.

In the second, imperative sexual needs are raised to a superhuman pitch. The protagonists are again Saul, Lilith and the Nubian. Saul is in a woody place in a storm, demoralized, his wagon half-sunk in a quagmire. He has been cowed by his glimpse of a unicorn, a girl bound to its back, and following it a black naked host, the army of a decaying race, enacting a kind of Rape of the Sabines on his people. Almost wiped out for lack of women, they have been forced to breed with animals. Saul is quite lost when Tel—the Nubian—emerges from the storm, helps him lift the wheels from the quagmire, and drives him home to Lilith. On the way, Saul speculates about the nature of Tel, who, unknown to him, is the prince of this race. (pp. 466-70)

Tel has already caught a glimpse of Lilith, and turned away, a man who has followed barren ways too long. He enters the house with Saul, and there declares his nature, and that of his people, to Lilith. . . . The curious thing is that though Tel is directing this Rape of the Sabines, his attitude to Lilith is one of terror; he might be lost in appalled contemplation of the Female God. (p. 471)

These dramatic fragments, with their study of barrenness, their fear of extinction, can obviously be related to Rosenberg's primary experience as an isolated person dangling between two societies, and to his later war-experiences. But the myth of Tel and his decaying race, with the urgency of their love in the face of extinction, suggests a communal experience transcending one brilliant man's inevitable rootlessness. It may be that, living in a community of men sharing the same hard knowledge of a wasteful isolating war and who, no doubt, after early battle-trials accepted him as one of themselves, Rosenberg came into the power that informs his later work. His invocation of England, as in certain of the Trench poems, has more the feeling of England conceived as a great living entity than is to be found in the work of any other poet of his generation. He spoke for a community.

Rosenberg's position, as a greatly endowed writer with a Jewish background, the son of Tolstoyans and pacifists seeking out battle-trials, resembles that of the amazing Russian-Jewish writer, Isaac Babel, in the Red Cavalry. Babel had to endure the anomaly of being a Jew among Cossacks, to bear the strain of two disciplines, two terribly disparate modes of thought and feeling, to learn how to kill. He made his art out of his burden, but sometimes the joints of his imagination almost crack under the strain. In Rosenberg the particular Jewish background and the more general English and war-experience reinforce one another, and this without self-conscious eclecticism.

The vaguely Hebraic background, already referred to, of the dramatic fragments, is made more explicit in a group of three poems on Jewish themes, written in the trenches, and exploring the same themes of barrenness and extinction.

In **"The Burning Of The Temple"** Rosenberg invokes the wrath of Solomon. This is no exercise in Biblical nostalgia: it is Solomon's wrath that is invoked, not his wisdom, in three curt stanzas. . . . [There] is an implicit scorn—identical with that of Moses for Israel in Egypt—of the inertia permitting the Temple's destruction. **"The Destruction of Jerusalem By The Babylonian Hordes"** is a variation on the same theme, while **"Through These Pale Gold Days"** resumes, in contemporary terms, the theme of **"Moses"**: how to touch the rude heart of the mauled, sweaty horde. These Hebrew poems, of the same period as his Trench poems, testify to the noble solidity of Rosenberg's vision. It was possible for him to live at the center of several conflicting faiths, to penetrate to the heart of competing mythologies. First there is creative energy, that Power to remake the world, encountered in **"Moses"** and traced to its Amazonian source in **"Daughters Of War"** and **"Dead Man's Dump."** Against this there is inertia, as in **"The Burning of the Temple"** or the Israelite bondmen of **"Moses,"** and Power leading to extinction or chaos when left uncontrolled by a shaping intelligence, as in **"The Lusitania"** and the **"Unicorn"** fragments. (pp. 471-72)

An essay on Rosenberg ought not to end without acknowledging the imperfect nature of most of his work. During his great creative period, from late 1915 to April 1918, he was immersed in the trench warfare which transformed his poetry without allowing him the leisure finally to unify it. Its conflicting characteristics, of fragmentariness and cragginess, repel the lazy-minded. Rosenberg has a capacity to startle and disappoint at once, an awkward combination of delicacy and clumsiness, the relationship to language of a great poet combined with an archaicism of language never fully discarded. Language for him was a form of latent energy, not to be used for the mere passive recording of experience, but rather as an instrument in its exploration and control. Once he peeled off the top layer and penetrated to the deepest level, language became activated energy at the service of the imagination and the will. By a paradox, his penetration to this level has been in part concealed by blunders any smooth amateur could avoid. The residual dead diction is due in the main to Rosenberg's early death; he hadn't the time to organize his discoveries. Another cause is probably his friendship with poets of an older generation, honorable craftsmen who admired his work without understanding his aims.

It would be tragic if these faults permanently concealed Rosenberg's true force. His was a strong nature, with an always active will to dominate experience and extract from it a rigorous discipline. He disliked Turgenev and thought him "immoral" because of the impression he gave of the poverty of life. . . . It is impossible to consider him the victim of his own background or of a war which, though it destroyed him, enlarged his understanding. He had worked on himself, till he reached the point where English poetry was fit for heroes. He might have given a decadent England standards to judge itself by, and led a generation between two wars. As it is, he emerges as a lonely eminence. (pp. 473-74)

Dennis Silk, "Isaac Rosenberg (1890-1918)," in Judaism *(copyright © 1965 by the American Jewish Congress), Vol. 14, No. 4, Fall, 1965, pp. 462-74.*

BERNARD BERGONZI   (essay date 1965)

[*An English novelist, scholar, and essayist, Bergonzi has written extensively on the works of H. G. Wells, T. S. Eliot, and other major figures in twentieth-century literature. In the excerpt below, Bergonzi states his belief that Rosenberg's only peer among the war poets was Wilfred Owen. While he agrees with D. W. Harding (see excerpt above) in his assessment of the classical qualities manifested in Rosenberg's later verse, he disagrees with Harding's statement that the obscurity of Rosenberg's early work is the result of exploration and experiment. He states that the earlier work "is marred by a quality that could be called groping as much as exploration."*]

Rosenberg was distinguished from the other war poets, first, by his Jewish origins, and then by his urban and working-class background, which meant that he had no English pastoral nostalgia to set against front-line experience. And since he went through the war as a private he saw that experience in a different perspective from the junior officer. But above all, Rosenberg is distinguished by the nature of his poetic talent. Most of his contemporaries had been formed in the Georgian mould, and had to adapt their basically conventional verse forms to sustain a weight of new experience: one sees the process very clearly in Sassoon; but Rosenberg was from the beginning an experimenter, or perhaps an explorer, in his use of poetic language. His pre-war poems are numerous enough to show his originality of approach, and even if the war had not intervened there is every reason to suppose that he would have continued his explorations. Unlike some of his slightly younger contemporaries, Rosenberg was not made into a poet by the war, but it both brought his gifts to a sudden maturity and cut them short. (p. 110)

One central aspect of Rosenberg's exploratory habit of language has been . . . precisely defined by D. W. Harding, in a valuable essay on Rosenberg [see excerpt above]. . . . [Rather] often Rosenberg wasn't at all sure what he wanted to say when he was writing a poem: . . . [Harding's] comparison of a sculptor plastically working on his statue and letting the conception grow accordingly isn't altogether exact, since clay and words are, of course, very different media. Certainly, one is much more aware of *process,* of composition as something continuous rather than a single act, in reading Rosenberg's poetry than with any of his contemporaries. But taking a less favourable view than Professor Harding's, I would be inclined to say that a great deal—perhaps most—of Rosenberg's earlier work is marred by a quality that could be called groping as much as exploration. A lot of this work seems to me incoherent and often desperately obscure. But this is no more than to say that it was the apprentice work of a dedicated and potentially powerful talent.

The impact of the war had an immediately sharpening effect on Rosenberg's poetry: his poem, **'On Receiving News of the War'**, written in Cape Town in 1914, offers a good example of Rosenberg's capacity for linguistic compression and for conveying meaning non-discursively through symbolic images. . . . The rather cryptic final stanza suggests that Rosenberg, though seeing the catastrophic nature of war much more clearly than most of his contemporaries, was also inclined to regard it as a possibly regenerative disaster; as Rilke, for instance, had in the *Fünf Gesang.* One recalls Rilke's image,

'Hot, an iron-clad heart from an iron-clad universe' . . . in the final stanza of another of Rosenberg's poems, **'August 1914'**:

> Iron are our lives
> Molten right through our youth.
> A burnt space through ripe fields
> A fair mouth's broken tooth.

Here Rosenberg manipulates very skilfully the multiple associations of his images; each of them can be construed both literally and figuratively. War has transformed 'our lives' to iron by the imposition of a cruel and inexorable pattern; but the first two lines also suggest the slaughter by iron—shell-splinters, say—of 'our youth', namely the young soldiers engaged in fighting. Similarly, the 'burnt space through ripe fields' is both a literal picture of what must have been a common sight in France in the late summer of 1914, and a compressed image of the destruction wrought by war on the amenities and traditions of normal human behaviour. Again, 'a fair mouth's broken tooth' can be a slight but disfiguring physical mutilation resulting from battle, or more extensively a symbol of the brutalizing effect of war on any manifestations of human beauty.

Rosenberg is set apart from other poets of the Great War, in the first place, by a certain detachment and impersonality; in D. W. Harding's words, 'he tried to feel in the war a significance for life as such, rather than seeing only its convulsion of the human life he knew'. One might go further and say that there was always an element of aestheticism in Rosenberg's vision; whereas Owen aimed at fusing the poetry and the pity, Rosenberg kept them separate. There is a significant passage in one of his pre-war essays:

> It is a vain belief that Art and Life go hand in hand. Art is as it were another planet, which does indeed reflect the ways of life, but is, nevertheless, a distinct and separate planet.

The symbolist notion of a separate and self-contained world of art could not have been phrased more concisely.

There is a good example of Rosenberg's aestheticism in a poem called **'Louse Hunting',** in which the stress is not on the misery of the lice-infested soldiers but rather on the grotesque visual patterns they make in trying to kill the lice (Rosenberg also treated this theme in a wryly ironical fashion in **'The Immortals'**). Undoubtedly the fact that he was also a painter influenced Rosenberg's development as a poet.

Rosenberg had, above all, a two-fold vision of the war: he was aware both of the human suffering it involved, and the unsurpassed human effort, which he regarded as a kind of absolute value, which it called forth. And this set him apart from traditional patriots and from the poets of anti-war protest. Although, as his letters show, Rosenberg could not regard the war as in any way justifiable, he accepted it imaginatively as a totally embracing way of life. There was nothing in his previous existence that could serve him as a sanative norm in the way that rural England did for many of his contemporaries (if anything, it was Jewish history and tradition that filled this role for Rosenberg); and as a private soldier he was more deeply immersed in the war than the officer-poets. At the same time, his detachment was unimpaired by the appalling sense of responsibility for others that they had to bear, and which is one of the dominant motives of Owen's poetry. The contrast is clearly brought out if one compares Rosenberg's **'Marching'** with Sorley's 'All the Hills and Vales Along': in the latter

there is an implicit separation between the speaker and the marching men—'the chaps Who are going to die perhaps'—who are enjoined, in a blend of compassion and irony, 'So be merry, so be dead'. Rosenberg's poem, on the other hand, is written from the standpoint of one of the marching men. . . . The precisely observed and isolated visual detail of the opening lines indicates the painter's eye. Then, in the second part, we have the packed, rapidly succeeding metaphors that characterize much of Rosenberg's verse. The poem allows for the viability of the heroic mode, inasmuch as the men 'husband the ancient glory'; the mythological forge of Mars continues to function, but the changed nature of modern war seems to be recognized, and the hovering impatient presence of death is also acknowledged. In the richly complex closing lines, which resist complete explication, Rosenberg combines a number of diverse strands. The 'blind fingers' are blind because they are Fate's; but also because of the muddle directing the course of the war which is constantly sending men to death. The 'iron cloud', incorporating one of Rosenberg's favourite epithets, is both a generalized symbol for war and a more exact indication of some specific phenomenon, perhaps an artillery bombardment, which rains 'immortal darkness'. This last phrase is deliberately ambiguous: it may mean that death can bestow immortality; but also that the darkness of death is itself 'immortal' (i.e. unending). In conjunction with the 'strong eyes' of the final line, one has both an idea of the unseeing but defiant eyes of some heroic statue secure in its immortal reputation, and of the 'strong' (that is, vigorous and active) eyes of men prematurely closed by death: one may compare Ezra Pound's 'Quick eyes gone under earth's lid'. And 'blind' in the antepenultimate line adds force to the juxtaposition of 'darkness' and 'eyes', and suggests a further possibility, namely that the 'immortal darkness' fallen on the 'strong eyes' is not that of death but of blindness.

D. W. Harding has referred to the way in which Rosenberg fuses two apparently disparate attitudes, which as he puts it, 'express a stage of consciousness appearing before either simple attitude has become differentiated'. Certainly Rosenberg's imagination seems to have functioned dialectically, and this may have been both cause and effect of his great attachment to the poetry of Donne. . . . The dialectical habit of mind, and the specific influence of Donne, are very apparent in one of Rosenberg's best, and best-known, poems, **'Break of Day in the Trenches',** in which the dialectical movement is objectified by the figure of the rat, moving freely between the British and German trenches. The basic structure of the poem recalls Donne's 'The Flea'. The soldier in the trench is juxtaposed between two modest natural objects. . . . Yet he does not employ them primarily for solace, as a means of escape from the destructive presence of war in the manner of, say, Blunden. The rat's function is to emphasize by his very freedom the arbitrary separation between the two front lines, and by his low, ugly vitality to point up the fact of human death. . . . The poppies were, of course, to become a celebrated emblem of the British war dead following the popularity of John McCrae's 'In Flanders Fields.' . . . Here, Rosenberg is emphasizing their intimate connection with the dead; the magnificent image, 'Poppies whose roots are in man's veins', refers to the way in which the poppies are, as it were, growing out of the innumerable bodies of the dead, whose red blood seems to have flown out of their veins and into the flowers. The poppies are a short-lived flower—they 'drop, and are ever dropping'—but their transience is scarcely more than that of the men who are constantly dropping in their midst. Nevertheless, the one poppy singled out for attention at the beginning of the poem is, for the moment, 'safe', in the precarious haven of the soldiers ear: they are, perhaps, destined to drop together. This is an unusual but effective alignment of man and nature, and shows Rosenberg's originality of insight. The poem ends with all the multiple associations of the pregnant word, 'dust'; the dust that whitens the poppy is the same dust that covers the dead and to which they will, in the end, turn.

Rosenberg's finest poem, and his most complete crystallization of war experience, is without doubt **'Dead Man's Dump'**; A. Alvarez has described it as the greatest poem by an Englishman to have been produced by the war, and I am inclined to agree. . . . [Realism] is transformed into symbolism and, as in his other trench poems, Rosenberg does not dwell on the details of violent death and mutilation. In D. W. Harding's words, 'he thinks only in terms of death which comes quickly enough to be regarded as a single living experience'. **'Dead Man's Dump'** is indeed an exploration of death as an absolute experience, which at the same time has something of the complexity and gradations of life. One notices from the beginning how Rosenberg's language fuses realism and symbolism. . . . [The] first two lines are direct, realistic observation, but in the third line, the comparison of the coils of barbed wire to 'crowns of thorns' is both visually apt and richly associative. In the reference to stakes 'like sceptres' which are supposed to stay the enemy flood one is, I think, meant to recall Canute, and no doubt, too, the fact that his attempt to stay the actual flood of the sea was fruitless: so too the wire may fail in its protective function. One sees at this point how Rosenberg has already moved farther away from the particular and the concrete, towards a generalized significance; it is, however, part of his strength that his perceptions are always rooted in the concrete, and he always returns to it. . . . If one compares [his depiction of dead soldiers] with the huddled corpses in the opening stanza of Sassoon's 'Counter-Attack', one can gauge how very different Rosenberg's intentions were. In the third stanza we find a remarkable statement of the idea glanced at in **'Break of Day in the Trenches'**, that there is a relation between man and nature which is brought to fruition when the dead return to the soil. . . . (pp. 110-18)

In the fifth stanza there is a kind of awe at the absoluteness of the experience of death fused with a sense of loss and pity; the last two lines recall some of the dominant images of **'August 1914'**, here used with greater freedom. . . . Professor Harding has said of this stanza, 'It is noteworthy here that Rosenberg is able and content to present contrasted aspects of the one happening without having to resort to the bitterness or irony which are the easier attitudes to such a contrast.' To those who are accustomed to think of the best war poetry as essentially a poetry of protest and revolt, Rosenberg's detachment and impersonality may seem disturbing, even a little inhuman. Whilst recognizing this, one must also point out that he moves to a degree of transcendence that takes him far away from his starting point in the realities of front-line activity; in such poetry we have a profound exploration of the concept of death, startling in its imaginative intensity, which goes beyond simple description, no matter how deeply felt, of the casualties of battle. . . . In the middle stanza, Rosenberg shows both a painter's eye and an ontological insight: if one were looking for an Arnoldian touchstone, the inexplicable but moving phrase, 'Joined to the great sunk silences', would surely qualify as an index of poetic authenticity. The poem moves towards the sombre paradox of its conclusion when the just-dead try to cry out to the living—and succeed. . . . (pp. 118-19)

There is another poem in which Rosenberg attempts to penetrate death as a self-contained and absolute way of life, transcending that of the living—**'Daughters of War'**. Here he abandons any attempt at realism, and builds his poem on a symbolic structure which shows the fallen swept up by the **'Daughters of War'**, who are seen as both Amazons and Valkyries. . . . Rosenberg believed this to be his best poem, and it contains some characteristically fine lines and images; but it seems to me to lack both the unity and the exactness of **'Dead Man's Dump'**. Above all, it suffers from being wholly in a symbolic mode, instead of displaying the strength which comes from counterpointing the symbolic against the realistic.

Rosenberg's war poems are not numerous, and I think that those I have referred to are the best of them, though there are others that would require mention in a more extended discussion, such as **'In War'** and **'A Worm Fed on the Heart of Corinth'**. Some critics, notably Jon Silkin, have seen signs of a major achievement in Rosenberg's verse plays, *Moses* and the fragmentary *The Unicorn*. This is something I find hard to accept; it is certainly true that he may have been feeling his way in these compositions towards larger themes than he had so far attempted, but their language seems to me obscure and clotted, typical of the groping effect that Rosenberg's poetry manifested when he was in less than perfect control of his medium. Some of the individual speeches are impressive, but the plays themselves fail to convince, above all, as drama. Because of the nature of his approach to composition, which produced something of a hit-or-miss effect, Rosenberg's successes are scattered, and his failures to move into meaning and coherence are rather numerous. But the superb quality of his successes is a sufficient sign of the talent that the war destroyed. Above all, Rosenberg is distinguished from most of his contemporaries who wrote about their experiences as combatants by seeming to have already mastered the war in poetic terms, instead of being mastered by it. For most of the poets who survived, the war remained the central experience of their lives, exercising profoundly traumatic effects and continuing to influence their attitudes in later years. This is true, above all, of Sassoon, and to a considerable extent of Graves and Blunden; and, among novelists, of Henry Williamson. If Rosenberg had survived, in all probability the war would have been only one potential subject, and perhaps not the most important, in his activity as a poet; I do not think it would have had the same dominating effect on his imagination as it had on some of his contemporaries.

But to prophesy that Rosenberg might have achieved a degree of literary greatness had he survived is idle. His imperfections were large and must be recognized, but for all that he seems to me to have had the most interesting potentialities, as opposed to realized achievements, of any of the war's victims. And it is time his stature was recognized, for he has been shabbily treated in the past: he was excluded from Robert Nichols's 1943 anthology of poets of the Great War, and received only a contemptuously fleeting mention in Edmund Blunden's British Council pamphlet, *War Poets 1914-18* (1958). The point must be insisted on: his only peer is Wilfred Owen. (pp. 119-21)

Bernard Bergonzi, "Poets IV: Rosenberg and Owen," in his Heroes' Twilight: A Study of the Literature of the Great War *(© 1965 by Bernard Bergonzi; reprinted by permission of the author), Constable and Company Ltd., 1965, pp. 109-35.**

MARIUS BEWLEY (essay date 1970)

[*Bewley discusses the importance of Rosenberg's Hebrew roots to his poetry, as do Jack Lindeman (see Additional Bibliography) and Frieda Clark Hyman (see excerpt above). Like Dennis Silk (see excerpt above), Bewley believes that power and spiritual conquest were the central themes of Rosenberg's most important works.*]

There is, certainly, a confusing unevenness in . . . [*The Collected Poems of Isaac Rosenberg*], an occasional fragmentary quality that is superficially disengaging. His best efforts are contained in a handful of *Trench Poems* which must be set off against a considerably larger number of poems written at different stages in his creative immaturity. This period of artistic uncertainty and more or less conventional poetics was more than usually protracted in Rosenberg's case; and that for a number of reasons, most of which can be traced to the discouragements of poverty.

In view of all this, it is sad, but not surprising, that Rosenberg has been left to languish among the Georgians. He is, of course, entitled to that classification by virtue of his inclusion, by a single poem, in Edward Marsh's 1916-17 Georgian anthology. His most influential friends had been Georgians; his small correspondence includes letters to Gordon Bottomley, Edward Marsh, Lascelles Abercrombie, and R. C. Trevelyan—all of them names that made Georgian literary history, and have been long out of fashion. But Rosenberg developed into something else, and left the suburbanized garden plots of Georgian poetry far behind him. (p. 282)

Rosenberg belongs to that small group of poets who had sensed how essentially different the war that began in 1914 was from all others. Their greater awareness was not merely rational but intuitive, and their poetry is an attempt to explore and analyze the monstrous experience. In their hands war poetry came to mean something different from what it had commonly meant before. For them war no longer comprised a fragment of experience, but its totality. They no longer tried to evaluate it in the perspective of peacetime assumptions, to accept the apology of official slogans, or absorb the war's effect on the individual by dreaming of an imminent return to the status quo. They understood that, for them at any rate, the tyranny was absolute. (p. 286)

Most of the poets who won recognition during World War I developed a protective subjectivity like Alan Seeger, or, like that truly typical Georgian, Rupert Brooke, continued to experience the war in the cracked molds of old attitudes, and under the colors of a faded glamor. When mentioning the few names that one can positively bring forward, names like Edward Thomas, Wilfred Owen, and Isaac Rosenberg, one must remember that their profound perception of the nature of the crisis represented, necessarily, only a partial understanding, and that their insights were more personal than social. And so it is difficult to generalize, even about a group of three. But they did begin and end with this in common (and this they shared with a few others, such as Siegfried Sassoon): equally, they hated the sham and hypocrisy of the war, and they saw through it with a surprisingly radical vision. (pp. 286-87)

For every person who has read a poem of Rosenberg's, a few hundred must have read something of Wilfred Owen's. And yet Rosenberg is the greater poet. Both men were rather like unguilty angels who had fallen with the rout into pandemonium, and their verse is an attempt to survey creatively their new midnight universe. Owen may have carried a little more of the old heaven with him, but Rosenberg understood better

the brutal anonymity of the war, and the true dimensions of the tragedy. Owen never quite became more than a good Georgian, and while it would be rash to speculate about the course of his literary career had he lived, his work has none of that rampant, impatient eagerness to reach beyond itself which is so frequently startling in the other poet's work. There was something Wordsworthian about the Georgians, but it was a Wordsworth stripped of stature; and it is stature that one never quite discovers in Owen's own poems. His hatred of war is too exclusively a hatred of its physical effects on the lives of the young Englishmen under his command. (p. 288)

Rosenberg's poetry does not stop short of the pity and tenderness in Owen's, but passes beyond it into something new. He is aware that the suffering of war is too great to be comforted, and he cannot mistake pity for succor; in his poetry, suffering achieves something like classical composure. Details are lost in bold simplicity of form, and his victims. have a heroic moral strength, a stoicism which invites the mind not to the frustrating pity of helplessness, but to something like the re-creative pity of the ancient stage.

As an example of this attitude one may look at a short passage from **"Dead Man's Dump,"** one of the greatest poems of World War I. It is directly, even starkly, concerned with suffering, and yet its terrible picture of agony never hinders the poise, the freedom of inquiry that is maintained throughout. In this poem, so impersonal and detached in comparison with much of Owen's poetry, there is a hard, almost shocking, concreteness and immediacy of imagery that makes Owen seem vague and general by contrast. . . . (pp. 288-89)

One is not so much aware of the single, the private, death here, as one is aware of the representative and universal quality in the death which is described. All "the older dead" and all who will die seem to participate symbolically in this one soldier's death. The ineffectual resentment we might otherwise feel is guarded against by very carefully handled suggestions of inevitability, and, even as we watch, the action reaches and seems to continue beyond that point where human tenderness can follow, down into an antique, stoic underworld of "great sunk silences." This soldier is less a private person than a point at which the fate of men in war becomes for a moment visible.

And it is significant that no facile, gratuitous commentary on that fate is offered in the whole eighty-six lines of **"Dead Man's Dump."** The poem's strength lies in the composure it maintains when faced by human pain, in its refusal to indulge an easy grief or extend an invitation to tears. It shows a sure control of words moving through dangerous emotions at disciplined speeds and leading the reader, by their very restraint and poise, into a fuller understanding of human dignity.

But Rosenberg did not pass from writing derivative poetry in civilian life to verse of this stature in a single day. One may arrive at a better understanding of the peculiar impersonality of *Trench Poems* if one looks first at the play *Moses*. Its strength is not the strength of the later poems, but it is a necessary step towards them and in some respects nothing Rosenberg wrote later exceeds it in interest.

Rosenberg wanted to find some intelligible correlation between the private agony and the tremendous destructive energy released in modern war, some way of imparting full weight to the unknown lives being snuffed out in pain and hence some way of guaranteeing his own identity against destruction. He sought, therefore, to create in Moses the idea of a human consciousness and will great and energetic enough to oppose war successfully. This conception of energy and power became an integral part of Rosenberg's imagination. It not only provided him with a theme and symbols: more important, it helped to strengthen the texture of his writing.

Rosenberg's concept of power has obvious affiliations with his Jewish background, and its genesis goes back far into his own life—back into those dreary years of poverty and sickness. One can trace its development in several disguises in his earlier work and letters. But Rosenberg never attempted to exploit the compensatory comforts of art, and he never developed his notion of power, such as it was, as an anodyne for the pains of experience. (pp. 289-91)

[The] first impact of the war on Rosenberg conferred a universal significance on what had been merely private struggle before, and gave new scope and depth to his writing.

Moses was the first fruit of this enlarged frame of mind. Yet as things stand, the conception with which Rosenberg struggles in the play remains a little inchoate. Moses emerges as a figure of great force, but lacks a proportionate moral definition. . . .

For all its violence of language, the action of *Moses* is static. This is not necessarily a defect, for it is undeniably a play to be read. It is inconceivable on the stage. The play is in two scenes, and occurs at that point in Moses' career when he has not yet disclaimed Pharaoh but is about to do so. Moses is seen throughout as more god than man—a source of energy to all who come in contact with him. (p. 291)

In the beginning Moses is not aware of his potential power. He is still a victim of Egyptian sensuality and indolence. The consciousness of what he can be awakens slowly in him but when it comes it is a tremendous spiritual revelation. . . . (p. 293)

Moses is Rosenberg's largest attempt to educe creatively the idea of a new kind of consciousness which would characteristically express itself in (the words are his) ''virility'' and ''original action.'' This conception is available to the reader through a prose paraphrase of the play; it is far more important that the effects of this idea are felt in many passages as the strength of the verse itself.

However much the action flags, Rosenberg's verse has a dramatic quality locally that calls for special elucidation. Here is a short speech from the first scene:

> Moses: Fine! Fine!
> 　See in my brain
> 　What madmen have rushed through,
> 　And like a tornado
> 　Torn up the tight roots
> 　Of some dead universe.
> 　The old clay is broken
> 　For a power to soak in and knit
> 　It all into tougher tissues
> 　To hold life,
> 　Pricking my nerves till the brain might crack
> 　It boils to my finger tips,
> 　Till my hands ache to grip
> 　The hammer—the lone hammer
> 　That breaks lives into a road
> 　Through which my genius drives.

This passage contains the whole idea of the play in germ: an awakening sense of power, and the determination to grasp it. It is characteristic of this play that each speech has a tendency

to become a microcosm reflecting the central conception in its full breadth and vigor. In this passage one remarks the strength of the verbs, which are not only violent but operate with kinesthetic effect: tight roots are torn up by a tornado, the hands ache to grip the hammer, nerves are pricked, the brain threatens to crack, and so on—figures full of tensions and resistances. As Moses symbolizes the desire for (in Rosenberg's own phrase) ''original action,'' it is impressive that this desire should so tangibly incarnate itself here in a series of kinesthetic verb operations. These power images actually seem to release an energy within the verse which stands in apposition to the formally articulate desire. Furthermore, one notes that while the response one brings to the imagistic series is cumulative in effect, there is a rising curve of intensity, as towards a dramatic catastrophe. The first two images—the madmen and the tornado—clear the stage (carefully localized to the arena of the brain) for the influx of the new vision of power. The image of the broken clay is transitional and leads into the fully developed power image, the hammer which breaks lives into a road, and serves as climax to this particular sequence. Then, the ultimate image of regality closes the sequence—genius out-Pharaohing Pharaoh in a procession down a royal highway.

It is part of Rosenberg's high status as a poet that the power concept which he developed in *Moses* did not constitute a settlement that fostered the delusion of permanence, an investment whose dividends might be drawn on at leisure. He believed in energy as a bowstring might: taut, he was a singing resistant thing; but relaxed, he was abject and useless. Nevertheless, there was always the temptation to accept an easier solution, a reconciliation with the past, with what Charles Sorley had called ''imaginative indolence,'' rather than to preserve the perpetual tension demanded by the exacting kind of consciousness Rosenberg sought. (pp. 293-95)

His poem **''Returning We Hear the Larks''** represents his tireless resistance against what appear to him to be temptations to capitulate. It is his best known poem, and Beth Zion Lask correctly says, ''Had he written nothing else, this one poem could have stood to serve his fame.'' (pp. 295-96)

The opening situation is a stark statement of human insecurity, but the sudden burst of song which, after an initial moment of terror, the soldiers endure with joy, is, within the compass of the poem, something in the nature of a spiritual experience. The line which carries the main burden of that experience, ''Joy—joy—strange joy,'' curiously resembles one of the ejaculatory lines in a secret memorandum of Pascal's commemorating an intense mystical experience: under the heading FIRE he had written ''Joy, joy, joy, tears of joy.'' The two following lines in Rosenberg's poem confirm the mystical nature of the experience. There is the religious intonation of the interjection ''Lo!,'' the ecstatic, evocative shrillness of ''heights of night,'' the solemn mystery of the ''unseen larks.'' Finally, in the following line, there are the beneficent suggestions of music, rain, and prayer.

From the viewpoint of their poetic integrity these lines present the experience as a valid one, certainly nothing to mistrust or regret. Nevertheless, a moment after the larks cease singing, a moment after the experience has passed, Rosenberg does question its validity in the last seven lines, which he marshals against the first part of the poem. Rosenberg seems almost to have preferred death, which might have dropped from the heavens, to the song that did, and he accuses it, in two closing similes, of concealed treacheries.

He had once written before the war: "It is all *experience;* but good God! It is *all* experience, and nothing else." During the war he had finally achieved a kind of organization of that experience, and gained a measure of control over it by informing his consciousness with a new energy and confidence. Once the immediate exultation of the larks' song had passed, everything the music meant to Rosenberg—and perhaps it had better be left vague—represented a temptation from the past to slacken his hold, to subside into "that terrible middle-class sloth of outlook and appalling 'imaginative indolence.'" At the beginning of the war, confronted with its first sights of injustice, he had asked in his poem **"God,"** "Who rests in God's mean flattery now?" Certainly he did not wish to be guilty of doing so himself.

And yet one cannot help noting that the final seven lines of the poem do not carry the conviction poetically that the first part does. They lack the spontaneous immediacy of the opening. There is a profound poignancy about **"The Larks"** which arises from an ambiguity of which Rosenberg himself was not yet wholly aware. Do the siren larks sing from a past which Rosenberg is courageous enough to resist, inviting him to a spiritual surrender? Or are they ministers of a grace which still seems beyond the reach of his powers, which so far he has neither the courage nor the means of attaining? Probably both answers are partly true. At any rate, Rosenberg's poised indecision in this poem constitutes a brilliant examination of the bases of the spiritual security he was endeavoring to construct for himself.

Although one can occasionally trace an ironic inflection in *Moses,* irony was not a favorite instrument of Rosenberg's genius. His mind lacked the cynicism necessary for a mocking mode of expression. But one of his *Trench Poems,* **"Break of Day in the Trenches,"** owes its success to the presence of something at its center approximating irony. Even here, however, the irony is without sarcasm, and almost without bitterness. There is a pervading stillness in the poem, an accomplished nervelessness. In some ways this is the saddest and most human of all his poems. It contains two points of consciousness: the poet who speaks, and who no longer seems to have any intense reaction to what he undergoes, and a rat who is credited with a personal and critical outlook. . . . The positions of men and rats [are] quietly exchanged. It is the rat who has become civilized (and for that reason only is "droll"). And it is the rat who [becomes] the judge of men who appeal to him for knowledge of themselves. (pp. 296-98)

Some particular mention should also be made of the poem **"Louse Hunting."** In twenty-five short lines it describes a delirious episode in a barracks at night. Naked soldiers, driven to frenzy by the biting of the lice, leap into a wild vermin-hunting dance by candlelight. Rosenberg invests the scene with Gothic depth, evoking the terror and fascination of a Walpurgisnacht. (pp. 298-99)

After the metaphorical richness of *Moses,* the hard spareness of the images in *Trench Poems* may come as a surprise. Continued contact with the war inevitably led Rosenberg's poetry from the somewhat ideal experience of *Moses* into the harder realm of actual endurance. Some of the color and music fades to be replaced by steel, but there is a close relationship, nonetheless, between the earlier play and the later poems. And several of the *Trench Poems* reproduce with some directness the argument of *Moses.*

In **"Soldier: Twentieth Century,"** Rosenberg returns to his conception of a "great new Titan" strong enough to subdue the forces which an evil world has raised against him. . . . (p. 299)

When Rosenberg's concept of power is stated as directly as here and in *Moses,* there is a certain ambivalence in its meaning. If, indeed, the saving power of the individual which he would oppose to the destructive force of war is primarily an affair of the consciousness, a kind of inviolable spiritual integrity, why is it expressed so predominantly in physical terms?

Part of the answer is involved in Rosenberg's sense of race, and his strong attraction towards those men in Jewish history who were deliverers from both spiritual and physical tyranny. Redemption from the apathy of life and the horror of war was hardly imaginable to him as possible under one aspect only. It was natural that a sensibility deeply impressed by Moses and Maccabaeus should find, when confronted with crisis, a militant, even a fierce symbolism and imagery congenial. But no rifles flowered in Rosenberg's poetry, and the conquest he envisaged always remained essentially a spiritual one.

Rosenberg's very last poems show how deeply he was coming to rely on the traditions of the Jews when he died. One of these poems deals with the burning of the Temple, another with the destruction of Jerusalem by the Babylonians, and the last poem included in the volume deals with the Jewish persistent sense of exile. It is clear that in dealing with Old Testament themes he discovered a norm of reference and a moral security he could find nowhere else. He reveals in his last poem [**"Through these pale cold days"**] his growing insistence on Jewish positives. (p. 300)

The Semitic faces in the first quatrain [of **"Through these pale cold days"**] look out across the following lines towards the sources of Hebraic tradition and life, only to discover that their long separation from them has brought spiritual death. It was in a return to these sources, what in *Moses* he had called "the roots' hid secrecy," that Rosenberg looked for the authority to reject the sterility of modern life, of which war was only the most hideous expression.

The probable course of Rosenberg's literary career, and what its influence on the literature of the 'twenties would have been had he lived may be an amusing form of speculation to anyone who admires his poetry, but that sort of game cannot substantially help a reputation that must, after all, rest on work done. In *The Complete Works* we do have an emphatic assertion of really great talent. (p. 301)

Marius Bewley, "The Poetry of Isaac Rosenberg" (originally published in a different version in Commentary, *Vol. 17, No. 1, June, 1949), in his* Masks & Mirrors: Essays in Criticism *(copyright © 1949, 1952, 1955, 1958, 1959, 1962, 1963, 1964, 1965, 1966, 1967, 1968, 1970 by Marius Bewley; reprinted with the permission of Atheneum Publishers, New York),* Atheneum, *1970, pp. 281-301.*

IRVING HOWE (essay date 1975)

[*A longtime editor of the leftist magazine* Dissent *and a regular contributor to* The New Republic, *Howe is one of America's most highly respected literary critics and social historians. He has been a socialist since the 1930s, and his criticism is frequently informed by a liberal social viewpoint. Howe is widely praised for what F. R. Dulles has termed his "knowledgeable understanding, critical acumen and forthright candor." Howe has written: "My work has fallen into two fields: social history and literary criticism. I have tried to strike a balance between the social and the literary;*

to fructify one with the other; yet not to confuse one with the other. Though I believe in the social approach to literature, it seems to me peculiarly open to misuse; it requires particular delicacy and care." In the following excerpt Howe discusses the various social and literary influences that helped shape Rosenberg's poetry. In discussing Rosenberg's use of Jewish materials, Howe states that the poet used them in a detached and fresh way— as "myth rediscovered." Like F. R. Leavis (see excerpt above), Howe sees similarities between Rosenberg's world view and that of D. H. Lawrence.]

[Rosenberg's] work shows the stamp of night-school culture, but often, thereby, a grotesque originality; he wrote English as if it were a new language. To become an artist meant for him a radical sundering from his environment, not as the familiar sentimental or sullen rejection of Jewishness, since Jewish motifs flourish in his work, but as a decision to transplant himself into the great tradition of English poetry. Keats staring into the sweet shop became a Whitechapel boy staring at Keats.

Sent to the Somme as a private in the First World War (the other English "war poets" were officers, gentlemen), Rosenberg fell in battle on April 1, 1918. Before his death he had completed a group of poems about army life. **"Trench Poems,"** which seem to me without equal, for their kind, in English poetry.

Rosenberg would be praised in the '20s and '30s by T. S. Eliot [see annotated bibliography] and F. R. Leavis [see excerpt above]; first-rate critical pieces by Marius Bewley (*Masks and Mirrors*), Denys Harding (*Experience into Words*), and Dennis Silk (in *Judaism*, Autumn, 1965) [see excerpts above] would follow; recently Joseph Cohen has written the most complete account of Rosenberg's life; but the poems themselves—all together filling a small book and the best of them a few pages— have never held the attention of readers as have the war writings of Rupert Brooke, Siegfried Sassoon and Wilfred Owen. No glamorous fatality hangs over Rosenberg's head: he was just a clumsy, stuttering Jewish doughboy.

Rosenberg's early poems are thick with the language of Shakespeare and Keats, also with pre-Raphaelite decoration. These speak more of an overmastering intent to become a poet, a need to overcome a scrappy education through fierce appropriations, than they do of the usual borrowings and discipleship. The style of these early poems ranges from heaving rhetoric to romantic lyricism, but what marks Rosenberg as a significant writer at this point is just those barbarisms of phrasing such Georgian friends as Gordon Bottomley and Edward Marsh found hard to take. The early Rosenberg is always driving himself to say more than he has to say, because he thinks poets must speak to large matters. Later he learns that in a poppy in the trenches or a louse in a soldier's shirt, there is enough matter for poetry.

I find it a cause for wonderment that Rosenberg escaped from or banished the immigrant Yiddish culture in which he was formed. An early **"Ballad of Whitechapel"** reads like a bad translation of the "sweatshop" Yiddish poets starting to write in London and New York during the 1890s; it is one of the few instances where Rosenberg is content with pathos. He seems to have decided not to confront directly that tract of adolescent experience which has obsessed so many Jewish writers. Though the sensibility of humanist *Yiddishkeit* enclosed his youth, he simply ignored it in his work. When he does turn to Jewish motifs, they are drawn from Biblical sources but in a manner oddly abstract, even mythical. His verse play, **"Moses,"** ranges from a surplus of rant to glimmers of sub-

limity; it launches a vision of Jewish rebirth (Moses, he said, "symbolizes the fierce desire for virility and original action"); but it is less the projected rebirth of a nation than a summoning of energies for self-assertion. For Rosenberg's poetry—this helps distinguish it from the other "war poets"—is marked by a strong prophetic urge which he could never quite bring under control or into focus. At best, it leads him to a recognition that he is living in a moment of historical disintegration. (pp. 195-97)

In the four or five years before going into the army, Rosenberg had begun to write poems in which this sense of historical disintegration, as acute in its way as that of D. H. Lawrence, would be realized through images not always coherent or settled but very powerful in fragments, stanzas, lines. Never having mastered the art of writing a good poem, he was preparing himself to write a few great ones.

One of the most astounding of these earlier poems is **"The Female God,"** where his gifts for intense dramatism and expressionist phrasing come into mature play. . . . (p. 197)

The fury that men have felt in our time, and no doubt before it, at what they see as their entrapment by "the feminine principle," the suffocating dampness of sensual need, is here enlarged to a kind of metaphysical vision. The "female god" who has dethroned the ancient masculine God, comes to seem "rose-deaf"—"rose": lovely, enchanting; "deaf": unresponsive, imperial.

About Rosenberg's Jewish poems I can only say here that he anticipated what may be a course for poets in the future. Once milieu and memory are exhausted, Jewishness can take on the strangeness of a fresh myth, or at least a myth rediscovered; the Bible loses its tyranny of closeness and becomes a site to be ransacked. Rosenberg wrote as if he were *free* to do what he wished with Biblican materials, not exactly a common condition among Jewish writers, and while **"Moses"** and **"The Unicorn"** are failures, they point to major possibilities. In **"The Jew"** he compressed these possibilities into eight lines. . . . (p. 198)

Except perhaps for the last line, **"The Jew"** shows Rosenberg's gift for packed phrasing: "a lamp in his blood," the moral vision carried by the race; the commandments as "moon," not sun, because the moon reflects and moral life requires reflection; and the wonderful play in the fourth line twisting the terms of the previous two.

Finally Rosenberg's talent came to fruition in the **"Trench Poems."** In the letters he sent home from the trenches, Rosenberg gripes as much as anyone else, but in the poems it is as if he himself were no longer there, no longer afflicted and imperiled. Hating the war, calling the soldier's life "slavery," he nonetheless proposed to "saturate myself with the strange and extraordinary new conditions of this life, and it will all refine itself into poetry later on." From a merely human point of view, it is both impressive and chilling: as if all experience must finally be put to the service of poetry. Yet that does seem to have been Rosenberg's idea. "Iron are our lives / Molten right through our youth," he wrote in the poem, **"August, 1914,"** and from the "iron" he made his handful of great poems.

In the best of the **"Trench Poems"**—**"Returning, We Hear the Larks," "Dead Man's Dump," "Break of Day in the Trenches"** and **"Louse Hunting"**—he focuses upon a commonplace event, a lull in the fighting, the weariness after a dangerous moment. Some men have come back, in **"Returning, We Hear the Larks,"** from a night mission. . . . (pp. 198-99)

"A strange joy" follows, for the night is "ringing with unseen larks" and "music showering on our upturned list'ning faces." The conclusion is overpowering in its acceptance of the sheer arbitrariness of survival. . . .

In **"Break of Day in the Trenches,"** the poet pulls "the parapet's poppy / To stick behind my ear," and then encounters "a queer sardonic rat." He speaks directly: "Droll rat, they would shoot you if they knew / Your cosmopolitan sympathies." The rat and the poppy become symbols of the intermingling, the indistinguishability of existence and perishing. . . . (p. 199)

Reflecting upon these poems I have found myself turning back to T. S. Eliot's doctrine of the impersonality of poetry. "What happens [in a poem]," writes Eliot, "is a continual surrender of [the poet] as he is at the moment to something which is more valuable. The progress of an artist is a continual self-sacrifice, a continual extinction of personality."

Rosenberg seldom reached, perhaps he did not live long enough to reach, that middle plane of achievement which entails the tokens of a formed *persona*. In most of his poems he fell short of a distinct poetic personality, and in a few went beyond it. In his early poems there is a false or assumed personality, a Whitechapel Keats; in the **"Trench Poems"** there is a transcendence of mere personality: no individual voice, no complaint, no sadness, no opinions, no irony, no rebellion, indeed, an utter submergence of the grief that must lie behind the poems, quite as if some drained being were writing, rather than a mere afflicted man. This saturation in the life available to him, this submission to what little he could have, enabled Rosenberg to achieve the moral poise of an absolute dramatism, that creative faith in the value of rendering which is really beyond argument.

Rosenberg began with the common stock of Romantic diction, and then, as I hear it, borrowed heavily from Hardy. There are some lines from **"Dead Man's Dump"** describing corpses on the battlefield . . . which share the rhythm and diction of Hardy's "Transformations." In the end, however, one should acknowledge a margin of originality in Rosenberg's language, a fusion of ill-heard and thereby, at times, recharged poeticism with harsh urban speech. In a few poems, a moment of the world is held by the grip of truth. (pp. 200-01)

> *Irving Howe, "The Poetry of Isaac Rosenberg" in* The New Republic *(reprinted by permission of* The New Republic; © *1975 The New Republic, Inc.),* Vol. 173, No. 14, October 4, 1975 *(and reprinted in his* Celebrations and Attacks: Thirty Years of Literary and Cultural Commentary, *Horizon Press, 1979, pp. 195-201).*

JEAN LIDDIARD (essay date 1975)

[*In the excerpt below from her biographical and critical study of Rosenberg entitled* Isaac Rosenberg: The Half-Used Life, *Liddiard discusses the basis of Rosenberg's ambivalent attitude toward God and religion, as revealed in the poems.*]

As in all the poems in [*Youth*] the numinous quality of the world is so strongly presented that the impression is one of explosive forces barely held in check; the opposing elements are sometimes evenly matched to create stillness, as [in **"None**

have seen the House of the Lord"**]** where the firm pacing rhythm and oriental imagery frame the passion for intimate union in formal magnificence. Rosenberg has "slinked past God" in his emergence from childhood; now he feels forced to return to Him; but he is not simply giving way to nostalgia for his secure early faith. He is equipped and ready to do battle with the God of his fathers; the creative powers of the poet challenge the powers of the Creator. This constantly recurs, light-heartedly in the love poems, grandly in the plays, darkly in the war poems. So his heroes become Promethean and in the case of Moses, highly unorthodox. Rosenberg's God is unorthodox. He is the source of all power, of the dynamic forces that create and charge the universe, of which man's creative power is one. However the struggle between God and His creation cannot be a simple matter of victory and defeat. There is no force of darkness, no Satan, in Rosenberg's universe; the nearest to it is chaos. God himself contains and must be responsible for all that is in His creation. The poet first engages with Him over being cast out from the security of his faith: "Yea! He hath fled as far as the uttermost star. . . ." But where the Christian poets, Donne, Marvell, Crashaw and Francis Thompson, who were Rosenberg's models for this kind of poetry, justify the ways of God to man through man's own complicity in his fall from grace, and rest their hopes of salvation on Christ, Rosenberg naturally does not. Indeed his response is to turn on God and call Him to account, not unlike his Hebrew forefather Job. Rosenberg in his South African lecture on **"Art"** refers to Blake's drawing from the Book of Job, "The Song of the Morning Star", and also imitates Blake's deliberate simplicity in several lyrics. . . . (pp. 136-37)

Rosenberg identifies with God not only as a human soul longing to be united with Him, but as a fellow creator; he can see from God's point of view as well as his own. For God the wise man and the fool fished up to heaven are both material to His purpose. This creative identification with God enables Rosenberg to treat Him very freely in his poetry; God uses him, so he will use God. This has often distressed orthodox reviewers of his poems, especially the poem called **"God"**, published in *Moses A Play*. (pp. 137-38)

Rosenberg cannot disguise, from himself or God, his reaction to the evil of the world, nor affect an acceptance he does not feel. He rejects the orthodox Jewish tradition of resignation to an unknowable will, and rounds on the orthodox God of that tradition, who will not act or even respond to the "one, fearless", who "turned and clawed like bronze". It is intended to be provocative, a way of breaking through frustration, and of course it indicates continuing religious feeling; a non-believer would not feel so betrayed. As always for Rosenberg, it is the inertia of frustration which is so unbearable. On 16 September 1912, to Alice Wright, he writes of Milton's ability to deal with exactly that problem:

> When Milton writes on his blindness, how dignified he is! how grand, how healthy? What begins in a mere physical moan, concludes in a grand triumphant spiritual expression, of more than resignation, of conquest. But I think the concluding idea very beautiful. I like the sonnets very much, an uncommon artistic expression of the artist's common lament.

Rosenberg also wants "more than resignation . . . conquest". The dignified tone of Milton's sonnets which he admires is one he tries to achieve in his own poems, dealing with the appalling suffering of war. But at this stage he is still fighting

God with His own creative weapons. In two poems from *Youth,* "**The One Lost**" and "**God Made Blind**", a jealous terrible God is defeated by human cunning and human love; and in *Moses A Play* "**Sleep**", less raw than these, presents the God as both glamorous and frightening. . . . The concise suggestion of the scale and gleaming enchanted stillness of the Gods gives the poem a peculiarly haunting atmosphere, but the tensions of the hostility to them prevents it from drifting into post-Romantic fantasy.

The theme of a God both resisted and desirable recurs perhaps because Rosenberg found it difficult to reconcile the opposing elements of his own temperament. It was not only the stresses of creative work and the lack of enough opportunity to realize his gifts; there were also the conflicting needs for friendship, for appreciation, "real intimacy—love", and his reserve, his need for personal freedom and independence and the arrogance of which he was sometimes accused. *Youth* explores these oppositions: the flesh and the spirit, "**Love and Lust**"; the affirmation of his own powers and the relating of them to their source, a creative God who also destroys; immediate human experience with its inadequacies and a belief in ultimate fulfilment. The last two he deals with more fully in *Moses A Play* and his last poems and plays; the first, "**Love and Lust**" is appropriate to *Youth*. . . . [The characteristic of the poems included in *Youth,* as well as others written at the same time,] is frequently the paradox of the lover's separateness from his love, in spite of their union; even the necessity of that separateness for the poet to be fully aware and responsive to the experience—a typical stance of Rosenberg's which extends also to his war poetry. . . . (pp. 138-39)

Even in the poems celebrating fulfilment, like "**Wedded**" (2), . . . the sense of just having come to rest is strong—the poem is vibrant with motion that has barely ceased. . . . At the heart of the experience there is often ambivalence, as in the "death" of the final line.

The ambivalence of love, especially its physical aspect, he relates to his ambiguous God—desirable and perceived through the human senses, but offering fulfilment that lies tantalizingly beyond them. The fierceness of physical sensation, the resentment of the spirit at its lack of freedom, the fascination of the divine and its apparent unconcern for human striving, come together in a curious poem, "**The Female God.**" . . . (p. 140)

This female power is the only force that opposes "the ancient God"—she is linked to the creative power and the beauty desired (and feared) by the creative imagination. In one of the fragmentary drafts of his last unfinished play, "**The Unicorn**", Rosenberg tackles this as a major theme, although his ultimate intentions are not clear. (p. 141)

The whole group of poems concerning God or a Goddess are interesting for their originality; they are part of his exploration of forces beyond man which yet reflect and respond to man's needs and desires. Rosenberg is working towards his own mythical structure in which to place and comprehend his personal human experience. This is why the theme of savage cosmic forces and superhuman beings returns so strongly in his war poetry when he is confronted with human experience so extreme and specific that it could overwhelm all but the simplest response. Through the mythological element he could extend his experience beyond the personal moment.

This of course was a very ambitious aim for any poet—it was to take Yeats as many years as Rosenberg lived to do it successfully. What is surprising about Rosenberg is not that he

failed to cohere and complete this achievement, but that he succeeded at all. "**The Female God**" has all his faults: over-elaborate images that dissipate rather than reinforce their effect; an uneasy mixture of idioms—the biblical "Yea" and the curt direct speech of the last two lines, which give a faint effect of bathos. . . . (pp. 141-42)

Yet there is a sense of scope, a range of suggestiveness (in the hair images especially), that saves the poem (and other similar poems) from banality or pomposity. (p. 142)

> *Jean Liddiard, in her* Isaac Rosenberg: The Half Used Life *(© Jean Liddiard 1975; reprinted by permission of the author), Victor Gollancz Ltd, 1975, 287 p.*

HAROLD BLOOM　(essay date 1979)

[*In* The Anxiety of Influence *(1973), Bloom formulated a controversial theory of literary creation called revisionism. Influenced strongly by Freudian theory, which states that "all men unconsciously wish to beget themselves, to be their own fathers," Bloom believes that all poets are subject to the influence of earlier poets and that, to develop their own voice, they attempt to overcome this influence through a process of misreading. By misreading, Bloom means a deliberate, personal revision of what has been said by another so that it conforms to one's own vision: "Poetic influence—when it involves two strong, authentic poets—always proceeds by a misreading of the prior poet, an act of creative correction that is actually and necessarily a misrepresentation. The history of poetic influence . . . is a history of anxiety and self-serving caricature, of distortion, of perverse, wilful revisionism." In this way the poet creates a singular voice, overcoming the fear of being inferior to poetic predecessors. Bloom's later books are applications of this theory, extended in* Kabbalah and Criticism *(1974) to include the critic or reader as another deliberate misreader. Thus, there is no single reading of any text, but multiple readings by strong poets or critics who understand a work only in ways that allow them to assert their own individuality or vision. In addition to his theoretical work, Bloom is one of the foremost authorities on English Romantic poetry and has written widely on the influences of Romanticism in contemporary literature. In the following discussion of Rosenberg's career, Bloom appraises his subject as "the best Jewish poet writing in English that our century has given us."*]

Rosenberg was a poet-painter directly in the Pre-Raphaelite tradition. His poetry developed out of Blake, Keats, Rossetti and Swinburne, and the hard-edged phantasmagoria of the Pre-Raphaelite mode is wonderfully present in his best poems and fragments, all written in the last two years of his life. But Rosenberg, who knew some Yiddish, and who hoped until the day of his death to join the Jewish Battalion that Jabotinsky had organized, was clearly an English poet with a Jewish difference. This difference transcends the biblical diction that he shared with Blake and Swinburne, and even the consciously Jewish subject matter of much of his best work. A violent Expressionist in his poetic style, struggling against a literary tradition that only partly sustained him, Rosenberg remains the best Jewish poet writing in English that our century has given us. His finest poetry is of high intrinsic interest, but its limitations have the additional value of suggesting why British and American Jewish poetry has been surprisingly inadequate, with some distinguished exceptions.

Rosenberg's immediate advantage, his undoubted genius aside, is that he worked in ignorance of the poetic Modernism that burgeoned from 1915 on. The idiom of his precursors, except for its lack of intensity, was in no way opposed to the prophetic visions that demanded voicing in his poetry, which would not have accommodated itself to the strictures of Eliot and Pound. But because he had no true quarrel with the diction of Georgian poetry, and indeed greatly admired poets such as Lascelles Abercrombie and Gordon Bottomley, Rosenberg's Jewishness gave him a sharper sense of influence-anxiety than that manifested by such contemporaries as Edward Thomas and Wilfred Owen, to cite only the other two really distinguished poets killed in World War I.

Rosenberg's malaise is shown by his deliberate turn to Emerson and to Whitman, whose "Drum-Taps" is an immediate influence on Rosenberg's best and most famous war poems. (pp. 1, 21)

In 1916, Emerson's effect can be felt in **"Expressionism,"** Rosenberg's first real poem, followed soon afterward by **"Chagrin,"** which also concerns the poet's need to break into an expressionistic sublimity, and which begins with the vision of the poet as a rebellious son of a divine king, trapped by his own beauty. . . .

The sudden bursting-forth of Rosenberg's genius comes soon after this, in the astonishing **"Break of Day in the Trenches,"** with its restrained yet frightening irony, and with equally powerful phantasmagorias of the Western Front: **"Louse Hunting," "Returning, We Hear the Larks," "Dead Man's Dump"** and the undervalued **"Daughters of War,"** which is worthy of late Yeats. Though these "trench poems" are Rosenberg's most famous, and are strong work by any standards, they do not seem to me his major accomplishment. I would locate that in his biblical poems and dramatic fragments. These include prophetic lyrics such as **"The Burning of the Temple," "The Destruction of Jerusalem by the Babylonian Hordes"** and Rosenberg's death poem, written for the Jewish Battalion. . . .

Finer even than these lyrics are the dramatic fragments, **"Moses," "The Amulet"** and **"The Unicorn,"** the latter two centering upon the kabbalistic figure of Lilith, Adam's demonic first wife. In one of Rosenberg's fragments, Lilith says of Adam: "He is a widower since I died to him." Haunted by the realities of trench warfare, searching in his poetry for his true origins in Jewish tradition, the womanless Rosenberg undoubtedly saw himself as an abandoned Adam, a widower for whom tradition had died. His yearning and his poetic triumph, however truncated, is summed up for us by the most beautiful of his fragments, [**'A Worm Fed on the Heart of Corinth,'**] a prophetic lyric worthy of Blake. . . .

It is difficult to overpraise this, and difficult also not to wince at its moral burden. The interplay between "incestuous," "amorphous," "famous," "shadowless," and "amorous" is the cognitive kernel of the poem, with the other four words pressuring "famous" into meaning something like satanic infamy. Here at least, Rosenberg fused his traditions, as few Jewish poets writing in English have done since. The strategies of Modernism and of post-Modernism alike seem to impede Jewish poets in their perhaps hopelessly contrary quest for a poetic language adequate both to Jewish tradition and to Anglo-American literary conventions. Rosenberg, whose death was so tragically early, may have had the benefit of doing his work at exactly the right time, before the Modern tradition's advent and its subsequent shadows of belatedness combined to afflict Jewish and other poets with truly acute self-consciousness. (p. 21)

Harold Bloom, "A Fusion of Traditions," in The New York Times Book Review (copyright © 1979

by The New York Times Company; reprinted by permission), July 22, 1979, pp. 1, 21.

IAN PARSONS   (essay date 1979)

[*The chairman of Chatto & Windus and director of several other publishing firms, Parsons was the only publisher to show interest in Rosenberg's work during the 1930s, when the poems had been long out of print and anthologists were ignoring their existence. Parsons was largely responsible for encouraging D. W. Harding to prepare the* Collected Works *of 1937. The excerpt below is from the introduction to the 1979 edition of the* Collected Works, *considered the most complete and authentic edition to-date. Parsons's article contains an in-depth discussion of Rosenberg's use of imagery and his literary style.*]

That a good deal of Rosenberg's poetry, and especially his dramatic verse, is difficult to grasp, must be admitted. He himself was well aware of it. 'Most people', he wrote to Sydney Schiff in June 1915, 'find my poems difficult', and added, 'My technique in poetry is very clumsy I know.' (p. xvii)

The fact is that words flew into Rosenberg's mind as birds fly into a tree; they settled there, sometimes in patterns of indescribable beauty, but sometimes they failed to coalesce and remained disparate, glittering but inchoate.

But the difficulties and complexities, such as they are, sprang neither from confusion of thought nor any lack of the means of expression; still less, as Rosenberg himself said, 'from blindness or carelessness'; they were the result of an extraordinary compression of language ('I am always afraid of being empty'), and of his own particular and highly individual vision. Moreover he possessed, from very early on, the complementary gift of being able to clothe his ideas in language as original and startling as his vision. There are few poets whose work is more impressively free from the banal epithet and the dead phrase. Indeed, so many of his images are new and unfamiliar that one is apt at first to be puzzled by their strangeness; by the apparent abruptness, too, with which sometimes they are introduced. But gradually, with continued reading, one comes not only to appreciate their signal force and appropriateness, but to grasp the associations which link them to, and illuminate, their context.

One of the most astonishing statements made about the poets of the First World War, and by a Cambridge don at that, was that Owen and Rosenberg 'were killed before they had anything to write about except war'. It is not true of Owen, and it is ludicrously untrue of Rosenberg. . . . On the contrary, Rosenberg began writing poetry very early, in 1905 when he was barely 15 years old, and virtually never stopped. Moreover one cannot help being struck by the technical assurance of some of these juvenile poems, despite their occasional naïveté. They display, to a degree exceptional in so inexperienced a writer, what T. S. Eliot called 'an authoritativeness of manner'. . . . And although in the immediately following years, his growing familiarity with English and other poets inevitably led him to reflect some of their accents and to echo some of their cadences, he fairly rapidly outgrew these influences. Swinburne is clearly present in a number of these early poems, including **'Dawn Behind Night', 'Lines Written in an Album',** and **'Bacchanal';** Hardy is equally so in **'The Dead Past',** and Keats and Rossetti are certainly behind some of the 1911-12 love poems. But increasingly Rosenberg was finding his own idiom, and over the next two years produced a score of poems that are essentially *sui generis.* Among them were **'Glory of Hueless Skies',**

'**Apparition**', '**A Warm Thought Flickers**', '**At Night**' and the superb '**Midsummer Frost**'. Written in a variety of metres and rhyme-schemes, these poems have in common a peculiar freshness of outlook (no 'Georgian' echoes here), an originality of conception and imagery, and a command of metaphor that would be remarkable in a much older man. Above all they have already, as I have said, begun to take on the unmistakable tone and flavour of his mature poetry. Nobody but Rosenberg could be thought the author of . . . '**Midsummer Frost**'. . . . (pp. xvii-xix)

To this period also belong several poems of marked originality, in both conception and form, such as '**The Mirror**' and '**Significance**'. . . . (p. xix)

These poems were followed . . . by a series of major poems written in South Africa or shortly after his return to this country in the Spring of 1915. They included love poems with a much broader range of emotion and depth of feeling than he could compass earlier, like '**I Have Lived in the Underworld too Long**', '**Her Fabled Mouth**' (written when he must have been reading the Elizabethan and Jacobean poets), '**The Exile**', and the sensuous, almost erotic '**Sacred, Voluptuous Hollows Deep**'. Perhaps the best, and certainly the most technically accomplished, was the first of the two poems he called '**Wedded**'. . . . Surely one of the most humanly revealing and moving poems of this kind ever written.

There were many other short poems—'**A Girl's Thoughts**', '**If You are Fire**'—of a simplicity and lyric grace that give the lie to the assumption that all Rosenberg's middle period work was 'difficult'. (pp. xix-xx)

There are several others, written about the same time, of an equal simplicity and directness. Some of them (and many of the fragments) combine a bracing succinctness of diction with an exhilarating astringency. (p. xx)

And let nobody imagine that he was without humour. The prose piece called *On a Door Knocker* is proof of that, and the same cockney sense of comedy informs several of the poems. . . .

Nor can one read far in Rosenberg's poetry without becoming aware of the fact that he was a painter-poet. Adjectives and images involving colour abound, and the sharp, observant eye of the draughtsman is everywhere apparent. (p. xxi)

It was on his return from staying with his married sister in Cape Town that Rosenberg embarked on his most ambitious work to date, his verse play *Moses*. The large number of extant drafts of it, or parts of it, show that it gave him many hours of labour, and when he published it the following year, at the end of May 1916, he was still not wholly satisfied with it. Understandably, in my view, for though it has always attracted critical attention at a high level and undoubtedly contains passages of surpassing beauty, it still seems to me a flawed work in which form and content never quite join hands.

Moreover it encouraged a misconception to which Laurence Binyon gave currency that Rosenberg 'aspired to become a representative poet of his own nation' [see additional bibliography]. I do not believe that he did. Of course, he was a Jew, and was brought up in a conventional Jewish home, with all that that means in the way of traditional influence and cultural background. But he never really attempted to learn Hebrew, had only little Yiddish, and only small interest in Judaism as such. No, his vision was cosmic rather than sectarian, personal and unique rather than specifically Jewish. True, he was profoundly influenced by Hebrew mythology and legend, especially as enshrined in the Bible; but it was his own myths that he wove round the archetypal characters that he drew from those sources. (pp. xxi-xxii)

[The] radical change in his whole way of life that being in the Army entailed had a correspondingly profound effect on his character, and ultimately of course on his poetry. From the end of 1915 onward his poems increasingly reflect his changed circumstances and surroundings. . . . This was the period leading up to the great poems of 1916-17, half-a-dozen of which—including '**Break of Day in the Trenches**', '**Returning, we Hear the Larks**', and the superlative '**Dead Man's Dump**'—have been widely anthologised and form the basis on which, for most people, Rosenberg's reputation as a poet rests. Acclaimed by poets as far back as the twenties and the thirties (Bottomley, Binyon, Sitwell, Sassoon, Muir) and by critics from that day to this (Leavis, Harding, Isaacs, Silkin, Silk and Hobsbaum) they are in no need of praise from me.

There are, in fact, only two or three things that I would like to say about them. The first is that, splendid and deservedly famous though they are, I do not think they should be allowed to detract from the merits of the very large number of other memorable poems which Rosenberg wrote. . . . Secondly, I do not think any useful purpose is served by making detailed comparisons between the war poems of Owen and Rosenberg. The differences are so great, not only because of differences in their circumstances (Owen was an officer, Rosenberg a private) though these to some extent conditioned the material on which they worked, but in the whole tone and idiom of their poems. So that what they had in common seems to me far less significant, in terms of poetry, than what distinguishes them. Like Owen, Rosenberg saw very clearly the horrific nature of the war in which they were both caught up, and the extent of the sacrifice that was to be incurred. But the bitter indignation, the *saeva indignatio* that, chastened and restrained by pity, is a dominant characteristic of Owen's war poems, has no place in Rosenberg's. In some extraordinary way, he managed to detach himself emotionally from the terrible things that were going on all round him, to expose himself to them and to record them minutely but objectively, and then to transmute them into poetry of the highest imaginative quality, set in a much broader context than his own personal plight. Thus it is that solicitude, rather than Owen's compassion, is the emotion they so movingly convey. . . . (pp. xxiv-xxvi)

I would only like to add the recommendation that anybody who wants to know the truth about Isaac Rosenberg's character should sit down and read his Letters straight through from beginning to end. They will find it a rewarding and ennobling experience. For Rosenberg was as incapable of duplicity as he was of meanness or malice, and his steadfastness and integrity shine through these letters with a brightness that increases as the years pass. They were features of his character that neither the rigours of life in the ranks (which were hurtful enough for a diminutive recruit, and a Jew to boot) nor the ardours and endurances of the trenches, could qualify or dim. Indeed, what one notices with growing admiration is the manner in which the hardships and dangers of life at the Front served only to heighten the intensity of his interest in poetry, other people's as well as his own, and his concern for the welfare of his friends. . . . [His] own miseries and misfortunes are retailed graphically but without a trace of self-pity. Through it all he retained, miraculously, not only his sense of humour but an unquenchable optimism. Writing to Marsh at the end of April 1917 about 'his mistress, the flighty Muse', he says that though she has absconded with luckier rivals 'surely I shall hunt her and chase her somewhere into the Summer and sweeter times'. And a few months later he writes to Bottomley, 'I live in an immense trust that things will turn out well'. (pp. xxvi-xxvii)

Ian Parsons, "Introduction" (text © Ian Parsons, 1979; reprinted by permission of the author and Chatto & Windus), in The Collected Works of Isaac Rosenberg: Poetry, Prose, Letters, Paintings and Drawings *by Isaac Rosenberg, edited by Ian Parsons, Chatto and Windus, 1979, pp. xv-xxvii.*

LES MURRAY   (essay date 1980)

[*A frequent contributor to Australian literary journals, Murray provides an astute discussion of Rosenberg's career in the following review of* The Collected Works of Isaac Rosenberg.]

In the years since Isaac Rosenberg's death on the Western Front in April 1918, his reputation has grown steadily—and yet it . . . has undergone a sixty-year spurt. No less than three biographies appeared in 1975, and there have been recent efforts to put him up as the greatest of the lost English poets of the First World War. I believe a new Penguin anthology of the War poets, edited by John Silkin, gives Rosenberg pride of place over Owen, Sassoon, Blunden, Graves and all the rest; this book is either just out or is about to appear. I think these efforts are misplaced, if honourable, and that they might well embarrass the man himself, if he could hear of them. (p. 52)

Probably the only good thing the war did for Rosenberg was that it resolved his indecision over whether to concentrate on painting or on poetry; poems can be scribbled with a pencil stub on scrap paper in a dugout, but painting under such conditions is impossible. A few small sketches survive from his war service, but all of his relatively few surviving paintings date from before he went into the Army. Several are reproduced in Ian Parsons' [*The Collected Works of Isaac Rosenberg*], but I do not feel able to judge their worth; I know from experience that there's no such thing as a reproduction of a painting. The art critic Maurice de Sausmarez wrote of them that they had "a quality that is intensely personal and suggests the probable direction of a later development. This quality is not easy to characterize, but includes a simplification that moves towards compression of experience rather than towards the schematic, a design which is not arbitrarily imposed as in some of Stanley Spencer's work, but is distilled and inseparable from the content. The symbol always retains the sensuousness of the original experience and he mistrusts an art that uses 'symbols of symbols'."

This is also a very good description of what is best in his poetry. To cite just one example, [there] is the second stanza of "Midsummer Frost", a poem written in 1914 but revised several times before its publication in the following year. . . . (pp. 52-3)

Beneath all the fag-ends of a worn-out poetical diction, there is something alive in this, a genuine imagination finding terms for inner experience, recreating it in images rather than in formulae. The image of the heart 'hidden as a root from air or a star from day' is pure Rosenberg, alive and infinitely more daring than the tame decorums of most contemporary Georgian poetry; it foreshadows the beautiful image, used in two of his poems written in 1917 ("Soldier: Twentieth Century" and "Girl to Soldier on Leave") of a figure hidden like 'a word in the brain's ways'. As a whole, "Midsummer Frost" is a failure; the first two stanzas are fascinating, with the real grip

and involute strangeness of poetry, the rest of the poem loses tension, loses focus, loses itself in unresolved verbiage. As so often happens, the sense of a powerful, evolving personal style peters out almost as soon as it is created. The poet obviously detected this himself and wrestled with it; time after time, the useful notes which the editor supplies with very many of the poems and fragments record repeated rewritings, re-castings, pleas for advice or comment from the half-dozen or more people to whom he would send his drafts and who served as his sounding-boards. In what is really quite a small output if we remember that he was writing seriously for twelve or thirteen years before his untimely death at the age of twenty-eight we see poem after poem marred by the scheme, the arbitrarily imposed design, the retreat into received sentiment, archaism, pallid atmospherics. . . .

What is more heartening is the wide variety of attempted forms to be found in the same smallish output. There is even a small impressionist sketch ['Green Thoughts Are'] from 1915 that has something of the vivid freshness of a Welsh englyn or a Japanese tanka. . . .

It is interesting to note that, apart from the very early and unsuccessful "Ballad of Whitechapel", this is the only glimpse of East End life, perhaps of his own childhood, in Rosenberg's whole corpus. (p. 53)

It is also one of only seven or eight poems of Rosenberg's which I would consider complete, finished pieces. More even than most poets, he is a writer of starts, passages, middles, fragments, and more than most poets he has to be read in a spirit of retrieval, of sorting out the magical from the overcompressed, the off-key and the muddled. He has little sense of poetic logic, though he strove to master it. Even the best of his war poems, the four or five on which his reputation has grown, are shaky, with dead lines, patches of bathos and frequent tendencies to melodrama.

The whole conception of ["Dead Man's Dump"] in my opinion, is essentially melodramatic; it is rescued only by precariously successful writing strung between some truly excellent bits. . . .

Melodrama of conception ruins several other poems of the war period altogether poems such as "In the Trenches", "The Dying Soldier", "In War", and disastrous bathos wrecks the mock-portentous "The Immortals". "Break of Day in the Trenches" succeeds, shakily, because it attempts no very high flights, but really the only satisfyingly complete, all-of-a-piece war poems are two or three quite short ones, the successfully philosophical "A Worm Fed on the Heart of Corinth", "The Troop Ship" perhaps, though it is little more than an impression, and "August 1914". . . .

I am a little worried by the youth/tooth rhyme [in "August 1914"]; Rosenberg is far from immune to the bad habit of inserting a word, or writing a whole line, for the sake of a rhyme, but, in view of the quality of the rest of the poem and the marvellous image of the ripe fields, the last line can probably be allowed to pass muster. The famous "Returning, We Hear the Larks" has a more serious weakness in its ending, an image about girl's hair which has not been properly worked out and integrated in the poem; we see that it is a Medusa image, but it has been left conventional and disjointed, not tautened into poetry. This is a great pity, because the conception of the poem is sound and original, and the balancing of joy and deadly threat summons up a vivid sense of a moment in the nightmare life of the trenches, a moment when an unexpected grace comes out of the natural world at dawn and seems to bless stumbling, tired men full of profound relief at still being alive.

Given the circumstances under which Rosenberg wrote his war poems, my strictures may seem harsh; I doubt I'd have done half as well, in his place. I also understand the problems of the slow-developing kind of poet, the poet who experiments widely in order to find his way. There is ample evidence, in the letters, that Rosenberg regarded it as essential to get poems and concepts down and fixed, even in an imperfect way; shaping and refining could come later, after the war. (p. 54)

It is legitimate, I suppose, to wonder how much faith Rosenberg thought he could invest in the prospect of a calm life after the war in which all of its horrors and depths could be refined into great art, and how much he was driven by the reality of terrible danger to get something down on paper, even if patchy and imperfect, something to stand against extinction. Like many of us, he was half in love with the big-poem-yet-to-be-written, and conscious of the provisional nature of nearly all actual poems. It takes time, perhaps a lifetime, to see what is lasting and timeless in one's own work and what isn't, to realise that the great project is *in there*, wound through the texture of what one has done. Rosenberg didn't have that sort of time; he died with youth's belief in an available future, profoundly shaken perhaps, but still necessary to his thinking about his art. If he is sometimes praised nowadays rather in the spirit of the process theory of poetry, the poem as a mimesis of disorder rather than a wrestling with it to discover deeper order, I think that is anachronistic and rather corrupt, an attempt to recruit him to modernist, revolutionary purposes he never espoused and probably never heard of. It is probable that, if he had survived, he would have become a very important poet indeed, perhaps more important than any of the other English poets of the war generation, but it is also likely that his unsureness and lack of an instinctive sense of poetic design would have plagued him for many more years. Despite everything, I do believe his best passages point to a distinctive power in him which might have allowed English poetry to renew itself in a native way through his development. This may be what attracts English critics and poets to his cause, a wish that English poetry had been able to cross over into the modern era in its own terms, without the alien and wrenching effects of Eliot's and Pound's Franco-American modernism, that powerful but suspect strain which English poets have aped and resisted ever since.

But this is a nostalgia for national prestige in art, and resentment at relegation: it's about the Empire. In the long run, Rosenberg might have made the transition to peace better than Wilfred Owen, and might have found more to say. His wide range of experimentation with different modes and subjects before the war suggests it. Compared with the classic, coherent war poems which Owen achieved, however, his look patchy and tentative, and we are forced into valuing potential above performance if we place him above Owen. I think it is more justifiable to see him as ultimately superior to the rest, even Graves. Given a longer run, I'm pretty sure he would have left Graves far behind.

Ian Parsons mourns the lost potential of Rosenberg, but does not stretch it into speculative polemic [see excerpt above]. He has the more modest purpose of showing that his subject should not be thought of simply as a poet of the war, but as one who achieved distinctive and lasting things in the pre-war period, things quite different from and in advance of what most of his Georgian contemporaries were doing. There is some merit in

this claim, in that he certainly *tried* many quite distinctive things, poems about a female godhead, about a dead and rotting god, about gigantic, quasi-Blakean figures, and there is the rather fervidly erotic **"Night"**, which reads like a tussle with a deep and potent anima. There are many traces of this figure in his other poems, and we could start what the Germans call *culture-historical* hares if we began to speculate on its significance. To grow too involved in a poet's half-realised or unrealised themes, though, it to court the academic preference for ideas above poetry, that ambitious vice which has been the curse of criticism in this century. In my opinion, the nearest thing to a satisfyingly worked-out poem from Rosenberg's pre-war period is the delicate **"In Half Delight of Shy Delight"**, in which the young girl is seen 'still plaiting her men-unruffled curls.' . . . (pp. 54-5)

A slighter poem from the period which achieves simplicity without slipping into trite tum-te-tum is **"A Bird Trilling its Gay Heart Out"**. Otherwise, we are once again left with fragments and retrievals.

From the letters, it is clear that Rosenberg carried with him into his wartime period a great many continuities and poetic interests from the past; he probably never thought of the war as his prime theme, in the way that Owen did. The letters show that he held on, naturally enough, to a lot of poetic coggage which he would have had to discard if he had survived; in particular, he remained interested in his huge, fragmentary and nearly unreadable **"Moses"**, a sort of historico-mythical verse play on which he worked for years. An extract from this, the **"Ah Kolue"** speech, was the only poem of Rosenberg's which ever appeared in Marsh's annual *Georgian Poetry* anthology. It is hard to escape the feeling that, faithful as he was to his Jewish identity and heritage, the Hebrew tradition (got at second hand, since he did not read Hebrew) was never a very fruitful source for his poetry, though he dipped his bucket there many times, and was planning an epic or verse play on Judas Maccabaeus for the postwar period; a lot of his experience of war, and a lot of his thinking about it, was to have gone into this project. I have a feeling he would have met with a good deal of frustration, if he had lived to attempt this. The garment might not have fitted the body. His Hebraic poems always have a worked-up, costume-drama feel to them. He was, after all, a modern Jew, admittedly only a generation away from the *stetl*, but drawing nearly all of his cultural sustenance from English society and English art. His contribution, and it is a real and precious one, is to English poetry. His tragedy was part of a greater tragedy of Western man whose dimensions no one in his time could discern; he helped us to feel and imagine something of its inwardness. To that extent, he helped to bring our age into consciousness of itself. (p. 55)

Les Murray, "Isaac Rosenberg," in Quadrant *(reprinted by permission of* Quadrant, *Sydney, Australia),* Vol. XXIV, No. 3, March, 1980, pp. 52-5 *(and to be reprinted in his* Persistence in Folly, *Angus & Robertson, 1984).*

ADDITIONAL BIBLIOGRAPHY

Binyon, Laurence. Introduction to *Poems,* by Isaac Rosenberg, edited by Gordon Bottomley, pp. 1-50. London: William Heinemann, 1922.
    A laudatory discussion of Rosenberg's life and work.

[Blunden, Edmund]. "Rosenberg's Poetry." *The Times Literary Supplement,* No. 2530 (28 July 1950): 470.

A review in praise of *The Collected Poems of Isaac Rosenberg.* Blunden, himself a preeminent war poet, wrote of Rosenberg: "When it was his chance to see the tormented scene of war as a fighting man, he was not driven from his course as an imaginative herald; his grandeurs broke forth even from the squalor and the barbarism of battle; but he, too, had the touch of pity, or "Dead Man's Dump" would be less of a masterpiece."

Cohen, Joseph. "Isaac Rosenberg: The Poet's Progress in Print." *English Literature in Transition* 6, No. 3 (1963): 142-46.

Research paper. Cohen is the author of *Journey to the Trenches,* a study of Rosenberg's life and work. In this article, he relates the publishing history of the various editions of Rosenberg's works.

——. *Journey to the Trenches: The Life of Isaac Rosenberg, 1890-1918,* New York: Basic Books, 1975, 224 p.

A major biographical and critical study of Rosenberg's life and work.

Eliot, T. S. "A Brief Treatise on the Criticism of Poetry." *The Chapbook* II, No. 9 (March 1920): 1-10.

An essay on the poor quality of contemporary poetry criticism, which makes brief mention of Rosenberg as an unjustly neglected poet. Frequently cited in other essays on Rosenberg, Eliot's article reads, in part: "Let the public, however, ask itself why it has never heard of the poems of T. E. Hulme or of Isaac Rosenberg, and why it has heard of the poems of Lady Precocia Pondoeuf and has seen a photograph of the nursery in which she wrote them."

Gregory, Horace. "The Isolation of Isaac Rosenberg." In his *Spirit of Time and Place,* pp. 155-61. New York: W. W. Norton & Co., 1973.

Informative biographical and critical essay. Gregory believes that Rosenberg's social and artistic isolation were perhaps responsible for the "seriousness and independence" with which he contemplated his art, and for his conviction that "art intensifies life."

Grubb, Frederick. "War and Peace: The Embattled Truth; Wilfred Owen and Isaac Rosenberg." In his *A Vision of Reality: A Study of Liberalism in Twentieth Century Verse,* pp. 73-96. New York: Barnes & Noble, 1965.*

Compares Rosenberg to Blake and states that Rosenberg's poetry has more enduring value than that of any of the war poets other than Edward Thomas and Wilfred Owen.

Lewis, C. Day. "Isaac Rosenberg." *The London Mercury* XXXVI, No. 214 (August 1937): 386-87.

Reviews *The Collected Works of Isaac Rosenberg.* Lewis, himself a prominent figure among the leftist Oxford poets of the 1930s, praises Rosenberg's works, concluding that "We remember him by lines and phrases rather than by whole poems: in many of his best poems there is the effect of a fog rolling aside for a moment to reveal a brilliant world in movement, and then the fog rolls up again. There is little doubt that, if he had lived, he would have achieved the necessary integration between form and imagination."

Lindeman, Jack. "The 'Trench Poems' of Isaac Rosenberg." *The Literary Review* 2, No. 4 (Summer 1959): 577-85.

Discussion of the "Trench Poems" and the manner in which they reflect Rosenberg's "three loyalties": to the human race, to England, and to Judaism.

Muir, Edwin. "Poetry." In his *The Present Age from 1914,* edited by Bonamy Dobrée, pp. 43-128. London: Cresset Press, 1939.*

Brief summary of the war poets. Muir praises Rosenberg's dramatic verse, stating: "If he had lived he would have been a major poet or nothing."

Pinto, Vivian de Sola. "Trench Poets, Imagists and D. H. Lawrence." In his *Crisis in English Poetry: 1840-1940,* edited by Basil Willey, pp. 137-57. London: Hutchinson & Co., 1951.*

Comments on the unfair neglect Rosenberg's work has suffered.

Press, John. "Isaac Rosenberg." In his *Poets of World War I,* pp. 46-53. Windsor, England: Profile Books Ltd., 1983.*

Biographical and critical essay. The critic discusses Rosenberg's life and character, and briefly describes Rosenberg's treatment of the themes of death, sexuality, and spiritual regeneration in his poems and plays.

Robson, W. W. "The Poet from Cable Street." *The Times Literary Supplement,* No. 3833 (29 August 1975): 958-60.

Biographical and critical essay. Robson discusses the influences that shaped Rosenberg's art, including his family background, his schools, and his friends and patrons. This article also reviews the three biographies of Rosenberg written by Joseph Cohen, Jean Moorcroft Wilson, and Jean Liddiard.

Wilson, Jean Moorcroft. *Isaac Rosenberg: Poet & Painter.* London: Cecil Woolf, 1975, 220 p.

A helpful biography. Wilson's concluding chapter discusses the ways Rosenberg's works were affected by the events of his life.

Constance (Mayfield) Rourke

1885-1941

American critic, historian, essayist, and biographer.

Rourke was a pioneer in the field of American cultural history. Her *American Humor: A Study of the National Character* provided a fresh perspective on America's artistic heritage, and furnished a rebuttal to such critics as Van Wyck Brooks and T. S. Eliot, who asserted that America had no cultural traditions other than those that it had imported from Europe. In consequence, they claimed, American artists labored on barren ground. Rourke devoted years of travel and study to formulate a reply to these charges. The success of her efforts can be measured in part by the response of Van Wyck Brooks himself, who recanted his own theory and wrote in the introduction to Rourke's posthumous volume, *The Roots of American Culture, and Other Essays*, that she had "brought together proofs of a rich creative life in our past" and found indications "of distinctive native American elements."

Rourke was born in Cleveland, Ohio, in 1885. Her father died of tuberculosis when she was three years old, at which time Rourke's mother took over full responsibility for her education and support. Rourke studied at the Sorbonne and at Vassar, where she later taught for five years. As a young woman, she had a wide circle of friends, but the bond to her often difficult and demanding mother was the most important tie in her life. Many critics feel that the mother-daughter relationship described in Rourke's *Troupers of the Gold Coast; or, The Rise of Lotta Crabtree* mirrors, in many ways, her own deep attachment to her mother. She was also devoted to the city of Grand Rapids, Michigan, where she lived most of her life. Rourke viewed Grand Rapids as an ideal American community, replete with rich local traditions to nourish its artists and a history of support for the arts. Rourke's first major work, *Trumpets of Jubilee: Henry Ward Beecher, Harriet Beecher Stowe, Lyman Beecher, Horace Greeley, P. T. Barnum*, appeared in 1927. *Trumpets of Jubilee* examines the careers of these five individuals who, in their time, caught the public imagination and left an impact on American popular culture. All of the themes that Rourke developed in her later work are touched upon in this early study, including her theory that the American tradition is essentially theatrical in nature.

Rourke's reputation as a cultural historian was established by *American Humor*, which is still widely studied. This work was the result of Rourke's extensive "living research," in which she traveled throughout the United States, listening to the stories of old lumberjacks, riverboat captains, vaudeville actors, miners, and mountaineers, and examining every surviving example of folk art that she could uncover. In the resulting volume, Rourke advanced her theory that an American cultural tradition indeed exists, and that it is based on humor. She believed that this humor arose as a result of conflicts on many fronts between the Old and the New Worlds and cited as an example the clash of cultures between American colonists and Europeans, who regarded the "Yankees" as unlettered rustics. She maintained that much of American humor is devised for purposes of concealment, and that in its most typical form this humor represents an attempt to disguise the true nature of persons and situations. The black-face makeup of

the minstrel and the dead-pan delivery of the typical American narrative both function as masks. In *American Humor*, Rourke identified five pervasive American folk figures: the Yankee peddler, the backwoodsman, the strolling player, the minstrel, and the comic poet. Each of these five archetypes, she wrote, embodies one important aspect of the American character. In *American Humor* and in her later works, Rourke embraced Johann Gottfried von Herder's theory that frontier traditions give rise to folk art and, eventually, to fine art. Rourke's theory, technique, and unpretentious style led Stanley Edgar Hyman to call her approach "both analytic and synthetic" and describe it as "one of the most promising activities in American criticism."

Rourke died in 1941 as the result of a fall from an icy front porch in Grand Rapids. She had been at work on what was to have been a three volume "History of American Culture." Van Wyck Brooks edited her incomplete essays and voluminous notes and published them as *The Roots of American Culture* a year after Rourke's death. Critics agree that this book is flawed as a result of the unfinished state in which it was published. However, several essays in it are repeatedly singled out for praise: "The Shakers," "Voltaire Combe," and "Traditions for a Negro Literature."

Rourke's other works include the biographies *Troupers of the Gold Coast, Davy Crockett*, and *Audubon*. In discussing *Trou-*

pers of the Gold Coast, commentators often criticize Rourke for adopting a theatrical style of writing which, they believe, undermines the work's scholarly value. *Davy Crockett* and *Audubon* have also been attacked for stylistic failings. Rourke wrote these works for juveniles, but their comprehensive bibliographies reveal the extensive research that went into their preparation. Critics feel that had Rourke presented her material differently, she could have appealed to a broader audience and gained scholarly acceptance for what are essentially very scholarly works. In her biography of painter Charles Sheeler, Rourke overcame these early faults, and this work has been unanimously praised by critics for its exceptional insights and astute analysis of the manner in which folk art forms are adapted for use in the fine arts.

Rourke's work was often denied scholarly recognition during her lifetime due to her deliberately affected bibliographic casualness and folksy style. However, she believed that these techniques "spared her the intellectual's risk of isolation," and "kept her at the center of American life." *The Nation* said of Rourke that "her underlying purpose was to bring to the American present a greater and more informed awareness of the American past, especially in the arts; for it was her conviction that specific integrated knowledge and understanding of the past was indispensible to the creative worker in any field."

(See also *Contemporary Authors*, Vol. 107.)

PRINCIPAL WORKS

Trumpets of Jubilee: Henry Ward Beecher, Harriet Beecher Stowe, Lyman Beecher, Horace Greeley, P. T. Barnum (biographies) 1927
Troupers of the Gold Coast; or, The Rise of Lotta Crabtree (biography) 1928
American Humor: A Study of the National Character (history and criticism) 1931
Davy Crockett (biography) 1934
Audubon (biography) 1936
Charles Sheeler: Artist in the American Tradition (biography and criticism) 1938
*The Roots of American Culture, and Other Essays (essays) 1942

*This work was completed by Van Wyck Brooks.

LEONARD WOOLF (essay date 1927)

[*Woolf is best known as one of the leaders of the "Bloomsbury Group" of artists and thinkers, and as the husband of novelist Virginia Woolf, with whom he founded the famous Hogarth Press. The Bloomsbury Group, which was named after the section of London where the members lived and met, also included Clive and Vanessa Bell, John Maynard Keynes, Lytton Strachey, Virginia Woolf, Desmond MacCarthy, and several others. The group's weekly meetings were occasions for lively discussions of philosophy, literature, art, economics, politics, and life in general. Although the group observed no formal manifesto, Woolf and the others generally held to the tenets of philosopher G. E. Moore's* Principia Ethica, *the essence of which is, in Moore's words, that "one's prime objects in life were love, the creation and enjoyment of aesthetic experience, and the pursuit of knowledge." In the excerpt below, Woolf reviews* Trumpets of Jubilee.]

[The recently-published autobiography of P. T. Barnum] is an amalgamation of the various autobiographies published by Barnum during his lifetime. Those who embark upon it should not miss another book just published, **"Trumpets of Jubilee,"** by Constance Mayfield Rourke. . . . Barnum and Miss Rourke between them supply 1,300 large pages of reading matter, which will last a good many people through their summer holidays. Miss Rourke has had a very good idea, and has carried it out with considerable ability. She has written the lives of Lyman Beecher, his daughter Harriet Beecher Stowe, his son, Henry Ward Beecher, Horace Greeley, the founder and editor of the *Tribune*, and Barnum. The title of her book might well have been "The Big Drummers," for the connection between her five biographees is that they all had a genius for big drum beating, an instinct for shouting "Walk up, walk up, ladies and gentlemen," in just that tone of voice which would make the great public flock into their church, lecture-room, museum, or circus, or rush to buy their "Uncle Tom's Cabin." Miss Rourke's book is not exactly easy reading, and her style is somewhat fatiguing; but I found it extraordinarily entertaining, full of information which was new to me, and packed with details which show the incredible vagaries of the human soul.

> Leonard Woolf, "The Big Drummers," in The Nation and The Athenaeum, *Vol. XLI, No. 18, August 6, 1927, p. 609.**

MARK VAN DOREN (essay date 1934)

[*Van Doren, the younger brother of Carl Van Doren, was one of America's most prolific and diverse writers of the twentieth century. His work includes poetry—for which he won the Pulitzer Prize in 1939—novels, short stories, drama, criticism, social commentary, and the editing of a number of popular anthologies. He has written accomplished studies of Shakespeare, John Dryden, Nathaniel Hawthorne, and Henry David Thoreau, and served as the literary editor and film critic for the* Nation *during the 1920s and 1930s. Van Doren's criticism is aimed at the general reader, rather than the scholar or specialist, and is noted for its lively perception and wide interest. Like his poetry and fiction, his criticism consistently examines the inner, idealistic life of the individual. In the words of Carlos Baker, Van Doren brings to his best work "a warmth of epithet, a crisp precision of definition, and a luminousness of poetic insight." In the excerpt below, Van Doren offers a guarded but generally admiring review of* Davy Crockett. *He acknowledges the difficulties faced by the author who seeks to write a factual biography of a legendary historical figure.*]

"Davy Crockett" is essentially a study of that ringtailed, roaring American language which seems to have been at the peak of its richness a little more than a century ago. It was heard in the Western clearings and up back trails, but more particularly it was heard along the great rivers, the Ohio and the Mississippi, which were the thoroughfares of a swarming, many-colored culture. (p. 193)

Miss Rourke has been quite as much interested in the legend of Crockett as in the man himself, or at any rate she has permitted herself to quote and paraphrase liberally from the almanacs and chapbooks which continued for twenty years after his death to fabricate things he might have said. The things he might have said and done are so little different from the things he did say and do, and the whole body of lingo is so interesting and typical in itself, that Miss Rourke rightly enough represents it all. There are those, indeed, who would have forbidden her to make use even of Crockett's own autobiographies, long considered spurious. But she has been at some pains to prove that the earliest of these, known as the ''Narrative,'' was written by him with the help of one Thomas Chilton; she is willing to accept portions of the ''Tour'' as authentic; and she does not hesitate to take incidents from the posthumous ''Exploits'' in order to round out her tale of the hero who died at San Antonio. No reader should quarrel with such a method when it is employed by so able and intelligent a writer as Miss Rourke, who among other things knows how to quote supremely well; so well, indeed, that we are spared the suspicion, unless we suddenly come to and begin to think for ourselves, that much of the tall talk she praises must have been unbearably dull, and that Crockett himself must have had his tiresome hours. Neither, surely, was he quite the fellow whom Miss Rourke makes him out to be. He was probably a little less important, a little less noble, if one can judge by the ''Narrative'' which Miss Rourke herself authenticates; for in that book the buzz of his tongue grows sometimes very tedious, as no doubt it did in Washington, in Jackson's day. But the privilege of idealization is one again that no rational reader will deny so charming a writer as Miss Rourke. She has done something not easy to do. She has preserved a horsefly in amber. (pp. 193-95)

> Mark Van Doren, ''A Coonskin Classic,'' in The Nation (*copyright 1934* The Nation *magazine, The Nation Associates, Inc.*), *Vol. CXXXVIII, No. 3582, February 28, 1934 (and reprinted as ''Books, 1921-1938: A Coonskin Classic,'' in his* The Private Reader: Selected Articles and Reviews, *Henry Holt and Company, 1942, pp. 193-95*).

STEPHEN VINCENT BENÉT   (essay date 1936)

[*Benét was an American man of letters whose poetry and fiction is often concerned with examining, understanding, and celebrating American history and culture. The comic short story* ''The Devil and Daniel Webster'' *and the Pulitzer Prize-winning Civil War epic* John Brown's Body *are his best-known works. In the excerpt below, Benét offers an enthusiastic assessment of Rourke's* Audubon.]

[Miss Rourke's life of Audubon] is also a life of the wilderness, a life of the earlier America he saw and lived in and loved. . . . [It] was a green Paradise for a man like Audubon—and for other men, too, who had neither his genius nor his eyes. And its shape remains at the back of our minds, and colors our beliefs and our thinking. Miss Rourke knows the frontier, and that there were many frontiers from Audubon's to Big Harp's. It has been described as a place where you could find almost anything and usually did. . . .

The question of Audubon's birth and parentage, Miss Rourke discusses, perhaps, as fully as is possible from the rather confused evidence. Audubon himself is reported to have said ''My own name I have never been permitted to speak. Accord me that of Audubon, which I revere, as I have cause to do.'' . . . I think Miss Rourke would like him to be the lost Dauphin, if it were possible, and she presents very fascinatingly the speculations that might be in favor of it, though, of course, she is far too sound a biographer to present them as anything but speculations and possibilities. But I seem to detect (perhaps unjustly) a slight wistfulness in her tone when she speaks of it—and it is a wistfulness I share. For, if it could be proved, it would be one of the great, engaging melodramas of history. Not that it is necessary. The necessary thing is the ''Birds of America'' with its more than a thousand birds, its almost five hundred species—the ''Ornithological Biography,'' the ''Vi-

viparous Quadrupeds'' the journals, the letters, the portraits, the sketches, the plates. You have only to look at one of the plates reproduced in this volume to see what Audubon did. And, in this life, Miss Rourke has done for him what he did for the birds of his new country. She has painted him in his habitat and alive. (p. 2)

> *Stephen Vincent Benét, ''Audubon and the American Wilderness,'' in* New York Herald Tribune Books (© *I.H.T. Corporation; reprinted by permission*), *November 1, 1936, pp. 1-2.*

VAN WYCK BROOKS   (essay date 1942)

[*Brooks is noted chiefly for his biographical and critical studies of such writers as Mark Twain, Henry James, and Ralph Waldo Emerson, and for his influential commentary on the history of American literature. His career can be neatly divided into two distinct periods: the first, from 1908 to 1925, dealt primarily with the negative impact of European Puritanism on the development of artistic genius in America. Brooks argued that the puritan conscience in the United States, carried over from Europe, produced an unhealthy dichotomy in American writers and resulted in a literature split between stark realism and what he called ''vaporous idealism.'' During this early period, Brooks believed that in reality America had no culture of its own, and that American literature relied almost exclusively on its European heritage, a view which Rourke frequently attacked. After 1925, and his study of Emerson, Brooks radically altered his view of American literary history, conforming in many ways with Rourke's conceptions of American culture. Brooks began to see much in America's past as unique and artistically valuable, and he called for a return in literary endeavors to the positive values of Emerson, as opposed to the modern pessimism of such writers as T. S. Eliot and James Joyce. By the time of Rourke's death, Brooks was sympathetic to her viewpoint. He edited her final work and wrote the following summary of her career.*]

Constance Rourke began to write at a moment when the American mind was intensely concerned with itself, past, present and future, a moment of self-recognition that was marked by a number of writers who were bent on exploring the culture and resources of the country. . . . With her deep roots in the Middle West, she pondered over the statement, so frequently made by other critics, that America had no esthetic tradition of its own. Was it true, she asked herself, that we had failed to produce a culture in which the arts could flourish? If this was true, it was serious, it was ominous indeed, for no art had ever reached a point where it could speak a world-language without an inheritance of local expression behind it. Occasional peaks of achievement did not alter this rule. As Constance Rourke said later in her study of Charles Sheeler, ''Art has always taken on a special native fibre before it assumes the greater breadth;'' and therefore an American esthetic tradition was a desideratum that was not to be lightly given away. It was so fundamental that it was not to be surrendered unless there were positive proofs that it did not exist. And how far had American criticism explored this subject? As for the tradition itself, if this could be shown to exist it might make all the difference for the future of our art and all the difference, meanwhile, for the creative worker. What would not our artists gain in maturity and confidence if they felt that they were working ''in a natural sequence''?

It was in some such terms as these that Constance Rourke posed her problem, well knowing that if she could solve it successfully and fully the consequences might be important for American art. Meanwhile, she had been drawn to the theories

of Herder, of which Whitman had seen the implications, theories that had been distorted in the interests of antiquarianism
but never, as she felt, truly explored. According to Herder,
the folk-forms were essential in any communal group, they
were the texture of the communal experience and expression,
and the fine arts sprang out of the folk-arts and one had to look
to these in order to find the source of any culture. Here Constance Rourke found herself challenged at the outset. That
America had no folk-art was the general opinion: it was all but
universally believed that we had no folk-expression aside from
vestigial remains of European culture. Constance Rourke was
not deterred by this belief, and she felt that our dominant
conception of culture was wrong. Culture, according to this
idea, was something to be imposed from without by a process
known as the "transit of civilization." It was John Fiske who
used this phrase, and it was Fiske's conception that "carriers"
were to bring us piecemeal the culture of Europe; and it was
assumed that if we dipped deeply enough into the main streams
of European culture we might ultimately hope to witness their
rise in this country. In the meantime, we were the victims of
a "cultural lag;" and Constance Rourke opposed this theory
because it led us to disregard the ways in which every culture
has actually developed. It goes without saying that she did not
wish to isolate us from these main streams of European culture.
She welcomed them all, but that was another matter. She merely
said that the question was not whether we might "catch up"
with Europe, the question was one of finding a center of our
own, and the center of every culture has always existed within
the social organism of the country itself. Was it true, then, to
return to Herder, that we really had no folk-forms? Was it not
rather the case that we had a long folk-life behind us which
had found inevitable expression in forms of its own? Had not
the critics ignored the creative forces that have always existed
in this country? And could these not be shown to constitute an
esthetic tradition?

To prove the existence of this tradition, to reveal it in manifold
ways was Constance Rourke's purpose in all her writings. She
felt that if she could assemble materials enough, the tradition
would declare itself through them, and she wished to make our
natural inheritance accessible in order that it might nourish the
workers of the future, placing them in possession of characteristic native forms which they might use to advantage as
points of departure. Her work was thus mainly exploratory,
and she threw herself into it with a zest that took her into every
corner of the country. (pp. vi-ix)

[When her studies were completed and her conclusions drawn,]
Constance Rourke had assembled proofs of a rich creative life
in our past, and she had found indications in it of distinctive
native American elements. Derived as it may have been from
Europe, our early culture diverged from Europe in accordance
with our native experience and needs.

Her history would have attempted to show how far this was
true, and some of the papers [included in *The Roots of American
Culture and Other Essays*] already show it. She points out, for
instance, how colonial Annapolis, which was sometimes called
the American Bath, differed in its easy spaciousness from the
English Bath. She shows how American Calvinism diverged
from English Calvinism and formed a wholly new cultural
pattern, how all our original patterns of thought and feeling
were gradually "pulled into new dimensional forms." It was
so in our early theater, in our early music. The motivating ideas
from Europe were shaped to our own distinctive ends, and
Constance Rourke shows how the fumblings of our nascent

culture sprang from a life and experience that were peculiar to
the country. . . . I have been able to salvage only a few fragments from the great mass of her half-written manuscripts and
notes, but these are enough to show, I think, how important
the work would have been for artists and writers and students
of American culture. As they stand, these fragments, side by
side with her other books, reveal the rich stores of tradition
that lie behind us, the many streams of native character and
feeling from which the Americans of the future will be able
to draw. (pp. xi-xii)

> *Van Wyck Brooks, in his preface to* The Roots of
> American Culture, and Other Essays *by Constance
> Rourke, edited by Van Wyck Brooks (copyright 1942
> by Harcourt Brace Jovanovich, Inc.; renewed 1970
> by Alice D. Fore; reprinted by permission of the
> publisher), Harcourt Brace Jovanovich, 1942, pp.
> v-xii.*

JOSEPH WOOD KRUTCH   (essay date 1942)

[*Krutch is widely regarded as one of America's most respected
literary and drama critics. Noteworthy among his works are* The
American Drama since 1918 *(1939), which analyzes the most
important dramas of the 1920s and 1930s, and "Modernism" in*
Modern Drama *(1953), in which he stressed the need for twentieth-
century playwrights to infuse their works with traditional humanistic values. A conservative and idealistic thinker, he was a
consistent proponent of human dignity and the preeminence of
literary art. His literary criticism is characterized by such concerns: in* The Modern Temper *(1929) he argued that because
scientific thought has denied human worth, tragedy has become
obsolete, and in* The Measure of Man *(1954) he attacked modern
culture for depriving humanity of the sense of individual responsibility necessary for making important decisions in an increasingly complex age. In the following excerpt, Krutch provides a
general discussion of Rourke's career and a favorable review of*
The Roots of American Culture, and Other Essays.]

Up to her untimely death last year Constance Rourke was
engaged upon a history of American culture planned in three
volumes. . . . From what Van Wyck Brooks calls "the great
mass of her half-written manuscripts and notes" he has been
able to salvage eight fragments, [published as *The Roots of
American Culture and Other Essays*] . . . a volume of modest
size. Of the five which run to any considerable length two,
"The Roots of American Culture" and **"American Art: A
Possible Future,"** are generalized and speculative; three, **"The
Rise of Theatricals," "Early American Music"** and **"The
Shakers,"** are in considerable part factual.

All are interesting, well—and sometimes wittily—written. But
they are fragments; fragments extensive enough to reveal clearly
both the author's point of view and the fact that she spread the
net of her research both very widely indeed and deep into
seldom-explored seas; sufficiently fragmentary, nevertheless,
to leave unanswered the questions how and how well she would
have been able to solve the problems of scale, selection and
integration. Occasionally one feels that on the scale indicated
by the treatment of certain subjects, not three, but three hundred
volumes would have been required. Occasionally, also, it seems
that certain picturesque incidents and personages are less specifically American than they are assumed to be. And in passing
it may also be remarked that the decision—made either by Miss
Rourke or Mr. Brooks—to omit, absolutely all reference to
authorities or sources greatly diminishes the value of the fragments to any one who would like to pursue a subject where
the author left it off.

Miss Rourke, as readers of her previous books are aware, belongs to that school of cultural historians which takes its leading conceptions from the anthropologists rather than from the conventional historians of literature or art. That means, to begin with, that by ''culture'' is not meant ''the best that has been thought and said,'' but the whole complex of thoughts, habits, ideals and institutions which constitute a way of life. . . .

Such an historian does not ask when did Pope or Rousseau or Handel reach America. He asks instead what rhymes did the backwoodsman make or what songs did the Shakers sing. And by so doing he opens up a whole new field of study.

Miss Rourke does not, of course, deny that foreign influences exist or that they are important. What she resists is the absolutist conception of art as something fundamentally distinct from the writing, building or singing which goes on below the level of self-conscious artistic creation and therefore as something of which the very conception must be passed on from one country to another after the fashion, to use the standard simile, of ''the torch.'' She quotes, as a satisfactory expression of what she rejects, a phrase of John Fiske's, who spoke of the ''transit of civilization,'' and she rejects along with it the whole idea that American culture must await the day when we have achieved sufficient leisure, wealth and stability to first import and then assimilate an effective leaven from elsewhere. . . .

Both theories have their dangers. The proponent of the one is likely to see ''influences'' everywhere; the other to underestimate them. Even more important, perhaps, is the fact that the student who fixes his attention on the ''transit of culture'' is likely to present the literary or artistic history of our country as a desert relieved by only a few cases, while the search after the American tradition is likely to find himself buried beneath the multiplicity of his materials. Miss Rourke occasionally seems to minimize unduly ''influences'' even when she does not deny them. To her, for example, it seems not so very much more than a curious coincidence that our plays about the Indian should so commonly idealize him just at the time when the conception of the ''noble savage'' was reaching our shores although, as a matter of fact, a pretty good case could no doubt be made out for the contention that the Indian of our early literature is the noble savage. Where another sort of historian would stress the fact that Royal Tyler probably has ''The School for Scandal'' well in mind when he wrote ''The Contrast,'' Miss Rourke brushes aside as unimportant whatever he may have learned from Sheridan. So, also, it might be questioned whether or not one of the most vivid and entertaining of her passages, a rapid portrait of that great eccentric, Junius Brutus Booth, reveals in him anything exclusively American. He has a more spacious stage on which to play, but why are his antics any more American than those of his great immediate predecessors in England—John Phillip Kemble, who regularly got majestically tight in the best company, or Edmund Kean, whose intoxications had a more Dionysian character?

These criticisms are, however, very minor and the value of Miss Rourke's work is hardly diminished by them or by any doubts one may have as to the truth or falsity of her theory as such. The important fact, aside from the sheer interest of her writing, is the fact that she presents a picture of American cultural life so much livelier than the one to be got from conventional historians. Whether early America was or was not a cultural desert by Matthew Arnold's definition, at least its people were not leading lives which seemed dull or barren to them. They were not waiting drearily for the emergence of

culture. They were dancing and fiddling and singing and writing and declaiming at a great and lively rate.

Joseph Wood Krutch, ''Constance Rourke, Explorer of Our Folk Arts,'' in New York Herald Tribune Books *(© I.H.T. Corporation; reprinted by permission), August 9, 1942, p. 3.*

ALFRED KAZIN   (essay date 1942)

[*A highly respected American literary critic, Kazin is best known for his essay collections* The Inmost Leaf *(1955) and* Contemporaries *(1962), and particularly for* On Native Grounds *(1942), a study of American prose writing since the era of William Dean Howells. Having studied the works of ''the critics who were the best writers—from Sainte-Beuve and Matthew Arnold to Edmund Wilson and Van Wyck Brooks'' as an aid to his own critical understanding, Kazin has found that ''criticism focussed many— if by no means all—of my own urges as a writer: to show literature as a deed in human history, and to find in each writer the uniqueness of the gift, of the essential vision, through which I hoped to penetrate into the mystery and sacredness of the individual soul.'' In perhaps the most discussed review of Rourke's works, Kazin praises* The Roots of American Culture, and Other Essays, *but perceives Rourke to have failed in establishing the connection between America's early culture and that of the present day.*]

When Constance Rourke died in 1941, she left a few essays and fragments of what was to have been her central work, the book toward which all her affectionate and meticulous studies in American art and the American character had been preparatory: a three-volume ''essay'' elucidating the richness and distinction of neglected native sources in American culture. The biographer of Audubon and Davy Crockett and Charles Sheeler, the historian of frontier theatricals in **''Troupers of the Gold Coast,''** the student of American folklore in **''American Humor''** and of nineteenth-century American personality in **''Trumpets of Jubilee,''** editor in her last years of the WPA Index of American Design, she had for thirty years made America her subject, with an attachment to American data that was as imaginative as her feeling for style; and in this last unfinished testament of her devotion she had outlined an affirmation of our cultural resources that she meant as a challenge to our traditional and Europe-fascinated conception of the origin and the place of the arts in America.

What she was aiming at in this last book was a radical revaluation of the conception that the arts in America have had to be derived from European forms, that we have been ''carriers,'' in John Fiske's word, from the Old World to the New. Out of her studies over the whole range of American art and folklore, her sensibility to what was original in the American texture, she had come to the conviction that this assumption of America's necessary lag behind Europe in the arts, the very assumption that we have had to go to Europe for the life of art at all, sacrificed what we had most to give ourselves out of our own past. Following Herder's theory that the fine arts can grow best only out of the native folk arts, she staked out a field for herself in the folk art of early American communities and went back to them to extract the native inheritance—to oratory and design, the frontier legends, the decorative art of the Pennsylvania Dutch, the spare small houses of early New England ''that had almost the quality of abstract sculpture,'' early shipbuilding and city planning, the communal art of groups like the Shakers, the dramatic elements in the Indian treaties, early religious music, and much else. Here in our buried but accessible past, as she felt, in the graphic enduring evidences that lay almost under our feet in America, was a wealth of esthetic insight and craft, of lost spiritual gifts in the arts, of spaciousness and strength, that we had passed over in false humility or ignorance, and out of a mechanical submission to the European example. Here, in work as precise as the delicately-carved Shaker furniture, as colorful as the early theatricals, as lusty as the frontier tales, as spiritually intense as the early music, was a distinctive tradition—a good thing *and* our own.

A folklorist of philosophic breadth rather than an antiquary or nationalist, Constance Rourke did not mean that these native forms were enough for us, that we had now to break away from Europe, as it were, and collect our vestiges. For herself, she enjoyed collecting American vestiges, primitives and designs, as she enjoyed the frontier legends of which she wrote so exquisitely in **"American Humor,"** the early theatricals, and everything that had the clean firm lines of early American creations. What she sought was a richer self-awareness of our native character and potential, a sense of our creative identity, a conception of culture not limited merely to literature or the yearning after the abstract European graces. "The classic has nothing to do with grandeur." In the phrase she applied to the enduring character in the paintings of the forgotten Voltaire Combe, she sought "the irreducible element"—our native element, the irreducible and the ineradicable that gave character to us. This irreducible element was what she had explored in Audubon and Davy Crockett, in the great folk creation of the Yankee, in the welding of many foreign strands into an original creation; and tracing its lines, its addiction to myth, the qualities she found in the Puritan ceremonials, the Pennsylvania Dutch barns, the Texas tall tales, the classic ring of Sam Houston's speeches, the effect of American climate and atmosphere, she went deep into the subterranean sources of American community life. A student and exponent of folk culture, she could at the end have said, in D. H. Lawrence's words: "Men are free when they are in a living homeland . . . free when they belong to a living, organic, believing community, active in fulfilling some unfulfilled, perhaps unrealized purpose."

Seeking this irreducible element, Constance Rourke worked all her life in the tentative and the unexplored with the same quiet exhilaration that she had described in Audubon before his birds—"He habitually saw the world at daybreak." She was an observer, a seeker of essence; poles removed from those who offered us only a derivative culture, she was equally removed from the complaisant antiquaries and historical romancers who have lately exploited our panicky cultural nationalism. She sought what so many modern Americans have lost, what so many Europeans have established as the first principle of a human existence—the sense of locality, the simple happiness of *belonging* to a particular culture; she had no interest in isolating us from the European patrimony. To understand this is to understand how fundamentally simple and yet rare was her curiosity, how deeply she had grasped the inner truth and the pain of the modern American alienation. "Belief makes the mind abundant," Yeats said; Constance Rourke knew something about the lack of belief and continuity, the damaging void in the modern American spirit.

Beyond that effort to locate and define a native inheritance, however, she did not go; and it was just here that she failed us. For having restored what had often not been even known, she took it for granted, as in her last chapter here on **"American Art: A Possible Future,"** that the way ahead was in some sense clear; that we had as definable a future as we had available a tradition. A creative worker in folklore, she confused the plea-

sure she took in her own explorations, even the subtle grace she conferred upon them in all her books, with an imminent opportunity in art for others. But while the past she recovered lives in some measure in her books, it lives as the refraction of her curiosity and sympathy, as a series of touching and comic vignettes on the page; it is an image, a story told, not ready ground on which we can stand. In this Constance Rourke, though scrupulously unsentimental, unwittingly paralleled what Van Wyck Brooks has done in his elegies to the classic glories of Concord, what so many biographers and historians have lately done in their effort to search out an American tradition to sustain us against the moral insecurity of the times. They have assumed that to recover an example is to make it available and fertile for us; they have assumed that to recover the past bodily and uncritically, as in the massive American records of our day, is to confer its abstract glow concretely.upon us. Constance Rourke was not thinking, like Brooks, of John Greenleaf Whittier's sweetness of character; she was gathering examples of craft. But having found an esthetic tradition of our own, she inevitably assumed that we had only to enjoy it, to catch its leading impulses, to let it direct us fruitfully.

Where Brooks has ceased to be interested in criticism, Constance Rourke, for all her skill in esthetic analysis, had not yet approached its contemporary ground: restoring our inheritance, she could only give us lofty vistas. Brooks has failed us since "The Life of Emerson" by making too facile, too treacherously emotional, an equation between past and present; Constance Rourke failed us by not drawing the wealth of patterns and skills she had uncovered into *our* "natural sequence" now, our contemporary predicament and need. . . . We know now that we have an inheritance, that we have our irreducible element. But that is all we shall know—the legend, the museum, the light golden haze given back—until it has become works as well as faith. We have our irreducible element, but we shall never know what it is we have until we can use it without piety or the endless frightened supplications to the past. Commemoration, somehow, is never enough. (pp. 259-60)

Alfred Kazin, "The Irreducible Element," in The New Republic *(reprinted by permission of the author),* Vol. 107, No. 9, August 31, 1942, pp. 259-60.

STANLEY EDGAR HYMAN   (essay date 1948)

[*As a long time literary critic for* The New Yorker, *Hyman enjoyed a prominent position in American letters from 1940 to 1970. He is most famous for his belief that much of modern literary criticism should depend on knowledge received from disciplines outside the field of literature; consequently, many of his best reviews and critical essays rely on his application of theories gleaned from cultural anthropology, psychology, comparative religion, and other disciplines. In the following excerpt, Hyman provides a detailed survey of Rourke's career and compares her work to that of other American folklorists.*]

When Constance Rourke died in 1941, at the age of fifty-six, she had only begun to find her direction. She had published six books and was at work on a monumental three-volume *History of American Culture,* for which all the other books were merely preliminary exploration. A few years before, in **Charles Sheeler,** she had hit on what will probably emerge as her chief contribution to contemporary criticism, a method of analyzing formal art in terms of its roots in folk tradition. At the same time she was engaged in finding, organizing, interpreting, and popularizing an American folk tradition that would be available to future artists. Her work was thus both analytic and synthetic, and the two strands together constitute one of the most promising activities in American criticism, unfortunately carried on since her death by no one.

Her first book, *Trumpets of Jubilee,* . . . is a study of five persons of wide popular appeal in America in the middle years of the last century: Lyman Beecher, Harriet Beecher Stowe, Henry Ward Beecher, Horace Greeley, and P. T. Barnum. It is to some extent biography, to some extent social history, and to some extent, in the section on Mrs. Stowe, the only literary figure in the group, genuine criticism (including a shrewd analysis of why *Uncle Tom's Cabin* had a power none of her other novels achieved, and a very perceptive comparison with Hawthorne). Some of the social history gets down to underlying causal factors, but a good deal of it is simply a skimming of the surface, a reporting on vagaries of furniture and costume, and the folk material in the book,—an interpolated fragment of "Old Dan Tucker," some fine tall tales—is of the latter order, a kind of superior local color. The book is least satisfactory in regard to the Beecher clan, since Miss Rourke never quite manages to define their appeal; most generally satisfactory in the Barnum section, a brilliant study of the man as a focus for an age's giantism; and perhaps most dramatically effective in the portrait of Horace Greeley, a deeply moving story sharpened into tragedy by the only editorializing Miss Rourke permitted herself in the book, an ironic picture of the social pretensions of the Greeley children after their father's death. As a book it is rather a mixed performance, but all the strains of the later work are in it, struggling to break through the crust of traditional social history.

The next book, *Troupers of the Gold Coast,* published a year later, is Miss Rourke's least ambitious work. It is an undistinguished, pleasant, and superficial attempt to create the atmosphere of old-time theatrical trouping, and it has something of the tone of a scrapbook full of faded theater programs, a button off Edwin Booth's jacket, and a garter worn by Adah Menken. It is not a book that anyone without golden childhood memories of Lotta Crabtree or Lola Montez would bother reading. The book has nothing that could fairly be called either social or cultural history, and of folk material only a dozen fragments of folksongs and popular songs of the period, and a few brief pages on the "characters" of early San Francisco: the Great Unknown, "George Washington," the Fat Boy, Guttersnipe, Rosie, two dogs named Bummer and Lazarus, and the Emperor Norton. It has no critical method, and in fact no criticism.

American Humor, subtitled *A Study of the National Character,* appeared in 1931, an ambitious unraveling of one strand in the cultural history of the United States. The book divides American folk-related culture into a number of separate studies (frequently obtaining what Kenneth Burke calls "perspective by incongruity" through the use of shrewd juxtapositions): the Yankee and backwoodsmen as American types; the minstrel show; trouping performers and religious cultists as two types of American "strollers"; Lincoln and the comic writers; the classic American writers; the Western humorists; James and Howells as facets of the American artist; contemporary writers through the twenties. The formal literary figures are treated as outgrowths of the folk culture, sometimes with a certain distortion—Hawthorne becomes a teller of folk tales, *Moby Dick,* with its comic Biblical names and nautical puns, a cousin to the joke-books of the day—but sometimes the distortion is a brilliant restoration, like the recognition of Lincoln as a literary figure. Miss Rourke is constantly hovering on the verge of a

deeper concept of folk culture, a matter of archetypal myth and ritual, which she learned from Jane Harrison's *Ancient Art and Ritual* but never quite manages to apply. She notes that Mike Fink was "a Mississippi river-god, one of those minor deities whom men create in their own image and magnify to magnify themselves," and that Crockett "became a myth even in his own lifetime," and after his death assumed "an even bolder legendary stature than before." She sees the process, though, as essentially a euhemerizing one, a fairly civilized folk somehow "mythologizing" a historical character within a few years, instead of recognizing the dynamic development implicit in Miss Harrison's view, whereby historical characters with what might be called "myth-attracting" features acquire older mythic attributes and stories.

Miss Rourke notes that a "legendary assumption of wisdom" has "appeared persistently among American comic characters," but is unable to go on and interpret it as a complex transference from ancient oracles to Old Zip Coon (if not directly from an African prototype). She mentions "the primary stuffs of literature": "the theatre that lies behind the drama, the primitive religious ceremony that has been anterior to both, the tale that has preceded both the drama and the novel, the monologue that has been a rudimentary source for many forms." She is able to recognize these ancient patterns underlying American pseudo-folk-poetry, but the understanding of processes of the "folk work" like transmission, independent origin, accretion, continuity, and alteration that would have enabled her to define the relationship is beyond her. . . . What Miss Rourke manages to do in the book is define the "primitive base," consisting of "songs and primitive ballads and a folk-theater and rude chronicles," often "full of coarse and fragmentary elements, full of grotesquerie or brutality," on which our literature, like any other, rests, and insist on that relationship as her central theme and concern:

> Through the interweaving of the popular strain
> with that of a new expression on other levels
> a literature has been produced which, like other
> literatures, is related to an anterior popular lore
> that must for lack of a better word be called
> folk-lore.

The conclusion of the book formulates the synthetic function: few artists have worked without a rich traditional store, the task of criticism is "discovering and diffusing the materials of the American tradition" in which the artist may steep himself.

Miss Rourke's next two books were attempts at diffusing that traditional store. The first was *Davy Crockett,* . . . and the second *Audubon.* . . . The *Crockett* is Miss Rourke's only thorough failure. Written in the condescending popular style of a juvenile for teen-age readers, the book is a jumble of the real Crockett and the legend; a sequence of dramatized anecdotes, including Crockett's children speaking "tall talk" around the house, strung-together Crockett fables from the *Almanacs,* with little interest in the real man and his significance. The sort of thing Miss Rourke is reduced to is sneaking in Crockett's vote in defense of Biddle and the Bank, buried in a sentence about something else with no attempt made to explain it. *Davy Crockett* is unscholarly, unanalytic, "folksy" in the worst sense of the word, and generally an unreadable and poor book. *Audubon* two years later somewhat redeemed the record. Although straight biography with no attempt at criticism or analysis, the book is at least, unlike the *Crockett,* interesting and well written, and Miss Rourke confined her gullibility to accepting as a strong possibility the legend that Audubon was the little lost Dauphin, and telling an extremely dubious etiological myth of his inventing the combination of pastel and water-color technique he used by a lucky movie accident one day. Both books made available to American writers aspects of American frontier tradition, the pioneering man of action and the pioneering artist, but unfortunately made them available in a form any serious writer could be pardoned for ignoring.

Constance Rourke's first book of genuine folk criticism was *Charles Sheeler*. . . . In Sheeler she found a serious artist (although not so good a one as she believed) who had discovered an American folk tradition for himself, the functional form of the Shaker artisans, and who had consciously grounded his work in it, to the work's great benefit. Looking at Sheeler's paintings and photographs (many of them reproduced as evidence in the book), she discovered the basic principle that had eluded previous popularizers of the folk tradition, that a tradition is not in subject but in *form,* that the secret does not lie in painting a hillbilly building a silo, but in painting *as a* hillbilly builds a silo. (This was the key realization that helped her to such later insights as that the writers who said we had no native theatrical tradition were wrong. They hadn't known where to look. She looked in the public ceremonial of the Indian treaty, in the dialectic play of the Calvinist sermon, and found it.) On the strength of this discovery in Sheeler, she affirmed her principles with a new certainty. "Possibly our soil has not been too shallow for a full creative expression," she wrote; and she showed Sheeler studying architectural and handicraft form in Bucks County, discovering Shaker buildings and furniture and the Shaker motto "Every force has its form," and finally emerging as a "pathfinder in the use of American traditions in art," American without being provincial, modern and still rooted in the past, responsive at once to Shaker barns and primitive Negro sculpture.

A further level of abstraction that would have found the formal relation between Shaker barns and African sculpture was beyond Miss Rourke's power. She was always on the verge of relating her American material to the great stream of world folk culture (she noted, without further exploration, that behind a graveyard tall story in *Life on the Mississippi* is the Osiris myth, that the legends of Crockett's birth are taken over from Hercules, his fire-bringing from Prometheus, his silver bullet from the Scandinavian, other features from Celtic and American Indian lore), but she lacked the background, the learning, perhaps the imagination, to do that job successfully. What she settled for was the narrower ambition of creating a specifically American and democratic folk tradition to oppose to the sophisticated and undemocratic European formal tradition defined by men like Eliot. She explained the difficulty of the job: "we sometimes seem to be hunting for a tradition . . . but traditions are often hard to discover, requiring a long and equable scrutiny; they are hard to build, consuming an expanse of time which may pass beyond a few generations." Even a few more years of life might have enabled her to do a good part of that building.

The Roots of American Culture, Constance Rourke's last book, published posthumously in 1942, consists of brief sections from the manuscript of her *History of American Culture,* several of which had previously appeared in magazines, salvaged and edited with a preface by Van Wyck Brooks. The material is very fragmentary: an essay on **"The Roots of American Culture,"** a long study of early American theatricals, a piece on early American music, one on the Shakers, a "note" on folklore, a study of an obscure naturalistic artist named Voltaire

Combe, a survey of the extent of genuine Negro folk culture in the minstrel shows, and a piece on a possible future direction for American painting. The art and music criticism, by dealing with the relatively obscure, avoids the necessity of having to be technical with a somewhat untrained eye and ear, but the theatrical study reveals a real sense of the theater, and she has a sureness about folk forms that must have distinguished her work in the Index of American Design.

By far the best essay, and one that shows most fully her developed critical method, is the short piece on the minstrel shows called **"Traditions for a Negro Literature."** Against the opposition of writers like S. Foster Damon, who claimed that no legitimate Negro material exists in the minstrel show (and the presumable opposition of the George Pullen Jackson, Guy Johnson, Newman Ivey White school, who claim that no Negro art exists anyway not stolen from white art), Miss Rourke opposed fact. She demonstrated that all the classic white minstrel compositions were borrowings: that Dan Emmett's "Old Dan Tucker" was either Negro-derived or wholly of Negro origin, with a Negro-type tune, a Negro shouting choral effect, and a content of cryptic Negro animal fables about the jaybird and the bulldog; that "Turkey in the Straw" is certainly a Negro dance song; that "Dixie" begins with a characteristically Negro Biblical legend; that Dan Rice's "Clar de Kitchen" is an animal fable in which the Negro triumphs, and so on. She further showed that the ritual forms and conventions of the minstrel show, its dance routines, its cries, in addition to its musical and anecdotal material, were all Negro or Negro-derived. Having performed that analytic job, using the first part of her method, the tracing of formal art to its folk roots, Miss Rourke went on to do the synthetic half of the job, the organization of a folk tradition for artists to use, by showing that much of the Negro material preserved in a distorted and offensive form in the minstrel shows has been preserved nowhere else, and that it could be lifted from the minstrel setting, cleansed and refurbished, to furnish a vital tradition for American Negro literature. (Miss Rourke does not make use of, or perhaps was not familiar with, one of the best illustrations of her case, the minstrel song "De Blue-Tail Fly," which under the accretions of cheap minstrel dialect is a serious and very fine song of slave protest and rebellion.)

Because of the specialized nature of her subject, Miss Rourke did not take up what is probably the basic question about American Negro folk material, its complicated relationship to primitive African myth and ritual, and by extension the basic problem of her field, the general relationship of art to rite. In another part of the book, however, the section, "The Indian Background" in the long essay **"The Rise of American Theatricals,"** Miss Rourke found the problem precisely at the heart of her topic and manages in a few pages to be remarkably suggestive. She claims that the Indian treaties are the earliest American drama, and one of the sources, along with the European tradition, of later American drama. . . . The fifty Indian treaties known to have been printed, Miss Rourke points out, form a cycle with "epic proportions as well as an epic theme," and are "poetry of a high order." These are not only our first plays, she insists, but also inevitably our best early plays: "That the treaties could be matched in poetic or imaginative values by individual effort in their own time was hardly to be expected: they were traditional, communal, they expressed values that had long been accumulated."

Here she is very close to the same discovery about which she hovered in *American Humor:* that the important relationship of art literature to folk literature lies, not in the surface texture of folk speech, but in the archetypal patterns of primitive ritual, the great myths. Again, in **"A Note on Folklore"** in the book, she recognizes that something basic is lacking in her subject, the use by American writers of folk material, that it tends to be a "placing of quaint bits end to end," but she fails to perceive what it is that is lacking, and the piece falls off into inconsequence.

The thing Miss Rourke *did* discover in the book, a basic critical concept continuing her discovery in *Charles Sheeler* that a tradition lies not in content but in form, is her recognition that the American folk tradition is not primarily naturalistic but abstract: the abstraction of a Jonathan Edwards sermon, a Navajo blanket, a John Henry feat, and a Vermont hooked rug; and that it is Marin who is painting in it, not Norman Rockwell. A number of other fragmentary elements of promise are buried in the book: a recognition (borrowed from Ruth Benedict) of the importance of Gestalt "configurations" in studying cultures; a plan for the serious teaching of American folk literature in the colleges; a study of how a people like the Shakers can acquire something like the communality of a "folk" in one generation. But these were promises she did not live to fulfill. (pp. 127-33)

Miss Rourke's work was unquestionably limited. She lacked Jane Harrison's learning and her focus on the ritual drama as hub; Raglan's familiarity with the breadth of the material; the pluralism and integrative ability of Thomson and Troy; the acquaintance with a relatively primitive people, or true "folk," of Mary Austin; even Parrington's basic toughmindedness. She began with every handicap: a concept of folklore as local color and sentimental theatrical memories; an unexplored field in the hands of ignoramuses specializing in the guitar and the ten-gallon hat; a country whose true folk tradition lacks all homogeneity, consisting of Indian and Negro survivals and European imports, all modified beyond recognition to fit their new contexts. Despite all these handicaps, her work represents a steady development toward more and more significant criticism: discovering her analytic and synthetic functions in *American Humor,* as well as the relationship between folk and art literature; synthesizing a tradition of folksy content in *Crockett* and *Audubon;* discovering that a tradition lies in form rather than content in *Sheeler,* and that her true method was the folk analysis of formal art; realizing that the American folk tradition is abstract and has basic ritual elements in her unfinished *History of American Culture,* and on that basis doing her most significant jobs of analysis (the Indian roots of American drama) and synthesis (the minstrel tradition reconstructed for a Negro literature).

Miss Rourke's relationship to Van Wyck Brooks may be worth mention here. The only book of his she has ever quoted specifically is *The Pilgrimage of Henry James,* in her James chapter in *American Humor,* and that to accept some of its incidental judgments and demolish its basic conclusion, that James broke with the American tradition by concentrating on the international scene rather than the meal in the firkin. She has attacked Brooks by indirection in her discussion of Twain in *American Humor* ("It is a mistake to look for the social critic—even manqué—in Mark Twain"), and attacked his manifestoes in the *Freeman* at some length in *Charles Sheeler* for calling for the mechanical creation of a hierarchical school of American artists rather than the free use of American materials arising out of concrete needs and situations. Even *The Roots of American Culture,* which Brooks assembled and introduced with a respectful and proprietary preface, contains in the title essay a sharp attack on Brooks's central position (although Brooks is not named), what De Voto has tagged "the literary fallacy," when she writes: "The governing idea that ours is a literary culture, or any similar preconception, may throw our judgments awry." (pp. 140-41)

Much of Constance Rourke's special approach and significance is typified by the basic quarrel with Brooks over Henry James. As one endeavoring to create a valid and usable American tradition, she felt it absurd to throw James to the enemy, and she worked passionately to renaturalize him. The point of her James chapter in *American Humor* is that James is, as Howells said, basically and fundamentally in the American tradition, never more so than when he lived abroad and concerned himself with the international scene. In the last analysis she was not only the isolater of folk sources and roots in formal art, the synthesizer of a living folk tradition for other artists to come, the educator of provincial critics like Van Wyck Brooks, the popularizer of obscure and misapprehended figures and cultural phenomena in our past—Audubon, Voltaire Combe, the minstrel show, Horace Greeley; she was also a democrat and a patriot, in a deeper and better-informed sense than the ranters and the book-burners. . . . She knew the secret that the true artist has two homes: his native land and the globe. (p. 141)

Stanley Edgar Hyman, "Constance Rourke and Folk Criticism," in The Antioch Review *(copyright © 1947, copyright renewed © 1974, by The Antioch Review Inc.; reprinted by permission of the Editors), Vol. 7, No. 3, September, 1947 (and reprinted in a slightly different form in his* The Armed Vision: A Study in the Methods of Modern Literary Criticism, *Alfred A. Knopf, 1948, pp. 127-41).*

KENNETH S. LYNN (essay date 1963)

[*Lynn is a prominent American historian and literary critic who has written extensively on the lives and works of major American literary figures, including Mark Twain, William Dean Howells, and Theodore Dreiser. One of Lynn's main critical concerns is the stripping away of the myths that surround America's authors through close, unprejudiced consideration of existing biographical information. In the following excerpt, Lynn examines Rourke's achievement in* Trumpets of Jubilee *and summarizes her career.*]

Thronging. It was one of Constance Rourke's favorite words. She loved, as Whitman did, the sense of being a part of the American crowd, and the best of her books make us feel the throb of a collective excitement. While her literary attention centered on individuals—in whose personal eccentricities she clearly rejoiced—the one was always taken to be the symbol of the many. As she wrote in the foreword to *Trumpets of Jubilee,* her first book, popular leaders like Lyman Beecher, Harriet Beecher Stowe, Henry Ward Beecher, Horace Greeley, and P. T. Barnum were "nothing less than the vicarious crowd, registering much that is essential and otherwise obscure in social history, hopes and joys and conflicts and aspirations which may be crude and transitory, but none the less are the stuff out of which the foundations of social life are made"; even when she went on to deal with writers like Nathaniel Hawthorne and Emily Dickinson—who could scarcely be described as having the popular touch of a Barnum or a Beecher—she nevertheless conceived of them in a social way: as interpreters of a people's quest for national identity.

When *Trumpets of Jubilee* appeared in 1927, Constance Rourke's insistence on the vital connection between the American artist and his society was a lonely position indeed; as for dealing sympathetically with popular leaders, "it is a habit in these days to scorn popularity." Ever since the Civil War, so she was to acknowledge in *American Humor* . . . , American critics had been carrying on what one of Henry James' characters had called the "wretched business" of quarreling with their country. The masterworks of post-Civil War writing had all voiced in their various ways the alienation of their authors from the accepted values of the Gilded Age. In the artistic generation to which Constance Rourke belonged—that truly remarkable group of poets, painters, literary critics, and social commentators who were born between the end of the 1870s and the mid-1890s and who came of age in the first decade and a half of the twentieth century (Miss Rourke was twenty-one in 1906)—the attitude of the American artist toward his society became even more intransigent. Where Henry Adams, Henry James, and Mark Twain had been deeply troubled by their inability to feel at home in their society, the iconoclasts of the new generation gloried in their separateness. The word of the day was *new,* and contempt for the conventional was vast. (pp. 157-58)

The unique achievement of Constance Rourke's first book is that she alone, among all the other members of her generation who were bent on exploring the cultural resources of the country, was willing to honor the spokesmen of an older America for their own sake as well as for the sake of present and future American artists. Yet she was no more a pious antiquarian, who approached the past hat in hand, so to speak, than she was a debunker or a myth-maker. At once sympathetic and objective, she was a superb cultural historian; by her quiet but compelling example, she has had a continuing influence on writers concerned with the American past for more than thirty-five years. (p. 162)

First and last, she took a balanced view; as she wrote in the foreword to *Trumpets of Jubilee,* her aim was to let "a little of the singular life of the . . . [past] . . . crowd through, with its constricted spaciousness, its stirring trouble, and loud laughter." Except for Barnum, all the major figures in *Trumpets of Jubilee* endure a public trial and humiliation in one form or another. (p. 164)

Laughter, however, as well as trouble, is given its due. Constance Rourke's appreciation of Yankee wit, which is more fully manifested in *American Humor,* seasons her treatment of Lyman Beecher and immensely humanizes him; in a decade when the term *Puritan* became a synonym, in Charles Beard's phrase, for anything that interfered with "the new freedom, free verse, psychoanalysis, or even the double entendre," Constance Rourke insisted on the sly humor, the homely ways, and the boisterous passion of Lyman Beecher. With her folk-detective's instinct for finding older forms beneath newer ones, she conceived of Beecher's sermons—and those of his son Henry even more so—as a kind of theatrical performance that ranged from high tragedy to low comedy. Indeed, she conceived of all the dramatis personae of *Trumpets of Jubilee* as theatrical performers, for she adored the theater, as Whitman did, as the most social of all the arts—the place where the one and the many confronted one another most directly. The theater had the "constricted spaciousness" that she felt was the key to American culture and therefore all things theatrical became a primary source of her metaphors. The very title, *Trumpets of Jubilee,* leads us to anticipate a circus—with cosmic overtones. In her second book, *Troupers of the Gold Coast, or The Rise of Lotta Crabtree* . . . , she indulged her delight in the-

atricality in less oblique terms, but whomever she wrote about, whether [*Davy Crockett* or *Audubon*] . . . , the gaudy theatricality of her subject's imagination was the quality that most stirred her own. In her own way she was Barnumesque, and the reader comes away from her studies of American life with the feeling that he has just witnessed the Greatest Show on Earth.

Which is not to say that she was not discriminating or that she lacked standards—quite the contrary. Unlike many students of the popular arts, Constance Rourke was equally at home in discussing the fine arts. If her study of *Charles Sheeler: Artist in the American Tradition* . . . is valuable for the connections it establishes between an individual artist's practice and the aesthetic expression of a communal group (in this case the Shakers), the book is also important for what it says about the intrinsic merits of Sheeler's work. To state the case in literary terms, Constance Rourke was a critic of texts as well as of contexts, and when she undertook to defend some of the masterpieces of an earlier America against the jeering sophisticates of the 1920s, she did so with an authority that only those who have read the best of what has been thought and said can command.

Writing with that combination of descriptive specificity and visionary sweep which constituted her personal signature, Constance Rourke helped bring us to an awareness of a tradition that, as she wrote in *American Humor,* was "various, subtle, sinewy, scant at times but not poor." (pp. 164-65)

Kenneth S. Lynn, "Introduction to the Harbinger Edition" (© 1963 by Harcourt Brace Jovanovich, Inc.; reprinted by permission of the publisher), in Trumpets of Jubilee: Henry Ward Beecher, Harriet Beecher Stowe, Lyman Beecher, Horace Greeley, P. T. Barnum *by Constance Rourke, Harcourt Brace Jovanovich, 1963 (and reprinted as "The Trumpets of Jubilee," in* Visions of America: Eleven Literary Historical Essays *by Kenneth S. Lynn, Greenwood Press, Inc., 1973, pp. 157-66).*

GENE BLUESTEIN (essay date 1972)

[*Bluestein offers an in-depth study of Rourke's best-known work,* American Humor.]

[In *American Humor,* Constance Rourke] developed a method of literary and cultural analysis which was, in the strictest sense, neither folkloristic nor historical, but a unique combination of disciplines. . . . Despite its relatively short existence, Miss Rourke insisted America had its own tradition, unique in its development and rich enough to control and color the flow of formal art which issued from it.

In the first of what was to be a trio of characterological studies, Miss Rourke discerned the lineaments of the American as they emerged in the figure of the Yankee. By the end of the eighteenth century, she noted, he was easily identified as the peddler, a lone, shrewd figure who had already become more than regional, taking on aspects of myth and fantasy. . . . Puritanism may have provided body to the Yankee myth, but to Miss Rourke's eye it contained too dark a view to be responsible for his fanciful humor and irreverence. . . . Similar traits of swapping and dissembling might be traced to the Yorkshireman, but Miss Rourke emphasized the mixing of strains from other sections of the British Isles and even France. The background was complex and she was neither simplistic nor provincial in her evaluation of its sources.

Her discussion of the seventeenth century was sparse, for although there were distinct outlines of permanent influence in the life and thought of the period, it was the Revolutionary War era which, "with its cutting of ties, its movement, its impulses toward freedom, seemed to set one portion of the scant population free from its narrow matrix." . . . Just at this point, when the Yankee began to emerge as a national symbol, Miss Rourke noted also the emergence of a major theme in American cultural history and a characteristic literary strategy. The tension between Europe and America, which later critics have identified as the "international theme," is apparent from the very beginning of our national history. . . . The insight was a crucial one for it illuminated a problem that many critics had either overlooked or misinterpreted. The contrast between Europe and America (especially between England and the United States) in politics, manners, and literary theory led some scholars to place the conflict outside the configurations of American experience. The nature as well as the significance of the antagonism were thus easily misread as manifestations of American chauvinism or British pomposity. By placing the opposition of Old World and New squarely in the mainstream of American thought, Miss Rourke skirted the pitfalls of either extreme position, at the same time affirming its significance as an American rather than a strictly regional antagonism. Much of the criticism leveled by both sides was accurate. But the important point, she insisted, was that the American character was formed under the pressure of criticism from abroad, a circumstance which helped to explain some of its special qualities and the literary strategies in which it was represented. (In a later section of *American Humor* she identified the international theme as a major one in the work of both Mark Twain and Henry James.) (pp. 67-9)

The second major phase of this steady accretion of national characteristics bore the clear imprint of the backwoodsman. Miss Rourke noted the interesting fact that as the Yankee had emerged from the embroilments of the Revolutionary War, so the frontiersman made his appearance during the War of 1812. In both cases the pressure of a military and political conflict demanded a forceful image capable of fusing diverse aspects of the national imagination. But a more significant insight is her insistence that the backwoodsman's ancestry was similar to the Yankee's, rooted in Calvinism and drawing upon the same ethnic stocks. . . . [The backwoodsman was] "a new beast" spawned by the rivers and forests of the West. Miss Rourke was fully aware of the implications held by her descriptions of this new stage in the synthesis of old and new elements. There was a dark stain at the heart of this development. Horror, terror, and death were ever present in the frontier experience; the tales and legends of the frontiersman repeated an earlier motif which mingled magical outcroppings of birth with clear intimations of terror and death, resulting often in a middle ground that Miss Rourke identified as the grotesque. In all this, however, the comic sense functioned as before, providing a resilience which "swept through them in waves, transcending the past, transcending terror, with the sense of comedy itself a wild emotion."

The actors in this part of the unfolding drama of creation were diverse and flamboyant, uniting in their own persons the elements of reality and the fantastic. . . . This was important documentation for Miss Rourke's argument that a usable folk tradition did indeed exist in this country.

One of her major methodological accomplishments is exemplified in her ability to identify the juxtaposition of folk and popular traditions within which the American character developed. Folklore exposes the deepest level of national traits and values; it is an anonymous tradition rooted in oral story telling and is passed down from person to person until the layers of truth and fiction become one, indistinguishable from each other. Popular art exists on a more conscious level, often utilizing folk themes but easily recognizable as the work of a particular individual. She saw more clearly than any other critic the peculiar tendency in America for folk and popular traditions to merge rather than to exist separately in isolated areas, as is often the case in Europe. We discover often a figure so close to folk tradition that he can recreate on a popular level what seems essentially folk in its style. Mark Twain and Woody Guthrie are of this sort, and so was James Audubon, whose ornithology Miss Rourke related to the huntsman's close knowledge of nature. (pp. 70-1)

The third major figure whose character became permanently etched into the emerging portrait of the American was the Negro. . . .

Constance Rourke began her discussion with a description of the vogue of minstrelsy, a subject which at the time was almost entirely unexplored. (p. 72)

Miss Rourke saw in the phenomenon of minstrelsy a major source of several important elements which added to the still unfinished portrait of the American. The first was a satirical humor that often blossomed into full-scale burlesque. . . . Negro folklore abounded in animal fables and nonsense songs that introduced a "bolder comic quality" than had been expressed in earlier American humor. But Miss Rourke identified in black tradition something more than a simple primitivism. Beneath the careless and often preposterous humor there was a tragic substratum which filled a gap in the configuration of American traits. The Negro had known defeat and it "could be heard in the occasional minor key and smothered satire" of his music and song. Like the earlier prototypes of the American, the Negro wore a mask, but unlike them his conscious satire was rooted in a vision of the human condition which the flourishes of his fantasy never obscured. That sense of the limitation and ultimate defeat of man which might have been the contribution of Calvinism to the American character, Miss Rourke's argument suggests, came rather through the experience of the Negro, though blunted and refracted for the popular mind by white minstrelsy. Indirectly though forcefully, a third figure was added to the Yankee and the Backwoodsman, merging like the earlier ones into the generic type. (p. 73)

The first part of *American Humor* was an attempt to discover the sources of the American character by examining the underlying folk tradition which, as Herder had proposed, would reveal its authentic forms. After establishing her triptych Miss Rourke turned to environmental and institutional forces which helped to shape the larger patterns of American literature. Her central concern was with the influence of the frontier on native theater and religion.

Each of the three character types had strong associations with theater, a term which Miss Rourke opposed to the drama. The theatrical, she pointed out, "is full of experiment, finding its way to audiences by their quick responses and rejections. On the stage the shimmer and glow, the minor appurtenances, the jokes and dances and songs, the stretching and changes of plots, are arranged and altered almost literally by the audience or in their close company; its measure is human, not literary." . . . The last phrase contains the major insight, for it helps to explain the curious resistance in American literature to the classical and neo-classical conception of the sublime. As she noted later in connection with our novelists and poets, the movement is away from traditional forms which emphasize a high style and the hegemony of tragedy. The center of gravity was comic and as in earlier experiences it was a levelling agent with marked antagonism toward ''highbrow'' traditions. (pp. 74-5)

''This lawless satire'' of the thirties and forties ''was engaged in a pursuit which had occupied comedy in the native vein elsewhere. . . . Comedy was conspiring toward the removal of all alien traditions, out of delight in pure destruction or as a preparation for new growth.'' . . .

Miss Rourke did not make this frontier hypothesis in an articulate formulation, but it is so close to the main lines of Turnerian speculation that it merits attention. Over and over again the frontier has been defined by important critics and writers as the area in which the legacy of the Old World was wiped clean and the meaning of America written afresh. For Constance Rourke it was comedy which purged the old traditions and provided the basis for the new. As in the classical formulation by Frederick Jackson Turner, it was a process by stages through repeated contact with an unsophisticated but vital frontier existence. But where Turner emphasized the pragmatic and anti-intellectual propensities of the frontiersman, Miss Rourke saw a new mythology springing from the depths of the American wilderness. The difference is perhaps that, as a historian, Turner was too often unaware that he had shifted his ground to typological or mythical approaches. Miss Rourke's approach was almost always folkloristic and she was consequently sensitive to categories of analysis which were only implied in Turner's formulation.

Thus her discussion of the frontier led directly to the consideration of the religious revivals which she identified ''in a fundamental and not irreverent sense'' as belonging to the theatrical developments of the same period. The frontiersmen were ''of the race which produced the leaping, heel-cracking comic figures who proclaimed their identity with the lightning and the alligator. They joined in the orgiastic forest revivals on the Red River and Gaspar River, shouting and pleading to be bathed in the blood of the lamb, and bending, writhing, jerking, falling, barking, and creeping over the ground like the creatures of the wilderness.'' . . . This is a conception of the frontier distinct from Turner's though it follows his general line that, as Miss Rourke put it, the ''restraining bonds were broken of that rigorous faith that seemed a solid American inheritance from the older civilizations.'' (pp. 76-7)

As I noted earlier, one of Constance Rourke's main tasks was to provide evidence of a rich source from which an American literary tradition could be seen to flow. By exploring both folk and popular developments she more than made the point. ''Far from having no childhood,'' she could argue, ''the American nation was having a prolonged childhood.'' What she had shown was that despite its lack of a feudal or antique past, America had its own period of primitive accumulation upon which, and in general accordance with Herderian theory, a formal art tradition could be built. All of its preparation, however, led American literature to a unique expression ''derived from the life out of which it sprang.'' If its natural level was not the sublime, even its comedy demanded special definition. . . . Although its central function was to unify the heterogeneous elements of our experience, its technique was poetic, ''keeping that archetypal largeness which inheres in the more elementary poetic forms, with the inevitable slide into figure and that compact

turn with unspoken implications which is the essence of poetic expression.''

Here the most valuable of Miss Rourke's critical observations comes into clearest focus. It is essentially a revision of Herderian theory which, on the one hand, avoids a mechanical application of the idea to American conditions and, on the other, helps to explain the distinct configurations of our native tradition. The materials brought together during our period of germination, she maintains, existed on several levels. Hence ''this comic poetry could not be called folk-poetry, but it had the breadth and much of the spontaneous freedom of folk-poetry; in a rough sense its makers had been the nation. Full of experiment and improvisation, it did not belong to literature; but it used the primary stuffs of literature, the theater that lies behind the drama, the primitive religious ceremony that has been anterior to both, the tale that has preceded both the drama and the novel, the monologue that has been arudimentary source for many forms.'' . . . The primary phase in America was never, in Herderian terms, purely folk but already a hybrid concatenation of folk and popular. (pp. 77-8)

Constance Rourke stopped just short of making a major statement about the relationship of her analysis to the characteristic attitudes of American writers toward the idea of genre. . . . In the closing section of the book she does provide a somewhat sketchy analysis of the main lines of our literary tradition which flow from the sources she was the first to identify as crucial to our literary development. But as I have tried to show, she does not conceive of our literary figures as ''outgrowths of folk culture.'' To the contrary, her comment was that ''though he drew upon traditional material, Hawthorne could not rest at ease as the great English poets have rested within the poetic tradition that came to them through the ballads and romances, or as the great English novelists have drawn upon rich local accumulations of character and lore.'' . . . What she could explain was Hawthorne's predilection for the ''romance,'' which led him to transmute ''regional legends into inner moods,'' or as in *The Scarlet Letter,* to slip into an ''irreverent rude comedy far from the conscious Puritan habit.'' (Miss Rourke may have had in mind that truly humorous scene, redolent with hints of Elmer Gantry and other lecherous clerics, in which Dimmesdale, fresh from his forest encounter with Hester, almost seduces the most virginal of his parishioners.)

Constance Rourke's insights led her to an understanding of the constant attack by American writers on established canons of taste and style. And it is important to underscore the influence of Herder's thought on her work. Like Emerson and Whitman she went directly to the heart of his meaning, observing that ''a mild nostalgia quickly took the place of Herder's bold creative concept of the folk as a living wellspring of poetry and song. This was brought about mainly through the selective work of Schlegel and the Grimms, whose explorations of folklore and folk-song had great value but who developed to an extreme the romantic concept of primitive or folk-life which had first been touched upon by Montaigne. Antiquarianism began to cast its long insidious spell, and inquiries as to the folk-arts came to be regarded as minor excursions into the petty or the quaint.'' No criticism can ever completely contain either the sources or the effects of art, as no literature can finally fulfill its own expectations. But our debt to Constance Rourke stems from her awareness of the major strategy which Americans have utilized to establish their own sense of identity and coherence. Though it is an approach closely approximating Herder's, she noted the significant function of comedy as a way of blunting the criticism of European ''high'' cultures. Moreover, it makes us aware of the persistent use of the mask or persona as the characteristic response to foreign criticism. The barbarism of the American (who is easily tagged as the redskin) reveals itself to be a more complex state than many critics have perceived, partly because it is itself a literary strategy, partly because the folk sources from which it derives are more sophisticated than the palefaces have allowed themselves to recognize. (pp. 79-80)

> *Gene Bluestein, ''Folklore and the American Character,'' in his* The Voice of the Folk: Folklore and American Literary Theory *(copyright © 1972 by the University of Massachusetts Press), University of Massachusetts Press, 1972, pp. 65-90.**

JOAN SHELLEY RUBIN (essay date 1980)

[Rubin examines the manner in which Rourke's technique and style enabled her to enliven America's past.]

When the reviewers acclaimed **American Humor** in the spring of 1931, they hailed not only the book's interpretation of native culture but also its delightfully lively style. ''Miss Rourke,'' wrote her friend Eda Lou Walton in the *Nation*, ''is one of the few truly scholarly critics who write a beautiful prose. She is able so naturally to fuse her documentary evidence with her critical exposition as to convince any reader that her book . . . was written for pure pleasure.'' . . . A glance at any of Rourke's writings is enough to corroborate [this observation]. Carefully wrought descriptions of Crockett's surroundings enrich her discussions of his life on the frontier; striking metaphors explain the character of the Yankee, backwoodsman, and minstrel; imagined conversations enliven the story of Barnum, Greeley, or the Beechers. . . . Yet Walton, Brooks, and others, considering Rourke's prose, have never gone beyond praise. Her special amalgamation of scholarship and popular style was inextricably related to her concern for American culture. It deserves examination not simply as an illustration of beautiful writing but as a strategy for achieving the mythmaking, tradition-conscious, unified society Rourke valued.

The opening section of **American Humor** provides a good example of Rourke's style generally:

> Toward evening of a midsummer day at the latter end of the eighteenth century a traveler was seen descending a steep red road into a fertile Carolina valley. He carried a staff and walked with a wide, fast, sprawling gait, his tall shadow cutting across the lengthening shadows of the trees. His head was crouched, his back long; a heavy pack lay across his shoulders.
>
> A close view of his figure brought consternation to the men and women lounging at the tavern or near the sheds that clustered around the planter's gate. ''I'll be shot if it ain't a Yankee!'' cried one. The yard was suddenly vacant.

This passage, which is like a glimpse into the past through a pair of binoculars, is a refreshing beginning to a scholarly work on the themes and patterns of American humor in folklore and literature, for its style could hardly be called academic. Instead, Rourke has undertaken to spin a yarn. She is telling a story—and creating a myth. Her fictionalized narration has several components: the use of the vague, passive ''was seen'' that

removes the reader's expectations of historical accuracy; the inclusion of details of appearance, movement, and setting (''the lengthening shadows of the trees'') designed to establish an impression of fantasy rather than to bolster an argument; the reliance on direct quotation to supply dramatic effect. The nature of the stylistic device becomes clearer when one considers other ways of beginning the book. For example, Rourke might have written, ''The Yankee, the backwoodsman, and the minstrel have formed the basis for American humor. The Yankee was traditionally a peddler who traveled throughout the countryside; he was frequently the object of suspicion by local townspeople.'' She might have documented the statement by estimating the number of peddlers on the road in 1800 or describing a typical trade route. Walter Blair's discussion of the Yankee in his *Native American Humor* (1957) indicates the alternative Rourke rejected: ''The term 'Yankee,' in widespread use to denote an American, dates back to about 1775. . . . His simplicity, his penury, and his cautiousness are details of a sketchy portrait. . . .'' But Blair's straightforward and rather dry treatment was incompatible with Rourke's purposes. Arguing that the Yankee was a mythical creature, she adopted a form that guaranteed the persistence of that myth. Her use of the language of fiction both corroborated and insured the validity of her argument. We see her . . . as a mythmaker herself, this time employing style to amplify the Yankee's mythical attributes and create them anew. Perhaps by recording myths in the manner of the mythmaker, Rourke could crystallize them once and for all, so that they remained part of a permanent tradition.

The same reliance on fictional style as a way of revitalizing myth appears in Rourke's treatment of Audubon. . . . (pp. 135-37)

Apart from creating vivid characters, Rourke used style as an instrument of mythmaking in her less admirable practice of tentative phrasing. The words ''seems'' and ''as if'' appear frequently throughout **American Humor**. For example, she wrote: ''The Revolution, with its cutting of ties, its movement, its impulses toward freedom, seemed to set one portion of the scant population free from its narrow matrix.'' Similarly, Rourke observed: ''But queerly enough, the backwoodsman indulged in conduct resembling that of the Yankee when under the fire of criticism, as if after all there were a tacit bond between them.'' . . . Faced with her repeated use of words like ''seems,'' ''as if,'' and ''as though,'' the impatient reader may want to ask what *really* happened. But Rourke's failure to write concretely may be read as a further sign of her desire to create myth. Her language lends an aspect of imprecision and unreality to her writing, removing her discussion from the realm of fact to that of possibility.

Sometimes Rourke's interest in mythmaking even led her to take liberties with her sources. In **Audubon**, for example, she doctored the story of a meeting between Audubon and Daniel Boone to heighten the drama and romance of the episode. Though the originals of Audubon's journals have not survived, making it impossible to retrieve his own account of the event, there are interesting discrepancies between Rourke's version and the works she cited in her bibliography. Audubon's *Ornithological Biography*, Maria R. Audubon's *Audubon and His Journals*, and Lucy Audubon's *The Life of John James Audubon* all report that Boone and Audubon returned from a shooting match and retired to their room for the night, whereupon Audubon asked the famous hunter to talk about some of his adventures. After Audubon had gotten into bed and Boone had made himself comfortable on the floor, Boone related the tale of his narrow escape from some Indians when his squaw captors became drunk on whisky. . . . This anecdote, colorful enough, becomes even more so in Rourke's book. She removed the encounter between Audubon and Boone to a campfire, where the two men sit with other hunters. Interpolating a direct quotation and "tall talk," she has one of the audience say: "Tell us how you flusterated the Injuns, Dan'l." Boone complies, using "Injun" for "Indian" throughout his speech. Rourke has deliberately romanticized the setting of Boone's narration, transforming it from a private conversation to a public performance and adding fanciful lingo to emphasize Boone's and Audubon's mythic stature. Only after describing the campfire scene did she retire Boone to his blanket on the floor.

By this effort, as well as her fictionalized, evocative, and sometimes vague prose, Rourke saw to it that Americans would have enough myths to sustain an adequate culture. But myth-making, especially out of the material of the frontier, could be a touchy enterprise. Though Rourke added backwoods language to the Boone story, she left out backwoods violence, for in her sources, although not in her retelling, Boone says of the squaws: "I now recollect how desirous I once or twice felt to lay open the skulls of the wretches with my tomahawk." Like her transformation of Davy Crockett into a middle-class hero, the omission bespeaks a concern with the acceptability of native traditions. Rourke's double-edged definition of culture meant that she had to strike another of her delicate balances: between a view of frontier life as exciting enough to fuel the imagination, but not so raw and rough that it entirely flouted conventional standards for civilization. If her style helped to create a sufficient number of myths, it also made sure that those myths would pass muster.

A comparison of part of Bernard DeVoto's writings on the frontier with Rourke's contemporaneous treatment illuminates that stylistic strategy. Both DeVoto and Rourke discussed the Western boatman, for example, but in very different terms. . . . DeVoto's emphasis is on what he called "frontier hardness," a view supported by his language and by the relentless rhythm of his sentences. (pp. 139-42)

DeVoto celebrated the "masculine," uninhibited features of the boatman's personality. His remark that the words of the "Shawneetown" song [sung by the laboring boatmen] were "far decenter than most" is an insider's comment, as if he were giving his audience a wink of the eye, for he knows the other songs. And why not revel in this raw, raucous heritage? The boatmen were alive, vibrant, outrageous, captivating—and in the tales that developed about them, funny.

Yet when Rourke took up the same subject, she did so in a way that bore little resemblance to DeVoto's. Discussions of the boatman occur in both *Davy Crockett* and *American Humor*. "The red-shirted riverboatmen," Rourke said in *Davy Crockett*, "kept up a running repartee with men ashore or on other boats along the river. Like the wagoners they consorted together, had their own lingo, their own way of bantering, their wit, which was quick, and their songs, which were both rowdy and sentimental. Thousands of them were now afloat on the western rivers, noisy, quarrelsome, full of sport, gathering for short holidays at taverns when a journey was ended, and then away again up or down the rivers." Later in the passage, Rourke commented, "on open easy water the boatmen would sing out—" and quoted the first two lines of the Shawneetown song. "The air was full of boatmen's songs and full of talk," she added. "Flatboats passed, plying the rivers as shops or 'dog-

geries,' drawing alongside the arks to sell food or spirits or fancy notions to travelers." The first thing to notice in Rourke's description is the contrast between the characteristics she ascribed to the boatmen and the traits DeVoto enumerated. Most striking, of course, is the way Rourke has dropped out the sex: there are no "brothels" or "wenches" in her version, and she has introduced the sentimental Shawneetown song as typical. What DeVoto confronted as "obscene," Rourke transmuted into "rowdy." Her relativistic definition of culture had its limits, and whoring was beyond them. But there is more going on here than Rourke's neglect of details that did not meet certain cultural requirements. The difference between Rourke and DeVoto is not simply a question of content—that he includes sex while she does not. Even when they are talking about the same scenes, the same behavior, Rourke's account comes out less graphic, more lyrical, and so more comforting. The phrase "on open easy water" has the ring of serenity. DeVoto's boatmen drink; Rourke's gather "for short holidays at taverns." "War" for DeVoto is a "quarrel" for Rourke. Her boatmen are playful, cheerful, and rather innocent: they are "full of sport," they "banter" and "consort." This abstract, almost quaint language (also apparent in "spirits or fancy notions") softens the "frontier hardness" that delighted DeVoto but that Rourke, retaining some allegiance to a hierarchical view of culture, could not accept. It is important to observe that Rourke had achieved the softer effect stylistically: the image of the benign boatmen arises from her choice of words as well as from her selective focus. (pp. 142-44)

Rourke's depiction of the boatman can serve as an emblem of the way she approached frontier humor in general. An even better illustration of her stylistic tactics emerges by comparing the newspaper humor of the old Southwest to her treatment of it. . . . (p. 145)

[Rourke's section on the Southwestern writers in *American Humor*] begins with an example of the genre, a description of Ovid Bolus from Baldwin's *Flush Times*. Rourke's choice is significant, for out of all the newspaper sketches she might have quoted, she selected a passage concerning neither sex nor crude horseplay nor violence but rather the much more respectable pastime of lying. Beyond its palatable content, moreover, an excerpt from *Flush Times* had an additional advantage. Baldwin, more than most of his fellow journalists, was indebted to the essay style. He wrote in conventional literary English, not in the rough talk of an illiterate mountaineer or wandering sharper. Thus the quotation fits smoothly between Rourke's own polished paragraphs without disturbing either the reader's stomach or his ear. "Dialect was differentiated with a fine gift for mimicry," Rourke noted at the end of her discussion. But there is a difference between declaring the existence of dialect in a sentence dominated by the passive voice and letting the reader confront it directly in quotations. In *American Humor* as a whole, Rourke did not shun dialect altogether, but its incidental place in the book is far out of proportion to its frequency in native humor itself. The result—a function simply of the fact that Rourke's language so outweighs the language of her subject matter—is that the reader never glimpses for more than a moment the raw exuberant style of much American comic material. (pp. 150-51)

Her style in *American Humor* served her need to gloss over material that seemed improper and outside the bounds of good taste. Because she no doubt satisfied similar inclinations in readers who deplored "masculine" humor, we may even see her, to use Ann Douglas's phrase, as an agent of the "feminization'' of American culture about which Harold Stearns complained.

Yet Rourke had more pressing missions. Though she might displease a few like DeVoto who enjoyed a bawdy story or an account of a physically discomfiting prank, she could appeal to the widest possible audience, letting nothing stand in the way of a rapport with all of the ''folks.'' That desire for broad diffusion of a common—and acceptable—heritage was Rourke's most compelling reason for mitigating the rougher aspects of frontier life. It also underlay the form and language of virtually everything else she wrote. Style, an instrument of mythmaking, was simultaneously an instrument of what Rourke called ''possession.'' For tradition, to be ''usable,'' had to arise out of feelings that the entire community instinctively shared. . . . [The] past became ''usable'' when it was ''possessed'' as emotional experience.

Rourke's [conception] of ''possession'' reflects the impact of her experience with progressive education: the process conformed to a progressive teacher's model of learning. ''Instinctive possession,'' Rourke wrote, was a matter of ''saturation,'' of ''getting a sense of [tradition] into [the] minds and eyes and at the ends of [the] fingers, without any immediate purpose.'' In other words, one learned about native culture in the same spontaneous, individually tailored way one might learn from a follower of Dewey about geography or farm products. (pp. 154-55)

Rourke's understanding of ''possession'' bore another similarity to progressive educational theory: it displayed the vagueness and mysticism attending some teachers' pronouncements about self-expression. This is Rourke's most serious failing, a result of the same uneasiness about the way one actually arrived at an adequate culture that informed her ambivalence toward the ''practical'' arts. Her repeated use of the passive voice and of abstract language to describe ''possession'' is symptomatic of the imprecision attending her idea of how tradition functioned. Reconsider her remarks in her essay **''The Decline of the Novel''**: [Our tradition] is rich enough if it can only *be fully seen*. Out of a living perspective those epics, sagas, allegories, tales in which the imagination offers something for men to live by might *come into* . . . startling force and enlargement. . . .'' Brooks furnished a glimpse of Rourke's mysticism in his introduction to **The Roots of American Culture** by noting her view that once the materials of our past were assembled ''the tradition would declare itself through them.'' One may well ask whether the declaration is automatic, and how one progresses from a sense of tradition to a vital art. Alfred Kazin raised just those questions in an article about Rourke after her death, concluding that despite her important contributions, ''commemoration, somehow, is never enough'' [see excerpt above]. (pp. 155-56)

[Rourke's] understanding of the exigencies of ''possession,'' with respect to both children and adults, demanded not only a ''strict and simple narrative form'' but a prose style with a wide net, even if it meant submerging her painstaking research. Hence the device of fictionalization that Rourke used to describe the Yankee peddler at the beginning of **American Humor** also characterized the Crockett and Audubon biographies. . . . [The] scholarship is underplayed in favor of a tone of casual storytelling, as if the writer were recalling the lives of her friends from memory. The absence of footnotes or references in the text either to primary or secondary documents enhances the storytelling mode, marking Rourke as a popular writer outside the constraints of scholarly convention. (pp. 161-62)

As Rourke well knew, the use of image-laden language was a way of roping one's audience into the past, a method of bridging the distance between past and present by playing to a feeling of kinship among all people throughout history. Novelistic or dramatic style said to the reader: here is a heritage to which you are personally, emotionally connected.

Rourke adopted the device of fictionalization to varying extents in all but one of her books. Limited in **American Humor,** it wholly dominated **Davy Crockett** and **Audubon,** as well as the earlier **Troupers of the Gold Coast.** Though **Trumpets of Jubilee** was more scholarly, Rourke hoped her nineteenth-century ''portraits'' (the term is hers) would convey a sense of the ''color'' and ''tone'' of the lives of the Beechers, Greely, and Barnum. . . . Intending **Trumpets of Jubilee** to recreate the mood of the past, Rourke tinged the book with a fictional quality. The exception was **Charles Sheeler: Artist in the American Tradition,** which differs radically from Rourke's other writings because it is about a living artist, and rests on direct quotation from Sheeler rather than evocation of an earlier time. Yet even in her draft for ''A History of American Culture'' the requirements of exposition did not prevent Rourke from introducing elements of fictional style. Her introduction, for example, begins with the story of a group of imaginary travelers in Europe who discuss the fate of art in America. No doubt Rourke intended to create an exact counterpart to *The Wine of the Puritans,* itself an argument cast in fictional form. (pp. 162-63)

[Rourke] used Brooks's terminology in a letter to Alfred Harcourt about her ''History of American Culture'': ''This sounds highbrow and formal—you can't imagine how informal and intelligible it promises to be.'' That promise—to disguise her painstaking scholarship and to appeal to a wide audience—diminished Rourke's role as intellectual and deprived her of recognition she deserved. . . . The failure of academics to award all of Rourke's writing scholarly value has persisted up to the present time, and demonstrates, as Brooks might have said, that the division between ''high-brow'' and ''low-brow'' still exists. . . . Yet damaging though it was to Rourke's reputation as a scholar, her popular style had an important positive result. It placed her at what she saw as the center of American life, freeing her from the intellectual's risk of isolation. There were limits to the closeness Rourke welcomed—her friendships, after all, thrived on distance, and her position as critic demanded detachment—but within those boundaries she was more comfortable ''getting along with everyone'' than identifying herself as cut off from the ''folks.'' Indeed, it may be that popular style enabled Rourke to satisfy through writing yearnings for intimacy that she felt unable to express in personal relationships.

Rourke's style, like that of any novelist or poet, was not accidental. Her use of the language of fiction, which one might misunderstand as merely picturesque, needs to be considered as functional. Like her definition of culture and her understanding of myth, her approach to writing was a way of correcting Brooks's description of a divided America. It enabled her to create new myths and monitor the acceptability of old ones, to diffuse traditions and to participate in them. Constructing a bond of feeling that encompassed writer, subject, and audience, she could achieve unity on an emotional level not only throughout society generally but in particular between herself and the common man. (pp. 169-70)

Joan Shelley Rubin, in her Constance Rourke and American Culture *(© 1980 The University of North*

Carolina Press), *University of North Carolina Press,
1980, 244 p.*

SAMUEL I. BELLMAN (essay date 1981)

[*In this, the conclusion to his study* Constance M. Rourke, *Bellman
impartially assesses his subject's contributions to American literary history.*]

[Van Wyck Brooks] has erred, I strongly feel, in putting together this fragmentary cultural history [*The Roots of American
Culture*], for it weakens somewhat Rourke's essential argument
and highlights the shortcomings in her approach to her subject.
He did her a disservice by publishing her poorly worked-out
ideas and flimsy reasonings. There is, however, considerable
merit in the long analytical piece, **"The Rise of Theatricals,"**
although in view of all the culture barriers, her argument that
Indian treaties were our first dramas seems misleading. **"Early
American Music"** and **"The Shakers"** are generally informative and well-presented. The illustrative fable of an almost
unknown nineteenth-century painter [**"Voltaire Combe"**] . . .
is interesting for what it says about American life and art from
the early 1800s to the early 1900s. But in my view there are
certain things seriously wrong with the book as a whole.

First, an air of unreality floats over the work, largely because
of Rourke's steady insistence that the American artist needs to
work out of a body of communal tradition. Endless reiterations
and vast generalizations on this matter fill the book; many of
them occur in the very weak essays, **"The Roots of American
Culture"** and **"American Art: A Possible Future."** There is
altogether too much begging of the question throughout. Rourke
seems wishfully unrealistic in seeing cultural archaeologists
like herself as playing a vital role in the careers of American
artists, supplying them with necessary raw materials taken from
a common body of folkways. Thus: "A sensitive historical
criticism would seem a major necessity [for these artists], broadly
grounded in native research as well as in esthetics. A prodigious
amount of work is still to be done in the way of unearthing,
defining, and synthesizing our traditions, and finally in making
them known through simple and natural means." But—most
artists do not work in so history-conscious and programmatic
a way.

Then there are glaring omissions in her consideration of art
forms emerging from communal tradition. For instance, not
nearly enough is made of popular music, "white" forms or
"black" forms, since colonial times for the former and the
nineteenth-century minstrel shows (and the much earlier juba-
dancing of plantation slaves) for the latter. Nothing is said of
famous magazine illustrators, whose elegant covers, posters,
and pictorial sketches influenced American popular taste from
the earlier nineteenth century onward. And what of the numerous popular-art media—children's literature, comics, radio, cinema, graphic layouts for advertising—with interesting
roots in old-time tradition? True, these essays, mere bits and
pieces of Rourke's proposed *History,* do not pretend to provide
thorough coverage. Yet Rourke seems largely unaware of the
complex variety of expressions of popular art and thought that
have long been available to us. And, so much space in the
book is devoted to repeating the same simple notion to such
modest purpose, that additional substantive materials would
have been welcome.

Another shortcoming involves semantic confusions and blur-
rings. I have not found in Rourke's work an adequate distinction between popular-art forms and fine art. I have never felt

that she worked from a set of standards that specified the rigid
requirements of the latter, as opposed to relaxed guidelines for
the former. Her *Charles Sheeler* and portions of her other writings do show an awareness of the techniques of the fine, or
high, artist, but my point is that in the essay collection assembled by Van Wyck Brooks some such distinction and set of
standards would have been most helpful. Rourke does admit
that possibly the pioneer's "folk-handicrafts" have been over-
valued, though she acknowledges their "lasting creative values" and what they reveal "of visual and tactile skills." Yet
she will simply go on to say that "the typical pioneer or frontiersman was master of those daily and primitive arts that have
often afforded an ancestry for the fine arts." There are one or
two other brief hints along the same line, but nothing of a
substantive nature.

This is in **"American Art: A Possible Future."** In **"The Roots
of American Culture,"** she traces the philosophy of "the popular or folk-arts" from Montaigne to Herder and carries it
practically to her own time. To near-contemporary observers
whatever "is quaint or exaggerated is folk" and "possible
relationships of the folk-arts to the fine arts [have not] seemed
basic." Attempting here to explain the development of "dominant forms of expression" in the life of the folk—they result
primarily from "popular acceptances"—she says little about
the determinants of a group's art forms, save those stemming
from religion or superstition. A similar superficiality is seen
in her vague comments and misleading bias regarding art forms
of the folk, as opposed to "peaks of achievement," masterpieces, such definitive indexes of cultural quality as the fine
arts and genius, and the widespread notion that the arts are
luxuries.

Lastly, there are a number of errors and the like, which Brooks
should have caught. For example, Rourke would make very
much of the Gestalt concept of the dynamic configuration, as
applied to culture. She obtained this view from Ruth Benedict,
quotes her on the subject, quotes another famous anthropologist
(Robert H. Lowie) in a similar connection, and refers a number
of times to this important idea, without using the word "Gestalt." Things all hang together in a culture as elsewhere, is the
idea here; one component cannot be removed from the dynamic
whole and considered in isolation. Yet, when speaking of the
work of the American painter Charles E. Burchfield, she will
apparently overlook all she has said about the configurational
(Gestalt) view of things, and in fact all she has said about the
shaping forces of the American character, to make this strange
generalization. "If, as has been said, his deserted mansions
stand aloof from the earth on which they are planted, this
separation from environment has been a large part of our experience."

On another matter, Rourke, being very interested in the abstract
(in art and thought), a mode she handles very shakily, comments that in the seventeenth and eighteenth centuries, "Puritan
and non-Puritan alike were influenced . . . by the tendency
toward the abstract in Calvinistic theology, and equally by the
general turn toward abstraction which came in England with
the Reformation and took many speculative forms." This baf-
fler, which is followed by the amazing judgment that "the
journeyman builder" (whether or not he was a Puritan) obtained from "abstract values . . . an undefined pleasure" and
"even took a sensuous delight in the elimination of ornamental
detail," occurs in **"American Art: A Possible Future."** In the
title essay of the book, Rourke sees the Reformation as having
had seemingly self-contradictory effects: it gave "dignity to

the common man,'' while at the same time being influential ''in detaching art from the ruck of common life.'' This resulted in the individual's being ''given sole responsibility for his eternal fate.'' To take up only this last point, Rourke had spent a great deal of effort in *Trumpets of Jubilee* pointing out that many people after the Reformation—those under the influence of Calvinist-predestination theology, for example—were psychologically afflicted because they felt they were given no responsibility for their eternal fate.

But Rourke also sees the Reformation, especially through the medium of Calvinism, as having had this effect on the individual: ''he was cast into a complex and bewildering inner sphere, that of analytical self-scrutiny.'' And this kind of probing of the self, she has no doubt, ''would have developed if Luther and Calvin had never lived.'' She entertains the view (''it may even be argued,'' is the way she puts it) ''that the Reformation arose because of an inevitable drift of the exploratory human spirit toward inner complexities rather than that the Reformation created them.'' Possibly the most amazing feature of this sweeping away of fact and logic here is this. Shapers of human destiny (for good or ill), ''representative men,'' are not really taken into account. Historical changes, like the production of much of our art, seem to derive from the masses. Though Rourke does say, a little further along in this essay, that she is not exalting ''the common arts or common themes over the luxury arts,'' it is hard to escape the conclusion that her stress is generally on what comes from the people at large. (pp. 131-35)

Some more startling remarks might be mentioned. In her extended discussion (**''The Roots of American Culture''**) of important colonial towns such as Salem, Massachusetts, and Annapolis, Maryland, Rourke has a good deal of interest to say about the general layout, the architecture, and the pictorial art. She describes a painting ''of a lovely Annapolis lady with a volume of Locke on her lap,'' which ''suggests ideas that had a far-reaching influence upon the philosophy of the Revolution''; it ''reveals a typical concern of the ladies of Annapolis.'' This cultural thesis predicated on the portrait of a lady becomes an introduction to what reads like one more insubstantial line of reasoning. ''If the ladies were as noted for their interest in intellectual matters, they were also famous for their devotion to fashion and gay apparel,'' etc. Which leads to a brief discussion of ''a quaint and ancient custom [preserved] from the medieval courts. The gentlemen tilted for ladies' favors on horseback with lances and rings. Even now in Maryland this custom survives.'' No source for this information is cited, nor is it made clear how this is relevant to a tracing of our cultural roots. (p. 135)

The Roots of American Culture, I feel, is an extremely uneven work, in a way that none of Rourke's other books is, not even *Troupers of the Gold Coast* or *Davy Crockett.* Whatever her projected three-volume work on the History of American Culture would have been like, at least in one very important sense, this *Roots of American Culture* essay-volume is not entirely of her own doing. (p. 136)

Constance Rourke emerges from her sizable body of cultural studies of American art and American life, from her placid, semiretired existence in Grand Rapids with her aging and overly demanding mother in an unusually close relationship—as a striking example of one of the typical figures she has made so much of in *American Humor:* the comic poet. A great deal is involved in my calling *her* an American comic poet. There was her quick, lyrical responsiveness to geographic regions

and to the kinds of settlers (English, Scotch, Irish, European) who migrated there. Then, her straining imagination, which sensed fantasy and rhapsody in so many places that would leave others cold: an imagination at once responsive to giants, to the lure of legend, to the mystery of the all-promising theatrical stage; an imagination that enabled her to create her own (better-than-actual) world out of the wilderness of historical and familial tradition. And, there was her profound and joyous attachment to the people at large. Fittingly, given her predilections, she would title an important chapter in *American Humor,* which devotes considerable space to Walt Whitman and his poetry, ''I Hear America Singing.'' But the poet in the popular view has long been taken as an impractical, unrealistic individual whose thoughts run helter-skelter. And even in this regard, discounting slightly for interpretive bias, I feel that Rourke fits the broad description of comic poet. (p. 137)

Her greatest achievement as a writer, in my opinion, is her calling into being the spirit of our people, the American character: her suggesting its broad, yet deeply rooted outlines, even in the face of certain very doubtful judgments. . . . In the manner of an evocative, fanciful poet—a vatic interpreter or soothsayer (of sorts)—she discerned a deep truth about our diversified culture. Making a world, or making what may seem to be multiple worlds—with sets of prototypical figures: comic stereotypes, folk-hero giants, popular-success leaders like those in *Trumpets*—out of the wilderness of our earlier cultural history, is not a mere matter of simple imaginative creation. The poetic maker, the *poietes,* must do a special job: continually create this world-scene, sustain it with unceasing labor, lest it become lost. Thus I attach special meaning, at the risk of overinterpreting, to Rourke's reiterated concern in her various writings: there is still a great deal of work to be accomplished; ''so much remains to be done.''

As to Constance Rourke's contributions to our literature: her *American Humor,* I feel, for all its arguable judgments, remains her best piece of writing. Here, to a greater extent than in any other work, she provided students of American culture not only with an important new way of looking at the subject, but with a special vocabulary of applied terms for framing that view. This book . . . is—with all its paradoxical restraint in style, imaginative sweep in design, and eccentricity in execution— the product of a comic-poetic mind; and as such it remains ever fresh, in a manner of speaking, and bafflingly ambiguous.

Trumpets of Jubilee, though in style at least it often reflects more of Calvinism's severity and ponderousness than of the lightness of spirit suggested by the title, is also a marvelously evocative book. While it is clear that her five biographical subjects—three Beechers, Greeley, and Barnum—emerge *from* the people and, as huge popular successes, are very much *of* the people, they must also be considered as outstanding representative persons in their own right. Here, as she would do with folk-hero giants, Rourke conveyed the thrill she experienced when dealing with pop-up figures who thrust themselves sharply out of the printed page of legend and record, under the very eye of the reader. These five, in their own little world of new-era jubilation, show us the capacity for growth that is part of the American character: growth from frontier-community rawness to urban sophistication, growth out of Calvinistic mind-hobbling into a trumpeting freedom to entertain hopes of a better day.

What I take to be Rourke's second-best piece of writing is to be found in this book: her marvelous chapter on the life and hard times of Harriet Beecher Stowe, slave-woman (in effect) to masculine Calvinism, particularly as exemplified by her husband Calvin. In this saga of the bondage and qualified liberation of the famous daughter and sister of that rout of Calvinist ministers of the Beecher clan, Rourke showed how that lady came to be transmuted into Uncle Tom. And, an added source of pleasure, Rourke gave us insights into the affinity she herself felt with Harriet Stowe.

A third piece of writing that I feel deserves high praise is Rourke's *Charles Sheeler,* based to an extent on his own statements. . . . Aside from its interesting and informative bits of art history from the late 1800s to well into the twentieth century, *Charles Sheeler* shows how one gifted artist-photographer worked with and within existing forms to create his own aesthetic renderings of line-and-space configurations.

This recap of Rourke's most important contributions (in my opinion) to our literature, in effect to the unearthing of our cultural roots, serves as finale to the story of her lifetime of purposeful, faith-keeping research and recording. Her determined spirit lives on, in her still available books (*American Humor, Trumpets of Jubilee,* and *The Roots of American Culture*) at the very least. And since ''more remains to be done'' than she could ever have dreamed, more even than her projected three-volume history could ever have included, I believe that someday important additions will be made to her pioneering studies. (pp. 145-47)

ADDITIONAL BIBLIOGRAPHY

Marshall, Margaret. ''Constance Rourke: Artist and Citizen.'' *The Nation* CLII, No. 25 (21 June 1941): 726-28.
    A eulogistic personal remembrance, with notes on Rourke's research techniques. This article reveals the importance Rourke attached to the idea of the artist as an active participant in community life.

————. ''Constance Rourke in the Critics' Den.'' *The Nation* CLV, No. 17 (24 October 1942): 418-20.
    A defense of Rourke against her critics, and a laudatory review of *The Roots of American Culture.*

Mumford, Lewis. ''The Cultural Bases of America.'' *The Saturday Review of Literature* XXV, No. 33 (15 August 1942): 3-4.
    An enthusiastic overview of Rourke's career and a review of *The Roots of American Culture.*

Wertheim, Arthur F. ''Constance Rourke and the Discovery of American Culture in the 1930s.'' In *The Study of the American Culture: Contemporary Conflicts,* edited by Luther S. Luedtke, pp. 49-59. DeLand, Fla.: Everett/Edwards, 1977.
    A survey of Rourke's work, which traces her critical influences and draws parallels of influence between her books and the nationalistic introspection of America's economically depressed 1930s.

Carl (Friedrich Georg) Spitteler

1845-1924

(Also wrote under pseudonym of Felix Tandem) Swiss poet, novelist, essayist, autobiographer, short story and novella writer, journalist, editor, and critic.

Spitteler was one of Switzerland's foremost poets writing in German. Known primarily for his epic poetry, he was described by Romain Rolland as "the Homer of our age" and "the only master of the epic since Milton." Throughout his work, Spitteler combined myth and realism to create a unique cosmos that reveals his essentially pessimistic world view and allegorically depicts the soul's struggle to transcend the mundane aspects of life. In 1919 Spitteler was awarded the Nobel Prize in literature in recognition of two of his major works, *Prometheus und Epimetheus: Ein Gleichnis (Prometheus and Epimetheus: A Prose Epic)* and *Olympischer Frühling*.

Spitteler was born in Liestal, Switzerland. While attending secondary school in the city of Basel, he developed an interest in the arts and studied under the renowned historian Jakob Burckhardt. It was Burckhardt who introduced Spitteler to the works of the Italian Renaissance poet Ludovico Ariosto, whose long narrative poems later served as the inspiration for Spitteler's own epic works. From 1863 to 1868 he studied law and theology at the universities of Basel, Zurich, and Heidelberg. By the time of his theology examination, however, Spitteler had rejected orthodox Christian doctrine and declined to fulfill his ministerial obligations. It was a time of confusion and disillusionment for Spitteler, and in 1871 he left Switzerland for Russia, where he lived for nearly eight years. There, he worked as a tutor in the home of a Russian general while he wrote a major portion of his prose poem *Prometheus and Epimetheus*. Returning to his homeland, he completed and published the epic work with hopes that it would foster his reputation. Much to his disappointment, *Prometheus and Epimetheus* was completely ignored by critics and readers, who found the epic form unfashionable. It was not until many years later, after he earned the esteem of critics with his epic *Olympischer Frühling*, that this first literary endeavor was finally praised and favorably compared, in theme and poetical framework, to Friedrich Nietzsche's *Thus Spake Zarathustra*, which it had preceded by two years. Following the publication of *Prometheus and Epimetheus*, Spitteler worked as a journalist and as a teacher until 1892, when a large inheritance from his wife's family allowed him to devote full attention to his craft. In 1914, his growing literary reputation was arrested when he delivered *Unser Schweizer Standpunkt*, a political lecture that chastised the German government for its invasion of Belgium and urged Switzerland to maintain its neutrality during World War I. While the lecture endeared Spitteler to the French and influenced their critical reception of his works, the Germans refused to print any of his works in textbook anthologies. Spitteler received the Nobel Prize at the age of seventy-four, and thereafter lived a quiet life in Switzerland until his death.

Nearly all of Spitteler's important works rely on some variation of the Promethean theme that superhuman willpower and divine understanding can enable the aspirant to endure and eventually transcend life's tragedy and suffering. In his early epic, *Prometheus and Epimetheus*, Spitteler allegorically

renders this theme in the mythological story of two brothers—farsighted Prometheus, the "great rebel of injustice and the authority of power," and undiscerning Epimetheus, the practical ruler who seeks immediate gratification from life. Written in rhythmic prose based on biblical models, Spitteler's *Prometheus and Epimetheus* portrays characters from the Bible and Greek mythology in a timeless setting. Some critics believe that the epic is needlessly complicated and difficult to comprehend, while others praise the work for its readability and entertainment value. *Prometheus der Dulder*, Spitteler's last important work in the epic mode, is a major artistic development of his earlier epic. While the stories of the two epics are essentially the same in theme and subject, the later epic employs a poetic scheme of rhyming couplets, and throughout the work Spitteler maintains a shorter, tighter composition. Charles Baudouin echoes the critical consensus when he states that *Prometheus der Dulder* "is no mere working over of the original prose epic." Critics agree that *Prometheus der Dulder* represents a mature distillation of the poet's thought.

Olympischer Frühling is considered Spitteler's masterpiece and was the first work to bring the poet popular success in Switzerland and Germany. In *Olympischer Frühling*, Spitteler again borrowed his situations from Greek mythology. Although the work is based on the legend of the fall of Kronos and the Titans and the rise of Zeus and the Olympians, Spitteler created new adventures for the gods and mortals of his epic. Throughout *Olympischer Frühling,* Spitteler contrasted human weaknesses with the supernatural strength of the gods, and he again expressed the idea that only individuals who renounce happiness and the conventions of society can overcome the tragedies of earthly existence. The characters in the epic poem appear with familiar mythological names, but with unique personalities given to them by Spitteler. Thus, for example, Hera is a mortal woman instead of a goddess, Ananke is a masculine persona rather than feminine as in Greek legends, and Ajax, a mortal, becomes an Olympian god. An interesting, though uncommon view of *Olympischer Frühling* is held by Baudouin, who believes that the poetic portrayal of the rise of Zeus to ruler of the cosmos is a symbolic representation of the "redemption of the world by beauty." Most critics refer favorably to this poem as a demonstration of Spitteler's imaginative powers. Some commentators note, however, that he does not sustain the poetic images throughout this work. Nevertheless, Spitteler is widely praised for the evocative and beautiful language of *Olympischer Frühling,* which possesses, as James F. Muirhead states, "a Keats-like beauty of diction."

In addition to his poetry, Spitteler also wrote several prose works. Of these, the best known are his novels *Conrad der Leutnant, Imago,* and *Die Mädchenfiende: Eine Kindergeschichte (The Two Misogynists). Conrad der Leutnant,* Spitteler's experiment with Naturalism, is set in a loveless family environment and depicts an intense power struggle between the protagonist, Conrad, and his arch-antagonist, his father. While most critics agree that *Conrad der Leutnant* is not a major contribution to Naturalist fiction, the novel is an indication that Spitteler was capable of working in a realistic style, independent of myth. According to Spitteler, *Imago* "explains" his first work *Prometheus and Epimetheus,* in the context of the nineteenth-century, middle-class world. This autobiographical novel is considered by some critics and psychologists to be one of the earliest studies in psychoanalysis because of its examination of the conscious and subconscious conflicts between an artist's creative needs and his adherence to bourgeois values that inhibit those needs. Impressed by Spitteler's *Imago,* Sigmund Freud borrowed its title for the name of the first professional journal devoted to psychoanalysis. Working in a lighter vein, Spitteler wrote *The Two Misogynists,* an idyllic tale of two school aged children based on the author's own childhood experiences. Though it is a minor work, critics regard it as a delightful and realistic depiction of childhood.

For the most part, Spitteler dedicated his career to writing epic poetry and purposely repeated a single theme. Critics comment that the philosophical aspects of his writing are often difficult to comprehend, but most agree that his works possess beautiful poetic language and novel mythical tales of adventure. Although Spitteler's creative thought is sometimes compared to that of Nietzsche, commentators usually make a telling distinction between the two writers: they regard Nietzsche as a poetic philosopher and Spitteler as a philosophical poet. Nietzsche respected the Swiss poet's work, commenting that "Spitteler is the most subtle of all writers when he has to deal with aesthetic matters." Spitteler's disdain for the modern novel, which he believed supplanted the higher art form of the epic, and his dedication to writing epic poetry, kept him out of the mainstream of nineteenth and twentieth-century literary movements. Yet he remains significant as one of the few modern authors to attempt and succeed in recreating the spirit of the classical epic narrative.

(See also *Contemporary Authors,* Vol. 109.)

PRINCIPAL WORKS

Prometheus und Epimetheus: Ein Gleichnis. 2 vols. [as Felix Tandem] (prose poem) 1880-81
  [*Prometheus and Epimetheus: A Prose Epic,* 1931]
Extramundana (poetry) 1882
Schmetterlinge (poetry) 1889
Gustav (novel) 1892
Conrad der Leutnant (novel) 1898
Lachende Wahrheiten (essays) 1898
  [*Laughing Truths,* 1927]
Olympischer Frühling. 4 vols. (poetry) 1900-05; also published as *Olympischer Frühling* [revised edition], 1910
Balladen (poetry) 1905
Glockenlieder (poetry) 1906
Imago (novel) 1906
Gerold und Hansli, die Mädchenfiende: Eine Kindergeschichte (novella) 1907; also published as *Die Mädchenfiende: Eine Kindergeschichte,* 1920
  [*The Two Misogynists,* 1922; also published as *Two Little Misogynists,* 1922]
Meine Beziehungen zu Nietzsche (essay) 1908
Meine fruhesten Erlebniss (autobiography) 1914
Unser Schweizer Standpunkt (lecture) 1915
Prometheus der Dulder (poetry) 1924
Selected Poems of Carl Spitteler (poetry) 1928
Gesammelte Werke. 10 vols. (poetry, novels, novellas, lecture, autobiography, essays, and short stories) 1945-58

CARL SPITTELER   (essay date 1898)

[*Although Spitteler received much early negative criticism for his attempts to revive the epic narrative, he viewed it as the highest form of literature and spent most of his literary career writing in that mode. In this excerpt taken from his* Laughing Truths, *a collection of sometimes whimsical, sometimes incisive essays, Spitteler calls for a return to the epic form in literature.*]

The maxim that the Epic is no longer permissible in modern times is one of the most precious gems in the thesaurus of every man of culture. If one ventures to knock shyly at the portals of the brain and beg for a friendly explanation of why this is the case, one is met by a peevish murmur to the effect that the primitive days of the nations, the youth of mankind, and a naïve outlook on the universe form the only tolerable atmosphere for the Epic. Besides, the conclusion goes practically without saying, as is proved by the total absence of this form of art to-day, accompanied by the brilliant development of the romance, the true epic of the nineteenth century. In fact, it is an eternal and fundamental truth.

Thus, since the Homeric period furnished the above-mentioned conditions, the epic was then all right. Since they are lacking to-day, the epic is now all wrong. Verbum sap.

Good. The idea is plausible. But nobody seems to find it necessary to prove the assumption that the alleged fact is a knock-down blow, that the Homeric age really did afford the required conditions. That is, presumably, another eternal and fundamental verity. Or what would be the good of the popular catchwords that enable us to dispense with thinking, knowledge, learning, and other annoyances of that kind? And, of course, when we have not the most primitive ideas of what a given era was, it is clear that it must have been a primitive era.

I do not need here to give a historical lecture. But if the cavalier manner in which Homer handles his gods betokens a naïve outlook on the universe; if the exceedingly blasé and degenerate culture of the Ionic Asia Minor represents a state of infancy; if never-ending bewailing of the present, homesick longing for the past, and despair of the future are signs of the youth of humanity, then I claim the right to assert that the nineteenth century is an example of childhood. . . . (pp. 53-4)

This shows that the left leg of the fundamental verity is rather lame. Let us next deal with the right leg.

"Primitive condition, childhood, youth of humanity," "naïveté of outlook on the universe", "bloom, maturity, old age of nations". Who would venture to argue here as if these were known quantities? What if I asserted that humanity was never young and that no era was ever naïve? And this is just what I do assert. Is there really a biology of nations? Does anyone know when a people is young or when it is old? Is there anyone who would venture to decide dogmatically whether (*e.g.*) the Germans or Russians of to-day are an old or a young race, or whether they are at the beginning, in the middle, or at the end of their career? And so on.

And more. Or rather still less!

We do not even know what a "nation" or a "people" is. Is it determined by its mother-tongue and traditions, or by its constitution, politics, fatherland, and boundaries, or by its habits, customs, festivals, and religion? Do we know a single law of the life of nations, even if it be assumed that there can be laws of life for an abstract collective personality like a "people"? Such considerations show that all the wisdom about naïve views of the universe, or the childhood and youth of mankind, or the youth and age of nations, is sheer foolishness.

Moreover, the fate of this eternal and fundamental verity is just the same as that of all other such verities. If we take the trouble to make a closer examination, we shall always discover, low down in the right hand corner, a proper name in small characters, with "fecit" and a date appended. The eternal and fundamental verity that the epic belongs to youthful nations only has taken a course at the University of Tübingen and speaks the Swabian dialect. Before the days of [Cornelis] Vischer no one knew the first thing about it. Even in the eighteenth, as in all previous centuries, the epic was still regarded as the dearest and highest aim of every poet. Lessing put it in the first place, Goethe essayed it, Schiller yearned to it. And what has become of the famous sun of Homer? I suppose it has suffered an eclipse.

I am no more blind than other people to Vischer's merits. But the proposal that, out of affection for this Swabian Isaiah, we should propagate by a process of natural selection the owlish idea of trading the epic for the romance, is surely a piece of the most egregious tomfoolery.

Should we then wait for the epic until the gracious return of primitive conditions, naïve views of the universe, and the youth of mankind? Then we'll have to wait until the evening of time. For this state of affairs will never return, for the very good reason that it has never been there before. (pp. 54-6)

Carl Spitteler, "The Forbidden Epic" (originally published under a different title, in his Lachende Wahrheiten, *1898), in his* Laughing Truths, *translated by James F. Muirhead (reprinted by permission of G.P. Putnam's Sons), Putnam's, 1927, pp. 53-6.*

CHARLES BAUDOUIN (essay date 1920)

[*A French writer and psychologist, Baudouin was also the editor of the literary journal* Le Carmel, *to which Spitteler contributed. In the following excerpt, he offers a critical examination of Spitteler as a creator of "mythic epic"—a distinct combination of subjective contemplations inherent to myth and the objective adventures of an epic.*]

Few of Spitteler's prose works can be adequately appraised unless they are regarded as commentaries on his major poems. Particularly does the remark apply to *Imago,* which is puzzling if read without this key. But, as soon as we understand the genetic relationship between *Imago* and *Prometheus und Epimetheus,* the whole of the first-named book is illuminated by the idea, and we see that *Imago* is a great work.

In Spitteler's lyrics, the true personality of the author is more plainly disclosed than in the novels. Wherein lies the chief interest of *Schmetterlinge*? We learn from this book how a great poet endows everything he touches with greatness; how he lends greatness to that which, if handled by others, might appear paltry. In Spitteler's verses, the butterfly becomes one of the powers of the woodlands, becomes a fairy, a goddess. This transfiguration is assisted by the poet's use (for titles to some of his poems) of the mythological names which Linnaeus and others have given to various species: Proserpina, Mnemosyne, Hera, etc. These gracious names, may they not unconsciously have contributed to reawaken in Spitteler, the artist in words, the love of butterflies which had irradiated his childhood? However this may be, some of the poems in the volume assume the form of myths, legends of the creation. (pp. 50-1)

Thus it is that Spitteler's native genius, surging up continually, displays itself, almost unwarrantably, in a field where there might seem to be no place for mythical treatment. It is in the domain of the mythical epic that Spitteler is perfectly at home. When he goes elsewhere, for a time, it is by way of relaxation—chasing butterflies.

The "mythical epic," we have said. But, really, we are confounding two distinct things, the myth and the epic poem. Spitteler, who has notions of his own concerning the problems of aesthetics, and who is described by Nietzsche as "the most subtle of all writers when he has to deal with aesthetic matters," distinguishes clearly between them. The myth precedes the epic. It issues from a meditative contemplation of the world and of life; it is the echo of this contemplation in the soul; it is austere, and charged with cosmic melancholy. The epic, on the other hand, has an objective trend; it is fantasy, adventure, the joy of creating and of relating; it is an act, rather than a passive thing like an echo. In this sense, *Prometheus und Epimetheus* is predominantly myth, whereas *Olympischer Frühling,* is predominantly epic. If I understand Spitteler's thought aright, this distinction is closely akin to that drawn by Nietzsche between Dionysian art (participation in the mystery and suffering of the world) and Apollonian art (imposing a plastic form of luminous serenity upon this content of mystery and suffering). Spitteler is both musician and painter. The musician rules in the former of these domains, and the painter in the latter; but they are good neighbours, and are always ready for a chat.

The mention of *Prometheus und Epimetheus* raises the question of the relationship between Spitteler and Nietzsche. It is extremely probable that *Prometheus und Epimetheus* (1880-1881) had an influence upon *Also sprach Zarathustra* (1883), an influence which manifested itself alike in respect of the heroic content and in respect of the quasi-biblical form. Spitteler has himself discussed his relationships to Nietzsche. The two recluses must have come in contact at the University of Basle, where Spitteler was finishing his studies at the date when Nietzsche was teaching. But they did not become acquainted at this time. Later, they corresponded. Spitteler acclaimed *Der Fall Wagner* in an article in which he went so far as to say: "Nietzsche is a giant; he will therefore not take it amiss if we expect him to be great." In 1912 was published Ragaz's study of the relationships between *Prometheus und Epimetheus* and *Also sprach Zarathustra*. Then came the issue of Nietzsche's letters to Overbeck, and these show how high an opinion Nietzsche had of Spitteler. Whether there was or was not a strong direct influence, there can be no doubt as to the kinship between the two men's minds. (pp. 51-3)

[In *Prometheus und Epimetheus,* the] reader will have realised that, of the ancient Greek myth, Spitteler preserves little more than the names and the pure essence. Prometheus is still the strong man, the rebel against heaven, the exiled benefactor of mankind. But the tale has been refashioned, so that its episodes are utterly different from those of the old legend of Prometheus. Such a method of treatment undergoes generalisation in *Olympischer Frühling.* Here all the gods meet us bearing the old names—but they are new gods. Spitteler has no respect for mythological tradition. If he utters the familiar Greek syllables, this is only because they charm the ear. His gods are his own; they are the gods of his own household. Thus, in like manner, the Virgins of the Flemish painters were Flemings, fair and ruddy. Spitteler's Olympus is not on the Greek mountain of that name; it is in Jura or the Alps.

The procession of the gods, awakened from their sleep in the dark recessus of Erebus, climbs the Morgenberg [Mount Morning], ascending towards the serene beauty of the summit in springtime. But these mountain climbers are of a very different sort from the tourists who visit Switzerland. (p. 55)

What we witness . . . is the ascent of the gods, the slow but everlasting redemption of the world by beauty.

The redemption of the world! Though Carl Spitteler is a Swiss, and although his imagery is full of the vital juices of his native land, his inspiration is by no means that of a "national poet." It is human and superhuman; it is metaphysical; it is cosmical. His world is the whole world. Nature, for him, is animate throughout; and this nature speaks to him. Pan is close to him, as to all the great poets; and some of the thousand secret energies of the god are communicated to the artist's soul. For Spitteler, the "universe" is not an empty word from which all the colour has been washed out. In his youth he made acquaintance with "Weltschmerz," with those pangs of the poet and the metaphysician which (for want of a succinct vernacular term) we may describe as "cosmic suffering." He has known the state of mind in which we share the misery of all created beings, and in which we feel that the animals are our brothers in pain. This is the condition in which pity becomes a danger to those who feel it. Nietzsche, affrighted by his seer's vision, said of it: "The farther we see into life, the farther do we see into suffering."

Such were the characteristics of the anguish from which the thought-process took its rise both in Schopenhauer and in Nietzsche. Those who suffer from this anguish are constrained by a vital necessity to seek deliverance from it at any price. The artist will find deliverance in the beautiful. (p. 56)

If we cover suffering with a veil of lovely illusion, we have, ere long, not illusion but creation, a transmutation into gold; for this beauty gives birth to a very real joy. Such is Nietzsche's theme in *Die Geburt der Tragödie aus dem Geiste der Musik.* An analogous thought is the source of Wagner's art (though not, perhaps, of his tragedies in particular); and it is the source, likewise, of the art of Spitteler. And here we seem to have a metaphysical version of the same idea. Is not the world itself (the world of visible creation) the "maya," the illusion, in which God or the gods, the supreme artists, veil from their own eyes the sight of original sin? In the beginning was evil. May we not consider the creation to have been a deliverance by the beautiful? This is the fundamental tone of *Olympischer Frühling.*

The deliverance is progressive, being effected in the course of the eighteen thousand verses of the poem. When the mountain has been climbed, there is an orgy of celestial joy, of free aërial fantasy. The gods are making holiday, and show themselves at times to be in a merry mood. Aphrodite is mischievous, and plays pranks on the men. The action takes place in distinct episodes, each being complete in itself, a poem with a colour of its own. (pp. 56-7)

Spitteler is a good French scholar; he reads and loves our French classics; in his own writings he has achieved a synthesis of two cultures. His thought shows him to be the kinsman of Schopenhauer and of Nietzsche; and the Dionysian reverberation of his writings represents the outcome of the Teutonic tradition. But his Apollonian clarity, the purity of his versification, the supreme beauty of his visions—all these are Latin. Hence Spitteler's work is typically Swiss; but it is also something wider, it is European. "A European poet," he wrote to me; "that is the best description. I have never been a Swiss poet or a German poet; but, rather, a European, an international, an intertemporal poet. It was only by the accident of birth that I came to use the German language as my medium of expression." (p. 60)

> *Charles Baudouin, "Carl Spitteler" (originally published under a different title in* Revue de l'Epoque, *October, 1920), in his* Contemporary Studies, *translated by Eden Paul and Cedar Paul, G. Allen & Unwin, 1924 (and reprinted by Books for Libraries Press, 1969; distributed by Arno Press, Inc.), pp. 44-61.*

[ROMAIN ROLLAND]   (essay date 1925)

[*Rolland was a French man of letters and noted pacifist who is best known for his novel* Jean-Christophe, *a ten-volume life of a musical genius. Throughout his career, Rolland was inspired by the lives of heroic men and wrote biographies of Ludwig von Beethoven, Mohandas K. Gandhi, and Leo Tolstoy, among others. A distinguished musicologist and critic, he also wrote many dramas that demonstrate his theory of a "theater of the people," devoted to the inspirationally heroic and to social change. His artistic credo, according to W. Hunter Beckwith, centered on the principle that "all art manifestations should convey moral truth, which for him seems to be faith in humanity, a pantheistic religion, and continued insistence on the virtues of great artists." In the following excerpt, Rolland discusses the merits of Spitteler's works.*]

At first *Prometheus and Epimetheus* gripped me strongest, precisely because of its racy harshness, its chaotic aspect the pungent power of its penetrating juices that well forth as from the trunk of a broad-branched oak. Here a luxuriant jungle of myths, similes, and parables, there reveling in symbols that might have been borrowed from a mediaeval bestiary—or again, oh joy! the incomparable beauty of that symphony, that Swiss pastoral, *Pandora!* It suggested Beethoven, in all the fiery inspiration of his youth, yet already rich in experience, with Herculean hands shaping the plastic material to his will as in his last quartettes.

Then I followed down the stream and saw, as from the mouth of the rugged mountain canyon of *Pandora*, the broadening valley below, "black shadows vanishing in the sunshine flood," to where, circled by its mighty garland of mountain pinnacles, the stream widens in silvery beauty toward the sea, winding broad and peaceful through the land of the gods—the *Olympian Spring*. No longer is the theme dominated by the personal tragedy of Prometheus. No longer does the ear catch the cry of conquered anguish. The hot, pungent, aromatic originality of his maiden work has vanished. Here one detects mature control and mastery, the guiding intellect in its full creative power. But what luxuriance of dreams, visions, inventions, both lofty and beautiful, and all new and unhackneyed, welling up spontaneous, vigorous, and pure as a fresh mountain spring! The glory of June in the mountains and the star-strewn firmament above! A whole new world of myths and gods! It is intoxicating.

For more than forty years, as long as I have known Switzerland, I have dreamed of a great Swiss poet who should be not only a national minstrel, like Gottfried Keller, but also an interpreter of Nature's mighty moods, of her clouds, her eternal snows, her dashing mountain torrents, her crags and abysses. Here he is at last. . . . [Considering his *Olympian Spring*,] I am filled with an ecstasy of joy and well-being such as I have scarcely ever derived from a literary work. With what shall I compare it? I think of Ariosto, of Dante, of Mozart. The magic of this art seems to transform the words themselves into scents and colors. But new visions constantly draw us forward, new landscapes of the earth and of the soul, a whole empire of dreams extending from one pole to the other. The poem unfolds like a cycle of brilliant symphonic variations. As I write these words I think again of Beethoven, of his mysterious art of drawing from a single theme endless variations, a whole series of musical bas-reliefs representing every phase of feeling and beauty. It is thus that I see the twelve great variations of the *Hohen Zeit* in the *Olympian Spring*, an ocean of music, fathomless, boundless. I have just opened the book again. It is difficult to tear myself away from it. I would sail upon that ocean for years and years. Why ever return? Life is there in all its abundance, with its depths and shadows, but also with its light eternally playing upon the laughing waves.

Long after this Olympic symphony, with its brilliant orchestration, I read the third epic, *Prometheus the Endurer*. I found him again the hero of the earlier period, but far more tragic, because here stripped of the adornments of a luxuriant dream-life, the drawing more classic, more condensed, in the fewest possible lines, bared of every unessential—but with no sacrifice of rich experience both bitter and ennobling, boundless peace attained through boundless suffering. I know nothing that is at the same time so mournful and so cheerful as the final song, *Der Sieger*. Since the first Prometheus, age has crept over him and the victor knows the ashen taste of fame. Man wins here

the highest victory—complete self-mastery, without fear and without hope. (pp. 515-16)

Intoxicating only for the strong, and they are not many. We can understand the hostility with which the mediocre greet this poem. It is almost better that such a masterpiece should remain uncomprehended, unknown, to the common herd. For it would extinguish their hope—and this ardor of the soul, which such a masterpiece brings in hope's stead, is too intense for the weak hearts of average men.

Spitteler is the greatest of the Swiss. Never before has his country produced such an heroic figure in the world of art and thought. The Homer of our age, the greatest German poet since Goethe, the only master of the epic during the three centuries since Milton died! But far lonelier than either in the art of his age. I envision him like a solitary, towering mountain in the Alps, an entire mountain from foothills to summit, and each can take from him what he can appreciate—the flowers of his meadows, the fruits of his orchards. Each can find in him the spring to slake his thirst, the shade for noontide repose and dreams. But while you quaff from the spring and repose in the shade, high, high above you tower into the distant blue abyss the black aisles of his pine forests and his inaccessible snow-peaks. (p. 517)

> [Romain Rolland], *"A Bard of an Elder Age, a Symposium: In Memory of Carl Spitteler"* (originally published under a different title in Neue Zürcher Zeitung, April 26, 1925), in The Living Age (copyright 1925, by the Living Age Co.), Vol. 325, No. 4222, June 6, 1925, pp. 511-17.

ERNEST BOYD   (essay date 1925)

[*An Irish-American writer and translator, Boyd was a prominent literary critic known for his erudite, honest, and often satirical critiques. In the candidly wrought essays which form his important studies of Irish literature,* Ireland's Literary Renaissance *(1916) and* The Contemporary Dramas of Ireland *(1917), Boyd evaluated Irish literary works apart from English literature. He was also a respected translator, especially of French and German works, and his* Studies in Ten Literatures *(1925) demonstrates his knowledge of modern foreign literature. In the following examination of Spitteler's poetry and prose, Boyd maintains that Spitteler's* Prometheus and Epimetheus *anticipated the Nietzschean doctrine of the transvaluation of values.*]

[Spitteler's] earliest attempts at composition were, he tells us, submitted to the Swiss poet Gottfried Keller, who found them "lamentable as to form, but unusual in content," and so long did Spitteler strive to perfect his work that he was thirty-six years old before he ventured to publish his first book. The two volumes of *Prometheus und Epimetheus* appeared in 1880 and 1881 over the expressive pseudonym "Felix Tandem," and a quarter of a century was to elapse before a second edition was issued in the author's own name. (pp. 199-200)

No *résumé* can give an adequate idea of the beauty and profundity of this work, in which the transvaluation of all values was preached to a generation as yet unfamiliar with the Nietzschean doctrine. From the beginning we find that extraordinary faculty which has enabled the poet to clothe the most abstract ideas in a garment of delicate imagery, and to breathe life into the teachings of an abstruse mysticism. Where Nietzsche is the poetic philosopher, Spitteler is the philosophic poet, in the best sense of the word. The former was the evangelist of a new gospel, the latter has aimed solely at the creation of beauty, without a thought for his didactic mission. Spitteler is content to please, while Nietzsche's purpose was to convince, and herein lies the fundamental difference between Zarathustra and Prometheus. The one announces a potential superman, the other represented man at his highest and best, when his actions accord with the dictates of a noble soul. (p. 203)

A couple of years after the publication of *Prometheus und Epimetheus* his second book followed, under the title *Extramundana*. The writing of the earlier book had developed in Spitteler a sense of mythology which was not part of his original epic genius: "Even as a twenty-two-year-old student I was convinced that epic poetry was to be my life-work," he said once, in reply to those who had argued that the epical quality of *Prometheus und Epimetheus* indicated it as the work of mature age. But the thirteen years devoted to its composition brought with them an expansion of his talent which was expressed in his second volume. *Extramundana* was nothing less than an attempt to rewrite the story of the creation in verse. The author has since dismissed the experiment with a contemptuous reference which does not altogether do justice to its many fine pages. Nevertheless, his criticism of a too elaborate allegory, "cold and rhetorical," refers to much that will drive away all but his more enthusiastic admirers. There is a banality of thought, and a carelessness of form, which partly confirm Spitteler's description of the book as a piece of "hasty botch work."

For six years, from 1883 to 1889, no publisher could be found to accept the manuscripts of a poet who refused to write for the age of realism in which he lived. Finally, however, Spitteler persuaded his original publisher in Jena to issue *Schmetterlinge,* his first essay in rhyming verse. The transition to this form from the beautiful rhythmic prose of *Prometheus und Epimetheus* was the blank verse of *Extramundana.* So uncertain was Spitteler of his power of versification that he struggled for a long time with a rhyming dictionary, yet no trace of such labor will be found in these graceful poems, whose actual subjects are the butterflies of Switzerland. They have more, however, than an appeal to the poetic entomologist, for they give us the first of those memories of childhood and youth which Spitteler later developed in his prose stories. As soon as the poet sought his themes in his own country the Swiss element, as distinct from the German, became noticeable in his work, and *Schmetterlinge* served as a natural prelude to the four volumes of prose which now followed. (pp. 203-05)

In their order of publication these four works are, *Friedli der Kolderi, Gustav, Konrad der Leutnant,* and *Die Mädchenfeinde.* (p. 205)

Friedli der Kolderi, his first work to be published in Switzerland, consisted of seven of the most varied examples of prose narrative, four "feuilletons," two fairy tales, and the "study," which gives its title to the book. This last is by far the most remarkable, being an interpretation of Swiss character after the manner of the modern Russians. As a sketch of folk life it may rank with the best that Keller has written. It is composed of the simplest elements, yet, in its own way, it leaves an impression as lasting as any of the Russian story-tellers.

The idyllic little tale, *Gustav,* and the children's story, *Die Mädchenfeinde,* are both charming elaborations of autobiographical material. The young student of medicine who has failed at his examinations, to the great distress of his parents, returns to his home cherishing the dream of becoming a great composer. His philistine relations have little confidence in his

genius, but one of his compositions eventually reaches a distinguished musician and all ends well, as befits an "idyl"—another of Spitteler's experiments. If the gods have been less prompt to intervene in the reality of his own case than in the picture of *Gustav,* the personal interest of the story is not thereby diminished. The precocious misogynists of *Die Mädchenfeinde* are the occasion of a delightful picture of the child world, in which the problems of existence are faced with the same, if smaller, weapons as afterward serve in the struggles of manhood. It was characteristic of Spitteler that the *nouvelle* should have suggested to him this exposition of the psychology of childhood. Experimenting with a new *genre,* he succeeded in achieving the maximum of external dissimilarity, while preserving the fundamental identity of method employed by its recognized exponents.

A volume of satirical verse, *Literarische Gleichnisse,* preceded Spitteler's next and most important essay in contemporary prose fiction, *Konrad der Leutnant.* In this book the author undertook to meet his enemies the Realists on their own ground. . . . Spitteler decided to surprise his literary opponents by providing them with a new formula, which he illustrated in *Konrad der Leutnant.* "Before writing another epic I wanted to prove to myself that I could employ even the Naturalistic style, if I so desired. I chose the difficult form of the 'description' (*Darstellung*), in order to make my prose writing less easy." The subtitle of *Konrad der Leutnant* is *Eine Darstellung,* which term is defined by the author as follows: "By 'a description' I understand a special form of prose narrative, with a peculiar purpose, and a particular style which serves as a means to that end. The object is to obtain the highest possible intensity of action, the means are: unity of person, unity of perspective, consecutive unity of time." In other words, the principal character is introduced immediately the story opens, and remains throughout the central figure, only those events being related of which he is conscious, and as he becomes aware of them. The action develops uninterruptedly, hour by hour, no interval being passed over as unimportant or unessential. Naturally, such a narrative can cover only a comparatively short period of time.

The story of Lieutenant Conrad is told in the space of twelve hours, and relates how the young officer comes into conflict with the jealous authority of his father, the proprietor of the Peacock Inn at Herrlisdorf. (pp. 205-07)

In its bare outline *Konrad der Leutnant* offers no unusual interest, although the picture of rural manners is drawn with Spitteler's customary insight, and gives a value to the story which admirers of Keller will appreciate. Perfect is the characterization Kathri, who is the female counterpart of Conrad, and to whom a natural affinity draws him in the course of that tragic day. The whole household lives before us, as the members in turn cross the path of the central character, each contributing to the unfolding of his destiny. But the main interest of the book is, of course, technical. The mechanism of the *Darstellung* itself will suffice to hold the reader, apart from the intrinsic worth of the narrative. Spitteler has certainly given an ingenious demonstration of the logical development of literary Naturalism. The disadvantages of the method need hardly be emphasized, for we have long since seen the fallacy of the theory which gave birth to the school. Not every detail in *Konrad der Leutnant* is interesting, since no life can possibly be composed of uniformly valuable elements. The author, like all Realists, labors under the obligation of completeness, which imposes a vast fund of unprofitable material. Spitteler, however, is here frankly an experimentalist, and is entitled to some concessions to the success of his experiment. It is not improbable that he wished to effect a *reductio ad absurdum* of the Naturalistic doctrine, while incidentally proving his capacity as a Realist. . . . [While] welcoming this effort to make Spitteler more widely known, one cannot but regret the choice of an interesting, but unrepresentative, volume.

The year 1898, which saw the publication of *Konrad der Leutnant,* was marked by the appearance of a work which came as near to finding immediate recognition as is possible for Spitteler. *Lachende Wahrheiten,* a collection of critical essays, was, strange to say, the occasion of this unusual experience. . . . These "laughing truths" revealed Spitteler as a critic who knew how to combine a gentle freedom of manner with considerable aesthetic originality and a graceful style. The essays are *causeries,* rather than formal expositions of literary doctrine, although the remarkable discussion of the ballad leaves nothing to be desired from the point of view of exact knowledge. Stimulating as his theories appear, their translation into practice was more helpful, as when Spitteler's next book, *Balladen,* was published—after a long silence—in 1905.

The following year Spitteler made public a work which undoubtedly belongs to the same period as *Prometheus und Epimetheus.* In spite of the twenty-five year's interval, *Imago* stands in evident relationship to the author's first volume, with whose second edition its appearance coincided. The book is thinly disguised autobiography, and within the limits imposed by the fiction it may be regarded as a fairly reliable account of the events which attended the creation of *Prometheus und Epimetheus.* (pp. 208-10)

"An acute crisis of the soul" was the reason alleged by Spitteler for his decision to publish *Prometheus und Epimetheus* after thirteen years brooding over it. The choice of "Felix Tandem" as a pseudonym indicated the nature of his emotion at having emerged from a spiritual conflict which had given him the power to affirm his artistic personality. The points of resemblance between that early work and *Imago* extend beyond the identity of mood out of which they were written. There is a similarity of rhythm in the prose of both which is not found elsewhere in Spitteler, and a like tendency to clothe emotional impulses in a personal form. But the book has an interest quite distinct from its relation to the poet's entry into literature. As a novel of contemporary manners in provincial Germany, *Imago* deserves to be read by all who can share Spitteler's almost savage delight in candid analysis. The long chapter entitled, "In the Hell of Gemütlichkeit," is an exposure of essentially German conditions. Even that virtue of *Gemütlichkeit,* which Germany's worst enemies and best friends agree in conceding to her, does not soften the heart of Spitteler. He has many bitter things to say of the pseudo-culture of such typical institutions as the "Idealia *Verein,*" and his comments upon the social distractions of the middle classes are as unfriendly as his reflections upon "the dogma of the mystery of German womanhood." At bottom Spitteler's strictures are directed against the provincial philistine as he universally exists, but the German setting of *Imago* lends a special piquancy to his satire at the present time. Once again the ideas of Nietzsche and Spitteler coincide, in this commentary on German society, which has inexplicably escaped the attention of translators.

Spitteler's masterpiece, the great epic, *Olympischer Frühling,* . . . after ceaseless revision, received its final form in 1910. In what may be accepted as the definite version, the poem consists of five parts, divided into thirty-three cantos, in rhymed iambic couplets. From the wealth of epic material which had haunted Spitteler from his youth *Olympischer Frühling* alone achieved adequate expression. His first conception, *Johannes,* "a romantic epopee," has neither been published nor altogether abandoned by the author; unlike *Atlantis* and *Die Hochzeit des Theseus,* which were both adapted to ballad form and included in *Balladen.* It is a remarkable testimony to the intellectual quality of the man and the writer, that Spitteler should have devoted practically a lifetime to the creation of such a work. *Olympischer Frühling* is not a lifeless reconstruction of antiquity, but an original mythology, into which the poet has breathed the life of his own spirit. The classical nomenclature is preserved; we read of Zeus, Hera, Apollo, and Dionysos, but they are human gods and very close to our age. In fact, a dissociation of ideas is necessary before we can comprehend these figures who, in spite of their names, are moderns, living in a world familiar with the cinematograph, the steam-engine, and the airship! The classical student must rid himself of his preconceptions, if he would avoid mistaking for anachronisms these elements in Spitteler's mythology. (pp. 211-13)

Carl Spitteler has effectively disposed of the theory that epic poetry is possible only to a young people. *Olympischer Frühling* is a demonstration of arguments advanced in *Lachende Wahrheiten,* when, in the essay *Das verbotene Epos,* the poet combated the judgment which excluded the epic from modern literature [see excerpt above]. With wonderful skill and imagination Spitteler has combined the elements of humor and thought, of action and song, so that, for all its length, the poem is as diversified and as interesting as the epopees of the classical age. A deep note of pessimism runs through this, as through all his works, but it is not the bitter despair of mere personal disillusion, and just suffices to give *Olympischer Frühling* the mark of contemporary philosophy. Moreover, in the second version, the key of resolution in the face of experience is made more perceptible by the rewriting of the last canto, which describes the lofty faith of Herakles in his task of regeneration. The despondent nihilism of the earlier edition has been abandoned.

Spitteler's style is absolutely his own, being an expression in the German language of the spirit most remote from that which we know as Teuton. His idiom is national in its affection for the strong accents of that older tongue which survives on the lips of German-speaking Swiss, for Spitteler is never afraid to draw upon the verbal treasure of his own country. Here, indeed, we have a clew to the fundamental difference between the author of *Olympischer Frühling* and his German contemporaries. Carl Spitteler is Swiss, and as such he shares the privilege of Switzerland to serve as the point of fusion between Germanic and Latin culture. The Swiss spirit has been moulded by these two dissimilar linguistic and intellectual traditions, and the literature of Switzerland has always expressed this compromise. Often the result has been to render somewhat colorless the writings of men who were neither wholly French nor wholly German, but in Spitteler this compromise has found its happiest illustration. Superficially the form of his work is German, but its content is essentially Latin, and this has reacted upon the manner of its expression, giving the latter a suppleness and plasticity not characteristic of the Teutonic genius. An adequate translation of Spitteler's epic in verse is hardly conceivable, so intimate is the relation between the style and language of *Olympischer Frühling.* The poet's masterpiece must, for many reasons other than linguistic, remain the possession of a few, but not so the epic prose of *Prometheus und Epimetheus.* This remarkable work only demands a sympathetic interpreter in order that a wider audience may learn to admire, in its earliest and most original manifestation, the great genius of Carl Spitteler. (pp. 216-17)

> Ernest Boyd, "Carl Spitteler" (originally published in a slightly different form in The Egoist, Vol. VI, Nos. 3 and 4, July and September, 1919), in his Studies from Ten Literatures (copyright 1925 by Charles Scribner's Sons; reprinted with permission of Charles Scribner's Sons), Charles Scribner's Sons, 1925 (and reprinted by Kennikat Press, Inc., 1968), pp. 199-217.

JAMES F. MUIRHEAD   (essay date 1930)

[*Muirhead is the translator of several of Spitteler's works, including* Prometheus and Epimetheus, Laughing Truths, *and* Selected Poems of Carl Spitteler. *In the following excerpt, he focuses on Spitteler's major epic works and examines their conformity to the traditional epic style.*]

Though all his works are worthy of attention, it is as epic poet that Spitteler must stand or fall. The three epics ['**Prometheus and Epimetheus,' 'Olympian Spring,'** and **'Prometheus der Dulder'**] . . . occupied a very large proportion of his time and energy. The theme of 'Prometheus,' as a symbolic figure, was almost as continuous and important a factor in Spitteler's career as 'Faust' was in Goethe's. The interval of fifty years between the publication of **'Prometheus and Epimetheus'** . . . and **'Prometheus der Dulder'** . . . is not much less than that between the composition of the first scenes of 'Faust' (1774) and the appearance of the 'Second Part of Faust' (1831). In each case the poet was working on his theme up to within a few months of his death.

Spitteler has fortunately left us a very clear exposition of his conception of the epic, written some time before 1898, when it appeared in a volume of collected essays under the title of **'The Forbidden Epic'** [see excerpt above]. This may be described as a protest against the current idea that in our day the epic has been wholly supplanted by the novel. (p. 37)

Spitteler's epics conform thoroughly to the usual acceptance of epic as meaning a sustained and dignified narration of heroic adventure, generally under supernatural guidance. While, however, accepting the traditional or conventional machinery of the epic, Spitteler uses it with great elasticity. His epics may be read simply as fascinating narratives, with no other end in view than poetic and romantic pleasure. But it is also easy to bring them into allegorical touch with ordinary human life; and at times there seems almost a prophetic quality in the keen satire of many episodes. Humour is one of Spitteler's pronounced characteristics, and it is rare indeed to find it so inextricably intertwined with tragic happenings, romantic emotion, and picturesque description. Some readers may possibly find there is a little too much of this, especially in his habit of personifying everything, from a worm, a plant, or a cloud, to a fatuity, a thought, or a conscience. The more familiar one is with Spitteler, the more used one becomes to these personifications; and I confess I have reached the stage where their quaint appositeness almost invariably reconciles me to their fantastic quality.

A background of supernal beings seems almost an integral factor of the typical epic. Witness the works that occur to us at once as epics great beyond all question: The 'Iliad,' the 'Odyssey,' the 'Aeneid,' 'Paradise Lost,' Tasso's 'Jerusalem Delivered,' the 'Lusiads,' the 'Niebelungenlied,'—not to mention the Sagas or the religious epics of the East. Spitteler is quite in line with the orthodox tradition. But he has not, like the other modern poets, contended himself with a transferred or allegorical use of classical or other legend. He has created a cosmogony or mythology of his own, producing single-handed and, as it were in one gesture, what in other cases it has taken ages to evolve. The plot of his longest epic, **'Olympian Spring,'** is based on the downfall of Kronos and the Titans, followed by the reign of Zeus and the Olympians. But the Greek myth is treated with the utmost freedom, as little more than a general framework for new episodes invented by Spitteler himself. The names of the Greek gods are commonly used, but their new relation to their protoypes barely retains their general position in legend and often varies their qualities and adventures. Hera appears as the mortal Queen of the Amazons, wedded by force of circumstances to Zeus, who would otherwise have been at best her second choice. Ananke becomes masculine. Ajax is promoted to be an Olympian. Innumerable new characters are added, with such convincing names as the Seven Lovely Amaschpand, Hyphaist the Dwarf, Pelarg, Theopomp, Koproz, the Ape Greulich, and the like. Similar remarks may be made about the two Prometheus epics, though here the hero retains his essential character of champion of humanity against the tyranny of the Gods. The theft of fire, however, is not referred to. Pandora, far from being a mischief-maker, with a box full of winged curses, is a divine maiden, dominated by sympathy for mankind and ready to endow them with a panacea for all their ills—an attempt frustrated only by their own folly and that of their credulous sovereign, Epimetheus. Behind Prometheus, at once a part of himself and an external force, is his Mistress Soul, which prompts him to refuse the Conscience offered him by the Angel of the Lord, and may be taken to represent the direct or personal inspiration which every man, in his highest moments, feels to be his paramount and imperative guide. Epimetheus, on the other hand, a thoroughly well-meaning individual, accepts the conventional Conscience, which is the condition of his receiving the kingship of mankind, and ultimately comes to complete shipwreck.

In treating classical mythology in this manner, Spitteler is acting quite consciously and deliberately. He admits that the epic poet ought not to make Andromache rage and storm like Ajax, but he argues that he is quite at liberty to represent his chief figures as vague, wavering personalities. Careful analytical characterization is not his *rôle*. His attitude towards psychology is, on the whole, one of repugnance; his supreme law is to transmute spiritual states into objective appearances. Ulysses, when abused, simply shakes his head, instead of going through a spiritual struggle for the behoof of the reader. When Rinaldo's unresponsive inamorata finally falls in love with him on seeing that his love for her was cooling off, Ariosto does not, like a novelist, give an analytical account of the transformation. He simply invents two wonder-working springs. "He who can invent after this fashion is an epic master." For Spitteler the problems of the epic poet and the writer of romances are diametrically opposite. They only have one point in common, the unfolding of a record in narrative form. They may, it is true, be both advancing along the same road; but this involves no closer resemblance than that between the mounted knight and the snail he overtakes on the highway.

Spitteler writes his epics as the bard or skald tells his tales. They represent direct and momentary inspiration rather than the coherent erection, stone by stone, of some vast and clearly envisaged edifice. No doubt, as is the case with all inspired writers, he often builded better than he knew; and in the outcome we may recognize that there is nothing really irrelevant or out of place. But it is idle to try to grasp, as we read, the exact meaning of every episode, the concrete links connecting paragraph with paragraph. Far more enjoyment will ensue if we read his epics in the spirit in which he himself replied to a request for enlightenment: "If you find these scenes beautiful, you have understood them and I have nothing to explain; if you do not find them beautiful, so much the worse for me, but I cannot give you any better explanation." (pp. 39-43)

One of the most interesting of these commentaries is that of Dr. Jung, who treats Spitteler's **'Prometheus'** more or less in connection with Goethe's fragmentary drama on 'Prometheus' and with 'Faust.' I note it here, however, rather as a recognition of Dr. Jung's general reputation among psychologists than as a sign of any very thoroughgoing agreement on my own part. Dr. Jung identifies Prometheus with the typical introvert, while his brother Epimetheus is the equally typical extravert. Neither is wholly right or wholly wrong. The ideal or perfect man results from a combination of the two, a consummation which Dr. Jung considers to be indicated by the final reconciliation of the two brothers. To most readers the so-called introvert will seem to contribute by far the larger share of virtue to the combination, as the forgiveness extended by Prometheus to his brother is the result of an almost divine magnanimity, which throws utterly into the shade the somewhat whining penitence of the erring king. In Pandora and her part Dr. Jung sees the spiritual counterpart in the unconscious of the *rôle* of Prometheus himself in the conscious. It is interesting to compare with this Spitteler's novel entitled **'Imago'** . . . , which in his own words "gives the record of an actual life-experience, while **'Prometheus'** shows what the poet has made of it. **'Imago'** explains **'Prometheus.'**" (p. 44)

Another writer who is inevitably recalled by the Prometheus epic of Spitteler is Nietzsche, were it only for the fact that the earlier version of **'Prometheus'** is written in a hieratic, biblical, rhythmical prose not unlike that of 'Also Sprach Zarathustra.' [It should be noted that Spitteler's work appeared two or three years *before* that of Nietzsche.] The difference between the two prose-poems is, however, really essential. Zarathustra is a preacher, addressing his audience directly. The significant truths of Prometheus are presented to us incidentally, in a series of narratives, parables, allegories, and pictures. Though both are rebels against conventional Christianity, Spitteler clings to the divine quality of pity which Nietzsche rejects with scorn. And Spitteler's Superman is not above the laws of ordinary morality.

A point on which Spitteler lays great stress in his compositions is the use of the direct address. Prof. Sellar (among other authorities) tells us that Homer stands out among epic poets for the way he makes his characters known to us through speech as well as through action. His epic genius was reinforced by his dramatic genius. Spitteler's resemblance to the Greek bard in this point is no doubt one of the reasons which impelled Romain Rolland to call him the modern Homer [see excerpt above]. Dialogue and soliloquy are constantly used by Spitteler to elucidate his points; and to these he adds, as Homer did, the charms of apposite oratory. (pp. 45-6)

I have already mentioned humour as one of the most characteristic features of Spitteler's muse. This is as apparent in his epics as elsewhere—a rare feature in epic poetry, in spite of Samuel Butler's essay on 'The Humour of Homer.' Perhaps we may find his nearest parallel in the 'Orlando Furioso,' with

which he was very familiar. And it may be said of him, as it has been said of Ariosto, that he does not compromise his dignity by his jests, and that his sense of humour is not indulged in to the detriment of his sense of the pathetic or the tragic. One sometimes feels as if Spitteler's whimsical touches in serious passages *ought* to shock our sense of fitness, but to one reader at least they almost invariably have the effect of driving home the serious intention. They seem to come to the rescue of the nervous ganglion just in time to prevent its utter exhaustion. Unfriendly critics might argue that they resemble the stimulants given to sufferers on the rack so that the torture may be prolonged under favourable conditions. Spitteler's humour is not only fanciful, but often shows an irony at once bitter, gay, and witty. Whole episodes are pervaded with humour throughout, as (*e.g.*) the canto of **'Olympian Spring'** narrating the stolen visit of that naughty hussy Venus to the earth. One of Spitteler's most sympathetic critics has written that "the reader could never have imagined that great poetry could have so little solemnity"; and I wholly subscribe to what I take to be the meaning of this remark if I am allowed to insert an epithet such as "wearisome" or "high-brow" before the term "solemnity." The humour of Spitteler is not aggressive or obtrusive; but I am convinced that he held the view that humour almost vies with beauty as a consolation and solvent of the tragedy of existence. (pp. 46-8)

If it is objected that Spitteler's **'Olympian Spring'** is essentially different from any of the generally recognized great epics . . . , the assertion could hardly be denied. But its unlikeness consists, not in any neglect of the fundamental epical qualities of these poems, but in a difference of external form due to Spitteler's special poetic gift and to the age in which he wrote. I do not know whether there are admirers of 'Marmion,' 'The Idylls of the King,' 'Childe Harold,' or 'The Prelude' who would be ready to go to the stake for the thesis that these are truly great epics; but I do know that Spitteler's followers, many of them familiar with the works cited, would be ready to face at least the pillory of the Republic of Letters in defence of a similar assertion about **'Olympian Spring.'** One of these is, of course, M. Romain Rolland; and, though I have no title to speak for him, I think I may claim another among your own honourable Fellows in the person of Prof. J. G. Robertson [see excerpt below], who wrote an admirable appreciation of Spitteler as far back as 1921. They would, I am convinced, agree that Spitteler possesses in full measure the requisites of an epic poet as laid down by himself. (pp. 48-9)

James F. Muirhead, "Carl Spitteler and the New Epic" (1930), in Essays by Divers Hands, n.s. Vol. X, 1931, pp. 35-57.

ARTHUR ELOESSER (essay date 1931)

[*Eloesser gives a succinct and, for the most part, negative critique of Spitteler's epic work. He maintains that Spitteler's best work was in his nonmythic stories that deal with contemporary life.*]

Spitteler's attitude towards the world was that of a comic melancholy, but he had not better success when he tried to represent cosmic man in direct intercourse with the gods [in his *Prometheus*] than Robert Hamerling and Wilhelm Jordan had had before him. Though superior to them in intelligence, he failed, as they had done, owing to a deficient command of imagery and a view of life that was the reverse of Homeric, and so, in spite of himself, transformed his epic, though inspired by a spirit of revolt, into a *Messiade*. While Epimetheus descends into the lower world of virtuous, practical philanthropy that is pleasing to God, Prometheus preserves his soul, in spite of the tragic curse of suffering, insult, and privation; for his desire is for gods who shall grow greater and greater. The poem is a sort of amplification of Goethe's youthful rhapsody. Whereas Nietzsche's *Zarathustra* created an exalted world of thought all his own, Spitteler's is a conglomeration of abstract mythologies, in which the Bible, the antique and the modern worlds all make their voice heard with an imposing confidence. "Meanwhile Mythos groaned and sighed beside his two brethren," says the poem, and the unconscious irony of this verse applies equally well to thousands of others, in which Pandora, Doxa, Maia, Behemoth, Ashtareth, Beelzebub, and Leviathan all expend their eloquence upon a Prometheus who, moreover, neither creates nor acts. This admirer of Ariosto had conceived his *Olympischer Frühling (Olympian Springtide)* as an epic comedy, analogous to that which had once floated before the imagination of Schiller in the shape of an ideal play of intellectual freedom and sovereign mirth. But, after all, the fact that the gods conduct themselves no better than men and are capable of behaving in a most burlesque fashion in their intimate relations had long ago been established by others, from Lucian down to Wieland and Offenbach. But once Spitteler set out to modify and renovate the myths there was no satisfying him. His Olympus consorted indiscriminately with Walhall or with Niflheim, and his Hera might equally well have been a character out of Wagner or Strindberg. Nor is Nietzsche very far away, though Spitteler had not intended to summon him; while the approach of psychoanalysis is foreshadowed, even before Freud had reduced it to a system. Spitteler's head contained plenty of ideas, but they lacked stability, and his conceptions failed to clothe themselves in human form. By the time these thousands of verses have gone clattering past, one is left incapable of seeing or hearing anything. These two great epics were received with the profoundest respect, as often happens to works that hardly anybody has read to the end.

"Clearness of perception abandons men of intellect least of all when they are in the wrong," says Goethe. Spitteler produced his best work in a few little stories of living people, in which he thought he was wronging his "extramundane talent" by crushing it in the "hated vice of laborious prose." *Conrad der leutnant (Conrad the Lieutenant)* maintains its position as a powerful picture of humble life in Switzerland, bordering upon the "pedagogical provinces" of Gotthelf and Keller. It treats of a struggle for supremacy in the management of the family property between two generations and is clearly conceived, charged with vigour, and worked out to a tragic issue. If the father kills the son, this is because Spitteler wished to show that he, too, was capable of working in the naturalistic manner; but, he asked: "Can the naturalists write an epic too?"— though, since he had spent eight years in the land of Tolstoy, he should hardly have asked the question. While still in Russia, he had already written the story *Imago,* a piece of genuine experience that was intended as an explanatory prelude to his *Prometheus.* In it the Muse says to the poet: "This shall be my blessing. Now art thou sealed with the seal of pathos and dost bear the stamp of greatness. I demand of thee a self-confidence that shall never abandon thee, whether in error or in truth, in insult or in ill report; and I forbid thee ever to be unhappy in thy life." The poet is in love with a lady of the middle class, who is also honorary president of the "Idealia" society, in which the Philistines seek edification in music and poetry and, forgetful of divine things, worship the false gods of art. Imago is the poet's ideal conception of the true woman, an aery image that is his supernal possession. Here again,

understanding, reason, emotion, and imagination are all to be found, but the pathos is tempered by irony, experience and poetry are bound together, as with a floating gossamer, by fine threads of humour, while hieroglyphic symbols of the dreams engendered by the creative and erotic faculties are drawn into the brilliant play of intellect. This Spitteler in little is full of charm; but when he set up as an epic rhapsodist and, though a mere leader of shadow battles, claimed equal footing with the earth-shaking Nietzsche, he failed to justify any of the vast pretensions that were advanced on his behalf either by himself or in Alemannian literary circles.

As an epic rhapsodist Spitteler was a belated survival, who refused to recognize the inevitable triumph of the novel and its democratic development into a permanent record of the social agitations, cultural upheavals, spiritual revaluations, and intellectual enterprises of a whole age, but continued to stand aside in aristocratic aloofness from the common current of creative work, which, in spite of all its contradictions and antagonisms, shared in the same general tendencies. (pp. 266-68)

Arthur Eloesser, "The Novel about 1900," in his Modern German Literature, *translated by Catherine Alison Phillips (copyright 1933 by Alfred A. Knopf, Inc.; reprinted by permission of the publisher; originally published as* Die Deutsche Literatur vom Barock bis zur Gegenwart, *Bruno Cassirer, 1931), Knopf, 1933, pp. 211-307.**

E. M. BUTLER   (essay date 1935)

[*Butler discusses Spitteler's major epic,* Olympischer Frühling, *as both a work of genius and as an enigma in twentieth-century literature.*]

Carl Spitteler's achievement belongs entirely to the kingdom of poetry. His *Olympian Spring-Time,* a work of genius hitherto unequalled in this age, has cosmic magnitude and tragic vision. Whether consciously or not, he actually represented what Nietzsche had described in *The Birth of Tragedy:* a dark, Dionysian universe against which radiant Apolline gods and goddesses stand out in glorious relief. If pure pleasure is to be the criterion of a work of art, one can only acknowledge that his bold transplantation of Greek mythology into modern soil has been successful. Not only this, but he performed this miracle by means of another: the triumphant reinstatement of the epos in its ancient rights, a literary form which has lost its appeal to-day, being almost entirely superseded by the prose novel. Further than that he made use of a metre which sounds when described like the last word in artificiality: a six-stressed, iambic rhythm, rhyming in couplets, which ought to be (but happily is not) the seventeenth-century German alexandrine. Think of the boredom, as Robert Faesi pertinently suggests, which threatens one from an epos of 18,000 verses of this nature about some dozen Greek gods. But boredom is put to flight by the interest of the action, the spacious grandeur of the whole design, the characters and fates of the heroes, the glory of the conceptions, the power of the language, and the solid realism behind it all. This realism of Spitteler's is his chief point of contact with Homer; for his plot is original; and his Olympian gods and goddesses, undimmed by archaeology and untrammelled by research, live a life of their own in the world Spitteler created for them. They are more sharply individualised than Homer's deities; they sin more flagrantly, and they suffer far more acutely. Above and beyond human justice which Zeus indeed is called upon to dispense, they are shown to be in the grim clutches of fate; and the abyss beneath their feet is revealed in all its horror both to them and to us. They are thus transformed from gods into heroes—Spitteler's great originality lies in this; for the insistence of a fate beyond their power to propitiate is profoundly tragical and gives the necessary emotional value of contrast to their triumphant and victorious actions. Aeons in Erebus, a short period of light and life, and then Erebus again for countless ages; this is the perpetual cycle to which they are doomed. The old gods fall, the young gods rise and reign, only to fall again into darkenss when their hour has struck. . . . (pp. 317-18)

Against this terrible background the Olympian gods and goddesses, who awaken in Erebus and ascend upwards to Olympus in the radiance of a new dawn, shed the glory of sunrise all round them, a light which becomes fiercely dazzling in the second part of the poem, *Hera the Bride*. Like the *Illiad* this magnificent central action is the story of a wrath, and of how it was finally and tragically overcome. But it is the wrath of a woman and not of a man which is the mainspring of the action; the anger of the beautiful, baleful Olympian queen with her mortal taint, her fierce Amazon blood, her elemental passion of hatred and love for the glorious hero Apollo. (p. 321)

The glorious variety of the third part lacks the intense human interest of the second and the wonder and mystery of the first. But the adventures of Boreas, Poseidon, Ajax, Apollo, Hermes, Pallas Athene and Aphrodite; the tales told of olden days, in particular *Dionysus the Seer;* the humour, the beauty, the vision, the riotous imagination, and the ever-recurring sadness make of the whole a fitting climax for the spring-time of the Olympian gods. Moira's mercy, which had allowed them this pause for happiness and adventure, comes to an end owing to the mischievousness of Aphrodite in the fourth part; and the fifth part called *Zeus* heralds, although it does not represent, the approaching downfall of the new dynasty, much as the *Iliad* foreshadows the imminent destruction of Troy. When Heracles is sent down by Zeus to regenerate the ignominious human race, the gods of the *Olympian Spring-Time* are already beginning to wither away; and it is perhaps because of their earlier radiance that the final word about the experience as a whole is this: one has been uplifted and indeed transported by a mind of the most colossal range and power; but the unforgettable vision has left us exactly where we were before.

This is not because of any inherent weakness of Spitteler's. The poem has faults both in detail and construction; the humour is sometimes too boisterous; there are grotesque passages, and some tedious digressions. But these blemishes are too insignificant in such a riot of splendour to mar the total impression. Nevertheless the ultimate response to Spitteler's mythological cosmos is denial of its reality. His gods and goddesses seem real, and his universe terribly true, yet the vital tribute of belief will never be paid to the macrocosm of this remarkable work of genius. Poetry, no less than science, philosophy and religion, has for its ultimate aim the interpretation of the universe and life. But to attempt this by means of an artificial mythology is to mistake the nature of reality, a fundamental error for which no amount of creative genius and inventive power can entirely compensate. Spitteler's *Olympian Spring-Time,* for all its realism, is without the final sanction of reality. Arresting, exotic and sterile, it is perhaps the strangest of all the strange gifts German poetry has presented to our unmythological age. (pp. 321-22)

> *E. M. Butler, "The Aftermath," in her* The Tyranny of Greece over Germany: A Study of the Influence *Exercised by Greek Art and Poetry over the Great German Writers of the Eighteenth, Nineteenth and Twentieth Centuries, Cambridge University Press, 1935 (and reprinted by Beacon Press, 1958, pp. 301-36).**

GUSTAV MUELLER (essay date 1955)

[*Mueller praises Spitteler's accomplishment, calling him "the greatest of all philosophical poets."*]

[For his three epics, Spitteler] received, rightly, the Nobel prize. No schoolish learning, no second-hand scholarship, but a congenial kinship with the poetic creativity and philosophical originality of the Greeks guided him to his Olympus. The Greek names stand for living characters and are genuine symbols. ("Prometheus": Truth and goodness entail suffering and persecution.) One has to compare him with Dante and Homer to get his measure: Dante's bitterness of hell and sweetness of paradise and his intense personal integrity are like Spitteler's— but Spitteler is unencumbered by conventions and his chapters are composed and sing like classic sonatas; the rich movement of their visual-plastic imagination are like Homer's . . . and there is humor and "modern" philosophical reflection. What have I dared to say? Homer plus Dante equals Spitteler? Indeed, I am shuddering at my very own impious heresy—but I won't recant! (This does not mean that I am blind to Spitteler's faults— giants are entitled to gigantic faults.) (p. 294)

I have said but little; to say much would require a philosophical treatise. I am merely confessing: To me Spitteler is the greatest of all philosophical poets. His penetrating insight into the sorry scheme of things natural and social is transfigured into immense mythical visions; his existentialist reduction of man and all his finite values in confrontation with death is balanced by an absolute spiritual affirmation of the compassionate soul, but without any "happy end"; his abysmal contempt for the natural sciences and their technological mass civilization is overarched by the smile of an aesthetic world-view. Schopenhauer, Nietzsche, and Jacob Burckhardt are close neighbors—on Burckhardt particularly there are precious details in his conversations with Spitteler. (p. 295)

> *Gustav Mueller, "Carl Spitteler Reborn," in* Books Abroad *(copyright 1955 by the University of Oklahoma Press), Vol. 29, No. 3, Summer, 1955, pp. 294-95.*

GILBERT HIGHET (essay date 1960)

[*A Scottish-born writer and critic, Highet was a classical scholar and distinguished educator. As a literary personality on a weekly radio program in New York, he used a witty, urbane manner to present a variety of literature—from Greek and Latin classics to contemporary works—in an interesting and understandable form. Although Highet was sometimes harshly criticized for his popularizing techniques, his important studies* The Anatomy of Satire *and* Juvenal the Satirist *were scholarly works that received wide recognition in the literary community. In the following excerpt, he examines Spitteler's life and career, paying special attention to* Olympischer Frühling.]

We think of the Swiss as practical people, optimistic on the whole, and full of simple Christian piety. Carl Spitteler was impractical, a mystic, a convinced pessimist, and (although religiously minded) not a regular Christian in any sense. Nevertheless, his work seems to breathe the inmost spirit of Switzerland: not that of the prosperous little watchmaking cities, nor the cozy villa-colonies round the lakes, full of bankers and coupon-cutters, but the country as it appears from the air. To the eyes of the train-traveler or the walker, Switzerland is beautiful; but from the air it appears, as it is, a hard rough country. Much of it is cruel, inhospitable mountain ranges, much of the rest is cold, half-barren highland territory. Its greatest beauties are peaks, the Matterhorn and the Jungfrau and the Eiger, on which no human life can survive unaided for more than a few hours; and the winter season, deep in snow, is fabulously lovely, but its loveliness is close to death. That is the aspect of Switzerland which Carl Spitteler knew and presented in his poetry.

His greatest work was an epic poem, *Olympian Spring*. Hardly anyone in any western language has succeeded in writing epic poetry, for at least a century. But Spitteler paid no attention to contemporary fashions in literature. He belonged to no school. He had no disciples. He created a classic which stands by itself, and is virtually ageless.

Olympian Spring means 'The Youth of the Olympians.' It is a poem about the birth and adventures of the gods. They are, at least in name, the deities whom we know from Greece: Zeus the ruler, Apollo the spirit of light and poetry, Aphrodite the embodiment of beauty and love, Hephaestus the misshapen craftsman, and so forth. That sounds conventional: something like Keats's youthful fragment *Hyperion*. But if it had been conventional, it would probably never have won the Nobel Prize, and certainly would not have been worth reading or rereading. At best, it might have been like those imposing and shallow paintings by classicizing artists of the eighteenth century—'Council of the Gods,' 'Apotheosis of Hercules.' Far from it. Spitteler's Olympians have the names of Homer's gods, and some of their attributes; but they do not all have the same characters as their prototypes, and their adventures are quite original. Even their relationship to heaven, to fate, to the human world, and to one another is notably different. Since all myths contain symbolic meanings, the result of Spitteler's remolding of the Olympian pantheon is that his gods, although Greek, carry and embody his own personal vision of life. (pp. 251-53)

It is a very ambitious work. An epic on such a theme must be large, rich, and spacious. It fills over six hundred pages, some twenty thousand lines, divided into five main sections and each of these again into three or four or more shorter episodes. It is in rhyming couplets, but instead of the usual five-beat measure, Spitteler has chosen a strong swinging six-beat pattern which allows him more scope for his powerful rhetoric and for the big compound words into which he packs so much imagery.

The language is Swiss German. Not pure German, because it contains many dialect words and ejaculations, used for effects of simplicity and gaiety. . . . (p. 253)

Not only Swiss dialect words, but many German slang words and phrases (usually with a strong working-class flavor) are introduced in lighter descriptions or in conversations: for instance, the angry gods tell Ares not to interfere in an argument but to 'keep his own nose clean,' and the noise of a big banquet is summed up as 'tiddlediddledum and brouhaha.' These are not isolated examples. Sometimes long passages of satire (comparable to Milton's description of Limbo or the naughtier parts of Ariosto) are filled with words and cries and turns of phrase which are not only coarse but downright vulgar. This will strike some readers as being one of the most serious faults in the poem. Often the gods do not sound like gods at all, not even

like noble men and beautiful women, but like drunken farmers and quarreling fishwives. When a god curses or a goddess storms, even their anger should be noble.

On the other hand, there are many passages of purely poetic description which are broken by no such error of taste. Spitteler was Swiss and lived most of his life in Switzerland. His imagery, therefore, has the bright and super-childlike clarity of Alpine landscapes, and often shares the grandeur of the Alps. His figures cannot be called heavy or clumsy. Often they sound as interesting as the new chords used by Debussy or Strauss, and especially when two or three come together they make his imagery and his atmosphere brilliantly clear. Thus he can describe a thick and violent thunderstorm in the two words 'stormclouds heavenhightowering,'' or speak of dancing water as 'fountaineddywhirls,' a word full of delicate liquid consonants.

Another essential of poetry is at his command—rhetorical variety. The difficulty of writing any long book, but particularly a long poem in the epic manner, is that one tends to fall into unconscious repetitions of sentence-structure, to build all one's paragraphs along similar lines, to succeed one bald statement with another bald statement and another bald statement, to find favorite rhythms which will jog along comfortably to the end, and thus to betray something like an ineradicable poverty of thought. Spitteler avoids this with ease. He is an eloquent poet. What he is going to say at the foot of any page, although it follows logically and imaginatively, cannot be guessed from what he says at the top of the same page. He shifts his point of view, carrying the reader with him: sometimes to stand beside the gods and watch their conflicts, feel their angry gestures and hear their violent words, sometimes far above until we hear the little clouds talking to one another in the sky. He is careful to avoid the monotonous succession of sentences describing simple actions, which lulls the reader to sleep. Instead, he varies action with conversation, he describes objectively or he asks the reader for comment, he laughs with surprise or shouts with horror as the story develops. Within a single page he will put two sentences and an ejaculation into one line, and run a single sentence down through four big couplets. It is this gift of eloquence which again and again reassures us, when we are bewildered by the strangeness of Spitteler's myths or half-shocked, half-bedazzled by the cruelty of his mysticism, that he is not a woolly eccentric but a man who has thought long, seriously, and in the end successfully about the highest problems.

For his thought is very strange. Even the story he tells is strange. No one who knows the Greek myths could bear to read six hundred pages which merely told them all over again. What Spitteler does is to take the outline of one of the major myths—the tale that Zeus and the other gods displaced the older dynasty of Kronos and ruled the world from Mount Olympus, not without frequent rivalries and even quarrels—and to rewrite it with radically altered emphases, with many new adventures and motivations, and with a strangely enlarged view of the universe as background. We do not meet the Olympians first as divine children. Zeus is not born on Crete, or concealed from his cannibal father by cymbal-clashing priests. Pallas does not spring fully-armed from his head after he becomes king. Aphrodite is not born of the foam. No, they are immortals, and so they are never born. We first see them lying in the underworld, sleeping a sleep which seems to have had no beginning. Like veins of gold a thousand miles deep in the earth, they could slumber unseen in the dark forever. But their time has come. The prince of the underworld awakens them, sets them free, guides them out of the rain-soaked gloom of hell, and sends them on their way up to Mount Olympus. (pp. 253-55)

Like all good allegories, *Olympian Spring* has many meanings. It would scarcely be worth reading, despite its power, if it merely explained a single theory of the world through the gestures of a set of personifications. But the rise of the gods can be taken to symbolize many processes which we know, and it will help us to understand them better. It is like the growth of the human spirit, from helpless speechless childhood through energetic and careless youth, and then, through conflict, suffering, and the grudging acceptance of necessity, into maturity. Or again, it is like the appearance in history of a nation or a creed, starting from nothing except the darkness in which primitive forces lie asleep, then spreading out into a hundred manifestations of strength and beauty until at last it settles down—sometimes into cruel selfishness, sometimes, with better guidance, into self-forgetfulness, and work for the redemption of others. It is an allegory of the progress of reason, or of the growth of civilization, or of the course of history; these, and many other things. It is a wise poem.

The artist who stands closest to Spitteler is probably Richard Strauss. There are some remarkable coincidences between their works. Strauss's *Alpine Symphony* sounds like the music for the first section of Spitteler's epic; his *Hero's Life* is closely paralleled in the bitter episode where the Flatfootfolk create, out of sewer-gas, a rival Sun to displace the sun of Apollo from heaven; *Thus Spake Zarathustra* and *Death and Transfiguration* have much of Spitteler's lofty mysticism; the humor and variety of the High Time reappear in *Tyl Ulenspiegel's Merry Pranks* and in *Don Quixote;* the fiendish cruelty of *Salome* and *Electra* would not be strange to the creator of Moira and Gorgo. Even in their faults they are similar, for the vulgarity of Strauss's *Domestic Symphony* can be paralleled from some passages in *Olympian Spring,* for instance, the humiliation of Aphrodite. And in their technique it is easy to see resemblances: both love strange-sounding compounds, new chords, echoes of the myriad sounds of nature (Strauss makes clarinets bleat like sheep, Spitteler makes words croak like frogs and scream like eagles), and unexpected changes of rhythm. The Swiss are fond of comparing Spitteler to the mystical artist Böcklin, and indeed some of his grand evocations of the spirits of wild nature do resemble Böcklin's pictures in their majestic breadth of vision. But he moves much more, his thought is more active, his characters do not rest, but struggle and suffer with superhuman energy. Böcklin takes us into a world of contemplation. Spitteler into a world of action. Even in the first words of each new episode, the sensitive reader can hear the pulse of a forthright courage recalling the opening themes of Strauss's *Don Juan* and *Hero's Life.*

His thought would seem completely individual, if it were not strangely paralleled by another writer who was an exact contemporary of his. This was Friedrich Nietzsche. The two men worked quite independently, and did not study each other's books. Once Spitteler wrote a review of Nietzsche, and Nietzsche retorted with a typical snarl; but they never met, and did not mold each other's ideas. Yet both preached a pessimism derived from Greece, and used comparable symbols to make it clear (for instance, Apollo struggling with the subhuman forces of unreason). Both believed that life, although beautiful at times, was fundamentally bad and cruel. Both, apparently, thought the ordinary man was helpless and pitiful or contemptible, fit only to be ruled or redeemed by heroes. And both, it

should be mentioned, had a profound distrust of women: recognizing the irresistible power of woman's beauty, they hated woman for her treachery and cruelty, perhaps despised her for her weakness. But Nietzsche was a smaller, shriller man than Spitteler, and he insisted on this more savagely, with something of that imbalance which was at last to ruin him. It would seem that both Spitteler and Nietzsche drew much of their thought from Jacob Burckhardt, who in turn had partly derived it from Schopenhauer and partly worked it out in his own meditations on the meaning of art and history. (pp. 261-62)

But it would be wrong to suggest that most of Spitteler's ideas were derived from any other philosopher or poet. He thought hard and long before reaching his mystical creed: at first while he was studying for the Christian ministry, then when he was resolving to abandon it, and later during the eight long years he spent as a tutor in Russia. He continued to think throughout his life, with something of the slowness and the irresistible power of his own mountains and glaciers. The chief merit of *Olympian Spring* is a very rare and great one: like an Alpine landscape, it not only feeds our imagination but raises our thought to a new level above the noise and dust of the workaday world. (p. 263)

Gilbert Highet, "A Neglected Masterpiece: 'Olympian Spring'," in The Antioch Review *(copyright © 1952, copyright renewed © 1980, by the Antioch Review Inc.; reprinted by permission of the Editors and Publishers of* The Antioch Review), *Vol. XII, No. 3, September, 1952 (and reprinted in a revised form as "Spitteler's Epic: 'Olympian Spring'," in his* The Powers of Poetry, *Oxford University Press, New York, 1960, pp. 251-63).*

M. A. McHAFFIE AND J. M. RITCHIE (essay date 1960-61)

[*Conrad der Leutnant is considered one of Spitteler's most artistically successful novellas. This foray into Naturalism was unusual for Spitteler, who disliked the modern narrative. In the excerpt below, McHaffie and Ritchie discuss the narrative technique of the work.*]

Most historians of literature classify Spitteler as a cosmic poet, a literary curiosity writing epics in an age in which they are no longer appropriate, and dismiss his prose works in a few lines. **Conrad der Leutnant**, if it is mentioned at all, is disposed of as minor and insignificant. Spitteler himself considered it largely as an experiment in the naturalistic vein. . . . Later, he described the story as one of his 'künstlerischen Legitimationspapiere' ['papers proving he was an author'] and it is certainly worth more than the perfunctory attention it generally receives. A mere glance at the story reveals a mastery of the telling phrase and brilliant imagery which is completely modern, and the technique which Spitteler employs marks a significant step in the development of prose narrative. (pp. 45-6)

In the short theoretical statement which prefaces **Conrad**, Spitteler explains the new type of prose narrative he calls 'Darstellung'. The technical devices to be employed are clearly defined: unity of person, unity of perspective, constant progression in time. The main character is to be introduced in the first sentence and henceforth only what he observes is to be reproduced, and reproduced as he observes it. The action is to be recounted hour by hour, and no period of time passed over as unimportant. The action is therefore of necessity restricted to a few hours. From this, one can see that the author of this stylistic exercise imposes considerable restrictions upon himself. This is true also of the subject matter for 'Darstellung'.

Only one type of subject matter, namely dramatic, is suitable, and even then only such as will permit all the important motifs to be introduced naturally into the story immediately before the climax ('Entscheidung'). Should the subject matter be not only dramatic but tragic, involving several people, then an additional part is necessary after the death of the main character. . . . This additional part obeys the same rules as the first, with the perspective shifted to the next most important character.

All this sounds very formidable, but it is a measure of Spitteler's skill that the theoretical ballast is not obtrusive in the story, and that it is possible to read **Conrad** without worrying about problems of perspective. However, it is significant that Spitteler did indulge in these theoretical preliminaries, and it is rewarding to ask why he chose to impose such restrictions on himself. He states his aim in the preface: namely, 'denkbar innigstes Miterleben der Handlung' ['the most intimate experience']; in other words, the purpose of the new technique is to lower the barrier, to reduce the distance between the reader and the main character. This process is not the kind of thing one normally associates with the naturalists, but one can see why **Conrad** is often described as naturalistic. Spitteler deliberately confines himself to the laws of reality. . . . He is propounding something very close to the naturalistic technique of the 'Sekundenstil' when he declares that he will present the action 'lebensgetreu Stunde für Stunde' ['true to life, hour by hour'] instead of retaining the right of the author to select only what is significant. The only selection he permits himself is the naturalistic selection of one particular slice of life. One can read **Conrad** as a treatment of the naturalistic theme of the clash between the older and the younger generation, or, since this is obviously not merely a conflict between father and son, but also between mother and son, brother and sister, sister and fiancée, as a kind of drama of the domestic interior in the naturalistic vein, a picture of family life surpassing in bitterness anything offered in e.g., *Die Familie Selicke,* and far removed from any treatment of the family one will find in earlier nineteenth-century German works. (pp. 46-7)

Conrad is twenty-three years old. He has been an 'Industrieschüler' ['industrial student'] and has distinguished himself in military service. Behind him lies a period of happiness and comradeship, during which he has earned the approval of his superior officers and been publicly praised before the whole regiment. In the present, to which the story binds us, he has left the city behind and returned to his father's prosperous inn. The young officer is a nobody in his father's eyes, and his past success arouses not admiration but mockery and insolence. . . . Reasons are suggested for the antagonism between father and son: the father is a self-made man without the educational advantages which Conrad has enjoyed: he has had to build up, acre by acre, the property which Conrad will one day inherit: he has been only a 'Wachtmeister in the army, not an officer. But fundamentally the situation does not need to be motivated in this way. The enmity between Conrad and his father does not depend on external circumstances, it is a permanent state of mind. Hate is the only link between father and son. Conrad's thoughts revolve ceaselessly round his father . . . . (p. 47)

The situation would by itself suffice to make life . . . unbearable for Conrad, but it is further complicated by the fact that Conrad's mother is hopelessly neurotic. . . . For her as for his father, Conrad can do nothing right. . . . With his sister Anna, Conrad appears at first to be on better terms, but each

is equally capable of turning on the other. It is Anna who introduces him to Cathri, and the two women seem to be the best of friends, but when Conrad displays interest in Cathri, Anna immediately becomes as poisonous as the 'Hexenbase' ['sorceress'] and attacks Cathri viciously. . . . Only one character offers Conrad real warmth and affection, untinged by any desire to change or improve him, and she is a person from whom he cannot accept it, the local prostitute Jucunde. Conrad is a man at the end of his tether. No one person is responsible for his death. He is destroyed, not by his father alone, but by the narrow oppressive world in which he lives.

All the characters involved are creatures of uncontrollable impulse, not responsible for what they think and say. . . . So, for example, in a heated dispute . . . , Conrad temporarily routs his father by telling him that he had found his name scratched on the window of a brothel; but he had not meant to say these things. . . . He finally goes to his death, apparently as the result of a momentary impulse. (pp. 47-8)

Spitteler directs the naturalistic technique, not at outward reality, but at the inmost reaches of the mind. Everything is seen and heard through the eyes and ears of Conrad, and the result is an impressionistic, photographic and phonographic record of the world he experiences from moment to moment. There are little or no descriptive passages of the traditional type, and the action is largely carried forward by dialogue, which means the introduction of a lively, non-literary, spoken German. Too much dialogue can of course be monotonous, but Spitteler avoids the risk of becoming boring. He shows remarkable ingenuity in varying the psychological colouring of the dialogue. . . . Frequently the dialogue ceases and the reader is inside Conrad, eavesdropping on his thoughts, moods and feelings as they change from moment to moment in the few hours before his death. (p. 48)

The story has a clear line of development, a logical chain of motivation, Spitteler confines himself exclusively to the real world and the reader is completely convinced of the authenticity and accuracy of everything which has been narrated. But the narrative is completely objective. Since Spitteler has adopted one unchanging perspective and we therefore see the events only as they are experienced by the main character he cannot introduce generalization and author's comments to point the significance of the action. He offers no opinions, no clue as to how the reader ought to interpret these events. It is not he, but the characters who speak. Everything is hermetically sealed off. No chink is left in the armour through which it can be opened up. The reader must simply accept these events as they impinge on the consciousness of Conrad. He is not invited to join the author in reviewing the life of a human being from a height, he is invited to participate in the life of that human being for the few hours before his death.

To achieve this aim, Spitteler is prepared to accept the severe limitation of horizon we have observed. At the same time, this technique of limitation has its advantages. Loss of width is compensated for by a gain in depth. Reality is caught by means of this narrow mesh of time and place. The atmosphere of this particular family is captured—everything and everybody is involved in it. . . . The story conveys the feeling which Kafka was to intensify not so many years later, the feeling of being shut in, confined, the feeling that there is no escape from inevitable disaster. Conrad's attempt at escape from the explosive situation at home leads him to the 'Stationswirtschaft' ['station hotel'] and to the quarrel with the man who will later kill him. This feeling of being shut in is one result of the singleness of perspective. We are made to realize not only the psychological position of these people who are trapped within their narrow little world, but also the fact that each man is a prisoner within himself. The restriction in time is also significant. Only the present matters. Conrad has had a past life, he has dreams and hopes for the future, but the technique inevitably shows him as a slave of the moment, a creature of moods, thoughts, feelings and impulses which are constantly changing. This results in an intensification of the psychological treatment, which is the point of the experiment. The reader is drawn inside Conrad and made to experience exactly what he sees and hears and feels.

The change of perspective which Spitteler warns us to expect after the death of the main character is managed very skilfully. He does not simply switch the reader over from Conrad to Cathri. The change is much smoother and subtler. It already begins before Conrad's death. We leave him despairing, a mere machine moving to punish the stonethrower, and it is through the eyes of those left behind on the terrace that we observe his further movements. We are not on the spot when he is fatally stabbed, and the manner in which the wound is dealt is left deliberately obscure. But we are on the spot for the family's reaction to his death. In the short space of time which the story covers, there is, of course, no development of character, no startling 'Wendepunkt' ['turning point'], no moral transformation. Conrad's death changes nothing. (pp. 49-50)

In a story which he calls *Le Dernier Jour d'un Condamné,* Victor Hugo sets out to do exactly what Spitteler is attempting in **Conrad,** i.e., he tries to give the reader insight into the thoughts passing through the mind of a man who is going to die within a few hours. To achieve this, Hugo has his main character keep a diary, not only of his last day, but also of his last hour, and, literally, of his last minute. This, as Hugo realized, is a fantastic assumption, but it is the kind of thing which those employing the type of single perspective based on literary fictions like the diary or the letter are forced into, and which becomes increasingly improbable the nearer one gets to the death of the person concerned. *Werther* is an obvious example. Goethe has dealt with the difficulty by inventing the editor who takes over as Werther sinks deeper into the lethargy of suffering, to narrate what Werther no longer has the energy or the coherence to express, and to wind things up after his death. The kind of technique Spitteler employs in **Conrad** means that the fiction of the diary or letter can be abandoned. No one would wish to claim that **Conrad** is a masterpiece, or of comparable artistic merit to *Werther,* nor, on the other hand, is it merely an interesting experiment or an exercise in naturalistic prose. It is a story of considerable technical accomplishment and power, and it points towards much that is to come in both style and subject matter. It shows how a naturalistic 'Sekundenstil' technique, when applied to internal instead of external reality, results in an impressionistic style and a psychological depth which one does not normally associate with the naturalists. By the very rigidity of the perspective, it tends to stress the essential isolation of the individual and the impossibility of communication. . . . Is it so far from this to Kafka? (pp. 50-1)

M. A. McHaffie and J. M. Ritchie, "Narrative Techniques in Spitteler's 'Conrad der Leutnant'," in German Life & Letters, *Vol. XIV, Nos. 1 & 2, October, 1960-January, 1961, pp. 45-51.*

J. G. ROBERTSON (essay date 1968)

[*A respected scholar of German literature, and the author of numerous essays and books in his field, Robertson specialized in the study of Johann Wolfgang von Goethe's works, which have often been compared with the epics of Spitteler. In the excerpt below, Robertson offers a biographical and critical overview of Spitteler's career.*]

Spitteler's first published work, ***Prometheus und Epimetheus: ein Gleichnis,*** is without a predecessor in literature; unless we may claim Goethe's allegorical *Pandora* as a work of a kindred type. The reader who approaches it with classical preconceptions will find no satisfaction, for Spitteler's figures owe nothing but their names to antiquity. It is written in prose, a stately, Biblical prose, which again is without conspicuous analogues in German literature. The two brothers, Prometheus and Epimetheus, leave the common herd of men and settle in a lonely valley, shut off from all intercourse with their fellows. And after twelve years the angel of God bids men prepare to receive their king. The kingship is first offered to Prometheus, but on the condition that he "acquires a conscience", that he renounces his unlovely defiance of his fellow-men, that he yields his independence of soul. But Prometheus refuses; the gentler, weaker Epimetheus acquiesces, and is made a ruler of men. . . . (p. 93)

Meanwhile Prometheus in sullen defiance goes up into a high mountain, to live in sole obedience to his own goddess, Soul; and that nothing may come between him and his high mistress, he destroys the young of his faithful dog and his lion—all but a single puppy—these being, doubtless, symbols of the hopes and despairs which bind man to his common humanity. While Epimetheus basks in the sunshine of popular favour, Prometheus passes with his faithful dog and lion—the one faithful in love, the other in hate—through the Valley of the Shadow, becomes a prey to inner dissension, misery and despair. (pp. 93-4)

The second part of the epic leads us still deeper into the mystic maze of allegory: the little thread of "story" disappears; but the poet's style has become freer, less artificially archaic: there is more promise of what is to come. Spitteler turns now to Epimetheus and shows his incapacity for ruling, his subjection to the instincts of the herd, the hollowness of his ambitions, and the final betrayal of his holy trust. New myths are introduced which open up fresh vistas. Most beautiful of all is the descent of Pandora to the world; Spitteler's epic genius is nowhere more convincing than when he is describing a journey; it may be only his own journey from Liestal to Bern as a child of three, or that of the children in **Mädchenfeinde** from Langenbruck to Solothurn, or, as here, Pandora's, or the great progress of the gods from Erebos to Olympos—the epic touch is always present. Pandora comes down with her gift of happiness to mankind, but no one recognizes it, except a little child. The epic closes with Prometheus' great-hearted redemption of his erring brother, and their return to the old home in the valley. It is confessedly difficult to penetrate the heavy veil of allegory; at times the symbolism is childishly, mediaevally transparent; and again, thought seems to be struggling vainly to find plastic expression. **Prometheus** is undoubtedly pessimistic, deeply pessimistic; but Spitteler's pessimism has even less of a philosophic, Schopenhauer-like stamp than that of Leopardi or Grillparzer, or of *Tristan und Isolde;* it is a purely subjective pessimism of balked personal aspiration. Prometheus is a new Pastor Brand, a symbol of the right of genius to be true to itself, even at the risk of anti-social anarchy. The greatest achievement of this age in German literature, *Also sprach Zarathustra,* owes not a little to Spitteler's **Prometheus;** the strong individualism and the contempt of the herd are definitely Nietzschean, and the lion and the dog remind one of

Zarathustra's companions in his solitude, the serpent and the eagle; above all, Nietzsche has borrowed from his Swiss predecessor his stately beauty of language. But while Nietzsche is the thinker who seeks artistic symbols for ideas, Spitteler is, in the first instance, the artist who visualizes and creates. I doubt, however, whether even the reader of to-day, who has the benefit of a rapidly growing Spitteler literature, will get much beyond old Gottfried Keller's judgment of *Prometheus:* "What the poet wishes to say I do not know after reading his work twice; but in spite of all obscurity and indefiniteness I feel it all with him, feel the deep poetry that it contains." The veil is lifted a little in *Extramundana* . . . , a quite extraordinary work, in which, under the form of seven myths, the poet wrestles once more with the baffling life-enigma. But, as Spitteler himself felt in later life, there was a danger here of his becoming inextricably entangled in the abstract and the abstruse.

Prometheus und Epimetheus was followed by a very varied literary production, a kind of tentative experimenting in almost every kind of literature. Poetry is represented by four little volumes: [*Schmetterlinge, Literarische Gleichnisse, Balladen, Glockenlieder*]. . . . Only the first and the last are really lyric; Spitteler's ballads show a hankering after epic breadth, and his *Literarische Gleichnisse* harp rather persistently on the old problem of *Prometheus. Friedli, der Kolderi* . . . and *Conrad der Leutnant* . . . , are prose stories of a more or less objective type—the latter, indeed, an experiment in Franco-Russian realism. Other stories, *Gustav* . . . and *Imago* . . . , are definitely autobiographical. Spitteler always despised the novel, and it would seem as if his contempt had reflected back upon him. There is a surprising lack of distinction, both in the form and style of his stories; it makes one think of an actor who excels in impersonating heroic rôles, but fails when he has to present ordinary, everyday people. I do not even except *Imago*, to which writers on Spitteler ascribe particular importance. It is a story of the return of the native—no doubt, Spitteler's own return from Russia—and his disenchantment when he finds again the love he had idealized in his exile; but there is too much abstraction in Spitteler's treatment of the theme; his heroine is rather a repetition of the goddess Soul in *Prometheus* than a creature of flesh and blood. Not merely does one miss reality in the novel: there is a lack of passion, even idealized passion, in it. Goethe once deplored that the German poet Platen escaped greatness by his want of love. There might be some justification in applying this stricture to Spitteler: he is no love-poet; his lyric poems rarely deal with erotic emotions; and the wooing of Hera in the *Olympische Frühling* is a very loveless affair. Of all Spitteler's prose works my preference goes to *Mädchenfeinde* . . . , a delightfully fresh little story which opens up wide vistas, although it only tells about three schoolchildren.

In 1900 Spitteler inaugurated the twentieth century with the first volume of his *Olympischer Frühling*. . . . It is an epic in five books, thirty-three cantos and between eighteen and nineteen thousand lines. Here, as in his previous works, he deliberately flouted his public, one might say; for who wanted to read an epic in the twentieth century? The epic, he was told on every side, was dead; to attempt to revive it as a vehicle of serious poetic thought, was merely putting back the hands of the clock. But Spitteler has sinned more grievously than in the mere choice of an unpopular form of poetry; he, a modern poet, has made his theme the gods of Greece. Wagner, it is true, had made the gods of the north popular by grafting on them a very modern philosophy; but Greek mythology—that

was merely going back to an effete classicism! And to crown all: Spitteler has written his epic in a six-foot rhyming verse which only differs from the alexandrine in the freedom of its caesura; and that more than a hundred years after Goethe and Schiller had agreed that the alexandrine, with its recurrent jingle, was an impossible thing in German! Thus, taken all in all, it would have been difficult to conceive anything less likely to catch the ear of the public. But the *Olympische Frühling* could not be ignored as *Prometheus* had been, and in the course of these twenty years steadily widening circles, not restricted to Germany and Switzerland, have fallen under its spell. (pp. 94-8)

With each succeeding book, Spitteler's mastery over his art becomes more assured, his flights of fancy more daring, his humour subtler; with a Böcklin-like lavishness he empties his palette on his imagined world—imagined, and yet in its landscape background strangely true. It has been pointed out that the nature which the poet describes is—except in the first part, when he goes to the high Alps—that of the Jura, with which he was most familiar. Wonderful, too, is the skill with which he adapts his naturally monotonous metre to the varying moods of his narrative; and his racy Swiss dialect-words, which must often send a foreign reader in despair to the Swiss *Idiotikon*, stimulate like the breath of his own mountain air. Occasionally Spitteler even allows himself forcible neologisms and violations of the German tongue itself. But the quality I would place highest in his work is its extraordinary plasticity: everything is visualized, not mentally constructed; his gods are created, not merely described; this is a quality absent in none of the great epics. He has an extraordinary genius, too, for converting the most commonplace of individual experiences—and his imagery more often than not goes back to impressions of his earliest childhood—into sublime world-happenings. The terrible machine of necessity, for instance, was the child's first impression of a spinning-loom, and the Homeric battle of Ajax with the Giants a memory of the rough labourers in his uncle's brewery. Spitteler himself tells us: "The cherry-tree of Aphrodite, the walnut-tree of Pandora, the grass of Baldur, the corn of Noontide grew on my grandfather's fields. They have stood the transference well, even to Olympos."

The Gods of Greece have often passed across the stage of Northern literatures. . . . But here, in this poem of the twentieth century, they return again to the Western world: return, not as the stately gods of Winckelmann's colourless antiquarianism, or the guardians of the placid beauty of Goethe and Schiller's classicism, but as very living humanized beings—impetuous, humorous, naïvely happy, naïvely cruel, less often wise than cunning. They come burdened with the heritage of a whole century of European pessimism, and yet ready to face the future with a jubilant optimism and a prophetic joy. (pp. 100-02)

It is for later generations to grasp the true proportions and significance of this work, to appreciate it at its final value; we are still too near to it. . . . To many Spitteler has long been regarded as a kind of sleeping Barbarossa, who would some day awaken to assume the unclaimed sceptre in German poetry; others, again, confidently proclaim the *Olympische Frühling* a "Divine Comedy" of the new century. It is for the future to decide. Meanwhile it is certainly no exaggeration to say that the literature of the German tongue and the literature of Europe have no more grandiose, no stronger poetic work to show in the new century than this wonderful epic. (p. 102)

J. G. Robertson, "Carl Spitteler," in Contemporary Review, *Vol. CXIX, No. 1, January, 1921 (and re-*

printed in a revised form in his Essays and Addresses on Literature, *Books for Libraries Press, 1968; distributed by Arno Press, Inc.*), pp. 89-102.

WERNER GÜNTHER (essay date 1970)

[*Günther's essay, from which the following survey is taken, is considered an important critique of Spitteler's works.*]

Spitteler did not regard man and his soul with much seriousness, but, in fact, only what Goethe called "heiliger Ernst" can raise life on to the eternal plane. Certainly, Spitteler had a powerful imagination at his command, but it was from this, his most valuable asset, that he removed the driving force—the belief in the dignity of man. If he possessed basic insights of great worth, but failed to fill this framework with living poetry, it was due to deficiencies in his intuitive faculty, and hence in the source from which this is fed—that is, the quality of humanity. In Spitteler, both these qualities lacked a firm root, and were therefore too weak to combine effectively in order to resist non-artistic forces. Both as man and as poet he was a creature of contradiction. His greatness lies in the amount he managed to squeeze out of this rather barren nature.

The most perfectly tuned strings of his lyre were, obviously those where the least room was given to any anti-artistic strains. Generally speaking, we can distinguish three factors which helped in this. First, his work is capable of achieving an enchanting purity whenever the cosmic vibrations in his soul produce images which stem from a genuinely serious conception of human life, and whenever human forces are facing one another with defiance or serenity, notwithstanding the tragic surroundings in which they may exist.

In a second way, purity is often attained through Spitteler's child-like nature. . . . Indeed, perhaps no word can get nearer to the true Spitteler, and if this is remembered, much of his work becomes clearer. Even in his poetry, he often plays like a child, and yet the cosmic visionary and the child form complementary opposites, acting and reacting together, witnesses to the breadth of his nature.

The third realm in which Spitteler is at home is that of the sophisticate, the man-of-the-world. Although he strikes a discordant note in his rather limited, puppet-like portrayal of the lower classes (e.g. in **Conrad der Leutnant,** on the other hand he finds precisely the right tone when describing the atmosphere of a court, as for instance the ultra-refinement of Versailles in **Der Neffe des Herren Bezenval.** It was no accidental that he found such brilliant words to write of the French classical era. The aristocratic manners which he acquired in Russia suited his temperament perfectly, endowed as he was with wit, elegance and natural self-assurance.

It is an idle question to ask whether Spitteler wrote better poetry in his introvert or his extrovert vein. The true poet, as he creates, must also be introspective, for at that time he is inhabiting an imagined world, belonging only to himself; according to the degree in which he can adapt this world to normal reality, he may become more outward-looking. Even as a "realist", Spitteler remained an introvert.

A far more important question than this for the critic is that of the choice of theme. Spitteler gained much by restricting the number of subjects he treated to a minimum, and one cannot reproach him at all for this. Richness of artistic imagination, so Jacob Burckhardt had taught him, shows itself not in the number of themes one can invent, but in the mastery of one important motif, treated in various different ways. His Promethean epics, **Imago, Gustav, Der Neffe des Herrn Bezenval, Conrad der Leutnant,** all pertain to the theme of greatness, or the recognition of greatness. It is also touched upon in **Mädchenfeinde,** as well as in several scenes of **Olympischer Frühling.** Greatness, in his view and not only artistic greatness entails the renunciation of happiness, especially of happiness through love, and is bought at a terrible price. This theme, which had occupied the Romantics, had been clearly formulated by Schopenhauer, and subsequently appeared in many forms. It is certainly the stuff of tragedy, and has enormous artistic potential, but it is still nevertheless doubtful whether Spitteler did the right thing in devoting so much of himself to it. For quite clearly, in his case, the theme stems far less from the joy and suffering of a warm human heart than from the defiance and self-assurance of his own ego. With so much preoccupation with the self, the danger was that he could easily slip into a consciously intellectual or over-personal art-form. This is the case with, for instance, the novel **Imago,** where Spitteler definitely succumbs to the temptations of writing biography. His treatment of human experience is most effective and memorable in those works where he clothes it in mythology (e.g. **Prometheus**) or else sets it in an idyllic, if rather bitter atmosphere (as in **Gustav** or **Mädchenfeinde**).

Spitteler's genuine pathos reveals itself most clearly in **Prometheus und Epimethus.** . . . It is easy to list the faults of this early poem: its imbalance, the decline of artistic standards in the second half, the lack of inner motivation in certain episodes, imprecision in the drawing of Prometheus' character, the rational element: above all, the allegories, the excessive length of the work and the monotonous iambic metre, maintained with iron discipline, to the point where it obstructs the search for fresh imagery. It is much more difficult to say why, despite all its faults, the book remains a work of art (if not an "eternal" work as Romain Rolland claims [see excerpt above]). (pp. 199-201)

To sum up Spitteler's first work, one is tempted to employ the words spoken by Pandora when she meets a shepherd boy, who is painting on a canvas the fields, mountains and woods, the clouds and the birds:

> And all drawn with few strokes, somewhat childish and groping, with no certainty; here and there an object changed its form, bushes and hedges becoming lambs; but always there reigned an inward strength, and soul led the gentle lines from the dark foreground with its rough shadows towards the distant, fragrant, hazy land. . . .

Written in his old age (in 1924), **Prometheus der Dulder,** by his own admission a "second book on the same theme", has only the dark and bitter shadows of the foreground, but lacks the "distant, fragrant, hazy land" behind. The earlier work is more appropriate to its theme, and therefore more solid. One may perhaps describe the change as the move from "poet" to "artist", but in doing so, the usual connotations of value judgment must be removed from these terms. For in this case, in calling him an "artist" we mean that the original creative or "poetic" impulse (which is more or less unconscious, and automatically finds the right verbal expression for its message) has yielded to a *conscious* application of artistic methods: in other words, as the intuitive power decreases, the so-called outer form assumes more importance. In a perfect work of art, the distinction is removed and "artist" and "poet" become one, although one can still—e.g. with Gotthelf—sometimes accuse the poet of "artistic" errors. Naturally, there are almost as many transgressions as there are works of art, for the perfectly blended work is an extreme rarity. In Spitteler's *Dulder,* the effect of the more intellectual approach is felt in three fields: the versification, the "realistic" style, and the overall structure.

In the first **Prometheus**, the hero, escaping from the noisy feast, seems almost lost in the "secret" which drifts up out of the valleys; hour after hour he strides up and down, till the snow buries the land under a soft white carpet and the forest looms black and white under the stars. He is trembling with expectation, listening, peering, staring at the entrance to the forest. When the austere woman suddenly appears, the scene continues in silence. Yet underneath, life is bubbling through its veins.

In the second **Prometheus,** the defiance and restlessness of the hero—who takes a much more active, central role—are depicted in a more plausible fashion. However, it often happens that, to achieve this, too many words are required, and what he says does not make the scene any more impressive; the Goddess, too, loses much of the bewitching power of her beauty, by talking too hastily and too long, and the lines which describe her entry are too roundabout and vague, hindered by the demands of rhyme. The magic has gone.

However, in **Dulder,** too, there are many moments of individual beauty. The quest for a wider symbolism certainly bears much fruit, especially in the various secondary motifs which have been well chosen and delightfully executed; we can point, for instance, to the seductive fan which the Angel of God played with, as if casually, as he asks Prometheus a second time to renounce his soul; or the "bird of doom", who glides like a ghost from the forest as the Goddess Soul hurls her curse upon the Angel, on his kingdom, Epimetheus and the whole cowardly race of man; or, finally, there is the Goddess's vision of the future: "I hear the river of life, gushing through the caverns . . .", etc., to which Prometheus, slurring his words like a drunkard, gives not only the reply to which the Goddess counsels him: "Ich!", but the committed "Ich Alle!"

What we have said so far offers enough pointers as to how **Olympischer Frühling** should be judged. Here Spitteler, following all kinds of "experimental works" and practice "on the silent piano", attempted to bridge the gulf between mythology and symbolism on the one hand and realistic poetry on the other. He was trying to fill a cosmic vision with human colour and life. The undertaking required great caution, to say the least, and the result was bound to contain weaknesses. The reasons for this are easily enumerated: first, because Spitteler was tempted to confuse the epic element with mere adventure stories; secondly, because the deeper human insights were too readily lost sight of, obscured by the bitterness of the poet's general outlook; and thirdly, because, in any case, the work could never really hold together, the "realistic" element being conceived far too much in terms of the external, thus robbing the world of the Gods of a large part of its mythical flavour. Even apart from all this, there is still another problem inherent in the basic idea: how could he produce a satisfactory ending, after all the high-spirited wedding celebrations of the new set of Gods? We know how uncomfortable the poet felt about this problem. In the final version of 1910, he split the ending into two sections, "Ende und Wende", originally the last quarter of the first version, becoming "Der hohen Zeit Ende" and "Zeus"; but the division is purely superficial.

Yet how should he finish off the work? With the fall of the Gods at the end of the modern era? That would require a much

longer epic—and where would he find the material for it? Spitteler had long before cut himself off from the greatest source of fresh (and real!) experience: the world of man is forbidden to the Gods. Although there was nowhere else to find the material he required for effective poetic conflicts, it would have gone against his basic premises to come too close to the human sphere. . . . Zeus himself learns to his cost what it is to become involved with the "human breed", and henceforth his wish is to suffocate the entire human "horde" in a gigantic cloak and to set a hound upon the lord of the earth! We are left wondering, then, what good Hercules, the "complete human being", can do as he strides towards earth.

Spitteler, sensibly enough, restricted himself to showing us only the Olympic "spring". What might happen in the "summer" and the "autumn" we cannot tell—nor, perhaps could the author. After the exciting high nuptials, is what follows simply a sort of Olympic banality, no longer worth recording? The theme, which has begun splendidly enough, tails off into nothing. The "basic impulse" of **Olympischer Frühling,** the "need for unlimited elbow-room for the creative imagination" carried in it the seeds of its own destruction. When, towards the middle of the work, the "hohe Zeit", the huge "spring feast of the earth", begins, the ground suddenly falls away from under the poet's feet. What for Spitteler was the central core—the string of colourful adventures—appears to the sensitive reader as no more than richly imaginative ornamentation, while the part which for us has the most artistic weight—i.e. the opening poems **Auffahrt** and **Hera die Braut**—was almost, so the poet tells us, absent-mindedly omitted, at a time when he was without the advice of his friend Jonas Fränkel.

What raises **Die Auffahrt** to such poetic heights can be summed up in three main principles. For one thing, the theme of the ascent of the Gods, from Erebos, up the "Morgenberg", to Mount Olympus, with their detour through Heaven, springs from a blissful vision: there is a flavour of pure art about this journey. Then again, the scenery here is still clearly described and easily imagined: mostly an Alpine landscape seen through fresh eyes. And finally, most important: while the Gods are generally unnamed, we can conceive of them as one unit, and their opponents likewise. Because of this, Spitteler's poetic vision is able to emerge at full strength, not yet diverted or disturbed by other conflicting forces. Is it not remarkable that out of almost a thousand crudities of language in **Olympischer Frühling,** an exceedingly small number fall in the first half? For here the poet, much more than the artist, was at work. (pp. 203-06)

Genuine pathos, where the particular and the universal become fused, is also to be found in the occasional poem where Spitteler, having achieved a certain level of poetry, manages to sustain it; not, however, in the "visual" lyric of **Schmetterlinge,** nor yet in the more acoustic one of the **Glocken—und Gras-lieder,** where one sees and hears little more than the occasional sally into higher poetry. In the **Balladen** and the **Literarische Gleichnisse,** more undulating strains are to be perceived, though the latter will certainly not be appreciated first and foremost for their lyricism. Even here, however, one still finds no wholly perfected pieces. Only rarely does Spitteler manage to achieve the tonal contrasts of the true literary ballad, so well demonstrated by Goethe.

It is chiefly in the two stories, **Gustav** and **Die Mädchenfeinde,** that the childlike playfulness of Spitteler's "idyllic" temperament reveals itself. In **Gustav** . . . , the theme of greatness is developed out of a not unalluring idyll, which one would scarcely connect with the early satirical *Kleinstadtroman* (never published by Spitteler) on which it is based. A girl imparts to a young artist, who has failed as a medical student, the most precious gift a woman can give to a man—the belief in his vocation. The work certainly has many charming touches, but its basic structure lacks maturity, thus hampering any real refinement of language.

Artistically much more important is the Novelle, *Die Mädchenfeinde.* . . . Only at intervals is this story of a boys' world threatened by the intrusion of the poet's adult personality. As a whole, its evenness of tone, its sureness of touch in the depiction of the child mind, and the power and spontaneity of its epic pictures compel admiration. In his **"Früheste Erlebnisse"**, Spitteler conjures up the prime of his early years with love and moderation, tinged with a sort of bashfulness. In *Die Mädchenfeinde,* boyhood is transmitted on to a higher, more idealised, yet still semi-realistic plane. Thus the idyll, a delightful vision of youthful souls awakening, is embedded in an apparent commonplace of events and in a landscape intimately familiar to the poet. The Novelle is a summer's ramble, a summer's rapture. Yet, over the nimble alertness, the innocence and artlessness of child experience, there hovers the reflection of another ramble, of another, somehow deeper sensual rapture: the gently gliding entry into maturer human experiences. The story strides with consummate skill up the narrow ridge where the innocent child world is overtaken by disillusioned adolescence. Adults play a part in the story only in so far as the plot requires them, and yet they provide a meaningful framework, since the experiences of the youngsters overflow into their domain. The obvious antithesis to the world of child joy is the crazy student. Through this human oddity Spitteler has expounded with extraordinary acuteness his pet theme of the suffering artistic genius.

The mundane temperament of the poet at last reveals itself in engaging fashion in the long story *Der Neffe des Herrn Bezenval.* . . . This is a historical novel set at the time of the French Revolution. Just as in Conrad Ferdinand Meyer's *Amulett,* a young Swiss arrives in Paris and gets himself entangled in love and politics. The theme is the development of a somewhat gauche but morally upright young idealist into a fully aware adult, who finally sacrifices himself for the sake of his convictions.

In *Conrad der Leutnant* Spitteler is dealing with a world far outside his natural sphere. The story was an "art gageure", a challenge to the despised guild of naturalists. It was an attempt to attack his opponents with their own weapons, having first refined them—or so he believed. Refined, that is, not in terms of psychological analysis, which Spitteler considered inartistic and anyway superficial, but through the acceptance of the formal laws of classical tragedy—in particular the French.

With this technique, it is only immediately before the dénouement that he unites the main dramatic themes, imposing upon himself the unity of character and perspective, as well as a regular time-sequence, in order to achieve the most intense involvement possible in the plot. There are two main reasons why the attempt was doomed to failure. As a poet, Spitteler had little feeling for ordinary human love. The popular heart remained amazingly alien to his own. The individual was after all for him not sufficiently noble to warrant any creative interest, *sui generis.* This being so, how could the material he chose ever have provided him with a poetic stimulus? Moreover, Spitteler's self-imposed principles only increased the disparity. For the figures do not live in their own right, but only

in order to do justice to a preconceived idea of plot and character. From the outset they are treated like puppets. For the problems of authority and the generation-gap to be presented clearly, and so that the plot will develop in a terse and compact fashion, Conrad's father, who is immersed in ineluctable gloom, must appear to his son and daughter as a loathsome monster. And Conrad himself in his rank of lieutenant must appear as almost childishly obsessed in his hunger for power. Any subtle nuance in the story's fabric is thus precluded, and one is immediately struck by the glaring artificiality, even affectedness, of the work. Between the two main characters, father and son, no single spark of intimacy is ever kindled. There is therefore no basis on which tragic suspense can breed.

Imago, by Spitteler's own admission, was "not just a work of art, but . . . 'life-blood'". Yet he was "nauseated by this Sisyphus-like toil in prosaic filth". How, one may ask, can life-blood become nauseating? How can "life-blood" transform itself into prosody? If Spitteler preferred to present his innermost spiritual life in a "veiled and disguised" way, why then so sudden and naked a confession? Some personal thorn, some extra-artistic motive must surely have been at work. Was it some insuppressible grudge, a wound that refused to heal—an almost pathological need for revenge? This suspicion is now confirmed by what we know of the work's origins: there could anyway be no other answer to the question. *Imago* was an unfortunate book not only for the author but also for the sensitive reader—in fact, one of the most unedifying among the better-known works of contemporary literature. "The love story of Felix Tandem" (Spitteler published his first two works under this pseudonym) "in the year when he wrote Prometheus." This is Spitteler's own definition. Certainly a love story of a very strange kind! One lover between two women, one earthly, one unearthly, both with the same face, and after a fight in which he makes a fool of himself, he devotes himself completely to the unearthly. Prometheus with fainting fits—so one might just as well dub it! Not a Prometheus in an imaginary, mythical world, but a Prometheus "among the democrats", in a bourgeois environment. However, what once—in Prometheus' human weakness and stupidity, is developed in *Imago* into a biting satire of bourgeois society: "Idealia" as a mirror image of a complacent bourgeoisie flowing with "ideals" but in fact selfish and narrow.

This satire is not charmingly presented, but quivering with scorn and resentment. Resentment is the word, perhaps, which most accurately characterises the work. Resentment on the one side, delusions of grandeur—one cannot avoid the expression—on the other. And this implies the presence of an element which makes the work profoundly unartistic: the personal, the all too personal. The satire is born out of resentment, as is the hero's anguish when he is prevented from loving the woman. The hero is simply not a human being, but the marionette-like creation of the poet's resentful, almost monomanic, mind—a mind which here turns the vacuum of a growing sense of inferiority and aversion into a euphoria of artificial characters, without ever finding a way to translate its own "life-blood" into any redeeming artistic form.

In his essay on Spitteler, C. A. Bernouilli pronounced that *Imago* was at best an instinctive and violent "Aufschrei" ["outcry"], and at worst a completely artificial creation. One is bound to go along with this verdict, adding, too, that there are strains in this "outcry" which cast a shadow on the poet's human decency. (pp. 208-11)

Werner Günther, "Carl Spitteler," translated by E.M.W. Maguire (originally published in an ex-

panded form in his Dichter der neueren Schweiz, *Francke Verlag, 1963), in* Swiss Men of Letters: Twelve Literary Essays, *edited by Alex Natan (© 1970 Oswald Wolff (Publishers) Limited, London), Wolff, 1970, pp. 193-212.*

MARGARET McHAFFIE   (essay date 1977)

[*McHaffie discusses the novel* Imago *as a continuation of the Prometheus theme found throughout Spitteler's work.* Imago *is regarded by psychologists as one of the early studies of "unconscious" motivations revealed by psychoanalytic techniques.*]

If the preoccupation with Prometheus is clearest in Spitteler's first and last published works, it is not confined to them. It is also present in his novel *Imago*. However disparate the form, there are close links between the two Prometheus works and the novel. All of them have a strongly autobiographical element, and all of them are statements of the theme first expressed in *Prometheus und Epimetheus:* the fate of the exceptional man whose integrity compels him to resist the lure of easy fame and happiness and to assert himself against the demands of accepted authority. The Prometheus works are set in a timeless world of quiet valleys, snowclad mountain peaks, and the landscape of Heaven; both are peopled by angels and a motley assembly of figures from the Bible and from Greek mythology. *Imago* transfers Spitteler's basic theme to the Switzerland of the late nineteenth-century, and sets it in the drawing-rooms, dining rooms, and cafés frequented by affluent middle-class characters. The link between *Prometheus und Epimetheus* and *Imago* is nevertheless very close. Viktor, the protagonist of the novel, is unmistakably a self-portrait of the Spitteler who between 1879 and 1880 was at last forced to finish a publishable version of *Prometheus und Epimetheus*. . . . (pp. 68-9)

Imago is an account of this emotional crisis, which was largely caused by Spitteler's hopeless love for Ellen Brodbeck. He had earlier renounced the possibility of marrying her because he believed that personal happiness was incompatible with his vocation as a poet and the obligation to attain greatness. On his return to Switzerland in 1879, he found that he still loved her and that the sight of her with her husband and child was well-nigh unbearable. 'Das Leid unerwiderter Liebe' ['the pain of unrequited love'] compelled him, after thirteen years of hesitation, to produce the first part of *Prometheus und Epimetheus*. The work was intended to be both a compensation for his renunciation of happiness and a vindication of his choice. *Imago* records the emotional conflicts and torments which were at once the price that he paid for his devotion to poetry and the means of releasing him from the indecision about versions and motifs which had bedevilled his work on Prometheus for so long. (p. 69)

Though the name Prometheus does not occur in the novel, Spitteler is at pains to make the connection between himself and his fictional counterpart clear. The Viktor who returns to his native Switzerland after some years abroad is working on something which sounds very like *Prometheus und Epimetheus,* and parts of the novel, especially the more sentimental parts, are narrated in a highly mannered prose reminiscent of the earlier work. Motifs from *Prometheus und Epimetheus,* as for instance the ascent of the Lion into Heaven, appear in the novel as part of Viktor's imaginative experience. Viktor has had in the past the talents and interests in drawing, painting, and music which Spitteler had once had and had renounced for poetry. Viktor's devotion to his 'strenge Herrin' recalls, as it is meant to, Prometheus's devotion to his soul, and the completed work

which Viktor carries with him when he leaves his native town is alluded to in terms which once again evoke *Prometheus und Epimetheus*. . . . In a novel where all the other recurring characters have a surname, Viktor has none. The lack of surname underlines both his difference from the others and the significance of his first name. At the end of *Imago* the protagonist is victorious. The story of unhappy love, suffering, pain, and incipient madness has, as it were, a happy ending. . . . Viktor is released from his torment immediately after the completion of his work by the assurance that he has made the right choice, that he was right to renounce both happiness in love and the talents which had distinguished him in his youth.

Spitteler was less fortunate. In 1881, he hoped for the fame and recognition which the 'strenge Herrin' promises Viktor. He was aware that the first part of *Prometheus und Epimetheus* fell short of the goal which he had set himself in 1862 when he decided to become a poet. Throughout the years since then, his ambition had been to make his debut as a writer with a work of art comparable with Beethoven's first Trios. The sense of urgency created by the emotional crisis over Ellen Brodbeck would allow him to wait no longer for this perfection. He regarded the first part of *Prometheus und Epimetheus* as 'bloß eine vorläufige Skizze' ['a mere preliminary sketch'] which he would later revise. . . . Not until 1905, with the confidence gained from the enthusiastic reception of *Olympischer Frühling* and the reissue under his own name of *Prometheus und Epimetheus* was he at last able to overcome his bitterness, shape his unhappy experiences of more than twenty years earlier into a novel, and give its protagonist the triumphant name Viktor. *Imago* is a literary monument to Carl Felix Tandem and to his long neglected first work.

The memory of what he had endured for the sake of that first work occasions in *Imago* lapses into sentimentality which betray Spitteler's sense of the pathos of his past experience and his pity for his vulnerable former self. On the other hand, the passage of time had, by 1905, given him the necessary detachment to introduce a marked element of self-irony into the portrayal of Viktor and his problems. The irony is still perceptible in the laconic summing-up which Spitteler proffers for his novel in the essay *Mein Schaffen und mein Werk:* '**Imago: Inhalt: Tasso unter den Demokraten.**'

The arrogance implied in a formulation which evokes the memory of Goethe's drama is mitigated by Spitteler's ironical treatment of the theme. At the beginning of the novel, Spitteler's unhappy poet has so far nothing to show that he is a poet. While his former schoolfellows have already long since achieved respectable and lucrative professions and are in a position to patronize him, he, at the age of thirty-four, has only 'einen Wechsel auf die Zukunft'. He suffers in a Swiss 'Kleinstadt' ['small town'] not at the courts of Ferrara and Belriguardo. The unattainable beloved is not the Princess Leonore but a Frau Direktor with a weakness for whipped cream, a fondness for amateur theatricals, and a predilection for cultural gatherings of an undemanding kind. Without making light of the pain which his Tasso-figure suffers, Spitteler tells his story in a frequently mordant and mocking tone which makes the sentimental passages tolerable, and sometimes moving.

The novel begins with Viktor's arrival in his native town in September and ends in January as the train carries him off once more to an unnamed destination abroad. What he experiences in those few months illuminates the relationship between the artist and the world in which he has to live as a human being. For the most part, it is tense and uncomfortable. In *Imago,* very few of the characters have the perception to recognize the potentialities of the aspiring artist or the peculiar dangers to which he is exposed. Only the discerning Frau Steinbach, his foreign friends, and his dying former teacher believe in the importance of the rich, strange world of his imagination and in the greatness which Viktor senses in himself. Spitteler depicts Viktor as a cosmopolitan aristocrat of the spirit caught 'in der Hölle der Gemütlichkeit' ['in a hell of sociability'] among complacent, patriotic, middle-class characters who find his views odd and his appearance and behaviour eccentric. He worships art and beauty. They indulge in artistic pursuits as a pastime. In the meetings of their 'Kulturverein Idealia' Viktor discovers for himself what Tonio Kröger discovers at Herr Knaak's dancing lessons: there is no real possibility of mutual understanding, 'denn sein Sprache war nicht ihre Sprache'. Spitteler makes the difference not only figurative but literal as well. Viktor and the inhabitants of his native town do not, in any sense, speak the same language. They, as Swiss, naturally speak their dialect. He, after some years abroad, no longer does. Viktor corrects the assumption which Theuda's husband makes at their first meeting that he is, because of the difference of his speech, 'ein Fremder' ['a foreigner'], but Direktor Wyß's assumption is, on another level, quite true. Viktor has become an uneasy, rather scornful outsider in the town in which he was born. His devotion to art has alienated him from the way of life which most of the people among whom he now finds himself affirm. (pp. 69-73)

The theme of **Imago** is the theme of Prometheus railing against the imperfections of the world. The novel is both a record of a painful emotional experience in Spitteler's life and the story of a nineteenth-century artist. It portrays a man with the temperament and the imagination of a poet struggling among the banalities of bourgeois society; it is the story of Tasso among the democrats. In his depiction of Viktor's withdrawal from the drabness and deceptions of reality and his need for beauty, poetry, and greatness, Spitteler is moved by an impulse not dissimilar to the impulse which, in nineteenth-century Basle, prompted his mentor, Burckhardt, to recreate the world of the Renaissance. **Imago** is not a great novel, but it is a very interesting one. It has not been without its distinguished admirers. Sigmund Freud was one. Freud's respect for Spitteler's portrayal of emotional turbulence is reflected in the fact that he gave his Journal on the application of psychoanalysis to the Humanities the title **Imago**. The novel is remarkable for its psychological insights, its irony, and the wit with which much of it is formulated. If it is occasionally flawed by sentimental passages and an archness of tone not greatly to modern taste, it is nevertheless a not unimpressive example of the artist's ability to give shape and more than personal significance to the chaos of his own experiences. (p. 76)

Margaret McHaffie, "Prometheus and Viktor: Carl Spitteler's 'Imago'," in German Life & Letters, Vol. XXXI, No. 1, October, 1977, pp. 67-77.

ADDITIONAL BIBLIOGRAPHY

Boesche, Albert Wilhelm. "The Life and Works of Carl Spitteler." In *The German Classics of Nineteenth and Twentieth Centuries: Masterpieces of German Literature Translated into English, Vol. XIV*, edited by Kuno Francke, pp. 493-515. Albany, N.Y.: J.B. Lyon Co., 1913-14.

    Early discussion of Spitteler as one of the "four greatest modern representatives of German literature in Switzerland."

Jung, C.G. "The Problem of Types in Poetry: Carl Spitteler's *Prometheus and Epimetheus*." In his *Psychological Types or the Psychology of Individuation*, pp. 207-336. New York: Harcourt, Brace and Co., 1926.*

    Psychological profile of Prometheus and Epimetheus, which examines the two respectively as introvert and extravert. Jung also compares Spitteler's Prometheus to Goethe's Faust.

Knight, A.H.J. "Some Reflections on Spitteler's *Prometheus and Epimetheus*." *Modern Language Review* XXVII, No. 4 (October 1932): 430-47.

    Thorough discussion of the prose epic *Prometheus and Epimetheus*.

Lo Cicero, Vincent. "A Reappraisal of Spitteler's View of Schopenhauer." *The Germanic Review* XXXIX, No. 1 (January 1964): 37-49.

    Cogent examination which reappraises the critical contention that Spitteler's world view was pessimistic and similar to that of Schopenhauer.

Marble, Annie Russell. "Carl Spitteler." In her *The Nobel Prize Winners in Literature*, pp. 205-12. New York: D. Appleton and Co., 1927.

    Biographical sketch.

Muirhead, James F. "Carl Spitteler." *The London Mercury* 16, No. 91 (May 1927): 53-61.

    Biographical and critical commentary with emphasis on Spitteler's epic works, *Prometheus and Epimetheus, Prometheus der Dulder,* and *Olympischer Frühling*. Muirhead is the translator of several of the poet's works.

Sachs, Hanns. "The Unconscious in Carl Spitteler's Characters." In his *The Creative Unconscious: Studies in the Psychoanalysis of Art,* rev. ed., pp. 324-34. Cambridge, Mass.: Sci-Art Publishers, 1951.

    Interesting discussion of how Spitteler reveals the "unconscious" motivations of his characters through methods similar to those used in psychoanalysis. Sachs, psychoanalyst and editor of *Imago* (a journal so-named by Sigmund Freud after Spitteler's novel), had earlier praised the poet's *Imago* as "a manual for the phenomenon of the 'Oedipus-complex'."

Wallace Stevens

1879-1955

American poet, essayist, and dramatist.

Stevens is one of the most important American poets of the twentieth century. Although he most often referred to himself as a Romantic, his work is not definable in terms of any single poetic movement; he was, rather, an elegant stylist and aesthetic philosopher whose works delicately fuse elements of Imagism, Symbolism, Modernism, and Romanticism to "affect," as critic Henry W. Wells has noted, "what others proclaim: the creation of a new style or 'language' for verse." This "new style"—which is evident in even the earliest of Stevens's poems—combines popular American idioms, comic irony, a learnedly obscure vocabulary, and poetic meters that seemed to evolve from natural syntax and the sound of words. Thematically, the poems reflect the concerns of a philosopher. Stevens was preoccupied with the conflict between imagination and reality, and addressed this subject throughout his career. In such early works as "Sunday Morning" and "The Emperor of Ice-Cream," as well as "An Ordinary Evening in New Haven"—one of his last poems—Stevens explored this theme of "the difference that we make in what we see." Because of this central concern, his work exhibits a greater degree of artistic wholeness than that of many other authors whose work is more easily divisible into distinct periods and styles.

Stevens was born in Reading, Pennsylvania to a family of Dutch origins. In later years, his fine ear for the sounds of common speech often led him to employ characteristic phrases from the Pennsylvania Dutch vernacular in his poetry; these appear humorously intermingled with French phrases, nonsense words, and regional expressions from other parts of the United States. Stevens attended Harvard University from 1897 to 1900, and was subsequently admitted to the New York University Law School. In 1904 he began practicing law in New York City, and was married five years later. In 1916 he left New York and went to work for the Hartford Insurance Company in Connecticut, where he remained successfully employed until his death in 1955. Stevens's career as a professional businessman has long puzzled his biographical and critical commentators, but Stevens himself dismissed the issue of his dual careers by stating that he believed "it gives a man character as a poet to have this daily contact with a job."

Stevens's first poems appeared in *Poetry* magazine in 1914, but dissatisfaction with his work led him to delay publishing a collection until 1923, when *Harmonium* appeared. The initial critical response to *Harmonium* was limited. A few critics noted the "gaudiness," witty sophistication, and sensuousness of Stevens's verse, and labelled him a literary hedonist. Others considered him an escapist for ignoring the "wasteland crisis" in America. Stevens never denied the charges of escapism. Unlike T. S. Eliot and Ezra Pound, he did not believe that poetry need become a reflection of the mood of an era, but preferred to concern himself solely with questions of aesthetics and the functioning of the creative imagination. Following the publication of *Harmonium*, Stevens wrote no poetry for six years. Critics such as Edmund Wilson and John Gould Fletcher had foreseen that some of the more irrational and solipsistic ideas advanced by Stevens in *Harmonium* represented the sort

of withdrawal from life that would inevitably lead to just such an artistic impasse; in reviewing *Harmonium*, Wilson had written that Stevens must "either expand his range to take in more human experience, or give up writing altogether." It was 1935 before Stevens's next book, *Ideas of Order*, appeared. *Ideas of Order* and *Owl's Clover*, the book that followed, are more rhetorical in tone and contain fewer emotionally and sensually charged images than *Harmonium*. In these volumes Stevens reexamined the philosophical position that he had taken in poems such as "The Snow Man" from *Harmonium*, in which he had asserted that "the universe is silent" and that nothing exists but individual consciousness. Instead he arrived at the belief that an objective reality does exist, but that it lacks any intrinsic purpose except those imposed by human values.

Most critics designate *Notes toward a Supreme Fiction*, published in 1942, as Stevens's finest work. In it, Stevens resolved his speculations about the interaction between reality and the creative imagination through his concept of the "Supreme Fiction." For Stevens the "Supreme Fiction" or the "Grand Poem" represented an ideal fusion of reality and subjective imagination into a single entity. Each artist, then, creates an individual form of ultimate reality by uniting imagination with the external world. What results is a kind of secular myth representing "the merging of life and the creative act." In *The Necessary Angel: Essays on Reality and the Imagination*, published in 1951, Stevens offered a prose explanation of this theory in "The Noble Rider and the Sound of Words." In this essay, Stevens proclaimed his belief that poetry "is an interdependence of the imagination and reality as equals." This statement not only illuminates what Stevens meant by his concept of the "Supreme Fiction," it also summarizes the theme of most of his later poetry. In his mature works, such as *Esthétique du mal* and *The Auroras of Autumn*, Stevens reiterated and perfected the aesthetic philosophies that he had evolved in *Harmonium, Ideas of Order*, and *Notes toward a Supreme Fiction*. As critic Alfred Corn has observed, Stevens's later poems all reenact his career-long process of "pilgrimage from Nothing to Something." They are Stevens's elaborations on the role of metaphor in transforming "the real but empty thing" into something "unreal but fulfilling." In 1955 Stevens won the Pulitzer Prize in poetry for his *Collected Poems*.

Some critics have found Stevens's solution to twentieth-century metaphysical uncertainties to be rarefied and impersonal. The most frequent criticism of Stevens is that his poetry is overly abstract and does not portray recognizably human characters and situations. However, Stevens's interest was not in individual personalities or social issues, but in aesthetics and in the preservation of poetry in what he deemed an unimaginative age. Moreover, he believed that these interests must be the subjects of his poetry, since they derived naturally from his "sense of the world." "A man's sense of the world," Stevens wrote in his essay "Effects of Analogy," "is born with him and persists, and penetrates the ameliorations of education and experience of life." Thus, Stevens reasoned, to depart from his true subjects would render him, as a poet, "artificial and laborious."

Critics agree that Stevens's lifelong interest in the workings of the poetic imagination, and his exalted view of poetry as something that helps people live, place him in the Romantic tradition. However, they also recognize that he is indebted to the French Symbolists for his irony, his skepticism, and his theories of analogy. Similarly, the colorful, concrete images he employed in his poems reveal Imagist affinities, while his abstractions, erudition, and aesthetic accord with certain highly theoretical movements in the visual arts reflect Modernist tendencies. These diverse influences are united in his work by his unique style and his continuing ambition to effect transformations of reality through metaphor. The poetry that grew out of this ambition represents one of the major accomplishments in modern literature.

(See also *TCLC*, Vol. 3 and *Contemporary Authors*, Vol. 104.)

PRINCIPAL WORKS

Harmonium (poetry) 1923
Ideas of Order (poetry) 1935
Owl's Clover (poetry) 1936
The Man with the Blue Guitar, and Other Poems (poetry) 1937
Notes toward a Supreme Fiction (poetry) 1942
Parts of a World (poetry) 1942
Esthétique du mal (poetry) 1945
Transport to Summer (poetry) 1947
The Auroras of Autumn (poetry) 1950
The Necessary Angel: Essays on Reality and the Imagination (essays) 1951
Collected Poems (poetry) 1954
Opus Posthumous (poetry, dramas, and essays) 1957

Letters (letters) 1966
The Palm at the End of the Mind (poetry and drama) 1971

MORTON D. ZABEL   (essay date 1931)

[*Zabel was a poet, critic, and prominent scholar. From 1928 to 1937 he was associate editor, then editor, of Harriet Monroe's magazine,* Poetry, *which was the only journal at that time devoted solely to contemporary poetry. Throughout this period, he wrote extensively on English and American poetry. In the following excerpt, Zabel discusses the polarities in Stevens's verse between richness and simplicity.*]

Precision of the instrument is too infrequent in modern poetry to earn its masters anything less than the high distinction which . . . *Harmonium* . . . shows Wallace Stevens to possess. Yet the properties of his work, externally considered, might easily discredit him in the intemperate judgement. They are devices whose facile manipulation has won for a great share of contemporary verse a just—if usually ill-reasoned—contumely. Since Stevens has passed safely beyond the need of any comparison with his contemporaries, it is enough to note on this score that the "modern" devices which appear in these calmer days as the trickery of a topical vaudeville had behind them in his case the authority of instinctive symbolism and method; that they proceeded from an interior vision and necessity; and that for him this style was not a conjuror's garment but an expression for ideas of no given date, and of which he remains in many cases our only exact recorder.

The dimensions of his poetry are narrow. . . . Mr. Stevens' frugality of output is notable. Notable, however, only by contrast with the extravagance of his materials and the sensuous capacities they imply. The baroque attenuation, the lavish movement, the riot among colors and flowers, the panoply of limbs and lustres and tropical boskage, the fragile laces that edge seas terrifying, "snarled and yelping," the pomp of fat living and indulgent grossness—these mounting festivals of the senses that might emphasize in Parisian art its ineptitude and in the Oriental its austerity are vestiges of a romantic imagination whose scope is usually widest and whose technical impatience least bridled. But Mr. Stevens faced his resources with the diffidence of a critical eclecticism. For him the "barbaric glass," the "rosy chocolate And gilt umbrellas," "bananas hacked and hunched . . . from Carib trees," "effulgent, azure lakes," "the marguerite and coquelicot, And roses," "the cry of the peacocks" and the "forest of the parakeets," the "flowers in last month's newspapers" and the "forms, flames, and the flakes of flames," were at once a luxury for the senses and an assault upon the mind and integrity that nerves them.

Beyond the sense's capacity for creating wealth in experience, and the mind's capacity for containing it, lies the terrifying consequence of these appetites—confusion, the reward of intellectual gluttony and physical satiation. Conscious of this threat to sanity, Stevens' poetry established its polarity in richness and in simplicity: in "our bawdiness Unpurged by epitaph" on the one hand, and on the other in that crystalline clarity of vision and judgment which, schooled by the "imagination which is the will of things," "guards and preserves the spirit,'' sees eye to eye with the blackbird ''among twenty snowy mountains The only moving thing.'' . . . (pp. 148-50)

The sensibility that retains the uses of richness without endangering the precious security of simplicity makes little use of ascetic discipline for its own sake. Nor, in attempting a compromise between ''mildew of summer and the deepening snow'' will the sensibility risk a neutralization of its powers, a mere ''up and down between two elements,'' what Mr. Stevens calls ''the malady of the quotidian.'' Rather it will seek a balance which values the counterweights that maintain its poise. . . . This balance is the triumph of intelligence. Its reality in the sphere of the senses becomes for Mr. Stevens a symbol of its necessity in the sphere of thought and conduct. Between indulgence and austerity lies a luxury finer than either, the luxury of the two harmonized: of bravado and terror disciplined in fortitude, and of chaos and rectitude reconciled in order. . . . (pp. 150-51)

This hair-line correspondence is at once the clue to the sensuous logic of his style, and to the realism which saves his imagery from imaginative extravagance, his wit from verbal exercise, and his morality from the illusory intellectual casuistry which betrayed most of his colleagues. As the most perverse of his conceits holds to its roots in sincerity, so the most circuitous of his deductions refers directly to the actual conflict or moral challenge that initially demanded its unraveling. Mr. Stevens' method—on a different scale of emotional adjustment and sympathies—is almost exactly like Miss Moore's, although he has sought a fundamentally simpler resolution of the disparity between perception and intellectual habits than Miss Moore has in poems like *A Grave, A Fish,* and *Marriage.* His book's resources of exactitude in imagery and rhythm, its supple variety of measures, and its creative virtuosity are at length referable to a set of pure principles which make his work a unity as well as a model of clear intention. Imputed derivations from the methods of France, China, and Skeltonic English still leave intact a personality which shares its brilliance with only a few contemporaries. It is a personality whose lucid fitness of phrase and imagery clarifies today—as it did in an earlier more excited decade—the discord and prolixity of literary experience. (pp. 153-54)

Morton D. Zabel, ''The 'Harmonium' of Wallace Stevens,'' in Poetry (© *1931 by The Modern Poetry Association), Vol. XXXIX, No. 3, December, 1931, pp. 148-54.*

HARRIET MONROE   (essay date 1932)

[*As the founder and editor of* Poetry, *Monroe was a key figure in the American ''poetry renaissance'' which took place in the early twentieth century.* Poetry *was the first periodical devoted primarily to the works of new poets and to poetry criticism, and from 1912 until her death Monroe maintained an editorial policy of printing ''the best English verse which is being written today, regardless of where, by whom, or under what theory of art it is written.'' Monroe was one of the first to publish Stevens's poems, with some of his verse appearing in* Poetry *as early as 1914. In this review, Monroe discusses Stevens's role as a philosopher and humorist.*]

The delight which one breathes like a perfume from the poetry of Wallace Stevens is the natural effluence of his own clear and untroubled and humorously philosophical delight in the beauty of things as they are. Others may criticize and complain, may long for more perfect worlds or search subliminal mysteries—for him it is enough to watch the iridescent fall of sunlight on blue sea-water and pink parasols, and meditate on the blessed incongruities which break into rainbow colors this earth of ours and the beings who people it. To him the whole grand spectacle is so amazing that no melodramatic upheaval of destiny could possibly increase his sense of awe and wonder, or disturb his philosophic calm. He is content to live profoundly in the beauty of a universe whose lightest, most transient phenomena are sufficient evidence, to a mind in tune with it, of harmonies magnificent to infinity.

For this reason his poems, even those which seem slight, become hints of this immutable perfection. Like a Japanese carver discovering a god in a bit of ivory, Wallace Stevens, in such a poem as the *Paltry Nude* or *Peter Quince at the Clavier* presents the ineffable serenity of beauty.

Man's interference with this serenity—an interference ineffectual in any ultimate sense—is the central theme of his longer poems. In the one-act play *Three Travellers Watch a Sunrise,* a poem exquisite and deeply moving beyond analysis, this interference brings about tragedy; but even tragedy is shown as ineffectual to contradict beauty, whose processional march of splendor demands agony along with joy. In *The Comedian as the Letter C* the interference brings the more bewildering frustration of comedy; but even this falls whimsically into the scheme, for beauty invincible and immortal accepts frustration just as music accepts discord—and, lo and behold, the symphony moves on enriched. The hero of *Carlos Among the Candles* may be confused and amazed, but he goes on lighting the candles and illuminating with beams from the human imagination the inexhaustible beauty of the world. (pp. 39-40)

[There] was never a more flavorously original poetic personality than the author of [*Harmonium*]. If one seeks sheer beauty of sound, phrase, rhythm, packed with prismatically colored ideas by a mind at once wise and whimsical, one should open one's eyes and ears, sharpen one's wits, widen one's sympathies to include rare and exquisite aspects of life, and then run for this volume of iridescent poems.

I should like to take my copy to some quiet sea-flung space in Florida, where a number of the poems were written. The sky, perhaps, is cobalt, with mauve-white clouds; the sea is sapphire, flicking into diamonds under the wind; the sand is a line of purplish rose, and there are gaudy bathers and loiterers on the beach. And here is a poet undaunted by all this splendor, a poet as sure of delight as nature herself, as serenely receptive of beauty. The bleak despairs of lesser men visit him not at all—his philosophy embraces the whole fantastic miracle of life. . . . (p. 41)

For the philosopher and the satirist temper the poet's rage in Wallace Stevens. Whether he ever writes his masterpiece or not—and that is always uncertain through the turmoil of conflicting claims which besets us all today—he is of the race of the great humorists, using the word in its most profound sense, the sense in which Cervantes, Shakespeare, Synge, Lincoln may be counted as great humorists. In such men agony sinks into depths dark, hidden and unconfessed. The hard black stone is there, but laughter washes over it, covers it up, conceals it. Tragedy is comedy with such men—they are aware of the laughter of the gods and the flaming splendor of man's fight against it. This poet is one of them; his work, however incomplete as yet, is haughty with their lineage.

Always, in his lightest play of whimsicalities as well as in his most splendid assertions of beauty, one feels this deeper note, this sense of ultimate vanities and ecstasies contending, in the human atom, against infinities that threaten it with doom. The play of whimsicalities may seem a mere banter of word-bubbles, as in **Ordinary Women;** the assertions of beauty may be as magical in pomp of color and sound as **Le Monocle de Mon Oncle** . . . or as **The Paltry Nude Starts on a Spring Voyage.** . . . But in either extreme of lovely or whimsical utterance one feels the larger rhythms, one measures the poet's sweep by spaces beyond our earthly inches.

Perhaps **The Comedian as the Letter C** is the most complete assertion of cosmic humor which Mr. Stevens has as yet confessed to the world. It is at least the presentment, probably more or less autobiographical, of the predicament of man in general, or of highly sensitized man—let us say the artist—in particular, as he tries to live gloriously, and finds his soul caught in the meshes of life's allurements. Many poets have made a tragedy of this situation, shouting their agonies of rebellion and despair in more or less effective verse. Mr. Stevens is perhaps more keenly inspired in making of it a comedy searching and profound, a comedy whose azure laughter ripples almost inaudibly over hushed and sombre depths.

His little human unit—this "Socrates of snails," this "wig of things," this "sovereign ghost," . . . in short, this Crispin, who was "washed away by magnitude," is he not our modern exemplar of frustration, as Don Quixote was in his day? (pp. 42-4)

We must hope that the poem is not strictly autobiographical, that Mr. Stevens, unlike his baffled hero, will get his story uttered—to such a degree at least, as may be within the reach of poor mortality. For this poet, like a super-sensitized plate, is aware of color-subtleties and sound-vibrations which most of us do not detect, and of happiness in fine degrees which most of us do not attain. He derives, so far as one may trace the less obvious origins, from no one; but like Napoleon he may say, *"Je suis ancêtre!"* ["I am an ancestor"] for shoals of young poets derive from him. Quite free of literary allegiances to period or place, he distils into a pure essence the beauty of his own world. And beauty's imperishable perfection among shifting mortal shows is the incongruity at the heart of life which this poet accepts with the kind of serene laughter that covers pain. (p. 45)

> *Harriet Monroe, "A Cavalier of Beauty," in* Poetry *(© 1924 by The Modern Poetry Association), Vol. XXIII, No. 6, March, 1924 (and reprinted in a slightly different form as "Wallace Stevens," in her* Poets and Their Art, *revised edition, the Macmillan Company, 1932, pp. 39-45).*

WALLACE STEVENS   (lecture date 1948)

[*Stevens made few statements about his theory of poetry. His volume of essays* The Necessary Angel, *from which the excerpt below was taken, is thus a valuable aid to understanding his poetry, for the essays it contains represent the nearest thing available to a detailed statement by the poet of his ideas on the imagination and his theories of poetics.*]

[Analogy] is primarily a discipline of rightness. The poet is constantly concerned with two theories. One relates to the imagination as a power within him not so much to destroy reality at will as to put it to his own uses. He comes to feel that his imagination is not wholly his own but that it may be part of a much larger, much more potent imagination, which it is his affair to try to get at. For this reason, he pushes on and lives, or tries to live, as Paul Valéry did, on the verge of

consciousness. This often results in poetry that is marginal, subliminal. The same theory exists in relation to prose, to painting and other arts. The second theory relates to the imagination as a power within him to have such insights into reality as will make it possible for him to be sufficient as a poet in the very center of consciousness. This results, or should result, in a central poetry. Dr. Whitehead concluded his *Modes of Thought* by saying:

> . . . the purpose of philosophy is to rationalize mysticism. . . . Philosophy is akin to poetry, and both of them seek to express that ultimate good sense which we term civilization.

The proponents of the first theory believe that it will be a part of their achievement to have created the poetry of the future. It may be that the poetry of the future will be to the poetry of the present what the poetry of the present is to the ballad. The proponents of the second theory believe that to create the poetry of the present is an incalculable difficulty, which rarely is achieved, fully and robustly, by anyone. They think that there is enough and more than enough to do with what faces us and concerns us directly and that in poetry as an art, and, for that matter, in any art, the central problem is always the problem of reality. The adherents of the imagination are mystics to begin with and pass from one mysticism to another. The adherents of the central are also mystics to begin with. But all their desire and all their ambition is to press away from mysticism toward that ultimate good sense which we term civilization. (pp. 115-16)

Poetry is almost incredibly one of the effects of analogy. This statement involves much more than the analogy of figures of speech, since otherwise poetry would be little more than a trick. But it is almost incredibly the outcome of figures of speech or, what is the same thing, the outcome of the operation of one imagination on another through the instrumentality of the figures. To identify poetry and metaphor or metamorphosis is merely to abbreviate the last remark. There is always an analogy between nature and the imagination, and possibly poetry is merely the strange rhetoric of that parallel: a rhetoric in which the feeling of one man is communicated to another in words of the exquisite appositeness that takes away all their verbality.

Another mode of analogy is to be found in the personality of the poet. But this mode is no more limited to the poet than the mode of metaphor is so limited. This mode proposes for study the poet's sense of the world as the source of poetry. The corporeal world exists as the common denominator of the incorporeal worlds of its inhabitants. If there are people who live only in the corporeal world, enjoying the wind and the weather and supplying standards of normality, there are other people who are not so sure of the wind and the weather and who supply standards of abnormality. It is the poet's sense of the world that is the poet's world. The corporeal world, the familiar world of the commonplace, in short, our world, is one sense of the analogy that develops between our world and the world of the poet. The poet's sense of the world is the other sense. It is the analogy between these two senses that concerns us.

We could not speak of our world as something to be distinguished from the poet's sense of it unless we objectified it and recognized it as having an existence apart from the projection of his personality, as land and sea, sky and cloud. He himself desires to make the distinction as part of the process of realizing himself. Once the distinction has been made, it becomes an instrument for the exploration of poetry. By means of it we can determine the relation of the poet to his subject. This would be simple if he wrote about his own world. We could compare it with ours. But what he writes about is his sense of our world. If he is a melancholy person he gives us a melancholy sense of our world. (pp. 117-19)

A man's sense of the world is born with him and persists, and penetrates the ameliorations of education and experience of life. His species is as fixed as his genus. For each man, then, certain subjects are congenital. Now, the poet manifests his personality, first of all, by his choice of subject. Temperament is a more explicit word than personality and would no doubt be the exact word to use, since it emphasizes the manner of thinking and feeling. It is agreeable to think of the poet as a whole biological mechanism and not as a subordinate mechanism within that larger one. Temperament, too, has attracted a pejorative meaning. It should be clear that in dealing with the choice of subject we are dealing with one of the vital factors in poetry or in any art. Great numbers of poets come and go who have never had a subject at all. What is true of poets in this respect is equally true of painters, as the existence of schools of painters all doing more or less the same thing at the same time demonstrates. The leader of the school has a subject. But his followers merely have his subject. Thus Picasso has a subject, a subject that devours him and devastates his region. (p. 120)

What is the poet's subject? It is his sense of the world. For him, it is inevitable and inexhaustible. If he departs from it he becomes artificial and laborious and while his artifice may be skillful and his labor perceptive no one knows better than he that what he is doing, under such circumstances, is not essential to him. It may help him to feel that it may be essential to someone else. But this justification, though it might justify what he does in the eyes of all the world, would never quite justify him in his own eyes. There is nothing of selfishness in this. It is often said of a man that his work is autobiographical in spite of every subterfuge. It cannot be otherwise. Certainly, from the point of view from which we are now regarding it, it cannot be otherwise, even though it may be totally without reference to himself. There was a time when the ivory tower was merely a place of seclusion, like a cottage on a hill-top or a cabin by the sea. Today, it is a kind of lock-up of which our intellectual constables are the appointed wardens. Is it not time that someone questioned this degradation, not for the purpose of restoring the isolation of the tower but in order to establish the integrity of its builder? Our rowdy gun-men may not appreciate what comes from that tower. Others do. Was there ever any poetry more wholly the poetry of the ivory tower than the poetry of Mallarmé? Was there ever any music more wholly the music of the ivory tower than the music of Debussy?

The truth is that a man's sense of the world dictates his subjects to him and that this sense is derived from his personality, his temperament, over which he has little control and possibly none, except superficially. It is not a literary problem. It is the problem of his mind and nerves. These sayings are another form of the saying that poets are born not made. A poet writes of twilight because he shrinks from noon-day. He writes about the country because he dislikes the city, and he likes the one and dislikes the other because of some trait of mind or nerves; that is to say, because of something in himself that influences his thinking and feeling. So seen, the poet and his subject are inseparable. There are stresses that he invites; there are stresses that he avoids. There are colors that have the blandest effect on him; there are others with which he can do nothing but find fault. In music he likes the strings. But the horn shocks him. A flat landscape extending in all directions to immense distances placates him. But he shrugs his shoulders at mountains. One young woman seems to be someone that he would like to know; another seems to be someone that he must know without fail. (pp. 121-22)

The second way by which a poet manifests his personality is by his style. This is too well understood to permit discussion. What has just been said with respect to choice of subject applies equally to style. The individual dialect of a poet who happens to have one, analogous to the speech common to his time and place and yet not that common speech, is in the same position as the language of poetry generally when the language of poetry generally is not the common speech. Both produce effects singular to analogy. Beyond that the dialect is not in point.

A man's sense of the world may be only his own or it may be the sense of many people. Whatever it is it involves his fate. It may involve only his own or it may involve that of many people. The measure of the poet is the measure of his sense of the world and of the extent to which it involves the sense of other people. We have to stop and think now and then of what he writes as implicit with that significance. Thus in the lines of Leonidas:

> Even as a vine on her dry pole I support myself now
> on a staff and death calls me to Hades

we have to think of the reality and to read the lines as one having the reality at heart: an old man at that point at which antiquity begins to resume what everything else has left behind; or if you think of the lines as a figuration of despair on the part of the poet, and it is possible to change them into such a figuration, to read them as lines communicating a feeling that it was not within the poet's power to suppress.

Still another mode of analogy is to be found in the music of poetry. It is a bit old hat and romantic and, no doubt at all, the dated forms are intolerable. In recent years, poetry began to change character about the time when painting began to change character. Each lost a certain euphrasy. But, after all, the music of poetry has not come to an end. Is not Eliot a musical poet? . . . [Yesterday,] or the day before, the time from which the use of the word "music" in relation to poetry has come down to us, music meant something else. It meant metrical poetry with regular rhyme schemes repeated stanza after stanza. All of the stanzas were alike in form. As a result of this, what with the repetitions of the beats of the lines, and the constant and recurring harmonious sounds, there actually was a music. But with the disappearance of all this, the use of the word "music" in relation to poetry is as I said a moment ago a bit old hat: anachronistic. Yet . . . Eliot was musical. It is simply that there has been a change in the nature of what we mean by music. It is like the change from Haydn to a voice intoning. It is like the voice of an actor reciting or declaiming or of some other figure concealed, so that we cannot identify him, who speaks with a measured voice which is often disturbed by his feeling for what he says. There is no accompaniment. If occasionally the poet touches the triangle or one of the cymbals, he does it only because he feels like doing it. Instead of a musician we have an orator whose speech sometimes resembles music. We have an eloquence and it is that eloquence that we call music every day, without having much cause to think about it.

What has this music to do with analogy? When we hear the music of one of the great narrative musicians, as it tells its tale, it is like finding our way through the dark not by the aid of any sense but by an instinct that makes it possible for us to move quickly when the music moves quickly, slowly when the music moves slowly. It is a speed that carries us on and through every winding, once more to the world outside of the music at its conclusion. It affects our sight of what we see and leaves it ambiguous, somewhat like one thing. somewhat like another. In the meantime the tale is being told and the music excites us and we identify it with the story and it becomes the story and the speed with which we are following it. When it is over, we are aware that we have had an experience very much like the story just as if we had participated in what took place. It is exactly as if we had listened with complete sympathy to an emotional recital. The music was a communication of emotion. It would not have been different if it had been the music of poetry or the voice of the protagonist telling the tale or speaking out his sense of the world. How many things we should have found like in either case! (pp. 123-26)

It is time, therefore, to attempt a few generalizations, slight as the data may be. Accordingly, our first generalization is this: Every image is the elaboration of a particular of the subject of the image. If this is true it is a realistic explanation of the origin of images. . . . In the lines from Leonidas:

> Even as a vine on her dry pole I support myself now on
> a staff and death calls me to Hades

the particular is the staff. This becomes the dry pole, and the vine follows after. There is no analogy between a vine and an old man under all circumstances. But when one supports itself on a dry pole and the other on a staff, the case is different. [This illustration is] . . . not enough to establish a principle. But [it is] . . . enough to suggest the possibility of a principle.

Our second generalization, based on even slighter data, and proposed in the same experimental way, is this: Every image is a restatement of the subject of the image in the terms of an attitude. . . . If there is any merit to what was said about the sense of the world, that also illustrates the principle.

Our third generalization is this: Every image is an intervention on the part of the image-maker. One does not feel the need of so many reservations, if of any, in the case of this principle. But then of the three it is the one that matters least. It refers to the sense of the world, as the second principle did, and it could be said to be a phase of the second principle, if it did not refer to style in addition to the sense of the world. The second principle does not refer to style.

It is time, too, to attempt a few simplifications of the whole subject by way of summing it up and of coming to an end. . . . The venerable, the fundamental books of the human spirit are vast collections of . . . analogies and it is the analogies that have helped to make these books what they are. The pictorializations of poetry include much more than figures of speech. We have not been studying images, but, however crudely, analogies, of which images are merely a part. Analogies are much the larger subject. And analogies are elusive. Take the case of a man for whom reality is enough, as, at the end of his life, he returns to it like a man returning from Nowhere to his village and to everything there that is tangible and visible, which he has come to cherish and wants to be near. He sees without images. But is he not seeing a clarified reality of his own? Does he not dwell in an analogy? His imageless world is, after all, of the same sort as a world full of the obvious analogies of happiness or unhappiness, innocence or tragedy, thoughtlessness or the heaviness of the mind. In any case, these

are the pictorializations of men, for whom the world exists as a world and for whom life exists as life, the objects of their passions, the objects before which they come and speak, with intense choosing, words that we remember and make our own. Their words have made a world that transcends the world and a life livable in that transcendence. It is a transcendence achieved by means of the minor effects of figurations and the major effects of the poet's sense of the world and of the motive music of his poems and it is the imaginative dynamism of all these analogies together. Thus poetry becomes and is a transcendent analogue composed of the particulars of reality, created by the poet's sense of the world, that is to say, his attitude, as he intervenes and interposes the appearances of that sense. (pp. 127-30)

Wallace Stevens, "Effects of Analogy" (1948; copyright 1948 by Wallace Stevens; reprinted by permission of Alfred A. Knopf, Inc.), in his The Necessary Angel, *Knopf, 1951 (and reprinted by Vintage Books, 1965), pp. 105-30.*

LOUISE BOGAN (essay date 1950)

[*Bogan was a distinguished American poet whose work is noted for its subtlety and restraint, evidencing her debt to the English metaphysical poets. She served for many years as the poetry critic at* The New Yorker *and is the author of* Achievement in American Poetry: 1900-1950, *a respected volume of criticism. In the following review of* The Auroras of Autumn, *Bogan discusses Stevens's preoccupation with poetry about poetry. She also concurs with the commonly voiced complaint that Stevens's characters seem bloodless, and that his emotions are unduly constrained.*]

Wallace Stevens is the American poet who has based his work most firmly upon certain effects of nineteenth-century Symbolist poetry. The title of his latest volume, **The Auroras of Autumn,** indicates that his powers of language have not declined; here is one of those endlessly provocative, "inevitable" phrases that seem to have existed forever in some rubied darkness of the human imagination—that imagination with whose authority and importance Stevens has been continually occupied in his later period. This preoccupation was once implicit in what he wrote; his images performed their work by direct impact. Stevens' later explicit, logical, and rather word-spinning defense of the role of the imagination has weakened or destroyed a good deal of his original "magic." The whole texture and coloration of his later verse is more austere; his subjects are less eccentric; even his titles have quieted down. What has always been true of him is now more apparent: that no one can describe the simplicities of the natural world with more direct skill. It is a natural world strangely empty of human beings, however; Stevens' men and women are bloodless symbols. And there is something theatrical in much of his writing; his emotions seem to be transfixed, rather than released and projected, by his extraordinary verbal improvisations. Now that he is so widely imitated, it is important to remember that his method is a special one; that modern poetry has developed transparent, overflowing, and spontaneous qualities that Stevens ignores. It is also useful to remember (as Apollinaire knew) that since the imagination is part of life, it must have its moments of awkwardness and naïveté, and must seek out forms in which it may move and breathe easily, in order that it may escape both strain and artificiality. (pp. 382-83)

Louise Bogan, "'The Auroras of Autumn'" (originally published in The New Yorker, *Vol. XXVI, No. 36, October 28, 1950), in her* A Poet's Alphabet:

Reflections on the Literary Art and Vocation, *edited by Robert Phelps and Ruth Limmer (copyright © 1970 by Ruth Limmer as Trustee; reprinted by permission of Ruth Limmer, literary executor, Estate of Louise Bogan), McGraw-Hill Book Company, 1970, pp. 382-83.*

SISTER M. BERNETTA QUINN, O.S.F. (essay date 1952)

[*Quinn was a personal friend and correspondent of Stevens. The following excerpt deals with the theme of metamorphosis in Stevens's work as it is developed through such motifs as individual perception, or "the difference that we make in what we see", and the action of the perceiving mind as well as the eye. For other discussions of this topic, see the excerpts below by John J. Enck and Ronald Sukenick.*]

What is constant in Wallace Stevens's poetry, as well as in his theory of poetry, is emphasis on change, or—as he expresses the principle with greater nicety in the first of **"Three Academic Pieces"**—on metamorphosis. He concerns himself first of all with the structure of reality; secondly, with the way in which man knows his world; and finally, with the transfigurations of that world as imagination acts upon it. Each succeeding year of his critical prose and his verse further defines metamorphosis as it functions in the areas of metaphysics, epistemology, and aesthetics, the latter term including life itself considered as the highest of the arts.

A primary aspect of metamorphosis in Stevens is the effect of the senses on extra-mental reality. No one sees quite the same rose as anyone else does; there is, in fact, a semantics of perception, wherein sense "is like a flow of meanings with no speech/And of as many meanings as of men." What connotation is to a word the action of the senses is to a physical object. In **"Sombre Figuration"** Stevens remarks that reality is that about reality which impresses us: "As a church is a bell and people are an eye, / A cry, the pallor of a dress, a touch"; such a point of view relates him to impressionistic painting, a kinship made doubly clear by his habit of giving lyrics titles which might equally well apply to pictures (**"Study of Two Pears," "Girl in a Nightgown," "Landscape with Boat," "Woman Looking at a Vase of Flowers," "Man Carrying Thing," "Large Red Man Reading,"** to mention only a few). This variety of synecdoche is a consequence of the selection made by the senses from the ineffably multiple phenomena comprising the flux which overwhelms human consciousness from instant to instant. . . . The "difference that we make in what we see" is more transforming than any rhetoric, so that as one of the three theories propounded in **"Metaphors of a Magnifico"** suggests, there are as many realities as observers. The word Stevens uses for the difference made by the subject in the object is description, which is "a little different from reality"; it is neither what is described nor an imitation of it, but rather something artificial that exists in no place, only in the spirit's universe, that intangible "locale" of all seeming. This somewhat elusive view of appearance is elaborated upon in the fifth section of **"Description without Place."** . . . The term Stevens makes synonymous with such description is *revelation*, the Biblical connotations of which he underlines in the sixth part of the poem; there, too, he speaks of description as the double, though not too closely the double, of our lives—artificial, visible, intense.

The fullest illustration of "the difference that we make in what we see" is the early and widely anthologized lyric, **"Sea Surface Full of Clouds,"** the various sections of which ring a single setting through five changes. The setting in question is a November seascape near Tehuantepec, at daybreak. Arranged in six tercets, each part of the poem delineates a view of the ocean that reflects the highly colored Mexican sky; Stevens works out his five-paneled picture with exquisite balancing of syntax, delicately adjusted shadings of diction, using for every twelfth line an explanatory sentence in French to indicate how the shifting selves of the observer re-model this "fluent mundo" of sea and cloudy heavens, how in turn they evolve protean cloud-blossoms in marine gardens.

One of the poet's finest accounts of the process of perception is in **"Woman Looking at a Vase of Flowers."** . . . To the subject of the lyric, the bouquet becomes thunder, summer, the sides of peaches and pears; the abstract red and blue turn into particulars. Colors and shapes powerfully stir the woman; she is conscious of related impressions, which have a metamorphic nature: "The wind dissolving into birds, / The clouds becoming braided girls. . . ." These comparisons point out that the mind as well as the eye has its metamorphoses.

The spectator walking about New Haven on an ordinary evening regards certain chapels and schools as transformed men, openly displaying in their new identities the secrets they hid while human. . . . In Ovid's *Metamorphoses* trees frequently are not really trees but victims of love; stones, rivers, stars, not actually inanimate settings of man's life but men and women removed to lower realms of existence. Stevens adapts the principle of mutation to accord with the exigencies of his twentieth-century world by making the buildings of a Connecticut city exteriorizations of its inhabitants, at least in the mind of one beholder.

Besides the transformations effected by perception, things are changed by the words used to refer to them; nomenclature adds to the image on the retina, the vibrations on the ear drum. In **"Certain Phenomena of Sound"** Sister Eulalia is created of her name, just as is the dark-syllabled Semiramide. . . . (pp. 230-33)

Some objects, on the other hand, resist the catalysts of language and sense. . . . From the testimony of [the poem **"The Motive for Metaphor"**] Stevens apparently considers summer as a fullness of expression too much itself to need or sustain metaphor, unlike the half-seasons of autumn and spring, which some persons prefer to a complete reality. . . . Although ordinarily man can, at least in theory, make things over, some objects, like the two pears in a lyric from *Parts of a World*, impose their own qualities so violently that they "are not seen / As the observer wills," but as they are. Other examples wherein two forces pull in opposite directions, victory going to the real over the fictive, are the rising sun, calm sea, and moon hanging in the sky of **"Notes toward a Supreme Fiction,"** which Stevens declares "are not things transformed. / Yet we are shaken by them as if they were." The perceiving agent is symbolized often by the wind, called Jumbo in the poem of that name, a "companion in nothingness" who although a transformer is himself transformed. (pp. 234-35)

The relation of subject to object is a metaphysical problem Stevens likes to meditate upon, as shown by the sixty-page lyric, **"An Ordinary Evening in New Haven."** In the second section, he supposes that "these houses are composed of ourselves," with the result that New Haven becomes "an impalpable town," its bells, "transparencies of sound"; if this be true, then it follows that New Haven is "So much ourselves, we cannot tell apart / The idea and the bearer-being of the idea.'' Further on he advises us to consider ''Reality as a thing seen by the mind, / Not that which is but that which is apprehended.'' If these suppositions are valid, man might be regarded as a magician who makes phenomena real. The flowering Judas, dark-spiced branches of trees, cat-bird's gobble are ''real only if I make them so.'' (**''Holiday in Reality''**)

A final step in this tracing of the metamorphoses undergone by the objective world is the way in which a whole age takes character from one powerful figure. The term *Elizabethan* as applicable to the golden period of the Sixteenth Century is too dulled by use for flaming details of its origin to leap in the minds of average men, but Stevens, with characteristic alertness, looks afresh at the hackneyed phrase *Elizabethan age* and sees Elizabeth as a green queen in a summer of sun, the greenness and sunlight created by her own splendor. . . . There are various kinds of queens—red, blue, green, argent—each of whom bestows an identity upon her *milieu*.

Just as metamorphosis links the objective and the subjective worlds, so it connects the realm of reality with the realm of the imagination. In fact these are not two realms at all, but one—the realm of resemblance. Everything in our environment is, in certain respects, like everything else, bound together in an inescapable relationship which is the basis of appearance. In **''Three Academic Pieces''** Stevens shows how this truth operates by analyzing the colors of a seascape. . . . It is easy to see how like things resemble each other (man and man, woman and woman, year and year); it is not so easy to apply this principle to dissimilar objects, such as sand and water, palm tree and sky. But Stevens's ingenuity in using color as a bond is persuasive enough to let the illustration stand as a foundation for his aesthetic theory.

Resemblance is omnipresent in Nature; poetry, however, must supply resemblances to its fictions if these are to be truly supreme. Fortunately, it has two ways of doing so denied to Nature, as the essay goes on to explain. . . . For the second way, Stevens gives as an example music and that which music evokes in us; for the last he has in mind two abstractions. (pp. 236-38)

There are different degrees of excellence in poetry considered as metamorphosis, depending upon the things compared. . . . [If] these are two unlike things of adequate dignity, the resemblance transfigures, sublimates them. The common property is made brilliant. When the human mind moves from some exquisite earthly scene, such as a moonlit evening on a Caribbean island, to the thought of Paradise, both ideas gain in glory. In such a manner poetry transfigures, though not always so ambitiously. . . . The silver cord, golden bowl, pitcher, and wheel are parts of the tangible world though used in this passage as symbols to effect metamorphosis or resemblance or poetry—[in his essay] Stevens makes no attempt to differentiate among the three. The destruction of the body, which these represent figuratively, borrows an imaginative glory from them, just as they, inanimate creatures, acquire a new luster from their association with human death. Poetry satisfies our desire for resemblance but more than that, by the activity of the imagination in discovering likeness, it intensifies reality, enhances it, heightens it.

One more point, in a discussion of how poetry is metamorphosis in the writing of Wallace Stevens, is that art, by erasing the defects of its original, results in the ideal, in the universal unlimited by the particular, though drawn from it. In his most complete poetic statement on aesthetics, **''Notes toward a Supreme Fiction,''** which concludes *Transport to Summer*, Stevens presents the poem as transmuting life to Eden-like perfection: ''The poem refreshes life so that we share, / For a moment, the first idea. . . .'' Later in the same work he rephrases the proposition thus: ''The freshness of transformation is / The freshness of a world.'' Stevens works in the opposite direction from the Platonic theory. For Plato a poetic figure about a plum (A) was a copy of a real plum (B) which might perhaps have a bad spot on its underside and which itself was copied from the perfect plum (C) existing in the world of ideas. For Stevens, C drops out and A is superior to B. He is, indeed, closer to Aristotelian imitation, in spite of his repugnance for the term *imitation* as expressed in **''The Realm of Resemblance.''** To Aristotle mimesis was not a mere copying of the object as it existed in nature; it was a resemblance worked out into perfection in so far as the maker was able to do so. All aspects of the object extraneous to its perfection were eliminated. The supreme fiction must give pleasure, it must change, but it must also be abstract—the Stevensian word for ideal.

One characteristic of the world of Wallace Stevens is the fluidity of essence. Besides the union of opposites in Nature, there is also a mysterious transference of essences. Now that the concept of essence is no longer taken for granted—at least in several schools of modern philosophy—this interference with quiddity requires less suspension of disbelief than it would have in earlier periods. One instance of such mutation occurs in the middle section of **''Notes toward a Supreme Fiction''**: the water of the lake, says the poet, was ''Like a momentary color, in which swans / Were seraphs, were saints, were changing essences.'' In **''Variations on a Summer Day,''** the rocks of the cliffs are heads of dogs that turn into fishes and plunge into the sea; this, of course, happens only in the imagination though the desideratum is ''To change nature, not merely to change ideas.'' (pp. 241-43)

[One] illustration of the fluidity of essence is the poem **''The House Was Quiet and the World Was Calm,''** in which ''The reader became the book; and summer night / Was like the conscious being of the book,'' a progression which identifies the reader with the summer night. . . . Stevens surprises by using the indicative where accepted grammar would demand the subjunctive, as if to obliterate the distinction between wish and fulfillment; the scholar hears the words of the book spoken ''as if there was no book.'' The poet goes on to say that truth itself is summer, the night, the reader—a blending of essences reminiscent of Eliot's ''music heard so deeply that you are the music'' in the *Quartets*. (p. 244)

To disbelieve in the separateness of things is to court pantheism. Wordsworth, to whom Stevens has been compared, is popularly (whether justifiably so or not) associated with this type of thinking. Amidst the irritations, tedium, and discouragements of life, the desire to become some unsusceptible object is not an uncommon one, the desire to be, for example, a sun-drenched rock on a sweep of Hawaiian beach, a thinking stone soothed by sea-wind and palm-shadows, detached from all burdens of humanity. Such tales as Niobe's are perhaps due to the longing to escape from grief; escapism, incidentally, is a term to which Stevens has never objected. No one can better suggest this imaginary metempsychosis. After commenting on how closely Stevens approaches romantic pantheism, John Malcolm Brinnin, in his contribution to the Stevens issue of *Voices* (Spring, 1945), goes on to say: ''If it is possible to understand how it feels to be a pear, a green light on the sea, a bowl of flowers, Stevens manages, with necromantic conviction, to say that he does.''

Once man understands the nature of his world and of poetry he will, particularly if he is an artist, re-fashion reality in such a way as to achieve happiness in what will then become a terrestrial paradise. . . . According to this view, imaginative activity is a way of rendering man divine, in the sense that he shares God's creative power. . . . (pp. 245-46)

In **"The Figure of the Youth as Virile Poet,"** Stevens . . . makes poetry synonymous with apotheosis. . . . The relevance of this to the Stevensian doctrine of resemblance, or metamorphosis, is obvious. In **"A Pastoral Nun"** Stevens underlines the connection of poetry, apotheosis, and resemblance by pointing out that the first two resemble each other in that "Each matters only in that which it conceives."

Re-molding reality is not confined to men; even a rabbit can create through imagination a more satisfactory world than that of actuality, or so Stevens would convince us in one of his empathetic excursions into other than human consciousness, **"A Rabbit as King of the Ghosts."** Here the rabbit reduces the cat from a monument to a bug in the grass, little and green, whereas he himself grows to "a self that fills the four corners of the night." Everything in his environment now exists only for him—the trees, the vastness of night; he becomes more and more important in the cosmos until his head rises beyond the atmosphere of earth into space itself. The poem as a whole is a satiric expression of anthropomorphism.

This creative power, this sorcerer's gift capable of producing a terrestrial paradise, does not function automatically; it is an act of will, since imagination is the will of things. (pp. 246-47)

At the present time, realization of the resources of the imagination is intermittent, confined to "moments of awakening, / Extreme, fortuitous, personal," which correspond to Eliot's intuitional flashes in the *Quartets*. But the day will come when earth will constitute all the heaven that a savage race hungers for, a primal paradise regained through courage. It does not seem to bother Mr. Stevens that he probably will not be around to enjoy it; for him, there is always the solace of the blue guitar. (pp. 247-48)

Man is indeed the captain of his soul, the master of his fate, though he seldom acts as if he were; if he did, he would achieve freedom, as Stevens declares in **"The Latest Freed Man."** . . . **"On the Road Home,"** . . . in *Parts of a World,* accentuates Stevens's relativism by saying that freedom comes only after man discovers there is no absolute truth. After the denials of the speaker and his companion, the grapes grow fatter, the tree changes from green to blue ("Then the tree, at night, began to change / Smoking through green and smoking blue"), the night becomes warmer, closer. Everything takes on a new plenitude of being, as the six superlative adjectives in the last four lines indicate: *largest, longest, roundest, warmest, closest, strongest.*

Set against the imagination as shaping spirit is the desire of Stevens, expressed with equal vividness, to face things as they are. Indeed, his devotion to things as they are is hard to reconcile with his wish to remould them to what they should be. It may be that these two contradictory views are merely another instance of his Heracleitan opposites which fuse into a third and perfect singular—but on the other hand their incompatibility may constitute a crucial lack of clarity in his aesthetic, though perhaps the clash might better be described as a sign of countries of the mind yet to be explored. Subtle as Stevens's propositions are and admirable as is the intricacy with which

he has devised them in over a quarter of a century, there appear to be basic difficulties in his position, which suggest that the center which he seeks is still in the future tense.

On the side of things as they are, Stevens advocates a complete acceptance of the present, not an evasion such as that practiced by the "metamorphorid" Lady Lowzen of **"Oak Leaves Are Hands."** . . . Under [Stevens's] witty treatment is serious criticism: nothing but the past and the future exists for Lady Lowzen, who is adept at making these come alive and take on shimmering iridescence but who has no distinctive character of her own, as well as no belief in the reality of her Indian (Hydapsia, Howzen) environment. Stevens shows her metamorphorid nature by distorting *Flora* to *florid,* by using the word *bachelor* to keep even her sex from definiteness, by parodying *ancestral halls to hells.* As Miss MacMort, Flora had waited, spider-like, preoccupied with the splendid past of her family as symbolized in heraldic designs. A subtle overtone here is the etymology of Flora's maiden name: MacMort, the son (daughter) of death. Now, unsatisfied with being Lady Lowzen, she still dreams of the romantic past and the exciting future, her imagination a prism through which these two tenses pass. In the present she has no interest; her metamorphic powers do not touch it.

The problems raised by conflicting aspects of Stevens's theory of the imagination are not minor ones, though since their solution is "work in progress" one cannot at the present time criticize the theory with any conclusiveness. It would appear to be indisputable, however, that Stevens is a meliorist in the sense that he considers the human race to be moving forward toward a time when the faculties which comprise the psyche will be understood fully and will be used to the maximum of their powers. Then statements about the "change immenser than / A poet's metaphors in which being would / Come true" can be made in the indicative rather than in the subjunctive.

Is such a Utopian position tenable? The philosopher by profession would probably answer that one cannot (and never will be able to) think by imagining, since nothing is more unsuccessful in philosophy than an attempt to obliterate the distinctions between the abstract and the concrete. Poetry, he would say, deals with the concrete, the particular; philosophy, with the abstract, the universal—to which Stevens might reply by quoting from his description of the primitive man, held up as paragon, who "Imagines, and it is true, as if he thought / By imagining, anti-logician, quick / With a logic of transforming certitudes." (**"Sombre Figuration"**) And perhaps the philosopher in refutation might then point to the description of heaven in **"Sunday Morning"**—an oriental paradise characterized by suspended motion except for the plucking of lutes—as an example of what happens when one demands that the supra-sensible be clothed in sensory images. Despite Plato, Lucretius, Santayana, the marriage of poetry and philosophy is ordinarily not a happy one.

However, there is every reason to believe that one of Stevens's delicately testing intelligence will never rest content with his discoveries, whether in aesthetics or metaphysics; his mind is too fine to turn to stone by regarding all questions as answered. Undoubtedly the present stage of inquiry is "a moving contour, a change not quite completed." The spirit of Wallace Stevens is the spirit described in the tenth section of **"An Ordinary Evening in New Haven":** "It resides / In a permanence composed of impermanence." This is as it should be in one whose thought has metamorphosis at its heart. A mosaic of a man, even a major artist, is like a mosaic of the weather; in the very fluidity of both there is permanence of a sort. . . . Yet, like the weather, a man can only be described from day to day. (pp. 248-52)

> Sister M. Bernetta Quinn, O.S.F., "Metamorphosis in Wallace Stevens," in The Sewanee Review (reprinted by permission of the editor; © 1952, copyright renewed © 1980, by The University of the South), Vol. LX, No. 2, Spring, 1952, pp. 230-52.

RICHARD ELLMANN   (essay date 1957)

[Ellmann is the author of the definitive biography of James Joyce. He has also written widely on early twentieth-century Irish literature, most notably on William Butler Yeats and Oscar Wilde. In the following excerpt, Ellmann discusses the role that death plays in Stevens's poetic vision.]

In contemplating the poetry written by executives of large insurance companies, it is hard not to be curious about their treatment of the great fact of death upon which their ample livelihood depends. Lugubrious as the subject is, it offers a way into the obliquities of Wallace Stevens. Death appears importunately several times in Stevens' first volume, **Harmonium,** and less frequently thereafter, but a better beginning is his early play, **"Three Travellers Watch a Sunrise,"** because in it the principal bit of stage property is a corpse. It is the corpse of a dead lover, murdered by his girl's father; and the question in the play is how the three Chinese travelers, who have come out to watch the sunrise and not to look at corpses, will take the discovery of the body. It soon becomes apparent that they do not mind it a bit; they sympathize with the grief-stricken girl, but the corpse itself they treat as one more matter to be included in their surveyal of the scene. The sun, they say, will shine on the corpse as on another new thing. . . . (pp. 203-04)

They have no horror of death and no fear of it; but rather take it as part of some larger order which they have long since learned to accept as essential. The green of life and the red of grief or death are both preferable to blackness. The sun shines not indifferently but intimately upon death as upon life. A corpse contributes to the variety of the landscape. Probably Stevens put this point of view, which is his own, into the mouths of three Chinese because it seemed to him vaguely oriental. But his setting is not China but Eastern Pennsylvania, his Chinese are Chinese Americans, and we would be wrong to follow his equivocal hint in assuming that he advocates that the West accept the acceptance of the East.

If we look at his poems about death, we will find that he has decisive personal views about it. The early poems are even a little truculent. In **"The Death of a Soldier,"** he tells us that the soldier "does not become a three-days personage, / Imposing his separation, / Calling for pomp," and in **"Cortège for Rosenbloom,"** a more difficult poem, he defends the view of death which he has labeled Chinese by challenging its opposite, by challenging, that is, the notion that death is something apart and isolated. The ceremony of conventional mourning, its stilted decorum, its withdrawal of the dead man from the natural world, its figmental afterlife, are all satirized here. *Que faites-vous dans cè galère,* what are *you* doing in this mortician's heaven? the poet seems to be asking "the wry Rosenbloom" whose body is so absurdly apotheosized. The name of Rosenbloom suggests both an ordinary man and someone who springs like a flower out of nature and should not be separated from it. . . . The mourners [at Rosenbloom's fu-

neral] are infants because their concepts of man are undeveloped and founded on a dislike of man's real nature; hence they love their extrahuman illusions. . . . The real nature of man, Stevens is suggesting to us, is comprehended only in terms of an adult, human culture; Rosenbloom himself is an intense poem, is strictest prose, and prose and poetry are set against infants and insects. No wonder the mourners jumble the essence of Rosenbloom. This cortège, then, in the simplest terms, is the wrong way to conduct a funeral. What is the right way? **"The Emperor of Ice-Cream"** is the right way. Here the poet is hortatory, not descriptive, and his tone is buoyant and defiant. It defies the mourners of Rosenbloom, who would like to treat this corpse with the usual ceremony, but the poet will have none of their services. Instead he summons the living, and, to emphasize his point, he makes clear that everyone living is welcome, and especially those who proceed by nature with scant ceremony; this time the season is summer, as favored in Stevens' verse as winter is disfavored. . . . The way to treat death is to wear ordinary clothes, not turbans or boots of fur. It is to whip up some ice-cream in the kitchen, not to be finical; it is to spread flowers, not to toll the bell or ululate. Death, as we learned from the Chinese, is not horrible. The horny feet may protrude, and if they do, it is just as well. Do not call the embalmers. "Let be be finale of seem"—that is, away with the panoply of empty conventional mourning and empty conventional myths of death and afterlife. Let us accept being, which like the sun's rays comprehends death with life.

The last battlement before us is the line, "The only emperor is the emperor of ice-cream." There are two going interpretations of this line, one that the emperor is life, the other that he is death. When Stevens was informed of this difference of critical opinion, he said, in effect, "So much the better!" and refused to judge between them. If we take the emperor to be life, and the poet's whole sympathy to be with the living, then why does the poem deal so precisely and deliberately with the corpse in the second stanza? Why not push it out of the way instead of displaying it? And can a wake, even an ice-cream wake, be completely detached from death? On the other hand, if the emperor is to be identified with death, why bring in the cigar-rolling, ice-cream-mixing muscular man? Is concupiscence desirable at funerals?

I think we may reach a little nearer if we remember that the characteristics of ice-cream are that it is tasty, transitory, and cold. Life may be tasty and perishable, but it is not cold. Death may be cold but scarcely transitory, unless we assume that Stevens believes in an afterlife, which he doesn't, or tasty, unless we assume he has a death-wish, which he doesn't. Whoever the emperor is, he is realer than the run-of-the-mill emperors, the kaisers and Erlkönige, and his domain seems to include both life and death. The coldness of ice-cream suggests the corpse, as its sweetness suggests life's concupiscence. Stevens has said that his only daughter had a superlative liking for ice-cream, and is reported to have said also that she asked him to write a poem about it. Whether she did or not, there is a childlike quality about the poem—its absence of taboo, its complete, simultaneous, unruffled acceptance of conventional contraries—party food and horny feet. The child examines both without distaste. Both are included in the imperial domain. Ice-cream, then, is death and life.

But we must not think of death and life as a dual monarchy loosely joined by an indifferent ruler. The emperor is more than his ice-cream empire; he is the force that inspires and makes it one. Here again I call Stevens for my rather uncommunicative witness. He commented of the poem that it contained something of the essential gaudiness of poetry; this gaudiness must affect our estimate of the emperor. It is the more appropriate when we remember that in the poem **"Metaphor as Degeneration,"** Stevens asserts that *being* includes death and the imagination. My candidate for the emperor of ice-cream, then, is the force of being, understood as including life, death, and the imagination which plays in this poem so gustily upon both. The emperor creates ice-cream, expresses himself through death and life, conceives of them as a unity, and is immanent in both of them.

If the volume *Harmonium* has an integrating theme, it is this deliberate acceptance of death with life. Stevens will have none of heaven or immortality; these fictions, always of questionable value, are worn through. In both **"Sunday Morning"** and **"Le Monocle de Mon Oncle"** Stevens endeavors to show just what place death has in being. The first is an argument with a woman who, on Sunday morning, is prompted to think of Christ's sacrificial death and of the heaven which Christ opened to man by dying for him. The poet asks, "Why should she give her bounty to the dead?" and calls to her mind the beauty of the landscape. . . . The threat of something contrary to love, of obliteration, is what gives love its force. If there were no door there would be no room, but we are interested in the room, not the door. Then the poet mocks heaven and its attempt to abstract life from being and leave death behind. . . . It is in the context of death that we see our earthly mothers of beauty—our loves, who are waiting sleeplessly because, like the heroine, they are anxious with the problem of perishability. . . . Here, in more mellifluous phrases, are the same elements as in **"The Emperor of Ice-Cream"**; the men are supple, in the other poem muscular; here they are turbulent, boisterous, in orgy, there they are eaters of concupiscent curds. The sun to which they chant cannot be taken only as the power which creates life, for Stevens emphasizes that the singers are men who perish like dew; it has to be also the power that moves in death. Let us say tentatively that it is what Dylan Thomas calls the force that through the green fuse drives the flower and blasts the roots of trees. Here we not only accept being, we worship it. And because life is such a good thing, death, upon which it depends, must be a good thing too. But death is only a small part of being; instead of speaking of life and death as if they were equals, we might speak of a god whose death is no more than a cue for his instant rebirth.

Stevens returns to the problem of death in another fine poem in *Harmonium*, **"Le Monocle de Mon Oncle."** It is characteristic of this poet, who wrote English as if it were French (just as Carlyle wrote English as if it were German), that he puts his most serious thoughts into a courtly dialogue between a man and a woman. . . . We have to imagine the dialogue as beginning before the poem starts, when the woman, having left her bed with her hair in disarray, says to the poet that now that she is middle-aged there is *nothing* left for her but old age and death and after that, she hopes, heaven—that starry *connaissance* for lovers once young. The problem of the poem then is to win her over to accepting death and denying an afterlife. The speaker begins by associating himself with her feeling of age and regret, but ends by insisting that we should concern ourselves, even in old age, with life rather than with death. . . . For earth's honey, like ice-cream, is vested in perishability. He next establishes that life and love continue even though individuals depart, and finally demonstrates that life, which has offered strong passions to the young, offers to the aged the power to value its ephemeral, perishing moments.

In his later poetry Stevens continues his efforts to make death subordinate to life. His attitude does not alter, but his emphasis in later poems falls less on rebuking others for erroneous ideas of death than on attempting to portray his own idea. He endeavors to find a picture of death which will not terrify us and will not separate it from life. Some of these treatments of death, such as **"The Owl in the Sarcophagus,"** where he finds death to be made up of three modern mythological personages—peace, sleep, and memory; **"The Airman's Death,"** where the airman sinks into a profound emptiness which yet is somehow made close and a part of us; and **"Burghers of Petty Death,"** where actual death seems a little thing beside the feeling of death that sometimes pervades the mind, are not so seductive as his early arguments. In **"Esthétique du Mal,"** Stevens tries in the seventh section to come to grips with the problem entirely in pictorial form, and this poem is more winning. Like **"Cortège for Rosenbloom,"** it begins by anchoring the hero in nature like a rose. . . . (pp. 204-16)

This death is deathless in the sense that it is close to nature, close to life, close to the community of men living and men dead. It has nothing to do with the great looming abstraction of capitalized Death. The woman smoothing her hair [in the fourth stanza] might seem altogether detached from the soldier, but the soldier has never left the living and her gesture is a part of his being. This conception begins with the physical nearness of living and dead, but implies a metaphysical bond as well.

In Stevens' later verse there are many suggestions that death is what we make of it. **"Madame la Fleurie"** is a poem about a man who read horror into nature, and instead of seeing her as a lady with flowers conceived of her as a bearded queen, wicked in her dead light. He died in this falsification, and the result is that there are no blue jays for him to remember, now that he is dead; he is not like the soldier whose death is merely an extension, in a different tempo, of his life.

I suggested earlier that to Stevens the sun is the primal force which, as in Dylan Thomas, creates and destroys. I think we should correct this now to indicate that the destructive force is much less important for Stevens than for Thomas, that they are nearly opposites. For in Thomas, who sees the body as a shroud, and life as either a rapturous ignorance of death or a knowing horror of it, the main revelation is that death pervades life, while in Stevens it is that life pervades death. In Thomas the glory of life is stolen from death. Stevens' vision, for it is almost that, is of living and unliving—a term which seems closer to his ideas than dead—men joined together in admiration, whether vocal or mute, of being. Being is the great poem, and all our lesser poems only approximate its intensity and power.

The sun is this primal force of being, reflected alike by living and unliving, by people and by things. Our dualisms disguise their single origin. It can be called God or the Imagination (**"Final Soliloquy of the Interior Paramour"**), though these terms are also only metaphors for what is ultimately a mystery to be worshiped rather than fathomed. The beauty that the sun creates antedates human life; long before we came on the earth the sun was covering the rock of reality with leaves, but once arrived here, we too participate in it. The sun is the Ulysses to which we and the world are the faithful Penelope. Its force is constant, and anchors in repetition all the changes which occur in the world, as the everchanging gleams of sunshine stem always from the same burning source. It is bodiless, unreal in that sense, yet it fills bodies with light and inspirits them.

"It is the ever-never-changing-same," Stevens writes in **"Adult Epigram,"** and elsewhere he says it is the will to change which underlies all changes. We are, he writes in **"An Ordinary Evening in New Haven,"** in a permanence composed of impermanence.

Many of Stevens' poems can be read as accounts of the interaction of imagination and reality, but they have a theme which underlies that. **"Peter Quince at the Clavier,"** for instance, seems to be about an Abt Vogler building up a mountain of music from a few hints in experience, but the theme which was, I think, even more important to Stevens, is summarized in the lines,

> The body dies; the body's beauty lives.
> So gardens die, in their green going,
> A wave, interminably flowing.

The wave is a frequent metaphor for the force elsewhere saluted as the sun. As Stevens says in one of his essays, "A wave is a force and not the water of which it is composed, which is never the same." Sometimes he epitomizes this force as a river called Swatara, or simply as an unnamed river in Connecticut that flows nowhere like the sea; sometimes it is a changing giant (**"Things of August"**), sometimes a bodiless serpent (**"St. John and the Back-Ache," "The Auroras of Autumn"**). But the force can also be found in a creature like the blackbird in **"Thirteen Ways of Looking at a Blackbird,"** a poem which we would be well advised to read not as a declaration that there are thirteen ways of looking at a blackbird but that there is a blackbird behind all these impressions. I do not think it has been remarked that Stevens is unsympathetic to only one of the thirteen ways, Number XI, in which the protagonist is not "I" but "He." . . . The error of the man in the glass coach—and glass is almost always a bar to sight in Stevens' poems—is that he sees the blackbird merely as death; the further proof of his error is that he has *not* seen the blackbird, has seen only his own dark mind, the shadow of his equipage. And so, like the man in **"Madame la Fleurie,"** he abstracts the blackbird from nature and sees only fear in it.

Most of Stevens' poems are based upon images which somehow participate in this primal force of being, and it is the existence of the force in them that he is concerned to demonstrate. The sense of **"The Worms at Heaven's Gate"** is almost destroyed by its isolation in anthologies, where it seems to mean that the sardonic worms are handing up bits of a corpse with ironic comments on their deterioration. For Stevens the beauty does continue, it survives corruption, and the worms, not sardonic at all, can only talk of beauty, not of death.

In the individual person, the self, as Stevens says in **"The Plant on the Table,"** is the sun. This self should be dominated by the imagination, a solar light within the mind. In expressing our imagination we express the force of being. But in the individual man the light may be deflected. The imagination may look not upon the rest of being, but only upon itself; so, like Chieftain Iffucan, it may disparage the world of nature, or, like the other bantam in pine woods, solipsistically fail to recognize that we are all parts of a common world and bound together by the shared light of the sun. The danger of such narcissism is that it leads to empty hallucinations, such as that denial of being which is heaven, that denial of beauty which is modern religion, that denial of the imagination which is reason, that denial of life which is nostalgia. The trouble with all these is that they are petrifying, they produce bad statues instead of men, the creative fire is thwarted in them. The

imagination should queen it over the mind, with reason as her obsequious butler and memory as her underpaid maid-of-all-work. But she must always see the teeming earth, not the empty sky, as her domain. If she doesn't, the world becomes fixed and inert instead of malleable and suffusable. The imagination is constantly reshaping and reforming reality; it is not the poet's exclusive preserve—everyone has it—but the poet uses it more steadily and powerfully and with more recognition of its value. It is the imagination, like the sun, which keeps the world from being black. Memory and reason can aid instead of impeding it, by confirming the imagination's felt bond with all existence.

We can see why Stevens' poetry is so different from that of Eliot. Although Stevens occasionally takes note of our age as a leaden time, this is not at all a principal theme. In no sense does Stevens sigh for lost beliefs; rather he is elated that old hallucinations are over now so that the imagination can get a fresh start. They have prevented us from living in the physical world, and the great poverty for man is not to live there. The major man—Stevens' modest version of the superman—is the man who brings most sunlight to most rock, most imagination to most reality, and is closest to the primal force.

Although there is an obvious similarity between Stevens and Yeats in that they both worship in the church of the imagination, Stevens conceives of the primal force as existing independent of man and prior to him, while Yeats often suggests that it begins with man and is altogether human. In Stevens the imagination is impersonal and anonymous; it reminds us of Ortega y Gasset's contention that much modern art is dehumanized; but for Yeats the imagination works always through proper names. I find, more brashly, a second imperfect parallel in Stevens and his fellow American, the muscular one, Ernest Hemingway. When we think of Hemingway's stories about death, and particularly of "The Snows of Kilimanjaro," what strikes us is that the rather ignoble hero is given in the end a noble hero's death, and for a moment we may be baffled and ask why this man who has made such a mess of his talents and of his marriages should be treated by his creator so well. It is because, with all his defects, he has remained true to his eye; the great virtue in Hemingway is not to live the good life, but to see, as the great virtue in Stevens is to imagine. Even if the hero of "The Snows" has not done anything else, he has seen, and so mastered reality. In Wallace Stevens, the soldier, wounded also by life, is also saved by what he has found in it. Death, in both Stevens and Hemingway, comes beneficently to those who have expressed the primal force of vision, who have lived in the sun.

Most of Stevens' poetry is an essay in the intricacies of contentment, the mind and nature conspiring to render more lovely and awesome the force of being. There are sensual poems about plums, and philosophical poems about the mind's embrace of the plum, and a few, but only a few, poems about plumlessness, a state which depends upon plums for recognition. Stevens objects to those poets who make their pleas to the night bird, who dwell upon discontent. His interest in grief, anger, and other unpleasant emotions is cursory. He does not evade tragedy, but he does not regard it as very important. An atmosphere of elation pervades his work as he surveys the marvels of the world; he insures us against death by assigning it so minor and integral a place in being. He is too fascinated by the endless procession of beauties to pay much mind to the retirements of particular individuals. He confronts us with a table of fragrancies and succulencies, solemnly reminds us that all of these, like us, are islanded between the nothingness that precedes form and the rot that ends it, and then urges us to fall to. (pp. 216-22)

> *Richard Ellmann, "Wallace Stevens' Ice Cream" (copyright © 1957 by Richard Ellmann; reprinted by permission of the author), in* The Kenyon Review, *Vol. XIX, No. 1, Winter, 1957 (and reprinted in* Aspects of American Poetry, *edited by Richard M. Ludwig, Ohio State University Press, 1962, pp. 203-22).*

JOHN CROWE RANSOM   (essay date 1964)

[*An American critic, poet, and editor, Ransom is considered one of the most influential literary theorists of the twentieth century. Consistently in the vanguard of American scholarship, he began his career—with Robert Penn Warren, Donald Davidson, Allen Tate, and several others—as a member of the Fugitive group of Southern poets during the 1920s. The stated intent of the Fugitives was to create a literature utilizing the best qualities of modern and traditional art. Ransom regularly published poetry in the group's now-famous periodical* The Fugitive *(1922-1925), which he cofounded. After 1928, the four major Fugitives joined eight other writers, including Stark Young and John Gould Fletcher, to form the Agrarians, a group dedicated to preserving the Southern way of life and traditional Southern values. The Agrarians were concerned with social and political issues as well as literature; in particular, they attacked Northern industrialism and sought to preserve the Southern agricultural economy. In 1930, Ransom wrote the definitive "Statement of Principles" for the Agrarian anthology* I'll Take My Stand, *arguing for the South's return to a farming culture. A longtime professor of English at Vanderbilt University, Ransom left the South for Ohio in 1937, assuming the post of Professor of Poetry at Kenyon College. There, he founded and edited* The Kenyon Review, *a quarterly journal to which he attracted major contributors and himself contributed essays which evidence his unique critical theories and his drift from Agrarianism. Ransom is credited with originating the term "New Criticism," which forms the title of his most important work, published in 1941. Examining the critical theories of T. S. Eliot, I. A. Richards, and William Empson, Ransom proposed, in* The New Criticism, *a close reading of poetic texts and insisted that criticism should be based on a study of the structure and texture of a given poem, not its content. A pioneering New Critic, Ransom had many peers and successors in the movement, notably Warren, Tate, R. P. Blackmur, and Cleanth Brooks, who applied the criteria of New Criticism to prose as well as poetry. Although the various New Critics did not subscribe to a single set of principles, all believed that a work of literature had to be examined as an object in itself through a process of close analysis of symbol, image, and metaphor. For the New Critics, a literary work was not a manifestation of ethics, sociology, or psychology, and could not be evaluated in the general terms of any nonliterary discipline. In* The New Criticism, *Ransom outlined a system of critical thought that dominated the American academic scene for nearly three decades. In the excerpt below, Ransom appreciatively surveys Stevens's career.*]

When Stevens' first book, **Harmonium,** came into my friends' hands and mine, at Nashville in 1923, we did not fail to exclaim excitedly over the emergence of a new poet who spoke as having authority. But it was a phenomenon for which we could not quite make out the forward drift and destination, nor the antecedent history. When informed that an insurance man was the author, we were all the more mystified; we said that he must have two selves, and the second bore no relation to the first. (p. 234)

If we did not see in Stevens' first book his destination as a poet, we saw it sufficiently in his next book ten years later, and increasingly in many books, till we knew that he had put his ideas into order and was satisfied. He is not to be appreciated unless we approach him as a philosophical poet; and, more specifically, as a priest-like poet, who labored long in finding his credo, but then confirmed it and left it for a testament to his successors to inherit and use as they might see fit. (p. 235)

The poems of **Harmonium** number 85 and fill 113 pages; a big first book. The poet turned forty in 1919, but we will allow time for composition and publication. It appears that at about forty he came very suddenly into his poetic maturity. He found himself gifted with a prodigious power of word and phrase; having for his very own a powerful and masculine idiom, which wants never to lapse into sentimental or rhetorical conventions; equal to a thousand occasions, and to the technical forms into which they may be cast.

Since it is a first book it is likely to be a miscellany, and we are apt to suppose that many of the poems must have been written only to exhibit the poet to himself as a virtuoso, exulting in his mastery; not as yet necessarily in possession of his grand theme and program. But we shall see that this disposition of the poems had better not be taken for granted. (p. 237)

One gay and showy poem comes early in the book, and another even more astonishing one comes near the end. The early one is **"The Ordinary Women."** . . . We follow with ravished ears the rush of this narrative, but afterward it is hard to grasp the occasion, and some of the action. These are the Florida women, and there is no local lord to throw open his palace to them. I think the palace must be the fancy night club by the sea; the Sunset Club, or even "The Palace" itself. The women have saved up enough money for the evening, and there they go, in a group. As for the action inside the palace we are probably confused as to where in heaven they decipher a marriage-bed. I can only think of the bright constellation of Cassiopeia on her couch; the faithful wife and over-zealous mother in the Greek mythology. We should not boggle over the women wasting their time staring from bay-windows at the heavens. In Stevens' world the people on a clear night must always look up at the sky; for Stevens is a nature-poet remarkably according to Kant. If the people are indoors they probably import nature into the house by powerful simile and metaphor. (But they must know already the nature they import; it is of prime importance that there be times when nature seems very human. If we say, "King Richard has the heart of a lion," we must already have seen the lion or his picture, or have heard about him, and said of him, "This is the King of the beasts." We will touch on that later.) We shall find few poems in Stevens that leave nature out entirely. But another characteristic of Stevens is his occasional talk about the "ordinary" people; here they are the ordinary women. He does not use this word disparagingly, but affectionately; it means sturdy, natural, and decent.

The other virtuosity is greater than this, and later. It is **"Sea Surface Full of Clouds."** . . . My reader should look for himself at the three sections which belong between these two. The five of them have more identity than difference; in the time and the place, for example, producing the exactly uniform first lines; in the phrasing of analogous lines and tercets, and the order of progression from one to another. The key passages which bear the main burden of the poem seem to be as follows: the kind of chocolate and the kind of umbrellas which the morning light makes upon the deck; then the great question of who performed this miracle of turning the reflected clouds into sea-blooms on the sea, and the poet's ecstatic response in idiomatic French that his own good genius did that; and finally the effect produced when the sky clears and sky and sea take on their heavenly blue. But in the last section the poem breaks down, and the poet replies to the question sadly that it was his evil spirit that figured the scene too clownishly. But still in French; the poet did not like before, and does not like now, to use the first person in his own tongue, but the facile sententious French is very capable. Four times the poet worked his miracle; now his confession is an honest one, and he can afford it. He could not help it: beneath the poet's normal suavity there was always a clown lurking, and he was sure to break out somewhere. Perhaps Stevens had come to the conviction that he could make a proper nature-poem of 100 lines or so about any subject, and then dared himself to make one about chocolate and umbrellas. He came very close.

Now let us take up the topic of . . . the forty-year-old lover [who] undergoes a conversion and becomes the poet.

The poet gives us his own account of the matter in **"Le Monocle de Mon Oncle."** . . . If the title looks like clowning, it comes from a witty clown; it is not too inept. . . . In reading the poem I suggest that the person addressed at the beginning in four celestial phrases having two big nouns each is Queen Venus, incarnated in the Evening Star; and it is at the end of II that he addresses specifically the woman beside him. . . . The rejection of Venus, the election of poetry; the new poet manages his compound situation extremely well. The uncle may now remove his monocle.

But if Venus is the patroness of love, Florida, the land where it is always summer, is the place. There is another poem called **"O Florida, Venereal Soil"** . . . where the place is personified as the temptress. He begins with a stanza about "a few things for themselves," which are hateful features of the place, and continues with one about "the dreadful sundry" who are some of the persons of the place. . . . Florida, like Venus, is rejected; not at once, but later. The first poem of the following book in the **Collected Poems** is **"Farewell to Florida."** . . . Here too are many specified rejections as he stands on the deck of the high ship that is taking him home to winter. . . . (pp. 238-44)

I do not know when Stevens left Florida "for good." But **Harmonium** is all Florida; and many later poems will revert to Florida. (p. 244)

This poet . . . has one negative mission to discharge, and I will finish this section with some poems in which he goes about it. There is a little war he has to make, sometimes gently and sometimes in a rowdy style, for war is a great embarrassment to all our philosophies. He did not like the idea of the resurrection of the body; and that was according to the letter of the orthodoxy of the Christian churches, but not to that of the Synagogue. Stevens conceived his mission first as a mission to the Gentiles.

Now some poems about the finality of death. . . . [In **"The Jack-Rabbit,"**] the countryman knows when he sees a buzzard circling in the sky that the jack-rabbit's time is nearly up, and that his death will be absolute. The grandmother knows that her time is nearly up, for she is already preparing her winding-sheet, and it will be absolute too. The grandmother and the man do not mind speaking of the event for it is "expected." But at least the man shouted to warn the jack-rabbit.

One of the most brutal death-poems, which Stevens thinks sometimes ought to be brutal, is **"The Emperor of Ice-Cream."** . . . That is everybody's poem now, but still worth comment. One of the ordinary women has died. Her women friends set out the body in her best dress, while the men bring flowers and make the ice-cream. They are going to honor her by an all-night wake with suitable refreshments. Who cut the thread of life? They can't say; let them call him the emperor, whose face they never saw. Let the ice-cream be his sign; he gives life and death, but life though it is short is very sweet. "The only emperor is the emperor of ice-cream."

The gentlest and most persuasive and fullest poem among the very many poems which Stevens wrote about death is the famous **"Sunday Morning."** . . . It is also the most perfected and formal poem. (pp. 245-46)

But most poems on this theme come in later books, and most of those are about the deaths of soldiers. Stevens lived through many dreadful wars. The soldier-poem in **Harmonium** is called simply **"The Death of a Soldier."** . . . This is a quite perfect small poem. There will be many others in succeeding books; the reader will have a wide choice. (pp. 246-47)

[By the mid-point of his career] the poet had acquired a devoted following in the universities, and had lectured by invitation before academic audiences; the Extracts [in **"Extracts from Addresses to the Academy of Fine Ideas"**] stand for the Addresses he would have liked to make. But they would have had to be made in his own professional medium of verse; which was hardly to be expected. The rhetoric of the prose platform is much simpler than the rhetoric of poetry, especially if it is Stevens' poetry. (And the Extracts may well be rather more valuable to his readers than any like number of whole addresses.) The members of the imagined Academy of Fine Ideas would have consisted of the Platonists who worship the Pure Idea, and are the religious of the churches, or even the religious who have fallen out of the churches; or the Platonists who are the religious of the Synagogue, or even the religious who have fallen out of the Synagogue, who by virtue of their ancient Scriptures may be called the proto-Platonists, whose God in his second commandment forbade them to make any graven image of him; which by the nature of the case would have been wide of the mark. (pp. 247-48)

In his natural voice [the poet] offers a ruthless display of a poet's way of reasoning, not by making a logical chain of his ideas, but by a simple succession of the oracular or prophetic images which preceded them and contained them. Evidently these Extracts would have been the climactic moments of the Addresses, which as wholes would have been long and consecutive and easy.

I will try to recapitulate briefly in easier language the arguments of the five Extracts; not without believing that some readers will correct me here and there.

In Extract I the Messieurs live in a paper-world, and the paper is—theology; the construction by logic of a world upon which human eye has never lit. In II there is much darting about. The clever Secretary for Porcelain remarks that a catastrophe, or earthquake, though it may cause 10,000 deaths, can be glazed over as easily as a piece of pottery; by referring doubtless to the all-wise dispensations of the Pure Idea. But the poet accuses the academicians of laughing at the primitive eye which cannot see beyond its own world. That laughter is the chief of evils. In III the lean cats of the arches of the churches are the old priests, handsome and presentable as priests can be; but nowadays all men are priests of some sort, and their theologies are hopelessly at variance.

Extract IV astonishes us. It is a complete departure from the sequence of Extracts; a mere anecdote about a natural man, who walked into the land to see if the winter was broken, and who, if he found it so, would be back in his own proper and jubilant self. It is a nature-piece, and for an opulent poet it is a masterpiece in one unusual respect: it has not chosen one single ornament of language, one single figure of speech, to furbish its simple recital. It will serve by way of a small intermission as the poet-evangelist's anecdote of Everyman comforting his own spirit.

But Extract V is one long metaphor which amounts to a parable. The disputes of the four or five or six evangelists are turned into a TV Western show, where they become assassins and shoot each other down until only one remains standing. It brings our series of Extracts to a climax, so that I thought I could stop the exhibit there. The survivor is the poet-evangelist. But even after the shooting there is something strange; a quirk in his mind which it is altogether honest for him to confess. Even now, even in himself, there stirs this "singular romance, / This warmth in the blood-world for the pure idea." Nevertheless his proper song is of the visible glories of his own world, and the people like that song the best. (pp. 251-52)

Why does Stevens so often express an antipathy to the churches and priests? I suggest that Stevens, unlike most men, was fully and professionally committed to two economies already, and could spare no further time and strength for another one. But, if we should have to define his philosophical views on the whole, he would be a philosophical naturalist, perhaps a logical positivist; yet well acquainted as a healthy natural man with the moral imperative and willing to let it manage for itself. Finally, he did not approve the supernatural sanctions which the churches asserted, that is, the heaven or hell hereafter, though with increasing latitude of conviction; which had to be based upon the human images that they bestowed upon the unknown Pure Idea. He was entirely with Kant in this last view.

Before he finished, Stevens abandoned his feud with the churches. There is none of it in his last book, *The Rock,* incorporated in the *Collected Poems* of 1954 without previous publication. On the contrary there is the poem **"To an Old Philosopher in Rome,"** . . . where with perfect sympathy he addresses George Santayana, the lifelong philosophical naturalist who had nevertheless chosen to spend his last years in the Holy City. (pp. 253-54)

"Notes Toward a Supreme Fiction" . . . is the title of what must be Stevens' masterpiece as a philosophical poem. He is a philosopher who never stops being a poet. He employs two strategies, though they are likely to merge into each other before we know it. Never less than prodigal in the evocation of spectacular images or situations, he develops them in extended passages of almost pure poetry scarcely soiled by argumentative terms; all the same, they embody and objectify the argument. But even when he resorts to argument he is witty, or he is eloquent; able to play with the argument because his terms have more than single denotations. They exceed their logical functions, and their excess means that they are trying to secure a better footing in the world of the particulars. (p. 256)

The argument of the poem is clear. It has three uniform parts, with subdivisions, amounting to 210 lines for each part, the whole poem coming to 630 lines, plus a short dedication and an epilogue. The first part has for its title IT MUST BE ABSTRACT; it must state the general truth, the universal idea or concept of a poem. Then, IT MUST CHANGE, meaning that it must define the idea each separate time in fresh sensible terms, in justice to the fertility of the poet's mind and the infinity of the natural appearances. (The major man or major poet is he "that of repetition is most master." He never repeats under the same forms.) Finally, IT MUST GIVE PLEASURE, and the pleasure will not be from the satisfaction of the bodily needs and appetites (and will not belong to the first economy), nor will it come from the moral satisfaction (nor belong to the second economy). Its unique pleasure is nothing less than an ecstatic and all-pervading joy, which seems absolute and unqualified. (pp. 257-58)

The faith of Stevens is an aesthetic faith, not a theological faith, if it manages without the giant; whom we should identify with the God or First Idea who in order to objectify Himself created nature, and finally mankind. Man is the one conscious and responsible creature, and the responsibility laid upon him was to keep his Creator's commandments.

Now it is impossible not to be aware that Stevens was perfectly familiar with the poetry and faith of Walt Whitman, who in his turn was familiar with the transcendental philosopher Emerson, who thereby became the mediator between his own mentor Kant and the poet Whitman. Stevens and Whitman have a loose identity. Stevens' method of argument was like Whitman's method, to proceed by trailing a vast succession of images after him such as could never have got into the intellectual processes of Kant's philosophy. But Stevens' sequences are far more careful and articulate than Whitman's; and his technique as a poet compares with Whitman's as a finished and subtle art compares with a primitive art, and he does not lend himself to social schemes. (pp. 258-59)

There are certain chosen and thematic natural objects which occur again and again in Stevens' verse. I used to think of them as his God-images; they seemed to come to mind always as supernatural providences which were tonic when one's courage was draining away, or comforting when one was weary and disconsolate. They are images of objects in one's world which are specially revered, and possessed, and reverted to, as symbols of the healing power of the natural world.

There are two such objects in Stevens, each celebrated in many passages and poems. One is the sun, and the other is the rock. On the whole, the sun was the symbol chosen from the skies and weathers of Florida when that was the poet's element. The great rock was the usual symbol when New England became his element. (pp. 259-60)

In the middle of his seventies the poet and the poetry had to come to a close. The last book is almost perfectly serene; the jocosity is gone, and even the wit has nearly passed. (p. 263)

He did, however, in a roundabout manner deliver an epilogue; a modest one, titled **"The Planet on the Table,"** . . . which he wanted to utter at the end of his formidable book. It is in the third person, but it would tell what Ariel had spoken in effect. In Shakespeare's play, Ariel is designated as an airy spirit. Prospero is his master in some sense, a man of large and pressing affairs, like the ego or primary self in Stevens' own personality; and Ariel is the younger or alter ego, who sings at Prospero's bidding. It is not quite the relation of Stevens' own two selves. Yet it is the fact that Stevens the poet was invited in 1954, a year before his death, to spend the following academic year at Harvard delivering the Norton Lectures; but the businessman in Stevens was persistent in not wanting to be betrayed, and the poet did not really want to destroy his blood-brother, and declined the invitation. (p. 264)

John Crowe Ransom, "The Planetary Poet," in The Kenyon Review *(copyright 1964 by Kenyon College), Vol. XXVI, No. 1, Winter, 1964, pp. 233-64.*

HENRY W. WELLS (essay date 1964)

[Wells's essay discusses the originality of Stevens's poetry. Wells points out that while Stevens belonged to no school of poetics, he nonetheless achieved what many of them merely proclaimed: the creation of a new language and style for verse.]

It would be hard to exaggerate the unusual position occupied by Wallace Stevens in American poetry. Although he won for himself a high place in our literature during the years that witnessed the appearance of many eminent names in verse—Frost, Robinson, Eliot, Pound, Crane, Williams, and, possibly in a lower category, Elinor Wylie, Robinson Jeffers, E. E. Cummings, Allen Tate, Karl Shapiro, and a host of others—he belonged to no group and defied classification. Although it is clear that he knew English poetic rhetoric from Shakespeare to the present, that he possessed an intimate knowledge of French verse and had some command of the general field of European literature, none of his own writing is in the least imitative. Little in the earlier American poets influenced his own art, though he was much influenced by American thought and culture. His creative mind asserted itself in striking individuality and a rare degree of independence. (p. 3)

The most casual glance at his pages shows that he possesses rare qualities. Though he by no means flaunts eccentricity or oddity of style and thought, as does that excellent poet, E. E. Cummings, likewise a New Englander with fresh turns of mind, Stevens' originality proves notably quiet and profound. He does not to any extent worth serious mention tease the bourgeoisie, after the manner of the American Bohemians or the European avant-garde, nor formally declare a new era in poetry, as do Eliot or Pound. He proposes no new laws for others; he merely cultivates new and fastidious standards for himself. It is not for any mannerisms that he is chiefly known, though, for example, the witty and often self-deprecatory titles chosen for his poems might be thought to reveal a mannerism. His originality runs much deeper than that.

Perhaps more than any other American poet of his times, he insists on the importance of intellectual thought in poetry and writes accordingly. Another of his leading principles of composition is compactness or "density" of expression, though this all-important principle in his writing he silently assumes and almost never mentions in his own critical observations. In his poetry is a maximum use of metaphor, symbolism, and general compactness; from this chiefly derives the "difficulty" of his expression. In a quiet way, to a degree exhibited by no other poet of his period, he affects what others proclaim: the creation of a new style or "language" for verse, one almost as far removed from the general idiom of communication as possible, although very frank, terse, and direct expressions, quite unrhetorical and unadorned and by no means uncolloquial, are occasionally found as one of the many features of his style. He is more thoughtful, imaginative, and elegant, not to mention eloquent, than most or possibly any of his contemporaries. Making understanding still more difficult, his works rise from his moods as well as from his mind and tongue and hence the reader of any of his poems must first of all discern by intuition and a sympathetic reading what the mood of any

of his pieces may be. If from one point of view the poems are philosophical essays, from another they resemble musical compositions. They call for an approach that, if not essentially new, must nevertheless seem both fresh and somewhat elusive to the great majority of his readers and even to those best prepared to meet him on his own shifting grounds.

Stevens' works pose many problems and hand no ready key to his readers. Their variegated surface notwithstanding, they present a remarkably organic body of writing, from his earliest years to his last; few poems or pages of poems could be mistaken for those from another hand. To an exceptional degree certain thoughts and attitudes recur and even a fair number of symbols used in a personal manner are to be found. Occasionally one of his poems explicitly refers to another. The chief difficulty presented is not, however, a private or esoteric system but, on the contrary, that he is not a systematic thinker. Hence no formula guides us through the luxuriant labyrinth of his art and the paradoxes of his irony. A born ironist, he repeatedly writes poems that seem to contradict each other. He can be tragic or comic, grave or witty, gentle or harsh, sweet or acidulous, conservative or radical. His moods are almost Shakespearean in their infinite variety. Since many readers rely more than they are probably willing to admit on presuppositions, they find Stevens baffling: he confuses them for the really irrelevant reason that they cannot place him. This is as he should be, not as they should be. The explanation is simply that he is too large to be pocketed or pigeonholed. He writes with complete integrity, for the enlargement of his reader's heart, mind, and pleasure, not for the convenience of his reviewers, critics, or apologists.

In one highly important respect Stevens must seem not only elusive but virtually deceptive. In this regard, too, a prejudice may easily be formed. If his own repeated statements in his poems themselves are weighed literally and on their face value, it may appear that he is not the astonishingly versatile genius and free-playing mind which in actuality he is, but rather a narrow spirit chained to a single obsession. Much the greater part of his verse is to an important degree poetry about poetry. To such an extent does this aesthetic problem loom over him that it is not unfair to say that he writes poetry under an emotional compulsion which is also an intellectual compulsion: a need to explore the thesis that art is a supreme manner of grappling with reality. Stevens' mind is haunted by this metaphysical problem. . . . Such speculation by the intelligent and dedicated artist is certainly rationally justified. He seeks a rationale for his work, a mystique to warrant it in his own eyes. Most artists have had some warrant for their work at hand, as Shakespeare's lines on drama and acting, put into the mouth of Hamlet, so well indicate. But to be so far obsessed with this outlook that a large, possibly the largest, part of a poet's work grapples specifically with the subject, seems a species of mental and spiritual inversion, an almost incestuous relation between the poet and his productions. It suggests that he overlooks his audience, who have no such professional orientation, and speaks in soliloquy with himself. The condition looks unwholesome but insofar as it casts a blemish on Stevens' work, his times must share a part of the blame.

This is a very common condition in modern poetry. . . . Ezra Pound is forever pounding us with his ideas of art. T. S. Eliot's *Four Quartets* has art in its title and "the word" proves a large part of its subject matter. . . . The subject threatens endlessness. Its explanation is, doubtless, a virtually inescapable condition confronting the modern poet, self-conscious in his isolation from the general public, persuaded that he must carry the burden which theology has so recently laid aside, aware that he is talking in a new language by no means that of the market-place, and that he must in some measure justify his seeming eccentricity and explain to the masses of men, or even to his colleagues or to himself, what he is doing.

With Stevens the incentives seem even deeper than those indicated thus far. To all appearances he was born both a poet and a philosopher in aesthetics. Born, so to speak, a conjoined twin, he found himself in a difficult and occasionally embarrassing position. His poetry at times grew too philosophical and lost its spontaneity; his philosophy at times grew too vague and lost its cutting, rational edge. Divided within himself, he was all the more human in that he was not altogether a happy man. Here it must be added that finicky and almost affected as some of his early pervfervid rhetoric appears, he is, in fact, one of the most lusty, robust, and firm-grained writers in American literature, and perhaps the most gifted of all in expressing the joy of life. His thought can be either deeply comic or tragic. But a great streak, running bias like a fault over a face of rock, appears as a gash across his soul.

It should be remembered, however, that other poets, possibly greater than he, show such disproportion and disfeaturing. Undoubtedly Lucretius was a man haunted by an obsession, as fanatic in urging his atomic theory of the universe as Stevens in urging his metaphysical theories of art and imagination. The artist so conditioned is not invariably thwarted by his bias, though the man is almost always in some degree wounded. It may provide an irresistible impulse to composition, a fervor that the poet must at times share with the priest. For a lifetime Stevens was engaged in his priestly task of expounding the relations of art and reality. Of course it cannot be said that he solved the basic problems or even brought them into clear focus. But it can emphatically be said that in the course of his dedicated quest he created some of the finest poetry written in our century. His compulsion resembles the stem of a tree, his achievements in poetry may be likened to its fruits and flowers. . . . Here lies one of the major problems for his careful reader. Overimpressed by Stevens' own description of his poems as essays in the theory of poetry, the reader too easily minimizes or even overlooks his deep humanity and comprehensive outlook on many phases of life that proliferate from this hard and at times almost repellent stem. The reader may well be unaccustomed to these conditions. He must, however, become at home with them if he is to begin the serious study and keener enjoyment of Stevens' poems. (pp. 4-8)

The forms which [Stevens'] poetry assumes and the thoughts which it contains call for general comment; the poetry does not as a rule invite elucidation of detail. The scrutiny must, to be sure, be exceedingly close, often to an almost microscopic degree, but general conclusions, not masses of information, can alone throw light of any consequence upon the values of his art. . . . The problem is as unlike a crossword puzzle as possible; it is a question of style, psychology, habits of thought. (p. 10)

There are, perhaps, only a half dozen instances in all Stevens' works where a critic would seriously care to raise the question of possible pedantry, willful obscurity, or an artless personalism in allusions. Sometimes Stevens employs a proper name in a poem or title that might almost as well have been any other name. "From Havre to Hartford," he wrote once; but another French city would have done almost as well. The location of Havre probably weighs less with him than the allit-

eration. With a meticulous instinct for his art, he usually constructs each poem in such a manner that it shall be a self-explanatory microcosm. The exposition will presumably lie not upon the surface but within the framework of the poem. . . . Hard thought and a strenuous imagination are needed to extract the riches from Stevens' mines. The language may possibly appear dark in its imaginative style, but not to any serious degree in respect to its allusions or semantics. (pp. 11-12)

Stevens' strong personal characteristics notwithstanding, he must, I think, be commended for a greater scope than that of T. S. Eliot, dominated by the opposing spirits of frustration and reconciliation, or that of W. B. Yeats, with his gyres, his violence, and his antitheses, or Edith Sitwell, with her masks of fantasy and devotion. In elegance he is unsurpassed. (pp. 17-18)

> *Henry W. Wells, in his* Introduction to Wallace Stevens *(copyright © 1963 by Indiana University Press), Indiana University Press, 1964, 218 p.*

JOHN J. ENCK (essay date 1964)

[*Enck discusses the underlying philosophical system of Stevens's work. He states that unlike other philosophical systems, Stevens's has no validity outside the poetic universe—but "within it seems to have supplied him a system of faculties." Many of Enck's comments on the role of the imagination in Stevens's work are similar to the conclusions reached by Sister M. Bernette Quinn, O.S.F. (see excerpt above), and Ronald Sukenick (see excerpt below).*]

[Stevens's] fully evolved outlook does have a coherence. Its validity hardly matters outside his poetic universe; within it, it seems to have supplied him a system of faculties. He rarely indulges in the philosophic method: generalization, logic, fullness, and universality. Rather, he resembles the essayist who sketches his opinions graciously as personal preferences. This manner excuses him from rectifying inconsistencies, which worry him little, and tolerates manipulating subtly his preferred, granted rather simple and old-fashioned, opposites from the anecdotes to the late poems. For him, then, man's non-physical faculties constitute one side and the physical world, including man's body, the other. Such a scheme does not terminate in a vicious dualism. One might arrange these two areas on a scale which implies degrees of evolution but not necessarily values. (The terms are not always Stevens'.)

[Logic]

Thinking	Order
Imaginative	Things
Practical	Quotidian
Subhuman	Rock

[Skeleton]

Communication between these areas varies, and sometimes, it seems, messages get through to the wrong level. Also, he arrived at such a division gradually; although the full diagram should apply to **"The Rock,"** only a segment describes *Harmonium*. Ideally, it works in the following way.

The column on the right causes slight difficulty. The rock consists of matter, nearly undifferentiated, intractable, almost unformed, a needed base, a blank substance which subsumes the rest. It may correspond with similar materials in the philosophies of Plato and Plotinum, although Stevens imposes no moral judgments upon it. The quotidian consists of items handled daily for commerce or secondary pleasures or just to keep one alive. It covers red cherry pie in a restaurant, birds and animals, an insurance policy, or an exploding bomb. The quotidian substances have no intrinsic value, although excessive prices may be put upon fashionable ones because they can symbolize nearly anything. In the social world they are prized for what they will accomplish, and this condition extends to people when treated as anything other than ends. Many of these very items can escape from use and exist by themselves or in a proper company of their species. They may then become things and exhibit truly poetic characteristics. Things range from a blackbird across (not up or down) to the fictive hero, from a dead soldier to an idea. Order belongs to the laws, not quite empirical, upon which the continuation of the rest depends: the construct behind the theory of the atom from Heraclitus to Hiroshima. None of this partakes of anything divine nor, particularly, human. The principle is not man's contrivance and exists independent of him, whether he has discovered it or not, whether he has employed it or not. Corruption of uses may disrupt any area, the quotidian being especially susceptible, but such violations cannot destroy any true essence. Stevens' consciousness of man's skill in perverting ends accounts for the dual aspect throughout all his values, particularly for the exalted ones, until he has worked out their full implications. Freedom from a dedicated belief means that nothing dare be taken on faith. "Truth"—whatever it is—belongs to no single category nor, it would seem, the sum total. These four areas impress themselves upon men differently, and here the trouble in most theory and all practice begins. The imperfect communication represents no original sin nor fall of man. The Garden of Eden, had there been any, would have had to endure the same kinds, if probably not degrees, of confusions which afflict the present.

One may as well start with the practical, to move to the column on the left. . . . Stevens holds nothing against it, really, as long as it keeps its place, not a very elevated but regrettably an important one. The practical handles the quotidian. It tends orchards, bakes, sells, and, with most people, eats red cherry pie. It cannot formulate very much and need not have gone beyond the eighth grade in school, although it may have persisted to an LL.B. or Ph.D., and that pomposity causes part of the trouble. It fails to recognize that things in themselves—properly *by* themselves—exist and that from them the imagination can contrive valid artifacts. Apparently every man should have all four faculties, although no one has them developed in the same proportions. From an exaggerated sense of its powers, the practical supplies public statues of generals, as well as most generals, to say nothing of advertising campaigns, amplified music, organized sports, and all charlatans. Although suffering from delusions of adequacy, it possesses a pride and thus probably scorns the rock or, perhaps, finds that, having no practical value, the rock lacks existence. The subhuman it dismisses as childish or uncivilized. Its attitude toward the imaginative and things ranges from ignorance to hate, and it mismanages order, which it can barely comprehend except when applied by science as inventions. The scorn for intellect, thinking, reflects its engrained prejudices. Most traits of personality, and the more prevalent emotions, arise from this area, and consequently, in Stevens' terms, poetry can do little with character and daily desires. Indeed, poetry makes little of practical manifestations except for satire. Otherwise, it simply recoils in disinterested boredom. However one judges Stevens' attitude toward the practical, it does not rest merely on fastidiousness but shows a genuine concern for the welfare of the imaginative.

The imaginative has so many guises that no one can exhaust them; all the poems themselves cannot do that. Apparently it alone encompasses by intuition the other three areas on the left as well as, of course, all those on the right. Often it appears that the subhuman, the practical, and thinking abandon their proper functions and charter a triumvirate to overthrow the imaginative, but they have no greater chance of prevailing than do Caliban, sailors, and noblemen against Prospero. From the imaginative come all the arts and, for this discussion, particularly, poetry. Basically poetry is the imaginative treating things, and Stevens' fondness for Imagism may derive from such an outlook. The imaginative sees and enhances things nearly in defiance of their quotidian aspects, and as a result Stevens' poetry borders on surrealism, a result comparable with Max Ernst's appropriating catalogues. Likewise, his poetry must prize words because principally through vocabulary can one separate things from their quotidian bondage. For such a reason, too, poetry is "abstract"; it treats not specific daily configurations but discrete entities freed of impure functions and adjuncts. It seeks to get at an essential nature devested of its stale garb and clothed in a new magnificence. The imaginative aspires to encompass order which always eludes it because no individual objects can survive there and because it offers static paradigms while poetry requires the constant change of interplay among things. (Music, it would seem, may almost annex order, and Stevens always stresses this component of verse.) As for the rock, it challenges the imaginative; neither one can wrest all advantages from the other and banish it. Poetry, and all the arts, do not directly communicate things (nor order, nor the quotidian, nor the rock) but attributes which reveal themselves in no other fashion: a poem, or a piece of music, has no single meaning. On the other hand, the imaginative must have things and order, at least, to work with, and if it seeks independence, if it makes its muse fictive music, it betrays itself by aspiring beyond its station. Stevens always insists that the imaginative depends upon reality and that it does reach limits. Finally, the imaginative may observe the interchange between thinking, the practical, and subhuman with the outside, although such a commerce, to him, lacks poetry and belongs, perhaps, to drama and novels.

Thinking, likewise, has limits; because it deals in conceptual matters, it can make little of the rock. Ideally it would arrange values for the quotidian, like a superior parent with a child. It reassures when it becomes scientific but may veer toward sentimentality when it promises goods beyond its powers. In treating things, thinking grows philosophic or theological. The damage it may do things, in light of the imaginative, arises from its addiction to first causes and a hankering for a neat teleology. In this drive it may impose a system where none exists for a violent order and prevent the imaginative from functioning freely. Between thinking and order there can be no direct communication. Could there be, man would walk in unbearable clarity; his habits grace, his gestures art, his sounds music, his deeds charity. Through logic thinking may attempt such a direct assault on order, but it must fail as a satanic enterprise. Thinking must approach order through the imaginative, and in this view Stevens can see logic as illogical, the longest way round as the shortest way home, disorder as order, and an evening's thought as a day of clear weather. If thinking and the imaginative ever could join forces, they might abridge logic, but, so far, they agree like Darby and Joan, at best. When it regards literature, thinking clumsily insists upon moral allegory. As with all the other instances of rivalry between faculties, which should bolster each other, Stevens accepts the condition and does not rail against it. Together they might compose that central diamond, but it cannot become a habitation. The imaginative, thus, cannot work miracles, cannot redeem the supposed evils contrived by other faculties, cannot practice metamorphosis, but it provides the sole refuge from many ills.

The subhuman comes and goes in these poems, and one can make only limited guesses about it. Its force would seem largely negative. Like thinking, it can never encompass order. Intimations about order lead to superstitions, to the worship of false deities: Ananke in Africa or the imago of modern Europe. It may preach an impossible order based on fundamentalist phantasies about an unknowable heaven or hell; it cannot understand the rock, either. Linked to the material world by a skeleton, it would deny any human life if joined with the bones. Because they help compose man, something human may cling to them, so far can the imaginative extend. When the subhuman observes the quotidian, it unleashes the vulgarities of primitive desire corrupted by industrialization, but its lack of restraints may have a pathos which the more genteel practical lacks. If it joins with the imaginative to grasp things, the results provide an antidote to prevailing complacency through valid poems, such as **"Domination of Black"** or **"Like Decorations in a Nigger Cemetery."** Such bizarre pieces may express an essential violence understandable in no other way. The subhuman does not match the Freudian concept of the Id, although they share some affinities, nor does it quite perpetuate Jung's postulate of a racial memory. It has little more than any other faculty to do with the emotions. For Stevens, emotions may reside anywhere as an accompaniment of communications between faculties, although pleasure, particularly, belongs to the noting of resemblances and from this pursuit composes poems. (pp. 235-40)

Far from being a withdrawn connoisseur, Stevens stands in his landscape through all weathers to record its constancy within changes. In this world the ordinary light and what it connects give his imagination all he needs except, of course, the necessary darkness. Ultimately he appears one of the least specialized and most consistent poets. The multiple pleasures which spring from these abstracted things and shifting resemblances order his whole poetic: native and cosmopolitan, vigorous and aloof, uncompromising and witty, primordial and elegant, idiomatic and stylized. (pp. 244-45)

> *John J. Enck, in his* Wallace Stevens: Images and Judgments *(copyright © 1964 by Southern Illinois University Press; reprinted by permission of Southern Illinois University Press), Southern Illinois University Press, 1964, 258 p.*

RONALD SUKENICK   (essay date 1967)

[*Sukenick's essay examines the concept of metamorphosis as it is expressed in Stevens's poetry. Sukenick believes that "in Stevens's conception, history is a process in which no idea of reality is final, poetry is a progressive metamorphosis of reality, and reality itself is an entity whose chief characteristic is flux." For further discussion of the same theme, see the excerpts above by Sister M. Bernetta Quinn and John J. Enck.*]

The imagination for Stevens is not a way of creating, but of knowing. The imagination creates nothing, in the sense that it presents us with nothing that is not already in the world to be perceived. He in one place defines it as "the sum of our faculties," and characterizes it by its "acute intelligence." . . . He goes on to compare the imagination with light. "Like light," he says, "it adds nothing, except itself." The imagination, in other words, brings out meaning, enables us to see more. It does not create but perceives acutely, and the object of its perception is reality. What it perceives in reality is the credible. The credible, of course, is that which can be believed, and may be distinguished from absolute fact. The credible must be based on absolute fact, but is perceived by the imagination and may be beyond the range of normal sensibility. . . . The nature of poetic truth is not that it is true in the sense that absolute fact is true, but that it says something about reality we can believe—which, of course, is not to say it is untrue. It moves us from a state in which we cannot believe something about reality to one in which we can believe something about reality, and consequently puts us, to use Stevens' phrase, in "an agreement with reality." . . . (p. 16)

Stevens writes that "the poet must get rid of the hieratic in everything that concerns him and must move constantly in the direction of the credible." . . . When a poet gives to us something about reality that we can believe which before had been incredible, he adds, again in Stevens' phrase, to "our vital experience of life." . . . The poem expresses that vital experience precisely because, as I have pointed out, in it the ego has reconciled reality with its needs so that reality is infused with the concerns of the ego. "A poem is a particular of life thought of for so long that one's thought has become an inseparable part of it or a particular of life so intensely felt that the feeling has entered into it." . . . The poet is able to add to our vital experience of life because of the heightened awareness of life that results from the intensity of his thought and feeling. In his essay **"Three Academic Pieces,"** Stevens gives an example in another connection which is applicable here as illustration of the process of the imagination:

> It is as if a man who lived indoors should go outdoors on a day of sympathetic weather. His realization of the weather would exceed that of a man who lives outdoors. It might, in fact, be intense enough to convert the real world about him into an imagined world. In short, a sense of reality keen enough to be in excess of the normal sense of reality creates a reality of its own. . . .

The poet, then, gives us a credible sense of reality which brings us into vital relation with it.

Since the poet's vision is an intensified one, his description of reality in the poem is correspondingly heightened. It is "A little different from reality: / The difference that we make in what we see." . . . Here there is a pertinent analogy with Wordsworth, for whom the interaction of Nature and the imagination produced a new experience of reality resident in the poem. Stevens' idea is developed in **"Description Without Place."** . . . Description is revelation in that it is an imaginative perception of the thing described: it is neither the thing itself, nor a pretended reproduction of the thing. It is a new thing, not reality but a real artifice, so to speak, with its own reality that makes actual reality seem more intense than it ordinarily is. "The poem is the cry of its occasion, / Part of the res itself and not about it." . . . The poem is not about the thing (the "res"), but is the articulation of one's experience of the thing, an experience in which the articulation—the writing of the poem—is itself an essential part. To this should be added Stevens' statement in **"The Noble Rider and the Sound of Words"**: "A poet's words are of things that do not exist without the words." . . . (pp. 16-18)

With this in mind, regard a poem like **"The Death of a Soldier."** . . . The poem discovers a persuasive way of regarding a random and meaningless death as important and dignified. It perceives something in the soldier's death, not something that was not there in the fact of death, but something not seen except when looked at in a particular way, the particular way the poem looks at it. This is the good of rhetoric, to provide the perception that comes through saying things in particular ways.

The sense of reality is given in poetry through what Stevens calls "resemblance," or the similarities between things. The imagination creates resemblance in poetry through metaphor. . . . Poetry, through resemblance, makes vivid the similarities between things and in so doing "enhances the sense of reality, heightens it, intensifies it." . . . Therefore, "The proliferation of resemblances extends an object." . . . This is one theoretical source for Stevens' preoccupation, in poetic practice, with variations rather than progressive form, for it follows that saying a thing in another way is not merely repetition but also an extension of the original statement. In his essay **"Two or Three Ideas,"** Stevens translates the first line of Baudelaire's "La Vie Antérieure," "J'ai longtemps habité sous de vastes portiques," in three different ways. . . . One of the points he is trying to make in doing so is that our sense of reality changes and that this change is reflected in terms of style by the way we say things about it. "The most provocative of all realities is that reality of which we never lose sight but never see solely as it is. The revelation of that particular reality or of that particular category of realities is like a series of paintings of some natural object affected, as the appearance of any natural object is affected, by the passage of time, and the changes that ensue, not least in the painter." . . . (pp. 18-19)

For Stevens, poetry is a way of saying things in which the way of saying yields the meaning and in which the way of saying is more important than, but indistinguishable from, the thing said. "The 'something said' is important, but it is important for the poem only in so far as the saying of that particular something in a special way is a revelation of reality." . . . It is not only written language but also its sound that gives us, in poetry, a credible sense of reality: "words, above everything else, are, in poetry, sounds." . . . We seek in words a true expression of our thoughts and feelings which "makes us search the sound of them, for a finality, a perfection, an unalterable vibration, which it is only within the power of the acutest poet to give them." . . . This kind of truth is that of true rhetoric: the appropriateness of a particular way of putting things is what persuades us of the truth of that way of putting things. True rhetoric, which is the poet's obligation, "cannot be arrived at by the reason alone," and is reached through what we usually call taste, or sensibility; hence Stevens speaks of the morality of the poet as "the morality of the right sensation." . . . When the right sound is discovered, it gives pleasure: when Stevens speaks of listening to the sound of words, he speaks of "loving them and feeling them." . . . The pleasure given by the right sound, apart from this sensuousness of language, is that of the gratification that occurs when the imagination, through language, brings one into a favorable adjustment to reality. "The pleasure that the poet has there is a pleasure of agreement with the radiant and productive world in which he lives. It is an agreement that Mallarmé found in the sound of *Le vierge, le vivace et le bel aujourd'hui.*" . . . Thus Stevens can regard language as a god, a savior, in face of a bitter reality. . . . For Stevens, "There is a sense in sounds beyond their mean-ing," . . . and that sense of sound beyond meaning is an essential of language as it is used in poetry.

Stevens does not hesitate to reduce or obscure the discursive meaning of the language he employs in order to get at that sense in sounds. That is why he writes, "The poem must resist the intelligence / Almost successfully." . . . Again, he writes: "A poem need not have a meaning and like most things in nature often does not have." . . . This line of thought probably came to Stevens from the French Symbolist tradition, in which there is a conscious division between the creative and communicative functions of language, and in which, therefore, the creative value of words depends on their suggestiveness rather than on their strict meaning, so that obscurity and lack of specificity become virtues. "[Poems] have imaginative or emotional meanings, not rational meanings. . . . They may communicate nothing at all to people who are open only to rational meanings. In short, things that have their origin in the imagination or in the emotions very often take on a form that is ambiguous or uncertain." This would account for some of Stevens' obscurity as intentional, as I think is the case in the insistently cryptic **"Thirteen Ways of Looking at a Blackbird."** Certainly it could account for his freedom in coinage and, further, in his employment of nonsense. "I have never been able to see why what is called Anglo-Saxon should have the right to higgle and haggle all over the page, contesting the right of other words. If a poem seems to require a hierophantic phrase, the phrase should pass." . . . Usually Stevens' nonsense, while it has no rational meaning of its own, does create a meaning in its context which it communicates, as in **"An Ordinary Evening in New Haven,"** . . . where the sound of the phrase, "the micmac of mocking birds," in description of the lemons, helps to distinguish the character of "the land of the lemon trees" from that of the cloddish "land of the elm trees." . . . (pp. 19-21)

Frequently, however, Stevens' obscurity is not due merely to the use of language for effects that exclude rational meaning. Despite Stevens' calculated use of obscurity, his poetry has been from the beginning largely one of thought and statement. **"Sunday Morning"** is a meditative poem and in it, and in such poems as **"The Comedian as the Letter C"** and **"Le Monocle de Mon Oncle,"** the initial and perhaps chief problem of explication lies in penetrating the rhetoric to determine the thought it contains. In the volumes following *Harmonium* the poetry, especially in the long poems, is increasingly discursive. It is evident both from his poetic practice and from his prose that Stevens came to hold the poetry of thought as an ideal. . . . (p. 21)

In fact, there is a sometimes unresolved division between the discursive and imaginative functions of language that exists throughout Stevens' poetry. **"Thirteen Ways of Looking at a Blackbird"** represents only one extreme of this division, at which it appears to be assumed that the communication of specific discursive meaning is incompatible with the esthetic effects of language. It is perhaps a sense of strain between the discursive and imaginative functions of language that motivates R. P. Blackmur's comment in his essay, "On Herbert Read and Wallace Stevens": "Does it not seem that he has always been trying to put down tremendous statements; to put down those statements heard in dreams? His esthetic, so to speak, was unaware of those statements, and was in fact rather against making statements, and so got in the way." It is exactly this strain that makes itself felt when the referents of Stevens' language become uncertain, when his syntax fails, and his verse becomes unintelligible. Stevens uses obscurity in order to be suggestive, but he also uses it when the context requires that he be explicit. The blue and the white pigeons of **"Le Monocle de Mon Oncle"** are intelligible as contrasting states of mind and, though their meaning is indefinite, they suggest certain things about that contrast. But the "Blue buds or pitchy blooms" of **"The Man with the Blue Guitar,"** . . . seem to be specific kinds of intrusion into the blue of the imagination—a specific meaning for the phrase is implied, but is not communicated. The "three-four cornered fragrances / From five-six cornered leaves" of **"An Ordinary Evening in New Haven,"** . . . is in the same way puzzling rather than suggestive. On a larger scale, explication of section VI of the first part of **"Notes toward a Supreme Fiction"** . . . is problematic: a specific idea is indicated in the section but the statement fails to communicate it because the referent of the language is unspecified. One must guess at what is "not to be realized," what "must be visible or invisible." Sometimes uncertainty of meaning in Stevens' poems is caused by private reference, as in **"The Man with the Blue Guitar,"** . . . which Stevens has glossed as referring to a popular song. . . . License for such private reference, however, comes out of his emphasis on the imaginative or creative aspect of language. If Stevens uses the phrase "dew-dapper clapper-traps" . . . to describe the lids of smoke-stacks . . . , it is because he likes the way it sounds regardless of its obscurity. Unintelligibility in Stevens' poetry occurs characteristically when the communication of specific discursive content is frustrated by the use of those effects of language beyond meaning which Stevens conceives to be most essentially poetic. (pp. 22-3)

> *Ronald Sukenick, in his* Wallace Stevens: Musing the Obscure; Readings, an Interpretation, and a Guide to the Collected Poetry *(reprinted by permission of New York University Press; copyright © 1967 by New York University), New York University Press, 1967, 234 p.*

FRANK LENTRICCHIA (essay date 1968)

[*Lentricchia examines the naturalistic basis of Stevens's poetry. He says that Stevens did not see "poetry and science as two discrete and equally valuable modes of knowledge, but a distinction between rational and empirical knowledge. The former he assigned to philosophy, and the latter not to science alone, but, curiously, to poetry also . . ."* because *"poetic truth is an agreement with reality."*]

The suggestion that Stevens' temperament and theory of poetry are naturalistically based does not fit most current critical concepts of the poet. We understand that naturalism as a literary movement means the novel, and more specifically, novels like those of Émile Zola, Frank Norris, Theodore Dreiser, or James T. Farrell. Stevens wrote no fiction, of course, and we need only glance at his poetry to know that it is not in any ordinary sense "realistic." The idea of naturalism can be a meaningful one, however, if we consider it . . . philosophically (1) as a materialistic view of reality and (2) as a deeply skeptical attitude toward any theory of poetry wherein the imagination is given unique cognitive or constructive powers. To see naturalism in this way is to see it as a position antithetical to the core of neo-Kantian as well as romantic thought. Applied to Stevens' theoretical writings, the antithesis does not, unfortunately, illuminate all those elusive and involuted passages in his prose, but it does take us quickly to the theoretical issues that bothered him most.

The theme of time, process, flow, and decay is a pervasive one in Stevens' poetry, and no less so in his essays where the naturalistic world view becomes a basis for his theory of poetry:

> To see the gods dispelled in mid-air and dissolve like clouds is one of the great human experiences. It is not as if they had gone over the horizon to disappear for a time; nor as if they had been overcome by other gods of greater power and profounder knowledge. It is simply that they came to nothing. Since we have always shared all things with them and have always had a part of their strength and, certainly, all of their knowledge, we share likewise this experience of annihilation. It was their annihilation, not ours, and yet it left us feeling that in a measure, we, too, had been annihilated. It left us feeling dispossessed and alone in a solitude, like children without parents, in a home that seemed deserted, in which the amical rooms and halls had taken on a look of hardness and emptiness. What was most extraordinary is that they left no mementoes behind, no thrones, no mystic rings, no texts either of the soil or the soul. It was as if they had never inhabited the earth.

Behind the passage lies the shattering impact of Darwin, Marx, and Freud on modern thought. There is more here, however, than an abstract, academic understanding of the history of ideas since 1859. What emerges from the passage is a personally felt awareness of isolation, loss, and the finality of time which is alien to Coleridge's feeling for the harmony of self and nature. As an existentialist might have put it, the face of reality has become irrational, enigmatic, and man confronts nature now, not as the continuum of self, but as the "other." Epistemologically, the end of romantic idealism heralds the death of the organic reciprocity of imagination and nature. The self that used to be understood as a manifestation of spirit is but a discrete and insignificant particular since its transcendent projection has been shorn away, or "annihilated," as Stevens wrote. The idealistic universe is dead.

In an essay uncharacteristically marked by social and political sensitivity, Stevens alluded to World War II with the familiar Darwinian image of struggle. He saw the conflict the world was witnessing as "only a part of a warlike whole," and he found particularly frightening, not the absence of spirit or the gods, as he put it—that was a matter for the classroom—but the immediate and unremitting pressure of war on the individual consciousness. . . . The impact on Stevens of what he called the "pressure of reality," in a political and sociological sense, as well as in a philosophical one, is unmistakable. . . . Clearly one "era in the history of the imagination" (the romantic) had ended and a new one had begun.

In our time, idealistic views of the theory of knowledge become precious relics. Subject and object are not spiritually continuous, but are separated by an unbridgeable chasm. Stevens held that the self-existent and self-explanatory world of matter stands alone, independent of our perception of it; thus, the act of dynamic imaginative perception of reality is not the center of the highest act of knowledge as it was for Coleridge. The stuff of knowledge is the stuff of external reality, an "objective" given, and one "knows" by observation, compilation, hypothesis, and, finally, by empirical verification of one's hypothesis. As Ernst Cassirer has put it, the singular goal of the logical positivist (a latter-day naturalist) in epistemology is to try to reproduce ''the true nature of things as they are.'' Obviously mind and language, in the positivist's view, are only passive (secretarial) instruments for recording and checking the truth, not instruments for making and shaping it. In Darwin's world ''truth'' is the inherent value of the ''real.'' As Stevens puts it, ''All our ideas come from the natural world''; ''The ultimate value is reality.'' And as the common-sense naturalist: ''Kant says that the objects of perception are conditioned by the nature of the mind as to their form. But the poet says that, whatever it may be, *la vie est plus belle que les idées.*'' These are some of Stevens' naturalistic biases, and they extend to his view of poetry and the imagination:

> He [the poet] finds that as between these two sources [of poetry]: the imagination and reality, the imagination is false, whatever else may be said of it, and reality is true: and being concerned that poetry should be a thing of vital and virile importance, he commits himself to reality, which then becomes his inescapable and ever-present difficulty and innamorata. . . . He has strengthened himself to resist the bogus.

One expects such statements from the hard-nosed naturalist, who looks at all idealistic views of mind as the useless theories of those who have not had the good fortune to be naturalists, but not from a man who spent many of the important hours of his adult life writing poetry.

There is no real contradiction, however. When Stevens calls imagination ''the bogus'' he is not suggesting that the imagination is unimportant, but simply that it is not centrally involved with cognition. In his opinion, the cognitive activity in man belongs exclusively to scientific and empirical method; the function of poetry must not be confused with the cognitive perception of truth. What is at issue here is the opposition between idealists and naturalists on mind's relationship to reality. Stevens, for example, explicitly denies the validity of the ''metaphysical imagination'' of the romantics, a term he gets from Cassirer, because, as Cassirer put it in a passage that Stevens cites, the romantic imagination claims to be the one avenue to ultimate reality and the source of all value. A romantic poem functions, finally, as an ''opening'' or a window to the structure of idealistic reality. (pp. 121-25)

For Stevens the naturalist, the prosaic world of sense is the only world, and the one penetrated by the romantic imagination is an illusion. As for idealism's cognitive claims, he explicitly agrees with the positivist A. J. Ayer, and says that they are literally nonsense because only propositions that are capable of being empirically verified have cognitive value. Here, in the alliance with Ayer, is the unbridgeable gulf between the philosophical idealism of Coleridge and the philosophical naturalism of Stevens. Coleridge's world of spirit simply does not exist as far as Stevens feels he can know. The world of finite experience being everything, the values of an idealistic transparency of poetic form become something of a pleasant dream. No, Stevens will have nothing to do with romanticism: ''. . . we must somehow cleanse the imagination of the romantic,'' he wrote, suggesting that for our time an adequate theory of imagination must take account of philosophical naturalism's redefinition of the context in which we live. And yet, in spite of his naturalism, Stevens never hesitated to admit that he would happily embrace romantic theory were it intellectually honest to do so. A comment in an essay he wrote in 1951 indicates that he felt deeply the need for coherence and continuity: ''. . . if

we ignore the difference between men and the natural world, how easy it is suddenly to believe in the poem as one has never believed in it before, suddenly to require of it a meaning beyond what its words can possibly say.'' Stevens desires to affirm the core belief of romanticism at the very moment that he denies its credibility; in his poems the romantic ''dream'' and the naturalistic ''fact'' become the polar coordinates of thematic conflict, over and over again. In his essays he seems to say between the lines: ''Wouldn't it be pretty to believe in the romantic dream?''

In a naturalistic view of epistemology, and in a naturalistic world of materialistic process, how then is the poetic imagination framed? The answer is implicit in the question. The modern imagination feeds on empirical reality just as Wordsworth's fed on infinity. ''In poetry at least the imagination must not detach itself from reality,'' one of Stevens' notebook aphorisms reads. Similarly, Stevens paid John Crowe Ransom what he would consider the highest of compliments: ''Mr. Ransom's poems are composed of Tennessee.'' If, on the other hand, the imagination loses vitality and relevance as it ceases to immerse itself in the real, as Stevens suggested it would, and if the real is in constant flux, then the vital imagination, and the vital poetry, will always attach themselves to ''a new reality.'' Because the imagination by itself is not much, because it is bogus, or false, as he suggested, it ''has the strength of reality or none at all.'' . . . Within this world, new poems and only new poems can embody the qualities of vitality and freshness demanded by the naturalistic basis of Stevens' poetic. The writing of new poems becomes a necessity, not essentially a way of knowing, but a way of living fully and honestly within an ever-changing self that is trapped by an ever-changing world of material flow.

Finally, I think, the import of Stevens' naturalistic view of the imagination is concentrated in a question he once posed: ''Why should a poem not change in sense when there is a fluctuation of the whole of appearance?'' The question is a rhetorical one, of course, and suggests that the poem is significant only insofar as it is located in the perceived world (''the whole of appearance'') and faithful to it. Stevens' theory of reality and his view of the creative process imply, in the last analysis, a flat disbelief in any theory of poetry which assigns to the imagination a unique power of knowing in either a transcendental or even a purely finite way. Predictably, when Stevens approached the problem of whether or not poetry has a cognitive function as such, his naturalist theories and attitudes offered him a solution. His major distinction was not, as has often been maintained by recent neo-Kantian critics, a distinction between poetry and science as two discrete and equally valuable modes of knowledge, but a distinction between rational and empirical knowledge. The former he assigned to philosophy and the latter, not to science alone, but, curiously, to poetry also. Now, if ''poetic truth is an agreement with reality,'' and reality is defined by flow or process, then poetic ''truth'' cannot be static; in a world of perpetual change only the new poem, theoretically, can ''agree'' with the shifting face of reality. But, one might object, it has already been argued that the imagination is not a cognitive faculty. That is true: the imagination *by function* is not a cognitive faculty. The poet, unlike the scientist, does not pretend to give us a body of propositions that are capable of being verified. The ''truth'' of poems is their recognizable relationship to a particular space-time locus; genuine ''modern'' poetry, for Stevens, is always emblematic of a poet living in a (literally) godforsaken world, of a poet who draws on the particulars of place as a starting point because he cannot draw on spirit. In a naturalistic universe, *materia poetica* (a favorite Stevens phrase) is found wholly within the limits of finitude: ''. . . the real is only the base—but it is the base.'' (pp. 125-28)

Frank Lentricchia, ''The Explicit Poetics of Wallace Stevens,'' in his The Gaiety of Language: An Essay on the Radical Poetics of W. B. Yeats and Wallace Stevens (copyright © 1968 by The Regents of the University of California; reprinted by permission of the University of California Press), University of California Press, 1968, pp. 119-47.*

LOUIS UNTERMEYER (essay date 1969)

[*A poet during his early career, Untermeyer is better known as an anthologist of poetry and short fiction, an editor, and a master parodist. Horace Gregory and Marya Zaturenska have noted that Untermeyer was ''the first to recognize the importance of the anthology in voicing a critical survey of his chosen field.'' Notable among his anthologies are* Modern American Poetry *(1919),* The Book of Living Verse *(1931),* New Modern American and British Poetry *(1950), and* A Treasury of Laughter *(1946). Untermeyer was a contributing editor to* The Liberator *and* The Seven Arts, *and served as poetry editor of* The American Mercury *from 1934 to 1937. In the excerpt below, Untermeyer discusses Stevens's style. He refers to Stevens as ''one of the most original impressionists of the times''—a poet who deals in ''disintegrated fantasy'' and ''fictitious reality.''*]

The most casual reading of [*Harmonium*] discloses that Stevens is a stylist of unusual delicacy. Even the least sympathetic reader must be struck by the poet's hypersensitive and ingenious imagination. It is a curiously ambiguous world which Stevens paints: a world of merging half-lights, of finicking shadows, of disembodied emotions. Even this last word is an exaggeration, for emotion itself seems absent from the clear and often fiercely colored segments of the poet's designs.

Considered as a painter, Stevens is one of the most original impressionists of the times. He is fond of little blocks of color, verbal mosaics in which syllables are used as pigments. Little related to any human struggle, the content of *Harmonium* progresses toward a sort of ''absolute'' poetry which, depending on tone rather than on passion, aims to flower in an air of pure estheticism. His very titles—which deliberately add to the reader's confusion by having little or no connection with most of the poems—betray this quality: **''Hymn from a Watermelon Pavilion,'' ''The Paltry Nude Starts on a Spring Voyage,'' ''Frogs Eat Butterflies, Snakes Eat Frogs, Hogs Eat Snakes, Men Eat Hogs.''** Such poems have much for the eye, something for the ear, but they are too fantastic and dandified for common understanding. (p. 237)

Like William Carlos Williams, to whose *Collected Poems* Stevens furnished an introduction, Stevens is interested in things chiefly from their ''unreal'' aspect. He is, nevertheless, romantic. A romantic poet nowadays, says Stevens, ''happens to be one who still dwells in an ivory tower, but who insists that life there would be intolerable except for the fact that one has, from the top, such an exceptional view of the public dump and the advertising signs. . . . He is the hermit who dwells alone with the sun and moon, and insists on taking a rotten newspaper.'' That is why Stevens can write of **''The Worms at Heaven's Gate''** with no disrespect to Shakespeare, make a study in esthetics of the contents of a cab, and entitle a poem on death (''the finale of seem'') **''The Emperor of Ice-Cream.''**

''Sunday Morning'' and **''Sea Surface Full of Clouds''** are blends of disintegrated fantasy and fictitious reality. These poems are highly selective in choice of allusions, inner harmonies, and special luxuriance of sound. They burst into strange bloom; they foliate in a region where the esthetic impulse encroaches on the reasoning intellect. **''Thirteen Ways of Looking at a Blackbird''** and **''Domination of Black''** have a delicacy of design which suggests the Chinese; **''Peter Quince at the Clavier''** and the exquisite **''To the One of Fictive Music''** (Stevens' most obviously musical moment) reveal a distinction which places ''this auditor of insects, this lutanist of fleas'' as one who has perfected a kind of poetry which is a remarkable, if strangely hermetic, art.

After a twelve years' silence Stevens published *Ideas of Order* . . . in a limited edition. The format of the book and its private publication emphasizes the limitation as well·as the elegance of the contents. Here, as in *Harmonium*, Stevens seldom writes poetry about the *Ding an sich*, but almost always about the overtones which the thing creates in his mind. Here the candid surface breaks into cryptic epigrams, and the scenes are recorded in a deft but elusive phrase. Often enough a poem refuses to yield its meaning, but **''Academic Discourse at Havana''** and **''The Idea of Order at Key West''** surrender themselves in an almost pure music.

The Man with the Blue Guitar . . . , with a bow to Picasso, places its emphasis on man as artist and on the complicated relations between art and life. It is a far cry from the delight in luxuriance for its own sake which Stevens once called ''the essential gaudiness of poetry.'' There is little mischievous playing with the sound of words, as in the much-quoted line (from **''The Emperor of Ice-Cream''**) which had the ''roller of big cigars'' whip

> In kitchen cups concupiscent curds.

There is, instead, an increasing concern with the problem of a society in chaos and the difficult ''idea of order.'' Stevens has sacrificed some of the barbaric piling up of effects; his work is no longer a pageant of colors, sounds, and smells. The riotousness has been replaced by a grave awareness of the plight of man. Without losing the wit and delicacy of what Allen Tate has characterized as ''floating images,'' Stevens has gained compassion. A new preoccupation with man's bewilderment and despair strengthens Stevens' later work. . . .

[*Parts of a World* and *Transport to Summer*] enlarge Stevens' position as a poet. The esthete has become an essayist, although he remains poet-philosopher of ''the ultimate elegance.'' (pp. 237-38)

As always there is opulence, a sensory delight, in everything which Stevens touches. The opening of the early **''Sunday Morning''** has the flat but brilliant colors of a Matisse, especially one of that master's odalisque series. The later poetry is no less lush even when it is less spectacular. (p. 238)

It is apparent that Stevens concerns himself more and more with ''the beauty of innuendoes'' [as he stated it in **''Thirteen Ways of Looking at a Blackbird''**] than with ''the beauty of inflections''; his lines, sliding from one dissolving metaphor to another, are built on ambiguities that fall into indefinite and shifting designs. Much of his later writing is devoted to poems about poetry and the poetic process. *Three Academic Pieces* . . . is almost wholly concerned with the subject of metaphor, to the multiple meanings seen by the imagination, and the profuse ingenuities which permit the artist to escape the limitations of ordinary existence. In an essay, *From Poe to Valéry* (1948) T. S. Eliot wrote: "There is, first, the doctrine, elicited from Poe by Baudelaire, 'A poem should have nothing in view but itself'; second the notion that the composition of a poem should be as conscious and deliberate as possible, that the poet should observe himself in the act of composition—and this, in a mind as sceptical as Valéry's, leads to the conclusion, so paradoxically inconsistent with the other, that the act of composition is more interesting than the poem which results from it." Much of this is true of Stevens. But Stevens would maintain that the poet's role is to lead men out of their sordid world into the world of the imagination, "the supreme fiction," that escape is not evasion but entrance into a wider and richer sphere than the "violent order" which is our disorder. . . .

Critics differed widely concerning Stevens' importance as philosopher, designer, and creator. Some commentators maintained that Stevens was obsessed with nuances, superficial shades of color, infinitesimal gradations. Others declared that Stevens had added new dimensions to American poetry. . . .

In spite of the growing chorus of praise there were many who continued to object that Stevens' poetry was without drama and, though characters were occasionally introduced, without human beings. Yet Stevens had the last word with the conviction that a work of art is primarily a work of art, a moment arrested out of chaos, and that "Poetry is the subject of the poem." (p. 239)

> *Louis Untermeyer, "Wallace Stevens (1876-1955),"*
> in Modern American Poetry, *edited by Louis Untermeyer (copyright 1950 by Harcourt Brace Jovanovich, Inc.; renewed 1978 by Louis Untermeyer; reprinted by permission of the publisher), revised edition, Harcourt Brace Jovanovich, 1969, pp. 237-39.*

HELEN HENNESSY VENDLER (essay date 1969)

[*Vendler discusses the manner in which Stevens's style, themes, and metrical forms were developed through the act of composing such lengthy poems as* The Man with the Blue Guitar, Owl's Clover, Notes toward a Supreme Fiction *and* The Auroras of Autumn.]

Stevens, like Keats, believed in writing long poems, and defended the practice to Harriet Monroe in 1922: "The desire to write a long poem or two is not obsequiousness to the judgment of people. On the contrary, I find that prolonged attention to a single subject has the same result that prolonged attention to a senora has, according to the authorities. All manner of favors drop from it. Only it requires a skill in the varying of the serenade that occasionally makes me feel like a Guatemalan when one particularly wants to feel like an Italian." . . . For the rest of Stevens' life, long poems alternated with short ones, and while it may be that Stevens will be forever anthologized as the poet of **"The Snow Man,"** his own sense of balance required verse on a large scale. (p. 1)

Though Stevens never wrote anything approaching the length of *The Faerie Queene* . . . , his own long poems can have the same naturalizing power, and in fact they do. We become most acclimated to Stevens in reading them, and they form the illumined large to which the lyrics, volume by volume, attach themselves. In each period of Stevens' life as a poet, they are characteristic, and to read them in sequence is one way, if not the only way, of tracing both his states of feeling and his enterprises and inventions. It is also true that his greatest poems, by almost any judgment, are the longer ones, whether one

agrees with Yvor Winters' preference for **"Sunday Morning,"** Harold Bloom's for *Notes toward a Supreme Fiction,* Daniel Fuchs' for *Esthetique du Mal,* or yet choose, as I am sometimes inclined to do, *The Auroras of Autumn.*

Through the long poems Stevens discovered his own strengths. It was, for instance, not until 1942, in *Notes* that he settled on his final metrical form. Even then, he deserted that form to write *Esthetique du Mal* in 1944, and returned to it only in 1948, with *The Auroras of Autumn.* Those triads, as everyone has recognized, somehow organize his mind in its long stretches better than any other alternative, and yet to reach them he had to experiment with blank verse, couplets, ballads, terza rima, sonnetlike forms, and so on. This is the most obvious instance of Stevens' patient experimentation toward his own voice, but others come to light in reading the long poems. They are all directed toward a proper mode for his austere temperament, which is as different as can be from the temperament of Whitman or Wordsworth or Keats or Tennyson, those poets from whom he learned and to whom he is often compared. Neither is his sense of the world that of the French poets, however much he learned from them in his Harvard years. His manner was slow in evolving, and it evolved through his sense of himself and through a search for his own style. . . . (pp. 2-3)

Most criticism of Stevens has been concerned, understandably, with his "choice of subject"—variously defined. Some readers have seen his subject as an epistemological one, and have written about his views on the imagination and its uneasy rapport with reality. Others have seen his subject as a moral one, a justification of an aesthetic hedonism. Still others have seen his subject as a native humanist one, the quest of the American Adam for a Paradise in the wilderness. Stevens of course offers justification for all these views, and it is perhaps partial, in view of his many letters and essays on reality and the imagination, to prefer one of his more wayward statements, as usual objectively put, of what his own subject was, and how it developed through his life. Nevertheless, this brief summation seems closest in spirit to the Stevens one finds in the greatest poems: "One's cry of O Jerusalem becomes little by little a cry to something a little nearer and nearer until at last one cries out to a living name, a living place, a living thing, and in crying out confesses openly all the bitter secretions of experience." . . . This confession needs to be completed by the third stage of that repeated cry: after O Jerusalem, after the cry to something near, comes that final unseeking cry of the very late poems, notably **"The Course of a Particular."** A year or so earlier, Stevens had written that the poem was the "cry of its occasion, / Part of the res itself and not about it," but he could not rest in this partial identification of cry and creation. At last [in **"The Course of a Particular"**] the cry is entirely simple. . . . This is, of Stevens, "the text he should be born that he might write," to paraphrase his own line in *Description without Place.* One can hardly doubt that the leaves, as well as being leaves, are Stevens too, and that he has gone beyond crying out to Jerusalem, beyond crying out even to a living name or place or thing, beyond all directed cries at all. Utterance is utterance, and the exertion to make it something more has disappeared. Stevens recapitulates in this poem all his previous efforts—his efforts to be part of the universe, his efforts to create divinities, heroes, and human beings, all his fantasia—and dismisses those attempts at self-transcendence in the presence of this pure sound. This is "the authentic and fluent speech" he told Harriet Monroe . . . he hoped eventually to perfect for himself, a syllable intoning "its single emptiness." . . . (pp. 3-5)

But before the authentic came many trials of the less and the more authentic, and before the fluent came episodes of the halting and the borrowed, times when Stevens wanted to feel like an Italian and felt instead like a Guatemalan, as he wryly said. All these "trials of device" are recorded in his major poems, and underneath them all is the fatal stratum he will at last discover in *The Auroras of Autumn,* that blank which Harold Bloom rightly traces back to Emerson's *Nature:* "The ruin or the blank that we see when we look at nature, is in our own eye." . . . If we find, in reading Stevens, that he tries and discards mode after mode, genre after genre, form after form, voice after voice, model after model, topic after topic, we also find a marvelous sureness mysteriously shaping his experiments. The story does not have an entirely happy ending: *An Ordinary Evening in New Haven* represents a decline from *Notes toward a Supreme Fiction* and *The Auroras of Autumn,* as even Stevens himself seems to have recognized when he called it "this endlessly elaborating poem" and wished that it could have been written by "a more severe, more harassing master" who could propose "subtler, more urgent proof" than he could himself. . . . On the other hand, there are short pieces written in Stevens' last years which are the equal of anything he ever wrote, and, some would say, the best poems he ever wrote. Each poem is of course autonomous: "We never arrive intellectually," as Stevens said, "but emotionally we arrive constantly (as in poetry, happiness, high mountains, vistas)." . . . But each is also a stage in a sequence of development.

We keep, in reading Stevens, a double attitude, seeing the major poems both as things in themselves and as steps in a long progress toward his most complete incarnations of his sense of the world: "What is the poet's subject? It is his sense of the world. For him, it is inevitable and inexhaustible. If he departs from it he becomes artificial and laborious and while his artifice may be skillful and his labor perceptive no one knows better than he that what he is doing, under such circumstances, is not essential to him." . . . This is Stevens speaking, no doubt, of his own writing, and if we call him at times artificial and laborious we may be forgiven since he was there before us. There was no way for him to leap over those artifices; he had to go on by way of them: "The truth is that a man's sense of the world dictates his subjects to him and that this sense is derived from his personality, his temperament, over which he has little control and possibly none, except superficially. It is not a literary problem. It is the problem of his mind and nerves. These sayings are another form of the saying that poets are born not made." . . . The long poems give us very clearly Stevens' world, and naturalize us in it, so that we may be forgiven also if we say he invites this, he avoids that, he shrinks from this, he is shocked by this, he is indifferent to something else, he is consoled by these things. This is not censure, it is classification in the human world. (pp. 5-7)

After *Notes toward a Supreme Fiction,* Stevens discovers no new forms for long poems, and *An Ordinary Evening in New Haven* may seem only an extension implicit in the earlier poems, though with its episodic looseness, its lack of forward motion, and its ruminativeness, it enacts old age contemplating itself in sporadic proliferations, in "long and sluggish lines," as Stevens heavily described them. Sometimes this November voice in Stevens cannot even articulate itself into verse, and must content itself with those feelings, deep but inchoate, which the pine trees intimate in **"The Region November,"** or which the leaves express in **"The Course of a Particular."** As Stevens speaks in the voice of extreme old age, he and the interior paramour are finally stripped to the total lifelessness foretold

by the total leaflessness. . . . This is a version, conceived in wretchedness, of the plain sense of things, "a theorem proposed" about life in this brutally geometric end of reductive memory. If Stevens had ended only with this naked style, we would see it as the fitting gasp of the final poverty, the victory of Madame La Fleurie.

But if, as Stevens said, a change of style is a change of subject, so perhaps a change of subject may be regarded as a change of style. Though there are no more "long" poems after *An Ordinary Evening in New Haven,* certain late poems, taken together, make up what we may call Stevens' poem of infancy, as his west touches his east. He had begun his poetic life as a "marvellous sophomore," already armored with well-traveled sophistication, knowing all the languages and poetries of the world. Now after his summer credences and his autumnal littering leaves, he has come to the "inhalations of original cold, and of original earliness" . . . which, though they lie in midwinter, are yet intimations of the pristine. On the threshold of heaven, Stevens rediscovers earth, and writes a sublime poetry of inception.

The work which best shows the progress from the bitter geometry of age into an unbidden perception of the new is a poem which has gone, in the calendar of Stevens' year, beyond the deaths of October, November, December, and January, into the tenuous midwinter spring of February, with its hint of budding in magnolia and forsythia, its "wakefulness inside a sleep." Stevens begins in the toneless naked language of tedium. . . . Old age, seemingly prehistoric in its survival, is in fact inhabiting a pre-history, as the soul, not yet born, waits to be reincarnated. One morning in March it will wake to find not ideas about the thing, that intellectuality of old age, but the youthful thing itself. At that moment, in the first scrawny cry of the first returning bird, the poet's tentative infancy of perception will sense a signal of the approach of the colossal sun. Though this "bubbling before the sun" is as yet "too far / For daylight and too near for sleep," . . . Stevens is not daunted from imagining a possible for its possibleness, even in the leaden misery of winter.

In the great late poem **"A Discovery of Thought"** the perfect ideal is realized—the self is reincarnated as a child who, though newborn, remembers his previous existence and can speak his infant language, not in the rowdy summer syllables of ohoyo, but with "the true tone of the metal of winter in what it says." This extraordinary creature, Stevens' last mythical invention, is the child one becomes in second childhood, in that sickness where the eyes dim, where the body is a chill weight, and the old winning fairy tales of bearded deities become irrelevant. The wintry habitat of the man in second childhood is superbly real. . . . But in the midst of February's deathly wind and mist, there is a tinkling of hard ice and a trickling of melting ice which co-exist, as a continual metamorphosis thwarts finality. . . . And though the scene is populated with "blue men that are lead within" holding leaden loaves in their hands, nevertheless "when the houses of New England catch the first sun" we think that "the sprawling of winter" (like the wilderness commanded by the jar) "might suddenly stand erect." . . . In the strict ending of the poem, which gathers itself together after the great freedom of the sprawling lines of description, Stevens defines in three ways, with verse of metaphysical density, that speech of the antipodal creature:

The accent of deviation of the living thing
That is its life preserved, the effort to be born
Surviving being born, the event of life. . . .

The remembered continuity between past life and present life accounts for the deviation in the accent of this miraculous creature who remembers his previous incarnation; he remembers the trauma of being born and has no infantile amnesia; his life, like the life of the pines in *An Ordinary Evening in New Haven,* is "a coming on and a coming-forth," an e-vent, and he does not forget its prehistoric origins. Knowing everything, this infant creature is everything, and he represents Stevens' final image of perfection, one step beyond the naked majesty of poverty in which he had left the old philosopher in Rome. If the high stoic elegies of Stevens' plain sense of things make a fitting close to his withering into the truth, these short late poems, equally truthful, are those liquid lingerings into which the angel of reality transforms, for a moment, the bleak continuo of life's tragic drone. (pp. 309-14)

> *Helen Hennessy Vendler, in her* On Extended Wings: Wallace Stevens' Longer Poems *(copyright © 1969 by the President and Fellows of Harvard College; excerpted by permission), Cambridge, Mass.: Harvard University Press, 1969, 334 p.*

DANIEL J. SCHNEIDER (essay date 1975)

[In this essay, Schneider attempts to codify and explain Stevens's system of symbols. Schneider argues that Stevens was systematic, and that his symbols proliferated from four main divisions (north-south, sun-moon, summer, winter).]

Analysis of a symbolism created by a vigorous imagination is never easy, . . . and when, as in Stevens's poetry, symbolic patterns are developed deliberately over some fifty years, critics may find themselves so dazzled by the proliferations of the meanings—by what Marianne Moore has called the "interacting veins of life between his early and later poems"—that they may decide to content themselves either with very crude descriptions of the symbolic system or with the reflection that, after all, given the complexity of the system, no adequate description of it is possible. Criticism of Stevens's poetry, after some forty years of assiduous scholarship, today tends to rest satisfied with these two disturbing solutions to its difficulties. . . . Eugene Paul Nassar's study of Stevens's symbolism [*Wallace Stevens: An Anatomy of Figuration* (see Additional Bibliography)] demonstrates that sensitive classification can significantly enlarge our grasp of what Stevens is doing. But even Nassar, I think, does not go far enough; and a thorough study of the whole complex of Stevens's symbolism is obviously needed if we would grasp and appreciate the range and beauty of Stevens's vision.

The need for such a study is emphasized by the fact that some of Stevens's most frequently employed symbols continue to be interpreted as mere images—or as instances of Stevens's delight in ambiguity. The existing interpretations of **"Life is Motion"** are a case in point. Without exception critics have joined Elder Olson in finding the poem about as simple as the thesis stated in its title: "An uncomplicated affair," writes one critic, a poem that "satirizes the ungainly frontier and its animal spirits as Bonnie and Josie celebrate the marriage (of flesh and air) in Oklahoma with an operatic 'Ohoyaho.'" Even the critic who perceives that *air* is associated with the imaginary in Stevens's poetry concludes that in **"Life is Motion"** "we witness . . . a correspondence of person and place, and see how they are unified." One may grant criticism the right to dispense with what Marius Bewley has called the "wide range of reference to the other poems" in Stevens's work, but can one ignore that the "marriage of flesh and air" is but one more

variation of the theme Stevens was fond of orchestrating throughout his life: the marriage of reality and the imagination? An insensitivity to the symbolic import of many of Stevens's most persistent images and epithets—*Negro, bill, serpent, bronze, point, round, tip, wood, dove, rise, fall,* etc.—continues to blur our awareness of what is going on in the poetry. (pp. 160-62)

[In] reading the poems of a man whose work is all of a piece, we may certainly look for and expect the most remarkable kinds of subtleties. . . . I wish to stress—what cannot be stressed too strongly—the intricacy of Stevens's symbolic manipulations. A passage from **"Notes toward a Supreme Fiction"** illustrates the complexity of Stevens's later poetry. . . . In these lines we witness three related events: as the chanting Arabian imposes his astronomy upon the uncharted heavens, so the wood dove chants and the ocean howls. It is as if man, the lower animals, and the inorganic world were engaged in a common endeavor to sing the same song. (Samuel French Morse has said that the lines suggest "the universal existence of the poetic impulse.") But students of Stevens's symbolism may also recognize that the poet is here disclosing, in line after line, the conjunctions of reality and the imagination—conjunctions so close that it becomes virtually impossible to sever the two or to say whether one is contemplating, at a given moment, the real or the imagined.

Stevens begins with pure imagination. The Arabian astronomer, like the astronomer in **"A Candle A Saint,"** is one of "the sleepers" who make of the world a dream, a madman whose madness is woven of the same stuff as the madness of the night. He appears "at night" because that is the time for imaginative extravagance. His "damned hoobla-hoobla-hoobla-how" is an incantation of the imagination, a kind of magic, "damned" not only because it is amusingly infuriating but also because it is like the magic of salvation and damnation. Is the astronomer a scientist or a magician? Stevens means, of course, that he is both, since astronomy is but a kind of magic of the imagination. Yet for all the frenzy, the physical world does not dissolve into the Arabian's fictions: Stevens reminds us that the astronomy is inscribed upon an "unscrawled" future, a reality which is, after all, undifferentiated, unsymbolized, evading all fictive formulae.

The line "And throws his stars around the floor" requires very close analysis. That the Arabian throws *his* stars underscores the basic theme of Stevens's poetry, the theme of the interdependence of reality and the imagination, for the courses of the stars in the Arabian's astronomy are, ambiguously, the courses of the Arabian's fictions and the courses of the stars themselves, the *Ding an sich.* But why does he throw them around "the floor"? And why *around* the floor rather than *upon* it? Here a knowledge of the symbolic system is indispensable. A close study of *floor* reveals that the word invariably meant, for Stevens, reality—the earth itself, on which man stands and from which he tries to rise. Close associates of *floor* are *hill* and *rock,* and when Stevens employs these terms he generally introduces also a submerged metaphor of varnishing: moonlight or paint or some other fictive varnish is applied to the bare floor, or a brilliant creature passes over the floor, thus metamorphosing the barren reality. As for the preposition *around,* it is one of the many terms of geometry (others are *line, point, ring, circle, cone, sphere, angle* and *ellipses*) that Stevens characteristically employs in order to stress imaginative ordering of the chaos of the material flux, and a close study of Stevens's use of the preposition discloses that he had its symbolic meaning in mind when he was writing his earliest poems. Thus the line "And throws his stars around the floor" means (1) that the Arabian astronomer, in an act of extravagant imagination, imposes his fictions around—that is, in fictive patterns upon—reality; (2) that this creature of the imagination throws real stars in fictive patterns over reality; or (3) that the creature of the imagination throws real or fictive stars indiscriminately, profusely, in the fury of his imagining, over reality. In a poetry whose theme is the interdependence of reality and the imagination, such variety of interpretation is to be encouraged, not evaded.

We turn to the wood dove chanting his hoobla-hoo. Why "by day"? Why a dove? Or, why a wood dove? Why "used to"?

If the creature of the pure imagination, the Arabian astronomer, chants "at night," time of the moon's and imagination's ragings, the wood dove, less imaginative, chants "by day." It is reality's time, as a number of Stevens's poems make clear. For if the imagination is perforce associated with sleep and dream, reality is associated with the familiarity and ordinariness of daytime, as well as with the wakefulness of animals that must be alert in order to survive. As for the dove, it is, as close readers of Stevens will recognize, one of his most frequently employed symbols of the imagination; yet here Stevens calls it a "wood-dove"—the term *wood* symbolizing reality, which resembles a wood in its darkness and tangled disorder. Thus *wood* stresses either that the habitat of the imagination is reality or that the bird belongs half to the reality of the wood, half to the imagination symbolized by *dove*. The dove chants her song, but by virtue of her limited imagination she is capable of only one hoobla-how to the Arabian's three, and she chants in the reality of "day" and of the "wood." Or rather, she "used to" chant, for another one of the strange relations that Stevens here perceives is the relation of events in the memory to events in immediacy: to bring past and present together is after all one of the chief occupations of the imagination as it constructs its fictive "descriptions without place."

We have, then, this much: as the Arabian, a figure of the imagination, imposes his fictions upon reality, so the wood dove, a creature half of reality and half of the imagination, performs a similar act. We move finally, on this scale of descending imaginative power, to the third member, the ocean, symbol of pure reality. If Stevens is amused by the first two instances of imaginative activity, his scrutiny of pure matter's poetic behavior is pure irony, as if he were to say, "Ho! Even the ocean imagining the world!"

That the ocean is a symbol of the material flux will be clear to readers of such well-known poems as **"The Comedian as the Letter C"** and **"Sea Surface Full of Clouds."** Close readers of Stevens will also note that he often characterizes reality as being wet, guzzly, juicy, flowing, dripping, or oozing, whereas the imagination, in contrast, is often dry and fixed. Here Stevens also stresses the ocean's materiality by employing the adjective *grossest*. Yet even this gross machine of ocean displays an "iridescence" that Stevens invariably associates with the imagination. As for the rise and fall of the waves, whatever that may signify on a nonsymbolic level, it is, as symbol, a deliberate rendering of a kind of imaginative ordering of reality. The symbolic associates of *rise and fall* in Stevens's poetry are *up and down*, *to-and-fro*, and *undulation*, all of which are employed either to render the vital interdependence of reality and the imagination or to suggest the movement of the poet's rhythms. Moreover, *rising* and *falling*, taken separately, are almost invariably employed by Stevens to symbolize imagi-

native transformations, *rising* being associated with the poetic metamorphoses that enable one to throw off the great weight of reality, and *falling* (as well as its associates *running down* and *descending*) referring to the descent of imaginative riches from heaven.

Small wonder, then, that Stevens concludes these lines with the statement "Life's nonsense pierces us with strange relation." The relation he is speaking of is obviously more than the presence of "hoo" in each of the three events. It is the presence in all three of the conjunction of reality and the imagination. And these events "pierce" us in the sense that they awaken our awareness of the world: we experience the "momentary existence on an exquisite plane" that Stevens regarded as the characteristic effect of poetry.

Here we may [turn] . . . to the critic who writes that *moon* does not always equal the imagination. I grant that *moon* may on occasion symbolize more than imagination (and it can always be argued that the moon in a given poem is just the moon, as Blake's Tiger is, in a sense, just a tiger); but I have little doubt that *one* of the symbolic meanings of the word is always the imagination and I can find no evidence to refute that contention. It may be that the terms I have here been studying—*floor, around, wood, day, rise,* and *fall*—do not always equal what they equal in the passage I have explored. An image used as image in the early poetry sometimes does not appear as symbol until ten or twenty years later; moreover, the whole bent of Stevens's effort is to exhibit the interdependence of reality and imagination, and in consequence he creates, as I shall presently show, huge families of terms that symbolize *both* reality and imagination. But despite these intricacies, the major clusters of his symbolism are not difficult to isolate and codify (as I believe I have already shown), and it is only by means of codification that many of the problems presented by the poetry can be solved.

Stevens himself has provided an important clue to help us in our task of codification. In **"Effects of Analogy,"** after discussing several kinds of analogy in poetry, he offers as his first major conclusion, "every image is the elaboration of a particular of the subject of the image," and goes on to say, "if this is true, it is *a realistic explanation of the origin of images*" (italics mine). In a closely related essay, **"Three Academic Pieces,"** he writes that the proliferation of such analogies "extends an object" and intensifies the sense of reality, and that the intensified sense of reality creates, in turn, other resemblances, new analogies; the proliferation of resemblances, which is also a proliferation of images, might thus proceed indefinitely as long as the subject remains constant. Theoretically, given the subject and the first particular that enters the poet's mind, we should be able to infer all the images subsequently elaborated. If, for example, a writer's subject is Puritanism and his first particular a rock, we might expect images of hardness and coldness to proliferate from this particular, while images of softness, fluidity, and warmth might suggest an opposed attitude, less rigid and ascetic. Again, the rock is gray and we might expect a proliferation of other somber images, which would then elicit a host of opposed images of gaudiness. Since the images of color would breed still other images, the proliferations would continue until the poet had done with Puritanism as his subject.

In practice, of course, the proliferation of images is far more complicated than this illustration suggests. The imagination may uncover its richest images through associations so devious that the intellect can scarcely trace them. . . . This being so, a poet's images can be traced to their source only with difficulty. Nevertheless, if "every image is the elaboration of a particular of the subject" and if, as Stevens asserts, this is "a realistic explanation of the origin of images," it should be possible to lay bare many of the associational patterns by which the poet comes to include any given image in his work. (pp. 167-72)

For Stevens there are basically two different realities—a posited objective world of matter in motion (a fearful world which is violent, ever-threatening, and destructive) and a subjective reality which is abundant, rich, sensuous, "green and gay." Also there are basically two different imaginations in his poetry—a false and a true, the former cold and artificial, closely related to the reason, the latter rich, vital, and productive. As Stevens's attitudes toward reality and the imagination shift, his imagery inevitably changes. If reality in one poem provides the poet with his deepest satisfactions, in the next it is a horror. If the imagination is often the bountiful patron and guardian angel, it sometimes provides nothing comparable to the satisfactions of a reality undissolved in mental categories, and when it is divorced from human experiences the imagination becomes as ugly and alien as brute fact. "Merely going round" *is* a final good in Stevens's work, and the symbolism subtly reflects his shifting moods.

When we understand, then, that Stevens's "up and down between two elements" is actually an up and down between four (or more), our next step is to identify the particulars from which the imagery seems inevitably to spring. The frequent occurrences in his poetry of *sun, moon, South* and *North, summer* and *winter* suggest that these are generative particulars, and we can derive from them virtually the whole body of the symbolism. Thus *sun,* whatever other connotations the word may have, is a symbol of reality, and associated symbols of warmth and vitality proliferate directly from it, along with contrasting symbols of coldness and lifelessness. Then, since the sun is red or golden, vivid colors come to be associated with reality, whereas the imagination is symbolized by the cold, pale hues of moonlight. Again, since *South* is a symbol of reality, whatever is contained in the South may also stand for reality; so there occurs a proliferation of symbols of southern countries, tropical zones, jungle animals, plants, and the like. These call up their opposites in the realms of the imagination: northern countries, civilized places, civilized creatures. And so Stevens's imagination proceeds, engendering new symbols of which each one, being consubstantial with the others in its family, may stand synecdochically for the entire realm of which it is part. In the end Stevens creates the vast system of symbols which, being "in harmony with each other," constitute "a poem within, or above, a poem." . . . (pp. 172-73)

Since Stevens's chief concern in his poetry is to exhibit the incessant conflict between his two, or four, realms—that is, since "the poetry of a work of the imagination constantly illustrates the fundamental and endless struggle with fact"—the relationships between the symbols may be viewed most clearly if we study the major antithetical patterns developed: remembering always that under the pressure of changes in attitude, the symbolic meanings must change. What we must try to do is in a sense to place ourselves inside the mind of the poet: to understand his ways of piecing the world together, to absorb his memory so that we may know how, having established a basic symbolism in the early poems, he is able, under the pressure of feelings of attraction and revulsion, to modify this symbolism, discovering new meanings in symbols whose use had once been limited. (p. 173)

Daniel J. Schneider, "'The War that Never Ends': Patterns of Proliferation in Wallace Stevens's Poetry," in his Symbolism, the Manichean Vision: A Study in the Art of James, Conrad, Woolf, & Stevens *(reprinted by permission of the University of Nebraska Press); © 1975 by the University of Nebraska Press), University of Nebraska Press, 1975, pp. 154-203.*

ROBERT N. MOLLINGER   (essay date 1976)

[*In the following excerpt, Mollinger discusses Stevens's changing ideas on humanity's relationship to the cosmos. Mollinger finds that Stevens's beliefs progressed from a reductionist view to romanticism, and finally, to humanism.*]

In much of the critical literature on Wallace Stevens' central man, hero, and major man, there is confusion in the use of these terms. Usually considered as synonyms referring to the same concept, they are used as if they were interchangeable. However, the "central man" is not equivalent to the "major man." To Stevens the "central man" is the more general, abstract term; in most of the poetry the central man is used to denote that man who epitomizes the essential aspects of man. The central man is the essential man, and Stevens' search for him appears throughout the poetry. For instance, in **"The Man With the Blue Guitar"** the poet attempts to "play man as he is," and in **"Like Decorations in a Nigger Cemetery"** "man the abstraction" is meditated. Stevens' view of the central man is not constant, however; in Stevens' search for the central man the poet vacillates between positive and negative attitudes toward man. These specific conceptions and attitudes are denoted by the use of terms other than the "central man." At times a romantic ideal "hero" is seen as the central man; at times the common man, best exemplified by Crispin in **"The Comedian as the Letter C,"** is seen as the central man; and at times Stevens considers the "major man," a humanistic ideal, as the central man. Thus the "hero" and "major man" are specific conceptions and embodiments subsumed under the "central man."

"United Dames of America" exemplifies Stevens' search for the central man, here denoted as the "central face," and suggests that this search can lead to at least two possible, and contradictory, conceptions of man. The speaker in this poem listens to the words of an orator who provides one criterion for the definition of mankind. . . . It is not the quantity of men which determines the character of a group; it is the quality of the individuals who make up the group that is important. In this instance Stevens is speaking in general terms, but he does apply this formula specifically, for example, to politicians: "As the man the state, not as the state the man." . . . Thus Stevens realizes that he must determine the qualities of this individual man who characterizes the mass, or as the orator puts it, the paradigm which the mass produces, in order to describe the essence of man. The word "paradigm" introduces two possibilities in defining the essence of the mass. On the one hand, the paradigm may be just the pattern that the mass has produced or a typical example showing all the general characteristics of it; on the other hand, the paradigm may be the model of the group, the highest achievement or the ideal of man that it has produced. The word "singular" supports this dual interpretation. It could mean just the average individual, exemplified later in the poem by the "dame," and could also mean the highest, most distinguished, most excellent man, exemplified by the "naked politician."

Stevens' different views of the central man seem to depend on his view of the world in general, a view that continually changes: "I suppose that the way of all mind is from romanticism to realism, to fatalism and then to indifferentism, unless the cycle re-commences all over again." . . . For Stevens romanticism means an attitude which emphasizes the idealistic—in the sense of both utopian and mental—aspects of the world. By fatalism (which can include indifferentism) Stevens means an attitude which focuses on the naturalistic, deterministic qualities of the universe. Realism is an acceptance of both the romantic, idealistic elements and the fatalistic, naturalistic elements of reality. To a great degree these attitudes toward the world appear in Stevens' works in separate periods: his mood changes from an early fatalism to a romantic idealism, and then again to a late realism. Stevens' conception of man also shows this progressive movement throughout his poetry. In the early poetry, marked by a fatalistic mood, the central man appears as the common man. In the middle period (1936-1942), marked by romanticism, the central man appears as the hero. In the late poetry, marked by a realistic mood, he appears as the major man.

Stevens' conception of the central man in the early poetry of *Harmonium* . . . is exhibited best in **"The Comedian as the Letter C."** In this poem Stevens attempts to define the central essence of reality as naturalistic—the universe is valueless, indifferent to man, and quotidian or common—and further proposes a fatalistic attitude as the only viable one in such a universe. This pessimistic fatalism is probably encouraged also by his view of the central man, which he also attempts to define in this poem. . . . In [a] letter to Hi Simons about his motivation in writing **"The Comedian as the Letter C,"** Stevens makes clear that the essence of man, the central man, will be shown to be the common man of the mass. Crispin, then, is not representative of the modern poet, as most critics hold, but rather he is Stevens' perception of the common man: "The long and short of it is simply that I deliberately took the sort of life that millions of people live, without embellishing it . . .". . . . (pp. 66-8)

Denigrating Crispin by his ironic jabs at him throughout the poem, Stevens is concerned with presenting Crispin, and thus the central man, as a base commoner. In the first section of **"The Comedian as the Letter C,"** *The World without Imagination,* Stevens abstracts the essence of Crispin from the false imaginative masks with which Crispin hides his real self. Just as the sea destroys the fictive conceptions of nature, it destroys man's illusions of grandeur; "What counted was the mythology of self, / Blotched out beyond unblotching." Crispin romantically magnifies himself into a Socrates, a musician, a preceptor; but the poet knows better and ironically pinpoints Crispin's real stature as a "Socrates / Of snails, musician of pears," and a nincompated pedagogue. Man is a knave, or at best, a thane, and Crispin, after facing the naked reality of the sea, must face the naked reality of himself: "some starker, barer self / In a starker, barer world. . . ." Socrates stripped down to his essence, devoid of a fictive covering of a controlling intelligence, is a "skinny sailor." The "insatiable egotist" is really a "short-shanks," and his egotistical flights are destroyed. The world without imagination is the world and man seen without the distortions of romance and myth. Stripped of imaginary coverings, man sees himself and reality as it is, abstracted to the base; Crispin is really the "merest miniscule," the letter *c*. In his letters Stevens states that the *c* is a cipher for Crispin; thus Crispin is a nonentity. *C*, as a letter, is the base or foundation of the name Crispin; *c*, as the merest miniscule, makes Crispin a cipher, a zero, a nothing.

Recognizing that Crispin is base, Stevens continually debases him with epithets throughout the poem. For instance, sensing an "elemental fate" in the savagery in America, Crispin is called an "affectionate emigrant." Being an emigrant from his old world and thus an immigrant into this new reality, he is naive in the ways of the new world, and, as affectionate, he is overly fond of the new and thus slightly foolish in his fondness. Elsewhere in the poem Crispin is variously referred to as a "valet," and ironically derided by such labels as "connoisseur of elemental fate," "poetic hero," and "marvelous sophomore." In the naturalistic world portrayed in **"The Comedian as the Letter C"** man can only be viewed as almost lifeless. The quotidian, sapping Crispin, devitalizes him of his essential fluids and shows him to be animal-like—braying and blubbering. In fact, Crispin is figuratively dead. The only appropriate music is requiems and dirges—"an inactive dirge, / Which . . . Should merely call him dead." . . . He is seen as impotent and insignificant, and the malady of monotony, showing the essence of man to be that of an almost dead clown, infects Crispin and is fatal: "Jovial Crispin, in calamitous crape." . . . (pp. 68-9)

Though most emphasized in the early poetry, this negative, pessimistic view of the central man carries over into **"The Man with the Blue Guitar"** and is clearly defined here. At the end of the poem the speaker strongly asserts man's essence as he sees it, common and comic. . . . The essence of man is seen as comic: he is seen as strutting on stage with false confidence, his chest puffed out. The essence of man is seen as common: as Stevens says in his letters, he is an employee of the Oxidia Electric Light and Power Company. . . . Man is a puppet, having no real control over his life: he is a fantoccine or marionette, like the manikin of Crispin-valet in **"Anecdote of the Abnormal."** Thus this view of man is comparable to that taken by Stevens in **"The Comedian as the Letter C."** Just as the fantoche's chest is puffed out, Crispin utters imperative haws of hum; just as the fantoche is absurdly dressed in a shawl which the wind catches, Crispin is in bellowing breeches; just as the fantoche ends up as a common laborer, Crispin ends up as a common householder. Crispin is sapped by the quotidian; the fantoche is surrounded by the same. This earthly world is banal, with dirty smokestacks begriming man's existence. The poet seeks both a figure to believe in and worship in early parts of the poem, but he realizes at the end that man is just common and unheroic and has only earthly existence. . . . (pp. 69-70)

Describing a naturalistic universe and man as an apelike clown in it in *Harmonium* . . . in the early parts of *Ideas of Order* . . . , and in parts of **"The Man With the Blue Guitar."** . . . Stevens takes the position of a fatalistic naturalist: Crispin and similar figures are portrayed as animalistic and mechanistic. Puppets at the mercy of the universe, they are constantly made fools of. Stevens, in these early poems, recognizes the paradigm of man, the central man, not as an ideal, but as the typical man of the mass. The central man is the common man.

Throughout most of *Ideas of Order, The Man with the Blue Guitar* . . . , and *Parts of a World* . . . , Stevens rejects the fatalistic approach to the world evidenced earlier and generally accepts the romantic imagination. His conception of the central man also changes from his earlier one. Not being satisfied with his perception of the common vulgar man as the central or essential man, Stevens wants to go beneath this commonness and discover something more essential. In **"A Fading of the Sun"** of *Ideas of Order* he recognizes that man may be in some sense immortal and that there is a savior. This savior would have human characteristics; in fact, it would be a glorification of the human. Stevens is hinting at proposing a new sense of the central man: "In *A Fading of the Sun* the point is that, instead of crying for help to God or to one of the gods, we should look to ourselves for help. The exaltation of human nature should take the place of its abasement." . . . Entertaining two attitudes toward man, exaltation and abasement, Stevens now suggests that the former should be adhered to. This exaltation will be based on the discovery of a positive essence of man—the heroic. Instead of debasing man, as Stevens does in his figure of Crispin, he exalts man as a hero. Throughout this middle period, 1935 to 1942, the central man is seen as ideal or perfect and is variously referred to as a superman and supreme fiction. (pp. 70-1)

["Asides on the Oboe"] presents the first extended, though vague, attempt to describe the central man as the hero, and in this poem Stevens accepts fully the romantic ideal, the hero, as the only possible salvation. This poem and his comments during this period illustrate his firm commitment to the romantic hero at this time: "The spirit of negation has been so active, so confident and so intolerant that the commonplaces about the romantic provoke us to wonder if our salvation, if the way out, is not the romantic." . . . Similar to the hero portrayed in the earlier volumes, the hero as the central man is promoted in this poem as the final belief to replace the obsolete fictions, myths and gods, which man formerly believed in, and, though he is both a religious idea and a human ideal, he is more supernatural than natural. His words are described in religious terms as immaculate and he is pictured as transcending man. . . . Normal man cannot stand as a god, but one can imaginatively conceive of a superman who can, and being perfect, this ideal transcends man as a god would: "we project the idea of God into the idea of man." . . . At first appearing fictive—"impossible"—this supernatural ideal becomes "possible" because man chooses to believe in its existence.

At times in the first section of the poem the hero seems contradictorily to be a merger of the natural and the supernatural. On the one hand, as a "man of glass," he reflects all men and is a part of man; on the other, as a "human globe," he is all-inclusive, extravagantly large, and beyond man. The metaphorical description of the hero as a "million diamonds" combines both meanings. The central man sums us up by including as an abstraction all our qualities and by being our summit or ideal. But since diamonds are brilliant, rare, and the most valuable gems, the supernatural or perfect is emphasized rather than the natural. In section III the speaker, wondering about the relation of man to the hero during a time of war, makes clear that the hero is not human but a perfect, transcendent being. . . . We found the sum of men, first, by seeing the evil essence of man evident in war, and, second, by discovering the central man as our summit or ideal. The syntax of the last sentence indicates that the emphasis is on the discovery of the central good; the perception of evil was expected. Thus the central man is not wholly human here; in his central goodness, he is beyond the human. What "we" have discovered is a transcendent good, not the good in our own mundane selves. He is a superhuman to whom the speaker turns to escape the central evil: "If the future . . . also comes to nothing, sha'n't we be looking round for someone superhuman to put us together again, some prodigy capable of measuring sun and moon, some one who, if he is to dictate our fates, had better be inhuman, so that he is without any of our weaknesses and cannot fail?" . . .

In the last stanza of the poem the speaker becomes one with the central man, the prodigy of the imagination, not as an act of acceptance of the human, but as an act of belief in a superhuman: "But we and the diamond globe at last were one." Since the prologues are over, the speaker chooses his final belief. This belief is neither in ordinary man nor in poetry as such, as most critics state, but in an ideal creation of the imagination and of poetry, the hero. Speaking with "Asides on the Oboe" in mind, Stevens makes clear in a letter to Hi Simons that the hero is not to be equated with the imagination: "I ought to believe in essential imagination, but that has its difficulties. It is easier to believe in a thing created by the imagination. A good deal of my poetry recently has concerned an identity for that thing." . . . (pp. 72-4)

In summary, it has been seen that Stevens moves from a vague, obscure abstraction of the hero as central man in *The Man with the Blue Guitar* to the creation of a full-blown ideal figure with transcendent, divine qualities in *Ideas of Order* and *Parts of a World*. The romantic hero, created in reaction to such figures as Crispin, is first believed in as one would believe in a supreme fiction, but this belief becomes more sincere when, in "Examination of the Hero in a Time of War," the poet explains to himself that this belief is based on an intuitive, emotional perception of the heroic in man. As the poet's belief in the hero solidifies, it brings him peace: "To meditate the highest man . . . Creates, in the blissfuller perceptions, / What unisons create in music." . . . (p. 75)

[In the late poetry—*Transport to Summer, The Auroras of Autumn* and *The Rock*] there is the attempt to reconcile the two images of man presented in the previous poetry. The central man perceived as a comic and commonplace person and presented especially in "The Comedian as the Letter C" and the central man conceived as the ideal hero and appearing particularly in *Parts of a World* are reconciled in a new image of man. Just as Stevens attempted to reject his early fatalistic view of man, he rejects in his later poetry his romantic view of the hero. Still seeking the central man, Stevens finds him as a union or compromise of the common, comic man and of the ideal hero. He settles on a humanistic view of the central man between the fatalistic and romantic ones.

In "Study of Images II" . . . Stevens suggests the possibility of an image of man which would include his previous images. On the one hand, he portrays a positive image of women—"the pearly women"; on the other, a negative one—"witches." But he visualizes a possible union of the two. . . . This union of selves, or the merger of two images of the self, is one of the dominant motifs in the late poetry. Again, in "Things of August" the speaker recognizes the complete image: "When was it that the particles became / The whole man . . . ," and in "Repetitions of a Young Captain" the union is imagined more concretely by a soldier seeking his true self between the self as ideal hero, symbolized by the air, and the self as common nonhero, represented by the earth: "A few words of what is real or may be / . . . The soldier seeking his point between the two."

This new image of the central man is generally referred to as the "major man." In the longer and major poems of this period Stevens defines his view of the major man by limiting his ideality. In "Repetitions of a Young Captain" he views wartime soldiers as possible heroes: "Millions of major men against their like. . . ." And though on the one hand he admits that this ideal view of soldiers is an image in his mind, he suggests on the other hand that what he is saying contains true knowledge: "a know-and-know." In **"Notes toward a Supreme Fiction"** the definition of the major man is clearer. The speaker wonders at first if the common man can be viewed as the ideal hero: "Can we compose . . . MacCullough there as major man?" . . . MacCullough is imaged as a "crystal hypothesis," similar to the diamondlike hero of **"Asides on the Oboe."** However, man as the ideal hero is rejected here: "But the MacCullough is MacCullough, / It does not follow that major man is man." The common man is just the common man; the ideal hero is not man. Here the concept of the major man seems to be equivalent to the concept of the hero. But in [a later] . . . section of the poem, the concept of the major man is refined. . . . The speaker here rejects the romantic elements of the major man or hero; he rejects the making of a man into a god, the apotheosis of man into the romantic divine hero. Rejecting the romanticism of the hero prepares the way for the postulation of the major man as a new image of the central man.

Excluding the more ideal elements in his central man, Stevens includes the more common and natural ones. In **"Notes toward a Supreme Fiction"** the major man is seen as a heroic part of the common masses, and the idea of man, the major abstraction, is the common mass: "The major abstraction is the commonal." Since the heroic is part of the commonal, both the common people and all people, the central man can be embodied completely in a common man: "The man / In that old coat, those sagging pantaloons . . .". . . . The "pantaloon man," then, is Stevens' final embodiment of the central man and the essence of man. The speaker of **"Notes toward a Supreme Fiction"** calls on the ephebe not to go beyond the pantaloon man to make the final elegance, the ideal. He need not go beyond him, nor console him, because within the pantaloon man are all the qualities necessary for putting together, "confecting," a more perfect man: "It is of him, ephebe, to make, to confect / The final elegance. . . ." (pp. 75-7)

The images of the total man of glubbal glub, the political tramp, and the pantaloon man are reminiscent of earlier images of common men such as Crispin, the old fantoche of **"The Man with the Blue Guitar,"** and the hidalgo of **"A Thought Revolved."** However, just as Stevens purges the ideal image of man of its romantic elements, he eliminates from this image of the common the fatalistic elements. These new images are not mocked, scorned, or treated ironically. Man is not viewed as a ridiculous comic, and his condition is not viewed as tragic just because he is common. Previously the commonplace entailed comic absurdity and tragic pessimism; now it is accepted by itself. . . . (pp. 77-8)

Major man becomes a humanistic ideal and the final embodiment of Stevens' central man. Rejecting the romantic elements of the common man, Stevens in the late poems concerns himself with the realistically human. He now sees a new dignity in man. While Crispin had no dignity, Stevens' new idea of the central man has dignity: "How simple the fictive hero becomes the real . . ." . . . . Though Stevens still seems to envision a heroic ideal, it is now a more realistic one. His hero is no longer a constructed mental idea but rather an ideal of perfection apprehended in man. By seeking the perfectibility of man in the natural world, Stevens can be considered a true humanist. In the late poetry it is not the ideal hero which consoles man but the actual, living common man. In **"Esthétique du Mal"** the speaker seeks consolation for human pain. First he recognizes that pity from any supernatural creature leads to self-pity on the part of man; then he realizes that the "true sym-

pathizers" are within the actual, are other humans. . . . Compared to gestures by the supernatural, constructed by the romantic imagination, human gestures are small; but since they are all man has, they suffice and are effective. Human tenderness is now of the ultimate value in a wholly human world. It is this human world, inhabited by central men who are both capable and common, to which Stevens dedicates himself in his late poetry. . . . (p. 78)

> *Robert N. Mollinger, "Wallace Stevens' Search for the Central Man," in* Tennessee Studies in Literature, *Vol. XXI (copyright © 1976, by the University of Tennessee Press; reprinted by permission of The University of Tennessee Press), 1976, pp. 66-79.*

FRANK DOGGETT AND ROBERT BUTTEL (essay date 1980)

[*The following excerpt, written on the occasion of Stevens's centenary, reflects on the changing critical response to Stevens and the enduring value of his poetry.*]

In the centennial year of Wallace Stevens' birth, Stevens' art still seems fresh and elusive, but less precious and less eccentrically modern than it did more than fifty years ago when his first book appeared. Since then, the rich and memorable language of *Harmonium* has been augmented by the equally memorable, if more abstract, phrases in the later books. It is now assumed that the imagery derives from eternal or universal human situations and reverberates with echoes of philosophic implications. The poetry still imparts its special quality of withheld thoughtfulness. The effect of its subtly qualified, seemingly abstruse statements is to suggest that the poet may be amused, even skeptical of their never quite formulated profundities. Along with this implicit questioning, each poem's discourse contemplates in exacting language the shadings of its idea. "Words are thoughts," Stevens says, and with this concept of language his poetry, as so many critics have noted, involves a movement of thought, an activity of mind. This activity is stimulated by intimations beyond the plain statements in poems. The poems exert the fascination of what may be recognized as theory and what may be realized at the same time as the poet's intuition of a person in a time, a season, and a place, a setting.

Stevens has taken his place among the other cherished figures of our literature as part of an inheritance rather than as the isolated phenomenon he seemed to be in earlier days. Many critics now regard him as one of the major figures in the romantic tradition, and his relationship to Wordsworth and Keats . . . will be easily accepted by most of his readers. Yet he has not receded into a general background of romantic poetry. He is still the individualist, the master of his own style. Stevens' individuality attracts and overcomes parody. And because he is inimitable, his influence has been minimal for a poet of his monumental reputation. (pp. xi-xii)

[Stevens] believed devoutly that poetry should help us live our lives. As he sought relentlessly the "blissful liaison" between mind and nature, as he shed, one after the other, easy refuges for the imagination and stretched the mind to the furthest reaches of what it might be possible to know without falsification, he demonstrated the mind's ability to arrive at points of accord, however fleeting, with reality. "Poetry as manifestation of the relationship that man creates between himself and reality"—this is how he defines the role of poetry in one of his *Adagia*, and this role attaches to poetry, as his own poems prove again and again, a profound human significance. One measure of that significance is the depth of response among readers who come to know the poetry. Another is the diversity of that response; the poems in their rich complexity accommodate varying interpretations and allow readers to reach new syntheses of understanding as they assimilate these interpretations. The noble accents and human implications of Stevens' thought, as well as the inescapable rhythms of his poems, are what give his work the important place it holds today and assure that it will be read long after the occasion of his centenary. (p. xvii)

> *Frank Doggett and Robert Buttel, in a preface to* Wallace Stevens: A Celebration, *edited by Frank Doggett and Robert Buttel (copyright © 1980 by Princeton University Press; excerpts reprinted by permission of Princeton University Press), Princeton University Press, 1980, pp. xi-xviii.*

ALFRED CORN (essay date 1982)

[*In the excerpt below, Corn discusses Stevens's quest for The Supreme Fiction—the fusion of imagination and reality into one entity.*]

Wittgenstein enjoins us not to speak of those things that do not belong to discourse: ''Whereof we cannot speak, we must remain silent.'' And yet wonderfully often speakers or writers manage to find ways of talking approximately or indirectly about experience that they actually hold to be outside or above the reach of words. Ways of overcoming the obstacles to speech vary; they are part of the set of stylistic and contextual qualities that confer identity and identifiability on a writer. Of course the unsayable or ''ineffable'' itself is not the same category for all potential speakers (few of whom, in any case, will be writers). In certain religious faiths, it is accounted a sin to make any mention of the name of God, or of the divine; thereof, the righteous will keep silent. In other instances, both religious and secular, verbal expression is not held to be sinful or contaminating but merely inadequate and paltry, compared to some areas of private experience. This group includes most of the writers thought of as being concerned with the ineffable. It includes, for example, the later Stevens; but the early Stevens is often best understood as belonging to yet another contingent. This third group includes the temperaments who find imaginative writing (in a nontrivial sense) impossible: because they see no transcendent sanctions that could be drawn on to form truthful statements in literature. For them, the universe is silent, and thus silence is truer than any utterance. To invent is to fabricate, to fabricate is base or invalid, and so there is truly nothing to write.

It is tempting to call this last obstacle to speech ''negative ineffability''; and it is one that determines much of Stevens's early poetry. The negative mythological figure for the world of *Harmonium* is the Snow Man, who perceives ''Nothing that is not there, and the nothing that is.'' If there had been no other figures in the pantheon Stevens invented for his poetry, he could not have written many more poems. But Stevens began to imagine other altars, engaging in an extended poetic pilgrimage and entertaining many ideas on the nature of truth, of the imagination, and the philosophical status of poetic utterance. Why Stevens didn't from the start understand poems as ''fictions,'' and statements in them as hypothetical, has to do both with his own skeptic's temperament . . . and with modernist developments in American poetry during the first two decades of this century. . . . In any case, the notion that the poet ''nothing affirmeth and therefore never lieth,'' clearly

failed to satisfy Stevens: poems must be true, otherwise they are of no importance.

Poems must be true because, with the death of God, the arts must come to replace religion. In a letter to Barbara Church (which is dated August 12, 1947, but reflects beliefs he developed during his student days at Harvard fifty years earlier) Stevens said, ''As scepticism becomes both complete and profound, we face either a true civilization or a blank; and literature ought to be one of the factors to determine the choice. Certainly, if civilization is to consist only of man himself, and it is, the arts must take the place of divinity, at least as a stage in whatever general principle or progress is involved.'' What did living in a universe empty of deity mean for Stevens? The blankness, cold, and misery mentioned in **''The Snow Man''** are metaphoric ways of conveying it, and a more succinct formulation is found in his *Adagia:* ''Reality is a vacuum.'' Against human mortality, suffering, and meaninglessness, Stevens proposes the imagination as a redemptive force, to push back (here he inverts the metaphor) against the ''pressure of reality.'' The imagination is also the psychological faculty that allows poems to be written; indeed, the proportional equation ''silence is to speech as death is to life'' stands at the center of Stevens's poetic vocation. If one can write poems, one may find a sanction for human existence, and so may live.

Stevens's view of the ''imagination as value,'' a conviction he repeats in many prose contexts and draws on as the emotional substance for so many poems, could be seen as absolute, no less comprehensive than a belief in the divine. Just as frequently, however, he expressed an opposing view: ''The ultimate value is reality.'' When poetry fails to reflect reality, it presents merely a ''dead romantic,'' a ''falsification.'' Stevens is never clear and precise as to how the false imagination is to be distinguished from the true, the dead romanticism from the live; but, in general, he seems to look for a marriage, a mystic union between the imagination and reality, without explaining how wedlock is to be effected. (Readers will recall, in this connection, the fable of the ''mystic marriage'' between the captain and the maiden Bawda in *Notes Toward a Supreme Fiction*.)

It is apparent that, although Stevens was drawn to philosophical issues and discourse, he did not demand of himself the development of a system organized and expressed with philosophical rigor: ''What you don't allow for,'' he said, ''is the fact that one moves in many directions at once. No man of imagination is prim: the thing is a contradiction in terms.'' This is as much a program as a description: Stevens wishes to *postpone* the hasty formulation of a system, to forestall final conclusions. He wishes to rest neither in the imagination nor in reality because rest is undesirable; is hard to distinguish from philosophical or psychological stasis or perhaps paralysis; and life is supremely a question of movement and change. In a letter to Sister Bernetta Quinn (April 7, 1948) he says: ''however, I don't want to turn to stone under your very eyes by saying 'This is the centre that I seek and this alone.' Your mind is too much like my own for it to seem to be an evasion on my part to say merely that I do seek a centre and expect to go on seeking it. I don't say that I do not expect to find it. It is the great necessity even without specific identification.''

Even if philosophical or religious finality were attainable, Stevens recognizes that the ''never-resting mind'' would not accept any such finality: ''Again, it would be the merest improvisation to say of any image of the world, even though it was an image with which a vast accumulation of imaginations had been content, that it was the chief image. The imagination itself would not remain content with it nor allow us to do so. It is the irrepressible revolutionist.'' The view of truth (and life) that emerges from these statements is one shared by many modern philosophers of mind: truth is not a set of propositions but is a psychological process. For Stevens, there is (and should be) a constant oscillation between the categories reason/fact and imagination/fable. A poetry or a life content with either of these opposing terms will not constitute fulfillment. Poets (considered exemplary for all of us) will always be seeking, voyaging, and questing, so long as they are alive.

This summary of philosophic and poetic ideas, though it is partial and perhaps supererogatory for the Stevens scholar, may retrace for nonspecialists the steps taken during Stevens's long career. In early Stevens, the ground is, generally, bare reality, the wintry landscape of nothingness seen by the Snow Man; the *figure* is the imagination that comes to free the mind from its subjection to reality. In the later Stevens it is more often the imagination that is the ground, all-pervasive and easily available. Reality then comes to seem the figure brought in as a contrast, a ''refreshment,'' a cleansing away of the dull fictional film habitually covering our view of things. The emblematic figure typically summoned by Stevens in 1922 is the **"One of Fictive Music"**; for the later Stevens, it is the **"Necessary Angel"** of reality. But, more and more often, Stevens begins to call for a fusion of reality and imagination into one entity, variously referred to as the Grand Poem, the Supreme Fiction, the Central Mind, or the Central Imagination. This hypothetical category comes to seem in some sense possible to Stevens, even though it always remains a projection. There is a constant future-tenseness to Stevens's visionary insight; he gives notes *toward* the Supreme Fiction, *prologues* ''to what is possible.'' A title Stevens considered for his first book was *The Grand Poem: Preliminary Minutiae;* and the early Stevens could say, ''The book of moonlight is not written yet nor half begun,'' and, ''Music is not yet written but is to be.''

The implication is that Stevens believes the great book can be written and that he will do it. By 1943 and the writing of *Notes,* it is apparent that the projective character of his vision has crystallized as doctrine. In an essay composed that same year he says, ''The incredible is not a part of poetic truth. On the contrary, what concerns us in poetry, as in everything else, is the belief of credible people in credible things. It follows that poetic truth is the truth of credible things, not so much that it is actually so, as that it might be so.'' (pp. 225-29)

Although Stevens's *summum bonum* belongs to futurity, his adumbrations of it remind one of other poets' efforts to recount mystic experiences actually undergone, remembered wordlessly, and termed ineffable in the usual sense. Here it will be useful to consider some of Stevens's reflections on ultimate value, which, in this instance, he terms ''nobility'':

> I mean that nobility which is our spiritual height and depth; and while I know how difficult it is to express it, nevertheless I am bound to give a sense of it. Nothing could be more evasive and inaccessible. Nothing distorts itself and seeks disguise more quickly. There is a shame of disclosing it and in its definite presentations, a horror of it. But there it is. The fact that it is there is what makes it possible to invite to the reading and writing of poetry men of intelligence and desire for life. I am not thinking of the ethical or the sonorous or at all of the man-

ner of it. The manner of it is, in fact, its difficulty, which each man must feel each day differently for himself. I am not thinking of the solemn, the portentous or demoded. On the other hand, I am evading a definition. If it is defined, it will be fixed and it must not be fixed. As in the case of an external thing, nobility resolves itself into an enormous number of vibrations, movements, changes. To fix it is to put an end to it. [**"The Noble Rider and the Sound of Words,"** in *The Necessary Angel*]

''Vibrations, movements, changes'': much of Stevens's poetic style is covered by these terms, and they constitute part of the difficulty of his ''manner.'' The whole passage, with its strenuous effort to get at the inexpressible, suggests that Stevens's first intuitions concerning the nature of a supreme and always future fiction may have come to him out of his struggle with style and expression itself. The title of the essay from which this passage is drawn refers not only to nobility, but also to ''the sound of words.'' Consider then another passage from the same essay in *The Necessary Angel,* one where Stevens discusses our feeling for words themselves.

> The deepening need for words to express our thoughts and feelings which, we are sure, are all the truth that we shall ever experience, having no illusions, makes us listen to words when we hear them, loving them and feeling them, makes us search the sound of them, for a finality, a perfection, an unalterable vibration, which it is only within the power of the acutest poet to give them.

A paradox present in this apologia for words and their sounds, words at their most *physical,* in short, is that the principal result is immaterial and nonverbal. Stevens says as much in another essay (**"Effects of Analogy"**): ''There is always an analogy between nature and the imagination, and possibly poetry is merely the strange rhetoric of that parallel: a rhetoric in which the feeling of one man is communicated to another in words of the exquisite appositeness that takes away all their verbality.''

The inference, then, is that our surest clue, our only available insight, into the nature of the ''central imagination'' are words and their sound. Unlike most poets of mystic insight, Stevens does not deplore the inadequacies of his medium; he celebrates it and becomes its hierophant. Is it appropriate to call this a ''verbal sublime''? There is at least one major precedent for it in literature—the poetry of Mallarmé. Other affinities between the two poets have been noted: the view of the poet as a sacramental figure; the recourse to music as the best analogy for poetry; and the belief (Mallarmé's belief) in a final Book that the world was meant to become, a Book not yet written. (This must be one of the sources of Stevens's Supreme Fiction.) In actual fact, the French poet Stevens most often mentions is not Mallarmé, but Paul Valéry, who, however, belongs to the same tradition. . . . This view of the sacramental role of the poet, whose poems may be considered incantations or prayers, is not foreign to Valéry's own poetics and fits well with something he once said about prayer and unknown tongues (his prototype, obviously, was Roman Catholic liturgical Latin): . . . ''That is why one should pray only in unknown words. Return the enigma to the enigma, enigma for enigma. Lift up what is mystery in you to what is mystery in itself. There is in you something equal to what goes beyond you'' [''Comme le Temps est calme,'' translation mine]. . . . For his part, Stevens said (in the *Adagia*), ''Poetry is a search for the inexplicable,'' and ''It is necessary to propose an enigma to the mind.'' Although he did not write his poems in Latin, no small number of the incantations Stevens proposed to his mind (and ours) employ French words; and much of his vocabulary (in the poems) is composed of archaism, coinages, and sound-words either onomatopoetic in nature, or modeled on Elizabethan singing syllables (''hey-derry-derry-down,'' etc.), or similar to scat-singing in jazz (''shoo-shoo-shoo,'' and ''ric-a-nic,'' for example). The point is, no doubt, to invent that ''imagination's Latin'' Stevens speaks of in *Notes Toward a Supreme Fiction*. It is in this sense, perhaps, that he wished to be understood when he said, ''Personally, I like words to sound wrong.'' An overstatement; but it is certainly true that Stevens has one of the most noticeable styles in our poetry; and it could be said that he wrote an English that often sounds as if it were another language. How is the poet to overcome universal silence? One way is to make a joyful noise.

In view of his high claims for poetry, it appears that nothing can be more serious than poetic style. In his essay **''Two or Three Ideas,''** he proposes that, as poems and their style are one, so men and their style are one; the same may be said of ''the gods.'' Then why not interchange *all* the terms? The style of men, and their poems, and their gods, are one; thus, style is an index of the divine. The task, as Stevens saw it, was to discover and compose a style that would serve as just such an index. Already noted is Stevens's reliance on a special diction to give the effect of ''otherness,'' of enigmatic mystery, an effect appropriate to a supreme, future fulfillment. Beyond that, the poet must include in his repertoire accents of grandeur and nobility. Stevens draws on several sources for these. Anyone who has heard him read, or has heard recordings of his reading, will have immediately noted the resemblance of his elocutionary style to that of the Protestant minister—the intonations of prayer, the accents of exhortation. By the same token, the language of Stevens's poems is often Christian in flavor: ''Sister and mother, and diviner love. . . .'' Stevens is like other Romantic poets in adapting Christian rhetoric to his purposes, and, of course, he borrows directly from Wordsworth, Shelley, Keats, and Whitman themselves. More surprising, however, is his enormous reliance on Shakespeare, and not merely for personae like Peter Quince and Marina. He tends to draw on Shakespeare's high rhetoric for certain moments of large, visionary utterance. When, in **''Final Soliloquy of the Interior Paramour,''** he writes, ''We say God and the imagination are one . . . / How high that highest candle lights the dark,'' it is impossible not to think of Portia's lines in Act V of *The Merchant of Venice:* ''How far that little candle throws his beams! / So shines a good deed in a naughty world.'' Stevens's recasting is no disgrace to its source; and part of the power of these lines lies in the connection the reader makes between the sense of Shakespeare's greatness and the philosophical amplitude of the issues being treated in this poem.

Stevens has come so far from ''the nothing that is'' as to speak of deity, God, with a capital letter. The gradual pilgrimage from Nothing to Something recapitulated in his career as a poet is a process enacted constantly (though on a much smaller scale) in his later poems. The typical embodiment of the change is metaphor, which he describes variously as ''metamorphosis,'' ''transformation,'' ''transmutation,'' and even ''apotheosis.'' Metaphor is the agency by which a real but empty thing is imaginatively transformed into something ''unreal'' and ful-

filling. The poem as a whole is to be taken as an extended metaphor. (pp. 229-32)

The metaphor of the passage from winter to spring as representing the shift from one ontology to another is very frequent in Stevens, and, in fact, is the basis for . . . **''Not Ideas About the Thing, But the Thing Itself.''** Recalling that ''metaphor,'' by its etymology, can suggest the notion of ''transport'' (itself a term with several possible meanings), one is given a clue to part of the intention in a volume like *Transport to Summer* . . . , which may be understood as a book-length embodiment of the central doctrine of metaphysical transformation. The volume opens with a summer poem, **''God Is Good. It Is A Beautiful Summer Night''** (to be read, ''God=Good=Summer''), but, not resting with that, goes on to include poems oscillating back and forth between summer and winter settings, and ends with *Notes,* which includes the same constant pendulum swing, beginning with autumn and ending with the ''Fat girl, terrestrial, my summer, my night.'' If it is desirable to isolate a central controlling ''structure'' in the Stevensian imagination, no doubt it is the idea of metaphoric transformation that must be proposed. At the lower end of the scale, this provides the endless variety of tropes invented by Stevens in the poems; at the next level, it presents the poem under the aspect of transfiguration or apotheosis; and then, the *volume* of poems as a change from the wintry mind to the *summum bonum* of summer. It is fair to say, too, that Stevens's long poetic career moves generally from a predominantly ''wintry'' metaphysics to a more positive and reassuring stance. And, if seasonal change is the most frequent *temporal* metaphor for revelation in Stevens, the most frequent *spatial* one is **''Pilgrimage.''** . . . (p. 233)

The metaphorical transformation of reality, then, was actually a kind of religious pilgrimage for Stevens. And its completion he viewed as an apotheosis, but one that must be undertaken again and again—it is never final. The exact nature of deity is not to be stated; Stevens is content with formulae such as the ''central imagination'' or the ''central poem.'' The act of writing offers the only clue Stevens has to the nature of the divine, and the intuitions of poetry all have to do with a directional transformation, from thing to figure, from fact to fable. A poem such as **''A Primitive Like an Orb,''** which touches on all these ideas, can be read almost as a catechism for Stevens's beliefs about poetry and its relationship to the divine. (p. 234)

The universal vacancy so apparent to Stevens in the first phase of his career has come to be replaced by a sense and a rhetoric of fullness. A primary source of his conviction as to the certitude of that fullness is the feeling emanating from that very rhetoric, in poems lesser than the ''essential poem.'' The obstacle to utterance is removed, for Stevens, by the transforming power and cosmic harmony manifest in *poesis* itself. (p. 235)

Alfred Corn, ''Wallace Stevens: Pilgrim in Metaphor,'' in The Yale Review *(© 1982 by Yale University; reprinted by permission of the editors), Vol. 71, No. 2, Winter, 1982, pp. 225-35.*

ADDITIONAL BIBLIOGRAPHY

Baird, James. ''Transvaluation in the Poetry of Wallace Stevens.'' In *Studies in Honor of John C. Hodges and Alwin Thaler: Tennessee*

Studies in Literature Special Number, pp. 163-74. Knoxville: University of Tennessee Press, 1961.*

    Discussion of Stevens's contribution to modern poetic theory.

Bly, Robert. "Wallace Stevens and Dr. Jekyll." In *American Poets in 1976,* edited by William Heyen, pp. 4-21. Indianapolis: Bobbs-Merrill Co., 1976.

    Philosophical and speculative essay. American poet Robert Bly examines Stevens's work in terms of the artist's failure in his attempts to reintegrate the dark side of man's nature (his visionary, sensual self) with his "light" personality (his intellectual, idealistic self).

Bornstein, George. "The New Romanticism of Wallace Stevens." In his *Transformations of Romanticism in Yeats, Eliot and Stevens,* pp. 163-230. Chicago: University of Chicago Press, 1976.

    Study of the varying responses to Romanticism of three major twentieth-century poets.

Borroff, Marie. *Language and the Poet: Verbal Artistry in Frost, Stevens and Moore.* Chicago: University of Chicago Press, 1979.*

    Scholarly technical study of the language of modern poetry. In the chapters on Stevens, Borroff provides a structural and etymological analysis of Stevens's use of diction.

————. "Sound Symbolism as Drama in the Poetry of Wallace Stevens." *ELH* 48, No. 4 (Winter 1981): 914-34.

    Examination of Stevens's use of language "in its phonetic rather than its conceptual aspect."

Bromwich, David. "Wordsworth, Frost, Stevens and the Poetic Vocation." *Studies in Romanticism* 21, No. 1 (Spring 1982): 87-100.*

    Comparative study. Bromwich traces the implicit attitudes of the poets towards their vocation and their environment as these are expressed in William Wordsworth's "Responsibility and Independence," Robert Frost's "Two Tramps in Mud Time," and Stevens's "The Course of a Particular."

Bump, Jerome. "Stevens and Lawrence: The Poetry of Nature and the Spirit of the Age." *The Southern Review* 18, No. 1 (January 1982): 44-61.*

    An examination of the nature poetry of Wallace Stevens and D. H. Lawrence.

Burney, William. *Wallace Stevens.* New York: Twayne Publishers, 1968, 190 p.

    In-depth survey of Stevens's works. Burney's study provides close readings of the major poems and also discusses the prose and the plays.

Frye, Northrop. "Wallace Stevens and the Variation Form." In *Literary Theory and Structure,* edited by Frank Brady, John Palmer, and Martin Price, pp. 395-414. New Haven: Yale University Press, 1973.

    An analysis of structure in Stevens's poetry. Frye discusses Stevens's use of a type of poetic form resembling a musical theme and its variations.

Lehman, David. "Three Meditations on Wallace Stevens." *Shenandoah* XXXII, No. 2 (1981): 85-101.

Discussion of Stevens's varying attitudes toward reality as evidenced by "A Study of Two Pears" and "Someone Puts a Pineapple Together." Lehman also examines the ways Stevens's attitudes toward religion diverge from Freudian theory.

Lieber, Todd M. "Wallace Stevens: The Hero in an Age of Disbelief." In his *Endless Experiments: Essays on the Heroic Experience in American Romanticism,* pp. 243-64. Columbus: Ohio State University Press, 1973.

    Lieber discusses Stevens's work as the culmination of "the tendency of American Romanticism . . . to make the heroic journey the drama of the creative self."

Litz, A. Walton. *Introspective Voyager: The Poetic Development of Wallace Stevens.* New York: Oxford University Press, 1972, 326 p.

    Examination of the early poems (1914-1937).

Miller, J. Hillis. "Stevens's 'Rock' and Criticism As Cure: I and II." *The Georgia Review* XXX, Nos. 1, 2 (Spring 1976; Summer 1976): 5-31, 330-48.

    Etymological reading of Stevens's "The Rock."

Morse, Samuel French. *Wallace Stevens: Poetry As Life.* New York: Pegasus, 1970, 232 p.

    Biographical and critical study. Morse's book is the only Stevens biography to appear to-date. In this volume Morse attempts to "bring the life and the poetry into relationship."

Nassar, Eugene Paul. *Wallace Stevens: An Anatomy of Figuration.* Philadelphia: University of Pennsylvania Press, 1965, 229 p.

    Important and highly influential critical study. Nassar examines the nuances of meaning connected with various figures that recur constantly in Stevens's poetry, in an attempt to find a pattern in Stevens's use of symbolism.

Simons, Hi. "The Genre of Wallace Stevens." *The Sewanee Review,* LIII, No. 4 (October-December 1945): 566-79.

    An examination of Stevens's treatment of "distinctively philosophical" subject matter in his poems.

Stern, Herbert J. *Wallace Stevens: Art of Uncertainty.* Ann Arbor: University of Michigan Press, 1967, 206 p.

    Philosophical study. Stern argues that Stevens's poetry reflects an aesthetic consistency that other critics have failed to perceive.

Webb, Eugene. "The Ambiguities of Secularization: Modern Transformations of the Kingdom in Nietzsche, Ibsen, Beckett and Stevens." In his *The Dark Dove: The Sacred and Secular in Modern Literature,* pp. 34-87. Seattle: University of Washington Press, 1976.*

    Study of the role of myth in modern literature.

Woodward, Kathleen. "Wallace Stevens and 'The Rock': Not Ideas about Nobility But the Thing Itself." In her *At Last, the Real Distinguished Thing: The Late Poems of Eliot, Pound, Stevens and Williams,* pp. 99-132. Columbus: Ohio State University Press, 1980.*

    Traces the evolution of the concept of the hero in Stevens's poetry.

Zukofsky, Louis. "For Wallace Stevens." In his *Preposition: Collected Critical Essays of Louis Zukofsky,* pp. 24-38. Berkeley and Los Angeles: University of California Press, 1967.

    Personal impressions of the poetry and philosophy of Stevens by the poet Zukofsky.

(Giles) Lytton Strachey

1880-1932

(Also wrote under pseudonym of Ignotus) English biographer, critic, essayist, short story writer, poet, diarist, and dramatist.

Strachey is best known as a biographer whose iconoclastic reexaminations of historical figures revolutionized the course of modern biographical writing. He conceived a type of biography that integrated established facts, speculative psychological interpretations, and imaginative recreations of his subjects' thoughts and actions which resulted in lively, perceptive, and above all human biographical portraits. In his major biographies—*Eminent Victorians, Queen Victoria,* and *Elizabeth and Essex: A Tragic History*—Strachey disclosed previously overlooked complexities of personality in some of the most prominent and revered figures of English history.

Born in London, Strachey was the eleventh child of a large, upper-class family. His father was a respected military general and an administrator to India. It was Strachey's domineering mother, however, who was the major influence in his life, inspiring in him, through her teachings, an enthusiasm for the French language and literature. As early as age five he was encouraged to write verse, which was read aloud at family gatherings. His primary and secondary education was conducted at private schools and by private tutors until 1899, when he enrolled at Trinity College, Cambridge. There, Strachey formed important personal and literary relationships that endured throughout his life. Among his friends at Cambridge were Thoby Stephen, Leonard Woolf, Clive Bell, and John Maynard Keynes. With Strachey, they formed the nucleus of the coterie later known as the "Bloomsbury Group"—so-named after that section of London where members lived and met. The group also included Virginia Woolf; her sister, Vanessa Bell; Desmond MacCarthy; Roger Fry; and occasionally E. M. Forster. Bloomsbury's Thursday evening meetings were occasions for lively discussions of philosophy, literature, art, economics, politics, and life in general. Although the group observed no formal ideology, it was founded on philosopher G. E. Moore's *Principia Ethica,* the essence of which is summarized in Moore's statement that "one's prime objects in life were love, the creation and enjoyment of aesthetic experience, and the pursuit of knowledge." For Strachey, members of the Bloomsbury Group provided companionship and were his confederates in rejecting the remaining social conventions of the Victorian era.

In 1905 Strachey failed to obtain a fellowship at Trinity College, having submitted an unacceptable paper on the subject of the controversial English statesman Warren Hastings. Thwarted in his plans for an academic career, Strachey worked as a literary critic and essayist for several journals and became the drama critic for *The Spectator,* which was owned and edited by his cousin, St. Loe Strachey. During this time, Strachey polished his writing style and formulated his theories on the art of biography. His astute critiques of several French writers, and an especially brilliant essay on Jean Baptiste Racine, brought him to the attention of H.A.L. Fisher, a publishing representative. Commenting that Strachey was "one of those rare Englishmen who knew French from the inside," Fisher commissioned him to write a survey of French literature. The result

was Strachey's first book, *Landmarks in French Literature.* Marked by his gift for incisive summary, the work was well received, but it did not bring him the fame he hoped to achieve. Despondent that he was not as artistically successful and productive as his friends among the Bloomsbury Group, Strachey decided that history might be his forte and turned his literary efforts to writing "silhouettes" of famous historical figures. Deploring the prevalent hagiographical bent of contemporary biographers and adhering to his dictum that "discretion is not the better part of biography," he wrote *Eminent Victorians.* Though Strachey's bold interpretation of the lives of Florence Nightingale, Cardinal Henry Edward Manning, Dr. Thomas Arnold, and General Charles George Gordon stirred controversies within the literary establishment, the work was a major success. Thus, having found his literary niche, he devoted his time to writing two other major biographies: *Queen Victoria,* a humanizing portrait of the Queen and Prince Albert, and *Elizabeth and Essex,* an interesting, though artistically flawed, Freudian analysis of Queen Elizabeth. In addition, Strachey wrote many biographical essays for periodicals, which were eventually collected in *Portraits in Miniature, and Other Essays,* and he became a respected literary critic of eighteenth and nineteenth-century French and English literature. Suffering from ill health for most of his life, Strachey died at the age of fifty-two.

Eminent Victorians is Strachey's most critically discussed work. In his well-known preface to that work he expounded his theories of biography, maintaining that it should be more than a dull compilation of facts manipulated to venerate historical figures. Rather, Strachey believed that it is the biographer's business "to lay bare the facts of the case as he understands them . . . dispassionately, impartially, and without ulterior intention." His portraits of Nightingale, Manning, Arnold, and Gordon in *Eminent Victorians* combine literary artistry with selective biographical facts to produce new insights into personalities formerly assumed to be well understood. This biographical work is tightly written, colored by striking metaphors, and maintains Strachey's characteristically detached point of view. In addition, *Eminent Victorians* consistently employs an ironic tone which serves to deflate the reputations of his subjects. Michael Holroyd indicates that upon closer scrutiny Strachey's "detachment was part of a literary mannerism, skilfully employed so as to bring into sharper relief his irony and power of denigration." For all its success, however, *Eminent Victorians* was also harshly criticized by literary critics and historians who objected to Strachey's selective use of facts and his tendency to judge biographical subjects by modern standards, rather than in the context of their own era. Regardless of such criticism, *Eminent Victorians* became a model for a new kind of biography that was imitated throughout England and America.

Strachey's most popular biography, *Queen Victoria*, is often referred to as his most traditional work. Although he intended to reveal the mediocrity of Victoria's character, critics agree that Strachey became totally enraptured by his subject. In a series of vignettes, he depicted the Queen as a sympathetic figure administering to her advisors, to her public, and to her husband, Prince Albert. While Strachey's characteristic irony is less pervasive in *Queen Victoria*, he consistently raised rhetorical questions which allow readers to draw their own conclusions about the motivations behind Victoria's behavior, often interrupting his narrative to ask the reader such questions as "What was to be done?" or "What was going through her head?" Commentators remarked that, compared to *Eminent Victorians*, Strachey adhered more faithfully to historical fact in *Queen Victoria* and they have praised his psychological insight into the characters of Victoria and her courtiers. Strachey's next biography, *Elizabeth and Essex*, is often considered a historical drama rather than a historical biography, and it is generally regarded as the least successful of Strachey's major works. Critics comment that as a biographer Strachey simply did not have enough historical facts to combine with his "fictive facts" to make the portrait believable. Virginia Woolf commented that "the facts and fiction refuse to mix. . . . Elizabeth never became real in the sense that Queen Victoria had been real." Despite this artistic flaw, *Elizabeth and Essex* is considered important for its innovative use of Freudian psychoanalysis. In his attempt to reveal the motives of Queen Elizabeth's behavior—from her political decisions to her choice of lovers—Strachey imaginatively reconstructed incidents of Elizabeth's early childhood. In a laudatory appraisal of *Elizabeth and Essex*, Sigmund Freud regarded Strachey's psychoanalysis of Queen Elizabeth to be correct.

Most critics agree that Strachey raised biography to an art form. While his use of historical facts was often contrived and unscholarly, he is generally praised for his artful and entertaining portraits. As a debunker, Strachey exposed the human frailties of prominent figures and maintained an irreverent stance toward the conventions of the past. According to Hol-

royd, "Strachey's influence as a biographer has matched that of Plutarch and Boswell." Though his literary reputation has diminished somewhat in recent times, he is still considered a pioneer in the realm of modern biography.

PRINCIPAL WORKS

Landmarks in French Literature   (criticism)   1912
Eminent Victorians: Cardinal Manning, Florence Nightingale, Dr. Arnold, General Gordon   (biography)   1918
Queen Victoria   (biography)   1921
Books and Characters: French and English   (criticism)   1922
Elizabeth and Essex: A Tragic History   (biography)   1928
Portraits in Miniature, and Other Essays   (biography and essays)   1931
Characters and Commentaries   (criticism)   1933
The Collected Works of Lytton Strachey. 6 vols.   (biography, history, criticism, and essays)   1948
*Ermyntrude and Esmeralda: An Entertainment   (short story)   1969
Lytton Strachey by Himself: A Self-Portrait   (diary)   1971
The Shorter Strachey   (biography, essays, and criticism)   1980

*This work was written in 1913.

THE SPECTATOR   (essay date 1912)

[*In the review excerpted below, Strachey's first published work,* Landmarks in French Literature, *is praised as a perceptive and scholarly contribution to literary criticism.*]

Mr. G. L. Strachey, in his *Landmarks in French Literature*, has accomplished an extremely difficult task with considerable success. As an introduction to the study of a fascinating subject his book is a thoroughly sound and useful piece of work, admirably concise, and characterized throughout by a careful and scholarly appreciation of the peculiar qualities of the French genius. We do not, however, agree with all Mr. Strachey's verdicts on individual authors, and we differ from him in particular with reference to Montaigne and Voltaire. (p. 444)

Mr. Strachey is a very sound guide in his purely literary criticism, and shows a keen appreciation of style and form. All his criticism of French poetry is full of insight and sympathy, and this is particularly true of what he says with regard to Racine. . . . While we admire most his handling of French poetry, we fully recognize his soundness in dealing with the other branches of literature, the splendid rhetoric of Bossuet, the laughter of Rabelais, and the ruthless portraiture of Saint-Simon. We regret that Mérimée is not mentioned among the writers of the nineteenth century, but such omissions are perhaps inevitable in a book of this kind. We shall only repeat what we have said in its praise. Such work must of course be very largely its own reward; but still it is in the interest of Providence that there should be some exceptions to this rule, and Mr. Strachey's book deserves a place among the exceptions. (pp. 444-45)

"French Literature," in The Spectator (© 1912 by The Spectator), *Vol. 108, No. 4368, March 16, 1912, pp. 444-45.*

EDMUND GOSSE   (letter date 1918)

[*Gosse's importance as a critic is due primarily to his introduction of Henrik Ibsen's "new drama" to an English audience. He was among the chief English translators and critics of Scandinavian literature and was decorated by the Norwegian, Swedish, and Danish governments for his efforts. Among his other works are studies of John Donne, Thomas Gray, Sir Thomas Browne, and important early articles on French authors of the late nineteenth century. Although Gosse's works are varied and voluminous, his intellectual style is somewhat casual, with the consequence that his commentary lacks depth and is not considered to be in the first rank of modern critical thought. However, his broad interests and knowledge of foreign literatures lend his works much more than a documentary value. In this letter to the editor of* The Times Literary Supplement, *Gosse objects to and refutes Strachey's depiction of Lord Cromer in* Eminent Victorians.]

Sir,—The volume by Mr. Lytton Strachey entitled **"Eminent Victorians"** has been received publicly and privately with a chorus of praise. The author, who possesses wit and vigour, expends these qualities in a pyrotechnical display of satire. He reduces the demigods of our youth to the Gog and Magog of Bartholmy Fair. It is very amusing, and gratifying to those who grudge the dead their prestige. But even what is sparkling should be just. The late Lord Cromer is the object (among others) of Mr. Strachey's sardonic humour, and as Mr. Strachey is being accepted as an oracle, Lord Cromer's friends can but expostulate.

Mr. Lytton Strachey says of Lord Cromer that "he found it easy to despise those with whom he came into contact," that he was unmoved and cold, that "a sub-acid smile was the only comment he allowed himself." I know not what intimacy Mr. Strachey enjoyed with Lord Cromer, but he has painted a picture of him which is a caricature, and not a good-natured one. In his description our friend is hardly to be recognized. The conversation of Lord Cromer was copious; it was generally stimulating, and often delicious. It combined warmth of feeling with vivacity of expression. Lord Cromer was accessible and responsive. He was a sober, but essentially an ardent, patriot.

Mr. Lytton Strachey says:—"The East meant very little to him; he took no interest in it." There was nothing in which he took so much interest. It was seldom out of his mind; it furnished four-fifths of his conversation, in the course of which he never wearied of dwelling on minute points of difference between the Eastern and the Western temperament. The most important of his later writings, his "Political and Literary Essays," is full of evidence of this preoccupation. . . .

Mr. Lytton Strachey pursues Lord Cromer with his sarcasms in still further directions. He writes with extreme ability and in a most attractive style. It is therefore all the more important to check his statements before they are crystallized into history.

> Edmund Gosse, "The Character of Lord Cromer," in The Times Literary Supplement (© Times Newspapers Ltd. (London) 1918), No. 858, June 27, 1918, p. 301.

LYTTON STRACHEY   (essay date 1918)

[*In his much-discussed preface to* Eminent Victorians, *excerpted below, Strachey sets forth his theory of literary biography. This preface has been referred to by Leon Edel as "a manifesto on the writing of history Lytton-style."*]

It is not by the direct method of a scrupulous narration that the explorer of the past can hope to depict that singular epoch [the Victorian age]. If he is wise, he will adopt a subtler strategy. He will attack his subject in unexpected places; he will fall upon the flank, or the rear; he will shoot a sudden, revealing searchlight into obscure recesses, hitherto undivined. He will row out over that great ocean of material, and lower down into it, here and there, a little bucket, which will bring up to the light of day some characteristic specimen, from those far depths, to be examined with a careful curiosity. Guided by these considerations, I have written [*Eminent Victorians*]. I have attempted, through the medium of biography, to present some Victorian visions to the modern eye. They are, in one sense, haphazard visions—that is to say, my choice of subjects has been determined by no desire to construct a system or to prove a theory, but by simple motives of convenience and of art. It has been my purpose to illustrate rather than to explain. It would have been futile to hope to tell even a *précis* of the truth about the Victorian age, for the shortest *précis* must fill innumerable volumes. But, in the lives of an ecclesiastic, an educational authority, a woman of action, and a man of adventure, I have sought to examine and elucidate certain fragments of the truth which took my fancy and lay to my hand. (pp. v-vi)

Human beings are too important to be treated as mere symptoms of the past. They have a value which is independent of any temporal processes—which is eternal, and must be felt for its own sake. The art of biography seems to have fallen on evil times in England. We have had, it is true, a few masterpieces, but we have never had, like the French, a great biographical tradition; we have had no Fontenelles and Condorcets, with their incomparable *éloges*, compressing into a few shining pages the manifold existences of men. With us, the most delicate and humane of all the branches of the art of writing has been relegated to the journeymen of letters; we do not reflect that it is perhaps as difficult to write a good life as to live one. Those two fat volumes, with which it is our custom to commemorate the dead—who does not know them, with their ill-digested masses of material, their slipshod style, their tone of tedious panegyric, their lamentable lack of selection, of detachment, of design? They are as familiar as the *cortège* of the undertaker, and wear the same air of slow, funereal barbarism. One is tempted to suppose, of some of them, that they were composed by that functionary, as the final item of his job. The studies in this book are indebted, in more ways than one, to such works—works which certainly deserve the name of Standard Biographies. For they have provided me not only with much indispensable information, but with something even more precious—an example. How many lessons are to be learnt from them! But it is hardly necessary to particularise. To preserve, for instance, a becoming brevity—a brevity which excludes everything that is redundant and nothing that is significant—that, surely, is the first duty of the biographer. The second, no less surely, is to maintain his own freedom of spirit. It is not his business to be complimentary; it is his business to lay bare the facts of the case, as he understands them. That is what I have aimed at in this book—to lay bare the facts of some cases, as I understand them, dispassionately, impartially, and without ulterior intentions. To quote the words of a Master—"Je n'impose rien; je ne propose rien: j'expose." (pp. vi-vii)

> Lytton Strachey, in a preface to his Eminent Victorians: Cardinal Manning, Florence Nightingale, Dr. Arnold, General Gordon, G. P. Putnam's Sons, 1918, pp. v-vii.

WILLIAM LYON PHELPS (essay date 1922)

[*Phelps spent over forty years as a lecturer at Yale. His early study* The Beginnings of the English Romantic Movement *(1893) is still considered an important work and his* Essays on Russian Novelists *(1911) was one of the first influential studies of the Russian realists. From 1922 until his death in 1943 he wrote a regular column for* Scribner's Magazine *and a nationally syndicated newspaper column. During this period, his criticism became less scholarly and more journalistic, and is notable for its generally enthusiastic tone. In the excerpt below, Phelps assesses several of the essays collected in Strachey's* Books and Characters.]

This handsomely printed volume [**"Books and Characters"**] contains fifteen essays. . . . They are all interesting, for I do not believe that Mr. Strachey could be dull if he tried; they are interesting in their subjects, in their style, and in their indication of the development of the author. Since Augustine Birrell published the first series of "Obiter Dicta," in 1884, I do not recall any book of literary essays that made a like sensation until the appearance of **"Eminent Victorians."**

In the book before us we see that the brilliant irony, the incisive wit, the pictorial imagination, and the flair for the concrete symbol—all of which were evident on every page of **"Eminent Victorians"**—were not from the first particularly characteristic of their author's manner. They increased with his increase in years. Almost any competent reviewer could have written **"The Poetry of Blake,"** which agreeably fills fifteen pages of this volume; and one who should begin with it would say, "Where is the Strachey we know?" Then, if one should turn to **"Lady Hester Stanhope,"** one could hardly repress an exclamation of glad recognition. . . .

In addition to conventional phrases, there are, in the earlier pieces, rhapsodical passages, which would seem to indicate that the author, in the course of his pilgrimage through this world, had passed the familiar stages that lead from enthusiasm to irony. He may count it an intellectual advance; but I wonder if he does not sometimes wish he might recapture the first, fine, careless rapture.

There are sentences in the essay on Racine . . . and in the one on Sir Thomas Browne . . . which are so wildly enthusiastic that if they were written now, and by some one else, I surmise that it might be unfortunate for their author if they came under Mr. Strachey's eye. He, of course, would not be the first to treat with satire what he formerly treated with reverence. . . . (p. 5)

Probably no one has ever written a better account of the extraordinary and absurd friendship between Voltaire and Frederick, who to me, at all events, seems to need the appellation "the Great" rather more than greater men, whose wine needs no bush. This essay was written in 1915, and Mr. Strachey remarks in the opening paragraph: "Just as modern Germany dates from the accession of Frederick to the throne of Prussia, so modern France dates from the establishment of Voltaire on the banks of the Lake of Geneva." (pp. 5, 10)

The least valuable paper in this volume is that called **"Shakespeare's Final Period,"** dated 1906. Had Mr. Strachey confined himself to poking fun at sentimental biographers and critics who insist that "King Lear" represents the dramatist's own heartbreak and "The Tempest" his final calm, for neither of which commonly accepted statements is there a scintilla of evidence, he would have done well; but the "creative" part of his article is as fanciful as the positions he attacks. . . .

The long essay on Mme. du Deffand . . . and the short one on Mr. Creevey . . . are masterpieces. They give the very age and body of the time his form and pressure. The picture of the blind old woman queening it in her salon, and then falling in love as pitiably as only old ladies know how to do, is in Mr. Strachey's best style; and the foot-loose, vivacious Creevey, chronically hungry for food and gossip, lives again in these pages. Both these biographies end with a touch of twentieth-century melancholy, almost of self-pity, which does not make them any the less impressive.

Mr. Strachey is too wise to write in only one vein. Many readers of **"Eminent Victorians,"** on hearing that he was engaged on a life of Queen Victoria, looked forward to it with a relish easy to imagine. If he treated Victorians as he treated the Master of Rugby, what would he do with Victoria? It is certain that he disappointed these worthies. His method is of course dramatic; he selects just the material sure to be sensational; but when we finish the last page of that biography we feel that Victoria was a ruler as well as a queen. And, in disengaging the character of the Prince Consort from the royal household, he performed for that able and industrious statesman a lasting service.

Not for anything would I miss a new book by Lytton Strachey. I am already looking forward to the next one, for no matter what the subject, it cannot fail to be full of matter and manner. Some day I hope he will write a biography of Rousseau—he is possibly the only man in the world who could come nearest to the mystery. (p. 10)

> *William Lyon Phelps, "A Strachey of Many Moods," in* The New York Times Book Review *(copyright © 1922 by The New York Times Company; reprinted by permission), July 30, 1922, pp. 5, 10.*

RAYMOND MORTIMER (essay date 1922)

[*Mortimer, a friend of Strachey, offers a review of* Books and Characters *and gives general criticism on Strachey's style, stating that it is characteristically vivid, detached, and dramatic. While Mortimer comments that Strachey liked to "sketch a man's appearance and deduce from it his character," D. S. Mirsky believes that such a statement is a reversal of Strachey's artistic method (see excerpt below).]*

The author of *Queen Victoria* and *Eminent Victorians* has invented a new manner, if not a new *genre,* of history; and in face of the imitations, often so vulgar, that are already appearing, the word Stracheyesque seems an inevitable addition to our critical vocabulary.

The first characteristic of Mr Strachey's art is the startling vividity with which he paints his personages. They satisfy the eye. You feel you can walk round them. His Lord Melbourne, his Disraeli, are as real as any characters in fiction. They are almost too lifelike, one feels, too good to be true. But they are hypotheses that work: and work neatly and gracefully, so that if we sometimes suspect that the whole truth would be something very different, what matter? Is not Mr Strachey—are we not all—too sensible and philosophic to take History for more than a sober, daylight fiction, as Mr Santayana calls it? The trouble comes with certain other figures, Manning, for instance, and Gladstone. Mr Strachey's touch remains delicate, his technique unfaltering, but something is missing. And what but a little sympathy on the showman's part with the moral standpoint and inspiring faith of his puppets? Where there is no belief in law, a lawyer seems a ridiculous figure; where there is no belief in God, a saint is frankly grotesque. And it is the weakness of Mr Strachey's histories that he is a worshipper of Reason, who can no more understand the attraction and power of other faiths than he can the stupider instincts of the brute creation.

The second characteristic of Mr Strachey is his attitude of ironic detachment. In view of this it is natural that he should be accused of lacking seriousness. He would appear to approach his subjects without a prejudice, a prevention, or a moral theory; and often after a detailed statement of the facts, sometimes given in the actual words of the character concerned, he will leave them *sans commentaire*. But, *le malin*, does he not make them speak for themselves? For the facts are selected with an ingenuity which we sometimes fear to be disingenuous, and a Latin fondness for *oratio obliqua* only makes his satire more devastating. Lack of principles may amount in itself to a principle; and Mr Strachey, with all his greater subtlety, is perhaps at heart as much a partisan as Gibbon or Voltaire. In vain does he write of men as if they were animals, and he a naturalist; though detached, he is still not impartial. For obviously some sorts of animals are more attractive and comprehensible to him than others.

The third characteristic of this historian is that he has the expert eye of a theatrical producer for dramatic effect. He makes costume eloquent; he makes every situation tell; and if in *Eminent Victorians* he is writing too evidently for the sake of "effects," in *Queen Victoria* he sets his scene and arranges his lighting with subtler and more art-concealing art. Indeed it sometimes seems that while Clio serves to grace his measure, Thalia is his real flame. For he stages the drama of history as a comedy of manners; his particular delight is in the unexpected and the preposterous; and his sentimental passages are flavoured with a delicate cynicism which makes them most enchanting things in his work. He remains detached, and so succeeds in writing history that is dramatic without being romantic. Does not such detachment constitute the difference between classic and romantic art?

A favourite method of Mr Strachey's is to sketch a man's appearance and deduce from it his character. When reading him, we naturally tend to reverse the process. The phantasm of the author thus evoked from the pages of his biographical studies is a figure half Creevey, half Voltaire; a disillusioned happy little man, with small penetrating eyes, very neat, very urbane, clean-shaven, of course, and probably plumpish. And he seems, in these books, to gaze with attentive curiosity through the bars of the Menagerie of History at the pompous antics of all these ridiculous Victorian creatures, wagging their vast vaticinatory beards, and taking the Union Jack, the Deity, and themselves with fantastic and equal seriousness.

But now Mr Strachey turns his attention to a more polite zoological department; and leads us to the Monkey House of the Eighteenth Century to observe the inhabitants as they gregariously chatter and quarrel round the cleverest of apes, Voltaire, and tease into madness the lonely, pathetic, farouche, incomprehensible bear, Jean-Jacques Rousseau. It is evident that Mr Strachey prefers such simian society to that of the solemn-eyed goats and monogamous penguins in the Victorian enclosure.

The new book [*Books and Characters*] is a collection of papers written at intervals during the last seventeen years, and arranged in the historical order of their subjects. But to show the development of Mr Strachey's interests, I will catalogue them in the order in which they were composed. The years 1905 to 1908 give essays on Voltaire's tragedies, Shakespeare's last period, Johnson's Lives of the Poets, Blake, Rousseau, Beddoes, and Racine. This may be considered the first period of Mr Strachey's work; and the papers, with the exception of that on Rousseau, are all chiefly concerned with the criticism of literature. Then in 1913 there is an essay on Mme du Deffand, followed in turn by Voltaire in England, Henri Beyle, Voltaire and Frederic, and lastly, in 1919, by Lady Hester Stanhope and Mr Creevey. All the papers in this group are primarily biographical and portray individual and social character. There only remains to mention a quite exquisite little pastiche of a Voltairean dialogue between Moses, Diogenes, and Locke: it is undated and has not appeared before.

This book then shows the transference of Mr Strachey's activity from the study of style to that of character. Also here, in contrast with the books he wrote later, he is chiefly occupied with persons and books sympathetic to him. Thus it is pleasant, though surprising, to find that his appreciation of language should lead him to write so enthusiastically of Beddoes, though his description of him as a belated Elizabethan seems to me at least one-sided. This essay will certainly drive every reader to penetrate the Gothic gloom and macabre magnificence of Death's Jest-Book, in which they will find one of the most impressive and continuous cataracts of romantic poetry in English. (pp. 338-40)

All the essays are written in the witty and precise style we have come to expect from Mr Strachey, but it is easy to see his standpoint becoming more definite, and his idiosyncrasies more marked. The two latest papers have exactly the same quality and texture as the big work on Queen Victoria. Still I consider that the finest character study in this collection, that of Mme du Deffand (and how fine it is!) is the one inspired by the greatest sympathy; and the best literary criticism is that of her, and I fancy Mr Strachey's favourite author, Racine. This is the most important essay in the book, and an invaluable, because unique, contribution to English critical literature.

Mr Strachey always obviously enjoys reversing accepted opinions. But it is unfair to call iconoclast the artist who has revealed that the insipid Lady of the Lamp was really a splendid and remorseless Amazon, and has substituted for the priggish alabaster Albert of official history, a melancholy, misunderstood, too humane and too romantic Prince. Never though has he fought more admirably than against the Vulgar Errors and ignorant provincialism of English critics of Racine. (pp. 340-41)

No one could be a better guide than Mr Strachey through the obstacles which make the approach to Racine so arduous to English readers. But first a warning; it is useless for any one to open a Racine without a pretty sound understanding and appreciation of the French language. The first thing necessary is a sensitive ear. And it is lack of ear in the reader which is the most formidable obstacle rather than any difficulty with the classical conventions the use of which Mr Strachey so eloquently explains and defends. (p. 341)

Raymond Mortimer, "Mr Strachey's Past," in The Dial (copyright, 1922, by The Dial Publishing Company, Inc.), Vol. LXXIII, No. 3, September, 1922, pp. 338-42.

D. S. MIRSKY (essay date 1923)

[*Mirsky was a Russian prince who fled his country after the Bolshevik Revolution and settled in London. While in England, he wrote two important and comprehensive histories of Russian literature,* A History of Russian Literature *and* Contemporary Russian Literature. *In 1932, having reconciled himself to the Soviet regime, Mirsky returned to the U.S.S.R. He continued to write literary criticism, but his work eventually ran afoul of Soviet censors and he was exiled to Siberia. He disappeared in 1937. In the excerpt below, Mirsky gives an early, though balanced critique of Strachey's literary method and surveys the biographer's major works.*]

Writing a few months ago in *The Dial* about Mr. Strachey's last book, Mr. Raymond Mortimer attempted "to reverse the process" by which Mr. Strachey is accustomed "to sketch a man's appearance and deduce from it his character" [see excerpt above]. (p. 175)

Mr. Mortimer has truly "reversed" Mr. Strachey's method. . . . And as the simplest sort of definition is a negative one, my first definition of Mr. Strachey's method will be that it is just the opposite of the method displayed by Mr. Raymond Mortimer.

There are two ways of writing history which I may call the mythological and the novelistic way. The mythological way is to work in generalisations, to simplify history into a formula, to think in types and moulds—it is the method of deducing from the "ironical detachment" of Mr. Strachey's books the penetrating smallness of his eyes. This method is by far the easier, and has always been used in preference to the other method. It is the method of many very great historians, of Macaulay, of Rénan, of Mommsen: it is also the method of the world at large, of the collective memory of Mankind—the method that created the ancient Mythologies, and the smaller but no less instructive modern myths, such as the myths of the Lady with the Lamp, or of the Prince Consort. It is precisely in destroying these convenient and popular simplifications and substituting for them characters that are complex, unique, and not reducible to short formulae, that Mr. Strachey has shown that he does not belong to the mythological school of history.

The other method, which I have called the novelistic, which rejoices, not in the potential simplicity, but in the actual complexity, of Nature, appears later in history and is displayed more seldom. In fact, I do not know of any great historian who ever used it on any large scale. Periods, nations, civilizations are too much of a generalisation for a historian of this disposition; but a biographer, of course, if he pretends to be anything but a mere recorder or anecdote-monger must have something of this quality. And this is why the art of biography is really a modern art. The greatest book in this line is, and will probably for ever remain, the *Mémoires* of the Duc de Saint-Simon. And this is, of course, the only author to whom Mr. Strachey is essentially indebted. It would be, however, falling into the mythological rut to describe Mr. Strachey as a Saint-Simon *redivivus*. Saint-Simon was simple, unsophisticated, a violent and unabashed partisan. But it was his very simplicity that made his vision so perplexingly complex. Mr. Strachey is far too complex and sophisticated himself to produce anything approaching Saint-Simon in created complexity. He compares Saint-Simon's style to a "tropical forest—luxuriant, bewildering, enormous—with the gayest hummingbirds among the branches, and the vilest monsters in the entangled grass." But Mr. Strachey would have had to be a second Dickens to find all this in the brown-brick squares of Bloomsbury.

Mr. Strachey's literary work falls into three distinct periods. The first (1905-1912) during which he was interested in lit-

erature, chiefly French, includes about half the papers in *Books and Characters,* and his first publication in book form the *Landmarks in French Literature.* During the second (1913-1915) he was mainly attracted by literary biography, and the age of Voltaire. With the third period his interest becomes absorbed in the lives of unliterary men and women, and begins to gravitate round the central figure of Queen Victoria. This includes his two best-known books and two short essays in *Books and Characters* on Mr. Creevey and Lady Hester Stanhope.

So before adventuring himself into the intricate mazes of human life, Mr. Strachey had feasted on the rich dishes of imaginative literature, and feasted with far less ironical detachment than he later turned out to possess. The difference of Mr. Strachey's attitude towards literature and life (may it be only a difference of age?) is striking. He seems to find literature a more serious, but a much less enjoyable thing than Reality. He is almost solemn when he deals with Beddoes or Sir Thomas Browne; he is quite enthusiastic when he speaks of Racine or Saint-Simon, but I very much doubt whether in all sincerity this enjoyment of *Phèdre* or of *Urn-Burial* is quite as keen as his enjoyment of the diary of Mr. Creevey, or of the adventures of "the boy Jones."

Mr. Strachey is (or rather was, for since that little book on French literature which appeared in 1912 he has written nothing strictly critical) a very solid and respectable critic. His taste is catholic, and his appreciations keen and just. The book on French literature is a little masterpiece of its kind; the distribution of matter is so well balanced, the few quotations so appropriate and representative, his comprehensive sympathy for the complex genius of France so thorough, that it may be put up as a model of this sort of writing. And it contains pages that are more than respectable. The paragraph on Saint-Simon is quite as good as anything I know in the way of descriptive criticism. For Mr. Strachey's is this most difficult kind of criticism which is not to give an interpretation or a commentary on the author in question, but to describe in words of your own the effect which the writer produces and the way he goes about it. Mr. Strachey gives us really a quintessential extract of Saint-Simon! (pp. 175-77)

To me (it may be the foreigner speaking in me) Mr. Strachey's principal claim to critical pre-eminence is his essay on Racine [in *Books and Characters*]. For an English critic to appreciate the greatest of French poets is so rare an accomplishment that alone it would suffice to place such a critic above all the rest. I do not know whether Mr. Strachey's dexterity in wielding Racine quotations is not lost on most of his readers, but, for myself, I know of no greater and purer poetical thrill than when one of the great passages of Racine suddenly breaks on me. . . . I can forgive anything to an Englishman who speaks understandingly of Racine. But there are in Mr. Strachey's critiques some things that do need forgiving. He has a dangerous mannerism of beginning and ending his articles with certain rhetorical flourishes, a mannerism which will have its full development later, but which is apparent in his earliest papers. These beginnings and ends are like the rubrics of a mediaeval scribe, and are rather ridiculous on the very modern background of Mr. Strachey's middle parts. A very characteristic one occurs in the end of the (excellent otherwise) essay on Sir Thomas Browne (who is a dangerous model and one not to be lightly imitated), and I cannot help being greatly diverted by the idea of the gentleman painted by Mr. H. Lamb sitting between the paws of the great sphinx and rolling forth to the sands of the desert the magnificent cadences of *Hydriotaphia* or of the *Garden of Cyrus*.

There is a certain topsy-turvyness in Mr. Strachey's outlook typical of the general topsy-turvyness of things in modern times. Life and literature seem to have changed places. Literature, of course, is the only worthy and serious pursuit in the world, the only thing worth really troubling about, and the great literary creators are the only people who may be approached seriously—note the respect with which he incidentally speaks of Charlotte Brontë in *Queen Victoria,* quite as if he were a mediaeval monk suddenly mentioning a saint in a story dealing with profane worldlings. But however respectable the craft of letters, no literature can be as entertaining as real life. The world is what Mr. Strachey must have for his entertainment if even literary work be his standard of holy living. "What shall it profit a man, one is tempted to exclaim, if he gain his own soul and lose the whole world?" says Mr. Strachey in his essay on *The Poetry of Blake*. Blake was certainly a genius and not to be spoken of lightly as you may speak of mere politicians, such as Gladstone. But poor Blake never realised that for all his marrying of heaven and hell he was hopelessly on the wrong track. If he really wanted to discover that existence was good, he ought to have turned his back on both those unearthly regions, and plunged head forward into the diaries of Mr. Pepys. He would have found there something much more worth living for than anything in either of the Canticles of Dante.

This I think is the line of argument which led Mr. Strachey away from great books to correspondences and diaries, not always great, but always amusing. The first result of this peregrination was the series of essays written about 1914 on Voltaire and his contemporaries. These articles are of course very good, but they are not yet Mr. Strachey in full. Voltaire himself, had he been a third party to the quarrel, might have given a more spirited account of his relations with Frederick and much in the same manner as Mr. Strachey has done. Voltaire, in fact, is easy to write about. The subject is, in itself, so full of character and amusement that it is hardly very difficult to make the best of it. A cool and clear wit will suffice, and a tolerable gift of narrative.

There is a notion current about Mr. Strachey that he is essentially akin to the eighteenth century and the French genius (which is not quite the same as the eighteenth century). There is an exaggeration in this and, I think, misrepresentation. The air of the eighteenth century—or what is conventionally supposed to be the air of the eighteenth century—is a clear and thin air with no "atmosphere" to speak about, a *lumen siccum,* if ever there was. Mr. Strachey's art is as decidedly "modern," an atmosphere of variously reflecting density, a doubtless *lumen humidum.* Of course, the thing loosely called "modernity" *was* started in the eighteenth century, and Mr. Strachey has many interesting things to say on the subject, but it is not the eighteenth century of Voltaire. Two great writers so very different and still akin to each other in that they are the two spring fountains of modernity—Saint-Simon and Rousseau—are the real grandfathers of Mr. Strachey's art. For it is in Saint-Simon and Rousseau first of all men (except Shakespeare, of course) that the modern conception of personality makes its appearance—in the state of unconscious creation in Saint-Simon and of a painfully self-conscious idiosyncrasy in Rousseau. Personality is the beginning and end of Mr. Strachey's vision of the world, and personality was discovered by the Duc de Saint-Simon and by the author of the *Confessions.* In this sense, Mr. Strachey may belong to the eighteenth century. (pp. 177-79)

It has been said that Mr. Strachey has revived the art of biography. If this be meant in the sense that he has revived the art of portraying live characters from documental evidence, the statement is misleading—there was no art to revive. The art of such portrayal has never existed, at any rate in anything like the perfection it has received at Mr. Strachey's hand. Mr. Strachey is not with the biographers but with the autobiographists and memoir-writers and with the novelists of the nineteenth century. For the art created by Saint-Simon and Rousseau became the art of the novelists rather than of anyone else, and the masters before whom Mr. Strachey must incline are Thackeray, Tolstoy, Dostoievsky, not any one of his professional predecessors. But if biography be considered as one of the forms of the *narrative* art in general, the art of telling a story from documental evidence, then Mr. Strachey is really a reviver. For his interest is equally distributed between his subject and his form, and if his chief delight lies in the humanity he describes, his readers' delight is equally due to the skilful craftsmanship of his writings. Historians and biographers have of late times been too much attracted by scientific ideas to care much about their writing, and if there were historians who really thought of doing literary work, it was those who were least of all interested in the accuracy of the facts they had to do with—these were the generalising and constructive historians, of the Taine type, who thought much less of discovering the truth than of making a plausible and striking outline of anything. The historian of detail depended on documents, and the further he kept a meddling hand from them the more he was respected.

Now, it seems that Mr. Strachey's ambition lies something the same way, or at least for some reason or other he wants to make it out that it does so. He takes for his motto in *Eminent Victorians* the words: "Je ne propose rien, je ne suppose rien; j'expose." This is a deal too modest. The last verb ought to be "je compose" or at least "je dispose." For with all his respect of fact and relish of detail, Mr. Strachey takes great and sometimes exaggerated pains to tell his story elegantly. And nothing can be said against his great skill in this matter. The story is always told in the best possible way, and even when the story is practically incidental and only for clearness' sake indispensable, Mr. Strachey tells it in the fewest words but to the greatest effect. His accounts of the Tai-ping rebellion and of the Mahdi's beginnings are lucid, accurate and amusing, and the construction of his biographies is always masterly. But Mr. Strachey has certain deep-rooted faults of style, and I cannot admire his way of beginning and ending. (pp. 180-81)

It is, however, ungenerous to grumble about such shortcomings when we get so many good things besides. These are abundant in *Eminent Victorians,* but *Queen Victoria* is brimful of them. Mr. Strachey's reputation was made by *Eminent Victorians,* but it rests on *Queen Victoria. Eminent Victorians* is the first flights of youthful ability (if youth were a thing easily associated with our idea of Mr. Strachey); *Queen Victoria* is the fuller growth of maturity. The distance between the two books is almost as great as from [William Thackeray's] *Book of Snobs* to *Vanity Fair.* In the first book Mr. Strachey's genius does something curiously like running riot—he has not yet mastered his single faculties. And he displays, besides violent personal feeling in his *Dr. Arnold* and *Cardinal Manning,* other more agreeable angularities, such as a more farcical sense of comedy, than appears in *Queen Victoria.* There is something verging on farce, for instance, in the account of Lord Panmure, the Bison, "casting wistful eyes towards the happy pastures of the Free Church of Scotland," and his obstinate opposition to Miss

Nightingale. Nor is Mr. Strachey deficient in the higher aspects of his art; he boldly uses metaphor and poetical simile when he stands in need of it, but he is at his best in his metaphors when they are used in a strictly businesslike way, when closing on his subject he discovers that it cannot be defined to the end in ordinary terms, and boldly strikes out—as in the splendid paragraph on Gladstone in *The End of General Gordon*. . . . (p. 182)

Being admittedly an iconoclast, a destroyer of accepted idols, Mr. Strachey often, however, moves in the grooves of a too easy polemic, and in this direction sometimes exaggerates his negative work. This he does not so much in the main story as in direct assertions, which are not always borne out. He has expressions, for example, which may lead the reader to expect Queen Victoria to turn out a regular tyrant in petticoats, and has himself to retract a little in the end of the volume, and to explain that, after all, Queen Victoria was not quite as despotically inclined as George III. These disproportionate expressions, together with the occasional rhetorical clausulae, are, I think, the only artistic shortcomings of *Queen Victoria*. I do not know whether it answers all the exigencies of strict historical documentation, but I have no doubt that it is one of the most readable books ever written, and a book full of human knowledge and human interest. And for grasp of personality combined with narrative power Mr. Strachey can stand his own against no matter what great novelist.

After all, the ultimate quality of the book (and of *Eminent Victorians*, in a lesser degree) is neither wit nor picturesqueness nor wealth of appropriately chosen detail. It is atmosphere. Something indefinable, something like a less obtrusive and less immovable Wagnerian *leitmotif* accompanies every one of Mr. Strachey's characters whenever they make their appearance on his puppet-stage. Something which has been the privilege of some of the greatest novelists—Dickens and Dostoievsky—whose characters we recognise by the first word they utter, by the very intonation of their voices, hopelessly irreducible to literary tricks. Mr. Strachey's way of conveying the atmosphere of his characters is also ultimately irreducible. But they move about each in their own atmosphere, carrying it about with them like a mysterious aura. To give names to these atmospheres, to speak of the solid vitality of Queen Victoria, the romantic charlatanism of Disraeli, the sad conscientiousness of Prince Albert, would be useless. Such things are the secret of the artist. This is hardly a Latin characteristic, and the *lumen humidum* of Mr. Strachey is essentially in the line of English tradition.

And what is Mr. Strachey's personal attitude towards his Victorian actors? Is it really ironic detachment? Hardly quite so. It might have been so originally, as it certainly was with Voltaire and Frederick. But somehow, I think, in the process of studying this nineteenth century, so bewilderingly rich in human documentation, and after all so intensely human and so unusually emotional, he seems to have discovered that human life is something more than an entertaining puppet show, that it was curiously easy to be moved by sympathy, and that the prolonged familiarity of these beings was sure to leave deep sentimental traces. Human frailty and the vanity of human activities, even in their ridiculously self-important Victorian conscientiousness, even in people who could sincerely admire Landseer and Winterhalter, and had retained of Religion all its boredom without retaining anything of its glamour, were poignantly pathetic, and as self-confident bad taste is perhaps the most pathetic form of Man's frailty and consequently his near-

est approach to the greatest Christian virtue, humility, it is only just that Mr. Strachey should have finished his book on a note artistically false, and for that very reason, perhaps, all the more humanly true. (pp. 183-84)

> *D. S. Mirsky, "Mr. Lytton Strachey" (reprinted by permission of the Literary Estate of D. S. Mirsky), in* The London Mercury, *Vol. VIII, No. 44, June, 1923, pp. 175-84.*

EDWIN MUIR   (essay date 1926)

[*Muir was a distinguished Scottish novelist, poet, critic, and translator. With his wife Willa, he translated works by various German authors unfamiliar to the English-speaking world, including Gerhart Hauptmann, Hermann Broch, and, most notably, Franz Kafka. Throughout his career Muir was intrigued by psychoanalytic theory, particularly Freud's analyses of dreams and Jung's theories of archetypal imagery, both of which he often utilized in his work. In his critical writings, Muir was more concerned with the general philosophical issues raised by works of art—such as the nature of time or society—than with the particulars of the work itself, such as style or characterization. In the essay excerpted below, he credits Strachey with changing the form of biography and humanizing it through his use of irony.*]

In *Eminent Victorians* Mr. Strachey did two things for biography: he humanized it by irony, he gave it form. He went out in search not of great figures and noble characters, but of human nature, and he always found it. Having found it, he set it out in his own terms. All his characters passed through his eighteenth-century workshop, and emerged in the ironically appropriate costumes he had devised for them. They emerged, if not in their own shape, then in some shape which revealed it. For the time being their author's puppets, they played over again the game which they had played far more intensely, sometimes in tears and agony, in the actual world. Mr. Strachey held the strings which moved this puppet play, and they were constantly being manipulated, but very rarely did we catch sight of them. The figures seemed to be going through the ballet of their own lives, a ballet simplified and stylized to the last detail; and it was only in the conventionalization of the costumes and attitudes that one recognized the choreographer.

There was drama in that spectacle, but it was a drama which had taken place a long time before, and existed now only as a memory and a conscious play. The figures "remembered" for the hundredth time when they had to make such and such a gesture, when they had to laugh, weep, show lively apprehension, anticipation, repentance, doubt, affection. They did not feel; they imitated the passions, sorrowful or happy, which happened to come their way in the game.

It is this effect of distance and illusion which gives Mr. Strachey's work its rare poetic quality, and makes him a distinguished artist. He writes in two moods: the consciously ironical in which he satirizes the pretensions and hypocrisies of men, and the involuntarily ironical in which he sees the drama of existence as a transitory, illusory process which has happened so often that it has now but an apparent reality. Only where his deliberate irony is quiescent does this more profound irony come into play. His portrait of Arnold of Rugby, for example, is excellent satire; but his portraits of Manning, Florence Nightingale, and Victoria are something more. *Queen Victoria* was commended for being less ironical than *Eminent Victorians*, but the truth was that in it Mr. Strachey's irony had only released the lesser themes of the satirist to seize upon life itself. With the abrogation of his conscious gift for ironical presentation the true bias of his profoundly ironical mind was re-vealed, and the complete compass of his imagination released.

The strange thing is that through this irony he arrived, without formulating them, at conclusions not unlike those of men for whom one can detect in his works no sympathy: the metaphy-sicians, mystics, and saints. Life as Mr. Strachey portrays it is an illusion; he can portray it as nothing else; and his work is most profound precisely where the sense of illusion is most unmistakably given: where he shows Manning mounting the little back stair of the Vatican or walking in state to West-minster; where he describes the distant and tiny figure of Gor-don standing on the toy ramparts of Khartoum, gazing over a desert which only to him is illimitable; where he records the remote sorrows, domestic and State, of the little woman who sat on England's throne. We remember the incidents in his books which destiny seems to be arranging for their uncon-scious effect: Newman weeping outside the house at Little-more, Disraeli bearing flowers to the Queen. These incidents, trivial or moving, have a significance almost symbolical, as if in them the complete essence of a character were expressed. If a choreographer were to put these characters in a ballet he would fix them in precisely the postures Mr. Strachey has fixed them in. A mystic would do the same. On the life of this world a complete scepticism and a profound mysticism may come to the same conclusions. (pp. 119-23)

[Mr. Strachey] seems at first glance to be completely outside the current of modern literature; and a clever writer calls him a Voltaire who has reached the age of two hundred odd years. There is little resemblance between the author of **Queen Victoria** and the author of *La Pucelle*. Mr. Strachey's sensibility is modern; his imagination is romantic; only by his cool ration-ality does he belong to the eighteenth century. His **Cardinal Manning** and **Queen Victoria** would have appeared very novel if not quite incomprehensible to Dr. Johnson; their sceptical imagination and compassionate irony would have disturbed the lexicographer's mind. The truth is that Mr. Strachey has a very modern temperament and sensibility, and that he would be more completely at a loss than almost any other writer if he were transported into the eighteenth century. If he appears out of place in our time it is not because his intelligence is un-modern; it is because his temperament is unique. He is an inimitable writer, but he belongs as certainly to this age as Lamb did to his. (pp. 126-27)

> Edwin Muir, *"Lytton Strachey," in his* Transition: Essays on Contemporary Literature *(copyright © 1926 by The Viking Press, Inc.; copyright renewed © 1954 by Edwin Muir; reprinted by permission of Viking Penguin Inc.), The Viking Press, 1926, pp. 117-27.*

SIGMUND FREUD (letter date 1928)

[*An Austrian neurologist, Freud is the father of psychoanalysis. The general framework of psychoanalytic thought, explained in his seminal work* The Interpretation of Dreams *(1900), encom-passes both normal and abnormal behavior and is founded on the tenet that all behavior is motivated by antecedent causes. Freud's interrelated theories on the unconscious (primitive impulses and repressed thoughts), the libido hypothesis (sexual energy that follows a predetermined course), the structure of personality (id, superego, ego), and human psychosexual development (sequential stages of sexual development) have been widely used in the treat-ment of psychopathology utilizing four main analytic techniques: free association, dream analysis, interpretation, and transfer-ence. Although Freud was sometimes harshly criticized for his innovative theories, especially for such ideas as infantile sexuality*]

and the Oedipus and Electra complexes, he was for the most part greatly respected as a thinker and teacher. In addition, Freudi-anism has had significant influence on various schools of philos-ophy, religious and political ideas, and artistic endeavors such as surrealism in art, atonal music, and stream of consciousness literature. Thus, along with such important thinkers as Karl Marx, Friedrich Nietzsche, and Albert Einstein, Freud is considered one of the most important shapers of modern thought. After reading Strachey's Elizabeth and Essex, *Freud wrote Strachey a letter praising him for his use of psychoanalysis to reveal the psychology of his biographical subjects.*]

I am acquainted with all your earlier publications, and have read them with great enjoyment. But the enjoyment was es-sentially an aesthetic one. This time [in *Elizabeth and Essex*] you have moved me deeply, for you yourself have reached greater depths. You are aware of what other historians so easily overlook—that it is impossible to understand the past with certainty, because we cannot divine men's motives and the essence of their minds and so cannot interpret their actions. Our psychological analysis does not suffice even with those who are near us in space and time, unless we can make them the object of years of the closest investigation, and even then it breaks down before the incompleteness of our knowledge and the clumsiness of our synthesis. So that with regard to the people of past times we are in the same position as with dreams to which we have been given no associations—and only a layman could expect us to interpret such dreams as those. As a historian, then, you show that you are steeped in the spirit of psycho-analysis. And, with reservations such as these, you have approached one of the most remarkable figures in your country's history, you have known how to trace back her char-acter to the impressions of her childhood, you have touched upon her most hidden motives with equal boldness and dis-cretion, and it is very possible that you have succeeded in making a correct reconstruction of what actually occurred. (pp. 336-37)

> Sigmund Freud, *in a letter to Lytton Strachey on December 25, 1928 (reprinted by permission of Sig-mund Freud Copyrights Ltd), in* Lytton Strachey, a Critical Biography: The Years of Achievement (1910-1932), Vol. II *by Michael Holroyd, Heinemann, 1968 (and reprinted in his* Lytton Strachey and the Blooms-bury Group: His Work, Their Influence, *Penguin Books, 1971, pp. 336-37).*

ERNEST BOYD (essay date 1928)

[*An Irish-American writer and translator, Boyd was a prominent literary critic known for his erudite, honest, and often satirical critiques. In the laudatory essay excerpted below, Boyd disagrees with those commentators who maintain that Strachey's intention was to blight the reputations of his biographical subjects.*]

Ever since Lytton Strachey published **"Eminent Victori-ans"** . . . , we have witnessed an extraordinary rise in the popularity of biography. It seemed as if he had given a new lease of life to a form of literature which had previously, in his own words, "been relegated to the journeymen of letters" [see excerpt above]. It is only necessary to read most of the newer biographers to find how little they have improved upon their predecessors. Journeymen they were and journeymen they remain, despite the substitution of the "modern," Strachey-esque manner for the pious pomposities of the old-fashioned biography.

In certain quarters it was the fashion to charge Lytton Strachey with being responsible for this changed conception of the biographer's function. He was accused of being cynical, frivolous, iconoclastic, and people were heard to declare that his method was too easy, too unscholarly ever to displace the sounder method of his predecessors. Mr. Strachey has, I think, triumphantly refuted this contention. In the space of ten years he has written only three books, apart from a volume of reprinted essays: **"Eminent Victorians," "Queen Victoria"** and now **"Elizabeth and Essex."** . . . All three are works of patient scholarship, differing from the productions of most scholars only in so far as they are written with an exquisite feeling for the graces of the English language. They are obviously not the work of a "smart" person, prepared at any time to demolish a reputation. That Mr. Strachey has left to the innumerable horde of his imitators.

Even more noticeably in **"Elizabeth and Essex"** than in **"Queen Victoria"** has he departed from the attitude which made **"Eminent Victorians"** famous. I well remember with what curiosity I looked forward to his book on the Queen, and with what interest I realized that she did not appear in his pages like another figure, more elaborately drawn, from his first book. Mr. Strachey very evidently had been captured by his subject, and if irony was by no means absent, there was also respect. In fact, at one point I felt that he was being too discreet. It will be remembered that little or nothing is revealed of Queen Victoria's sentiments at the time of the Franco-Prussian War. These could not, I fancy, have been lacking in a certain interest in view of the prevailing feeling about Germany at the moment when **"Queen Victoria"** appeared.

"Elizabeth and Essex" disposes once and for all of the notion that Lytton Strachey is just a witty iconoclast. Careful research, an immense documentation and a felicitous style combine here in a narrative as exciting as any novel. The author does not himself adopt the license of his imitators. He does not imagine his facts, nor put into the mouths of his people words for which there is no warrant. His sources are authentic and are so skilfully used that the vast labor entailed is not apparent to the uninitiated. To quote his own description of Bacon's essays, the book is written "in a succession of gnomic sentences from which every beauty but those of force and point" has been strictly banished.

The story of Elizabeth and Essex has all the fascinations of Tudor romance. The enigmatic interplay of these two figures is set against the colorful and teeming background of Elizabethan politics, from which poison, dagger and rack are never absent. The Virgin Queen was a study for the modern pathologist or psychiatrist. Her "mysterious organism" was "the pivot upon which the fate of Europe turned." Mr. Strachey unfolds this story in brilliant chapter after brilliant chapter, unravelling the tangled threads of amorous intrigue and political machination. At the exact nature of Elizabeth's relations with Essex we can only guess. Alternately favored and rebuffed, adored and defied, Essex is led to the block by circumstances over which perhaps the Queen herself had no control.

That, indeed, is part of the charm of Lytton Strachey's picture of those times. He sees people and events with the eyes of a contemporary and when he makes any comment it is to warn the reader not to look at the period with the eyes of today. . . .

There is real drama in the relations between Elizabeth and Essex, and Mr. Strachey fortunately has the ability to convey all that lies in the situation without indulging in those psycho-analytical smirks which are now considered necessary. He portrays the two and presents them more or less as they must have seemed to themselves and to their contemporaries. Despite the bond between them, Elizabeth resisted Essex in circumstances where it would have been more natural for her to take his advice. His efforts to get an appointment for Bacon make an interesting and typical story. Vacillating as the Queen was, her tergiversations with Essex make a problem in which one feels that the human, the feminine factor plays an even greater part than in the general affairs of state.

Bernard Shaw once denounced in characteristic terms the Elizabethan drama, with its blood, incest and murder. It is interesting to contrast his approach to that period with Lytton Strachey's. The latter is urbane and understanding, where the former is indignant and full of protest. With a deft phrase, a paragraph or two, Strachey expounds situations as remote from him as from Shaw. But his manner of dissociating himself is entirely different. He is the incarnation of the present day attitude at its best. He is neither hero-worshiper nor reformer.

Above all, he writes as beautifully as he thinks. One longs to quote but he is not a creator of "purple patches." The style is the man: a highly sensitive, extraordinarily dexterous mind, which is reflected in writing which is a joy to the ear and to the intelligence. Lytton Strachey is most effective where he is most intelligent. That is surely the rarest of literary phenomena. Usually when the words sparkle, the ideas hardly bear examination. Lytton Strachey has made the appeal of intelligent prose as captivating as poetry.

Ernest Boyd, in a review of "Eminent Victorians," "Queen Victoria," and "Elizabeth and Essex" (reprinted by permission of The American Play Company, Inc.), in Outlook and Independent, *December 26, 1928, p. 1415.*

EDMUND WILSON (essay date 1932)

[*Wilson, considered America's foremost man of letters in the twentieth century, wrote widely on cultural, historical, and literary matters, including several seminal critical studies. He is often credited with bringing an international perspective to American letters through his widely read discussions of European literature. Wilson was allied to no critical school: however, several dominant concerns serve as guiding motifs throughout his work. He invariably examined the social and historical implications of a work of literature, particularly literature's significance as "an attempt to give meaning to our experience" and its value for the improvement of humanity. Though not a moralist, his criticism displays a deep concern with moral values. Another constant was his discussion of a work of literature as a revelation of its author's personality. In* Axel's Castle *(1931), a seminal study of literary symbolism, Wilson wrote: "The real elements of course, of any work of fiction are the elements of the author's personality: his imagination embodies in the images of characters, situations and scenes the fundamental conflicts of his nature." Related to this is Wilson's theory, formulated in* The Wound and the Bow *(1941), that artistic ability is a compensation for a psychological wound; thus, a literary work can only be fully understood if one undertakes an emotional profile of its author. Wilson utilized this approach in many essays, and it is the most often attacked element of his thought. However, although Wilson examined the historical and psychological implications of a work of literature, he rarely did so at the expense of a discussion of its literary qualities. Perhaps Wilson's greatest contributions to American literature were his tireless promotion of writers of the 1920s, 1930s, and 1940s, and his essays introducing the best of modern literature to the general reader. In his critique of several of Strachey's works, Wilson finds*] *that Strachey was an inimitable biographer and a major influence on the public's changing attitude towards the Victorian era.*]

Lytton Strachey's chief mission . . . was to take down once for all the pretensions of the Victorian Age to moral superiority. His declaration in the preface to *Eminent Victorians,* "Je n'impose rien; je ne propose rien: j'expose" [see excerpt above], was certainly not justified by the book that followed. His irony here was so acid that it partly dehumanized his subjects. The essays on Manning and Dr. Arnold, though the technique gives an effect of detachment, have a force of suppressed invective; and the essays on Florence Nightingale and Gordon, written with the same metallic accent, make the subjects less sympathetic than they probably deserve to be. In attempting to destroy, for example, the sentimental reputation that had been created for Florence Nightingale, he emphasized her hardness to such a degree as to slight her moral seriousness and the deep feeling for suffering that drove her. Only at moments does he let these appear: "O Father," he quotes her as writing, "Thou knowest that through all these horrible twenty years, I have been supported by the belief that I was working with Thee who wast bringing everyone, even our poor nurses, to perfection"; and "How inefficient I was in the Crimea, yet He raised up from it trained nursing." Such a woman must have been more than the mere demon of energy that Lytton Strachey tried to make her appear.

But from *Eminent Victorians* on, the ferocity of Strachey abates. Queen Victoria is already a different matter. In this book, both Victoria and Albert become human and not unattractive figures. He is said to have approached them originally in the mood of *Eminent Victorians* and then found himself relenting. Victoria is not caricatured as Florence Nightingale is: she is presented simply as a woman, living, for all her exalted position and her public responsibility, a woman's limited life. To Strachey's Victoria, the role of queen is a woman's personal experience, a matter of likes and dislikes, of living up to social obligations. This is the force of the famous deathbed scene, which has been imitated so often by people who have tried to reproduce the cadences without understanding the point: that Victoria has lived through the Victorian Age, has stood at the center of its forces, without knowing what it was all about.

But in Strachey's next biography, *Elizabeth and Essex,* he produces a somewhat similar effect without the same ironic intention. *Elizabeth and Essex* seems to me the least satisfactory of Strachey's books. His art, so tight and so calculated, so much influenced by the French, was ill-suited to the Elizabethan Age. His Elizabeth, though a fine piece of workmanship like everything he did, is worse than metallic, it is wooden. It concentrates so narrowly on the personal relation between the Queen and her favorite that we wonder, glancing back to the earlier book, whether it really was Victoria who lacked interest in the politics and thought of her time, whether it was not perhaps Strachey himself. Certainly Elizabeth lived in a larger intellectual world than Victoria, yet we get almost none of it in Strachey. In general, we do not feel that the individual fates of the characters are involved with the larger affairs of history. The personal story is told with insight, but then, after all, Michelet tells a thousand such stories, taking them in his stride. And we here, for the first time with Strachey, become disagreeably aware of the high-voiced old Bloomsbury gossip gloating over the scandals of the past as he ferrets them out in his library. Lytton Strachey's curious catty malice, his enjoyment of the discomfiture of his characters, is most unpleasantly in evidence in *Elizabeth and Essex.* His attitude toward women—

Florence Nightingale, Mme. du Deffand, Queen Victoria or Queen Elizabeth—was peculiar in this, that he was fascinated by their psychology without feeling any of their attraction, and rather took pleasure in seeing them humiliated. The feminine subjects he chose were certainly lacking in feminine charm, and he seemed to do everything possible to make them unappetizing. His study of Queen Elizabeth in the light of modern psychology brings her character into sharper focus, but the effect of it is slightly disgusting; it marks so definitely the final surrender of Elizabethan to Bloomsbury England.

The revolt against Victorian pretences thus ends in faintly scabrous psychology; and in his next book Lytton Strachey recapitulates his view of history—a view with which Flaubert and Anatole France, Henry Adams and T. S. Eliot have already made us familiar and which assumes that modern society, in relation to the societies of the past, represents some sort of absolute deterioration. In *Portraits in Miniature,* which seems to me one of Strachey's real triumphs, he gives glimpses, through a series of thumb-nail sketches of for the most part minor historical and literary personages, of the evolution of modern society from the Elizabethan to the Victorian Age. These personages, by very reason of their special interest or small capacity, supply cultures particularly clear of the social and intellectual bacteria at work during the periods in which they lived. The first specimen is Sir John Harrington, the Elizabethan inventor of the watercloset; then we are shown some seventeenth-century types: an amateur scientist, a truculent classical scholar, an ambitious university don, the leader of an uncouth Protestant sect, and a few eighteenth-century types: a French abbé who consorted with the philosophers, a French magistrate and country gentleman who insisted on his rights, a lady of sensibility; and we end with Mme. de Lieven, whose liaison with the bourgeois Guizot marks for Strachey the final surrender of the splendid aristocratic qualities he had admired in Queen Elizabeth. A second series of miniatures reviews the British historians from the eighteenth-century Hume to the Victorian Bishop Creighton, and suggests a similar moral. The industrial, democratic, Protestant, middle-class world is a comedown, says Strachey by implication, from Queen Elizabeth, from Racine, from even Voltaire (these last two are favorites of Strachey's, on whom he has written more than once). When one considers the great souls of the past, the present seems dreary and vulgar—the Victorian Age in particular, for all its extraordinary energy, was a disgrace to the human spirit. This is the whole of the message of Strachey; and when he had said it as pointedly as possible in the fewest possible words, he died.

But not only did Strachey in his writings point an historical moral: he illustrated one himself. In his gallery of English historians, he himself should fill out the series. Certainly one of the best English writers of his period, he makes us feel sharply the contrast between Shakespeare's England and his. Shakespeare is expansive and untidy and close to the spoken language. Lytton Strachey, whose first-published book was a history of French literature, is so far from being any of these things that one of his chief feats consists in having managed to achieve in English some of the effects of French. His biographical method, though novel in England, was already an old story in France. Sainte-Beuve was the great master of it, and Strachey's ironic tone has something in common with his. The weaknesses as well as the virtues of Strachey's style are the result of his imitation of French models. He is lucid and cool and precise, but he is terribly given to clichés. The penalty of trying to reproduce in English the chaste and abstract vocabulary of French is finding one's language become pale and banal. No wonder the age of Shakespeare turned rigid and dry in Strachey's hand. And by the time he had reached *Portraits in Miniature,* he was importing belatedly to England a point of view that since the middle nineteenth century had become a commonplace in France.

The real force and audacity of Lytton Strachey are therefore seen best, as I have indicated, at the beginning of his career. In *Eminent Victorians,* which was published just at the end of the war, he stripped forever of their solemn upholstery the religion, the education, the statesmanship and the philanthropy of the society which had brought it about. The effect in the English-speaking countries was immediate and swiftly pervasive. The biographers turned at once to the easy game of exposing accepted celebrities, and this soon became a bore and a nuisance. The harshness of *Eminent Victorians* without Strachey's wide learning and bitter feeling, the intimate method of *Queen Victoria* without his insight into character, had the effect of cheapening history, something Strachey never did—for, though he was venomous about the Victorians, he did not make them any the less formidable. He had none of the modern vice of cockiness; he maintained a rare attitude of humility, of astonishment and admiration, before the unpredictable spectacle of life, which he was always finding "amazing" and "incredible." But neither the Americans nor the English have ever, since *Eminent Victorians* appeared, been able to feel quite the same about the legends that had dominated their pasts. Something had been punctured for good. (pp. 551-56)

> *Edmund Wilson, "Lytton Strachey" (originally published in* The New Republic, *Vol. LXXII, No. 930, September 22, 1932), in his* The Shores of Light: A Literary Chronicle of the Twenties and Thirties, *Farrar, Straus and Young, Inc., 1952, pp. 551-56.*

V. S. PRITCHETT   (essay date 1933)

[*Pritchett is highly esteemed for his work as a novelist, short story writer, and critic. He is considered one of the modern masters of the short story, and his work is a subtle blend of realistic detail and psychological revelation. Pritchett is also considered one of the world's most respected and well-read literary critics. He writes in the conversational tone of the familiar essay, a method by which he approaches literature from the viewpoint of a lettered but not overly scholarly reader. A twentieth-century successor to such early nineteenth-century essayist-critics as William Hazlitt and Charles Lamb, Pritchett employs much the same critical method: his own experience, judgement, and sense of literary art are emphasized, as opposed to a codified critical doctrine derived from a school of psychological or philosophical speculation. His criticism is often described as fair, reliable, and insightful. In the following review of* Characters and Commentaries, *Pritchett assesses Strachey's strengths and weaknesses as a biographer and historian.*]

Lytton Strachey was among the most civilized of men, and few of us are civilized enough to forgive him a superiority which does not flatter us. We have, of course, our consolations—who has not? We can remark that it is simple to be civilized if you make your world small enough. We can quote the first sentence of an essay on Militarism and Theology (to be found in this collection of his literary remains [*Characters and Commentaries*], "Ultimately the world is governed by moderate men," and reflect that there was nothing moderate about Lytton Strachey. To be an artist is to be immoderate.

And we can dig further among his reviews of eighteenth century English literature in this book for the information that in that century alone did English writers wield power, and silence their betters with their brains. . . .

But the old England returned when the aristocratic civilization went, and moderation came back and Lytton Strachey will not rule. His civilization does not stand. His brief influence, theatrical at one time because of the imitators on whose account his reputation unjustly suffered, already wanes. Already we discuss whether he had scholarship whether he was the last of the bourgeois or the first of the revolutionaries and a great many silly things besides. It is better to open this miscellaneous collection of essays and reviews dating from 1903 onward and to get down as closely as possible to the facts.

The first of the revolutionaries? The last of the bourgeois? It seems to us he was rather the last of the naughties. In Strachey we had a survival from the age which drew his most damaging mockeries; and a most misleading survival because he timed his entry noticeably late. For the naughtiness of the 'nineties was given a new lease of life with him and a rather more solid lease. He was an excellent exponent of how to pursue Art for Art's sake without losing passionate convictions. His trick of depressing the pedal of picturesque horror and of pulling out the high fluting stop of aesthetic fervor prolonged the airs of fin de siècle into our times; but under cover of this he drew forth another note, the accents of Reason reasserted from the last civilized century and of Criticism rescued from life and Matthew Arnold. With all the malice and grace of a desultory reading he set about the work of providing the Victorian age with criticism.

Having the aesthete's eye for the picturesque and the intellectual's instinct for the damning, Strachey was most adulated and most damned for his guerrilla brilliances. But to dismiss him as the irresponsible aesthete and cynic is absurd. In ridiculing Gordon he was attacking Imperialism; and who will not say that after their course of Strachey the eminent Victorians are becoming more estimable for being relieved of their dubious godhead? To those who still find him cynical I recommend the papers in the third section of this book, for example, those entitled, **"Avons-nous changé tout cela"** (an essay on tolerance), **"Bonga-Bonga in Whitehall"** and **"Militarism and Theology."** And there is the last sentence of the paper on Lord Morley. "The heartless, irreverent, indecent eighteenth century produced the French Revolution. The Age of Victoria produced—what?" Insolent, rhetorical, disingenuous; but note the date at the foot of the essay and ponder. It is 1918. In these papers Strachey is no mere aesthete. He is the hater of war, oppression, bigotry and stupidity. He is the pacifist, the radical fire-eater rather than the literary dilettante. And his voice, for all its coolness, its calculated hesitations and soothing innuendo, has an unmistakable passion.

On his favored ground, the eighteenth century—about which he had fewer illusions than many modern worshipers of that intellectual refuge have—his genius for evocation and appreciation are at their best. He is less the critic than the guide. In his criticism one feels a weakness: he has had too much pleasure.

It is as well to note that his refuge is not an eighteenth century refuge, but a modern citadel. Its weakness is first its class weakness: why should we assume that the values of an enlightened liberal bourgeois culture will endure any longer than the aristocratic Age of Reason? If we are tolerant, as he suggests, about those things which no longer have importance to us, why should we esteem the tolerance on which his civilization rests? Another weakness is in the matter of religion. That Strachey has an aesthetic sympathy for certain kinds of religious belief is clear. But religion meant for him obscurantism, unreason and superstition, it awakened all his spite and malice. The view was superficial and crude and it accounts, I think, for a certain hollowness in his work.

V. S. Pritchett, "Last of the Naughties," in The Christian Science Monitor *(reprinted by permission from* The Christian Science Monitor; © *1933 The Christian Science Publishing Society; all rights reserved), December 2, 1933, p. 7.*

GUY BOAS (essay date 1935)

[*Boas was an English writer, educator, editor, and critic. In the following excerpt from his* Lytton Strachey, *he discusses Strachey's first collection of literary criticism,* Landmarks in French Literature.]

It may be argued that Strachey was greater as a critic of books than as a biographer of men, for the controversial element which he invariably aroused as a biographer is not stirred by his literary criticism. In dealing with literature, though he was often pungent and always vital, he advanced no challenging theories, discovered no awkward scandals, and, except perhaps in his essays on Carlyle and Creighton, who, being Victorians, could not fail to excite his mischief, he did not indulge in impertinence. It was, indeed, a paradoxical fact that Strachey, who in biography delighted, at least so it was alleged, to be contradictory and wayward, turning reputations topsy turvy and introducing grotesque absurdities into the discussion of earnest problems, worshipped in the realm of letters at the calm sane shrines of Racine and Boswell, Pope and Hume, and if he was naturally in sympathy with the scepticism of Voltaire and Gibbon, his enthusiasm for the extreme lucidity of their classical prose was at strange variance with his reputation for mental enormities and ultra-subtle perversity.

Except for a few short essays contributed to Reviews and an Introduction to an edition of Mrs. Inchbald's *A Simple Story,* Strachey published nothing before his **Landmarks in French Literature**. . . . This small volume is a masterpiece of compression, and displays a penetrating understanding and a sensitive appreciation of French letters of which few Englishmen are capable, and which still fewer have been able to express with Strachey's velvet touch. I am inclined to wonder whether **Landmarks in French Literature,** published unobtrusively in *The Home University Library* over the name of G. L. Strachey, six years before that writer sprang into fame as Lytton Strachey, author of **Eminent Victorians,** is not Strachey's best book. It is not often that one can apply the simple word 'beautiful' appropriately and with absolute sincerity to a book, but to this one I should apply it. Also it belongs to that small number of volumes which seem to carry a finality and sense of completeness about them which is in contradistinction to their size: Sir Walter Raleigh's *Shakespeare* is a book of this kind, Sir Henry Hadow's *Wagner* another, and Strachey's **Landmarks in French Literature** makes the same effect.

Thus Strachey's first published love was of France, and to the end one feels that French intellect, French clarity, and that peculiar element of atmosphere of which one is conscious the moment one steps on French soil, were dearer to him than roast beef, Sloane Square, or the Canterbury Cricket week. More-

over, it was France at its most French which he loved, the France that existed before the Revolution, aristocratic, leisured, fastidious, the France of Madame de Sévigné, of Molière, of the *Grand Monarque*. Strachey quotes Talleyrand as remarking that only those who had lived in France before the Revolution had really experienced *la douceur de vivre*. Strachey would have rejoiced to have lived in that pre-Revolution France: as it was, the nearest he could get to experiencing at second hand *la douceur de vivre* was by steeping himself in the literature of that earthly paradise.

There is a passage in **Landmarks in French Literature** describing the Versailles of Louis Quatorze which pictures to perfection the lost world for which Strachey yearned and to whose standard of distinguished brilliance he strove in everything he wrote to approximate. . . . (pp. 4-5)

Later in his book Strachey treats Rousseau and Diderot with understanding, but his pen does not glow again with the same ardent rapture with which he apostrophizes the literary splendours of seventeenth-century France, Molière, Racine, La Fontaine, Boileau, Bossuet, La Rochefoucauld, and La Bruyère: these are the names which fire him to ecstasy, the products and representatives of that age of exclusive culture with which Strachey's highly individual spirit was by nature in harmony and love.

It is the same with the scattered essays which constitute Strachey's critical work on English literature [**Books and Characters**]. However smart and novel and more than up-to-date his biographical theories might be considered, when he set himself to examine an English author it was not the works of James Joyce or Stephen Spender, nor even of Robert Bridges which occupied his attention; the only modern work of importance which Strachey seems to have reviewed was Hardy's *Satires of Circumstance* which he found 'baffling'. (p. 6)

It was to the plays of Shakespeare that Strachey devoted his faculties and affection, to the prose of Sir Thomas Browne, the poetry of Pope, the criticism of Dr. Johnson, the biography of Boswell, the histories of Hume and Gibbon and Macaulay and Carlyle and Froude. . . . [It] might well have been that so daring and electric a mind as Strachey's might have evolved a new theory as to the importance, shall we say, of some incoherent post-war poet, or the unimportance of Milton or Spenser. Surely he who was supposed to have thrown a cardinal, a general, a headmaster, and a lady-with-a-lamp in the mire, might have been expected to unmask the *Faery Queene* or lay bare absurdities in *Paradise Lost*. But Strachey did nothing of this. It is true he inserted a few typical details in the course of his lives of great writers: 'Mr. Gibbon', we are informed, 'was always slightly overdressed'; Hume one evening at a party in Paris 'appeared in a charade as a Sultan between two lovely ladies'; Creighton's sole lapse from lifelong equanimity was on a railway station when he repeatedly inquired, 'Where's my black bag?'; but when it is with the works of these writers that he is dealing he praises and appreciates with equal sanity and eloquence, makes no attempt to question the judgements of Time, and shows no signs of aspiring to 'the heroic folly or the clownish courage of the New Criticism'. He advances a novel Shakespearian theory, but it is not unconvincing. He maintains that the three plays of Shakespeare's 'Final Period', *Cymbeline, The Winter's Tale,* and *The Tempest* were written not in an ultimate mood of grave and benign serenity, as Professor Dowden thought, but when the dramatist was 'half enchanted by visions of beauty and loveliness, and half bored to death; on the one side inspired by a soaring fancy to the singing of ethereal songs, and on the other urged by a general disgust to burst occasionally through his torpor into bitter and violent speech'. I was myself somewhat surprised by this view, which I first heard from Strachey's own lips when he came to one of our undergraduate literary societies at Christ Church, Oxford, soon after the War, and read us this essay as a paper. I contested the view then, and we had an amusing talk after the meeting, when he admitted that his essay appeared first in a magazine which after this contribution never issued again. Now, however, that I have had fifteen more years in which to study the plays, I am inclined to think that Strachey's appreciation both of the splendours and the blemishes of these three plays is a more congruous view than the vague and sentimental conception which he challenged.

Though Strachey gloried in the soaring fancies and elusive subtleties of Shakespeare's mature plays, though he enjoyed and understood the curious art of Sir Thomas Browne, and wrote an admirable essay on the mysticism of Blake, that which he prized most dearly in literature was lucidity. He was never happier, in two senses of the word, than when he was extolling the quality of clarity in one of the great lucid authors. There is a revealing passage in his essay on Pope in which, having quoted some of Pope's early couplets in order to show how his later work gained in weight, he comments on the early lines as follows:

> Everything is obvious. The diction is a mass of *clichés;* the epithets are the most commonplace possible. . . . But what a relief to have escaped for once from *le mot propre,* from subtle elaboration of diction . . . from complicated states of mind. How delightful to have no trouble at all—to understand so very, very easily every single thing that is said!

'To understand so very, very easily every single thing that is said.' This is Strachey's cardinal doctrine. No one can deny that he practised what he preached, and it is natural to find him hailing with special enthusiasm this quality wherever he finds it in literature. . . . (pp. 6-8)

[One is prompted] to recur to the question whether the treasury of English letters would not have been enriched by a store of even purer gold had Strachey devoted his energies entirely to literary criticism, whether his claim to immortality would not have been surer had he devoted the twenty more years, which might have been his according to the Psalmist's allowance, to praising great writers rather than to dissecting, as I understand he was preparing to do when he died, the lives of Browning, Matthew Arnold, and General Booth, or by drawing a full-length portrait, perhaps, as suggested to him by Professor Raleigh, of Benjamin Jowett.

I think a good case can be made out that things would have been even better so, though I am not unmindful that the answer is that we might then have possessed a second Professor Raleigh, but not a Lytton Strachey. (pp. 8-9)

> *Guy Boas, in his* Lytton Strachey *(reprinted by permission of Oxford University Press), Oxford University Press, London, 1935, 21 p.*

ANDRÉ MAUROIS   (essay date 1935)

[*Maurois was a French man of letters whose versatility is reflected in the broad scope of his work. However, it was as a biographer that he made his most significant contribution to literature. Following the tradition of Lytton Strachey's "new" biography, Maurois believed that a biography should adhere to historical facts regardless of possibly tarnishing the images or legends of biographical subjects. Furthermore, he believed that biography should delve into the psychological aspects of personality to reveal its multiplicity, its contradictions, and its inner struggles, and that a biographical work should be an interpretive expression of the biographer. Most of Maurois's works have been translated into English and many of his biographies were widely read in America, including* Ariel: The Life of Shelley *and* Proust: A Biography. *In the following discussion of Strachey's literary style, Maurois maintains that Strachey only appears to be detached, for his real attitudes can be found beneath "a fine web of epigrams."*]

Strachey's style is finely shaded, to the point sometimes of preciousness. He sketches, he tests, he scores out, he glosses. He masters the indefinite and the complex. His best portraits are those of characters like Prince Albert or Robert Cecil, whom he can paint as they should be painted, in grey against grey. . . . (p. 223)

Nearly always his dissections lead, not to conclusions but to questionings. His favourite words seem to be *subtle* and *perhaps.* When he is just about to drop a character, in despair of getting any closer to him, he still has twinges of regret or repentance, and he will add one last paragraph, generally beginning with "And yet. . . ." There, with marvellous skill, he will undo the new-made joints of the structure he has so patiently erected. . . . [It] is just in this feeling for the infinitely small in the order of passion and character that Strachey often reminds one of Proust. From Proust also he seems to have that rare and delicate touch of style which blends familiarity with perfection and nonchalance with vigour. Like Proust, too, Strachey is above all a poet, that is to say, a man who, by fresh images, can recreate a living world. There is a truly poetic beauty in Strachey's description of the death of Queen Victoria, the last stanza of a completed poem; it might call to mind the funeral march of Siegfried, the recurring themes of the cycle, at the end of the *Götterdämmerung.* (pp. 223-24)

Every historian, Strachey maintains, should have his point of view. He certainly had his. His detachment is only in appearance. His hates and loves—his hates especially—are emphatic. By hiding them under a fine web of epigram, he increases their strength of attack. He declared once that he neither imposed nor suggested, but only exposed. But this was only a half-truth. He suggested because he withheld; he imposed because he omitted. "Pick the card for yourself," says the conjurer, handing us his pack: but how careful he has been in arranging the cards so as to guide our choice!

What is Strachey's point of view? His originality lies in the fact that he introduced the ideas and tone of an eighteenth-century Frenchman into an England which was still very Victorian. The French translator of **Eminent Victorians**, M. Jacques Heurgon, has quoted a significant passage which explains how Lytton Strachey, to many of the younger Englishmen, stood as a guide to their thought. ". . . today," he wrote, "the return is once more towards the Latin elements in our culture, the revulsion from the Germanic influences which obsessed our grandfathers, the preference for what is swift, what is well arranged, and what is not too good." In other words, Strachey represented an English reaction against Carlyle, against Gladstone, and therein his function was more than that of a biographer. He extirpated emphasis, both of style and of feeling, from a whole generation.

He might almost be labelled a Voltairean, or perhaps, even more precisely, a disciple of Anatole France. He hated mysticism almost as much as eloquence. . . . (pp. 237-38)

So entirely does Strachey feel himself a man of the eighteenth century, that he even reproaches Stendhal for having that admiration for romantic attitudes which, in Frenchmen of the Empire period, consorts so strangely with logic and precision. (p. 238)

But however much of an eighteenth-century Frenchman Lytton Strachey may have been, he was so in a very English way. It would be a very rough-and-ready approximation to compare him to Voltaire. His mockery is less direct. Voltaire has wit, Strachey has humour. To a puritan people, reserved and passionate, as the English are, humour is a more reassuring form of the comic, because it is more hidden. How can one be angry when nothing hostile has actually been said? Why be indignant over a piece of mimicry? Still less over a quotation? When Strachey wishes to demolish something or somebody, he is often content simply to quote. For instance, he tells us how Cardinal Manning, in his diary, pledged himself to eat no cake during Lent, but added in the margin: "save dry biscuits." Voltaire would have elaborated this with ironic or violent commentary. To Strachey the stinging quotation sufficed to show the weakness of a faith that haggled over self-denial. He is inimitable when he gravely enunciates something which he knows to be absurd, or when he plays with dangerous epigrams. Of Dr Arnold he says: "He believed in toleration, too, within limits; that is to say, in the toleration of those with whom he agreed." Or of Cardinal Manning: "Certainly he was not a man who was likely to forget to look before he leaped, nor one who, if he happened to know that there was a mattress spread to receive him, would leap with less conviction." (pp. 239-40)

[Although] French in his style and Voltairean in some of his prejudices, he remains at bottom extremely English. A Cambridge don has remarked that the most important event in the history of English biography was the conquest of Lytton Strachey by Queen Victoria. But the conquest was easy. It counted for something that Strachey sprang from one of the great Whig families. He could depict with true understanding those solid, silent characters, seemingly proof against all enthusiasms, whose sound sense ensures the permanence of England and saves her from all freakish dangers. His famous portrait of Lord Hartington is handled humorously, but with respect. In Queen Elizabeth, an ambiguous and frightening character, he admires those barriers and negations which make her so strongly English. If he retains any kindliness towards a Church, it is towards the Anglican, as bearing all over it the marks of human imperfection. Nearly always, after manhandling some eminent Victorian, he sets him on his feet again. Dare it be said that he himself was, in great measure, an eminent Victorian? (pp. 240-41)

André Maurois, "Lytton Strachey," in his Prophets and Poets, *translated by Hamish Miles (copyright ©1935 by Harper & Brothers; reprinted by permission of the author and the author's agents, Scott Meredith Literary Agency, Inc., 845 Third Avenue, New York, NY 10022; originally published as* Magiciens et logiciens, *B. Grasset, 1935), Harper & Brothers Publishers, 1935 (and reprinted in* Points of View: From Kipling to Graham Greene *by André Maurois, Frederick Ungar Publishing Co., 1968, pp. 215-42).*

VIRGINIA WOOLF   (essay date 1939)

[Woolf is one of the most prominent literary figures of the twentieth century. Like her contemporary James Joyce, with whom she is often compared, Woolf is remembered as one of the most innovative of the stream of consciousness novelists. Concerned primarily with depicting the life of the mind, she revolted against traditional narrative techniques and developed her own highly individualized style. Woolf's works, noted for their subjective exploration of characters' inner lives and their delicate poetic quality, have had a lasting effect on the art of the novel. A discerning and influential critic and essayist as well as a novelist, Woolf began writing reviews for The Times Literary Supplement *at an early age. Her critical essays, which cover almost the entire range of English literature, contain some of her finest prose and are praised for their insight. Along with Lytton Strachey, Roger Fry, Clive Bell, and several others, Woolf and her husband Leonard formed the literary coterie known as the "Bloomsbury Group." In her essay "The Art of Biography," she regards Strachey's* Queen Victoria *as the best of his biographies and* Elizabeth and Essex, *referred to as Strachey's "experiment" in art, as the least successful.]*

The figure of Lytton Strachey is so important a figure in the history of biography that it compels a pause. For his three famous books, *Eminent Victorians, Queen Victoria,* and *Elizabeth and Essex,* are of a stature to show both what biography can do and what biography cannot do. (p. 222)

[The] anger and the interest that his short studies of Eminent Victorians aroused showed that he was able to make Manning, Florence Nightingale, Gordon, and the rest live as they had not lived since they were actually in the flesh. Once more they were the centre of a buzz of discussion. Did Gordon really drink, or was that an invention? Had Florence Nightingale received the Order of Merit in her bedroom or in her sitting-room? He stirred the public, even though a European war was raging, to an astonishing interest in such minute matters. Anger and laughter mixed; and editions multiplied.

But these were short studies with something of the over-emphasis and the foreshortening of caricatures. In the lives of the two great Queens, Elizabeth and Victoria, he attempted a far more ambitious task. Biography had never had a fairer chance of showing what it could do. For it was now being put to the test by a writer who was capable of making use of all the liberties that biography had won: he was fearless; he had proved his brilliance; and he had learned his job. The result throws great light upon the nature of biography. For who can doubt that after reading the two books again, one after the other, that the *Victoria* is a triumphant success, and that the *Elizabeth* by comparison is a failure? But it seems too, as we compare them, that it was not Lytton Strachey who failed; it was the art of biography. In the *Victoria* he treated biography as a craft; he submitted to its limitations. In the *Elizabeth* he treated biography as an art; he flouted its limitations.

But we must go on to ask how we have come to this conclusion and what reasons support it. In the first place it is clear that the two Queens present very different problems to their biographer. About Queen Victoria everything was known. Everything she did, almost everything she thought, was a matter of common knowledge. No one has ever been more closely verified and exactly authenticated than Queen Victoria. The biographer could not invent her, because at every moment some document was at hand to check his invention. And, in writing of Victoria, Lytton Strachey submitted to the conditions. He used to the full the biographer's power of selection and relation, but he kept strictly within the world of fact. Every statement was verified; every fact was authenticated. And the result is a life which, very possibly, will do for the old Queen what Boswell did for the old dictionary-maker. In time to come Lytton Strachey's Queen Victoria will be Queen Victoria, just as Boswell's Johnson is now Dr. Johnson. The other versions will fade and disappear. It was a prodigious feat, and no doubt, having accomplished it, the author was anxious to press further. There was Queen Victoria, solid, real, palpable. But undoubtedly she was limited. Could not biography produce something of the intensity of poetry, something of the excitement of drama, and yet keep also the peculiar virtue that belongs to fact—its suggestive reality, its own proper creativeness?

Queen Elizabeth seemed to lend herself perfectly to the experiment. Very little was known about her. The society in which she lived was so remote that the habits, the motives, and even the actions of the people of that age were full of strangeness and obscurity. 'By what art are we to worm our way into those strange spirits? those even stranger bodies? The more clearly we perceive it, the more remote that singular universe becomes', Lytton Strachey remarked on one of the first pages. Yet there was evidently a 'tragic history' lying dormant, half-revealed, half-concealed, in the story of the Queen and Essex. Everything seemed to lend itself to the making of a book that combined the advantages of both worlds, that gave the artist freedom to invent, but helped his invention with the support of the facts—a book that was not only a biography but also a work of art.

Nevertheless, the combination proved unworkable; fact and fiction refused to mix. Elizabeth never became real in the sense that Queen Victoria had been real, yet she never became fictitious in the sense that Cleopatra or Falstaff is fictitious. The reason would seem to be that very little was known—he was urged to invent; yet something was known—his invention was checked. The Queen thus moves in an ambiguous world, between fact and fiction, neither embodied nor disembodied. There is a sense of vacancy and effort, of a tragedy that has no crisis, of characters that meet but do not clash.

If this diagnosis is true we are forced to say that the trouble lies with biography itself. It imposes conditions, and those conditions are that it must be based upon fact. And by fact in biography we mean facts that can be verified by other people besides the artist. If he invents facts as an artist invents them—facts that no one else can verify—and tries to combine them with facts of the other sort, they destroy each other.

Lytton Strachey himself seems in the *Queen Victoria* to have realized the necessity of this condition, and to have yielded to it instinctively. 'The first forty-two years of the Queen's life', he wrote, 'are illuminated by a great and varied quantity of authentic information. With Albert's death a veil descends.' And when with Albert's death the veil descended and authentic information failed, he knew that the biographer must follow suit. 'We must be content with a brief and summary relation', he wrote and the last years are briefly disposed of. But the whole of Elizabeth's life was lived behind a far thicker veil than the last years of Victoria. And yet, ignoring his own admission, he went on to write, not a brief and summary relation, but a whole book about those strange spirits and even stranger bodies of whom authentic information was lacking. On his own showing, the attempt was doomed to failure.

It seems, then, that when the biographer complained that he was tied by friends, letters, and documents he was laying his finger upon a necessary limitation. For the invented character lives in a free world where the facts are verified by one person only—the artist himself. Their authenticity lies in the truth of his own vision. The world created by that vision is rarer, intenser, and more wholly of a piece than the world that is largely made of authentic information supplied by other people. And because of this difference the two kinds of fact will not mix; if they touch they destroy each other. No one, the conclusion seems to be, can make the best of both worlds; you must choose, and you must abide by your choice.

But though the failure of *Elizabeth and Essex* leads to this conclusion, that failure, because it was the result of a daring experiment carried out with magnificent skill, leads the way to further discoveries. Had he lived, Lytton Strachey would no doubt himself have explored the vein that he had opened. As it is, he has shown us the way in which others may advance. The biographer is bound by facts—that is so; but, if it is so, he has the right to all the facts that are available. If Jones threw boots at the maid's head, had a mistress in Islington, or was found drunk in a ditch after a night's debauch, he must be free to say so—so far at least as the law of libel and human sentiment allow. (pp. 223-26)

Virginia Woolf, "The Art of Biography" (1939), in her The Death of the Moth and Other Essays *(copyright 1942 by Harcourt Brace Jovanovich, Inc.; renewed 1970 by Marjorie T. Parsons, Executrix; reprinted by permission of the publisher; in Canada by the Author's Literary Estate and The Hogarth Press), Harcourt Brace Jovanovich, 1942 (and reprinted in her* Collected Essays, *Vol. 4, The Hogarth Press, 1967, pp. 221-28).*

MAX BEERBOHM (essay date 1943)

[*Though he lived until 1956, Beerbohm is chiefly associated with the fin de siècle period in English literature, more specifically with its lighter phases of witty sophistication and mannered elegance. His temperament was urbane and satirical, and he excelled in both literary and artistic caricatures of his contemporaries. "Entertaining" in the most complimentary sense of the word, Beerbohm's criticism for* The Saturday Review—*where he was a long-time drama critic—everywhere indicates his scrupulously developed taste and unpretentious, fair-minded response to literature. Beerbohm, who captured Strachey's long, lean, angular physique in several artistic caricatures, praises Strachey as a biographer of the first rank, defending him against those critics who would label him a mere "debunker."*]

Lytton Strachey was not a great writer, not a great man, and not old enough to have become a Grand Old Man. But his gifts and his repute amply sufficed to ensure reaction against him very soon after the breath was out of his body. I think it was Ben Jonson who spoke of "the backward kick of the dull ass's hoof". That is not a pretty expression. But it is neither silly nor vulgar. The vulgar term, "a debunker", the term that the average writer or talker cursorily applies to Strachey, is not only vulgar, it is also silly.

That he was not a hero-worshipper, or even a very gallant heroine-worshipper, may be readily conceded. Also, he was perhaps not a very warm-hearted man. (As to that, I really don't know.) Assuredly he was not an artificer and purveyor of plaster saints or angels. He was intensely concerned with the ramifications of human character, and greatly amused by them. He had a very independent mind, and was an egoist in so far as he liked finding things out for himself and using his own judgement on what he found. Perfect justice is a divine attribute. Lytton Strachey, being merely a human being, had it not. He had, like the rest of us, imperfect sympathies. Great strength of character, keen practical sense and efficiency, for example, did not cause his heart to glow so much as one might wish they had. They seemed rather to give him a slight chill. Though he recognised the greatness of Florence Nightingale, the necessary grit that was at the core of it rather jarred on him; while its absence from the character of Sidney Herbert gave great tenderness to his portrait of that statesman. Nor did his love of exercising his own judgement move him to dissent from that of Purcell, the biographer of Cardinal Manning. He was essentially, congenitally, a Newman man. Who among us isn't? But I think his preference rather blinded him to the fair amount of grit that was latent in the delicacy, the poetry of that great priest and greater writer. In the character of Dr. Arnold there was such a wealth of grit, and a strenuousness so terrific that one may rather wonder how Strachey could bear to think of him and write of him. The portrait fails, I think, because it is composed throughout in a vein of sheer mockery. It is the only work of his that does not seek, does not hesitate, does not penetrate, and is definitely unfair. It is the only work of his that might, so far as it goes, justify the application to him of that term which shall not again soil my lips and afflict your ears.

The vein of mockery was very strong in him certainly, and constantly asserted itself in his writings. A satirist he was not. Mockery is a light and lambent, rather irresponsible thing. *"On se moque de ce qu'on aime"* is a true saying. Strachey was always ready to mock what he loved. In mockery there is no malice. In satire there may be plenty of it. Pope was full of it. But he was rather an exception. Your satirist is mostly a robust fellow, as was Aristophanes, as were Juvenal and Swift; a fellow laying about him lustily, for the purpose of hurting, of injuring people who, in his opinion, ought to be hurt and injured. He may, like Aristophanes, have an abundant, a glorious gift for mockery. But fundamentally he is grim. He is grimly concerned with what he hates in the age to which he belongs. I do not remember having found anywhere in the works of Lytton Strachey one passing reference to any current event. He was quite definitely, and quite impenitently, what in current jargon is called an escapist. (pp. 10-12)

Strachey was by temperament an Eighteenth Century man. In the Age of Reason, and of Wit too, he felt far more at home than in the aftermath of the Industrial Revolution, and in the first fine careless rapture of the Internal Combustion Engine. Even we, in spite of our coarseness, deplore these great phenomena, and wish they had never happened, and grieve that mankind will not in any foreseeable future be able to shake them off and be quit of them. Strachey, like the good Eighteenth Century Englishman that he was, had close contacts with France. Indeed I feel that he was even more at ease in French than in English literature and life. It was in that handbook on French literature that he made his début. In the volume entitled ***Books and Characters*** . . . and in his last work, ***Portraits in Miniature*** . . . , there is constant truancy to France. Racine, Voltaire, Rousseau, Mme. de Sévigné, the Abbé Morellet, Mme. du Deffand, the Président de Brosses—with all of these he is on terms of cosiest intimacy. To our native Victorians he was rather in the relation of a visitor, an inquirer, an inquisitor. I don't think he was—as Desmond MacCarthy had gathered from him that he was—"horrified" by them. He disliked the nineteenth century in comparison with its forerunner, but it appealed to him far more than could the twentieth. . . . Perhaps Strachey was rather ashamed of the hold the Victorians had on

him in virtue of their proximity. And perhaps it was for this reason, and to shake off these insidious rivals to his dear ones of the Eighteenth Century, or perhaps it was merely in a sudden spirit of adventure, that he plunged off into the court of Queen Elizabeth. Anyway it was a brave thing to do. ***Elizabeth and Essex*** . . . is a finely constructed work, but seems to me to be essentially guesswork. A very robustious, slapdash writer might convince me that he was in close touch with the souls of those beings whose actions and motives are to me as mysterious as those of wild animals in an impenetrable jungle. You rightly infer that I am *not* a Sixteenth Century man. And I make so bold as to say "Neither was Lytton Strachey."

"A finely constructed work" I have said. But what work of Lytton Strachey's, large or small, was not admirably firm in structure?—*totus, teres atque rotundus*. (pp. 13-15)

As biographer, he had, besides his gift for construction, the advantage of a splendid gift for narrative. He was a masterly teller of tales, long or short, tragic or comic. He could, as it were, *see* the thing he had to tell, *see* the people concerned in it, see them outwardly and inwardly, and make us share gratefully his vision. Who could have made so much as he of such things as the adventures of "the boy Jones" in Buckingham Palace, of the inception and the building of the Albert Memorial, of Mr. Gorham's vicissitudes in the Court of Arches and the Judicial Committee of the Privy Council? As the finest example of his narrative gift—I had almost said his dramatic gift—I would choose perhaps his treatment of what led to the tragedy of the dereliction and death of General Gordon. The tremendous tale, charged with the strangely diverse characters of the eminent men involved in it—Gladstone, Hartington, Baring, and Gordon himself—is told with the subtlest strength, oscillating steadily, with the swing of a pendulum, between Downing Street and the Soudan. For a while we are in the one place, then we are with equal vividness in the other, alternately, repeatedly; and great is the cumulative effect of this prolonged strophe and antistrophe. To those of you who are, as I am, fond of thrills, but have never read these pages, I would say earnestly, "Read these pages."

The element of criticism was implicit, and often explicit, in all Lytton Strachey's biographical work. From time to time he indulged in criticism undiluted. As a literary critic alone he would have been worthy to be remembered. The best kind of critic—the helpfully interpretative, the almost creative critic—is very passive before he becomes active. Such an one was Strachey. With an intellect of steely quality there was combined in him a deep sensibility and receptivity. He had felt before he thought. And two at least of his critical works—his long essay on Racine, and his Leslie Stephen Lecture on Pope—happened to be of cardinal, of crucial effect. Racine had never had high repute upon these shores; and the Romantic Movement had reduced Pope to a small shadow among our own poets. It was Strachey's silver trumpet that woke the young men of two decades ago to high appreciation of those two worthies. And by the way, literature apart, aren't there in the Elysian Fields two other worthies who have reason to be grateful to the supposed iconoclast?—Queen Victoria and the Prince Consort? The Prince in his life-time had never been popular; and after Sir Theodore Martin's saccharine biography he had become a veritable mock. I never heard a kind word for him. The Queen, who in my childhood and youth had been not only revered but worshipped, was, soon after her death, no longer in public favour. Her faults had become known, and her virtues were unheeded. This is not so now; and is not so by reason of Lytton

Strachey's fully judicial presentment of her with all the faults over which her virtues so very much preponderated. And it is, by the same token, through him that we know the Prince not as just dreadfully admirable, but as some one to be loved and to be sorry for.

But after all—and perhaps you are saying "Oh, if only it *were* all!"—it is as a writer, in the strict sense, as a user of that very beautiful medium, the English language, that I would especially extol Lytton Strachey. (pp. 18-20)

> *Max Beerbohm, in his* Lytton Strachey, *Cambridge University Press, 1943 (and reprinted by Haskell House Publishers, Ltd., 1974), 27 p.*

E. M. FORSTER   (lecture date 1944)

[*Forster was a prominent English novelist, critic, and essayist, whose works reflect his liberal humanism. His most celebrated novel,* A Passage to India, *is a complex examination of personal relationships amid the conflicts of the modern world. Although some of Forster's critical essays are considered naive in their literary assessments, his discussion of fictional techniques in his* Aspects of the Novel *is regarded as a minor classic in literary criticism. Forster, a peripheral member of the "Bloomsbury Group," enjoyed a literary friendship with Strachey. In this excerpt, he gives Strachey's biography* Queen Victoria *a glowing evaluation. However, John Halperin (see excerpt below) contends that Forster was incorrect regarding Strachey's methods as a historian.*]

[*Queen Victoria*] came out at the beginning of our period, it is an achievement of genius, and it has revolutionized the art of biography. Strachey did debunk of course; he hated pomposity, hypocrisy and muddle-headedness, he mistrusted inflated reputations, and was clever at puncturing them, and he found in the Victorian age, which had taken itself very, very seriously, a tempting target for his barbed arrows. But he was much more than a debunker. He did what no biographer had done before: he managed to get inside his subject. Earlier biographers, like Macaulay and Carlyle, had produced fine and convincing pictures of people; Lytton Strachey makes his people move; they are alive, like characters in a novel: he constructs or rather reconstructs them from within. Sometimes he got them wrong; his presentation of General Gordon has been questioned, so has his brilliant later work on Elizabeth and Essex. But even when they are wrong they seem alive, and in the **Queen Victoria** his facts have not been seriously challenged; and, based on dry documents, a whole society and its inhabitants rise from the grave, and walk about. That was his great contribution. He was a historian who worked from within, and constructed out of the bones of the past something more real and more satisfactory than the chaos surrounding him. He is typical of our period, and particularly of the twenties—throughout them his influence is enormous; today it has declined, partly because people are again taking themselves very, very seriously, and don't like the human race to be laughed at, partly because Strachey had some tiresome imitators, who have brought his method into discredit. However that doesn't matter. Reputations always will go up and down. What matters is good work, and **Queen Victoria** is a masterpiece. It is a pageant of the historical type, but as the grand procession passes we—you and I, we little readers, are somehow inside the procession, we mingle unobserved with royalty and statesmen and courtiers and underlings, and hear their unspoken thoughts.

Even a frivolous passage, like the one about the Boy Jones, has its historical function. Lytton Strachey was a gay person

who loved fun and nonsense, and he knew how to make use of them in his work. Through the episode of the enigmatic Boy Jones, an undersized youth who repeatedly entered Buckingham Palace and hid there in the year 1840, was discovered under sofas, and confessed that he had "helped himself to soup and other eatables, sat upon the throne, seen the Queen, and heard the Princess Royal squall," Strachey recreates the domestic confusion existing there, and makes the period come alive. Then he passes on to more serious topics.

What was he serious about? Not about political ideals or social reform. Like T. E. Lawrence, he was disillusioned though in another way. He believed, however, in wit and aristocratic good manners, and he was implacable in his pursuit of truth. He believed, furthermore, infidelity between human beings. There, and there only, the warmth of his heart comes out. He is always moved by constant affection, and the Queen's love for the Prince Consort, and for his memory, makes the book glow and preserves it from frigidity. Strachey's belief in affection, like his fondness for fun, is too often forgotten. . . . [In the famous passage describing the Queen's death, he] begins by being the dignified historian; then he dismisses his subject tenderly, and launches the Queen as it were on an ebbing tide, carrying her backwards through the manifold joys of life till she vanishes in the mists of her birth. (pp. 280-82)

> *E. M. Forster, "English Prose between 1918 and 1939" (originally a lecture delivered at the University of Glasgow in 1944), in his* Two Cheers for Democracy *(copyright 1951 by E. M. Forster; renewed 1979 by Donald Parry; reprinted by permission of Harcourt Brace Jovanovich, Inc.; in Canada by Edward Arnold Ltd.),* Harcourt Brace Jovanovich, 1951, pp. 272-84.

DOUGLAS SOUTHALL FREEMAN   (lecture date 1953)

[*Freeman was one of America's most distinguished biographers and historians. His massive, Pulitzer Prize-winning biographies* R. E. Lee *and* George Washington *are considered the definitive works on two of the greatest figures in the history of the United States. These multivolume studies, along with the author's other major work,* Lee's Lieutenants: A Study in Command, *evidence what Virginius Dabney described as Freeman's "well-nigh unparalleled military understanding, plus enormous industry and capacity for research." A few weeks before his death, Freeman delivered an address to the Chicago and Richmond Civil War Round Tables. In his speech, part of which is excerpted below, he attacked Strachey's biographical methods.*]

I have often looked at Lytton Strachey's five-page account of what was happening in the mind of Essex after a famous interview with Queen Elizabeth. Five pages he devotes in his "psychography," so-called, to the thoughts of Essex at that particular time. Although I lived twenty years with General Lee and have lived for ten years with General Washington, I am prepared humbly to submit to you that I do not know what either of them ever was thinking at a given moment unless he happened to have written it down himself. We cannot be too sure. Of all the frauds that ever have been perpetrated on our generation, this "psychography" is, in my opinion, the worst. How dare a man say what another man is thinking when he may not know what he himself is thinking! That is the fate of a good many of us.

> *Douglas Southall Freeman, in an extract from an address delivered to the Chicago and Richmond Civil War Round Tables in Spring, 1953, in* Lee *by Douglas Southall Freeman, edited by Richard Harwell*

*(copyright © 1961 Estate of Douglas Southall Free-
man; reprinted with permission of Charles Scribner's
Sons), Charles Scribner's Sons, 1961, p. xii.*

R. A. SCOTT-JAMES (essay date 1955)

*[In his discussion of aspects of Strachey's literary style, Scott-
James finds that the essence of Strachey's work is "to make
history, and especially biography, interesting."]*

Strachey is a writer whose work gains by being read in its
entirety. When we do so we realize that there is a whole world
of his creation, a world filled with people, all of them individual, with features and tricks of speech and even clothes
which he has made memorable. It is not inconsistent to add
that they are puppets, with the slight ridiculousness of puppets,
whom he has set moving with strings, making them dance their
odd dances in the society of other puppets. He does not give
us the sense of any God, or Cosmic Order or overwhelming
Destiny behind the show; the show is enough for him. Though
he is able to master the intellectual arguments of a Hume or
lightly expound the doctrines of Papal Infallibility, he is not a
philosopher or much interested in philosophy; he is interested
in people, especially sophisticated people, and the way they
behave. He is by no means indifferent to moral values, but the
standards by which he judges them are peculiarly his own. The
people he admires and likes are those who do things for their
own sake and not for the sake of something else. He cannot
bear busy-bodies, however efficient they are, like Florence
Nightingale and Mr. Gladstone. He likes people who are interested in beauty and the arts, who value friendships, and
delights to look at them when they are in love or flying into
a passion or talking gaily in salons or going to 'supper parties
and water-parties, concerts and masked balls, plays in the little
theatre and picnics under the great trees of the park'.

How enjoyable such scenes are! And the style he employs has
to suit the subject and reflect the mood. No starchy, periodic
style would do, or any which suggested straining after recondite
meanings. Let there be 'heavenly lucidity', balance, precision,
the 'tone of a polished conversation'. It is perhaps because he
cultivates the easy manner of conversation that he uses so many
clichés—'genius for frienship', 'glorious heritage', 'hideous
fiasco'—and tolerates colloquialisms—'Manning was an Archdeacon; but he was not yet *out of the wood*'. He does not shrink
from 'sticking in the mud'—people use such expressions in
familiar talk. But though the occasional carelessness or inel-
egance may slightly disturb us, his style in general is fastidious,
expressive, and very pleasing to the ear. At all costs he refuses
to be dull. Sometimes he holds our attention by a few exact
and telling details—'Her short, stout figure, with its folds of
black velvet, its muslin streamers, its heavy pearls at the heavy
neck, assumed an almost menacing air.' And sometimes, carried away by mellifluous words, he paints a radiant scene
almost to the point of flamboyance—he is not willing to miss
the opportunity of enchanting the more romantic of his readers.
And the slight prick of a paradox ensures that the attention
will not wander, and the more so if the paradox contains a
truth. 'What really bound her to him was the fact that they so
rarely met.' 'It is by his very perfection, by the very completeness of his triumph, that Racine loses.' He is as witty as
Oscar Wilde, but there is gravity behind his wit. He makes us
smile, not laugh. He is as paradoxical as Chesterton, but less
blatant, never hilarious. Often he prods us by suddenly reaching
a conclusion the opposite of that he has been leading us to
expect. 'So one might have supposed; but the contrary was the

case.' His books should not be recommended to those who like
to read themselves to sleep.

To make history, and especially biography, interesting—that
is the essence of Strachey's work. Every one of his biographies,
long and short, reads like a novel or short story, with this
difference, that unlike the majority of novels and short stories,
it is usually done with sensitive art, and in a manner which
gives full scope to irony and wit. . . . Life 'as he understands
it'—that is his material. Like every true artist he endeavours
to give an account of the world as his imagination has conceived
it, and his world of the past is peopled with all sorts of complex,
odd characters, expressing themselves stupidly and divinely,
dressing up and behaving, thinking thoughts which can be read,
hiding or indecently exposing their emotions, and after a time
so dying as to give him a congenial deathbed scene. What an
amusing world! What a grim, smiling, scowling, loving, hating, but always *behaving* world it is that he serves up to us so
lightly for our entertainment, adding, as showman, his own
spice of comment, delicate, humane, sententious, provocative,
witty, or slightly impertinent. (pp. 30-2)

R. A. Scott-James, in his Lytton Strachey *(© Profile
Books Ltd. 1955), British Council, 1955, 39 p.*

JAMES STRACHEY (letter date 1956)

*[Strachey's brother and sister-in-law, James and Alix, studied
with Sigmund Freud, translated most of his works into English,
and were themselves psychoanalysts. In this letter to Martin Kallich, author of* The Psychological Milieu of Lytton Strachey *(see
excerpt below), James Strachey clarifies several points regarding
his brother's use of psychoanalysis in his work.]*

Though I had begun to take an interest in psycho-analysis just
before the first World War, it was not until 1920 that my wife
& I went to Vienna to study under Freud. By that time **Eminent
Victorians** had of course been out for two years, and **Queen
Victoria** was largely written. I think it is safe to say that none
of the *E.V.* character sketches were influenced in the slightest
by Freud; and the same may also be assumed of *Q.V.*

My brother did not read German, and till well into the 1920s
[Freud's] works were only accessible in English in extremely
indifferent (& indeed incorrect) translations. He had read a
very few of these, and was on the whole sceptical to begin
with. The great psychological influence on him at the *E.V.* &
Q.V. period was undoubtedly Dostoevsky—who, after all, reveals a lot of the same material as Freud, and whom Freud
himself regarded as the greatest of novelists.

As regards **Elizabeth & Essex** the position was slightly different. By the time he wrote it he had learnt a good deal more about
psychoanalysis from talks with us. And he accepted pretty
completely the account we (and especially my wife) gave him
in some detail of what seemed to us the probable underlying
attitude of Elizabeth to the execution of Essex. His account of
this in the later part of the book (as well as earlier passages
preparing for it) is indeed purely psychoanalytic. This of course
was why he dedicated the book to us.

While I was in Vienna I gave Freud the two earlier books and
he particularly enjoyed them. Lytton sent him a presentation
copy of *E. & E.* and Freud wrote a long letter of thanks in the
course of which he said he thought Lytton's account of the
story was quite correct [see excerpt above]. (p. 359)

As is generally known, my brother was to a very large extent homosexual. Traces of his views on that subject are to be found in his published works; but in those days nothing more open would have been permissible. His attitude to sexual questions more generally was strongly in favour of open discussion. But he was never inclined to undue solemnity. There is a large amount of unpublished material—including a very great deal of delightful correspondence—which I hope will become accessible with the gradual advance of civilized opinion. For this advance we owe a good deal, I believe, to Lytton's own influence (though this is not generally known) on his contemporaries, and, of course, more than anything to that of Freud. (pp. 359-60)

James Strachey, in a letter to Martin Kallich on October 2, 1956, in American Imago *(reprinted by permission of the Wayne State University Press; copyright 1958 by The Association for Applied Psychoanalysis, Inc.), Vol. 15, No. 4, Winter, 1958, pp. 359-60.*

CHARLES RICHARD SANDERS (essay date 1957)

[*Sanders is the author of the biographical and critical work* Lytton Strachey: His Mind and Art, *as well as several critical essays on Strachey. In this excerpt, he offers an analysis of the biographer's distinctive style.*]

From first to last Strachey's style was clearly marked, recognizably individual, and, in almost every sentence, impressive. (p. 302)

We cannot read Strachey, in the first place, without being impressed by the sameness which stamps itself upon every page. His sentences are all the product of a steadfast mind and a clear, definite purpose. It is not merely that his point of view is fixed and that his habits of expression are formed. It is not merely that he is obviously determined to say nothing that is not sensible. Fully as important are certain qualities of style, possibly to him ideals of style, which he never allows himself to forget. One of these is lucidity. We simply cannot imagine Lytton Strachey lapsing into obscurity or dallying lazily with the ambiguous. Another quality of style for which he constantly sought was penetration. He was not satisfied with mere exposition; there must also be revelation. Style must possess and stimulate insight. He also wished for precision, for diction that was clean, exact, and crisp. Another striking quality of style which he desired and which his writings possess in unusual measure is maturity. His is the kind of maturity that treats his readers as highly intelligent adults. (pp. 305-06)

Other qualities which Strachey desired in his style were color, humor, appeal to the ear, and appeal to the imagination. Humor he valued highly, both because he found it delightful in itself and because it provided his style with a highly effective balance wheel. Through the use of color, appropriate verbal sounds, and well-chosen images he was able to enrich his style, to increase its range, and to endow it with some of the potencies which are to be found in poetry.

All these qualities of style are woven into the warp of Strachey's style and give it constancy. Not to be overlooked also among such qualities is that of good form—the kind of good form which can result only from obedience to the generally accepted conventions of good writing. (pp. 306-07)

His skill is nowhere seen at better advantage than in some of his narrative passages. He enjoyed stories, particularly those which go to make up history, and he always told them well. His narrative style is nearly always vigorous, direct, economical, and vivid. It never loses its sense of direction or point; and it rarely misses an opportunity to gather humor along the way. It is admirable even in his extremely early writings. (p. 307)

Strachey was too much interested in literary craftsmanship to ignore the possibilities of the paragraph. He did not, therefore, like many modern journalists and short-story writers, commit himself to the use of the short paragraph exclusively. . . . He did not like, to borrow a figure from Coleridge, a series of short panting paragraphs but preferred one that could take a deep breath of thought. (pp. 310-11)

Strachey's interest in effective sentence construction, like his interest in all other matters pertaining to style, appeared early. (p. 311)

As we examine Strachey's sentences, in his later work as well as in the early essays, two facts impress us. One is the constant and persistent care with which he shaped almost every sentence that he wrote; the other is the great variety of patterns which he used. It would not be easy to prove that he preferred any device of sentence construction or any form of the sentence. His style flows so easily from sentence to sentence that one is scarcely conscious of the numerous shifts from device to device and from pattern to pattern. Here, as in dealing with paragraphs, he followed the principle of achieving variety within uniformity. Like all other masters of prose style, he accomplishes much by varying the length of his sentences. (p. 312)

Contrast is another device of which Strachey is fond. The following sentence combines it with cataloguing and parallelism: "Such were the daily spectacles of colored pomp and of antique solemnity, which—so long as the sun was shining, at any rate—dazzled the onlooker into a happy forgetfulness of the reverse side of the Papal dispensation—the nauseating filth of the highways, the cattle stabled in the palaces of the great, and the fever flitting through the ghastly tenements of the poor." He may combine contrast with balance and with the emphasis which can be given to a word by placing it at the end: "Voltaire was a scoundrel; but he was a scoundrel of genius." (p. 313)

Strachey was very fond of the question as a device of style. Here, for one thing, was another way of varying the sentence patterns and of relieving the monotony that might be produced by a series of affirmations. Strachey knew that the occasional flashing of a question was a great help in keeping readers awake. But it was equally useful for purposes of insinuation and emphasis. (pp. 314-15)

His mind was also one that delighted in expressing itself through the concrete and the specific. His extensive use of quotations is related to this fact. He realized their value in literary criticism and objected to discussions of literature that were limited to abstractions and generalities and that did not give examples of the literature being discussed. (p. 316)

This habitual preference for the specific and concrete became united with a marked dramatic instinct in the quotations which Strachey used in his biographical writing. He believed that his characters would soon let us know what they were if they were allowed to talk. If they were wise, their words would reflect their wisdom. If they were stupid or absurd, their words would give them away. (pp. 316-17)

Strachey, like Fielding, found the world full of humor which, like manna from Heaven, had only to be discovered in order to be enjoyed. Much of the humor in his writings is of this kind: the slapstick of the mountainous Hume, at a party of laughing young ladies, attempting to sit in a chair much too weak and suddenly subsiding to the ground, and of old Lord Rolle tripping over his mantle and falling down the steps at Victoria's coronation. . . . (pp. 319-20)

The kinds of humor to be found in Strachey's works are greatly varied. Much of it springs from irreverence toward objects which custom, convention, and orthodoxy have accepted as holy. (p. 321)

Bathos, with its sudden descent from the sublime to the ridiculous, is one of Strachey's favorite devices. He was thoroughly familiar with its use for comic purposes in such writers as Pope and Byron. He used it frequently and nearly always with great brilliance. . . . In *Queen Victoria* Strachey does not like Baroness Lehzen, a pompous, pretentious, managing woman. With bathos he reduces her to her proper stature: "The pastor's daughter, with all her airs of stiff superiority, had habits which betrayed her origin. Her passion for caraway seeds, for instance, was uncontrollable." (pp. 323-24)

Another device which Strachey uses often, irony, does not always achieve a comic effect. Frequently, Strachey's purpose in employing it is that of suggesting a philosophical pondering of the strange ways in which human affairs unfold. . . . In *Elizabeth and Essex* the implications of some of the irony are darkly tragic. In sending her lover Essex to his death, Elizabeth feels moving within her the spirit of her father, who had had his own wives executed. . . . (p. 324)

A fondness for long words of classical origin soon makes itself manifest after one begins to read Strachey. These words reflect his delight in French literature, in Sir Thomas Browne's prose, and in the diction which characterized much of the literature of eighteenth-century England. Such words as *intensity, lucid, pellucid, lurid, curious, singular, vitriolic, extraordinarily, astonishing, virulence, sardonic, peccant, villatic, salubrious, dithyrambic, vituperation, volubility* are among his favorites. Some, like *lurid, astonishing,* and *extraordinarily,* used with vividness and emphasis in mind, are perhaps overworked. Others, like *intensity* and *lucid,* may suggest qualities which Strachey prized very highly. (p. 326)

Edmund Wilson [see excerpt above] and others have accused Strachey of being terribly given to clichés. In a sense their accusation is well grounded. It would be hard to excuse Strachey for writing that Michelet "shows us the spectacle of the past in a series of lurid lightning-flashes." Appropriate though it is to Michelet, the whole statement is stale and unimpressive. (pp. 326-27)

Strachey does not, however, fall into unjustifiable triteness often. Although he likes upon occasion to use words, phrases, and even longer groups of words which have been repeated many times, he knows well the significance of a context. He has learned thoroughly Wordsworth's great teaching that the value and effectiveness of words is dependent chiefly on their relation to other words. (p. 327)

Strachey's fondness for nicknames also arises in part from his realization of the value of occasional informality. He knew too that nicknames are nearly always picturesque and may often suggest through metaphor significant traits of characters. . . . He knew when to give details and when to give a concise,

general statement, when to employ elaboration and when to use restraint, when to confine himself to the language of abstraction and when to appeal to the senses. Considerations of brevity he never forgot. He did not like realistic novels packed with details—details which cluttered the mind or filled it with tedium.

That his style possesses poetic qualities has been observed almost from the beginning of his literary career. The pleasure which he found in reading poetry and in writing it is reflected in his prose. If there are many times when his style appeals chiefly to our fundamental sanity, our common sense, and our sense of reality, there are many others when it appeals just as strongly to our imagination and to our sense of beauty. His mind was well supplied with figures, and he was skillful in selecting those which would do his work best. (p. 330)

> *Charles Richard Sanders, in his* Lytton Strachey: His Mind and Art *(© 1957 by Yale University Press, Inc.), Yale University Press, 1957, 381 p.*

MARTIN KALLICH   (essay date 1961)

[*In the excerpt below, taken from his* The Psychological Milieu of Lytton Strachey, *Kallich discusses Strachey's use of Freudian analysis in* Elizabeth and Essex. *According to Kallich, Strachey was influenced by Freudian ideas, which were frequently discussed by British intellectuals at the turn of the century. He states that Strachey was "aware of the unconscious as a source of deep insight into the inner life; and he also learned how to structure personality by exhibiting its dual nature and to dramatize it by emphasizing internal conflicts."*]

Originally, Strachey set out to write candid biographies. Becoming more and more convinced of the correctness of the Freudian principle as the basis for the explanation of psychic traits, he relied more obviously on certain sexual motifs in his portrayals of character. The degree of candor intensified until, in *Elizabeth and Essex: A Tragic History,* the sex motive is so prominent, especially in the analysis of Elizabeth's assumed neurosis, that part of the work reads like a parody of a clinical analysis. In this respect, *Elizabeth and Essex* differs from *Queen Victoria,* in which the analytical psychological insights are successfully integrated into the narrative and the sense of art preserved.

Elizabeth and Essex thus represents a climax of a certain trend in Strachey's development as a biographer—that is, in it Strachey consciously and deliberately adopted Freudian theses and experimented with imaginative psychoanalysis, and so, perhaps, went to extremes when dealing with sexuality. The numerous references to sexuality attest to Strachey's wish to be scientifically frank and objective—he refers to virginity, sexual intercourse, castration, private parts, homosexuality, hermaphroditism; and he makes use of such psychoanalytic themes as neurosis, compensation, hysteria, and childhood traumas. (p. 102)

The parts of the narrative that reveal Strachey's clinical insights deal only with the character of Queen Elizabeth. As drawn by Strachey, her complex character stands out in bold relief against the relatively flat two-dimensional surface portraits of Raleigh, Bacon, Cecil, and Philip of Spain. Even Essex, a major figure in the biography, is denied the kind of deep analysis that is given his supposed mistress.

Francis Bacon is generally treated simply and superficially as an insincere and untrustworthy character—an intellectual snake, "profound in everything but psychology." . . . Strachey attempts to complicate and deepen his portrait by indicating several traits; but a catalogue is not an analysis. (pp. 103-04)

Bacon is thus seen as a complicated nature, as Strachey lists the several traits that comprise his character—speculation, pride, ambition, fastidiousness, sensitivity, opulence and luxurious living. He is also a man of prose—dominated, like the serpent, by intellect, not feeling. . . . Too cunning, therefore, for his own good, Bacon is never able to penetrate beneath the surfaces of situations. . . . His behavior in the Essex episode was execrable: he was mean and paltry, shiftily self-seeking. Lastly, he is decadent—Strachey cannot help trying to shock his readers. Bacon kept handsome and disreputable young men near him, finding "in their equivocal society an unexpected satisfaction." . . . Strachey quotes Bacon's mother who fulminates against one male lover—a "bloody Percy" who was being kept "as a coach companion and bed companion." . . . (pp. 104-05)

Strachey's cruel dissection of Bacon's unpleasant character is skilful, but it is not deep. Bacon is caricatured; he may be considered even more than Philip of Spain or Robert Cecil the villain of a melodrama. More shrewd than Bacon, Robert Cecil, on the other hand, is treated somewhat sympathetically. Yet Strachey's portrait of him is not the more convincing. Like Bacon, he has one outstanding trait; but unlike Bacon, whom Strachey does *not* despair of understanding, Cecil is an *enigma*, in the manner of the figures appearing in *Eminent Victorians*. The impression that his deformity produced when set against his apparently mild manner was, Strachey says, "the uneasiness produced by an enigma: what could the combination of that beautifully explicit countenance with the shameful, crooked posture really betoken?" With "a discerning eye" Strachey speculates on what went on in "his inner spirit" and conjectures that "the clue to the enigma" was simply a crafty and cautious patience that worked only when compelled by circumstance, and then only with a minimum of positive action. (p. 105)

As for King Philip II of Spain, he too is caricatured and simplified like the other minor characters. Always is he seen industriously mixing religion and worldly matters as he plans the destruction by means of numerous armadas of the heretic English nation and its hated Protestant Queen. Philip's motivation is deliberately dramatized and complicated in the Dostoevski manner by means of the typically brilliant Stracheyan rhetoric. . . . (p. 106)

As for Essex, Elizabeth's handsome and ambitious lover, like every other male at the English court, including his enemy Raleigh, he was attracted to the Queen by the usual power considerations. In general, the Earl of Essex, according to Strachey's overall psychological interpretation, is pictured as a muddle-headed man of action—his confusion and the eventual self-destruction that it caused being determined by three conditions over which he had little or no control. One originated in outer cultural circumstances, social and political; another in inner psychological forces; and the last in an unusual and dangerous relationship with a woman whose grandeur and power he, as a man, intensely resented.

Strachey thinks of Essex as a last representative of the virtues and vices of the Lancastrian nobility, a spirited and chivalrous figure representing the romantic spirit of the ancient feudalism which had been almost entirely destroyed by the English Reformation under Henry VIII. Unlike the practical-minded Bacon, Essex was thus unrealistic, old-fashioned, extravagantly gallant, rash, misguided—and foolish: "he was not a realist, he was a romantic—passionate, restless, confused." (pp. 106-09)

Essex . . . was not only confused because of outward cultural circumstances; he was also confused because of inner psychological pressures. That is, he suffered from a "double nature" . . . ; this is a psychological insight for which Strachey is noted. . . . (p. 107)

For an epoch that required the caution and dissimulation of Machiavellian policy for survival, Essex's temperament—his "frank impetuosity"—was far too honest and open. He was vehemently precipitate, frank, proud, easily angered by fancied slights, and thus incapable of dissimulation, unlike his mistress the Queen, who was obviously far more clever and self-disciplined than he and in whom dissimulation was second-nature. . . . Energetic and aggressive, he loved physical action; but, following the dictates of his double nature, he also enjoyed the meditation of a retreat in solitude. But, apparently, he did not meditate and keep his own counsel carefully enough; for he could not discipline his emotions. He was not circumspect; he was a simple-hearted, egocentric personality, easily duped by flattering friends: "he was not very strong in the head," Strachey crudely remarks on his chief defect of character, echoing a similar comment on General Gordon. . . .

The third source of confusion in Essex's mind is found in a peculiar relationship between a man and a woman, a man who assumed because of the predominant cultural ideals of the time that power should be his because of his sex, and a woman who because of an accident of birth actually had the power. (p. 108)

The curious relationship between this dashing young man and the old Virgin Queen undoubtedly fascinated Strachey, always intrigued by the puzzle of personality and human behavior. The narrative of *Elizabeth and Essex* represents approximately fifteen years, the last in the life of the protagonists—Essex being a youth of nineteen when admitted to intimacy with the Queen, then fifty-three.

Strachey cannot believe that the young man could have sincerely loved the old Queen. . . . To Strachey, ever sceptical, ever willing to guess at motives below the surface, it is "that ambiguous relationship." . . . And to Essex it was such, too, as Strachey interprets him. That is, Strachey believes that his defiant and unsubmissive attitude towards the Queen re-enacts the archetypal war between the sexes. (p. 109)

Thus the relationship between the young man and the old woman was ambiguous, unstable, and stormy. Essex's masculine inability to submit to the whims of the monarch, a female, resulted in numerous furious disputes which were patched up in equally fervid reconciliations. . . .

[When] he had permitted his masculine defiance to get out of hand, it was the beginning of the end for young Essex. For Elizabeth now began to distrust him, to question his protestations of adoration. On his side, being stubborn and proud, he could not admit he was wrong; he could not bring himself to apologize to the Queen for his disobedience and intemperate behavior. Moreover, he did not know what to do, for he was "disturbed, uncertain." At this point in the narrative, Strachey falls back on what has become with him a useful psychological cliché—the split personality. . . . (p. 110)

In the second chapter of *Elizabeth and Essex* Strachey presents a long analysis of the character of the old Queen, who, as we have already noted, at the age of fifty-three and for fifteen years thereafter, had a strange relationship with a young man, the Earl of Essex. The psychological problem that Strachey sets up for himself is to account for Elizabeth's virginity and her ambiguous love-hate attitude towards the opposite sex, both assumed as crucial in determining her character as well as her political policy.

Elizabeth's chief trait was prevarication: she could scarcely make a decision; and when she did, because she was very unsure of herself, likely as not she would countermand it. The basic source of her ambiguities, her "curious temperament" . . . was a secret—Strachey insists—even unknown to the Queen herself. But with the direct intervention of psychoanalysis this secret can be fathomed. (pp. 111-12)

Strachey's problem of understanding the psychology of his Elizabethan subjects is made even more difficult by their remoteness in time. How can they who lived over three hundred years ago be known from within, when the evidence is so meager? The age in which they lived—its outward appearances and literary expressions may be familiar; but the motivational impulses certainly are not. (p. 112)

Of course, one way that Strachey solves the problem of evidence is by using intimate letters as documentary sources. And so he is enabled to discover the usual contradictions in the age itself, contradictions reflected in the individual people who have made it up. . . . His picture of the age is thus familiar—it is a standard Strachey portrait of contradictions and self-conflicts, of "complicated contrasts" and "bewildering discordances." . . . Strachey catalogues these antitheses—subtlety and naiveté, delicacy and brutality, piety and lust, filth and splendor, savagery and exquisiteness, lovely lyrics and barbaric bear baiting, and lastly hermaphroditism! "The flaunting man of fashion whose codpiece proclaimed an astonishing virility, was he not also, with his flowing hair and his jewelled ears, effeminate?" . . . These sensational contradictions make it difficult for us living hundreds of years after to understand the age.

But Strachey is not content merely to balance the antitheses—his method in *Eminent Victorians;* clearly under the influence of modern psychology, he believes that they are symptomatic of something deeper and more fundamental, and the image he uses is suggestive of his method and approach through an understanding of what he believes is basic—the unconscious sexual instincts. (p. 113)

In his last full-blown biography *Elizabeth and Essex,* Strachey's psychological insights into the personality of Queen Elizabeth are the standard but controversial Freudian variety. Strachey's observations on Essex, and the host of minor characters—the menacing and ambitious Raleigh, the hypocritical Francis Bacon, the splenetic but sincere Anthony Bacon, the crafty and secretive Cecil, the obsessed and absurdly pious Philip II of Spain—are not marked by any unusually noteworthy psychological insights. In general, Strachey seizes upon one or two outstanding traits for these secondary figures and, depending upon the importance of the character, plays his variations upon them; that is, he makes use of his usual formula, as developed in *Eminent Victorians,* for understanding curious ambiguities and inconsistencies, and thereby suggests the mystery and enigma of personality. The balanced rhetoric of paradox obscures the essential shallowness of the insight into these minor characters. With Francis Bacon, Strachey attempts only briefly a true Freudian complication as he intimates homosexuality. But this

scandalous detail is only introduced for shock effect—it serves no structural purpose in the reading of Bacon's sinuous mind.

Even the portrait of the Earl of Essex, confused by a double nature, is standard Strachey—a popular, easy psychology, one that does not penetrate very deeply into complicating unconscious motives. Strachey speculates little if at all on the nature of Essex's childhood, probably neglected, or his relations with his wife, who apparently loved him faithfully despite his supposed amour with the Queen. Nor does Strachey specify the reasons for Essex's anxiety, his periodic breakdowns, of which a good deal is made in the narrative. Strachey thus presents a picture of a dual personality suffering intense contradictions—equally attracted by power politics and by peaceful solitude; but, allowing his emotions to override his reason, Essex contributed to his own destruction. The density of this insight is deceptive—produced only by rhetoric. Again, in Essex's case, Strachey adopts the pattern of psychological insights that he had developed for the characters in *Eminent Victorians.*

Strachey's most telling applications of analytical psychology are made upon the strange personality of Queen Elizabeth. When contrasted with the elaborate and deep insights into her character, those into Essex and the secondary characters are felt to be relatively shallow and imperceptive. Only her life has the orthodox earmarks of the Freudian approach to depth psychology—the assumptions that the sex instinct is an unconscious determinant of basic personality traits, and that the hazards and anxieties of childhood (traumas, including a sudden and violent loss of a parent and accidental but crucial associations of sexual experience with great possible danger to her life), as they interfere with normal development, may become causes of psychological damage, of regressive behavior. Some of Elizabeth's girlhood experiences distorted her psychic life and made her, when adult, *hysterical, neurotic* (terms that Strachey employs for the first time in his long biographical narratives); but she compensated her frigidity, her denial of sexual expression, by becoming a lascivious and dangerous virgin, ambiguously coquettish in her attitude toward courtiers and countries alike. Thus a compulsive prevaricator, she could not make a forthright decision; and when, as in the case of young Essex, her last great lover, she did at last make a forthright decision, it was neither rational nor intelligent, as it was basically motivated by fear and hysteria. Because of the mental distortions induced by an irrational unconscious, she could not read his character correctly; and seeing him *not* as an essentially bewildered and weak person who was helpless before his enemies, his own folly and double nature, but as a menacing man in the archetypal war between the sexes, she revenged, through him, the death of her mother who had died at the hands of another male, her cruel father. In this manner, one might say, Strachey puts the tragic history of the relationship between Elizaeth and Essex on a sexual basis—Elizabeth's virginity as opposed to Essex's manhood.

This psychoanalytical view of Elizabeth, "that perverse, that labyrinthine character," . . . makes sense. Only Strachey's speculations on another problem, her baffling sexual dualism, seem dubious and inconsistent and therefore poorly integrated with the other details. But whether Strachey's conclusions are true it is impossible to state categorically—Elizabeth being long dead and these speculations into her unconscious impossible of verification through actual clinical psychoanalysis.

Those who reject the psychoanalytic hypotheses may conclude with the sceptical Max Beerbohm that *Elizabeth and Essex* is "essentially guesswork" [see excerpt above]. But Virginia

Woolf's reaction is far more generous and her appreciation of the intention of Strachey's work far more perceptive. Like the academic historians, she admits that because *Elizabeth and Essex* was not based on authenticated fact, it was a failure [see excerpt above]. . . . (pp. 123-26)

Others who are convinced of the validity of Freud's theories may feel that there must be an answer to the unusual and difficult personality problems concerning Queen Elizabeth and that the solution can be found in the psychoanalytical framework. Strachey himself is unhesitantly, almost clinically frank in his use of the modern psychoanalytic approach to the personality of Elizabeth. As is known, he must have distrusted his own ability to deal intelligently with the personality of Elizabeth, for he had consulted with the analysts James and Alix Strachey when faced with the problem of reconstructing the psychological history of the Virgin Queen's character formation. Their assistance probably accounts for the clinical tone of parts of the narrative, making *Elizabeth and Essex* one of his most candid biographies. The air of medical objectivity provided by the introduction of intimate sexual details in turn reinforces the feeling in the reader that the insights, even though highly speculative, are consistent, convincing, and perhaps, also, correct (until additional data concerning Elizabeth's unconscious can be accumulated). (pp. 126-27)

> *Martin Kallich, in his* The Psychological Milieu of Lytton Strachey *(copyright © 1961, by Martin Kallich; reprinted with the permission of Twayne Publishers, a Division of G. K. Hall & Co., Boston), Bookman Associates, 1961, 162 p.*

GABRIEL GERSH   (essay date 1967)

[*In his assessment of Strachey's literary method, Gersh states that Strachey is best remembered for broadening the scope of biography by "introducing the standards of aesthetic judgement and psychoanalysis."*]

[Lytton Strachey] widened the range of biographical writing by introducing the standards of aesthetic judgment and psychological analysis, and for that he has a niche in the history of English letters. As a biographer, he had a genius for compression and refinement of fact—his careful cleaning of historical portraits revealed new tints and tantalizing subtleties—and for evoking in the reader the sense of the past, making him feel at ease in the strange climate of buried generations. His supreme distinction was his style. It was easy, supple, but precise: never mandarin or musclebound, it helped him to give the necessary illusion of authority, continuity, and impartiality. He practised what he described as an attack on the flank or in the rear, with a "sudden, revealing searchlight into obscure recesses, hitherto undivined." And he supported his attack with a vast weight of evidence, facts carefully sifted, arranged with deadly effect and pointed with irony. He had a sense for the essential and the apparently essential detail, for the trivial image that gave his portraits its authentic touch. His sardonic detachment was the result of years of reading, but he never let the evidence get out of hand. He marshalled the minor figures of the cast with an impresario's skill, picking them out for posterity in a few colorful phrases. His method was to stress an important trait in every character, introduced like a Wagnerian *leitmotif* into the general score of historical narrative, and set them all limping with a different Achilles heel. And he painted in vivid colors, with an almost hallucinatory clearness, the victim's features and dress, making them the signs of temperament and action.

The result of Strachey's art was to give the panjandrums of the past the appearance of reality. But it is necessary to stress that it was only an appearance, an illusion of detachment. For he was not impartial. He deliberately eliminated whole segments of life from his historical canvas, for he was determined to give to all his writing the sublime economy of art, and the history had to be trimmed to fit. It was, after all, the figures in the landscape that he stressed—the men, not the movements. He presented historical situations against the background of personal conflicts and individual wills—and he chose always the bizarre, the intellectual, the paradoxical. "Human beings are too important to be treated as mere symptoms of the past," he wrote, but it was quite a different matter to conceive history, as he wrote elsewhere, as "the indescribable complexities, the incalculable extravagances of a myriad consciousness."

This is one fundamental weakness of Strachey's work, and it is important to examine the weakness because of the high finish of the style, the siren enchantments of his method. His books are very readable, and are streaked with greatness, but as a historian he must be discounted and as an artist he had several flaws. Strachey remains a miniaturist in spite of his handling of *Queen Victoria,* and although he seems to lay bare a hundred hearts, he does not penetrate far into historical fact. The brilliance of his puppets is always abnormal; they are incredibly unique, and are always made to play a leading role in history. Therefore, he says that Turgot's dismissal made the French Revolution inevitable, and that Lady Mary Wortley Montague was "the most vital force in the mechanism of the eighteenth century's social life." His hero, Voltaire, "the most famous man in the world," is presented as "the commander-in-chief in the great war against medievalism." . . . (pp. 397-98)

In that same essay, Strachey wrote: "The ironical Fates were at work again. By a strange chance, no sooner was medievalism dead than industrialism was born." This foreshortening and telescoping of historical fact is common in his writing and amounts to little more than phrase-making. For he seeks to fit the background to his figures, and with superb stage-management, to make history revolve around the hub of his fascinating victims, endearingly remote, monsters of charm and intellect. His introduction of "the ironical Fates," for instance, is a revealing phrase he often uses. He writes in *Queen Victoria,* for example, of Stockmar's "pre-ordained destiny," and invoked the Fates to explain Cardinal Manning's development, while Florence Nightingale was controlled by a Demon. He had no philosophy of history, so that the Fates were used, with a coy scepticism, to fill the void in this thinking.

Strachey remained essentially a literary critic. He longed for the eighteenth century, for the imagined perfections of French salons, which he regarded as a high watermark in European civilization. It was before industrialism—he was against that—and democracy, a society of cultivated persons firmly based on injustice. As in Athens, one could enjoy good conversation and take the slaves for granted. He despised the present century, and the common people in any century: he was insulated from their concerns, too insulated in experience ever to be a great historian. And it was as an artist in history perhaps that he would have preferred to be judged.

What are we to think of a twentieth-century writer, who, in dreaming of a century which he sees as an "enchanted island of delight and repose," is completely indifferent to the sea of misery in which that island is set? He liked to think, moreover, of the days of Versailles, "gay lords and proud ladies dancing together under the stars." But he did not think of the grimy bodies, the strong odors, the filthy beds and floors—how they talked in the salons, but never how they smelt! And although the virtues of cleanliness were doubtless exaggerated by the Victorians, the toilets of Versailles are as much a part of historical reality as General Gordon's supposed taste for brandy. That was another cardinal weakness in Strachey's equipment. His concern for imaginative truths did not extend to the lives of the majority or the basic facts of history. He ignored social and economic facts entirely. And even in his personal judgment he often missed the mark—as in his underestimation of Disraeli, "the absurd Jew-boy, who set out to conquer the world," Matthew Arnold ("he would be a critic"), Elizabeth and Dr. Arnold.

Despite his literary skill and his tolerant eclecticism, there were dangerous limitations. He could not understand religious piety, though he sympathized with Newman's mysticism, which had a romantic patina; he despised men of action, or regarded them with amused contempt; he had a personal aversion to writing about sexual relations—love is omitted in his work, except in the gross disparity in the personal relations between Essex and Elizabeth, Walpole and Madame du Deffand; he despised the compromises of politicians, and could not understand the concerns of economists; and he had a hatred for "the singular limitations of average passions and human thoughts." As a historian he was, in brief, an intellectual snob, corrupted by nostalgia—and nostalgia is not enough to keep history alive.

Like Carlyle, Strachey was, moreover, carried away by the efficiency of his own style. It was the triumph of style over subject, for he could not resist the compelling image, the dab of rouge, the sly stab in the back, the final glowing overstatement. As a connoisseur of the absurd and eccentric, he liked to be entertaining at all costs—to be evenly urbane, and to take nothing seriously except books and characters.

For Strachey's essential failure is that he had no philosophical backing, no proper standards of judgment but those of the ivory tower. The context into which he put his characters was a purely formal one, designed on aesthetic principles from the material of history. (He distrusted high purpose, theories of history, the anonymous miracles of historic process.) Style and scepticism were, he considered, enough to give meaning and order to the figures in the frieze. But they were not. They showed that he cared too much for art and too little for history. (pp. 398-99)

> *Gabriel Gersh, "Lytton Strachey: Pathfinder in Biography," in* Modern Age *(copyright © 1967 by the Intercollegiate Studies Institute, Inc.), Vol. 2, No. 4, Fall, 1967, pp. 394-99.*

THE TIMES LITERARY SUPPLEMENT　(essay date 1969)

[*The following excerpt is a short review of Strachey's short story* Ermyntrude and Esmeralda. *The bawdy story was expressly written for the entertainment of Strachey's friends and not published until 1969.*]

Before settling down to write **Eminent Victorians** Lytton Strachey threw off this diminutive novel or *facétie* as he called it. **Ermyntrude and Esmeralda** consists of an exchange of letters between two Edwardian young ladies who were completely ignorant of the facts of life, frantically curious about them and evidently eager to experience them. Inevitably one of the writers has a handsome brother with a tutor who has a taste for Grecian habits. The whole is briskly written and could most fairly be described as moderately enjoyable. The weakest part

is the description of the servants, who are really dummies except below the girdle. This perhaps illustrates how Strachey, and indeed Bloomsbury as a whole, judged by supremely superficial standards things and persons which they did not understand. We have only to compare Strachey's "Henry" with Henry Green's Raunce in *Loving*—"there was many an occasion when I went up to Mamselle's boudoir to give her a long bonjour"—to realize the power of imagination in Mr. Green and its absence in this squib of Strachey's.

We are told that Bloomsbury when they read this book were convulsed with giggles. That may well have been the case. Lytton Strachey might have been wise to remember some words of a man whom he admired (Horace Walpole): "I do not love to expose my limping skeleton to giggledom." The little book was written for Henry Lamb who, unlike the gentry of Bloomsbury, was no giggler. Alas! we shall never know what that fine, perceptive man with his discriminating judgment of books thought of this little production. How refreshing to see that Strachey's **Queen Victoria,** in which genius banishes giggledom, is enjoying its twenty-first printing.

> *"A Bloomsbury Squib," in* The Times Literary Supplement *(© Times Newspapers Ltd. (London) 1969; reproduced from* The Times Literary Supplement *by permission), No. 3535, November 27, 1969, p. 1357.*

MICHAEL HOLROYD　(essay date 1971)

[*Holroyd's* Lytton Strachey: A Biography *(see Additional Bibliography) and* Lytton Strachey and the Bloomsbury Group: His Work, Their Influence *form the definitive biographical and critical account of Strachey's life and art. Holroyd's work is indebted to Strachey's brother, James, who allowed Holroyd access to the vast collection of Strachey's private papers. The following excerpt is a survey of Strachey's major works.*]

Landmarks in French Literature is disposed in seven chapters, each one scoring the crescendo and diminuendo of a separate epoch and literary movement. As he charts each individual landmark, pin-points it and neatly connects it with what is destined to succeed, Strachey weaves a graceful series of literary-historical contours that give the book its cohesive texture. The pattern is simple but immediately effective. In every chapter he erects a temple at which to worship; and then, after the architectural climax has been reached, introduces a figure who opposes the foregoing *Zeitgeist* and heralds the new emergent spirit of creation. By these means the link between one literary age and the next is drawn with fluency and eloquence. (pp. 131-32)

The structure of his criticism makes no pretensions to originality, but it imposed a convenient neatness and unity of tone upon the book and conveyed the impression of constant development. The many merits which this skilful organization helps to bring out are freely displayed on almost every page. Above all else, his compression and terse, though never austere, economy of verbal description is, in many passages, quite masterly. At his best, Strachey conveys in the briefest possible space the peculiar charm of each author, the unique flavour of his work, the literary influences which he first inherited and later exerted, the teachings of the various critic-philosophers, the obsessive themes of the novelists, poets, dramatists. On the more academic side he also elucidates the particular prose style into which each successive movement infused its thoughts and emotions, the historical background from which it naturally evolved and against which it must be set, and the quality of enjoyment which its chief exponents can liberate in the sensitive twentieth-century reader. Although, inevitably, no one will find himself in exact agreement with all Strachey's canons—his contention, for example, that the pen portraits of Saint-Simon are never caricatures because 'his most malevolent exaggerations are yet so realistic that they carry conviction' is surely an unnecessary piece of special pleading—or applaud the omission of some French writers—the exclusion of Prosper Mérimée and Gérard de Nerval are certainly controversial—yet as an example of pure literary craftsmanship, *Landmarks in French Literature* could hardly be bettered. (pp. 132-33)

Eminent Victorians is Strachey's best full-length work. Though it does not maintain the uniform texture of *Landmarks in French Literature,* though it does not quite achieve the immaculate synthetic cohesion of *Queen Victoria,* though it does not perhaps conjure up the Victorian age as vividly as *Elizabeth and Essex* does the Elizabethan, yet it touches reality more closely than any of these. For the impact between Strachey and his biographical subjects was of greater urgency and took place at a more intense level of experience during the war years, and while he was still unknown, than at any other period of his career. His four eminent Victorians are rendered with the acuteness of true caricature. They are not photographs in literature, and some of the lines of character in their make-up bear only misshapen resemblance to the originals. But seen as creatures of parody and extravagance, each one constructed round a few easily recognizable and strongly developed traits, they each convey the impression of an authentically lifelike countenance.

In *Landmarks in French Literature,* Strachey had treated his writers exclusively as pioneers or reactionaries to the historical exposition of the book, and had appraised their literature, in terms of tendencies and schools. Now he claimed to be doing away with these trappings of prestige and the ephemeral whims of fashion, to be presenting individuals as interesting in their own right. . . . The widespread and collective reaction to *Eminent Victorians* when it came out belies this admirably strict individualistic approach. It is possible that Strachey, not gifted with any great depth of self-knowledge and holding the opinion that art must depend on consistency, really believed that his four sitters symbolized for him nothing beyond themselves. But the distortions which he manipulated on all four of them are consistent with George Simson's view that *Eminent Victorians* represents his greatest and most prolonged onslaught upon the evangelicalism that was the defining characteristic of Victorian culture, and which, Strachey believed, had been indirectly responsible for the First World War. Once again the reader is given a dramatized conflict between the powers of light and darkness. Extolling the virtues of reason, simplicity, moderation and tolerance—qualities which he himself possessed in a high degree—he shows us how, to a greater or lesser extent, his Victorian quartet sacrificed these attributes by becoming, as Lord Annan succinctly puts it, 'the dupes of two false moral systems: ecclesiastical Christianity and the religion of success'.

In order to disperse the sacrosanct myths enveloping Cardinal Manning, Florence Nightingale, Doctor Arnold and General Gordon, he was compelled to marshal a good deal of his critical attention on them as non-representational beings. Yet in all four studies, the parallel oversimplification resulting from his monochromatic biographical technique impoverishes the rich complexity of human life. (pp. 167-69)

The change in tone and literary style between *Eminent Victorians* and *Queen Victoria* gives some indication of the post-war development in Strachey's character, and shows the greater refinement he brought to this biographical method. His real originality and force are best seen in the pages of *Eminent Victorians*. In *Queen Victoria,* written at a happier period of his life, the astringent, incisive style has softened into a kindlier mood of mellow and affectionate nostalgia. The pace is gentler too, more explorative though less acute, and the basis of the construction has shifted from a quartet of one-act dramas to a single organic unit composed of a series of interconnected chapter-scenes, more akin to a subjective novel. (p. 243)

In *Queen Victoria,* Strachey came nearer to portraying a hero and heroine, and the artistic means by which he chose to represent them were of a quite different order. All pretence at a strictly impersonal attitude is now abandoned, and a more subjective spirit of romance is invoked. Strachey livens up his amiable portraits with just a hint of entertaining malice. His heroes were far from perfect, he is constantly reminding us. They had their full share of faults. Everything apparently conspires to a fair distribution of disqualifications. Yet the skill, of course, lies in apportioning the favoured characters with only the more diverting and endearing frailties, so that the untrained reader is led to believe, even against some of the evidence, that he has discovered for himself that Victoria was really quite a sweet little lady, and that the grossly underrated Albert possessed a considerable talent. (pp. 247-48)

Queen Victoria has claims to be considered a more mature work than *Eminent Victorians*. To a very large extent, Strachey relinquished his air of bland superiority; and the methods he used to convey a mellow and enfolding atmosphere were less arbitrary than those he had previously employed in uncovering a hidden core of diabolism. The scholarship is more thorough; the tone more finely controlled; and the writing no less lucid. His irony is lowered so that it flows like a sub-current flavouring the whole biography, and giving it its distinctive poise and harmony. In this sense, his prose style is more subtle than in his earlier book, the extreme quietness and depth of both the irony and wit being absorbed as a necessary part of the narrative. (pp. 248-49)

Another reason why, in the opinion of some critics, *Queen Victoria* carries greater conviction than *Eminent Victorians,* is that the narrative appears to have been more scrupulously put together. With the greater choice of material at his disposal, there was no need for Strachey to search after peculiar significance in trivial episodes, to manipulate quotations or to present as accredited truth some evidence which had only dubious foundation in fact. Several apocryphal anecdotes and sayings are repudiated in footnotes; and when, for example, he recounts how Albert refused to open his door to Victoria so long as she demanded entrance as Queen of England, only consenting to admit her as his wife, Strachey, though not wishing to omit the story, describes it fairly and openly as 'ill-authenticated and perhaps mythical, yet summing up, as such stories often do, the central facts of the case'. At the same time, partly perhaps because of this greater scrupulousness, *Queen Victoria* remains a much less witty and irreverent book than *Eminent Victorians*. (p. 250)

Elizabeth and Essex has been called Strachey's only work of fiction. In form, in planning, and partly in its illustrations, it bears an interesting resemblance to Virginia Woolf's *Orlando* (the experiences of whose hero with the same queen are those of Essex himself); but the structure of this tragic history is nearer to that of a five-act play than a novel. The long meditations attributed to the main characters have their origin in the monologues of Elizabethan drama, where the protagonist often occupies the stage alone, delivering in rhetorical poetry the passions and perplexities that divide his soul. (p. 289)

Elizabeth and Essex is Strachey's *Antony and Cleopatra.* . . . Passion is the overriding theme of *Elizabeth and Essex.* Essex was a typical Court favourite, and in Strachey's pages his sensual temperament and genius for friendship are brought out in a manner that helps to emphasize his similarity to Antony. Like Antony he leaves and returns to his Queen; and like Antony he dies a violent death. Elizabeth is no Cleopatra; but each in her own way was 'a lass unparallel'd'—the Queen of England's infinite variations of temper forming an obvious dramatic equivalent to the 'infinite variety' of the Queen of Egypt. (p. 291)

Elizabeth and Essex was largely a calculated biographical experiment, incorporating much autobiographical interest. Unlike *Queen Victoria,* the story is not compactly arranged around the main regal figure, but carried along in a looser episodic form. The difference in construction, narration and mood between this book and his earlier ones underlines the full flexibility of Strachey's style. It has been said that his writing is indebted to, among many others, La Bruyère, Anatole France, Gibbon, Saint-Beuve, Saint-Simon, Walter Pater and Voltaire. But although his prose was certainly a composite affair, it was also highly personal. Very characteristic, in all his biographies, is his use of indirect speech which serves to recount the facts as seen from the viewpoint of the characters themselves, which enables him to interpret the secret thoughts of these characters, and to impersonate their tricks of speech. There are many examples of this technique in *Elizabeth and Essex.* (pp. 291-92)

Probably the most noticeable feature of Strachey's prose style is his regular employment of the stereotyped phrase. Many critics have carped unduly at this aspect of his writing, for the most obvious combination of words is not necessarily the hallmark of inferior prose or second-hand thinking. By making use of a very simple vocabulary and humdrum, colloquial epithets, Strachey was sometimes able to summon forth a feeling of personal intimacy that could never have been beguiled by more recondite methods. (p. 294)

'To be brief', wrote George Santayana, 'is almost a condition of being inspired.' In Strachey's tightly drawn pages, the neat conversational clichés fit perfectly, like old gems made new and luminous by their improved setting. But in his weakest and most flamboyant strain, overloaded with picturesque adjectives and adverbs, he seems to be unsuccessfully trying to avoid the banal. This failure may in part be the penalty he paid for trying to reproduce in English the chaste and abstract vocabulary of the French. But if style ultimately reveals the man, then the flat and simulated passion of these more high-flown, ambitious passages only shows how oddly his desire outran his performance. (pp. 294-95)

Both biographies [*Queen Victoria* and *Elizabeth and Essex*] were love stories, but love stories of a very different order. In his treatment of Victoria's strong sexuality, Strachey had been decorously unobtrusive. In dealing with Elizabeth's sexual make-up, he adopted a far more salacious and erotic tone, full of suggestive allusion and innuendo. In the opinion of one reverend gentleman—who belongs to a body of men especially well-suited to nosing out such matters—he also showed himself in this last biography 'preoccupied with the sexual organs to a degree that seems almost pathological'. This is a great ex-

aggeration. But undoubtedly there is some libidinous imagery in *Elizabeth and Essex,* and several dark passages that contain sly and vibrant animal overtones. (pp. 296-97)

This preoccupation with sexual themes and deviations is decked out with certain Freudian overtones. Significantly, Strachey dedicated his book to [his brother and sister-in-law,] James and Alix Strachey, who were by this time pupils of Freud and who were to produce the standard English translation of all Freud's works. Despite his wartime tuition, Strachey did not read German at all proficiently, and until well into the 1920s Freud's writings were available in English only in extremely indifferent—and even incorrect—translations. Strachey had read a very few of these, and to begin with, was mainly sceptical as to their value. None of his character sketches in *Eminent Victorians* were influenced in the slightest by Freud, and nor was the portrait of Queen Victoria. The great psychological influence on his earlier work had been Dostoyevsky—who, of course, reveals a lot of the same material as Freud, and whom Freud himself regarded as the greatest of all novelists. (pp. 298-99)

Michael Holroyd, in his Lytton Strachey: A Critical Biography: The Years of Achievement (1910-1932), *Vol. II (copyright © 1968 Michael Holroyd; reprinted by permission of Holt, Rinehart and Winston, Publishers), Holt, Rinehart and Winston, 1968 (and reprinted in his* Lytton Strachey and the Bloomsbury Group: His Work, Their Influence, *Penguin Books, 1971, 400 p.)*

DONALD H. SIMPSON   (essay date 1974)

[*Simpson examines each essay within Strachey's most controversial work,* Eminent Victorians. *In addition, he provides an overview of the work's early critical reception.*]

Strachey regarded his essays [in *Eminent Victorians*] as variations on a theme—Manning, *allegro vivace;* Florence Nightingale, *andante;* Arnold, *scherzo;* and Gordon, *rondo.* [Michael] Holroyd summed up the common theme as "one dominating quality—a sense of ambition, inflated beyond reason by religious superstition" and Strachey's considerable gifts were devoted to conveying this.

Strachey wrote with great artistry, producing a volume that was compellingly readable, often very amusing, but, over all, negative in purpose and impact. His method involved a presentation based on one dominating characteristic in the subject, supported by carefully selected evidence. There were various means to this end.

Firstly, the achievements of the Eminent Victorians were built up beyond even the claims of their admirers so that the contrast with the feet of clay that were to be revealed would be all the greater. Florence Nightingale, for example, was credited with excessive achievements in purveying the hospitals and reforming nursing methods during the Crimean War. Gordon's leadership of the "Ever-Victorious Army" was depicted as the transformation of "an ill-disciplined, ill-organised body" into an almost magically conquering one whereas it had already achieved considerable success before he assumed command.

All four of the subjects had strong religious convictions. Strachey's approach to these was phrased in an atmosphere of flippancy "where nothing needs to be proved since everything depends on the proof being taken for granted," *e.g.* "The years that followed showed to what extent it was safe to depend upon St Peter.'' Since religious doubts and problems were irrelevant to Strachey's thinking, he was unable to realise that Arnold's theological difficulties about certain Christian doctrines or Manning's reaction to the Gorham judgment could be taken seriously.

An air of bathos was conveyed by mixing serious ideas with irrelevant factors. Names provided one opening. ''St Guthlake, Brother Drithelm, St Amphibalus, St Wulstan and Cunibert the Hermit'' are part of a list in a paragraph aimed at building up the picture of Newman as a credulous and somewhat ridiculous simpleton. Names such as Wegg-Prosser, Gell, Burbidge, Walrond and Simpkinson were inserted for no valid reason save a certain comic implication. Strachey was even more given to introducing physical defects and mannerisms—Gordon (on the doubtful authority of Chaillé-Long) was described as ''tripping,'' Clough as ''This earnest adolescent, with the weak ankles and the solemn face,'' and Arnold, whose ''outward appearance was the index of his inward character'', had legs ''shorter than they should have been.'' Even if these were correct, Strachey knew as well as his readers that comic names and physical shortcomings did not in themselves invalidate ideas or actions; but the skill of the writing is such that the impression of absurdity is conveyed. (p. 88)

The impression of the narrative is strengthened by the use of adjectives. **''Cardinal Manning''** abounds in hints of intrigue—Manning went ''up the little winding staircase in the Vatican and through the humble door'' to visit Monsignor Talbot. Later in the same paragraph, ''the winding stair'' is repeated, followed by ''the low-arched door.''

Strachey referred in his preface to lowering a little bucket into the great ocean of material to ''bring up to the light of day some characteristic specimen.'' His was no random fishing; he directed a keen light of purpose into the ocean depths and selected what was not necessarily characteristic but what might, by suitable presentation, support his thesis. . . . Analyses of this practice must inevitably deal with details and can therefore seem trivial, but when so much of Strachey's effect depended on the manipulation of fragments of information and dialogue, an assessment of the general picture drawn from them must depend to some extent on such specific study.

In handling such material, Strachey used a degree of emphasis to highlight certain aspects of character, while omitting or passing rapidly over those facts which did not accord with his view of the individual concerned. Arnold was a great lover of the peace of the countryside, but this was minimised by Strachey since it clashed with the image of a restless, narrow-minded busybody. Florence Nightingale took a personal interest in nurses under training throughout a long period of her later life, but human sympathies would mar the picture of a pitiless ''tigress'', so this was transformed into ''indulged in sentimental friendships with young girls'' and attributed to her senility (described with a chillingly acid relish and some inaccuracy in the final paragraph of the essay). Cardinal Manning was shown as self-seeking and ambitious; and as his interest in social problems, and zealous work even in extreme old age, would diminish the impact of this limited interpretation, this aspect of his life had to be given a demoniac quality (''A kind of frenzy fell upon him'').

The characteristics of the Eminent Victorians were further accentuated by dramatic contrasts with others—the forceful scheming Manning and the amiable pathetic Newman (''The Eagle and the Dove''), the domineering Florence Nightingale

(''the terrible commander who had driven Sidney Herbert to his death''), and the eccentric Gordon contrasted with the callous self-seeking Evelyn Baring.

Turning to the individual essays, the two themes of the longest of them, **''Cardinal Manning''**, were the irrelevance and triviality of the Christian religion and the ambition of Manning—the ''superstitious egotist.'' Anglicans and Roman Catholics alike were presented as contemptible. (pp. 88-90)

Manning himself was depicted throughout as moved solely by ambition, both as a showy and worldly Archdeacon (''cutting brilliant figures on the ice'' on the basis of a passing reference in Purcell's biography that he had learned to skate) and in his remarkable career after his conversion to Rome. The episode which it is difficult to interpret in terms of unalloyed ambition is the conversion itself, since Manning then seemed assured of a distinguished career in the Church of England. Strachey—without any insight into the religious conflict—could only fit this into his preconceived pattern by implying that, at his interview with the Pope in 1848, Manning was promised promotion if he went over to Rome. (p. 89)

Andante is a curious subtitle for the second essay, since Strachey saw Florence Nightingale as possessed by a demon. His account of her life and character has been subjected to the most meticulous analysis of any of the Eminent Victorians by Rosalind Vaughan Nash, Miss Nightingale's cousin, who had worked with Sir Edward Cook on the authorised biography (1914) and had abridged it in 1925. She noted examples of Strachey's distortion or inaccuracy in using facts from Cook's biography—many trifling in themselves, but building up to the picture of an obsessive and unnatural interest in nursing from childhood, a superhuman achievement at Scutari, and an invariably aggressive attitude to others. An episode which in its original form suggested a resolution to tackle a difficult task was retold to make it an attempt to brow-beat a doctor. (pp. 89-90)

Dr Arnold—*Scherzo* was treated with comparative brevity, and was shown largely in isolation, without a conflict theme. It was more of a caricature than the others, but Holroyd defended it as such; ''Lytton needed to invent or suppress no major facts in order to produce the preposterous impression he wanted'', but it is an extreme example of selectivity. The element of personal malice may be due in part to Strachey's own school experiences, and partly to the contemptuous hostility he and his friends felt towards Mrs Humphry Ward, Arnold's granddaughter.

Perhaps too much attention has been given to the somewhat ludicrous matter of Arnold's short legs, which were introduced as part of ''the index of his inward character.'' Sir Edward Marsh claimed that Strachey had admitted to him that he invented this, though other sources suggest that he believed that he had read it somewhere. More serious is the lack of balance in the account of Arnold's character. Strachey found his moral earnestness completely unacceptable, and tellingly illustrated its intellectual limitations. He also made the valid point that Arnold was not as revolutionary an educational theorist as had been claimed for him at times; but he was blind to the strength of Arnold's personality and the influence he exerted through it. His hopes for Christian reunion were certainly in advance of much of the thinking of his age; he had intellectual curiosity; and he felt an inner tension between the claims of Christian goodness and theological dogma which, if he did not always follow it to its logical limits, stimulated a questing spirit in some of his pupils. . . . To read in his letters of his love of the Lakes, of a walk in the rain and a swim on the way home, and of his family happiness, is to realise how much has been left out. Mrs Ward's comment was, "The coarse caricature of my grandfather, Arnold of Rugby, which the book contains, does not trouble me much. He will, I think, survive it." (pp. 90-1)

The final portion of *Eminent Victorians*, **"The End of General Gordon"**, provoked two extreme reactions. To some, the unheroic portrayal of a military leader matched a mood of growing disillusion with a war nearing the end of its fourth year. To others, the denigration by a conscientious objector of a soldier who died at his post seemed particularly offensive. It was based on varied sources, some of them dubious—as he admitted (as something of an afterthought); the authenticity of the *Memoirs* of Li Hung Chang had been disputed, and Colonel Chaillé-Long's writings require discrimination in their use.

Chaillé-Long was the main source of the most controversial point of Strachey's essay—Gordon's drinking. (p. 91)

During the 1890s, Chaillé-Long produced increasingly fantastic versions of events in Africa, and as an old man, in 1912, he wrote *My Life in Four Continents,* in which Gordon was accused of kicking his servant (duly repeated by Strachey), advocating swindling the Khedive, and finally being in his tent during the night attack. On this occasion the story was that he had not only a Bible but "a bottle of cognac and sherry"—Strachey added the adjective "open" to the bottle. Thus, on this very dubious testimony, he not merely alleged that Gordon was a heavy drinker but that he was guilty of dereliction of duty under its influence.

Strachey gave this essay the title *Rondo*—which is defined as a "piece of music with leading theme to which return is made." This is no bad description of the drink theme. . . .

Dr Bernard Allen, Lord Elton and others who have defended General Gordon have never asserted that he was a total abstainer but have argued on the evidence of those who knew him, and the unquestionable facts of his physical fitness under trying climatic conditions, that Strachey's version is untenable. Further evidence comes from letters collected by the late Sir Hesketh Bell, chiefly from those who knew Gordon in Mauritius, where the smallness of the British community would have made any heavy drinking common knowledge. Holroyd assembled a few quotations to support Strachey, but they are very thin evidence indeed to justify his use of the word "dipsomaniac". (p. 92)

Whatever the later criticisms of individual aspects, *Eminent Victorians* attracted widespread attention on its publication. . . .

Despite some dissenting voices, which rather pleased Strachey, the general approval raised the question of a successor. . . .

[*Queen Victoria*] has a much greater precision in citing sources, and even notes when there is no authentic origin for an anecdote which has an air of credibility. Strachey did however tend to assert deductions as facts, *e.g.* a paragraph on Prince Albert's relations with the Queen began categorically: "He was not in love with her", whereas the sources noted do not necessarily bear that interpretation. . . .

It is however noteworthy that, writing a bare twenty years after the Queen's death, when only her early letters had been published, and having to rely largely on memoirists such as Creevey

and Greville, he produced so life-like and rounded a portrait. . . .

There was considerable surprise at the sympathy shown by Strachey for the Queen herself. Though he depicted her with many human failings, and included some extracts from her letters and journals which seem particularly commonplace out of context, the over-all picture is surprisingly genial. (p. 93)

Queen Victoria portrayed the Queen from a limited viewpoint in a series of essays, primarily showing her relations with her family and her ministers. The politicians depicted—Melbourne, Peel, Palmerston, Gladstone and Disraeli—were shown from a restricted aspect—their policies and principles emerge only in the context of their relation to the Queen—but with considerable skill. The tendentiousness of *Eminent Victorians* did not vanish but was somewhat modified, and Max Beerbohm has pointed out the skill with which Strachey adapted his prose style to the varied characters of these men [see excerpt above]. (pp. 93-4)

Since their first warm reception, they have been assessed and reassessed many times and in contrasting ways. "Strachey's work sounds like the flop of a large man who has tried to dive and failed", wrote C. S. Lewis. Edmund Wilson noted "his curious catty malice" [see excerpt above], but Edwin Muir declared "Every stroke of irony in his books is weighed not for its effectiveness but for its justice", and G. M. Trevelyan wrote "you have not only historical sense . . . but *judgement*."

On the whole, *Queen Victoria* was more widely applauded than *Eminent Victorians,* though Strachey himself preferred the latter.

It became clear, too, to both hostile and friendly critics, that these books were to have a considerable influence on biographical method and style. . . .

Strachey himself, however, would never have been a significant influence if his own work had not had positive qualities to which his weaker imitators could not aspire. In his view, biography demanded construction, balance, and literary skill. He saw his subjects as human beings, to be made alive by the use of their own words, and if in place of the stained-glass window portraits of "official biography" he substituted images of the Max Beerbohm school, it gave a challenge to others to produce life-like portraits. (p. 94)

Donald H. Simpson, "Lytton Strachey & the Facts,"
in Encounter *(© 1974 by Encounter Ltd.), Vol. XLII,*
No. 1, January, 1974, pp. 87-94.

LEON EDEL   (essay date 1979)

[*An American critic and biographer, Edel is a highly acclaimed authority on the life and work of Henry James. His five-volume biography* Henry James *(1953-73) is considered the definitive life and brought Edel critical praise for his research and interpretive skill. John K. Hutchens has summarized Edel's views on the ideal literary biographer as follows: "He is . . . a sensitive critic as well as a scrupulous collector of facts, searches a writer's work not only for its own esthetic sake but for what it says about the writer's inner life, uses the psychoanalyst's techniques but is not confined by them, and by-passes the orthodox biographer's subservience to chronology in favor of grouping for dramatic emphasis outside a fixed-time schedule." Edel himself has added, "My aim in biography is to achieve tightness of synthesis and a clear narrative 'line.' In criticism I like directness and lucidity." His* Bloomsbury: A House of Lions *is the story of the "Bloomsbury Group" and its principal figures, including Lytton Strachey.*

In this excerpt, Edel examines the reasons for the popular success of Strachey's Eminent Victorians.]

Lytton's manifesto on history and biography [contained in his preface to *Eminent Victorians* (see excerpt above)] can be summarized: there is no excuse for dull biographies, those two-volume memorials with their funereal tone and tombstone size. History is an art, not a compilation written by journeymen. Biography has to be analytic, lively, human, and composed with becoming brevity. In modern times, with massive archives, it is no longer possible to write histories of a given age: instead, one can lower a small bucket into the great sea of documents and books and come up with characteristic specimens and symptoms; in a word, the whole can be deduced from the parts. In this way Lytton, by publishing only four "characters" out of the Victorian era, characterized the era. His book was an instant success during those final months of the long First World War. (p. 227)

Why did *Eminent Victorians* capture the imagination of war-weary England? Taine's theory of the race, the environment and the moment—*la race, le milieu et le moment*—as combining to produce a significant work may very well be applied to Lytton Strachey's book. Strachey challenged and mocked Church and State and the military. He did this not in criticism of the immediate war effort, but within the safety of the past—the recent past which England still remembered. It was a consolation and a relief for Britons to see that in this war they had shown the same toughness, the same resilience, and had made the same mistakes. Lytton had said that Voltaire grinned most when he was in earnest, and the grin of *Eminent Victorians* made it an earnest as well as an amusing book. His readers were prepared to overlook Lytton's mannerisms, his inaccuracies, his wantonly imagined details, and to accept his characterizations. The Church harbored ambitious and power-seeking individuals; the military had generals with an exalted notion that Bible and sword were the justification for their existence; the schools had great schoolmasters of platitudinous proportions. In his vivid portrait of Florence Nightingale, Lytton also paid homage to the toughness of English women and their ability to confound Downing Street. From now on he would paint English queens—Victoria, Elizabeth—who had in them the very stuff that produced the Victorian Miss Nightingale. Moreover, the essay on "The Lady with the Lamp" exalted the common soldier and spoke on behalf of his fate in compassionate and humane terms. England was at this moment filled with soldiers who knew the pain of their wounds and had experienced the benefits of Miss Nightingale's revolution. The urgencies of war had exposed Britain to all its institutions, and Strachey held up these institutions in the light of gentle (and at times even savage) ironies. Thus he fulfilled for his readers Taine's dictum: the English race, the beloved land, and this crucial moment helped create one of the greatest literary successes of the century.

There were few readers who realized that Lytton Strachey had done more than present a palimpsest of British history in which Britons could read their present into the past. He had written his book in a new kind of ink—the ink of Vienna, of Sigmund Freud. . . . Lytton Strachey was the first practitioner of "psycho-history," and he did it with direct use only of what in Freud was relevant to his own work. The Viennese master himself could applaud him. When *Elizabeth and Essex* appeared, Freud wrote a letter to Lytton saying that he had read all his works and that he considered the book on Elizabeth an exemplar of the psychoanalytic method applied to history [see

excerpt above]. Lytton had worked within "the incompleteness of our knowledge and the clumsiness of our synthesis," but he had worked with "boldness and discretion." Historians, unlike analysts, working with the personages beyond living confrontation, were in the same position as "dreams to which we have been given no associations." Lytton had nevertheless been able to trace back Elizabeth's character "to the impressions of her childhood." He thus "touched on her most hidden motives." And Freud ventured to add that possibly Lytton had succeeded in making "a correct reconstruction of what actually occurred." (pp. 227-28)

Where lay the success of *Eminent Victorians* beyond the fact that it seemed to touch *la race, le milieu et le moment*? There were the Stracheyesque stance, the high irony, the intimate effect of using diaries as if they were the private thoughts of the characters and a host of new biographical devices including skillful *collage* and *pastiche*. And then there was the extraordinary economy of the prose, the flair with which vast amounts of dull material were reduced to a brilliant paragraph or sentence of description. Lytton Strachey had dared to do what other biographers feared: to interpret his materials courageously, to say what things meant. Biographies crammed with fact, he observed, were tasteless; a fact had no meaning unless some attempt was made to interpret it. Lytton's book—and we must not blame him for his imitators—gave rise to a whole series of "debunking" biographies in which the famous were knocked off their pedestals. But he also had disciples: André Maurois in France, Van Wyck Brooks in America. Brooks borrowed an entire methodology from Strachey—not always with happy results, but with considerable public success. What Strachey understood, for all his abrasiveness, was the principle of human volatility; he knew that the ego seeks at all costs its basic defenses; and he knew what other biographers had not learned—that a biographical subject is consistently ambiguous, irrational, inexplicable, self-contradicting; hence, it truly lends itself to irony and to delicacies of insight and sentiment. (p. 229)

Leon Edel, "Eminence of Lytton," in his Bloomsbury: A House of Lions *(copyright © 1979 by Leon Edel; reprinted by permission of Harper & Row, Publishers, Inc.), J. B. Lippincott Company, 1979, pp. 219-31.*

JOHN HALPERIN   (essay date 1980)

[*In the following assessment of* Eminent Victorians, *Halperin disagrees with those critics who maintain Strachey's biographies are works of art. He asserts that Strachey was an unreliable historian who used his own version of history to refute and mock past principles and conventions.*]

In an essay called "English Prose between 1918 and 1939" (1944), E. M. Forster takes some trouble to describe Lytton Strachey's method as an historian [see excerpt above]. He worked from *within*, says Forster, and so brought his characters psychologically alive. By managing to get inside his subjects he was able to bring whole societies to life, and in so doing he revolutionized the art of biography. According to Forster, Strachey was implacable in his pursuit of truth.

But which truth and whose? Forster acknowledges that Strachey was uninterested in politics—no doubt a serious flaw in an historian; and he admits that Strachey must have gotten some of his biographical subjects wrong—most likely, General Gordon.

As usual, Forster himself is wrong; for if Strachey ever got anyone right, it was General Gordon. Certainly there is little else that he got right in *Eminent Victorians*. As Leon Edel has remarked of Strachey, "One may expect that the reverse of what he says is usually the truth"; his most characteristic vein is that of "malice and subterfuge." Strachey's motive in *Eminent Victorians* was to mock, to startle, to debunk—and to make himself famous. All of these things the book managed to do. But it did not manage to become history. (p. 433)

It has been suspected for many years that Strachey was not a dependable historian. The questions worth asking and answering now are—what exactly did he do to the historical record, and why did he do it? (p. 434)

Surely Virginia Woolf is right when she says (in her essay "The Art of Biography" [see excerpt above]) that Strachey succeeded when he treated biography as a craft and failed when he treated it as an art. . . . The biographer, she says—reaching a conclusion very different from Strachey's—is *not* an artist; at least, he shouldn't be.

Strachey's method as biographer, to use Mrs. Woolf's terms, is that of an artist rather than that of a craftsman. Bloomsbury's ideas about "significant form" govern his approach to history. His work is less objective than "autonomous," a work of art with its own internal coherence and logic but with only some relation to what lies outside it—in this case, historical truth. Just as Roger Fry believed that paintings need express only themselves—need not, above all, be representational—so Strachey's biographies are less representational, less reproductions of exterior reality, than artistic creations, like novels, true only to themselves and to what the artist sees. Strachey's own philosophy of historiography (set forth in an essay in *The Spectator* in 1909) allows the historian to be—indeed, declares that he must be—an artist. Art, Strachey says here, is the great interpreter; through the artist's personal revelation only may bare facts be transformed into readable history. History, he says, is less a science than a branch of literature; good history writing is as personal as poetry and requires literary method.

All this talk about art is palaver. Strachey wrote about history as art, but he wrote history as polemics. His very personal approach to his subjects assured the destruction of "pure" historiography. He did not believe in placing historical facts before the reader and letting him form his own conclusions. His method rather was to select his presentable facts in order to force the reader to reach the same conclusions he himself had reached before he began to write. He usually had in his head the plan of a book, including what he was going to say, long before he began reading and research on his topic. He took more interest in his characters than in their milieux and unfairly, I think, applied to them and to older customs and beliefs the modern standards of a less reverent age. In his books the events of past history often seem little more than a series of farcical imbecilities, trivial eccentricities, bigotries, and crimes resulting from a human nature consistently imperfect. In Strachey's tendency to focus too much on personality and too little on the outside forces shaping personality, we can once again see the influences of Bloomsbury's theories of form. For if Bloomsbury was anything, it was antihistorical. Strachey's biographies are chiefly interesting as an expression of his age's perception of others—whether the English Renaissance, as in *Elizabeth and Essex*, or the 19th century, as in *Queen Victoria* and *Eminent Victorians*. (pp. 434-35)

"Je n'impose rien; je ne propose rien: j'expose," says Strachey in the preface to *Eminent Victorians*. Like almost everything else in the book, this is pure fabrication. Strachey got some of his facts right (principally in the account of General Gordon), but most of the rest of the time he distorts or simply changes what he knows to be the truth. Certainly he understands Cardinal Manning's cruelty, cunning rigidity, megalomania, and hardheartedness. Equally well does he understand Florence Nightingale's passion for medical reform, her hatred of bureaucracy and bungling, her genius for organization. In both of these studies he perceives the ways in which simple human affection and warmth have been obliterated by the cold ambition of aspiring natures. But he wants us to laugh at Victorian earnestness and devotion to duty, and in order to get us to do this he revises and flattens many of the facts of the lives of both. The account of Dr. Arnold is fabrication from first to last. The story of Gordon is brilliantly incisive—though even here Strachey was unable to resist some distortion of history.

Eminent Victorians is an attack upon Victorianism—more than anything else upon fanatical evangelicalism, which Strachey and many of his contemporaries felt had been chiefly responsible for making the Great War possible. It is for this reason that *Eminent Victorians* begins with a study of a famous Victorian cleric—even though the equally famous schoolmaster, Dr. Arnold, was born 13 years earlier than the Cardinal and died half a century earlier.

After a series of loaded rhetorical questions, the portrait of Manning commences its improbable, incredulous, preposterous path. Very like Butler in *The Way of All Flesh* (much more than G. E. Moore's *Principia Ethica*, the Bible of Bloomsbury), Strachey is so eager to condemn that he sometimes forgets to do the most important thing of all in satire—that is, to bring his subject-target to life through plausible description. No one could have been as diabolical as Manning is said to be . . . , no one, not even Machiavelli's *Prince*, could always be so prescient, so politically astute. (pp. 436-37)

To Strachey, Florence Nightingale was less objectionable than Manning, but again in his account of her he used those aspects of her character he found repellent to illustrate characteristics of the age he abhorred. He attacks her for repressing her erotic feelings and for her indifference to human relationships while he praises the energy with which she fought, all of her life, bureaucracy and convention. Strachey's picture is that of a sort of Amazon whose humanitarianism was based on a system rather than real feeling, whose sexual instinct became sublimated in good works. As so often in Strachey's biographies, there is some truth in this picture, but again a good many facts are wrong—because of deliberate distortion or careless historiography. One result of his distortions has been to turn a genuine 19th-century epic into a 20th-century mock-epic. For Florence Nightingale *was* a great woman; in Strachey's hands she appears less great than eccentric. (pp. 439-40)

"Nowhere," Dr. Arnold once said, "is Satan's work more evidently manifest than in turning holy things to ridicule." Strachey's "caricature essay" (the phrase is Edel's) on Thomas Arnold isn't even remotely accurate. It is not only inaccurate—it is irresponsible and malicious. Strachey's dislike of Arnold undoubtedly stems in part from his own unpleasant school experiences at Abbotsholme, in part from his dislike of the pious biography of Arnold by Dean Stanley and of the more popularized account of Rugby given by Thomas Hughes in *Tom Brown's Schooldays*, a best seller of the 1850's. Strachey's response was to exclude all documentary eidence from his discussion of Arnold and to construct a caricature rather than a portrait. Strachey's defenders betray their ignorance of the facts when they try to justify the portrait of Arnold. (pp. 441-42)

One of Strachey's rare virtues in *Eminent Victorians* is that he manages to capture and portray the stubbornness, the fanaticism, of both Gordon and Gladstone. Both were rigid and violent in their prejudices, and upon finding themselves on opposite sides of an issue which involved the potential loss of human life, blood must inevitably have been shed. Strachey for once did not have to invent; the neuroses and megalomania were there in his subjects. He did not need to change historical facts in order to indict the government of the most staunchly religious English statesman of the 19th century; that government indicted itself. **"The End of General Gordon"** is the best of the portraits in *Eminent Victorians* not only because of the brilliance of its narrative but also because of the unusually few distortions of fact. Perhaps Strachey blames Gordon a bit less than he should—for Gordon, as Holroyd says, was in truth a half-crazed romantic, a manic-depressive fatalist, high on brandy and the Bible throughout much of his life. To portray him as a 19th-century Don Quixote, both comic and heroic, a man more sinned against than sinning, is to ignore the fact that much of the trouble in the Sudan came about as a result of Gordon's own absurdities. But of course Strachey would take the side of a rebel against Victorian authority. (pp. 452-53)

Holroyd's claim that "Strachey's influence as a biographer has matched that of Plutarch and Boswell" is, of course, far-fetched; but controversy has kept *Eminent Victorians* alive for over six decades now and will probably continue to keep it alive. In his preface to the book [see excerpt above], Strachey advocates detachment as a necessary attitude of mind for the would-be historian; we have seen that his biographies, if they lack anything, lack detachment. Still, in his philosophy of historiography, in his pronouncements upon biographical form, Strachey has had some influence, and his books undoubtedly will continue to be read if for no other reason than that they are entertaining to read. (p. 454)

John Halperin, "'Eminent Victorians' and History," in The Virginia Quarterly Review *(copyright, 1980, by* The Virginia Quarterly Review, *The University of Virginia), Vol. 56, No. 3 (Summer, 1980), pp. 433-54.*

IRA BRUCE NADEL (essay date 1981)

[*Nadel is a writer, editor, and educator whose most recent literary interest has been in the evolution of biography as a literary genre. In the following excerpt, he examines Strachey's use of metaphor in* Eminent Victorians. *According to Nadel, metaphor (the "subtler strategy") enables Strachey to "maintain the brevity and aesthetic detachment he required for* Eminent Victorians." *Specifically discussed are military and animal metaphors within the work.*]

[The] appearance of *Eminent Victorians* in 1918 altered the tone, style and structure of biography through its self-conscious approach to biographical writing. Its most important contribution was its proof that compressing a life did not detract from the quality of a biography. And the most immediate and direct form of compression Strachey used was metaphor, which dramatically illustrated rather than explained the character of his subjects. Metaphor, the "subtler strategy," maintained the brevity and aesthetic detachment Strachey required for *Eminent Victorians,* in addition to providing a means of harmonizing the disparate individuals and their lives. Through the use of

metaphor Strachey both summarized past practices and anticipated new developments in the theory and writing of biography. (p. 146)

From his earliest considerations of biography, Lytton Strachey understood the value of metaphor. This may have originated in his early interest in poetry, especially Shakespeare and Milton, as well as in the prose of Gibbon and Macaulay. The French provided other models, notably Fontenelle and Condorcet both of whom Strachey cites in the "Preface" to *Eminent Victorians.* Whatever the source, Strachey continuously sought the clearest and most direct metaphors for his subjects: "let us have the pure essentials—a vivid image, on a page or two, without explanation, transitions, commentaries or padding," he declared in his essay on John Aubrey. Metaphor became the major stylistic embodiment of "the pure essentials," compressing opposite characteristics of his subjects into single figures of speech. With his emphasis on the relation rather than the accumulation of details, Strachey naturally found metaphor congenial because it permitted the vividness, richness of meaning, and feeling discursive prose generally denied, and facilitated the unity and harmony so necessary for the aesthetic telling of a life.

The opening paragraph of *Eminent Victorians* initiates the military metaphors that dominate the work. Describing the "subtler strategy," Strachey outlines the action of the new biographer who will "attack his subject in unexpected places . . . fall upon the flank, or the rear . . . [and] shoot a sudden, revealing searchlight into obscure recesses." . . . Following his own orders, Strachey then manoeuvres a series of battle metaphors to express the sense of attack, pursuit and combat that fittingly summarizes the aggressive manner of his biography. The military metaphors in the text in fact shift from battle (Manning and Newman) to administration (Nightingale, Arnold), to, finally, defeat (Gordon). That Strachey chose a military metaphor as the essential one for the book establishes the work's quintessential Victorianism. For as Michael Timko has argued, the central cultural symbol of the Victorian period was "engagement, in both the sense of battle and quest."

Animal metaphors compose the second major group of metaphors in *Eminent Victorians* and they, too, support another aspect of the work that makes it more a condensation than an exposé of Victorian ideas. Timko again explains: "the consistent use of bestial imagery serves to emphasize the awareness of the Victorians of the need to find irrefutable evidence to prove the humanity . . . of human beings." . . . In response to Darwin's work, which seemed to jeopardize their fundamental humanity, the Victorians desperately sought to define their humanness in the face of "a demonstrated participation in the bestial nature," an endeavour which was complicated by questions concerning man's ability to know things about himself and his world. . . . In his adoption of the various bestial images that appear in *Eminent Victorians.* Strachey displays the essentially Victorian character of his work in terms of its verbal texture and patterns of imagery. (pp. 147-48)

The cause of Strachey's fascination and involvement with military metaphors is complex. It is clearly an extension of the Victorian sense of engagement but also a reflection of the very war taking place at the time Strachey wrote *Eminent Victorians.* As early as 1908 Strachey began to find battle imagery attractive, especially to express the conflict between the educated and the philistines. France was a model to him of civilization; the correspondence of Voltaire and D'Alembert a catalyst. What Michael Holroyd calls the spirit of "revolutionary ferment" grew until it culminated in the aggressive attitude and, I would add, the language of *Eminent Victorians*. Social and financial freedom from his family coincided for Strachey with the war, and confirmed his ability to sustain the radical spirit which was symbolized by his break with the *Spectator*. His pacificism during the First World War did not prevent him from employing its images metaphorically to mark his independence from the preceding generation of Stracheys.

Supplementing the military metaphors in *Eminent Victorians* are those drawn from animals which mix the bestial with the natural. Birds are particularly favoured: Manning is an eagle, Newman a dove; Nightingale "hatches" as a swan, becomes an eagle and is finally transformed into a tigress; Gordon is a hawk. Later, cranes and turkey-cocks embody aspects of Gordon's character and he is said to resemble an exotic bird as he peers northward through his telescope on the fortress roof at Khartoum. Ironically, he becomes the grim attraction for the very hawks he admired when the Mahdi orders his head to be displayed between two tree branches on a public highway after his murder. Other animal metaphors in the biography include a bison (Lord Panmure), a stag (Sidney Herbert), a terrier, (Dr Hall) and one particularly pathetic image, "a thoroughbred harnessed to a four-wheeled cab" (Newman). . . . (pp. 149-50)

An additional, implied metaphor Strachey employs might be identified as 'Titanic.' The Fates, Chaos, Demi-Gods and Prophets are all found in the text as metaphors of the 'Titanic' forces Strachey promotes around his subjects to enhance their stature before he undermines them with irony. Manning's ambition struggles with and then defeats the Fates . . . ; Florence Nightingale brings a semi-Miltonic power to the disorder at Scutari. Possessed by a "demon" she has a "visionary plan" as she confronts the Hell at Scutari, but gradually "the reign of chaos and old night began to dwindle." . . . Arnold reigns like an Old Testament prophet who "involved in awful grandeur, ruled remotely . . . from an inaccessible heaven." . . . General Gordon's life acquires classical references: it is a "tragic history" governed by Fate and Fortune, although he possesses a certain divine aura: "walking at the head of his troops, with nothing but a light cane in his hand, he seemed to pass through every danger with the scatheless equanimity of a demi-God." . . . (p. 150)

Collectively, these metaphors, with their emphasis on grand and epical adventures, develop into a pattern that the subtext—the ironical tone and witty exposé of weaknesses, prejudices and inadequacies—undermines. This contrasting duality of meaning and metaphor in the work extends the formal operation of metaphor, which is to link the similar with the dissimilar, as well as join the referential with the expressive. By subtly dismantling the Titanic metaphors, Strachey displays the meaning of the lives he narrates, and identifies the thematic nature of his work. *Eminent Victorians,* then, not only uses metaphor to express its possibilities but analyzes metaphor to show its limitations.

There is also, however, a personal dimension to the use of metaphor in the book. While it operates stylistically to unite the public and private selves of his subjects, metaphor also joins the divisions of self within Strachey's own character. His personal conflicts over sexual issues ("'what pity one can't now and then change sexes!'" he once wrote to Clive Bell), and social behaviour (his outward shyness and diffidence was at odds with his growing self-confidence) found resolution through his use of metaphor. The military metaphors expressed his sense of independence and resistance, the animal, his determination to assert his own liberal humanism, and the Titanic, his growing sense of self-assurance as both a writer and individual.

Within *Eminent Victorians* there are other devices, of course, that sustain and contribute to the sense of unity such as shifts in narrative technique, the mixture of times, and the conflation of sources. But metaphor, most clearly and consistently, infuses the language of the biography with the experience of unity in diversity. (pp. 150-51)

Strachey did not diminish his use of metaphor in his later writing; he continued to use it whenever it would enhance, dramatically and imaginatively, his work, recognizing and exploiting its power to illuminate rather than to "confuse." In *Queen Victoria* a small crystal pebble functions as the metaphor for the Queen, while a serpent acts as the metaphor for Bacon in *Elizabeth and Essex*.

In metaphor Strachey found a way to combine copiousness of meaning with brevity of style. The effect of an arresting image replacing a tedious detail was not lost on his prose. In his biographical writing, metaphor functioned as a textual trope of compression and a personal trope of expression. Through its objectivity, impartiality was present; through its originality, imagination overshadowed history; through its stylistic variety, fictions emerged from the restrictions of discourse. The result was the fashioning of biography into art. A prelude to that development and a postscript to this essay is George Eliot's remark that "all of us, grave or light, get our thoughts entangled in metaphors and act fatally on the strength of them." (p. 151)

Ira Bruce Nadel, "Strachey's 'Subtler Strategy': Metaphor in 'Eminent Victorians'," in Prose Studies *(© Frank Cass & Co Ltd 1981; reprinted by permission of Frank Cass & Co Ltd), Vol. 4, No. 2, September, 1981, pp. 146-52.*

ADDITIONAL BIBLIOGRAPHY

Bell, Clive. "Lytton Strachey." In his *Old Friends: Personal Recollections*, pp. 25-41. London: Chatto & Windus, 1956.
    Fond reminiscences by one of Strachey's closest friends, with some critical comments on Strachey's biographical style. Bell and Strachey first met at Cambridge and maintained a lifelong friendship, each a vital part of the Bloomsbury Group.

Clemens, Cyril. "Lytton Strachey." *The Dalhousie Review* XX (April 1940): 29-35.
    Overview of early critical reactions to Strachey's works.

Dobrée, Bonamy. "Lytton Strachey." In his *The Post Victorians*, pp. 577-89. London: Ivor Nicholson & Watson, 1933.
    Balanced criticism of Strachey's technique of revealing the less flattering or unsympathetic human characteristics of his subjects.

Hartwell, Robert Metcalf. "Lytton Strachey." *University of California Chronicle* XXXIV, No. 4 (October 1932): 409-41.
    Detailed biographical and critical study analyzing Strachey's principal works.

Holroyd, Michael. Introduction to *Ermyntrude and Esmeralda*, by Lytton Strachey, pp. 9-12. New York: Stein and Day, 1969.
    A brief account of Strachey's short story *Ermyntrude and Esmeralda*, the bawdy satire that he wrote for the entertainment of friends.

——. *Lytton Strachey: A Biography*. Rev. ed. New York: Penguin Books, 1979, 1144 p.

Definitive biography. Holroyd's biography, along with its companion volume *Lytton Strachey and the Bloomsbury Group: Their Work, Their Influence* [see excerpt above], form a comprehensive portrait of Strachey's life, the times in which he lived, and his close association with some of the era's important literary figures. Holroyd's work is indebted to Strachey's brother, James, who allowed Holroyd access to the vast collection of Strachey's private papers. Holroyd's initial meeting with James Strachey (a noted psychologist and translator of Sigmund Freud's works) is delightfully recounted in the preface to this biography.

Huxley, Aldous. "The Author of *Eminent Victorians*." In his *On the Margin: Notes and Essays*, pp. 136-42. New York: George H. Doran Co., 1923.

Characterizes Strachey as a twentieth-century Voltaire who combines the French writer's "old irony" with a "newly-found sympathy" in his biographies.

Johnstone, J. K. "Lytton Strachey." In his *The Bloomsbury Group: A Study of E. M. Forster, Lytton Strachey, Virginia Woolf, and Their Circle*, pp. 267-319. London: Secker & Warburg, 1954.

General discussion of Strachey's three major works: *Eminent Victorians*, *Queen Victoria*, and *Elizabeth and Essex*.

Kronenberger, Louis. "Lytton Strachey." *The Bookman*, New York LXXI, No. 4 (July 1930): 375-80.

Discusses the artistic nature of Strachey's biographies. Kronenberger calls Strachey a literary eclectic whose work combines both romantic and classical elements.

Levy, Paul. Introduction and Afterword to *The Really Interesting Question and Other Papers*, by Lytton Strachey, edited by Paul Levy, pp. ix-xiv, 171-72. New York: Coward, McCann & Geoghegan, 1972.

Commentaries on this collection of previously unpublished esoteric works, which includes some of Strachey's undergraduate essays, later political writings, and short stories.

MacCarthy, Desmond. "Lytton Strachey and the Art of Biography." In his *Memories*, pp. 31-49. London: MacGibbon & Kee, 1953.

Discussion of Strachey's "interpretive" style of biography. This chapter addresses some of the criticism regarding Strachey's use of biographical facts, the moral aspects of his writing, and the lack of sympathy within his works. MacCarthy was also a longtime friend of Strachey's and a Bloomsbury member.

Quiller-Couch, Arthur. "The 'Victorian Age'." In his *Studies in Literature*, 2d ser., pp. 279-302. New York: G. P. Putnam's Sons, 1922.*

Faults Strachey for "sneering" at the Victorian Age. While Quiller-Couch acknowledges the artistic qualities of Strachey's *Queen Victoria*, he believes Strachey did not fully understand the Victorian era, and that the biographer was especially ungracious in his mocking treatment of Prince Albert's Great Exhibition of 1851.

Redford, Bruce B. "The Shaping of the Biographer: Lytton Strachey's 'Warren Hastings, Cheyt Sing, and the Begums of Oude'." *The Princeton University Literary Bulletin* V, No. 1 (Autumn 1981): 38-52.

Examination of Strachey's 1905 fellowship dissertation for Trinity College, Cambridge, which was not accepted, thus ending Strachey's hopes for an academic career.

Sanders, Charles Richard. *The Strachey Family 1588-1932: Their Writings and Literary Associations*. Durham, N.C.: Duke University Press, 1953, 337 p.

Genealogical study of the Strachey family; examines, through anecdotes, their personalities, friendships, associations, and familial propensity for literary pursuits. Sanders is also the author of *Lytton Strachey: His Mind and Art* (see excerpt above).

Strachey, James. Preface to *Spectatorial Essays* by Lytton Strachey, pp. 7-10. New York: Harcourt, Brace & World, 1965.

Explains how Strachey became *The Spectator's* first drama critic.

Swinnerton, Frank. "Bloomsbury: Bertrand Russell, Roger Fry and Clive Bell, Lytton Strachey, Virginia Woolf." In his *The Georgian Literary Scene: 1910-1935*, rev. ed., pp. 265-94. London: Hutchinson, 1969.*

Offers both positive and negative criticism on Strachey's prose style, which Swinnerton believes was inspired by French literature.

Van Doren, Carl, and Van Doren, Mark. "Essayists." In their *American and British Literature since 1890*, pp. 248-70. Chautauqua, N.Y.: Chautauqua Press, 1926.*

Short critique that regards Strachey as a reviver of the art of biography.

Woolf, Leonard. "Cambridge." In his *Sowing: An Autobiography of the Years 1880-1904*, pp. 107-220. New York: Harcourt, Brace & Co., 1960.*

Personal recollections of Strachey during Woolf's university days at Cambridge, where the two formed a lasting friendship.

Mark Twain

1835-1910

(Pseudonym of Samuel Langhorne Clemens; also wrote under pseudonyms of Thomas Jefferson Snodgrass, Josh, Muggins, Soleather, Grumbler, and Sieur Louis de Conte) American novelist, short story and novella writer, journalist, essayist, memoirist, autobiographer, and dramatist.

Twain, considered the father of modern American literature, broke with the genteel traditions of the nineteenth century by endowing his characters and narratives with the natural speech patterns of the common person, and by writing of subjects hitherto considered beneath the consideration of serious art. Twain is often regarded as a humorist and children's writer, though very serious subjects are treated in such perennially popular books as *The Adventures of Huckleberry Finn*, *The Adventures of Tom Sawyer*, and *A Connecticut Yankee in King Arthur's Court*. Initially a clowning humorist, Twain matured into the role of the seemingly naive Wise Fool whose caustic sense of humor forced his audience to recognize humanity's foolishness and society's myriad injustices. Later, crushed by personal tragedy, economic hardship, and ill health, Twain turned on "the damned human race," portraying it as the totally corrupt plaything of a cruel God.

Clemens grew up in the Mississippi River town of Hannibal, Missouri, whose landmarks and people later served as models for the settings and characters of many of his novels, particularly *The Adventures of Tom Sawyer*. At age twelve Clemens quit school and became a journeyman printer; by the time he was seventeen his first sketches were appearing in the newspapers he typeset. During the late 1850s Clemens piloted steamboats on the Mississippi, a livelihood he enjoyed until the Civil War closed the river to commercial traffic. After brief service in the Confederate militia, Clemens traveled west, working as a silver miner and reporter in Nevada and California. During this period he began writing under the byline of Mark Twain, a navigational term indicating two fathoms of water. In 1865 he published his first important sketch, "Jim Smiley and His Jumping Frog," in a New York periodical. The story was widely popular and was reprinted two years later in Twain's first book, *The Celebrated Jumping Frog of Calaveras County, and Other Sketches*, a collection which appeared just as the author set out on a cruise to southern Europe and the Middle East. The letters Twain wrote to two American newspapers detailing the clash of New and Old World cultures proved immensely popular and two years later were collected as *The Innocents Abroad; or, The New Pilgrim's Progress*. The success of this book and Twain's growing fame as a comic lecturer established him as America's leading humorist, although some readers considered his frontier wit uncouth. Twain published several other collections of sketches in his life, the most notable being *Roughing It* and *A Tramp Abroad*.

In 1870 Twain married Olivia Langdon and, after settling in Hartford, Connecticut, published his first novel, *The Gilded Age*, written in collaboration with Charles Dudley Warner. The novel's title became a commonly used term to describe America's post-Civil War industrial boom. The popular children's book *The Adventures of Tom Sawyer*, the first of four novels set in Twain's native Mississippi Valley, appeared in

1876. Immediately afterward he began work on *Tom Sawyer*'s sequel, a novel concerning Tom's friend Huckleberry Finn. This novel was written in three intermittent bursts of inspiration during the next eight years. Though critically misunderstood and banned from public libraries upon its appearance in 1885, *The Adventures of Huckleberry Finn* came to be recognized by later critics as a masterpiece. The meaning of the book, which details a young boy's encounters with the barbarities of civilization, has been debated for nearly a century, most notably by Lionel Trilling, T. S. Eliot, and Henry Nash Smith. Lewis Leary has spoken for many critics when he wrote that the book "poses what has been called the inescapable dilemma of democracy—to what degree may each single and separate person live as an unencumbered individual and to what extent must he submit to distortions of personality required by society?" In the company of the runaway slave Jim, Huck escapes from the hypocritical "starchiness" of St. Petersburg, Missouri, and drifts down the Mississippi on a free-floating raft. The symbolism of the river, Huck's relationship to Jim, and the author's attitude toward the predominantly unsympathetic characters encountered along the journey have been the subject of numerous interpretations. In recent decades, much critical controversy surrounding *Huckleberry Finn* has centered on the "Phelps Farm" section, which constitutes the final twelve chapters of the book. This section, which reintroduces Tom Sawyer into the narrative and tells of the two boys' attempts to rescue the recaptured Jim, has been called by some critics a major and crippling flaw in Twain's otherwise magnificent tale. Others have attempted, with some success, to defend Twain's insertion of the "Phelps Farm" episode into the work. Whatever their differences, critics agree that Twain never again wrote a book equal in power to *Huckleberry Finn*.

Several bad investments plunged Twain into bankruptcy during the 1890s. In a few years he had paid off his tremendous debts, and in so doing had published several important books, including *The Tragedy of Pudd'nhead Wilson, and the Comedy Those Extraordinary Twins* and the biographical novel *Personal Recollections of Joan of Arc*, the latter published under the pseudonym Sieur Louis de Conte to test his readers' response, hence, his own skill. Out of the hardships of the 1890s and the tragedies of the 1900s, which included the death of his wife and two of his three daughters, Twain's natural sarcasm deepened into a fatalistic despair over the nature of God and humanity, and his work became more introspective and polemical. His growing pessimism had been evident as early as the novel *A Connecticut Yankee in King Arthur's Court*, and dominated his finest short story, "The Man That Corrupted Hadleyburg," which presents evil as a necessary adjunct of good. In the years just before his death he worked on his "gospel" of determinism, *What Is Man?* and the fragments assembled posthumously as *The Mysterious Stranger*, which presents life as "a grotesque and foolish dream." The first of several editions of Twain's autobiography appeared in 1924.

Scholars recognize in Twain a man divided in outlook between comic and tragic perceptions of existence. Throughout his career Twain looked back yearningly to his happy youthful days on the Mississippi, finding in his memories spiritual rejuvenation and inspiration. At the same time he was deeply pessimistic about the future. His longing for an idealized past as a haven from an increasingly hostile present is evident in most of his major works of fiction. Critics have sought to explain this fatalistic division in outlook, and two major theories have risen from the debate. The first, expounded by Van Wyck Brooks in *The Ordeal of Mark Twain*, sees in Twain a genius beset from childhood with a deep guilt complex and stifled by America's crude frontier atmosphere, his writings edited into prettified respectability through the efforts of his wife and his friend William Dean Howells. The influence of Olivia Clemens and Howells has been greatly discounted by Bernard DeVoto, whose *Mark Twain's America* and *Mark Twain at Work* demonstrate the positive effects of frontier life on Twain's development and attribute his pessimism to the many personal tragedies he suffered during the last decades of his life.

As DeVoto and other critics have noted, Twain can be found on both sides of every issue: immortality, war, and the social problems of the South, to name but three. His importance to world literature lies not in the power of his ideas, but in the universality of his characters' dilemmas and the accessibility of his works to readers of all ages.

(See also *TCLC*, Vol. 6; *Contemporary Authors*, Vol. 104; *Dictionary of Literary Biography*, Vol. 11: *American Humorists, 1800-1950*; Vol. 12: *American Realists and Naturalists*; and *Yesterday's Authors of Books for Children*, Vol. 2.)

PRINCIPAL WORKS

The Celebrated Jumping Frog of Calaveras County, and Other Sketches (sketches) 1867

The Innocents Abroad; or, The New Pilgrim's Progress (sketches) 1869
Roughing It (sketches) 1872
The Gilded Age [with Charles Dudley Warner] (novel) 1874
The Adventures of Tom Sawyer (novel) 1876
Ah Sin [with Bret Harte] (drama) 1877
A Tramp Abroad (sketches) 1880
The Prince and the Pauper (novel) 1882
Life on the Mississippi (memoirs) 1883
The Adventures of Huckleberry Finn (novel) 1884
A Connecticut Yankee in King Arthur's Court (novel) 1889
The American Claimant (novel) 1892
The Tragedy of Pudd'nhead Wilson, and the Comedy Those Extraordinary Twins (novel and sketch) 1894
Personal Recollections of Joan of Arc [as Sieur Louis de Conte] (novel) 1896
The Man That Corrupted Hadleyburg, and Other Stories and Essays (short stories and essays) 1900
Extracts from Adam's Diary (short story) 1904
What Is Man? (essay) 1906
Extract from Captain Stormfield's Visit to Heaven (novella) 1909
The Mysterious Stranger (novel) 1916
Mark Twain's Autobiography (autobiography) 1924

W. D. HOWELLS (essay date 1869)

[*Howells was the chief progenitor of American realism and the most influential American literary critic during the late nineteenth century. He was the author of nearly three dozen novels, few of which are read today. Despite his eclipse, he stands as one of the major literary figures of the nineteenth century: he successfully weaned American literature away from the sentimental romanticism of its infancy, earning the popular sobriquet "the Dean of American Letters." Through realism, a theory central to his fiction and criticism, Howells sought to disperse "the conventional acceptations by which men live on easy terms with themselves" that they might "examine the grounds of their social and moral opinions." To accomplish this, according to Howells, the writer must strive to record impressions of everyday life in detail, endowing characters with true-to-life motives and avoiding authorial comment in the narrative. In addition to many notable studies of the works of his friends Mark Twain and Henry James, Howells perceptively reviewed three generations of international literature, urging Americans to read Émile Zola, Bernard Shaw, Henrik Ibsen, Emily Dickinson, and other important authors. In this review of Twain's* The Innocents Abroad, *Howells comments favorably on the book's generous portions of ironic humor and the author's portrayals of human nature.*]

[Will the reader] credit us with a self-denial proportioned to the vastness of Mr. Clemens's very amusing book if we spare to state why he is so droll or—which is as much to the purpose—why we do not know? This reticence will leave us very little to say by way of analysis; and, indeed, there is very little to say of *The Innocents Abroad* which is not of the most obvious and easy description. The idea of a steamer-load of Americans going on a prolonged picnic to Europe and the Holy Land is itself almost sufficiently delightful, and it is perhaps praise enough for the author to add that it suffers nothing from his handling. . . . It is out of the bounty and abundance of his own nature that he is as amusing in the execution as in the conception of his work. And it is always good-humored humor, too, that he lavishes on his reader, and even in its impudence it is charming; we do not remember where it is indulged at the cost of the weak or helpless side, or where it is insolent, with all its sauciness and irreverence. The standard shams of travel which everybody sees through suffer possibly more than they ought, but not so much as they might; and one readily forgives the harsh treatment of them in consideration of the novel piece of justice done on such a traveller as suffers under the pseudonym of Grimes. It is impossible also that the quality of humor should not sometimes be strained in the course of so long a narrative; but the wonder is rather in the fact that it is strained so seldom.

Mr. Clemens gets a good deal of his fun out of his fellow-passengers, whom he makes us know pretty well. . . . (pp. 107-08)

Of course, the instructive portions of Mr. Clemens's book are of a general rather than particular character, and the reader gets as travel very little besides series of personal adventures and impressions; he is taught next to nothing about the population of the cities and the character of the rocks in the different localities. Yet the man who can be honest enough to let himself see the realities of human life everywhere, or who has only seen Americans as they are abroad, has not travelled in vain and is far from a useless guide. (pp. 108-09)

The didactic, however, is not Mr. Clemens's prevailing mood, nor his best, by any means. The greater part of his book is in the vein of irony. . . . At Tiberias our author saw the women who wear their dowry in their head-dresses of coins. "Most of these maidens were not wealthy, but some few have been kindly dealt with by fortune. I saw heiresses there, worth, in their own right—worth, well, I suppose I might venture to say as much as nine dollars and a half. But such cases are rare. When you come across one of these she naturally puts on airs." . . . In this vein of ironical drollery is that now celebrated passage in which Mr. Clemens states that he was affected to tears on coming, a stranger in a strange land, upon the grave of a blood-relation—the tomb of Adam; but that passage is somewhat more studied in tone than most parts of the book, which are written with a very successful approach in style to colloquial drolling. As Mr. Clemens writes of his experiences we imagine he would talk of them; and very amusing talk it would be: often not at all fine in matter or manner, but full of touches of humor—which if not delicate are nearly always easy—and having a base of excellent sense and good feeling. There is an amount of pure human nature in the book that rarely gets into literature. . . . Almost any topic, and any event of the author's past life, he finds pertinent to the story of European and Oriental travel, and, if the reader finds it impertinent, he does not find it the less amusing. The effect is dependent in so great degree upon this continuous incoherence that no chosen passage can illustrate the spirit of the whole, while the passage itself loses half in separation from the context. (pp. 109-11)

Under his *nom de plume* of Mark Twain, Mr. Clemens is well known to the very large world of newspaper readers; and this book ought to secure him something better than the uncertain standing of a popular favorite. It is no business of ours to fix his rank among the humorists California has given us, but we think he is, in an entirely different way from all the others, quite worthy of the company of the best. (p. 112)

W. D. Howells, "The Innocents Abroad" (originally published in The Atlantic Monthly, *Vol. XXIV, No. 146, December, 1869), in his* My Mark Twain: Reminiscences and Criticisms *(copyright, 1910, by Harper & Brothers), Harper & Brothers Publishers, 1910, pp. 107-12.*

MATTHEW FREKE TURNER   (essay date 1876)

[*Twain impresses the critic as little more than a jester who profanes sacred things and parodies valuable works.*]

There is no mistake at all about Mark Twain's cleverness, but his fun does not appeal to one as does that of Artemus Ward; it is drier, harder, less to the point, and not nearly so fresh and racy. It is a great deal more diffuse; Mark Twain will take a page to bring his jest home—Artemus Ward will do it in a line, in a phrase, in the misspelling of a single word. There is, perhaps, a little too much of the professional jester about Mark Twain. He takes his pen in hand to write a funny paper: his jokes are often forced and far-fetched. Artemus Ward never seems to seek for a jest; his jokes come spontaneously, as if by accident. . . . Mark Twain's humour is drier; he follows the old rule that Charles Lamb disapproves—he never laughs at his own jokes.

A common form that his humour takes is to treat a subject from an entirely extravagant point of view, and yet to write with most perfect moderation and propriety of language; and, be it observed, Mark Twain's English, when he does not purposely introduce colloquial Yankeeisms, is excellent. Of this kind of humour is his **"Cannibalism in the Cars."** Perhaps no happier combination of the ghastly and the humorous has been made since Swift's famous proposition about cooking babies. The paper is too long, and the humour a trifle, perhaps, too grim for quotation.

There is one sort of fun much employed by Mark Twain; against which I strongly protest. It is where he turns solemn or sacred subjects into ridicule. It may be a tempting resource to a professional jester, in search of a subject, to exercise his wits upon topics which only require to be treated with levity to make some light-brained people laugh; but it is quite unworthy of such a writer as Mark Twain. . . . At any rate, I counsel Mark Twain, if he is anxious for the suffrages of decent readers, in his own and this country, to leave profanity alone.

Of the same low type of humour is the account of **"The Killing of Julius Caesar,"** in the style of a Western newspaper describing the result of a "difficulty in a bar-room." . . . (pp. 208-09)

This is surely very poor indeed. The idea is no better a one than would occur to a used-up Western Editor, and the execution is as low and vulgar as well can be. Still worse, and almost entirely destitute of fun, is the Biblical story of Joseph, told as the frequenter of a bar-room might tell it to his pot companions, over his Bourbon whisky or Lager beer.

Not a bit better are the parodies. When will jesters understand that parodies and travesties of works of true merit are the very poorest forms that wit or humour can take? . . . To burlesque what is in itself contemptible, and yet popular, is, of course, another matter. (p. 210)

[Twain] is a veritable literary "sapper," and does not hold at all with the Sunday-school books, which tell us how the good little boy got his reward, and the wicked little boy came to a bad end. (p. 211)

It will be seen that Mark Twain is, by no means, a genial, kindly humourist, like his predecessor, Artemus Ward; that, though he hits the same blots, his mode of attack is altogether different.

Mark Twain is a jester, and very little more. When he is not on the trail of some joke, he is apt to be insufferably tedious. Herein, I apprehend, lies the difference between a breaker of jests and a true humourist; between our Dickenses and Thackerays, our Sternes and Goldsmiths, and such men as Hook and the younger Coleman. (p. 212)

> *Matthew Freke Turner, "Artemus Ward and the Humourists of America," in* The New Quarterly Magazine, *Vol. VI, No. 11, April, 1876, pp. 198-220.**

[WILLIAM ERNEST HENLEY]   (essay date 1880)

[*Henley was an important figure in the counter-Decadent movement of the 1890s and the leader of an imperialistic group of young British writers—including Rudyard Kipling, H. Rider Haggard, and Robert Louis Stevenson—who stressed action, virility, and inner strength over alienation, effeminacy, and despair: characteristics they attributed to the Decadents. As editor of the* National Observer *and the* New Review, *Henley was an invigorating force in English literature, publishing and defending the early works of such writers as H. G. Wells, Thomas Hardy, and Bernard Shaw. As a poet, he was a pioneer in the use of free verse, though he also wrote many poems that combine realistic social observation and description with traditional forms. His most famous poem, "Invictus," demonstrates his* braggadocio *style and optimistic spirit, two qualities apparent in much of his work. In the following favorable review of* A Tramp Abroad, *Henley concludes that Twain's popularity is well deserved.*]

A new book by the American humourist who calls himself Mark Twain is sure to find readers; more than that, it is sure to deserve them. Mr. Clemens, in truth, is the most successful and original wag of his day; he has a keen, sure sense of character and uncommon skill in presenting it dramatically; and he is also an admirable story-teller, with the anecdotic instinct and habit in perfection, and with a power of episodic narrative that is scarcely equalled, if at all, by Mr. Charles Reade himself. He has seen men and cities, has looked with a shrewd and liberal eye on many modes of life, and has always something apt and pointed to say of everything; finally, he shares with Walt Whitman the honour of being the most strictly American writer of what is called American literature. Of all, or almost all, the many poets, novelists, essayists, philosophers, historians, and such like notables (orators excepted) America has produced, the origins are plainly European. . . . Mark Twain is American pure and simple. To the eastern motherland he owes but the rudiments, the groundwork, already archaic and obsolete to him, of the speech he has to write; in his turn of art, his literary methods and aims, his intellectual habit and temper, he is as distinctly national as the fourth of July itself.

No doubt in Mark Twain there is something too much of the abstract reporter as American needs and usages have modified and finished that interesting entity; no doubt there is something too much of the professional jester. He is immoderately given to "layin' around" after matter for paragraphs, with the manner and air of a smart ignoramus, not unconscious of his defects, but rejoicing in them and preferring them. Again, it is impossible for him to be serious for more than two minutes at once about anything. . . . Luckily he is in his way a literary artist of exceptional skill, so that, his vices notwithstanding, he is not often offensive and hardly ever tedious. . . . It is the peculiarity of Mark Twain that, while he is always bent on being

funny—deliberately and determinedly funny—he almost always succeeds in his intent. He has a certain dry, imaginative extravagance of fun that is neither more nor less than a literary intoxicant, so irresistible is its operation and so overwhelming its effect.

His new book, '**A Tramp Abroad**,' is the record of a walking tour through certain parts of Europe. No one who knows Mark Twain will be surprised that the walking tour was got through every how but on foot. Of uniform excellence '**A Tramp Abroad**' is not; but it is very vigorously and picturesquely written throughout; it contains some of the writer's happiest work; it is a worthy sequel to books of such uncommon point and freshness as '**Roughing It**' and '**The Innocents at Home**.' In the second chapter Mark Twain is already at work, and at his best and brightest, too, as those who read his adventure with a raven will feel. This adventure reminds him of Jim Baker's theory of animal linguistics, and particularly of that theory in connexion with the blue jay. . . .

The fun and tenderness of the conception, of which no living man but Mark Twain is capable, its grace and fantasy and slyness, the wonderful feeling for animals that is manifest in every line, make of all this episode of Jim Baker and his jays a piece of work that is not only delightful as mere reading, but also of a high degree of merit as literature. It is the best thing in the book though the book is full of good things. . . . (p. 529)

[We] shall take our leave of Mark Twain and his most excellent book. Only let his next be as good, and his peculiar public may vaunt their fortune against that of the admirers of any other living prose writer, English or American. (p. 530)

> [*William Ernest Henley*], *in a review of "A Tramp Abroad," in* The Athenaeum, *No. 2739, April 24, 1880, pp. 529-30.*

S. L. CLEMENS   (letter date 1888)

[*In the following letter "to a clergyman who cannot be identified," Twain attempts to explain his method of composition.*]

I am not sure that I have methods in composition. I do suppose I have—I suppose I *must* have—but they somehow refuse to take shape in my mind; their details refuse to separate & submit to classification & description. . . .

However, let us try guessing. Let us guess that whenever we read a sentence & like it, we unconsciously store it away in our model-chamber,—it goes, with the myriad of its fellows, to the building, brick by brick, of the eventual edifice which we call our style. And let us guess that whenever we run across other forms—bricks whose color or some other defect offends us, we unconsciously reject these, & so one never finds them in our edifice. If I have subjected myself to any training processes—& no doubt I have—it must have been in this unconscious or half-conscious fashion. . . . I think it likely that the training most in use is of this unconscious sort & is guided, & governed, & made by & by unconsciously systematic by an automatically working taste—a taste which selects & rejects, without asking you for any help, & patiently & steadily improves itself without troubling you to approve or applaud; yes, & likely enough, when the structure is at last pretty well up, & attracts attenion, *you* feel complimented—whereas you didn't build it, & didn't even consciously superintend.

Yes, one notices, for instance, that long and involved sentences confuses him & that he is obliged to re-read them to get the sense. Unconsciously, then, he rejects that brick. Unconsciously he accustoms himself to writing short sentences as a rule. At times he may indulge himself with a long one, but he will make sure that there are no folds in it, no vagueness, no parenthetical interruptions of its view as a whole; when he is done with it, it won't be a sea-serpent, with half of its arches under the water; it will be a torchlight procession.

Well, also, he will notice, in the course of time, as his reading goes on, that the difference between the *almost*-right word & the *right* word is really a large matter—it's the difference between the lightning-bug & the lightning. After that, of course, that exceedingly important brick, the *exact* word—however, this is turning into an essay, & I beg pardon.

So I seem to have arrived at this:

Doubtless I have methods, but they beget themselves; in which case I am only their proprietor, not their father.

> *S. L. Clemens, "My Methods of Writing" (originally a letter to an unidentified recipient on October 15, 1888), in Mark Twain Quarterly, Vol. VIII, No. 3, Winter-Spring, 1949, p. 1.*

ANDREW LANG   (essay date 1891)

[*A Scottish man of letters, Lang was a distinguished anthropologist, historian, poet, and writer of fairy tales. In such works as* Custom and Myth *(1884),* Ritual and Religion *(1887), and* The Making of Religion *(1898), he combined his Greek scholarship and astute literary judgement to write influential works on totemism and the folk origins of religion. Lang has also been praised as an accomplished historian and biographer. A friend and associate of such romance writers as H. Rider Haggard and Robert Louis Stevenson, Lang was a key figure in the late nineteenth century revival of romance literature, writing sympathetic criticism of his friends' works and collaborating on the novel* The World's Desire *with Haggard. He was a prolific magazine critic who sometimes reviewed the same book in different periodicals under different names. In the excerpt below, Lang discusses Twain's strengths and weaknesses as a writer of both humorous and serious work.*]

If you praise [Mark Twain] among persons of Culture, they cannot believe that you are serious. They call him a Barbarian. They won't hear of him, they hurry from the subject; they pass by on the other side of the way. Now I do not mean to assert that Mark Twain is "an impeccable artist," but he is just as far from being a mere coarse buffoon. Like other people, he has his limitations. Even Mr. Gladstone, for instance, does not shine as a Biblical critic, nor Mark Twain as a critic of Italian art nor as a guide to the Holy Land. I have abstained from reading his work on an American at the Court of King Arthur, because here Mark Twain is not, and cannot be, at the proper point of view. He has not the knowledge which would enable him to be a sound critic of the ideal of the Middle Ages. An Arthurian Knight in New York or in Washington would find as much to blame, and justly, as a Yankee at Camelot. Let it be admitted that Mark Twain often and often sins against good taste, that some of his waggeries are mechanical, that his books are full of passages which were only good enough for the corner of a newspaper. Even so, the man who does not "let a laugh out of him"—like the Gruagach Gaire—at the story of the Old Ram, or of the Mexican Plug, or of the editing of the country newspaper, or of the Blue Jay, or at the lecture on the German language, can hardly have a laugh in him to let out. Chesterfield very gravely warns his son that it is wrong and vulgar to laugh; but the world has agreed to differ from Chesterfield. To "Homo

Ridens" Mark Twain is a benefactor beyond most modern writers, and the Cultured, who do not laugh, are merely to be pitied. But his art is not only that of a maker of the scarce article—mirth. I have no hesitation in saying that Mark Twain is one among the greatest of contemporary makers of fiction. For some reason, which may perhaps be guessed, he has only twice chosen to exercise this art seriously, in **"Tom Sawyer"** and in **"Huckleberry Finn."** The reason, probably, is that old life on the Mississippi is the only form of life in which Mark Twain finds himself so well versed that he can deal with it in seriousness. Again, perhaps his natural and cultivated tendency to extravagance and caricature is only to be checked by working on the profound and candid seriousness of boyhood. These are unlucky limitations, if they really exist, for they have confined him, as a novelist, to a pair of brief works, masterpieces which a fallacious appearance has confounded with boys' books and facetiae. Of the two, by an unheard-of stroke of luck, the second, the sequel, is by far the better.

> *Andrew Lang, "The Art of Mark Twain," in* The Illustrated London News *(© 1891 The Illustrated London News & Sketch Ltd.), Vol. XCVIII, No. 2704, February 14, 1891, p. 222.*

WILLIAM ARCHER   (essay date 1900)

[*A dramatist and critic, Archer is best known as one of the earliest and most important translators of Henrik Ibsen and as a drama critic of the London stage during the late nineteenth and early twentieth centuries. Archer valued drama as an intellectual product and not as simple entertainment. For that reason he did a great deal to promote the "new drama" of the 1890s, including the work of Ibsen and Bernard Shaw. Throughout his career he protested critical overvaluation of ancient drama, claiming that modern works were in many ways equal to or better than Elizabethan or Restoration drama. Similar in prescience to his dramatic criticism is his* Poets of the Younger Generation, *one of the first critical studies of many important modern English poets, including A. E. Housman, Arthur Symons, and William Butler Yeats. In the following review, Archer strongly praises Twain's* "The Man That Corrupted Hadleyburg."]

Parables have their fates, like other forms of literature. Not every parable is found to possess the adhesive quality above adverted to. For one "Pilgrim's Progress" or "Candide" that "catches on" to the mind of the world, there are scores that drop off and are swept into the waste-paper bin. I shall be greatly surprised if this is the fate that awaits **"The Man that Corrupted Hadleyburg."** Mark Twain has before now shown himself a shrewd, penetrating, and even subtle psychologist. His new apologue reveals no new aspect of his genius. It is, moreover, a parable pure and simple, with no suspicion of art-for-art's-sake about it. Were we to take it as a story, as a representation of life, its cynicism would be intolerable. It would leave Maupassant nowhere. But taken simply for what it is—a fable designed to drive home an ethical lesson—it seems to me to possess such constructive skill and literary vigor as may well give it a place among the parables that stick tight to the popular imagination.

Perhaps you wonder to find Mark Twain among the moralists at all? If so, you have read his previous books to little purpose. They are full of ethical suggestion. Sometimes, it is true, his moral decisions are a little summary. Often, nay, generally, his serious meaning is lightly veiled in paradox, exaggeration, irony. But his humor is seldom entirely irresponsible for many pages together, and it often goes very deep into human nature. Let me merely remind you of that exquisite page—one of how many!—in **"Huckleberry Finn,"** where Huck goes through his final wrestle with his conscience as to the crime of helping to steal Jim out of slavery. . . . [It] is one of the master-passages in a masterpiece of fiction. Yet if the reader should ever find it crop up as a finger-post at one of the cross-roads of life, I think he may safely follow its guidance.

To return to **"The Man that Corrupted Hadleyburg."** I am not going to discount it by attempting to tell its story. Indeed, I could not if I would, even in six times the space that remains to me; for though it runs to only sixty pages, its construction is so ingeniously complex that it would take something like half that space to make even a comprehensible sketch-plan of its mechanism. A more tight-packed piece of narrative art it would be hard to conceive. A Sardou melodrama is not fuller of thrilling peripeties; and there are touches in it which remind one of a greater dramatist than Sardou. The thing it most nearly resembles in recent literature is Stevenson's delightful "Bottle-Imp"; but there is this difference, that Stevenson did not invent his fable, whereas Mark Twain did. And with all its earnestness of purpose and bitterness of tone, it is full of humor. The great meeting of the citizens of Hadleyburg is a scene of sustained and delectable comedy, not without a vein of real human pathos in the futile struggles of poor Richards and his wife to drag themselves out of the quicksand in which they are floundering.

And what is the moral of the apologue? In essence it is simple and even commonplace; in form it is somewhat daring. Mark Twain suggests an emendation in the text of the Lord's Prayer: the dropping of the negative particle in the petition, "Lead us not into temptation." We ought to pray, he says, to be led into temptation, for virtue that has never stood the test is a mere baseless opinion of self-righteousness. . . . Not otherwise did Mephistopheles argue in the first chapter of another and older apologue—the Book of Job, to wit. Mark Twain's message, you see, can scarcely lay claim to novelty. Another American philosopher has told us that "they didn't know everything down to Judee." But they knew one or two things that the world has but imperfectly learnt during all these centuries; and this thing Mark Twain has translated into modern terms of almost Swiftian sternness. (pp. 413-15)

> *William Archer, "'The Man That Corrupted Had-*
> *leyburg'—A New Parable," in* The Critic, *New York,*
> *Vol. XXXVII, No. 5, November, 1900, pp. 413-15.*

HENRY ADAMS   (letter date 1901)

[*An American autobiographer, historian, essayist, and novelist, Adams's work is less pertinent to the history of literature than it is to the history of ideas. In the latter context, Adams embodies for many a particularly modern viewpoint, one which sees the world becoming less stable and coherent than it once was and which predicts that this trend will continue, never to be arrested. Adams developed this doctrine most thoroughly in his best-known work,* The Education of Henry Adams. *In the following excerpt from a letter to Elizabeth Cameron, Adams praises* Extracts from Adam's Diary, *a portion of which originally appeared in the April 1901 issue of* Harper's Monthly Magazine.]

By the way, speaking of Satan, please note Mark Twain's *Diary of Adam.* There are one or two good jokes in it, but of these I am not an expert judge. What charms my historical soul is the point of view, which is unconsciously the same as that of the twelfth-century mystery, and of Milton, and they were all unconscious. Is it not curious that the man should always have instinctively represented himself as a tool and a fool in contact with the woman? Mark Twain's Adam is really a very inter-

esting person. His affectation of science is keenly true,—no one knows about that more than I do. The Eve is not studied, of course; the paper is a study of Adam alone; and it is marvelous true; in fact, to own up, it is me myself; a portrait by Boldini. (pp. 326-27)

> *Henry Adams, in an extract from a letter to Elizabeth*
> *Cameron on April 8, 1901, in his* Letters of Henry
> Adams (1892-1918), *edited by Worthington Chaun-*
> *cey Ford (Copyright 1938 by Worthington C. Ford.*
> *Copyright © renewed 1966 by Emily E. F. Lowes.*
> *Reprinted by permission of Houghton Mifflin Com-*
> *pany),* Houghton Mifflin, 1938, pp. 324-27.

G. K. CHESTERTON   (essay date 1910)

[*Regarded as one of England's premier men of letters during the first half of the twentieth century, Chesterton is best known today as a colorful* bon vivant, *a witty essayist, and creator of the Father Brown mysteries and the fantasy* The Man Who Was Thursday. *Much of Chesterton's work reveals his childlike* joie de vivre *and reflects his pronounced Anglican and, later, Roman Catholic beliefs. His essays are characterized by their humor, frequent use of paradox, and chatty, rambling structure. In the following excerpt, published shortly after Twain's death, Chesterton discusses the characteristics of the famous American's humor.*]

We are always told that there is something specially sinister in the death of a great jester. I am not so sure about the point myself, seeing that so many thousand human beings, diplomatists, financiers, kings, bankers, and founders of philosophies, are engaged in functions far more ultimately fruitless and frivolous than really making the smallest schoolboy laugh. If the death of a clown makes pantomimes for a moment tragic, it is also true that the death of a statesman makes statesmanship for a moment highly comic; the irony cuts both ways. But in the case of Mark Twain there is a particular cause which at once emphasises and complicates this contrast between the comic and the serious. The point I mean is this: that while Mark Twain's literary merits were very much of the uproarious and topsy-turvy kind, his personal merits were very much of the stoical or even puritanical kind. While irresponsibility was the energy in his writings, an almost excessive responsibility was the energy in his character. The artistic European might feel that he was, perhaps, too comic when he was comic; but such a European would also feel that he was too serious when he was serious.

The wit of Mark Twain was avowedly and utterly of the extravagant order. It had that quality of mad logic carried further and further into the void, a quality in which many strange civilizations are at one. It is a system of extremes, and all extremes meet in it; thus houses piled one on top of the other is the ideal of a flat in New York and of a pagoda in Pekin. Mark Twain was a master of this mad lucidity. He was a wit rather than a humorist; but I do not mean by this (as so many modern people will certainly fancy) that he was something less than a humorist. Possibly, I think, he was something more than a humorist. Humour, a subtle relish for the small incongruities of society, is a thing that exists in many somewhat low society types, in many snobs and in some sneaks. . . . A man may enjoy humour all by himself; he may see a joke when no one else sees it; he may see the point and avoid it. But wit is a sword; it is meant to make people feel the point as well as see it. All honest people saw the point of Mark Twain's wit. Not a few dishonest people felt it.

But though it was wit it was wild wit, as wild as the pagoda in China or the other pagodas in New York. It was progressive, and the joke went forward by arithmetical progression. In all those excruciating tales of his, which in our youth made us ill with laughing, the idea always consisted in carrying some small fact or notion to more and more frantic lengths of deduction. If a man's hat was as high as a house Mark Twain would think of some way of calling it twenty times higher than a house. If his hat was smashed as flat as a pancake, Mark Twain would invent some startling and happy metaphor to prove that it was smashed twenty times flatter than a pancake. His splendid explosive little stories, such as that which describes how he edited an agricultural paper, or that which explains how he tried to decipher a letter from Horace Greeley, have one tremendous essential of great art. I mean that the excitement mounts up perpetually; the stories grow more and more comic, as a tragedy should grow more and more tragic. (pp. 10-12)

As such [Mark Twain's humour or wit] was truly mountainous, and almost apocalyptic. No writer of modern English, perhaps, has had such a genius for making the cow jump over the moon; that is, for lifting the heaviest and most solemn absurdity high up into the most starry adventures. He was never at a loss for a simile or a parable, and they were never, strictly speaking, nonsense. They were rather a kind of incredible sense. They were not suddenly inconsequent, like Lewis Carroll; rather they were unbearably consequent, and seemed capable of producing new consequences for ever. Even that fantastic irreverence and fantastic ignorance which sometimes marked his dealings with elements he insufficiently understood, were never abrupt departures, but only elaborate deductions from his idea. It was quite logical that when told that a saint's heart had burst his ribs he should ask what the saint had had for dinner. It was quite logical that his delightful musician, when asked to play music appropriate to the Prodigal Son, should play, "We all get blind drunk when Johnny comes marching home." These are things of real wit, like that of Voltaire; though they are not uttered with the old French restraint, but with a new American extravagance. (p. 12)

Somebody in an advanced Socialist paper that I saw the other day said that Mark Twain was a cynic. I suppose there never was a person so far removed from cynicism as Mark Twain. A cynic must at least mean a man who is flippant about serious things; about things that he thinks serious. Mark Twain was always serious to the verge of madness. He was not serious about St. Francis; he did not think St. Francis serious. He honestly supposed the marvels of St. Francis to be some ecclesiastical trick of Popes and Cardinals. He did not happen to know that the Franciscan movement was something much more certainly popular than the revolution that rent America from England. He derided King Arthur's Court as something barbaric. He did not happen to know that the only reason why that dim and highly dubious Court has made a half-entry into history is that it stood, if it ever stood at all, for the remnant of high civilization against the base advance of barbarism. He did not happen to know that, in his time, St. Francis stood for the ballot-box. He did not happen to know that, in his time, King Arthur stood for the telephone. He could never quite get rid of the American idea that good sense and good government had begun quite a little while ago; and that the heavier a monumental stone was to lift the more lightly it might be thrown away. But all these limitations of his only re-emphasise the ultimate fact: he never laughed at a thing unless he thought it laughable. He was an American; that is, an unfathomably solemn man. Now all this is due to a definite thing, an historical

thing, called Republican virtue. It was worth while to issue the Declaration of Independence if only that Mark Twain might declare his independence also. (p. 14)

[Mark Twain] was radiant with a rectitude none the less noble for being slightly naive; he carried everywhere those powerful platitudes that are like clubs of stone. With these he hammered Calvinism in his youth and Christian Science in his old age. But he was not an "advanced" thinker, not a mind in revolt; rather he was a conservative and rustic grandfather older than all such follies. But this strength in him and his country truly came from a great spirit which England resisted and has forgotten; the spirit which, when all is said, made it no nonsense to compare Washington to Cincinnatus; the austere love of liberty and of the ploughshare and the sword. (p. 15)

> G. K. Chesterton, "Mark Twain" (originally pub-
> lished in T. P.'s Weekly, Vol. XV, No. 390, April
> 29, 1910), in his A Handful of Authors: Essays on
> Books and Writers, edited by Dorothy Collins (re-
> printed by permission of Miss D. E. Collins), Sheed
> and Ward, Inc., 1953, pp. 10-15.

H. L. MENCKEN (essay date 1913)

[*From the era of World War I until the early years of the Great Depression, Mencken was one of the most influential figures in American letters. His strongly individualistic, irreverent outlook on life and his vigorous, invective-charged writing style helped establish the iconoclastic spirit of the Jazz Age and significantly shaped the direction of American literature. As a social and literary critic—the roles for which he is best known—Mencken was the scourge of evangelical Christianity, public service organizations, literary censorship, boosterism, provincialism, democracy, all advocates of personal or social improvement, and every other facet of American life that he perceived as humbug. In his literary criticism, Mencken encouraged American writers to shun the anglophilic, moralistic bent of the nineteenth century and to practice realism, an artistic call-to-arms which is most fully developed in his essay "Puritanism As a Literary Force," one of the seminal essays in modern literary criticism. A man who was widely renowned or feared during his lifetime as a would-be destroyer of established American values, Mencken once wrote: "All of my work, barring a few obvious burlesques, is based upon three fundamental ideas. 1. That knowledge is better than ignorance; 2. That it is better to tell the truth than to lie; and 3. That it is better to be free than to be a slave." In the following excerpt, Mencken offers high praise of Twain, whom he considered one of the major influences on his own work.*]

I believe that **"Huckleberry Finn"** is one of the great masterpieces of the world, that it is the full equal of "Don Quixote" and "Robinson Crusoe," that it is vastly better than "Gil Blas," "Tristram Shandy," "Nicholas Nickleby" or "Tom Jones." I believe that it will be read by human beings of all ages, not as a solemn duty but for the honest love of it, and over and over again, long after every book written in America between the years 1800 and 1860, with perhaps three exceptions, has disappeared entirely save as a classroom fossil. I believe that Mark Twain had a clearer vision of life, that he came nearer to its elementals and was less deceived by its false appearances, than any other American who has ever presumed to manufacture generalizations. I believe that, admitting all his defects, he wrote better English, in the sense of cleaner, straighter, vivider, saner English, than either Irving or Hawthorne. I believe that four of his books—**"Huck," "Life on the Mississippi," "Captain Stormfield's Visit to Heaven,"** and **"A Connecticut Yankee"**—are alone worth more, as works of art and as criticisms of life, than the whole output of Cooper, Irving,

Holmes, Mitchell, Stedman, Whittier and Bryant. I believe that he ranks well above Whitman and certainly not below Poe. I believe that he was the true father of our national literature, the first genuinely American artist of the blood royal.

H. L. Mencken, "Credo" (originally published in The Smart Set, Vol. XXXIX, No. 2, February, 1913), in his A Mencken Chrestomathy (copyright 1924 by Alfred A. Knopf, Inc. and renewed 1942 by H. L. Mencken, reprinted by permission of the publisher), Knopf, 1949, p. 485.

CARL Van DOREN (essay date 1921)

[Van Doren is considered one of the most perceptive critics of the first half of the twentieth century. He worked for many years as a professor of English at Columbia University and served as literary editor and critic of The Nation *and* The Century *during the 1920s. A founder of the Literary Guild as well as author and editor of several American literary histories, Van Doren was also a critically acclaimed historian and biographer. Howard Moss wrote of him: "His virtues, honesty, clarity and tolerance are rare. His vices, occasional dullness and a somewhat monotonous rhetoric, are merely, in most places, the reverse coin of his excellence." In the following excerpt, Van Doren surveys Twain's works.]*

Mark Twain was more than a shrewd, barely literate backwoodsman. He had a tumultuous rush of expression; he had, moreover, thanks to Artemus Ward and his fellows, a literary form already prepared for him. Being expected, as a humorist of that type, to employ burlesque, he employed it to make fun of ecstatic travelers, particularly of those whose ecstasy followed the guidebook rather than their own taste and always rose with the reputation of the thing seen. Being expected, too, to be irreverent for humorous effect, he laughed at everything that did not seem to him overpoweringly sacred, and even from sacred moods often extricated himself with a jest. These were the conventions of his order. And as he was individually a husky, unashamed Westerner, when he found much in ancient art and scenery that, to his limited appreciation, fell below what he had heard of it, he said so in a loud voice irritating to fastidious ears. His public, however, was not fastidious. Relieved by the absence of that note of breathlessness which had oppressed it in earlier travel books, it gasped and then roared. Here was a writer who scratched the surface of American culture and found beneath it the rough, insouciant, skeptical, hilarious fiber of the pioneer. Undoubtedly *Innocents Abroad* flattered the mob with the spectacle of free-born Americans romping through venerable lands and finding them on so many counts inferior to America. The practical jokes of the book have lost much of their power to entertain; nor do the purple pages on which Mark Twain set down, in beadrolls of glorious names, his sense of the might and thunder of antiquity now sound so eloquent as they probably sounded in the sixties. But sweep and vigor and jolting contrasts and pealing laughter have not deserted the book. It remains an essential document in the biography of Mark Twain and in the history of American civilization.

If confessed mendacity playing around facts can transform them into fiction, both *Innocents Abroad* and *Roughing It,* published in 1872, approach the novel. Contemporary readers thought of them as reasonably true, allowing the author, however, the large license of the successful liar. Now that Mark Twain is no longer in the news his actual exploits concern his readers less and less in comparison with the permanent elements contributed to his work by his elaborating imagination. These elements play a larger part in *Roughing It* than in *Innocents Abroad.* Having "taken down" the Old World as measured by the New, he now set up the New in a rollicking, bragging picture of the Great West where he had acquired his standards of landscape and excitement. His account, shaped to look like autobiography, takes him from St. Louis across the plains to the Rockies and on to California and Hawaii. But, unlike the story of the *Innocents,* this was not written day by day with the events still green in the mind. They had had time to ripen in the imagination and to take on a significance which the deepest impression can never have at the first moment. *Roughing It* is uneven in tone and in excellence; the exposition falls below the description, which is ordinarily florid, and neither can equal the narration, particularly when it runs lustily across the plains with the rocking stage-coach or when it carries the narrator through his maiden adventures in the mining camps. Although he too frequently falls into the burlesquing habits which still clung to him from his days of Nevada and California journalism, he also rises decisively above them, and above all his predecessors in popular humor, with chapters of genuine poetry, of an epic breadth and largeness, commemorating free, masculine, heroic days. (pp. 163-65)

The year after his marriage he went to Hartford, where he lived for seventeen years, with intervals of lecturing and occasional sojourns in Europe. At Hartford lived also Mrs. Stowe and Charles Dudley Warner; and with Warner, who to the Mark Twain of that period seemed an important man of letters, he collaborated in a novel, *The Gilded Age,* which appeared in 1873. The more conventional elements in the book, the Easterners, Philip Sterling and Henry Brierly, and their loves and fortunes, are Warner's; the more original, the sections portraying Western life and satirizing Congress and Washington, are Mark Twain's. His, too, is the masterly conception of Colonel Beriah Sellers, the man of hope, who lives constantly in the expectation of an avalanche of unearned increment in his direction. From the collaboration of two such different authors nothing unified could come. Warner's chapters are usually tame; Mark Twain's are often noisy and busy with his old burlesque. Neither man shrank from melodrama or hesitated to set it side by side with the most scrupulous realism. But the materials of *The Gilded Age* are a dozen times better than its art. Perhaps all the more truly because of its lack of balance and perspective does the book reproduce the jangled spirit of the time, its restlessness, its violence, its enthusiasms so singularly blended of the sordid and the altruistic. Colonel Sellers, who has the blood of his creator in him, typifies an entire age which had newly begun to realize the enormous resources of the continent and was mad, was ridiculous, with the fever of desire for sudden riches. The age *was* gilded. (pp. 166-67)

Life on the Mississippi belongs with the most precious American books. The second part, indeed, which reports a journey Mark Twain made in 1882 to visit old scenes, rises in parts little above good reporting, though all of it conveys a sense of the deeps of many memories beneath the adventures it recounts. But the first twenty chapters flash and glow as even the highest passages of *Roughing It* had not done. Herein are set down with a crowded accuracy warmed by eloquence and affection the impressions of Mark Twain's eager youth, of his old aspirations toward the river, of his struggle to attain mastery over it, of his consummate hours as pilot. The splendor of those days had grown upon him, not faded, and he who had once entered into their events with the flushed passions of an epic hero now wrought at them with the accomplished strength of an epic poet. (pp. 167-68)

The Adventures of Tom Sawyer took Mark Twain from epic to comedy. . . . [The] general quality of realism . . . characterizes *Tom Sawyer* throughout. To a delicate taste, indeed, the book seems occasionally overloaded with matters brought in at moments when no necessity in the narrative calls for them. The boyish superstitions, delectable as they are in themselves, tend to lug *Tom Sawyer* to the documentary side of the line which divides documents from works of art. Nor can the murder about which the story is built up be said to dominate it very thoroughly. The story moves forward in something the same manner as did the plays of the seventies, with exits and entrances not always motivated. And yet a taste so delicate as to resent these defects of structure would probably not appreciate the flexibility of the narrative, its easy, casual gait, its broad sweep, its variety of substance. Mark Twain drives with careless, sagging reins, but he holds the general direction. Most of his readers remember certain episodes, particularly the whitewashing of the fence and the appearance of the boys at their own funeral, rather than the story as a whole. To inquire into the causes of this is to find that the plot of *Tom Sawyer* means considerably less than the characters. . . . Boys of Tom's age can follow his fortunes without discomfort or boredom. At the same time, there are overtones which most juvenile fiction entirely lacks and which continue to delight those adults who Mark Twain said, upon finishing his story, alone would ever read it. At the moment he must have felt that the poetry and satire of *Tom Sawyer* outranked the narrative, and he was right. They have proved the permanent, at least the preservative, elements of a classic.

Tom Sawyer cannot be discussed except in connection with its glorious sequel *The Adventures of Huckleberry Finn.* . . . *Huckleberry Finn* has remarkable unity. To tell a story in the first person was second nature to Mark Twain. . . . And his sense of identity with the boy restricted him to a realistic substance as no principles of art, in Mark Twain's case, could have done. With the first sentence he fell into an idiom and a rhythm flawlessly adapted to the naïve, nasal, drawling little vagabond. . . . It has been remarked that Huck appears rather more conscious of the charms of external nature than his Hannibal prototype, Tom Blankenship, doubtless was; and of course, strictly speaking, he rises above lifelikeness altogether by his gift for telling a long yarn which has artistic economy and satiric point. But something like this may be said of all heroes presented in the first person. Mark Twain, though for the time being he had relapsed to the shiftless lingo of his boyhood companion, was after all acting Huck for the sake of interpreting him; and interpretation enlarges the thing interpreted. Tom Sawyer acquires a new solidity by being shown here through the eyes of another boy, who, far from laughing at Tom's fanciful ways of doing plain tasks, admires them as the symptoms of a superior intelligence. After this fashion all the material of the narrative comes through Huck's perceptions. Mouthpiece for others, Huck is also mouthpiece for himself so competently that the whole of his tough, ignorant, generous, loyal, pyrotechnically mendacious nature lies revealed.

And yet virtues still larger than the structural unity thus imparted make *Huckleberry Finn* Mark Twain's masterpiece. In richness of life *Tom Sawyer* cannot compare with it. (pp. 168-72)

Mark Twain, in the midst of many vicissitudes remembering the river of his youthful happiness, had seen the panorama of it unrolling before him and also had been moved to record it out of sheer joy in its old wildness and beauty, assured that merely to have such a story to tell was reason enough for telling it. (p. 174)

A Tramp Abroad . . . written about a walking trip which Mark Twain made in 1878 through the Black Forest and to the Alps with his friend the Rev. Joseph H. Twitchell, continued his now expected devices in humorous autobiography, without any important innovations. Certain episodes and certain descriptive passages emerge from the general level, but even they only emphasize the debt his imagination owed to memory. Writing too close to his facts he could never be at his richest. In 1882 he published his first historical novel, *The Prince and the Pauper,* avowedly for children and yet packed with adult satire in its account of how by a change of clothes Prince Edward, later Edward VI of England, and Tom Canty, a London beggar boy, underwent also a change of station and for an instructive period each tasted the other's fare. By some such dramatic contrast Mark Twain, the radical American, preferred always to express his opinion of monarchical societies; like the older patriots, he set hatred for kings as the first article in his political creed. Of this important side of his nature the most characteristic utterances are to be found in *A Connecticut Yankee in King Arthur's Court* . . . , which deserves also to be considered one of the most thoroughly typical books yet produced by the American democracy. . . . Let us see, he said in effect, how this longing for the past would work out if gratified. What about the plain man under Arthur? What about plumbing and soap and medicines and wages and habeas corpus? What filth and superstition and cruelty did the pomps of feudalism not overlay? Mark Twain behaves as the devil's advocate in the *Yankee,* candidly ascribing to the sixth century the abuses of other older ages as well as its own. Perhaps, since he habitually read Malory's *Morte d'Arthur* and had a natural tenderness for its chivalric postures, he even exhibits a special animus arising from civil war within himself. At any rate, he let himself run almost without check among sixth-century scenes as he imagined them, ridiculing follies with a burlesque as riotous as that in *The Innocents Abroad,* and adding to it the more serious anger which had grown upon him. (pp. 175-77)

His decisive preference for [*Personal Recollections of Joan of Arc*] among all his books may perhaps be ascribed to the unusual labor to which he was put by an unprecedented task; it may also be ascribed to a lifelong interest in Joan which, beginning as a boy's sympathy for a girl's tragic fate, finally amounted to a genuine reverence for the Maid which saw in her the symbol of innocence undone by malice and corruption. Like his fierce essay *In Defense of Harriet Shelley* . . . and his movingly tender *Eve's Diary* . . . , *Joan of Arc* illuminates that region in Mark Twain's nature which practised a sort of secular Mariolatry. . . . The book constitutes his answer to the charge brought up by the *Innocents Abroad* and the *Yankee,* that he lacked reverence for names made sacred to men by good report; it is proof that he commanded the accents of adoration. In its own right, however, it must rank below an imaginative achievement like *Huckleberry Finn* because it is less thoroughly grounded than that book in any real experience. Over too many chapters of *Joan of Arc* droops the languid haze which accompanied all the historical romances of the American nineties. Only in the final third, which deals with the trial and which masterfully employs the original records, does Mark Twain knit his passion with his facts in the degree which breaks down the boundaries ordinarily only too able to divide romance from reality.

After *Joan of Arc* he wrote nothing equal to it in dimension and ambition. . . . His sweetness had begun to grow weary and turn more and more insistently to thought which was neither sweet nor gay. His pessimism appears unmistakably in *Following the Equator*. . . . Though now a national figure, by popular suffrage *the* national man of letters, he had for some years suffered from a diffusion, if not a diminution, of his power. *The American Claimant* . . . , returning to Colonel Sellers of *The Gilded Age* for material, and *Tom Sawyer Abroad* . . . and *Tom Sawyer, Detective* . . . , had none of them fulfilled expectations naturally aroused. Even the better novel *Pudd'nhead Wilson* . . . defied the efforts he put into it and escaped his control as he wrote. Part of it moved off into unrestrained farce and had to be issued separately as *Those Extraordinary Twins;* part of it developed into the seriously conceived tragedy of Roxana and her son—but a tragedy founded on the conventional device of infants changed in the cradle. It adds something to Mark Twain's documentary value by its picture of Virginians in the West and by its principal character, Pudd'nhead Wilson. . . . Pudd'nhead is . . . memorable as the village atheist, whose maxims, printed at the head of each chapter in this book and also in *Following the Equator,* so frequently express the tired disillusionment which was becoming Mark Twain's characteristic mood. (pp. 177-80)

The human individual, he argued in *What Is Man?* . . . is a mere automaton, without choice as to his birth or as to any impulse or thought or action, good or bad. Each decision follows irresistibly from precedent circumstances and so on back to the protoplasmic beginnings. Beliefs and resolutions cannot control behavior, which follows instinctively from the temperament with which the individual is endowed and which operates under the sleepless rule of the master-passion, the desire for self-approval. Punishment and censure are consequently meaningless; so is remorse. Mark Twain, who had no more than an amateur's learning in ethical systems, believed his doctrine of scientific determinism to be far more novel and contributory than it was. As a matter of fact, not the logical but the personal aspects of his contentions are impressive. By them he unconsciously defended himself from the savage, the morbid attacks of self-condemnation and remorse from which he repeatedly suffered for all his peccadilloes. Only by assuring himself that no one deserves such blame could Mark Twain quiet his raging conscience. (pp. 181-82)

Such philosophic nihilism did not constantly possess Mark Twain during the disturbed last dozen years of his life. In *The Man That Corrupted Hadleyburg* . . . he produced a corrosive apologue on the effects of greed, which here overthrows all the respectable reputations in a smug provincial town. Only one of them wins pity; the others appear not as moral automatons but as responsible thieves and hypocrites. And similarly *The $30,000 Bequest* . . . traces in a foolish couple the fatal influence of the anticipation of wealth. What Mark Twain had once thought hugely comic in Colonel Sellers he had now come, after his own hot hopes and disappointments, to regard as one of the first of follies, if not of offenses. In neither story, however, are the negligent or malicious higher powers shown at work, unless it is through the poor frailties of the men and women. *Captain Stormfield's Visit to Heaven* . . . took a very substantial sailor to heaven as the *Connecticut Yankee* had taken a skeptical mechanic to Arthur's Court. That Mark Twain originally thought his whimsy blasphemous and suppressed it so long shows how orthodox—and how unimaginative—was the social stratum from which he derived and which might actually have winced at light references to jasper walls and pearly gates.

For intellectual energy *Stormfield* cannot be mentioned in the same breath with *The Mysterious Stranger,* written during the dark night of Mark Twain's spirit in 1898 and issued posthumously. . . . The scene lies ostensibly in sixteenth-century Austria but actually, to all intents, in the Hannibal of Tom and Huck. Boys like these make up the central group; the narrator, Theodor Fischer, is as much Mark Twain as Tom Sawyer ever was. To them comes at times a supernatural playmate calling himself Philip Traum but rightly Satan, nephew of the mightier potentate of that name. Though he plays terrible pranks upon the villagers, he seems beneficence itself as compared to them, with their superstition and cowardice and cruelty. And all the time he acts, for the three boys, as commentator upon the despicable human race, "a museum of diseases, a home of impurities," which "begins as dirt and departs as stench"; which uses its boasted moral sense to know good from evil and then to follow evil. The sole redeeming fact in human life, Philip assures Theodor in the end, is that *"Life itself is only a vision, a dream. . . . Nothing exists save empty space—and you. . . ."* (pp. 182-83)

> Carl Van Doren, "Mark Twain," in his The American Novel *(reprinted with permission of Macmillan Publishing Company; copyright 1921 by Macmillan Publishing Co., Inc.; renewed 1949 by Carl Van Doren),* Macmillan, 1921, pp. 157-87.

BERNARD SHAW   (essay date 1924)

[*Shaw is generally considered the greatest and best-known dramatist to write in the English language since Shakespeare. Following the example of Henrik Ibsen, he succeeded in revolutionizing the English stage, disposing of the romantic conventions and devices of the "well-made play," and instituting the theater of ideas, grounded in realism. During the late nineteenth century, Shaw was also a prominent literary, art, and music critic. In 1895, he became the drama critic for* The Saturday Review, *and his reviews therein became known for their biting wit. During his three years at* The Saturday Review, *Shaw determined that the theater was meant to be a "moral institution" and an "elucidator of social conduct." The standards he applied to drama were quite simple: Is the play like real life? Does it convey sensible, socially progressive ideas? Because most of the drama produced during the 1890s failed to approach these ideals, Shaw usually assumed a severely critical and satirical attitude toward his subjects. Although he later wrote criticism of poetry and fiction—much of it collected in* Pen Portraits and Reviews (1932)—*Shaw was out of sympathy with both of these genres. He had little use for the former, believing it poorly suited for the expression of ideas, and in his criticism of the latter he rarely got beyond the search for ideology. As Samuel Hynes has noted, Shaw was driven by a rage to better the world. A Fabian socialist, he wrote criticism which was often concerned with the humanitarian and political intent of the work under discussion. In a preface to his drama* Saint Joan, *Shaw notes Twain's idiosyncratic interpretation of the Maid of Orléans in* Personal Recollections of Joan of Arc, *comparing the American's approach to that of Andrew Lang, author of* The Maid of France: The Life and Death of Jeanne d'Arc.]

[For many years] the literary representations of The Maid were legendary. But the publication by Quicherat in 1841 of the reports of her trial and rehabilitation placed the subject on a new footing. These entirely realistic documents created a living interest in Joan which Voltaire's mock Homerics and Schiller's romantic nonsense missed. Typical products of that interest in America and England are the histories of Joan by Mark Twain and Andrew Lang. (p. xxxviii)

Mark Twain's Joan, skirted to the ground, and with as many petticoats as Noah's wife in a toy ark, is an attempt to combine Bayard with Esther Summerson from Bleak House into an unimpeachable American school teacher in armor. Like Esther Summerson she makes her creator ridiculous, and yet, being the work of a man of genius, remains a credible human goody-goody in spite of her creator's infatuation. It is the description rather than the valuation that is wrong. Andrew Lang and Mark Twain are equally determined to make Joan a beautiful and most ladylike Victorian; but both of them recognize and insist on her capacity for leadership, though the Scots scholar is less romantic about it than the Mississippi pilot. But then Lang was, by lifelong professional habit, a critic of biographies rather than a biographer, whereas Mark Twain writes his biography frankly in the form of a romance.

They had, however, one disability in common. To understand Joan's history it is not enough to understand her character: you must understand her environment as well. Joan in a nineteenth-twentieth century environment is as incongruous a figure as she would appear were she to walk down Piccadilly today in her fifteenth century armor. To see her in her proper perspective you must understand Christendom and the Catholic Church, the Holy Roman Empire and the Feudal System, as they existed and were understood in the Middle Ages. If you confuse the Middle Ages with the Dark Ages, and are in the habit of ridiculing your aunt for wearing "medieval clothes," meaning those in vogue in the eighteen-nineties, and are quite convinced that the world has progressed enormously, both morally and mechanically, since Joan's time, then you will never understand why Joan was burnt, much less feel that you might have voted for burning her yourself if you had been a member of the court that tried her; and until you feel that you know nothing essential about her.

That the Mississippi pilot should have broken down on this misunderstanding is natural enough. Mark Twain, the Innocent Abroad, who saw the lovely churches of the Middle Ages without a throb of emotion, author of **A Yankee at the Court of King Arthur,** in which the heroes and heroines of medieval chivalry are guys seen through the eyes of a street arab, was clearly out of court from the beginning. Andrew Lang was better read; but, like Walter Scott, he enjoyed medieval history as a string of border romances rather than as the record of a high European civilization based on a catholic faith. Both of them were baptized as Protestants, and impressed by all their schooling and most of their reading with the belief that Catholic bishops who burnt heretics were persecutors capable of any villainy; that all heretics were Albigensians or Husites or Jews or Protestants of the highest character; and that the Inquisition was a Chamber of Horrors invented expressly and exclusively for such burnings. Accordingly we find them representing Peter Cauchon, Bishop of Beauvais, the judge who sent Joan to the stake, as an unconscionable scoundrel, and all the questions put to her as "traps" to ensnare and destroy her. And they assume unhesitatingly that the two or three score of canons and doctors of law and divinity who sat with Cauchon as assessors, were exact reproductions of him on slightly less elevated chairs and with a different headdress. (pp. xxxix-xlii)

Mark and Andrew would have shared her innocence and her fate had they been dealt with by the Inquisition: that is why their accounts of the trial are as absurd as hers might have been could she have written one. (p. xlvii)

> *Bernard Shaw, in a preface to his* Saint Joan: A Chronicle Play in Six Scenes and an Epilogue *(copy-*

right, 1924, by George Bernard Shaw; copyright renewed © 1951 by the Literary Estate of Bernard Shaw; reprinted by permission of The Society of Authors on behalf of the Bernard Shaw Estate), Brentano's, 1924 (and reprinted by Brentano's, 1926), pp. v-lxxxiv.*

UPTON SINCLAIR   (essay date 1925)

[*An American novelist, dramatist, journalist, and essayist, Sinclair was a prolific writer who is most famous for* The Jungle *(1906), a novel which portrays the unjust labor practices, filth, and horrifying conditions of Chicago's meat-processing industry, and which prompted passage of the Pure Food and Drug Act of 1906. A lifelong, outspoken socialist, Sinclair addressed the excesses of capitalist society in most of his works and demanded, in his critical theory, the subservience of art to social change. Although most of his fiction is dismissed in the United States for its obtrusive didacticism, Sinclair is one of America's most-read authors outside of North America, his works being particularly popular in the Soviet Union. In the excerpt below, Sinclair embraces Van Wyck Brooks's perception of Twain as a tormented genius and laments Twain's wasted talent, judging him to be a coward and a fraud.*]

Provincial America in the decades following the Civil War based its religion upon the dogma that it was the most perfect nation upon God's footstool. The whisky-drinking, tobacco-chewing, obscenity-narrating, Grand Old Party-voting mob would tolerate no criticism, not even that kind implied by living differently. To it an artist was a freak, whom it punished with mockery and practical jokes. There were only two possible ways for him to survive; one was to flee to New York and be lost in the crowd; the other was to turn into a clown and join in laughing at himself, and at everything he knew to be serious and beautiful in life. This latter course was adopted by a man of truly great talent, who might have become one of the world's satiric masters if he had not been overpowered by the spirit of America. His tragic story has been told in a remarkable study, "The Ordeal of Mark Twain," by Van Wyck Brooks.

For something like forty years Mark Twain lived as an uncrowned American king; his friends referred to him thus—"the King." His was a life which seemed to have come out of the Arabian Nights' enchantment. His slightest move was good for columns in the newspapers; when he traveled about the world he was his country's ambassador at large—his baggage traveled free under consular dispensation, and in London and Vienna the very traffic regulations were suspended. When he went to Washington to plead for copyright laws, the two houses adjourned to hear him, and the speaker of the House turned over his private office to the king of letters. He made three hundred thousand dollars out of a single book, he made a fortune out of anything he chose to write. The greatest millionaires of the country were his intimate friends; he had a happy family, a strong constitution, inexhaustible energy—what more could a human being ask?

And yet Mark Twain was not happy. He grew less and less happy as time passed. Bitterness and despair began to creep into his writings; sentences like this: "Pity is for the living, envy is for the dead." Stranger yet, it began to be whispered that America's uncrowned king was a radical! In times of stress some of us would go to him for help, for a word of sympathy or backing, and always this strange thing was noticed; he was full of understanding, and would agree with everything we said; yes, he was one of us. But when we asked for a public action, a declaration, he was not there. (pp. 327-28)

The worm which was gnawing at his heart was not revealed, until in the course of time his letters were given to the public. Now we know the amazing story—that Mark Twain lived a double life; he, the uncrowned king of America, was the most repressed personality, the most completely cowed, shamed, and tormented great man in the history of letters. (pp. 328-29)

[His wife and daughters] went over everything he wrote and revised it according to the standards of the Elmira bourgeoisie. They suppressed the greater part of his most vital ideas, and kept him from finishing his most important works. When he wrote something commonplace and conventional they fell on his neck with delight, and helped to spend the fortune which it brought in. When he told the truth about America, or voiced his own conclusions about life, they forced him to burn it, or hide it in the bottom of a trunk. His one masterpiece, **"Huckleberry Finn,"** he wrote secretly at odd moments, taking many years at the task, and finally publishing it with anxiety. Mrs. Clemens came home from church one day, horrified by a rumor that her husband had put some swear words into a story; she made him produce the manuscript, in which poor Huck, telling how he can't live in the respectable world, exclaims: "They comb me all to hell." Now when you read **"Huckleberry Finn,"** you read: "They comb me all to thunder!"

Mark Twain had in him the making of one of the world's great satirists. He might have made over American civilization, by laughing it out of its shams and pretensions. But he was not permitted to express himself as an artist; he must emulate his father-in-law, the Elmira coal-dealer. The unhappy wretch turned his attention to business ventures, and started a huge publishing business, to publish his own and other books. He sold three hundred thousand copies of General Grant's Memoirs, and sold hundreds of thousands of copies of other books, utterly worthless from the literary point of view. (p. 330)

Going back to Mark Twain's books, we can read these facts between the lines, and see that he put his balked and cheated self, or some aspect of this self, into his characters. We understand how he poured his soul into Huck Finn; this poor henpecked genius, dressed up and made to go through the paces of a literary lion, yearns back to the days when he was a ragged urchin and was happy; Huck Finn and Tom Sawyer represent all that daring, that escape from the bourgeois world, which Sam Clemens dreamed but never achieved. He put another side of himself into Colonel Sellers, who imagined fortunes; and yet another side into Pudd'nhead Wilson, the village atheist who mocked at the shams of religion. Secretly Mark Twain himself loathed Christianity, and wrote a letter of cordial praise to Robert Ingersoll; but publicly he went to church every Sunday, escorting his saintly wife, according to the customs of Elmira!

The more you read this story the more appalling you find it. This uncrowned king of America built up literally a double personality; he took to writing two sets of letters, one containing what he really wanted to say, and the other what his official public self was obliged to say. He accumulated a volume of "unmailed letters," one of the weirdest phenomena in literary history. (p. 331)

He wrote a War Prayer, a grim satire upon the Christian custom of praying for victory. "I have told the whole truth in that," he said to a friend; and then added the lamentable conclusion: "Only dead men can tell the truth in this world. It can be published after I am dead." He explained the reason—this financier who had fortunes to blow in upon mechanical inventions: "I have a family to support, and I can't afford this kind of dissipation." . . .

Of course a man who wrote like this despised himself. It was the tragedy of Tolstoi, but in a far more humiliating form; Tolstoi at least wrote what he pleased, and did in the end break with his family. But Mark Twain stayed in the chains of love and respectability—his bitterness boiling and steaming in him like a volcano, and breaking out here and there with glare and sulphurous fumes. . . .

In the effort to excuse himself, this repressed personality evolved a philosophy of fatalism. Man was merely a machine, and could not help doing what he did. This was put into a book, **"What is Man?"** But then he dared not publish the book! (p. 332)

He, America's greatest humorist, had a duty laid upon him; he saw that duty clearly—how clearly we learn from a story, **"The Mysterious Stranger,"** a ferocious satire upon the human race, published after his death. In this book Satan asks: "Will a day come when the race will detect the funniness of these juvenilities and laugh at them—and by laughing at them destroy them? For your race, in its poverty, has unquestionably one really effective weapon—laughter. Power, money, persuasion, supplication, persecution—these can lift at a colossal humbug—push it a little—weaken it a little, century by century; but only laughter can blow it to rags and atoms at a blast. . . . As a race, do you ever use it at all? No; you lack sense and the courage." Such was the spiritual tragedy going on in the soul of a man who was going about New York, clad in a fancy white costume, smiled upon and applauded by all beholders, crowned by all critics, wined and dined by Standard Oil millionaires, dancing inexhaustibly until three or four o'clock in the morning, and nicknamed in higher social circles "the belle of New York." (pp. 332-33)

Upton Sinclair, "The Uncrowned King," in his Mammonart: An Essay in Economic Interpretation *(copyright, 1924, 1925 by Upton Sinclair), 1925, pp. 326-33.*

STEPHEN LEACOCK   (essay date 1934)

[*A respected Canadian professor of economics, Leacock is best known as one of the leading humorists of the first half of the twentieth century. Of Leacock, George Ade has written: "He inherits the genial traditions of Lamb, Thackeray, and Lewis Carroll and has absorbed, across the Canadian border, the delightful unconventionalities of Oliver Wendell Holmes and Mark Twain, with possibly a slight flavor of Will Rogers." Leacock is the author of biographies of Twain and Charles Dickens, and among his humorous books* Nonsense Novels *is generally considered his best. In the following excerpt, Leacock compares and contrasts the works of Dickens and Twain.*]

Charles Dickens, who ceased to be Boz, and Mark Twain, who ceased to be Samuel Clemens, . . . represent the highest reach of the written humor of the nineteenth century. Perhaps they represent more than that. For it is at least open to argument whether certain phases of art did not reach their highest point at that time, leaving Dickens and Mark Twain representing the world's supreme reach in their own field. The nineteenth century was the era of the printed word, just as the twentieth is becoming the era of the flickering shadow and the metal voice. (p. 121)

If it is true that Charles Dickens and Mark Twain stand preeminent in history in the field of humor and almost contemporary in time, it is all the more notable that the work of each is quite distinct from that of the other. They only meet at that highest reach where humor has passed from the mere fun of words and things to the sad pathos of life itself and we smile at the incongruity of our little lot. (p. 122)

The fact is that the basis of Mark Twain's work was utterly different from that of Dickens. He found it in the contrast of an old civilization with a new. It was the Far West of Nevada and the Rockies and California that inspired Mark Twain. He was able to look back from the altitude of Virginia City and see the older world as it was; presently he went off to Europe on the *Quaker City,* and the trip and the point of view which it gave him inspired all his later work. He was able to turn on Europe—on its forms and ceremonies, its monuments and its mummies (dead and living), its hauteur and its humbug, the "eye of innocence" of the Westerner. And to this eye, contrasts and incongruities are revealed never suspected before. Hence the kings and the mummies and the knights and the mediaeval pictures and such become "funny." The previous ideas of the significance of such things are dissolved in the prism of this mode of thought, and break into their contrasting and incongruous elements. A knight in armor becomes a man in hardware, a monk pictured in a stained glass window with uplifted eyes is "trying to think of a word." The killing of Julius Caesar is "localized"—as done in Nevada journalism. The form of it all is irreverent, but the effect as wholesome as the sweeping of a fresh wind through a dank swamp.

There is nothing of this in Dickens except perhaps when he applies the cheery ignorance of a British cockney to the interpretation of France and Italy. . . . But there is no depth in Dickens's picture. He is not "interpreting" Europe as Mark Twain is. Mark Twain as the Yankee at the Court of King Arthur is profound in the satire—right or wrong—of his observation. Dickens as the Cockney at the Court of Versailles is just sniggering—as a cockney would.

The fact is that the starting point of Dickens's humor was of another kind. His humor started mainly from the presentation of queer comparisons. This at its best is admirable technique. Bill Nye once spoke of a bow-legged man as having "legs like twenty-five minutes after six." The utter incongruity of the relationship between time and legs, thus brought into harmony, is fit to rank with scientific discovery. Now, Dickens had an extraordinary gift for seeing likenesses between everything and everything else, especially between animate and inanimate objects: for him clocks wink, jugs grin, clothes dance and whisper on the clothes line, talking to the wind. (pp. 123-24)

Mark Twain, too, had his own particular verbal forms and verbal effects, and admirable indeed they were. He kicked loose, after his earliest crude attempt at writing, from the supposed humor of bad spelling. Henceforth he used bad spelling only as a transcription for the bad language in the mouth of his characters. If he wrote "Yessiree!" it was because he meant "Yessiree." Nor did puns make any particular hit out west, or with Mark Twain. But he found and created delight in the misuse of words, not by himself but his characters, where a sound seems to convey the right meaning but doesn't. Witness the case of old Mr. Ballou of **"Roughing It,"** who said that the horses were "bituminous from long deprivation," and who drank half a cup of coffee made with alkaline water and then threw it away, saying that it was "too technical for him."

Take as a further example the solemn reconstruction of Shakespeare by the Duke on the raft (in **"Huckleberry Finn"**) when the Duke is preparing Hamlet's soliloquy to be given by him as a recitation in a Mississippi village. What he makes is not a parody; that is not the point. The contrast lies as between reconstruction from memory and inspired composition. (pp. 126-27)

Each of the two great humorists had his characteristic faults and characteristic shortcomings. The humor of Dickens is disfigured by the sentiment and sentimentality so often linked with it in his works. (p. 127)

Dickens at his worst runs to drivel. Not so Mark Twain. He never bothered much about the poor; at least he never cried over them. The West had made him tough. He denounced injustice and political wrong, but he did it in flaring invective, in raw coarse language, not in sobs. But Mark Twain had his own special failing in prolixity. Especially as he grew older he was reckless in his egotistical demand on the reader's time and attention. When he wanted to convey the impression of an interminable harangue, he made an interminable harangue; in order to ridicule the boredom of a long story he recites the whole long, boring story. Witness in the **"Connecticut Yankee in King Arthur's Court"** the long tales put into the mouth of the girl Alisande to show how tiring she was. She certainly was, but so was Mark Twain.

But neither the humor of Dickens nor that of Mark Twain would have attained to the eminence which it holds and deserves if it did not contain far higher elements than these. There is, as has been said, a still higher plane to which humor can attain. This is seen when the contrasts and incongruities and misfits upon which humor rests are those of life itself: the contrast between what we might be and what we are, between the petty care and anxieties of to-day and the nothingness to which they fade to-morrow, between the fever and the fret of life and the final calm of death.

In retrospect all our little activities are but as nothing, all that we do has in it a touch of the pathetic, and even our sins and wickedness and crime are easily pardoned in the realization of their futility. Thus do we look back in life to the angers and the troubles of childhood. Thus might omniscient wisdom look on the fates and follies of mankind. In this divine retrospect humor and pathos become one, and the eyes of laughter brim with tears. The highest point of Dickens's art is reached when he presents to us a crook like Alfred Jingle, and makes him almost lovable, a villain like Squeers and extracts amusement from him, a damp, oleaginous horror like Mrs. Gamp and calls forth laughter. This "divine retrospect" was the real marvel of Dickens's genius. No one ever achieved it as he did. That is why his books rise before the mind even larger in remembrance than in perusal. This soft light of retrospect that looks back on the sins and sorrows of life, as we do on the angers of childhood, with the same understanding and forgiveness, this is humor at its greatest. Mark Twain, too, reaches it— pre-eminently with Huckleberry Finn and Nigger Jim. The little outcast boy, floating down the broad flood of the Mississippi on his raft, the clarity of his unsullied soul—and with him Nigger Jim, who embodied the docility, the forgivingness of the Negro race—there are wonderful characters, and this is a searching indictment of our civilization. But the soft haze in which it lies, the very shadows on the waters, rob it of all anger. Huckleberry Finn could have stepped across into the pages of Dickens to talk with Alfred Jingle in the debtors' prison; or could have carried Jingle away on his raft to join with the Duke and the King in re-editing Shakespeare. For at this point the art of the two writers has run into one. Thinking of such work as this, one wonders whether, in our age of flickering shadows and raucous voices, it can ever be done again. Perhaps the time is past. (pp. 127-29)

Stephen Leacock, "Two Humorists: Charles Dickens and Mark Twain," in The Yale Review (© 1934, copyright renewed © 1962, by Yale University; reprinted by permission of the editors), Vol. XXIV, No. 1, September, 1934, pp. 118-29.

THEODORE DREISER (essay date 1935)

[*Considered among America's foremost novelists, Dreiser was one of the principal American exponents of literary Naturalism. He is known primarily for his novels* Sister Carrie (1901), An American Tragedy (1926), *and the Frank Cowperwood trilogy (1912-47), in each of which the author combined his vision of life as a meaningless series of chemical reactions and animal impulses with a sense of sentimentality and pity for humanity's lot. Deeply concerned with the human condition but contemptuous of traditional social, political, and religious remedies, Dreiser associated for many years with the American socialist and communist movements, an interest reflected in much of his writing after 1925. Adopting Van Wyck Brooks's position—that Twain was a thwarted genius—Dreiser attacks the sentimental perception of Twain as a lovable clown. The critic sees Twain's pessimism as the only honest aspect of his work.*]

A psychologic as well as literary enigma that has much troubled me, as it has many another who has surveyed American literature, is Mark Twain. Middle West American of quite humble Tennessee and Missouri village and farm backgrounds—with a few parent- and relative-owned slaves to complicate the picture—he remains to this hour, in the minds of most Americans, not the powerful and original and amazingly pessimistic thinker that he really was, and that several of his most distinguished contributions to American letters prove—but rather, and to this hour, the incorrigible and prolific joker and, at best, humorist who, up to the time of his death and since, has kept the world chuckling so continuously that it has not even now sobered sufficiently to detect in him the gloomy and wholly mechanistic thinker. (p. 615)

But how came this to be? Were there two Twains from the beginning, as one and another critic has asked since reading *What Is Man* and *The Mysterious Stranger*? (pp. 615-16)

The financial interest or investment in his earlier conventional works and their reputation is still very great.

In the meantime, however, we have had *Joan of Arc*, which when published anonymously in 1895 was so different from the accepted work of Twain himself at the time that it was suggested by Twain that it be published under a nom de plume. . . . Yet, as different as it was, the general opinion was favorable, and so he acknowledged it. . . .

Just the same, shortly thereafter . . . he wrote, although he withheld from publication until 1916—six years after his death—two works entirely out of harmony with anything he had previously written: *The Mysterious Stranger* and *What Is Man?* In the meantime, that is between 1898 and 1910, when he died, while these other works were on the shelf, he published such volumes as *A Double-barrelled Detective Story, King Leopold's Soliloquy, Eve's Diary, Christian Science*, plus the much more daring, although much more humorous and therefore much safer, *The Man Who Corrupted Hadleyburg*—the first real break in his public humor, salving of a naughty, naughty world. Also, *Captain Stormfield's Visit to Heaven*, equally laughable. But

with *What Is Man?* and *The Mysterious Stranger* out, although ignored, there still remain other things which will see the light—when? In this reactionary day? I doubt it. (p. 617)

In *The Mysterious Stranger* he has conceived life from the depths of a giant despair. What I am earnestly seeking to convey is that by no means has Mark Twain been properly evaluated. In America, as it is intellectually running even at this time, I doubt if he can be. There is, as I have said, a financial interest in his reputation *as is,* which has to be and will be (never fear) taken into consideration.

Next, for all the labors of Hollywood and the young anarchists of sex in literature and art, compositions such as *1601* and his yet unpublished short stories will await a secret and a numbered issue—if so much. And for all the revelation of the laboratories that point to a mechanistic universe and the entire determinist philosophy, never fear that *What Is Man?* or *The Mysterious Stranger* will be given either wide publicity or achieve serious mental consideration in America if elsewhere. And there are several reasons for that: dogmatic religion, as well as social and moral convictions on every hand—these latter lying entombed or enwombed in the first—and next, the never ending benightedness of the mass—schools or no schools, universities or no universities, biological and physical laboratories, or no biological and physical laboratories. (pp. 619-20)

What interests me, however, is this seeming duality of Twain, for, of course, there were not any two Mark Twains, just one. From the beginning, there was only the conventionally environed Twain who did not arrive, for instance, at the reading of Pepys's *Diary* until he was forty, and whose amazed curiosity as to Spencer, Darwin, Huxley, following his first trip abroad (*Innocents Abroad* . . .), led naturally, in interruptedly—that is by way of fame—to introduction to the literary pundits of the East, marriage into a conservative and well-to-do family, the Langdons of Elmira, New York, the undying friendship and guidance of the conservative and even moralistic William Dean Howells, Charles Dudley Warner, Thomas Bailey Aldrich, and, naturally, Harper and Brothers, to name but a few. Also to such modified social protests (with brakes) as *The Prince and the Pauper, A Connecticut Yankee in King Arthur's Court,* etc. But not to the *Personal Recollections of Joan of Arc* or at long last to *The Man Who Corrupted Hadleyburg, The Mysterious Stranger,* or *What Is Man?* As I have said, these last two, though written in 1898, were not published in his lifetime. And his old-time contemporaries never lived to see them.

But of what was Twain so terrified? (pp. 620-21)

My suspicion is that it was the secondary social and conventional forces enveloping him after his early success and marriage, and playing on this sympathetic, and, at times, seemingly weak humanist, that succeeded for a time in diverting him almost completely from a serious, realistic, and I might say Dostoevskian, presentation of the anachronisms, the cruelties, as well as the sufferings, of the individual and the world which, at bottom, seem most genuinely to have concerned him. . . . [He] could not have been unaware of the degradations, the deprivations, the inequalities, and the sufferings of the majority of the men and women about him or in the world. (pp. 621-22)

The best he did for the Negro at any time was to set over against Harriet Beecher Stowe's Uncle Tom, the more or less Sambo portrait of the Negro Jim who, with Huckleberry Finn, occupied the raft that was the stage of that masterly record of youthful life, *Huckleberry Finn.*

But why? For most certainly in addition to, and in spite of, his humorous bent, he was a realist at heart, and a most extraordinary one. One need only thumb through the *Innocents Abroad,* or *Roughing It,* or *Tom Sawyer,* or *Huckleberry Finn,* or *The Gilded Age,* to find page after page, character after character, scene after scene, drawn movingly as well as brilliantly enough, and this, in spite of his Brobdignagian humor, from the life about him. I hardly need remind you of the fortunes and misfortunes of the Colonel Mulberry Seller's family where, despite the colossally comic aspects of the colonel's ambitions and his methods (*There Are Millions in It*), the pathos of his career, and that of his wife and children, rings sonorously and sadly.

Again, in *Roughing It* consider its virility and its importance as a reconstruction of a fantastic and yet absolutely real phase of American history—an unforgettable and most important section of our national life. True, belly-shaking caricature plays over a cold sense of fact, yet the tragedy of the silver-boom town is as apparent as its comedy and takes permanent and accurate shape for the benefit, I hope, of an inquisitive posterity. In *Huckleberry Finn* consider the Granger-Sheperdson feud. And, in spite of the wholly humorous report of it, the tragic implications of it all. A single turn of the pen at any point in this narrative, and you would have a story which would startle, terrify, as well as thrill and entertain, the most avid seekers of realistic truth. The same is true of Colonel Sherburn's reception of and speech to the crowd that came to lynch him. No humor there, as you will note: only the hard, cold reality of a courageous man's confrontation of a reasonless, meaningless mob. It could as well have come out of Balzac, of Tolstoi, of Saltykoff. Here is no yielding to the necessity for humor, nor the exaggeration of jest, for Twain in his soberer moods was always the realist—and a great one. Yet, for reason of that bent of his toward caricature and towering exaggeration, almost wholly uppermost in his youth and early manhood, he was slow in coming to the more balanced aspects of his later work. One wishes at times that, like Shakespeare, he could have balanced the fantastically ridiculous with the truly tragic, and in some lovely American picture have dealt with what he knew to be the true features and factors of the period in which he lived.

Inquiry and reflection have caused me to assume as follows: To begin with, he was as a child, and in so far as a liberal—yes, even a conventional—education was concerned, but poorly dealt with. No public schooling after his eleventh year. Next, swirling about him were those western and middle-western Americans of his day, semi-lunatic with bonanza religious as well as financial and "moral" dreams. Ah, the twisted sociologic, as well as psychologic, forces playing upon a nature at once sensitive, kindly, and at the same time exaggeratedly humorous! The jest! The jest! And about him—in the American newspaper and upon the American platform—those reigning American models of his day: Artemus Ward, Josh Billings, Bill Nye, Petroleum V. Nasby. And all so stupendously successful. America could afford to laugh. As yet it was sufficiently free and happy to permit it so to do. And not only these, but consider the crudities and nonsensicalities of his own Missouri small-town world, Florida, Missouri! Hannibal, Missouri! Read of them in *Huckleberry Finn.* And related to him, even nondescript farmers, some of them owners of ill-kept and ill-trained slaves with whom, and with the children of whom, he, as a schoolboy and small-town loafer, played. And after that, the youthful life of a Mississippi pilot's apprentice, with all the crude midwestern river life that registered on the quivering, if jest-loving, sensibilities of a world genius of twenty—a stripling Falstaff as well as Dickens combined. Yet, never a novelist—never. He could not write a novel. Consider only *The Gilded Age!* Rather, your humanist annalist, but without the complete and tragic life of any single defeated mortal burned deep in his heart. Why? He who could write of the Mysterious Stranger? And the sorrows of Joan of Arc? Why?

But after these early days, swift success, stupendous, worldwide fame! The laughter of England, America, Germany, France. Our simple and almost boobish genius thrust willy-nilly into the company of wealth, reputation, title, conventional and mental assumption and punditry, in its most aggravated forms. And with handclapping and backslapping everywhere. Oh, our darling Mark—the great American World Genius! (pp. 622-24)

Yet, in spite of all the glamour, here was the other Twain thinking betimes of *What Is Man?* and *The Mysterious Stranger,* and, in his heart, hating his limitations. . . .

But because it was so glamorous and so grand, and he hated to hurt people, and there was his publisher's investment in his books, and what his good friends thought of him, he did not dare to revolt! He feared what they would say. That ostracism awaited him, as it awaits every man who will not march with the crowd. And so, eventually—pain and morbidity. (p. 625)

Not that I am calling on Twain to be anything that he was not. It is he, himself, who has indicated in all that he feared to publish in life that he was really calling on himself to do differently and to be different. But convention—convention, the dross of a worthless and meaningless current opinion—this was the thing that restrained him. (p. 626)

Yet below all this, and that on which his feet were resting, was the solid rock of his own temperament and understanding. And with this as his point of vantage and departure, and despite the impact of the meretricious life that was spinning about him, came the final conviction that most of what he saw and was so busy with mere sound and fury, signifying nothing—tinsel and tawdry make-believe which could only detract from his true stature. The truth of it is apparent, and not only that, but confessed, in his *Autobiography,* and in those really deathless works which his tinsel contemporaries never knew. I refer again to *The Mysterious Stranger* still sold, if you will believe it, as a Christmas book for children, and *What Is Man?* read by a corporal's guard of the initiated, in the course of, let us say, a year, if so often. (pp. 626-27)

Theodore Dreiser, "Mark the Double Twain" (copyright © 1935 by the National Council of Teachers of English; reprinted by permission of the publisher and the author), in English Journal, *Vol. XXIV, No. 8, October, 1935, pp. 615-27.*

BOOTH TARKINGTON (essay date 1939)

[*Tarkington was a popular Midwestern writer who worked in the realistic tradition of William Dean Howells and Mark Twain. He is best remembered today for his adventure-filled, wholesome young-adult fiction, most notably the* Penrod *series and* Seventeen, *which are considered classic portraits of the all-American boy at the turn of the century. In such works as the Pulitzer Prize-winning novels* Alice Adams *and* The Magnificent Ambersons, *Tarkington also contributed significantly to American literature in his portrayal of early twentieth-century Midwestern mores and in his fictional accounts of the personal and social consequences of industrialization. In the following excerpt Tarkington discusses Twain's two most famous characters, Tom Sawyer and Huckleberry Finn.]*

An exalted realist, criticizing *Treasure Island,* said that pirates were rare; he had never met anybody who had even seen one. I think I recall that Stevenson's reply was to the effect that he himself had been one in his boyhood and that all the boys he had ever known were pirates frequently. *Tom Sawyer* supports the great Scotchman's defense; but Mark Twain was so generous to the boys in *Tom Sawyer* that he let them do more than merely play at being pirates. He gave them adventures that all boys, in their longing dreams, make believe they have. He made extravagant, dramatic things happen to them; they were pitted against murderers, won their ladyloves, and discovered hidden gold. He made them so real that their very reality is the stimulus of the adult reader's laughter; but he embedded this reality in the romance of a plot as true to the conventional rules of mid-nineteenth century romantic novelwriting as it was to the day-dreams of the boy Mark Twain himself had been.

Mark Twain, writing *Tom Sawyer,* transposed himself backward through time into the boy he was in Hannibal, felt and knew again all that the boy had felt, said again what the boy had said, and then, with a masterly craft, evoked the portrait of that boy on paper. Moreover, this portrait is none the less true for the unreal background of plot against which it is seen, and I think the reason for this truthfulness is that the fantasis of romantic events seemed real to Mark Twain as he wrote, and that he had no doubt of its reality since it was built out of stuff fashioned in the mind of the boy. That is to say, although Mark Twain spoke of Tom Sawyer as a composite, the portrait is mainly of Mark Twain as a boy: it is essentially autobiographical, though by no means literally the record of Mark Twain's own youthful adventures and circumstances.

But into the story there is early the advent of a personage who was warmly sympathetic to Mark Twain yet exterior to him in no sense autobiographical. This first appearance of one who has been for more than half a century an inmate, so to speak, of every American household where there is any reading was accomplished with astonishing simplicity. There should have been meteors and portents; but Huckleberry Finn strolled into the consciousness of his fellow-countrymen modestly and wholly unaware of his own greatness. (pp. vii-viii)

In *Tom Sawyer* [Mark Twain] kept Huckleberry within bounds and subordinate to Tom; yet it is obvious that the author was more and more deeply fascinated by Huckleberry, and that the fascination increased and increased until it became irresistible and so made itself into an irresistible book, greater than its progenitor.

I think it was Stevenson who selected as the two great dramatic moments in all English fiction the dropping of the burden of Christian in *Pilgrim's Progress* and the discovery of Friday's footprint by Robinson Crusoe, and that this selection was supported by the opinion that mental images of these two moments were more universally implanted in the memories of readers than were any others. Stevenson may have been right about this and yet it is probable that in the memories of American readers, at least, three other imaginary pictures would compete in universality: Eliza crossing the ice, Ben Hur winning the race, and Tom Sawyer whitewashing the fence. But by the same test—that of being present interestingly in the minds of readers of all kinds—it seems to me that Huckleberry Finn is the great national figure of his period and that no other "char-

acter" of all fiction of that time lives now so vividly, or with anything like such triumph of humor and warm reality, as he does now in this later and greatly changed generation. (pp. ix-x)

> *Booth Tarkington, in an introduction to* My Cousin Mark Twain *by Cyril Clemens (copyright, 1939 Rodale Press), Rodale Press, 1939, pp. vii-xi.*

BOYD GUEST   (essay date 1945-46)

[Guest examines Twain's attitudes toward women as revealed in his life and writings, in an essay which itself reveals the critic's own doubts about women's suffrage and other feminist goals embraced by Twain.]

As an observer, interpreter, and reflector of the great cross-section of American life during the period in which he lived—and because of his versatile interests—Mark Twain's attitude toward women is important in estimating the general question of "woman's rights." If he represented the spirit of "youth" to his wife, his attitude toward women was also that of the youth filled with the sentiment of the chivalric tradition plus youth's recognition of, and respect for, equality. He felt that "Woman is all that she should be—gentle, patient, long-suffering, trustful, unselfish, full of generous impulses."

In the first volume of Mark Twain's *Autobiography,* A. B. Paine writes: "The boy could be tender and kind, and was always gentle in his treatment of the other sex." . . .

The most signal example of his gay, gallant attitude toward women occurred when he gave **"Woman an Opinion"** as a toast at an early banquet of the Washington Correspondents' Club: "I love the sex. I love all the women, irrespective of age or color." . . .

Throughout his life, Mark Twain retained the Westerner's innate attitude of chivalry toward women. His *Joan of Arc* indicates his interest both in women and in the age of gallantry. The murder of Joan of Arc affords for Mark Twain a startling contrast to the ideals of the chivalric period. Too, he comes to the rescue of the lady when he writes **"In Defense of Harriet Shelley,"** roundly denouncing Dowden's *Life of Shelley,* which put the cause of the separation of Harriet and Shelley upon Harriet. Clemens argues that Shelley was totally responsible. When he was seventy years old he wrote: "Girls are charming creatures." (p. 1)

Admiration for his wife led him to many generalized statements in praise of woman. For instance, when writing of Mrs. Clemens' nursing her grandfather, he praises the *endurance* of woman. . . . (p. 2)

Clemens was torn between a sense of justice and the chivalric ideal. Realistically he saw that all men could not be trusted to deal fairly with women; so he was willing to enter the fight for women's rights. That decision places him on the side of the positive, conscious feminists, and no doubt afforded much solid influence among the host of Americans who admired him. . . .

In **"Queen Victoria's Jubilee,"** Clemens mentions the development of woman's rights during the life-time of the Queen. . . . This meant progress to Clemens; therefore, he was in sympathy with the emancipation of women.

Clemens became vehement in his espousal of woman's rights when he wrote **"The Temperance Crusade and Woman's**

Rights." . . . He discredits the power of prayer of the Crusaders because he hates to see them surrender to God credit which they deserve themselves. He supported their successful program of picketing. . . . And then reappears the conflict in Clemens between justice and chivalry, with justice winning through expediency, not choice: "I cannot help glorifying in the pluck of these women, sad as it is to see them displaying themselves in these unwomanly ways." . . . (p. 3)

In a later speech on the rights of women, delivered January 20, 1901, at the annual meeting of the Hebrew Technical School for Girls, held in Temple Emmanuel, he said: "Referring to woman's sphere in life, I'll say that woman is always right." . . . Clemens always expressed great confidence in the moral value and influence of women, but that confidence has not been justified in woman's employment of the ballot.

The only evidence one can find that Clemens spoke adversely about women's rights is in **"The Sandwich Islands,"** but even in this, his humorous whimsicality betrays the utmost insincerity. . . . (p. 4)

> Boyd Guest, "Twain's Concept of Woman's Sphere," in Mark Twain Quarterly, Vol. VII, No. 2, Winter-Spring, 1945-46, pp. 1-4.

EUGENE O'NEILL (essay date 1953?)

[*O'Neill is generally considered America's foremost dramatist. His plays consistently examine the implacability of an indifferent universe, the materialistic greed of humanity, and the problems of discovering one's true identity. Because O'Neill's plays are bleak portraits of a world without ultimate meaning, critics have come to regard him as the most pessimistic of American dramatists. He is credited with creating the traditions of twentieth-century American drama and is considered as integral to modern world literature as Bertolt Brecht and August Strindberg. In the following brief tribute, published long after his death in 1953, O'Neill comments on Twain's central role in American literature.*]

Mark Twain is the true father of all modern American literature. In his work, the living spirit of America, the essential personality and quality of the American, is expressed in more varied elements than ever before or since his time. In his books, as in no others, the American, who could be born of no other soil than this America, lives with unique American gusto and color.

> Eugene O'Neill, "Eugene O'Neill's Tribute" (1953?; courtesy of Collection of American Literature, The Beinecke Rare Book and Manuscript Library, Yale University), in Mark Twain Journal, Vol. XVI, No. 3, Winter, 1972, p. ii.

LESLIE A. FIEDLER (essay date 1955)

[*Fiedler is a controversial and provocative American critic. While he has also written novels and short stories, Fiedler most effectively expressed his ideas and insights in his literary criticism. Emphasizing the psychological, sociological, and ethical context of a work, rather than its literary qualities, Fiedler's criticism often views literature as the mirror of a society's consciousness. Similarly, he believes that the conventions and values of a society are a powerful determinant of the direction taken by its authors' works. The most notable instance of this critical stand in Fiedler's work is his reading of American literature, and therefore American society, as an infantile flight from "adult heterosexual love." This idea is developed in his most important work,* Love and Death in the American Novel, *along with the view that American*

literature is essentially an extension of the Gothic novel. Although Fiedler has been criticized for what are considered eccentric pronouncements on literature, he is also highly valued for his adventuresome and eclectic approach, which complements the predominantly academic tenor of contemporary criticism. In The Tragedy of Pudd'nhead Wilson, *which Fiedler praises, a slave is freed and a community's racism revealed. To the critic, the incident becomes "a particular instance of some universal guilt and doom."*]

The most extraordinary book in American literature unfortunately has not survived as a whole; but its scraps and fragments are to be found scattered through the work of Mark Twain: a cynical comment ascribed to a small-town lawyer and never printed, the wreck of a comic tale framed by apologies and bad jokes, and finally the *Pudd'nhead Wilson* that has come down to us, half melodramatic detective story, half bleak tragedy. What a book the original might have been, before *Those Extraordinary Twins* was detached and Pudd'nhead's *Calendar* expurgated—a rollicking atrocious melange of bad taste and half understood intentions and nearly intolerable insights into evil, translated into a nightmare worthy of America.

All that the surrealists were later to yearn for and in their learned way simulate, Twain had stumbled on without quite knowing it. And as always (except in *Huckleberry Finn*) he paid the price for his lack of self-awareness; he fumbled the really great and monstrous poem on duplicity that was within his grasp. The principle of analogy which suggested to him linking the story of the Siamese Twins, one a teetotaler, the other a drunk, Jekyll and Hyde inside a single burlesque skin—to a tale of a Negro and white baby switched in the cradle finally seemed to him insufficient. He began to worry about broken plot lines and abandoned characters, about the too steep contrast between farce and horror; and he lost his nerve. . . . Down the well went the burlesque supernumeraries and finally out of the story; and the poor separated twins remain to haunt a novel which is no longer theirs.

But something in Twain must have resisted the excisions; certainly they were made with a striking lack of conviction, and the resulting book is marred by incomprehensible motivations and gags that have lost their point with the unjoining of the once Siamese twins. The two stories were, after all, one, and the old book a living unity that could not be split without irreparable harm.

Yet *Pudd'nhead Wilson* is, after all, a fantastically good book, better than Mark Twain knew or his critics have deserved. Morally, it is one of the most honest books in our literature, superior in this one respect to *Huckleberry Finn;* for here Twain permits himself no sentimental relenting, but accepts for once the logic of his own premises. . . . It is a book which deals not only with the public issue of slavery, after all, long resolved—but with the still risky private matter of miscegenation, which most of our writers have chosen to avoid; and it creates in Roxy, the scared mulatto mother sold down the river by the son she has smuggled into white respectability, a creature of passion and despair rare among the wooden images of virtue or bitchery that pass for females in American literature. . . .

Perhaps the best way to understand *Pudd'nhead* is to read it as a complement to *Huckleberry Finn*, a dark mirror image of the world evoked in the earlier work. . . . *Huckleberry Finn* also is steeped in horror, to be sure; but it is easier to know this than to feel it. . . . [It] has so poetic a texture, so genuine though unmotivated a tone of joy—that one finds himself eternally doubting his own sense of its terrible import. In *Pudd'n-*

head, however, the lyricism and the euphoria are gone; we have fallen to a world of prose, and there are no triumphs of Twain's rhetoric to preserve us from the revealed failures of our own humanity. (p. 17)

Just as the grotesque in *Pudd'nhead* tends to break free from the humorous, so the tragic struggles to shed the nostalgic which swathes it still in *Huckleberry Finn.* In the earlier book, it is possible to believe that the flight toward freedom and childhood is more than a flight toward isolation and death. There is always waiting in a bend of the river Aunt Sally's homestead: a utopia of childhood visits and Southern home-cooking. (pp. 17-18)

By the time he was attempting to detach *Pudd'nhead* from the wreck of his larger book, Twain had decided that the only unthreatened utopia is death itself. . . . Twain no longer finds in freedom the pat happy ending waiting to extricate his characters from their moral dilemmas and himself from the difficulties of plotting. He does not abandon the theme of liberty, but renders now the full treacherous paradox, only half of which he had acknowledged earlier. . . .

The resolution of *Pudd'nhead* is, of course, double; and the revelation which brands the presumed Thomas à Becket Driscoll a slave, declares the presumed Valet de Chambre free. We are intended, however, to feel the "curious fate" of the latter as anything but fortunate; neither black nor white, he is excluded by long conditioning from the world of the free, and barred from the "solacing refuge" of the slave kitchens by the fact of his legal whiteness. (p. 18)

· · · · ·

In [*Pudd'nhead*], we see Twain's mythicized Hannibal for the first time from the *outside;* in [*Huckleberry Finn* and *Tom Sawyer*], we are already inside of it when the action begins, and there is no opportunity to step back and survey it. But Pudd'nhead comes as a stranger to the place of Twain's belonging; and the author himself takes advantage of this occasion to pan slowly into it, giving us an at first misleadingly idyllic description of its rose-clad houses, its cats, its sleepiness, and its fragrance—all preparing for the offhand give-away of the sentence beginning, "Dawson's Landing was a slaveholding town . . ." . . .

In *Pudd'nhead Wilson,* Hannibal is felt from the beginning not as a Western but as a *Southern* town. The river is no longer presented as the defining edge of the natural world, what America touches and crosses on its way West; but as a passageway into the darkness of the deep South. . . .

A comparison inevitably suggests itself with *Huckleberry Finn* in which the southward motion had served to symbolize (in contempt of fact) a motion toward deliverance. But here the direction of the river that Twain loved is felt only as the way into the ultimate south, the final horror—the absolute pole of slavery. The movement of the plot and the shape of the book are determined by this symbolic motion toward the sea, now transposed from a dream of flight to a nightmare of captivity. It is after she herself has been threatened with such a fate and in order to preserve her son from it, that Roxy switches the children in the cradle. But there is no way to escape that drift downward toward darkness to which the accident of birth has doomed her and her son; by virtue of her very act of evasion she sets in motion the events that bring both of them to the end she had dreaded.

It is not only as a slave-holding town that Dawson's Landing belongs to the South, but also in terms of the code of honor to which everyone in the book subscribes. Patrician and Negro, American and foreigner, free-thinker and churchgoer, all accept the notion that an insult can only be wiped out in blood, and that the ultimate proof of manhood is the willingness to risk death in such an attempt. The real demonstration of the unworthiness of the false Tom is his running to the courts for redress in preference to facing a duel. . . .

In *Huckleberry Finn,* the society which Huck finally rejects, his "sivilization," is essentially a world of the mothers, that is to say, of what Christianity has become among the females who sustain it just behind the advancing frontier. . . .

In *Pudd'nhead Wilson,* however, society is defined by the fathers, last defenders of the chivalric code and descendants of the cavaliers. Four in especial represent the world to which Pudd'nhead aspires: York Leicester Driscoll, Percy Northumberland Driscoll, Pembroke Howard and Col. Cecil Burleigh Essex—the names make the point with an insistence that is a little annoying. This is a world continuous with that of Renaissance gallantry, connected with the Court of Elizabeth, which represents for Twain on the one hand a romantic legend, and on the other a kind of lost sexual Eden. . . . (p. 16)

One half of the story of Thomas à Becket Driscoll (really the slave Valet de Chambre) is the account of his failing this world of the fathers, first in gambling and thieving, then in preferring the courts to the field of honor, finally in becoming out of greed and abject rage, a quasi-parricide. Twain spares us, perhaps from some reluctance to surrender to utter melodrama, more probably from lack of nerve, the final horror. The logic of the plot and its symbolic import both demand really that Tom be revealed at last as the bastard of the man he killed; but we are provided instead with a specially invented double of the dead Driscoll as the boy's begetter, a lay figure called Cecil Burleigh Essex.

In all of the book, only a single mother is allowed the center of the stage—the true mother of the false Tom, the slave girl Roxana. Just as in *Huckleberry Finn,* Nigger Jim is played off against the world of Aunt Polly-Aunt Sally-Miss Watson, so in this reversed version a Negress is set against the society defined by Driscoll, Howard, and Essex. This is, of course, a just enough stroke, which satisfies our sense of the historical as well as our desire for the typical. If the fathers of the South are Virginia gentlemen, the mothers are the Negro girls, casually or callously taken in the parody of love, which is all that is possible when one partner to a sexual union is not even given the status of a person.

The second and infinitely worse crime of Tom is the sin against the mother, the black mammy who threatens him with exposure; and the most moving, the most realized sections of the book deal with this relationship. . . .

In *Pudd'nhead,* this tearful romance of the boy as a heartless jilt, becomes involved with the ambiguous relations of black and white in the United States, with the problems of miscegenation and of "passing," and is lifted out of the sentimental toward the tragic. Twain's own judgment of sexual relations between the races is not explicitly stated; but there seems no doubt that he thought of the union between Roxy and Essex as a kind of fall—evil in itself and the source of a doom on all involved. . . .

A further reach of complexity is added to the theme by the symbolic meanings inevitably associated with the colors white and black, meanings which go back through literature . . . and popular religion . . . to the last depths of the folk mind. No matter how enlightened our conscious and rational convictions may be in these matters, we are beset by a buried ambivalence based on this archetypal symbolism of light and dark. Twain himself in this very novel speaks unguardedly of the rain trying vainly to wash soot-blackened St. Louis white; and the implication is clear: black is the outward sign of inward evil. In this sense, the Negro puzzlingly wears the livery of the guilt we had thought the white man's. But *why?* It is a question which rings through the white man's literature in America; and the answer returns in an ambiguity endlessly compounded. . . .

Perhaps the supreme achievement of this book is to have rendered such indignities not in terms of melodrama or as a parochial "social problem" but as a local instance of some universal guilt and doom. The false Tom, who is the fruit of all the betrayal and terror and profaned love which lies between white man and black, embodies also its "dark necessity"— and must lie, steal, kill and boast until in his hybris he reveals himself as the slave we all secretly are. This tragic inevitability is, however, blurred by the demands of the detective story with which it is crossed. The tragedy of Tom requires that he expose and destroy himself; the melodrama of Pudd'nhead Wilson requires that he reveal and bring to justice the Negro who has passed as white; and Twain decided finally that it was Pudd'nhead's book—a success story. Yet there remains beneath the assertion that a man is master of his fate, the melancholy conviction that to be born is to be doomed, a kind of secularized Calvinism. . . .

Pudd'nhead is Tom Sawyer grown up, the man who has not surrendered with maturity the dream of being a hero; but it must be added that he wants to be a hero on his own terms, to force himself upon a hostile community without knuckling under to its values. . . . (p. 17)

He begins as a pariah, the sage whose wisdom is taken for folly: an outsider in a closed society, a free thinker in a world of conformism, a gadgeteer and crank, playing with palmistry and fingerprints. But he is also, like his creator, a jokester. . . . Yet like his creator he wants to succeed in the world he despises; and he yields to it half-unwittingly even before it accepts him, adjusting to its code of honor, its definition of a Negro— while writing down in private or reading before a two man Free Thinkers' Society his dangerous thoughts.

Typically enough, it is as a detective that he makes his comeback. (pp. 17-18)

[However], the revelations of David Wilson (the name "Pudd'nhead" is sloughed off with his victory) restore civil peace only between him and the community which rejected him: for the rest, they expose only bankruptcy and horror and shame, the stupidity of our definition of a Negro and the hopelessness of our relations with him. Wilson's disclosure of Roxy's hoax coalesces with Twain's exposure to America of its own secret self; and the double discovery is aptly framed by Wilson's Calendar entries for two of our favorite holidays.

The chapter which contains the courtroom revelation is preceded by the text, "*April 1*. This is the day upon which we are reminded of what we are on the other three hundred and sixty-four." The implication is clear, whether conscious or not, not fools only but slaves! And it is followed by another, even grimmer, "*October 12, the Discovery*. It was wonderful to find America, but it would have been more wonderful to miss it." The Discovery! It is a disconcerting ending for a

detective story, which should have faith in all disclosures; but it is the aptest of endings for an American book, the only last word possible to a member of the Free Thinkers' Society. Beyond such bleak wisdom, there is only the cry of Roxy at the moment of revelation, "De Lord have mercy on me, po' miserable sinner dat I is!" But this is forbidden to Mark Twain. (p. 18)

> *Leslie A. Fiedler, "'As Free As Any Cretur . . .',"*
> *in* The New Republic *(reprinted by permission of*
> *The New Republic; © 1955 by The New Republic,*
> *Inc.), Vol. 133, Nos. 7 and 8, August 15 and 22,*
> *1955, pp. 17-18; pp. 16-18.*

LAURIAT LANE, JR.   (essay date 1955)

[*Lane posits the greatness of* Huckleberry Finn, *arguing that it holds many themes in common with great novels, and that it draws heavily upon epic tradition.*]

Of all forms of literature, the novel is in many ways the hardest to describe with any precision. Its relative newness as a form and its varied and complex nature combine to make this so. Whenever we try to view such a full and living book as *The Adventures of Huckleberry Finn*, some of it always escapes our gaze. . . . Each time we read *Huckleberry Finn* we read a certain book, and each time we read it we read a different book. No one of these books is the real *Huckleberry Finn;* in a sense, they all are.

At the heart of *Huckleberry Finn* lies a story about real human figures with genuine moral and ethical problems and decisions, figures placed in a society which we recognize as having everywhere in it the flavor of authenticity—the whole combination treated, for the most part, as directly and realistically as possible. I would like to move beyond this primary description or definition of *Huckleberry Finn,* however, and suggest that the novel may contain other elements equally important to a full appreciation. I would like to extend the novel in three directions, in space, in time, and in degree: in space, by considering some of the ways in which the book extends beyond its position as one of the masterworks of American fiction and becomes, if the term be allowed, a world novel; in time, by considering how much *Huckleberry Finn* resembles a literary form much older than the novel, the epic poem; and in degree, by considering just how much *Huckleberry Finn* transcends its position as a realistic novel and takes on the forms and qualities of allegory. (p. 1)

The first real novel and the first world novel is, by almost universal consent, Cervantes' *The Adventures of Don Quixote.* The most important thing which *Don Quixote* has bequeathed to the novels after it (apart of course from the all-important fact of there being such a thing as a novel at all) is the theme which is central to *Don Quixote* and to almost every great novel since, the theme of appearance versus reality. This theme is also central to *Huckleberry Finn.*

Even on the simplest plot level the world of *Huckleberry Finn* is one of deception. The very existence of Huck at all is a continual deception—he is supposed to be dead. This falseness in his relations with the world at large merely reflects the difference between his standards and those of the outside world. Huck's truth and the truth of the world are diametrically opposed. Throughout the novel his truth is always cutting through the surfaces of the world's appearance and learning the contrary reality beneath. At the climax Huck tells himself, "You can't pray a lie—I found that out.'' That is to say, the lie of appearance is always far different from the truth of reality, and to the truly heroic and individual conscience no amount of self-delusion can ever bridge the gap lying between.

In the final section of the book, the theme of appearance versus reality reaches almost philosophical proportions. Both because of the way in which Jim's escape is carried out and because of the underlying fact of there being no need for him to escape at all, the situation is one of total dramatic and moral irony. At the end, however, Twain relaxes the tone, straightens out the plot complications, and lets the moral issue fade away. He avoids, in fact, the logical conclusion to the kind of disorder he has introduced into his world-in-fiction, a world in which the distinction between appearance and reality has, from the reader's point of view, been lost forever. For if we cannot tell appearance from reality, if the two do become totally confused and impossible to distinguish, the only answer can be the one Twain eventually came to in his most pessimistic work, *The Mysterious Stranger;* that all is illusion, and nothing really exists. In *Huckleberry Finn,* Twain does not yet reach this point of despair. By centering his action within the essentially balanced mind of the boy, Huck, he keeps his hold on reality and manages to convey this hold to the reader. But the main issue of the novel, between the way things seem and the way they are, is nevertheless one that trembles in the balance almost up to the final page.

Huckleberry Finn also gains its place as a world novel by its treatment of one of the most important events of life, the passage from youth into maturity. The novel is a novel of education. Its school is the school of life rather than of books, but Huck's education is all the more complete for that reason. Huck, like so many other great heroes of fiction—Candide, Tom Jones, Stephen Dedalus, to mention only a few—goes forth into life that he may learn. One of the central patterns of the novel is the progress of his learning.

Yet another theme which *Huckleberry Finn* shares with most of the world's great novels is that of man's obsession with the symbols of material wealth. The book opens with an account of the six thousand dollars Huck got from the robbers' hoard and ends on the same note. Throughout the intervening pages gold is shown to be not only the mainspring of most human action, but usually the only remedy mankind can offer to atone for the many hurts they are forever inflicting on one another. And as Mr. Lionel Trilling has remarked, in a certain sense all fiction is ultimately about money.

The world novel may also convey a total vision of the nation or people from which it takes its origin. It not only addresses the world in a language which is uniquely the language of that nation or people, but it brings before the view of the world at large many character types which are especially national. In *Huckleberry Finn* we recognize in Jim, in the Duke and the Dauphin, in Aunt Sally, and in Huck himself, typically American figures whom Twain has presented for inspection by the world's eye. *Huckleberry Finn* gains much of its justification as a world novel from the fact that it is an intensely American novel as well.

In his essay on ''The Poetic Principle'' Poe remarks that ''no very long poem will ever be popular again.'' In part, no doubt, Poe bases this remark on his own special definition of poetry. But he is also recognizing that during the eighteenth and nineteenth centuries the epic poem was gradually dying out as a literary form. Or, to be more precise, it was gradually merging with another form, the novel. (pp. 1-3)

One quality of the epic poem is simply scope. Some novels confine themselves to treating exhaustively and analytically a limited segment of life. But others seem to be constantly trying to gather all life into their pages and to say, within a single story, all the important things that need to be said. Such novels derive much of their strength from the epic tradition, and *Huckleberry Finn* is such a novel. It has geographical scope. It ranges down the length of the great river and cuts through the center of a whole nation. As it does so, it gains further scope by embracing all levels of society, from the lowest to the highest. And it has the added scope of its own varying qualities, ranging from high comedy to low farce, from the poetic tranquility of life on the raft to the mob violence and human depravity always waiting on the shore.

Epic poetry gives literary form to the national destiny of the people for whom it is written. *Huckleberry Finn* gives literary form to many aspects of the national destiny of the American people. The theme of travel and adventure is characteristically American, and in Twain's day it was still a reality of everyday life. The country was still very much on the move, and during the novel Huck is moving with it. Huck's movements also embody a desire to escape from the constrictions of civilized society. Such a desire is of course not uniquely American, but during the nineteenth century Americans took it and made it their own. The American of that time could always say, as did Huck at the very end of the story, ''I reckon I got to light out for the territory ahead of the rest, because Aunt Sally she's going to adopt me and sivilize me, and I can't stand it. I been there before.'' Another specially American theme is that of the Negro, and Huck is faced with this problem throughout the story. Starting with the typically American prejudices and easy generalizations about Jim, he is gradually shocked into an increasingly complex awareness of Jim as a human being. And although Huck's relations with Jim do not so much embody a national attitude as suggest how the nation may purge itself of one, the theme of the Negro is still one which achieves epic stature in *Huckleberry Finn.*

The epic hero is usually an embodiment of some virtue or virtues valued highly by the society from which he has sprung. Huck has many such virtues. He holds a vast store of practical knowledge which makes itself felt everywhere in the story. He knows the river and how to deal with it; and he knows mankind and how to deal with it. And he has the supreme American virtue of never being at a loss for words. In fact Huck, though he still keeps some of the innocence and naïveté of youth, has much in common with one of the greatest of epic heroes, Odysseus, the practical man. Jim also has some of the qualities of an epic hero. He has strength and courage, and he possesses the supreme virtue of epic poetry, loyalty. It is part of Twain's irony that in Huck and Jim we have, in one sense, the two halves of an epic hero. In Huck, the skill and canniness; in Jim, the strength and simple loyalty.

In the society along the shore we see traces of other epic values, values which have survived from a more primitive world. The Grangerford-Shepherdson feud strikes the modern reader as a senseless mess, but as Huck says, ''There ain't a coward amongst them Shepherdsons—not a one. And there ain't no cowards amongst the Grangerfords either.'' Huck sees the essential folly behind this courage, but the reader, one degree further removed from the harsh reality, is allowed the luxury of a double vision. Similarly, Colonel Sherburn, destroying a lynching mob merely by the courage of his presence, illustrates another epic theme, the bravery of one against many.

One final quality which *Huckleberry Finn* derives from its epic ancestry is its poetry. The novel is full of poetry. Not just the passages of lyric description, which mark a pause between the main actions and give a heightened and more literary tone just as they often did in the traditional epic, but also the many similes and turns of speech Huck uses, which, if they are not quite Homeric, are certainly unforgettable. And much of the exaggerated language of the frontier world, one not far removed in kind from that of the primitive migrations, is also a natural part of the epic style. (pp. 3-4)

Although all novels are in a certain sense descended from *Don Quixote*, it is also true that in another sense all novels, and especially English ones, are descended from Bunyan's *Pilgrim's Progress*. The main difference between the allegorical novel as we know it today and Bunyan's narrative of the human soul is that whereas in *Pilgrim's Progress* we have an allegory that tends to turn into a novel, in most modern instances we have a novel that tends to turn into an allegory. As the author, whether he be Melville or Mann or Twain, develops and elaborates his original materials, he may become aware of certain meaningful connections which are tending to establish themselves between the physical objects and the physical narrative he is describing and the related spiritual values and conflicts. Drawing on a tradition which has existed for a long time in literature and which is a natural part of the artistic process in any form, the author finds himself writing allegory. And this is what happened to Mark Twain. Writing as he was a great novel, his masterpiece in fact, he organized and related certain physical materials to certain metaphysical conditions so that their relationship became meaningful in a special way—became, in short, allegory.

Huckleberry Finn is the story of a journey, a real journey. If we are to find any meaning in Huck's journey beyond the literal level, we must seek it first in the medium through which Huck journeys, in the great river down which he drifts during much of the story. And Huck's movements take on at least the external form of a basic symbolic pattern, one seen in such poems as Shelley's *Alastor*, Arnold's *The Future*, and Rimbaud's *Bateau Ivre*, a pattern stated most directly in *Prometheus Unbound*, "My soul is an enchanted boat." Implicit in this pattern is the suggestion that the river journey can have a distinctly metaphysical quality, that it can be, in fact, a journey of the soul as well as of the body. This suggestion is not at all arbitrary. Of all forms of physical progression, that of drifting downstream in a boat, or on a raft, is the most passive one possible. The mind under such conditions is lulled, as Huck's mind is, into the illusion that it has lost all contact with reality and is drifting bodilessly through a world of sleep and of dreams. Thus the nakedness of Huck and Jim when they are alone on the raft becomes a symbol of how they have shucked off the excrescences of the real world, their clothes, and have come as close as possible to the world of the spirit.

All journeys, even allegorical ones, must have a goal. What is the goal of Huck's journey? We find the answer in what happens while Huck and Jim float down the river. The pattern is, very simply, one of an ever-increasing engagement of the world of the raft, of the spirit, with the world of the shore, of reality. As the book progresses, more and more Huck tells about events that take place on the banks, and less and less he tells about those that take place out on the river. No matter how hard Huck and Jim try to escape, the real world is always drawing them back into it. Finally, in the Duke and the Dauphin, themselves fleeing for the moment from the harsh reality of the river's shores, the real world invades the world of the raft, and the latter loses forever the dream-like and idyllic quality it has often had for the two voyagers. The climax of Huck's lyric praise of the river comes significantly just before this mood is shattered forever by the arrival of the Duke and the Dauphin.

Parallel to this pattern of the ever-increasing engagement of the world of the shore with that of the raft is a pattern which begins with Huck's pretended death, a death which is actual to all the world but Huck and Jim. The symbolic fact of his death accomplished, Huck must find an identity with which he can face the real world. His assumption of various such identities forms a significant pattern. The various masks he assumes, starting with that of a girl, as far removed from the reality as possible, gradually draw back nearer the truth. Huck's final disguise, as Tom Sawyer, is only slightly removed from his real self. When he is about to reveal this real self and is instead taken for Tom, Huck almost recognizes the meaning of his journey. For he says to himself, "But if they was joyful, it warn't nothing to what I was; for it was like being born again, I was so glad to find out who I was."

This, then, is the allegory of *Huckleberry Finn.* Dying symbolically almost at the opening of the novel, Huck journeys through the world of the spirit, ever working out a pattern of increasing involvement with the world of reality and with his own self, both cast aside at the beginning of the journey. Only when he is finally forced to assume this real self in the eyes of the world, through the sudden arrival of Aunt Polly, is he allowed to learn the all-important truth Jim has kept from him throughout the novel, that his Pap "ain't comin back no mo." We cannot say that Huck has undergone a total initiation and is now fully prepared to take on adulthood, but neither can we doubt that he has undergone a knowledgeful and maturing experience. And at the end of the story he is about to undertake another journey, this time to the west, in search of further experience and further knowledge. (pp. 4-5)

Lauriat Lane, Jr., "Why 'Huckleberry Finn' Is a Great World Novel," in College English *(copyright © 1955 by the National Council of Teachers of English; reprinted by permission of the publisher), Vol. 17, No. 1, October, 1955, pp. 1-5.*

WILLIAM VAN O'CONNOR   (essay date 1955)

[An associate of Robert Penn Warren and Cleanth Brooks, O'Connor was a practitioner of the New Criticism, an influential movement in American criticism which paralleled a similar movement in England led by I. A. Richards, William Empson, and T. S. Eliot. Although the various New Critics did not subscribe to a uniform set of principles, all believed that a work of literature must be examined as an object in itself through close analysis of symbol, image, and metaphor. For the New Critics, literature is not a manifestation of ethics, sociology, or psychology, and cannot be evaluated in the general terms of any nonliterary discipline. In the following excerpt, written in answer to that of Lauriat Lane, Jr. (see excerpt above), O'Connor cites what he perceives as numerous flaws in Huckleberry Finn.*]*

From the late nineteenth century to World War I, and even after, there was much discussion of the great American novel. Eventually the idea died, apparently of its own inanity. But in recent years the idea, though not the phrase, has returned to life, for we are informed, from a variety of critical positions, that *The Adventures of Huckleberry Finn* is the truly American novel.

A novel wants to be circumscribed to live in its own terms, to fulfill itself imaginatively. On the other hand, it speaks to a people and to their beliefs about themselves. Huck is said to live for us somewhat as Roland lives for France or Arthur for England. If Huck is firmly enshrined in myth it would be futile to try to dislodge him. But his place in an American myth would not of itself be assurance that *Huckleberry Finn* is a great novel. (p. 6)

[There] are a number of flaws in *Huckleberry Finn,* some of them attributable to Twain's refusal to respect the "work of art" and others attributable to his imperfect sense of tone. The downstream movement of the story (theme as well as action) runs counter to Jim's effort to escape. Life on the raft may indeed be read as implied criticism of civilization—but it doesn't get Jim any closer to freedom. One may also ask (it has been asked before) why it never occurred to Jim, or to Huck, to strike out for the Illinois shore and freedom. It is possible that Twain felt Tom's highjinks were necessary not merely to prepare for the disappearance of Huck but to shift attention away from his conflicting themes.

For the downward movement of the novel, of course, the picaresque form serves its subject very well, allowing for innumerable and rapid adventures, afloat and ashore, and for the sort of ponderings that are peculiar to Huck. The picaresque form is also a clue to the kind of unity the book does have, a melodramatic mixture of reality and unreality and of comedy and horror. It is frequently theatrical in a good sense of the word. But the unity depends on Huck's mind, and too often there are bits of action, dialogue, and observation which are not appropriate to him. There are two sorts of theatricality in the novel, melodrama and claptrap.

Huck's relationship with his father is melodrama. So is the shooting of Boggs, or the tar and feathering of the Duke and King. A proof of their being melodrama is the ease with which one moves from a scene of violence to a humorous dialogue. For example, the encounter of Huck and Jim with the thieves and murderers aboard the *Walter Scott* is followed by the minstrel show, end-men sort of humor of "Was Solomon Wise?" Verisimilitude offers no problem when reality merges with unreality or horror dissolves innocently into comedy, but sometimes Twain's sense of proper distance, the degree and nature of the stylization he is employing, fails him and the action becomes gruesomely real. An instance of this is Huck's telling of the murders in "Why Harney Rode Away for His Hat." The starkness is too unrelieved. The scene does not respect the premises nor the general tone of the novel, and, even though it might work in another novel, it does not work here.

A good deal is made, quite justly, of Huck's affection for Jim, and the example commonly given is Huck's apology to Jim after having tormented him with a lie about there having been no storm. . . . But Twain sometimes loses sight of Huck's moral sensitivity. An instance is in Chapters XVII and XVIII.

Near the close of Chapter XVI the raft is run over by an upstream steamboat. In the darkness, after he and Jim have dived into the water, Huck cannot see Jim and his calls go unanswered. Huck then strikes out for shore. The following chapter, "The Grangerfords Take Me In," is a humorous introduction to the Grangerford family. Huck stays with the Grangerfords for many days, perhaps weeks, getting involved in their affairs, notably as courier between the lovers Miss Sophia Grangerford and Harney Shepherdson. No thought about Jim enters Huck's head! It doesn't occur to him to search for the

old Negro. Jack, Huck's "nigger servant," finally invites him to see a "stack o' water-moccasins" in a swamp, a trick for leading him to the spot where Jim is hiding. . . . There is not much indication that Huck is greatly relieved or moved at finding Jim alive: "I waked him up, and I reckoned it was going to be a grand surprise to him to see me again. . . . He nearly cried he was so glad. . . ." Huck says nothing about being glad himself. Perhaps we are to read this passage ironically, as an instance of a boy's self-centeredness and believe that true affection lies beneath it. This might be so, but it doesn't explain away Huck's absence of grief over Jim's "death," or his failure to search for him if alive, or his general indifference to Jim's fate.

Technically, too, the device for getting rid of Jim so that Huck can move into the Grangerford-Shepherdson world is awkward and unconvincing. Jim tells Huck he had heard him call for him when they were swimming toward shore but hadn't answered for fear of being detected. Presumably one reply would have quieted Huck and made detection much less likely. And if Huck had been allowed to help Jim hide, or even to maintain some awareness of him, he would be the Huck known to us in "Fooling Old Jim."

Huck's parody (Chapter XVII) of the activities of Emmeline Grangerford, poetess, is extremely amusing, but the "voice" is more nearly Twain's than Huck's. Many other things are put into the mouth of the twelve or thirteen year old Huck that, sometimes only weakly humorous themselves, are Twain himself speaking. . . . In "An Arkansas Difficulty," where Twain is giving a sense of life in a small river-town, he makes Huck relate an observation on "chawing tobacker" that one would expect to find as "filler" in a nineteenth-century newspaper or magazine. Most incongruous of all, perhaps, is Huck's account of the Duke's rendition of Hamlet's soliloquy.

A more self-conscious artist would not have allowed such discrepancies to mar the tone of his novel. The truth is that Twain, however gifted a raconteur, however much genius he had as an improviser, was not, even in *Huckleberry Finn,* a great novelist.

A glance at Twain's biography reveals attitudes that, if they were related about another "major" writer, would appear highly damaging. In *My Mark Twain* William Dean Howells reported: "He once said to me, I suppose after he had been reading some of my unsparing praise of [Jane Austen]: '*You* seem to think that woman could write,' and he forbore withering me with his scorn. . . ." Howells also wrote: "I fancy his pleasure in poetry was not great, and I do not believe he cared much for the conventionally accepted masterpieces of literature." (pp. 6-8)

Huckleberry Finn is involved with the mystique of America. The chief symbols are the Boy and the River. Huck is the break not merely with Europe but with civilization, the westward push. Self-sufficient and yet dependable, he is the proper kind of individualist. He is also youth, a rugged Peter Pan who lives eternally. Huck belongs also with Cooper's Leatherstocking and Faulkner's Ike McCaslin, symbolic figures who reject the evils of civilization. (A weakness in all of them is that they do not acknowledge the virtues of civilization or try to live, as one must, inside it.) Huck is, finally, a sentimental figure, not in himself of course, since he is a boy, but in the minds of those who unduly admire his departure for the territory.

The River, as Eliot says, is time and timelessness, "a strong brown god" with his own thoughts about the machine, the hurry and fuss of cities, the illusions and struggles that make us lie, steal, or cheat. But the River is also the Mississippi as it borders the state of Missouri, the very heart of America. If Twain helped create a mythic river, the mythic river also helped Twain find his place as a legendary writer. Having such a place, he is sometimes, by sheer association, given more: he is made into the "Lincoln of American literature." (p. 8)

The association of Lincoln and Twain may seem appropriate at first glance—but only at first glance. Presumably Howells meant that both men discovered their need for comedy in the pathos and tragedy of the human condition, that both men were sons of a frontier society. To a degree, then, the comparison holds. But to allow for a detailed comparison, Lincoln should have to have written novels, or Twain to have been a politician, statesman, or writer of speeches. Insofar as Lincoln the writer and Twain the writer can be compared, Lincoln is the greater. Lincoln's wit, also in a vernacular idiom, is frequently more subtle than Twain's and may be expected to be more lasting. Lincoln's ability in writing an analytical prose, flexible and closely reasoned, and his ability in writing a serious and, when the occasion required, solemn rhetoric were also greater than Twain's. The seriousness and solemnity in Twain are of innocence betrayed, as in the concluding paragraph of *The Mysterious Stranger*. Lincoln's seriousness is that of a man dealing with the world, in its own terms when forced to, but also above it, urging it to create its destiny in ways that make for the fullest sense of achievement and dignity. If Lincoln had written novels, he would, without doubt, have been a greater novelist than Twain. His virtues include Twain's and surpass them. (p. 9)

Probably it is a time and a place, with a language appropriate to them, that appeals to the followers of Twain. In a series of letters addressed to Van Wyck Brooks, Sherwood Anderson made many references to Twain, to the midwest, and to *the book*. In Brooks's introduction to the letters one reads:

> I can remember how struck I was by his [Anderson's] fresh healthy mind and his true Whitmanian feeling for comradeship, his beautiful humility, his lovely generosity, and the 'proud conscious innocence' of his nature. This was his own phrase for Mark Twain's mind at the time he was writing *Huckleberry Finn*. . . .

This passage, in language reminiscent of Anderson's own, of Hemingway's too, but a little thin and nostalgic to have been Twain's, is obviously intended as wholly a compliment. If one wonders why an American quality, innocence, and superior writing go together, there is Anderson's reasoning on the matter: "He [Twain] belonged out here in the Middle West and was only incidentally a writer." Presumably craftsmanship, wide experience, or even thought in any complexity inhibit a truly American writer. Innocence, that strange word in American life, helps to account for Twain's place, and the place of *Huckleberry Finn,* in the hierarchy of American literature. (pp. 9-10)

The difficulty we have in conceiving what Huck might be as an adult is an indication of the limited usefulness of Huck as a symbol. If we refuse to over-value him as a symbol, we may be less inclined to over-value the novel, or to over-value the language in which it is written. (p. 10)

William Van O'Connor, "Why 'Huckleberry Finn'
Is Not the Great American Novel," in College English *(copyright © 1955 by the National Council of*
Teachers of English; reprinted by permission of the
publisher), Vol. 17, No. 1, October, 1955, pp. 6-
10.

FREDERICK ANDERSON (essay date 1961)

[*Frederick Anderson compiled* Mark Twain: The Critical Heritage *in 1971 and has edited and introduced other works by and about Twain. In the following excerpt, he criticizes the play* Ah Sin, *a collaborative effort by Twain and Bret Harte, concluding that it displays poor dramatic technique.*]

The existence of a text of *Ah Sin*, Bret Harte and Mark Twain's play set in a mining camp on the Stanislaus River, has only recently become known. The production of the play in 1877 was a failure, the work was never published, and scholars have relied on contemporary reviews for information about the only collaborative venture by two of the West's foremost writers. Even a casual reader will discover the cause for this neglect, since while *Ah Sin* is not the poorest work by either man, it is not far from it. Nevertheless, a play about the West by two authors whose experiences in the area provided material for some of their most effective writing deserves examination. (p. v)

Although Clemens was responsible for the final revisions, much, perhaps most, of the initial material in the play came from Bret Harte. The names and to some extent the characterizations of all the figures in the play except Silas Broderick, Ferguson, and the Tempest family were already known to Bret Harte's readers. (pp. x-xi)

Clemens's chief contribution to *Ah Sin* was his effort to render accurately the rhythms and vocabulary of actual speech since Harte's dialogue in this play, as in most of his writing, was conventionally stilted and romantic. Clemens's skill in the use of the vernacular was seriously tested by Harte's rhetoric, as is shown by the evolution of the following passage. Harte originally had Judge Tempest remark, "I know not what to say." Clemens revised this specimen of unlikely speech to "Well, I don't know of anything further to say." Such revisions permeate the fragments of the early manuscript and repeatedly show Mark Twain's efforts to move from the formalized speech of the nineteenth century stage toward realistic language and characterization. These efforts were too few and made too late to salvage a play which was written well within the dramatic conventions of the period and however considerable Clemens's revisions may have been, his statement that he had "left hardly a foot-print of Harte in it anywhere" is exaggerated.

The uneasy and sporadic collaboration between Harte and Clemens is reflected in the play's chaotic and sometimes incoherent succession of events, the implausibly feeble motives which bring these events about, and the sketchily developed characterizations. Moreover, since neither man was a trained dramatist, their conception of the enterprise wavered from tragedy and melodrama to comedy and farce with no successful attempt to develop or sustain a consistent mood. Advertisements and programs identified this nondescript production with desparate ambiguity as "a dramatic work in four acts." (pp. xi-xii)

"When our play was finished, ["] said Clemens, in a curtain speech on the night of the New York opening, "] we found it was so long, and so broad, and so deep—in places—that it would have taken a week to play it. I thought that was all right;

we could put "to be continued" on the curtain, and run it straight along. But the manager said no; so he cut out, and cut out, and the more he cut out the better the play got. I never saw a play that was so much improved by being cut down; and I believe it would have been one of the very best plays in the world if his strength had held out so that he could cut out the whole of it." (p. xvi)

Frederick Anderson, in a preface to "Ah Sin": A Dramatic Work by Mark Twain and Bret Harte, edited by Frederick Anderson (copyright 1961 by The Mark Twain Company and The Bret Harte Company; reprinted by permission of The Mark Twain Company and The Bret Harte Company), The Book Club of California, 1961, pp. v-xvi.

CLYDE L. GRIMM (essay date 1967)

[*In the following excerpt, Grimm contends that Twain's adaptation of the novel* The American Claimant *from a farcical play sheds light on his political and social positions. Disenchanted with democracy, Twain idealized the possibility of earning social position by superior breeding and noble demeanor.*]

Although Mark Twain's *The American Claimant* . . . is a hastily and crudely fabricated novel, it is an interesting and significant work for at least two reasons. First, having been adapted by Twain from a farce drama written in collaboration with William Dean Howells, the novel provides an opportunity for study of Twain's imaginative conversion of pointless humor into meaningful satire. Second, because it reiterates with little ambiguity political and social themes which recur throughout Twain's work, the novel provides a clearer as well as more mature statement on cultural issues with which Twain had been concerned for years.

The play from which the novel grew has a curious history of its own, certain aspects of which warrant recapitulation. Twain and Howells never intended more than to amuse themselves and, they hoped, a large audience by creating a ridiculously impractical schemer who would strut and fret his hour upon the stage in a series of ludicrous antics signifying nothing. (p. 86)

After having shown continued but ineffectual interest for several years, Howells proposed in April 1883 that they make definite plans to write the play in October and assured Twain that their idea had "the making of a good comedy in it without doubt." However, when in November and December of that year the two authors finally put the play together in short but intense flurries of effort, they produced what Howells less than enthusiastically called "an extreme farce." The inferiority of "extreme farce" to "good comedy," though difficult to assess precisely, no doubt contributed to Howells' eventual loss of confidence in the play and his withdrawal from arrangements to stage it. (p. 87)

Perusal of the play confirms Howells' objection that there is nothing to it but character and situation. The main "plot" focuses on Sellers the zany inventor, who amid impoverished surroundings displays a variety of fantastic gadgets from which he hopes to make a fortune; ironically, a modest, practical device in which he has shown little interest ultimately proves successful and redeems him. In one underplot Sellers lays claim to an English earldom but gratuitously renounces it in the end. A second underplot, the conventional romance, brings together with unusually little difficulty Sellers' daughter and the young English heir, who also gratuitously renounces his claim. The claimant idea contributes nothing essential to the action and as an addition to Sellers' eccentricity is superfluous. Another alleged weakness, the materialization idea [a scheme for reviving the dead] provides some incidental satire and also some farcical humor when Sellers twice expresses horror at the thought that a living girl is in love with what he supposes to be a "materialized" ghost. As for its contribution to Sellers' alleged lunacy, his belief in materialization does not appear any more incredible or insane than his confidence in a fire-making fire extinguisher, which none of the play's critics objected to and which Daniel Frohman even considered its only amusing element. Neither materialization nor any of Sellers' other inventions or delusions seems inappropriate for "extreme farce," which after all seldom invites serious rational scrutiny. The play suffers most from the formal weaknesses sensed by Howells and Herne: its thinness of plot and the arbitrary employment of supporting elements. (p. 89)

Although he borrowed little verbatim, Twain nevertheless retained all of the basic elements of the farce. . . . [He] radically altered his view of the story material and its significance and . . . transformed it from meaningless farce into thoroughgoing political and social satire. In doing so, he showed remarkable ingenuity in adapting and integrating those elements which Howells and the others had most objected to. He revamped the claimant plot by expanding Sellers' role as a would-be English peer and also by adding for ironic contrast a fully developed complementary plot tracing the English heir's attempts to become an American democrat. Sellers' "lunacy" remains the same in terms of his devotion to fantastic projects but gains special significance in the new context. Even the materialization scheme becomes an effective vehicle for satire. Yet in spite of its ingenious thematic unity, the novel suffers from Twain's haste in putting it together in only "71 days." For example, the new episodes devoted to the young Englishman's adventures, comprising roughly a third of the novel, are crudely inserted as a virtual block in the middle of the Sellers material. The satire in these episodes especially but in others as well is heavy-handed, as Twain's telling predominates over his showing.

Notwithstanding its shortcomings as art, however, *The American Claimant* is significant for the light it throws on Twain's political and social thought. Repeating themes and devices which appear in many of his earlier works, it invites comparisons which illuminate major cultural issues which preoccupied him for many years and indicates the direction in which, at the age of fifty-six, he sought or had found resolutions. Most apparent and interesting is Twain's recapitulation of the theme of disenchantment with democracy which he had employed just a few years earlier in *A Connecticut Yankee in King Arthur's Court*. . . . The disillusioned figure in *The American Claimant* is not, however, like Hank Morgan, a native American raised on common-sense utilitarianism and democratic political principles; rather he is a young English nobleman, Viscount Berkeley, who has been raised as the heir to the Earldom of Rossmore. Twain assigns Berkeley the "candor, kindliness, honesty, sincerity, simplicity, [and] modesty" which suggest innate nobility of character antecedent to social status or political rank. . . . He has been infected with the radical political theories of Lord Tanzy of Tollmache (whose Germanic name connotes insanity) and has determined to renounce his aristocratic station, emigrate to America and make his way by ability alone. The lesson taught by his subsequent adventures is two-fold: first, that in spite of its professed equalitarianism American democracy is a corrupt sham which perpetuates inequality and changes only its bases and the processes by which it is established; second, that the abstract principle of equality, no matter how sincerely adopted and earnestly pursued, will not produce the sentiment or feeling of equality, because it is contrary to human nature. (pp. 90-1)

Democratic leveling perverts the meaning of "equality" and by mocking the labels for superior intelligence, character, education and conduct tends to obliterate legitimate moral distinctions or gradations among human beings.

Berkeley finds, moreover, that the equalitarianism implied by this specious use of language is only nominal after all, for inequality and deference to rank or status are widespread in America. (p. 92)

Almost from the beginning of his tenure in America, Berkeley had been aware of a discrepancy between the principles he idealistically espoused and the sentiments he actually felt. . . . Berkeley thus resumes his inherited identity as an aristocrat much as Prince Edward and King Arthur do in earlier novels. It is important to note that in his case as in theirs the rank or title signifying superiority is accompanied by real distinction of character, breeding and conduct and therefore, unlike the titles and ranks adopted or conferred in America, has a legitimate moral basis.

This need not suggest that Twain sanctions the ordinary or traditional concept of hereditary aristocracy; in fact, . . . he repudiates it. Yet he does dramatize a concept of natural aristocracy, in which innate nobility and superior breeding entitle one to social distinction. Not only do men naturally fail in the practice of equalitarianism, they also naturally fail to display an equal capacity for or inclination toward intelligent, moral behavior. Reminiscent of James Fenimore Cooper's, Twain's chief criticism of democracy in America is not that men seek and society confers distinction but that the natural aristocrat is dispossessed and ignored in favor of ridiculous, corrupt and even brutal shams.

The remaining episodes of the novel, which are dominated by Colonel Sellers, develop these themes with variations peculiar to his special temperament and background. Though some pure farce remains, Twain did a remarkably thorough job of converting pointless elements from the play into meaningful and cohesive satire for the novel.

One of the most significant revisions concerns the claimant idea. . . . In the novel Sellers once again believes himself to be the rightful earl, having inherited his claim upon the death of his distant Arkansaw relative Simon Lathers, the former "earl." But of greatest significance is that Berkeley's father, the Earl of Rossmore, admits that a mistake in succession occurred years ago and, though he does not believe the courts would uphold it, confirms the moral right of the American claimant. What this radical change may suggest of Twain's attitude toward his own family's claims is conjectural, but its effect on the characterization of Sellers is quite plain. Sellers in the novel cannot be ridiculed for believing himself an heir or claimant to the peerage; Twain made him, in at least one sense, a legitimate pretender. Thus, whatever else may remain laughable about Sellers, this particular element of his characterization invites serious consideration.

As a matter of fact, no matter how ridiculous many of his antics appear, Sellers is one of the most "sympathetic" adult characters Twain created. (pp. 93-5)

Neither the crassness and cynicism of the age nor his personal disappointments alter his character, his temperament or his basic outlook. . . . Imagination is the key to Sellers' personality, as it is to the personalities of a number of other Twain characters. . . . Sellers consciously chooses to indulge an image of himself and his surroundings commensurate with his own high moral ideals and aspirations. (pp. 96-7)

In any case, the new context demands a thoroughgoing reappraisal of Sellers' eccentricities as having a good deal more significance than they display in the farce. One peculiarity shared by both Sellers and his daughter is a culturally split personality. The Colonel's co-existent obsessions with Franklinian inventions and with dreams of an earldom suggest that he is a product of two different cultures. . . . Most important, however, is that both Sellers and Berkeley display genuine nobility of character which distinguishes them from the common level of men who represent democratic culture and which vindicates their natural instincts, justifying both Berkeley's resumption of his aristocratic station and Sellers' aspiration to it. (p. 97)

Twain does not, however, limit his satire to the shams and pretensions of the Gilded Age alone; he enlarges the scope and significance of his criticism of American culture by broadening its historical perspective. He does so by once again transforming none-too-promising materials retained from the farce. The first of these is the "deadly chromos" which adorn the Sellers household. . . . (p. 98)

Dixon Wecter has noted one of Andrew Jackson's vanities which may have been Twain's inspiration both for the chromo device . . . above and for another use of chromos in the Berkeley episodes of the novel; Wecter reports that "an artist named Earl was hired to live at the White House during the eight years of his Administration, and do nothing but paint one picture after another of the President." Such a fact would have been widely publicized in Whig circles, both during and after Jackson's tenure in office, and Twain, whose family's affiliation with the Whig party is well documented, would almost certainly have known of it. The chromo of Jackson on Sellers' wall might well have been inspired by one of Earl's portraits and intended as a direct satiric allusion. (p. 99)

Twain further enlarges the historical perspective of the novel by adapting Sellers' materialization scheme. Although the incidental satire achieved by this device remains much the same in the novel as in the play . . . , Sellers' mistaken identification of the young Englishman as a materialized ghost, while continuing to provide farcical humor, functions in the novel as satire also and contributes much to the development of primary themes. Twain expanded the function of this device by first of all complicating the confusion of identities. Early in the novel Berkeley escapes from a hotel fire dressed in the clothes of a notorious one-armed frontier bank robber, One-Armed Pete, who is burned to death in the fire. Dressed as a cowboy, Berkeley receives the deference of both ordinary citizens and government officials but mistakenly assumes that it is again due to his English rank. In fact, however, they defer to him not as a European noble but as a peculiarly American equivalent—the "noble" Westerner. . . . Properly identified—by his moral stature, not by his clothes—Berkeley absolves not only himself but also the centuries-old culture of which he is a product. (pp. 100-01)

In fact Berkeley and Pete are related only as antitheses, and when they are viewed as representatives or symbols of their respective cultures this antithesis becomes of greatest significance. Like the contrast in *A Connecticut Yankee* between the original, sixth-century Knights of the Round Table and the "converted," nineteenth-century knights of the Yankee's stock exchange, this contrast in *The American Claimant* suggests that the development of democratic culture in America represents historical degeneration, not "progress" as Americans are accustomed to boast. One-Armed Pete, the frontier "knight" or literal "robber baron," symbolizes democracy's inversion of the social order and of the moral values upon which it is based; Berkeley, on the other hand, represents the European institutions and culture from which America revolted. Though its distribution of rank may be imperfect, Europe nevertheless produced Berkeley, whose moral distinction matches his social rank and to that extent at least vindicates the culture which makes possible such a match.

In America, however, disparity between moral stature and social rank is the rule. . . . Sellers cannot escape the "inhaled" influences of his native environment nor can he satisfactorily resolve the conflict between them and his natural instincts. . . . His compulsion to sustain romantic ideals and to strive for some measure of satisfaction on his own terms, as opposed to those prevailing in his environment, makes him an admirable and even heroic figure.

Sellers' absurdities, like those of Don Quixote, require that a distinction be made between spirit and manner; he is ridiculous not because of his romantic temperament, noble spirit and idealistic vision but because of the elaborate, archaic and incongruous manners and forms with which he identifies proper expression of these. In contrast to her father's ingrained and irremediable quixotism, Sally Sellers toward the end of the novel "reforms" by adopting a healthier, more mature view of aristocratic distinction, which of course complements Berkeley's reformed view of equalitarianism and democracy. (pp. 101-02)

Twain seems, therefore, to have revealed much of himself in his characterizations of Berkeley and Sellers, both of whom display this same dualism. . . . Judging by *The American Claimant*, what Twain had concluded was that for a person of the innate character and temperament of a Colonel Sellers the conditions of American life create a frustrating disparity between noble motives and opportunities for their fulfillment, which he can prevent from ending in despair only by indulging in absurd pretenses and illusions. From his revised and mature perspective—perhaps already that of despair—Twain could no longer treat these absurdities as farce but was compelled to display their tragicomic aspect instead. (pp. 102-03)

> *Clyde L. Grimm, " 'The American Claimant': Reclamation of a Farce," in* American Quarterly *(copyright 1967, Trustees of the University of Pennsylvania), Vol. XIX, No. 1, Spring, 1967, pp. 86-103.*

ROBERT PENN WARREN (lecture date 1974)

[*Warren is considered one of the most distinguished men of letters in America today. Consistently in the intellectual vanguard of American scholarship, he began his career—with John Crowe Ransom, Donald Davidson, Allen Tate, and several others—as a member of the Fugitive group of Southern poets during the 1920s. The stated intent of the Fugitives was to create a literature utilizing the best qualities of modern and traditional art. After 1928, the four major Fugitives joined eight other writers, including Stark Young and John Gould Fletcher, to form the Agrarians, a group dedicated to preserving the Southern way of life and traditional*

Southern values. The Agrarians were concerned with social and political issues as well as literature; in particular, they attacked Northern industrialism as they sought to preserve the Southern farming economy. Warren, Ransom, and Tate eventually left Agrarianism and went on to become prominent founders of New Criticism, one of the most influential critical movements of the mid-twentieth century. Although the various New Critics did not subscribe to a single set of principles, all believed that a work of literature had to be examined as an object in itself through a process of close analysis of symbol, image, and metaphor. For the New Critics, a literary work was not a manifestation of ethics, sociology, or psychology, and could not be evaluated in the general terms of any nonliterary discipline. Warren's work is strongly regional in character, often drawing its inspiration from the land, the people, and the history of the South. Warren's deep interest in history and his conception that art is a vital force in contemporary society, informs all of his work. In the following excerpt, Warren discusses Twain as an artist representative of the nineteenth-century disillusionment brought on by the collapse of the Jeffersonian concept of democracy.]

[Mark Twain] most deeply embodied the tensions of his time. (p. 15)

[His] relation to the issues of his age is full of extraordinary ambivalences. For instance, he repudiated the historical past (including his father and the South), but the telling and retelling of his personal past, directly or indirectly, became his chief stock-in-trade. Then, in this telling of the personal past, emerged new ambivalences and new tangles. (p. 16)

The ambivalences, the tensions, were central to Twain's being, but in his most famous book, *Adventures of Huckleberry Finn,* one of the impulses seems to have been to resolve them. The basic conflict in the novel is, of course, between the life on the river, where Huck finds innocence, brotherhood with man, and communion with nature, and life ashore, where, stage by stage, he discovers the corruption of society, a process that comes to climax when conscience itself is exhibited as the creature of society, embodying its most cruel mandates. As Huck gradually develops a new "consciousness" to replace the old "conscience," the reader's expectation rises that Huck may find for himself—and for the reader—a way to redeem life ashore, to create a life in which the "real" of the shore and the "ideal" of the river may meet, or at least enter into some fruitful relation.

But nothing of the sort occurs. At the end, Huck finds himself conniving in the famously brutal joke, at Nigger Jim's expense, that undercuts all the moral discovery on the river. To cap the climax, he finds himself caught in the very trap of society from which he had sought escape on the river, with his only comfort now in the vague notion that he may cut out for the "territory"—even though Twain well knew what the "territory" would become in the course of winning the West. So we are left with the irremediable split—and presumably an unredeemable world and a self that, as long as it is of that world, is unredeemable, too.

It is *A Connecticut Yankee at King Arthur's Court* that most nakedly exhibits the unresolvable issues that had lain behind the struggle to complete the earlier novel. Now when Twain began *A Connecticut Yankee* he had in mind little more than a savage joke at the expense of the romantic cult of medievalism and more indirectly at the expense, probably, of the late Confederate States, under whose flag Samuel Clemens had briefly and ineffectually borne arms. But soon, to the savage jest at the expense of the past, there was joined, not a "hymn" to boyhood and innocence, but a "hymn" to modernity.

Hank Morgan, a superintendent at the Colt Arms Company, who, in his technician's pride, asserts that he can "invent, contrive, create" anything, sets out to introduce the natives of Arthurian Britain, in which he mysteriously finds himself, to the blessings of technological civilization. This mission of humanitarian improvement goes hand in glove, however, with Hank's program to become the "Boss"; that is, in an unconscious parody of imperialism and strange forerunner of Conrad's *Heart of Darkness* the role of humane civilizer and that of the exploiter merge. Or, to leap from the Belgian Congo of the late nineteenth century to the Western world of the late twentieth, the establishing of a rational order demands centralized authority, and ironically the effort to free man may end in a new form of tyranny. (pp. 18-20)

If *A Connecticut Yankee* is fraught with dire forebodings about democracy in general and, more appallingly, about modern industrial-technological democracy in particular, that grimness is as nothing compared to what was to come, after our Philippine operetta of imperialism, in **"To a Person Sitting in Darkness."** (p. 21)

[Twain came] to agree with Hank that the human race was "muck." Or if not muck, it was wicked vermin, as in *The Mysterious Stranger,* where Satan, who, to please the boy Theodor, having molded and vitalized some little creatures of clay, picks up a couple who had got to fighting and with his fingers crushes them and flings the miniscule bodies aside and then wipes away the blood smear on his handkerchief—meanwhile pursuing his conversation. Man's infinite capacity for folly and infinite capacity for wickedness, in the face of all his shabby pretenses, is Twain's final theme, and the fact that American democracy is, by his standards, one of the shabbier pretensions gets almost forgotten.

No, this is not Twain's final theme. The final theme even more drastically undercuts the whole concept of a democratic—or any other kind of—social order, and therefore renders irrelevant any criticism of, or hope for, man. All is illusion, a "fever-dream."

If nothing is real, there is no guilt. And there are no problems of politics, society, justice, or history. Except those of spooks. Who, of course, have no "self" to cast a vote "spoken on their honor and their conscience." (pp. 21-2)

> *Robert Penn Warren, "America and the Diminished Self," in his* Democracy and Poetry *(copyright © 1975 by Robert Penn Warren; excerpted by permission; originally presented as a Jefferson Lecture of 1974, Harvard University), Cambridge, Mass.: Harvard University Press, 1975, pp. 1-37.**

JAMES E. CARON (essay date 1982)

[*Caron links the seemingly disparate elements of* Pudd'nhead Wilson *into a single expression of Twain's pessimistic vision.*]

Despite the fact *Pudd'nhead Wilson* gained its name from a character in the book, David Wilson, many critics have denied, belittled, or ignored his significance to the story. In effect, Wilson has been held to the role of someone who moves the plot along but has no intrinsic importance—a mere lever. This view of Wilson also maintains that the aphorisms at the head of each chapter are not attributable to him, nor are they related to the story itself. These judgments dismiss Wilson as a pudd'n-head (accepting Dawson's Landing's values without reflection) while implying Twain's inability to achieve artistic integrity.

On the other hand, some readers of the book take Wilson seriously and have shown his intelligence and importance. Nevertheless, the task of comprehensively relating the aphorisms to the narration has been generally neglected. I believe an examination of the relationship of the aphorisms to the story will not only demonstrate their commentary upon the action and enlargement upon the themes but will show Wilson's central position in the work. Furthermore, the Calendar's function is evidence of Twain's success as a literary "surgeon"; it illustrates the integrity of his artistic vision, including the appropriateness of the book's complete title, *The Tragedy of Pudd'nhead Wilson.*

Insisting upon David Wilson's authorship of the aphorisms is admittedly a less than precise notion. Most critics see them as Twain's, not Wilson's, but it is unsatisfactory simply to reverse this judgment and claim they are Wilson's. . . . The story itself has the local color of Dawson's Landing; the aphorisms project the community of America and also the community of mankind. This effect of multilevel community allows for a resonance of meaning in which the narration often implies a national or universal significance by virtue of the aphorisms. The David Wilson whom the reader encounters in the story may have no overt correspondence with these larger implications which insist upon Twain's authorship, but the narrative clearly shows Wilson's possession of intelligence, irony, and humor—the bases of the Calendar's satiric, pessimistic vision. Even if we cannot fully separate Twain and his character insofar as the aphorisms are concerned (so that he and Wilson strike the reader as Siamese-twin writers of the Calendar), it is crucial to see Wilson's narrative presentation as essentially harmonious with the thought and tone of the Calendar.

The relationship of the aphorisms to the narrative is a complex one, as the idea of the moral framework and the levels of community suggest. Although many of the aphorisms comment upon specific incidents in the story, they do so in varying degrees of obliqueness, often enlarging upon the book's themes in the process. . . . My effort to demonstrate a consistent relationship between Calendar and narration will use three ideas, each with its own cluster of aphorisms and each with its own degree of embodiment in the story: (1) various forms of fiction-making, (2) the perversity of humanity and existence, and (3) unexpected connections. (pp. 452-54)

John Gerber seems correct when he declares that much of the critical dissatisfaction with *Pudd'nhead Wilson* is due to its being judged by novelistic standards when it is not a novel at all. Gerber refers to the story as a "fabulation," closer to oral tradition than to novelistic realism. . . . No doubt Gerber is correct in suggesting the European tradition of storytelling as a possible precedent for *Pudd'nhead Wilson*'s design, but there is another tradition closer to Twain: the American tall tale.

Although the tall tale is not realism, it often grew from a nucleus of events which were amazing but plausible. There is no sharp line dividing the realistic story from the tall-tale variety since the tall tale's technique is to use realistic detail to provide plausibility for its fantastic conceptions. Typically, the narration proceeds with a succession of details that is progressively exaggerated until a preposterous climax—the "snapper"—is reached. . . . The obvious fictional techniques of the *Pudd'nhead Wilson* narration, as well as the thematic treatment of lies highlighted by the aphorisms, are part of Twain's strategy for revealing a "tall tale" quality in the antebellum South. The fundamental imbalance of a slave-based aristocracy functions as an artful lie woven into the history of America. Slavery and aristocracy are like the preposterous conceptions of the tall tale, and the unquestioning acceptance of both is created by people's upbringing and social customs. . . . Once *Pudd'nhead Wilson* is thought of as having a tall tale's form, the absurd logic of the ending (freeing Tom in order to enslave him) makes sense as the snapper of the story, and its function as the moment of recognition gives a clue to the story's tragic dimension.

Using the tall tale as a metaphor to portray the old South is ironically appropriate since that portion of the country was the nursery for the narrative form. . . . As the "tall" part of the Southern tale, slavery is symbol and theme, for it exemplifies a way of life. (pp. 454-56)

The town's contentment and its chief citizens' stainless nobility are moral qualities based upon the economic fact of slavery. . . .

"Habit is habit, and not to be flung out of the window by any man, but coaxed down-stairs a step at a time." The habit of slavery and the aristocracy it supported were part of America from the beginning, even in its democratic constitution.

"One of the most striking differences between a cat and a lie is that a cat has only nine lives." The cat's various lives probably refer to the various forms a lie may take as well as the cat's possible longevity. . . . On an institutional level the pragmatic concerns of framing a constitution led to a democracy in which a slave is counted as three-fifths of a person in apportioning the number of congressmen. Such an arrangement is political sleight of hand from one point of view but eminently practical from another. (p. 457)

Chapter 11 has two aphorisms. . . . The second aphorism seems anything but related to the story: "As to the Adjective: when in doubt, strike it out." Nevertheless, it is relevant to the idea of fiction-making. The saying may be interpreted as a grammatical warning against embellishment, exaggeration, or complete fabrication. (p. 458)

Chapters 13 and 15 could be subtitled "Everyone has his or her own good reasons for creating fictions." The lie of slavery taints everyone to some degree. (p. 459)

America as the new Eden was one of the oldest views of the new world, and Wilson's Calendar uses the implied universal dimension in that concept. With references to the Garden and comments upon life itself, the aphorisms provide a second general proposition: existence and people are perverse. With a slight twist to Genesis, the aphorism for chapter 2 rewrites the biblical story. Adam took the apple, not because he wanted it but because it was forbidden. . . . By assigning such motivation to the primary act of disobedience, perversity as an archetypal quality of human nature is suggested. (pp. 460-61)

Even life itself is seen as some kind of perverse event. . . . (p. 461)

By presenting slavery in . . . metaphysical terms Twain not only questions the legitimacy of the institution, but also, with hints of predestination, aims at an even bigger slaveholder: the Deity. (p. 462)

The attack against the perverseness of the cosmic design and its Designer continues with the aphorism for chapter 4, which speaks of special providences. . . . This blend of slavery and predestination which manages to satirize the divine as well as the human is a good example of the considerable power Twain can achieve by carefully modulating the narration by means of the aphorisms.

False Tom is the most obvious example of the perverseness of human nature. As a baby Tom preferred the tongs above all things for a toy. . . . Such behavior is especially apparent in relation to Roxy. First of all, Tom refuses to give her money when she returns to see him, perversely denying the bonds of affection to which Roxy might appeal as his former nurse (cf. the first aphorism for chapter 8). But even when their true relationship is revealed, Tom's behavior is the same, for he repays Roxy's greatest sacrifice for him—allowing herself to be resold into slavery to pay for his gambling debts—by selling her down the river. "If you pick up a starving dog and make him prosperous, he will not bite you. This is the principal difference between a dog and a man" (ch. 16). (pp. 462-64)

"Gratitude and treachery are merely the two extremities of the same procession. You have seen all of it that is worth staying for when the band and the gaudy officials have gone by." . . .

What the aphorism suggests is a third general proposition: the notion of unexpected connections. An obligation can inspire treachery as easily as gratitude. . . . To be more specific in the terms *Pudd'nhead Wilson* provides, it is a fascination with the idea of a common bloodstream between two entities appearing to be radically different: miscegenation. Like slavery, miscegenation is both theme and symbol. (p. 464)

Another example of a common ground for apparently disparate things is given in chapter 14 when the narrator is describing Roxy's laughter. . . . The highest and the lowest, the happiest and the most miserable possess the gift of such perfect laughter. As gratitude and treachery are linked by being the ends of the same procession, so too are the angels and the slaves linked by their mutually perfect laughter—though it is perfect for different reasons. The angels' laughter is perfect as a reflection of their perfect bliss, the slaves' as a hammer to shatter their perfect misery. . . . "Only Laughter," observes Satan, "can blow it [a colossal humbug] to rags and atoms at a blast. Against the assault of Laughter nothing can stand." (p. 465)

How is Wilson tragic, and what happens to laughter in such a tragedy? (p. 466)

If an organic relationship between the aphorisms and the narrative is admitted, then the possibility that Twain meant those aphorisms to reflect the character of David Wilson must be taken seriously. Wilson is possibly as much a prudent head as he is a pudd'nhead, not just a plot mechanism and not just a blind supporter of slavery and the Southern aristocracy.

In the narrative he behaves like an *eiron* (the self-deprecating man), ironic towards himself as well as others. . . . The problem, however, rests with the community; the people also cannot read Wilson's calendar correctly. "But irony was not for those people; their mental vision was not focussed for it. They read those playful trifles in the solidest earnest." . . . (pp. 466-67)

The results of these misreadings are Wilson's position on the fringe of society and the nickname "Pudd'nhead." Yet the decision "to live down his reputation and work his way into the legal field" . . . should not be misconstrued as a desire to be like the average citizen of Dawson's Landing. Through his aphorisms, Wilson maintains an ironic distance from the community as he seeks to rise in it. . . . As the aphorisms indicate, Wilson is smart enough to realize the pervasiveness of different lies as well as the relative view of morality and reality such fiction-making represents. . . . Far from being merely a piece of machinery, David Wilson is in fact an archliar.

Pudd'nhead Wilson uses many stock devices of comedy—a slave is freed, social order is restored, Wilson is apparently integrated into the society, villainy is unmasked, mistaken identities are recognized—but there is something very uncomedic about the ending. A slave is freed but another person is bound over and sold, and a closer look at the moral freedom of the first mocks the concept. When the morality of the social order is questionable to begin with, its restoration is of dubious value. (pp. 466-67)

The full tragic nature of the pudd'nhead's final position in the community can best be seen by considering the Judge's relation to Wilson. In a story dealing with dualities and twins, Wilson is a twin to the Judge. A hint of this can be gathered from the town's Society of Freethinkers: Wilson and the Judge are the only members. More obvious is Wilson's replacement of the Judge as chief citizen. The Judge's final role is the *pharmakos* or outcast who is ritually sacrificed to cleanse the community and to rebalance its morality. Wilson, of course, plays the role of the outcast from the beginning, but in his case the role is tragic since he *remains* a kind of sacrifice and outcast, even at the moment of his greatest triumph. (p. 468)

Wilson's status as permanent sacrifice is understandable through the absurd logic by which Tom is pardoned for murder and then sold down the river, a logic which turns a moral debt into a monetary one. . . . Only a mind tuned to irony and its aspect of self-mockery can get the complete joke because the laugh is on *everyone*. Wilson can be seen as being aware of this final turn of the screw if we accept the ironic vision of the aphorisms as his. Of course this perception forever separates Wilson from the rest of the community. When directed at him, the joke contains a further twist because he is now part of Dawson's Landing despite and because of his irony. His superiority puts him at the top, yet simultaneously shows him the moral worthlessness of that position, making him a continual sacrifice to the provincial mentality of Dawson's Landing.

In a sense Wilson has fooled himself. By exercising his independence, staying in Dawson's Landing, and becoming a success, he has lost the moral freedom he had enjoyed by being on the fringe of society. His ambition and superior capabilities have made him the chief citizen by the story's end; yet, with his participation in the enslavement of false Tom, Wilson has become more like the citizens of Dawson's Landing than he would care to admit. This is why he deserves the name of pudd'nhead. Everyone makes him or herself a moral pudd'nhead by compromising with the various lies society inevitably produces. The self-election of the townspeople to this "office" is plainly symbolic. Wilson's story is one of success in antebellum Southern society, but it moves towards a tragic dimension because he is aware of the loss sustained in achieving his success. . . . The final image of the story, then, is one which has been left out: Wilson's face etched with a grimace of silent self-mockery as he is serenaded.

That silence suggests a question: if Wilson sees the larger problems of Dawson's Landing, why doesn't he speak out? why doesn't he act? The answer is that Wilson already knows what Hank Morgan never learned: the attempt to effect moral reform often results in new evils, and it is best not to try, especially if one wants to be socially successful. Even if it is conceded that the pudd'nhead is not all pudd'nhead, the result is the same—status quo. The only channel open for Wilson's moral energy is the one he had all along, namely his aphoristic calendar, limited in its audience and limited by the invective

that occupies as much space as the satire. Nevertheless, it is the only place left for any kind of laughter. (pp. 468-70)

James E. Caron, "Pudd'nhead Wilson's Calendar: Tall Tales and a Tragic Figure," in Nineteenth-Century Fiction *(© 1982 by The Regents of the University of California; reprinted by permission of The Regents), Vol. 36, No. 4, March, 1982, pp. 452-70.*

JOHN SEELYE (essay date 1982)

[*Seelye is an American novelist whose most notable works include* The True Adventures of Huckleberry Finn, *a rewriting of Mark Twain's classic according to the preferences of modern critics, and the nonfictional* Prophetic Waters: The River in Early American Life and Literature. *Seelye has also published several critical studies on the works of Herman Melville, Booth Tarkington, Mark Twain, and other American literary figures. In this study of* Tom Sawyer, *Seelye examines the eternal boyhood of Twain's young hero.*]

[Because Tom Sawyer remains] a boy, we are inclined to shrug him off as a lesser creature, as an instance of arrested development, especially when he is compared to the much beloved Huck Finn. Yet it won't do to turn Tom Sawyer away with a shrug. He bears careful attention. Like Hamlet he deserves studying.

As Louis Rubin, Jr., long ago observed, the reputation of Mark Twain's first boys' book would be far greater had the author never written the sequel. . . . To judge the earlier novel with the canons of adult literature is unfair, for Mark Twain himself declared to William Dean Howells that it was "professedly and confessedly a boy's and girl's book"—at least by the time he had cut out all the "dirty" parts; and it should be evaluated on the author's terms. (p. 408)

Tom Sawyer is literally in charge of the plot, becoming an early example of the *auteur* principle. A prankster from the start, by the middle of the book he has mounted a huge hoax, a scenario which will bring the residents of St. Petersburg to the threshold of tragedy only to yank them back into comic relief and laughter. . . . As both a mischief-maker and an author of self-starring dramas Tom Sawyer is a subliminal projection of Sam Clemens, firmly rooted in obscure depths from which the book bearing his name draws considerable power. To dismiss the book as not being great adult literature may be easy, but few readers, of any age, can set *Tom Sawyer* aside once they start to read it.

By contrast *Huckleberry Finn* has a much slower and less intriguing development, in which a suspenseful plot is set aside for a leisurely episodic one. In both novels the influence of Charles Dickens is obvious, but the element of cliff-hanging gothicism is more nearly dominant in *Tom Sawyer*. . . . Like Dickens, Mark Twain had an undeniable skill at scaring the daylights out of us, and he was in this regard a man with a golden arm, to which were affixed a hand and fingers of sterling silver.

Mark Twain (again like Dickens) resorted for his effects to sometimes shabby tricks. . . . And yet, paradoxically, the staginess and the sleights-of-hand are engaging to children, who are willing to take their wonders where they find them; nor can we detach the theatrics from the melodrama which lends both books their special power. . . . [How] few are the books of children that have managed to endure beyond the decade in which they were written. *Tom Sawyer* is one of that select company, and the boy would appreciate the honor—no small accomplishment.

If in the marvelously flexible voice of Huck Finn there is abstracted the eternal innocence that was the romantics' notion of childhood, then in the shape of Tom Sawyer there is centered a darker, yet more vital force, the demonic power we associate also with Dickens. He expresses an urge that mingles love and hatred, creativity and destruction, energies identified with poltergeists and juvenile delinquents, an urge expressive of the midpoint between childhood and adolescence—puberty. (pp. 409-10)

In his old age Clemens as Mark Twain raged against Theodore Roosevelt for his imperialism and political theatricality, but when the old man in the white suit attacked the president for being a "fourteen-year-old" and a "show-off," he was more self-revealing than he knew. Mark Twain's Roosevelt was but Tom Sawyer grown older, and Tom Sawyer old was also Sam Clemens, on both a literal and figurative level. That demonic power of which I have spoken is in literature often expressed through melodrama, a genre dealing in the terrific opposition of emotional forces; and if Tom Sawyer's world is rife with the anxieties of puberty, it is also explosive with melodramatic encounters. Adolescent anxieties and volatile melodrama express the soul of the man who was known by his friends for his fits of rage and was called Youth by his wife. (p. 411)

[It] is *Tom Sawyer* which of all Mark Twain's books for children most resembles a play in its shape. This novel is so theatrical in form and mood that an apocryphal tradition exists that it was once framed as an actual drama.

First of all, where so many of Mark Twain's books, fiction or otherwise, are travel books, the adventures of Tom Sawyer take place near town, and all of the hero's excursions, whether to Jackson's Island or McDougal's Cave, eventually end with his return home. Consequently the action of *Tom Sawyer* has the conventional limits of a stage play. . . . As Dixon Wecter and others have shown us, *Tom Sawyer* is rich in autobiographical details—the matter of (and with) Hannibal—most of which are transformed only slightly to meet the exigencies of fiction. That those exigencies are nearly neoclassical in rigidity suggests one good reason why we should give *Tom Sawyer* a closer look.

The theatrical aspect of the novel is introduced in the opening pages. . . . At a critical point, as on the stage, Tom is dragged out of a closet, and by a clever boy's stratagem he escapes punishment. The first scene ends when Tom streaks over the backyard fence with the agility of a small animal, and he will be seen performing this trick several times in succeeding chapters, ending with his flashing vault over Judge Thatcher's fence after he has thrown a rock through the window whence came his shower of shops. The image of Tom scrambling repeatedly over a fence is a lovely bit of theater. . . . (pp. 412-13)

Much of what follows is likewise the stuff of theater, whether the comedy of grade-school graduation ceremonies or the sentimental set piece of Muff Potter's pathetic praise of his loyal little friends. (p. 413)

The original seed for this aspect of *Tom Sawyer* may be found in Mark Twain's notebook for 1866, a list of childhood superstitions recalled from his youth. . . . [Throughout the book,] childish games turn into often grim reality. Thus the repetition of superstitious matter leads directly to the first appearance of Injun Joe, whose murder of Dr. Robinson and false testimony

against Muff Potter will provide one of the chief threads if not the most important strand of the plot. Thenceforth the matter of childish superstitions is tied to the melodramatic stuff of dime novels—and melodramas, a darkening action providing counterpart to the sentimental love story centered by Becky Thatcher; these apparently disparate directions are finally joined by the climactic episode in McDougal's Cave.

Another strand is provided by Tom's penchant for playacting. . . . (p. 414)

What follows next is among the least satisfactory (though one of the most memorable) parts of the book, involving the torn frontispiece of Mr. Dobbins's anatomy book and ending with the extended parody of schoolhouse ceremonies. Containing sublimated sexuality that verges on the sadomasochism associated with Victorian pornography, it ends with a burlesque that quotes the turgid romantic prose Mark Twain associated not only with sentimentalism but with the feminine "literary" sensibility of his day. During this sequence Becky Thatcher is at her most unattractive, and the love between the two children is expressed by mean and hurtful tricks. That is, having been returned from the theatrical (and male) world of Tom's imagination to the domestic (female) world of St. Petersburg—from a zone of unrestrained boyhood to an erotic comedy of manners in which lies and deception characterize boy-girl relationships—we are brought very close to psychic depths beyond the sounding of children.

On the superficial (i.e. chivalric) level, Tom does the "right" and gallant thing, and takes Becky's whipping for her. The lovers are reconciled, and the schoolroom sequence closes with the comic ceremonies. But the series of adventures that follow are shared not by Tom and Becky but by Tom and Huck, a darkening melodrama haunted by the specter of Injun Joe much as the village theater is centered by the loving and tearful Aunt Polly. As it was on Jackson's Island, the bond being celebrated is the male one, a union which the drunken derelict Muff Potter blesses by his symbolic laying-on of hands through the bars of his cell window. . . . Reaching out through his bars, he is a symbol of "good" badness in restraint. . . . [The] action of the last part of the book is a symbolic extension of the world of pirates and Indians which Tom earlier established on Jackson's Island, a world made up entirely of boys and men. (pp. 415-16)

Dixon Wecter tells us that the original Injun Joe was a respectable member of the lower levels of Hannibal society, but Indians hoping for good press may count on little help from Mark Twain. From *Roughing It* onward, the American aborigine is presented as a subspecies of Yahoo, largely because Sam Clemens's own experience with Indians was limited to degenerate tribes in Nevada and California. (p. 416)

Injun Joe . . . is much more than a sexual menace: he is evil personified, who does bad things because he likes to. . . . Injun Joe is mostly a psychological presence, not a physical being. This is true of most of the characters in the book, who are known by a few symbolic properties—Aunt Polly's thimble or Becky's golden braids—or, most important, by their costumes. (p. 417)

What is most fascinating about Injun Joe, however, is not what repels but what attracts, for the boys are drawn to him, even as they are tensed to flee, by the outlaw's association with the fabulous treasure he has found. . . . On one part of the stage, as it were, the outlaws stumble upon the gold, while on another the boys, like frightened angels, witness the event unseen, an audience of two that has no desire to enter the action below, but that entertains a powerful wish to get hold of the gold. (p. 418)

In the cave episode . . . Mark Twain gives the complex mixture of terror and desire with which Injun Joe is associated yet another and deeper dimension, evoking age-old myths and plunging his young hero into shadows much darker than any summoned up on the stage. . . . It is a nightmare world focused by the lost children and haunted by the specter of Injun Joe, the pastoral yet tragic tale of the babes in the woods reset in a distinctly American yet universal scene, a limestone cave that evokes primordial caverns, measureless to man but all too familiar to children.

Walter Blair first pointed out that *Adventures of Tom Sawyer* is composed of different stories that take their separate narrative ways, often independent of one another. Like the distinct divisions between the various zones of Tom Sawyer's world, from Aunt Polly's parlor to the hidden chambers of the cave, these narratives may be seen as essentially disjunctive, and in terms of literary craft they are; but in the final episode of the novel Mark Twain manages to bring most of them together in a way that testifies to the unconscious artistry that was his greatest gift. . . . This climactic joining of strands results in a transcendent example of children's literature, which ends with the vastly satisfying discovery of the hidden gold, converting the nightmare of menace into a dream of wish-fulfillment.

Before going on to explore the depths of the cave episode, we must first put *Tom Sawyer* into context, the better to understand the implications of the story's conclusion. If *Tom Sawyer* is put in the shade by the book by Mark Twain that followed it, its shadowy aspect can be all the more appreciated by looking at the novels for boys written by other authors which preceded it, chief among them being Thomas Bailey Aldrich's *The Story of a Bad Boy* (1869). Aldrich's Tom Bailey (as the boy's name suggests) is like Tom Sawyer an autobiographical projection, and like Mark Twain's Tom he is a maker of ornate mischief, having a superabundance of natural energy which is pitted against the conformist rigidity of a New England village. P. T. Barnum in his *Autobiography* (1855) had portrayed his own Yankee youth in much the same light, and there is more than a touch of Barnum in Tom Bailey, who like Tom Sawyer is something of a showman, given (like Barnum) to staging elaborate hoaxes. (pp. 419-20)

We may, as does Walter Blair, list all the points *Tom Sawyer* shares with the boys' books already in circulation by 1876, but it is the difference that is most important, and the difference turns on the last chapters of the book. Tom Sawyer, having saved Judge Thatcher's daughter from a terrible fate, would have been rewarded by Horatio Alger with a modest position in the judge's law office. . . . But Tom's reward far exceeds that of most Alger heroes, for his share of the treasure, six thousand dollars, transforms him into a well-heeled citizen. (pp. 421-22)

Having promoted himself from rapscallion to rich boy, Tom does not have to assume the responsibilities normally attending the transformation from bad to good—quite the reverse. Instead he goes to work on his next theatrical production, converting the cave into a stage-set for his robbers' gang. . . . Though Mark Twain ends the book by promising a sequel in which he would portray his characters after they had grown up (an idea expressed in his earliest notes for the book that became *Tom Sawyer*), he never did carry out the promise, but went on to

further celebrations of Tom Sawyer as an unredeemable (as opposed to Huck Finn, the eternal) child.

Leslie Fiedler, who has defined for all time the Good Bad Boy, speaks (despite his habitual iconoclasm) for many other critics when he suggests that Judge Thatcher's prediction is correct, that Tom Sawyer "can only grow into goodness, *i.e.* success, for his 'badness' is his boyhood and he cannot leave one behind without abandoning the other." But my point reverses Fiedler's logic, for Tom does not grow up to be a judge or a soldier because he just doesn't grow up. Louis Rubin makes a similar point when he declares that Tom Sawyer was incapable of becoming (in T. S. Eliot's words) " 'an eminently respectable and conventional member' of 'conventional society.' " Yet Rubin grants Tom a measure of maturity by projecting an adulthood in which he becomes a writer—becomes, that is to say, Mark Twain.

I wish to take Rubin's logic one step further (or backward) and suggest that Tom Sawyer remains forever a boy, being the immaculate conception of a man who himself only imperfectly grew up. . . . Mark Twain, who spent much of his adult life trying to convince the world that he was as much a responsible businessman as an artist, created two boys who in quite different ways embody irresponsibility. . . . (pp. 422-23)

Set against the dominant myth of success as celebrated by Horatio Alger, the story of Tom Sawyer is clearly subversive. . . . (pp. 423-24)

Much as Tom himself can never settle for a humdrum life of work and wage, so his *Adventures* soon runs out of village materials, and both book and boy head for the familiar gothic graveyard and the forest beyond. . . . The connotations of woods and oak tree suggest that Tom is a pagan whose world is the wildwood beyond the boundaries of town, and the drama enacted deep down below seems part and parcel likewise of ancient adventures acting out even older mysteries. (pp. 424-25)

Tom Sawyer is never absorbed into the dominant culture . . . Tom's romantic "illusions" are often verified, as with his recovery of the treasure. . . . Only in the sequel does Tom become a victim of his illusions—in *his* adventures all dreams come true. Suspended between the worlds of nightmare and wish-fulfillment, *Adventures of Tom Sawyer* is a book of dreams—which is why it is preeminently a book for children.

Once again it is the gold that turns the trick. . . . Tom's flight brings him perilously close to Injun Joe also, with ultimately delightful results for himself and Huck. In the figure of the half-breed all mysteries converge, a coincidence that entails more than a convenience of plot. Up on Cardiff Hill Injun Joe is the conventional villain of melodrama, his evilness enhanced by his mixed blood, the half-breed being a miscegenetic type depicted in much nineteenth-century American literature as being inherently vicious. But down in the cave Injun Joe becomes something much deeper, a nightmare apparition associated with myth and fable. (pp. 426-27)

As ogre, then, he is the kind that is not slain but outwitted. . . . Tom Sawyer alone has the knowledge and the wit to find the gold. In effect he acts out an age-old plot, a "real" adventure in which he steals the treasure from the thief, thereby merging his heroics with the archetypes whose adventures supply the original stuff of the oldest children's stories, fairy tales that are fragments of ancient pagan myths.

Mark Twain makes a subtle point when he shows that Tom Sawyer, who cannot even under duress commit the simplest bit of Scripture to memory, has easily memorized the adventures of Robin Hood so he can play by the book. Playing by the book is Tom Sawyer's greatest game, one that will be reduced to two-dimensionality in *Adventures of Huckleberry Finn;* but in his own *Adventures* it is a guide to his essential character. Inside the village, whether in the schoolroom or parlor, he constantly resists playing by the rules. . . . But out in the forest, on the island, or eventually in the cave it is Tom who makes up the rules, and everyone must play by them. . . . In this light—the green light—Tom Sawyer can be seen, if only for a flickering moment, as a devotee of Pan. Even though Tom is driven to reducing his reading to rules, as rules they become a version of chivalric code, the kind associated not with knights but with outlaws, whose code is distinctly their own.

This merely reinforces the most important point of the book, which is that Tom Sawyer, unlike the good bad boys who precede him (whether T. B. Aldrich's Tom Bailey or Horatio Alger's Ragged Dick), remains unregenerate, forever committed to the world of play. Though celebrated as a hero by the town, he refuses to accept the terms of the final act in all hero stories, whether spun by ancient bards or by Sir Walter Scott. Having found the gold he should also get the girl; but Becky, like Joe Harper before her, drops from sight thenceforth, as the courtship ritual is converted to Tom's courting of Huck, male bonding certifying the essential subversiveness of the story. (pp. 427-28)

It is time therefore that we stop insisting that Tom Sawyer, boy and book, be other than what they are. . . . But do not expect him ever to change: like him or loathe him, he forever remains Tom Sawyer, rooted deep in waters dangerous to uninformed pilots, whether critics or merely readers who make the mistake of traveling upstream from *Adventures of Huckleberry Finn.* We may dismiss Tom Sawyer as a case of arrested development, but the novel that bears his name is not so easily put down; and where children are concerned, that is the truest test of literature. Not a few of us grownups, like Tom Sawyer (and Mark Twain), are unredeemed children in that regard too. (pp. 428-29)

> *John Seelye, "Introduction" (© 1982 by The University of the South; reprinted by permission of Viking Penguin, Inc.; originally published as "What's in a Name: Sounding the Depths of 'Tom Sawyer'," in The Sewanee Review, Vol. XC, No. 3, Summer, 1982), in The Adventures of Tom Sawyer by Mark Twain, Viking Penguin, to be published in 1984.*

ADDITIONAL BIBLIOGRAPHY

Blair, Walter. "When Was *Huckleberry Finn* Written?" *American Literature* XXX, No. 1 (March 1958): 1-25.
> Offers convincing evidence that *Huckleberry Finn* was written in three periods, during 1876, 1880, and 1883.

Brashear, Minnie M. *Mark Twain: Son of Missouri.* 1934. Reprint. New York: Russell & Russell, 1964, 294 p.
> Emphasizes the positive influence on Twain of eighteenth-century European literature and his childhood in Hannibal.

Brazil, John R. "Perception and Structure in Mark Twain's Art and Mind: *Life on the Mississippi.*" *The Mississippi Quarterly* XXXIV, No. 2 (Spring 1981): 91-112.
> Explains the difference between the "Old Times on the Mississippi" and the appended sections of *Life on the Mississippi* in

terms of Twain's struggle to find a common language that would reflect both his boyish romanticism and his mature practicality.

DeVoto, Bernard. *"Mark Twain's America"* and *"Mark Twain at Work."* Boston: Houghton Mifflin Co., 1967, 491 p.
> Combines two of DeVoto's important critical works in one volume. The first, written in response to Van Wyck Brooks's *The Ordeal of Mark Twain,* presents a portrait of American frontier life and humor of the mid-nineteenth century, showing this background to have been beneficial to Twain's development. The second book, written after scrutiny of Twain's manuscripts, examines the composition of *Tom Sawyer* and *Huckleberry Finn.* The last chapter outlines the personal tragedies that shaped Twain's final writings.

Fuller, Daniel J. "Mark Twain and Hamlin Garland: Contrarieties in Regionalism." *Mark Twain Journal* XVII, No. 1 (Winter 1973-74): 14-18.*
> A short study of the widely different uses made by Twain and Garland of their midwestern backgrounds.

Hill, Hamlin. *Mark Twain: God's Fool.* New York: Harper & Row, 1973, 308 p.
> Detailed biography of the last decade of Twain's life based on unpublished material from the papers of Mark Twain. Hill portrays Twain's last years as a tragedy of declining artistic powers and growing bitterness.

Jones, Alexander E. "Mark Twain and the Determinism of *What Is Man?*" *American Literature* XXIX, No. 1 (March 1957): 1-17.
> Traces Twain's evolving philosophy and its culmination in *What Is Man?* Jones finds the work to be Twain's gospel of hope rather than pessimism.

Jones, Howard Mumford. "The Pessimism of Mark Twain." In his *Belief and Disbelief in American Literature,* pp. 94-115. Chicago: University of Chicago Press, 1967.
> An explication of Twain's beliefs regarding the nature of God and humanity, finding Twain's pessimism representative of a late nineteenth-century trend in philosophy and religion.

Kaplan, Justin. *Mr. Clemens and Mark Twain: A Biography.* New York: Simon and Schuster, 1966, 424 p.
> A well researched biography, emphasizing conflicting aspects of Twain's personality.

Kipling, Rudyard. "An Interview with Mark Twain." In his *From Sea to Sea, Vol. II,* pp. 304-18. Leipzig: Bernhard Tauchnitz, 1900.
> A lively interview covering a wide variety of subjects.

Krause, Sydney J. "Twain's Method and Theory of Composition." *Modern Philology* LVI, No. 3 (February 1959): 167-77.
> A short study of Twain's seemingly haphazard techniques of composition, focusing on his practices of "spontaneous writing" and extensive revision.

Masters, Edgar Lee. *Mark Twain: A Portrait.* New York: Charles Scribner's Sons, 1938, 259 p.
> Assesses Twain's life and works.

Neider, Charles. *Mark Twain and the Russians: An Exchange of Views.* New York: Hill and Wang, 1960, 32 p.
> An exchange of letters between Neider and Russian journalist Y. Bereznitsky, the latter charging that Mark Twain's writings are subject to official suppression in the United States.

———. *Mark Twain.* New York: Horizon Press, 1967, 214 p.
> A collection of essays, many of which were originally introductions to various works of Mark Twain.

Paine, Albert Bigelow. *Mark Twain: A Biography; The Personal and Literary Life of Samuel Langhorne Clemens.* 4 vols. New York: Harper & Brothers Publishers, 1912.
> The authorized biography, containing much valuable material on Twain, though criticized by some scholars as idealized.

Rubin, Louis D., Jr. "*Tom Sawyer* and the Use of Novels." In his *The Curious Death of the Novel; Essays in American Literature,* pp. 88-99. Baton Rouge: Louisiana State University Press, 1967.

An examination of the literary components of *Tom Sawyer.* The book is used as a model for understanding the construction of novels.

Tenney, Thomas Asa. *Mark Twain: A Reference Guide.* Boston: G. K. Hall, 1977, 443 p.

Annotated bibliography which thoroughly covers criticism on Twain through 1976.

Trilling, Lionel. "*Huckleberry Finn.*" In his *The Liberal Imagination: Essays on Literature and Society,* pp. 104-17. New York: Viking Press, 1950.

An essay on *Huckleberry Finn,* examining, with acknowledgement to T. S. Eliot (see *TCLC,* Vol. 6), Huck as a servant of the brown river-god, the Mississippi.

Turner, Arlin. *Mark Twain and George W. Cable: The Record of a Literary Friendship.* East Lansing: Michigan State University Press, 1960, 141 p.

Contains the two writers' opinions of each other and of many other subjects, in letters written during their joint lecture tour of 1884-85.

Wagenknecht, Edward. *Mark Twain: The Man and His Work.* 3d rev. ed. Norman: University of Oklahoma Press, 1967, 302 p.

An essential biographical and critical study of Twain and his outlook, demonstrating extensive knowledge of Twain criticism through 1960, and including valuable footnotes and bibliographies.

Émile (Adolphe Gustave) Verhaeren

1855-1916

Belgian poet, dramatist, short story writer, and essayist.

Today considered the most important poet in Belgian literature, Verhaeren was especially venerated during his lifetime
for his energetic spirit, his lofty socialism, his lyrical tributes
to common folk, and for his open faith in scientific and industrial progress. Early in his poetic career he had passed
through a physical, mental, and spiritual crisis which resulted
in the collections *Les soirs*, *Les débâcles* (subtitled "moral
deformation"), and *Les flambeaux noirs*. While these contain
some of the darkest and most aberrant poetry of nineteenth-
century Decadence, Verhaeren emerged from this period with
the collection *Les apparus dans mes chemins*, which concludes
with the wholesome and joyful "Saint Georges" ("St. George"),
and he thereafter epitomized the literary celebrant of early
twentieth-century optimism. His poetry was translated
throughout the world and was especially admired in Russia,
Japan, and in Germany, the latter claiming Verhaeren as an
essentially Teutonic poet who by chance wrote in the "decadent" French language. However, after his death Verhaeren's
message of optimism did not have the same meaning for subsequent generations that it had for his own. His work is now
of interest more for its beautiful imagery and its exploitation
of the *vers libre* form than for its social enthusiasm.

Verhaeren was born in Saint-Armand, a Flemish town near
Antwerp. Like many Belgian writers, Verhaeren had a strong
Flemish cultural background but was conversant in only the
French language. His early education took place in Brussels,
and he later studied at the College Saint-Barbe, a Jesuit school
at Ghent. There he was a classmate of Maurice Maeterlinck
and Georges Rodenbach, who later became two of the most
renowned of the Belgian Symbolists. Leaving the College Saint-
Barbe, Verhaeren reluctantly went to work in his uncle's oil
factory for a short time before entering the University of Louvain to study law. At Louvain, Verhaeren became involved in
local literary circles and edited the little magazine *La semaine*.
Having attained his degree, he went into practice with a law
firm in Brussels. The head of this firm, Edmond Picard, was
also among the chief figures of the "Young Belgium" movement—a group of writers who generally favored Naturalism
in prose and Parnassianism in poetry, but whose central purpose was the establishment of a more sympathetic atmosphere
for literature and the arts in a society dominated by commercial interests. At the encouragement of Picard, Verhaeren began publishing his poems in *La jeune Belgique* and *L'art moderne*, and he helped found the journal *Societé nouvelle*. During
this time *Les flamandes*, Verhaeren's first collection, was published and gained considerable attention for what is regarded
as typically Flemish earthiness. After practicing law for a short
while, Verhaeren devoted himself wholly to literature and for
a number of years lived outside of Belgium, mostly in London.
At this time he also suffered his "crisis," during which the
poet rejected every emotional support, including his childhood
faith of Catholicism, and masochistically aggravated his already pained state of mind. Although the cause of the crisis
is not specified by his biographers, tentative explanations focus
on three possible origins of the trauma: loss of religious belief,

digestive ailments, and the general climate of late nineteenth-
century malaise abetted by recent translations of the works of
the pessimistic philosopher Arthur Schopenhauer. In the early
1890s Verhaeren's life became more stable; he returned to
Belgium, married, and began working for the cause of socialism. In the next two decades he produced what are judged
his greatest works: *Les campagnes hallucinées*, *Les villes tentaculaires*, *Les villages illusoires*, *Les forces tumultueses*, *La
multiple splendeur*, and *Les rythmes souverains*. Verhaeren became internationally famed as a singer of industrial progress.
During the First World War he chronicled the destruction of
the Belgian cities and countryside and wrote anti-German poems
and propaganda. Driven out of German-occupied Belgium,
Verhaeren died in a railway accident at Rouen, France.

Throughout Verhaeren's career his poetry went through a
number of phases distinguishable by their varying moods and
styles and at the same time unified by the poet's characteristic
intensity of expression and sincere devotion to the subject at
hand. In his first collection, *Les flamandes*, the "Flemish
women" of the title are an organizing symbol for a series of
lusty and picturesque views of Flemish life, a boisterous tableau of images that form a poetic counterpart to the paintings
of David Teniers and Pieter Brueghel. For his next collection,
Les moines, Verhaeren spent some time in a cloister to explore
the mystical aspect of what is commonly thought of as the

radically dual spirit of the Flemish, represented on the one hand by the Brueghelesque commotion of Ghent and on the other by the mist-shrouded silence of Bruges. Verhaeren wrote: "Mysticism and sensualism have formed and developed my being all my life. This double force has influenced both my life and art." The next three collections—*Les soirs, Les débâcles,* and *Les flambeaux noirs*—are a trilogy sharply demarcated among the poet's works as the product of his crisis years. The artistic result of Verhaeren's psychic upheaval was a group of nightmarish poems in which his suffering and derangement are pictured with the same startling vividness as the Flemish revels in *Les flamandes.*

While critics have praised Verhaeren's early collections for their determination and poetic genius, the postcrisis works are considered more typical of the Belgian author's spirit. Having broached the depths of introversion, Verhaeren now examined and celebrated the world outside of himself, especially its most humble characters and settings. In *Les campagnes hallucinées* and *Les villes tentaculaires,* the subject of the poet's songs is the charm and vigorous way of life of rural Belgium. While exalting in verse the physical joy and nobility of country folk, he also laments their exodus to the cities, which at this point are viewed as "tentacular" monstrosities depleting an ancient natural world. Later Verhaeren came to admire the power of urban industry and saw the technological advancement of cities as a unifying force in human life. *Les visages de la vie, Les forces tumultueses, La multiple splendeur,* and *Les rythmes souverains,* called Verhaeren's "most precious books" by Stefan Zweig in 1910 and universally accepted by the poet's admirers as his greatest works, are the most abandoned expression of this confidence in a future of social and scientific progress, a confidence approaching religious fervor. An anecdote tells how once, while riding in a train as it passed the smoke and flames of a factory complex, Verhaeren rushed to the windows, exclaiming: "How beautiful!" To an extent, World War I undermined Verhaeren's belief in the inevitability of a worldwide utopia conceived by science and fulfilled by industry. His later collections include a number of poems berating Germany for singlehandedly putting an end to humanity's dream.

In addition to his major poetry, Verhaeren also wrote several collections of love poems—*Les heures claires (The Sunlit Hours), Les heures d'après-midi (Afternoon), Les heures du soir (The Evening Hours)*—and four dramas: *Le Cloître (The Cloister), Les aubes (The Dawn), Philippe Deux (Philip II),* and *Hélène de Sparte (Helen of Sparta).* The latter works are considered unsuccessful excursions into theater by a fundamentally lyrical talent, more interesting as statements of Verhaeren's social ideology than as dramatic works. Verhaeren also wrote some works of short fiction, *Cinq récits (Five Tales),* which are moodpieces exemplary of the abundance of Gothic literature produced by Belgian authors. Despite his fiction and dramas, however, critics judge Verhaeren's genius to have been exclusively poetic, with his later collections bringing him popularity and contemporary critical acclaim. After the First World War, regard for Verhaeren's work declined, and his importance in world literature now derives from his long-held position as Belgium's greatest poet.

(See also *Contemporary Authors,* Vol. 109.)

PRINCIPAL WORKS

Les flamandes (poetry) 1883
Les moines (poetry) 1886

Les soirs (poetry) 1887
Les débâcles (poetry) 1888
Les flambeaux noirs (poetry) 1890
Les apparus dans mes chemins (poetry) 1891
Les campagnes hallucinées (poetry) 1893
Les villages illusoires (poetry) 1895
Les villes tentaculaires (poetry) 1895
Les heures claires (poetry) 1896
   [*The Sunlit Hours,* 1916]
Les aubes (drama) 1898
   [*The Dawn,* 1898]
Poems of Émile Verhaeren (poetry) 1899; also published as *Poems of Émile Verhaeren* [enlarged edition], 1915
Les visages de la vie (poetry) 1899
Le cloître (drama) 1900
   [*The Cloister,* 1915]
Philippe Deux (drama) 1901
   [*Philip II* published in *The Plays of Émile Verhaeren,* 1916]
Les forces tumultueses (poetry) 1902
Toute la Flandre. 5 vols. (poetry) 1904-11
Les heures d'après-midi (poetry) 1905
   [*Afternoon,* 1917]
La multiple splendeur (poetry) 1906
Les rythmes souverains (poetry) 1910
Les heures du soir (poetry) 1911
   [*The Evening Hours,* 1918]
Hélène de Sparte (drama) 1912
   [*Helen of Sparta* published in *The Plays of Émile Verhaeren,* 1916]
La Belgique sanglante (essays) 1915
   [*Belgium's Agony,* 1915]
Les ailes rouges de la guerre (poetry) 1916
The Plays of Emile Verhaeren [first publication] (dramas) 1916
The Love Poems (poetry) 1917
Oeuvres de Verhaeren. 9 vols. (poetry) 1919-33
Cinq récits (short stories) 1920
   [*Five Tales,* 1924]

Translated selections of Verhaeren's poetry have appeared in the following publications: *Six French Poets* and *Contemporary Belgium Poetry.*

STÉPHANE MALLARMÉ (letter date 1888)

[*Mallarmé was one of the leading poets and theorists of the Symbolist movement in French literature. Verhaeren's earlier poetry collections, to which Mallarmé refers in his 1888 letter below, are also those closest in spirit to Symbolism, sharing its traits of philosophical despair, hallucinatory imagery, extraordinary mental states, and verbal experimentation.*]

I am . . . interested in your handling of verse. No one has been more instrumental than yourself in establishing one of poetry's latest and most important conditions. Like a blacksmith, you take your verse from the forge of our time-honored language. You melt it down and give it any form you wish. Sometimes you stretch it out beyond its usual length at the end of a stanza—and even then it is still poetry. Let me congratulate you on that particular point. So it is that the poet disappears (this is without question the great discovery in modern poetry) and the verse itself projects its own passions through its leaps and bounds; its ecstasy lives alone through its own rhythms; and so verse is born, rather than being imposed or brutally thrust upon us by the writer. It all works out beautifully in this poetry of yours. A gleam here or there, a sudden surge of music, begin to create the poem and seem to linger in a hesitating line, like a forgotten sunset cloud. And there are other poems lashed by the torrents of their own storm, eternally, superbly, loudly renewed whenever we dream. . . .

> *Stéphane Mallarmé, in a letter to Émile Verhaeren on January 22, 1888, in his* Mallarmé: Selected Prose Poems, Essays, & Letters, *edited and translated by Bradford Cook (© 1956, The Johns Hopkins Press, Baltimore 18, Md.), The Johns Hopkins University Press, 1956, p. 101.*

RÉMY DE GOURMONT   (essay date 1896)

[*French poet, novelist, and philosopher, Gourmont was also among the leading contemporary critics of Symbolist authors. His* The Book of Masks, *from which the essay below has been excerpted, is one of the seminal studies of this literary and artistic movement.*]

Of all the poets of today, narcissi along the river, Verhaeren is the least obliging in allowing himself to be admired. He is rude, violent, unskillful. Busied for twenty years in forging a strange and magical tool, he remains in a mountain cavern, hammering the reddened irons, radiant in the fire's reflection, haloed with sparks. (p. 35)

If we discover his dwelling and question him, he replies with a parable whose every word seems scanned on the forge, and, to conclude, he delivers a tremendous blow of his heavy hammer.

When he is not laboring at his forge, he goes forth through the fields, head and arms bare, and the Flemish fields tell him secrets they have not yet told anyone. He beholds miraculous things and is not astonished at them. Singular beings pass before him, beings whom everybody jostles without being aware, visible alone to him. (pp. 35-6)

He has seen Death, and more than once; he has seen Fear; he has seen Silence. . . . (p. 36)

The characteristic word of Verhaeren's poetry is *halluciné*. The word leaps from page to page. An entire collection, the *Campagnes hallucinées* has not freed him from this obsession. Exorcism was not possible, for it is the nature and very essence of Verhaeren to be the hallucinated poet. "Sensations," Taine said, "are true hallucinations." But where does truth begin or end? Who shall dare circumscribe it? The poet, with no psychological scruples, wastes no time over troubling himself to divide hallucinations into truths or untruths. For him they are all true if they are sharp and strong, and he recounts them frankly—and when the recitation is made by Verhaeren, it is very lovely. (pp. 36-7)

With Verhaeren, beauty is made of novelty and strength. This poet is a strong man and, since those *Villes tentaculaires* which surged with the violence of a telluric upheaval, no one dares to deny him the state and glory of a great poet. Perhaps he has not yet quite finished the magic instrument which for twenty years he has been forging. Perhaps he is not yet master of his language. He is unequal; he lets his most beautiful pages grow heavy with inopportune epithets, and his finest poems become entangled in what was once called prosaism. Nevertheless, the impression of power and grandeur remains, and yes: he is a great poet. (pp. 37-8)

> *Rémy de Gourmont, "Verhaeren," in his* The Book of Masks, *translated by Jack Lewis (originally published in* Le livre des masques, Vol. I, 1896), J. W. Luce and Company, 1921 (and reprinted by Books for Libraries Press, 1967; distributed by Arno Press, Inc.), pp. 35-40.*

GEORG BRANDES   (essay date 1904)

[*Brandes was a Danish literary critic and biographer whose extensive writings on such authors as Henrik Ibsen, August Strindberg, and Søren Kierkegaard helped make their works better known outside of Scandinavia. He was one of the first critics to understand and encourage the innovative drama of Ibsen, and he virtually "discovered" Friedrich Nietzsche, providing the first serious critical attention that the German philosopher received. In his major critical work,* Main Currents in Nineteenth-Century Literature, *Brandes viewed French, German, and English literary movements as a series of reactions against eighteenth-century thought. Brandes said of himself that he was more than a critic but less than a philosopher. In a letter to him, Nietzsche called Brandes a "missionary of culture." This is perhaps the best definition of Brandes's function within literature. He possessed the ability to view literary movements and the individuals who contributed to those movements within the broader context of virtually all of nineteenth-century literature.*]

[Verhaeren's] first book of poems, *"Les Flamandes,"* depicted exuberant, joyous and substantial Flanders, with her farmsteads, public-houses and fairs; the women have the same luxuriant health as Rubens and Jordaens impart to them. As a pendant to this Flanders, in *"Les Moines"* he depicts pious Flanders, the Flanders of the Blessed Virgin, whose praises are sung by those who have renounced the world, the life of the cell, monastic dreams, the quiet life by rule that is passed in prayer, divine service and ecclesiastical pageants; the Flanders that Memling recorded for posterity. (p. 812)

Though Verhaeren's verse, in his first books, still exhibits the strict regularity of rhythm and rhyme of earlier French poetry, he has by degrees thrown off every obligation of metre, frequently making use of similar sounds instead of rhyme, and he is always satisifed to rhyme for the ear, irrespective of orthography. It is a fact that should be highly appreciated that he nevertheless obtains extraordinary effects of sound in his treatment of language, a powerful, virile euphony, always sonorous, occasionally harsh. His dramas are written in this verse, interspersed now and again with speeches in rhythmic prose.

In his drama, *"Le Cloître"* . . . , he reverts to his early theme, monastic life, but here it is interpreted in another spirit. The strongest and wildest passion finds expression in this piece, and the most varied types of monks are represented with masterly firmness and assurance. There is something grand about the theme. We perceive from the first, in the monastery into which we are introduced, only the varied ambitions, piety, mutual ill-will and rivalry of the monks. (p. 813)

Between 1893 and 1898 Emile Verhaeren wrote a trilogy, the subject of which was one that touched him, a child of the country, closely, and that he had for a long time taken very much to heart, namely, the fatal absorption of the inhabitants of the country by the town, which, in his native land, had gradually caused the country to grow desolate and the villages deserted. . . .

The last link in his trilogy, the drama called *"The Dawn" (Les Aubes),* is perhaps the most remarkable and important work that he has yet produced. . . .

The scene of action is outside the domain of historical reality, as is always the case in Verhaeren's writings. There is a war; a hostile army approaches the huge town of Oppidomagne, driving the fugitives from the burning villages before it towards the capital. We make acquaintance with various sections of the population, the swarm of beggars and the fugitive, embittered peasants. We are prepared for the coming of a man whom everyone is thinking of and talking about, Jacques Hérénien, the great popular tribune, who wishes to bring the body of his father, an old peasant, to the cemetery in the town. He comes, and we get some impression of the enormous esteem in which he is held. (p. 814)

Years after reading this play for the first time, a recollection of something striking remains, but, singularly enough, you forget the particulars. You retain the memory of Hérénien's personality in indistinct outline, and without any definite impression of his characteristics. This may certainly be laid partially to Verhaeren's charge.

Everything here stands and falls with the personality of the tribune and the impression of greatness he is able to impart. Verhaeren found himself face to face with the problem ever present in poetry: How is the impression of greatness to be produced? It is done most simply and easily through the importance attributed by others to an individual, their respectful, enthusiastic and affectionate behavior towards him, or, on the other hand, their envy, hatred and malice; in the second place, through their blunt declarations of his worth. Then, finally— and this is of course the main thing—by his own words and actions. Now Hérénien speaks in a manly and enthusiastic style; we perceive his power over other men's minds; everything he says has a lyrically rhetorical swing; but the stamp of greatness is undeniably somewhat effaced. Voltaire, who had disciples in the armies of France's enemies, was very much more simple. Frederick II of Prussia, who had admirers in the armies of his enemies, was very much more blunt. Even Gambetta, whose influence was greatest as an orator, was not so serious all the time.

One feels in this drama that Verhaeren has fought for political, no less than for artistic, freedom; in 1892 he was working with Eekhoud and Vandervelde in Brussels for the development of the House of Representatives, he established an Art Department, and went in eagerly for the cause of popular education. For him, as for many another man of the day, the great man is he who can make the idea of peace an established fact. The difficulty of utilizing the hero of the peace drama dramatically, however, lies in the difficulty of individualizing that idea. There has only been one man in our own day who has shown genius and new tactics in this direction, Jean de Bloch the Pole, who attempted to combat war financially; but his originality was not of the sort adapted to the character of the popular tribune or a hero of tragedy. Nevertheless it was in the elaboration of the tribune's personality that Verhaeren should have fought his chief battle. But, being in his heart of hearts a lyrist, he did not take sufficient pains over it, and although *"Les Aubes"* is certainly one of the most remarkable dramatic works of our day, it has not become the redeeming word that a masterpiece is. (p. 815)

> *Georg Brandes, "Emile Verhaeren As a Dramatist,"* in The Living Age *(copyright 1904, by the Living Age Co.), Vol. CCXLII, No. 3142, September 24, 1904, pp. 812-15.*

STEFAN ZWEIG (essay date 1910)

[*As a critic, Zweig is best known for his studies of Honoré de Balzac, Charles Dickens, Fedor Dostoyevski, and Friedrich Nietzsche. His critical study of Verhaeren, from which the following excerpt on the later poetry collections has been taken, was the first major examination of the Belgian poet's life and works, and it is indicative of his renown among German readers and critics.*]

Verhaeren's work was in his youth and prime a flame exceedingly hot, lawless, free, and flaring like the very years of his youth and prime. Now, however, in the work of his fifties, now that passion has cooled, the yearning is revealed to find the goal of this passion, the inherent lawfulness of this unrest. (p. 179)

This transition from youth to age is in Verhaeren, to use Nietzsche's phrase, a transition from the Dionysiac to the Apollinarian, from a plethora to harmony. His yearning is now *vivre ardent et clair*, to live passionately, but at the same time clearly to preserve his inner fire, but at the same time to lose his unrest. Verhaeren's books in these years grow more and more crystalline; the fire in them no longer blazes openly like a flaring pyre, but glitters and sparkles as with the thousand facets of a precious stone. The smoke and the unrest of the fire die down, and now the pure residues are clarified. Visions have become ideas, the wrestling earthly energies are now eternal immutable laws.

The will of these last years, of these last works, is the will to realise a cosmic poem. In the trilogy of the cities Verhaeren had laid hold on the universe as it lies around us to-day; he had snatched it to him and overcome it. In passionate visions he had shaped its image, achieved its form, and now it stood beside the actual world as his own. But a poet who would create the whole world for himself, the whole infinite vista of its possibilities by the side of its actualities, must give it everything: not only its form, not only its face, but its soul as well, its organism, its origin, and its evolution. He must not merely apprehend its pictorial aspect and its mechanical energy, he must give it an encyclopaedic form. He must create a mythology for it, a new morality, a new history, a new system of dynamics, a new system of ethics. Above it or in it he must place a God who acts and transforms. He must fashion it in his poetry not only as something that is, not only as something in the present, but as something that has been and is becoming, something that is part and parcel of the past and of the future too. It must ring out the old and ring in the new. And this will to create a cosmic poem is to be found in Verhaeren's new and most precious books—*Les Visages de la Vie, Les Forces Tumultueuses, La Multiple Splendeur, Les Rythmes Souverains*—books which by their mere title announce the effort to include the dome of heaven in their vast embrace. They are the pillars of a mighty structure, the great stanzas of the cosmic poem. They are no longer a conversation of the poet with himself and contemporary feeling; they are a pronouncement addressed to all the ages. *S'élancer vers l'avenir* is the longing they express: a turning away from all the pasts to speak to the future. The lyric element in them steps beyond the boundary-line of poetry. It kindles the neighbouring domains of philosophy and religion, kindles them to new possibilities. For not only aesthetically would Verhaeren come to an understanding with realities; not by poetry only would he overcome the new possibilities; he would fain master them morally and religiously as well. The task of these last and most important books of verse is no longer to apprehend the universe in individual phenomena, but to impress its new form on a new law. In *Les Visages de la Vie* Verhaeren has in individual poems glorified the eternal forces, gentleness, joy, strength, activity, enthusiasm; in *Les Forces Tumultueuses* the mysterious dynamics of union shining through all forms of the real; in *La Multiple Splendeur* the ethics of admiration, the joyous relationship of man with things and with himself; and in *Les Rythmes Souverains* he has celebrated the most illustrious heroes of his ideals. For life has long since ceased to be for him mere gazing and contemplation. . . . (pp. 181-83)

Description, poetic analysis, has gradually grown into a hymn, into 'laudi del cielo, del mare, del mondo,' into songs of the whole world and of the ego, and of the harmony of the world's beauty in its union with the ego. The lyrical has here become cosmic feeling, knowledge has become ecstasy. Over and above the knowledge that there cannot be anything isolated, that everything is arranged and obeys the last uniform law of the universe, over and above this knowledge rises something still higher—over the contemplation of the world rises faith in the feeling of the world. The glorious optimism of these works ends in the religious confidence that all contrasts will be harmonised; that man will more and more be conscious of the earth; that every individual must discover his own law of the world in himself, the law that makes it possible for him to apprehend everything lyrically, with enthusiasm, with joy.

Here Verhaeren's poetry far exceeds the boundary-line of literature; it becomes philosophy and it becomes religion. Verhaeren was from the very first an eminently religious man. In his childhood Catholicism was the deepest feeling of his life, but this Catholicism had perished in the crises of his adolescence, his religious feeling had given way to the rapt contemplation of all new things, to ecstasy inspired by the aspect of life. But now, when Verhaeren returns to the metaphysical, the old yearning is reawakened. The old gods are dead for him; Pan is dead, and Christ too. Now he feels the need of finding a new faith, a new certainty, a new God for the new sensation, this identity of I and world. The new conflicts have created a longing in him for a new equilibrium; his stormily religious feeling, determined to believe, needs new cognition. The image of the world would be incomplete without the God who rules it. All his yearning goes out to this God, and it finds its fulfilment. And this knowledge gives him the highest joy life can have, the loftiest pride life can bestow. . . . (pp. 183-85)

To chisel this new face of God is the aim of his last and most mature works, in which the obstinate 'no' of his youth has become the loud exulting 'yes' of life, in which the great possibilities of old have become an unsuspected opulent reality. (p. 185)

The artist is responsible for his talent, because it is his task to express it. Now the higher the idea of art is understood, the more art feels its task to be the task of bringing the life of the universe into harmony, so much the more must the feeling of responsibility be intensified in a creative mind.

Now, of all the poets of our day Verhaeren is the one who has felt this feeling of responsibility most strongly. To write poetry is for him to express not himself only, but the striving and straining of the whole period as well, the fearful torment and the happiness that are in the birth of the new things. Just because his work comprises all the present and aims at expressing it in its entity, he feels himself responsible for the future. For him a true poet must visualise the whole psychic care of his time. For when later generations—in the same manner as they will question monuments concerning our art, pictures concerning our painters, social forms concerning our philosophers—ask of the verses and the works of our contemporaries the question, What was your hope, your feeling, the sum of your interpretation? how did you feel cities and men, things and gods?—shall we be able to answer them? This is the inner question of Verhaeren's artistic responsibility. *And this feeling of responsibility has made his work great.* Most of the poets of our day have been unconcerned with reality. Some of them strike up a dancing measure, rouse and amuse people lounging in theatres; others again tell of their own sorrow, ask for pity and compassion, they who have never felt for others. Verhaeren, however, heedless of the approval or disapproval of our time, turns his face towards the generations to be. . . . (pp. 254-55)

It was, in the last instance, this magnificent feeling of responsibility which did not permit him to pass by any manifestation of our present time without observing and appreciating it, for he knows that later generations will ask the question how we sensed the new thing, which to them is a possession and a matter of course, when it was still strange and almost hostile. His work is the answer. The true poet of to-day, in Verhaeren's eyes, must show forth the torment and the trouble of the whole psychic transition, the painful discovery of the new beauty in the new things, the revolt, the crisis, the struggles it costs to understand all this, to adapt ourselves to it, and in the end to love it. Verhaeren has attempted to express our whole time in its earthly, its material, its psychic form. His verses lyrically represent Europe at the turning of the century, us and our time; they consciously contemplate the whole circuit of the things of life: *they write a lyric encyclopaedia of our time, the intellectual atmosphere of Europe at the turning of the twentieth century.* (pp. 255-56)

Stefan Zweig, in his Émile Verhaeren, *translated by Jethro Bithell (Reprinted by permission of Houghton Mifflin Company. Originally published as* Émile Verhaeren, *1910), Houghton Mifflin, 1914, 274 p.*

FEDERICO OLIVERO   (essay date 1914)

[*Olivero examines the collections written during Verhaeren's crisis period.*]

[The poems of *Les Soirs, Les Débacles,* and *Les Flambeaux noirs*] were written during that period of the Romantic movement, when the poetical current, not only in France but also in the neighboring countries, was dividing into two streams, one of which continued the traditional course, while the other swerved aside and went rambling through the forest of Allegory and Mystery. What gives Verhaeren's lyrics their peculiar character is the combination of Hugo's and Lamartine's style with the philosophical thought of Laforgue and the symbolic *précieusités* of Verlaine and Mallarmé. Having revived the impassioned fervor and the mystic melancholy of *Les Feuilles D'Automne* and *Les Harmonies Poétiques* in *Les Flamandes* and *Les Moines,* the Poet suffered from perplexity in composing some poems afterwards published in *Les Bords de la Route;* but there was a new strain in his soul and he began to record with a forcible style a set of original, wild, deep impressions. *Les Soirs* are essentially a mirror of the utter dejection and hopeless gloom of his spirit; *Les Débacles* reveal the disease of his soul, and *Les Flambeaux noirs* show us the symbols of a darkened mind, the last stage of his spiritual illness.

In *Les Soirs* he limits himself to sing the tragic splendor of sunsets, the desolate grandeur of midnight skies; his poetical world does not seem to know either the balmy freshness of dawn or the golden radiance of noon; the blood-red flare of a perpetual afterglow broods over the horizon of his dismal dreamland. The lonely marshes—their rotting waters glittering with metallic iridescence through bristling tufts of rushes—reflect, as a broken mirror, the sinister glare of the dying sun; no breath of life is blowing upon this wilderness, no breeze wrinkles the imprisoned river, stretching far in scattered pools to a sky of greenish vapors and dazzling crimson clouds. (p. 63)

It is not the sweet and strange twilight of Verlaine; it is the grim closing of night, when drear bars of red light linger in the darkening West. Sometimes it is a silent, ice-bound landscape,—the Realm of Death,—where iron cliffs raise, from the snow-fields, their sharp peaks to a sky glistening with the everlasting, fiery eyes of stars,—a sky symbolizing Eternity. To intensify the luminous atmosphere of his pictures, to infuse the dream of intense light haunting his soul into his descriptions,—which appear to him always too pale to represent exactly his visions,—he accumulates gold and scarlet and purple with an effect of fantastic gorgeousness, wrapping in a golden radiance his fairy islands. . . . He lavishes the richest colors of his palette in his endeavor to paint the emblems of his ardent and wild soul, the smouldering ruins of his heroic ideals, the sunset of his hope, as Baudelaire did trying to portray the changing hues of his tragic hallucinations. . . . As some contemporary artists, with whom he shares the tendency to deal with *macabre* subjects, as Odilon Redon and Henri de Groux, he likes violent contrasts of light and shadow,—tumultuous fights between gloomy clouds and sunbeams piercing as fiery swords the monsters of dark vapors,—oceans, all pitch-black chasms and glittering amber foam,—cyclopean towns of ebony and gold. We do not perceive any delicate penumbra, any transparent shade in his pictures; they are like dusky frescoes on which dazzling spots of colored light would be dancing and playing, as when the crimson shafts of the setting sun are sifted through wind-tossed trees. And from these murky lands, from these blazing horizons, strange sounds arise, long reverberating in his soul: magic, alluring songs of wizards and sibyls, shouts of mad terror, the clamor of routed armies, the crash of burning towers, the echo of clanging bells, voices of agony and distress, the cry of suffering nature. (pp. 64-5)

His mind is haunted by funereal images; night is to him the vault where are lying the unknown heroes who died on their lonely roads to glorious goals,—the stars burning around the gigantic catafalque as glimmering tapers in the mournful gloom. Nature shows him only symbols of universal death; the moon—a maiden wan in her golden coffin—is brought down the ebony staircase of black clouds to the tomb waiting for her in the depths of a dismal lagoon. And his own face, his haggard, careworn countenance, does it not look as the sepulchre of his blighted hopes, of his sumptuous dreams all turned to dust? Autumn is to him no time of slow and melancholy decay, but a bright outburst of life, the supreme and fullest bloom of the Rose of Nature, the apotheosis of the magnificent forces ruling the world, and yet the dominion of an imperial, solemn Form, whose head is crowned with the ruby studded diadem of Death. (pp. 65-6)

When Verhaeren has to express his essential emotions—a hopeless sadness, a wild sorrow—he has only to draw upon a large treasure of images accumulated during his long hours of solitary and intense contemplation; and the outcome of the mystic wedding of his soul with the external world is a morbid and deep poetry of nature, his mournful ideas pervading all things with a strange, vehement life, his peculiar feelings casting on the landscape a lurid shadow, where no sense of joy, not even a sweet melancholy, can survive. The trees, in their mantles of dusty gold, seem to go as weary pilgrims towards a never approaching goal, on the plains lying dead under the autumnal clouds hanging motionless in a leaden sky;—the woods, when the blast is not wringing their gnarled boughs, shudder with the terror of eternal pain,—the cliffs raise their impotent wrath, their dumb despair, to the sunset glowing with a bitter, vain passion; and no one shall know the mystery of the tortured stones, and no one shall tell when an unseen hand will close the lids of the stars' diamond eyes. . . .

When, like a sad Narcissus sitting on the bank of a weird pool, he explores his pale reflection in the dark mirror of Nature, he only perceives the dizziness of terror in his look, the bitter smile of despair on his lips. Even the gorgeous blossoming of a garden in spring-time is to him but a symbol of the vain magnificence of his dreams, of his fruitless effort, of his ineffectual yearning towards happiness, and also of his solitary and proud disdain. Beauty is dying, lonely, forsaken, along the gleaming alleys; no hand plucks the fine flowers, their perfumes vanish on the incense-laden breeze, their chalices burst open as caskets of jewels only to reflect the purple of the desolate evening. (p. 67)

In the last part of this lyrical trilogy the darkness is deepening; the images taken directly from nature yield the place to sinister, quaint emblems wrought by the poet's mind, the mystic voices of things are hushed by the obscure warning of destiny. The artist is startled by ghastly visions, born in the fever of his brain and intertwined in bizarre arabesques; his spirit is lost in a maze of idle reasonings, in a labyrinth of contradictory arguments; the dead silence of his soul is broken by fitful whispers of dark forebodings; only the queer flowers of insanity glimmer here and there in the spiritual night. As in the sickly psychological conditions analyzed by Poe in *Ulalume* and *Berenice,* where mean, insignificant objects acquire a symbolic value, a deep and wide meaning, in his diseased soul everything becomes the mystic token of unseen presences, assuming a strange and great significance. His anguish changes into a torturing doubt, into a wild rush of his thoughts for certainty, for light and truth; his sadness rises to anger and despair, to the maddening dread of a child lost in a gloomy forest, to the wrath of a blindman trying to escape from a house on fire, until his reason breaks under the strain and dies in the hopeless struggle. (pp. 68-9)

The atmosphere of his dreams is heavy, stifling as the blue, poisonous air of Maeterlinck's *Serres chaudes;* his spell-bound visionary soul has no power to disentangle herself from the net of beautiful, horrid and incoherent images, subtly woven by a black magic. Baudelaire's influence is to be detected in the dark melancholy of his general tone, but especially in the dreadful phantoms hovering above that *Mare Tenebrarum* in which his soul is drowning; in *Heures mornes, Le Depart, Un Soir,* he leads us to a land of darkness and horror, suddenly lit up by red flashes of lightning, by glaring crimson stars, by a flaring torch, the dusky, limitless, desolate land, once visited by Baudelaire and De Quincey in their opium trances; the lines of the French poet, . . .

> On the background of my nights the finger of
> all-knowing God
> Draws, without respite, a many-shaped
> nightmare.

are the keynote of several eerie poems contained in **Les Débacles** and **Les Flambeaux noirs.** Bloody idols of ebony and gold rise on pedestals of basalt in the blazing twilight; idols of black marble stare at him in moonlit caves, the gleam of fateful stars in their eyes of precious stones, which have the fascination of Medusa's baleful look. Satanic guiles embodied in ghastly forms, they allure his soul with their wicked irresistible smile; they descry his inmost thoughts; they drag him to unsufferable torments; a cruel serenity sits on their foreheads, the serenity of inexorable destiny. (p. 70)

Vainly he has endeavoured to wring their mystery, their secret, out of the mouths forever dumb; vainly he has questioned the awful figures, whose enigmatic, unfathomable eyes glitter as phosphoric jewels in the gloom. Among these terrible forms of *Welt-schmerz,* all that man has done goaded either by necessity or by the desire to increase the amount of joy allotted to him, appears to the poet aimless and vain. Both the crumbling hamlet, so utterly sad and forlorn in the gathering night, when the last songs are dying, monotonous and tragic, on the lonely roads,—and the monstrous town, where the streets, swarming with haggard, weary people, twist and writhe as snakes around the harbors and docks and the grimy, resonant walls of huge workshops, the big city wrapped in yellow fogs, where mankind, withered and wizened, bows to the lust of gain, to the hideous golden idol,—both these manifestations of human labor seem to the poet symbols of a useless fight against the iron laws of an inflexible destiny. (p. 72)

In his first poems he had sung the undaunted power of his race, Artevelde and the Flemish heroes, the wild beauty of mediaeval times, of ages of war and freedom; he had descended into the forgotten tombs of the kinds of old, and, descrying among the royal dust the ruby ring and the jewelled helmet, had exalted the renown of his native country. (p. 73)

But, afterwards, he shut out of his mind the dream of ancient glory, and having turned his look to modern times he felt with keen grief the loss of any noble ideal, he was struck with pity and disgust at the sight of the ghostly throng without confidence in life, without fervor, without hope.

And now, analyzing his own soul, he discerned his spiritual ruin; since the enjoyment of life,—a mirage of opal and gold, held, glistening and enticing, before our fascinated eyes by the wicked sorcerer, the World,—is mere vanity, a sullen pessimism rules with unrestrained sway over his mind. Nevertheless, though he is aware of the bitter deception lurking under the brilliant illusion, he also knows that he will not be able to dispel his eager longing for joy, his yearning towards bliss, his unquenchable thirst for happiness; and he tries to love his desires in spite of their treachery, conscious that these aspirations are life itself. (pp. 73-4)

Besides he knows that he is not fit for the deadly battle which is fought in the world uninterruptedly, without truce, and from his tower of pride he looks in somber dejection on the triumphal pagentry of life. In these hours of despondency his soul is sometimes stirred by mystic, vehement aspirations towards the Absolute, the Eternal. He had before, in **Les Moines,** clearly expressed these tendencies; he was then leading us through a blessed land of peaceful joy, through holy gardens where the lilies of chastity emerge from the brambles of pain, where the apparitions of dreaming angels illuminate, as a divine sunrise, the woods and the golden shores of the ideal country. (p. 74)

He had contemplated in cloisters built among black desolate mountains the ascetic faces, the pure, azure eyes looking at him under the wimple of the hood; in the still atmosphere of lonely valleys, of untrodden meadows, he had heard the whisper of lilies growing in the religious silence. Then the Gothic cathedrals, lit by the glow of barbaric jewels, by the sumptuous light filtered through the stained-glass windows,—slender and bright as a figure painted by a Flemish Primitive, through which the soul burns visibly,—had shone in his rapturous spirit. But now this background of blazing gems is dimmed by the dark ghosts of remorse; there is in him an ardent desire for renunciation, a wild love of suffering; from the swamps of Despair his mind soars on untiring wings to the sapphire sky of Hope; he would like to quench his burning fever, to still the violent throbbing of his impassioned heart among the stone flowers of austere crypts, in the solemn, immense shadow of gloomy churches, where only a crucifix gleams under the violet beam alighting on it from the dusky rose-window. (pp. 75-6)

The style he adopts to represent his wildest moods, his hard struggles against the all-prevading gloom, the fight in his soul between the ideal and the lowest instincts, between *l'Ange et la Bête,* recalls Baudelaire's rough power of images; thus in **Eperdument** and in some strophes of **Les Débacles** we perceive the influence of *Les Fleurs du Mal* in the violent chiaroscuro, in the flowing rhythm, in the sincerity and energy of the form. But, as regards the inmost spirit of Verhaeren's poetry, the French poet breathes a mystic life into his lines, when his nostalgic soul remembers the everlasting bowers of light, the celestial flowers she lay among. Elsewhere these fierce emotions yield to a softer mood; and the sweet, passionate tenderness of *Sagesse* strikes us in a deeper way, coming, as it does, after tumultuous discords of anguish and smarting pain. Verhaeren's poetic utterance feels also the influence of Hugo's magniloquent, bombastic diction; the harmony of his verse is now and then marred by a tendency to a rhetoric declamatory style; he shouts instead of singing. The jarring impression derived from his accumulations of loud consonantal sounds, clashing with a sharp clang in his tormented form is indeed sought by the artist trying to convey and faithfully reflect the turmoil of his exasperated feelings, of his deep emotions; strongly personal are the accords of a note, very often the sounds *oir, or, ent,* struck at the beginning of a poem, with the subsequent sounds, thus creating a solemn melody, as a plain-chant, which goes on in beautiful modulations throughout the lyric. The poet is fond of dwelling on a particular idea, on a unique musical effect; consequently repetitions of single words and phrases are often employed, and a rhyme is frequently accompanied by a long train of resonances; this bent of his technique culminates in the use of the refrain.

The influence of J. K. Huysmans may also be noted, either regarding the mystic side of Verhaeren's poetry or his evocations of the grand, painful effort of mankind, of the struggle going on in the whirlpool of the big industrial towns; in *A Rebours* we find the portrait of a soul, the analysis of a psychological condition showing striking analogies with our poet's spiritual state. . . . (pp. 76-8)

Les Flamandes and **Les Moines** are written in quatrains and sonnets, the influence of the Parnasse school being still clearly visible in the treatment of these metrical forms; but it is in the *vers libre* that Verhaeren's art shows itself at its best, and to this free arrangement of the lines, so particularly dear to the symbolists, he will stick in his later poems. Several among the lyrics of **Les Débacles** are written in this way, the most suitable to the rush and fervor of the poet's fiery inspiration. He also uses distichs, triplets and quatrains; when the strophes of four lines cannot contain all his ideas, and the frequent stops would break the tumultuous flow of his thought, he links the quatrains together, thus forming a long stanza of sometimes a score of lines. Conversely, when the intellectual impulse is too slight to fill a long strophe he resorts to the narrower limits of the distichs and triplets, occasionally binding them together with a refrain.

With this lyrical trilogy the poet has first given us a complete image of his true self, of the personality, which we only get glimpses of in *Les Flamandes* and *Les Moines*. Here at last he passes the boundaries of the magic circle traced around him by the combined influences of old and of contemporary artists, and enters his own ground, where he can build a fit dwelling for his soul, a somber and powerful work of art, a palace sad with the gloom of Romanic crypts and barbaric fantastic carvings, mystic with the high soaring of slender Gothic columns and aërial arches. (p. 80)

> *Federico Olivero, "Émile Verhaeren's Lyrical Trilogy: 'Les Soirs,' 'Les Débacles,' 'Les Flambeaux noirs',"* in Poet Lore *(copyright, 1914, by Poet Lore, Inc.; reprinted by permission of Heldref Publications, a publication of the Helen Dwight Reid Educational Foundation), Vol. XXV, No. 1, Winter, 1914, pp. 63-80.*

JETHRO BITHELL   (essay date 1915)

[*In his anthologies of Belgian poetry from both Flemish and French-language authors, Bithell supplied English readers with what is still the most extensive profile of that country's literature. Likewise, Bithell's* Contemporary Belgian Literature, *from which the following survey of Verhaeren's works has been excerpted, remains the most comprehensive study of this subject.*]

[*Les Flamandes*] was hailed with abuse (one critic said the young poet had "burst like an abscess," and another called him the "Raphael of dirt"), but—it was hailed, and henceforth Verhaeren had a name.

Verhaeren himself has in his riper years more or less disowned this first book of his. He is wrong; and those critics of his are wrong who regard it as a mere collection of *juvenilia*. It has faults; but they are only the faults of unrestraint, and there is unrestraint in Verhaeren's ripest work. The poems are packed with vigour—in Verhaeren's own language they are gorged with sap, they are explosions of energy. The only question for the critic is whether they are not too pictorial. But *Les Flamandes* is not more a succession of pictures than many another Flemish book which is praised as such. Verhaeren's idea at the time he wrote it was to produce in verse exactly such pictures as Teniers, Jordaens, and other Flemish artists had produced on canvas, in other words, genre pictures. (pp. 119-20)

Verhaeren was . . . unconsciously occupied by the idea of the superman; only, instead of placing the superman in the future, he found him in the past. The old Flemish artists were supermen, because they were such tremendous eaters and drinkers, because they created masterpieces between two drinking-bouts. (The idea is naïve; but Verhaeren, it may be said at once, is essentially naïve.) Apart from the idea, however, the poems are rich with the very thing that makes a poem—with the something we have no word for and which the Germans call *Stimmung*. There is a mood of the greatest artistic refinement in some of the poems (*L'Abreuvoir*, for instance—a picture of cattle being watered at sunset), and even where the diction is

coarse to the last limit of decency there is a brazen strength in the raw images which lifts the poem above vulgarity. (pp. 120-21)

There is not a trace of coarseness in *Les Moines*. . . . Here the exaltation is ascetic. After the "explosion of life" that *Les Flamandes* had been for Verhaeren, a reaction had come. Not exactly a religious reaction (the faith of his fathers had gone for ever), but a return to the romance of the ritual, to the symbols of mystic fervour.

In *Les Moines* actual experiences of monastery life are drawn upon: the poet has spent three weeks in the monastery of Forges, near Chimay. He shared the life of the monks, and it was hoped in the monastery itself that he would remain. But all the evidence available shows that Verhaeren, having collected his stock of impressions, was very glad to get away to more substantial fare than the monks' table afforded; and there is further evidence that he made up for lost feasts by very copious eating. The result was a ruined digestion, which is perhaps the main cause of the appalling pessimism which blackens the pages of the next collections of his poems.

The German theorists have taken up the poet's legend here, and from the poems of his three books [*Les Soirs, Les Débacles,* and *Les Flambeaux Noirs*] . . . , made out a case for what they call his "pathological period." He was evidently ill for a long time; but one may doubt whether the exasperated despair and the pretence of madness which make the atmosphere of the books have more than a literary genuineness. The fact is that this kind of thing was the fashion at the time. One has only to read the reviews of those days to find a pessimism and maladies quite as excruciating as those of Verhaeren. . . . The truth is, Schopenhauer was in the air. . . . Some of the poets had actually read him. . . . It was the *fin-de-siêcle*ism of which we have read so much. (pp. 122-24)

In the poems of Verhaeren's trilogy, however, there is a sustained coherence of the impression which lends an air of reality to the philosophical structure which critics have reared by taking a passage here and there. Stefan Zweig's analysis of the poet's longing for death and approach to madness is itself a poem. The German critic rightly points out the leitmotiv of the trilogy: the will to suffer ("To suffer for oneself, alone, but voluntarily"). But this very insistence of the will betokens vigorous intellectual activity: here is none of the apathy of disease. The poet carefully notes all the phases of his exasperation, notes them with inspired imagery, in rhythms new to French poetry. . . . He whips himself into an illusion of madness, watches the corpses of his reason floating down the Thames, and cries out: "When shall I have the atrocious joy of seeing madness attacking my brain nerve by nerve?" (pp. 126-27)

It may well be that Verhaeren in this trilogy has created the classic epic of disease. This may still be true even if it should be proved by some future biographer that Verhaeren never had a pathological period except on paper. Certain it is that individual poems are magnificent in their metallic imagery, their raw colouring (as with great dabs of red and black and gold), the daring onomatopoeia of their rhymes. What a landscape this tortured visionary, this "sick wolf," unrolls! (pp. 128-29)

["**Les Villes**," one of the poems of *Les Flambeaux Noirs*,] is a first expression of the new ideas which were to end his pessimistic phase. Verhaeren is by his very nature an optimist; it is a need of his nature to be able to believe and to worship with fervour. . . . [There] is something of an astonished child about Verhaeren. Everything is wonderful to him; these streets of London, for instance, through which we pass mechanically, are to him colossal manifestations of human power; motor-cars, shops, factories, canals, museums, the passing of crowds—"poured as from a bent full bottle's neck"—railway stations, docks, ships—what ordinary, meaningless words these are to us, and to him what storehouses of romance! (pp. 130-31)

Verhaeren's task has been to teach us to look at the change without fear, knowing that whatever mechanical inventions accelerate the pace of living the human organisation can adapt itself infinitely, and that if the world changes, man will change too. All is well; because it cannot be otherwise. (pp. 132-33)

[Verhaeren] had turned to the past for the inspiration of his Flemish genre-scenes and the pathetic figures of his monks. But in the cosmopolitan searchings which followed he had learned to look at the world with different eyes. He had discovered new ideals of beauty. The beauty of a thing does not lie in its outward form, but in the power it expresses. For Verhaeren, henceforth, the motive spring of poetry is energy. Poets had sought harmony; Verhaeren now seeks energy. To the old poets a roaring factory was repulsive, grotesque; to Verhaeren the panting in multiplied effort of the machinery has the rhythms of stupendous poetry. Viewed from this standpoint, all that had bewildered him in the modern City becomes intelligible, and inevitable in the progress of man to godhead; he sees that a modern poet must not only be reconciled with modern conditions but must discover their epic grandeur, and hail mechanical inventions as the poets of old hailed great victories. Following unconsciously in the track of Walt Whitman (his great forerunner whom he had not read), Verhaeren now turns his cosmic pain into cosmic joy, and strikes out into new paths of poetry which are destined to be the great highways of the verse to be.

The books in which Verhaeren sang his inspired vision of the new city are *Les Campagnes Hallucinées* . . . and *Les Villes Tentaculaires*. . . . These are, probably, his most important, as they are his most suggestive, books. *Les Campagnes Hallucinées,* "the hallucinated countryside," describes the desertion of the country for the town. The villagers can always at night see the glare of the city on the horizon, and Verhaeren personifies this City as an octopus stretching out its tentacles to drain the life's blood of the country. It is a magnificent and lurid vision. (pp. 133-35)

But, while showing us things as they are, the poet proclaims their necessity. The City, loathsome as some of its manifestations are, is necessary; for the City is progress. The Country, with its idylls and its old-time peace and beauty, *must* die, or only exist at a slave's ransom, for it is the foe of progress. In herself the City concentrates energy, "red strength and new light," to inflame with fever and fecund fury the brains of those (heroes, scholars, artists, apostles, adventurers) who pierce the wall of mystery that glooms the world, discover new laws, and subdue the vast forces of life imprisoned in matter.

This—the necessary conquest of the Country by the City—is the main idea of Verhaeren's riper work. It proved a very fertile idea, and led, in a further series of famous books [*Les Visages de la Vie, Les Forces Tumultueuses, La Multiple Splendeur, Les Rythmes Souverains, Les Blés Mouvants*] . . . , to the development of various poetic themes—the beauty of mechanical things, the gospel of admiration, salvation by ecstasy, and other doctrines. . . . (p. 139)

Les Villages Illusoires . . . is a part of the series in so far as it symbolises, in some of its poems, Verhaeren's reconciliation

with the world. But it is rather different in style to the other books—less inspired perhaps, but more restrained and more full of the matter of poetry as traditionally conceived. It is the only book of Verhaeren's in which he is a symbolist; but his symbols are so clear and broadly outlined that they need no interpretation. There is, for instance, the poem of the ferryman, who struggles manfully against the storm to reach the opposite bank whence he is pitifully hailed, only to find, when his oars are broken and his rudder is gone, that he is still where he started from. Beaten as he is, however, he has not let go of the green reed between his teeth. How inspiriting is this picture of will-power that clings to hope! More desolate in the murk of its landscape is the symbol of the fishermen hopelessly befogged in the night of ignorance and selfishness: the dank fog chokes everything and buries the moon. . . . (p. 140)

Verhaeren is essentially a masculine poet, and women do not understand him. Many of his poems which deal with women and love are violently, outrageously erotic; but they are not love-poems. It was not till after his marriage that Verhaeren wrote love-poems; and from these [*Les Heures Claires, Les Heures d'Après-midi, Les Heures du Soir*] . . . violence is excluded. (p. 142)

Verhaeren is a lyrist pure and simple. Wherever he has tried his hand at anything else than poems he has, comparatively speaking, failed. His art criticism, especially his book on Rembrandt, is often interesting as a revelation of himself. His literary criticism is generous and all-embracing; he has no eyes for faults or littleness, but his complete intelligence of all literary genres inspires him with illuminating touches. His dramas have not conquered the stage, and they never will, though several of them have been performed with a fair measure of success. Even Arthur Symons' translation (*The Dawn*) could not make *Les Aubes* . . . more than passably interesting, though it has some importance in the chain of Verhaeren's work as completing *Les Campagnes Hallucinées* and *Les Villes Tentaculaires* by showing the final reconciliation of the town and the country, after a siege of Oppidomagnum. At the present moment, too, *The Dawn* has points of interest in its prophecy of the ending of war by the triumph of socialism: only when war disappears, says the great tribune (apparently modelled on Verhaeren's friend and fellow-worker Émile Vandervelde) who is the hero of the tragedy, will all other injustices disappear too—the hate of the country for the city, of poverty for gold, of distress for power. Only when races learn to embrace each other will the world cease to bristle with nations, armed and tragic and deadly, on the frontiers. *Le Cloître* . . . has dramatic moments of some power. . . . In *Philippe II* . . . Verhaeren had (after De Coster) a great opportunity of contrasting the black asceticism of Spain with the rubicund joy in life of Flanders; he shows us Philip, a religious maniac, spying on his son, while he himself is spied upon by the monks of the Inquisition. *Hélène de Sparte* is fine in conception: he would show us Helen returned to Sparta with a heart sick of the love she has inspired and endured, longing to end her days in peace, "a woman who tends a hearth with slow and gentle hands"; but peace is denied her (for she is Beauty)—all hands stretch out to seize her, lust flames around her, and when she cries out for death the satyrs of the woods and the nymphs of the rivers assail her, and Jupiter himself snatches her up to the sky.

Verhaeren is a world-poet; his theme is the cosmos. But for one part of his work at least his native province of Flanders claims him as her own and calls him her national poet. *Toute la Flandre* is a series of five books [*Les Tenderesses Premières, La Guirlande des Dunes, Les Héros, Les Petites Villes à Pignons, Les Plaines*] . . . in which he celebrates his native land in the present and in the past. *La Guirlande des Dunes* has now (like Lemonnier's *Le Petit Homme de Dieu*) an absorbing and pathetic interest. The dunes that in these poems are a "garland" are now soaked with blood; multitudinous cannon have thundered for months over these canals; and "this sad but sweet corner" is now a desert. One poem rolls out the saga of the immemorial towers of Nieuport and Lisweghe and Furnes, the towers that rise out of the sea-mists "like widows weeping in the winds of old winters." Wars with the rolling thunder of their guns raged round them, very long ago, and yet they stand. . . . They symbolise, these hoary, battle-stained towers, the indestructible heroism of Flanders, the measureless mourning of her departed days, all the history of a tenacious land. (pp. 143-47)

Critics have not sufficiently realised the fact that Verhaeren is so astonished by the beauty of action, of mechanical force, that he stands outside it. He sees it with the eyes of the spectator, of the painter. It has so much the greater effect on him as he has not the depth of a philosopher, but the naïveté of a wondering child. To him it is all a miracle. The mightier poet of the new world will have grown up in it, and will have eyes for manifestations which are less obvious. (p. 149)

> *Jethro Bithell, "Émile Verhaeren," in his* Contemporary Belgian Literature, *Frederick A. Stokes Company, Publishers, 1915, pp. 108-49.*

AMY LOWELL (essay date 1915)

[*Lowell was one of the leading proponents of Imagism in American poetry. Like the Symbolists before her, some of whom she examined in* Six French Poets, *Lowell experimented with free verse forms. Under the influence of Ezra Pound, Lowell's poetry exhibited the new style of Imagism, consisting of clear and precise rhetoric, exact rendering of images, and greater metrical freedom. Although she was popular in her time, standard evaluations of Lowell accord her more importance as a promoter of new artistic ideas than as a poet in her own right. The following excerpt from* Six French Poets *is a survey of Verhaeren's major poetry.*]

[Verhaeren] ranks now, not only as the prophet of a new era, but as the authentic voice of a dead era. The Belgium he portrays has been devastated by war, and so completely crushed that at the moment it can hardly be said to exist. . . . Future ages will not only study [Verhaeren] as a great poet, but as an accurate portrayer of life in Belgium before the war. His artistic value, for many years at least, is bound to be overshadowed by his historic value. He stands out as the finest flower of a ruined country, and as such can never again be contemplated as merely walking step by step with the writers of any other country, no matter how great. (pp. 3-4)

A pleasant anecdote is told of [Verhaeren] . . . , how one rainy day he clumped into [Camille] Lemonnier's lodgings (never having met Lemonnier, by the way), and blurted out, "Je veux vous lire des vers!" ["I want you to read these verses!"] And what he read was the manuscript of his first book, *Les Flamandes.*

Lemonnier encouraged him, criticised him, and, shortly after, the book was published. Then the storm broke, and howled about Verhaeren. The book was strong, vivid, brutal. It was as violent, as coarse, as full of animal spirits, as the pictures of Breugel the Elder, Teniers, or Jan Steen. As one of the critics said, "M. Verhaeren pierced like an abscess." (p. 13)

And really it is a startling book, written with a sort of fury of colour. The red, fat flesh tints of Rubens have got into it, and the pages seem hot and smoky with perspiration. The desire to paint seems engrained in the Flemish character. . . . In his poem, *Les Vieux Maîtres,* Verhaeren speaks of [the] old masters as painting "les fureurs d'estomac, de ventre et de débauche" ["the passions of the stomach, of the belly and of debauchery"]. The description applies equally well to his own poems in this book. They are marvellously done, blazing with colour and blatant with energy.

Metrically, *Les Flamandes* is not particularly interesting, being written in the ordinary French alexandrine. The interest of the book lies in its treatment of subjects. Many of the most remarkable poems must be read in their context, but there is a series of interiors, little Flemish *genre* pictures, which show the vivid style in which the whole is written. . . . Notice [in *La Cusine,* for example,] how wonderfully bright and sparkling it all is,—"the snapping of light in the glasses" and the fire "crumbling itself into sparks." How excellently the word "crumbling" gives the up and down effect of firelight!

Les Flamandes appeared in 1883, and it was not until 1886 that Verhaeren's next book, *Les Moines,* published by quite a different firm, came out. Why Verhaeren changed his publisher, we do not know. Why he changed his whole manner of writing can be guessed.

I have said [elsewhere] that the Flemish character is made up of two parts, one composed of violent and brutal animal spirits, the other of strange, unreasoning mysticism. (pp. 13-15)

Whether Verhaeren wrote *Les Moines* to satisfy the need of expression for this gentler side of his nature, whether his painter's eye was fascinated by the pictorial value of old monasteries and quiet monks, or whether he wished to prove to the world that he could do things that were not violent, it is impossible to say. . . . [Certainly] to show the world that he has more than one string to his lute is a very natural desire in a young poet.

Les Moines is a sad book, a faded book. The monasteries are here, but bathed in the light of a pale sunset. (p. 16)

It is a book of delicate etchings, pensive and melancholy, and again written in French alexandrines. In this book, more than in *Les Flamandes,* Verhaeren seems to be feeling his way.

Then Verhaeren broke down. . . . Herr Zweig, in his exhaustive biography, spends a great deal of time in telling us how he had to have the door-bell taken off because he could not bear its ringing, and how the people in the house had to go about in felt slippers. Herr Zweig is delighted with *Les Soirs, Les Débâcles,* and *Les Flambeaux Noirs,* published respectively in 1887, 1888, and 1890, because he considers them so remarkable a portrayal of an unusual state of mind, and says they must be "priceless to pathologists and psychologists." I suspect that if Herr Zweig lived in America he would not be so interested in the description of what is to us quite a common occurrence. I do not suppose there is a person who will read these lines, who has not either been there himself or had a friend who has. (p. 17)

I will [consider] two poems from *Les Soirs,* not because of their interest to the pathologist and psychologist, but because they are such remarkable pictures, and because they show that wedding of sound to sense which is to become one of Verhaeren's most characteristic powers. . . . See how long and slow the cadence is [in *Londres*], and the heavy consonants make the poem knock and hum like the Westminster bells he mentions. It almost seems as though Big Ben must have been striking when he wrote the poem.

This intermixture of sound with pure painting is one of Verhaeren's most remarkable traits. In . . . *Le Moulin,* we have another sombre landscape, but the whole movement is different; from the first line we are conscious of sound, but it is no longer the insistent beating which underlies *Londres;* it is a sort of sliding, a faint, rushing noise. Anyone reading the first stanza aloud cannot fail to be conscious of it. It is this presence of sounds in his verse, quite apart from the connotations of his words, which gives Verhaeren's work its strange, magic reality, and makes it practically impossible to translate. (pp. 18-19)

Before we leave these three books, I want to [consider] one more poem, *La Morte,* which is a sort of end dedication to *Les Flambeaux Noirs.* Here, at last, Verhaeren begins to use that extraordinary *vers libre* for which he is afterwards to be so noted. Some poets seem capable of expressing themselves perfectly in the classic alexandrine, some can use both old and new forms according to the content of the poem. . . . But the alexandrine has never seemed to fit Verhaeren. (p. 20)

Verhaeren's *vers libre* is always rhymed. And in a language so abounding in rhyme as the French, that is no handicap to the free poet. Not only does Verhaeren use end rhymes, he cannot resist the joy of internal rhymes. But I am anticipating, for in *La Morte* . . . there are very few internal rhymes, although his fondness for alliteration and assonance begins to be noticeable. For the rest, *La Morte* is a beautiful, foggy picture, sad, but with a kind of sadness which is already beginning to enjoy itself in a sombre sort of way. In other words, Verhaeren is beginning to get well, but he is not quite willing to admit it yet. (p. 21)

In one line of this poem Verhaeren has given us the real cause of his illness. His reason has died, he says, "from knowing too much." Or, to paraphrase this, his sanity has fled before the vision of a more extended knowledge. The mystic and the modern man have been struggling within him. It is this struggle which has forced so many French poets back to the Catholic Church. But Verhaeren was made of more resisting stuff. The struggle downed him, but did not betray him. He fell back into no open arms; by sheer effort he pushed himself up on his feet. (pp. 23-4)

He came out of his illness, as is usually the case with strong people, a sane, more self-reliant man. . . .

In 1891, Verhaeren published two volumes of poems, with two different publishers. One, *Les Bords de la Route,* is a collection of poems written at the time of *Les Flamandes* and *Les Moines;* the other, *Apparus dans Mes Chemins,* marks the beginning of a new epoch. Verhaeren is feeling the zest of life again, but it is a more spiritual zest than before, if one can use the term for such a very materialistic spirituality. Verhaeren is waking up, as it were, like a man stretching his arms, not yet fully awake. *Saint Georges* is probably the best known poem of the volume. . . . (p. 24)

And now we have come to Verhaeren's great period; to the books which have made him the greatest poet of Belgium, and one of the greatest poets of the world. . . . In [*Les Campagnes*

Hallucinées, Les Villages Illusoires, and *Les Villes Tentaculaires,*] we have all Verhaeren's excellencies in rich profusion. Here are the towns, with their smoking factories, crowded streets, noisy theatres, and busy wharves; here are the broad, level plains of Flanders starred with windmills, the little villages and farms, and the slow river where fishermen come. . . . Verhaeren had found himself. At a time when France was in the midst of *Symbolisme;* when nature, divorced from the pathetic fallacy, made little general appeal; when every-day life was considered dull, and not to be thought about if possible;— Verhaeren wrote of nature, of daily happenings, and of modern inventions. He not only wrote, he not only sang; he shrieked, and cut capers, and pounded on a drum.

Writing in French, Verhaeren has never been able to restrain himself within the canons of French taste. His effervescing nature found the French clarity and precision, that happy medium so cherished by the Gallic mind, as hampering as he would have found Greek artistic ideals had he lived several centuries earlier. He *must* put three rhymes one after the other if he felt like it; he *must* have a couple of assonances in a line, or go on alliterating down half a page. There was nothing in his nature to make the ideas of the *Symbolistes* attractive to him; he would none of them. The mysticism of which I have spoken modified itself into a great humanitarian realization. He believed in mankind, in the future. (pp. 25-6)

A Frenchman would have felt constrained to put some definiteness into these hopes. To give some form to what certainly amounted to a religion. Verhaeren was troubled by no such teasing difficulty. He simply burned with a nebulous ardour, and was happy and fecund. This is one of the reasons why Verhaeren's poetry is so much better understood and appreciated by Englishmen and Americans—Anglo-Saxons in short— and by Germans, than any other French poetry. There is a certain Teutonic grandeur of mind in Verhaeren which is extremely sympathetic to all Anglo-Saxons and Germans. Where the French intellect seems coldly analytic and calm, Verhaeren charms by his fiery activity.

One of the devices which Verhaeren employs with consummate skill, is onomatopoeia, or using words which sound like the things described. (This is at once wedded to, and apart from, the sort of sound I have mentioned above.) He carries this effect through whole poems, and it is one of the reasons for the vividness of his poems on nature.

An excellent example of this is *La Pluie* from *Les Villages Illusoires.* . . . The long sweeping *l's* of the first stanza give the effect of the interminable lines of rain in an extraordinary manner, and the repetition of [la pluie]. . . adds a continuous drawing out, a falling—falling—falling—as it were. Even apart from the beauty and surprise of the rhymes, the movement of this poem, and its pictorial quality, make it one of Verhaeren's masterpieces.

He has done this same thing in a number of other poems in this volume, such as *La Neige, Le Silence, Le Vent.* (pp. 27-30)

Two other poems in this book I cannot pass by. They are pictures of village life, full of feeling and understanding, and rich in that pictorial sense which never deserts Verhaeren. The first one, *Le Meunier,* is made up of the beauty of terror— terror worked up, little by little, from the first line to the last. Verhaeren is no mere descriptive poet. Neither is he a surface realist. His realism contains the psychologic as well as the physiologic. Spadeful by spadeful, the earth rattles down on the coffin, and with each spadeful the grave-digger's terror grows, with the silence of the night, and the gradual pervading, haunting, of the personality of the dead miller, all about, till "the wind passes by as though it were someone," and the grave-digger throws down his spade and flees. After that, "total silence comes." It is all, and it is enough. (pp. 30-1)

Very different is **Les Meules Qui Brûlent**. A splendid impressionist picture, with the burning hay-ricks starting up, one after the other, out of the blackness. (p. 35)

One strange thing about Verhaeren is his true greatness. No matter how onomatopoeic he becomes, no matter how much he alliterates, or whatever other devices he makes use of, he never becomes claptrap. . . . No matter what Verhaeren does, his work remains great, and full of what Matthew Arnold calls "high seriousness." (pp. 37-8)

A brooding Northerner, Verhaeren sees the sorrow, the travail, the sordidness, going on all about him, and loves the world just the same, and wildly believes in a future in which it shall somehow grind itself back to beauty. **Les Villes Tentaculaires** is full of this sordidness, a sordidness overlaid with grandeur, as iridescent colour plays over the skin of a dying fish. But it is also full of the constant, inevitable pushing on, the movement, one might call it, of change.

One poem from **Les Villes Tentaculaires** [serves] as illustration. . . . (pp. 38-9)

The dramatic intensity of this poem [**La Bourse**] equals that of **Le Meunier**. And this is Verhaeren's third great gift: the dramatic. I have already spoken of his visualizing gift, of his power of reproducing sound in words; the third side of his greatness is the sense of drama. In spite of the decoration in **La Bourse**, in spite of [certain] lines . . .—beautiful, but painfully prone to stick out of a poem like knobs on an embossed wall-paper—the poet has managed to keep them in their place, so that they do not interfere, but rather add to the drama of the whole.

Verhaeren is not a didactic poet. He does not suggest a way out. He states, and hopes, and firmly believes; that is all. And always remember, in thinking of Verhaeren's work in the light of his philosophy, that he is first of all an artist, a painter, and he must always take a painter's delight in pure painting. For those people who prefer a more clear, more classic style of poetry, Verhaeren has no charm. He is nebulous and redundant. His colours are bright and vague like flash-lights thrown on a fog. But his force is incontestable, and he hurls along upon it in a whirlwind of extraordinary poetry. (pp. 43-4)

That Verhaeren must have married sometime before 1896 is clear, because **Les Heures Claires**, published in that year, is the first of a series of love poems, of which [**Les Heures de l'Après-midi** and **Les Heures du Soir**] . . . are the other volumes.

Verhaeren's love story has evidently been tranquil and happy. The poems are very sweet and graceful, but it must be confessed not of extreme importance. They are all written in regular metre, which seems almost typical of their calm and unoriginal flow. (p. 44)

We have reached the last stage of Verhaeren's career. The stage of powers ripening, growing, solidifying. His part is taken; he has learnt his peculiar medium, and formulated his ideas. His final volumes, many though they are, merely show him writing still remarkable poems along the lines he has cho-

sen. There is no diminution of his genius, and his fecundity is extraordinary. (p. 45)

Verhaeren has lost nothing of his great vigour, and that the rage for justice which made him a socialist still burns in him. (pp. 45-6)

What Verhaeren has done for poetry is this. He has made it realize the modern world. He has shown the grandeur of everyday life, and made us understand that science and art are never at variance. He has shown that civic consciousness is not necessarily dry and sterile, but can be as romantic as an individual. And he has done all this without once saying it directly, by force of the greatest and most complete art. (p. 47)

> *Amy Lowell, "Émile Verhaeren," in her* Six French Poets: Studies in Contemporary Literature *(copyright, 1915, by The Macmillan Company), Macmillan, 1915, pp. 1-47.*

JURGIS BALTRUŠAITIS   (essay date 1916)

[*The following excerpt is indicative of Verhaeren's stature among his readers in Russia. The critic states: "Verhaeren, particularly with us in Russia, has long since been accorded the glory of a poet of modernity." This admiration for Verhaeren's modernity is contradicted by the later criticism of P. Mansell Jones and Kristiaan Versluys (see excerpts below).*]

The genius Verhaeren must in every conceivable degree be considered as the first of contemporary artists, not only for the incomparable mastery of his art, but, far more significantly, for the extraordinary fullness of his inner experience. To be sure, it would be possible to name two or three more poets of our age who have attained in their art approximately the same spiritual height, but in comparison with the poetry of the great Belgian all their attainment seems to be only that of one of the borderlands, a more or less essential portion, while only in Emile Verhaeren has the modern soul been revealed in all the entirety of its creative ferment, of its inner right to a new life and readiness for this life.

Verhaeren, particularly with us in Russia, has long since been accorded the glory of a poet of modernity. Though perfectly accurate and just, such a definition is still far from exhausting all the sides of his creative image, and does not express the most basic and paramount element of his art. This concept of modernity, as it is applied to the poet, has in view chiefly his wonderful song about the city and his immortal eulogy of the fly-wheel and the steel hammer with which our time is forging its fortune and building its destiny. The first singer of Belgium, with her most rich productivity, had of course to assign an exceptional place in his art to the gigantic thunder and clang of the machine and to all the pertinacity of labor. But in this he is only the Belgian, only the artist who is expressing the basic structure and spirit of his native land. Far more important and more significant are that all-pervading passion with which Verhaeren, in somewhat liturgical fashion, celebrates the triumphant will of all life, and that exultant appeal for its building of landmarks and for the justification of our little lives by stubborn toil in the name of the future, without which the passing day remains only passing, and modernity only modernity. And in this the magical poet of Belgium becomes at once one of the most inspired of artists, the spokesman for all humanity and the singer of the sole truth of the universe.

And so not merely modernity as such, but modernity as a strong, iron, ascending rung on the unbroken ladder of human creation and struggle, has become not the glorification of our pressing and unanimous heroic task, since by dint of this, in the sweat of our brow we exalt the design of the cosmos, not yet comprehended, and serve its gradual establishment as the foundation and order of our lives! Why, it is enough to read if no more than the wonderful **'Smithy''** or **"The Scheldt"** **(L'Escaut)** (in the collection **"All Flanders"** [Toute la Flandre], **"The Heroes"** (Les Heros),** or if only the one little poem **"Tunnel,''** a work of genius in its compactness and power,— to be convinced that the images of our daily life make up only the flesh, the outer content of Verhaeren's poetry, while its spirit, more loftily and broadly than our doings and events, both in its essence and in its artistic tasks, has its value altogether, so to speak, on cosmic standards. In the eternal event, all the power of our daily struggle and all the heterogeneity of our waking lives concern the poet only insofar as they breathe with the living premonition and the living realization of the coming victory of humanity. . .

Being imbued in his inward experience with such a lofty feeling for the cosmos in its unique wholeness, Verhaeren in his works unexpectedly shifted the seemingly inviolate and unshakeable axis of art, and into the realm of poetry entered and became the content of genuine poetry all the petty concerns of our daily lives, even what, before Verhaeren, had been considered too inconsequential, ordinary and crude. Because from the transforming and magical touch of his creative will these petty and crude details became important and significant and entered inseparably into the great fabric of the cosmos and breathed with its mysterious breath, like the leaves of a majestic tree, or, in the expression of the poet himself, "like the separate sparkles of one and the same light."

This same fundamental spirit of Verhaeren's art and his inner inclination must explain also all the peculiarities of his images, as well as his peculiar creative devices. As though in a concern that the small thing, as a separate entity should be constantly apprehended in connection with the great, as a unity, the poet loves to endow the small thing with the marks and attributes of the great, and the great thing with the tokens of the small, and quite doubles the images, in an effort to increase their outer capacity, to give the finite the dimensions of infinity or to force the static to turn into action. Is it not for his reason that the sun, in Verhaeren, is "like a golden penny," that his ships are like "furious stallions on the green and white meadows of the sea," that the beating of the human heart often seemed to him "a gigantic fist" in which was clenched "the strain of fury and savage hate"?

From this source comes even the very form of the works of this incomparable poet. What else indeed, if not a concurrence with the primeval rhythms of the cosmos, can explain the fact that we are affected with such a mighty power, so imperiously, by the flow of Verhaeren's verse, always indivisible from its content, by the entire irresistible solemnity of his speech and the thrilling clarity of his creative passion?

The great poet's inspiration captured more clearly than could we many a sunny song from the hidden, and to us silent, mystery of the cosmos; it divined the inner truth of the universe and trustingly yielded to this forbidden truth his own human heart, a heart lacking in an understanding of the great and the small (elements in the universe). This is why Verhaeren's solemn appeal to praise, to the creative hammer and to the cult of ecstasy will ring through the ages so integrally and so convincingly. (pp. 50-2)

Jurgis Baltrušaitis, "To the Memory of Emile Verhaeren," translated by W. Edward Brown (originally published under a different title in Russkoje slovo, *Vol. 18, No. 267, December 1, 1916), in* Lituanus: The Lithuanian Quarterly, *Vol. 20, No. 1, Spring, 1974, pp. 49-52.*

ARTHUR SYMONS   (essay date 1923)

[*While Symons initially gained notoriety as an English Decadent of the 1890s, he eventually established himself as one of the most important critics of the modern era. As a member of the iconoclastic generation of fin de siècle aesthetes that included Aubrey Beardsley and Oscar Wilde, Symons wholeheartedly assumed the role of the world-weary cosmopolite and sensation hunter, composing verses in which he attempted to depict the bohemian world of the modern artist. He was also a gifted linguist whose sensitive translations from Paul Verlaine and Stéphané Mallarmé provided English poets with an introduction to the poetry of the French Symbolists. However, it was as a critic that Symons made his most important contribution to literature. His* The Symbolist Movement in Literature *(1899) provided his English contemporaries with an appropriate vocabulary with which to define their new aesthetic—one that communicated their concern with dreamlike states, imagination, and a reality that exists just beyond the boundaries of the senses. Symons also discerned that the concept of the symbol as a vehicle by which a "hitherto unknown reality was suddenly revealed" could become the basis for the entire modern aesthetic. A proper use of the symbol "would flash upon you the soul of that which can be apprehended only by the soul— the finer sense of things unseen, the deeper meaning of things evident." This anticipated and influenced James Joyce's concept of an artistic "epiphany," T. S. Eliot's "moment in time," and laid the foundation for much of modern poetic theory. Symons translated Verhaeren's drama* Les aubes, *and in the essay excerpted below offers an appraisal of Verhaeren's poetry.*]

The poetry of Emile Verhaeren, more than that of any other modern poet, is made directly out of the complaining voices of the nerves. Other writers, certainly, have been indirectly indebted to the effect of nerves on temperament, but Verhaeren seems to express only so much of a temperament as finds its expression through their immediate medium. In his early books *Les Flamandes, Les Moines* . . . , he began by a solid, heavily colored, exterior manner of painting *genre* pictures in the Flemish style. Such poems as **"Les Paysans,"** with its fury of description, are like a Teniers in verse; not Breughel has painted a kermesse with hotter colors, a more complete abandonment to the sunlight, wine and gross passions of those Flemish feasts. This first book, *Les Flamandes,* belongs to the Naturalistic movement; but it has already (as in the similar commencements of Huysmans) so ardent a love of color for its own sake, color becoming lyrical, that one realizes how soon this absorption in the daily life of farms, kitchens, stables, will give place to another kind of interest. And in *Les Moines,* while there is still for the most part the painting of exteriorities, a new sentiment, by no means the religious sentiment, but an artistic interest in what is less material, less assertive in things, finds for itself an entirely new scheme of color. . . . But it is not until *Les Soirs* that we find what was to be the really individual style developing itself. It develops itself at first with a certain heaviness. Here is a poet who writes in images: good; but the images are larger than the ideas. . . . Everything must be done *immensément.* The word is repeated on every page, sometimes twice in a stanza. The effect of monotony in rhythm, the significant, chiming recurrence of words, the recoil of a line upon itself, the dwindling away or the heaping up of sound in line after line, the shock of an unexpected caesura, the delay and the hastened speed of syllables: all these arts of a very conscious technique are elaborated with somewhat too obvious an intention. There is splendor, opulence, and, for the first time, ''such stuff as dreams are made of.'' Description is no longer made for its own sake; it becomes metaphor. And this metaphor is entirely new. It may be called exaggerated, affected even; but it is new, and it is expressive. (pp. 229-31)

In *Les Débâcles,* a year later, this art of writing in colored and audible metaphor, and on increasingly abstract and psychological subjects, the sensations externalized, has become more master of itself, and at the same time more immediately the servant of a more and more feverish nervous organization. . . . And the contemplation of this *fiévreux* is turned more and more in upon itself, finding in its vision of the outer world only a mirrored image of its own disasters. (pp. 231-32)

Two years later, with *Les Flambeaux Noirs,* what was nervous has become almost a sort of very conscious madness: the hand on one's own pulse, the eyes watching themselves in the glass with an unswerving fixity, but a breaking and twisting of the links of things, a doubling and division of the mind's sight, which might be met with, less picturesquely, in actual madness. There are two poems, **''Le Roc''** and **''Les Livres,''** which give, in a really terrifying way, the very movement of idea falling apart from idea, sensation dragging after it sensation down the crumbling staircase of the brain, which are the symptoms of the brain's loss of self-control. . . . (pp. 232-33)

In these poems of self-analysis, which is self-torture, there is something lacerating, and at the same time bewildering, which conveys to one the sense of all that is most solitary, picturesque and poignant in the transformation of an intensely active and keen-sighted reason into a thing of conflicting visionary moods. At times, as in the remarkable study of London called **''Les Villes,''** this fever of the brain looks around it, and becomes a flame of angry and tumultuous epithet, licking up and devouring what is most solid in exterior space. Again, as in **''Les Lois''** and **''Les Nombres,''** it becomes metaphysical, abstract, and law towers up into a visible palace, number flowers into a forest. . . . That art of presenting a thought like a picture, of which Verhaeren is so accomplished a master, has become more subtle than ever; and . . . for the most part menacing speculations in the void, take visible form before us, with a kind of hallucination, communicated to us from that (how far deliberate?) hallucination which has created them. Gradually, in **''Les Apparus dans mes Chemins,''** in **''Les Campagnes Hallucinées,''** in **''Les Villages Illusoires,''** in **''Les Villes Tentaculaires,''** the hallucinations become entirely external: it is now the country, the village, the town, that is to say, the whole organized world, that agonizes among cloudy phantoms, and no longer a mere individual, abnormal brain. And so he has at once gained a certain relief from what had been felt to be too intimately a part of himself, and has also surrendered to a more profound, because a more extended, consciousness of human misery. Effacing himself, as he does, behind the great spectacle of the world, as he sees it, with his visionary eyes, in his own violent and lethargic country, he becomes a more hopeless part of that conspiracy of the earth against what man has built out of the earth, of what man has built out of the earth against the earth, which he sees developing silently among the grass and bricks. All these books are a sort of philosophy in symbols, symbols becoming more and more definite. . . . **''Les Cordiers,''** the old man spinning his rope against the sky, weaving the past into the future . . . and, finally, the many-tentacled towns, drawing to themselves all the strength and sap

of the earth: **''Les Spectacles,'' ''La Bourse,'' ''Le Bazar,''** the monstrous and material soul of towns.

Contrast these poems with those early poems, so brutal, so Flemish, if you would see at a glance all the difference between the naturalistic and the symbolistic treatment. The subject-matter is the same; the same eye sees. . . . But at first there is merely an eye that sees, and that takes the visible world at its own valuation of itself. Later on, things are seen but to be readjusted, to be set into relation with other, invisible realities, of which they are no more than the wavering and tortured reflection. And with this poet, in his later manner, everything becomes symbol; the shop, the theater, the bank, no less than the old rope-maker weaving the horizons together. (pp. 233-37)

Verhaeren's second play, *Le Cloître,* is much finer in every way than his first, *Les Aubes,* but it does not convince us that he is a dramatist, in the strict sense of the word. The only French poet of the present day who has really vivid energy, his energy is too feverish, too spasmodic, too little under the control of a shaping intellect, to be of precisely the quality required for the drama. The people of these brief and fiery scenes are like little broken bits of the savage forces of the world, working out their passionate issues under the quiet roofs of the cloister. All their words are cries, coming out of a half-delirious suffering; and these cries echo about the stage in an almost monotonous conflict. It seems to us that the form which suits Verhaeren best is the form which he has temporarily abandoned—a kind of fiery reverie, seen finally in his last book, *Les Visages de la Vie* . . . ; and in all these poems, **''La Foule,'' ''L'Ivresse,'' ''La Joie,''** and the rest, we see the poet sending his soul into the universe and becoming a vehement voice for all that he finds most passionate in it. It is, in its way, dramatizing of emotion, but, if one may say so, an abstract dramatizing. It is the crowd, not Dom Balthazar; joy itself, not some joyous human being for which he finds words; and his merits and his defects make him a better spokesman for disembodied than for embodied souls. Since the early period of Flemish realism he has been, while making his language more and more pictorial, making his interests more and more internal. He no longer paints landscapes, but the scenery of the soul, and in the same vast and colored images. He magnifies sensation until it becomes a sort of hallucination of which he seems always to be the victim. Now all this is so very personal, so clearly the vision of a not quite healthy temperament, that his neurotic monks in the cloister, with their heated and vehement speech, seem more like repetitions of a single type than individual characters. But he has certainly come nearer to dramatic characterization than in the *Shadowy Dawn,* and he has founded his play on a more emotionally human basis; on a basis, it would seem, partly suggested by the story which Browning tells in *Halbert and Hob.* And, taken as a poem, it is full of vigorous, imaginative writing, in which the religious passion finds eloquent speech. And, after all, is not this one of the most interesting, and not even one of the least successful, attempts at what a more extravagant imitator has lately called *La tragédie intérieure*? The actual tendency of art is certainly toward an abandonment of the heroic and amusing adventures which constituted so much of the art of the past, and a concentration upon whatever can be surmised of that soul which these adventures must doubtless have left so singularly indifferent. . . . Verhaeren falls into the movement, trying to give a more lyrical form to this new kind of drama, trying to give it a narrower and fiercer intensity. What he has so far achieved is a melodrama of the spirit, in which there is poetry, but also rhetoric. Will he finally be able to find for himself a form in which the "inner tragedy" can be externally presented without rhetoric? Then, perhaps, the poetry will make its own drama. (pp. 237-40)

Arthur Symons, "Emile Verhaeren" (originally published in a slightly different form in The English Review, *Vol. XXVI, March, 1918), in his* Dramatis Personae *(copyright, 1923 by The Bobbs-Merrill Company; copyright renewed © 1951 by the Literary Estate of Arthur Symons; used with permission of the publisher, The Bobbs-Merrill Company, Inc.), Bobbs-Merrill, 1923, pp. 229-40.*

ALDOUS HUXLEY   (essay date 1923)

[*Huxley was an important English novelist and social critic whose best-known work is* Brave New World. *In his essay on Verhaeren, Huxley derogates what are usually considered the Belgian poet's virtues, particularly his celebration of the "animalism" of the Flemish peasantry, and compares him unfavorably with the French poet Arthur Rimbaud.*]

The flag-maker is a man of energy and strong vitality. He likes to imagine that all that surrounds him is as large, as full of sap and as vigorous as he feels himself to be. He pictures the world as a place where the colours are strong and brightly contrasted, where a vigorous chiaroscuro leaves no doubt as to the true nature of light and darkness, and where all life pulsates, quivering and taut, like a banner in the wind. From the first we find in Verhaeren all the characteristics of the tailor of banners. . . . [In his earliest book of verse, *Les Flamandes*,] we find him making copious use—or was it abuse?—as Victor Hugo had done before him, of words like "vaste," "énorme," "infini," "infiniment," "infinité," "univers." Thus, in **"L'Ame de la Ville,"** he talks of an "énorme" viaduct, an "immense" train, a "monstrueux" sun, even of the "énorme" atmosphere. For Verhaeren all roads lead to the infinite, wherever and whatever that may be.

Infinity is one of those notions which are not to be lightly played with. The makers of flags like it because it can be contrasted so effectively with the microscopic finitude of man. Writers like Hugo and Verhaeren talk so often and so easily about infinity that the idea ceases in their poetry to have any meaning at all. (pp. 155-57)

[In] certain respects, Verhaeren, in his view of life, is not unlike Balzac. This resemblance is most marked in some of the poems of his middle period, especially those in which he deals with aspects of contemporary life. *Les Villes tentaculaires* contains poems which are wholly Balzacian in conception. Take, for example, Verhaeren's rhapsody on the Stock Exchange. . . . (p. 157)

One cannot read these lines without thinking of Balzac's feverish money-makers, of the Baron de Nucingen, Du Tillet, the Kellers and all the lesser misers and usurers, and all their victims. With their worked-up and rather melodramatic excitement, they breathe the very spirit of Balzac's prodigious film-scenario version of life.

Verhaeren's flag-making instinct led him to take special delight in all that is more than ordinarily large and strenuous. He extols and magnifies the gross violence of the Flemish peasantry, their almost infinite capacity for taking food and drink, their industry, their animalism. In true Rooseveltian style, he admired energy for its own sake. All his romping rhythms were dictated to him by the need to express this passion for the

strenuous. His curious assonances and alliterations . . . arise from this same desire to recapture the sense of violence and immediate life.

It is interesting to compare the violence and energy of Verhaeren with the violence of an earlier poet—Rimbaud, the marvellous boy, if ever there was one. Rimbaud cut the stuff of life into flags, but into flags that never fluttered on this earth. His violence penetrated, in some sort, beyond the bounds of ordinary life. In some of his poems Rimbaud seems actually to have reached the nameless goal towards which he was striving, to have arrived at that world of unheard-of spiritual vigour and beauty whose nature he can only describe in an exclamatory metaphor:

Millions d'oiseaux d'or, ô future vigueur!

But the vigour of Verhaeren is never anything so fine and spiritual as this "million of golden birds." It is merely the vigour and violence of ordinary life speeded up to cinema intensity.

It is a noticeable fact that Verhaeren was generally at his best when he took a holiday from the making and waving of flags. His Flemish bucolics and the love poems of *Les Heures,* written for the most part in traditional form, and for the most part shorter and more concentrated than his poems of violence and energy, remain the most moving portion of his work. Very interesting, too, are the poems belonging to that early phase of doubt and depression which saw the publication of *Les Débâcles* and *Les Flambeaux Noirs*. The energy and life of the later books is there, but in some sort concentrated, preserved and intensified, because turned inwards upon itself. Of many of the later poems one feels that they were written much too easily. These must have been brought very painfully and laboriously to the birth. (pp. 158-60)

Aldous Huxley, "Verhaeren," in his On the Margin: Notes and Essays *(copyright 1923, 1951 by Aldous Huxley; reprinted by permission of Harper & Row, Publishers, Inc.; in Canada by Mrs. Laura Huxley and Chatto & Windus), George H. Doran, 1923, pp. 155-60.*

GERALDINE P. DILLA   (essay date 1924)

[*Dilla discusses Verhaeren's later poems of patriotism and war.*]

Emile Verhaeren experienced the war in most of its phases, and he had the understanding heart of the true poet; therefore the record of his last two years has great permanent value. (p. 20)

Les Ailes Rouges de la Guerre is a collection of remarkable originality, comprehensiveness, and excellence. It expresses in impassioned verse the great ideas and significance of the war as well as its details; it pictures experiences of the countryside and the city as well as those of the individual soldier and villager. Its thirty-four poems are representative both in form and style of Verhaeren's earlier work. Many are in Alexandrines, but more are in his own *vers libre*. This last, however, is not at all what we call free verse in English. His is an intricate form in strophes of varied length with a finely-wrought relation between the strophes and the sections of the whole poem. The lines vary in length; the rime-scheme is irregular with occasional assonances and alliteration. The sound not only harmonizes with the sense but has a beauty of its own; therefore this form becomes one of exquisite art.

Surely with Verhaeren the style is the man, for the numerous epithets applied to his poetry only indicate that it is the artistic expression of his broad intelligence and sympathetic emotion. His verse shows boundless vitality, fiery activity, exuberance, intensity, extreme sensitivity to impressions, splendor, tenderness, and high seriousness,—all combined with immensity in scope and plan. He achieves fine effects through strong contrasts of idea and color, and through the cumulation of details. Especially notable is his art of presenting thoughts like pictures, and making his pictures vivid by methods similar to those the impressionists used in their painting, such as the juxtaposition of component elements. But before the great ideas for which Verhaeren stands in literature, these peculiarities and excellences of his style sink into relative unimportance.

Emile Verhaeren was first and foremost the exponent of universal ideals in European poetry. Though he began as the singer of an essentially national life—that of all Belgium, for he was Flemish in blood and Walloon in language and associations, he became the prophet of internationalism. He felt the unifying power of modern inventions, of modern urban life, and of higher ideals of statecraft; and he expressed this yearning for an amicable unity of states while the world was floundering in exaggerated nationalisms. But he was not the same kind of internationalist as M. Romain Rolland. Verhaeren's irrefutable answer to the great Frenchman's *Au-Dessus de la Mêlée* appeared thus in the *Revue de Paris:* "One must not try to hold a scale when the enemy is brandishing a sword." One of his first war poems, **"Bleeding Belgium,"** shows this spirit of internationalism assailed by the war. . . . (pp. 21-2)

Such a poem as **"Au Reichstag"** shows this ideal of internationalism—"the fraternal heart of a new Europe." Verhaeren recounted the fine promises of the social democrats to stop war, which were unfulfilled by their quick return to the old helmeted death. . . . As he says in **"Bruges and Anvers,"** "You who dreamed of a European soul,—here is your ideal falsified and baffled. Germany seeks to confiscate to her profit what was the most beautiful ideal one can imagine in history."

But no writer could be more intensely patriotic, or more intelligently so, than Verhaeren. He was a real son of Belgium, intimately conversant with her moods, hopes, people, and history. His early volumes, like *Toute la Flandre,* expressed in powerful poetry her varied life; his monographs on painting interpreted her art; his prominent part in the movement represented by "La Jeune Belgique" from 1883 on helped to create that marvelous flowering known as the Belgian Renascence, which he described in affectionate reminiscence in the essay on Louvain. He understood not only the two races whose union he symbolized, but also the two aspects of the Belgian mind—mysticism and the love of pleasure. (pp. 24-5)

The ardor of Verhaeren's reverent patriotism is evident everywhere, and especially in **"Un Lambeau de Patrie"** which describes the few bleak flooded miles of his fatherland unconquered through the war. (p. 25)

Verhaeren could not do otherwise than express his righteous indignation on the invasion of Belgium. "Germany, the Exterminator of Races," is "the maker of twilight" not only in Belgium but in Armenia and Poland. In **"Le Cri,"** he asserts that the cry which resounds so tragic today, and spreads abroad from plain to plain is a just cry, although it is a cry of hate. It is no longer the great call of marvellous love that formerly re-echoed among the people; it is now the just cry of hatred. And the poet is stirred to powerful satire, as in [his] striking portrait of the megalomanic emperor, **"William II."** . . . (p. 26)

One of the Verhaeren's strongest indictments of Germany appeared first in *Les Annales* of Paris and later in *Belgium's Agony*—*"L'Allemagne Incivilisable."* There he discussed the type of mind that is obedient, patient, reverent of authority, and for that very reason incapable of the highest flight of invention, spontaneity, originality and liberty. He said that Germany was essentially feudal, and although it may have possessed a culture, it did not have civilization. His impassioned address to the German people, a late poem entitled **"Au Peuple Allemand,"** shows Verhaeren's attitude most clearly. . . . (p. 28)

France was Verhaeren's refuge during some of his last months, and to her he paid exquisite tribute in **"France et Allemagne,"** a long poem where the two nations are compared and where Paris, which charms the soul of man, is said to have continued the civilization of Athens and Rome and to have added Christian grace to classic beauty. Equally enthusiastic is his praise of England, which seemed "like a vast and solid ship of granite that ruled the waves in fog and in solitary strength." In a letter he wrote how greatly England had raised herself in the eyes of Europe and in his own esteem by her regenerating energy and loyalty in the war, and in **"Angleterre"** he proclaimed this same fine admiration. His beautiful poem in memory of that best-known English poet-martyr appeared in the *Fortnightly Review* of April 1916. **"Rupert Brooke"** is an exquisite portrait of him who "being a poet, resolved to be a soldier," and it tells the story of his burial at Scyros. (p. 29)

[Verhaeren] is the only one among modern poets in French who is really popular with his countrymen of all ranks. From *Les Flamandes* through all his books to *Les Ailes Rouges de la Guerre* he never lost his close sympathy with the lives of the common people. In **"L'Ame Paysanne"** he shows a phase of the war felt only by those who live in close touch with the sensitive and mute love of the land so intimately a part of the Belgian and French country-folk. . . . (p. 30)

A sympathetic perception and love of a great modern city is still rarer in a poet. But Verhaeren so intelligently appreciated democratic ideals, modern inventions, great industries, and the resultant masses of population in cities that he has been called the poet of modernity. He not only pictured the outward aspects but interpreted their esthetic and ethical significance, in such poems as those on the first aeroplanes, the hospitals, the factories of war, and on Hamburg. He had, moreover, a real democratic faith in the power and ability of the mass of people. In these and other respects he has been compared with Whitman, but the Belgian poet is so unmistakably the greater artist and thinker that the resemblances are only superficial.

Most of the poems in *Les Ailes Rouges de la Guerre* are lyrical or descriptive; each one gives vivid pictures and ideas. **"Le Monde s'arme"** is a concise but comprehensive description of the beginning of the war when the world armed "from the depths of the sea even to the stars"; **"Les Exodes"** is the picture of the refugees. With the same tender intimacy and fine restraint of his *Les Heures d'Après-Midi,* **"La Patrie aux Soldats Morts"** realizes the tragedy of the young soldiers who died "when the light of day appears most sweet to them." The poem **"Ypres"** tells the history of the weavers who worked through the ages and built the Halles in their honest pride; it describes the splendor of the Cloth Hall, the belfry, and the cathedral, as well as the civic glory of Ypres, now burned and leveled to the ground. The noble **"La Cathédral de Reims"** cannot be better characterized than as an adequate poetic memorial to its great subject. (pp. 30-1)

Naturally in his last writings, Verhaeren's love of life and keen sense of its beauty are not so evident as in the earlier; but his largeness of vision is not lost. In *Parmi les Cendres* he said that Flanders and Wallonia have known days as sombre as the present. "Burgundy, Spain, and Austria each have by turn oppressed and dismembered them. They are not dead; they have always revived."

Here one must recall Verhaeren's socialism and his idea of war, which had been announced long before when in *Les Aubes* the socialist Hordain said: "If fatherlands are fair, sweet to the heart, dear to the memory, armed nations on the frontiers are tragic and deadly; and the whole world is yet bristling with nations." Again, in the words of Hérénien, the great tribune: "The hour of doing justice to the fundamental injustice, war, has come in its turn. Only with it will the others disappear too: the hate of the country for the city, of poverty for gold, of distress for power."

But heroism in war has had no more impassioned singer than Verhaeren. In *Poèmes Légendaires de Flandre et de Brabant,* with its dedication to Belgium written less than two months before the poet's death, the hero of Liège takes his place with the great national figures of Flemish history. (pp. 31-2)

> *Geraldine P. Dilla, "The Later Poetry of Emile Verhaeren," in* South Atlantic Quarterly *(reprinted by permission of the Publisher; copyright © 1924 by Duke University Press, Durham, North Carolina), Vol. 23, No. 1, January, 1924, pp. 20-34.*

JOHN W. CRAWFORD   (essay date 1924)

[*Crawford reviews the English translation of Verhaeren's* Cinq récits (Five Tales).]

A vision of terror-laden life, of nature stealthily hostile to men, of brother harboring secret hate of brother, is pitilessly sharp and clear, yet poignantly lyrical, in the **"Five Tales"** of Emile Verhaeren. Alien, disembodied threats take concrete shape in familiar streets and buildings and lurk in commonplace corners. Inns and quaint villages, smiling in pastoral quiet, reveal grotesque designs of fear and death. After the gentle dreaming day comes a night made hideously real with primeval menace, the roving ghosts of old forgotten awe.

The startling contrast, in Verhaeren's poems, between wistful, twilight simplicity, vague, half-pleasing sorrows and alien, implacable fate is implicit, likewise, in his prose. He conveys an exaltation of despair and suggests a stark panic. The mood swells irresistibly to crackling horror. It is as if he had snatched away the veil of complacent indifference with which the yawning abyss of the future is made endurable, even alluring, and forced unwilling eyes to stare into those terrible depths. Fleeting moments of anguish, that come to every one, are prolonged and intensified to the point of sheer, intolerable beauty and ecstatic, oblivious pain.

"The Inn of Gentle Death" is a magnificent accumulation of bald yet allusive statements. Brief sentence follows brief sentence. The language is absolutely transparent, yet rich with a subdued music of its own. It is always subordinate to the slow, restrained, but progressive development of the sardonic theme. The charming inn, with lustrous copper pots and cool neutral walls, dignified old tables and temperate, unhurried drinkers, might be the setting for a whimsical, touching idyl in a minor strain. The atmosphere of the taproom is completed amply, tersely, with a feeling of its endless continuity. The sole jarring note is added with an unerring skill; "the massive coffin-shaped clock, whose ciphered dial face lowered behind heavy glass, ticked off impassively its monotonous syllables." The clock makes itself known with a shock of premonition; this lovable old inn is not so kindly disposed toward the upstart humanity within its seemingly amiable walls as it first seemed to be. . . .

The "plot" is not so different from some cheap "thriller," but the story is a masterpiece of a poet's imagination.

A convincing picture of utterly unreasonable hysteria is given in **"One Night."** It is as subjective and personal as **"The Inn of Gentle Death"** is objective and detached. It is pure state of being, and is, in a sense, an anticipation of the expressionistic mode. Anxiety is multiplied and echoed in a thousand forms. House and belfries and churches become animate and strain to devour humanity, to fall upon and crush them, to come dancing out into the street in a nightmare of maddened lines and angles and masses. The very lights, which ought to be a reassurance, are fiercely leering eyes. It is a vivid embodiment of the terrifying question lurking behind accepted and known things.

"The Three Friends" is a vignette of hopelessness. The old women sit at tea and talk of trivial things, guessing at the sounds in the streets. All the while their mutual, furtive secret is a living presence in the room. They exist for the reader in all their loneliness and distrustfulness, with the vanished shadows of romantic love hovering over them and softening their querulous weakness with pitiful glamour and grandeur. The story itself is a tiny segment carrying a hint of a whole lifetime of each of them, and of the village in which they live. Mean and sordid old women, they are complaining in cracked, earsplitting voices of their ailments, regarding one another with respectful dislike, yet they are merely shells over secret and profound emotions, and they are immortally significant.

The runaway hearse which wrecked **"The Horse Fair at Opdorp"** is a device of almost theatrical gaudiness. The clinging, screaming street urchins and pompous, pursy churchwardens sway and rebound precariously as the sombre, black-and-silver vehicle, with its mockery of death lights and funeral trappings hurtles insanely through the streets of towns and lanes of countrysides. It is Death itself, as the reader follows its actual course, and is betrayed into childlike acceptance of its transformed and figurative career.

> *John W. Crawford, "Life Laden with Terror," in* The New York Times Book Review *(copyright © 1924 by The New York Times Company; reprinted by permission), November 23, 1924, p. 9.*

CHARLES BAUDOUIN   (essay date 1924)

[*Baudouin's* Psychoanalysis and Aesthetics, *from which the following excerpt has been taken, is a psychoanalytic study of Verhaeren's mind and art.*]

Verhaeren's evolution may be described as follows: up to the end of the crisis, towards the poet's thirty-fifth year, he is a thorough introvert, strongly attached to his "early affections," and suffering from a longing for the mother; later he becomes an extrovert, he acquires an interest in the outside world, he has conquered and is master of all the second terms of the coupled contrasts. Then he encounters love, which he understands as the intimate gift of self, as action; he finds he is a socialist, he realises the beauty of modern life, he "accepts" the "factory" (a double symbol, representing for him paternal authority and the reality of life). This is what we have named Verhaeren's "conversion." (p. 304)

[The] religious sentiment dragged down with it the whole of the poet's erstwhile equilibrium. Already in *Les flamandes,* and still more in *Les moines,* this ruin is foreshadowed: the acute crisis of the subsequent years was the expression of its emergence above the threshold of consciousness. The evil was accentuated because religious faith had provided a rationalisation of the tendency to introversion; it had, so to speak, justified the tendency. Henceforth there was to be a ceaseless contradiction between tendency and reason.

In especial does Verhaeren's strong ascetic tendency function henceforward in the void. In *Les débâcles* it has been reduced to an insensate desire for self-inflicted injury. It thus forms one of the main factors of the evil, for it leads Verhaeren to yearn for even more suffering, to wish "to diminish" himself yet further, and "to forge distresses for himself at his own anvil." (p. 306)

By entering upon social work, Verhaeren was led to "accept the factory," he was led to a belief in the present, to faith in human labour. A new ideal, a new meaning to life, serves to justify the tendencies and to bring them under control. Harmony has been achieved. (p. 307)

If Verhaeren's symbols appear twisted and obscure at a first glance, they are not so because of a desire on the part of the poet to be affected or to astonish his readers. It is precisely when they are obscure that they are fundamentally spontaneous; they are like dreams or nightmares which have been faithfully recorded, and they may be analysed with the same rigorous method as that employed in the analysis of dreams. Thus we find that the apparent inconsequence of one or other of the *Chansons de fou* is a disguised presentation of the profoundest complexes in the poet's psyche. Later, when Verhaeren's symbols become simpler and more lucid, when they evolve towards classicism, we have another proof of his sincerity. As the poet develops a wider interest in the world without, as he "objectivates" himself, he feels less impelled to sing of himself, and he tends towards an objective art which is to be a more faithful reflection of his new personality—a personality "which has fled the confines of self and has hastened to answer the call of the unanimous forces." Verhaeren consents even to run the risk of sacrificing originality to sincerity, for he gives up the visions, the special method of expression, and the rhythms which he had created, which were his signature, as it were, and of which he could be legitimately proud. Whereas other artists, less strong, cling desperately throughout life to the most mediocre of their eccentricities, since they see therein the guarantee of their artistic individuality, Verhaeren regally disdains a treasure of which the smallest jewel might make such seekers after originality weep with envy. Verhaeren loves running risks, he loves defiance; these are part of his heroism. He loves to exceed all his whilom exploits, as does his Hercules, even to the accomplishment of the impossible. Above all, he wishes to be sincere. When, therefore, the new soul he has created within himself demands of him a less spasmodic form of expression, an art less concentered in self, more objective and even, if needs must, less personal—straightway he adopts such an art and makes it his own. His decision hardly seems to be a voluntary one. Verhaeren's sincerity is his instinctive conscience as an artist. A new state of soul creates a new art.

This perfect artistic sincerity, this wholehearted obedience to the dictates of an inward monitor, is what has rendered our

analysis possible. The analysis, in its turn, confirms our conviction of Verhaeren's sincerity. In this way the work becomes a mirror of the soul—a symbolical mirror, it is true, but none the less faithful. All who knew Verhaeren, knew how simple and childlike he was; his whole life's work reflects his simplicity, his ingenuousness; and it is because it does so that it is so true. (pp. 307-08)

> *Charles Baudouin, in his* Psychoanalysis and Aesthetics, *translated by Eden Paul and Cedar Paul (copyright, 1924, by G. Allen & Unwin Ltd.; originally published as* Le symbole chez Verhaeren, *quatrième édition, 1924), G. Allen & Unwin Ltd., 1924, 328 p.*

RONALD SUSSEX (essay date 1955)

[*Sussex offers a laudatory summarization of Verhaeren's poetic themes.*]

The astonishing Belgian renaissance of the 1880's was no isolated outburst: it sprang from a long tradition, and it was no accident that both local and universal values found memorable expression in the great lyric poet thrown up by the movement—Emile Verhaeren. Even more than his contemporaries Maeterlinck, Van Lerberghe, Rodenbach and Lemonnier, Verhaeren seemed to gather up in himself the age-old tradition of his own people as well as the dreams and aspirations of modern humanity, the quiet poetry of humble life as well as the stormy rhythms of nature, the measured rural year as well as the huge convulsions of urban industry. (p. 52)

With what proud affection Verhaeren studied his people in its every manifestation, from the rebel burghers of the Gothic age to the baroque fecundity of Rubens, from the sluggish, toilsome winter month to the joyous amplitude of summer, from the devout tranquility of the *béguinage* to the sensual riot of the *kermesse.* He abhorred nothing that was Flemish: he was one with his kind, and it was through Flemish windows that he looked out upon the world.

Equally Flemish was his way with womankind. His first volume of verse, *Les Flamandes* . . . , was a fleshly, turbulent hymn to the superb animality of his people, whose appetites found pasture in the rich, copious foods that the seventeenth century *petits maîtres* loved to paint, as well as in the ample flesh of Flemish woman and the large families she mothered. This is an unethereal art, forceful and even crude in its emphasis, truculently earthy and carnal, but quite free of the decadent, satanic note popularized by Baudelaire. Yet this same poet could write, with deep and sincere feeling, of the devout, affectionate aunt who was a real mother to him and the interpreter of his childhood faith, and later, in accents hardly less religious (though no longer Catholic), could pen the exquisitely tender lyrics to his wife which make up the three volumes called *Les heures.* These volumes, along with the letters to his wife published by M. René Vandevoir in 1938, show an idealized, spiritual conception of love reminiscent of Rossetti, of Mrs. Browning and even of the *Vita Nuova.* Love so disciplined, and built upon utter sincerity, trust and loyalty, had none of the hues of death that troubled Ronsard and Donne, none of the destructive, self-torturing fury of Racine's Phèdre: the morning of love might yield place to the fulness of afternoon, then to the waning strength of evening, but time and mortality had no dominion over it. This co-existence of huge animal strength and of deep tenderness is very Flemish—Rubens himself exemplified it two centuries before.

No poet who is a good European can jettison the past, and Verhaeren, though this was not the habitual bent of his mind, *did* turn back to the history and tradition of his own people as well as of humanity as a whole. The slow, laboured progress of man towards the light seemed to him to be a pilgrimage led by heroes, the lighthouses of humanity. In the path already trodden by Emerson and Carlyle Verhaeren singled out for admiration those concentrations of human courage or intelligence who really lent meaning to what Hugo styled the *légende des siècles* [*legend of the centuries*]—the missionary-apostle of the Merovingian age, the feudal baron who fought back the Northmen, the painter who evoked new forms of beauty, the burgesses who defended elementary human rights against the exploiter, the explorer and the conquistador, the alchemist and the inventor. The gesture of Eve in refusing Paradise, of Hercules in battling with death, of Luther in defying Rome, of Rembrandt in his self-immolation to his art—these were the rich, historic moments in mankind's *chanson de geste* [*heroic song*]. Nor did Verhaeren's hero-cult rest there: he went beyond Emerson and Maeterlinck in lending heroic stature to the humble artisan, and, with profound moral insight, in robing his contemporary hero, not in armour, but in overalls.

It was this extolling of modern life, in a verse-form that pulsed with Verhaeren's elemental strength, which first brought him before the wider public. If one except the volumes of 'decadent' poems of the 'crisis' period (1886-89), the outcome of a highly fashionable and deliberately exploited neurasthenia, Verhaeren's poems of the early 1890's are the earliest in the manner which was later to be recognized as characteristically his. This was a decade of rural depopulation, of industrial discontent and intense poverty, but Verhaeren, though he could see all the energy of the countryside being drained away into the 'tentacular' modern city, and village life abandoned to paupers and idiots, could also see with a poet's eyes the great strength and promise that lay behind the ugly forms of mine-head and factory, of railroad and stock-exchange and laboratory. He could admire the 'Gothic' past and the triumphs of its historic faith, but would gladly let the dead past bury its dead—old Europe could well turn its back on all this, to plunge into the fermenting vat of the present. The city, for all its vice and rapacity, its demonic energy and its traffic in human flesh, was truly the crucible in which a shining future was being cast and shaped. For him, as for William Blake, the dark satanic mills of Metropolis hid the growing ramparts of the new Jerusalem—though in Verhaeren's thought this was to be no habitation for God, only for man. . . . With all his heart and mind and soul and strength Verhaeren believed, with Shelley, that the world's great age was beginning anew and the golden years returning. Hence the bitterness of his awakening, when 1914 shut the door on his hopes for the unity and brotherhood of mankind. The Europe he had dreamed into being, the Europe he had seen being forged on the anvil of progress, now fell apart, and his own little country offered tragic evidence of the desolate ruin that remained.

There was another Verhaeren, too—the man of the fields and woods and open air, the man in whose flesh pulsed the rhythm of all created things. This was the poet who could render the slow strength of the Scheldt or the fury of November on the dunes, the sun-lit colour and fragrance of the garden at Caillou-quibique or the crystal quiet of the starts. Like a true Fleming he could pass from the warm intimacy of a cottage hearth to the stormy unrest of the sea, from the tinkling of the first birdsong in February to the wild music of the Atlantic gales. Indeed, his native element seemed to be the wind, whose huge

tumult and disorder answered his own inner mood, whose violence awakened the fighter in him, whose pure breath loved and cleansed the body of him. Unlike Francis Jammes with his pastoral simplicity, or Henri de Régnier with his elegiac statuesqueness, Verhaeren was nearer to Hugo (his master) in the orchestration of nature's music: he knew and loved her every phase, and found in her not only solace and strength, but the matter of high poetry and noble thinking. The clear, tranquil pantheism of his later manner showed no self-doubt or anguish, but the faith of a man who trod the earth as a loved place, as one belonging there. (pp. 52-4)

Ronald Sussex, "The Good European," in ADAM *International Review (© ADAM International Review 1955), Vol. 23, No. 250, 1955, pp. 52-4.*

P. MANSELL JONES (essay date 1957)

[*Jones's* Verhaeren *is a complete critical survey of the poet's works. In the epilogue to his study, excerpted below, Jones expresses qualified admiration for Verhaeren's poetry, continuing to value its "moral stimulation" and vitality, while denying the high degree of "modernism" once attributed to his verse (see excerpt above by Jurgis Baltrušaitis). Viewed in the context of modern poetry, which includes T. S. Eliot's "The Waste Land," Verhaeren's works appear an inadequate expression of twentieth-century experience. For a similar critique of Verhaeren's modernity, see Kristiaan Versluys's essay excerpted below.*]

Reading [Verhaeren's] work through again, one can see his debts accumulate to Baudelaire, Rimbaud, Verlaine and Laforgue, to say nothing of Hugo whom he cultivated increasingly. But one also perceives how much in subsequent poetry is latent in the long and varied sequence of his experiments. (p. 49)

To begin with his first distinctive phase, Verhaeren's success in making poetry 'out of the complaining voices of the nerves', as Symons put it [see excerpt above]; his effort to match with imagery and rhythm those 'abysms of melancholy' from which, in Valéry's opinion, he must have suffered acutely, predate an unprecedented invasion of literature and the arts by irrational and neurotic types of fantasy, some of which may strike us as brilliant and revealing, while others leave us indifferent to their trivial and humourless extravagances. Cultivated most feverishly in France, such preoccupations have turned many writers and artists of talent from the time-honoured task of creating beauty to the intuitive analysis, through their special media, of ever more extreme forms of mental and moral aberration.

And here we should remind ourselves that in the middle years of his productivity Verhaeren, still prone to sombre hallucinations, practised what I have ventured to call the modern macabre style—that morbid blend of the grotesque and the corrupt which he took over, with elaborations of his own, from Baudelaire and Huysmans, combining with it elements derived from eccentric artists in the pictorial traditions with which he remained in creative contact. The originality of this composite style lies in the manner of its adaptation to actual situations, and at that Verhaeren could be strangely successful. His numerous experiments in the macabre may be found to have supplied important links between the distortions of late mediaeval and baroque art and the curiosities of contemporary fantasy.

At this point a distinction must be made to avoid misrepresentation. Although his work abounds in material for the psychologist, Verhaeren does not appear to have been touched by

Freudian theories. For this reason and also because he was at all times consciously an artist, producing work which, despite the *sauvagerie* of his temperament and the 'paroxysms' of his manner, never ceased to be effectively composed and 'controlled', he cannot be classed as a forerunner of those enemies of logic and artifice, the Surrealists, nor would it be wise to suggest that they felt any curiosity for his work.

Yet, with no desire to force a comparison, one cannot help detecting the recurrence of a certain tone in Verhaeren's phase of distress which becomes resonant in theirs, a distraught note, alien to harmony, balance or repose, which suggests that he too had moments of ominous perception into the confusions of his time, such as the Surrealists profess to have into the obscure chaos of today.

As for the question of modernity, Verhaeren's position looked secure forty years ago, when it would have seemed rhetorical to ask, was he not the first significant poet of the scientific and industrial era? Today what claims may have been his to originality in this sphere are largely ignored. Yet it was the author of *Les Villes tentaculaires* who, with a skill hitherto without precedent, succeeded in adapting to poetry the real operations of the laboratory, the rebarbative aspects of factory premises and the behaviour of operatives at work, in their relaxations and in revolt. He ruminated over the purposes of such activities and strove to appreciate their significance. Since his time the attitude of poets and artists has changed from one of confidence to one of distrust and foreboding. 'When I am in the company of scientists', wrote W. H. Auden recently, 'I feel like a curate who has strayed into a drawing-room full of dukes. If the attitude of poets towards our civilization is merely negative, this is mainly because they know that poets can do nothing to solve the problem of a machine culture and the people who might be able to do so seem hardly aware that these problems exist'. That looks like a failure of nerve. Actually, however, many poets and artists, including Auden, are anxiously concerned with our machine age, its conditions and its culture; and if their approach seems more cautious than Verhaeren's it is because they have reason to be more suspicious. Yet none appear to have advanced beyond him in the attempt to solve the technical problem involved in making lyrical reference to the implements and products of an aggressive materialism, which has revolutionized our social life and opened before it simultaneous prospects of power and disaster. It may be that contemporary poets are more indebted to his example than they are aware of being. I have disclaimed any intention of 'proving' influences. But anyone who has studied the way a literary influence works knows that it can affect subsequent writers without deliberate effort on their part and often despite a healthy disregard for precedents. I see little in contemporary poetry of a similar inspiration that surpasses Verhaeren's in ingenuity. Yet how often the relationship of science to poetry is discussed without mention being made of the name of a poet in whose work the long line of what in France has been called *la poésie scientifique* had reached a resounding ascendency before the end of last century. What Verhaeren achieved was not merely the appropriation of the nomenclature of apparatus and experiment and its adaptation in neat catalogues of rhymed description; much of that kind had been done before him. He abandoned the age-long practice of personifying natural forces and dramatizing their interactions. Instead, he adopted the terms by which science identifies forces and substances in the laboratory and in the lecture-room. Marinetti is said to have claimed Verhaeren as the 'spiritual father' of the school he founded. But it is hardly a compliment to his ex-perimental mannerisms to say that they served as models for the imitative frivolities of Futurism. A real fervour inspires the best of his modernist verse. Arbitrary details and operations become poetical through the feeling he has for them, and description is caught up and galvanized in the energy of his rhythms and images. (pp. 49-51)

In one of the most significant short poems of his later period—'Le Navire' (*Les Rythmes souverains*)—humanity is symbolized as a ship being steered by its captain over the troubled seas of time into the serenity of the future. . . . Here in the recognition of the unanimity of natural operations, the gradual advance in man's perception of their laws and his progressive adaptation of life to their sanctions, we recognize the basic principles and inspiration of the movement called Unanimism. From the tentative experiments of 1906 made by the group of L'Abbaye, and soon to be followed by the theories and applications of M. Jules Romains, poetry, drama and the novel in France have been periodically refreshed by a type of initiative which owes part of its impulse to the original examples of Whitman and Verhaeren. (p. 52)

For most of us today, the epoch of modern poetry dates from the appearance in 1922 of *The Waste Land*, or perhaps one should say, from the gradual realization in the ensuing decade of the significance of this difficult poem. What Verhaeren had in common with the Unanimists, namely collective vision and humanitarian sympathies, separated him from Eliot, whose deeper analysis—psychological in character and metaphysical in judgment—proved to be more satisfying to the intelligentsia of a world recovering from the unprecedented wastage of the biggest war in history. Strong new movements in literature and the arts can effect such diversions and achieve such injustices. Yet it is not improbable that the fuliginous tableaux of *Les Villes tentaculaires* had impressed thoughtful readers at the turn of the century with as deep a sense of cleavage in the modern soul as that which Eliot's poem exposed through a different approach and technique. (pp. 52-3)

How is our subject related to the dominant philosophical mood of today?

Verhaeren was no metaphysical; yet like some of our prominent metaphysicians he could not have placed essence before existence. If to be an existentialist meant to believe in life and to enjoy it, then he would be the greatest existential poet. But he is merely a great singer of existence, and so for the moment his message is effaced by a type of philosophy which recommends life with a grimace of courage, as if it were largely repulsive. His insistence on *orgueil* (self-reliance) and freedom has all the force which the Existentialists attach to these words—without the desperation. . . . Like Nietzsche, however, he had a strong sense of the tragic heroism involved in the acceptance of necessity. The supreme courage of the exceptional being who pits all the strength of his physical, mental and moral faculties against the overwhelming powers of circumstance stirred the poet to his depths, especially at the moment of paroxysm, when nerves and sinews are strained to the utmost and the magnificent rage of humain despair closes in conflict with the obscure violence of human destiny. . . .

But what of the tragedies involved in the common human lot of our time? The author of *Les Villes tentaculaires* sees soundness of life frustrated, beauty desecrated and innocence befouled. . . . (p. 54)

But as with many benevolent observers in the days of pre-war prosperity, his sense of menace tends to evaporate in the assumption that all things work together for good in accordance with 'l'instinct mieux défini de l'être humain' ['humanity's veritable higher instincts'], which laws are gradually being disclosed by science. Complacency is the last failing of which a mind and heart as sensitive and noble as Verhaeren's could be accused. It is none the less disturbing to find how completely the denunciations of **Les Villes tentaculaires** fade into the acclamations of the later volumes—save for the references to war which, like a thunderbolt falling from skies that seemed blue, shook the refugee profoundly but could hardly be said to have renewed the poet's inspiration.

More seriously still, like many another pantheist, Verhaeren shows no sense of the tragic mystery of evil, that inveterate perversity which Baudelaire perceived and denounced in himself and in other men. The later poet's genuine naïveté is here at a discount; he does not seem to have realized either the unaccountable malignancy of wickedness or its tenacious subtlety and resource. It stands, no doubt, to the honour of his fundamental sanity and reverence that Verhaeren betrays no prescience of the horrors of forced labour, organized torture and mass murder on the scale of unprecedented magnitude which many of his younger contemporaries lived to suffer or to witness within a few decades of his death. And it may go far to explain the relative neglect of his work to admit that while we may have no more conviction than he had of a personal deity we have none of his confidence in the divinization of man through science. . . . (pp. 54-5)

Still less may we be able to believe in the solution of the mystery of God, which he outlined in these words: 'Although sceptical and very hesistant in matters of belief, I never doubt one thing, that the *savants* will succeed—though I don't know when—in unveiling the real significance of life, in giving us the true understanding of the universe, the veritable knowledge of God. I am entirely, absolutely convinced of that'.

Adapting a phrase of Peter Quennell's, T. S. Eliot differentiated the kind of poet we need when he said of Baudelaire that he had the 'sense of the age'. How does Verhaeren meet this criterion? 'Our entire epoch is reflected in his work', said Stefan Zweig. But had Verhaeren the critical attitude which Eliot found in Baudelaire, and which we find in Eliot and in the later poems of Yeats? Verhaeren saw with incomparable breadth what Zweig again called 'all manifestations of the modernity of his day'. But did he see *through* them? Let us recall Baudelaire's famous theory of civilization: 'It is not in gas or in steam or in turning tables. It is in the diminution of the traces of original sin'. We must not of course expect theological discriminations from Verhaeren. But has he any criticism of comparable depth to offer? Such questions are unavoidable. They suggest that a large part of his report, for all its vivid realism, is not profoundly penetrating. No poetry is more vitalistic than his, but no vitalistic poetry was ever less complete as a criticism of life. Its moral stimulation is real, but it is an encouragement rather than a cure. (pp. 55-6)

> *P. Mansell Jones, in his* Emile Verhaeren *(reprinted by permission of The Bodley Head Ltd for Bowes & Bowes), Bowes & Bowes, 1957, 64 p.*

IAN HIGGINS (essay date 1973)

[*Higgins discusses Verhaeren's poetic theories and the manner in which they determine the function of the "verse speech" in Verhaeren's dramas.*]

H. R. Rookmaaker adapts Michaud in distinguishing three streams in both the literature and the painting of around 1890 in France. In literature, the first is *décadence*, the "poésie affective" of which Verlaine is the master; the second is *symbolisme*, the neo-Platonist "poésie intellectuelle" whose chief figure is Mallarmé; the third is that of *poésie fantastique*, centring on Rimbaud. (p. 1)

Verhaeren wrote poetry in both the first and the third manners distinguished by Rookmaaker, and in his constant drive towards expression of the law of change in the universe, something in itself inscrutable but whose effects are exemplified and whose workings are typified in phenomena, he is quasi-Symbolist (or *idéiste*, in [G. A.] Aurier's definition). But his monism excludes any neo-Platonism; and he retains a belief in the dignity and importance of man as the being which both realises the law as having specific value beyond the generic, and experiences the world as the object of an imperative to assume the workings of the law by acting on the world—that is, the urge to integrate the objective expression of the law and the subjective human expression of it. For him as for the Synthetists and the literary Symbolists, since the law can at best only be expressed, the practical problem is the choice of expression—the choice of a mode of symbolism or analogy. But compared with the work of the literary Symbolists, there is a complicating factor in Verhaeren, in the socialist commitment present in his thought from the early 1890s onward. There are more elements to balance: it is a question not simply of attaining in the mediation the right proportion and relation of self-expression to reference outside the self, but of doing so in a *prescriptive* mediation. The creation of the work of art is itself an act, but the work implies and invites action in a particular direction in the world outside itself: the problem for Verhaeren is to provoke in the reader or spectator a formulation of the socio-ethical meaning of the *idée* or law whose effects are exemplified, and workings typified, in the sensuous presence of the work—to synthesise description with prescription and demonstration so that the latter should have the same objective authority for the reader or spectator as does the world-as-perceived outside the work. Verhaeren's theoretic writings and his poetry and drama bring together the major artistic and intellectual currents of the time, and to study his inevitable theoretic failure will shed light certainly on Verhaeren, and I hope also on aesthetic problems of the Symbolist and post-Symbolist periods in France. (pp. 3-4)

When writing about poetry, Verhaeren rarely discusses technique other than in principle. His main concern seems to be with poetry as an instrument of self-realisation for both poet and public. At first, at the beginning of the 1890s, he sees poetry essentially as self-expression, free of collective considerations. Yet already there is a clear gap between him and much Symbolist theory. In an article of 1890, he rejects escape into "le rêve" ["the dream"], and welcomes the pain and contradiction of "la vie réelle" ["real life"]. This is because *rêve* tends towards a sterile changelessness, an attempt at escaping contingency. His poetry is an act of release, a safety-valve for his integral, physical, being. During the 90s, Verhaeren's view becomes more outward-looking, and the poems after 1900 reflect this. But the view of poetry remains essentially the same. The poem is a product of the whole being, and some form of harmony, physical and mental balance, is involved in creating the poem: it is an act, in which he momentarily achieves the self-realisation he perpetually needs and seeks. . . . So the individual consciousness bears on the world through the creation of the poem, and realises for itself a place in the world. How does the poet experience this consciousness?

Throughout his career, Verhaeren insists that rhythm is the most important material aspect of poetry. As one would expect from someone so interested in painting and sculpture, Verhaeren is a fertile creator of visual images and metaphors, but the most powerful experience of the materiality of a poem is for him in its rhythm. Rhythm often comes as if naturally at the head of the list of qualities of a particular poet he is discussing. In a lecture of 1901, he says that the true poet has the gift, at the very moment a thought arises in his brain, of conceiving it as a living entity, endowed with a rhythmic action; and that he cannot therefore but be a perfect master of rhythm. This insistence on seizing the idea as it first bursts into the consciousness is important. . . . The main characteristic of inspiration for Verhaeren is a rhythmic excitement of the entire being, and rhythmic expression of that inspiration is the main goal of the poet. . . . Verhaeren's poetry is meant to communicate and persuade, not simply to express, and not necessarily to prove; and rhythm is the principal means to this end. (pp. 4-5)

If Verhaeren wants his poetry to "persuade", what does he want to persuade his reader of? During the 1890s, the idea of collectivity occupied Verhaeren in a largely social form, but always closely associated with the individualism which one finds everywhere in his poetic theory. In 1893, he rejects Art for Art's sake, and all *a priori* formulae for poetry: he emphasises the individual poet's inspiration and concern to express himself totally, independent of schools or political doctrines, but says at the same time that self-expression is automatically expression of the world. . . . He goes further the following year, when he says that social commitment is perhaps a necessary condition for the self-fulfilment of the next generation of artists. He rejects the elaboration of programmes in poetry: the original source of the work is still the artist's spontaneous urge to self-expression. But without dropping the idea of collectivity, Verhaeren invokes the "âme de choix"—the genius, a vital figure in all his subsequent work. If such a man writes social poetry, Verhaeren says here, he does so without betraying his individual inspiration. Only, the development of the modern world seems to be such that individual inspiration will more and more involve awareness of a collective destiny.

Verhaeren develops this idea elsewhere by suggesting that collectivity is a scientific fact. Scientific research has revealed the exclusively material structure and unity of the universe. Man is realising himself more and more fully, becoming more like the God in whom he formerly believed. The poet is one who expresses his "exaltation lyrique" at this evolution into an unknown future; a part of the whole, he is as much its consciousness as any man, but unusual in his faculty for expressing the enthusiasm which that consciousness awakens. Again, he obeys no programme; he automatically expresses the collective experience. (pp. 5-6)

The great poet's inspiration is essentially a sense of his place in the collective destiny of the society he is writing for.

But such a contribution to the growth of universal self-consciousness is not the prerogative of poetry. Often Verhaeren writes of art in general rather than poetry, and often the poet is joined with the painter and the sculptor in a common destiny. . . . One article, **"La Sensation artistique"**, is of particular interest because it shows how close Verhaeren's experience of painting and sculpture is to his experience of poetic

inspiration. Good art procures for the spectator an experience of the cosmic exaltation which originally inspired its creator—just as happened to Verhaeren when he read out his poems. The same thing happens to the art-enthusiast when he *talks about* works he has enjoyed: he feels an urge to re-experience and also to communicate the rhythmic excitement which the *idée* has provoked in him. The kinship of this with poetic inspiration is clear. Characteristically, Verhaeren refers to the *sensation artistique* as a "frisson divin". The link between art and the divine, with the common denominator being beauty, shows how close aesthetics is for Verhaeren to considerations of man and his destiny, and recalls his idea that poetry inspires itself more and more from the spectacle of man's progress towards a state of "divinity". (pp. 6-7)

Although he often writes of art rather than of an art, one has to consider the different means of expression in painting, poem and sculpture. In the plastic works which Verhaeren discusses, language is denied the spectator. This may not matter as long as the communication is not meant to be persuasion; but as soon as it is—as with Verhaeren—the artist has to reckon with misinterpretation. The poem, on the other hand, uses a medium potentially familiar to all, with a conventional system of meaning which its user can accept, reject or modify in trying to persuade. (p. 10)

The temptation for the poet is then to rely on the conventional system of meaning in language to describe or evoke the circumstances and nature of his experience of inspiration, and in so doing to try and communicate it to his reader. This is what usually happens in Verhaeren's lyrical cosmic poems. The poet may then read his work to an audience, as Verhaeren liked to, and so take advantage of the physical contact this sets up between himself and his public. This relationship may stand a better chance of appearing to the audience as typifying the workings of the universal law which the poem is about. But the obstacle will remain that such a poem describes or evokes one man's experience of this law; although the poem itself, in its sensuous presence, exemplifies the effects and typifies the workings of the truth it is talking about, it is talking about it, whereas for example the sculpture does not. . . . One alternative, which Verhaeren often uses, is the narrative or epic poem. Here already his concern with history begins to imply the dramatic. But the problem here is the same: does the past speak for itself, or does it need the mediation of history? In such poems, Verhaeren's narrative is always lyrical and mediatory, so that the reader's immediate encounter is still with the poet or his persona.

The poet is therefore faced with an obstacle, which the sculptor does not have to reckon with. The sculptor makes stone or metal suggest something they otherwise might not have done. The poet of course makes ink suggest something which a bottleful might not have done, but the form he gives it has a conventional semantic content beyond its new shape, whereas the piece of marble remains a piece of marble, perhaps suggestive, but with no accretion of conventional significance beyond the formal resemblance it may have to something else. . . . The sculpture may be a more immediate manifestation of the *idée*, appearing to tend more towards exemplification than towards symbolic representation. (pp. 11-12)

Nevertheless, it would appear from what Verhaeren says about poetry that he thinks the potential persuasive power of a piece of marble or bronze is less than that of language in poetry, however great a genius the sculptor may be. The problem is to present the spontaneity and authenticity of an individual's inspired insight into man's role in universal evolution at the moment of its first irruption into his consciousness, and to combine this manifestation with the power of persuasion which a mastery of language would give him. A possible solution is a poetic drama, a linguistic, three-dimensional plastic phenomenon which is a work only in performance. The temporality of drama is different from that of the static plastic arts, in that the spectator's temporal experience depends on the actors. In the static arts the spectator creates the time, as his eye moves over the surface of the object; in the performed arts, the performer creates the time, so that there is a tension in the spectator's experience of the work: he apprehends it as an evolving external phenomenon, instead of supplying the evolution himself. Gauguin, for whom painting and music were near neighbours at the top of the hierarchy of arts because they both give the public's *rêve* full rein (he is typical of the Synthetists in this), nevertheless gives music a secondary place precisely because of the mode of its temporality: it seems fair to suggest, in the perspectives of Verhaeren's writings, that this kind of temporality could set drama above painting as an expression of universal law.

In addition, it is interesting that Verhaeren should call the spectator's reaction to the plastic work an exercise of his "rite personnel". Such a reference introduces temporality, and recalls both the collective and participatory nature of religious celebration and the origins of the theatre in such events. The theatre is characterised by the collective participation of the spectators and their intimate relationship—even if it is a relationship of alienation—with the celebrants, or actors. It contrasts in this respect with poetry, which tends to be read in solitude. (pp. 12-13)

So a further reason why Verhaeren should be drawn to the theatre may be discerned. As Zweig and others testify, the reading aloud of the finished poem is for Verhaeren the climax of its creation, which is not surprising in view of his emphasis on rhythm as the most important material characteristic of poetry. If the play showed someone experiencing the inspiration which characterises art, and if that person were gifted with a poet's powers of rhythmic verbal expression, then communication of such an experience might be possible on a relatively large scale, the speaker drawing the members of the audience into his experience so that they realised for a while the divine *grandeur* of their common identity, but each according to his *rite personnel*. The spectator's immediate encounter would not be with the playwright or his persona. Where the Verhaeren poem exists in two modes insofar as the original inspiration is its subject, this drama would present the spectacle of someone actually undergoing such an inspiration and realising it in expression. This expression might in theory, if endowed with the right qualities of rhythm and "exaltation", be felt by the spectator to communicate spontaneously the state of mind which has inspired it. The dramatic character would not address himself to the spectator, he would not need to describe the circumstances of his experience—the spectator would hear an immediate linguistic materialisation of it: the lyrical speech *would be* the experience as the character realised it, bringing it through his surprised consciousness into language, thus affording himself some understanding of it, delivering himself as the poet does of the pressure of his inspiration, and in so doing defining for himself once more a position in the world. (pp. 13-14)

This is largely what happens in Verhaeren's plays, and it is particularly apparent in the first three, which are in a mixture of prose and verse. All are set at a time of change, and all emphasise the rhythmic or cyclic nature of historical change: for Verhaeren, history is linear, but change is brought about by the same principle reasserting itself, a fossilised institution being destroyed through its internal contradictions. In each of the plays, the future of a community is at stake, and the characters are constantly made aware of their involvement in the collective evolution. Whatever their standpoint, their reaction when the historical process impinges on them particularly sharply is always in verse—a sudden heightening of the expression, with an element of the unpredictable and the undefinable, created by the prosody, going hand in hand with the rhythm and conveying the spontaneity and surprise of the character's reaction. (p. 14)

In Verhaeren's plays, the speech in verse is communication as well as expression. It is not necessarily a deliberate attempt at persuasion, although some are meant to persuade the other characters. It expresses the character's reactions, or sometimes his convictions, and other characters and the spectator witness the expression. The characters' reactions are also communicated through the verse speech to the other characters present, in that the verse usually generates an emotional and ideological momentum which carries the other characters along with it. The verse speech also communicates the reaction to the spectator; but at the same time it may communicate more to him than the speaker or the other characters would suspect: his reaction is experienced by the spectator as a function of a situation which is different from that of the characters in that he is outside theirs. So the verse speech invites the spectator to interpret and evaluate, in the same way as any dramatic speech, while at the same time admitting him into a greater intimacy with the character than is the case in naturalistic plays. (p. 19)

There is certainly an alternation in the nature and degree of participation in those of Verhaeren's plays which contain both prose and verse, though the stylisation of most of the prose prevents the plays degenerating into naturalistic illusionism. The power of the verse to induce a momentary vision from the character's point of view is enhanced by its contrast with the apparently more controlled prose, and the overall result is an intensification of the spectator's reaction: he sees each speech as a function of the others, and so his understanding of the situation is increased; but at the same time he appreciates or sympathises with the emotions both of the enlightened characters and of those who are wrong or destroyed. The verse brings the spectator to see the world and the individual in terms of one another, throwing each character's enthusiasm, doubt or fear into relief against the background of the ever-changing, still unfathomed world.

For Verhaeren, the universe is dynamic, a complex of rhythms, and the aim of art is to help both artist and public to a full awareness of the dynamism in terms of value. . . . What Verhaeren tries to do, in different ways, in his poems and poetic dramas, is to grasp the nettle of mediation and actually endow the rhythms of the physical world, embodied here as the rhythm of political change and the rhythm of oral utterance, with the superior denotative and connotative power of language, and so to persuade the public that his call to action is the valid one. The plays are increasingly sophisticated attempts at making the world exemplify what it expresses and express what it exemplifies. (p. 21)

Les Aubes, set in an imaginary land in the future, presents a peaceful socialist revolution: but the description is of a way the world is not, the issue appears to have been decided *a priori* by the prescribing mind of the play's creator—the mediation has been mediated, as in the poem. *Le Cloître,* set at an indeterminate time in an indeterminate country, presents the takeover of power in a monastery and the conflict between progressives and conservatives. It is a paradigm of how the law of change affects even the most closed of communities. But for this reason, and because of its vague setting, it may be felt to have little demonstrative power for the socio-political world outside the play and the monastery. *Philippe II,* however, is a sophisticated illustration of how the law has actually manifested itself in history. But still the law, being an abstraction, can only be evoked, linguistically, symbolically. *Hélène de Sparte* is the final attempt at the impossible synthesis of abstraction and reference, expression and exemplification. In presenting a political conflict in the past, Verhaeren has turned this time to myth, where the convention permits what cannot be tried in the historical play. The law, in the form of Zeus, plays a part. Verhaeren is careful, through elaborate staging and the roles played by the characters, to present Zeus as a projection of human consciousness. Yet precisely because of the attempt to exemplify the meaning in the work, the element of symbolism erupts on the surface. It is notable that, from an imaginary case-history of successful revolution, in *Les Aubes,* Verhaeren progresses to generalities in *Hélène de Sparte.* Zeus' intervention can be reduced to a general statement that the world perpetually changes: there is no suggestion of the right way of assuming this law in action. And indeed, the more such a symbolic mediation (as making Zeus speak) went into detail, the more it would draw attention to itself as mediation—exemplification would be seen completely to give way to expression. In *Hélène de Sparte* the world is both mediated and seen to need mediation, but the mediation by definition does not have the unquestionable integrity of the unmediated world. As communication, *Hélène de Sparte* is powerful; it may even communicate much of what it expresses: but in the end it lacks, as persuasion, the authority and prescriptive clarity which Verhaeren seems to have dreamed of for a committed art.

Verhaeren is clearly a product of his age, artistically and intellectually. He was also a great defender of modernity and experiment both in the arts and outside them. Does it not seem extraordinary, then, that despite his technical knowledge of painting and his friendship with so many painters of the day, he should have paid little or no attention to the Synthetists or the Fauves or the Cubists? The problem with Verhaeren is that as he matures he is less content with a "pure" aesthetics and purely painterly questions: his work is an early attempt to integrate ideological commitment to something in the world outside art with the gains in technique made by the writers and painters of the age. In the urge to express the universal law, there is always the tendency to abstraction, found in the various techniques of suggestion; but this is at the pole neither of pure expressionism nor of what Mondrian was to call "pure plastics". At the very moment when painters begin explicitly to concern themselves with the new problems brought to light notably by Mallarmé, Verhaeren parts company with them because he retains a belief in the importance of subject-matter and—dare one say it?—Anecdote. Aesthetically there is the same drive towards synthesis of expression and exemplification, the same dream of a self-expressive *évidence:* but apart from the irreducibility of mind and outside world, there is the problem in Verhaeren that aesthetics is inseparable from morality, and individual morality from collective.

A further problem is Verhaeren's consistent belief in the primacy of language in human experience of the world. This is an idea which occurs constantly in his poetry. Perception as recognition, and valuation, depend on language; and this is as true of the plastic arts as it is of the world outside them. One of the most striking features of **"La Sensation artistique"** is that the spectator is said to feel the need to express his reaction and communicate it to others. In Verhaeren, not only is language mediation of the world, but mediation of the world is essentially linguistic. It is therefore wholly consistent, in Verhaerenian perspectives, to ask the artist to assume the linguistic aspect of mediation and the mediatory aspect of language, in an attempt to provoke the public to a particular formulation of the world mediated. In other words, if it is impossible not to interpret the world, art should demand to be interpreted, and in a particular direction.

In the retention of subject-matter, and a relatively discursive poetic style, Verhaeren looks back to the past; in the search for a moral *évidence* inseparable from a phenomenological one, and the related hesitation as to whether expression or communication is the object of criticism, he looks forward to the debates over committed art of the mid-twentieth century. (pp. 22-3)

Ian Higgins, "Towards a Poetic Theatre: Poetry and the Plastic Arts in Verhaeren's Aesthetics" (copyright © by Forum for Modern Language Studies *and Ian Higgins), in* Forum for Modern Language Studies, *Vol. IX, No. 1, January, 1973 (and reprinted in* Literature and the Plastic Arts, 1880-1930: Seven Essays, *edited by I. Higgins, Scottish Academic Press, 1973, pp. 1-23).*

CLAIRE L. DEHON (essay date 1977)

[*Dehon discusses the leading characters in Verhaeren's dramas as allegorical types. She contends that by using characters who are not meant to be viewed as individuals, Verhaeren created works that function in the ancient manner of allegory as "a ritual, a magic event designed to arouse in the spectator a sense of his place in the universe."*]

[Verhaeren] offers much to interest a reader who is curious about the past and who wants to understand the evolution of the modern theater. . . . [His plays (*Les Aubes, Le Cloître, Philippe II,* and *Hélène de Sparte*)] are disturbing because they form an audacious mixture of elements. Apparently they borrow their elements from all kinds of sources: the myth of Helen from antiquity; the use of the alexandrine from the seventeenth century; the powerful images and exaggerated sentiments from Romanticism; the class of social struggle from the literature of the end of the nineteenth century. These ideas are mixed within a symbolist esthetic to create original plays which later gave birth to our contemporary theater.

The first of the plays, *Les Aubes,* reveals the horrors of war and the revolt of a populace drawn against its will into the conflict. Jacques Hérénien, the son of a peasant, leads the insurrection, and an enemy captain who is a disciple of his socialist theories arranges with him to prevent the troops from fighting. In accordance with their agreement, the besieged townspeople open the gates to the enemy army and overthrow their own government. Happy at his success, Hérénien plans to celebrate the victory, but the soldiers who are still loyal to the government assassinate him.

Next, leaving aside his preoccupation with social justice, Verhaeren turned to the more interior conflict of remorse. *Le Cloître* relates the story of a monk, Balthazar, who has retired to a monastery after having killed his father and let an innocent man be condemned in his place. Ten years later a man confesses to him that he has committed a similar crime. This incident inspires the monk to confess his own crime to the assembled monks, for in spite of the years of severe penance he does not feel himself to be absolved. Unfortunately the confession only serves to reveal his immense pride, as if his despicable crime and the violence of his remorse rendered him superior to others. Dom Marc, a young monk with mystical aspirations, reveals to Balthazar that he will be saved when he accepts human justice. Understanding that there is no other way to appease his conscience, he lets himself be led to the scaffold by a bloodthirsty mob.

The theme of conflict of religion, justice, and pride appears again in *Philippe II*, this time merged with a political interest. The subject is limited to the exposition of the crisis which impels this very devout king to renounce fatherly affection and cause his son, who has dared to stir up a revolt against the royal power, to be executed. Here, as in the earlier plays, much is made of violence and bloody death. Verhaeren liked such exaggerated depictions, for he believed that they illustrated the unending conflict between life and death.

They have the same purpose in *Hélène de Sparte,* but here they recall as well a fundamental principle of beauty already expressed by the painter Tebaldeo in *Lorenzaccio:* "L'art, cette fleur divine, a quelque fois besoin de fumier pour engraisser le sol et le féconder." Wars, murders, vice, human tragedies, all work together towards the flowering of beauty. Ménélas and Castor are assassinated because Beauty requires such a holocaust to maintain her fascination, but also because the pursuit of the ideal consumes the impassioned artist. Hélène, the human incarnation of this concept, watches the tragedies arise beneath her feet without grasping the reason for them. Terrified by the inevitable events, she asks Zeus to take her away from this world where, she feels, she has only called forth misery and death. But before granting her request, the king of the gods explains her destiny in the cycle of life. Beauty awakens passions, some of which give birth to immortal works and others to esthetic fervor; still others destroy those who experience them. Thus, like Baudelaire, Verhaeren emphasizes the significance of beauty.

Unfortunately the public did not understand this message, seeing in this play as in the earlier ones only terrible events and unsympathetic characters. This judgment has not been modified, and Hérénien, for example, is often taken for a narcissistic demagogue. Such displeasing traits of character are, however, accepted with no difficulty if they are seen to belong to allegorical characters. . . . (pp. 390-92)

Verhaeren did not like the term "allegory," however; for him it recalled too strongly the bondage of the pre-Romantic artists. (p. 393)

Wishing to "sublimate" the real in ideas, the author rejected the term "allegory" since it implied . . . the rendering concrete of the abstract. Verhaeren appears not to have completely understood the creative mechanism of allegory, for even if Justice is a Roman woman in a tunic, the artist had to imitate the real in order to create her. A sculptor, a painter, a writer will always manage to give her original features if he wants to. Artistically, whether one departs from the real and subli-

mates it to arrive at the abstract, as Verhaeren hoped to do, or moves from the idea to the object as the Greeks did, the two intellectual and esthetic movements can only be expressed in a simplified form. Such a simplification takes place in the two cases because it is impossible to portray an abstract concept with complex features and still be understood by the public; and because the movement from the personal to the universal requires by definition this kind of simplification. The difference between the two is this: the allegory of Justice is traditionally represented in the form of a Roman woman, while in Verhaeren Justice appears in the form of the king Philippe II, the monk Balthazar, and the plebeian Hérénien. If an author chooses the universal allegory of Justice he is insisting on the uniqueness of the principle; while in using an allegory based on more personal elements, as Verhaeren does, he puts emphasis on the diversity of the idea.

Verhaeren's desire to include diversity is not absolute, for the three characters resemble one another despite the differences in their natures and their situations. Two reasons explain this phenomenon: first, the three heroes are incarnations of the same concepts; and, second, Verhaeren seems to have been obsessed by this kind of individual. Influenced by Nietzsche and by socialism, dreaming of a better world in which the "little man" would no longer be oppressed, the poet exalted the "chief," the leader of the people. This idea, found scattered through his poetry, dominates his theater. Clearly he hoped to reveal and explain his concept to the public, and for this reason he had to make use of allegory. (pp. 393-94)

Following the pattern of Zola, he used characters, events, time periods, settings, and even language in creating his allegories. And since the process of sublimation tends to simplify, different guiding ideas are brought in to amplify the plays. These works are based on the four virtues that Verhaeren considered essential in the superior human being: strength, justice, compassion, and beauty. (p. 394)

These exceptional individuals strongly resemble Nietzsche's superman; ideal constructions, they were the dream of a greathearted intellectual who was deeply wounded at the sight of human misery. (p. 395)

As a Romantic, Verhaeren was trying to achieve inner peace, which meant for him acceptance of the death of the body and faith in the survival of his work. Thus projecting his personal anxieties onto his characters, he identifies them with Christ, and the themes of Easter and Resurrection are introduced to fortify the concept of the leader. In the end, in order to demonstrate that the ideas rule over all humanity, Verhaeren chose—according to Stefan Zweig—subjects within the frameworks of society (*Les Aubes*), religion (*Le Cloître*), politics (*Philippe II*), and ethics (*Hélène de Sparte*).

These different milieux, as well as certain variations in character and situation, give each play its own uniqueness, although the guiding principles are to be found throughout Verhaeren's entire theatrical production. Their presence, even in varying degrees, tends to unify the personalities of Hérénien, Balthazar, and Philippe II, while most of the other characters resemble either "tempéraments," after Zola, or types, like that of the blind seer. There is neither psychological analysis nor evolution of personality, since these plays have a purpose other than to demonstrate the depth of the human soul. The three masculine characters stand out from all the others because they are heroes. The hero for Verhaeren is different from ordinary mortals, since his moral qualities, carried to the extreme, permit him to overcome all obstacles in his path. Hernani's ''Je suis une force qui va'' applies perfectly to the hero of Verhaeren. Led by an almost morbid resolution, which is sustained by a will that never fails, he can take action where others would draw back. Once his goal is determined, he moves toward it without hesitation as if blind to everything opposed to his destiny. Nothing stops him, even if his actions lead to scandal (*Le Cloître*), the death of his son (*Philippe II*), or his own death (*Les Aubes*). Men let themselves be conquered by this hero—or they become his irreconcilable enemies. In either case they are incapable of judging this creature, for they cannot attain a large enough perception to grasp the meaning of his deeds.

The first hero, Hérénien, embodies the type of popular leader, admired by an educated public as well as by peasants and workers. Everyone senses in him a strength, a sense of justice, an openness of which they themselves are incapable. An unshakable will pushes him to accomplish what he considers to be his mission on earth: to stop the war. His impetuosity, his self-confidence, his scorn for danger help him rise above the whims of public opinion. His assurance and vanity are expressed with such naiveté and candor that the spectator might accuse him of unbounded egotism. And in fact he lives in a vague dream of the joyful humanity he will have liberated. He seems to throw himself into the arms of death because of his excessive personality, but in order to round out his character he is forced to confront the soldiers still loyal to the Regency, and to die. Just as in the case of a Romantic hero like Julien Sorel, he cannot become completely himself until the moment of his death. The exhibition of the body in the public square and the adoration of the people transform him for a moment into Christ. After this the hero turns into a legend, abandoning his now useless body to become elevated into an Idea.

Exactly like Hérénien, Balthazar dominates the mob by his will, his pride, and his obstinacy. To achieve his destiny he must commit two extraordinary acts: he must assassinate his father and undergo an exemplary punishment, accepting the humiliation of the civil justice. Consumed by remorse, the monk finds no appeasement in submitting to the customary penances of the monastery. After the revelations of the young Marc, he gives up his ambition to become prior and forces his companions to repudiate him. It is of no importance that his action weakens the monastery, for Balthazar is an incarnation of Resurrection. He will leave with some readers the impression of an insane egotist thirsting for blood, but this impression is based too exclusively on appearances. The monk had to commit a murder and bear constantly the burning pain of remorse in order to leave behind him the memory of a sacrifice carried out in the name of human justice. It was necessary that he be brought low in order to be born again from his ashes like the Phoenix.

The character of Philippe II does not arouse sympathy, mostly because Verhaeren portrayed him with the traditional qualities of a totally sombre being, lightened by no humanitarian elements. An agent of the Inquisition, he organizes the pursuit of heretics and encourages all forms of espionage. He commits the horrifying crime of killing his son, and when he kneels by the body to pray the spectator is inclined to consider him a despicable hypocrite. But here also the surface aspect is misleading, for in fact Philippe is a new Abraham sacrificing his son to humanity, to kingship, to God. He needs an incomparable strength and courage to overlook his paternal feelings and do away with this corrupted offspring. His greatness results from his sacrifice as well as from his determination. To hesitate

or to complain would be inappropriate for a king so aware of his mission. Moreover, all three of the heroes know nothing of hesitation, doubt, or irresolution. Their exaggerated characters make of these men single-minded monsters who are distracted by nothing. Though they sometimes confide in women, for example, above all they use them in order to accomplish their tasks, without letting themselves be softened by feminine tears.

Their determination pushes them inexorably and they are not concerned if innocent victims are crushed. This almost inhuman fatality is shocking to the unprepared spectator. But we must put ourselves into the period and remember the exaggerations of the Decadent and Romantic writers. And to a historical explanation must be added an esthetic reason: these heroes correspond perfectly to the definition of an allegorical character, for they make abstractions concrete, embodying justice, pity, and strength. (pp. 395-97)

But each of the heroes represents ideas to different degrees and in different ways. If they embody justice, one is social justice (Hérénien); another, personal justice in conflict with society (Balthazar); and the third, the sense of justice that a responsible head of state must apply in order to govern well. Their pity allows them to help the less gifted (sometimes even against the latter's will), but they are revealed as more inspired than compassionate. In general, their personalities and their actions exaggerate what men should do to annihilate the absurdity of the human lot. Thus, in *Les Aubes,* someone had to be the first to dare to stop the war and persuade the soldiers in both camps to lay down their arms. Once this solitary gesture was made, a legend grew from it, and humanity could begin to make its way slowly toward a better future. (p. 398)

Conceived at the same time as the other plays but not finished until twelve years later, *Hélène* is different from them in its more classical tone. It brings up the idea of fatality as a blind force driving beings unable to understand what is happening to them. Hélène lets herself be led by events, having neither the will nor the moral force of the three earlier heroes. The other characters in the play are no more substantial: Ménélas is the tired old husband, Pollux the politician-profiteer, Electre and Castor the lovers. As for the crowd, just as in *Les Aubes* it is composed of diverse types rather than distinguishable individuals. All the characters illustrate the importance of beauty in human life, and at the same time another principle dear to authors at the end of the century. Along with Nietzsche and Zola, Verhaeren conceived of the human experience as an infinite spiral, and if beauty requires ugliness—as Tebaldeo claimed—in the same way life is replenished by its opposite. It is thus that "toute mort, toute défaite, tout revers de fortune est annulé par la victoire finale de l'éternel retour" ["Every death, every defeat, every setback is annulled by the final victory of the eternal return"] and in this way human destiny loses its appearance of absurdity. The mythological story allows these ideas to be expressed in a more comprehensible manner than personal allegories, as it reaches to a common cultural base. Hence the advantage of choosing a well-known legend and many contemporaries of Verhaeren used Greek myths to express their own feelings about fate. (pp. 398-99)

Verhaeren's use of time also makes his allegories both original and modern. In his work on Ionesco, Paul Vernois, using a simplified outline, compares the fates of the characters of Corneille, Racine, Montherlant, and Ionesco. We see Corneille's hero torn by passion and will, but rising towards a redeeming sacrifice, actions based on the notion of a linear time. Ionesco's hero, hesitating between escape and destruction, collapses without glory, and here time is conceived as circular. Verhaeren's characters contain something of both of these schemes. Torn between duty and feelings, the indifference of the crowd (*Les Aubes*), ambition (*Le Cloître*), paternal love (*Philippe II*), the desire for peace (*Hélène*), they rise towards a transcendent sacrifice. Their heroic transformation, however, does not resemble that of Corneille, because the notion of time has changed. Whether consciously or not, Verhaeren's theater abandons linear time for the concept of a cyclical human history. In *Les Aubes,* when the crowd weeps for the hero, a blind man announces that from this dawn others will arise. This inevitable recurrence of events appears also in *Le Cloître,* where the two parricides committed in similar circumstances indicate the existence of a cycle. In the same way Zeus, at the end of *Hélène,* announces poetically the physical principle that nothing is lost, nothing is created, but all is transformed. The exchange completes itself in this last play, as the use of the myth constitutes a true liberation from time. In fact the myth itself has long been meaningless for a Christian society, and as the author has added his own ideas of mankind to it he has lifted it out of its historical and social context; he has placed it outside of time.

This concept is of the highest importance in literary history, for to consider time as circular liberates man from its control and evokes a new notion of being. If a hero or an allegorical character can easily be replaced, he loses all individuality. Thus Verhaeren's theater while glorifying the superior man destroys the idea of selfhood. This new view of time and the hero, undoubtedly inspired by Nietzsche, will lead to other innovations. Once separated from the contingencies of time and individuality, the play no longer resolves a problem based on confrontation between characters but becomes a ritual, a magic event designed to arouse in the spectator a sense of his place in the universe. And allegory thus recovers its earliest function, that of destroying the evil forces that threaten humanity. (pp. 401-02)

> *Claire L. Dehon, "Allegory in the Plays of Emile Verhaeren," in* Philological Quarterly *(copyright 1977 by The University of Iowa), Vol. 56, No. 3, Summer, 1977, pp. 389-403.*

KRISTIAAN VERSLUYS (essay date 1980)

[*Versluys examines Verhaeren's depiction of the modern city in his "social trilogy"* (Les campagnes hallucinées, Les villes tentaculaires, *and* Les aubes), *concluding that the poet's ultimate faith in urban progress indicated a nineteenth-century, rather than a truly modern, sensibility. For a similar view of Verhaeren's modernity see P. Mansell Jones's essay excerpted above; for a contrasting view see Jurgis Baltrušaitis's essay, also excerpted above.*]

[Verhaeren's often quoted poem **"Les Usines"**] provides a typical sample of his art as it developed in the last decade of the nineteenth century when he wrote his so-called social trilogy consisting of the verse collections, [*Les Campagnes hallucinées* and *Les Villes tentaculaires,* and the verse drama *Les Aubes*] . . . . In these three works Verhaeren wrote poetry that stands out by its kinetic quality. (p. 298)

If . . . one reads Verhaeren's verses in a dramatic manner, one must feel how the chaotic use of poetic devices underscores the description of a chaotic city. The jolting rhythm, the irregular succession of assonances, of inner rhymes, rich rhymes, long lines, short lines, stanzas and refrains, repetitions, glaring

metaphors, resonant words, personalizations and expressions such as "là-bas" and "ici" that function as transposed oratorical gestures are the stylistic means used to support a vision of the modern city—the modern industrial seaport city as Verhaeren came to know it in Antwerp, Liverpool, Manchester and London in particular—a vision of the city that is looming up as a fearful, gigantic and living organism in constant motion, characterized by an atmosphere that is suffocating and a din that is infernal.

In Verhaeren's city, steamers bellow with a husky voice, trains rumble by, electric hammers bang incessantly and everywhere one can hear the constant subterranean rattling of the factory-machines. Through the crooked streets people hurry and scurry like frenzied phantoms. In hordes they hurl themselves forward—a million arms lifted at the same time, a million hands grabbing—in search of what Balzac outlined already as the city man's two ambitions: *or et plaisir* [*gold and pleasure*]. But while the novelist endowed his characters at least with a thin veneer of sociability and good manners, behind which, to be sure, they hide a most hideous ferocity, Verhaeren's masses move in a purely instinctual fashion, like animals in heat. "Rut" is a favored word with the poet, and it applies as well to the brokers in the stock exchange who are greedy for gold as to the patrons of the red light district, to whom it applies in a more literal sense.

In evoking this fierce violence of the city and its inhabitants Verhaeren testifies to a rare pictorial power. To the sole effect of vividness, however, much else that one expects in mature poetry has been sacrificed. In the heat of his passion, Verhaeren tends to lose all sense of nuance. He hyperbolizes too consistently. The pathos of his verses is unrelieved. He knows how to find the energetic word but neglects to look for the right word. He chooses his lexicon, in obedience to Verlaine, "sans trop de peine" ["without too much trouble"]. His verses are concentrated around one striking term: a descriptive adjective that indicates the mood, an active verb that conveys the by now sufficiently stressed impression of energy or a noun that is shocking, sometimes even crude. Grouped around these kernels is too large an accumulation of dead elements. In the best poems they serve as foil for the energetic term, but too often they are themselves without shine to such an extent that they absorb the light of the explosive words instead of serving as their mirror.

It is, however, not only lack of formal concern for the finished line that cost Verhaeren his once highly rated literary reputation. The modern reader is bound to be less irritated by this negligence than by the constant sacrifice of symbolistic allusiveness to achieve an effect of naturalistic vigor. In Verhaeren's poetry one rarely encounters a suggestion of the truly lyrical, a reference to the incommensurable, an awareness of something beyond the merely descriptive. This is true for all his work and it points to a general lack of poetic perceptivity. It is true in particular, however, for his city poetry.

Verhaeren's provincial background may have a lot to do with this. During his childhood, he lived in an idyllic Flemish village, which he never left except for an occasional trip with his father to nearby Antwerp. His formative years he spent between the protective walls of a Jesuit boarding school in the town of Ghent. He went to college in Louvain. Ghent and Louvain are sizable towns but by no means big cities. They belong to what Verhaeren termed "les villes à pignons", the gabled towns—provincial, picturesque, rich in history, a little dreamy and behind their time. It was not until after his college years that the poet started to travel widely and discovered the real metropolises of Paris and London. By that time, however, his attitudes were shaped and although in later life he stayed in several big cities for considerable periods of time, he never ceased to be a tourist, an onlooker. Ever the surprised observer, he was struck by the city's power and potential which is so emphatically reflected in his thundering verses. Over and again he rediscovered the city as something new, great and exciting, something so overwhelming that the observation of its outward appearance alone sufficed to fascinate him for a lifetime. (pp. 298-300)

Stefan Zweig . . . made a short-sighted claim, when he called Verhaeren "the poet of our age." To the modern reader it is obvious that Verhaeren's self-assertive individualism belongs to the nineteenth rather than to the twentieth century. His habit of stamping his image on everything he observes betrays a confidence that is no longer ours. For that very reason, Zweig was much nearer the truth where he compared Verhaeren to Walt Whitman. Both the American and the Belgian poet share indeed a trust in the subject to the detriment of the object. (p. 301)

Verhaeren . . . , who was thrown into the city without transition of preparation, came to regard the increasing urbanization in the nineteenth century as an alienating, disruptive force that threatened to bury man in what Lewis Mumford was later to call the modern *necropolis* or what Verhaeren himself has called, in an expression that has remained famous, *la ville tentaculaire.*

The image that dominates that part of Verhaeren's work we are dealing with is indeed that of the city as a monster that chokes its victims, a vampire that sucks the country dry. The massive flight from the Flemish villages that followed a severe agricultural crisis in 1886 became in Verhaeren's imagination a symbol of the irresistible attraction the town exerts over the country. It became his main theme in *Les Campagnes hallucinées.* . . . (p. 303)

In spite of this vision of the city as an omnivorous octopus, however, Verhaeren does not reduce the country-city dichotomy to a simple contrast between good and evil. The country has its own sources of damnation, its criminals, its perverts, its quacks, its superstitions, its orgies. It is blighted at least partly by its own fault, while the city, though evil and vile, has its own sources of redemption. From the countryman's perspective it possesses a great appeal. (pp. 303-04)

Verhaeren's view of the city, therefore, is divided. It is a place of present suffering, but at the same time one of future salvation. It resembles somewhat Wordsworth's ambivalent view of London in *The Prelude* even to the very fact that both poets are embarrassingly vague in their mentioning of the forces that will bring the dramatic turnabout in the city's role. One suspects that in making their optimistic prophecies both poets were engaged in wishful thinking. Verhaeren, at any rate, indulged in the pieties of both the romantic and the positivistic age. He tagged to his convincing indictment of the industrial city a number of poems in which he expresses his belief—a belief very similar to that expressed at the end of Vigny's "La Bouteille à la mer"—that once the Ideas—strength, justice, pity and beauty—will rule over mankind. Scientific research will provide an answer to all metaphysical questions and at the same time provide solutions for all human problems. This belief is stated without any substantiation and the link between salvation through science and the city as the place where this salvation will materialize is only a tenuous one. . . . (p. 304)

One looks in vain to *Les Aubes* for a more specific view of the beneficial forces that could put an end to urban evil. The play stages a siege of a modern city, which serves as the pretext for the discussion of three major problems: international war, the conflict between the city and the country and the struggle between the classes. The solution Verhaeren proposes to these complex issues is of a startling simplicity. In the person of the tribune Jacques Hérénien he introduces the charismatic leader, the new Christ announced in "L'Ame de la ville", without, however, succeeding in giving his main character even the least semblance of credibility. At all times, his magnificent achievements seem totally out of proportion to his talents. He loves the great gesture, he loves to face the crowd with his arms akimbo, he loves to throw at them the written proof of the sycophantic advances the leading classes made to him but which he triumphantly resisted. But his gestures are empty, pathetic. . . . His performance as an orator is negligible and though we are asked to believe that he has written a number of very influential books on political theory, he appears on the stage as intellectually undernourished. (p. 305)

[Verhaeren] must have felt that the modern problems of war and social inequality can no longer be solved after the fashion of Jacques d'Artevelde, the fourteenth-century Flemish orator from whom the hero of *Les Aubes* derives his first name, or Hérénien, the Roman tribune from whom he took his last name. The time of benevolent despots waving a magic wand is over. It may seem strange that a man who has been called the poet of modernity should not have understood that more fully. But, then, this lack of understanding lay all the time at the basis of Verhaeren's perception of the modern world. His design to submerge in his environment took the form of a *projection* of himself into his environment. Like Hérénien, he can say, "J'ai façonné, d'après mon plan, le monde" ["After my own plan I have fashioned the world"]. He had always spoken so loudly and emphatically about things that the things had had no opportunity to speak for themselves. In *Les Aubes,* as it were, they take their revenge. Hérénien is the typical Verhaerenman, who in a more direct fashion than the poet in his verses, tries to force his vision on the world. He is the *projection* come alive. It goes to show to what extent such a projection can lead to an estrangement from reality that even in a situation falsified to suit his needs—a modern war represented as a medieval siege—Hérénien cannot operate in a plausible fashion. At every moment the tale goes against its hero and its teller. *Les Aubes* is a textbook example of a literary work that disproves implicitly what it sets out to prove explicitly.

In spite of this, however, Verhaeren retains a certain historical value. His confusion was characteristic of the transitional era in which he lived, an era that witnessed the replacement of the rural order by an urban and industrial one. To perceive this change and to record it was already meritorious in itself, the more so as it represented an attempt to come to terms with external reality at a time when the poetic effort began increasingly to be directed towards the inner life. (pp. 306-07)

Kristiaan Versluys, "Three City Poets: Rilke, Baudelaire and Verhaeren," in Revue de littérature comparée *(© Didier-Érudition, 1980; reprinted by permission of Didier-Erudition, Paris), Vol. 54, No. 3, July-September, 1980, pp. 283-307.**

ADDITIONAL BIBLIOGRAPHY

Corell, Alice F. "The Contribution of Verhaeren to Modern French Lyric Poetry." *The University of Buffalo Studies* V, No. 2 (February 1927): 43-73.
　　Survey of the major poetry.

Crawford, Virginia M. "Émile Verhaeren: The Belgian Poet." *The Fortnightly Review* 66, No. 60 (November 1896): 715-26.
　　An early survey of Verhaeren's poetry.

Gosse, Edmund. "Four Poets: Émile Verhaeren." In his *French Profiles,* rev. ed., pp. 324-28. London: William Heinemann, 1913.*
　　A general discussion and survey of Verhaeren's works.

Lamberton-Becker, May. "Émile Verhaeren." *The Bookman,* New York XLIV, No. 6 (February 1917): 639-43.
　　Biographical and critical sketch.

Norrish, P. J. "Unanimist Elements in the Works of Durkheim and Verhaeren." *French Studies* XI (January 1957): 38-49.
　　Sees Verhaeren, along with sociologist Émile Durkheim, as a precursor of Jules Romain's artistic theory of unanimism, the study of human groups and of "the mysterious personalities and forces that arise when two or more people meet."

Randall, Huberta Frets. "Whitman and Verhaeren—Priests of Human Brotherhood." *The French Review* XVI, No. 1 (October 1942): 36-43.
　　Compares Whitman and Verhaeren as poets who shared "the same joyous belief in human nature and in the future of the human race, an optimism so overwhelming that no other poet could equal them."

————. "Linguistic and Stylistic Changes in the Poetry of Émile Verhaeren." *Symposium* IX, No. 1 (Spring 1955): 70-8.
　　Textual study of variant forms of the poems in *Les débâcles* through its successive editions from 1888-1923.

Redwood-Anderson, John. "My Friendship with Émile Verhaeren." *ADAM International Review* 23, No. 250 (1955): 33-51.
　　Memoir reprinting several letters from Verhaeren.

Rosenfeld, Paul. "Émile Verhaeren." In his *Men Seen: Twenty-Four Modern Authors,* pp. 240-60. New York: The Dial Press, 1925.
　　Descriptive survey of Verhaeren's poetry.

Sadler, Michael T. H. "Émile Verhaeren: An Appreciation." *Poetry and Drama* 2 (June 1913): 172-79.
　　Biographical and critical sketch.

Turquet-Milnes, G. "Verhaeren." In his *Some Modern Belgian Writers: A Critical Study,* pp. 46-73. New York: Robert M. McBride & Co., 1917.
　　Critical survey of Verhaeren's poetry and dramas.

Worthing, Beatrice. "Verhaeren and England." *ADAM International Review* 23, No. 250 (1955): 56-86.
　　Account of Verhaeren's stay in London. The essay reprints numerous letters from the poet to English friends and translators.

H(erbert) G(eorge) Wells

1866-1946

(Also wrote under pseudonyms of Sosthenes Smith, Walter Glockenhammer, and Reginald Bliss) English novelist, short story writer, historian, essayist, autobiographer, and critic.

Wells is best known today as one of the forerunners of modern science fiction and as a utopian idealist who foretold an era of chemical warfare, atomic weaponry, and world wars. *The Time Machine, The Invisible Man, The War of the Worlds, The Island of Doctor Moreau,* and several other works among Wells's canon, are considered classics in the genres of science fiction and science fantasy. *The Outline of History,* a history of the world written to demonstrate the needlessness of national boundaries and to offer hope for world peace, is Wells's most famous and controversial nonfictional work. As a polemicist, Wells's strident advocacy of free love and of socialism, as well as his attacks on what he considered the stifling moral constraints of society, are credited with contributing to the liberalization of modern Western culture.

Wells was born into a lower-middle-class Cockney family in Bromley, Kent, a suburb of London. Struggling to escape the unrewarding, below-stairs existence that defeated his parents, Wells attended London University and the Royal College of Science, where he studied zoology. One of his professors was the noted biologist T. H. Huxley, who instilled in Wells a belief in social as well as biological evolution. After graduation from London University, Wells wrote a biology textbook and tried his hand at writing fiction, contributing short stories to several magazines. The serialization of his short novel *The Time Machine* brought Wells his first substantial critical notice—he was hailed as a literary genius by a critic for the *Review of Reviews*—and launched his career. The writing of science fiction and science fantasies occupied the earliest part of his career and brought him great popular and critical attention. As his popularity grew, Wells was enabled by his burgeoning fame to meet Arnold Bennett, Joseph Conrad, and other prominent authors of the day, with whom he exchanged criticism and opinions on the art of writing. His own theory and style of writing was basically journalistic and was acquired while serving under editor Frank Harris as literary critic at *The Saturday Review.* Believing that it is important to continuously place copy before the reading public, even if one's concerns are soon outdated and forgotten, Wells gradually turned from fiction of entertainment to address the social and political problems of England and the world. Several socially concerned, comedic novels followed the science fiction works; in such novels as *The Wheels of Chance, Kipps: The Story of a Simple Soul,* and *The History of Mr. Polly,* Dickensian, lower-middle-class characters are depicted living at odds with the downtrodden society in which the author had himself been raised. A socialist, Wells joined the Fabian Society in 1903, but left the group after fighting a long, unsuccessful war of wit and rhetoric over some of the society's policies with his friend, the prominent Fabian and man of letters Bernard Shaw. Wells's socialist thought, combined with a belief in the gradual perfection of humanity through evolution and scientific innovation, is expressed in the serious fiction and prognostications that gradually succeeded the humorous character novels

during the first decade of the twentieth century. By 1914, through such works as *Anticipations of the Reaction of Mechanical and Scientific Progress upon Human Life and Thought, A Modern Utopia,* and *The New Machiavelli,* Wells was established in the public mind as a leading proponent of socialism, world government, free thought, and free love, and as an enemy of many elements of Edwardian thought and morality.

Before World War I, Wells's name was commonly linked with that of Shaw as an advocate of the new, the iconoclastic, and the daring. But the war and its aftermath of widespread disillusionment upset his optimistic vision of humankind. During the war, as evidenced by the essay *God the Invisible King* and the novel *Mr. Britling Sees It Through,* Wells turned temporarily to belief in God—a belief that he later vigorously repudiated. His postwar ideas on humanity's perfectibility were modified to stress the preeminent importance of education in bringing about progress. In his ambitious two-volume work *The Outline of History,* a work written to further the cause of world peace, Wells attempted to illustrate the commonality of the origins and histories of the world's peoples. The subject of much critical discussion, *The Outline of History* sparked one of the most celebrated literary debates of the 1920s, between Wells and his longtime antagonist, the Catholic polemicist Hilaire Belloc. Objecting to Wells's naturalistic, Darwinian view of world history, Belloc attacked the *Outline* as a simple-minded, nonscientific, anti-Catholic document. A war of mutual refutation was fought by both writers in the pages of several books and essays. Ironically, although much of the scientific community now affirms Wells's biological theses as presented in the *Outline*, during the mid-1920s the preponderance of scientific evidence supported the biological theories of Belloc, who, in the minds of many critics, bested Wells in their exchange of polemical broadsides. Throughout the 1920s and 1930s, Wells's works became progressively less optimistic about the future of humanity and increasingly bitter, as is evident in such satiric novels as *The Croquet Player* and *The Holy Terror*. The advent of World War II increased Wells's despondency about the future, and his last book, *Mind at the End of Its Tether*, foretells the destruction of civilization and degeneration of humanity. Wells died in London in 1946.

Critics believe that Wells's reputation as a writer of fiction rests upon his early science fiction and science fantasy tales, and on his humorous character novels. These works continue to be widely read and have been the subject of numerous adaptations in other artistic media. Perhaps the most successful such adaptation was the Mercury Theater's famous radio broadcast of *The War of the Worlds* on Halloween night, 1938, when many listeners across the United States panicked in the face of what they believed was an actual Martian invasion of the Earth. With their use of such fantastic devices as invisibility, time travel, and encounters with aliens from other worlds, Wells's scientific romances have also influenced the work of several generations of science fiction writers. Although the character novels, according to Wells's critics, lack psychological subtlety and are not as well constructed as his science fiction works, Wells is praised for the humor and sympathy for common individuals which is displayed throughout them. The publication of *The History of Mr. Polly* in 1910, according to many critics, marked the end of Wells's literary ascension. His novels had by that time taken on a pedantic nature, and many of his subsequent works, such as *Joan and Peter* and *The World of William Clissold*, examined contemporary social problems in a didactic way that drew the scorn of many critics of the era. However, *Tono-Bungay*, an ambitious portrayal of social and political decay, stands out among Wells's social novels and serves as a bridge between his character and expository fiction. The subject of numerous interpretations, *Tono-Bungay* has been called, by many critics, Wells's greatest novel. From the turn of the century until his death, Wells wrote social and political criticism and prognostications. Of these, *The War That Will End War* gave the world, through its title, a cynical catch-phrase for obstinate, benevolent naivete in the face of widespread human corruption—a criticism of much of Wells's social fiction and nonfiction. For all his concern over the future of the human race, critics remain uncertain as to whether Wells actually believed that humanity could be improved. There is evidence that, like the Time Traveller of his first major work, Wells believed that even if life is indeed a meaningless, dualistic struggle, "it remains for us to live as though it were not so."

In spite of the pessimism that pervades many of his last works, Wells is regarded as one of the most prominent champions of the early twentieth-century spirit of British liberal optimism. With the possible exception of Shaw, perhaps no other author of his day so effectively captured the exuberant sense of release from Victorian conventions and morals. The continued popularity of his books, the tremendous body of criticism devoted to them, and the liberalizing effect that much of his work had

on Western thought combine to make Wells one of the major figures in modern literature.

(See also *TCLC*, Vol. 6 and *Something About the Author*, Vol. 20.)

PRINCIPAL WORKS

Select Conversations with an Uncle, Now Extinct, and Two Other Reminiscences (short stories) 1895
The Time Machine (novel) 1895
The Wonderful Visit (novel) 1895
The Island of Dr. Moreau (novel) 1896
The Wheels of Chance (novel) 1896
The Invisible Man (novel) 1897
The War of the Worlds (novel) 1898
When the Sleeper Wakes (novel) 1899
Love and Mr. Lewisham (novel) 1900
Anticipations of the Reaction of Mechanical and Scientific Progress upon Human Life and Thought (essay) 1901
The First Men in the Moon (novel) 1901
Mankind in the Making (essays) 1903
The Food of the Gods, and How It Came to Earth (novel) 1904
Kipps: The Story of a Simple Soul (novel) 1905
A Modern Utopia (essay) 1905
The Future in America: A Search after Realities (essays) 1906
In the Days of the Comet (novel) 1906
First and Last Things: A Confession of Faith and Rule of Life (essay) 1908
New Worlds for Old (essay) 1908
The War in the Air and Particularly How Mr. Bert Smallways Fared While It Lasted (novel) 1908
Ann Veronica (novel) 1909
Tono-Bungay (novel) 1909
The History of Mr. Polly (novel) 1910
The Country of the Blind, and Other Stories (short stories) 1911
The New Machiavelli (novel) 1911
Marriage (novel) 1912
The War That Will End War (essays) 1914
The Wife of Sir Isaac Harmon (novel) 1914
The World Set Free (novel) 1914
Boon [as Reginald Bliss] (sketches) 1915
The Research Magnificent (novel) 1915
Mr. Britling Sees It Through (novel) 1916
God the Invisible King (essay) 1917
The Soul of a Bishop: A Novel (with Just a Little Love in It) about Conscience and Religion and the Real Troubles of Life (novel) 1917
Joan and Peter: The Story of an Education (novel) 1918
The Outline of History. 2 vols. (history) 1919-20
The Undying Fire (novel) 1919
Men Like Gods (novel) 1923
The World of William Clissold (novel) 1926
Mr. Blettsworthy on Rampole Island (novel) 1928
The Open Conspiracy (essay) 1928
The Autocracy of Mr. Parham: His Remarkable Adventures in This Changing World (novel) 1930
The Bulpington of Blup (novel) 1932
The Shape of Things to Come (essays) 1933
Experiment in Autobiography (autobiography) 1934
The Croquet Player (novel) 1936

The Holy Terror (novel) 1939
All Aboard for Ararat (novel) 1940
Guide to the New World (essay) 1941
Mind at the End of Its Tether (essay) 1945
George Gissing and H. G. Wells: Their Friendship and
    Correspondence (letters and criticism) 1961

I. ZANGWILL (essay date 1895)

[*An English man of letters, Zangwill was one of the outstanding Jewish literary figures of his era. His fame began with the novel* Children of the Ghetto: A Study of a Peculiar People *(1892), the first of several fictional portrayals of life in the Jewish ghetto. Through this sympathetic treatment of ghetto life, Zangwill is credited with preventing the passage of anti-Jewish legislation by Parliament. The author of other popular novels and dramas, Zangwill was also the founding editor of the humor magazine* Ariel: The London Puck, *a contributor to major English periodicals, and an influential spokesman for the Zionist cause. In the excerpt below, Zangwill reviews* The Time Machine *and* Select Conversations with an Uncle.]

In his brilliant little romance **The Time Machine** Mr. Wells has inclined to the severer and more scientific form of prophecy—to the notion of a humanity degenerating inevitably from sheer pressure of physical comfort; but this not very novel conception, which was the theme of Mr. Besant's *Inner House,* and even partly of Pearson's *National Life and Character,* Mr. Wells has enriched by the invention of the Morlocks, a differentiated type of humanity which lives underground and preys upon the softer, prettier species that lives luxuriously in the sun, a fine imaginative creation worthy of Swift, and possibly not devoid of satirical reference to "the present discontents." There is a good deal of what Tyndall would have called "scientific imagination" in Mr. Wells' further vision of the latter end of all things, a vision far more sombre and impressive than the ancient imaginings of the Biblical seers. The only criticism I have to offer is that his Time Traveller, a cool scientific thinker, behaves exactly like the hero of a commonplace sensational novel, with his frenzies of despair and his appeals to fate, when he finds himself in danger of having to remain in the year eight hundred and two thousand seven hundred and one, into which he has recklessly travelled; nor does it ever occur to him that in the aforesaid year he will have to repeat these painful experiences of his, else his vision of the future will have falsified itself—though how the long dispersed dust is to be vivified again does not appear. Moreover, had he travelled backwards, he would have reproduced a Past which, in so far as his own appearance in it with his newly invented machine was concerned, would have been *ex hypothesi* unveracious. Had he recurred to his own earlier life, he would have had to exist in two forms simultaneously, of varying ages—a feat which even Sir Boyle Roche would have found difficult. These absurdities illustrate the absurdity of any attempt to grapple with the notion of Time; and, despite some ingenious metaphysics, worthy of the inventor of the Eleatic paradoxes, Mr. Wells' *Time Machine,* which traverses time (viewed as the Fourth Dimension of Space) backwards or forwards, much as the magic carpet of *The Arabian Nights* traversed space, remains an amusing fantasy. . . . Mr. Wells might have been plausibly scientific in engineering his Time Machine through Space and stopping at the points where particular periods of the world's past history became visible: he

would then have avoided the fallacy of mingling personally in the panorama. But this would not have suited his design of "dealing in futures." For there is no getting into the Future, except by waiting. You can only sit down and see it come by, as the drunken man thought he might wait for his house to come round in the circulation of the earth; and if you lived for an eternity, the show would only be "just about to begin."

Mr. Wells' other book, published simultaneously, as if by the aid of the Time Machine, and entitled **Select Conversations with an Uncle,** confirms the impression of his powers, though it would not have produced it. It comprises about a dozen articles which appeared in the *Pall Mall Gazette,* and scintillate with the sort of humour which that organ is wont to "slate." There is wisdom as well as fantasy in some of these trifles, though others are too trifling. (pp. 153-55)

> I. Zangwill, "Without Prejudice," in The Pall Mall Magazine, *Vol. VII, No. 29, September, 1895, pp. 151-60.**

E. A[RNOLD] BENNETT (essay date 1902)

[*Bennett was an Edwardian novelist who is credited with bringing techniques of European Naturalism to the English novel. His reputation rests almost exclusively on* The Old Wives' Tale *and the Clayhanger trilogy, novels which are set in the manufacturing district of Bennett's native Staffordshire and which tell of thwarted lives lived amidst dull, provincial existence. In the following article he discusses* The First Men in the Moon *at some length, then* The Wonderful Visit, Love and Mr. Lewisham, *and the scientific romances.*]

[H. G. Wells] has hitherto somewhat suffered, in the public estimate, under the disadvantage of being wrongly labelled. It is a fact that his work is at least as diverse as that of any living prose-writer. In the seven years since he ascended into the literary firmament he has given forth "scientific romances" such as **The Time Machine, The Invisible Man,** . . . and **The First Men in the Moon;** satiric fantasias, such as **The Wonderful Visit** and **The Sea Lady;** a naturalistic romance, in **The Wheels of Chance;** a realistic novel of modern life, in **Love and Mr. Lewisham;** a couple of volumes of sketches and essays; about half a hundred "strange stories," in all veins, from that of Poe to that of Guy de Maupassant; and finally . . . **Anticipations,** which are as a lamp to the feet of the twentieth century. Nevertheless, and despite all this, if you mention the name of H. G. Wells to the man in the street, he is fairly sure to exclaim, "Oh, yes, the disciple of Jules Verne." Even critics who think to render the acme of praise call him "the English Jules Verne." And critics who wish to patronize refer to his "*pseudo*-scientific romances." (pp. 260-61)

The great difference between Jules Verne and Mr. Wells is that the latter was trained in scientific methods of thought, while the former was not. . . . Those who prefix "pseudo" to the scientific part of Mr. Wells's novels are not the men of science. On the contrary, one may pleasantly observe the experts of *Nature,* a scientific organ of unrivalled authority, discussing the gravitational phenomena of **The First Men in the Moon,** with the aid of diagrams, and admitting that Mr. Wells has the law on his side. The qualities of **The First Men in the Moon** are fourfold. There is first the mere human psychology. We begin with two human beings, Mr. Cavor the inventor, and Mr. Bedford the narrator. They are real persons, realistically described, and whether Mr. Cavor stands abashed before the Grand Lunar, or Mr. Bedford floats alone in infinite space, neither of them once loses his individuality or ceases to act or think in a perfectly credible and convincing way. Secondly, there is the scientific machinery of the narrative, always brilliantly invented, lucidly set forth, and certainly not yet impugned by science. Thirdly, there is the graphic, picturesque side of the affair, as examples of which I may refer to the splendid sunrise on the moon, the terrible lunar night, and that really wonderful instance of close creative thought, the exposition of the air-currents through the caverns of the moon. Fourthly, and to my mind most important, there is what I must call, for lack of a better term, the philosophic quality, that quality which is fundamental in all Mr. Wells's work, and which here is principally active in the invention of the natural history and the social organization of the moon. (pp. 263-65)

"What a strange life!" said the angel.

"Yes," said the vicar, "what a strange life! But the thing that makes it strange to me is new. I had taken it as a matter of course until you came into my life."

I had taken it as a matter of course! That is precisely the attitude of which Mr. Wells's attitude is the antipodes. With him, nothing is of course, and every one who converses with him at any length finds this out first. Under all the wit, the humour, the pathos, the wayward beauty of *The Wonderful Visit* may be perceived this firm and continuous intention—to criticize the social fabric, to demand of each part of it the reason for its existence, and in default of a reply, to laugh it out of existence.

The Wheels of Chance is a quasi-satiric romance from which the supernatural element is excluded. Its hero, Mr. Hoopdriver, . . . is the best-loved of all Mr. Wells's creations. But I can merely mention the book here as the precursor of the realistic novel, *Love and Mr. Lewisham,* the only novel, in the usual meaning of the term, which Mr. Wells has yet written, but which is surely to be followed by others. (pp. 269-70)

Here, therefore, even in the realistic novel of modern matter-of-fact, we are not allowed to get away from the scientific principles that man is a part of nature, that he is a creature of imperious natural forces, that he is only one link in the chain of eternal evolution.

In the "scientific romances," to which we may now at last come, the principle of evolution and a conception of "man's place in nature" are Mr. Wells's great basic facts. (p. 271)

Among all Mr. Wells's tales I remember but one, **"A Story of the Stone Age,"** which deals with the past. It is the future, it is evolution, it is innovation, which he preaches and will always preach. (p. 273)

Mr. Wells is a man of science in order, first and foremost, that he may be a prophet and map out the path so that humanity shall avoid détours. And prophecy is really what he has always been at when he has touched science. He may juggle with our ideas of time and space, as in *The Time Machine,* **"The Plattner Story," "The Crystal Egg,"** and **"The Accelerator"**; he may startle or shock us by the artistic presentation of a scientific "conjuring-trick," as in *The Invisible Man* and *The Island of Doctor Moreau;* he may awe us by sheer force of an original imaginative conception, as in **"The Star," "Under the Knife,"** and **"The Man Who Could Work Miracles."** But his real, preferred business has been to prophesy, to peer into the future. In *The Time Machine,* the Time-Traveller goes forward, not into "the dark backward and abysm." Mr. Wells's fancy was youthful in those days, and the Time-Traveller journeyed through

a million years or so; he saw a grim and terrible vision of the evolution of the "submerged tenth" and the "upper classes," a world murderously divided against itself. . . . (pp. 273-74)

The War of the Worlds was not a prophecy, but it was in the nature of a prophecy, a speculative, warning criticism, so far as it described an organization of intelligent beings more advanced than our own. And the same is to be said of *The First Men in the Moon.* In *When the Sleeper Wakes* and **"A Story of the Days to Come,"** Mr. Wells returned to prophecy in fiction. But it was a much quieter, soberer, humbler, and an infinitely more useful prophecy than that of *The Time Machine.* Instead of dealing with thousands and millions of years, he dealt with a century or so. And in *Anticipations of the Reaction of Mechanical and Scientific Progress upon Human Life and Thought,* he has abandoned the garb of fiction, and he definitely stands forth naked and unashamed as a prophet of the real. . . . His strongest points are his clear vision and his intellectual honesty and courage; his weakest point is his instinctive antipathy to any static condition.

And his forecast of the more immediate future, his creed? You may see it set out with surprisingly close texture of detail in *Anticipations;* and in a forthcoming series of essays, possibly more boldly creative in character than *Anticipations,* the instant means to the Great End may be shadowed forth as they present themselves to his mind. Suffice it to say here that Mr. Wells firmly believes in universal peace and in the high destiny of nature, *The Time Machine* of seven years ago notwithstanding. (pp. 274-76)

> *E. A[rnold] Bennett, "Herbert George Wells and His Work" (originally published in* Cosmopolitan Magazine, *Vol. XXXIII, No. 4, August, 1902), in* Arnold Bennett and H. G. Wells: A Record of a Personal and a Literary Friendship, *edited by Harris Wilson, University of Illinois Press, 1960, pp. 260-76.*

HAVELOCK ELLIS   (essay date 1904)

[*Ellis was a pioneering sexual psychologist and a respected English man of letters. His most famous work is his seven-volume* The Psychology of Sex (1897-1928), *a study which contains frankly stated case histories of sex-related psychological abnormalities and which is greatly responsible for changing British and American attitudes toward the hitherto forbidden subject of sexuality. In addition to his psychological writings, Ellis edited the Mermaid Series of sixteenth through eighteenth century English dramatists (1887-89) and retained an active interest in literature throughout his life. As a critic, according to Desmond MacCarthy, Ellis looked for the expression of the individuality of the author under discussion. "The first question he asked himself as a critic," wrote MacCarthy, "was 'What does this writer affirm?' The next, 'How did he come to affirm precisely that?' His statement of a writer's 'message' was always trenchant and clear, his psychological analysis of the man extremely acute, and the estimate of the value of his contribution impartial. What moved him most in literature was the sincere expression of preferences and beliefs, and the energy which springs from sincerity." Here he reviews* Mankind in the Making, *finding it an extremely accomplished book.*]

Although prophets are nowadays rare among us, Mr. Bernard Shaw is not absolutely alone. We have others, and among them not one is better worth listening to than Mr. H. G. Wells. As we have seen, a prophet may be defined as a person who is something of a scientist and something of an artist and altogether a moralist. In science, while Mr. Shaw has occupied himself with political economy, Mr. Wells has had the advantage of a training in physical and biological work; as in art, just as Mr. Shaw has amused himself with writing plays, Mr. Wells has developed a singularly original kind of fiction, and thereby attained a wide reputation, not only in England, but also in France, being indeed the only Englishman so far assigned a place in the "Célébrités d'Aujourd'hui" series. As a moralist, Mr. Shaw is more brilliant and accomplished, for from the outset he has clearly held before him this most conspicuous part of the prophet's duty. Mr. Wells has here been somewhat shy and reticent; though he has frequently put a certain amount of morality into his fiction he has usually been anxious that it should only be visible to those who know how to find it; even a prophet must live, he seems to have said to himself; it is only within the last few years, in the maturity of his power and reputation, that he has boldly stepped into the public arena conspicuously enfolded in the prophet's mantle. . . . It is thus that Mr. Wells comes before us in his recent and extremely able book, *Mankind in the Making*. (pp. 204-06)

We live in a land, as Mr. Wells puts it, into which there may be said to be a spout discharging a baby every eight seconds. All our statesmen, philanthropists, public men, parties and institutions are engaged in a struggle to deal with the stream of babies which no man can stop. "Our success or failure with that unending stream of babies is the measure of our civilisation." (p. 206)

To survey life and to reorganise it, on so broad and sweeping a scale as Mr. Wells attempts, necessarily brings him into a great many fields which have been appropriated by specialists. Mr. Wells quite realises the dangers he thus runs, but it can by no means be said that he has altogether escaped them. In this way he sometimes seems to be led into unnecessary confusions and contradictions. One may observe this in the discussion of heredity which is inevitably a main part of his theme. Mr. Francis Galton has proposed that we should seek to improve the human race as we improve our horses and dogs, by careful breeding, in order to develop their best qualities. Mr. Wells argues, quite soundly in my opinion, that this will not work out, that we do not know what qualities we want to breed, nor how we are to get them. But Mr. Wells rushes to the other extreme when, without exactly proposing it, he suggests that there may be nothing unreasonable in mating people of insane family with "dull, stagnant, respectable people," in the hope that the mixture will turn out just right. We do certainly know that as a rule mad people are most decidedly not examples of "genius out of hand," but, on the contrary, people who have got into a monotonous rut that they cannot lift themselves out of; they are far more dull and stagnant than the respectable people, and the suggested mixture is scarcely hopeful. (pp. 207-08)

Another more fundamental criticism occurs as we read Mr. Wells's pages, and one that more closely touches his prophetic mission. He appears before us as the apostle of Evolution; he states briefly, as a self-evident proposition, that "man will rise to be overman"; the New Republican is always to bear that in mind. But while such a belief is certainly an aid to an inspiring gospel of life, it can by no means be admitted that it is self-evident. On the contrary, from an evolutionary point of view, there is not the slightest reason to suppose that man will ever rise to be overman. . . . As regards man it might be plausibly maintained that the typical Man reached his fullest and finest all-round development, as the highest zoological species, in the Stone Age some ten thousand years ago, that the Superman

really began to arise with the discovery of writing, the growth of tradition and the multiplication of inventions some six or eight thousand years ago, and that we have now reached, not the beginning of the Superman but the beginning of the end of him. (pp. 208-09)

And here we are led to the only remaining criticism of the New Republic that I have to offer. One feels throughout Mr. Wells's prophesyings a certain note of what I may perhaps venture to call without offence, parochialism. The evolution of man, if it means anything, must affect the whole species, and not a single section. Mr. Wells confines himself exclusively to the English-speaking lands, and through a great part of his book he is very much occupied with tinkering at some of our cherished English institutions. The preacher who set out by proclaiming salvation for mankind invites us to contribute to the fund for the new organ. Not only is Mr. Wells's "mankind" thus narrowly limited, he even objects to the study of other nations. Ancient languages he taboos altogether; a knowledge of modern languages he regards as "a rather irksome necessity, of little or no educational value." (p. 210)

If, however, Mr. Wells is sometimes led into unwarrantable extremes of statement, it is generally easy to see that he is so led by his moralising purpose, and that he is legitimately exercising the prophetic function. How admirable a moralist he is may be clearly seen in the chapter entitled "The Cultivation of the Imagination." Here he deals with the question of the methods by which the boy or girl should be initiated into the knowledge of all that makes manhood and womanhood. It is a delicate question, but it could not well be discussed in a more sane, wholesome, frank, and yet reticent manner. In such a discussion Mr. Wells is at his best; he enables us to realise that we are perhaps advancing beyond "that age of nasty sentiment, sham delicacy, and giggles," as he calls the Victorian era; it is here that he shows how significant a prophet he is of the twentieth century. (p. 212)

Havelock Ellis, "Another Prophet: H. G. Wells" (originally published in Weekly Critical Review, *February 19, 1904), in his* Views and Reviews: A Selection of Uncollected Articles, 1884-1932, first and second series *(reprinted by permission of François Lafitte for the Literary Estate of Havelock Ellis), D. Harmsworth, 1932 (and reprinted by Books for Libraries Press, 1970; distributed by Arno Press, Inc.), pp. 204-12.*

BERNARD SHAW   (letter date 1906?)

[Shaw is generally considered the greatest and best-known dramatist to write in the English language since Shakespeare. Following the example of Henrik Ibsen, he succeeded in revolutionizing the English stage, disposing of the romantic conventions and devices of the "well-made play" and instituting the theater of ideas, grounded in realism. During the late nineteenth century, Shaw was also a prominent literary, art, and music critic. In 1895, he became the drama critic for The Saturday Review, *and his reviews therein became known for their biting wit and brilliance. Although he later wrote criticism of poetry and fiction— much of it collected in* Pen Portaits and Reviews *(1932)—Shaw was out of sympathy with both of these genres. He had little use for poetry, believing it poorly suited for the expression of ideas, and in his criticism of fiction he rarely got beyond the search for ideology. As Samuel Hynes has noted, Shaw was driven by a rage to better the world. A Fabian socialist, he wrote criticism which is often concerned with the humanitarian and political intent of the work under discussion. Shaw and Wells were uneasy friends throughout much of their professional lives, having met while*

serving on the staff of The Saturday Review. *In the following letter, in which reference is made to Mr. Hoopdriver of Wells's* The Wheels of Chance *and to Kipps of* Kipps: The Story of a Simple Soul, *Shaw questions his friend's intent in the science fantasy* In the Days of the Comet. *In this novel, the Earth is temporarily enveloped in a green gas produced as the tail of a comet passes through the atmosphere. Earth's population is, for a short time, rendered unconscious, to awaken refreshed and endowed with the qualities of honesty, benevolence, and forgiveness, as well as an openness to polygamous marital arrangements and a desire for a socialist world government. Hence, Shaw's literary allusions, in a letter that also urges Wells to become a more serious Fabian propagandist.*]

What is all this in the ***Comet*** about a *menage à quatre*? What does it mean? Why does the book break off so abruptly? Why not take some green gas and be frank? (p. 650)

You cannot go on spinning comets out of your head for ever. You have done Kipps; and you have done the Comet hero; and having done them you will dry up like Kipling unless by a continuous activity you push your experience further. You must get the committee habit: that is, you must learn the habits of the human political animal as a naturalist learns the habits of wasps, by watching them. And you must learn their possibilities by trying to accomplish definite political ends through them. . . . You must, in short, learn your business as a propagandist and peripatetic philosopher if you are ever to be anything more than a novelist bombinating in vacuo except for a touch of reality gained in your early life. We have all been throug[h] the Dickens blacking factory; and we are all socialists by reaction against that; but the world wants from men of genius what they have divined as well as what they have gone through. You must end either in being nothing, or in being something more than a man with a grievance, which is what your Comet chap is. I was accidentally and externally a clerk like him once; but really I was a prince. Your Kippses and people are true to nature, or rather to modern civilization, just as David Copperfield's dread of Littimer [confidential servant of Steerforth] and his adventures with his landlady are true to civilization; but David Copperfield is not a man at all: Dickens has never for a moment given himself away in that book; and your Hoopdrivers & Kippses & Comet man, though excellent as demonstrations, are mere masks behind which you hide yourself. You are always bragging that you have been Kipps & that you know. This is a quintessential lie: if you had been Kipps you wouldnt know. If you said "I am God: and I know," it would be more to the point. Well, now that Kipps is demonstrated, you must learn a new trade—the Fabian trade. And the product will be, not a suite of offices & a million subscribers, but an approfounded and disillusioned and more variously effective Wells. (pp. 652-53)

> *Bernard Shaw, in a letter to H. G. Wells on September 14, 1906? in his* Collected Letters: 1898-1910, *edited by Dan H. Laurence (© 1972 The Trustees of the British Museum, The Governors and Guardians of the National Gallery of Ireland, and Royal Academy of Dramatic Art; reprinted by permission of The Society of Authors on behalf of the Bernard Shaw Estate), Dodd, Mead & Company, 1972, pp. 650-53.*

HILAIRE BELLOC (essay date 1908)

[*At the turn of the century, Belloc was considered one of England's premier men of letters and a provocative essayist. His characteristically truculent stance as a proponent of Roman Catholicism*

and economic reform, and his equally characteristic clever humor drew either strong support or harsh attacks from his audience. But critics find common ground for admiration in his poetry; Belloc and his longtime friend and collaborator G. K. Chesterton have been lauded by W. H. Auden as the best light-verse writers of their era, with Belloc's Cautionary Tales *considered by some his most successful work in the genre. And in such collections as* On Nothing *(1908) and* On Everything *(1909), Belloc proved that he could write convincing and forceful essays on nearly any subject, as either controversialist or defender of the status quo, in a prose style marked by clarity and wit. Closely linked to Belloc's Catholic beliefs was his proposed economic and political program called Distributism, a system of small ownership harking back to Europe's pre-Reformation period and fully described in the controversial 1912 essay* The Servile State. *Because he looked to the past—particularly to the Middle Ages—for his ideals, Belloc has not been widely read by modern readers; his desire to return to the values of an authoritarian epoch, as well as recurrent flashes of anti-Semitic comment in his works, have contributed to his eclipse as an important literary figure. Belloc's reputation as a polemicist reached its zenith in 1926, when he attacked Wells's* Outline of History *as simplistic and anti-Catholic in* A Companion to Mr. Wells's "Outline of History" *(see TCLC, Vol. 6). This broadside prompted a year-long war of mutual refutation waged by Belloc and Wells in several books and essays. The following excerpt is taken from an essay written amidst an earlier battle between the two writers; this review is but one of many articles published in* The New Age *during the 1908 "Great War" of ideas, which was waged between the Catholic Distributists Belloc and Chesterton and the agnostic socialists Wells and Shaw. In this essay, Belloc uses a review of* First and Last Things *as a springboard for an attack upon Wells's thought.*]

My Dear Wells,—I foolishly and rashly took your book upon ***First and Last Things*** with a promise to do what is called "reviewing" it. For this task I am not competent. I am not sure that anybody is, but I am quite sure that I am not. A review is either a summary, telling people what is in the book, or a judgment of that book, or a mixture of both. Now your book upon the ***First and Last Things*** contains so much of a human being, and is so full and so free from repetition that I don't see how it would be possible to summarise it, except as one summarises a character or an historical period by reading over and over again, and by leaving one's judgment to the process of time. As for judging, which is the second part of "reviewing," I again confess myself incapable. I can only measure by certain clear standards where generalities are concerned; for instance, I can distinguish between what is known and what is guessed in physical science, and between the emotion produced by good verse compared with the emotion produced by any passionate patriotic revenge mixed up with good verse. But when it comes to the appreciation of something so organic as a personality and what that personality thinks, I can only express an opinion equally personal, and that would not be "reviewing."

What I had better do, I think, is to tell you how the book strikes one in the literature of our time. What its place is and will be.

You will agree with me, I think, that the distinction between men to-day is the distinction between those prepared to discover and to express the truth, and those not concerned in this matter. The former happen to be in modern England as we know it, a very small body indeed. . . .

Now you are one of these. If you find Paris is well built you say so. The discovery gives you pleasure, and the expression of the discovery gives you pleasure, and you are indifferent whether for the moment some rascally Jew millionaire is on his trial for treason in France or not. If you think you have discovered an honest speech-maker in the United States, you say so, and you are indifferent to the prejudices of intimate friends in the matter. And so forth. I am confident that if, by personal experience, you discovered that a man had actually lifted himself off the ground by force of will, and had done a piece of "levitation" you would record the fact with enthusiasm, and would take a great deal of trouble to impress it upon your fellow beings, and so forth.

Now the people who want to tell the truth to-day are the people who will count with our immediate posterity. The hypocrites won't count—you can smell around you the tawdry and malodorous relics of the reputations of dead Cabinet Ministers; the vast host that repeat phrases don't count. The few who discover and desire to express *do* count. Therefore, your book will most undoubtedly be regarded one year after another as the development of our time proceeds.

My next business is to lay down as a proposition which I shall not prove, but upon which the whole of this my appreciation depends, that the modern world is very rapidly settling down into two fairly clearly marked bodies of opinion. (p. 160)

One of them is Catholicism, the other is that which you see shaping around you.

I say wisely "bodies" of thought. Not theories, but things, not conclusions but enthusiasms alive with passion.

I remember in one of your books you represented some fashionable fellow or other, whom I think you talked of as a cleric of the "Huysman" sect. He, in that future society you were describing, stood for some paltry fad or other, some millinery, some archaeological amusement, such as may tickle wealthy women. You know, of course, when I say Catholicism I do not mean that. When I say Catholicism I mean what the people mean who sell flowers near Victoria Station, and what the little hump-backed man means who sells papers somewhat further on. (This is not libel, for the hump-backed man is poor.) For I had a game the other day, laying a bet as to whether those in communion with the See of Rome were properly described in current English as Catholic. I referred it to the popular voice, and discovered all the day down Victoria Street that when an ordinary Englishman says Catholic he means Catholic. On this account do I use that word, but if anyone prefers that in writing to you I should use the word Papist or Romanist, or R.C., or even that to me meaningless word "Christianity," I should be delighted to use it so that we know what is meant by the word. Well, then, to return. I say the world is falling into these two bodies of thought, and falling rapidly, and the proof is, that the transcendental dogmas unproved and unprovable of the anti-Catholic side in Europe are beginning to be accepted wholesale and in bulk, precisely as are accepted the dogmas of religion.

Now I confess the interest of your book to me is to guess upon which side of the sand-bank thought of your book's kind will fall.

Here, I beseech you, Wells, to wait a moment. I am not interested to discover whether the sources from which it springs are Catholic or not. They obviously are not Catholic. What I am interested in is the process of appreciation apparent in such thought and the development of it. . . . Perpetually do I find in [your book] marks of sympathetic or emotional attraction to that which has given all its life to the anti-catholic camp. On the question of immortality, for instance, you do not ask yourself whether men continue to live or do not continue to live after death, but rather whether you feel inclined that they should

do so. On that prime question whether things are a pyramid which grows from an apex or whether they are not rather a cube whose molecular structure is pyramidal; whether we should feel the dynamics of the universe to proceed from or towards personality; whether a certain direction *is up* or *down;* whether the Universe was made or makes, and in general, *whether there is a God*—on this prime question (whereupon all true thought reposes) you tell me that sometimes, looking at a view or at the night, you feel a mysterious communion with a great personality. In words far less admirable than your own, and with intelligences wholly inferior to yours, the very modernists say such things. But surely the problem with which the mind of man wrestles is not whether he likes it or feels that such a personality should be, but whether it *is*.

When you talk not of that with which you sympathise or of that which you feel, but of that which you intellectually accept (or as we Catholics should say, of your Faith), you give a certain number of postulates upon the one side, but you give also a certain number of postulates upon the other.

For instance, next to the prime question whether there is a God, comes the quarrel between nominalism and realism; the great awakening of the human mind after the Dark Ages fought out that quarrel, and the Church decided against nominalism. Now your book is nominalist, whereas we are realist. You are nominalist when you say that matter in its ultimate analysis is no longer matter, and you are nominalist when you say that general terms lead men astray. In general, the intellectual framework of the book is of the school, or rather, the army, opposed to ours; but every now and then, like a man choosing things in a shop because he likes them, and therefore choosing divers things, you strike a strong note upon our side. For instance, you distinguish in more than one place between what is known and what is guessed—that is a purely Catholic habit. To-day we Catholics alone maintain that sanity as a body. You show in more than one passage a distaste for the dreary, repeated assertions of things never seen: things the supposed existence of which reposes upon nothing less flimsy than a Jacob's Ladder of hypotheses; that distaste is a profoundly Catholic distaste. I think if it were put to you which meant more to you, beer or the chemical analysis of beer, you would say beer. I think if it were put to you whether you were more sure of oak than of the analysis of oak upon any scientific lines you would plump for oak. More: in that vastly most important point, the stuff of humanity, you are perpetually dragged by your powerful intelligence towards seeing men. You try to mix your Socialism with the fact, Man. It won't mix, but at any rate you try to do it, and no other Socialist to my knowledge does.

So I ask myself as I lay the book down for the third or the fourth or the fifth time, into which watershed the stream of thought you represent (and largely originate) will fall when we are all dead. It is a profound question, the answer to it is all important, and I do not pretend to furnish that answer; but of one thing, at the risk of repetition, I will again affirm that I am certain, and that is that it *will* fall upon one side or the other; there are only two. Their dualism and their antagonism will be increasingly apparent as we grow old, and perhaps before the end of our time they will have led to wars. (pp. 160-61)

Hilaire Belloc, "A Letter to Wells" (reprinted by permission of A D Peters & Co Ltd), in The New Age, n.s. Vol. II, No. 18, February 29, 1908, pp. 160-61.

H. G. WELLS (essay date 1908)

[*In the following essay, Wells sarcastically answers the charges levelled by Belloc in his review of* First and Last Things *(see excerpt above)*].

Quite apart from the pleasure I feel in being written about by an artist so strong and subtle and admirable as Belloc, I rejoiced to read his letter in *The New Age*, that organ of all that is most "advanced" in contemporary thought. As one who has adventured into "advanced" circles and tried to get some sort of collective effectiveness out of their mental activities, as one who has retired at last baffled and temporarily disheartened before their immense, their invincible incoherence, I can appreciate perhaps more vividly than anyone else the urgent need there is to say and say again and keep on saying until the unfamiliar idea works its way home, that there is a need of thinking about how one thinks before one sets out upon the higher thought, or advanced or progressive thought, or indeed any sort of thinking about things in general at all . . .

Lord! the time I have had! It has been like trying to walk up a luggage chute while some lunatic above was raining down trunks, hand-bags, hat-boxes, dead cats, live cows, and cabbages!

The incapacity of most of these people to keep up for five minutes the distinction between a theory of social reconstruction and the strategic and tactical necessities of a political campaign!

Their incapacity to realise that a propaganda of ideas is hampered by a Basis that entirely mis-states what you are trying to make people understand!

Their artful secondary reasons! Their earnest search for the true motives behind a proposition! Their sudden plunging resorts to suspicion!

Their conceptions of research! . . .

Well, that is by the way. There are two matters upon which Belloc dwells in his illuminating criticism. One, the reality of God, I cannot deal with here, because there is not available space enough nor time enough to go at all beyond stark initial propositions; the other, the (mentally) more fundamental issue, the issue between Nominalist and the Realist. I disagree with Belloc in his interpretation of the situation. I do not think there is to be that deep separation and conflict ahead of us that he foretells. Nominalist and Realist are, I think, convergent systems of attitude that are giving place to re-stated reconciling propositions. That he finds me, for example, astraddle and doubtful between the two channels he marks is just one of many considerations that disincline me to agree with him. I know it is tempting to sweep in the lines of a broad separation through all the twisting of human thought, to separate as Nominalists one great body from—I snatch at names haphazard—Heraclitus, through William of Occam to William James, and put over against them the intellectuals from Plato and Aristotle via Abelard, let us say, to Dr. MacTaggart. Only—it isn't so. Two sets of influences have subtly and profoundly altered the fundamental conceptions on which this opposition rests. One is the growing realisation of a factor of will in thought, due to the invasion of psychology by observation; the other, the perception of what I may call inter-specific, as well as intra-specific, individuals—that is to say, of "links"—which Darwinism brought home to the human mind. In place of absolute qualitative oppositions, it follows that we get quantitative differences, and the nature of the issue is changed altogether. . . .

Life is not only short but urgent, so that one must write of these things in a kind of shorthand, but I think that will convey my point to Belloc anyhow. (pp. 161-62)

H. G. Wells, "Nominalist and Realist" (reprinted by permission of The Executors of the Estate of H. G. Wells), in The New Age, *n.s. Vol. IV, No. 8, December 17, 1908, pp. 161-62.*

UPTON SINCLAIR (essay date 1911)

[*An American novelist, dramatist, journalist, and essayist, Sinclair was a prolific writer who is most famous for* The Jungle *(1906), a novel that portrays the unjust labor practices, filth, and horrifying conditions of Chicago's meat-processing industry, and which prompted passage of the Pure Food and Drug Act of 1906. A lifelong, outspoken socialist, Sinclair addressed the excesses of capitalist society in most of his works and demanded, in his critical theory, the subservience of art to social change. Although most of his fiction is dismissed in the United States for its obtrusive didacticism, Sinclair is one of America's most-read authors outside of North America, his works being particularly popular in the Soviet Union. Sinclair acclaims* The New Machiavelli *as one of the most incisive English novels of the day.*]

I personally consider the greatest of English living writers of fiction [to be] H. G. Wells. **"The New Machiavelli,"** I believe, is his masterpiece, one of the most powerful of English novels. It can be called a Socialist novel, provided that the word is understood in its broadest sense; it is an appeal for sex freedom rather than for economic freedom, but incidentally it takes into its view the whole of the modern movement for the emancipation of thought. It is a tremendous and moving piece of work, and its publication is a great event in English literature. I am willing to risk the prophecy that it will be the most-talked-of novel of the present season.

"The New Machiavelli" recites in elaborate and comprehensive detail the life story of a rising young English university man, who goes into public life. He comes in contact with all the various forces which are struggling in English society at the present time, and ultimately becomes the founder of a movement for the advocacy of social reform within the Conservative party. He becomes a member of Parliament, and is well on the way toward a Cabinet position, when his career is wrecked upon the rocks of our present-day marriage conventions. We have had such cases, both in this country and in England, but here for the first time we see the story from the inside. We see the man's marriage, and understand the causes of its growing unhappiness; we meet the second woman, who proves to be—our "yellow" newspapers have made the word "affinity" almost unusable, but there is no other word that can be substituted. Wells's purpose is to assert the dignity and nobility of true passion, to vindicate its rights, and to set forth its meaning in the scheme of nature. The epoch-making quality of his novel lies just here: that one follows the story, step by step, and is irresistibly moved to understand and to sympathize. The latter part of the book is simply terrific. It gathers headway and moves like an avalanche; it has the inevitability and the tragic power of one of the old Greek dramas. We see the man fling his career to the winds, and turn his back upon England, with its Philistinism and its Pharisaism, going away with the woman of his love. Some eminent English bishop is on record as having said that he would rather inoculate his daughter with smallpox germs than have her read **"Ann Veronica."** I shall wait with interest to hear what assortment of diseases the bishop will select to express his disapproval of **"The New Machia-velli."** (pp. 4-5)

Upton Sinclair, "Socialist Fiction" (reprinted by permission of the Literary Estate of Upton Sinclair), in Wilshire's, *Vol. XV, No. 2, February, 1911, pp. 4-5.**

REBECCA WEST   (essay date 1914)

[*West is considered one of the foremost English novelists and critics to write during the twentieth century. Born Cecily Isabel Fairfield, she began her career as an actress—taking the name Rebecca West from the emancipated heroine of Henrik Ibsen's drama* Rosmersholm—*and as a book reviewer for* The Free-woman. *Her early criticism was noted for its militantly feminist stance and its reflection of West's Fabian socialist concerns. Her first novel,* The Return of the Soldier (1918), *evidences a concern that entered into much of her later work: the psychology of the individual. West's greatest works include* The Meaning of Treason (1947), *which analyzes the motives of Britain's wartime traitors—notably, William Joyce ("Lord Haw-Haw")—and* Black Lamb and Grey Falcon (1942), *a record of the author's 1937 journey through Yugoslavia. West's literary criticism is noted for its wit, aversion to cant, and perceptiveness. Of her own work, West has commented: "I have always written in order to discover the truth for my own use, on the one hand, and on the other hand to earn money for myself and my family, and in this department of my work I hope I have honoured the truth I had already discovered. I have like most women written only a quarter of what I might have written, owing to my family responsibilities. I dislike heartily the literary philosophy and practice of my time, which I think has lagged behind in the past and has little relevance to the present, and it distresses me that so much contemporary work is dominated by the ideas (particularly the political and religious ideas) of the late eighteenth or nineteenth century, and those misunderstood." Early in her career, West was hotly antagonistic to Wells's works, sensing in them little more than sexist twaddle. Later, she and Wells became lovers and the parents of a son, Anthony West, the noted essayist. Below, writing during her period of adversity to Wells, West likens him to Cervantes's buffoonish Sancho Panza and Bernard Shaw to Don Quixote.*]

Criticism matters as it never did in the past, because of the present pride of great writers. They take all life as their province to-day. Formerly they sat in their studies, and thinking only of the emotional life of mankind—thinking therefore with comparative ease, of the color of life and not of its form—devised a score or so of stories before death came. Now, their pride telling them that if time would but stand still they could explain all life, they start on a breakneck journey across the world. They are tormented by the thought of time; they halt by no event, but look down upon it as they pass, cry out their impressions, and gallop on. Often it happens that because of their haste they receive a blurred impression or transmit it to their readers roughly and without precision. And just as it was the duty of the students of Kelvin the mathematician to correct his errors in arithmetic, so it is the duty of critics to rebuke these hastinesses of great writers, lest the blurred impressions weaken the surrounding mental fabric and their rough transmissions frustrate the mission of genius on earth.

There are two great writers of to-day who greatly need correction. Both are misleading in external things. When Mr. Shaw advances, rattling his long lance to wit, and Mr. Wells follows, plump and oiled with the fun of things, they seem Don Quixote and Sancho Panza. Not till one has read much does one discover that Mr. Shaw loves the world as tenderly as Sancho Panza loved his ass, and that Mr. Wells wants to

drive false knights from the earth and cut the stupidity and injustice out of the spiritual stuff of mankind. And both have to struggle with their temperaments. Mr. Shaw believes too blindly in his own mental activity; he imagines that if he continues to secrete thought he must be getting on. Mr. Wells dreams into the extravagant ecstasies of the fanatic, and broods over old hated things or the future peace and wisdom of the world, while his story falls in ruins about his ears.

Yet no effective criticism has come to help them. (pp. 19-20)

Mr. Wells' mind works more steadily than Mr. Shaw's, but it suffers from an unawareness of the reader; an unawareness, too, of his material; an unawareness of everything except the problem on which it happens to be brooding. His stories become more and more absent-minded. From **"The Passionate Friends"** we deduced that Mr. Wells lived on the branch line of a not too well organized railway system and wrote his books while waiting for trains at the main line junction. The novel appeared to be a year book of Indian affairs; but there were also some interesting hints on the publishing business, and once or twice one came on sections of a sympathetic study of moral imbecility in the person of a lady called Mary, who married for money and impudently deceived her owner. And what was even more amazing than its inchoateness was Mr. Wells' announcement on the last page that the book had been a discussion of jealousy. That was tragic, for it is possible that he had something to say on the subject, and what it was no one will ever know. Yet this boat of wisdom which had sprung so disastrous a leak received not one word of abuse from English criticism. No one lamented over the waste of the mind, the spilling of the idea. (p. 20)

Rebecca West, "The Duty of Harsh Criticism," in The New Republic (*reprinted by permission of* The New Republic; © *1914 The New Republic, Inc.), Vol. I, No. 1, November 7, 1914, pp. 18-20.**

HENRY JAMES   (letter date 1915)

[*As a novelist, James is valued for psychological acuity and a complex sense of artistic form. Throughout his career, James also wrote literary criticism in which he developed his artistic ideals and applied them to the works of others. James defined the novel as "a direct impression of life" and considered the quality of this impression—the degree of moral and intellectual development—and the author's ability to communicate this impression in an effective and artistic manner the two principal criteria for estimating the worth of a literary work. James admired the self-consciously formalistic approach of contemporary French writers—particularly Gustave Flaubert—an approach which contrasted with the loose, less formulated standards of the English novel. On the other hand, he favored the moral concerns of English writing over the often amoral and cynical vision which characterized much of French literature in the second half of the nineteenth century. His literary aim was to combine the qualities of each country's literature that most appealed to his temperament. After considering various fictional strategies, James arrived at what he thought the most desirable form for the novel to take. Basically objective in presentation—that is, without the intrusion of an authorial voice—the novel should be a well-integrated formal scheme of dialogue, description, and narrative action, all of which should be received from the viewpoint of a single consciousness, or "receptor." In James's novels, this receptor is usually a principal character who is more an observer than a participant in the plot. Equal in importance to the artistic plan of a novel is the type of receptor a novelist chooses to use. The type demanded by James's theory is a consciousness that will convey a high moral vision, humanistic worldview, and a gen-*]

erally uplifting sense of life. James admired much of Wells's fiction and wrote the author several glowing letters of praise. But Wells, who differed drastically with James in his conception of the role of literature, unexpectedly attacked his longtime friend in Boon, *a book of critical sketches. In this work, Wells, who considered the role of literature to be somewhat equivalent to that of sociopolitical advocacy, mocked James's literary theories and likened ''the Master,'' as a writer, to ''a magnificent but painful hippopotamus resolved at any cost, even at the cost of its dignity, upon picking up a pea which has gotten into a corner of its den.'' Upon reading a portion of* Boon, *James sent Wells the following sarcastic retort.*]

My dear Wells,

I was given yesterday at a club your volume **"Boon, etc.,"** from a loose leaf in which I learn that you kindly sent it me and which yet appears to have lurked there for a considerable time undelivered. I have just been reading, to acknowledge it intelligently, a considerable number of its pages—though not all; for, to be perfectly frank, I have been in that respect beaten for the first time—or rather for the first time but one—by a book of yours; I haven't found the current of it draw me on and on this time—as, unfailingly and irresistibly, before (which I have repeatedly let you know). However, I shall try again—I hate to lose any scrap of you that *may* make for light or pleasure; and meanwhile I have more or less mastered your appreciation of H. J., which I have found very curious and interesting after a fashion—though it has naturally not filled me with a fond elation. It is difficult of course for a writer to put himself *fully* in the place of another writer who finds him extraordinarily futile and void, and who is moved to publish that to the world—and I think the case isn't easier when he happens to have enjoyed the other writer enormously from far back; because there has then grown up the habit of taking some common meeting-ground between them for granted, and the falling away of this is like the collapse of a bridge which made communication possible. But I am by nature more in dread of any fool's paradise, or at least of any bad misguidedness, than in love with the idea of a security proved, and the fact that a mind as brilliant as yours *can* resolve me into such an unmitigated mistake, can't enjoy me in anything like the degree in which I like to think I may be enjoyed, makes me greatly want to fix myself, for as long as my nerves will stand it, with such a pair of eyes. I am aware of certain things I have, and not less conscious, I believe, of various others that I am simply reduced to wish I did or could have; so I try, for possible light, to enter into the feelings of a critic for whom the deficiencies so preponderate. The difficulty about that effort, however, is that one can't keep it up—one *has* to fall back on one's sense of one's good parts—one's own sense; and I at least should have to do that, I think, even if your picture were painted with a more searching brush. For I should otherwise seem to forget what it is that my poetic and my appeal to experience rest upon. They rest upon *my* measure of fulness—fulness of life and of the projection of it, which seems to you such an emptiness of both. I don't mean to say I don't wish I could do twenty things I can't—many of which you do so livingly; but I confess I ask myself what would become in that case of some of those to which I am most addicted and by which interest seems to me most beautifully producible. I hold that interest may be, *must* be, exquisitely made and created, and that if we don't make it, we who undertake to, nobody and nothing will make it for us; though nothing is more possible, nothing may even be more certain, than that my quest of it, my constant wish to run it to earth, may entail the sacrifice of certain things that are not on the straight line of it. However, there are too many things to

say, and I don't think your chapter is really inquiring enough to entitle you to expect all of them. (pp. 485-87)

Henry James, in a letter to H. G. Wells on July 6, 1915, in his The Letters of Henry James, Vol. II, *edited by Percy Lubbock (copyright 1920 Charles Scribner's Sons; copyright renewed 1948 William James and Margaret James Porter; reprinted with permission of Charles Scribner's Sons), Charles Scribner's Sons, 1920, pp. 485-87.*

WILLIAM LYON PHELPS   (essay date 1916)

[*Phelps spent over forty years as a lecturer at Yale. His early study* The Beginnings of the English Romantic Movement *(1893) is still considered an important work and his* Essays on Russian Novelists *(1911) was one of the first influential studies of the Russian realists. From 1922 until his death in 1943 he wrote a regular column for* Scribner's Magazine *and a nationally syndicated newspaper column. During this period, his criticism became less scholarly and more journalistic, and is notable for its generally enthusiastic tone. In the following excerpt, Phelps expresses his enjoyment of* The Wheels of Chance, *observing the emergence of Wells the artist.*]

Twenty years ago, while doing some reviewing for a New York journal, I received a package of new novels. The title of one of them caught my fancy, though I had never heard of the author. It was **The Wheels of Chance,** by H. G. Wells. He had been a maker of books less than a twelvemonth, though prophetically prolific, having published four separate volumes the first year of his career, 1895. It may be a damaging admission, but while I have a high respect for the ability of Mr. Wells, I have never enjoyed reading any one of his novels so much as I enjoyed **The Wheels of Chance.** One may roar with laughter at **Bealby** . . . , but there is no more delicacy in its humour than in a farce-film; whereas **The Wheels of Chance,** describing the bicycle adventures of Mr. Hoopdriver, the dry-goods clerk, has something of the combined mirth, pathos, and tenderness of Don Quixote. There is not a hint in this little book of Wells the Socialist, Wells the Reformer, Wells the Futurist, Wells the Philosopher—there is only Wells the artist, whom I admire more than I do the sociological preacher.

I am quite willing to admit that it is the more pretentious Wells who has become the world-figure, for a world-figure he undoubtedly is. Before the Great War, his books were in the window of every important book-shop in Germany, where he was studied rather than read. French and Russian translations poured from the press year after year. And yet I am not at all sure that he has made any real contribution to modern thought, whereas he has made a distinct contribution to modern literary art. He writes books faster than any one can read them; faster than any one publisher can produce them, as may be seen by a reference to his bibliography. Yet as a rule his work is neither shallow nor trivial.

In one respect he has never fulfilled the promise of **The Wheels of Chance.** There was a touch of spirituality in that playful comedy, a flash that has since been altogether obscured by the cloudy sky of materialism. It seems unfortunate that when Mr. Wells has so many gifts, so much talent, he has not the little more, and how much it is! He is a man of prose, downright, hard-headed, matter-of-fact. One could hardly expect him to write like Nathaniel Hawthorne, but it is a pity that he should be as far removed from Hawthorne as a railway timetable. How is it possible for a man to have so much humour and be so limited? Yet that kind comes only by prayer and fasting, words that have no meaning for Mr. Wells.

Many of his stories are like a dusty road, as Scott's are like a thick forest. We reach certain elevations and see ahead of us nothing but the long brown way, in the pitiless glare of the sun. That was my feeling all through *Ann Veronica*. I liked *Marriage* much better, though the wilderness-cure was a large order. I liked *The Wife of Sir Isaac Harman* better yet, for it contains an admirable commingling of the two authors living in the brain of Mr. Wells, the author of *The Wheels of Chance, Kipps* and *Bealby*—and the man who wrote *Ann Veronica* and *Marriage*. (pp. 252-54)

> William Lyon Phelps, "Twentieth Century British Novelists" (originally published as "The Advance of the English Novel," in The Bookman, Vol. XLIII, June, 1916), in his The Advance of the English Novel (reprinted by permission of Dodd, Mead & Company, Inc.; copyright, 1915 by Dodd, Mead and Company; copyright, 1916 by Dodd, Mead and Company, Inc.), Dodd, Mead, 1916, pp. 232-66.*

RANDOLPH BOURNE (essay date 1918)

[*An American essayist who wrote during the years of World War I, Bourne is recognized as one of the most astute critics of American life and letters of his era. During his short life, he contributed numerous articles to national magazines and became known as a champion of progressive education and pacifism, as well as a fierce opponent of sentimentality in literature. Bourne was on the original staff of* The New Republic *and was also a contributing editor of* The Dial *and* The Seven Arts, *until the latter was officially suppressed during the war for its pacifist position. In a tribute published in* The New Republic, *Floyd Dell listed the characteristics of Bourne's mind as "restless and relentless curiosity, undeterred by sentiment and never recoiling in cynicism; the mood of perpetual inquiry, and the courage to go down unfamiliar ways in search of truth." Wells puts youth at the helm in* Joan and Peter, *and Bourne concludes that it is all one needs to know of life in England for the last twenty-five years.*]

It is always a question whether Mr. Wells is an incomparably gifted observer of the sweep of events, or whether he uses the world of institutions and ideas primarily as symbols of his own insistent personality. Was his recent religious flare an attempt to beat to its goal a real world rapidly mysticizing under the strain of war, or was it a personal recoil against a sudden sense of helplessness? If we could answer these questions we should know whether it is England that has righted itself, abandoning the Mr. Britling who found conscious social control too much for him without the guiding hand of a divine comrade, returning to the old confident maker of new worlds for old; or whether it is only Mr. Wells's own robust spirit emerging from its so singularly unbecoming religious widowhood to the delights of pragmatic power again.

At least, this new novel ["**Joan and Peter**"] represents a complete convalescence. Its chief sensation is the relegation of God back to the innocuous rôle into which the late Victorian had got him. This book puts God familiarly but decisively in his place, and restores our responsible, curious, adventurous, experimental youth at the heart of the world's soul and the helm of its affairs. To young Peter, shattered in limb but wise from his war experience, progress is again religion: "work and learning are our creed." God, seen in his vivacious dream, is the Old Experimenter, tinkering about in his dusty workshop, as he tells Peter with a rather jolly cynicism: "If you have no will to change it, you have no right to criticize it." So it

becomes our task for the future to "take hold of the world, unassisted by God, with the acquiescence of God, and in fulfillment of some remote incomprehensible planning on the part of God." Fickle Mr. Wells! What has become of the Invisible King, the first President of the Republic of Mankind? Even Oswald, the noble old imperialistic idealist, finds God as a "name battered out of all value and meaning," and sinks back on a "Nameless and Incomprehensible, an Essence beyond Reality, a Heart of all Things, by which he lives and is upheld." God has been withdrawn from the Wellsian programme.

Thrown back on our own resources, we have a right to ask how this old unquenchable pragmatic optimism feels today in a world still blindly agonizing at war. Joan and Peter go ahead to build a "civilized life of creative activities in an atmosphere of helpful goodwill." After the war he is to take up biological research and she is to do house-building. Well, this return of Wells to the old ideas and aspirations finds virtue gone out of them. It is something to have gotten rid of a superfluous mysticism, but the morsels of uncritical pragmatism handed back taste a little stale and cold. What Wells misses is the slight skeptical weariness with which the living remnant of a younger generation is beginning to view the ease and blitheness of political pragmatists. Why has our scientifically trained and experimental generation in all countries put all its energy at the service of an industrialized statism? Why do so many of our former minds of democratic goodwill betray now so shallow an emotional comprehension of the forces our war is raising up that they seem like children who witness passionate scenes between their elders with only a naïve wonder what it can all be about? Wells is not exactly glib, but he gives no hint for the future how we are to tame or sublimate the terrible mob unreasons that have made the "social" and the "collective"—our old ideal fetishes—into so bitter a mockery. When he offers us his old instruments, made for the creative life of society, we are impatient and hold off, not through sheer pique or inertia, but because we are honest enough to be suspicious even of ourselves and all the valiant brandishings we have made.

But this morbid preoccupation with Wells as an antebellum prophet should not blind us to the triumphant achievement that "**Joan and Peter**" is. Never has he spread for us such a gorgeous sociological panorama. If he does the antebellum, he has done it with a superb bounce and competence that no one will ever surpass. This is not a novel; it is a library; it is a telescoped newspaper. It is everything that one needs to know about the public life of the significant classes in England for the last twenty-five years. You marvel at the flawless mechanism of his intelligence, which can take in this chaotic clashing mass of movements and events, and stream it out into a ribbon of vivacious narrative, imperturbable in interest on every page, always fresh and personal and assured. If there is less of the old piquancy, there is still a marvelous pertinency of characterization. And in spite of the panoramic sweep, it is always a story about persons, and never a mere chronicle or dialogue. His people are types, of course, but how admirably he gives the impression of clinching their essential qualities! From the parents and the aunts, living their enlightened radicalism of the early nineties in their safe and settled world, to the restless youths and girls of 1914, he passes in review all the dear dead satisfactions that shriveled in the blaze of war. (pp. 215-16)

The "education" of which "**Joan and Peter**" is the story is the training provided by this whole era, rather than by any of the schools or colleges, outrageous or admirable, to which they may go. There are charming chapters of their child-life; there is the free and eager wish for pleasure and excitement and knowledge in the years just before the war; there is the ironical fate of all these golden youths as they are sucked into it. How much Wells misses at times out of all this may be seen by comparison with a book like Cannan's "Mendel." Sex is still the slightly unclean thing that Wells puzzles chastely over. Joan is a brave young Diana—but is not a frank eroticism better than Wells's mixture of pudency and bold grappling? There are uncomfortable reminiscences of Wells's previous matings, and an actual eternal recurrence of the "You're my man, and I'm your woman!" Yet, after all, Wells does skirt just outside the range of priggishness and get all the discussion he wants into his impetuously moving story. Of course he has almost forgotten that there was ever such a thing as a proletarian. You could never imagine from his book that the future of England might belong to the Labor party. The proletarian-aristocrat, who stirs us in a person like Lenine, does not exist for Wells's imagination. He joins Mr. Gompers and Vachel Lindsay in repudiating the class struggle. He has relegated his middle-class God, but he has done nothing to his men. In the face of a cry for vast new desires and stirring new types, he has joined so many of his fellow pragmatists in looking back. The coming years, I am afraid, will turn him to stone. (p. 216)

Randolph Bourne, "The Relegation of God," in The Dial (copyright 1918, by The Dial Publishing Company, Inc.), Vol. LXV, No. 773, September 19, 1918, pp. 215-16.

VIRGINIA WOOLF   (essay date 1919)

[*Woolf is considered one of the most prominent literary figures of the twentieth century. Like her contemporary James Joyce, with whom she is often compared, Woolf is remembered as one of the most innovative of the stream of consciousness novelists. Concerned primarily with depicting the life of the mind, she revolted against traditional narrative techniques and developed her own highly individualized style. Woolf's works, noted for their subjective explorations of characters' inner lives and their delicate poetic quality, have had a lasting effect on the art of the novel. A discerning and influential critic and essayist as well as a novelist, Woolf began writing reviews for* The Times Literary Supplement *at an early age. Her critical essays, which cover almost the entire range of English literature, are praised for their insight and contain some of her finest prose. Along with Lytton Strachey, Roger Fry, Clive Bell, and several others, Woolf and her husband Leonard formed the literary coterie known as the "Bloomsbury Group." In this essay, she concludes that Wells treats unimportant things as though they are profound and lasting.*]

[If] we speak of quarrelling with Mr. Wells, Mr. Bennett, and Mr. Galsworthy it is partly that by the mere fact of their existence in the flesh their work has a living, breathing, everyday imperfection which bids us take what liberties with it we choose. . . . If we tried to formulate our meaning in one word we should say that these three writers are materialists. It is because they are concerned not with the spirit but with the body that they have disappointed us, and left us with the feeling that the sooner English fiction turns its back upon them, as politely as may be, and marches, if only into the desert, the better for its soul. Naturally, no single word reaches the centre of three separate targets. In the case of Mr. Wells it falls notably wide of the mark. And yet even with him it indicates to our thinking the fatal alloy in his genius, the great clod of clay that has got itself mixed up with the purity of his inspiration. . . . It can scarcely be said of Mr. Wells that he is a materialist in the sense that he takes too much delight in the

solidity of his fabric. His mind is too generous in its sympathies to allow him to spend much time in making things shipshape and substantial. He is a materialist from sheer goodness of heart, taking upon his shoulders the work that ought to have been discharged by Government officials, and in the plethora of his ideas and facts scarcely having leisure to realise, or forgetting to think important, the crudity and coarseness of his human beings. Yet what more damaging criticism can there be both of his earth and of his Heaven than that they are to be inhabited here and hereafter by his Joans and his Peters? Does not the inferiority of their natures tarnish whatever institutions and ideals may be provided for them by the generosity of their creator? (pp. 208-10)

If we fasten, then, one label on all these books, on which is one word materialists, we mean by it that they write of unimportant things; that they spend immense skill and immense industry making the trivial and the transitory appear the true and the enduring. (p. 210)

Virginia Woolf, "Modern Fiction" (originally published as "Modern Novels," in The Times Literary Supplement, No. 899, April 10, 1919), in her The Common Reader (copyright 1925 by Harcourt Brace Jovanovich, Inc.; renewed 1953 by Leonard Woolf; reprinted by permission of the author's Literary Estate and The Hogarth Press), Harcourt Brace Jovanovich, 1925, pp. 207-18.*

C. S. LEWIS   (letter date 1920)

[*Lewis is considered one of the foremost Christian and mythopoeic authors of the twentieth century. Indebted principally to George MacDonald, G. K. Chesterton, Charles Williams, and the writers of ancient Norse myths, he is regarded as a formidable logician and Christian polemicist, a perceptive literary critic, and—most highly—as a writer of fantasy literature. A traditionalist in his approach to life and art, he opposed the modern movement in literary criticism toward biographical and psychological interpretation. In place of this, Lewis practiced and propounded a theory of criticism which stresses the importance of the author's intent, rather than the reader's presuppositions and prejudices. Writing to his lifelong friend and correspondent Arthur Greeves, shortly after his own graduation from Oxford, Lewis discusses Wells's novel* Marriage.]

You will be surprised when you hear how I employed the return journey—by reading an H. G. Wells novel called '**Marriage**' . . . , and perhaps more surprised when I say that I thoroughly enjoyed it; one thing you can say for the man is that he really is interested in all the big, outside questions—and the characters are intensely real, especially a Mr Pope who reminds me of Excellenz. It opens new landscapes to me—how one felt that on finding that a new kind of book was waiting for one, in the old days—and I have decided to read some more of his serious books. It is funny that I—and perhaps you—read the old books for pleasure and always turn to contemporaries with the notion of 'improving my mind'. With most, I fancy, the direct opposite is so. (p. 264)

C. S. Lewis, in a letter to Arthur Greeves in February, 1920, in his They Stand Together: The Letters of C. S. Lewis to Arthur Greeves (1914-1963), edited by Walter Hooper (reprinted with permission of Macmillan Publishing Company; text copyright © 1979 by The Estate of C. S. Lewis), Macmillan, 1979, pp. 264-65.

H. L. MENCKEN (essay date 1921)

[*From the era of World War I until the early years of the Great Depression, Mencken was one of the most influential figures in American letters. His strongly individualistic, irreverent outlook on life and his vigorous, invective-charged writing style helped establish the iconoclastic spirit of the Jazz Age and significantly shaped the direction of American literature. As a social and literary critic—the roles for which he is best known—Mencken was the scourge of evangelical Christianity, public service organizations, literary censorship, boosterism, provincialism, democracy, all advocates of personal or social improvement, and every other facet of American life that he perceived as humbug. In his literary criticism, Mencken encouraged American writers to shun the anglophilic, moralistic bent of the nineteenth century and to practice realism, an artistic call-to-arms that is most fully developed in his essay ''Puritanism As a Literary Force,'' one of the seminal essays in modern literary criticism. A man who was widely renowned or feared during his lifetime as a would-be destroyer of established American values, Mencken once wrote: ''All of my work, barring a few obvious burlesques, is based upon three fundamental ideas. 1. That knowledge is better than ignorance; 2. That it is better to tell the truth than to lie; and 3. That it is better to be free than to be a slave.'' In a review of* Joan and Peter *which appeared in the December 1918 issue of* The Smart Set *(see TCLC, Vol. 6), Mencken dismissed Wells as a spent force in literature. In the following review of* The Outline of History, *Mencken discusses Wells as a well-read, reflective social thinker, but one who cannot overcome several forms of national and caste prejudice. Nevertheless, Mencken finds the work to be a colossal synthesis of human knowledge.*]

Two years and two months ago, addressing the chosen of God from this pulpit, I announced the decease and preached the funeral sermon of H. G. Wells as a novelist. Let that sermon stand. Wells the novelist is still dead—dead as Haman, dead as Friedrich Barbarossa, dead as the Constitution of the United States. But out of the tomb, wearing all the glittering raiment of the departed, there crawls the murderer, to wit, Wells the forward-looker, the popular philosopher, the advanced thinker, the amateur politician, the soothsayer in general practice. This literary felon I am bound to abhor, for Wells the novelist was a performer very much to my taste, but all the same I am not one to deny his talents. On the contrary, I believe that, within the limits presently to be set forth, he owns and operates one of the most active and penetrating intelligences in function in the England of today—that he is an enormously clever, well-taught, reflective, courageous and original fellow—a man with a head worth a pile of Chesterton heads as high as the Trafalgar monument, or a pile of Lloyd George or Asquith heads as huge as the Alps. (p. 218)

Wells, for all his intellectual suppleness and cunning, has prejudices . . . ; it is a common human bond between us, like our joint incapacity to move our ears. Many of these prejudices arise out of the simple fact that he is an Englishman—that he was brought up amid certain general ideas, certain ways of looking at things, certain fundamental assumptions. Others owe their origin to the special circumstance that, as Englishmen estimate such distinctions, he is an Englishman of the lower classes—one shut off from a large and important body of privileges and immunities—a man facing peculiar obstacles in his struggle toward power and eminence among his compatriots. To be an Englishman is to be born with an incurable prejudice in favor of certain notions in government, *e.g.*, debate, representation, majority rule, compromise, the whole machinery of parliamentarism. And to be of the lower classes in any civilized country is to be born with an even firmer prejudice in favor of certain other notions, *e.g.*, human equality, the

virtues of education, the eternal immorality of whatever is aristocratic, the substantial truth of the Sermon on the Mount. You will find both prejudices lavishly displayed from end to end of Wells's new and extremely shrewd and valuable work, *The Outline of History.* (pp. 219-20)

Wells, when he writes the history of the world in the terms of an Englishman who, whatever his intrinsic learning and intelligence, is still distinctly the inferior of, say, the Duke of Norfolk, Prof. Dr. Gilbert Murray, or even the Right Hon. Winston Churchill, is also writing it in the terms of an ordinary respectable American. This explains the lavish and usually wholly uncritical praise that has been heaped upon his book. It is a very interesting, intelligent and instructive book; it comes near being a genuinely great book; but there are still a number of fundamental defects in it as truthful history, and all of them arise out of Wells's inborn and ineradicable prejudices.

I shall not rehearse them in detail; you will read the *Outline* assuredly, and so discover them for yourself. Nevertheless, a few hints may be of service. There is, first of all, the prejudice of a typically democratic man against every tendency to transfer sovereignty from the people to an individual—the chronic incapacity of such a man to understand such regal egoists as Alexander, Julius Caesar, Charlemagne, Frederick the Great, and Napoleon I. Wells is not merely against all these great conquerors; he is extravagantly unjust to them; he simply cannot understand them. And in order to carry off his libel of them, he is forced into not a few obvious absurdities, *e.g.*, the doctrine that military genius is a thing of a very low intellectual order, and scarcely to be distinguished from a talent for ordinary crime. This, of course, is quite idiotic. . . . And by the same token he is grossly unfair to the sort of men who deduce philosophical ideas from the acts of such captains—for example, Bismarck and Machiavelli. Here the historian is always a slave to the democrat—that is, to the man who believes, not in salient and extraordinary men, but in the huge, brutish masses of ordinary men.

The same interloper appears every time Wells turns from the interpretation of the past to the forecasting of the future. The thing he dreams of is a sort of universal democracy, with all the affairs of the world ordered by the will of a vague and shifting majority. But he sees, of course, that the success of any such scheme must depend upon the possession of quick and accurate information by the people, and, more important still, upon their capacity to make use of it in a rational manner. Therefore, he is an enthusiastic advocate of popular education, and insists that it be made very much cheaper and more widespread than it is today. But here he overlooks a capital fact, and that is the fact that popular education, no matter what efforts are made to improve it, must inevitably remain but little more than a device for perpetuating the ideas that happen to be official—in other words, the nonsense regarded as revelation by the powers currently in control of the state. Education in the true sense—education directed toward awaking a capacity to differentiate between fact and appearance—is and always will be a more or less furtive and illicit thing, for its chief purpose is the controversion and destruction of the very ideas that the majority of men—and particularly the majority of official and powerful men—regard as incontrovertibly true. To the extent that I am genuinely educated, I am suspicious of all the things that the average citizen believes and the average pedagogue teaches. Progress consists precisely in attacking and disposing of these ordinary beliefs. It is thus opposed to education, as the thing is usually understood, and so there should be no surprise in the fact that the generality of pedagogues, like the generality of politicians and superpoliticians, are bitter enemies to all new ideas. (pp. 221-22)

Thus Wells's peruna fails to convince me; I doubt seriously that it would cure the patient. He believes in it simply because believing in it is an invariable part of the mental baggage of a democrat. Most of his other errors are due to his virtues as a British patriot. . . . The whole war section . . . is immeasurably above anything that any American of like origin and surroundings would be capable of. It will probably be years before an American historian shows a fifth of the decency that Wells shows. . . . Here Wells displays once more, conclusively and sickeningly, how much higher all discussions of public matters range in England than they do in America. I know of no American who could have planned a work so bold and comprehensive—a work involving so colossal a synthesis of human knowledge and opinion in a field so tangled and so wide. And I know of none who could have executed it with such unfailing learning, such charming persuasiveness, and, above all, so much of honesty, dignity and sense. (p. 223)

> *H. L. Mencken, "H. G. Wells 'Redivivus'" (originally published as "A Soul's Adventures," in* The Smart Set, *Vol. LXIV, No. 3, March, 1921) in his* "Smart Set" Criticism, *edited by William H. Nolte (copyright © 1968 by Cornell University; used by permission of the publisher, Cornell University Press), Cornell University Press, 1968, pp. 218-23.*

LEONARD WOOLF   (essay date 1926)

[*Woolf is best known as one of the leaders of the "Bloomsbury Group" of artists and thinkers, and as the husband of novelist Virginia Woolf, with whom he founded the famous Hogarth Press. The Bloomsbury Group, which was named after the section of London where the members lived and met, also included Clive and Vanessa Bell, John Maynard Keynes, Lytton Strachey, Virginia Woolf, Desmond MacCarthy, and several others. The group's weekly meetings were occasions for lively discussions of philosophy, literature, art, economics, politics, and life in general. Although the group observed no formal manifesto, Woolf and the others generally held to the tenets of philosopher G. E. Moore's* Principia Ethica, *the essence of which is, in Moore's words, that "one's prime objects in life were love, the creation and enjoyment of aesthetic experience, and the pursuit of knowledge." Deeply interested in promoting the growth of experimental, modern literature, the Woolfs founded the Hogarth Press in 1917 "as a hobby," and through the years their efforts enabled the works of many new, nontraditional writers, such as T. S. Eliot and Robert Graves, to appear in print for the first time. A Fabian socialist during the World War I era, Woolf became a regular contributor to the socialist* New Statesman *and later served as literary editor of* The Nation and the Athenaeum, *in which much of his literary criticism is found. Throughout most of his life, Woolf also contributed essays on economics and politics to Britain's leading journals and acted as an advisor to the Labour Party. Addressing the controversy between Wells and Hilaire Belloc regarding* The Outline of History, *Woolf aligns himself with Wells.*]

A great deal of amusement and instruction can be obtained from the booklet just published, **"Mr. Belloc Objects,"** by H. G. Wells. . . . The controversy which has arisen between these two distinguished writers is of far greater interest than is usually the case with such intellectual dogfights. Even the circumstances surrounding the origin of the controversy and of Mr. Wells's booklet are remarkable and worthy of record. Mr. Belloc wrote twenty-four long articles attacking Mr. Wells's **"Outline of History,"** and the series was published in three

Catholic papers. . . . The tone of these articles has the acrid superiority which Mr. Belloc adopts towards those who do not agree with his views on Roman Catholicism, drink, "European" civilization, and Jews, and I do not think that Mr. Wells exaggerates when he says that the articles are "grossly personal and provocative." But they also purported seriously and elaborately to prove Mr. Wells's ignorance and mis-statements with regard to what is known about the origin of species and in particular of man. Mr. Wells wrote six articles in reply, and sent them to the Catholic papers which had published the original attack, offering to give them, if necessary, without payment. In each case they were refused. . . . Mr. Wells, thereupon, offered his articles to various non-Catholic papers, both British and American, some of which, I believe, were journals of very large circulation. In every case the articles were rejected, and so Mr. Wells decided to publish them in book form.

You do not want to be a journalist to see, after reading this booklet, that the articles are first-class copy, even without Mr. Wells's name attached to them. In ordinary circumstances nine out of ten editors would have jumped at them, with a large cheque in both hands. Surely this is a very remarkable phenomenon in these days of alleged enlightenment. Here is a Roman Catholic writer attacking one of our most popular authors for giving, in a historical work, an account of the origin of man which has not received the *imprimatur* of the Roman Catholic Church, and when he wishes to defend himself, he finds the doors of the Press shut against him. The fact is at least worthy of record.

As to the controversy itself, I must admit to being considerably amused by the personal side of it. Here certainly Mr. Belloc has got as good as and more than he gave. But behind Mr. Belloc's pompous and offensive superiority and Mr. Wells's enjoyment of "cocking snooks" at it, lies a real issue. The issue, as I see it, is between obscurantism and a genuine attempt to state and face facts. I suppose that I am not impartial in this controversy, for I am definitely on Mr. Wells's side. I have heard people whose judgments I respect say many hard things of **"The Outline of History."** Anyone can pick holes in the book; anyone can pick holes in any book which attempts to give a bird's-eye view of the history of man from the time when there was no man until the nineteenth century. Whether such a book is worth writing and reading depends not on the holes in it, but on the shape and size of the holes. The holes in **"The Outline of History"** seem to me of the kind which do not prevent it being of remarkable value to any ordinary person, whether he be a Roman Catholic, a Protestant, or an agnostic, who wishes to know the main facts which constitute the outlines of human history. Mr. Wells, like all of us, has his prejudices and his ignorances, and they distort some of what he calls facts in his book. But he has sufficient knowledge, honesty, and scientific training and outlook not to allow them to distort the outline.

Probably some of the facts concerning the origin and history of mankind contradict the preconceived beliefs of every one of us, whether we be Christians or agnostics. Certainly the facts with regard to natural selection and prehistoric man are in conflict with the teachings of the Roman Catholic Church which were formulated in the Middle Ages. The issue raised by this controversy and the publication of Mr. Wells's articles, not in the Press, but in the form of a booklet, is whether ordinary people should be allowed to know the facts and should discuss their implications or whether the mediaeval system of obscurantism and of the Index Librorum Prohibitorum should be applied to all such dangerous subjects. Mr. Belloc, in his perpetual attacks upon scientists and historians, has shown himself to take his stand definitely on obscurantism and the Index. His methods in attacking **"The Outline of History"** are his usual methods. To pretend that Charles Darwin invented a preposterous and now exploded theory in order to "get rid of the necessity for a Creator" (surely no more false statement than this with regard to Darwin's motives and scientific integrity has ever been made by a controversialist!), to set up a bogus "European" or Latin or Catholic culture, whose scientists and historians are never quoted, though their works, unknown to benighted non-Catholic Britons, however learned and distinguished, always confirm the teachings of the Roman Catholic Church and Mr. Belloc—to do this is only a new variation upon what has now become a very familiar tune.

Perhaps the most interesting thing in Mr. Wells's booklet is his last chapter. Leaving the acrid region of detailed controversy, he tries to find a reason for his difference with Mr. Belloc. He suggests that fundamentally their difference arises from their belonging to two different types of mind with two entirely different visions of the universe. Mr. Belloc belongs to the old type of mind and school of thought in which the individual life is all that matters, and there is a vision of "a fixed and unprogressive humanity working out an enormous multitude of individual lives from birth to either eternal beatitude or to something not beatitude." To Mr. Wells life in the universe is "a steadily changing system," and the individual life is comparatively unimportant. It is an episode which ends, though life goes on.

> *Leonard Woolf, "Mr. Wells v. Mr. Belloc," in* The Nation and The Athenaeum, *Vol. XXXIX, No. 25, September 25, 1926, p. 735.*

CONRAD AIKEN   (essay date 1926)

[*An American man of letters best known for his poetry, Aiken was deeply influenced by the psychological and literary theories of Sigmund Freud, Havelock Ellis, Edgar Allan Poe, and Henri Bergson, among others, and is considered a master of literary stream of consciousness. In reviews noted for their perceptiveness and barbed wit, Aiken exercised his theory that "criticism is really a branch of psychology." His critical position, according to Rufus A. Blanshard, "insists that the traditional notions of 'beauty' stand corrected by what we now know about the psychology of creation and consumption. Since a work of art is rooted in the personality, conscious and unconscious, of its creator, criticism should deal as much with those roots as with the finished flower." In reviewing* The World of William Clissold, *Aiken suggests that Wells failed to define the modern liberal mind, and discusses the probable reasons.*]

In the course of his offensive-defensive preface to his new novel, **The World of William Clissold,** Mr Wells remarks that "it is a point worth considering in this period of successful personal memoirs that if the author had wanted to write a mental autobiography instead of a novel, there is no conceivable reason why he should not have done so. . . . Clearly he did not want to do so." This is sufficiently emphatic—Mr Wells puts his foot down hard on the idea that his book is to be received as a romance with a key, or a work of propaganda, or a disguised self-portrait. He is tired of being told, he says, that his characters, his very numerous characters (he makes a partial list of them, very few of whom one remembers by name) are mere aliases for H. G. Wells. He insists that they are "characters," as now he insists that William Clissold is a character. He

admits, but only to deprecate, a close resemblance of the views and opinions of William Clissold to his own views—how otherwise, indeed, could Mr Wells have conceived him? "How can one imagine and invent the whole interior world of an uncongenial type?"

This is all very true as far as it goes—but when one has read the two fat volumes of Mr Clissold's memoirs one begins disturbedly to wonder just *why* Mr Wells so "clearly did not want to" give this curious compendium the franker shape of a mental autobiography. One's wonder, in this regard, is two-fold. Did Mr Wells believe that only a *soi-disant* novel, a "full-dress" novel, could carry successfully, to the maximum number of readers, the ideas which he wished to put into general circulation? . . . Or, on the other hand, is it really possible that Mr Wells, after so prolonged an opportunity for self-discovery, aided, too, by the almost unanimous sharpsightedness of his critics in this matter, still fosters illusions as to his ability to write *novels?* Does he join with his publishers in believing his present work to be a masterpiece of fiction?

To believe that is to believe the incredible: and nevertheless Mr Wells insists that we believe it. Clearly, for him, William Clissold is a living and breathing person: and just as clearly, for his reader, William Clissold is nothing of the sort. One can perhaps partially account for the failure of Mr Wells to make him live and breathe by noting the really enormous difficulty of the task which he has set himself—and in noting this one can candidly admit that the attempt has been heroic and highly instructive. Mr Wells has tried, and has been the first to try—the first even to conceive—the portrayal, in a novel, of the entire intellectual, as well as emotional and physical, history of an individual. As he justly observes, a great and perhaps preponderant part of our lives is centred in that queer, random, never-ending process of self-education which is involved in the mere fact of our exposure to a highly organized and complex social scene, a scene in which changing ideas and increasing scientific knowledge play a profoundly important part. If one proposes, for example, to tell the story of Mr Z's life, why should one omit the fact that at the age of eighteen his whole conception of life was changed by his reading of Freud, Jung, Adler, and Havelock Ellis? Should not this vital experience be recorded as searchingly as possible? (pp. 503-04)

The question is one which no critic would presume to answer offhand. The idea is grandiose, magnificent: one would like hugely to see it done: one does not even dare to say that it is impossible: but one is completely sure that Mr Wells has not himself succeeded in it. His novel fails, as a novel, primarily because the mass of more or less familiar information, through which one has to wade in the course of Clissold's education, is too heavy and too sustained a burden for the slight narrative to carry. One encounters a vast treatise on economics, another on biology, another on sociology, a fourth on psychology, a fifth on the psychology and potential social uses of advertising, a sixth on the relations of the sexes, a seventh on financial hegemony as the road to a world state—and sandwiched between, pitifully compressed, a few tiny episodes of Clissold's personal history. That, one is certain, is not the way to do it. (pp. 504-05)

This is a question of proportion and arrangement, simply; and in this Mr Wells seems quite definitely to have made a huge technical mistake. If one cares for a useful parallel, one calls to mind the remarkable skill with which Tolstoi, in Anna Karenina, manages to give us a complete account of Levin's fluctuating views as to a possible agrarian policy for Russia. Tolstoi does not try to present all this in a single bolus: he breaks the mass into innumerable fragments and he presents it in innumerable ways—now as dialogue, now as reflection, now as action. He knows when to stop, and when to rest his reader by judicious use of contrast. Everywhere he sees the problem as a *novelist's* problem—he must keep the stream moving, he must keep *ideas* in their place as mere functions of a given personality. If the ideas interest us in their own right, they also and more importantly interest us as the ideas to which Levin's character and situation would inevitably have led him. Mr Wells fails to achieve this, for the good enough reason that he has little or no sense of character. His Clissold is a lay figure. We never actually see or hear him—even in those few episodes of direct action or dialogue which Mr Wells half-heartedly interpolates, as if now and then he had remembered his duty as a novelist, one never detects that gleam of the quintessential amid the various by which one recognizes a dynamic unity in a fictive person. Not only does Mr Wells fail in this, but he also fails, not infrequently, even to give his little scenes and dialogues that minimum of verisimilitude without which narrative becomes grotesque. The scene in which Clissold's mother informs her sons of the death of their father must be among the worst ever written by a novelist of repute. It indicates an almost complete absence of psychological insight.

One is driven back, finally, to one's original question: why should Mr Wells have gone to such pains at all? Why *not* have written, instead, a mental autobiography? There can be no virtue in ambiguity; Mr Wells has an interesting mind, one of the contemporary minds of which an unalloyed analysis would be intensely interesting; nor can one see that the device of projection has afforded any greater freedom of speech than Mr Moore, for example, found possible in his autobiographical trilogy. Mr Wells's comments on his contemporaries are neither exciting nor profound—their omission, even if necessary, would scarcely be felt. One almost suspects that they were introduced, like so many sugar-plums, for that part of the public which dotes on gossip. For the rest, all one can say is that **The World of William Clissold** is an astonishingly compendious outline of the modern liberal mind. Nothing is omitted. It is an admirable piece of propaganda for a world state, reared on an economic basis, and a pretty complete survey of modern thought. Mr Wells has a somewhat "levelling" touch—he often writes carelessly and he almost never writes with distinction; but his energy and his grasp, his ability to see the whole field and to look singly toward an ultimate, are sufficiently remarkable to make his book an exceptionally interesting experiment. No one who follows the evolution of the modern novel can afford to pass it by—it is one of those comparatively rare books of which the failure is definitely instructive: it is a lesson in a new technique. (pp. 505-06)

> *Conrad Aiken, "An Outline of the Modern Mind,"*
> *in* The Dial *(copyright, 1926, by The Dial Publishing*
> *Company, Inc.), Vol. 81, No. 6, December, 1926,*
> *pp. 503-06.*

EDMUND WILSON (essay date 1930)

[*Wilson, considered America's foremost man of letters in the twentieth century, wrote widely on cultural, historical, and literary matters, including several seminal critical studies. He is often credited with bringing an international perspective to American letters through his widely read discussions of European literature. Wilson was allied to no critical school: however, several dominant concerns serve as guiding motifs throughout his work. He invariably examined the social and historical implications of* a work of literature, particularly literature's significance as "an attempt to give meaning to our experience" and its value for the improvement of humanity. Though not a moralist, his criticism displays a deep concern with moral values. Another constant was his discussion of a work of literature as a revelation of its author's personality. However, although Wilson examined the historical and psychological implications of a work of literature, he rarely did so at the expense of a discussion of its literary qualities. Perhaps Wilson's greatest contributions to American literature were his tireless promotion of writers of the 1920s, 1930s, and 1940s, and his essays introducing the best of modern literature to the general reader. In the excerpt below, Wilson favorably reviews* The Autocracy of Mr. Parham.]

[*The Autocracy of Mr. Parham*] is an amusing and well aimed satire on a certain type of reactionary opinion which has lately been becoming fashionable. Wells has invented in Mr. Parham an all too lifelike comic character whom we recognize at once as the embodiment of something in the air: certain attitudes and ideas which the universities, English and American, the intellectuals of Bloomsbury, Antibes and the literary and artistic penthouses of New York, T. S. Eliot's Criterion and the American Humanists have been running to since the War. Mr. Parham is a young Oxford don who believes that the only salvation for society lies in a return to tradition and order. He is a man of learning and taste, and a parasite, a prig and a snob. . . .

I will not say that the encroachments of age have not dulled Wells's imagination in this book. The vision of the future with which more than half of it is occupied has little of the brilliance of Wells's early feats in this line: it is all a little like a long editorial. But what journalist, young or old, can write such editorials as Wells? And who else—even Aldous Huxley—feels so sensitively and so promptly the currents in the intellectual air, and guesses so accurately what they imply, in terms of money, social relations, politics and sex, in the human society from which they emanate? The first chapters of this book, before the dream begins, are as vivid, as funny and as shrewd as any satire Wells has ever written. One can only hope that his prophecies in the last part are not so true as they have sometimes been.

> *Edmund Wilson, "The Academic Fascist" (reprinted*
> *by permission of Farrar, Straus and Giroux, Inc.),*
> *in* The New Republic, *Vol. LXIV, No. 822, Septem-*
> *ber 3, 1930, p. 79.*

C. HARTLEY GRATTAN (essay date 1931)

[*An economist as well as a social and literary critic, Grattan was a prolific contributor of articles to national magazines and was considered a well-informed literary critic. His professional career began in 1924, when one of his essays appeared in H. L. Mencken's* The American Mercury; *afterward, like Mencken, he earned a reputation as an outspoken opponent of the moralistic New Humanism movement in American letters. Throughout much of his career, Grattan was also a recognized authority, through his many lectures and writings, on Australia and the southwest Pacific. In the excerpt below, Grattan addresses many of the weaknesses commonly attributed to Wells's thought and works.*]

That "exuberant, amiable Cockney Englishman," has never lacked detractors. From his earliest days the scared crows of criticism have cawed loudly at the successive pleas for change he has launched upon the world. No one of his novels has won unstinted praise, and it is only with the passing of the years that **Tono-Bungay** has become an undisputed masterpiece of twentieth century fiction. Even as I write that axiom I feel sure that a voice will be raised in contradiction before the ink is fairly dry upon it, and certainly no one will be found to say that Wells's non-fiction books have received anything approaching universal acceptance. . . .

It is significant that the class in which he has always placed his faith for the future is the middle class, the next above him, with a dash of regard for the aristocracy in his ideas about the directors of the society of the future. It is no wonder that Lenin remarked to Trotsky of Wells, "What a bourgeois he is! He is a philistine! Ah, what a philistine!" It is noticeable, too, that Wells is a complete Englishman in his reactions, in spite of his intellectual internationalism. . . .

His early writing was in the field of education; it appeared in educational journals; and all his life, whether writing fiction or not, he has been an educator.

His first success as a writer for the general press had come in 1891 when Frank Harris (how often Frank Harris appears in the life histories of Wells's contemporaries) printed an essay in *The Fortnightly Review*. Seriously addressed to his life work Wells turned out, in his amazingly prolific way, light essays, reviews and scientific articles. Then he struck his first real vein of gold and produced his scientific romances, of which the most famous is **The Time Machine**. He ran through that phase quickly enough, dropped it when its financial possibilities were still tremendous, and turned to the novel, nonfictional social criticism and prophecy. But whatever he wrote he was primarily a journalist and an educator, an educating journalist. . . . (p. 178)

He was at the top of his bent and produced his masterpiece, **Tono-Bungay,** in 1909. Restless as ever, he turned to the Fabian Society and politics when he showed no signs of running out of material and was quickly disillusioned. He put his irritation into disconcerting books, brought down an avalanche of disapproval, and was just steadying for a new phase when the War came.

The first gun crumpled Wells's objectivity and he became the chief architect of the liberal interpretation of the War (preserved for the amusement of future generations in **Mr. Britling Sees It Through**), pro-Ally, anti-German, war for a better world, prelude to utopia, Armageddon, etc., etc. The War ended and Allied "ideals" were on the junk heap in short order. Wells was deflated—but not for long! He was shortly out once more for the world state—not the League of Nations, with which he toyed, to be sure—but the world state. The great weapon for creating opinion in favor of this ideal was education, ergo **The Outline of History,** to rewrite all history as propaganda for this beloved world state. Exciting—what? Next, the Open Conspiracy—great capitalists gone idealist and acting, with H. G. Wells as master behind the scenes, as obstetricians of the world state. Hurrah! All aboard for H. G. Wells's heaven! So he shouts at 64, but who listens?

It is easy enough to see what H. G. Wells believes. Let's tabulate his underlying notions. He believes in progress, science, education and the inherent goodness of man. These four ideas are fundamental. From them everything else he has professed to believe foliates. They go together somewhat after this fashion: all history demonstrates that mankind is to achieve its destiny by changes in the environment known as progress. (Mankind as a biological fact has changed little for thousands of years and has shown itself infinitely adaptable to environmental changes.) In the past change has been haphazard, as productive of muddle and suffering as of order and happiness.

Within the last few centuries mankind has discovered an instrument, science, which makes it possible to control and direct change—to turn it into a movement toward Utopia. This is not generally understood. The old notions about the value of the past persist, muddle is preferred to order, so through education we must indoctrinate the young, and change as many of the old as have not petrified mentally, with the idea that science is the only trustworthy guide to salvation. With a generation of leaders laboring under that conviction Utopia will come in a jiffy.

What is Utopia? Why, the world state, governed by an intellectual aristocracy for the benefit of the many, a scheme combining the advantages of internationalism and nationalism, communism and capitalism, good and bad, black and white—in a few words, a state realizing the noble pipe-dreams of H. G. Wells. All outline-of-history history points in that direction. It's a sure bet—unless in a year or two H. G. Wells changes his mind, and then the gamblers on it will find themselves holding the bag and Wells off shouting for some new arrangement of the future. Every time Wells has had a peeve he has made a novel of it. Every time reality has contradicted his prophecy he has pointed out what duffers we all have been not to see that reality was what it was and vaunted his superior wisdom by producing a new scheme to exorcise reality, for Mr. Wells is as much a "superior purzon" as ever George Nathaniel Curzon was. But whatever the new pot at the foot of the rainbow may hold, the pot will be made of progress, science, education and the inherent goodness of man. Wells may change his mind about marriage, divorce, birth control, God visible or invisible, king or commoner, but he hangs resolutely to his fundamentals.

He has always dealt in futures. Even his most laborious study of the past was undertaken with an eye on tomorrow. A confirmed teleologist, he has never for one moment doubted that the world has a purpose. . . . Society in England since 1688 has become progressively more unstable, hence more easily moulded. In the Wellsian argument this undoubted fluidity is a major point in favor of Utopia. What is so loosely constructed can easily be made over. But in studying the future Wells has emphasized the fluidity of the present and missed its conservative complexities—in being dazzled by the logical possibilities of intelligently utilizing the fluidity in the interest of a better world, he has underestimated the force of tradition and human inertia. (pp. 178-79)

It is no trick at all for him, either, to caricature the aimless imbecility which characterizes so much of the activity in the modern world. To cite **Tono-Bungay** again, where better is the promoter limned? Edward Ponderevo is simply Mark Twain's Colonel Sellers realizing his dreams—he got the millions that were in "it." But even though the conditions which allowed the Ponderevo's to blow up such a balloon of wealth are imbecilic and the product of forces released in society but recently, Wells fails sufficiently to indicate the powerful vested interest a large class has in the continuation of the system.

Somewhere in Wells's mind is the idea that suddenly through an act of free will (he believes firmly in free will, a necessary basis for all Utopianism) or slowly through education, men will be diverted from their present evil ways and run smiling into a bright Utopia. One can only grin! It is his blindness to obstacles, his dazzlement with the future, which leads to Wells's fitful allegiance to "causes"—ranging from Fabianism to the Allied program in the War. When they don't achieve results, they are dropped and a nasty reference is made to them in a novel. For it is an ironic fact that with all his talk about cosmic perspectives and with all his ability to imagine cosmic tragedies—as in his short story *The Star*—his mind has remained glued to the *immediate* present. His Utopias are, as I remarked, tomorrow; his past, yesterday; his disorderly present, today! There can be no true realization of the complexities of social engineering on this basis. Van Wyck Brooks has called Wells an "artist in society." That is an acute observation which Mr. Brooks intended as a compliment, but which I take to symbolize Wells's weakness. An artist's material is, in the last analysis, something malleable to the fullest extent. He masters it and gives it form, and if he does not he is reproached for his inadequacy. Society is something else again, and the only imaginable being to whom it is material for artistic rearrangement is the supposititious God.

Wells has a typical modern mind of the pre-war variety. Most of the elements which it contains are present in the post-war minds, but in a modified fashion. The post-war minds have been disciplined and disillusioned. There is no longer a widespread belief in the inherent goodness of man. No critical thinker today is convinced that progress will *immediately* issue in anything at all. That education is a weapon universally useful is doubted on all sides. History is not interpreted teleologically, but as a record of man's known experience in the world and nothing else. That society is rickety, improvised in many of its aspects and susceptible of indefinite change is admitted, but there is a clearer realization of the deeper obstacles to change. The prohibition situation has driven this home to Americans. Utopia is discounted heavily as a mirage, a pink and purple dream, not to be expected around the next corner. Only science retains an undisputed hold over the modern mind, and even here there is a marked change. There is no longer much talk of liberation through mechanical inventions. The emphasis has shifted to the social sciences where the complexities of human society emerge. The optimistic "artist of society" has given way to the thoughtful social engineer to whom even hope is a transient emotion and whose normal state is a quiet pessimism relieved by confidence in the validity of his method.

And so H. G. Wells is losing his grip upon the thoughtful public. He does not speak the language of the rising generation. They read him only as an easy way to comprehend a dying type of mentality, and they are not stirred to action or belief by anything he may say. They cannot entirely enter into William Clissold's world, for his problems are not their problems and the world that made him they know only through Wells's novels. *The Open Conspiracy* seems a somewhat childish affair, ignoring a variety of problems of which they are conscious because confronted with the rising importance of the engineer in American society. So they shout in increasing numbers, "Good-bye, Mr. Wells, good-bye!" Mr. Wells shakes his head and writes another plea for the world state. "It'll come, young man, it'll come! If not in my lifetime, in yours." (pp. 179, 198)

> C. Hartley Grattan, "Good-Bye to H. G. Wells!"
> in Outlook and Independent *(copyright, 1931, by the*
> Outlook Company), *Vol. 157, No. 5, February 4,*
> *1931, pp. 178-79, 198.*

MALCOLM COWLEY   (essay date 1934)

[*Cowley has made several valuable contributions to contemporary letters with his editions of important American authors (Nathaniel Hawthorne, Walt Whitman, Ernest Hemingway, William Faulkner, F. Scott Fitzgerald), his writings as a literary critic for The* New Republic, *and, above all, for his chronicles and criticism of modern American literature. Cowley's literary criticism does not attempt a systematic philosophical view of life and art, nor is it representative of a neatly defined school of critical thought, but rather focuses on works—particularly those of "lost generation" writers—that he believes personal experience has qualified him to explicate and that he considers worthy of public appreciation. The critical approach Cowley follows is undogmatic and is characterized by a willingness to view a work from whatever perspective—social, historical, aesthetic—that the work seems to demand for its illumination. In the excerpt below Cowley discusses Wells's* Experiment in Autobiography, *concluding that it is a work of art and the best of his books.*]

Just at the moment when it seemed that he was going to fade out a little less spectacularly than Bennett, Galsworthy and Shaw, publishing a long series of volumes each one of which was reviewed a little more briefly and read a little less carefully than its predecessor—now, in his sixty-eighth year, [Wells] has come close to performing a miracle. He has written a book that stands with the best of his earlier work. For my own part, I vastly prefer this outline of Wells by Wells to his three ponderous outlines of human knowledge. **"Experiment in Autobiography"** is to be valued chiefly as a work of art; it is, I think, the best of his novels.

It is even a whole collection of novels, bigger and more satisfying than most of the current trilogies and tetralogies. It begins as a sort of "David Copperfield" story about a Cockney boy who lived among all sorts of bad smells and quaint characters and managed somehow to get an education. Then there is a second novel, the love story of a young science instructor who married his cousin and deserted her for one of his pupils, thereby putting an end to his teaching career. These early adventures are told without shame or reticence, but also without any attempt to dramatize the hero. A third section, "Fairly Launched at Last," is good in quite a different way. Wells was now (1895-1900) a rising young novelist, and the drama of his story was centered in his meetings with other writers and his interchange of ideas with them. He reminds us here of something we had almost forgotten: the vigor and ferment of intellectual life at the turn of the century, the passion with which ideas were put forward and debated, the feeling that all these projects would be realized in the better society of the future. Those were the great days of liberalism, and Wells makes them live again.

But his autobiography has also a final section, a chapter of fifty thousand words that deals with his career since 1900 and his picture of the world in which we live. This chapter is obviously and immensely inferior to everything that has gone before. Partly, I suppose, the sudden loss of richness and sympathy is explained by causes personal to the author. He has lived so much in public that he has almost ceased to have any private life (or at least any private life that he can write about candidly, without hurting the reputations of people still alive). He is dealing, moreover, with recent events that he hasn't had time to digest. Even so, I think that he could and would have done a better job if he had not been held back by the fear of saying the last word about himself and his world, and so being left at sixty-eight with no more books to write. The beginning of his autobiography is too good; it must have frightened him into making a weak conclusion.

There is, however, another and less personal reason for the positive dullness of the last chapter. Wells regards this book as being essentially a story about "the awakening of world citizenship in a fairly normal intelligence." From this point of view, the chapter in which his "citizenship" takes its final form ought to be the climax of an intellectual drama. But the climax is botched and unconvincing. His dream of an Open Conspiracy of millionaires and technicians that would take over the world and run it intelligently is a dream that has nothing to do with the shape of things as they are. Instead of serving as a reasoned guide to conduct, it ends by being a religion, one that consoles him for his personal inadequacies and one whose "releasing and enveloping relation to the individual *persona* is . . . almost precisely the same" as that of other religions. It is a faith that blinds him to everything real and threatening in the present situation—to the lassitude and fear for the future that are spreading through the Western world, to the bitterness of the ambitious young students who would like to rise like H. G. Wells but find that their path has been blocked, to the desperation of the working classes, the uneasy fear that attacks the rulers, the almost universal violence that is the most evident feature of life in these middle decades of the twentieth century. Wells is happy in his faith. He believes that civilization still is marching upwards and onwards, that the goal is now in sight, and that merely by education, without blood or class conflicts, we can attain the Great Good Place of which he dreams, where men like himself will "supply teaching, coercive and directive public services to the world."

Wells's Utopia belongs to the happy days before the War. Today it is less alive, and less skillfully embalmed, than Lenin's corpse in his tomb outside the Kremlin. Still, Wells himself lives on and ends by impressing us with his own sort of greatness. He is like the survivor of a prehistoric time, a warm, ponderous, innocent creature ill adapted to the Ice Age in which we live, and yet overshadowing the smaller animals that shiver behind rocks without ever venturing into the open. They have a bitter wisdom that he lacks, but they are not of his stature. (pp. 22-3)

> *Malcolm Cowley, "Outline of Wells's History," in* The New Republic *(©1934 The New Republic, Inc.), Vol. LXXXI, No. 1041, November 14, 1934, pp. 22-3.*

G. K. CHESTERTON (essay date 1936)

[*Regarded as one of England's premier men of letters during the first half of the twentieth century, Chesterton is best known today as a colorful* bon vivant, *a witty essayist, and creator of the Father Brown mysteries and the fantasy* The Man Who Was Thursday. *Much of Chesterton's work reveals his childlike* joie de vivre *and reflects his pronounced Anglican and, later, Roman Catholic beliefs. His essays are characterized by their humor, frequent use of paradox, and chatty, rambling structure. During the summer of 1908, Chesterton and his wife Frances rented a house in Rye, where Henry James and Wells also lived. In the following excerpt from his autobiography, Chesterton offers his opinion of Wells's thought and alludes to life in Rye and to the savage caricature of James in* Boon, *a book which ended the long friendship between James and Wells. Throughout their professional lives, Chesterton and Wells remained close friends, although each was vigorously opposed to the other's social, political, and religious thought.*]

In those days down at Rye, . . . I saw something of Mr. H. G. Wells, and learnt to appreciate that in him which I think made him rebel against the atmosphere of Henry James; though Henry James did really appreciate that quality in Wells. Indeed, Henry James expressed it as well as it could be expressed by saying, "Whatever Wells writes is not only alive, but kicking." It seems rather unfortunate that, after this, it should have been Henry James who was kicked. (p. 222)

I have always thought that [Wells] reacted too swiftly to everything; possibly as a part of the swiftness of his natural genius. I have never ceased to admire and sympathise; but I think he has always been too much in a state of reaction. To use the name which would probably annoy him most, I think he is a permanent reactionary. Whenever I met him, he seemed to be coming from somewhere, rather than going anywhere. He always had been a Liberal, or had been a Fabian, or had been a friend of Henry James or Bernard Shaw. And he was so often nearly right, that his movements irritated me like the sight of somebody's hat being perpetually washed up by the sea and never touching the shore. But I think he thought that the object of opening the mind is simply opening the mind. Whereas I am incurably convinced that the object of opening the mind, as of opening the mouth, is to shut it again on something solid.

The name of Mr. H. G. Wells has already inevitably suggested the name of Mr. Bernard Shaw. . . . (pp. 223-24)

As compared with Belloc or myself, Bernard Shaw was definitely in favour of the South African War. At any rate, he was very definitely in favour of the South African Peace, the particular Pax Britannica that was aimed at by the South African War. It was the same, for that matter, with Mr. H. G. Wells; then a sort of semi-detached Fabian. He went out of his way to scoff at the indignation of the Pro-Boers against the Concentration Camps. Indeed, he still maintains, while holding all wars indefensible, that this is the only sort of war to be defended. He says that great wars between great powers are absurd, but that it might be necessary, in policing the planet, to force backward peoples to open their resources to cosmopolitan commerce. In other words, he defends the only sort of war I thoroughly despise, the bullying of small states for their oil or gold; and he despises the only sort of war that I really defend, a war of civilisations and religions, to determine the moral destiny of mankind. (p. 225)

Those who now think too little of the Allied Cause [of World War I] are those who once thought too much of it. Those who are disappointed with the great defence of civilisation are those who expected too much of it. A rather unstable genius like Mr. H. G. Wells is typical of the whole contradiction. He began by calling the Allied effort, **The War That Will End War.** He has ended by saying, through his rather equivocal mask of Mr. Clissold, that it was no better than a forest fire and that it settled nothing. It is hard to say which of the two statements is the more absurd. It settled exactly what it set out to settle. But that was something rather more rational and modest than what Mr. Wells had settled that it was to settle. To tell a soldier defending his country that it is **The War That Will End War** is exactly like telling a workman, naturally rather reluctant to do his day's work, that it is The Work That Will End Work. We never promised to put a final end to all war or all work or all worry. We only said that we were bound to endure something very bad because the alternative was something worse. (pp. 246-47)

> *G. K. Chesterton, "Friendship and Tomfoolery" and "The Shadow of the Sword," in his* Autobiography *(1936 edition © Gilbert Keith Chesterton; 1969 edition © Dorothy Edith Collins; reprinted by permission of Miss D E Collins), Hutchinson & Co., Ltd., 1936 (and reprinted by Hutchinson of London, 1969, pp. 214-35, 236-58).*

EVELYN WAUGH (essay date 1939)

[*From the publication in 1928 of his novel* Decline and Fall *until his death in 1966, Waugh was England's leading satirical nov-*

elist. In such works as Vile Bodies, The Loved One *and* Scoop, *he skewered such targets as the bored young sophisticates of the 1920s, the American commercial trivialization of death, and the questionable values of the British press. Considered a major Catholic author after his conversion in 1930, Waugh is best known today for his novel* Brideshead Revisited, *which examines the lives of the members of a wealthy Catholic family. Much of Waugh's postconversion writings reflect the author's often maligned Tory values of the preeminence of wealth, privilege, and proper insouciance. In the excerpt below Waugh disdainfully reviews Wells's novel* The Holy Terror.]

Mr. Wells's latest novel [*The Holy Terror*] deals, like so many of its predecessors, with the immediate future. It traces the career from his birth to his death of the future World Dictator, who, it is to be presumed, is at this moment an undergraduate and will shortly begin hustling Mosleyite speakers off their stands in Hyde Park. It offers four possible directions of interest: a psychological study of the motives which lead a man to desire and achieve popular deification, a "success-story" showing the steps by which he attains his object, a speculative curiosity as to whether any such series of events as Mr. Wells describes is, in fact, likely to occur, and, closely allied to it, the curiosity as to why and how Mr. Wells, in mature years, has retained the exuberant and almost bumptious optimism of his extreme youth. The more earnest the reader, the more likely he is to be disappointed in all four directions; the casual reader, with ruthless skipping, may get considerable enjoyment, for Mr. Wells has still most of the instincts of a novelist, and when he has a story to tell, cannot tell it badly. But story-telling is very much more strenuous work than political dissertation, and Mr. Wells shows an inclination to take longer and longer naps while his characters are left to take care of themselves and their disembodied voices drone on in a manner that must be easy to write but is almost impossible to read.

Rud—Mr. Wells's hero—is an odious character. . . . The qualities which lead him to eminence are selfishness and luck. . . .

The "success-story" has been badly shirked. It begins admirably. Rud's first flirtings with the various extreme parties, his choice of colleagues, his first violent push for popularity are well told. Then at the interesting stage—the transition from party leader to World Dictator—Mr. Wells drops into generalisations and tells of his rise not as an intimate but as a remote historian—a historian of a loose and unscholarly kind—the author, in fact, of the *Outline of History*. There is the further grave disability that the minor characters are quite flat. Lord Horatio, the Leader of the Purple Shirts, offered grand opportunities for caricature which are neglected. The newspaper magnates are cyphers. There is also evidence that Mr. Wells's association with the cinema has been deleterious. The "shots" of Chiffan's domestic felicity are pure film technique of the most hackneyed kind—not even Hollywood; Elstree—and the death of Rud might be the climax to "Should a Doctor Tell?"

It is all too apparent that Mr. Wells's interest lies in the diffuse political discussions which form the bulk of the book and that the story is incidental—comparable in fact to the sumptuous illustrations in the *Outline of History*—put there at some expense to make the work saleable. The idea is the familiar one, that Prosperity and Peace are Just Round the Corner. Mr. Wells has believed this consistently for the best part of a lifetime; now when his liberal contemporaries are in panic, he refuses to budge. The glorious, egalitarian, sanitary, uninhibited world of applied popular science is still there; all that has been changed is the method of getting to it. Mr. Wells sees that the fashion

is now for gang rule and hero worship. Very well, here is the gang, here is a figurehead as contemptible as you can want—and yet in spite of—no, *because* of him the new world comes bouncing in like a football. It is Mr. Wells's way of filling the gap that he himself made in his conception of human destiny. The widely-accepted hypothesis of the Fall of Man and the Atonement—leaving aside the supernatural credentials on which they are held—did and still do explain the peculiar position of man in the universe. Remove them and, if you have a sanguine temperament, you must believe that only the most flimsy and artificial obstructions keep man from boundless physical well-being.

Mr. Wells still sees these obstructions as those which afflicted him with claustrophobia in his youth—religion, nationality, monogamy, the Classics, gentility, general lack of general information. And here, too, in a way, he has gotten something. He refuses to be misled by the preposterous distinctions of Left and Right, that make nonsense of contemporary politics. His hero Rud is able quite effortlessly to absorb both factions. There is, Mr. Wells sees, a single proletarian movement aimed at the destruction of traditional culture; the fact that it is at the moment split only shows the puerile cussedness of people who have not learned chemistry; remove the sentimental obsessions—the schoolgirl "crush" on the leader, the chivalrous concern for the under-dog—and there is basic agreement. Mr. Wells has never been interested in foreigners; at least he has never believed they are foreign in anything but language; the vast heterogeneity of mankind and the rival systems of logic by which they reason, have never perplexed him. Nor does he realise the vitality of the obstructionists. In fact he denies that there is any serious conflict at all. But at least he has done a service in clearing the issues as much as he has, and, if he can persuade the lower-middle-brow public for whom he writes that they are getting fussed about the wrong difficulty, this will be a highly salutary book; it is all the more regrettable that its intrinsic quality should be so meagre.

Evelyn Waugh, "Machiavelli and Utopia—Revised Version," in The Spectator *(© 1939 by The Spectator; reprinted by permission of* The Spectator*), Vol. 162, No. 5772, February 10, 1939, p. 234.*

T. S. ELIOT   (essay date 1940)

[*Perhaps the most influential poet and critic of the first half of the twentieth century, Eliot is closely identified with many of the qualities denoted by the term Modernism: experimentation, formal complexity, artistic and intellectual eclecticism, and a classicist view of the artist working at an emotional distance from his or her creation. He introduced a number of terms and concepts that strongly affected critical thought in his lifetime, among them the idea that poets must be conscious of the living tradition of literature in order for their work to have artistic and spiritual validity. In general, Eliot upheld values of traditionalism and discipline, and in 1928 he annexed Christian theology to his overall conservative world view. Of his criticism, he stated: "It is a by-product of my private poetry-workshop: or a prolongation of the thinking that went into the formation of my verse." In the following excerpt Eliot discusses Wells's abilities as a journalist.*]

No one can have failed to observe that since the beginning of this war two men, whom we had thought of as slowly and unwillingly retiring from public life, have emerged into a glare of prominence. I mean Mr. Churchill and Mr. Wells. They must be nearly contemporary; they were both men of celebrity, I remember, when I was a freshman. Both have spoken and written a great deal in the last thirty-odd years; neither possesses what one could call a *style,* though each has a distinct idiom: that of Mr. Wells being more like a durable boiler suit, and that of Mr. Churchill more like a court dress of rather tarnished grandeur from a theatrical costumier's. (p. 319)

My own generation does not seem to have produced either a great demagogue—such as have been Mr. Churchill and Mr. Lloyd George—or a great journalist—such as have been Mr. Wells, Mr. Shaw and Mr. Chesterton. I am not, in this context, using either term, 'demagogue' or 'journalist,' in any but the most favourable sense. Of men highly gifted for journalism—in this most favourable sense—there have been several. For instance, Mr. Wyndham Lewis, Mr. Middleton Murry and Mr. John Macmurray all have the necessary fluency, earnestness and desire to influence as large an audience as possible; and Mr. Lewis, at least, is unquestionably a writer of as great genius as Mr. Wells. Yet none of them has ever been listened to by more than a minority public; and as for the men of my time who have been able to capture a large audience, I believe they are all, by comparison with Mr. Wells, pygmies. By individual comparison of gifts alone, ample reason can be found for Mr. Wells's success. Mr. Wells started as a popular entertainer, and his advantages of education gave him the opportunity to exploit 'popular science' for a generation all ready to suspend disbelief in favour of this form of romance. To this paying activity he brought imagination of a very high order: some of his short stories, such as 'The Country of the Blind,' and certain scenes from his romances, such as the description of sunrise on the moon in *The First Men in the Moon,* are quite unforgettable. Later, he employed remarkable gifts as a recorder in chronicles of the sort of society in which he took his origins. Through being a popular entertainer, he found an opening as a prophet—the nearest parallel in the last few years is Miss Dorothy Sayers. None of my contemporaries of a distinction at all comparable to that of Mr. Wells has started by this popular appeal of entertainment. And I think that this is more than a personal difference; it is the difference of a generation.

The world into which Mr. Wells—and the late Arnold Bennett—arrived (the same world, really, as that of Lord Stamp) was a world of 'getting on.' For the ambitious youth of literary gifts and humble origins, the first thing—sensibly enough—was to make a living by giving the public its entertainment; when one had got sufficiently established, then one might be free, either to devote oneself to a work of literary art, or to preach openly to a public which is docile and respectful to success. In the course of this rough experience Mr. Wells probably learned a number of things about writing—about 'putting over' ideas to the large public—which his juniors have never learnt. He also suffered, because of his period, in a way in which younger men have not suffered. He exhibits, for example, a curious sensitiveness about his origins: in a recent contribution to the *Fortnightly* he rebukes the younger generation for grudging him in middle age the modest competence which is no more than his due in consideration of his straitened youth. I cannot help comparing him here with the man whom I consider the greatest journalist, in the best sense of the term, of my time: Charles Péguy. Péguy was a peasant, and makes you feel that he took a deep pride in his origins. But the difference between Mr. Wells and my own generation is of another kind. I cannot think of any good English writer of my generation who is either sensitive because of being humbly born, or who puts on airs because of being well born: the distinction is of no interest among writers. Perhaps it is partly that we have found ourselves in a position in which 'getting on' was always out of the question. There was nowhere to get

to. That kind of success, for a serious man of letters, is no longer possible.

The serious journalism of my generation is all minority journalism. That is more than a difference between Mr. Wells and my contemporaries; it is a difference between the worlds into which they were born. The crowd of season-ticket holders is still there—it is bigger than ever—reading Mr. Wells's latest in the first class as well as the third class compartment: he tells them what they are ready to accept, and part of what he says is true. His great imaginative gifts, and picture-book method, make very real to his public the situation that he describes; and as he does not reason, or draw upon any kind of wisdom inaccessible to the common man, he imposes no great strain upon the minds of his readers. And as his proposals are always in world terms, he does not ask of his readers individually any great exertion from which they would flinch. On the other hand—and this is perhaps something to be mentioned in common with Mr. Churchill after all—he is capable of a kind of bluntness which is far too rare among the loud-speaker voices of our time. Like Mr. Churchill, he is capable of putting his foot into it again and again; and this capacity for rudeness is more endearing, in the long run, than the cautious, diplomatic politeness of the people who are so careful never to put their feet into anything. There is something very refreshing about Mr. Wells's violent hostility to Christianity in general and to the Catholic Church in particular; and his words about the American attitude towards the war, and our attitude towards America, in the *Fortnightly* article already cited, are worth all the suave palaver and exasperating preachments to which other publicists treat that country.

There is, I believe, no place for a modern Wells to educate the public in more modern opinions. Our public is not yet in existence. We can only hope to provide thought of a very different kind and very different tendency, formed in very different categories, for a small number of thinking people prepared for new 'dogma' (in Demant's phrase). This is not to maintain an attitude of aloofness, but a realistic view of the limits of our possible effectiveness. We can have very little hope of contributing to any immediate social change; and we are more disposed to see our hope in modest and local beginnings, than in transforming the whole world at once. On the other hand, though the immediate aims are less glittering, they may prove less deceptive: for Mr. Wells, putting all his money on the near future, is walking very near the edge of despair; while we must keep alive aspirations which can remain valid throughout the longest and darkest period of universal calamity and degradation. (pp. 319-22)

T. S. Eliot, "Wells As Journalist" (reprinted by permission of Faber and Faber Ltd and Mrs Valerie Eliot), in The New English Weekly, *Vol. XVI, No. 16, February 8, 1940 (and reprinted in* H. G. Wells: The Critical Heritage, *edited by Patrick Parrinder, Routledge & Kegan Paul, 1972, pp. 319-22).*

GRAHAM GREENE (essay date 1940)

[Greene, an English man of letters, is generally considered the most important contemporary Catholic novelist. In his major works, he explores the problems of spiritually and socially alienated individuals living in the corrupt and corrupting societies of the twentieth century. Formerly a book reviewer at The Spectator, *Greene is also deemed an excellent film critic, a respected biographer, and a shrewd literary critic with a taste for the works of undeservedly neglected authors. Here he reviews* All Aboard for*

Ararat, *a novel of modern characters and events that parallel the biblical episode of Noah and the deluge.*]

Mr. Wells's new fable opens with the sad Mr. Noah Lammock, seated at his desk writing nothing. "The cold realisation of final defeat" has "closed about his heart." As God in this story identifies Mr. Lammock with Mr. Wells in spite of his protests—"I never wrote *The Time Machine*"—the reader may be forgiven for making the same mistake and seeing Mr. Lammock as that baffled idealist who planned *The Great Conspiracy,* and believed that airmen might yet save the world. It is a frank and delightful self-portrait; Mr. Lammock, once he gets involved in argument with the old gentleman from the lunatic asylum who claims quite rightly to be God, soon forgets his despair. He is quite prepared—on certain conditions, of course—to set sail in the Ark and start a new world. He is a near-heroic figure as he makes his final claim: "No man is beaten until he knows and admits he is beaten, and that I will never know nor admit." Never mind the arid core of his new world—"Atheist, Creative, Psycho-synthetic"; never mind the wooliness of his desires—"We want, on the one hand, an incessant, relentless process of the will and intelligence, protected in some way from disintegrating influences, and on the other hand we want a broad appeal to ordinary people which will anticipate and protect . . ." Even at his vaguest Mr. Wells retains an enormous creative drive, and his new book will be read by all those who remember with pleasure his short story, "**A Vision of Judgment,**" for its humour, and for the odd incongruous vein of poetic feeling which once, in the days of *Mr. Polly,* made Mr. Wells a novelist of genius. God discussing with wit his own Book and the morals of the first Mrs. Noah, God worried by his shadow, Satan, God pursued by the doctor and attendants of a lunatic asylum—there may be people who will be offended by Mr. Wells's Divinity, but if so they have missed entirely that curious love of a God who doesn't, in his view, exist, that tenderness for a phantom which has dug itself into Mr. Wells's brain.

Graham Greene, "The Second Deluge," *in* The Spectator (© *1940 by* The Spectator; *reprinted by permission of* The Spectator*), Vol. 165, No. 5860, October 18, 1940, p. 398.*

CHRISTOPHER ISHERWOOD   (essay date 1951)

[*Isherwood is an English-born man of letters who is known for his largely autobiographical accounts of pre-Nazi Berlin and for his detached, humorous observations on human nature and manners. As a young man during the 1930s, he was a member of the Marxist-oriented Oxford group of poets that included Stephen Spender and W. H. Auden. Isherwood and Auden collaborated on several plays, works of fantasy which combine verse with prose. Describing himself as a "born film fan," Isherwood has also experimented with cinematic and episodic techniques in his works of fiction. While living in California, he wrote movie scripts and* Prater Violet, *a novel about the film industry. Isherwood's* Berlin Stories, *adapted by John Van Druten for his* I Am a Camera, *was the basis for the stage musical and film* Cabaret. *He became a U.S. citizen in 1946. In the excerpt below he discusses Wells's creativity, pessimism, and beliefs about God and mysticism.*]

Wells felt that the novel in its traditional form was out of date. . . . Nevertheless, [he] was capable of fine writing, when he wasn't in too much of a hurry; and, throughout his career, he continued to produce novels.

As a matter of fact, Wells had all the gifts which go to make a 'traditional' novelist. He could create solid characters, write lively, naturalistic dialogue, and evoke the atmosphere of houses and places. His humour was Dickensian, lapsing sometimes into facetiousness but bold and warm at its best. These qualities are most apparent in *Kipps, Tono-Bungay* and *Mr Polly,* three books which drew largely upon the experience of Wells' own childhood and adolescence. Wells was always at his most vivid when he returned to that period; no doubt because he could look at it from a distance, objectively. He never gave himself time to do this in dealing with his later life. Everything had to be reported at once, as it happened—like the scribbling of a war correspondent in the midst of a still-smoking battlefield. There was no time to worry about form, or the technical problems of presentation; there was no question of excluding any portions of the given material because they didn't happen to 'fit'. Every bit of it had to go in.

The majority of Wells' realistic novels (I shall speak of his scientific fantasies later) deal with the impact upon their author of a person, or an idea, or a situation. The person is usually a woman, one of the many in Wells' life, very thinly disguised. The idea or the situation is presented subjectively, just as it struck Wells himself. This initial impact (the impact, for example, of World War I upon Wells in *Mr Britling Sees It Through*) is the author's point of departure into speculation and theorizing. 'What does it mean?' he asks himself aloud, 'what do I think about this?' (Wells isn't sure, because he is thinking even as he writes, thrashing the problem out before our eyes.) Along the lines of these speculations, which are like spacious corridors leading off in all directions, wander the minor characters. These are often brilliantly drawn, and their personal circumstances and doings engage our interest, even when they are somewhat irrelevant to the main theme. And then, beyond the open-ended, incomplete structure of the novel, we are aware of the surrounding contemporary world, with all the diversity of its business and its anxieties, ever present on the horizon of the author's consciousness.

It is a measure of Wells' genius that he was able to make these big untidy talkative books so alive and readable. From an artistic standpoint, most of them can only be described as failures; they simply don't 'compose'. But Wells achieved a larger kind of success; he showed how the tight classic form of the novel might be expanded to include a much wider area of reference. That he himself didn't know when to stop, that he expanded the novel until it burst, is not so important. You can't make experiments without explosions. He remains a great pioneer. (pp. 42-3)

Several of Wells' realistic novels were hugely popular, at the time of their publication, because of their topicality and the shock value of the problems they discussed. Today, his reputation is based chiefly upon the *Outline of History* and half a dozen of his scientific fantasies. Wells would not regret the survival of the *Outline;* it is a masterpiece. But he might well resent our preference for *The Time Machine, The Island of Dr Moreau, The Invisible Man, The War of the Worlds, The First Men in the Moon* and *The War in the Air.* No author cares to have his early works (these were all written before 1909) preferred to his later ones; Wells continued to write scientific fantasies throughout his life, but these, like the realistic novels, became increasingly discursive and were never very successful. Besides, he would probably complain that we have failed to understand the inner meaning of the stories themselves. We regard them as enjoyable thrillers—just as we regard *Gulliver's Travels* as a quaint book for children. (pp. 43-4)

When he looked into the future, Wells alternated between extremes of optimism and pessimism. The early scientific fantasies are deeply pessimistic; a fact which we usually overlook. There is the unutterable sadness of the Time Traveller's last glimpse of the dying world; the reversion of Moreau's fabricated humans into beasts; the wretched fate of the Invisible Man. Life and individual genius end in frustration and defeat. Nearly fifty years later, in his book *Mind at the End of its Tether,* Wells repeated this message: 'The end of everything we call life is close at hand and cannot be evaded.' Yet his own character was essentially optimistic. A natural Utopian, he continued, despite many disappointments, to cling to his vision of a World State; he was still fighting for it in his old age, in the midst of World War II. (p. 44)

In his youth, Wells hated God and violently denied His existence; for 'God', in those days, was the God of the Big House, the feudal Overlord. But *Mr Britling,* shaken by the horror of the First World War, found that some Ultimate Reality was, after all, necessary to his peace of mind; so Wells rediscovered Him as 'the Captain of Mankind', a sort of supernatural President of the future World State. This God appears in two further novels, *The Soul of a Bishop* and *The Undying Fire;* but it is doubtful if Wells found Him either comforting or convincing. Indeed, He appears to be little more than a metaphor. His chief quality is negative; He is fundamentally opposed to His Church and to all organized Religion. He makes a last bow, in the guise of a weary and cynical old man, in *Joan and Peter,* telling the young hero that, if he doesn't like the world, he must change it himself.

Wells' 'theological excursion' was doomed to failure because he could never quite escape from the dualistic religious concepts of his upbringing: God high in Heaven and we, His servants, hopelessly far beneath. Such dualism is nauseating to any man of Wells' temperament because it immediately confronts him with his old enemy, established authority. Wells might try to persuade himself that 'his'' God was different, but he couldn't. The truth was that he didn't really want a Captain of Mankind any more than he had wanted a feudal Overlord. He wasn't a follower. Indeed, he had a horror of 'Great men'.

Nevertheless—and this is Wells' tragedy—he was always dimly but poignantly aware that something was lacking, some vital spark that would bring his New Utopia to life. Under the influence of Plato's *Republic,* which he had read as a schoolboy, he imagined an Order of Samurai—a group of dedicated and sternly disciplined young people who would give their lives to the work of building the society of the future. His writings on this subject actually inspired the formation of enthusiastic groups which looked to him for leadership. Wells, to his great mortification, was unable to offer them any; he couldn't devise a practical programme. 'Toward the end of his life he remarked on the fact that just about the time he made this unsuccessful attempt at practical construction, Lenin, "under the pressure of a more urgent reality", was quietly and steadily drawing up an "extraordinarily similar plan"—the Communist party organization.' But, even if a revolutionary situation had existed in England at that period, and even if Wells had been a born revolutionary leader, he and his Samurai would have found themselves, sooner or later, in trouble. For a dedicated group demands a faith; without one, it cannot continue to function. Lacking genuinely spiritual inspiration, it will turn to some substitute idolatry, such as nationalism or the cult of a leader; and so the movement defeats itself and the World State can never be founded, much less sustained.

Wells was always proclaiming his faith in the capacities of Man. Yet he refused to take account of Man's highest capacity—that of knowing and drawing strength from what is eternal within himself. Some inhibition or deeply-seated fear, it would seem, made Wells unable to accept the validity of the mystical experience, or to recognize its central importance in the scheme of human evolution. Why he couldn't bring himself to do this, despite all his urgent self-questionings, I don't know. (pp. 45-6)

Christopher Isherwood, "H. G. Wells" (originally published in Tomorrow, *Vol. X, No. 5, January, 1951), in his* Exhumations: Stories, Articles, Verses *(reprinted by permission of Candida Donadio & Associates, Inc.; copyright © 1966 by Christopher Isherwood), Methuen & Co Ltd, 1966, pp. 38-46.*

W. SOMERSET MAUGHAM (essay date 1952)

[*Maugham was an English dramatist, short story writer, and novelist who is considered a skilled, cynical satirist. Best known for his autobiographical novel* Of Human Bondage, *Maugham also achieved popular success with such plays as* Caesar's Wife, The Breadwinner, *and* Our Betters. *In the excerpt below, Maugham discusses the reasons for Wells's diminished popularity.*]

[Wells] had no illusions about himself as an author. He always insisted that he made no pretension to be an artist. That was, indeed, something he despised rather than admired, and when he spoke of Henry James, an old friend, who claimed, as I have hinted, perhaps a little too often that he was an artist and nothing else, it was good-humouredly to ridicule him. "I'm not an author," H. G. would say, "I'm a publicist. My work is just high-class journalism." On one occasion, after he had been staying with me, he sent me a complete edition of his works and next time he came he saw them displayed in an imposing row on my shelves. They were well printed on good paper and handsomely bound in red. He ran his finger along them and with a cheerful grin said: "They're as dead as mutton, you know. They all dealt with matters of topical interest and now that the matters aren't topical any more they're unreadable." There is a good deal of truth in what he said. He had a fluent pen and too often it ran away with him. I have never seen any of his manuscripts, but I surmise that he wrote with facility and corrected little. He had a way of repeating in one sentence, but in other words, exactly what he said in the previous one. I suppose it was because he was so full of the idea he wanted to express that he was not satisfied to say it only once. It made him unnecessarily verbose.

H. G.'s theory of the short story was a sensible one. It enabled him to write a number that were very good and several that were masterly. His theory of the novel was different. His early novels, which he had written to earn a living, did not accord with it and he spoke of them slightingly. His notion was that the function of the novelist was to deal with the pressing problems of the day and to persuade the reader to adopt the views for the betterment of the world which he, H. G., held. He was fond of likening the novel to a woven tapestry of varied interest, and he would not accept my objection that after all a tapestry has unity. The artist who designed it has given it form, balance, coherence and arrangement. It is not a jumble of unrelated items.

His later novels, are, if not, as he said, unreadable, at least difficult to read with delight. You begin to read them with interest, but as you go on you find your interest dwindle and it is only by an effort of will that you continue to read. I think *Tono Bungay* is generally considered his best novel. It is written with his usual liveliness, though perhaps the style is better suited to a treatise than to a novel, and the characters are well presented. He has deliberately avoided the suspense which most novelists attempt to create and he tells you more or less early on what is going to happen. His theory of the novelist's function allows him to digress abundantly, which, if you are interested in the characters and their behaviour, can hardly fail to arouse in you some impatience. (pp. 222-24)

I think that is why his novels are less satisfactory than one would have liked them to be. The people he puts before you are not individuals, but lively and talkative marionettes whose function it is to express the ideas he was out to attack or to defend. They do not develop according to their dispositions, but change for the purposes of the theme. It is as though a tadpole did not become a frog, but a squirrel—because you had a cage that you wanted to pop him into. H. G. seems often to have grown tired of his characters before he was halfway through and then, frankly discarding any attempt at characterisation, he becomes an out-and-out pamphleteer. One curious thing that you can hardly help noticing if you have read most of H. G.'s novels is that he deals with very much the same people in book after book. He appears to have been content to use with little variation the few persons who had played an intimate part in his own life. He was always a little impatient with his heroines. He regarded his heroes with greater indulgence. He had of course put more of himself in them; most of them in fact are merely himself in a different guise. Trafford in *Marriage* is indeed the portrait of the man H. G. thought he was, added to the man he would have liked to be. (pp. 224-25)

"I've been saying the same things to people for the last thirty years," he said to me with exasperation, "and they won't listen." That was the trouble. He had said the same things too often. Many of his ideas were sensible, none of them was complicated; but, like Goethe, he thought that one must always repeat truth: *Man muss das Wahre immer wiederholen.* He was so constituted that never a doubt entered his mind that he was definitely possessed of *das Wahre.* Naturally people grew impatient when they were asked once more to listen to views they knew only too well. He had had an immense influence on a whole generation and had done a great deal to alter the climate of opinion. But he had had his say. He was mortified to find that people looked upon him as a has-been. They agreed with him or they didn't. When they listened to him it was no longer with the old thrill of excitement, but with the indulgence you accord to an old man who has outlived his interest.

He died a disappointed man. (p. 228)

> *W. Somerset Maugham, "Some Novelists I Have Known," in his* The Vagrant Mood: Six Essays *(copyright, 1949, 1950, 1952, by W. Somerset Maugham; copyright, 1933, by Doubleday & Company, Inc.; copyright, 1940, by the Curtis Publishing Company; copyright renewed © 1980 by the Literary Estate of W. Somerset Maugham; reprinted by permission of The Executors of the Estate of W. Somerset Maugham and William Heinemann Ltd), Heinemann, 1952 (and reprinted by Doubleday, 1953, pp. 202-50).**

KENNETH REXROTH (essay date 1958)

[*Rexroth was one of the leading pioneers in the revival of jazz and poetry in the San Francisco area during the 1940s and 1950s.*

Largely self-educated, he became involved early in his career with such left-wing organizations as the John Reed Club, the Communist party, and the International Workers of the World. During World War II he was a conscientious objector, and since that time has become antipolitical in his work and writing. Rexroth's early poetry was greatly influenced by the Surrealism of André Breton, but his later verse has become more traditional in style and content, though by no means less complex. However, it is as a critic and translator that Rexroth has gained prominence in American letters. As a critic, his acute intelligence and wide sympathy have allowed him to examine such varied subjects as jazz, Greek mythology, the works of D. H. Lawrence, and the Kabbala. As a translator, Rexroth is largely responsible for introducing the West to many Chinese and Japanese classics. In the excerpt below, Rexroth traces parallels between the ideas of Wells and Lawrence, finding that both were essentially concerned with "matrimony," or a "life of dialogue."]

A lot of tosh has been written about Wells as a "social" novelist, always trying to reform the world via preachy fiction. You would think he was a sort of Upton Sinclair at his worst or a bad "proletarian" novelist. It must be quite a shock for an innocent person, with an honestly empirical approach, to sit down and read his fiction from *The Time Machine* to *The Research Magnificent*, admittedly his best period. His novels are not social novels at all. True, they reflect the society of their time; Ann Veronica, for instance, is a feminist. But *Tono-Bungay* is no more "about" the evils of patent medicines than *Crime and Punishment* is "about" Russian detective methods. All the major Wells novels have exactly the same subject as those of a writer no one would dream of connecting with him— D. H. Lawrence; they are about matrimony, about the mysteries and difficulties and agonies and tragedies and—rarely—the joys of the search for a true "life of dialogue." Wells's characters seek constantly and painfully to realize each other as total persons, and they usually pitifully fail. It is only too true that the Social Lie is precisely the conspiracy of organized society to prevent precisely this, and so there is always implicit a running criticism and sometimes a specific criticism of the frauds by which men live. Wells says depreciatingly that his people are seldom realized. This is false modesty. They are not constructed as artistic artifacts. They struggle to realize each other, and so, in their success or failure, realize themselves poignantly for the reader. (p. 115)

> *Kenneth Rexroth, "Henry James and H. G. Wells" (originally published as "The Screw Turns on Mr. James," in* The Nation, *Vol. 187, No. 4, August 16, 1958), in his* Assays *(copyright © 1961 by Kenneth Rexroth; used by permission of Bradford Morrow for The Kenneth Rexroth Trust), New Directions, 1961, pp. 114-17.**

ALFRED KAZIN (essay date 1967-68)

[*A highly respected American literary critic, Kazin is best known for his essay collections* The Inmost Leaf *(1955) and* Contemporaries *(1962), and particularly for* On Native Grounds *(1942), a study of American prose writing since the era of William Dean Howells. Having studied the works of "the critics who were the best writers—from Sainte-Beuve and Matthew Arnold to Edmund Wilson and Van Wyck Brooks" as an aid to his own critical understanding, Kazin has found that "criticism focussed many— if by no means all—of my own urges as a writer: to show literature as a deed in human history, and to find in each writer the uniqueness of the gift, of the essential vision, through which I hoped to penetrate into the mystery and sacredness of the individual soul." In the excerpt below, Kazin discusses Wells's impressions of America as revealed in* The Future in America.]

When H. G. Wells arrived here in April, 1906, to collect material for a book on the United States, he was not yet forty, and was famous in the English-speaking world for his scientific romances *(The Time Machine, The War of The Worlds),* for his predictions of the coming technology *(Anticipations),* and for his first novels of lower middle-class life *(Kipps).* . . . Wells himself was a hyperactive mind, extraordinarily quick, unstoppable in conversation as he was on paper, "a spoiled child," said his friend Bernard Shaw. Wells thought of himself as a wholly new development in English literature, a novelist with a scientific training. He had risen from a draper's shop to the company of Thomas Henry Huxley through his capacity for assimilating, teaching and popularizing biology. From the theory of evolution he had absorbed so powerful a sense of man's possibility and the incalculable future that he went on to create a new kind of science fiction, not simply a prediction of twentieth-century engineering, like Jules Verne's, but fantasies of a time when intelligence would dominate social life completely, become a dramatic character in its own right.

Wells, when still in his twenties, had found a large public for his voyages into the future; they were read as entertainments but also were taken as a new social gospel founded on the power of "science" to create a better world. (p. 137)

Wells was perhaps never to grasp just how odd, creative, utterly personal and "otherworldly" this obsessive searching after the future was. He was a gifted writer in so many different fields, he came up with so many interesting ideas, saw so many patterns and consequences in the long sequence of human evolution, that, although he disclaimed any resemblance to Jules Verne, he could not help noticing that he had made certain correct predictions, and took credit for them. But this was a way of naming and regularizing his concern with the future, which was indeed so "otherworldly" that Wells was as possessed by it as a prophet by his religion, and which he was to turn against not like any other twentieth-century man who has lost his faith in illimitable progress, but like a believer who has lost his faith. Wells's "faith," even in this early stage of his career, was not *in* anything but his passion for reading the future, his excited, visionary sense of the endless flux that *he* kept always before his eyes and that *he* could read. His extraordinary conversation flowed into and made books; his books retained the sound and urgency of his conversation. Nothing so commonplace as predictions—in a time of many predictions—could have contained his interest in the future, could have expressed the quality of his interest in it. The future was in man's relentless, absorbed, constant determination of it. It was ultimately not so much ahead of man as a present intellectual passion for distinguishing between seeming and reality, for seizing on novelty and for unfolding patterns. Although Wells had created the "future" as a living, urgent topic for his readers, his greatest interest was in portraying history as constant movement. This was, of course, the movement of H. G. Wells's own mind. As the twentieth century wore on, grinding down his old self-confidence, Wells came to describe his life experience, as he did in *Experiment in Autobiography* . . . as "discoveries and conclusions of a very ordinary brain." But when he arrived in New York in 1906, he was a notably self-confident writer who felt that he was up to understanding anything. (p. 138)

The book Wells came to write was *The Future in America: A Search After Realities.* What, he was asking, can America show us of the necessary future, of the coming rational order? This was to be no book of mere impressions (although impressions naturally went to construct Wells's answers to his own questions). In the venerable, enormous, often comically extreme travel literature on the New World, Wells's book stands out because he always sees the contradiction between the possibilities of American life and its actual irrationalities. The usual English inquiry was—and is—trained on our failure to live up to our democratic professions. Wells, in a breezy, cocky, faintly Olympian style that suits the complacent rationalism of pre-1914 social theory, finds a violation not of our professed idealism but of our constructive possibilities. (pp. 138-39)

The Future in America shows him disturbed by the hatred of Negroes, the hysteria that could be so quickly whipped up against "agitators" and revolutionaries, especially when they happened to be new arrivals in the country. But as one can tell from his anxiety about the excessive number of immigrants (just then arriving in their greatest numbers at Ellis Island), and the particular indignation he felt when Maxim Gorky was savagely excluded from every hotel in New York for innocently disregarding the official moral code, Wells's sympathies naturally went to the exceptional men, not to the masses. . . .

Thus from the very beginning, Wells approached America with his characteristically excited, wholly speculative images of America as a field of energy and power, as an example of human motion and ambition on a new scale. (p. 139)

Wells had many sharp and sad things to say about the feeling against Negroes, about the passion for "getting and spending," about a messenger boy he saw in the subway still wearily doing his rounds at two in the morning. He did a sketch of "Hinkey-Dink" Kenna, a Chicago ward heeler, operating from a saloon. While on the subject of the "irresponsible American rich," he managed to get in a little crack at Henry James, in whose "later work . . . one sees them at their best, their refinement, their large wealthiness, their incredible unreality, I think of *The Ambassadors* and that mysterious source of the income of the Newsomes, a mystery that, with infinite artistic tact, was never explained; but more I think of *The Golden Bowl,* most spacious and serene of novels . . . But this is the quintessence, the sublimation, the idealisation of the rich American. Few have the restraint for this." He described Andrew Carnegie as "the jubilee plunger of beneficence, that rosy, greyhaired, nimble little figure, going to and fro between two continents, scattering library buildings as if he sowed wild oats . . . Nothing seems too wild to believe of him, and he fills the European imagination with an altogether erroneous conception of the self-dissipating quality in American wealth." He was quick to note every break in the official American facade, but despite his intellectual obsession with the "future," he was not always a good prophet. He thought that "the victory of private property was complete," and that in view of the opposition of the big capitalists and the courts, it would take a revolution to bring about an income tax. (He also assumed, hilariously enough, that since Americans were determined to make the most of their lives, "one has a vision of bright electrical subways, replacing the filth-diffusing railways of today, of clean, clear pavements free altogether from the fly-prolific filth of horses coming almost, as it were, of their own accord beneath the feet of a population that no longer expectorates at all; of grimy stone and peeling paint giving way everywhere to white marble and spotless surfaces, and a shining order, of everything wider, taller, cleaner, better. . . .")

Wells thought that the average American had "no sense of the state," his material self-concern was paramount. So, to conclude his book, he ended by describing his interview with

Theodore Roosevelt in the White House—the dreamer, planner, thinker who had such a powerful "sense of the state." The meeting of Wells and Roosevelt is described as a friendly, wholly philosophic dialogue between two intellectuals. The subject was Wells's *The Time Machine.* Although the book is not named, it is clear from the account of the discussion in the White House that this was the book they discussed. (pp. 141-42)

[The] contrast between James and Wells on the subject of America remains extraordinarily revealing of both. *The American Scene* [published the year after *The Future in America* appeared] is the book of a "native," and Wells's frankly the impressions of a visitor; *The American Scene* is the soliloquy of a novelist, prodigiously expressive, with a staggering visual imagination and unlimited intellectual fancy, who seems to be setting the "scene" with ideas for dozens of novels he *could* write. James's book is the response of a very great literary sensibility to the established surface, to the cherished, historic, appointed value, to whatever *is.* Where Wells is the eager, restless historic impressionist of things-as-they-can-be, as presumably they are about to be, as they could be and should be, James is concerned with the look of buildings, streets, statues, parks. (p. 143)

Yet Wells's almost mystical invocation of the future was, in the end, to prove as "personal" as was James's sense of the past. Wells returned to the United States in 1935 for a look at the New Deal, and his image of Franklin D. Roosevelt—". . . a ganglion for reception, expression, transmission, combination and realisation, which, I take it, is exactly what a modern government ought to be"—was, like his portrait of Theodore Roosevelt in *The Future in America,* not so much an exact description as a certificate of approval. The organized ideology in Russia had taken the power to create the future away from nineteenth-century literary imaginations like himself. Wells would not yet admit this. He saw in Stalin the intellectual statesman that he had seen in other heads of state who would talk his ideas with him. Like Shaw and the Webbs, Wells had waited so long for the "rational" and "modern" state that by the thirties he became impatient and saw it everywhere.

But just before the end he wavered. When he was near eighty, he took a doctorate in science at London University with a thesis on "personality." By the end of the Second World War, when he felt himself dying, he discovered, in his last book, "mind at the end of its tether." In the face of the atom bomb, reality was not rational and the rational was not the real. . . . The habitual interest in his life is critical anticipation. Of everything he asks, To what will this lead? And it was natural for him to assume that there was a limit set to change, that new things and events would appear, but that they would appear consistently, preserving the natural sequence of life. He did his utmost to preserve the trends, that upward spiral, toward their convergence in a new phase in the story of life, and the more he weighed the realities before him the less was he able to detect any convergence whatever. (pp. 143-44)

> Alfred Kazin, "H. G. Wells, America and 'The Future'" (reprinted by permission of the author), in The American Scholar, Vol. 37, No. 1, Winter, 1967-68, pp. 137-44.

DARKO SUVIN   (essay date 1979)

[*Suvin discusses Wells's work as crucial to the development of significant science fiction.*]

H. G. Wells's first and most significant SF cycle (roughly to 1904) is based on the vision of a horrible novum as the evolutionary sociobiological prospect for mankind. His basic situation is that of a destructive newness encroaching upon the tranquillity of the Victorian environment. Often this is managed as a contrast between an outer framework and a story within the story. The framework is set in surroundings as staid and familiarly Dickensian as possible, such as the cozy study of *The Time Machine,* the old antiquity shop of "The Crystal Egg," or the small towns and villages of southern England in *The War of the Worlds* and *The First Men in the Moon.* With the exception of the protagonist, who also participates in the inner story, the characters in the outer frame, representing the almost invincible inertia and banality of prosperous bourgeois England, are reluctant to credit the strange newness. By contrast, the inner story details the observation of the gradual, hesitant coming to grips with an alien superindividual force that menaces such life and its certainties by behaving exactly as the bourgeois progress did in world history—as a quite ruthless but technologically superior mode of life. This Wellsian inversion exploits the uneasy conscience of an imperial civilization that did not wipe out only the bison and the dodo: "The Tasmanians, in spite of their human likeness, were entirely swept out of existence in a war of extermination waged by European immigrants. Are we such apostles of mercy as to complain if the Martians warred in the same spirit?" (p. 208)

As Wells observed, the "fantastic element" or novum is "the strange property or the strange world." The strange property can be the invention that renders Griffin invisible, or, obversely, a new way of seeing—literally, as in "The Crystal Egg," "The Remarkable Case of Davidson's Eyes," and "The New Accelerator," or indirectly, as the Time Machine or the Cavorite sphere. It is always cloaked in a pseudo-scientific explanation, the possibility of which turns out, upon closer inspection, to be no more than a conjuring trick by the deft writer, with "precision in the unessential and vagueness in the essential"—the best example being the Time Machine itself. The strange world is elsewhen or elsewhere. It is reached by means of a strange invention or it irrupts directly into the Victorian world in the guise of the invading Martians or the Invisible Man. But even when Wells's own bourgeois world is not so explicitly assaulted, the strange novelty always reflects back on its illusions; an SF story by Wells is intended to be "the valid realization of some disregarded possibility in such a way as to comment on the false securities and fatuous self-satisfaction of everyday life."

The strange is menacing because it looms in the future of man. Wells masterfully translates some of man's oldest terrors—the fear of darkness, monstrous beasts, giants and ogres, creepy crawly insects, and Things outside the light of his campfire, outside tamed nature—into an evolutionary perspective that is supposed to be validated by Darwinian biology, evolutionary cosmology, and the fin-de-siècle sense of a historical epoch ending. Wells, a student of T. H. Huxley, eagerly used alien and powerful biological species as a rod to chastise Victorian man, thus setting up the model for all the Bug-Eyed Monsters of later chauvinistic SF. But the most memorable of those aliens, the octopuslike Martians and the antlike Selenites, are identical to "The Man of the Year Million" in one of Wells's early articles (alluded to in *The War of the Worlds*): they are emotionless higher products of evolution judging us as we would judge insects. In the final analysis, since the aliens are a scary, alternative human future, Wellsian space travel is an optical illusion, a variation on his seminal model of *The Time*

Machine. The function of his interplanetary contacts is quite different from Verne's liberal interest in the mechanics of locomotion within a safely homogeneous space. Wells is interested exclusively in the opposition between the bourgeois reader's expectations and the strange relationships found at the other end: that is why his men do land on the Moon and his Martians on Earth.

Science is the true, demonic master of all the sorcerer's apprentices in Wells, who have—like Frankenstein or certain folktale characters—revealed and brought about destructive powers and monsters. From the Time Traveller through Moreau and Griffin to Cavor, the prime character of his SF is the scientist-adventurer as searcher for the New, disregarding common sense and received opinion. Though powerful, since it brings about the future, science is a hard master. Like Moreau, it is indifferent to human suffering; like the Martians, it explodes the nineteenth-century optimistic pretentions, liberal or socialist, of lording it over the universe. . . . This science is no longer, as it was for Verne, the bright noonday certainty of Newtonian physics. Verne protested after *The First Men in the Moon*: "I make use of physics. He invents . . . he constructs . . . a metal which does away with the law of gravitation . . . but show me this metal." For Wells human evolution is an open question with two possible answers, bright and dark; and in his first cycle darkness is the basic tonality. The cognitive "match" by whose small light he determines his stance is Darwinian evolution, a flame which fitfully illumines man, his hands (by interaction of which with the brain and the eye he evolved from ape), and the "patch he stands on." Therefore Wells could much later even the score by talking about "the anticipatory inventions of the great Frenchman" who "told that this and that thing could be done, which was not at that time done"—in fact, by defining Verne as a short-term technological popularizer. From the point of view of a votary of physics, Wells "invents" in the sense of inventing objective untruths. From the point of view of the evolutionist, who does not believe in objects but in processes—which we have only begun to elucidate—Verne is the one who "invents" in the sense of inventing banal gadgets. For the evolutionist, Nemo's submarine is in itself of no importance; what matters is whether intelligent life exists on the ocean floor (as in **"In the Abyss"** and **"The Sea Raiders"**). Accordingly, Wells's physical and technical motivations can and do remain quite superficial where not faked. Reacting against a mechanical view of the world, he is ready to approach again the imaginative, analogic veracity of Lucian's and Swift's story-telling centered on strange creatures, and to call his works "romances." Cavorite or the Invisible Man partake more of the flying carpet and the magic invisibility hood than of metallurgy or optics. The various aliens represent a vigorous refashioning of the talking and symbolic animals of folktale, bestiary, and fable lore into Swiftian grotesque mirrors to man, but with the crowning collocation within an evolutionary prospect. Since this prospect is temporal rather than spatial, it is also much more urgent and immediate than Swift's controlled disgust, and a note of fairly malicious hysteria is not absent from the ever-present violence—fires, explosions, fights, killings, and large-scale devastations—in Wells's SF. (pp. 208-11)

With all his strengths and weaknesses Wells remains the central writer in the tradition of SF. His ideological impasses are fought out as memorable and rich contradictions tied to an inexorably developing future. He collected, as it were, all the main influences of earlier writers—from Lucian and Swift to Kepler, Verne, and Flammarion, from Plato and Morris to Mary Shel-

ley, Poe, Bulwer, and the subliterature of planetary and subterranean voyages, future wars, and the like—and transformed them in his own image, whence they entered the treasury of subsequent SF. He invented a new thing under the sun in the time-travel story made plausible or verisimilar by physics. He codified, for better or worse, the notions of invasion from space and cosmic catastrophe (as in his story **"The Star"** . . .), of social and biological degeneration, of fourth dimension, of future megalopolis, of biological plasticity. Together with Verne's *roman scientifique*, Wells's "scientific romances" and short stories became the privileged form in which SF was admitted into an official culture that rejected socialist utopianism. True, of his twenty-odd books that can be considered SF, only perhaps eight or nine are still of living interest, but those contain unforgettable visions (all in the five "romances" and the short stories of the early sociobiological-cum-cosmic cycle): the solar eclipse at the end of time, the faded flowers from the future, the invincible obtuseness of southern England and the Country of the Blind confronted with the New, the Saying of the Law on Moreau's island, the wildfire spread of the red Martian weed and invasion panic toward London, the last Martian's lugubrious ululations in Regent's Park, the frozen world of **"The New Accelerator,"** the springing to life of the Moon vegetation, the lunar society. These summits of Wells's are a demonstration of what is possible in SF, of the cognitive shudder peculiar to it. Their poetry is based on a shocking transmutation of scientific into aesthetic cognition, and poets from Eliot to Borges have paid tribute to it. More harrowing than in the socialist utopians, more sustained than in Twain, embracing a whole dimension of radical doubt and questioning that makes Verne look bland, it is a grim caricature of bestial bondage and an explosive liberation achieved by means of knowledge. Wells was the first significant writer who started to write SF from within the world of science, and not merely facing it. Though his catastrophes are a retraction of Bellamy's and Morris's utopian optimism, even in the spatial disguises of a parallel present on Moreau's island or in southern England it is always a possible future evolving from the neglected horrors of today that is analyzed in its (as a rule) maleficent consequences, and his hero has "an epic and public . . . mission" intimately bound up with "the major cognitive challenge of the Darwinist age." For all his vacillations, Wells's basic historical lesson is that the stifling bourgeois society is but a short moment in an impredictable, menacing, but at least theoretically open-ended human evolution under the stars. He endowed later SF with a basically materialist look back at human life and a rebelliousness against its entropic closure. For such reasons, all subsequent significant SF can be said to have sprung from Wells's *Time Machine*. . . . (pp. 219-21)

Darko Suvin, "Wells As the Turning Point of the SF Tradition," in The Minnesota Review *(© 1975 The Minnesota Review; reprinted by permission of the editors), n.s. No. 4, Spring, 1975 (and reprinted in a different form in his* Metamorphoses of Science Fiction: On the Poetics and History of a Literary Genre, *Yale University Press, 1979, pp. 208-21).*

ROBERT M. PHILMUS (essay date 1981)

[*Philmus compares Wells's* The Island of Doctor Moreau *to the satires of Jonathan Swift.*]

The Island of Doctor Moreau is the most sustained, and also the most Swiftian, of all Wells's SF satires. (p. 2)

Unmistakably, its inspiration is the final book of *Gulliver's Travels*. Its theme is not radically different from the one Wells began with. He is still dealing with what he elsewhere characterized as the uneasy balance between ''the natural man,'' or ''culminating ape,'' and ''the artificial man, the highly plastic creature of tradition, suggestion, and reasoned thought.'' . . . The antimony . . . informs a satiric fable, the subtle complexity of which arises from the dynamics of a vision of humanity that is not really explicable in the static terms of ahistorical generalizations about the essential Jekyll-and-Hyde-like duality of the individual. Wells's satiric emphasis on man as a superficially civilized animal is Swiftian; but so is his satiric method, the shifts in perspective which give his vision a stereoscopic quality. In effect, he ''darwinizes'' the Yahoos and Houyhnhnms. The beast man evolved from and the more nearly rational creature he may evolve into become the temporal boundaries of *Moreau*'s universe, whose conceptual possibilities Wells plays off against one another in order to explore the nature of the human species as it is at present. (p. 6)

The story of how Prendick and two other survivors, adrift in a dinghy for eight days, famished, and dying of thirst, at length agree upon a plan for human sacrifice, illustrates the feral instincts which privation can elicit in man. Equally significant is the fact that Prendick, the last to go along with their scheme for abandoning civilized restraint, alone escapes the fate that befalls his two companions when they attempt to carry out their murderous designs upon one another.

The immediately subsequent chapters, detailing what happens to Prendick before he arrives on Moreau's island, likewise serve by way of a prologue to the satire that follows, by exhibiting in particular the bestiality of which the human species is gratuitously capable. Not long after his rescue, Prendick regains consciousness. He also regains his strength, thanks to Montgomery, who has him drink something ''that tasted like blood.'' . . . But the doings on board the rescue ship do not help Prendick recover his psychological balance after an ordeal that had impelled him towards cannibalism. Indeed, they justify the name *Ipecacuanha*. The cruelty of the sailors and the brutishness of their captain have a kind of purgative effect: their actions eliminate any clear distinction between man and beast. Prendick thus arrives on Moreau's island having already lost any firm sense of the norms of civilized human behavior.

Everything that Prendick has undergone or been witness to in making the transition to a place ironically bearing the Rousseauesque designation Noble's Isle prepares him to misapprehend what he finds there. Leaving the compound, where Moreau and Montgomery have locked him out of their laboratory, he wanders off among the Beast Folk and presently forms a horrific idea about them. . . . Moreau, he imagines, has been—and still is—''animalising . . . men'' by means of vivisection. . . . (pp. 6-7)

Edward Prendick, with his Gulliverian credulousness, here [offers a] lurid interpretation [which], though it turns out to be erroneous, [fulfills a satiric intent: it] calls attention to the Beast People as ''grotesque caricatures of humanity.'' . . . That is, it emphasizes the similarities between them and civilized man. The acquired habits that differentiate him from beast—or from savage—find a parodic equivalent in their customs and rituals. Following Swift's example, Wells ridicules man's pretentions to civility by reducing its outward signs to an absurdly primitive form. The Law that Moreau's creatures chant, for instance, mechanically codifies and rigidly expresses the kind of religio-moral precepts and beliefs that society invokes to curb ''the

natural man.'' In content and purpose, it is a cretinized Decalogue. By translating the Decalogue into a series of elementary injunctions—''Not to go on all-Fours,'' etc.—and palpable threats—''*His* is the House of Pain,'' etc. . . . Wells points to simple-minded fear and superstition as the factors motivating man to repress his innate brutishness. At the same time, the fact that the Beast People are obviously uncomfortable with the Law and with all of the other accessories of civilized behavior exposes the artificiality of human ''tradition, suggestion, and reasoned thought.'' Indeed, the civilizing practices that man has adopted in the course of his evolution as a social being appear at this stage of the fiction to do little more than disguise his true—that is, biologically original—nature.

The chapter . . . in which Moreau explains to Prendick the how and why of his experiments adds a new dimension to the satire. In part, it reveals the absurdity of trying to reconcile Darwinian theory with the concepts of traditional theology. Moreau, by using the techniques of surgery and hypnotism to transform beasts into human-like beings, replaces Darwinian Nature. To be sure, the workings of natural evolution are not really purposive; but the sort of randomness to which they are subject likewise enters into his obsessive project in artificial evolution. (In response to Prendick's query as to ''why he had taken the human form as a model,'' Moreau ''confesse[s] that he had chosen [it] by chance.'' . . . The experimenter with living tissue is thus the Shaping God of Evolution. But as Creator and Law-Giver, the ancient and white-haired doctor is also the Jehovah of the Pentateuch. (Concerning his first effort at man-making, he tells Prendick: ''All week, night and day, I moulded him [i.e., a gorilla],'' and on the seventh day ''I rested.'' . . . This synthesis of theology and science, however, has disastrous consequences, especially for theology. As the deity presiding over evolution, Moreau dismisses the problem of why evil exists in the world by saying that he has ''never troubled about the ethics of the matter.'' . . . Compelled to be ''as remorseless as Nature,'' he remains deaf to the suffering of his creatures. Nor can the pain they must endure in the process of (artificial) evolution be explained theologically except by postulating an (at best) apathetic God. Certainly there is no accounting for that pain in any morally acceptable terms. It cannot even be justified as a means to an end: first, because the end proposed is never (to be) achieved; and secondly, because ''the material [that] . . . has dripped into the huts yonder'' . . . is all too often a dead end in itself.

Pain, in Moreau's view, characterizes a passing evolutionary phase. Plants and possibly ''the lower animals'' do not feel it; and ''it gets needless,'' he argues, as life progresses to the stage where reason supercedes it. His obsession—to sculpt a being which would act purely from rational motives—springs out of his belief that pain as an actuating force behind human behavior is ''the mark of the beast'' in man. . . . But Prendick, who shows himself inclined to judge by appearances, takes a different position. He regards expressions of pain and its concomitant, fear, as humanizing traits. As he holds the Leopard Man at bay, for example, he remarks: ''seeing the creature there is a perfectly animal attitude. . . . its imperfectly human face distorted with terror, I realised again the fact of its humanity.'' . . . Of course, this stance of Prendick's is by no means totally incompatible with Moreau's. The two agree that pain is the link between man and beast. But Moreau goes on to stress the need for man to sever that connection, to overcome his susceptibility to pain and thereby transcend his animal nature. Nor is this to say that his disagreement with Prendick is merely a matter of emphasis. It is also a matter of outlook;

and as such, it signals an ambivalence that (typically in Wells's SF) otherwise manifests itself in *Moreau* on a much larger scale.

In discussing with Prendick the theory underlying his experiments, Moreau directs the reader to the issue of what the human species might become. His disquisition, that is, introduces a shift in satiric focus, a shift that unmistakably declares itself almost the moment the doctor is killed by his last victim, the puma. Hitherto, Wells had concentrated satiric attention on "the artificial man," whose civilized habits he had ridiculed as being at best superficial—indeed, as being virtually tantamount to hypocrisy. But with Moreau's death, the satire turns against "the natural man." Man's civilized habits emerge at this point as civilizing traits: they represent a fragile protection against his potential bestiality. Just how necessary that protection is becomes clear once the Beast People begin freely reasserting their animal impulses. As their regression follows its inevitable course, the brutal rule of survival—of kill or be killed—usurps the place of Moreau's Law (to the undermining of which Prendick has been a contributor). At the same time, the Beast Folk lose all but the slightest vestiges of what had earlier been the ironic signs of their humanity.

Prendick slowly reverts to a kind of animal savagery as well. His first step backward is to cut himself off from the one other human being remaining on the island: Montgomery. His justification for doing so—"I felt that for Montgomery there was no help: that he was in truth half akin to these Beast Folk." . . .—reveals that Prendick, though by now an initiate into Moreau's secret, still imagines his nature to be essentially different from that of the rest of the inhabitants of Noble's Isle. However, the murder of Montgomery and the burning of the compound oblige Prendick to live among Moreau's creatures: and as they revert to type, he himself acquires a bestial aspect. (pp. 7-8)

After he contrives to escape from "the painful disorder" of the island, . . . the persuasion that had overwhelmed Gulliver takes hold of him: "I felt no desire to return to mankind." . . . But while he and Gulliver share the same response, and for a similar reason, their dread of being exposed to the brutishness of men derives from opposite experiences. Gulliver, having spent most of his Fourth Voyage among the Houyhnhnms, disdains men for their contrast to those perfectly rational creatures. Prendick, after a sojourn of almost a year among the Yahoos (as it were), comes to fear man's similarity to them. The sight of other men often reminds him of the Beast People, and he is frequently haunted by the nightmarish idea "that presently the degradation of the Islanders will be played over again on a larger scale." . . . But he takes comfort from the rather naive belief—hardly grounded in his own experiences or behavior—that all this is "an illusion, that these seeming men and women about me are . . . men and women for ever, perfectly reasonable creatures full of human desires and tender solicitude." . . . Less ironic, and also far more significant from the standpoint of Wells's inquiry into the limits of human plasticity, is the fact that Prendick looks to the stars for solace. For in them, as symbols of the future and of "the vast and eternal laws of matter," . . . resides the hope that man may become something other than the clothed and gabbling but mentally intractable ape *Moreau* discovers him still to be. (pp. 8-9)

> *Robert M. Philmus, "The Satiric Ambivalence of 'The Island of Doctor Moreau',"* in *Science-Fiction Studies (copyright © 1981 by SFS Publications), Vol. 8, No. 23, March, 1981, pp. 2-11.*

WILLIAM J. SCHEICK   (essay date 1981)

[*Scheick explains why* Star Begotten *was a revolutionary science fiction novel.*]

Despite a respectable reception at the time of its publication, H. G. Wells's *Star Begotten: A Biological Fantasia* . . . has been no favorite among literary critics or SF aficionados. In fact, today it is hardly known at all, even by experts on Wells. But Wells wrote it during the period of his late career when he was celebrating the maturation of his thought and artistry; and he apparently viewed the work as an advance in the direction of the ultra-SF novel, an elusive ideal toward which his previous SF novels, by a kind of asymptotic evolution, had been pointing. (p. 19)

[In] the 1930s Wells viewed the onset of his intellectual and artistic maturity as coincident with the rise of modernism; and significantly, in this regard, in *The Anatomy of Frustration* William Burroughs Steele begins his major work in 1922.

The early 1920s, in Wells's opinion, exhibited momentarily a keener perception of reality as a consequence of the shock of World War I. The war, Wells maintained, had shattered illusions which had been supported by the deceiving framework of façade of ideas characteristic of pre-war generations. During the 1930s, however, Wells feared that humanity was reverting toward these same illusions, deluding itself about security and peace by re-establishing the old order. In the fiction he wrote during the 1930s he remained true to the post-War vision embodied in his fiction of the preceding decade. Aesthetically this constancy was manifested principally through the artistic management of fictional structure in the novels he published in the 1930s. During these years Wells mastered a technique which he referred to as "the splintering frame," a manner correspondent to the shattering of the older framework of ideas by World War I.

Wells was, in his own words, "for a time the outstanding instance among writers of fiction in English of the frame getting into the picture." This image suggested to Wells an artistry derived from reality, a mimetic artistry evoking a dimension of reality beyond the deceptive distortion of "a rigid frame of values never more to be questioned or permanently changed." . . . "It required some years and a number of . . . experiments," he continued to explain in 1932 concerning his approach to fictional structure, "before I got it really clear in my own mind that I was feeling my way towards something outside any established formula for the novel altogether."

Not merely reactive, Wells also eventually recognized the need "to reconstruct the frame in which individual lives had to be lived, before [he] could concentrate upon any of the individual problems of fitting them into this frame." But this more encompassing frame would be less rigid than the shattered one from which it emerges and which it now circumscribes. It indeed would evince a specific identity, for in Wells's view speciation embodies the evolutionary process; and even in the matter of characterization Wells explained further: "I am taking more interest now in individuality than ever I did before." But in both instances, in Wells's practice, this new individuality meshes with the typical in such a manner as to point more clearly than previously towards an ideal.

More specifically, Wells's technique of "the splintering frame" employs certain fictional conventions in a way so as to frustrate reader expectations generally associated with these conventions, to draw attention to themselves as artificial devices, and finally to point away from the text as a self-contained finished artifact and towards the reader's experience as open-ended and infused with expanded dimensions for on-going development. Through this technique Wells sought to make the reader experience fictional "space" or form as at once timeless (the ideal) and timely (the individual), as relevant and relative. For Wells a novel is ideally a self-consuming artifact, a work with a distinct identity that finally should not exist for itself (i.e., art-for-art's sake) but should yield up its individuality in the process of exposing the reader to multiple realities in time, to time itself as a dimension that includes various unique species evolving toward an ideal mode as well as a variety of alternate possibilities for humanity, which at any given moment lives as if in a dream. Just as the text at once incorporates a unique and typical identity, so too should its readers sense within themselves the paradoxical blend of individuality and communal type.

In the light of these observations *Star Begotten* becomes most fascinating. It evinces a variety of "the splintering frame" practiced by Wells during the 1930s, and this structural management is designed to act dialectically with the framework readers had come to anticipate in a Wellsian SF novel. Nor are Wellsian ideas exempt from this revision, for references to *The War of the Worlds* . . . are accompanied by allusions to [*The Food of the Gods, A Modern Utopia,* and *The Outline of History*]. . . . (pp. 19-20)

[Wells] repudiates less than he revises, seeking to derive from the preparatory experimentation of his earlier years (1898 to 1920, the significant terminal date) a greater synthesis of his thought and his art. Unlike the Martians in *The War of the Worlds,* the aliens in *Star Begotten* remain unseen, are indeed only hypothetical; the force they evince—the transformation of humanity into a more advanced state—is less threatening than promising finally, so that the very concept of "invasion" is inverted in the later novel. Unlike *The Food of the Gods* and *A Modern Utopia, Star Begotten* presents only an abstract configuration of the future resulting from this possible benign invasion: "the trouble is that we have no material in our minds out of which we can build a concrete vision of things to come. How can we see or feel the future until we have made the future and are actually there?" . . . Unlike *The Outline of History,* the vague future predicted in *Star Begotten* is not the product of linear growth but of linear-like expansive parallel development, of the emergence of a more encompassing alternate possibility at once contingent upon yet distinct from the human past. This paradox, a later manifestation of Wells's notion of "opposite idea" as signifying "essential complement" rather than "antithesis" and of time as a fourth dimension of space, informs every level of *Star Begotten.* (p. 21)

The novel suggests that *Homo sideralis,* the species derived from the genetic changes effected by the alien-directed cosmic rays, is somehow simultaneously a biological sport and an evolutionary development within *Homo sapiens* . . . ; the two species are no more opposed than are spirit and matter, reality and dream—in neither of which are the two apparent oppositions mutually exclusive. . . . Just as the new genetic change will occur within human cells, just as the Martian brain will be housed in the earthly human body, just as mind exists within flesh or spirit resides within matter, *Homo sideralis* will evolve within *Homo sapiens.* Such argument by analogy implies that *Homo sideralis* is indeed "integral to this scheme of space and time." . . . (pp. 21-2)

Like *Homo sideralis, Star Begotten* combines something old and something new. It has adopted the concepts of a Martian

invasion, of prognostication, and of progress as presented by Wells from 1898 to 1920 for the purpose of modifying expectations generated by them to the extent that even the terror associated with the idea of an alien invasion is transformed into a hypothetical benign advent. In contrast to *The War of the Worlds,* this novel offers no real plot, no solution or real conclusion, not even the certainty that an invasion is indeed under way. And Wells is also careful to indicate that the entire notion of the genetic mutation of *Homo sapiens* in the novel is both original and antiquated, is in fact an adaptation of one of humanity's most well-known and cherished legends: the biblical Christmas story. (p. 22)

By demythologizing biblical types, and in the process depicting contemporary experience as a more broadly realized parallel dimension of the biblical narrative to be always more fully expanding in time, Wells confronts and exorcises reader expectations generated by these types. For instance, in contrast to the New Testament, *Star Begotten* focuses upon the parents, particularly Joseph, rather than upon the special child. . . . Potentiality for the transformation of humanity into more encompassing parallel dimensions of existence lies within every child. But since, *contra* the example of *A Modern Utopia,* a "concrete vision of things to come" cannot be rendered, Wells emphasizes the parents of the child, people living in the reader's dimension of reality and responsible for the education of the next generation.

Moreover, Wells ends his novel with the birth of the parents' self-awareness very shortly after the appearance of their child, in contrast to the New Testament version (especially according to Matthew), which begins with the birth of the Christ beneath the star in the East and details the career of the Messiah. *Star Begotten,* in short, remains unfinished, the promise of its title apparently unfulfilled. . . . Ideally, in Wells's view, the reader is to experience a birth of self-awareness concerning his own prospects as a parent, in the broadest sense, every one of whose children is potentially "star-begotten."

Ideally the reader should ascertain that just as Mary and Joseph Davis, like their biblical prototypes, are the people *within* or behind the event of the remarkable birth and just as the birth itself is the product of a genetic change *within* human cells amounting to the incarnation of Martian mind *within* human flesh, so too the dimension of human reality that is *Homo sideralis* lies but veiled . . . *within* each reader. By demystifying the biblical account of Joseph and Mary, Wells lifts the veil of Christian mythology and reveals a greater dimension of contemporary reality in their story; and this demystification includes as well an "opening out," unveiling or broadening of audience expectations concerning a Wellsian work of SF and of prognostication. The reader's anticipation of conventions in Wells's work are, in short, revised; like Joseph Davis, the reader "pass[es] from a hunt for monsters to an investigation of outstanding endowment, to the detection and analysis of what is called genius in every field of human activity." . . . (pp. 22-3)

Star Begotten is an SF novel which has undergone a genetic change, a modification from *within* the genre. Like Joseph Davis, it simultaneously incorporates a distinctive individuality and an expanded or revised generic typicality. Similarly to *Homo sideralis'* incarnation of Martian brains within human flesh, this novel exhibits the new, enlarged, more clarified (less veiled) mentality of Wells in the 1930s, a mentality "incarnated" within the invasion formula utilized in his early SF, specifically in *The War of the Worlds.* Indeed Wells's very example underscores his message that *Homo sideralis* potentially exists as a dimension within all humanity, for the description of the mutated species' mind as a "simpler, clearer and more powerful way of thinking" . . . echoes Wells's remarks pertaining to what he believed had occurred within his own mind after 1920. He was still H. G. Wells, even as *Star Begotten* was an SF novel; but this novel, like its author, also evinced a newness, a broadened dimension (expansively parallel, not strictly linear, in relation to its predecessors) implying an open-ended form rich in possibility for apparently countless new ideological and fictional beginnings, each expressive of an evolutionary advance toward the ideal SF novel.

Like that of *Brynhild* . . . and *Apropos of Dolores* . . . , then, the structure of *Star Begotten* is subtly managed by Wells to elicit expectations in the reader concerning such matters as plot and closure. These anticipations are in turn frustrated and revised, for the purpose of instating new ideological and artistic possibilities suggested by the text, by finally existing outside the text and in the world of the reader. This subtle management in the novel includes the narrative voice, which (in contrast to Wells's experiments with it in the 1920s) is left unagitated and unreflexive, even as the body of *Homo sapiens* is left intact during the alleged invasion of the Martians. Mutated is the genelike "ideological framework" . . . arising from within the cell-like or bodylike conventions of the Bible and of such SF novels of alien invasion as *The War of the Worlds*. Like *Homo sideralis*, *Star Begotten* is a half-breed work. It was for Wells a new species of SF novel, at once continuous with his early SF and distinct from it, simultaneously traditional or typical (the biblical analogue) and innovative or individual (the ideas the vehicular analogue carries). The ideological framework of the novel—never complete or capable of yielding narrative closure, "always beginning" as new ideas expanding pregnantly within old structures—constitutes the "new, simpler, clearer and more powerful way of thinking" embodied in Wells's fictional artistry during the 1930s. The structural open-endedness and "realism" of *Star Begotten* suggested to Wells the capacity of the SF genre to accommodate countless beginnings as each new clarifying ideological framework within such works generates from within itself successive enlargements of parallel dimensions of human possibility. In its demonstration of generic flexibility, *Star Begotten* was, for Wells, a new species of fiction, typically continuous with his early work while at the same time a distinctive revision contributing to the evolutionary advancement of the asymptotic ultra-SF novel. (pp. 23-4)

William J. Scheick, "Towards the Ultra-Science-Fiction Novel: H. G. Wells's 'Star Begotten'," in *Science-Fiction Studies* (copyright © 1981 by SFS Publications), Vol. 8, No. 23, March, 1981, pp. 19-25.

JOHN BARKER   (essay date 1982)

[*Barker discusses Wells's* Outline of History, *tracing the evolution of the author's humanistic vision of world history and examining the* Outline's *main argument that men and women of all nations share "a common human destiny upon this little planet amidst the stars."*]

Wells frequently seems our contemporary, although he precedes Toynbee by a generation. Political growth, cultural development, and social conflict remain as some substantial themes for reducing the whole of history to comprehension; but the closing illustration in most surveys of history today is seldom the usual political map of the world on Mercator's projection. We now find instead Wells's picture of the little speck of cosmic dust on which all mankind is travelling, the earth as photographed from space—"a morning star of hope," he called it, "our own warmer planet, green with vegetation and grey with water, with a cloudy atmosphere eloquent of fertility, with glimpses through its drifting cloud-wisps of broad stretches of populous country and narrow, navy-crowded seas." Wells's chosen viewpoint on the human epic has already become in large measure ours, and it seems almost certain to be our children's; for that reason alone, he is a very important historian for the late twentieth century.

To Wells the composite question (phrased by the astronomer Kepler) with which he introduced his novel, *The War of the Worlds*—"But who shall dwell in these worlds if they be inhabited? . . . Are we or they Lords of the World? . . . And how are all things made for man?"—offered both an intriguing start of an imaginative tale and a valid perspective on human history. For whom had the earth finally been made—for men, or perhaps for Martians? Proudest throughout his public career to call himself a scientist, he saw man as part of the physical universe and man's story understandable largely in relation to the conclusions the biological evidence showed. Nonetheless he discerned that more immediately a worse fate than extinction could be in store—a bartering by man of humanity and individuality for the sake of order and peace. A society of this kind, which he described most explicitly in *The First Men in the Moon*, with its utterly cerebral ruler and its degenerate population bred to perform certain specialized tasks—a society where thought was controlled, the past forgotten, and all was subordinated to technology and communal needs—was unmistakably anti-utopian. Utopia achieved, it seemed, could well be not the perfect life envisioned by some, but a nightmare. Twentieth-century experience would make such nightmares easier to project, most notably in Aldous Huxley's *Brave New World* and George Orwell's *Nineteen Eighty-Four*.

This alarming prospect led Wells to take a new stance which gave him the appearance of being an optimist, a one man brain trust who surveyed the chief forces for social and political change and pressed hard for global reconstruction. Recalling his first venture into public affairs in 1900 with *Anticipations*, he wrote that he had reviewed the pretensions of democracy and stated the widely unspoken thought of the late Victorians: "This will not work." He had then considered existing governments and ruling influences, and said as plainly: "These do not work," at a time when most active people were saying, "They will work well enough for a few years more." "And so," he went on, "through circumstances and simplicity rather than through any exceptional intelligence, I arrived ahead of everyone at the naked essential question, which everyone about me was putting off for to-morrow, 'What, then, will work?' And the attempt to answer that has been the cardinal reality of my thought and writing ever since." (pp. 302-03)

On the hot evening of August 4, 1914, he quickly wrote a newspaper article whose title epitomized his view and became a powerful slogan—**"The War That Will End War"**; and in 1918, as the victory bells pealed out ecstatically, he spoke out strongly for a League of Nations to ensure eternal peace, an idea his prospectus had held out in its many versions. Now if ever was the time for a new world to be built: But utopia's chances of survival, he saw, would depend on a new harmony among peoples, an outlook freed from the " 'King and Country' stuff" that had divided men into armed camps and nearly wrecked civilization. Ultimately, Wells thought, the war had been caused by "an educational breakdown," and planetary salvation now depended on mankind agreeing on a new history for all and teaching it. History would thus no longer be an implement for war; it would become a plowshare. "There can be no common peace and prosperity," he wrote, "without common historical ideas." (pp. 317-18)

When *The Outline of History,* over one-thousand-pages long, appeared in 1919, it was hailed as an incredible feat, and proved to be his greatest best seller; and, with a copy in almost every English-speaking home (often the only historical work) and translations far and wide, it gave him immediate respectability. Here was the vast and scattered past of all mankind marvelously caught in a single glance; here was history as science, clear, useful, and easily accessible; here was hope rising from the ashes with a blueprint for the future; and here emphatically was a story, gripping and memorable, without footnotes or references, its words plain enough to have been written on a standard typewriter. These credentials and Wells's special talents ensured the *Outline*'s astonishing reception, which swamped all criticisms of detail or interpretation, and charges of plagiarism; and it is doubtful that any history book before or since has had such a triumphant impact.

Wells had chosen the *Outline*'s theme long before. Ever since his schooldays at Mr. Morley's academy he had disliked mere dates, pedigrees, and enactments. He had outgrown history as the ascent of the white—or English—race with his adolescence; and Marxism seemed to him a mental epidemic of spite hindering truly creative revolution. Great men were only interruptions in the broad onward movement of human affairs; and, as for Christianity, he had, for example, spent a whole episode in *The War of the Worlds* showing how ineffectual it was. The great and obvious alternative—already the basis of his manifestoes—was history as progress, tied, as Huxley had trained him to see it, to a biological foundation. The *Outline* started with the origins of the globe itself, the record of the rocks, and the momentous movement of the first living things from water to dry land. "We do not know how life began upon the earth," Wells confessed, but he described with scientific imagination the great ages of plants, reptiles, and mammals, the climatic shifts, and the harsh process of natural selection. Evidence pointed to man's appearance about 600,000 B.C., when history in the strict sense could be said to begin; but man owed his heredity to the millions of years beforehand and remained subject to laws of nature operating since creation. What occurred in geological time was vital for a correct understanding of mankind's past and prospects. Enduring patterns of behavior had been set, including the habit of association, and there for Wells lay the force uniting history. Ever since reptiles had sheltered their eggs and protected their offspring, animal communities had increased their interdependence; and history had become one story of ever-expanding relationships, culminating in the airplane- and radio-linked humanworld of his day.

The future Wells looked forward to was the federation of mankind, and he noted every stage in human sociability. A surprisingly large and very readable part of the *Outline* describes the life of primitive man—the little Neanderthal tribes hammering flints and preparing skins at squatting places, the larger-brained Cro-Magnon race hunting, painting, perhaps taming the horse, and the beginnings of settled agriculture by Neolithic peoples who reached the highest form of political association till then in their Swiss-lake villages. "What was man thinking about himself and about the world in those remote days?"

Wells asked. Probably, he wrote, the first true men "took day and night, sun and stars, trees and mountains, as being in the nature of things—as a child takes its meal times and its nursery staircase for granted." But gradually a primitive religion of fears and propitiations emerged, and, with speech, a tribal mind came into existence whose monstrous ideas seem oddly far more savage than the simplicity and directness typical of the rock painters. "Hitherto a social consciousness had been asleep and not even dreaming in human history. Before it awakened it produced nightmares." Progress was also conceived by Wells as the growth of knowledge and the spread of enlightenment; and in man's upward march shameful practices had to be eliminated. . . . (pp. 318-20)

Trade, navigation, and money were all notable developments, but none surpassed writing—an invention of whose powers Wells was particularly aware. Writing had made intellectual growth possible, and given men accurate knowledge in common. For the first time, therefore, they had the chance to see their story as a worldwide human adventure.

The world today, however, was still only at the beginning of knowledge; but near the close of the pre-Christian era immense constructive ideas had emerged, in Greece and Palestine especially, and a crucially significant phenomenon had occurred. Mankind, Wells thought, had started to grow up from a predominantly barbaric past and reach out responsibly to greater and broader purposes. . . . The first experiment, Alexander's empire, was glorious but futile, but it revealed the oneness of human affairs and the practicability of a world law and organization; and, at the beginning of the third century B.C., the general result of the transformation in the ancient Mediterranean was that three of the great structural ideas that rule the modern mind had arisen—science, universal righteousness, and a human commonwealth. "The rest of the history of mankind," Wells wrote (and the view was irresistible to his ordinary readers), "is very largely the history of those three ideas . . . spreading out from the minds of the rare and exceptional persons and peoples in which they first originated, into the general consciousness of the race, and giving first a new color, then a new spirit, and then a new direction to human affairs."

From that point onward Wells defined progress as the further stages of these three ideas in action, and men were judged according to the help they had given. Authentic heroes were few in the crowded cast, villains numerous, and plain failures many for varying reasons. In the exercise of free intelligence Herodotus, Socrates, Plato, the boldly speculative friar Roger Bacon, Voltaire, Darwin, and of course Huxley, were among those who gained top marks; at the bottom, indeed outside the running, were the pedants of the Alexandrian library, the court of the Inquisition, and ecclesiastical opponents of the evolutionary theory. Wells admired Christ but not Christianity, despised Muhammad but approved Islam, and had mixed feelings for the Buddhist life of withdrawal; but all world religions complemented by inspiration and insight what history and science displayed—that men formed one universal brotherhood and shared "a common human destiny upon this little planet amidst the stars." (pp. 321-22)

[Woodrow Wilson] was one of Wells's failures, an impractical egotist, and the League of Nations by its very title was tailored to precedent. Instead of man ruling the earth at last, the war had produced in the League a "homunculus in a bottle." But, as the epic story of man's adventure, indeed of life itself, rose to a crisis amid prodigious questioning, Wells affirmed, "we are in the dawn of a great constructive effort." What, then, would work? Wells's answer, to which he believed all history had been moving (he had proved it) and human necessities pointed categorically, was a Federal World State. "Nationalism as a God must follow the tribal gods to limbo. Our true nationality is mankind." As the drama entered the present, he summoned all men to an "immense task of adjustment." . . .

The characteristics of the new utopia would be a common world religion, simple and natural; a world state sustained by universal, lifelong education; no armies, navies, or unemployed; world organization of scientific research, which "compared with that of today will be like an ocean liner beside the dugout canoe of some early heliolithic wanderer"; freedom of thought; and economic organization for the public good. . . . "Human history"—and Wells's words were widely quoted—"becomes more and more a race between education and catastrophe." (p. 324)

In certain respects *The Outline of History* complements Toynbee's great *Study,* and *vice versa,* both being born out of the First World War, both reacting to historical impoverishment, and both intensely anxious for the human race. Wells's work, on the other hand, was a whirlwind achievement aimed at a general audience, Toynbee's a most elaborate and learned inquiry; and Wells was a biologist, largely self-taught, Toynbee a highly educated classical scholar. For a shrunken globe Wells advocated an essentially political and social solution, the outcome he thought of natural forces; Toynbee came to see man's salvation lying in a higher religion, sketched exotically. In seeking to bring everything together and lift it to a higher level, the *Outline* vaguely descends from Humboldt's encyclopaedic *Cosmology* which had influenced Wells as a boy; but its greatest resemblance is surely to the writings of Voltaire in its claims to be scientific, its interpretation of the past as progress, in the size (and often similarity) of its prejudices, and in its insistence that history is for building a better life. "Human Ecology," Wells would call it, the working out of biological, intellectual, and social consequences, and he wished it to displace conventional historical studies, which to him were limited or trivial. Such an enlarged and purposeful form of analysis, basically uncomfortable with the past, naturally clashes with customary academic interests. Wells's disapproval of politics may be justly questioned, he neglected the arts, and social and economic developments are hard to fit into an evolutionary pattern. But these points on the whole were mostly missed by Wells's public, who were engrossed by the future too.

Undeniably the *Outline* had and continues to have great strengths—artistic merit as a whole, a powerful storyline holding it together, and, most of all, a central place in the vast drama for the common man, not as a silent multitude but personified in absorbing generalizations. To Wells, and to his young readers at the turn of the century, the common man was history's true hero—as he invariably was in Wells's novels. His labor had supported society, his talents had repeatedly burst through restrictions of priests and rulers, and, though his were the corpses strewn on battlefields while diplomats danced, a better future would be built through his good sense. Progress occurred through his initiative (a confidence Voltaire did not have) and was measured by improvement in his status. To be straightforward, the hero of the *Outline* was actually Wells himself, reliving his own breakthrough from dirty china shop to well-run country house—the last the most delightful setting of life to him, and providing him with his nostalgic model for a world of universal, cultivated gentlefolk. . . . Designed for all the world's peoples, the *Outline* succeeded in being the only

kind of total history most people can easily remember, with its down-to-earth statements, its novellike form, and its final illustration the future reference for all the human past—a map with "The United States of the World" scrawled across it in bold letters. Its content risked being superficial, but at last, it seemed, here was the heart of the matter called history, quite simply the real story; and to a secular age Wells's book appeared as an alternative to the Bible. (pp. 325-26)

> *John Barker, "Wells," in his* The Superhistorians: Makers of Our Past *(copyright © 1982 by John Barker; reprinted with permission of Charles Scribner's Sons), Charles Scribner's Sons, 1982, pp. 300-30.*

ADDITIONAL BIBLIOGRAPHY

Batchelor, John. "H. G. Wells." In his *The Edwardian Novelists*, pp. 119-49. New York: St. Martin's Press, 1982.
  Discussion of several major novels and how they deal with the theme of escape.

Bellamy, William. "H. G. Wells." In his *The Novels of Wells, Bennett, and Galsworthy*, pp. 114-43. New York: Barnes & Noble, 1971.
  A critical study of *In the Days of the Comet, Kipps, Tono-Bungay*, and *The History of Mr. Polly.*

Bergonzi, Bernard, ed. *H. G. Wells: A Collection of Critical Essays.* Englewood Cliffs, N.J.: Prentice-Hall, 1976, 182 p.
  Ten important essays on Wells and his work. Critics include Bernard Bergonzi, Robert M. Philmus, David Lodge, and others.

Brome, Vincent. *H. G. Wells: A Biography.* London: Longmans, Green and Co., 1952, 255 p.
  A biography containing interesting personal glimpses into Wells's life, and including many examples of the critical reception of his works.

——. "H. G. Wells As a Controversialist." *The University of Windsor Review* II, No. 2 (Spring 1967): 31-45.
  An account of Wells's quarrels with the Fabians, Josef Stalin, Henry James, and Hilaire Belloc.

Delbanco, Nicholas. "James and Wells." In his *Group Portrait*, pp. 137-79. New York: William Morrow and Co., 1982.
  Documents the famous quarrel between Wells and Henry James.

Farrell, John K. A. "H. G. Wells As an Historian." *The University of Windsor Review* II, No. 2 (Spring 1967): 47-57.
  Appraisal of *The Outline of History* and *The Shape of Things to Come*, finding the former suspect as a work of history because of oversimplification and lack of documentation, and the latter a surprisingly prophetic book.

Ford, Ford Madox. *Letters of Ford Madox Ford.* Edited by Richard M. Ludwig. Princeton: Princeton University Press, 1965, 335 p.
  Contains several letters from Ford to Wells that offer criticism of the latter's works.

Freeman, John. "H. G. Wells." In his *The Moderns: Essays in Literary Criticism*, pp. 53-101. 1917. Reprint. Freeport, N.Y.: Books for Libraries Press, 1967.
  A critical examination of Wells's canon, emphasizing his social and humorous novels and his nonfiction.

Hillegas, Mark R. *The Future As Nightmare: H. G. Wells and the Anti-Utopians.* New York: Oxford University Press, 1967, 200 p.
  Traces antiutopianism from Wells's early work through similar efforts by other important science fiction writers of the twentieth century.

Hynes, Samuel. "H. G. and G.B.S." In his *Edwardian Occasions: Essays on English Writing in the Early Twentieth Century*, pp. 18-23. New York: Oxford University Press, 1972.*

Comparison of the lives and beliefs of Bernard Shaw and Wells, both of whom the critic sees suffering from "*Weltverbesserung-swahn*—a rage to better the world."

Kagarlitski, J. *The Life and Thought of H. G. Wells*. Translated by Moura Budberg. London: Sidgwick & Jackson, 1966, 210 p.
    Wells interpreted by a Russian Marxist.

Kemp, Peter. *H. G. Wells and the Culminating Ape*. New York: St. Martin's Press, 1982, 225 p.
    Documents Wells's interpretation of human needs, including food, sex, congenial habitat, and survival.

Lodge, David. "*Tono-Bungay* and the Condition of England." In his *Language of Fiction: Essays in Criticism and Verbal Analysis of the English Novel,* pp. 214-42. London: Routledge and Kegan Paul, 1966.
    Examines *Tono-Bungay* as a work of art and 'condition of England novel.' According to Lodge, the novel explicates "the changing nature of English society in an era of . . . revolution."

Mackenzie, Norman, and Mackenzie, Jean. *The Time Traveller: The Life of H. G. Wells*. London: Weidenfeld and Nicolson, 1973, 487 p.
    A detailed and complete biography of Wells.

Macy, John. "H. G. Wells and Utopia." In his *The Critical Game,* pp. 269-76. New York: Boni and Liveright, 1922.
    An essay on Wells's vision of Utopia as set forth in *The World Set Free*.

Mirsky, D. S. "H. G. Wells and History." *The Criterion* XII, No. 46 (October 1932): 1-9.
    Views Wells as an exponent of "bourgeois" attitudes.

Parrinder, Patrick, ed. *H. G. Wells: The Critical Heritage*. London: Routledge & Kegan Paul, 1972, 351 p.
    A collection of important reviews and studies of Wells's work.

Shaw, Bernard. "H. G. Wells on the Rest of Us." In his *Pen Portraits and Reviews,* pp. 279-83. London: Constable and Co., 1932.
    A remembrance of Wells as a petulant, childish man of many talents. This essay contains Shaw's wry appraisal: "I never met such a chap. I could not survive such another."

Sinclair, Upton. "Some New Books: *Ann Veronica.*" *Wilshire's* XIV, No. 2 (February 1910): 16.
    Somewhat unfavorable review by an admirer.

———. "New Books: *Joan and Peter.*" *Upton Sinclair's* I, No. 9 (January 1919): 6.
    Favorable review.

Snow, C. P. "H. G. Wells." In his *Variety of Men*, pp. 63-85. New York: Charles Scribner's Sons, 1967.
    Snow's reminiscences of conversations with Wells, and a brief biography.

Suvin, Darko, and Philmus, Robert M., eds. *H. G. Wells and Modern Science Fiction*. Lewisburg, Pa.: Bucknell University Press, 1977, 277 p.
    A collection of essays concerning Wells's influence on, and comparative stature within, the modern science fiction world, and containing criticism of his early scientific romances.

West, Geoffrey. *H. G. Wells*. New York, W. W. Norton & Co., 1930, 287 p.
    Portrait written in consultation with Wells.

Wilson, Harris, ed. *Arnold Bennett and H. G. Wells: A Record of a Personal and a Literary Friendship*. Urbana: University of Illinois Press, 1960, 290 p.*
    An insightful collection of articles and letters by Bennett and Wells.

Appendix

THE EXCERPTS IN TCLC, VOLUME 12, WERE REPRINTED FROM THE FOLLOWING PERIODICALS:

ADAM International Review
The Adelphi
American Imago
American Quarterly
The American Scholar
The Antigonish Review
The Antioch Review
Appeal to Reason
The Athenaeum
The Atlantic Monthly
The Bookman, *London*
The Bookman, *New York*
Books Abroad
The Canadian Bookman
Cesare Barbieri Courier
The Christian Science Monitor
CLA Journal
College English
The Colored American Magazine
Commentary
Comparative Drama
Cosmopolitan Magazine
The Critic, *London*
The Critic, *New York*
The Dial
Encounter
The English Journal
The English Review
Essays by Divers Hands
Forum and Century
Forum for Modern Language Studies
Forum Italicum
The French Review
French Studies
German Life & Letters
The German Quarterly
The Germanic Review
G. K.'s Weekly
Hispania
The Hudson Review
The Humanities Association Bulletin
Illinois Quarterly

The Illustrated London News
The Illustrated Weekly of India
International Journal of Sexology
Italian Quarterly
James Joyce Quarterly
Judaism
Kentucky Foreign Language Quarterly
The Kenyon Review
Life and Letters, *London*
Lituanus: The Lithuanian Quarterly
The Living Age
The London Mercury
Mark Twain Journal
Mark Twain Quarterly
The Minnesota Review
Modern Age
The Modern Language Journal
Modern Language Quarterly
Monatshefte
MOSAIC
The Nation
The Nation and The Athenaeum
The New Age
New English Weekly
New Orleans Times-Democrat
The New Quarterly Magazine
The New Republic
New Statesman
The New Statesman & Nation
New York Evening Post
New York Herald Tribune Books
The New York Review of Books
The New York Times
The New York Times Book Review
The New Yorker
Nineteenth-Century Fiction
The North American Review
Novel: A Forum on Fiction
The Outlook
Outlook and Independent
The Pall Mall Magazine
Partisan Review

Philological Quarterly
PHYLON
Pioneer
PMLA
Poet Lore
Poetry
Prose Studies
Quadrant
Renascence
Revue de littérature comparée
The Romania Review
The Saturday Review, *London*
Science-Fiction Studies
Scrutiny
The Sewanee Review
The Smart Set
South Atlantic Quarterly
The Southern Review
The Southern Workman
The Spectator
Studies in the Twentieth Century
Symposium
The Tennessean, *Nashville*
Tennessee Studies in Literature
The Times Literary Supplement
Tomorrow
T. P.'s Weekly
TSE: Tulane Studies in English
Twentieth Century Literature
The Virginia Quarterly Review
Weekly Critical Review
The West Indian Review
Wilshire's
Wisconsin Studies in Contemporary
    Literature
Yale French Studies
The Yale Review

THE EXCERPTS IN TCLC, VOLUME 12, WERE REPRINTED FROM THE FOLLOWING BOOKS:

Adams, Henry. The Letters of Henry Adams (1892-1918). *Edited by Worthington Chauncey Ford. Houghton Mifflin, 1938.*

Allen, Clifford. Homosexuality and Creative Genius. *Edited by Hendrik M. Ruitenbeek. Astor-Honor, 1967.*

Anderson, Frederick. Preface to "Ah Sin": A Dramatic Work, *by Mark Twain and Bret Harte. Edited by Frederick Anderson. The Book Club of California, 1961.*

Appignanesi, Lisa. Femininity & the Creative Imagination: A Study of Henry James, Robert Musil & Marcel Proust. *Vision Press, 1973.*

Auchincloss, Louis. Reflections of a Jacobite. *Houghton Mifflin, 1961.*

Auden, W. H. Foreword to The Desire and Pursuit of the Whole: A Romance of Modern Venice, *by Frederick Rolfe. Cassell, 1934, 1953.*

Baker, Houston A., Jr. The American Self: Myth, Ideology, and Popular Culture. *Edited by Sam B. Girgus. University of New Mexico Press, 1981.*

Barker, John. The Superhistorians: Makers of Our Past. *Scribner's, 1982.*

Barzun, Jacques, and Taylor, Wendell Hertig. Preface to Trent's Last Case, *by E. C. Bentley. Garland, 1976.*

Baudouin, Charles. Contemporary Studies. *Translated by Eden Paul and Cedar Paul. Allen & Unwin, 1924, Books for Libraries Press, 1969.*

Baudouin, Charles. Psychoanalysis and Aesthetics. *Translated by Eden Paul and Cedar Paul. Dodd, Mead, 1924.*

Beerbohm, Max. Lytton Strachey. *Cambridge University Press, 1943, Haskell House, 1974.*

Bellman, Samuel I. Constance M. Rourke. *Twayne, 1981.*

Bentley, E. C. Those Days. *Constable, 1940.*

Bergonzi, Bernard. Heroes' Twilight: A Study of the Literature of the Great War. *Constable, 1965.*

Bewley, Marius. Masks & Mirrors: Essays in Criticism. *Atheneum, 1970.*

Bithell, Jethro. Contemporary Belgian Literature. *Stokes, 1915.*

Bluestein, Gene. The Voice of the Folk: Folklore and American Literary Theory. *University of Massachusetts Press, 1972.*

Boas, Guy. Lytton Strachey. *Oxford University Press, 1935.*

Bogan, Louise. A Poet's Alphabet: Reflections on the Literary Art and Vocation. *Edited by Robert Phelps and Ruth Limmer. McGraw-Hill, 1970.*

Bone, Robert. The Negro in America. *Rev. ed. Yale University Press, 1965.*

Boyd, Ernest. Studies from Ten Literatures. *Scribner's, 1925, Kennikat Press, 1968.*

Bradbury, Malcolm, and McFarlane, James, eds. Modernism: 1890-1930. *Penguin, 1974, The Harvester Press, 1978.*

Brawley, Benjamin. The Negro in Literature and Art in the United States. *Rev. ed. Duffield, 1929, Scholarly Press, 1972.*

Brée, Germaine. Gide. *Rutgers University Press, 1963.*

Brooks, Van Wyck. Preface to The Roots of American Culture, and Other Essays, *by Constance Rourke. Edited by Van Wyck Brooks. Harcourt Brace Jovanovich, 1942.*

Brown, Sterling. The Negro in American Fiction. *Associates in Negro Folk Education, 1937, Kennikat Press, 1968.*

Brown, Sterling. Negro Poetry and Drama. *Associates in Negro Folk Education, 1937.*

Brown, Sterling. Negro Poetry and Drama and The Negro in American Fiction. *Atheneum, 1972.*

Butler, E. M. The Tyranny of Greece over Germany: A Study of the Influence Exercised by Greek Art and Poetry over the Great German Writers of the Eighteenth, Nineteenth and Twentieth Centuries. *Cambridge University Press, 1935, Beacon Press, 1958.*

Cahill, Daniel J. Harriet Monroe. *Twayne, 1973.*

Chesterton, G. K. Autobiography. *Hutchinson, 1936, Hutchinson, 1969.*

Chesterton, G. K. A Handful of Authors: Essays on Books and Writers. *Edited by Dorothy Collins. Sheed and Ward, 1953.*

Churchill, Kenneth. Italy and English Literature: 1764-1930. *Macmillan, 1980.*

Cockshut, A.O.J. Man and Woman: A Study of Love and the Novel 1740-1949. *Collins, 1977, Oxford University Press, 1978.*

Davidson, Donald. ''The Spyglass'': View and Reviews, 1924-1930. *Edited by John Tyree Fain. Vanderbilt University Press, 1963.*

Day, A. Grove, and Knowlton, Edgar C., Jr. V. Blasco Ibáñez. *Twayne, 1972.*

Devlin, John. Spanish Anticlericalism: A Study in Modern Alienation. *Las Americanas, 1966.*

De Gourmont, Remy. The Book of Masks. *Translated by Jack Lewis. Luce, 1921, Books for Libraries Press, 1967.*

Dickson, Lovat. Radclyffe Hall at the Well of Loneliness: A Sapphic Chronicle. *Scribner's, 1975.*

Doggett, Frank, and Butlel, Robert, eds. Wallace Stevens: A Celebration. *Princeton University Press, 1980.*

Dos Passos, John. Rosinante to the Road Again. *Doran, 1922.*

Edel, Leon. Bloomsbury: A House of Lions. *Lippincott, 1979.*

Ellis, Havelock. Views and Reviews: A Selection of Uncollected Articles, 1884-1932, first and second series. *D. Harmsworth, 1932, Books for Libraries Press, 1970.*

Ellis, Havelock. Preface to The Well of Loneliness, *by Radclyffe Hall, Covici, Friede, 1928.*

Eloesser, Arthur. Modern German Literature. *Translated by Catherine Alison Phillips. Knopf, 1933.*

Enck, John J. Wallace Stevens: Images and Judgments. *Southern Illinois University Press, 1964.*

Eoff, Sherman H. The Modern Spanish Novel: Comparative Essays Examining the Philosophical Impact of Science on Fiction. *New York University Press, 1961.*

Ewart, Gavin. Introduction to The Complete Clerihews of E. Clerihew Bentley, *by E. C. Bentley. Oxford University Press, 1981.*

Forster, E. M. Two Cheers for Democracy. *Harcourt Brace Jovanovich, 1951.*

France, Anatole. On Life & Letters, first series. *Translated by A. W. Evans. John Lane, 1911, Dodd, Mead, 1924.*

France, Anatole. On Life & Letters, third series. *Translated by D. B. Stewart. John Lane, 1922.*

Freeman, Douglas Southall. Lee. *Charles Scribner's Sons, 1961.*

Fussell, Paul. The Great War and Modern Memory. *Oxford University Press, 1975.*

Gayle, Addison, Jr. Oak and Ivy: A Biography of Paul Laurence Dunbar. *Doubleday, 1971.*

Gide, André. The Journals of André Gide: 1928-1939, Vol. III. *Translated by Justin O'Brien. Knopf, 1949, Secker & Warburg, 1949.*

Gilkes, Michael. The West Indian Novel. *Twayne, 1981.*

Giovanni, Nikki. Afterword in A Singer in the Dawn: Reinterpretations of Paul Laurence Dunbar. *Edited by Jay Martin. Dodd, Mead, 1975.*

Goldberg, Isaac. Introduction to Blood and Sand, *by Vicente Blasco Ibáñez. Ungar, 1958.*

Greene, Graham. The Lost Childhood, and Other Essays. *Eyre & Spottiswoode, 1951.*

Gregory, Horace, and Zaturenska, Marya. A History of American Poetry, 1900-1940. *Harcourt Brace Jovanovich, 1946.*

Günther, Werner. Swiss Men of Letters: Twelve Literary Essays. *Edited by Alex Natan. Wolff, 1970.'*

Harding, D. W. Experience into Words: Essays on Poetry. *Chatto & Windus, 1963.*

Harris, Frank. Latest Contemporary Portraits. *Macaulay, 1927.*

Hatfield, Henry. Crisis and Continuity in Modern German Fiction: Ten Essays. *Cornell University Press, 1969.*

Hearn, Lafcadio. Essays in European and Oriental Literature. *Edited by Albert Mordell. Dodd, Mead, 1923.*

Hemingway, Ernest. A Moveable Feast. *Charles Scribner's Sons, 1964.*

Hesse, Herman. My Belief: Essays on Life and Art. *Edited by Theodore Ziolkowski. Translated by Denver Lindley with Ralph Manheim. Farrar, Straus and Giroux, 1974.*

Higgins, Ian, ed. Literature and the Plastic Arts, 1880-1930: Seven Essays. *Scottish Academic Press, 1973.*

Highet, Gilbert. The Powers of Poetry. *Oxford University Press, 1960.*

Holroyd, Michael. Lytton Strachey, a Critical Biography: The Years of Achievement (1910-1932), Vol. II. *Heinemann, 1968.*

Holroyd, Michael. Lytton Strachey and the Bloomsbury Group: His Work, Their Influence. *Penguin, 1971.*

Howe, Irving. Celebrations and Attacks: Thirty Years of Literary and Cultural Commentary. *Horizon Press, 1979.*

Howells, W. D. My Mark Twain: Reminiscences and Criticisms. *Harper & Brothers, 1910.*

Howells, W. D. W. D. Howells As Critic. *Edited by Edwin H. Cady. Routledge & Kegan Paul, 1973.*

Howells, W. D. Introduction to Lyrics of Lowly Life, *by Paul Laurence Dunbar. Dodd, Mead, 1896.*

Howells, W. D. Introduction to The Shadow of the Cathedral: A Novel, *by Vicente Blasco Ibáñez. Translated by Mrs. W. A. Gillespie. Dutton, 1919.*

Huxley, Aldous. On the Margin: Notes and Essays. *Doran, 1923.*

Hyman, Stanley Edgar. The Armed Vision: A Study in the Methods of Modern Literary Criticism. *Knopf, 1948.*

Ireland, G. W. André Gide: A Study of His Creative Writings. *Oxford at the Clarendon Press, 1970.*

Isherwood, Christopher. Exhumations: Stories, Articles, Verses. *Methuen, 1966.*

Isitt, Yvonne. German Men of Letters: Twelve Literary Essays, Vol. III. *Edited by Alex Natan. Wolff, 1964.*

Iyengar, K. R. Srinivasa. Lytton Strachey: A Critical Study. *Chatto & Windus, 1938, Kennikat, 1967.*

James, Henry. The Letters of Henry James, Vol. I. *Edited by Percy Lubbock. Scribner's, 1920.*

James, Henry. The Letters of Henry James, Vol. II. *Edited by Percy Lubbock. Scribner's, 1920.*

Johnson, James Weldon. Preface to The Book of American Negro Poetry. *Edited by James Weldon Johnson. Harcourt Brace Jovanovich, 1922.*

Jones, P. Mansell. Verhaeren. *Yale University Press, 1957.*

Kallich, Martin. The Psychological Milieu of Lytton Strachey. *Bookman Associates, 1961.*

Kayser, Wolfgang. The Grotesque in Art and Literature. *Translated by Ulrich Weisstein. Indiana University Press, 1963.*

Kazin, Alfred. The Inmost Leaf: A Selection of Essays. *Harcourt Brace Jovanovich, 1955.*

Kermode, Frank. Preface to Five Women, *by Robert Musil. Translated by Eithne Wilkins and Ernst Kaiser. Delacorte Press, 1966.*

King, Bruce, ed. West Indian Literature. *Archon, 1979.*

Lawrence, D. H. Selected Literary Criticism. *Edited by Anthony Beal. Heinemann, 1955.*

Lawrence, Margaret. The School of Femininity: A Book for and about Women As They Are Interpreted through Feminine Writers of Yesterday and Today. *Stokes, 1936, Kennikat Press, 1966.*

Lawson, Victor. Dunbar Critically Examined. *Associated Publishers, 1941.*

Lemaître, Jules. Preface to Cosmopolis, *by Paul Bourget. Maison Mazarin, 1905, Current Literature, 1923.*

Lentricchia, Frank. The Gaiety of Language: An Essay on the Radical Poetics of W. B. Yeats and Wallace Stevens. *University of California Press, 1968.*

Leslie, Shane. Introduction to In His Own Image, *by Frederick Baron Corvo. Knopf, 1925, Carlton House.*

Lewis, C. S. They Stand Together: The Letters of C. S. Lewis to Arthur Greeves (1914-1963). *Edited by Walter Hooper. Macmillan, 1979.*

Lewisohn, Adèle. Introduction to Edgar Allan Poe, *by Hanns Heinz Ewers. Translated by Adèle Lewisohn. Huebsch, 1917.*

Liddiard, Jean. Isaac Rosenberg: The Half Used Life. *Gollancz, 1975.*

Logan, J. D., and French, Donald G. Highways of Canadian Literature: A Synoptic Introduction to the Literary History of Canada (English) from 1760 to 1924. *McClelland and Stewart, 1924.*

Loggins, Vernon. The Negro Author: His Development in America to 1900. *Columbia University Press, 1931, Kennikat Press, 1964.*

Lowell, Amy. Six French Poets: Studies in Contemporary Literature. *Macmillan, 1915.*

Lowndes, Marie Belloc. Diaries and Letters of Marie Belloc Lowndes: 1911-1947. *Edited by Susan Lowndes. Chatto & Windus, 1971.*

Lucas, F. L. Authors Living and Dead. *Macmillan, 1926.*

Ludwig, Richard M., ed. Aspects of American Poetry. *Ohio State University Press, 1962.*

Luft, David S. Robert Musil and the Crisis of European Culture: 1880-1942. *University of California Press, 1980.*

Lynn, Kenneth S. Visions of America: Eleven Literary Historical Essays. *Greenwood Press, 1973.*

Lynn, Kenneth S. Introduction to Trumpets of Jubilee, *by Constance Rourke. Harcourt Brace Jovanovich, 1963.*

Macphail, Andrew. Introduction to In Flanders Fields, and Other Poems, *by John McCrae. G. P. Putnam's Sons, 1919.*

March, Harold. Gide and ''The Hound of Heaven.'' *University of Pennsylvania Press, 1952.*

Maugham, W. Somerset. The Vagrant Mood: Six Essays. *Heinemann, 1952, Doubleday, 1953.*

Maurois, André. Prophets and Poets. *Harper & Brothers, 1935.*

Maurois, André. From Proust to Camus: Profiles of Modern French Writers. *Translated by Carl Morse and Renaud Bruce. Doubleday, 1966, Weidenfeld and Nicolson, 1967.*

Maurois, André. Points of View: From Kipling to Graham Greene. *Frederick Ungar, 1968.*

Appendix

Mencken, H. L. A Mencken Chrestomathy. *Knopf, 1949.*

Mencken, H. L. "Smart Set" Criticism. *Edited by William H. Nolte. Cornell University Press, 1968.*

Meyers, Jeffrey. Homosexuality and Literature 1890-1930. *The Athlone Press, 1977.*

Michaud, Régis. Modern Thought and Literature in France. *Funk & Wagnalls, 1934.*

Mitgang, Herbert, ed. The Letters of Carl Sandburg, *by Carl Sandburg. Harcourt Brace Jovanovich, 1968.*

Monroe, Harriet. Poets and Their Art. *Rev. ed. The Macmillan Company, 1932.*

Muir, Edwin. Transition: Essays on Contemporary Literature. *Viking Penguin, 1926.*

Murch, A. E. The Development of the Detective Novel. *Philosophical Library, 1958.*

Nersoyan, H. J. André Gide: The Theism of an Atheist. *Syracuse University Press, 1969.*

O'Brien, Justin. The French Literary Horizon. *Rutgers University Press, 1967.*

O'Connor, William Van, ed. Forms of Modern Fiction: Essays Collected in Honor of Joseph Warren Beach. *Indiana University Press, 1959.*

Pacifici, Sergio. The Modern Italian Novel: From Pea to Moravia. *Southern Illinois University Press, 1979.*

Panek, Le Roy. Watteau's Shepherds: The Detective Novel in Britain, 1914-1940. *Bowling Green University Popular Press, 1979.*

Parrinder, Patrick, ed. H. G. Wells: The Critical Heritage. *Routledge & Kegan Paul, 1972.*

Phelps, William Lyon. The Advance of the English Novel. *Dodd, Mead, 1916.*

Phelps, William Lyon. The Advance of English Poetry in the Twentieth Century. *Dodd, Mead, 1918.*

Pike, Burton. Robert Musil: An Introduction to His Work. *Cornell University Press, 1961.*

Pritchett, V. S. The Living Novel & Later Appreciations. *Rev. ed. Random House, 1964.*

Pryce-Jones, Alan. Preface to Young Törless, *by Robert Musil. Translated by Eithne Wilkins and Ernst Kaiser. Pantheon Books, 1955, Noonday Press, 1958.*

Ramchand, Kenneth. The West Indian Novel and Its Background. *Barnes & Noble, 1970.*

Ramchand, Kenneth. Introduction to Jane's Career: A Story of Jamaica, *by Herbert G. de Lisser. Africana, 1971.*

Revell, Peter. Paul Laurence Dunbar. *Twayne, 1979.*

Rexroth, Kenneth. Essays. *New Directions, 1961.*

Rhodenizer, V. B. A Handbook of Canadian Literature. *Graphic Publishers, 1930.*

Robertson, J. G. Essays and Addresses on Literature. *Books for Libraries Press, 1968.*

Ronay, Gabriel. The Dracula Myth. *Allen, 1972.*

Ronay, Gabriel. The Truth about Dracula. *Stein and Day, 1972.*

Rosenberg, Isaac. The Collected Works of Isaac Rosenberg: Poetry, Prose, Letters and Some Drawings. *Edited by Gordon Bottomley and Denys Harding. Chatto and Windus, 1937.*

Rosenberg, Isaac. The Collected Works of Isaac Rosenberg: Poetry, Prose, Letters, Paintings and Drawings. *Edited by Ian Parsons. Chatto and Windus, 1979.*

Routley, Erik. The Puritan Pleasures of the Detective Story: A Personal Monograph. *Gollancz, 1972.*

Rubin, Joan Shelley. Constance Rourke and American Culture. *University of North Carolina Press, 1980.*

Rule, Jane. Lesbian Images. *Doubleday, 1975.*

Sanders, Charles Richard. Lytton Strachey: His Mind and Art. *Yale University Press, 1957.*

Sartre, Jean-Paul. Situations. *Translated by Benita Eisler. Braziller, 1965.*

Schneider, Daniel J. Symbolism, the Manichean Vision: A Study in the Art of James, Conrad, Woolf, & Stevens. *University of Nebraska Press, 1975.*

Scott-James, R. A. Lytton Strachey. *British Council, 1955.*

Secor, Walter Todd. Paul Bourget and the Nouvelle. *King's Crown Press, 1948.*

Shaw, Bernard. Saint Joan. *Brentano's, 1924.*

Shaw, Bernard. Collected Letters: 1898-1910. *Edited by Dan H. Laurence. Dodd, Mead, 1972.*

Sinclair, Upton. Mammonart: An Essay in Economic Interpretation. *1925.*

Singer, Armand E. Paul Bourget. *Twayne, 1976.*

Smith, Henry Nash, ed. Mark Twain: A Collection of Critical Essays. *Prentice-Hall, 1963.*

Spitteler, Carl. Laughing Truths. *Translated by James F. Muirhead. Putnam's, 1927.*

Starkie, Enid. André Gide. *Bowes & Bowes, 1953.*

Stevens, Wallace. The Necessary Angel. *Knopf, 1951, Vintage, 1965.*

Stevenson, Lionel. Appraisals of Canadian Literature. *Macmillan, 1926.*

Strachey, Lytton. Preface to Eminent Victorians. *Putnam's, 1918.*

Sukenick, Ronald. Wallace Stevens: Musing the Obscure; Readings, an Interpretation, and a Guide to the Collected Poetry. *New York University Press, 1967.*

Suvin, Darko. Metamorphoses of Science Fiction: On the Poetics and History of a Literary Genre. *Yale University Press, 1979.*

Sykes, Christopher. Preface to Stories Toto Told Me, *by Frederick Baron Corvo. Collins, 1969, St. Martin's Press, 1971.*

Symons, A.J.A. Introduction to The Desire and Pursuit of the Whole: A Romance of Modern Venice, *by Frederick Rolfe. Cassell, 1934, 1953.*

Symons, Arthur. Dramatis Personae. *Bobbs-Merrill, 1923.*

Symons, Julian. Mortal Consequences: A History—From the Detective Story to the Crime Novel. *Harper & Row, 1972.*

Tarkington, Booth. Introduction to My Cousin Mark Twain, *by Cyril Clemens. Rodale Press, 1939.*

Thomson, H. Douglas. Masters of Mystery: A Study of the Detective Story. *Collins, 1931.*

Twain, Mark. The Complete Essays of Mark Twain. *Edited by Charles Neider. Doubleday, 1963.*

Tymn, Marshall B., ed. Horror Literature: A Core Collection and Reference Guide. *Bowker, 1981.*

Untermeyer, Louis, ed. Modern American Poetry. *Rev. ed. Harcourt Brace Jovanovich, 1969.*

Van Doren, Carl. The American Novel. *Macmillan, 1921.*

Vendler, Helen Hennessy. On Extended Wings: Wallace Stevens' Longer Poems. *Harvard University Press, 1969.*

Wagner, Jean. Black Poets of the United States: From Paul Laurence Dunbar to Langston Hughes. *Translated by Kenneth Douglas. University of Illinois Press, 1973.*

Wells, Henry W. Introduction to Wallace Stevens. *Indiana University Press, 1964.*

West, Rebecca. Ending in Earnest: A Literary Log. *Doubleday, Doran, 1931.*

Wilkins, Eithne, and Kaiser, Ernst. Foreword to The Man without Qualities, Vol. 1, *by Robert Musil. Translated by Eithne Wilkins and Ernst Kaiser. Coward-McCann, 1953, Secker & Warburg, 1953.*

Williams, C. E. The Broken Eagle: The Politics of Austrian Literature from Empire to Anschluss. *Barnes & Noble, 1974.*

Williams, Kenny J. They Also Spoke: An Essay in Negro Literature in America, 1787-1930. *Townsend, 1970.*

Wilson, Edmund. The Shores of Light: A Literary Chronicle of the Twenties and Thirties. *Farrar, Straus and Young, 1952.*

Wilson, Harris, ed. Arnold Bennett and H. G. Wells: A Record of a Personal and a Literary Friendship. *University of Illinois Press, 1960.*

Woolf, Cecil. Introduction to Nicholas Crabbe; or, The One and the Many, *by Frederick Rolfe. Chatto & Windus, 1958.*

Woolf, Virginia. The Common Reader. *Harcourt Brace Jovanovich, 1925.*

Woolf, Virginia. The Death of the Moth and Other Essays. *Harcourt Brace Jovanovich, 1942.*

Woolf, Virginia. Collected Essays. Vol. 4. *Hogarth, 1967.*

Zweig, Stefan. Émile Verhaeren. *Translated by Jethro Bithell. Houghton Mifflin, 1914.*

Cumulative Index to Authors

This index lists all author entries in the Gale Literary Criticism Series and includes cross-references to other Gale sources. References in the index are identified as follows:

AITN: *Authors in the News,* Volumes 1-2
CA: *Contemporary Authors* (original series), Volumes 1-109
CANR: *Contemporary Authors New Revision Series,* Volumes 1-11
CAP: *Contemporary Authors Permanent Series,* Volumes 1-2
CA-R: *Contemporary Authors* (revised editions), Volumes 1-44
CLC: *Contemporary Literary Criticism,* Volumes 1-27
CLR: *Children's Literature Review,* Volumes 1-6
DLB: *Dictionary of Literary Biography,* Volumes 1-23
DLB-DS: *Dictionary of Literary Biography Documentary Series,* Volumes 1-4
DLB-Y: *Dictionary of Literary Biography Yearbook,* Volumes 1980-1982
NCLC: *Nineteenth-Century Literature Criticism,* Volumes 1-5
SATA: *Something about the Author,* Volumes 1-30
TCLC: *Twentieth-Century Literary Criticism,* Volumes 1-12
YABC: *Yesterday's Authors of Books for Children,* Volumes 1-2

Alepoudelis, Odysseus 1911-
  See Elytis, Odysseus

Algren, Nelson 1909-1981 ...... **CLC 4, 10**
  See also CA 13-16R
  See also obituary CA 103
  See also DLB 9
  See also DLB-Y 81, 82

Allen, Heywood 1935-
  See Allen, Woody
  See also CA 33-36R

Allen, Woody 1935-...............**CLC 16**
  See also Allen, Heywood

Allingham, Margery (Louise)
  1904-1966....................**CLC 19**
  See also CANR 4
  See also CA 5-8R
  See also obituary CA 25-28R

Allston, Washington
  1779-1843..................**NCLC 2**
  See also DLB 1

Almedingen, E. M. 1898-1971......**CLC 12**
  See also Almedingen, Martha Edith von

Almedingen, Martha Edith von 1898-1971
  See Almedingen, E. M.
  See also CANR 1
  See also CA 1-4R
  See also SATA 3

Alonso, Dámaso 1898-.............**CLC 14**

Alta 1942-......................**CLC 19**
  See also CA 57-60

Alther, Lisa 1944-.................**CLC 7**
  See also CA 65-68

Altman, Robert 1925-.............**CLC 16**
  See also CA 73-76

Alvarez, A(lfred) 1929-.........**CLC 5, 13**
  See also CANR 3
  See also CA 1-4R
  See also DLB 14

Amado, Jorge 1912-..............**CLC 13**
  See also CA 77-80

Ambler, Eric 1909-...........**CLC 4, 6, 9**
  See also CANR 7
  See also CA 9-12R

Amichai, Yehuda 1924-........**CLC 9, 22**
  See also CA 85-88

Amiel, Henri Frédéric
  1821-1881..................**NCLC 4**

Amis, Kingsley (William)
  1922-............**CLC 1, 2, 3, 5, 8, 13**
  See also CANR 8
  See also CA 9-12R
  See also DLB 15
  See also AITN 2

Amis, Martin 1949-..............**CLC 4, 9**
  See also CANR 8
  See also CA 65-68
  See also DLB 14

Ammons, A(rchie) R(andolph)
  1926-...........**CLC 2, 3, 5, 8, 9, 24**
  See also CANR 6
  See also CA 9-12R
  See also DLB 5
  See also AITN 1

Anand, Mulk Raj 1905-...........**CLC 23**
  See also CA 65-68

Anaya, Rudolfo A(lfonso)
  1937-......................**CLC 23**
  See also CANR 1
  See also CA 45-48

Anderson, Jon (Victor) 1940-.......**CLC 9**
  See also CA 25-28R

Anderson, Lindsay 1923-..........**CLC 20**

Anderson, Maxwell 1888-1959 .... **TCLC 2**
  See also CA 105
  See also DLB 7

Anderson, Poul (William)
  1926-......................**CLC 15**
  See also CANR 2
  See also CA 1-4R
  See also DLB 8

Anderson, Robert (Woodruff)
  1917-......................**CLC 23**
  See also CA 21-24R
  See also DLB 7
  See also AITN 1

Anderson, Roberta Joan 1943-
  See Mitchell, Joni

Anderson, Sherwood
  1876-1941...............**TCLC 1, 10**
  See also CA 104
  See also DLB 4, 9
  See also DLB-DS 1

Andrade, Carlos Drummond de
  1902-......................**CLC 18**

Andrews, Cecily Fairfield 1892-
  See West, Rebecca

Andreyev, Leonid (Nikolaevich)
  1871-1919..................**TCLC 3**
  See also CA 104

Andrić, Ivo 1892-1975 ....**CLC 8**
  See also CA 81-84
  See also obituary CA 57-60

Angell, Roger 1920-..............**CLC 26**
  See also CA 57-60

Angelou, Maya 1928- ....**CLC 12**
  See also CA 65-68

Anouilh, Jean (Marie Lucien Pierre)
  1910-................**CLC 1, 3, 8, 13**
  See also CA 17-20R

Anthony, Florence 1947-
  See Ai

Antoninus, Brother 1912-
  See Everson, William (Oliver)

Antonioni, Michelangelo 1912- .....**CLC 20**
  See also CA 73-76

Antschel, Paul 1920-1970
  See Celan, Paul
  See also CA 85-88

Apollinaire, Guillaume
  1880-1918................**TCLC 3, 8**
  See also CA 104

Appelfeld, Aharon 1932- ....**CLC 23**

Apple, Max (Isaac) 1941-..........**CLC 9**
  See also CA 81-84

Aquin, Hubert 1929-1977.........**CLC 15**
  See also CA 105

Aragon, Louis 1897-1982 ...... **CLC 3, 22**
  See also CA 69-72
  See also obituary CA 108

Archer, Jules 1915-...............**CLC 12**
  See also CANR 6
  See also CA 9-12R
  See also SATA 4

Arden, John 1930-..........**CLC 6, 13, 15**
  See also CA 13-16R
  See also DLB 13

Arguedas, José María
  1911-1969....................**CLC 10, 18**
  See also CA 89-92

Armah, Ayi Kwei 1939-.............**CLC 5**
  See also CA 61-64

Armatrading, Joan 1950-..........**CLC 17**

Arnim, Achim von 1781-1831 ..... **NCLC 5**

Arnow, Harriette (Louisa Simpson)
  1908-...................**CLC 2, 7, 18**
  See also CA 9-12R
  See also DLB 6

Arp, Jean 1887-1966...............**CLC 5**
  See also CA 81-84
  See also obituary CA 25-28R

Arquette, Lois S(teinmetz)
  See Duncan (Steinmetz Arquette), Lois
  See also SATA 1

Arrabal, Fernando 1932- ..... **CLC 2, 9, 18**
  See also CA 9-12R

Artaud, Antonin 1896-1948 .... **TCLC 3**
  See also CA 104

Arthur, Ruth M(abel)
  1905-1979....................**CLC 12**
  See also CANR 4
  See also CA 9-12R
  See also obituary CA 85-88
  See also SATA 7
  See also obituary SATA 26

Arundel, Honor (Morfydd)
  1919-1973...................**CLC 17**
  See also CAP 2
  See also CA 21-22
  See also obituary CA 41-44R
  See also SATA 4
  See also obituary SATA 24

Asch, Sholem 1880-1957.........**TCLC 3**
  See also CA 105

Ashbery, John (Lawrence)
  1927-..... **CLC 2, 3, 4, 6, 9, 13, 15, 25**
  See also CANR 9
  See also CA 5-8R
  See also DLB 5
  See also DLB-Y 81

Ashton-Warner, Sylvia (Constance)
  1908-.....................**CLC 19**
  See also CA 69-72

Asimov, Isaac
  1920-........ **CLC 1, 3, 9, 19, 26**
  See also CANR 2
  See also CA 1-4R
  See also SATA 1, 26
  See also DLB 8

Asturias, Miguel Ángel
  1899-1974...............**CLC 3, 8, 13**
  See also CAP 2
  See also CA 25-28
  See also obituary CA 49-52

Atheling, William, Jr. 1921-1975
  See Blish, James (Benjamin)

Author Index

Author Index

Cable, George Washington
1844-1925 . . . . TCLC 4
See also CA 104
See also DLB 12

Cabrera Infante, G(uillermo)
1929- . . . . CLC 5, 25
See also CA 85-88

Cain, G. 1929-
See Cabrera Infante, G(uillermo)

Cain, James M(allahan)
1892-1977 . . . . CLC 3, 11
See also CANR 8
See also CA 17-20R
See also obituary CA 73-76
See also AITN 1

Caldwell, Erskine 1903- . . . . . . CLC 1, 8, 14
See also CANR 2
See also CA 1-4R
See also DLB 9
See also AITN 1

Caldwell, (Janet Miriam) Taylor (Holland)
1900- . . . . CLC 2
See also CANR 5
See also CA 5-8R

Calisher, Hortense 1911- . . . . . . CLC 2, 4, 8
See also CANR 1
See also CA 1-4R
See also DLB 2

Callaghan, Morley (Edward)
1903- . . . . CLC 3, 14
See also CA 9-12R

Calvino, Italo 1923- . . . . CLC 5, 8, 11, 22
See also CA 85-88

Campbell, (Ignatius) Roy (Dunnachie)
1901-1957 . . . . TCLC 5
See also CA 104
See also DLB 20

Campbell, (William) Wilfred
1861-1918 . . . . TCLC 9
See also CA 106

Camus, Albert
1913-1960 . . . . . . CLC 1, 2, 4, 9, 11, 14
See also CA 89-92

Canby, Vincent 1924- . . . . CLC 13
See also CA 81-84

Canetti, Elias 1905- . . . . CLC 3, 14, 25
See also CA 21-24R

Cape, Judith 1916-
See Page, P(atricia) K(athleen)

Čapek, Karel 1890-1938 . . . . TCLC 6
See also CA 104

Capote, Truman
1924- . . . . CLC 1, 3, 8, 13, 19
See also CA 5-8R
See also DLB 2
See also DLB-Y 80

Capra, Frank 1897- . . . . CLC 16
See also CA 61-64

Carey, Ernestine Gilbreth 1908-
See Gilbreth, Frank B(unker), Jr. and
Carey, Ernestine Gilbreth
See also CA 5-8R
See also SATA 2

Carleton, William 1794-1869 . . . . . . NCLC 3

Carman, (William) Bliss
1861-1929 . . . . TCLC 7
See also CA 104

Carpentier (Y Valmont), Alejo
1904-1980 . . . . CLC 8, 11
See also CANR 11
See also CA 65-68
See also obituary CA 97-100

Carr, John Dickson 1905-1977 . . . . . . CLC 3
See also CANR 3
See also CA 49-52
See also obituary CA 69-72

Carrier, Roch 1937- . . . . CLC 13

Carroll, Lewis 1832-1898 . . . . NCLC 2
See also CLR 2
See also YABC 2
See also DLB 18

Carroll, Paul Vincent
1900-1968 . . . . CLC 10
See also CA 9-12R
See also obituary CA 25-28R
See also DLB 10

Carruth, Hayden
1921- . . . . CLC 4, 7, 10, 18
See also CANR 4
See also CA 9-12R
See also DLB 5

Carter, Angela 1940- . . . . CLC 5
See also CA 53-56
See also DLB 14

Carver, Raymond 1938- . . . . CLC 22
See also CA 33-36R

Cary, (Arthur) Joyce
1888-1957 . . . . TCLC 1
See also CA 104
See also DLB 15

Casares, Adolfo Bioy 1914-
See Bioy Casares, Adolfo

Casey, John 1880-1964
See O'Casey, Sean

Casey, Michael 1947- . . . . CLC 2
See also CA 65-68
See also DLB 5

Casey, Warren 1935-
See Jacobs, Jim and Casey, Warren
See also CA 101

Cassavetes, John 1929- . . . . CLC 20
See also CA 85-88

Cassill, R(onald) V(erlin)
1919- . . . . CLC 4, 23
See also CANR 7
See also CA 9-12R
See also DLB 6

Cassity, (Allen) Turner 1929- . . . . CLC 6
See also CANR 11
See also CA 17-20R

Castaneda, Carlos 1935?- . . . . CLC 12
See also CA 25-28R

Castro, Rosalía de 1837-1885 . . . . . NCLC 3

Cather, Willa (Sibert)
1873-1947 . . . . TCLC 1, 11
See also CA 104
See also DLB 9
See also DLB-DS 1

Causley, Charles (Stanley)
1917- . . . . CLC 7
See also CANR 5
See also CA 9-12R
See also SATA 3

Cavafy, C(onstantine) P(eter)
1863-1933 . . . . TCLC 2, 7
See also CA 104

Cavanna, Betty 1909- . . . . CLC 12
See also CANR 6
See also CA 9-12R
See also SATA 1, 30

Cayrol, Jean 1911- . . . . CLC 11
See also CA 89-92

Cela, Camilo José 1916- . . . . CLC 4, 13
See also CA 21-24R

Celan, Paul 1920-1970 . . . . CLC 10, 19
See also Antschel, Paul

Céline, Louis-Ferdinand
1894-1961 . . . . CLC 1, 3, 4, 7, 9, 15
See also Destouches, Louis Ferdinand

Cendrars, Blaise 1887-1961 . . . . CLC 18
See also Sauser-Hall, Frédéric

Césaire, Aimé (Fernand) 1913- . . . . . CLC 19
See also CA 65-68

Chabrol, Claude 1930- . . . . CLC 16

Challans, Mary 1905-
See Renault, Mary
See also CA 81-84
See also SATA 23

Chambers, James 1948-
See Cliff, Jimmy

Chandler, Raymond
1888-1959 . . . . TCLC 1, 7
See also CA 104

Chaplin, Charles (Spencer)
1889-1977 . . . . CLC 16
See also CA 81-84
See also obituary CA 73-76

Chapman, Graham 1941?-
See Monty Python

Chapman, John Jay
1862-1933 . . . . TCLC 7
See also CA 104

Char, René (Emile)
1907- . . . . CLC 9, 11, 14
See also CA 13-16R

Charyn, Jerome 1937- . . . . CLC 5, 8, 18
See also CANR 7
See also CA 5-8R

Chase, Mary Ellen 1887-1973 . . . . CLC 2
See also CAP 1
See also CA 15-16
See also obituary CA 41-44R
See also SATA 10

Chateaubriand, François René de
1768-1848 . . . . NCLC 3

Chayefsky, Paddy 1923-1981 . . . . CLC 23
See also CA 9-12R
See also obituary CA 104
See also DLB 7
See also DLB-Y 81

Chayefsky, Sidney 1923-1981
See Chayefsky, Paddy

Cheever, John
1912-1982 . . . . . . CLC 3, 7, 8, 11, 15, 25
See also CANR 5
See also CA 5-8R
See also obituary CA 106
See also DLB 2
See also DLB-Y 80, 82

Duras, Marguerite
1914-................CLC 3, 6, 11, 20
See also CA 25-28R

Durrell, Lawrence (George)
1912-..........CLC 1, 4, 6, 8, 13, 27
See also CA 9-12R
See also DLB 15

Dürrenmatt, Friedrich
1921-............. CLC 1, 4, 8, 11, 15
See also CA 17-20R

Dylan, Bob 1941-.........CLC 3, 4, 6, 12
See also CA 41-44R
See also DLB 16

Eastlake, William (Derry) 1917-.....CLC 8
See also CANR 5
See also CA 5-8R
See also DLB 6

Eberhart, Richard 1904- .... CLC 3, 11, 19
See also CANR 2
See also CA 1-4R

**Echegaray (y Eizaguirre), José (María
    Waldo)** 1832-1916...........TCLC 4
See also CA 104

Eckert, Allan W. 1931-............CLC 17
See also CA 13-16R
See also SATA 27, 29

Edgeworth, Maria 1767-1849 ..... NCLC 1
See also SATA 21

Edmonds, Helen (Woods) 1904-1968
See Kavan, Anna
See also CA 5-8R
See also obituary CA 25-28R

Edson, Russell 1905-.............CLC 13
See also CA 33-36R

Edwards, G(erald) B(asil)
1899-1976...................CLC 25

Ehle, John (Marsden, Jr.)
1925-......................CLC 27
See also CA 9-12R

Ehrenbourg, Ilya (Grigoryevich) 1891-1967
See Ehrenburg, Ilya (Grigoryevich)

Ehrenburg, Ilya (Grigoryevich)
1891-1967...................CLC 18
See also CA 102
See also obituary CA 25-28R

Eich, Günter 1907- ....CLC 15
See also obituary CA 93-96

Eigner, Larry 1927- ....CLC 9
See also Eigner, Laurence (Joel)
See also DLB 5

Eigner, Laurence (Joel) 1927-
See Eigner, Larry
See also CANR 6
See also CA 9-12R

Eiseley, Loren (Corey)
1907-1977.....................CLC 7
See also CANR 6
See also CA 1-4R
See also obituary CA 73-76

Ekeloef, Gunnar (Bengt) 1907-1968
See Ekelöf, Gunnar (Bengt)
See also obituary CA 25-28R

Ekelöf, Gunnar (Bengt)
1907-1968...................CLC 27
See also Ekeloef, Gunnar (Bengt)

Ekwensi, Cyprian (Odiatu Duaka)
1921-......................CLC 4
See also CA 29-32R

Eliade, Mircea 1907-.............CLC 19
See also CA 65-68

Eliot, George 1819-1880......... NCLC 4
See also DLB 21

Eliot, T(homas) S(tearns)
1888-1965....... CLC 1, 2, 3, 6, 9, 10,
                          13, 15, 24
See also CA 5-8R
See also obituary CA 25-28R
See also DLB 7, 10

Elkin, Stanley L(awrence)
1930-............ CLC 4, 6, 9, 14, 27
See also CANR 8
See also CA 9-12R
See also DLB 2
See also DLB-Y 80

Elliott, George P(aul)
1918-1980...................CLC 2
See also CANR 2
See also CA 1-4R
See also obituary CA 97-100

Ellis, A. E. ....CLC 7

Ellison, Harlan 1934- .... CLC 1, 13
See also CANR 5
See also CA 5-8R
See also DLB 8

Ellison, Ralph (Waldo)
1914-................... CLC 1, 3, 11
See also CA 9-12R
See also DLB 2

Elman, Richard 1934-.............CLC 19
See also CA 17-20R

Éluard, Paul 1895-1952 .... TCLC 7
See also CA 104

Elvin, Anne Katharine Stevenson 1933-
See Stevenson, Anne
See also CA 17-20R

Elytis, Odysseus 1911- ....CLC 15
See also CA 102

Emecheta, (Florence Onye) Buchi
1944-......................CLC 14
See also CA 81-84

Emerson, Ralph Waldo
1803-1882................... NCLC 1
See also DLB 1

Empson, William 1906- ...... CLC 3, 8, 19
See also CA 17-20R
See also DLB 20

Endo, Shusaku 1923- .... CLC 7, 14, 19
See also CA 29-32R

Enright, D(ennis) J(oseph)
1920-..................... CLC 4, 8
See also CANR 1
See also CA 1-4R
See also SATA 25

Ephron, Nora 1941- ....CLC 17
See also CA 65-68
See also AITN 2

Epstein, Daniel Mark 1948-........CLC 7
See also CANR 2
See also CA 49-52

Epstein, Jacob 1956-.............CLC 19

Epstein, Leslie 1938-.............CLC 27
See also CA 73-76

Erdman, Paul E(mil) 1932- ....CLC 25
See also CA 61-64

Erenburg, Ilya (Grigoryevich) 1891-1967
See Ehrenburg, Ilya (Grigoryevich)

Eseki, Bruno 1919-
See Mphahlele, Ezekiel

Esenin, Sergei (Aleksandrovich)
1895-1925.................. TCLC 4
See also CA 104

Eshleman, Clayton 1935-...........CLC 7
See also CA 33-36R
See also DLB 5

Espriu, Salvador 1913-.............CLC 9

Evans, Marian
See Eliot, George

Evans, Mary Ann
See Eliot, George

Evarts, Esther 1900-1972
See Benson, Sally

Everson, R(onald) G(ilmour)
1903-......................CLC 27
See also CA 17-20R

Everson, William (Oliver)
1912-................... CLC 1, 5, 14
See also CA 9-12R
See also DLB 5, 16

Evtushenko, Evgenii (Aleksandrovich) 1933-
See Yevtushenko, Yevgeny

Ewart, Gavin (Buchanan)
1916-......................CLC 13
See also CA 89-92

Ewers, Hanns Heinz
1871-1943................. TCLC 12

Ewing, Frederick R. 1918-
See Sturgeon, Theodore (Hamilton)

Exley, Frederick (Earl)
1929-................... CLC 6, 11
See also CA 81-84
See also DLB-Y 81
See also AITN 2

Fagen, Donald 1948-
See Becker, Walter and Fagen, Donald

Fagen, Donald 1948- and **Becker, Walter**
1950-
See Becker, Walter and Fagen, Donald

Fair, Ronald L. 1932-.............CLC 18
See also CA 69-72

Fallaci, Oriana 1930- ....CLC 11
See also CA 77-80

Fargue, Léon-Paul 1876-1947 .... TCLC 11
See also CA 109

Farigoule, Louis 1885-1972
See Romains, Jules

Fariña, Richard 1937?-1966 ....CLC 9
See also CA 81-84
See also obituary CA 25-28R

Farley, Walter 1915-.............CLC 17
See also CANR 8
See also CA 17-20R
See also SATA 2
See also DLB 22

Author Index

Author Index

Marley, Robert Nesta 1945-1981
See Marley, Bob
See also CA 107
See also obituary CA 103

Marquand, John P(hillips)
1893-1960................ **CLC 2, 10**
See also CA 85-88
See also DLB 9

Márquez, Gabriel García 1928-
See García Márquez, Gabriel

Marquis, Don(ald Robert Perry)
1878-1937................. **TCLC 7**
See also CA 104
See also DLB 11

Marryat, Frederick 1792-1848 .... **NCLC 3**
See also DLB 21

Marsh, (Edith) Ngaio
1899-1982................. **CLC 7**
See also CANR 6
See also CA 9-12R

Marshall, Garry 1935?- .... **CLC 17**

Marshall, Paule 1929-............ **CLC 27**
See also CA 77-80

Marsten, Richard 1926-
See Hunter, Evan

Martínez Ruiz, José 1874-1967
See Azorín
See also CA 93-96

Martínez Sierra, Gregorio 1881-1947
See Martínez Sierra, Gregorio and Martínez
Sierra, María (de la O'LeJárraga)
See also CA 104

Martínez Sierra, Gregorio 1881-1947 and
**Martínez Sierra, María (de la
O'LeJárraga)** 1880?-1974 .... **TCLC 6**

Martínez Sierra, María (de la O'LeJárraga)
1880?-1974
See Martínez Sierra, Gregorio and Martínez
Sierra, María (de la O'LeJárraga)

Martínez Sierra, María (de la O'LeJárraga)
1880?-1974 and **Martínez Sierra,
Gregorio** 1881-1947
See Martínez Sierra, Gregorio and Martínez
Sierra, María (de la O'LeJárraga)

Martinson, Harry (Edmund)
1904-1978.................. **CLC 14**
See also CA 77-80

Masefield, John (Edward)
1878-1967.................. **CLC 11**
See also CAP 2
See also CA 19-20
See also obituary CA 25-28R
See also SATA 19
See also DLB 10, 19

Masters, Edgar Lee
1868?-1950.................. **TCLC 2**
See also CA 104

Mathews, Harry 1930- .... **CLC 6**
See also CA 21-24R

Matthias, John (Edward) 1941-...... **CLC 9**
See also CA 33-36R

Matthiessen, Peter 1927- ..... **CLC 5, 7, 11**
See also CA 9-12R
See also SATA 27
See also DLB 6

Matute, Ana María 1925-............ **CLC 11**
See also CA 89-92

Maugham, W(illiam) Somerset
1874-1965............. **CLC 1, 11, 15**
See also CA 5-8R
See also obituary CA 25-28R
See also DLB 10

Maupassant, (Henri René Albert) Guy de
1850-1893................... **NCLC 1**

Mauriac, Claude 1914-............. **CLC 9**
See also CA 89-92

Mauriac, François (Charles)
1885-1970.................. **CLC 4, 9**
See also CAP 2
See also CA 25-28

Maxwell, William (Keepers, Jr.)
1908-........................ **CLC 19**
See also CA 93-96
See also DLB-Y 80

May, Elaine 1932-................. **CLC 16**

Mayakovsky, Vladimir (Vladimirovich)
1893-1930................... **TCLC 4**
See also CA 104

Maynard, Joyce 1953-............. **CLC 23**

Mayne, William (James Carter)
1928-........................ **CLC 12**
See also CA 9-12R
See also SATA 6

Mayo, Jim 1908?-
See L'Amour, Louis (Dearborn)
See also CA 109

Maysles, Albert 1926-
See Maysles, Albert and Maysles, David
See also CA 29-32R

Maysles, Albert 1926- and **Maysles, David**
1932-........................ **CLC 16**

Maysles, David 1932-
See Maysles, Albert and Maysles, David

Mazer, Norma Fox 1931-.......... **CLC 26**
See also CA 69-72
See also SATA 24

McBain, Ed 1926-
See Hunter, Evan

McCaffrey, Anne 1926- .... **CLC 17**
See also CA 25-28R
See also SATA 8
See also DLB 8
See also AITN 2

McCarthy, Cormac 1933-........... **CLC 4**
See also CANR 10
See also CA 13-16R
See also DLB 6

McCarthy, Mary (Therese)
1912-........... **CLC 1, 3, 5, 14, 24**
See also CA 5-8R
See also DLB 2
See also DLB-Y 81

McCartney, Paul 1942-
See Lennon, John (Ono) and McCartney,
Paul

McClure, Michael 1932-........ **CLC 6, 10**
See also CA 21-24R
See also DLB 16

McCourt, James 1941-............. **CLC 5**
See also CA 57-60

McCrae, John 1872-1918........ **TCLC 12**

McCullers, (Lula) Carson
1917-1967............ **CLC 1, 4, 10, 12**
See also CA 5-8R
See also obituary CA 25-28R
See also SATA 27
See also DLB 2, 7

McCullough, Colleen 1938?- ....**CLC 27**
See also CA 81-84

McElroy, Joseph 1930-............. **CLC 5**
See also CA 17-20R

McEwan, Ian 1948-................ **CLC 13**
See also CA 61-64
See also DLB 14

McGahern, John 1935-.......... **CLC 5, 9**
See also CA 17-20R
See also DLB 14

McGinley, Phyllis 1905-1978.......**CLC 14**
See also CA 9-12R
See also obituary CA 77-80
See also SATA 2
See also obituary SATA 24
See also DLB 11

McGivern, Maureen Daly 1921-
See Daly, Maureen
See also CA 9-12R

McGuane, Thomas (Francis III)
1939-.................... **CLC 3, 7, 18**
See also CANR 5
See also CA 49-52
See also DLB 2
See also DLB-Y 80
See also AITN 2

McHale, Tom 1941-1982 .... **CLC 3, 5**
See also CA 77-80
See also obituary CA 106
See also AITN 1

McIlwraith, Maureen Mollie Hunter 1922-
See Hunter, Mollie
See also CA 29-32R
See also SATA 2

McIntyre, Vonda N(eel) 1948-......**CLC 18**
See also CA 81-84

McKay, Claude 1889-1948........ **TCLC 7**
See also CA 104
See also DLB 4

McKuen, Rod 1933- .... **CLC 1, 3**
See also CA 41-44R
See also AITN 1

McManus, Declan Patrick 1955-
See Costello, Elvis

McMurtry, Larry (Jeff)
1936-............. **CLC 2, 3, 7, 11, 27**
See also CA 5-8R
See also DLB 2
See also DLB-Y 80
See also AITN 2

McNally, Terrence 1939- .... **CLC 4, 7**
See also CANR 2
See also CA 45-48
See also DLB 7

McPherson, James Alan 1943- .....**CLC 19**
See also CA 25-28R

Meaker, Marijane 1927-
See Kerr, M. E.
See also CA 107
See also SATA 20

Author Index

Author Index

Powell, Anthony (Dymoke)
1905-.............. CLC 1, 3, 7, 9, 10
See also CANR 1
See also CA 1-4R
See also DLB 15

Powers, J(ames) F(arl)
1917-...............CLC 1, 4, 8
See also CANR 2
See also CA 1-4R

Pownall, David 1938- ....CLC 10
See also CA 89-92
See also DLB 14

Powys, John Cowper
1872-1963...............CLC 7, 9, 15
See also CA 85-88
See also DLB 15

Powys, T(heodore) F(rancis)
1875-1953...................TCLC 9
See also CA 106

Pratt, E(dwin) J(ohn)
1883-1964...................CLC 19
See also obituary CA 93-96

Preussler, Otfried 1923-...........CLC 17
See also CA 77-80
See also SATA 24

Prévert, Jacques (Henri Marie)
1900-1977....................CLC 15
See also CA 77-80
See also obituary CA 69-72
See also obituary SATA 30

Price, (Edward) Reynolds
1933-...................CLC 3, 6, 13
See also CANR 1
See also CA 1-4R
See also DLB 2

Price, Richard 1949-...........CLC 6, 12
See also CANR 3
See also CA 49-52
See also DLB-Y 81

Priestley, J(ohn) B(oynton)
1894-...................CLC 2, 5, 9
See also CA 9-12R
See also DLB 10

Prince, F(rank) T(empleton)
1912-...................CLC 22
See also CA 101
See also DLB 20

Pritchett, V(ictor) S(awdon)
1900-...................CLC 5, 13, 15
See also CA 61-64
See also DLB 15

Prokosch, Frederic 1908-...........CLC 4
See also CA 73-76

Proust, Marcel 1871-1922 .... TCLC 7
See also CA 104

Pryor, Richard 1940- ....CLC 26

Puig, Manuel 1932-..........CLC 3, 5, 10
See also CANR 2
See also CA 45-48

Purdy, A(lfred) W(ellington)
1918-...................CLC 3, 6, 14
See also CA 81-84

Purdy, James 1923-..........CLC 2, 4, 10
See also CA 33-36R
See also DLB 2

Pushkin, Alexander (Sergeyevich)
1799-1837...................NCLC 3

Puzo, Mario 1920-............CLC 1, 2, 6
See also CANR 4
See also CA 65-68
See also DLB 6

Pym, Barbara (Mary Crampton)
1913-1980...............CLC 13, 19
See also CAP 1
See also CA 13-14
See also obituary CA 97-100
See also DLB 14

Pynchon, Thomas
1937-.......... CLC 2, 3, 6, 9, 11, 18
See also CA 17-20R
See also DLB 2

Quasimodo, Salvatore
1901-1968....................CLC 10
See also CAP 1
See also CA 15-16
See also obituary CA 25-28R

Queen, Ellery 1905-1982 .... CLC 3, 11
See also Dannay, Frederic
See also Lee, Manfred B(ennington)

Queneau, Raymond
1903-1976...............CLC 2, 5, 10
See also CA 77-80
See also obituary CA 69-72

Quin, Ann (Marie) 1936-1973.......CLC 6
See also CA 9-12R
See also obituary CA 45-48
See also DLB 14

Quinn, Simon 1942-
See Smith, Martin Cruz

Quoirez, Françoise 1935-
See Sagan, Françoise
See also CANR 6
See also CA 49-52

Rabe, David (William) 1940-..... CLC 4, 8
See also CA 85-88
See also DLB 7

Rado, James 1939-
See Ragni, Gerome and Rado, James
See also CA 105

Radomski, James 1932-
See Rado, James

Radvanyi, Netty Reiling 1900-
See Seghers, Anna
See also CA 85-88

Ragni, Gerome 1942-
See Ragni, Gerome and Rado, James
See also CA 105

Ragni, Gerome 1942- and **Rado, James**
1939-......................CLC 17

Rahv, Philip 1908-1973 ....CLC 24
See also Greenberg, Ivan

Raine, Kathleen (Jessie) 1908-.......CLC 7
See also CA 85-88
See also DLB 20

Rand, Ayn 1905-1982..............CLC 3
See also CA 13-16R
See also obituary CA 105

Randall, Dudley (Felker) 1914-......CLC 1
See also CA 25-28R

Ransom, John Crowe
1888-1974........ CLC 2, 4, 5, 11, 24
See also CANR 6
See also CA 5-8R
See also obituary CA 49-52

Rao, Raja 1909-..................CLC 25
See also CA 73-76

Raphael, Frederic (Michael)
1931-.................... CLC 2, 14
See also CANR 1
See also CA 1-4R
See also DLB 14

Rattigan, Terence (Mervyn)
1911-1977....................CLC 7
See also CA 85-88
See also obituary CA 73-76
See also DLB 13

Raven, Simon (Arthur Noel)
1927-........................CLC 14
See also CA 81-84

Rawlings, Marjorie Kinnan
1896-1953................... TCLC 4
See also CA 104
See also YABC 1
See also DLB 9, 22

Ray, Satyajit 1921- ....CLC 16

Read, Herbert (Edward)
1893-1968.....................CLC 4
See also CA 85-88
See also obituary CA 25-28R
See also DLB 20

Read, Piers Paul 1941-...... CLC 4, 10, 25
See also CA 21-24R
See also SATA 21
See also DLB 14

Reade, Charles 1814-1884 .... NCLC 2
See also DLB 21

Reaney, James 1926-..............CLC 13
See also CA 41-44R

Rechy, John (Francisco)
1934-................CLC 1, 7, 14, 18
See also CANR 6
See also CA 5-8R
See also DLB-Y 82

Redgrove, Peter (William)
1932-........................CLC 6
See also CANR 3
See also CA 1-4R

Redmon (Nightingale), Anne
1943-........................CLC 22
See also Nightingale, Anne Redmon

Reed, Ishmael 1938- .... CLC 2, 3, 5, 6, 13
See also CA 21-24R
See also DLB 2, 5

Reed, John (Silas) 1887-1920...... TCLC 9
See also CA 106

Reed, Lou 1944-..................CLC 21

Reid Banks, Lynne 1929-
See Banks, Lynne Reid
See also CANR 6
See also CA 1-4R
See also SATA 22

Remark, Erich Paul 1898-1970
See Remarque, Erich Maria

Remarque, Erich Maria
1898-1970....................CLC 21
See also CA 77-80
See also obituary CA 29-32R

Renault, Mary 1905-........ CLC 3, 11, 17
See also Challans, Mary

Renoir, Jean 1894-1979 ....CLC 20
See also obituary CA 85-88

Author Index

Author Index

Author Index

Tryon, Thomas 1926- . . . . CLC 3, 11
  See also CA 29-32R
  See also AITN 1

Tshushima Shūji 1909-1948
  See Dazai Osamu
  See also CA 107

Tunis, John R(oberts)
  1889-1975 . . . . CLC 12
  See also CA 61-64
  See also SATA 30
  See also DLB 22

Turco, Lewis (Putnam) 1934- . . . . . . CLC 11
  See also CA 13-16R

Tutuola, Amos 1920- . . . . CLC 5, 14
  See also CA 9-12R

Twain, Mark 1835-1910 . . . . . . TCLC 6, 12
  See also Clemens, Samuel Langhorne

Tyler, Anne 1941- . . . . CLC 7, 11, 18
  See also CANR 11
  See also CA 9-12R
  See also SATA 7
  See also DLB 6
  See also DLB-Y 82

Tyler, Royall 1757-1826 . . . . NCLC 3

Tynan (Hinkson), Katharine
  1861-1931 . . . . TCLC 3
  See also CA 104

Unamuno (y Jugo), Miguel de
  1864-1936 . . . . TCLC 2, 9
  See also CA 104

Underwood, Miles 1909-1981
  See Glassco, John

Undset, Sigrid 1882-1949 . . . . TCLC 3
  See also CA 104

Ungaretti, Giuseppe
  1888-1970 . . . . CLC 7, 11, 15
  See also CAP 2
  See also CA 19-20
  See also obituary CA 25-28R

Updike, John (Hoyer)
  1932- . . . . . . CLC 1, 2, 3, 5, 7, 9, 13, 15,
                          23
  See also CANR 4
  See also CA 1-4R
  See also DLB 2, 5
  See also DLB-Y 80, 82
  See also DLB-DS 3

Uris, Leon (Marcus) 1924- . . . . CLC 7
  See also CANR 1
  See also CA 1-4R
  See also AITN 1, 2

Ustinov, Peter (Alexander)
  1921- . . . . CLC 1
  See also CA 13-16R
  See also DLB 13
  See also AITN 1

Vaculík, Ludvík 1926- . . . . CLC 7
  See also CA 53-56

Valera (y Acalá-Galiano) Juan
  1824-1905 . . . . TCLC 10
  See also CA 106

Valéry, Paul (Ambroise Toussaint Jules)
  1871-1945 . . . . TCLC 4
  See also CA 104

Valle-Inclán (y Montenegro), Ramón (María)
  del 1866-1936 . . . . TCLC 5
  See also CA 106

Vallejo, César (Abraham)
  1892-1938 . . . . TCLC 3
  See also CA 105

Van Den Bogarde, Derek (Jules Gaspard Ulric) Niven 1921-
  See Bogarde, Dirk
  See also CA 77-80

Van der Post, Laurens (Jan)
  1906- . . . . CLC 5
  See also CA 5-8R

Van Doren, Mark
  1894-1972 . . . . CLC 6, 10
  See also CANR 3
  See also CA 1-4R
  See also obituary CA 37-40R

Van Druten, John (William)
  1901-1957 . . . . TCLC 2
  See also CA 104
  See also DLB 10

Van Duyn, Mona 1921- . . . . CLC 3, 7
  See also CANR 7
  See also CA 9-12R
  See also DLB 5

Van Itallie, Jean-Claude 1936- . . . . . . CLC 3
  See also CANR 1
  See also CA 45-48
  See also DLB 7

Van Peebles, Melvin 1932- . . . . . . CLC 2, 20
  See also CA 85-88

Van Vogt, A(lfred) E(lton)
  1912- . . . . CLC 1
  See also CA 21-24R
  See also SATA 14
  See also DLB 8

Varda, Agnès 1928- . . . . CLC 16

Vargas Llosa, (Jorge) Mario (Pedro)
  1936- . . . . CLC 3, 6, 9, 10, 15
  See also CA 73-76

Vassilikos, Vassilis 1933- . . . . CLC 4, 8
  See also CA 81-84

Verga, Giovanni 1840-1922 . . . . TCLC 3
  See also CA 104

Verhaeren, Émile (Adolphe Gustave)
  1855-1916 . . . . TCLC 12
  See also CA 109

Verlaine, Paul (Marie)
  1844-1896 . . . . NCLC 2

Verne, Jules (Gabriel)
  1828-1905 . . . . TCLC 6
  See also SATA 21

Vian, Boris 1920-1959 . . . . TCLC 9
  See also CA 106

Viaud, (Louis Marie) Julien 1850-1923
  See Loti, Pierre
  See also CA 107

Vicker, Angus 1916-
  See Felsen, Henry Gregor

Vidal, Gore
  1925- . . . . CLC 2, 4, 6, 8, 10, 22
  See also CA 5-8R
  See also DLB 6
  See also AITN 1

Viereck, Peter (Robert Edwin)
  1916- . . . . CLC 4
  See also CANR 1
  See also CA 1-4R
  See also DLB 5

Villiers de l'Isle Adam, Jean Marie Mathias Philippe Auguste, Comte de,
  1838-1889 . . . . NCLC 3

Visconti, Luchino 1906-1976 . . . . . . CLC 16
  See also CA 81-84
  See also obituary CA 65-68

Vittorini, Elio 1908-1966 . . . . . CLC 6, 9, 14
  See also obituary CA 25-28R

Vliet, R(ussell) G. 1929- . . . . CLC 22
  See also CA 37-40R

Voinovich, Vladimir (Nikolaevich)
  1932- . . . . CLC 10
  See also CA 81-84

Vonnegut, Kurt, Jr.
  1922- . . . . . . CLC 1, 2, 3, 4, 5, 8, 12, 22
  See also CANR 1
  See also CA 1-4R
  See also DLB 2, 8
  See also DLB-Y 80
  See also DLB-DS 3
  See also AITN 1

Voznesensky, Andrei 1933- . . . . . CLC 1, 15
  See also CA 89-92

Wagman, Fredrica 1937- . . . . CLC 7
  See also CA 97-100

Wagoner, David (Russell)
  1926- . . . . CLC 3, 5, 15
  See also CANR 2
  See also CA 1-4R
  See also SATA 14
  See also DLB 5

Wahlöö, Per 1926-1975 . . . . CLC 7
  See also CA 61-64

Wain, John (Barrington)
  1925- . . . . CLC 2, 11, 15
  See also CA 5-8R
  See also DLB 15

Wajda, Andrzej 1926- . . . . CLC 16
  See also CA 102

Wakefield, Dan 1932- . . . . CLC 7
  See also CA 21-24R

Wakoski, Diane
  1937- . . . . CLC 2, 4, 7, 9, 11
  See also CANR 9
  See also CA 13-16R
  See also DLB 5

Walcott, Derek (Alton)
  1930- . . . . CLC 2, 4, 9, 14, 25
  See also CA 89-92
  See also DLB-Y 81

Waldman, Anne 1945- . . . . CLC 7
  See also CA 37-40R
  See also DLB 16

Waldo, Edward Hamilton 1918-
  See Sturgeon, Theodore (Hamilton)

Walker, Alice
  1944- . . . . CLC 5, 6, 9, 19, 27
  See also CANR 9
  See also CA 37-40R
  See also SATA 31
  See also DLB 6

Walker, David Harry 1911- . . . . CLC 14
  See also CANR 1
  See also CA 1-4R
  See also SATA 8

Walker, Joseph A. 1935- . . . . CLC 19
  See also CA 89-92

Author Index

Wiebe, Rudy (H.) 1934- ..... CLC 6, 11, 14
See also CA 37-40R

Wieners, John 1934- .... CLC 7
See also CA 13-16R
See also DLB 16

Wiesel, Elie(zer) 1928- .... CLC 3, 5, 11
See also CANR 8
See also CA 5-8R
See also AITN 1

Wight, James Alfred 1916-
See Herriot, James
See also CA 77-80

Wilbur, Richard (Purdy)
1921- .... CLC 3, 6, 9, 14
See also CANR 2
See also CA 1-4R
See also SATA 9
See also DLB 5

Wild, Peter 1940- .... CLC 14
See also CA 37-40R
See also DLB 5

Wilde, Oscar (Fingal O'Flahertie Wills)
1855-1900 .... TCLC 1, 8
See also CA 104
See also DLB 10, 19

Wilder, Billy 1906- .... CLC 20
See also Wilder, Samuel

Wilder, Samuel 1906-
See Wilder, Billy
See also CA 89-92

Wilder, Thornton (Niven)
1897-1975 .... CLC 1, 5, 6, 10, 15
See also CA 13-16R
See also obituary CA 61-64
See also DLB 4, 7, 9
See also AITN 2

Wilhelm, Kate 1928- .... CLC 7
See also CA 37-40R
See also DLB 8

Willard, Nancy 1936- .... CLC 7
See also CLR 5
See also CANR 10
See also CA 89-92
See also SATA 30
See also DLB 5

Williams, Charles (Walter Stansby)
1886-1945 .... TCLC 1, 11
See also CA 104

Williams, (George) Emlyn
1905- .... CLC 15
See also CA 104
See also DLB 10

Williams, John A(lfred)
1925- .... CLC 5, 13
See also CANR 6
See also CA 53-56
See also DLB 2

Williams, Jonathan (Chamberlain)
1929- .... CLC 13
See also CANR 8
See also CA 9-12R
See also DLB 5

Williams, Paulette 1948-
See Shange, Ntozake

Williams, Tennessee
1914-1983 ...... CLC 1, 2, 5, 7, 8, 11,
15, 19
See also CA 5-8R
See also obituary CA 108
See also DLB 7
See also DLB-DS 4
See also AITN 1, 2

Williams, Thomas (Alonzo)
1926- .... CLC 14
See also CANR 2
See also CA 1-4R

Williams, William Carlos
1883-1963 ...... CLC 1, 2, 5, 9, 13, 22
See also CA 89-92
See also DLB 4, 16

Willingham, Calder (Baynard, Jr.)
1922- .... CLC 5
See also CANR 3
See also CA 5-8R
See also DLB 2

Wilson, Angus (Frank Johnstone)
1913- .... CLC 2, 3, 5, 25
See also CA 5-8R
See also DLB 15

Wilson, Brian 1942- .... CLC 12

Wilson, Colin 1931- .... CLC 3, 14
See also CANR 1
See also CA 1-4R
See also DLB 14

Wilson, Edmund
1895-1972 .... CLC 1, 2, 3, 8, 24
See also CANR 1
See also CA 1-4R
See also obituary CA 37-40R

Wilson, Ethel Davis (Bryant)
1888-1980 .... CLC 13
See also CA 102

Wilson, John 1785-1854 .... NCLC 5

Wilson, John (Anthony) Burgess 1917-
See Burgess, Anthony
See also CANR 2
See also CA 1-4R

Wilson, Lanford 1937- .... CLC 7, 14
See also CA 17-20R
See also DLB 7

Wilson, Robert (M.) 1944- .... CLC 7, 9
See also CANR 2
See also CA 49-52

Winters, (Arthur) Yvor
1900-1968 .... CLC 4, 8
See also CAP 1
See also CA 11-12
See also obituary CA 25-28R

Wiseman, Frederick 1930- .... CLC 20

Witkiewicz, Stanislaw Ignacy
1885-1939 .... TCLC 8
See also CA 105

Wittig, Monique 1935?- .... CLC 22

Wittlin, Joseph 1896-1976 .... CLC 25
See also Wittlin, Józef

Wittlin, Józef 1896-1976
See Wittlin, Joseph
See also CANR 3
See also CA 49-52
See also obituary CA 65-68

Wodehouse, P(elham) G(renville)
1881-1975 .... CLC 1, 2, 5, 10, 22
See also CANR 3
See also CA 45-48
See also obituary CA 57-60
See also SATA 22
See also AITN 2

Woiwode, Larry (Alfred)
1941- .... CLC 6, 10
See also CA 73-76
See also DLB 6

Wojciechowska, Maia (Teresa)
1927- .... CLC 26
See also CLR 1
See also CANR 4
See also CA 9-12R
See also SATA 1, 28

Wolf, Christa 1929- .... CLC 14
See also CA 85-88

Wolfe, Gene (Rodman) 1931- ...... CLC 25
See also CANR 6
See also CA 57-60
See also DLB 8

Wolfe, Thomas (Clayton)
1900-1938 .... TCLC 4
See also CA 104
See also DLB 9
See also DLB-DS 2

Wolfe, Thomas Kennerly, Jr. 1931-
See Wolfe, Tom
See also CANR 9
See also CA 13-16R

Wolfe, Tom 1931- .... CLC 1, 2, 9, 15
See also Wolfe, Thomas Kennerly, Jr.
See also AITN 2

Wolitzer, Hilma 1930- .... CLC 17
See also CA 65-68
See also SATA 31

Wonder, Stevie 1950- .... CLC 12

Wong, Jade Snow 1922- .... CLC 17
See also CA 109

Woodcott, Keith 1934-
See Brunner, John (Kilian Houston)

Woolf, (Adeline) Virginia
1882-1941 .... TCLC 1, 5
See also CA 104

Woollcott, Alexander (Humphreys)
1887-1943 .... TCLC 5
See also CA 105

Wouk, Herman 1915- .... CLC 1, 9
See also CANR 6
See also CA 5-8R
See also DLB-Y 82

Wright, Charles 1935- .... CLC 6, 13
See also CA 29-32R
See also DLB-Y 82

Wright, James (Arlington)
1927-1980 .... CLC 3, 5, 10
See also CANR 4
See also CA 49-52
See also obituary CA 97-100
See also DLB 5
See also AITN 2

Wright, Judith 1915- .... CLC 11
See also CA 13-16R
See also SATA 14

Cumulative Index to Nationalities

Hardy, Thomas **4, 10**
Henley, William Ernest **8**
Housman, A. E. **1, 10**
Housman, Laurence **7**
James, M. R. **6**
Kipling, Rudyard **8**
Lawrence, D. H. **2, 9**
Lee, Vernon **5**
Lewis, Wyndham **2, 9**
Lowndes, Marie Belloc **12**
Lowry, Malcolm **6**
Macaulay, Rose **7**
Mew, Charlotte **8**
Meynell, Alice **6**
Milne, A. A. **6**
Noyes, Alfred **7**
Orwell, George **2, 6**
Owen, Wilfred **5**
Powys, T. F. **9**
Richardson, Dorothy **3**
Rolfe, Frederick **12**
Rosenberg, Isaac **12**
Saki **3**
Sayers, Dorothy L. **2**
Shiel, M. P. **8**
Sinclair, May **3, 11**
Strachey, Lytton **12**
Sutro, Alfred **6**
Swinburne, Algernon
  Charles **8**
Symons, Arthur **11**
Thomas, Edward **10**
Thompson, Francis **4**
Van Druten, John **2**
Walpole, Hugh **5**
Wells, H. G. **6, 12**
Williams, Charles **1, 11**
Woolf, Virginia **1, 5**

FRENCH
Alain-Fournier **6**
Apollinaire, Guillaume **3, 8**
Artaud, Antonin **3**
Barbusse, Henri **5**
Bernanos, Georges **3**
Bourget, Paul **12**
Claudel, Paul **2, 10**
Colette **1, 5**
Éluard, Paul **7**
Fargue, Léon-Paul **11**
France, Anatole **9**
Gide, André **5, 12**
Giraudoux, Jean **2, 7**
Huysmans, Joris-Karl **7**
Jacob, Max **6**
Jarry, Alfred **2**
Larbaud, Valéry **9**
Loti, Pierre **11**
Péguy, Charles **10**
Proust, Marcel **7**

Rostand, Edmond **6**
Saint-Exupéry, Antoine de **2**
Teilhard de Chardin, Pierre **9**
Valéry, Paul **4**
Verne, Jules **6**
Vian, Boris **9**
Zola, Émile **1, 6**

GERMAN
Benn, Gottfried **3**
Borchert, Wolfgang **5**
Brecht, Bertolt **1, 6**
Ewers, Hanns Heinz **12**
Feuchtwanger, Lion **3**
George, Stefan **2**
Hauptmann, Gerhart **4**
Heym, Georg **9**
Heyse, Paul **8**
Kaiser, Georg **9**
Mann, Heinrich **9**
Mann, Thomas **2, 8**
Morgenstern, Christian **8**
Nietzsche, Friedrich **10**
Rilke, Rainer Maria **1, 6**
Sternheim, Carl **8**
Toller, Ernst **10**
Wassermann, Jakob **6**
Wedekind, Frank **7**

GREEK
Cafavy, C. P. **2, 7**
Kazantzakis, Nikos **2, 5**
Palamas, Kostes **5**

HUNGARIAN
Ady, Endre **11**

INDIAN
Tagore, Rabindranath **3**

IRISH
A. E. **3, 10**
Cary, Joyce **1**
Dunsany, Lord **2**
Gregory, Lady **1**
Joyce, James **3, 8**
Moore, George **7**
O'Grady, Standish **5**
Shaw, Bernard **3, 9**
Stephens, James **4**
Stoker, Bram **8**
Synge, J. M. **6**
Tynan, Katharine **3**
Wilde, Oscar **1, 8**
Yeats, William Butler **1, 11**

ITALIAN
Betti, Ugo **5**
Brancati, Vitaliano **12**
D'Annunzio, Gabriel **6**

Giacosa, Giuseppe **7**
Marinetti, F. T. **10**
Pavese, Cesare **3**
Pirandello, Luigi **4**
Svevo, Italo **2**
Verga, Giovanni **3**

JAMAICAN
De Lisser, H. G. **12**
Mais, Roger **8**

JAPANESE
Dazai, Osamu **11**
Natsume, Sōseki **2, 10**
Shimazaki, Tōson **5**

LEBANESE
Gibran, Kahlil **1, 9**

MEXICAN
Azuela, Mariano **3**
Nervo, Amado **11**

NEW ZEALAND
Mansfield, Katherine **2, 8**

NICARAGUAN
Darío, Rubén **4**

NORWEGIAN
Bjørnson, Bjørnstjerne **7**
Grieg, Nordhal **10**
Hamsun, Knut **2**
Ibsen, Henrik **2, 8**
Kielland, Alexander **5**
Lie, Jonas **5**
Undset, Sigrid **3**

PERUVIAN
Vallejo, César **3**

POLISH
Borowski, Tadeusz **9**
Reymont, Wladyslaw
  Stanislaw **5**
Schulz, Bruno **5**
Sienkiewitz, Henryk **3**
Witkiewicz, Stanislaw
  Ignacy **8**

RUSSIAN
Andreyev, Leonid **3**
Babel, Isaak **2**
Balmont, Konstantin
  Dmitriyevich **11**
Bely, Andrey **7**
Blok, Aleksandr **5**
Bryusov, Valery **10**
Bulgakov, Mikhail **2**
Bunin, Ivan **6**

Chekhov, Anton **3, 10**
Esenin, Sergei **4**
Gorky, Maxim **8**
Hippius, Zinaida **9**
Kuprin, Aleksandr **5**
Mandelstam, Osip **2, 6**
Mayakovsky, Vladimir **4**
Sologub, Fyodor **9**
Tolstoy, Leo **4, 11**
Tsvetaeva, Marina **7**
Zamyatin, Yevgeny
  Ivanovich **8**

SCOTTISH
Barrie, J. M. **2**
Bridie, James **3**
Gibbon, Lewis Grassic **4**
MacDonald, George **9**
Muir, Edwin **2**

SOUTH AFRICAN
Campbell, Roy **5**
Schreiner, Olive **9**

SPANISH
Baroja, Pío **8**
Benavente, Jacinto **3**
Blasco Ibáñez, Vicente **12**
Echegaray, José **4**
García Lorca, Federico **1, 7**
Jiménez, Juan Ramón **4**
Machado, Antonio **3**
Martínez Sierra, Gregorio **6**
Miró, Gabriel **5**
Ortega y Gasset, José **9**
Unamuno, Miguel de **2, 9**
Valera, Juan **10**
Valle-Inclán, Ramón del **5**

SWEDISH
Heidenstam, Verner von **5**
Lagerlöf, Selma **4**
Strindberg, August **1, 8**

SWISS
Spitteler, Carl **12**

WELSH
Davies, W. H. **5**
Lewis, Alun **3**
Machen, Arthur **4**
Thomas, Dylan **1, 8**

YIDDISH
Aleichem, Sholom **1**
Asch, Sholem **3**

Cumulative Index to Critics

Critic Index

Critic Index

Gould, Gerald
  May Sinclair 3:438

Gould, Jean
  Amy Lowell 8:234

Gourmont, Remy de
  André Gide 12:142
  Joris-Karl Huysmans 7:412
  Émile Verhaeren 12:458

Grabowski, Zbigniew A.
  Stanisław Ignacy Witkiewicz
    8:506

Graham, Eleanor
  A. A. Milne 6:313

Graham, Kenneth
  Henry James 11:342

Graham, Stephen
  Valery Bryusov 10:78
  Aleksandr Kuprin 5:296

Gramont, Sanche de
  Antonin Artaud 3:54

Grandgent, Charles Hall
  John Jay Chapman 7:187

Granville-Barker, Harley
  Laurence Housman 7:355

Granville-Barker, Helen
  Gregorio Martínez Sierra and
    María Martínez Sierra 6:275

Grattan, C. Hartley
  Ambrose Bierce 1:85
  Jack London 9:259
  H. G. Wells 12:500

Graver, Lawrence
  Ronald Firbank 1:232

Graves, Robert
  Samuel Butler 1:134
  Alun Lewis 3:284
  George Moore 7:488

Gray, Donald P.
  Pierre Teilhard de Chardin
    9:495

Gray, J. M.
  Arthur Symons 11:426

Gray, James
  Edna St. Vincent Millay 4:318

Gray, Ronald D.
  Bertolt Brecht 6:35
  Franz Kafka 6:222

Gray, Simon
  Tadeusz Borowski 9:20

Gray, Thomas A.
  Elinor Wylie 8:532

Grayburn, William Frazer
  Rebecca Harding Davis 6:152

Grebstein, Sheldon Norman
  Sinclair Lewis 4:256

Green, Benny
  Damon Runyon 10:434

Green, Dorothy
  Henry Handel Richardson 4:380

Green, Ellin
  Laurence Housman 7:360

Green, Julian
  Charles Péguy 10:406

Green, Martin
  Dorothy L. Sayers 2:532

Greenberg, Clement
  Bertolt Brecht 1:97

Greene, Anne
  James Bridie 3:139

Greene, Graham
  George Bernanos 3:126
  Louis Bromfield 11:78
  Samuel Butler 1:135
  Ford Madox Ford 1:282
  Henry James 2:256
  Dorothy Richardson 3:353
  Frederick Rolfe 12:270
  Saki 3:366
  Hugh Walpole 5:501
  H. G. Wells 12:505

Greene, Naomi
  Antonin Artaud 3:54

Greenslet, Ferris
  Ernest Dowson 4:85
  Lafcadio Hearn 9:121

Gregg, Richard A.
  Yevgeny Ivanovich Zamyatin
    8:549

Gregor, Ian
  Thomas Hardy 4:170
  D. H. Lawrence 9:216
  Oscar Wilde 1:505

Gregory, Alyse
  Sherwood Anderson 1:36
  Paul Valéry 4:487

Gregory, Horace
  Sherwood Anderson 10:43
  Vernon Lee 5:318
  Amy Lowell 1:378
  Harriet Monroe 12:221

Grey, Zane
  Zane Grey 6:177

Griffith, John
  Stephen Vincent Benét 7:82

Griffith, Marlene
  Ford Madox Ford 1:284

Griffiths, Richard
  Paul Claudel 2:105

Grigson, Geoffrey
  Wyndham Lewis 2:386
  A. A. Milne 6:319
  Dylan Thomas 1:467; 8:462

Grimm, Clyde L.
  Mark Twain 12:446

Gross, Harvey
  Thomas Mann 8:264

Gross, John
  William Ernest Henley 8:106

Gross, Seymour L.
  Ivan Bunin 6:52

Gross, Theodore L.
  F. Scott Fitzgerald 1:269
  Booker T. Washington 10:532

Grosshut, F. S.
  Lion Feuchtwanger 3:178

Grossman, Joan Delaney
  Valery Bryusov 10:95

Grossman, Manual L.
  Alfred Jarry 2:284

Grossman, William L.
  Machado de Assis 10:282, 288

Grossvogel, David I.
  Guillaume Apollinaire 8:13
  Bertolt Brecht 1:106

Grubbs, Henry A.
  Alfred Jarry 2:278

Gruening, Martha
  Wallace Thurman 6:447

Grummann, Paul H.
  Gerhart Hauptmann 4:197

Guerard, Albert J.
  Joseph Conrad 6:115
  André Gide 5:224
  Thomas Hardy 4:171

Guest, Boyd
  Mark Twain 12:438

Guha-Thakurta, P.
  Rabindranath Tagore 3:485

Guicharnaud, Jacques
  Paul Claudel 2:104

Guillen, Claudio
  Juan Ramón Jiménez 4:214

Guiton, Margaret
  Georges Bernanos 3:119

Gullace, Giovanni
  Gabrielle D'Annunzio 6:136

Gullason, Thomas A.
  Stephen Crane 11:148

Gullón, Ricardo
  Miguel de Unamuno 9:516
  Ramón del Valle-Inclán 5:482

Gumilev, Nikolai
  Konstantin Dmitriyevich
    Balmont 11:30
  Andrey Bely 7:46
  Valery Bryusov 10:77

Gunn, James
  Henry Kuttner 10:272

Gunn, Peter
  Vernon Lee 5:313

Gunther, John
  Arthur Machen 4:279

Günther, Werner
  Carl Spitteler 12:349

Gurko, Leo
  Sinclair Lewis 4:251

Gurko, Miriam
  Sinclair Lewis 4:251

Gustafson, Alrik
  Bjørnstjerne Bjørnson 7:111
  Nordahl Grieg 10:206
  Knut Hamsun 2:205
  Verner von Heidenstam 5:253
  Selma Lagerlöf 5:236
  Jonas Lie 5:325
  August Strindberg 1:448
  Sigrid Undset 3:516

Guthrie, William Norman
  Gerhart Hauptmann 4:192

Gwynn, Stephen
  Henri Barbusse 5:11
  W. H. Davies 5:198

Haber, Edythe C.
  Mikhail Bulgakov 2:71

Haber, Tom Burns
  A. E. Housman 10:258

Hackett, Francis
  Henri Barbusse 5:12
  O. Henry 1:349

Hadfield, Alice Mary
  Charles Williams 1:516

Hadgraft, Cecil
  Miles Franklin 7:268

Haggard, H. Rider
  H. Rider Haggard 11:242

Haight, Gordon
  Marie Belloc Lowndes 12:204

Hakutani, Yoshinobu
  Theodore Dreiser 10:197

Hale, Edward Everett, Jr.
  John Jay Chapman 7:186
  Edmond Rostand 6:376

Hall, J. C.
  Edwin Muir 2:483

Hall, James
  Joyce Cary 1:142

Hall, Robert A., Jr.
  W. S. Gilbert 3:213

Hall, Trevor H.
  Arthur Conan Doyle 7:228

Hall, Wayne E.
  A. E. 10:26
  George Moore 7:499

Halline, Allan G.
  Maxwell Anderson 2:5

Halls, W. D.
  Maurice Maeterlinck 3:328

Halperin, John
  Lytton Strachey 12:418

Halpern, Joseph
  Joris-Karl Huysmans 7:417

Haman, Aleš
  Karel Čapek 6:90

Hamblen, Abigail Ann
  Mary Wilkins Freeman 9:71

Hamburger, Michael
  Gottfried Benn 3:105
  Hugo von Hofmannsthal 11:305
  Georg Trakl 5:457

Hamilton, Clayton
  Alfred Sutro 6:420
  Leo Tolstoy 4:453
  Alexander Woollcott 5:520

Hamilton, G. Rostrevor
  Alice Meynell 6:302

Hammelmann, H. A.
  Hugo von Hofmannsthal 11:299

Hammond, Josephine
  Lord Dunsany 2:142

Hampshire, Stuart N.
  Oscar Wilde 8:498

Hanan, Patrick
  Lu Hsün 3:300

Hankin, Cherry
  Katherine Mansfield 2:458

Hankin, St. John
  Oscar Wilde 1:495

Critic Index

Critic Index

Maguire, Robert A.
Andrey Bely **7**:62

Mahlendorf, Ursula R.
Georg Heym **9**:142

Mahony, Patrick
Maurice Maeterlinck **3**:328

Mallarmé, Stéphane
Émile Verhaeren **12**:457
Émile Zola **6**:558

Mallinson, Jean
Charles G. D. Roberts **8**:326

Malmstad, John E.
Andrey Bely **7**:62

Malone, Andrew W.
Lord Dunsany **2**:143

Malone, Dumas
Douglas Southall Freeman
11:223, 225

Mandelstam, Nadezhda
Osip Mandelstam **2**:403; **6**:265

Manganiello, Dominic
Guiseppe Giacosa **7**:314

Mangione, Jerre
Hanns Heinz Ewers **12**:136

Mankin, Paul A.
Ugo Betti **5**:57
Jean Giraudoux **2**:172

Manley, Norman Washington
Roger Mais **8**:241

Mann, Erika
Thomas Mann **8**:254

Mann, Heinrich
Heinrich Mann **9**:316

Mann, Klaus
Thomas Mann **8**:254

Mann, Thomas
Anton Chekhov **3**:160
Joseph Conrad **1**:200
Franz Kafka **2**:291
Heinrich Mann **9**:322
Thomas Mann **8**:256
Friedrich Nietzsche **10**:373
Bernard Shaw **3**:396
Leo Tolstoy **4**:459
Frank Wedekind **7**:576
Oscar Wilde **1**:503

Manning, Clarence Augustus
Sergei Esenin **4**:108

Mansfield, Katherine
John Galsworthy **1**:293
H. Rider Haggard **11**:242
Joseph Hergesheimer **11**:262
Jack London **9**:258
Rose Macaulay **7**:421
George Moore **7**:476
Dorothy Richardson **3**:347
Hugh Walpole **5**:492
Edith Wharton **3**:558

Manship, J. P.
Paul Claudel **10**:129

Marble, Annie Russell
Verner von Heidenstam **5**:253
Władysław Stanisław Reymont
5:391

March, George
Thomas Mann **2**:412

March, Harold
André Gide **12**:160

Marcus, Jane
Olive Schreiner **9**:404

Marcus, Phillip L.
Standish O'Grady **5**:354

Marcus, Roxanne B.
Juan Valera **10**:509

Marcus, Steven
O. Henry **1**:351

Marder, Herbert
Isaak Babel **2**:30

Marias, Julian
José Ortega y Gasset **9**:346
Miguel de Unamuno **2**:563

Marinetti, F. T.
F. T. Marinetti **10**:309, 312

Marker, Lise-Lone
David Belasco **3**:90

Markert, Lawrence W.
Arthur Symons **11**:453

Markov, Vladimir
Konstantin Dmitriyevich
Balmont **11**:35

Marks, Elaine
Colette **5**:164

Markus, Liselotte
Anatole France **9**:51

Marlow, Norman
A. E. Housman **10**:254, 261

Marquerie, Alfredo
Jacinto Benavente **3**:101

Marquis, Don
Don Marquis **7**:438

Marrow, Arminel
Guillaume Apollinaire **8**:17

Marsden, Kenneth
Thomas Hardy **10**:223

Marsh, E.
Rupert Brooke **2**:50

Marsh, Fred T.
Damon Runyon **10**:424

Marshall, Margaret
James Bridie **3**:132

Martin, Edward A.
Don Marquis **7**:448

Martin, Jay
Hamlin Garland **3**:200

Martin, Ronald E.
Joseph Hergesheimer **11**:279

Marx, Leo
F. Scott Fitzgerald **6**:172

Masing-Delic, Irene
Valery Bryusov **10**:91

Maskaleris, Thanasis
Kostes Palamas **5**:382

Maslenikov, Oleg A.
Konstantin Dmitriyevich
Balmont **11**:32
Hilaire Belloc **7**:49
Zinaida Hippius **9**:155

Mason, Eudo C.
Rainer Maria Rilke **6**:364

Mason, Lawrence
Robert Benchley **1**:76

Masson, David I.
C. M. Kornbluth **8**:221

Masters, Edgar Lee
Theodore Dreiser **10**:164
Harriet Monroe **12**:215

Materer, Timothy
Wyndham Lewis **9**:243

Mathew, Ray
Miles Franklin **7**:269

Mathews, Jackson
Paul Valéry **4**:492

Mathewson, Rufus W., Jr.
Maxim Gorky **8**:90

Mathewson, Ruth
Raymond Chandler **1**:176

Matich, Olga
Zinaida Hippius **9**:164, 165

Matsui, Sakuko
Sōseki Natsume **10**:331

Matthews, Brander
James Weldon Johnson **3**:239
Mark Twain **6**:454

Matthews, J. H.
Paul Éluard **7**:253

Matthews, John F.
Bernard Shaw **3**:405

Matthews, T. S.
James Agee **1**:9

Matthiessen, Francis Otto
Mary Wilkins Freeman **9**:66
Henry James **2**:259
Sarah Orne Jewett **1**:362

Maude, Aylmer
Leo Tolstoy **4**:458

Maugham, W. Somerset
Arnold Bennett **5**:34
Aleister Crowley **7**:207
Rudyard Kipling **8**:193
H. G. Wells **12**:507

Mauriac, François
Jean Giraudoux **7**:321

Maurice, Arthur Bartlett
Arthur Conan Doyle **7**:216

Maurois, André
Paul Claudel **10**:124
Antoine de Saint-Exupéry **2**:516
Anatole France **9**:49
André Gide **12**:171
Rudyard Kipling **8**:186
D. H. Lawrence **9**:218
Katherine Mansfield **8**:277
Marcel Proust **7**:530
Lytton Strachey **12**:402

Mautner, Franz H.
Karl Kraus **5**:292

Maxwell, William
Samuel Butler **1**:138

May, Frederick
Luigi Pirandello **4**:349

May, Georges
Jean Giraudoux **2**:156

May, Rollo
Friedrich Nietzsche **10**:389

Mayne, Richard
Wyndham Lewis **2**:398

McArthur, Peter
Stephen Leacock **2**:377

McCarthy, Justin Huntly
August Strindberg **8**:406

McCarthy, Mary
Henrik Ibsen **2**:230
Eugene O'Neill **1**:389, 393
John Van Druten **2**:575

McCarthy, Patrick
Alice Meynell **6**:303

McClellan, Edwin
Sōseki Natsume **2**:490; **10**:330,
338
Tōson Shimazaki **5**:434

McClintock, James I.
Jack London **9**:273

McComas, J. Francis
C. M. Kornbluth **8**:212
Henry Kuttner **10**:265

McCormick, John
Sherwood Anderson **1**:62
F. Scott Fitzgerald **1**:270

McCourt, Edward A.
Rupert Brooke **2**:55

McDonald, E. Cordel
José Ortega y Gasset **9**:344

McDowell, D.
Boris Vian **9**:537

McDowell, Frederick P. W.
Ellen Glasgow **2**:185

McDowell, Margaret B.
Edith Wharton **3**:578

McElderry, Bruce R., Jr.
Max Beerbohm **1**:73
Thomas Wolfe **4**:522

McElrath, Joseph R., Jr.
Mary Wilkins Freeman **9**:78

McFarlane, Brian
Henry Handel Richardson **4**:381

McFarlane, James Walter
Bjørnstjerne, Bjørnson **7**:113
Georg Brandes **10**:73
Knut Hamsun **2**:206
Jonas Lie **5**:330
Sigrid Undset **3**:525

McFate, Patricia
Ford Madox Ford **1**:285
James Stephens **4**:418

McGreivey, John C.
Hamlin Garland **3**:204

McHaffie, Margaret **12**:345, 352
Carl Spitteler **12**:345, 352

McKay, D. F.
Dylan Thomas **1**:475

McKee, Mary J.
Edna St. Vincent Millay **4**:317

McKeon, Joseph T.
Antone de Saint-Exupéry **2**:526

McKitrick, Eric
Edgar Saltus **8**:350

McLaughlin, Ann L.
Katherine Mansfield **2**:456

Critic Index

Critic Index

Critic Index

Critic Index

Critic Index

Critic Index